COLLINS
COBUILD

DICTIONARY OF
IDIOMS

THE UNIVERSITY
OF BIRMINGHAM

COLLINS
COBUILD

HarperCollins*Publishers*

HarperCollins Publishers
77-85 Fulham Palace Road
London W6 8JB

COBUILD is a trademark of William Collins Sons & Co. Ltd.

©HarperCollins Publishers Ltd. 1995
First published 1995

10 9 8 7 6 5 4 3 2 1

ISBN 0 00 375030 2 (HB)

ISBN 0 00 370946 9 (PB)

Corpus Acknowledgements

We would like to acknowledge the assistance of the many hundreds of
individuals and companies who have kindly given permission for
copyright material to be used in The Bank of English. The written
sources include many national and regional newspapers in Britain and
overseas; magazine and periodical publishers; and book publishers in
Britain, the United States, and Australia. Extensive spoken data has
been provided by radio and television broadcasting companies; research
workers at many universities and other institutions; and numerous
individual contributors. We are grateful to them all.

Note

Typeset by Morton Word Processing Ltd.

Printed in Great Britain by HarperCollins Manufacturing

Editorial Team

Founding Editor-in-Chief
John Sinclair

Editorial Director
Gwyneth Fox

Editorial Manager
Rosamund Moon

Editors
Elizabeth Potter   Jenny Watson
Michael Lax   Miranda Timewell   John Todd

Computer Staff
Tim Lane
Zoe James

The Bank of English
Jeremy Clear
Sue Smith

Secretarial Staff
Sue Crawley
Michelle Devereux

Design and Production
Ted Carden
Jill McNair
Lynsey Roxburgh

Publishing Manager
Debbie Seymour

Managing Director, Collins Dictionaries
Richard Thomas

Acknowledgements

We would like to thank Jane Bradbury for her invaluable assistance in reading through the text of the dictionary and commenting at length on it.

Clare Marson, Héloïse McGuinness, Luisa Plaja, and Mike Stocks worked on this dictionary in its early stages, and we would like to thank them for their contributions. We would also like to thank Deborah Yuill and Keith Harvey for their contributions, and to acknowledge their research at COBUILD into idioms, in particular in setting up the COBUILD Idioms Testing Initiative: an investigation into learners' perceptions of idioms and the way in which learners use idioms dictionaries.

Dr Julia Penelope and Robin Rosenberg read the dictionary text as our informants on American English, and, together with Lucille Glassman and Debbie Posner, helped us on many points. Professor Malcolm Coulthard and Malcolm Goodale commented on the text and suggested improvements. We gratefully acknowledge all their contributions and advice.

Finally, we thank other members of the COBUILD team for their support, comments, and suggestions throughout the project.

Introduction

The COBUILD **Dictionary of Idioms**, like other COBUILD dictionaries, is based
on an extensive study of a large corpus of modern English texts, and so it is in a
unique position to describe idioms in current English. Idioms are one of the
most interesting and difficult parts of the English vocabulary. They are
interesting because they are colourful and lively, and because they are
linguistic curiosities. At the same time, they are difficult because they have
unpredictable meanings or collocations and grammar, and often have special
connotations. Idioms are frequently neglected in general dictionaries and in
classroom teaching, because they are considered marginal items which are
quaint but not significant. Yet research into idioms shows that they have
important roles in spoken language and in writing, in particular in conveying
evaluations and in developing or maintaining interactions. The COBUILD
Dictionary of Idioms sets out to give detailed coverage of these points.

About this dictionary

The COBUILD Dictionary of Idioms is primarily intended for teachers of English
and intermediate–advanced learners, although we hope that many other
people will find it interesting and useful. It deals with approximately 4400
English idioms, and illustrates them with a rich collection of examples which
are drawn from The Bank of English and which show how idioms are used in
real English. There is a workbook – the COBUILD Idioms Workbook – to
accompany the dictionary, written by Malcolm Goodale. It is designed for both
class work and self-study, and concentrates on 250 of the idioms explained in
the dictionary.

What is an idiom?

An idiom is a special kind of phrase. It is a group of words which have a
different meaning when used together from the one it would have if the
meaning of each word were taken individually. If you do not know that the
words have a special meaning together, you may well misinterpret what
someone is saying, or be puzzled by why they are saying something that is
untrue or irrelevant. For example, learners might not recognize the idioms
bite someone's head off and *out in the cold*. They would then have problems
understanding remarks such as 'Don't bite my head off just because you're bad
tempered' and 'They were going to play together and that left me out in the
cold, you know'. (These examples are taken from transcribed conversations in
The Bank of English.)

Idioms are typically metaphorical: they are effectively metaphors which have
become 'fixed' or 'fossilized'. In some cases, it is fairly easy to see how the
idiomatic meaning relates to the literal meaning. For example, *kill two birds
with one stone* means 'achieve two things at the same time', and the image in
the metaphor supports this meaning. In other cases, the literal meanings may
make no sense at all. For example, *move heaven and earth* literally describes
an action which is physically impossible. In a few further cases, the metaphors
in the idioms are peculiar, and their true origins are unknown, so it is very
difficult to see how or why the idioms have come to have their current
meanings. For example, there are several explanations of *kick the bucket* and
raining cats and dogs, but none is very satisfactory. While we do not explain
idiom histories in this dictionary, we occasionally make comments to explain
words which might puzzle learners, or to explain common allusions which are
often made in the context of an idiom.

The scope of the dictionary

The COBUILD Dictionary of Idioms covers a large number of the idioms which
people are likely to find in everyday English. It includes traditional English

idioms such as *spill the beans* and *a red herring*. It also includes a number of expressions which can be considered 'semi-idioms': some very common multi-word metaphors such as *the acid test* and *brownie points*; metaphorical proverbs such as *every cloud has a silver lining* and *in for a penny, in for a pound*; common similes such as *white as a sheet* and *old as the hills*; and some other expressions which have a strong pragmatic meaning, such as *famous last words* and *that's the way the cookie crumbles*. We have deliberately avoided including other kinds of fixed expression such as *in fact* and *at least,* or greetings and other fixed formulae such as *how do you do* and *excuse me*. Many of these are very common, but they are dealt with in detail in our general dictionaries, such as the Collins COBUILD English Dictionary.

Some of the idioms in the COBUILD Dictionary of Idioms also appear in other COBUILD dictionaries, but there they can only be given very brief entries, often without examples. Other idioms in the Dictionary of Idioms are too infrequent to be included in even the largest COBUILD dictionary.

Phrasal verbs – fixed combinations of verbs and particles, such as *give up, put off*, and *throw out* – are dealt with in the COBUILD Dictionary of Phrasal Verbs. However, expressions which are combinations of verbs, particles, and fixed or semi-fixed noun phrases are considered to be idioms rather than phrasal verbs. This means that you will find expressions such as *give up the ghost, put someone off their stroke*, and *throw the baby out with the bath water* in the COBUILD Dictionary of Idioms, rather than in the Dictionary of Phrasal Verbs.

Idioms and corpora

COBUILD has always been associated with the use of corpora in lexicography. All our dictionaries, grammars, and usage books are based on our examinations of the evidence in large computer-held corpora of English texts. Since 1991, we have been working with The Bank of English. This now contains 211 million words, and it is made up from substantial holdings of British and American English together with smaller holdings of other varieties of English. The texts in the corpus range from newspapers, magazines, fiction, and non-fiction to transcribed conversations and broadcasting.

The COBUILD Dictionary of Idioms represents what we have learned about idioms in The Bank of English. One of the first points to be made is that idioms are comparatively infrequent, and it is only by having a very large corpus that we have sufficient evidence to describe idioms accurately and with confidence. Nearly one third of the idioms in this dictionary occur less often than once per 10 million words of the corpus. The idioms in the highest frequency band occur in our data at least once per two million words of English. However, to set the matter in perspective, only a few of these occur as frequently as any of the words we have marked for frequency in the COBUILD English Dictionary. More detailed information about the frequency bands is given on page xvii.

Another point is that although idioms are often described as 'fixed', they are typically not fixed at all. Many idioms have two or more alternative forms, without any change in meaning: for example, *burn your bridges* and *burn your boats*, or *up the ante* and *raise the ante*. Sometimes, these different forms reflect differences between British and American English: for example, *burn your bridges* is used in both varieties, whereas the form *burn your boats* is used only in British English. In many cases, there are several different verbs which can be used in an idiom: for example, 'sit' is the verb most commonly found in the idiom *sit on the fence*, and so we have given this as the main form, but verbs such as 'stay' and 'be' can be used instead of 'sit'. There are slight changes in meaning, but these changes are predictable from the usual meanings of the verbs which have been substituted. Similarly, prepositions or syntax can vary: for example, *have your back to the wall* and *have your back against the wall*, or *feel something in your bones* and *have a feeling in your bones*.

The COBUILD Dictionary of Idioms shows these kinds of variation, listing the major variations at the beginning of each entry, and indicating any differences in usage between variations. We also indicate cases where the form of the idiom is very unstable and we show the range of possible wordings. For example, there are no fixed words at all in the idiom *wash your dirty linen in public*. We deal with it at the headword **dirty**, and we discuss the range of alternative forms.

A third point is that idioms have often been associated with conversation and informal language. However, the evidence in The Bank of English suggests that they are also very common in journalism and magazines, where writers are seeking to make their articles and stories more vivid, interesting, and appealing to their readers. Idioms are often used by both journalists and politicians as shorthand ways of expressing opinions or conveying ready-made evaluations. While such use of idioms is often criticized and dismissed as 'cliché', suggesting that the speaker or writer has nothing interesting or original to say, it is also true that idioms help speakers and writers to be fluent and to get their opinions across effectively.

The examples in the COBUILD Dictionary of Idioms are all authentic, and drawn from The Bank of English. Where necessary, we have edited them slightly to make them easier to read; however, most are cited in their original forms. Idioms are often used in fairly complex ways in context, and so the examples chosen are often much longer than in other COBUILD dictionaries, in order to demonstrate this fully. For instance,

> *The two sides went into these talks with positions that were not very far apart in terms of their political demands. Dotting all the i's and crossing all the t's may take some time, however.*

The idiom appears in the second sentence of the example. On its own, this sentence would only give a partial insight into the meaning of the idiom: that the process is time-consuming. The first sentence adds context which reinforces the fact that 'dotting the i's and crossing the t's' involves dealing with details rather than the main part of a piece of work.

Idioms, pragmatics, and context

Pragmatics is the study of the way in which people use language to achieve different goals – for example in making suggestions or offers, in thanking, in expressing emotions and opinions, or in making commitments. Idioms have important pragmatic functions in language. Because they have fairly general meanings, they are less often used purely to convey factual information and more often to convey attitude. They typically convey evaluations: they are used as ways of expressing approval and admiration, or disapproval and criticism. An idiom may have connotations and pragmatic meanings which are not obvious to people who are unfamiliar with that idiom, and so the real meaning of a statement may be missed. Similarly, someone may use an idiom without realizing it will be interpreted as critical or disapproving, and therefore unintentionally cause the wrong reaction in the person they are talking to. The COBUILD Dictionary of Idioms gives explicit guidance on this area, in order to help learners of English (and their teachers) understand idioms more fully and be able to use them more confidently.

In addition to conveying evaluations, idioms have other functions in texts and interactions. For example, idioms are used to give emphasis or to organize discourse, or in conveying thanks or refusals. Where these uses are shown in our data, we mention them explicitly in the dictionary explanations.

People often use idioms in order to create a sense of 'camaraderie' with the people they are speaking to or writing for: idioms make language seem more lively and interesting, more friendly and more informal. Because of this, idioms are generally considered informal and are often labelled as 'informal' or 'colloquial' in general dictionaries of English. In fact, idioms are often used in contexts which are not really informal at all. In this dictionary, we have only labelled as 'informal' those idioms which are very informal and which might cause offence if used in the wrong situations. As a general rule, learners should be careful how they use idioms in formal contexts and in formal writing.

British and American idioms

There are some distinctions between the idioms used in British English and the idioms used in American English, although the majority of idioms are common to both varieties. We have covered both British and American idioms in this dictionary, and we show where there are variations in form or usage. For example, speakers of British English say that people *take things in their stride*, whereas speakers of American English say they *take things in stride*.

The situation is complicated because idiom usage changes rapidly. Some idioms are not used in American English – *on a sticky wicket* and *chalk and cheese* – whereas others are rarely used in British English – *live high on the hog* and *spin your wheels*. However, many other idioms which were originally American have become fashionable in British English, in particular in journalism or the media. Other American idioms become known to British speakers because of the influence of American culture, for example films and music. In some cases, 'American' idioms are now so common in British English that it would be wrong to label them as only – or even mainly – used in American English. Even though some people may think of these idioms as American, they are now much more widely known and used.

The situation with Australian English is also complicated, since Australian English includes both 'British' and 'American' idioms. We have not attempted in this dictionary to give guidance on Australian English, and when we comment that an idiom is only used in British English or only used in American English, we are neither including nor excluding Australian English. We have, however, included a few Australian English idioms which our evidence suggests are used more widely now. We have taken a similar approach with other varieties of English.

Finally...

Since we published our first COBUILD dictionary, many people have written to us with comments and advice. This has proved invaluable, and we have benefited greatly from it. We are always pleased to hear from the users of our dictionaries, and we would be delighted to hear from you. You can e-mail us at editors@cobuild.collins.co.uk or write to us at the address below.

We hope that you find the COBUILD Dictionary of Idioms useful, easy to use, and above all interesting. We look forward to hearing from you with your reactions and suggestions.

Rosamund Moon, Editorial Manager

COBUILD
Institute of Research and Development
University of Birmingham Research Park
Vincent Drive
Birmingham B15 2SQ
Great Britain

How to find an idiom

To find an idiom in the COBUILD Dictionary of Idioms, you should go straight to the index at the end of the dictionary. This contains entries for every lexical word in every idiom in the dictionary, and it shows you under which headword in the dictionary you will find the idiom that you are looking for. See page 433 of the dictionary for more information on how to use the index.

Although you can find idioms by looking at the main text first, you may find it harder to locate them. You may not know what form of the idiom is given in the text, and you may not realize that it has variations.

By using the index first, you will be able to see immediately if the idiom is covered in the dictionary, what form it is given in, and where to find it in the main text.

Headwords in the dictionary

The idiom entries in the main dictionary text are each attached to a headword, which is normally one of the lexical words in the idiom. Headwords are arranged alphabetically. This is to help you find idioms as easily as possible. For example, the index will tell you that *spill the beans* is under the headword **beans**. You then need to find the headword **beans** in the main dictionary: it is the headword between **bean** and **bear**.

> battle
> bay
> bead
> be-all
> beam
> bean
> **beans**
> bear
> beast
> beat
> beaver
> beck
> bed

Note that if the word we choose as headword is a plural noun or a verb participle, then the headword will also be in that form, rather than in the base form of the noun or verb. This is why *spill the beans* is under **beans** rather than **bean**.

Generally, the word we choose as headword is a noun: for example, *rock the boat* is under the noun **boat** as headword, and *sit on the fence* is under **fence**. If there are two nouns, then the headword is the first noun: for example, *it's raining cats and dogs* is under the headword **cats** and *cost an arm and a leg* under **arm**. If the idiom contains no nouns, then an adjective is chosen: for example, *go easy on someone* is under the headword **easy** and *in black and white* is under **black**. If the idiom contains no nouns or adjectives, then the headword will be either a verb or an adverb.

There are four main exceptions to this general rule:

1. The word chosen as headword is normally a fixed word in the idiom: that is, it never varies. In some cases, the only noun in the idiom

varies, and so we have chosen to put the idiom under another word which is fixed. For example, *beat your breast* has a common variation *beat your chest*, and so you will find the idiom under the verb **beat**.

2. Occasionally, our rule for choosing headwords would mean that two idioms which contain similar words would end up in very different parts of the dictionary. In this case, we put them under the same headword. For example, we put both *a fair crack of the whip* and to *crack the whip* under the headword **whip**.

3. If an idiom contains two nouns, but the first noun is a very general word such as 'end' or 'top', then the idiom will be found at the second noun. For example, *the thin end of the wedge* is under **wedge**.

4. Finally, similes such as *white as a sheet* and *old as the hills* are always dealt with under their adjectives – **white** and **old** in these cases – rather than under their nouns. This is because they generally reinforce or emphasize the meaning of the adjective.

The order of idiom entries

Idioms are arranged in alphabetical order under each dictionary headword. Note that if the first word in an idiom is 'a' or 'the', it is not taken into account in the idiom sequence. Here, for example, are the idioms appearing under the headword **wolf**:

> cry wolf
> keep the wolf from the door
> a lone wolf
> a wolf in sheep's clothing

Note also that only the principal forms of idioms are alphabetized. This means that any variant forms given at the beginning of an entry for an individual idiom may appear to be out of alphabetical order. Here, for example, are the idioms appearing under the dictionary headword **feet**.

> dead on your feet
> feet on the ground
> find your feet
> get cold feet
>   have cold feet (variation)
> get your feet on the ground
> get your feet under the table
> get your feet wet
>   have your feet wet (variation)
> have feet of clay
>   clay feet (variation)
> itchy feet
> land on your feet
>   fall on your feet (variation)
> put your feet up
> rushed off your feet
> stand on your own two feet
>   stand on your own feet (variation)
> sweep someone off their feet: 1
> sweep someone off their feet: 2
> think on your feet
> under someone's feet
> vote with your feet

Guide to the Dictionary Entries

keel ◄◄
on an even keel

    If someone or something is **on an even keel**, they are calm or are progressing steadily, especially during or after a period of troubles or difficulties.

    She sees it as her role to keep the family on an even keel through its time of hardship.

fly the nest ◄
leave the nest

    When children **fly the nest** or **leave the nest**, they leave their parents' home to live on their own. Compare **fly the coop**; see **coop**.

    One day the children are going to fly the nest and have their own lives.

    When their children had flown the nest, he and his wife moved to a thatched cottage in Dorset.

pick holes in something ◄

    If you **pick holes in** something such as an argument or theory, you find weak points in it which disprove it or show that it is wrong. Verbs such as 'poke' and 'shoot' can be used instead of 'pick'.

    They say that the great science of the 21st century will be biology. Thus we do not need so many physicists as in the past. It is easy to pick holes in this argument.

    For him, a winning start to the European Championship campaign was not enough and yesterday he picked holes in the team's performance against Poland.

    The defense lawyers attempted to poke holes in the testimony of a prosecution witness.

get up someone's nose ◄◄

    If you say that something or someone **gets up** your **nose**, you mean that they irritate you a great deal. This is an informal expression, which is used mainly in British English.

    Imagine my surprise when I contacted the dealers and was told 'Sorry, it will not arrive until February 10.' What really gets up my nose is that all I want is a standard white car.

    This producer looks as if he's going to get up everybody's nose. He has only been here for a few hours and already he has been babbling about 'discipline' to Annie.

dictionary headword
idiom

explanation

example

idiom and common variation

cross-reference

frequency indicator

comment on minor variations of idiom

comment on usage – for example, level of formality or region of use

neck and neck ◄◄◄

In a race or contest, if two competitors are **neck and neck**, they are exactly level with each other, so that it is impossible to say who will win.

The latest opinion polls show both parties running neck and neck.

Leeds are currently neck-and-neck with Manchester United for the Championship.

□ You can use neck and neck before a noun.

Philippe Jeantot of France and the South African John Martin are involved in a neck and neck race to finish second across the line.

follow-on paragraph, showing syntactic variation (also used for showing slight changes in meaning or use)

plain as the nose on your face

If you say that something is as **plain as the nose on** your **face**, you are emphasizing that it is very obvious or easy to understand.

It's plain as the nose on your face that this company is wildly undervalued.

His humour can be as plain as the nose on your face.

indication in explanation of pragmatic function – idiom is used to give emphasis

feather your nest ◄

If you accuse someone of **feathering** their **nest**, you are accusing them of taking advantage of their position in order to get a lot of money, so that they can lead a comfortable life.

The politicians seem anxious to feather their nests at the expense of the people.

It wasn't done to feather his own nest, it was for his son.

indication in explanation of pragmatic function – idiom is used to criticize someone

under your own steam: 1

If you go somewhere **under** your **own steam**, you make your own arrangements for the journey, rather than letting someone else organize it for you.

Most hotels organise tours to inland beauty spots, but car hire is cheap enough to consider taking off into the hills under your own steam.

meaning numbers – to show idiom has two meanings

under your own steam: 2

If you do something **under** your **own steam**, you do it on your own and without help from anyone else.

He left the group convinced he could do better under his own steam.

Guide to the Dictionary Entries

Idiom headwords, forms, and variations

At the beginning of each idiom entry in the dictionary, we give a headword form for the idiom. Idioms are arranged in alphabetical order of these forms. We use 'someone', 'something', and 'somewhere' in idiom headwords to indicate that the idiom has to be completed with a word referring to respectively a person, a thing, or a place. Similarly, we use words such as 'you', 'your', 'yourself', and 'their' to indicate that an appropriate pronoun or possessive adjective should be supplied.

Where an idiom has variations, we give the commonest form as the idiom headword. If a variation is very common, or substantially different from the idiom headword, or reflects a British/American usage distinction, we give the variation as a second idiom headword. We also mention these variations in the explanations:

> When children **fly the nest** or **leave the nest**, they leave their parents' home to live on their own.

> If you say that it is possible to do something **at a pinch** or **in a pinch**, you mean it can just be done if it is absolutely necessary. 'At a pinch' is used in British English and 'in a pinch' is used in American English.

Where the variations are minor, we mention them in a sentence at the end of the explanation:

> If you **pick holes in** something such as an argument or theory, you find weak points in it which disprove it or show that it is wrong. Verbs such as 'poke' and 'shoot' can be used instead of 'pick'.

Occasionally, variations are dealt with in a follow-on paragraph, if they need special comment. For example, the entry for the idiom *a wolf in sheep's clothing* has the follow-on paragraph

> ☐ People sometimes describe someone as **a sheep in wolf's clothing** to mean that the person seems dangerous or powerful, but is really harmless or ordinary.

and the entry for *have feet of clay* has

> ☐ You can also say that someone has **clay feet**. This form is used mainly in American English.

More information about variations can be found in the examples, which are chosen to reflect the range of forms occurring in The Bank of English.

Explanations and meanings

The explanations or definitions in this dictionary, as in other COBUILD dictionaries, are written in full sentences. This enables us to define idioms in a natural way, by explaining them in context with their most typical structures and collocations: see the following sections. The language of the explanations is kept as simple as possible, and just over 2000 different words are used.

In addition to describing the meanings of idioms, explanations often give information about the contexts in which they are used. For example, the explanation for *neck and neck*

> In a race or contest, if two competitors are **neck and neck**, they are exactly level with each other, so that it is impossible to say who will win.

shows that the idiom is typically used in the context of races and contests – and is also used to describe competitors in the race or competition.

Idioms sometimes have two or more different meanings. We indicate this by giving a number after the idiom headword. There are often different variations associated with the different meanings. Similarly, they often have different usages or frequencies, and we give this information in the individual numbered entries.

Sometimes follow-on paragraphs are used to deal with slight changes in meaning or usage. For example, the main explanation of *change hands* is

> If something **changes hands**, one person or organization gets it from another, usually by buying it.

and the follow-on paragraph is

> ☐ When something is sold for a particular amount of money, you say that amount of money **changes hands**.

Inflections and grammar

We do not give explicit information about the inflection and syntactic behaviour of idioms. Instead, we give the information implicitly, by showing in the explanations and examples which words inflect and which structure or structures are typically associated with an idiom. By using these as guidelines, learners will be able to produce their own sentences with idioms.

For example, the following explanation

> If someone **dots the i's and crosses the t's**, they add the final minor details to a piece of work, plan, or arrangement.

shows that there are two verbs in the idiom which both inflect. The explanation for *skate on thin ice*

> If you say that someone **is skating on thin ice**, you mean that they have got themselves into a difficult situation which may have serious or unpleasant consequences for them.

shows that the verb 'skate' inflects, and also that the verb is typically used in the continuous.

Explanations give other information about structures. The explanation for the first meaning of *marching orders* begins

> If you are given your **marching orders**, you are made to leave something such as a job or a relationship.

It shows that the idiom is typically used after the verb 'give', typically in the passive, and also after a possessive adjective. This is supported by the structures shown in the examples.

Changes in syntax are sometimes shown in follow-on paragraphs. For example, at *neck and neck*, the main explanation

> In a race or contest, if two competitors are **neck and neck**, they are exactly level with each other, so that it is impossible to say who will win.

shows that the idiom is used after a verb; the follow-on paragraph shows a syntax change:

> ☐ You can use **neck and neck** before a noun.

This is reinforced by the example:

> *Philippe Jeantot of France and the South African John Martin are involved in a neck and neck race to finish second across the line.*

Changes in syntax sometimes involve changes in spelling or form. For example, the follow-on paragraph for the idiom *break the ice* deals with a related noun:

> ☐ **An ice-breaker** is something that you say or do to break the ice.

Collocations

Explanations give information about collocations as well as about syntax. For example, the explanation for the idiom *pick holes in something*

> If you **pick holes in** something such as an argument or theory, you find weak points in it which disprove it or show that it is wrong.

shows that the idiom is typically used with a human subject and that the 'something' in the idiom headword is typically expressed by a word which means 'argument' or 'theory'.

The explanation for *close to the bone*

> If you say that a remark or piece of writing is **close to the bone** or **near to the bone**, you mean that it makes people uncomfortable, because it deals with things which they prefer not to be discussed.

shows that the idiom is used about something which people say or write.

Examples also give information about collocations. The examples for *neck and neck* show that this idiom is often used in political or sports contexts:

> *The latest opinion polls show both parties running neck and neck.*

> *Leeds are currently neck-and-neck with Manchester United for the Championship.*

They also show that the idiom is typically used after a verb such as 'run' or 'be', as well as showing that the competitors can be mentioned together as the subject of the verb, or one can be mentioned as the subject of the verb and the other after the preposition 'with'.

Pragmatics

The dictionary explanations for idioms show where they have some special pragmatic function. For example, in the explanation of *hit the nail on the head*

> If someone makes a comment and you say that they **have hit the nail on the head**, you mean that they have described a situation or problem exactly.

the formula 'If you say that... you mean that...' shows that this idiom is used to convey an opinion or evaluation, and that it is something speakers or writers use about someone else, rather than about themselves. More precisely in this case, the idiom is used to convey an opinion about the accuracy of another person's comment.

The wording of the explanation

> If you say that something is as **plain as the nose on** your **face**, you are emphasizing that it is very obvious or easy to understand.

shows that this idiom is used to emphasize the opinion that you are conveying. Similarly, the explanation

> If you accuse someone of **feathering** their **nest**, you are accusing them of taking advantage of their position in order to get a lot of money, so that they can lead a comfortable life.

shows that the idiom is used to convey attitude as well as criticism or disapproval.

Finally, a few of the idioms in this dictionary are speech acts: that is, a speaker uses them to express good wishes or thanks, an acceptance or refusal, and so on. For example,

> People say **'break a leg'** to a performer who is about to go on stage as a way of wishing them good luck.

and in a more complicated example:

> You say **'be my guest'** to someone when you are giving them permission to do something, or inviting them to do something. This expression is sometimes used in a sarcastic way. For example, you might use it to invite someone to do something difficult or unpleasant.

Style, register, and usage

The dictionary explanations give information about the likely contexts in which idioms are used, in particular where there are restrictions.

One kind of restriction relates to geographical variety: that is, an idiom is used only or mainly by one group of English speakers. We show this by beginning the explanation with a formula such as 'In British English' or by adding a sentence to the explanation such as 'This expression is used mainly in American English'. More information about idioms in British and American English is given on page vii.

Another kind of restriction relates to genre: some idioms are used only or mainly in a particular kind of writing, such as journalism, novels, or other literary writing. We show this by adding a sentence to the explanation such as 'This expression is used mainly in journalism'.

A third kind of restriction relates to date and currency. Some idioms in the dictionary are described as old-fashioned. This means that they are generally used nowadays by older people rather than young people. However, they may also be found in journalism or literary writing, where the writer is trying to create a particular effect.

The final kind of restriction relates to levels of formality. In most cases this is because an idiom is only used in informal situations, or may cause offence as it is considered rude. These idioms should be used very cautiously. We show this by beginning the explanation with a formula such as 'In informal English', or by adding a sentence to the explanation such as 'This is an informal expression' or 'Many people consider this expression offensive'. In a few cases, we describe an idiom as formal. This means that it is mainly used in formal contexts, such as serious journalism and other kinds of formal writing. Unless an idiom is explicitly labelled as 'formal' or 'literary', learners should generally avoid using them in formal contexts and formal writing.

Spellings

Individual words in idioms may have two or more spellings: for example, they may be spelled differently in British and American English. We give this information at the end of the idiom entry. All the alternative spellings are listed in the index. We also give information about cases where variant spellings or forms result from misunderstandings of one of the words: for example, 'tow' is sometimes used instead of 'toe' in *toe the line*.

Note that when idioms are used adjectivally in front of nouns, they are often spelled with hyphens.

Cross-references

Cross-references are occasionally given at the end of an explanation for idioms. Some cross-references draw attention to other idioms which are very similar in form or which may be confused. For example,

> When children **fly the nest** or **leave the nest**, they leave their parents' home to live on their own. Compare **fly the coop**; see **coop**.

We have given this cross-reference because *fly the coop* seems similar in form to *fly the nest*, although it has a different meaning. *Fly the coop* can be found under the dictionary headword **coop**.

We also give cross-references where idioms are restricted to British (or American) English and have close counterparts in American (or British) English.

> If you say that someone **has a green thumb**, you mean that they are very good at gardening. This expression is used in American English; the British expression is **have green fingers**.

In this case, it is not necessary to check the other entry as the meaning is the same, and so we do not give its dictionary headword.

Frequency bands

The dictionary shows the relative frequencies of individual idioms and individual meanings of idioms, as they are found in The Bank of English. There are three frequency bands which are indicated by black triangles (◄) at the beginning of each entry. The commonest idioms are marked out with three black triangles, the next commonest with two, and the next with one. 30% of idioms do not receive any frequency marker at all: these are expressions which are current in English, but occur less often than once in each 10 million words of corpus text.

◄◄◄ Approximately 750 idioms and their variations in this dictionary have three black triangles: each occurs at least once in every 2 million words of the corpus. It is these idioms which should have priority for teachers and learners, as they are the idioms most likely to be encountered in English. Examples include *the acid test*, *hot air*, and *up in arms*.

◄◄ Approximately 750 idioms and their variations have two black triangles. These idioms are relatively common, but not as common as the idioms with three triangles. Examples include *a blind alley*, *not take no for an answer*, and *up the ante*.

◄ Over 1500 idioms and their variations have one black triangle. These idioms occur between 1 and 3 times in every 10 million words of the corpus. This means that although they are regularly encountered in English, they need not be given such priority as the higher bands. Examples include *a smart alec*, *have an ace in the hole*, and *upset the applecart*.

The COBUILD English Dictionary also gives frequency information for its headwords. In this case, there are five frequency bands, indicated by black diamonds in the Extra Column. Note that these bands do not correspond to those in the COBUILD Dictionary of Idioms. In fact, only a few high-frequency idioms in this dictionary are as common as the items in the COBUILD English Dictionary which are marked with a single black diamond.

A

ace

the ace in your hand

If you have **the ace in** your **hand**, you have something which you can use to gain an advantage when you need it. This expression is used in British English.

You have to convince your opponent that you have the ace in your hand. Especially in politics. Everyone bluffs in politics.

The paper concludes that the President's adoption of special powers to tackle the economic crisis and maintain public order is a last throw. The Guardian says he now needs five aces in one hand to succeed.

come within an ace of something
be within an ace of something

If you say that someone **comes within an ace of** something, you mean that they very nearly succeed in doing it. You can also say that they **are within an ace of** something. These expressions are used mainly in British English.

The defendant was intent on murder and he came within an ace of succeeding.

She had just watched her hero come within an ace of a place in the Wimbledon quarter finals, only to lose his grip on the game.

have an ace in the hole ◄

If you **have an ace in the hole**, you have something which you can use to gain an advantage when you need it. This expression is used in American English.

He doesn't usually risk that much unless he thinks he has an ace in the hole.

Luckily, we had one beautiful ace in the hole. What made our computer different and will continue to make it different from any of our competitors is that we own our own systems software technology. Nobody else does.

play your ace

If someone **plays** their **ace**, they do something clever and unexpected which gives them an advantage over other people.

She went on to say that he was also a very important criminal lawyer who had defended men on heavy charges. And then she played her ace. He also had a number of clients who were involved in the gold business.

With all this meddle, muddle and money wasted, who could be surprised if the union plays the aces?

aces

hold all the aces

If you say that someone **holds all the aces**, you mean that they are in a very strong position because they have more advantages and more power than anyone else.

When I was an adolescent, I thought girls held all the aces. When you call for a date, you are sitting there wide open. She can slam the door in your face.

They hold all the aces and are not going to make changes voluntarily because it wouldn't be in their own interests.

acid

the acid test ◄◄◄

If you refer to something as **the acid test**, you mean that it will show or prove how effective or useful something is. You can also say that something is **an acid test**.

The acid test for the vaccine will be its performance in African countries where malaria is raging more fiercely than in Colombia.

So far, I don't feel too bad but I'm waiting for my first really stressful day when things go wrong. That will be the real acid test.

The case, as a whole, is an acid test of the justice system.

acquaintance

a passing acquaintance: 1
a nodding acquaintance

If you have **a passing acquaintance** or **a nodding acquaintance** with someone, you know them slightly.

And of course, he can now claim – after his first summit as head of government – more than a nodding acquaintance with his fellow leaders.

□ You can also say that someone is **a passing acquaintance** or **a nodding acquaintance**.

After a while a man came in who was evidently a passing acquaintance of the family and stopped at their table to chat.

a passing acquaintance: 2
a nodding acquaintance

If you have **a passing acquaintance** or **a nodding acquaintance** with something, you know a little about it but not very much.

We chatted for a little about poetry, with which he showed considerably more than a nodding acquaintance.

act

a balancing act   ◄◄◄

If you say that someone is performing **a balancing act**, you mean that they are trying to please two or more people or groups or to follow two or more sets of ideals that are in opposition to each other.

Mr Alia is performing a delicate balancing act. He talks of reform, but clings to old certainties.

It's been a difficult balancing act for the Japanese government under pressure both at home and abroad.

Vice-Mayor Simitian called it a classic balancing act between individual rights and community rights.

catch someone in the act   ◄◄

If you **are caught in the act**, someone sees you doing something secret or wrong.

The men were caught in the act of digging up buried explosives.

The local authority has set aside £500 to spend on security cameras, hoping the residents will be able to catch vandals in the act on film.

a class act   ◄◄◄

If you say that someone, for example a sports player or a performer, is **a class act**, you mean that they are very good at what they do.

Koeman is a class act. He's got great control and can hit passes from one side of the pitch to the other with amazing accuracy.

I have been tracking Neil for a year, he is a class act and I've got a lot of respect for his ability.

Hiatt's songs have been recorded by class acts like Bob Dylan, Rosanne Cash, The Everly Brothers and Willie Nelson.

clean up your act   ◄◄◄

If a person or organization **cleans up** their act, they stop behaving badly or irresponsibly, and begin to act in a more socially acceptable way.

The Minister warned the press two years ago that privacy laws would be implemented unless newspapers cleaned up their act.

There is enormous corruption in the game, but the game does not want to clean up its act.

In the last couple of years I've cleaned up my act a bit. I just drink wine and beer mostly, hardly any spirits.

get in on the act
be in on the act   ◄◄◄

If you **get in on the act**, you start doing something which was first done by someone else, usually so that you can have the same success as them, or get some advantage for yourself. You can also say that you **are in on the act**, or use other verbs instead of 'get'.

Its reputation has reached the United States and American investors have been trying to get in on the act.

It is rather like the Greens in Britain in the eighties: everyone wants to get in on the act.

It's not enough to read the books, I want to be in on the act.

Even the lifeguards have been brought in on the act, policing the beach for reckless sunbathers.

get your act together   ◄◄◄

If you say that someone needs to **get their act together**, you mean that they need to take control of themselves and to organize their affairs more effectively so that they can deal successfully with things and can avoid failure.

Basically they're a bunch of bums and they ought to get their act together.

We're going to be 22 points down by Monday, and we've got to get our act together.

The State Opposition is beginning to get its act together after a long period of muddling through.

a hard act to follow   ◄◄◄

If you say that someone is **a hard act to follow**, you mean that they are so impressive or so effective that it will be difficult for anyone else to be as good or as successful. Adjectives such as 'tough' and 'difficult' can be used instead of 'hard'.

'Martina is an honest and forthright person,' she says. 'She's outspoken about her views and, obviously, she's very good at tennis. Even when she retires, I'll think she's number one.' Navratilova, it seems, will be a very hard act to follow.

He had a hard act to follow. His predecessor was a brilliant intellectual who also drew, as Chancellor, on long practical experience as an observer of the economic scene.

There's no doubt Ford's vision and hard work has played a major role in the museum's success. He'll be a tough act to follow.

action

a piece of the action
a slice of the action   ◄◄◄

If someone wants **a piece of the action** or **a slice of the action**, they want to get involved in an activity which seems exciting and likely to be very successful or profitable. 'A slice of the action' is used mainly in British English.

Essentially, the information industry wants a piece of the action, the right to distribute parts of the Library's collection itself.

Within five years, every car manufacturer was at it. The hatchback explosion had begun and everyone wanted a piece of the action.

Because the US airline industry is in such a

poor way, it is falling over itself to get a slice of the action elsewhere.

actions

actions speak louder than words ◄

If you say that **actions speak louder than words**, you mean that people show what they really think and feel by what they do, rather than by what they say. People sometimes use this expression when they want to criticize someone who says one thing but does something else.

Tom, who's a shy chap at heart, firmly believes that actions speak louder than words and has, therefore, been demonstrating his love and passion for Jean in the only way he knows how: through taking her dog to the vet, through lovingly washing her car each week, through decorating each room in her house.

He said the terrorists' actions speak louder than their words. Their terrorist acts continue unabated.

Adam

not know someone from Adam

If you say that you **don't know** someone **from Adam**, you mean that you do not know them at all, and would not recognize them if you saw them.

We'll have one contact, who is simply a voice on the phone to us. I don't know him from Adam.

I knew nobody. I took with me two names and telephone numbers. One was an Anglo-Argentine couple: friends of a friend, who didn't know me from Adam.

ado

much ado about nothing

If you say that people are making **much ado about nothing**, you mean that they are making a lot of fuss about something which is not as important or significant as they think it is. This expression is used mainly in journalism.

French newspapers described the international row as 'Much Ado About Nothing' and 'a banal fishing incident'.

After one year, I dropped out of the course because it was much ado about nothing really. It was all about style, not about content.

□ This expression is often varied.

Lately there's been much ado about the ducks belonging to my poultry-farming neighbour.

□ **Much Ado About Nothing** is the title of a play by Shakespeare.

agenda

a hidden agenda ◄◄◄

If you say that someone has **a hidden agenda**, you suspect that they are secretly trying

to achieve a particular thing while they appear to be doing something else.

The unions fear these tactics are part of a hidden agenda to reduce pay and conditions throughout the company.

The hidden agenda of the Government's prison privatisation policy seems to have been exposed.

It was typical of his forthright determination that while others debated wide issues and hidden agendas he saw a wrong and sought to right it.

air

be left hanging in the air
hang in the air ◄◄◄

If you say that a question or remark **is left hanging in the air**, you mean that people avoid discussing it because they do not want to deal with it or the issues involved.

Asked how many arrest orders she had received so far from her colleague in Spain she walked away and left the question hanging in the air.

The presenter made intelligent points but never challenged anybody, so we were left with a lot of questions hanging in the air.

He looked at neither of them but left his remark hanging in the air.

□ You can also say that a question or remark **hangs in the air**. This is a fairly literary expression.

'We are losing our sense of the eternal. I think it's a loss that has done a great deal of damage to modern art.' His words hung enigmatically in the air.

clear the air ◄◄◄

If you do something to **clear the air**, you deal openly with misunderstandings, problems, or jealousy, and try to get rid of them.

I get angry and frustrated with Hannah's spirited temperament, but I'm a great believer in expressing my feelings to clear the air.

Some groups in our community seem to suffer from discrimination. An independent enquiry could clear the air and sort out the problem.

□ You can also say that **the air clears**, or talk about **air-clearing**.

After that the air cleared and we were fine, I really enjoyed working with him.

An extended air-clearing between George and Martha reveals the sham and drudgery of their lives.

□ Journalists sometimes talk about **clear-the-air** meetings or **clear-the-air** talks.

He is determined to have a clear-the-air meeting with Murray this weekend and snapped yesterday: 'I have to get to the bottom of this mess.'

hot air ◄◄◄

If you describe what someone says or writes as **hot air**, you are criticizing it for being full of false claims and promises.

In a sense, all the rhetoric about heightened co-operation can be seen as just so much hot air. There are still endless disputes.

Parliament is often full of hot air, mock insults and fake hostility.

Now that the value of art, along with everything else, has tumbled, we are better placed to ignore the hot air and evaluate works for what they are.

in the air ◄◄◄

If something such as a change, idea, or feeling is **in the air**, people are aware of it or think it is going to happen even though it is not talked about directly.

I might never have said 'Yes', if it hadn't been for the sense that political change was in the air, and that the arts community should have its ideas prepared.

Great excitement was in the air that week in London and, as the newspapers reported, in Paris, Berlin and St Petersburg as well.

As the band plays, and with romance in the air, Mr. Li recalls how he came to Panzhihua.

into thin air ◄◄

If someone or something vanishes **into thin air**, they disappear completely and nobody knows where they have gone. Compare **out of thin air**.

Her husband snatched their two children and disappeared into thin air for years.

Needless worry can vanish into thin air once you accept the things you cannot change.

out of thin air
from thin air ◄◄

If something appears **out of thin air**, it appears suddenly and unexpectedly. You can also say that it appears **from thin air**. Compare **into thin air**.

A crisis had materialised out of thin air.

Auster spins stories out of thin air.

Thirteen years ago, with her children almost grown up, she found herself having to conjure a career from thin air.

pull something out of the air
pluck something from the air ◄

If you say that a suggestion or an amount is **pulled out of the air** or is **plucked from the air**, you mean that you cannot take it seriously because it has no basis or justification and has only been said casually. Other verbs are sometimes used instead of 'pull' or 'pluck'.

She pulled a figure out of the air, an amount she thought would cover several months' rent on an office.

The figure of 30 per cent is not plucked out of

the air; it is based on the fact that from 1975 to 1990 the earnings of university professors and lecturers dropped by over 25 per cent.

□ This expression is often varied. For example, you can talk about 'thin air' instead of 'air'.

I don't like pulling decisions out of thin air and getting them wrong.

up in the air ◄◄◄

If an important decision or plan is **up in the air**, it has not been decided or settled yet.

At the moment, the fate of the Hungarian people is still up in the air.

This project is very much up in the air.

In terms of a steady line-up and future plans, things are pretty much up in the air for the band.

walk on air
float on air ◄

If you say that you **are walking on air** or **are floating on air**, you mean that you feel very happy or excited because of something nice that has happened to you.

As soon as I know I'm in the team it's like walking on air.

I can't believe that I've won. I'm floating on air.

airs

airs and graces
put on airs and graces ◄

In British English, if you say that someone has **airs and graces**, you disapprove of them for behaving in a way which shows that they think they are more important than other people. You can also say that someone **puts on airs and graces**.

I have never liked him and his daughter is so full of airs and graces.

Ian is such a nice bloke. He has no airs and graces.

In Liverpool I can still be myself, I don't have to put on any airs and graces here.

put on airs ◄

If you say that someone **puts on airs**, you disapprove of them for behaving in a way which shows that they think they are more important than other people.

The occasional Englishman tries to put on airs but we let it pass. It's just comic when they try to pretend they're still the master race.

He put on no airs, but his charisma was enormous.

aisles

roll in the aisles

If you say that people in an audience or group **are rolling in the aisles**, you mean that they are laughing so much at something that they find it hard to stop. Verbs such as 'rock', 'reel', and 'laugh' are sometimes used instead of 'roll'.

It's all good knockabout stuff that has them rolling in the aisles.

On the evidence so far, it's unlikely that the story-lines will have us reeling in the aisles.

alec

a smart alec
a smart aleck   ◄

If you describe someone as **a smart alec** or **a smart aleck**, you dislike the fact that they think they are very clever and they always have an answer for everything.

They've got some smart alec of a lawyer from London to oppose bail, and by God they're not going to get away with it.

You'll end up no more than a smart alec and you're well down that road already.

□ You can use **smart alec** and **smart aleck** before a noun.

I hate smart-aleck kids who talk like dictionaries.

□ The form 'aleck' is the usual spelling in American English. People sometimes spell 'alec' and 'aleck' with capital initials, as names.

alive

alive and kicking   ◄◄◄

If someone or something is **alive and kicking**, they are still active or still exist, even though you thought they had stopped or disappeared a long time ago.

When David Puttnam left Hollywood in 1988, some saw it as the end of his career. But as Patrick found when he visited the set of 'War of the Buttons', Puttnam is alive and kicking and doing what he loves best – film making.

Romance is still alive and kicking for a couple who will be celebrating their 50th wedding anniversary this week.

eat someone alive: 1

If you say that someone or something **will eat** you **alive**, you mean that they seem to be a great threat to you, and may destroy you.

If a president does not combine the short-run and long-run objectives, he's going to be eaten alive by Wall Street.

He was certain Sid would be eaten alive by the hardened criminals at the jail.

eat someone alive: 2

If something such as an illness or a problem **is eating** you **alive**, it is causing you great pain or distress.

The pain ate him alive; the world was nothing but fire and pain.

I know and she knows that the nursing home is the only solution. But it is eating me alive.

eat someone alive: 3

If you **are eaten alive** by insects, you are repeatedly bitten by them.

We've been sleeping on the floor; we have no water. It's been easily 100, 125 degrees. We've been eaten alive by bugs.

'Can we go out?' 'Outside? The mosquitoes will eat us alive.'

skin someone alive: 1

If you say that someone is able to **skin** you **alive**, you mean that they are much stronger or more powerful than you and may exploit you or ruin you.

They are fiercely competitive. If they can skin us alive in business, they will.

Anyone who reads your finance pages will see that shareholders in some major banks have been skinned alive.

skin someone alive: 2

If someone threatens to **skin** you **alive**, they are threatening to punish you severely.

Who let the bloody dog out? You catch that animal, Ernie, or you'll get skinned alive.

all

that's all she wrote

You can say **'that's all she wrote'** when there is no more to say or when something is finished. This expression is used in American English.

That was all she wrote. He got hurt, and he didn't play much anymore.

If I read about any of this, it's all she wrote for you here. I don't have to tell you that.

alley

a blind alley   ◄◄

If you refer to a way of working or thinking as **a blind alley**, you mean that it is useless or is not leading to anything worthwhile.

Sooner or later they will have to realize that this is a blind alley and that they need to re-think their own strategies.

Did she regard teaching as a blind alley?

right up your alley   ◄

If you say that something is **right up** your **alley**, you mean that it is the kind of thing you like or know about. **Right up** your **street** means the same.

This should be right up my alley but, despite the film's undoubted virtues, it has an air of 'Look at me, aren't I good' that grated.

I thought this little problem would be right up your alley.

□ You can also say that something is **right down** your **alley**.

I'll need whatever information you can turn up within the week. I have other people looking into this from other angles. But this case seems right down your alley.

all-singing

all-singing, all-dancing ◄

If you describe something new as **all-singing, all-dancing,** you mean that it is very modern and advanced, with a lot of additional facilities. This expression is used more commonly in British English than American.

His rival, the Savoy, has beaten him to the development of an all-singing, all-dancing computer system which is the latest in hotel marketing.

As long as you don't expect the latest all-singing, all-dancing Japanese marvel, the camera represents an excellent buy – and one that I can recommend.

altar

sacrificed on the altar of something ◄

You say that someone or something **is being sacrificed on the altar of** a particular ideology or activity when they suffer unfairly and are harmed because of it.

The European Community remains adamant that the interests of its twelve million farmers can't be sacrificed on the altar of free trade.

Let us hope and strive to ensure that Palo Alto's quality education will not be sacrificed on the altar of ill-conceived social experimentation.

Two leading public servants had been sacrificed on the altar of ministerial incompetence.

☐ You can also say that someone or something is **a sacrifice on the altar of** a particular thing.

The men were, in a word, expendable sacrifices on the altar of the Cold War.

American

American as apple pie

If you say that something or someone is as **American as apple pie,** you mean that they are typical of American culture or an American way of life.

Zurmo's family has been in the gun business for 60 years. To him, guns are as American as apple pie.

British Petroleum always abbreviates its name to BP and passes itself off as no less American than Mobil, Exxon and apple pie.

angel

a fallen angel ◄

If you refer to someone as **a fallen angel,** you mean that although they were once virtuous or successful, they are now wicked or unsuccessful.

Without an away League win all season,

Leeds United quickly became the fallen angels of the Premier League.

angels

on the side of the angels ◄

If you say that someone is **on the side of the angels,** you mean that they are doing what you think is morally right.

In addition to being for gun control, the President's on the side of the angels when it comes to racial tolerance, the environment and Indian rights.

The idea perpetrated by Western leaders that we are on the side of the angels seems to me a dangerous fantasy.

answer

not take no for an answer ◄◄

If someone **won't take no for an answer,** they go on trying to make you agree to something, even though you have already refused.

Five reporters who wouldn't take no for an answer entered U.S. quarters without authorization.

Gerry, whose persistence has been known to wear down the resistance of many executives, refused to take no for an answer.

She told me that she had, of course, refused, but that he wouldn't seem to take no for an answer. He kept pressing her.

ante

up the ante: 1
raise the ante ◄◄

In a dispute or contest, if you **up the ante** or **raise the ante,** you increase the demands that you are making or the risks that you are taking, which means that your eventual losses or gains will be greater.

He relished NATO's political give and take, and fought over every word, sometimes upping the ante so as to get a better compromise.

These judges have raised the ante by challenging the authority of Chief Justice Rehnquist, whose position makes him the top judicial spokesman on changes in federal court procedures.

Whenever they reached their goal, they upped the ante, setting increasingly complex challenges for themselves.

up the ante: 2
raise the ante

If you are gambling or investing money in something and you **up the ante** or **raise the ante,** you increase the value of the stake or investment you are offering.

Its network television division upped the ante by paying an estimated $2 million a year for an overall deal.

My defeat came when I was unable to persuade my backer to raise the ante.

ape

go ape
go ape crazy
go apeshit   ◄

If someone **goes ape** or **goes ape crazy**, they start to behave in an uncontrolled or irrational way, for example because they are very excited or very angry about something. These are informal expressions.

The crowd went ape.

Is he never tempted to break away, to go ape for a period?

You don't get the chance to go ape crazy.

□ You can also say that someone **goes apeshit**. This is a very informal expression, which many people find offensive.

If we mentioned heroin she would literally go apeshit.

appetite

whet someone's appetite   ◄◄◄

If something **whets** your **appetite** for a particular thing, it increases your desire for that thing or other similar things. You can also say that something **whets the appetite**.

Winning the World Championship should have whetted his appetite for more success.

Her appetite already whetted by the book, she took a trip to England.

The series is entertaining, and it certainly whets the appetite.

□ Some people use the verb 'wet' instead of 'whet' in this expression, but it is generally considered incorrect.

apple

the apple of your eye   ◄

If you say that someone is **the apple of your eye**, you mean that you are very fond of them.

I was the apple of my father's eye.

Penny's only son was the apple of her eye.

a bad apple
a rotten apple
a bad apple spoils the barrel   ◄◄

If you refer to someone as **a bad apple** or as **a rotten apple**, you mean that they are very dishonest, immoral, or unpleasant, and that they have a bad influence on the people around them.

It's an opportunity for them to make clear that they are not going to tolerate a bad apple in the United States Senate.

In any profession, there's always the rotten apple, isn't there.

□ People talk about **a bad apple spoiling the**

barrel or **a rotten apple spoiling the barrel** when they are talking particularly about the bad influence which the person has. This expression is very variable.

Let's be positive, not negative. One bad apple doesn't spoil the barrel.

He says there are some rotten apples in our security barrel.

applecart

upset the applecart
overturn the applecart   ◄

If someone or something **upsets the applecart** or **overturns the applecart**, they do something which causes trouble or which spoils a satisfactory situation.

I would not tolerate someone upsetting the applecart and, if necessary, they would have to be removed from the decision-making process.

Their acquisition of nuclear arms could upset the whole Asian applecart.

She still has the power to overturn the applecart by the sheer force of her personality and vocabulary.

apple-pie

in apple-pie order

If someone says that everything is **in apple-pie order**, they mean that everything in a place is very neat, tidy, and well-organized. This is a fairly old-fashioned expression.

Apart from the scaffolding and plastic sheeting that still remained, they found everything in apple-pie order.

On the upper deck everything was very much in apple pie order.

apples

apples and oranges   ◄

If you say that two things are **apples and oranges** or that comparing them is like comparing **apples with oranges**, you are pointing out that these things are completely different in every respect. These expressions are used mainly in American English.

I think you're talking apples and oranges, and I don't think you can really look at it as an equity issue.

To compare one with the other is to make the mistake we were all warned about in third grade, not to compare apples with oranges.

apron

apron strings: 1

If you say that one person is tied to another's **apron strings**, you are criticizing the first person for remaining dependent at an age when they should be independent. If someone cuts the **apron strings**, they become independent from the other person.

When we think about times we have felt close to our mothers, hasn't some of that enhanced our growth rather than tying us tighter to their apron strings?

There is no doubting that he and his mother will remain as close as ever, even if the apron strings have lengthened.

At 21, I was still living the life I'd been living when I was 15. I just had to get away from that, to cut those apron strings.

apron strings: 2

If you say that a country or institution is tied to another's **apron strings**, you mean that the first country or institution is controlled by the second when you think it should be independent. If they cut the **apron strings**, they become independent from the other country or institution.

Today few big pension funds remain tied by company apron-strings.

The Prime Minister has the rough outline of a blueprint for Australia as an independent nation, free of British apron-strings.

area

a grey area ◀◀◀

If you refer to something as **a grey area**, you mean that it is unclear, or that it does not fall into a specific category of things, so that nobody knows how to deal with it properly.

The court action to decide ownership of Moon Shadow has highlighted the many grey areas in the law affecting stolen animals.

Tabloid papers in England have reached a stage where sportsmen must either be painted as heroes or villains. There is no grey area in between.

There is always going to be a gray area. No commander who has ever fought a battle was completely sure of victory on the eve of that battle.

□ 'Grey' is usually spelled 'gray' in American English.

ark

out of the ark
go out with the ark

If you say that something is **out of the ark**, you are complaining in a light-hearted way that it is very old-fashioned and outdated. This expression is used in British English.

Its steering was simply dreadful and its cramped-up short-arm driving position was straight out of the ark.

Your radio series must have come out of the ark, where did you find all those awful old jokes?

□ You can say that something **went out with the ark** when you want to say that it is completely outdated.

You know tyres are made from oil, they're not made from rubber any more; that went out with the ark.

arm

at arm's length: 1 ◀◀◀

If you keep someone **at arm's length**, you avoid being friendly with them or getting emotionally involved with them.

Brian felt more guilt than grief. He'd tried to get close, but his father had kept him at arm's length.

After years of keeping foreign companies at arm's length, France is pulling them into its embrace.

This time he was not entertaining us or holding us at arm's length, but unreservedly disclosing himself.

at arm's length: 2 ◀

You can say that one person or organization is **at arm's length** from another when they are not closely connected, for example because it would be improper for them to influence one another.

The prison service is moving towards becoming a self-regulating agency at arm's length from government.

Relations between the bank and the committee will be at arm's length until the report is delivered in July.

chance your arm ◀

If you **chance** your **arm**, you do something risky or daring in order to get something you want. This expression is used in British English.

Sport is about going out and giving it your best shot, chancing your arm for glory. What is there to be frightened about?

Instead of going on the dole I chanced my arm on a business.

cost an arm and a leg ◀

If you say that something **costs an arm and a leg**, you are emphasizing that it costs a lot of money. Verbs such as 'pay', 'spend', and 'charge' are sometimes used instead of 'cost'.

It cost us an arm and a leg to get here. But it has been worth every penny and more.

Generally, their experience of restaurants confirmed all the worst tourist horror stories: indifferent pub lunches of chicken and chips or equally unappetising pasta restaurants charging an arm and a leg.

give your right arm

If you say that you would **give** your **right arm** for something or to do something, you are emphasizing that you want it a lot, and you would do almost anything to get it.

I have had an extraordinarily lucky career, playing a good many of the parts that any self-respecting actress would like to play. There are not many parts I would give my right arm for.

I can do nothing but think about my ex-husband. I would give my right arm to be able to start again.

put the arm on someone

If you **put the arm on** someone, you try to force them to do what you want. This expression is used in American English.

You got Cotter to put the arm on Lillian. You guys cut a deal so that Lillian gives up something.

Women like you are not only writing checks, but you're putting the arm on other people to give as well.

twist someone's arm ◄

·If you say that someone **is twisting** your **arm** to make you do something, you mean that they are trying hard to persuade you to do it.

I had to twist their arm to get them to start working with me, but once they did, it went well from there.

I didn't twist your arm to make you come. You wanted to because you sensed a story.

□ You can also talk about **arm-twisting**.

He borrowed 70 per cent of the dividend-money from his banks, after some arm-twisting.

arms

up in arms ◄◄◄

If someone is **up in arms** about something, they are very angry about it and are protesting strongly.

More than one million shopkeepers are up in arms against the new minimum tax. They are threatening a day's closure in protest.

This is a very delicate situation. Frank feels he has been publicly humiliated, and his sponsors are up in arms.

Politicians from both sides of the House were up in arms at her strongest ever criticism of EU attempts to unite Europe.

with open arms: 1 ◄◄

If you greet or welcome someone **with open arms**, you show that you are very pleased to see them or meet them.

We got out of the trucks to greet them with open arms. We had gifts ready, we were high on the idea of the meeting.

People in Sidon welcomed them with open arms and rice and flowers.

They were very, very affectionate. There were open arms, lots of smiles, big kisses. It was

definitely the kind of greeting you save for someone special.

with open arms: 2 ◄◄

If you welcome an event or new development **with open arms**, you are very pleased that it has happened.

Watchdog organizations welcomed today's guidelines with open arms, some admitting that they had exceeded expectations considerably.

The store ranks as Palo Alto's fourth largest sales tax generator. Certainly many communities would welcome it with open arms.

The Council did the right thing in getting him to carry out the study. They have accepted it with open arms and will, they say, progress with it.

arrow

a straight arrow ◄

If you describe someone as **a straight arrow**, you mean that they are very conventional, honest, and moral. This expression is used mainly in American English.

I was very much a product of my environment. I was very traditional, a real straight arrow in lots of ways.

Several friends describe Mr. Menendez as 'a straight arrow' who rarely drank and was close to his family.

□ You can use **straight arrow** before a noun.

It was impossible to imagine such a well-scrubbed, straight-arrow group of young people rioting over anything – except perhaps the number of chocolate chips in the dining hall cookies.

arse

lick someone's arse ◄

If you say that one person **licks** another's **arse**, you are critical of the first person because they will do anything at all to please the second person, often because the second person is powerful or influential and the first person wants something from them. This is a very informal expression, which is used in British English. Many people find it offensive.

I don't feel bad about slagging U2 off since everybody else is licking Bono's arse.

□ You can call someone who does this **an arselicker**. You can refer to the activity of doing this as **arselicking**.

Everett, you're not the arse-licker everybody thinks you are.

Meanwhile, we were down on our hands and knees arselicking all day, because if you upset somebody you had nowhere else to go.

art

have something down to a fine art ◄

If you **have got** an activity **down to a fine art**, you know the best way of doing it because you have practised it a lot and have tried many different methods.

They've got fruit retailing down to a fine art. You can be sure that your pears will ripen in a day.

Shopping for food is the biggest problem, though she has it down to a fine art. 'I go to the cheapest shops and buy only frozen or canned goods. I cannot remember the last time I bought the kids fresh fruit or vegetables.'

ask

a big ask

If you say that something which you have been asked to do is **a big ask**, you mean that you cannot be expected to do it easily or willingly, because it is very difficult or involves making a sacrifice. This expression is used mainly in Australian English.

It's a pretty big ask to run faster in the second half of the race.

It was a big ask for six state premiers to surrender many of their rights and responsibilities to help the central government.

ass

chew your ass

If someone **chews** your **ass**, they tell you angrily that your behaviour has upset or annoyed them. This is a very informal expression, which is used in American English. Many people find it offensive.

Well, come on in then, don't stand there in the hall while the old man chews my ass.

awakening

a rude awakening ◄◄

If you have had **a rude awakening**, you have been forced to realize the unpleasant truth about something.

Such details as have emerged about the new economic package suggest that Russian citizens are indeed in for a rude awakening. Whatever other problems they faced in the past, they have become used to certain essential goods being heavily subsidised. Now all this will change.

Johnson told reporters at the time that some of these inventions were so valuable, he was confident he could make a quick profit. But, instead of quick profits, Johnson got a rude awakening.

axe

an axe hanging over something ◄

If you say that there is **an axe hanging over** something, you mean that it is likely to be destroyed soon. If you say that there is **an axe hanging over** someone, you mean that they are likely to lose their job soon.

The axe was hanging over 600 jobs at oil giant BP last night.

I wouldn't say there's an axe hanging over him but he's only got another season to put everything right.

□ 'Axe' is spelled 'ax' in American English.

get the axe: 1
be given the axe

If someone **gets the axe** or **is given the axe**, they lose their job.

During the 1981 recession, most layoffs hurt factory or construction workers. But this time, business managers, executives and technical staff are getting the axe.

It's being reported in Chicago that Bears' coach Mike Ditka will get the axe today.

get the axe: 2
be given the axe

If something such as a project or part of a business **gets the axe** or **is given the axe**, it is cancelled or ended suddenly.

There will be cuts of $170 billion in defense, and almost $120 billion in domestic spending. Any idea what specific programs will get the ax?

A few days previously, the Westoe Colliery, the last pit in the region, was given the axe.

□ 'Axe' is spelled 'ax' in American English.

have an axe to grind ◄◄◄

If you say that someone **has an axe to grind**, you mean that they have particular attitudes and prejudices about something, often because they think they have been treated badly or because they want to get a personal advantage.

Lord Gifford believed cases should be referred by an independent agency which, as he put it, doesn't have an axe to grind. 'It saddens me,' he said, 'that courts are being brought into such a political conflict.'

He didn't have a critical ax to grind. He was very open-minded about other people's work.

There has to be some forum where ministers can speak their mind frankly and honestly without fear of being reported in the diary of some political rival with an axe to grind.

□ Sometimes people claim that they **have no axe to grind** when they are denying that their strong opinions about something are based on personal reasons.

The unions insist they have no axe to grind, because they will represent operators wherever they work.

□ 'Axe' is spelled 'ax' in American English.

B

babe

a babe in arms

You can describe someone as **a babe in arms** to emphasize that they are very young. This expression is used more commonly in British English than American.

Cycling hero Chris Boardman was on a bike almost before he could walk. His mother Carol said last night: 'All the family have always cycled and Chris has been going to races since he was a babe in arms.'

Battered children who have never known anything other than violence begin their life sentence as a babe in arms.

babes

babes in the wood

You refer to people as **babes in the wood** or **babes in the woods** when they are naive, innocent, and inexperienced, and they are involved in a complex situation where they are likely to be exploited or have problems.

They come from a country that is monolingual and monocultural and has been for thousands of years. They're like babes in the woods when it comes to trying to deal with this multi-ethnic society that we all just take for granted.

By this time I wasn't such a babe in the woods, and one thing I insisted on was that they commit themselves contractually to a ten-week promotional tour.

baby

leave someone holding the baby ◄

If you **are left holding the baby**, you are made responsible for a problem that nobody else wants to deal with. This expression is used in British English. **Leave** someone **holding the bag** means the same.

If anything goes wrong on this, Agnes, it's you and I who'll be left holding the baby, not our clever friend.

More often than he liked, Taylor was left holding the baby.

throw the baby out with the bath water ◄

If you warn someone not to **throw the baby out with the bath water**, you are warning them not to reject something completely just because parts of it are bad, as you think that other parts of it are good.

Even if we don't necessarily like that, we're not going to throw the baby out with the bath water.

By excluding the only member of the squad with any real experience of Olympic tensions and strains, the selection committee have thrown the baby out with the bath water.

back

be glad to see the back of someone ◄◄

If you say that you **are glad to see the back of** someone or something, you mean that you are glad that they have gone because you do not like them. Adjectives such as 'pleased' or 'happy' are sometimes used instead of 'glad'. This expression is used more commonly in British English than American.

Nick said last night that Court was a 'vile man'. He added: 'We are glad to see the back of him.'

Most Tory backbenchers will be as pleased to see the back of him as will the people whose jobs and businesses his policies have destroyed.

□ You can also say that you **want to see the back of** someone when you want them to go away.

Two out of three voters want to see the back of the Chancellor and the President of the Board of Trade.

behind your back ◄◄

If someone says something about you **behind** your **back**, they say unkind and unpleasant things about you to other people. If someone does something **behind** your **back**, they do it secretly in order to harm you. Compare **go behind** someone's **back**.

I knew behind his back his friends were saying, 'How can he possibly put up with that awful woman?'

So we put up with him when he tried to convert us to his right-wing beliefs. And, I'm ashamed to say, we laughed at him behind his back.

He had discovered that it was safer to have the Press on his side than to have correspondents sneaking around behind his back asking embarrassing questions.

break the back of something: 1 ◄

If you **break the back of** a task, you deal with the most difficult parts of it or the main part of it.

The new government hopes to have broken the back of the economic crisis by the middle of this year. If it fails in this task, then the political consequences could be disastrous.

break the back of something: 2

To **break the back of** something means to do something which will weaken it and lead to its eventual destruction.

Arms cuts should not be implemented too quickly or they'll break the back of his country's armed forces.

The government made a big effort late last year to break the back of the black market.

break your back

If you say that you **are breaking** your **back** to do something, you are emphasizing that you are working extremely hard to try to do it.

When you're breaking your back to make an enterprise work, it's going to cut into your time with family.

He will try his best to rescue the treaty when Britain takes over the EU presidency next month, but he will not break his back.

get off someone's back ◄

If you tell someone to **get off** your **back**, you are telling them angrily to stop criticizing you and leave you alone. This is an informal expression. Compare **on** someone's **back**.

He kept on at me to such an extent that occasionally I wished he would get off my back.

For once in their money-grabbing little lives, why don't they get off our backs?

□ If you **get** someone **off** your **back**, you make them stop criticizing you.

I vowed then that I would get them off my back and out of my life if it was the last thing I did.

get someone's back up
put someone's back up ◄

If you say that someone or something **gets** your **back up**, you mean that they annoy you. In British English, you can also say that someone or something **puts** your **back up**.

What does get my back up is a girlfriend who gets too jealous if someone else finds me attractive.

I thought before I spoke again. The wrong question was going to get her back up.

The appointment took the whole office by surprise and at first seemed to put people's backs up.

get your own back ◄◄◄

If someone **gets** their **own back** on you, they take revenge on you because of something that you have done to them. This expression is used in British English.

All you're interested in is in getting your own back on Terence.

A disgruntled worker got his own back after rowing with his boss by locking the whole firm out of the computer system.

I was bullied at school and I want to get my own back.

go behind someone's back ◄

If you say that someone **goes behind** your **back**, you mean that they do something secretly or without getting your permission, often in order to deliberately upset you. Compare **behind** your **back**.

Leonard, you haven't been completely open with me. You think I wouldn't know when you go behind my back?

They go behind our backs, they withhold information, they talk down to us like idiots.

have your back to the wall ◄◄◄

If you say that someone **has** their **back to the wall** or **has** their **back against the wall**, you mean that they have very serious problems or are in a very difficult situation, which will be hard to deal with.

Battered by the economic situation and unable to provide any long-term answer to the terrorism, the fledgling Labour government had its back to the wall.

But why is it that when you have your back to the wall, you only seem capable of hearing advice when it's couched in aggressive terms?

I think there will be demonstrations. I think that the regime really has its back against the wall and that we are seeing the beginnings of a revolution.

□ You can also say **when** your **back is to the wall** or **with** your **back to the wall**.

Although traditionally held to be less bloodthirsty than men, when their backs are against the wall women fight as hard as anyone.

With my back against the wall, I agreed to a hard bargain.

off the back of a lorry ◄

If someone says that something has fallen **off the back of a lorry**, or that they got something **off the back of a lorry**, they mean that they have bought something that was stolen. This expression is used in British English.

We bought some really excellent wine from a woman who clearly caught the bottles as they fell off the back of a lorry.

The only evidence of any criminal tendencies is that Pete once bought the boys a bicycle cheap off the back of a lorry.

on someone's back ◄

If you say that someone is **on** your **back**, you are complaining that they are annoying you by criticizing you and putting a lot of pressure on you. Compare **get off** someone's **back**.

The crowd aren't forgiving, they can be a bit fickle, and as soon as you make a mistake they are on your back.

You can't go to a guy and talk about your

deep feelings because if everyone else knows you're weak, they're on your back straight away.

on the back of an envelope

If you say that a plan or idea was written **on the back of an envelope**, you are emphasizing that it is still unfinished and that it needs much more work and thought before it is ready.

He has made decisions sketched out on the back of an envelope without proper consultation again.

But the screenplay sounds as if it has been written on the back of an envelope and the whole thing has an improvised air about it.

□ A **back-of-an-envelope** calculation or account is a rough estimate rather than an accurate figure.

According to a back-of-an-envelope calculation by Mr Kirshner, a solar square of mirrors, 30 miles long by 30 miles wide, would provide enough energy to supply the whole state.

on the back of a postage stamp

If you say that all that someone knows about something could be written **on the back of a postage stamp**, you are emphasizing that they know very little about it.

What she knew about children would have fitted on the back of a postage stamp.

put your back into something

If you **put** your **back into** something, you work very hard to do it successfully.

Eighty miles across the mountains could be done in six days walking, if she put her back into it.

The garden is stunning and a marvellous example of what can be achieved when people are prepared to commit themselves and put their backs into something.

stab someone in the back
a stab in the back ◄◄◄

If you say that someone that you trusted **has stabbed** you **in the back**, you mean that they have done something which hurts and betrays you.

She seemed to be incredibly disloyal. She would be your friend to your face, and then stab you in the back.

I'm really surrounded by a very hypocritical bunch of people, who want to kiss me every time they see me and then they stab me in the back.

She felt betrayed, as though her daughter had stabbed her in the back, deliberately chosen the worst way to hurt her.

□ A **stab in the back** is an action which hurts and betrays someone.

Mandela has warned that lifting sanctions against South Africa would be a stab in the back for the liberation struggle.

□ **Back-stabbing** is talk or gossip which is intended to harm someone. You can also talk about **back-stabbing** remarks.

People begin to avoid one another, take sides, be drawn into gossip and back-stabbing.

turn your back on someone: 1 ◄◄◄

If you say that someone **has turned** their **back on** you, you mean that they have ignored you and refused to help you.

We appeal to this conference – do not turn your back on the poor. Do not turn your back on the unemployed.

We can't just turn our back on them because otherwise we join a whole list of other organizations who say they're there to protect children, but really are not.

When I first got sick, people really turned their backs on me.

turn your back on something: 2 ◄◄◄

If you **turn** your **back on** something, you stop thinking about it and paying attention to it, or you reject it. Compare **when** your **back is turned**.

One good thing about moving jobs – you can turn your back on your mistakes.

He intends to turn his back on his Communist past and form a completely new party with which to challenge for power.

The annual review of the marriage guidance organisation Relate has found that thousands of young people are turning their backs on marriage.

when your back is turned ◄

If something happens **when** your **back is turned**, it happens when you are away or involved with something else. You can also say that it happens as **soon as** you **turn** your **back**. Compare **turn** your **back on** something.

Sometimes, a child is actually frightened to go to school – not because of what goes on there, but because of what she fears might happen at home when her back is turned.

They are quite happy to question you, though, and are not averse to having a look through your personal items when your back is turned.

you scratch my back and I'll scratch yours ◄

People say '**you scratch my back and I'll scratch yours**' to mean that one person helps another on condition that the second person helps them in return. People also say '**I'll scratch your back if you'll scratch mine**'.

The chemist knew his business and, willing to play the game of 'you scratch my back and I'll scratch yours', charged Eve for only the ingredients he used.

For men, commitments are based on common interest: I'll scratch your back if you'll scratch mine.

□ This expression is very variable. For example, you can talk about people **scratching** each other's **backs**, or say that something happens on an **I'll scratch your back** basis.

When French and German ministers scratch each other's backs, their British counterpart often looks awkward.

But with out-of-reach nanny rates and playcentre space scarce, she makes do with friends, neighbours and 'I'll scratch your back' support.

□ **Back-scratching** is helping someone so that they will help you in return.

And they know that a bit of helpful back-scratching when the state needs their services can be amply repaid one day.

backs

live off the backs of someone

If you say that one group of people **is living off the backs of** another group, you are criticizing the first group because it is using the money and resources of the second group to survive, and it gives nothing in return.

For too long the fat and decadent rich have lived off the backs of the working-class.

It is a parasitic organisation. It has lived off the backs of the people. Its members have stolen and extorted money to sustain themselves and their activities.

backwards

bend over backwards
bend over backward ◄◄

If you **bend over backwards** or **bend over backward** to do something, you try very hard to do it and to help or please someone, even if it causes you trouble or difficulties. 'Lean' is sometimes used instead of 'bend'.

UN officials have so far found no evidence to support the rebels' claims, but they are bending over backwards to accommodate their concerns in order to get the peace process moving again.

We are bending over backwards to ensure that the safeguards are kept in place.

But I tell you, Mr. Dorkins, you've done your duty. You've leaned over backward. She has nothing to complain about.

know something backwards
know something backwards and forwards ◄

If you say that someone **knows** something **backwards**, you are emphasizing that they know it very well. This form of the expression is used mainly in British English; in American English, the usual form is **know** something **backwards and forwards**.

I thoroughly enjoy lecturing and know my subject backwards.

He will be very much in demand. He knows the business backwards.

Everybody had a role and, probably out of desperation, I made Joe an assistant prosecuting attorney. Joe came alive, got to know the play backwards and forwards.

bacon

save someone's bacon ◄

If someone or something **saves** your **bacon**, they get you out of a dangerous or difficult situation. This expression is used mainly in British English.

Your mother once saved my bacon, did you know that. She lent me money when I needed it.

Insect spray really saves my bacon because I react quite badly to mosquito bites.

bag

be someone's bag ◄

If you say that something **is** not your **bag**, you mean that you are not very interested in it or are not very good at it.

'Being an umpire is not my bag,' Mr. Anders says. 'I'd rather be a player.'

The Crowes ain't my bag, but they gain my respect. They love what they do.

If sentimental, feel-good, life-affirming movies are your bag, this is for you.

in the bag ◄◄

If you say that something is **in the bag**, you mean that you feel certain that you will get it or achieve it.

Between you and me, laddie, it's in the bag. Unofficially, the job's yours.

After the 1-1 draw with Internazionale, the 1993 championship is as good as in the bag for Milan.

leave someone holding the bag ◄

If you **are left holding the bag**, you are made responsible for a problem that nobody else wants to deal with. This expression is used more commonly in American English than British. **Leave** someone **holding the baby** means the same.

If a project goes bust, investors are left holding the bag.

And then he made another deal, and they were left holding the bag.

He was worried about leaving Mom to hold the bag financially.

a mixed bag ◄◄◄

If you describe something as **a mixed bag**, you mean that it contains things that are of very different kinds or qualities.

Gateway has a mixed bag of items on special offer. Dessert plums are down to 50p per lb.

Mild garlic sausage drops to just £1.39 and several Somerfield dairy products are down.

The papers carry a mixed bag of stories on their front pages.

The anthology of short stories by Scottish writers is a rather mixed bag. This unevenness of quality may be an inevitable consequence of selecting writers on the grounds of nationality, rather than simply on literary merit.

someone's bag of tricks ◄

If you refer to someone's **bag of tricks**, you mean that they have a set of special techniques or methods to use in their work.

'Unpretentious Delights' by Johnny Griffin is perfectly titled. Recorded live in Warsaw in 1978, it is a delightful offering with Griffin going through his bag of tricks to great effect.

Audiences seemed disconcerted by Welles' unconventional camera techniques, the jarring cuts between scenes, the shock effects that Welles pulled out of his bag of tricks.

bags

pack your bags ◄◄

If someone **packs** their **bags**, they suddenly leave where they live or work, or they withdraw from an agreement usually because of a disagreement.

But it was a stormy romance. Jesse's wayward attitude prompted Gwyneth to pack her bags on several occasions.

If things go wrong and our conditions are not met, we will simply pack our bags and leave.

The firm action taken by the British authorities in unceremoniously ordering three British competitors in the Barcelona Olympics to pack their bags is a welcome signal that cheating, at least by British sportsmen and sportswomen, will not be tolerated.

bait

fish or cut bait

You can tell someone to **fish or cut bait** when you want them to stop wasting time and make a decision to do something. This expression is used in American English.

Morale and stamina were said to be low after seven weeks of stalemate – the time had come to fish or cut bait.

take the bait
rise to the bait ◄

If you **take the bait** or **rise to the bait**, you react to something that someone has said or done in exactly the way that they wanted you to react.

When the talk turned to horses, she told him how she had fallen off as a child and lost her nerve. Hewitt immediately took the bait, offering to teach her to ride.

It's important not to rise to the bait and get cross.

baker

a baker's dozen

If you have **a baker's dozen** of things, you have thirteen of them. This is an old-fashioned expression.

It's the idea of Alan Else, series co-ordinator, who has picked out a baker's dozen of top events between April and September.

balance

in the balance ◄◄◄

If you say that a situation is **in the balance** or hangs or remains **in the balance**, you mean that it is not clear what is going to happen.

I heard that one of the judges had died unexpectedly and that the choice of his successor was in the balance, with Holroyd and a couple of others as the most likely candidates.

Mankind today faces unprecedented problems and the future will hang in the balance if joint solutions are not found.

The survival of Municipal Mutual Insurance, Britain's leading insurer of local authorities, remained in the balance, as hopes for a European rescue of the group turned away from Paris towards Belgium and Germany.

throw off balance ◄◄◄

If you **are thrown off balance** by something, you are confused or surprised by it. Verbs such as 'knock' and 'catch' are sometimes used instead of 'throw'.

She was trying to behave as if his visit hadn't thrown her off-balance.

His directness seemed designed to throw Michael off balance.

Mullins knocked me off balance with his abrupt change of subject.

ball

a ball and chain ◄

If you describe someone or something as a **ball and chain**, you mean that they restrict your freedom to do what you want.

If you listen to members of the same sex talking to each other, you're likely to hear a man describe his wife as a ball and chain.

Our national debt is an economic ball and chain dragging us down, keeping longer term interest rates high.

the ball is in your court ◄◄

If you tell someone that **the ball is in** their **court**, you are pointing out that it is their responsibility to decide what to do next in a particular situation.

The ball's now in your court. You have to de-

cide what you're going to do to get the most from your money, given the level of risk you feel you can tolerate.

The ball is now in his court. I, and indeed others, have told him quite clearly what we think. He has to decide.

a crystal ball ◄◄◄

If you say that someone is looking into **a crystal ball**, you mean that they are trying to predict the future.

So why look in the crystal ball for next year, when we can look at the record of what has happened.

What you really need to help you select your new car is a crystal ball to tell you how much it will be worth two, three or four years down the road.

Can I ask you now to do a bit of crystal ball gazing? How high do you think the price of oil could go?

□ A **crystal ball** is a glass ball used by some traditional fortune-tellers to predict the future.

drop the ball

If you say that someone **has dropped the ball**, you are criticizing them for something foolish or incompetent that they have done. This expression is used mainly in American English.

Lafferty, instead of really being helpful, had tried to pass off the new arrival's sponsorship duties to his staff, and the staff dropped the ball.

There are people who'd like to see me fall, I know that. But I'm not afraid. I won't drop the ball.

have a ball ◄◄◄

If you **have a ball**, you enjoy yourself and have a really good time.

The boys were sitting happily on the ground. The burner was blazing, the kettle was on and, going by the gales of laughter, they were having a ball.

Why not go out and see if there's some place we can dance? Let's go and have a ball.

I've enjoyed every minute of politics. I've had a ball.

a new ball game
a different ball game ◄

If you describe a situation as **a new ball game** or **a different ball game**, you mean that it has changed so much that people will have to change the way they deal with it or consider it.

'What happens if you find out, as seems probable, that we have a case of sabotage on our hands?' 'Then it's a new ball game, Bruce. We'll have to trace the crime itself back to its authors.'

Politically, we're not yet there and we don't

know the timetable of the crisis. But in the end of it, it will be a whole new ball game.

If military force were to be used, then that could be a completely different ball game.

on the ball

If you describe someone as **on the ball**, you mean that they are alert and deal with things in an intelligent way.

Some clubs struggle in their attempts to raise money. A few are on the ball and make a thoroughly professional job of it.

You can't bumble along in this business. You have to be on the ball.

play ball ◄◄◄

If you agree to **play ball** with someone, you agree to do what they have asked you to do, or you agree to work with them in order to achieve something that you both want. Compare **play hardball**; see **hardball**.

The Association of British Insurers has threatened to withdraw its support if the banks and building societies refuse to play ball.

The indirect message to Japan's foreign minister appeared to be that, if Japan would not play ball with Russia on economic co-operation, Russia would look for friends elsewhere.

'Boys, I want to say that I appreciate the way you've played ball with me,' she declared, 'and in return you can be sure that I aim to play ball right back.'

set the ball rolling
start the ball rolling ◄◄◄

If you **set the ball rolling** or **start the ball rolling**, you start an activity or you do something which other people will join in with later. You can also **get the ball rolling** and **keep the ball rolling**.

A fierce price war is now underway with all the big supermarket rivals cutting prices. Sainsbury set the ball rolling last week with 30 per cent discounts on a wide range of brands.

Lord Mackay started the ball rolling on judicial openness when he abolished rules barring judges from speaking in public.

Once you get the ball rolling, everyone wants to be involved.

take the ball and run with it
pick up the ball and run ◄

If you **take the ball and run with it**, you take an idea or plan that someone else has started and you develop it in order to see if it will be successful or useful. This expression is very variable. For example, you can also say that you **pick up the ball and run**.

Whatever he does in that hour is up to him. If he studies, fine. If he stares at the walls, well there's nothing we can do. He's the one who has to take the ball and run with it.

In a couple of months all our efforts will be

forgotten unless other people pick up the ball and run.

□ Other nouns are often used instead of 'ball'.

Political theorists picked up the idea of liberty and ran with it down novel and experimental constitutional paths.

Any competent programmer could do it on a home computer and I'm hoping that someone else will take this and run with it because I haven't had the time.

the whole ball of wax

If you refer to **the whole ball of wax**, you are referring to the whole of something or to a number of different things which form a whole. This expression is used mainly in American English.

Perry wanted it all, the whole ball of wax. He wanted the Society for himself.

Let's just say that without you and him, there's nothing at all. You two are the whole ball of wax. And your uncle sure as hell knows that.

ballistic

go ballistic ◄

If someone **goes ballistic**, they get extremely angry and start behaving in a very forceful or irrational way as a result. **Go nuclear** means the same.

They claim the singer went ballistic after one member of his band allegedly failed to show for a sound check on the recent American tour.

Can you imagine what the atmosphere will be like at breakfast if these pictures are as bad as they sound? The Queen will, quite simply, go ballistic.

balloon

the balloon goes up ◄

If you say that **the balloon has gone up**, you mean that a situation has become very serious or something bad has just happened. This expression is used mainly in British English.

On the Saturday the balloon went up. Henry said he would be going out to a conference and not returning until the Sunday afternoon. Sara told him to take all his things and not to return at all.

On the line was his solicitor warning that the balloon was about to go up.

ballpark

a ballpark figure
a ballpark estimate

A **ballpark figure** or **a ballpark estimate** is an approximate figure or quantity. These expressions are used mainly in American English.

But what are we talking about here – a few

thousand, millions, two bucks? Give me a ballpark figure.*

I think just in a ballpark estimate – about 60-40. Sixty would support, 40 percent would be opposed.

in the ballpark

If you say that someone or something is **in the ballpark**, you mean that their ideas, actions, or estimates are approximately right, although they may not be exactly right. This expression is used in American English.

As one recovering gambler puts it, as long as you stay honest with yourself, you're somewhere in the ballpark.

Doctor Adams pointed out that as a piece of subtle surgical equipment it cost about £5 – an underestimate, maybe, but in the right ballpark.

in the same ballpark

If you say that one person or thing is **in the same ballpark** as another, you mean that the first person or thing is comparable to the second, or is as good or important as the second. This expression is used in American English.

As a general investigative agency, they're not in the same ballpark as the FBI.

'We're not very nervous.' Mr. Gruber, Blockbuster's chief marketing officer, predicts that Super Club's outlets won't be 'in the same ballpark' as Blockbuster's larger superstores.

balls

break someone's balls

If you say that someone **breaks** your **balls**, you mean that they seem to take pleasure in creating a great deal of unnecessary trouble for you. This expression is often used to refer critically to women who seem to enjoy destroying the sexual confidence of men. You can replace 'break' with 'bust'. This is a very informal expression, which many people find offensive.

You learned that the guy who writes the ads for the bank isn't the guy who loans the money. They break your balls.

Men prefer a twitchy little eye-flutterer even if she is breaking their balls behind the scenes.

□ You can refer to someone who behaves in this way as **a ball-breaker**, and describe their behaviour as **ball-breaking**.

She thinks there's a misconception of her and Jen as ball-breaking, man-hating, unapproachable bitches.

Another professor raised a great laugh by characterizing Jane Eyre as a novel written by one sex-starved ball-breaker about another.

keep balls in the air
juggle balls in the air

If you have to **keep** a lot of **balls in the air** or **juggle** a lot of **balls in the air**, you have to deal with many different things at the same time.

They had trouble keeping all their balls in the air. In management terms, they were trying to do too much and things were starting to break down.

I really am juggling a hundred balls in the air at the same time and driving Alan completely potty with my scatterbrained way of doing things.

banana

slip on a banana skin
slip on a banana peel   ◄◄

If an important or famous person **slips on a banana skin** or **slips on a banana peel**, they say or do something that makes them look stupid and causes them problems. Other verbs with a similar meaning can be used instead of 'slip'. This expression is used mainly in British English.

Most of the nation would enjoy seeing mighty Liverpool slip on a banana skin in front of millions.

You can be walking across Westminster Bridge full of noble thoughts at one moment and slipping on a banana peel the next.

He was unaware of the banana skin on which his department's heel was about to skid.

□ You can refer to something that causes someone to look stupid or have problems as **a banana skin** or **a banana peel**.

We are hoping this is a new era for the club, but there have been a few banana skins lying around in the past when people have thought like that.

This is nothing compared with the criticism the president gets from those major insiders who watch in horrified fascination as he lurches from one banana peel to another.

band

a one-man band
a one-woman band   ◄◄

If you describe someone as **a one-man band**, you mean that they carry out every part of an activity themselves, without any help from anyone else.

Business was quiet on the night we visited – which was as well, as the chef was a one-man band, taking orders, and cooking and serving at table.

I'm a one-man band, Mr Herold. At present I haven't even got a secretary.

□ A woman who is like this is sometimes described as **a one-woman band**.

The hens need to be shut up at dusk and the gate of the goose enclosure closed and I am no better at being in two places at once than the next one-woman band.

□ **A one-man band** is a street entertainer

who plays several different instruments at the same time.

bandwagon

jump on the bandwagon   ◄◄◄

If you say that someone, especially a politician, **has jumped on the bandwagon**, you disapprove of their involvement in an activity or movement, because you think that they are not sincerely interested in it, but are involved in it because it is likely to succeed or it is fashionable. 'Climb on', 'get on', and 'join' can be used instead of 'jump on'.

One of the dangers of following fads is that there are always bound to be inexperienced people ready to jump on the bandwagon and start classes in whatever is fashionable, with little or no training or qualifications of their own.

Why are the 'stars' now jumping on the fashionable green bandwagon? Few people doubt their sincerity, although some people doubt their effectiveness.

Conservative Republicans are incredulous and angry at the sight of Federal Reserve chairman, Alan Greenspan, climbing aboard the Bill Clinton bandwagon.

□ You can also say that someone is **bandwagon-jumping**.

We welcome any campaign on domestic violence, but we don't like the bandwagon-jumping of this organization.

□ 'Bandwagon' is also used in many other phrases such as someone's **bandwagon is rolling**, to mean that an activity or movement is getting increasing support.

The Government's determination to push ahead with the sell-off of British Rail underlines its desire to keep the privatisation bandwagon rolling.

bang

bang goes something

If you say **'bang goes** something', you mean that it is now obvious that it cannot succeed or be achieved. This expression is used mainly in British English.

What will the country be like a decade into the 21st century? First the bad news: there will be more work to do, not less. Bang goes the fantasy of retirement at thirty-five.

Bang goes his influence, maybe his job, if the two countries reach a real understanding.

more bang for the buck
a bigger bang for the buck
more bangs for your bucks   ◄

If you get **more bang for the buck**, you get a bigger quantity or better quality of something than you would expect to get for the amount that you spend. You can also say that you get **a bigger bang for the buck** or **more bangs for** your **bucks**. All these expressions are used mainly in American English.

With this program you get more bang for the buck you've spent on computers.

I think it's very, very important for those governments to do whatever they can to get a bigger bang for the buck.

Put crudely, we want more bangs for our bucks – the days of being able to afford vast bureaux all over the world are over.

☐ You can also say that someone gets **little bang for the buck**, when they get less than they expected for the amount of money they spent.

The company is getting little bang for its buck.

not with a bang but a whimper ◄

If you say that something happens **not with a bang but a whimper**, you mean that it is less effective or exciting than people expected or intended.

The Cannes film festival approached its climax yesterday not with a bang but a whimper, as thousands of disappointed festival-goers left early.

☐ You can also say that something happened **with a bang and not a whimper**, or **with neither a bang nor a whimper**.

Should the monarchy go, it would be with a memorable bang and not a whimper.

The last Hampshire match at Dean Park ended not with a bang, not even with a whimper; just an old-fashioned draw.

bank

break the bank ◄◄

If you say that something will not **break the bank**, you mean that it will not cost a lot of money or will not cost more than you can easily afford. Something that **breaks the bank** does cost a lot of money or more than you can easily afford.

Porto Cervo is expensive, but there are restaurants and bars that won't break the bank.

With everyone counting the pennies, self-catering holidays are a good option because you can enjoy a refreshing change without breaking the bank.

Officials say the cost of the war could break the bank and they're looking to US allies for more financial support.

laugh all the way to the bank
cry all the way to the bank ◄

If someone is **laughing all the way to the bank**, they are making a lot of money very easily or very quickly. Other verbs are sometimes used instead of 'laugh'.

Investors who followed our New Year share tips are laughing all the way to the bank. The

gains, considering that we are only five months into the year, are astronomical.

Doctors are grinning all the way to the bank this week as Medicare statistics reveal that most medical specialists earn more than $300,000 a year.

☐ If you say that someone **is crying all the way to the bank**, you are saying in an ironic way that they are making a lot of money very easily or very quickly. You can also say that someone **is crying all the way to the bank** when they are not making much money.

An Oscar for Nolte could add another £10 million, leaving him crying all the way to the bank.

The bookies had already closed their satchels and were resigned to crying all the way to the bank and back.

baptism

a baptism of fire ◄◄

If your first experience of a new situation is very difficult or unpleasant, you can describe it as **a baptism of fire**.

They have given themselves a baptism of fire by playing what many would consider the four best teams in the world.

To most men, of whatever rank, it was their baptism of fire. The first lessons learned were not new, but they were viciously taught.

bark

your bark is worse than your bite ◄

If you say that someone's **bark is worse than** their **bite**, you mean that they seem to be much more severe or unfriendly than they really are.

My bark is definitely worse than my bite. When people get to know me, they'll tell you I'm just a big softy really.

☐ People often vary this expression. For example, you can suggest that someone is as severe or unfriendly as they seem by saying that their **bite is as bad as** their **bark**.

Wales' team will discover today that England's bite is as vicious as their bark.

Lautro showed it has some bite behind its bark when it fined Interlife Assurance £160,000.

barrel

have someone over a barrel ◄

If you are having discussions or negotiations with someone and you say that they **have** you **over a barrel**, you mean that they have put you in a position where you cannot possibly win. 'Have' is occasionally replaced with 'hold'.

The unions wish they had more options. Jobs are tight, they know that, and they feel management has them over a barrel.

And now this time they've got them over a barrel.

Mr Tice said owners held him over a barrel on weekly prices.

scrape the bottom of the barrel
scrape the barrel ◄

If you say that someone **is scraping the bottom of the barrel** or **is scraping the barrel**, you mean that they are using something or doing something that is not very good, because they cannot think of anything better to use or do.

The game designers were scraping the bottom of the barrel for ideas when they came up with this one.

I can accept him having a go at me, but now he is really scraping the barrel by effectively having a go at our players.

barrelhead

on the barrelhead
on the barrel

If you pay cash **on the barrelhead** or **on the barrel** for something, you pay for it immediately and in cash. These expressions are used in American English; the British expression is **on the nail**.

Customers usually pay cash on the barrelhead, so bad debts aren't much of a problem.

TV has decided to pay exactly what a sports event appears to be worth – cash on the barrel and not a dollar more.

barrels

give someone both barrels
with both barrels

If you **give** someone **both barrels** or let them have it **with both barrels**, you attack them fiercely, aggressively, and forcefully.

Greenwood took this up with Butler and gave him both barrels.

Let him have it with both barrels and then get out of the situation while you can.

base

get to first base: 1

If you cannot **get to first base**, you cannot begin to make progress with your plans.

We couldn't get to first base with any U.S. banks. They didn't want to take the risk.

We wonder why there are so few women in leadership – they get trivialised before they even get to first base.

get to first base: 2
get to second base

People use expressions such as **get to first base** and **get to second base** to refer to the degree of sexual intimacy they have achieved

with their girlfriend or boyfriend. These expressions are used mainly in American English.

It takes Declan, the obligatory ladies' man of the cast, until the third episode to get past first base with any of his prey.

On a date, would it be easier to get to second base with Laverne or Shirley?

off base ◄◄

If you say that someone's judgement or opinion is **off base**, you mean that it is mistaken or wrong. This expression is used in American English.

I don't think the church is off base at all in taking a moral stand on this.

They had a lot of assumptions that were very far off base, I think.

For him to blame his mother for this is really off base.

touch base ◄

If you **touch base** with someone, you contact them, often when you have not spoken to them or seen them for a long time.

Being there gave me a chance to touch base with and make plans to see three friends whom I had not seen for a year.

Afterward Forstmann had touched base with his partners and found that they, too, harbored a vague distaste for the tobacco business.

bases

touch all the bases
cover all the bases ◄

If you say that someone **touches all the bases** or **touches all bases**, you mean that they deal with or take care of all the different things that they should. You can also say that they **cover all the bases**. These expressions are used mainly in American English.

He has managed to touch all the bases necessary, and trade goes on.

This is an exceptionally good contract. It touches all of the bases of what the people said were the problems.

The boss covers all bases when he sets up a job.

basket

a basket case: 1 ◄◄

If you describe a country or organization as **a basket case**, you mean that its economy or finances are in a very bad state.

The popular image about Latin America a few years ago was that it was a basket case.

To understand this, it's necessary to go back to the seventies, when the Post Office was regarded as a basket case, doomed to decline by the growth of competition from phone, fax and modem.

a basket case: 2

If you say that someone is **a basket case**, you mean that they are crazy or insane. This is an informal expression.

Mary comes to work in tears every day, and you wouldn't believe the bags under her eyes. She's gained fifteen pounds, as well. I tell you, she's turning into a basket case.

You're going to think I'm a basket case when I tell you this, but we used to play games – this was when we were about twenty, not kids.

bat

go to bat for someone
go in to bat for someone

If you say that someone **goes to bat for** you, you mean that they give you their support or help. You can also say that they **go in to bat for** you. These expressions are used mainly in American English.

She was just fabulous in going to bat for me, in not being judgmental, in seeing me through and helping me work it out.

I wasn't ashamed to go in to bat for Matt. I had faith his acting talent would justify it.

like a bat out of hell

If you go somewhere **like a bat out of hell**, you go there very quickly.

I didn't see her face, but I knew it was a woman. She tore across the highway like a bat out of hell. I damn nearly ploughed right into her.

He said 'Thank you, sir,' and departed like a bat out of hell.

off your own bat

If you do something **off** your **own bat**, you choose to do it or decide to do it rather than being told to do it. This expression is used in British English.

'Who's put you up to this call? Someone's told you to talk to me.' 'I'm doing it off my own bat, John.'

I'm certain whatever she did, she did off her own bat. Please make that clear, whatever she did was nothing to do with me.

play a straight bat: 1

If you say that someone **plays a straight bat**, you mean that they try to avoid answering difficult questions. This expression is used in British English.

But last Saturday her interviewee played a straight bat, referring all inquiries to his solicitors before driving off.

He is playing a straight bat. Though he is not yet ready to say whether he wants the laws relaxed or scrapped, he says he recognises that there are 'strong arguments' for legalised brothels.

play a straight bat: 2

If someone **plays a straight bat**, they do things in an honest and simple way because they have traditional ideas and values. This is an old-fashioned expression, which is used in British English.

Amit, then 14, was very surprised to find that 'playing a straight bat' was not considered all that important in his new school.

right off the bat

If something happens **right off the bat**, it happens immediately or at the very beginning of a process or event. This expression is used mainly in American English.

It was just as well that he learned right off the bat that you can't count on anything in this business.

Right off the bat I had a problem that threatened to give me editor's block five minutes into my first day of editing.

bath

an early bath

If you are involved in an activity and you take **an early bath**, you stop doing it and leave before you have finished. This expression is used in British English. Compare **send** someone **to the showers**; see **showers**.

At test screenings of Platoon, The War of the Roses and Goodfellas at least a quarter of the audience had opted for an early bath.

Nineteen of the country's most experienced referees have been invited to take an early bath as part of English football's attempt to lower the age of its top officials.

□ This expression is more commonly used in talking about football and rugby. If a player has **an early bath**, they are sent off the pitch before the end of the game, because they have severely broken the rules.

take a bath

If a person or a company **takes a bath**, they lose a lot of money on an investment. This expression is used mainly in journalism.

It is America's third-biggest bank failure. Its depositors have been saved by their federal deposit insurance; its bond and stockholders have taken a bath.

Investors in the company took a 35 million dollar bath on the company, which entered bankruptcy proceedings 18 months ago.

baton

pass the baton
hand the baton
pick up the baton

If someone **passes the baton** to you or **hands the baton** to you, they pass responsibility for something to you,

Does this mean that the baton of leadership is going to be passed to other nations?

He has handed over the baton to Mr Mellor who, should he be brave enough to attend, will come face to face with many of his tormentors.

☐ If you **pick up the baton**, you take over responsibility for something.

The heyday for conservationists was the mid and late 1980s when councils really picked up the baton of public concern and became the standard bearers in the quality of life versus nature debate.

bats

have bats in your belfry

If you say that someone **has bats in** their **belfry**, you mean that they have peculiar ideas or are crazy. This is an informal expression.

This music's dated melodrama is its potency. Eldritch truly has bats in his belfry, a corpse's chill to his voice, and a funereal hyperbole throughout his music.

batteries

recharge your batteries ◄◄

If you **recharge** your **batteries**, you take a break from activities which are tiring or stressful so that you can relax and will feel refreshed when you return to those activities.

After playing in the Divisional Championship, I took a long break from the game to recharge my batteries.

He wanted to recharge his batteries and come back feeling fresh and positive.

battle

the battle lines are drawn ◄◄◄

If you say that **the battle lines are drawn** between opposing groups or people, you mean that they are ready to start fighting or arguing, and that it has become clear what the main points of conflict or disagreement will be.

The battle lines were drawn yesterday for the fiercest contest in the history of local radio. Forty-eight applicants submitted their proposals in the chase for eight London broadcasting licences.

Battle lines were already being drawn up for a future power struggle.

a battle of wills ◄

If you describe an argument or conflict as **a battle of wills**, you mean that the people who are involved in it refuse to give in to each other's demands.

It was a battle of wills, and Grace's was the stronger.

The police have been under enormous pressure to end a wave of kidnappings which has

triggered *a battle of wills between the State governor and the Federal government.*

a battle of wits ◄

If you describe a competition or disagreement as **a battle of wits**, you mean that each person involved in it uses their intelligence and mental ability to beat their opponents.

With chess you're involved in a battle of wits from start to finish.

He is cunning, crafty and clever. The kidnap was carefully planned and thought out and the tone of the letter he sent was not from an uneducated person. It's now a battle of wits between my officers and this man.

fight a losing battle ◄◄◄

If you **are fighting a losing battle**, you are trying to achieve something, but you are very unlikely to succeed.

Some fat people despair of ever losing weight. And according to recent research by doctors in Los Angeles, very obese dieters may indeed be fighting a losing battle.

Miss Bennett fought a losing battle against her depression.

The producer says the theaters have been fighting a losing battle with television, movies, and video cassettes.

join battle ◄

If you **join battle** with someone, you decide that you are going to try and beat them in an argument or contest.

This new company intends to join battle with Cellnet and Vodafone in the mobile telecoms market.

Heseltine led the challenge against the Prime Minister and now finds himself joining battle with two of the Conservative Party's most admired figures.

a running battle ◄◄◄

If you have **a running battle** with someone, you argue with them or fight with them over a long period of time.

Police have been engaged in running battles with people protesting against the sharp increase in the price of the country's staple food, maize meal.

At the same time, I kept up a running battle of letters, faxes and phone calls, trying to find the right organisation in Russia to grant permission for the trip.

For the past year, Philippine beer drinkers have inspired a running battle between two brewers.

win the battle, lose the war
lose the battle, win the war ◄

If you say that someone **has won the battle, but lost the war**, you mean that, although they have won a minor conflict, they have been defeated in a larger, more important one, of which it was a part. You can also say that someone **has won the battle, but hasn't won the war**.

The strikers may have won the battle, but they lost the war.

We will get our justice. They have won the battle but they haven't won the war. We will have our day in court.

□ You can also say that someone **has lost the battle** but intends to **win the war**, to mean that they have lost a small conflict but still think they can win the larger one.

If you do start smoking again it does not mean you are a failure. Learn from what went wrong and pick another day to stop again. You may have lost the battle, but you can still win the war.

bay

keep something at bay
hold something at bay ◄◄◄

If you **keep** something **at bay** or **hold** it **at bay**, you keep it from attacking you or affecting you in some other way. You can also **keep** people **at bay** or **hold** them **at bay**.

By salting the meat, bacteria were kept at bay, preserving the meat for future use.

Gretchen felt the intense regret that she had kept at bay for so long well up inside her.

Tooth decay can be held at bay by fluoride toothpaste and good dentistry.

A dozen American soldiers hold the crowd at bay until the helicopter lifts off.

bead

draw a bead on
take a bead on

If you **draw a bead on** a target or **take a bead on** it, you aim your weapon at it. These expressions are used mainly in American English.

There was only one spot where the light through the trees would have enabled him to draw a bead on his target.

The small pale eyes squeezed shut as if he were taking a bead on her.

be-all

not the be-all and end-all ◄◄

If you say that something is **not the be-all and end-all**, you mean that it is not the only thing that is important in a particular situation.

Results are not the be-all and end-all of education.

According to the prevailing wisdom, a career may be important to a woman as a source of fulfilment, but it is not the be all and the end all of existence.

beam

be way off beam ◄

If you say that something **is way off beam**, you mean that it is completely wrong or mistaken. Other words can be used instead of 'way'. This expression is used in British English.

The writer was so hilariously way off-beam in his criticism of soccer that every single reader will want to see the article for themselves.

Everything she says is a little off beam.

bean

a bean counter
count the beans ◄

If you refer to someone as **a bean counter**, you mean that they are only interested in narrow questions such as how much money a business makes and spends, without caring about wider issues, for example, people's welfare. You usually use this expression when you disagree with this approach.

The reason for America's failure is that we have bean-counters running our companies. The Japanese have engineering and manufacturing people.

Most cases of cancer of the cervix occur in younger women. Medical bean counters don't think it is cost-effective to detect cervical cancer in the older age groups.

□ You can refer to this type of approach as **bean counting**, or you can say that someone **is counting the beans**.

He is as prone as he ever was to sudden outbursts against the Hollywood establishment – the bean-counting producers, the idiot studio heads, the lawyers, the grandiose agents.

I'm not trivializing this, but no funds were lost and no customers were affected. We should count the beans better, that's all.

not have a bean

If you say that someone **hasn't got a bean**, you mean that they have very little money. This is a fairly old-fashioned expression, which is used in British English.

It's quite incredible to think that he now hasn't got a bean.

'Where do you suppose she got that amount of money from? Lorimer?' 'I hardly think so. From all accounts he hasn't a bean.'

When we married we hadn't a bean so we bought all our furniture second-hand.

beans

full of beans ◄

If you say that someone is **full of beans**, you mean that they are happy, excited, and full of energy.

Jem was among them, pink-cheeked and full

of beans after a far longer sleep than anybody else had got.

He is a likable extrovert, full of beans.

know how many beans make five

If you say that someone **knows how many beans make five**, you mean that they are intelligent and sensible. This is an old-fashioned expression, which is used in British English.

The major concern of most parents is that the children are taught the basics, so that when they graduate they can talk nicely, spell properly and know how many beans make five.

not amount to a hill of beans
not worth a row of beans

If you say that something **doesn't amount to a hill of beans** or **isn't worth a hill of beans**, you mean that it is completely worthless and insignificant. You can also say that something is **not worth a row of beans**.

In this world the problems of people like us do not amount to a hill of beans.

To skeptics, political polls aren't worth a hill of beans.

If you don't know what it is you want to say and why, interview training is not worth a row of beans.

spill the beans ◄◄

If you **spill the beans**, you reveal the truth about something secret or private.

He always seemed scared to death I was going to spill the beans to the cops.

As Michael's friend, I can spill the beans on lots of things. I know his opinions on everything.

He was badgering her to stay loyal to him and not spill the beans about their affair.

bear

like a bear with a sore head

If you say that someone is behaving **like a bear with a sore head**, you are criticizing them for behaving in a very bad-tempered and irritable way. This expression is used mainly in British English.

I mean, it was quite obvious, wasn't it, that she really didn't want to go, but there you were, like a bear with a sore head, tantrums all the time, little legs drumming on the floor.

Jane Ashdown said she sometimes wished Paddy would quit politics. 'But I wouldn't ask him to give it up. He'd be like a bear with a sore head.'

loaded for bear

If you say that someone is **loaded for bear**, you mean that they are ready and eager to do something. This expression is used in American English.

We could notify the mainland police, and they could conduct the search, and go charging in

there with guns and bullhorns, loaded for bear.

A young squadron commander named Joshua Painter led the briefing. He had eight aircraft loaded for bear.

beast

no use to man or beast
no good to man or beast

If you say that someone or something is **no use to man or beast** or **no good to man or beast**, you are emphasizing that they are completely useless.

Circumstances had compelled him, much against his will, to take no less than six beginners, some of them first-voyagers, of no use to man or beast.

beat

beat your breast
beat your chest ◄◄◄

If you say that someone **is beating** their **breast** or **is beating** their **chest**, you mean that they are very publicly showing regret or anger about something that has gone wrong. You usually use these expressions to suggest that the person is not being sincere but is trying to draw attention to himself or herself.

At this month's meeting of the party's Central Committee, the party leader beat his breast with ritual self-criticism.

He is very thoughtful with the players. He doesn't go around beating his chest all the time. He knows when a quiet chat is what's needed.

□ You can describe the action of doing this as **breast-beating** or **chest-beating**.

His pious breast-beating on behalf of the working classes was transparently bogus, but it was a clever public relations job.

The show is about pomp, pretension and chest-beating melodrama.

miss a beat: 1 ◄

If someone says or does something without **missing a beat**, they continue to speak or they do it without pausing, even though you might have expected them to hesitate.

In a second round of testimony on Capitol Hill, the first woman attorney-general designate was asked point-blank whether she should bow out. But, without missing a beat, she replied: 'I do not believe it is appropriate for me to withdraw my nomination.'

'Are you jealous?' 'Only when I'm not in control,' he says, not missing a beat.

miss a beat: 2

If you say that someone does not **miss a beat**, you mean that they always know what is going on and so they are able to take advantage of every situation.

Browns is a stylish emporium of the best of the international fashion collections. They haven't missed a beat since 1970, and if they don't have the dress you want, they'll order it.

This time we played like machines. The longer the game went the stronger we got, and we never missed a beat.

beaver

an eager beaver ◄

If you describe someone as **an eager beaver**, you mean that they are very enthusiastic about work or very anxious to please other people. You usually use this expression to show that you find their behaviour foolish or annoying.

George was like a sneaky kid. He lied, boasted, was an eager beaver without the ability to live up to his promises.

The Holdsworths were wearily climbing up the front steps. They must have left before dawn, the damned eager beavers!

□ **Eager-beaver** can also be used before a noun.

If fraud became an issue, he might interest an eager-beaver assistant attorney general in the case.

beck

at someone's beck and call ◄

If you say that someone is **at** another person's **beck and call**, you mean that they are always ready to carry out that person's orders or wishes, even when these orders or wishes are unreasonable.

You're a person in your own right, not just a mum or a partner, and your child must understand that you can't always be at his beck and call for every little thing.

The specialised banks are, in effect, government departments, at the beck and call of politicians and bureaucrats.

bed

get into bed with someone
be in bed with someone ◄

If you say that one person or group is **getting into bed with** another, you mean that they have made an agreement and are intending to work together. If they **are in bed with** the other person or group, they are already working together. You usually use this expression to show disapproval.

The BBC might have been criticised for getting into bed with Sky TV last summer, but it's easy to see now why they did.

He said that anyone who criticizes her is an enemy and is in bed with the government.

get out of bed the wrong side
get out of bed on the wrong side

If you say that someone **got out of bed the wrong side** or **got out of bed on the wrong side**, you mean that they are in a very bad mood without there seeming to be any obvious reason for it.

Sorry I was so unpleasant when I arrived this morning. I must have got out of bed the wrong side.

An immigration official who rolls out of bed on the wrong side can take an unreasonable dislike to a visitor who will be removed from these shores without the opportunity to appeal against the decision.

put something to bed

If you **put** a plan or task **to bed**, you achieve it or complete it successfully.

Before putting the agreement to bed, we still had to satisfy Fran Murray.

We were rushing like that to put the wages to bed by around dinner time Tuesday.

you have made your bed and will have to lie on it

If someone tells you **'you have made your bed and will have to lie on it'**, they are telling you in an unsympathetic way that you have to accept the unpleasant consequences of a decision which you made at an earlier time. 'In' is often used instead of 'on'.

Curiously it never occurred to her even to consider leaving Barry. Her strict religious upbringing had convinced her that marriage was for life – in her eyes she had made her bed and would have to lie in it.

□ This expression is very variable. For example, you can say to someone, **'you've made your bed, now lie on it'** or just **'you've made your bed'**.

She came home one evening, after yet another blazing row, to find that Ian and their two children had disappeared. Her parents responded, 'You've made your bed, my girl. Now lie on it.'

You wouldn't expect us to turn around and say 'Oh well, you know you've made your bed – you're the one that caused the problem.'

bee

the bee's knees ◄

If you say that something or someone is **the bee's knees**, you are saying in a light-hearted way that you like them a great deal. This expression is used in British English.

Back in the '80s it was the bee's knees but now it looks horribly out of date.

I bought this white sweatshirt – I thought I looked the bee's knees.

have a bee in your bonnet ◄

If you say that someone **has a bee in** their

bonnet about something, you mean that they feel very strongly about it and keep talking or thinking about it. This is often something that you think is unimportant. This expression is considered old-fashioned in American English.

I've got a bee in my bonnet about the confusion between education and training.

There was no arguing with the boy when he'd got this bee in his bonnet.

☐ People often vary this expression.

I'm getting too old now for bees in my bonnet. I used to get very het up about things.

Oh, come on, let that bee out of your bonnet. The case is over.

beeline

make a beeline for something ◄

If you **make a beeline for** something, you go straight to it without any hesitation or delay.

The boys head for computer games while the girls make a beeline for the dolls.

My only hope was to take refuge among the crowd, so I hid myself in the casino, but at a certain point I saw my persecutor making a beeline for me.

beer

not all beer and skittles

If you say that something **isn't all beer and skittles**, you mean that it is not always as enjoyable or as easy as other people think it is. This expression is used in British English.

Others are keen to make clear that City life is not all beer and skittles.

Living on your own isn't all beer and skittles. It can be lonely too.

It's not all beer and skittles when you get to be famous.

small beer ◄◄

If you say that something is **small beer**, you mean that it is insignificant compared with another thing. This expression is used in British English.

This film cost £6 million to make, small beer compared to the £43 million splashed out on the making of Arnold Schwarzenegger's Terminator II.

The present series of royal scandals makes the 1936 abdication look like pretty small beer.

Black films remain small beer; they are doing little to shape the movie business.

beggars

beggars can't be choosers

If someone says to you **'beggars can't be choosers'**, they mean that you should not reject an offer or a particular course of action, because it is the only one which is available to you.

'So would you be happy to work wherever you got a job?' 'Initially, yeah. I mean, I think initially you've got to take anything that comes around because beggars can't be choosers.'

There are part-time jobs in the paper, and beggars can't be choosers. But you have to weigh up whether or not they are financially viable, or actually worth less than income support.

begging

go begging ◄

If something **goes begging**, it is wasted or not used, even though people do not need to make much effort to use it.

Nearly half a million holidays for the busiest six weeks of the year are still going begging.

Paintings by pop artist Andy Warhol went begging for the second night in a row last night at Christie's auction house.

bell

ring a bell ◄

If something **rings a bell**, it is slightly familiar to you and you are aware that you have heard it before, although you may not remember it fully.

'Who?' he queried, 'Passing Clouds? I simply don't remember them. Their name doesn't ring a bell.'

The sergeant made notes while she talked. 'I'll check and see if we've anything on him,' he said. 'It doesn't ring a bell at the moment.'

ring someone's bell

If someone or something **rings** your **bell**, you find them very attractive, exciting, or satisfying. This is an informal expression, which is used mainly in American English.

Well, truthfully, after a couple of comedies that didn't exactly ring my bell, I thought I'd like to do something that is very unusual, that hadn't been seen before.

saved by the bell

People say **'saved by the bell'** when they are in a difficult situation and at the last possible moment something happens which allows them to escape from it.

There was another period of silence. It was broken by the sound of Eleanor's car pulling up outside the front door. 'Saved by the bell,' I said.

And we are saved by the bell. The telephone rings, for once a timely distraction.

bells

alarm bells ring
warning bells ring ◄◄◄

If something sets **alarm bells ringing** or if **an alarm bell** starts to **ring**, people begin to be aware of a problem in a situation. You can also talk about **warning bells ringing**.

The islanders' fight for compensation has set alarm bells ringing round the world.

That company had raised over five million dollars for its launch and promptly went broke. The alarm bells started ringing.

He didn't understand the half of it but warning bells were beginning to ring in the back of his mind.

bells and whistles ◄

If you refer to **bells and whistles**, you are referring to special features or other things which are not essential parts of something, but which are added to make it more attractive or interesting.

People also crave anxiety-free products – simple items without lots of fancy bells and whistles and complex instructions.

Computers, car phones, fax machines, voice mail – all these things might seem like so many bells and whistles to some.

bellyful

have a bellyful

If you say that you **have had a bellyful** of something, you mean that you find it very irritating or boring, and you do not want to experience it any longer. This is an informal expression.

I have had a bellyful of excuses. It's always someone else's fault.

belly-up

go belly-up ◄◄

If a company **goes belly-up**, it fails and does not have enough money to pay its debts.

Considering that it is not unknown for insurance companies to go belly-up in the current hard times, it is as well for customers to bear in mind that the cheapest cover is unlikely to be the best.

Factories and farms went belly up because of the debt crisis.

belt

below the belt ◄

If you describe what someone has done as **below the belt**, you mean that it is unfair or cruel.

Highly-sensitive information about another person can often be used as a weapon against them, and these kinds of blows below the belt are the surest way to destroy a friendship or love affair.

Depending on whose version you believe, the People's Party has suffered either a deep humiliation or a blow below the belt from its political rivals.

belt and braces

If you say that someone has a **belt and braces** approach to doing something, you mean that they take extra precautions to make sure that it will work properly. This expression is used in British English.

A trawl of the computer system should reveal if customers were charged too much. 'It is a belt and braces approach to weed out irregularities,' said the bank.

He described airport security as an overly belt and braces approach, at huge cost to industry.

tighten your belt ◄◄◄

If you have to **tighten** your **belt**, you must spend less and live more carefully because you have less money than you used to have.

Clearly, if you are spending more than your income, you'll need to tighten your belt.

He recently announced the club will have to tighten its belt next season, saying he will lower wages and sell players.

☐ You can also talk about **belt-tightening**.

The nation's second largest bank announced a series of layoffs and other belt-tightening measures today to counteract heavy losses.

Yesterday's vote means that Greeks are prepared to accept a period of belt tightening.

under your belt ◄◄◄

If you have something **under** your **belt**, you have already achieved it or done it.

He'll need a few more games under his belt before he's ready for international football.

After a few years, I had enough recipes under my belt to put them into a book.

Today, with the Nobel Peace Prize under her belt, she is a stateswoman of world renown.

bend

round the bend ◄◄

If you say that someone is **round the bend**, you think that their ideas or behaviour are very strange or foolish. This is an informal expression, which is used more commonly in British English than American. **Round the twist** means the same.

Before I got involved in this I actually used to look at mountaineers and think they were a little bit round the bend.

If anyone told me a few months ago that I'd meet a marvellous person like you I'd have said they were round the bend.

☐ If you say that someone goes or is driven **round the bend**, you mean that they start behaving or thinking very strangely or foolishly. This is often as a result of being very frustrated or irritated by someone or something.

It's a lovely little place to visit, but I can see this bloke going round the bend there after spending all his working life in Rome.

Can you make that tea before your fidgeting drives me completely round the bend.

benefit

give someone the benefit of the doubt ◄◄◄

If you **give** someone **the benefit of the doubt**, you decide to believe that what they are saying or doing is honest and right, even though it is possible that they are not telling the truth or that they are doing something wrong.

I am basically a trusting person. I make it a practice to give everyone the benefit of the doubt. So I suppose that's why it took me so long to catch on.

The electorate, usually ready to give Tory economic policies the benefit of the doubt, may be on the verge of thinking that Labour could do better.

berth

give someone a wide berth ◄

If you **give** someone or something **a wide berth**, you deliberately avoid them.

I wouldn't mess with people like that, not me. I give them a wide berth.

Having lived all my adult life in Africa I have a very healthy respect for snakes and have always tried to give them a wide berth.

bet

a good bet: 1
a safe bet ◄◄◄

If you tell someone that something would be **a good bet** or **a safe bet**, you are advising them that it would be a sensible or useful thing to do.

As sales of suits continue to decline, the jacket you can wear with several different pairs of trousers has to be a good bet.

When you're unfamiliar with your guests' likes and dislikes, poultry is a safe bet for the main course.

□ If you say that something would be **a better bet** or **a safer bet**, you mean that it would be more sensible or useful than another possibility. If you say that something is someone's **best bet** or **safest bet**, you mean that it is the most sensible or useful thing to do.

Of course, not everyone looking for their first property wants a flat. You should weigh the pros and cons carefully before deciding whether a house would be a better bet.

Basing a drama series on a book is a far safer bet than commissioning one from scratch.

If you really want to keep your home safe from robbery, your best bet is still to buy a dog.

a good bet: 2
a safe bet ◄◄

If you say that it is **a good bet** or **a safe bet** that something will happen, you mean that it is very likely to happen. If someone is **a good bet** or **a safe bet** for something, they are very likely to do that thing.

But they will not enjoy reading this book; it is a safe bet that few will read more than 100 pages.

Mr Menem remains a good bet for re-election.

With a collection of talented individuals now playing as a team, Leeds United look a good bet to reach the final for the first time since 1978.

bets

all bets are off ◄

If someone says '**all bets are off**', they mean that it is impossible to say how a particular situation may develop.

This election year all bets seem to be off. In fact, even the folks who make a living predicting what the voters will do find themselves on shaky ground.

It's Scorsese's first period drama, so all bets are off until we see how the cast cope in the costumes.

hedge your bets ◄◄

If you say that someone **is hedging** their **bets**, you mean that they are avoiding making decisions, or are committing themselves to more than one thing, so that they will not make a mistake, whichever way the situation develops.

The Rev Donald Reeves hedges his bets on whether Carey is the leader the Church needs in troubled times. 'I don't really know him so I can't really say.'

Political forecasters are hedging their bets about the likely outcome of this Saturday's Louisiana governor's race.

bib

your best bib and tucker

If you are wearing your **best bib and tucker**, you are wearing your best clothes, for example because you are going to a very important or formal event. This is an old-fashioned expression.

The Middle East peace conference kicks off on October 30th in Madrid with all the guests on the invitation list promising to turn up on time in best bib and tucker.

They had a guest so she got dressed in her best bib and tucker and she went downstairs.

big

get too big for your boots
get too big for your britches ◄

In British English, if you say that someone **is getting too big for** their **boots**, you are criticizing them for behaving as if they are much more important or clever than they really are. Other verbs can be used instead of 'get'.

Get too big for their boots, kids these days. Think the whole universe should revolve round them.

Nobody in England will ever allow us to become too big for our boots.

I was often accused of being too big for my boots.

☐ In American English, you say that someone **is getting too big for** their **britches**.

We both know your brother ain't the marrying kind. To say nothing of his being too big for his britches since he struck it rich.

bike

on your bike ◄

People say **'on your bike'** when they are telling someone to go away or stop behaving in a foolish way. This is an informal expression, which is used in British English.

It was a heated game, and when I got Alec I just said something like 'You're out mate, on your bike.' Alec had a few words back and so it went. But it was all friendly in the bar afterwards.

It would be appropriate to say Your Royal Highness first time, then we could call her Ma'am. On your bike, I thought. I'm not having that. She's only written two books. I've done stacks.

☐ This expression is often used to say that someone has been sacked from their job.

By the end of the week Neilsen had been told to get on his bike by new boss Jim Duffy.

'Get us promoted or get on yer bike!' That's Derby's ultimatum to their manager Arthur Cox after their disappointing season.

☐ This expression is sometimes spelled 'on yer bike', to represent an informal pronunciation of 'your'.

bill

bill and coo

If you say that two lovers **are billing and cooing**, you mean that they are talking together in an intimate and loving way. This an old-fashioned or literary expression, which some people use to indicate that they think this behaviour is inappropriate.

Jenny decided to end their marriage when she caught Paolo billing and cooing down the phone to an ex-girlfriend.

I just have to stand there grinding my teeth while they bill and coo.

a clean bill of health: 1 ◄◄

If someone is given **a clean bill of health**, they are told that they are completely fit and healthy.

He had a full medical late last year and was given a clean bill of health.

Great Britain coach Mal Reilly, delighted to receive a clean bill of health for his 19-man squad, names his side today.

a clean bill of health: 2 ◄◄

If something is given **a clean bill of health**, it is examined or considered and then judged to be in a satisfactory condition.

Fourteen seaside resorts failed to meet the environmental and safety standards, while 43 were given a clean bill of health.

The bottom line of that intensive study was that the chemical industry got an environmental clean bill of health.

fit the bill
fill the bill ◄◄◄

If someone or something **fits the bill**, they are exactly the right person or thing that is needed in a particular situation. You can also say that someone or something **fills the bill**.

I wanted someone who really knew their way around film-making and I knew that Richard would fit the bill.

Finding somewhere peaceful to paint was the main priority of artists Jenny Partridge and Nigel Casseldine when it came to finding a home – and their 17th-century house perched on a remote hillside certainly fits the bill.

'Tea? Coffee?' 'Coffee would just fill the bill.'

foot the bill ◄◄◄

If you have to **foot the bill** for something, you have to pay for it.

Police will have to foot the bill for the slight damage to both cars.

Though the government is supportive, companies foot most of the bill.

It is increasingly recognised that to expect the insurance industry to foot the entire bill for pollution would bankrupt it.

sell someone a bill of goods

If you **have been sold a bill of goods**, you have been deceived or told something that is not true. This expression is used in American English.

I began to realize that I'd been sold a bill of goods, that I wasn't in any way incompetent or slothful.

bind

a double bind ◄

If you are in **a double bind**, you are in a very difficult situation, because you have problems that cannot be solved easily or without causing more problems.

He was in a classic double bind, with the Chinese suspecting him and his Cabinet of supporting the guerrillas, while the guerrillas considered them mere tools of the Chinese.

Battered women especially are in a double bind. Leaving the batterer is, in many cases, more dangerous than remaining.

bird
the bird has flown

If you are looking for someone and you say that **the bird has flown**, you mean that they have escaped or disappeared.

He'd been told to follow the woman to work and sit outside the Health Centre till she came out again. Instead he'd wandered off God knows where, come back at her normal leaving time and found the bird had flown.

a bird in the hand
a bird in the hand is worth two in the bush

If you refer to something that you have as **a bird in the hand**, you mean that it is better to keep it than to try to get something better and risk having nothing at all.

Another temporary discount may not be what you want, but at least it is a bird in the hand.

□ This expression comes from the proverb **a bird in the hand is worth two in the bush**.

Some are convinced that nothing short of re-housing the entire collection in a new, perhaps purpose-built, structure will solve its problems. 'A bird in the hand is worth two in the bush,' counters Mr Partington.

a bird of passage

If you describe someone as **a bird of passage**, you mean that they never stay in one place for long.

Most of these emigrants were birds of passage who returned to Spain after a relatively short stay.

the early bird catches the worm
an early bird ◄

If you tell someone that **the early bird catches the worm**, you are advising them that if they want to do something successfully then they should start as soon as they can.

If you're going to make it to the Senate, you need to start right now. The early bird catches the worm.

Portobello and Bermondsey markets are rewarding for early risers; most of the serious buying there happens between six and eight o' clock in the morning and it is very much the case that the early bird catches the worm.

□ You can refer to someone who gets up early in the morning or who does something before other people as **an early bird**. Early

bird can also be used to describe things that are available to these people.

We've always been early birds, up at 5.30 or 6am.

The restaurant's 'early-bird specials' offer cheaper food to early-evening diners.

An early-bird discount is sometimes available at the beginning of the season.

eat like a bird

If you say that someone **eats like a bird**, you mean that they do not eat very much.

I wanted to see if there was still a lust for the life she once enjoyed – the champagne, the chauffeur-driven cars – but there wasn't a flicker. She ate like a bird, was inclined to refuse a glass of wine, and was only interested in talking about her work.

She always orders two larger chops and one smaller chop because her daughter eats like a bird and her husband eats a lot.

give someone the bird: 1
get the bird

If an audience **gives** an entertainer or sports player **the bird**, they shout at them to show their disapproval of them. You can also say that the entertainer or sports player **gets the bird**. These are old-fashioned expressions, which are used in British English.

He made a couple of mistakes and the crowd immediately gave him the bird. That got to him and things went from bad to worse.

Eddie had once been top of the bill. And then one evening, he got the bird.

give someone the bird: 2

If someone **gives** you **the bird**, they make a rude and offensive gesture with one hand, with their middle finger pointing up and their other fingers bent over in a fist, in order to show their contempt, anger, or defiance of you. This expression is used mainly in American English.

Chip took a break from telling sundry adoring females how beautiful their eyes were to surreptitiously give Alex the bird. Alex swiftly returned the gesture only to find himself embroiled in a heated slanging match.

a little bird told me

If you say that **a little bird told** you a piece of information, you mean that you are not going to say how you found out about it or who told it to you. This expression is considered old-fashioned in American English.

Incidentally, a little bird tells me that your birthday's coming up.

'I couldn't resist coming over to say hello,' she cooed. The black eyes stared at her, the mouth puffed cigar smoke in her direction. 'A little bird told me you're Lorelei le Neve.'

a rare bird ◄

If you describe someone or something as **a rare bird**, you mean that there are not many people or things like them.

The great crime reporters, unfortunately rather rare birds nowadays, consorted with criminals.

Diane Johnson's book is that rare bird, an American novel of manners.

birds

the birds and the bees ◄

People sometimes describe sex and sexual reproduction as **the birds and the bees**, usually because they find it embarrassing to talk about these things openly, or because they are trying to be humorous to hide the fact that they find it embarrassing.

At the age of 16 I remember having yet another discussion about the birds and the bees with my father.

That girl's as interested in the birds and the bees as she is in every blessed other thing you can think of.

birds of a feather
birds of a feather flock together

If you describe two or more people as **birds of a feather**, you mean that they are very similar in many ways.

I think I envied her relationship with our mother. She and my mother were birds of a feather. You felt something special between them that left you out.

We're birds of a feather, you and me, Mr Plimpton.

□ This expression comes from the proverb **birds of a feather flock together**, which means that people from the same group or with the same interests like to be with each other.

Birds of a feather flock together. Basically, people seek out neighborhoods that are most congenial to them.

for the birds

If you say that something is **for the birds**, you think that it is stupid, boring, or worthless.

This journal business is for the birds. It's a waste of time.

This idea that everybody can go to college and pay it off by public service is for the birds.

kill two birds with one stone ◄

If you **kill two birds with one stone**, you manage to achieve two things at the same time.

We can talk about Union Hill while I get this business over with. Kill two birds with one stone, so to speak.

He had been on his way to the vegetable man's van, both to purchase some cucumbers

for his mother and – two birds with one stone – to seek out Mr Halloran.

biscuit

take the biscuit ◄

In British English, if you say that someone or something **takes the biscuit**, you are expressing surprise or anger at their extreme behaviour or qualities. **Take the cake** means the same.

For dirty tricks I can assure you it is the medical practices that really take the biscuit.

I've heard some odd things in my day but that took the biscuit.

This ban takes the biscuit. The whole idea is ridiculous and bureaucratic and not fair on the children.

bit

champ at the bit
chomp at the bit ◄

If you **are champing at the bit** or **are chomping at the bit**, you are impatient to do something, but are prevented from doing it, usually by circumstances that you have no control over. The verb 'chafe' is sometimes used instead of 'champ' or 'chomp'.

Foremen had been champing at the bit to strike before next week's meeting.

He had three of Goldman's best clients chomping at the bit to get a piece of this deal.

I'd better get this thing sorted out, or you'll be chafing at the bit at all the wasted time.

get the bit between your teeth ◄

If you **get the bit between** your **teeth**, you become very enthusiastic and determined about doing a particular job or task. The verbs 'have' and 'take' can be used instead of 'get'.

You're persistent when you get the bit between your teeth, I'll say that for you.

It's going to be difficult against Leeds United but the lads have got the bit between their teeth.

It's about time the government took the bit between its teeth and made it compulsory for drivers to attend proper driving courses.

bite

bite off more than you can chew ◄

If you say that someone **has bitten off more than** they **can chew**, you mean that they are trying to do something that is far too difficult for them to manage.

It was fair to wonder if I could even memorize the text, much less perform it. John, who always suffered from nerves in the theatre, was terrified that I had bitten off more than I could chew.

Don't bite off more than you can chew simply because everything is going so well.

a second bite at the cherry
two bites of the cherry ◄

If you get **a second bite at the cherry** or have **two bites of the cherry**, you have a second chance to do something, especially something that you failed at the first time. You can also say that you have **another bite at the cherry**. These expressions are used in British English.

We might, if we push hard enough, get a second bite at the cherry in two years' time.

I've had two bites of the cherry. Which was rather nice because all the mistakes I made with the first one, I hope I haven't repeated.

Several senior England players keep bidding farewell only to come back for another bite at the cherry.

take a bite out of something ◄

If something **takes a bite out of** a sum of money or other quantity, it takes away a part of it. This expression is used mainly in American English.

There is going to be a continuing growth in state and local taxes, so that they are going to be taking a bigger bite out of people's income than they ever have before.

But some of us, myself included, frankly, think we ought to have additional cuts in order to take a bigger bite out of the deficit.

biter

the biter gets bit

You can say that **the biter gets bit** when someone suffers as a result of their own actions, especially when they were intending to hurt someone else. This expression is used in British English.

Sympathy seldom abounds when the biter gets bit.

'Monday's vote,' one insider said, 'was a question of the biter getting bitten.'

Garner's victory was a case of the biter being bit.

bitten

once bitten, twice shy
once bitten ◄

People say **'once bitten, twice shy'** when they are explaining that a recent and unpleasant personal experience has made them very cautious about getting involved in similar situations in the future. Sometimes people just say **'once bitten'**.

I'm certainly not looking for new boyfriends or thinking of having any more kids. Once bitten, twice shy.

Before I could kick him he had scampered off again. Once bitten, twice shy, probably.

Do not expect Tokyo's punters, once bitten, to come rushing back for more.

black

black and blue ◄◄

If a part of your body is **black and blue**, it is badly bruised.

I didn't realise how clumsy I am. I was black and blue for three months.

I spent that night in hospital and was released the next day with minor head and neck injuries. My face was black and blue.

□ If someone **is beaten black and blue**, they are physically attacked and badly bruised.

They pulled my hair out and beat me black and blue.

A distraught mother has been ordered to hand over her twin daughters to the husband she claims beat her black and blue.

black and white ◄◄

If someone sees things in **black and white**, they see complex issues in simple terms of right and wrong. If a situation appears **black and white**, it seems to be a simple question of right and wrong, although it may in fact be very complex. These expressions are often used to criticize people who treat complex things in a very simple way.

That is not, any more, an accurate portrait of much of British society. People do not see these things purely in black and white.

She is still a champion of oversimplification, seeing issues in black and white.

The thing is not as black and white as the media have said.

□ You can also talk about a **black and white** question or issue, or about seeing things in **black and white** terms.

People think this is a sort of black and white issue that's very simple and that you can just make a decision.

The media portray the news in black-and-white terms.

in black and white ◄◄

If you say that something is **in black and white**, you mean that you have written proof of it.

You know, we've seen it. It's written right here in black and white.

We have a strict, clear rule in black and white, that sexual harassment will lead to expulsion.

in the black ◄◄◄

If a person or organization is **in the black**, they do not owe anyone any money. Compare **in the red**; see **red**.

Building societies stand to pick up waves of deserters from the high street banks, if the leading banks opt to end free banking for current account customers who stay in the black.

Last year, the company was back in the black, showing a modest pre-tax surplus of £4.6 million.

not as black as you are painted

If you say that someone is **not as black as** they **are painted**, you mean that they are not as bad as other people say they are. This is an informal expression, which some people consider offensive.

They had a strong mutual dislike of each other. I once said to Hilda, 'She's not as black as you paint her.'

I personally think that you are not so black as you have painted yourself.

blank

draw a blank: 1   ◄◄

If you are trying to find someone or something and you **draw a blank**, you cannot find them. If you are trying to find out about something and you **draw a blank**, you fail to find out about it.

I searched among the bottles and under and behind and inside everything I could think of and drew a blank.

We asked if they'd been in. We drew a blank.

We know a lot about what it does in mammals, birds, fish and reptiles, but we tend to draw a blank when it comes to humans.

draw a blank: 2

If you **draw a blank**, you are unable to remember something or to answer a question you are asked. This expression is used mainly in American English.

They asked him what reform policies China still plans to pursue. Mr. Yao seemed to draw a blank. Finally an aide prompted him.

Why do we recognise a face, but sometimes draw a blank when it comes to the name?

draw a blank: 3

In a sporting contest, if a team or competitor **draws a blank**, they do not score any goals or points, or win any races. This expression is used mainly in British journalism.

Rangers drew a blank at Hibernian – the champions were held nil-nil.

He now leads Pat Eddery, who drew a blank, 79-68 in the title race.

blanket

a wet blanket: 1

If you say that someone is **a wet blanket**, you mean that they spoil other people's fun because they are boring or miserable.

She made a visible effort to shake her blues. 'I'm sorry if I've been a wet blanket.'

'Hey', said Thack, looking at Michael. 'Stop being such a wet blanket.'

a wet blanket: 2

If something throws **a wet blanket** over an event or situation, it makes it less successful or enjoyable than it would otherwise have been.

Barre is worried that the Clinton economic plan will throw a wet blanket over the recovery.

In the year since then, the long wet blanket of the law has smothered the life of the free festival movement.

bleed

bleed someone dry
bleed someone white   ◄◄

If a person, organization, or country **is bled dry**, they are made weak, for example by being forced to use up all their money or resources. You can also say that someone **is bled white**.

The English bled my parents' country dry just like they have bled Scotland dry.

He extorted money from me on a regular basis for five years. But he was careful not to bleed me dry.

The most ludicrous and tragic spectacle on earth is to see a powerful nation bleeding itself white to build up vast heaps of armaments to put down a menace that cannot be put down by military means at all.

blessing

a blessing in disguise   ◄◄

If you describe an event as **a blessing in disguise**, you mean that it causes problems and difficulties at first, but later it turns out to bring great benefits or advantages.

Franklin's illness proved a blessing in disguise, for it gave him strength and courage which he had not had before.

The defeat might be a blessing in disguise – she now avoids a quarter final clash with America's Linda Harvey-Wild.

Other observers feel the split may be a blessing in disguise for the organization.

blind

blind as a bat

If you say that someone is as **blind as a bat**, you mean that they cannot see very well.

Everyone knew that Mary Nolan had been blind as a bat for years – she'd even suffered a damaging fall not so long ago, too.

Without my glasses I was blind as a bat.

the blind leading the blind

You can describe a situation as **the blind leading the blind** when the person in charge is just as incapable of doing the task as the person who they are meant to be helping or guiding.

If Cedric was going to work with Eric, it would be the blind leading the blind.

Their attempts to help the Third World poor were rather like the blind leading the blind.

□ This expression is sometimes varied by replacing 'blind' with another adjective appropriate to the subject that is being talked about.

His work certainly shocked the critics at his 1976 exhibition at New York's Museum of Modern Art. One damned it as an example of 'the banal leading the banal'.

fly blind

If someone **is flying blind** in a situation, they do not have anything to help or guide them.

We will be flying blind into a world we don't know anything about.

With billions of dollars at stake, the two presidents weren't willing to boost their offer while they were flying blind.

swear blind ◄

If someone **swears blind** that something is true, they insist that they are telling you the truth, even though you are not sure whether or not to believe them. This expression is used in British English; the American expression is **swear up and down**.

He had a reputation for being a bit of a philanderer but he swore blind that he had met the right girl in me and said he wanted to settle down.

Ron Atkinson swears blind that he bears no grudges against Manchester United for sacking him, but the atmosphere at Villa Park reeked of vengeance last night.

blink

on the blink ◄

A piece of machinery that is **on the blink** is not working properly.

We had to have the washing done at the laundry because our machine was on the blink.

The first computer went on the blink last Sunday.

block

on the block ◄◄◄

If something is put **on the block**, it is offered for sale at auction. This expression is used in American English; the British expression is **under the hammer**.

Last week, after months of rumors, the company officially put itself on the block.

The team's money worries had forced them to put the club on the block.

put your head on the block
put your neck on the block ◄

If you **put** your **head on the block** or **put** your **neck on the block**, you risk your reputation or position by taking a particular course of action. 'Lay' can be used instead of 'put', and 'chopping block' can be used instead of 'block'.

When the Prime Minister called a by-election in his own constituency, he put his head on the block.

He really put his neck on the block there and it's great to see his bravery being rewarded.

I don't know whether I can do what you want or not, and I am not going to put my head on the chopping block.

a stumbling block ◄◄◄

A **stumbling block** is a problem which stops you from achieving something.

US plans to produce some new, advanced chemical weapons have presented a stumbling block.

Officials did not say what the proposals contained, but they reportedly address some of the main stumbling blocks in the negotiations.

Your inability to choose between material security and emotional needs is a major stumbling block to your happiness.

blocks

off the blocks: 1
out of the blocks
off the starting blocks ◄

Off the blocks, **out of the blocks**, and **off the starting blocks** are used in expressions which tell you how quickly someone starts to do something. For example, if someone is 'first out of the blocks', they start to do something before everyone else.

The Liberal Democrats were first off the blocks with their manifesto on Monday.

Ontario was not fast off the starting blocks in developing any systematic intervention aimed at land conservation.

off the starting blocks: 2
off the blocks
out of the blocks

If someone gets **off the starting blocks**, **off the blocks**, or **out of the blocks**, they succeed in starting to do something, often despite difficulties.

People thought I was totally mad and, if they think that, then you just can't get off the starting block.

'All we need is to get started,' said manager Graeme Souness beforehand. To help him off the starting blocks he had 31-year-old Whelan back after a six months' absence with a thigh injury.

blood

after your blood

If someone is **after** your **blood**, they want to

harm or punish you, because you have harmed them or made them angry.

Adam has upset Broderick who is after his blood.

The entire street-gang network of New York is after their blood.

bad blood ◄◄

If there is **bad blood** between two people or groups, they have hostile feelings towards each other because of the arguments or quarrels they have had in the past.

The situation has reached crisis point because of the bad blood between the two.

Ever since the days of the Revolution there had always been bad blood between the two arms of the Soviet security forces.

Mr Levy said his relations with officials have been very friendly. There is no bad blood.

bay for blood ◄

If you say that people **are baying for blood**, you mean that they are demanding that a particular person should be hurt or punished, because of something that person has done. This expression is used in British English.

The travel company had just buried itself with debts of more than £12m and thousands of disappointed holidaymakers were baying for blood.

A large number of shareholders are now baying for his blood and although he owns a massive 15 percent of his company, he will be lucky to survive.

The tabloids have bayed for the blood of the killer, insisting on a custodial sentence.

blood and thunder ◄

If you describe a speech or performance as **blood and thunder**, you mean that it is full of exaggerated feelings or behaviour. This expression is used in British English.

In a blood-and-thunder speech, he called for sacrifice from everyone.

There's enough blood, thunder and smouldering passion to keep you watching.

blood is shed: 1
blood is spilled ◄◄◄

When someone talks about **blood being shed** or **blood being spilled**, they mean that people are being killed in fighting. These expressions are used mainly in journalism and literary writing.

All the signs are that if blood is spilled the countries will be at war.

The Surinam Embassy in the Hague said no blood had been spilt.

This is the main region where blood is being shed.

blood is shed: 2
blood is spilled

People sometimes talk about **blood being**

shed or **blood being spilled** when hardship is caused as a result of a change taking place.

Given the political blood that was spilled over the deficit reduction package, few observers believe the Congress and the president will do an about-face and start spending more.

blood is thicker than water

When people say **'blood is thicker than water'**, they mean that someone's loyalty to their family is greater than their loyalty to anyone else.

Families have their problems and jealousies, but blood is thicker than water.

'If Colonel Roosevelt is a candidate,' he told a reporter, 'I will not run against him. You know blood is thicker than water.'

blood, sweat, and tears ◄◄

If you say that a task or project involves **blood, sweat, and tears**, you mean that it is very hard to carry out and needs a lot of effort or suffering.

Forget the battle honours: what about the toil? The blood, sweat and tears?

That day he started work at the company which his wife Pat had spilled blood, sweat and tears to form.

It's almost as if the end product – the songs themselves – are less important than the blood, sweat and tears that went into them.

□ People sometimes vary this expression by replacing one of the nouns with a noun relevant to the subject they are talking about.

It seemed absurd to be told to sum up a story that has taken years of blood, sweat and creativity in '25 words or less'.

have blood on your hands
have bloody hands ◄

If you say that someone **has blood on** their **hands** or **has bloody hands**, you are accusing them of being responsible for a death, or for the deaths of several people.

Members of a crowd that gathered outside his residence said he had blood on his hands.

I want him to know he has my son's blood on his hands.

America befriended dictators with bloody hands.

in cold blood ◄◄◄

If you say that one person killed another **in cold blood**, you mean that they did it in a calm and deliberate way, rather than in anger or self-defence. People often use this expression to express shock or horror at a killing.

They murdered my brother. They shot him down in cold blood.

She was executed in cold blood while her boyfriend looked on helplessly.

□ You can describe a killing as **cold-blooded**

or say that the person who did it is **cold-blooded**.

This is just another attempt to excuse the cold-blooded murder of an innocent woman.

The argument is self-defence, but it is clear to Blackburn that she is a cold-blooded killer.

in your blood ◄◄

If you say that something is **in** your **blood**, you mean that it is a very important part of you and seems natural to you, for example because it is traditional in your family or culture.

Trilok has music in his blood. 'I was born into a family of musicians.'

Politics is in his blood. He is the 18th-generation head of a family of feudal rulers in Kumamoto in southern Japan.

He has Africa in his blood, having lived, worked and travelled there for many years.

like getting blood out of a stone
like getting blood out of a turnip

If you have difficulty persuading someone to give you money or information, you can say that it is **like getting blood out of a stone**. In American English, you can also say that it is **like getting blood out of a turnip**.

The goods have to be returned to their rightful owner and getting money back from the seller is like getting blood from a stone.

'You do make it difficult, don't you?' Hebburn said at last. 'It's like getting blood out of a stone.'

☐ People sometimes vary these expressions, using other verbs instead of 'get'.

Congressman James Moran said 'There is no money. You can't squeeze blood out of a turnip.'

make your blood boil
someone's blood boils ◄◄

If you say that something **makes** your **blood boil**, you mean that it makes you very angry. When you are very angry about something, you can say that your **blood boils**.

This statement is untrue and makes my blood boil.

It makes my blood boil. He doesn't like the players yet he's always trying to interfere.

My blood boiled, but I tried to answer as simply and directly as possible.

make your blood run cold
make your blood freeze ◄

If you say that something **makes** your **blood run cold** or **makes** your **blood freeze**, you mean that it frightens or shocks you a great deal. When you are extremely frightened or shocked, you can say that your **blood runs cold** or your **blood freezes**. All these expressions are used mainly in novels.

The rage in his eyes made her blood run cold.

It makes my blood run cold to think what this poor, helpless child must have gone through.

Then his blood froze. For there in the crowd was the one face he didn't want to see.

☐ You can use **blood-freezing** before a noun, to indicate that something is extremely frightening or shocking.

It's a blood-freezing image of corrupted innocence.

new blood
fresh blood ◄◄◄

If you talk about **new blood** or **fresh blood**, you are referring to new people who are brought into a company or organization to make it more efficient, exciting, or innovative. Compare **young blood**.

The group is understood to be looking for a permanent replacement to bring new blood to the role of chief executive.

The July Ministerial reshuffle is a chance to freshen up the government and make way for new blood.

out for blood

If people are **out for blood**, they intend to attack someone, or to make them suffer in some other way.

They seem to be out for blood, and they're attacking everywhere where their enemy is.

scent blood
taste blood ◄

In a competitive situation, if you **scent blood**, you sense a weakness in your opponent and take advantage of it. If you **taste blood**, you have a small victory and this encourages you to think that you can defeat your opponent completely.

Right wing parties, scenting blood, have been holding talks aimed at building an alternative coalition.

The real opposition to the Government continues to be its own backbenchers who have now tasted blood for the first time.

☐ You can also say that someone gets **a scent of blood** or **a taste of blood**.

The market has got the scent of blood and, having sniffed it, they are going for it.

sweat blood ◄

You can say that you **are sweating blood** to emphasize that you are working very hard to achieve something.

I have been sweating blood over the question of what is right and feasible to do.

I sweat blood to write songs with tunes that you can remember.

young blood ◄

If you talk about **young blood**, you are referring to young people who are brought into a company or organization in order to provide new ideas or new talent. Compare **new blood**.

I left medicine anyway. I wasn't really cut out for it, and the family business was in need of young blood.

The selectors have at last shown some bravery and forward thinking and gone for some young blood, fielding a side whose average age is just 26.

□ You can refer to young people who are full of enthusiasm and fresh ideas as **young bloods**.

Ray Floyd proved he can still compete with the young bloods when he became the oldest winner of the US Open at 43.

blot

a blot on the landscape ◄

If you describe a building or some other structure as **a blot on the landscape**, you mean that it is very ugly and spoils a place which would otherwise be very attractive.

The power station is both a blot on the landscape and a smear on the environment.

While country churchyards have much to commend them, urban cemeteries, it seemed to me, were blots on the landscape, dank, ugly and with tombstones far gone in decay.

a blot on your escutcheon

If there is **a blot on** your **escutcheon**, you have damaged your reputation by doing something wrong. Other nouns with a similar meaning can be used instead of 'blot'. This is an old-fashioned expression, which is used in British English.

For the leaders, this is probably a blip rather than a blot on the escutcheon.

Over the past 70 years it is probably true that there has been only one serious stain upon the Conservative Party's escutcheon.

blow

soften the blow
cushion the blow ◄◄◄

If something **softens the blow** or **cushions the blow**, it makes an unpleasant change or piece of news seem less unpleasant and easier to accept.

Although attempts were made to soften the blow, by reducing what some people had to pay, the tax still met with widespread opposition.

Although it will reduce weekly pay packets by around £50, the firm is offering to cushion the blow with a £4,000 cash handout spread over two years and by guaranteeing jobs and minimum hours.

strike a blow for something
strike a blow against something ◄◄◄

If you **strike a blow for** something such as

a cause or principle, you do something which supports it or makes it more likely to succeed. If you **strike a blow against** something, you succeed in weakening its harmful effect.

If she wins a vote of confidence in parliament, she will become the country's first woman Prime Minister. Her appointment would strike a blow for women's rights in Poland.

Johan has struck a blow for equality against an obvious and intolerable anomaly in the law.

'We have struck a major blow against drug dealing and crack manufacture in London,' said Drugs Squad Inspector Richard Woodman.

blows

come to blows ◄◄

If two people **come to blows**, they disagree so much about something that they start to fight.

Two smartly-dressed women came to blows on a crowded commuter train yesterday, throwing rush-hour services into chaos.

Some residents nearly came to blows over this proposal.

blue

out of the blue ◄◄◄

If something happens **out of the blue**, it happens unexpectedly.

Could it be that these people were really unhealthy but just didn't know about it? Or did the disease really strike out of the blue?

Then, out of the blue, a solicitor's letter arrived.

Turner's resignation came out of the blue in the aftermath of his team's 3-0 defeat at Portsmouth.

bluff

call someone's bluff ◄◄◄

If someone has made a threat and you **call** their **bluff**, you put them in a position in which they would be forced to do what they have been threatening. You do this because you do not really believe that they will carry out their threat.

At a meeting with student representatives on October 12, Mr Lukanov warned that he would deal severely with any protest actions in the universities. Now that the students have called his bluff, it remains to be seen what Mr Lukanov can do.

The Socialists have finally decided to call the opposition's bluff, and it looks as if they have succeeded. One of the three main opposition parties, the Radicals, have broken ranks by declaring that they would, after all, take part in the electoral contest.

blushes

spare someone's blushes
save someone's blushes ◄◄

If someone **spares** your **blushes** or **saves** your **blushes**, they do something that saves you from an embarrassing situation. These expressions are used in British English.

Hundreds of men were spared their blushes yesterday when a court ruled that the names of a prostitute's clients should remain secret.

Andy Gray spared Tottenham's blushes last night, scoring a superb goal against Enfield.

If such a resolution was passed, it would increase the feeling that the Government had lost control. But it would be better to pass it and save the pits and 30,000 miners' jobs than save the blushes of a politically bankrupt Government.

board

above board ◄◄

If you describe a situation or business as **above board**, you mean that it is honest and legal.

If you are caught out in anything not strictly above board, you may find yourself having to provide the taxman with old bank statements and proofs of income going back years.

I have never taken a penny of any of the money we've raised for the ministry. And anyone who wants to inspect our books can see for themselves that we are totally above board.

If this export had been conducted in an honest and above-board fashion, the defendants would have had no difficulty in reclaiming VAT paid on the gold.

across the board ◄◄◄

If a policy or development applies **across the board**, it applies equally to all the people or areas of business connected with it.

It seems that across the board all shops have cut back on staff.

The compromise proposal reduces funding across the board for community development grants, student loans, mass transit and summer schools.

□ You can also talk about an **across-the-board** policy or development.

There is an across-the-board increase in the amount of meat eaten by children.

back to the drawing board ◄◄◄

If you say that you will have to go **back to the drawing board**, you mean that something which you have done has not been successful and you will have to start again or try another idea.

His government should go back to the drawing board to rethink their programme in time to return it to the Parliament by September.

Failing to win means going back to the draw-

ing board, identifying shortcomings and attempting to improve on them.

go by the board
go by the boards

If a plan or activity **goes by the board** or **goes by the boards**, it is abandoned and forgotten, because it is no longer possible to carry it out. 'Go by the board' is used in British English and 'go by the boards' is used in American English.

Although you may have managed to persuade him, while he was at school, to do some constructive revision before examinations, you may find that all your efforts go by the board when he is at university.

I think we probably all forget that President Lincoln suspended habeas corpus. There were a lot of civil rights went by the boards.

sweep the board ◄

If someone **sweeps the board** in a competition or election, they win all the prizes or seats. This expression is used in British English.

The women's team has been quite outstanding, sweeping the board in swimming, diving, cycling and weight-lifting and missing only one gold in the athletics.

The opposition has swept the board in Sofia, where the renamed Communists have failed to win a single seat.

take something on board: 1 ◄◄◄

If you **take** an idea, suggestion, or fact **on board**, you understand it or accept it. This expression is used in British English.

I shall be hoping that the council will take that message on board.

I listened to them, took their comments on board and then made the decision.

We've never really taken on board the fact that we're in the computer age.

take something on board: 2

If you **take a** task or problem **on board**, you accept responsibility for it and start dealing with it. This expression is used in British English.

All you have to do is phone, telex or fax us. Our co-ordinator will take your problem on board and solve it.

boat

float someone's boat

If something **floats** your **boat**, you find it exciting, attractive, or interesting.

I can see its appeal. But it doesn't float my boat.

in the same boat ◄◄◄

If you say that two or more people are **in the same boat**, you mean that they are in the same unpleasant or difficult situation.

We are all in the same boat as the miners. People all over Britain are being made redundant every week.

If baldness is creeping up on you, take heart – 40 per cent of men under 35 are in the same boat.

We were two mums in the same boat and able to make each other feel better.

push the boat out

If you **push the boat out**, you spend a lot of money in order to have a very enjoyable time or to celebrate in a lavish way. This expression is used in British English.

I earn enough to push the boat out now and again.

Keep an eye on James. He's likely to push the boat out among his friends.

rock the boat   ◀◀◀

If someone tells you not to **rock the boat**, they are telling you not to do anything which might cause trouble or upset a stable situation.

While he is careful not to rock the boat with any ill-timed criticism, there is clearly some frustration that he is not being used to maximum effect.

Diplomats are expecting so much instability in a power struggle after his death that they argue it's unwise to rock the boat now.

□ If someone **is rocking the boat**, their behaviour is likely to cause trouble or upset a stable situation. Behaviour like this can be described as **boat-rocking**.

Before the report was concluded, he pulled back on the subject. I suspect the other parts of the White House complained he was rocking the boat.

I'm outspoken, sometimes critical of the organization, which is seen as boat-rocking, upsetting a comfortable arrangement.

Bob

Bob's your uncle

When you are describing a process or series of events, you can say **'Bob's your uncle'** to indicate that it ends exactly as expected or in exactly the right way. This expression is used in British English.

What he is implying is that anyone can do it. You just tag along with a teacher for a while, and in a year, Bob's your uncle, you are a teacher too.

See this safety valve here? Well, if the boiler should ever get too hot, the safety valve releases all the excess steam, and Bob's your uncle. No problem.

body

body and soul   ◀◀◀

You can use **body and soul** to emphasize

that you are doing something with all your energy or to the best of your ability.

They worked body and soul to make this day a success.

She was now committed to the band, body and soul.

Nancy threw herself into lost causes with quixotic blindness, identifying body and soul with the suffering and misery she had seen in Spain, Mexico, and Harlem.

a body blow   ◀◀

If you receive **a body blow**, something happens which causes you great disappointment or difficulty. This expression is used mainly in British journalism.

The sport received a body blow when the schools programme was virtually halted.

The result will deliver a body blow to Conservative party confidence.

Already these tax concessions have been whittled away and could be abolished altogether by 1994. This will be a body blow to the manufacturers, but not a fatal one.

keep body and soul together
hold body and soul together

If you do something to **keep body and soul together** or to **hold body and soul together**, you do it because it is the only way you can earn enough money to buy the basic things that you need to live.

20-year-old Rafael says he's selling firewood to keep body and soul together.

For a while he held body and soul together by working as a migrant laborer.

over my dead body   ◀

If you reply **'over my dead body'** when a plan or action has been suggested, you are saying emphatically that you dislike it, and will do everything you can to prevent it.

They will get Penbrook Farm only over my dead body.

Tough-guy Arnold Schwarzenegger's wife has told him he will go into politics 'over her dead body'.

boil

come to the boil
bring something to a boil   ◀

If a situation or feeling **comes to the boil** or **comes to a boil**, it reaches a climax or becomes very active and intense. 'Come to the boil' is used in British English and 'come to a boil' is used in American English.

Their anger with France came to the boil last week when they officially protested at what they saw as a French media campaign against them.

The issue has come to a boil in Newark, where federal prosecutors have warned lawyers that if the chairman is indicted, the govern-

ment may move to seize the money that he is using to pay legal fees.

□ Someone or something can also **bring** a situation or feeling **to the boil** or **bring** it **to a boil**.

The opposition is sure to bring the dispute back to the boil in any election campaign.

The gifted propagandist brings to a boil ideas and passions already simmering in the minds of his hearers.

off the boil: 1 ◄

In sport, if someone goes **off the boil**, they are less successful than they were in the past. This expression is used in British English.

I concede that I went slightly off the boil last season.

Sandy Lyle says it pays to go back to the fundamentals when your game goes off the boil.

off the boil: 2

If a feeling or situation goes **off the boil**, it becomes less intense or urgent. This expression is used in British English.

If a relationship seems to be going off the boil, it is a good idea to appraise the situation.

Since the massive outbreak of 1972, discontent had rarely been off the boil; and minor revolts had continued throughout the Seventies.

on the boil: 1 ◄

If a situation or feeling is **on the boil**, it is at its point of greatest activity or intensity. This expression is used in British English.

A word here, a phrase there were enough to keep tempers on the boil almost to the end.

Across the border in Sweden, a similar debate is on the boil.

on the boil: 2

In sport, if a person is **on the boil**, they are performing very successfully. This expression is used in British English.

All three players are obviously on the boil at the moment in the Italian league.

bold

bold as brass

If you say that someone does something **bold as brass**, you mean that they do it without being ashamed or embarrassed, although their behaviour is shocking or annoying to other people.

Their leader, bold as brass, came improperly dressed, wearing a lounge suit while all the others were wearing black ties.

Barry has come into the game bold as brass, brash and businesslike.

bolt

a bolt from the blue
a bolt out of the blue ◄◄

If you say that an event or piece of news was like **a bolt from the blue** or **a bolt out of the blue**, you mean that it surprised you because it was completely unexpected. You use this expression mainly when talking about unpleasant things.

A Foreign Office spokesman had described the coup as 'a bolt from the blue'.

Mrs Thomas says the arrest had come 'like a bolt out of the blue'.

shoot your bolt

If you say that someone **has shot** their **bolt**, you mean that they have done everything they can to achieve something but have failed, and now can do nothing else to achieve their aims. This expression is used in British English.

The opposition have really shot their bolt; they'll never ever get any more votes than this.

Adeline shot her last bolt now. She opened her eyes very wide, and for an instant it was as if Amy was looking into her own imploring face. 'Please, Amy, don't go.'

bomb

go like a bomb

If you say that a vehicle or a horse **goes like a bomb**, you mean that it can move very fast. This expression is used in British English.

Once I had a Czechoslovakian motorbike. It was built like a tank, weighed a ton, went like a bomb and was pure joy to ride.

put a bomb under something

If you say that you want to **put a bomb under** an organization or system, you mean that you feel impatient with it because it is old-fashioned or inefficient, and you want to completely change the way it operates. Other verbs can be used instead of 'put'. This expression is used in British English.

One half of us admired and valued the BBC's high standards, the other half longed to put a bomb under it and propel it into innovation.

We are ready for radical change. I have said before, we need a bomb under the system.

bombshell

drop a bombshell ◄◄

If someone **drops a bombshell**, they suddenly give you a piece of bad news which you were not expecting.

Next day the bombshell was dropped on the front pages of the newspapers: the company had gone into voluntary liquidation.

My ex-wife is on the phone and she drops a bombshell. Sue, our daughter, is pregnant.

bone

a bone of contention ◄◄◄

A **bone of contention** is an issue or point that people have been arguing about for a long time.

The president's plan to phase out protectionism for Brazil's backward computer industry is being blocked, as are his efforts to enforce patent protection. Both issues have been major bones of contention with the US.

Pay, of course, is not the only bone of contention.

close to the bone
near to the bone ◄

If you say that a remark or piece of writing is **close to the bone** or **near to the bone**, you mean that it makes people uncomfortable, because it deals with things which they prefer not to be discussed.

Penny said 'Let's talk about Christina.' But for Buck, this was getting dangerously close to the bone.

This isn't strictly satire, it's far too close to the bone to be funny.

'We'd better end here because this is getting...' She did not finish the sentence, but I guess she was going to say 'too near to the bone'.

cut to the bone ◄◄

If resources or costs **are cut to the bone**, they are reduced as much as they possibly can be. Verbs such as 'pare', 'shave', and 'strip' are sometimes used instead of 'cut'.

We managed to break even by cutting costs to the bone.

The universities feel they have already been pared to the bone by government cuts.

Eric had taken on the competition by shaving his running costs to the bone and offering the lowest prices possible.

have a bone to pick with someone

If you say that you **have a bone to pick with** someone, you mean that you are annoyed with them about something, and you want to talk to them about it.

'I have a bone to pick with you.' She felt justified in bringing up a matter that she had been afraid to discuss before.

Both men had a legitimate bone to pick with a government which has cold-bloodedly persisted with policies that are hurting its own supporters more than anybody else.

bones

the bare bones ◄◄◄

If you refer to **the bare bones** of something,

you are referring to its most basic parts or details.

Russian politics may not settle down into a multi-party system for some time. But the bare bones of representative democracy are there.

We worked out the bare bones of a deal.

We needed to strip the flat down to its bare bones. It was a terrific engineering and architectural challenge. It also raised many design problems.

□ You can use **bare-bones** before a noun.

The mayor will then have to slash the city's already bare-bones budget, and this will put a serious dent into all the city's services.

feel something in your bones
have a feeling in your bones ◄

If you say that you can **feel** something **in** your **bones**, you mean that you feel very strongly that you are right about something, although you cannot explain why. Verbs such as 'know', 'believe', and 'sense' are sometimes used instead of 'feel'.

Joe, I have a hunch you're going to lose tonight. I just feel it in my bones.

No amount of rationalisation or special pleading can disguise what people across the country know in their bones. His departure is not just a sadness and a loss; it is potentially a crisis.

□ You can also say that you **have a feeling in** your **bones**.

I've got a feeling in my bones we're going to lose this by-election.

make no bones about something ◄◄

If you **make no bones about** something, you do not hesitate to express your thoughts or feelings about it, even though other people may find what you say unacceptable or embarrassing.

And ever since that morning in Malcy when he had learned that they were bringing her with them, Dave had made no bones about resenting her presence.

There will be changes in this Welsh team until we get it right. I make no bones about that.

These companies make no bones about the fact that they are there to promote social and economic development as well as to make money.

book

bring someone to book ◄◄

If someone **is brought to book**, they are punished officially for something wrong that they have done. This is a fairly formal expression, which is used in British English.

No-one has yet been brought to book for a crime which outraged Italy.

The school has been closed indefinitely following the incident. The nuns say they will not re-

open the school until the culprits are brought to book.

by the book
go by the book
play things by the book ◄◄◄

If you do something **by the book**, you do it correctly, and strictly according to the rules. You can also say that you **go by the book** or **play things by the book**.

Modern man is often dull, studious, careful, safe. He does everything by the book.

They could have taken a stranglehold on the game, but they seemed determined to go by the book and not rush things.

Although the manager of the shop wasn't aggressive, he played things by the book and was completely unforgiving. So I was taken down to the police station and charged with theft.

□ You can use **by-the-book** before a noun to describe a person or their way of doing things.

He was content to process information and follow a by-the-book approach, always working toward the end of something.

□ If something is done correctly and in the usual way, you can say that it **goes by the book**.

As it looks now, this campaign will not go by the book. It'll be nothing like we've ever seen before.

a closed book

In British English, if you say that something or someone is **a closed book** to you, you mean that you know or understand very little about them. Compare **an open book** and **close the book on** something.

Economics were a closed book to him. It constituted a strange, illogical territory where two and two didn't always make four.

close the book on something ◄

If you **close the book on** something, you bring it to a definite end. You often use this expression to talk about a difficult or unpleasant situation being brought to an end. Compare **a closed book**.

Chancellor Kohl, for his part, said the two countries had closed the book on their painful past.

Lawyers say they are happy to close the book on one of the most frustrating chapters of the company's history.

American taxpayers will contribute 7.1 billion dollars toward closing the books on the war.

in your book ◄◄

You can say '**in my book**' when you are stating your own belief or opinion, especially when it is different from the beliefs or opinions of other people.

People can say what they like, but in my book he's not at all a bad chap.

I wanted him to call the police. In my book a violent woman's just as dangerous as a violent man.

Over-involvement with the client was a major crime in her book.

an open book ◄

If you say that a person's life or character is **an open book**, you mean that you can find out everything about it, because nothing is kept secret. Compare **a closed book**.

They trot out a standard answer when questioned about the background of Desiree and her family. 'Their lives are an open book,' says a spokesman. 'They are good people and she has always been a good kid.'

Her long life is not a completely open book, but it is full of anecdotes and insights into her part in Hollywood history.

read someone like a book

If you say that you can **read** someone **like a book**, you mean that you find it easy to know what they are thinking and planning.

Very clever of them, that bit. They must have read me like a book.

There are a number of books on the market which suggest that it is possible to learn to read a person like a book.

throw the book at someone ◄

If a person in authority **throws the book at** someone who has committed an offence, they give them the greatest punishment that is possible for the offence that they have committed.

The prosecutor is urging the judge to throw the book at Blumberg.

'If this is found to be true then we will throw the book at the clubs involved,' Barry Smart, the chairman of the league, said yesterday.

you can't judge a book by its cover ◄

If someone says '**you can't judge a book by its cover**', they mean that you should wait until you know someone or something better before deciding whether you like them, because your first impressions may be wrong.

Before, children who couldn't rely on their own intelligence to boost their image resorted to such a mode of dress. But now the intelligent pupils feel able to express themselves. It just goes to show that you can't judge a book by its cover.

We may say that we don't believe in judging a book by the cover, but research has shown that we do, over and over again.

books

cook the books ◄

If someone **cooks the books**, they dishonestly change the figures in their financial accounts in order to deceive people. People sometimes do this in order to steal money.

She knew that when the auditors looked over the books there would be no hiding the fact that she had cooked the books and £3 million was missing.

Four years ago, he vowed to strike back after discovering that a promoter was cooking the books.

☐ You can also say that someone **cooks the books** when they dishonestly change other kinds of written evidence for their own purposes.

The National Population Commission admits that, in its recent trials in several areas, many officials cooked the books.

in someone's bad books

If you are **in** someone's **bad books**, you have done something that has annoyed them. This expression is used in British English.

Sir John was definitely in the Treasury's bad books for incorrect thinking on economic prospects.

Thomas gloomily speculated that he might be the next to get into Mrs Simpson's bad books.

in someone's good books   ◄

If you are **in** someone's **good books**, you have done something that has pleased them. This expression is used in British English.

I never really was that bothered about being in the teacher's good books.

While Becky was out, Jamie made an attempt to get back in her good books by doing all the housework.

boot

get the boot
give someone the boot   ◄◄

If someone **gets the boot** or **is given the boot**, they lose their job. These are informal expressions.

The chief reason he got the boot was because the Chancellor didn't trust him any more.

Davis was given the boot after just nine days of filming and replaced by Jonathan Kaplan.

☐ You can also use these expressions to talk about someone whose partner has ended their relationship, often in a sudden or unkind way.

Sean has been given the boot by his girlfriend after admitting he'd been unfaithful to her.

put the boot into someone: 1
put the boot in   ◄◄

If someone **puts the boot into** a person or thing, especially a very weak person or thing, they criticize them very severely or are very unkind about them. You can also say that someone **puts the boot in**. The verb 'stick' is sometimes used instead of 'put'. This is an informal expression, which is used in British English.

Instead of sticking the boot into those in pov-

erty, the Prime Minister should give everyone an equal share of the cake.

There's no one quite like an unpublished novelist for putting the boot into established reputations.

Maybe because of his diminutive stature, Mr Carman uses his outstanding ability with language to make up for it and put the boot in.

put the boot in: 2

If someone **puts the boot in**, they attack another person by kicking or hitting them. This is an informal expression, which is used in British English.

Policemen who are tempted to put the boot in occasionally will have to tread more carefully in future.

boots

die with your boots on

If you say that someone **died with** their **boots on**, you mean that they died while they were still actively involved in their work.

Unlike most Asian businesspeople who die with their boots on, he has very sensibly left the entire running of Seamark to his son, apart from the occasional word of advice.

Like the legendary cowboy who proudly professes he wants to die in the saddle with his boots on, he says when his turn comes 'I always pray that I'll die at work, gardening.'

☐ People sometimes replace 'boots' with another word which relates to a person's job or life.

His career lasted longer than his looks. Wrinkles and all, he died with his greasepaint on.

fill your boots

If you **fill** your **boots** with something valuable or desirable, you get as much of it as you can. This expression is used in British English.

Not everything in Japan looks bleak: having filled their boots with cheap capital in 1987-89, many companies remain liquid enough to do without bank loans.

lick someone's boots
lick someone's shoes

If you say that one person **licks** another person's **boots** or **licks** their **shoes**, you are critical of them because they will do anything at all to please the second person, often because the second person is powerful or influential and the first person wants something from them.

Even if you didn't have an official position you'd still be a big shot locally, everybody'd be licking your boots.

☐ You can call someone who does this **a bootlicker**.

By now Bob demanded that everyone in his immediate circle sound like a skilled bootlicker.

quake in your boots ◄

If you say that someone **is quaking in** their **boots**, you mean that they are very frightened or anxious about something that is about to happen. Verbs such as 'shake', 'shiver', and 'tremble' are sometimes used instead of 'quake'. **Quake in** your **shoes** means the same.

If you stand up straight you'll give an impression of self confidence even if you're quaking in your boots.

Someone had to tell the packed club that he wouldn't be appearing – you can imagine me shaking in my boots, but somehow I managed to survive.

step into someone's boots
fill someone's boots ◄

In sport, if you take over from another person who has been injured or who has given up their position, you can say that you **step into** their **boots**. If you are as successful as them, you can say that you **fill** their **boots**. These expressions are used mainly in British English. Compare **step into** someone's **shoes**; see **shoes**.

Michael Kinane, the leading Irish jockey, has turned down the chance to step into Steve Cauthen's boots and ride for Sheikh Mohammed next season.

It is sad that he's gone, but if ever there was a man to fill his boots, it's Kevin Keegan.

bootstraps

pull yourself up by your bootstraps ◄

If you say that someone **has pulled** themselves **up by** their **bootstraps**, you are showing admiration for them because they have improved their situation by their own efforts, without help from anyone else. Other verbs are sometimes used instead of 'pull'.

It was his ability to pull himself up by his bootstraps which appealed to Mrs Thatcher. She defied those with misgivings by making him deputy chairman.

It is what this country was invented to do – to change our lives. Lift yourself up by the bootstraps, young fellow. Make yourself upwardly mobile.

to your bootstraps

If you say that someone is, for example, British **to** their **bootstraps**, you are emphasizing that they have all the characteristics you would expect to find in a British person. This expression is used mainly in Australian English.

Lord McAlpine and all his friends are law and order men to their bootstraps.

Sir Robert Menzies was British to the bootstraps.

bottle

hit the bottle ◄

If you say that someone **is hitting the bottle**, you mean that they are drinking too much alcohol, usually because something very unpleasant or upsetting has happened to them.

One newspaper even said I'd started hitting the bottle. Complete rubbish.

Teenagers from authoritarian or uncaring families are twice as likely as other youngsters to be heavy drinkers. 'They will hit the bottle to rebel,' said researcher Geoff Lowe.

bottom

be at the bottom of something
lie at the bottom of something

If you say that a particular thing **is at the bottom of** an undesirable attitude or situation or **lies at the bottom of** it, you mean that it is the real cause of it.

Remember that pride is at the bottom of all great mistakes.

This decision quite probably lies at the bottom of the colony's current discontent.

the bottom falls out of something
the bottom drops out of something ◄

If **the bottom falls out of** a market or industry, people stop buying its products in as large quantities as before. You can also say .**the bottom drops out** of a market or industry.

But just as quickly, the bottom fell out of the American home video game market.

By the late seventies that process was nearly finished and then the bottom dropped out of the steel industry and heavy industry in general.

bump along the bottom ◄

If you say that a country's economy **is bumping along the bottom**, you mean that it has reached a low level of performance, and is not getting any better or any worse. This expression is used in British English.

New car sales are continuing to bump along the bottom of recession as the motor industry shows little sign that it is going to revive substantially this year.

People are beginning to sense that we are bumping along at the bottom, but we are not going any further down.

get to the bottom of something ◄◄◄

If you **get to the bottom of** a problem or mystery, you solve it by discovering the truth about it.

Moorhead Kennedy says the investigation is necessary to get to the bottom of the case, which has spawned rumors and innuendo for a decade.

The attack was quite severe. We intend to get

to the bottom of things and, if needs be, ensure that action is brought against those responsible for it.

The secrets of a truly happy couple are ultimately a private mystery, but we've tried to get to the bottom of it.

bounds

out of bounds: 1 ◄◄◄

If a place is **out of bounds**, you are not allowed to go there.

The area has been out of bounds to foreigners for more than a month.

I'll make it clear that the kitchen is out of bounds.

The site has been out of bounds to civilians for more than ten years.

□ You can use **out-of-bounds** before a noun.

Avoid signposted out-of-bounds areas.

out of bounds: 2

If a subject is **out of bounds**, you are not allowed to discuss it.

The private lives of public figures should be out of bounds to the press and public.

'We'll put the subject out of bounds.' 'You can't do that. You promised me when I was twelve that I could always talk to you about anything.'

bow

bow and scrape ◄

If you accuse someone of **bowing and scraping**, you mean that they are behaving towards a powerful or famous person in a way that you consider too respectful.

Whatever the aides may say about bowing and scraping, however, the royals expect it. They even indulge in it themselves.

I'm hoping my hereditary title will not put off prospective customers. It can be a drawback because some people feel they have to bow and scrape.

□ 'Bow' is pronounced with the same vowel sound as the word 'how'.

take a bow ◄

People sometimes write **take a bow** before or after a person's name when they want to congratulate that person or show their admiration for them. This expression is used mainly in British journalism.

There are only three of them – take a bow, Grant Lee Phillips on guitar and vocals, Paul Kimble on bass and drummer Joey Peters – but they sound like an orchestra.

When you've got the best camerawork and the best commentators – Martin Tyler, take a bow – it's hard to go far wrong.

□ 'Bow' is pronounced with the same vowel sound as the word 'how'.

box

a black box ◄

You can refer to a process or system as **a black box** when you know that it produces a particular result but you do not understand how it works.

Only a decade ago cancer was a black box about which we knew nothing at the molecular level.

'When we were faced with this question we were also faced with how very little is known about the nature of the resistance to the pest in American vine species,' says Walker. He describes the phenomenon as 'a black box'.

out of the box: 1 ◄

If you come **out of the box** in a particular way, you begin an activity in that way. If you are first **out of the box**, you are the first person to do something. This expression is used mainly in American English.

Are you anticipating that Clinton is going to come right out of the box with a whole series of fairly substantial decisions?

Arco is definitely first out of the box with an alternative gas for cars without catalytic converters.

out of the box: 2

If you buy something such as a computer or software and you can use it **out of the box**, you can use it immediately, without having to do or learn complicated things first.

The computer industry has yet to sell a PC which can be used by a novice, straight out of the box.

You can, thank goodness, also use Origin straight out of the box.

out of your box

If you say that someone is **out of** their **box**, you mean that they are drunk or affected by drugs, or that they are very foolish. This is an informal expression, which is used in British English.

The guy must have been seriously out of his box!

boy

a whipping boy ◄

If you refer to someone or something as **a whipping boy**, you mean that people blame them when things go wrong, even though they may not be responsible for what has happened.

Honecker may have become a convenient whipping boy for the failures of the communist regime.

This is the story of how America's favorite whipping boy became her favorite son.

Businessmen fear that they and the hard-won free-market reforms will be the whipping boys for the economic ills that confront the new administration.

your blue-eyed boy
your fair-haired boy ◄

If you say that a man is someone's **blue-eyed boy** or **fair-haired boy**, you mean that the person has a very high opinion of the man and gives him special treatment. You usually use these expressions to indicate that you think the person is wrong to have this opinion or to treat the man so favourably. 'Blue-eyed boy' is used mainly in British English and 'fair-haired boy' is used mainly in American English.

He'd lost interest in Willy by that time – I was the blue-eyed boy.

For ten years you've been everybody's blue-eyed boy. You're one of the best-known magistrates in the country.

Okay, okay. I won't do anything to hurt your fair-haired boy. And business is business. We'll work together as we always have.

boys

boys will be boys ◄

People say '**boys will be boys**' when they want to excuse the noisy or rough way a boy is behaving by saying that it is normal for boys to be noisy and rough. This expression is also used to comment on similar behaviour in adult men.

'Your troubles are just beginning,' they would say, shaking their heads. 'Boys will be boys.'

The idea that 'boys will be boys' – so it's okay to smoke and drink too much and do dangerous things with little regard for personal safety – has to change if we are to see any improvement in the death and disease statistics for men.

□ You can talk about a **boys will be boys** attitude or situation.

He is not some showbiz celebrity or soccer star whose private misdemeanours can be shrugged off with a 'boys will be boys' attitude.

one of the boys ◄◄

If you describe a man as **one of the boys**, you mean that he is accepted as belonging to a group of men who behave in ways which are considered typically masculine. People sometimes describe a woman as being **one of the boys** when she behaves in a way which allows her to be accepted as part of a group of men. Compare **one of the lads**; see **lads**.

His overly enthusiastic efforts to seem just one of the boys were sometimes embarrassing.

If she played at being one of the boys she was condemned for being unwomanly. If she didn't join in she was seen as aloof.

brains

pick someone's brains
pick someone's brain ◄

If you **pick** someone's **brains** or **pick** their **brain**, you ask them for advice or information, because they know more about a subject than you do.

I'd like to pick your brains about something. Nothing urgent.

She, in turn, picked my brains about London – as she'd never been outside of the US and was thinking about a trip to England.

rack your brains
rack your brain ◄◄

If you **rack** your **brains** or **rack** your **brain**, you think very hard about something or try very hard to remember it.

Reformers are racking their brains for a way to slow down these processes.

She racked her brains but could not remember enough to satisfy the clerk.

They asked me for fresh ideas, but I had none. I racked my brain, but couldn't come up with anything.

□ You can refer to this activity as **brain-racking**.

All your brain-racking is making absolutely no contribution to the world.

□ The old-fashioned spelling 'wrack' is occasionally used instead of 'rack' in this expression.

brass

a brass farthing

If you say that someone will not get **a brass farthing**, you are emphasizing that they will not get any money at all. You can also say that something does not matter **a brass farthing** to emphasize that it does not matter at all. These are old-fashioned expressions, which are now used mainly in British journalism.

The tragic fact is that most children in lone-parent families will not gain a brass farthing through this Act.

Labour can continue to adapt its policies ever-nearer to those of the Liberal Democrats. But none of it matters a brass farthing if local parties, in towns up and down the country, remain at war.

the brass ring

If someone is reaching for **the brass ring** in a competitive situation, they are trying to gain success or a big reward or profit. This expression is used in American English.

There are good and bad features to living among people who are all young, on the make and going for the brass ring professionally.

They had already won their respective regionals in LA, Chicago, Atlanta and New

York. This was it. The brass ring. The stuff that dreams are made of.

cold enough to freeze the balls off a brass monkey

In informal British English, people sometimes say **'it's cold enough to freeze the balls off a brass monkey'** to emphasize that the weather is extremely cold. This expression is often varied. Many people consider it offensive.

It was a cold snap in the middle of spring with winds bitter enough to freeze a brass monkey.

☐ People often refer to this expression indirectly, for example by saying it's 'brass monkey weather'.

get down to brass tacks

If people **get down to brass tacks**, they begin to discuss the basic, most important aspects of a situation.

The third congress of Angola's ruling party was due to get down to brass tacks today with a debate on the party's performance during the last five years.

☐ **The brass tacks** of a situation are its basic, most important aspects.

These two countries, by contrast, are long on rhetoric, but short on brass tacks.

bread

the best thing since sliced bread
the greatest thing since sliced bread ◄

If you say that someone thinks that something is **the best thing since sliced bread**, you mean that they think it is very good, new, and exciting. You can also say that they think it is **the greatest thing since sliced bread**. You usually use these expressions to indicate that you think that their opinion is wrong or foolish.

When your programme first started I thought it was the best thing since sliced bread. But over the last three months I think you have adopted an arrogant attitude.

We are being told on every side that marketing is the greatest thing since sliced bread.

bread and butter: 1 ◄◄◄

If something is your **bread and butter**, it is the most important or only source of your income.

'Who's your audience?' 'We play maybe a hundred colleges a year. That is our bread and butter.'

I think I'm more controlled at work. I have to be; it's my bread and butter.

☐ Your **bread-and-butter** business is the part of your business which produces the main part of your income.

It's not exactly thrilling but it's good bread-and-butter work all the same.

bread and butter: 2 ◄

The **bread-and-butter** aspects of a situation or activity are its most basic or important aspects.

On major bread-and-butter issues, there's little difference between them. Both candidates are super cautious and both portray themselves as moderates.

☐ You can also say that these basic or important aspects are **the bread and butter** of a situation or activity.

It's the bread and butter of police work, checking if anybody had seen anything suspicious.

bread and circuses

Bread and circuses is used to describe a situation in which a government tries to divert attention away from real problems or issues, by providing people with things which seem to make their lives more enjoyable.

Metternich proceeded to neutralise political dissent through a policy of bread and circuses backed up by a fearsome secret police.

Our only hope is to return to constitutional and moral government. If we don't, our children and grandchildren will curse us for squandering their prosperity in exchange for today's bread and circuses.

cast your bread upon the waters

If you **cast** your **bread upon the waters**, you do something good or take a risk, usually without expecting very much in return. This is a literary expression.

You should make time to offer assistance to anyone who needs it. It's a case of casting your bread upon the waters – who knows how the favour will be repaid.

know which side your bread is buttered ◄

If you **know which side** your **bread is buttered**, you understand fully how you are likely to benefit from a situation, and you know what to do or who to please in order to put yourself in the best possible situation.

Donald was a man who knew with utter clarity which side his bread was buttered on.

I'm in no doubt which side my bread is buttered for the present.

breadline

on the breadline ◄

People who are living **on the breadline** are extremely poor.

Too many men have children and then forget about them – leaving the children and the mothers living on the breadline.

They should be stripped of everything they own but the bare essentials. Let them feel what it is like to be on the breadline.

☐ You can use **the breadline** in other ways.

For example, someone who is just **above the breadline** has just enough money to survive on. Someone who is **below the breadline** cannot survive on the money they have.

Obviously I'd want to earn enough to keep me above the breadline.

Families scraping a living on low incomes and benefits are already living below the breadline.

break

give me a break: 1 ◀◀

You can say **'give me a break'** after someone has said or done something, to show that you think that they are being very annoying or ridiculous.

The news item ended with comments from 'South Australian feminists' who were 'satisfied' by the finding. Give me a break! Why do they have to quote feminists on a decision that concerns the rights of all women? Why can't they quote mothers, teachers, nurses, or dancers?

give me a break: 2 ◀

You can say **'give me a break'** to tell someone to stop criticizing or annoying you and leave you alone.

Anxious families on the crime-ridden Mayhill estate in Swansea, yesterday begged youngsters, 'Give us a break', after dozens of cars were wrecked by the gangs.

give someone an even break
get an even break
give a sucker an even break ◀

If you **are** never **given an even break** or you never **get an even break**, you do not get the same chances or opportunities to do something as other people. This expression is used mainly in American English.

He is loath to give the opposition an even break.

He kept talking about how she never got an even break from the family.

☐ If someone says **'never give a sucker an even break'**, they are saying light-heartedly or ironically that you should not allow less fortunate people to have the same chances and opportunities as yourself.

His philosophy may be summed up as 'Never give a sucker an even break'.

They had no idea of fair play or giving suckers an even break.

breast

make a clean breast of something

If you tell someone to **make a clean breast of** something, you are advising them to tell the whole truth about it, so that they can begin to deal properly with a problem or make a fresh start.

'I am sure that will be the best for you.' 'But how can I go home?' 'You'll have to make a clean breast of it, dear.'

If you make a clean breast of your problems, creditors, whether secured or unsecured, are much more likely to deal fairly and leniently with you.

breath

a breath of fresh air ◀◀◀

If you describe someone or something as **a breath of fresh air**, you mean that they are pleasantly different from what you are used to.

I think you're a great family and I'm glad I'm going to join you. After the stuffy conversation we have at our dinner table, this is like a breath of fresh air.

Basically, I was bored. Brian never wanted to do anything. Life was stagnant. So Mike, my present husband, was a breath of fresh air.

hold your breath ◀◀◀

If you say that someone **is holding** their **breath**, you mean that they are waiting anxiously or excitedly to see what happens next.

She had been holding her breath and hoping that the agreement would be signed.

The world is holding its breath, he said, as we begin to negotiate the future of our country.

☐ If you say that you **aren't holding** your **breath**, you mean that you are not expecting a particular thing to happen, and so you are not worried or excited about it. In a situation like this, you can also advise someone: **'don't hold your breath'**.

The Chancellor has predicted Britain will drag itself out of the slump – but don't hold your breath, because he doesn't know when.

in the same breath ◀◀◀

If you say that someone says something and then **in the same breath** they say something else, you are pointing out that they are saying two things which are very different or which contradict each other.

For politicians to demand firm immigration controls and argue against racism in the same breath is a deep contradiction.

In the same breath you say that you are terribly depressed, and in the next, list your good points, which I am sure are very real.

take your breath away ◀◀◀

If something **takes** your **breath away**, it amazes and impresses you because it is so wonderful.

'Tell me again about the picture.' 'It's beautiful. It's so beautiful it takes your breath away.'

He had never believed he would come to such power. The more he realized it, the more it took his breath away.

waste your breath ◄

If you tell someone that they **are wasting their breath**, you are telling them that there is no point in them continuing with what they are saying, because it will not have any effect.

He wanted to protest again, but the tone of her voice told him he was wasting his breath.

Before I could get very far he interrupted me to tell me that I was wasting my breath.

☐ You can also tell someone that what they are saying is **a waste of breath**.

He would admit to the thefts, but deny everything else, and her accusations would be a waste of breath.

with bated breath ◄◄

If you wait for something **with bated breath**, you look forward to it, or you wait in an anxious or interested way to see what happens next.

The institution is now waiting with bated breath to see if the results of the next few surveys confirm its current assessment.

They got the people in the villages interested in what was going to happen, so they were then watching with bated breath as the experiment began.

☐ Some people use the word 'baited' instead of 'bated' in this expression, but it is generally considered incorrect.

breeze

shoot the breeze

If you **shoot the breeze**, you talk with other people in an informal and friendly way.

Goldie does what she likes doing best: shooting the breeze about life, love, and her bad reputation.

'He's positively awkward on social occasions,' says a political acquaintance. 'If you're sitting around a big table in the members' dining room, he won't shoot the breeze like the rest of them.'

brewery

couldn't organize a piss-up in a brewery

If you say that someone **couldn't organize a piss-up in a brewery**, you mean that they are extremely incompetent and are not capable of organizing anything at all. This is a very informal expression, which is used in British English. Many people find it offensive.

She was fired after saying her boss couldn't organise a piss-up in a brewery.

☐ People often vary this expression, for example by replacing 'piss-up' with a more polite word or expression.

We all know the real reason for failure – the

Greens could not organise an alcoholic revelry in a brewery.

brick

built like a brick shithouse

If you say that someone is **built like a brick shithouse**, you mean that they are extremely tall, broad, and strong-looking. This is a very informal expression, which is used in British English. Many people find it offensive.

This guy was built like a brick shithouse, with a huge mustache and smoldering brown eyes.

☐ You can use **brick-shithouse** before a noun to describe someone who looks like this.

One phrase incessantly flies from the lips of his brick-shithouse accomplice Anthony Chapman: 'It's a larf'.

drop a brick

If you **drop a brick**, you say something tactless or inappropriate which upsets or offends other people. This expression is used in British English.

After his comments on the live TV ·programme, Mr Freeman was immediately aware that he had dropped a political brick of the worst kind.

As foreign policy adviser to Helmut Kohl, the German chancellor, Horst Teltschik sometimes dropped bricks but never a bombshell.

shit a brick

If you say that someone **is shitting a brick**, you mean that they are extremely frightened or worried about something. This is a very informal expression, which many people find offensive.

bricks

make bricks without straw

If you say that someone **is making bricks without straw**, you mean that they are doing a job, or are trying to do it, without the proper resources that are needed for it.

His job was apparently to make education bricks without straw – that is to say, to be inspiring without having much money. ··

You say that Kissinger in the end built intricate structures, but that he built them made of bricks without straw.

☐ This expression is sometimes varied. For example, if you say that someone is **making bricks without much straw**, you mean that they are doing a job, or are trying to do it, with very few resources.

Full marks to Hampshire for a spirited attempt to make bricks without much straw.

bridge

cross that bridge when you come to it ◄

If you say **'I'll cross that bridge when I come to it'**, you are saying that you intend to deal with a problem when, or if, it happens, rather than worrying about the possibility of it happening.

'You can't make me talk to you.' 'No, but the police can.' 'I'll cross that bridge when I come to it.'

We do not know what we will do when it happens here, but that bridge we'll cross when we get to it.

☐ This expression is often varied. For example, you can say **'I haven't crossed that bridge yet'** when you have not yet dealt with a particular problem.

We have not crossed that bridge yet. We are trying to get the criminal case dealt with.

There are still a few bridges to cross.

bridges

build bridges ◄◄◄

If you **build bridges** between opposing groups of people, you do something to help them to understand each other or co-operate with each other.

You felt it was your duty to help build bridges between the communities involved here.

We look for ways to build bridges between our two organizations.

☐ You can refer to this process as **bridge-building**.

Do all you can to develop an open mind which allows bridge-building between you.

Lovett took the initiative to arrange a bridge-building luncheon at which a compromise could be agreed.

brief

hold no brief for something

If you say that you **hold no brief for** a particular cause, belief, or group of people, you mean that you do not support it. This is a fairly formal expression, which is used in British English.

This newspaper holds no special brief for a committee that has done nothing to distinguish itself in the past.

He holds no brief for formal education, ethical, philosophical, or mathematical. The early needs of his ideal citizens will be amply filled, as were his own, by traditional myths and stories.

bright

bright as a button ◄

If you say that someone is as **bright as a button**, you mean that they are intelligent,

full of energy, or very cheerful. This expression is used mainly in British English.

She was as bright as a button and sharp as anything. If it had been her running the company, it might still be OK.

She was as bright as a button, but wanted not to appear too bright in case it put people off.

bright-eyed

bright-eyed and bushy-tailed

If you describe someone as **bright-eyed and bushy-tailed**, you mean that they are lively, keen, and full of energy.

But for now, go and sleep awhile. I need you bright-eyed and bushy-tailed tomorrow.

This will be a busy year, so you need to be bright-eyed and bushy-tailed to cope.

broke

go for broke ◄◄

If you **go for broke**, you decide to take a risk and put all your efforts or resources into one plan or idea in the hope that it will be successful.

Hong Kong people have no inhibitions about showing wealth. But they have a particular entrepreneurial skill. We tend to be more conservative in Singapore, whereas Hong Kong people go for broke.

In London's West End there is a reluctance to take risks with new plays while going for broke on musicals.

We have to go for broke for victory against Belgium in the World Cup next month.

☐ **Go-for-broke** can also be used before a noun.

Three astronauts plan to walk in space today in a go-for-broke effort to retrieve a communications satellite.

Mr Deng's reformist policies have enabled China to enjoy one of the world's fastest rates of economic growth over the past 15 years. His recent go-for-broke push for a market economy promises even better.

if it ain't broke, don't fix it ◄◄

If someone says **'if it ain't broke, don't fix it'**, they mean that things should only be changed or interfered with if they are faulty or wrong.

With regard to proposals for some grand reorganization of the intelligence community: If it ain't broke, don't fix it. And I believe it is not broke.

☐ This expression has several variations. For example, you can say 'isn't broken' instead of 'ain't broke' and 'why fix it?' instead of 'don't fix it'.

Her outlook is 'If it isn't broken, why fix it?' She puts up with a lot I wouldn't tolerate.

□ The word 'ain't' is a form of 'isn't' which is used in informal or non-standard English.

broom

a new broom
a new broom sweeps clean　　◀

You can refer to someone as **a new broom** when they have just started a new job in a senior position and are expected to make a lot of changes. Compare **make a clean sweep**; see **sweep**.

We had a new, exceptionally young headmaster and he was a very active new broom.

'At least someone might actually make a decision now,' said one frustrated producer. But there is the usual apprehension you get with any new broom.

□ You can use **new-broom** before a noun.

What's he really like, the jazz-loving, cigar-smoking new-broom Chancellor?

□ This expression comes from the proverb **a new broom sweeps clean**.

A new broom doesn't always sweep clean, it just brushes some of the worst dirt under the carpet for a while.

brown

brown as a berry

If you say that someone is as **brown as a berry**, you mean that they are very tanned because they have been out in the sun.

Steve Hobbs had just come back from his holiday. Brown as a berry he was, when he came round here the following Monday.

She rode out to the yacht in a launch with a basket of fresh vegetables to find Franklin brown as a berry and in his usual fine spirits.

brownie

brownie points　　◀◀

If you say that someone should get **brownie points** for doing something, you mean that they can expect to be rewarded or congratulated for it. You may also be suggesting that this is the only reason that they did it.

Mr Stein would almost certainly win extra brownie points for taking an ultra-cautious view and removing uncertainty from the share price.

There are no brownie points in the real world for smart, clever, formal marketing plans, until and unless they lead us to effective action in the customer market.

He has lost all the Brownie points he won for twice visiting the war-ravaged lands that used to be Yugoslavia. Criticising Red Cross workers, as he did yesterday, is neither helpful nor fair.

brunt

bear the brunt of something　　◀◀◀

If someone or something **bears the brunt of** an unpleasant or damaging event, they have to take the main force of its harmful effects. Other verbs are sometimes used instead of 'bear'.

In 37 years with British Rail, I saw how station staff always bore the brunt of public anger over fare rises.

When the sufferer is in pain, frustrated by their own weakness, you will bear the brunt of their anger, guilt and inadequacy.

He said that two buildings which took the brunt of the blast would probably have to be demolished.

brush

tar someone with the same brush　　◀

If some members of a group behave badly and if people wrongly think that all of the group is equally bad, you can say that the whole group **is tarred with the same brush**.

I am a football supporter and I often have to explain that I'm not one of the hooligan sort, because we all get tarred with the same brush.

The trouble is that in the public eye all of us will be tarred with the same brush.

□ In this expression, 'same' is often replaced with an adjective which refers to the group who behave badly.

At a rough guess, only 10 per cent of the inhabitants collaborated with the occupiers. But all have been tarred with the collaboration brush.

bubble

the bubble has burst
prick the bubble　　◀◀◀

If you say that **the bubble has burst**, you mean that a situation or idea which was very successful has suddenly stopped being successful. You can also say that someone or something **has pricked the bubble**.

The bubble has burst. Crowds at the team's World League games are down from last year's 40,000 average to 22,000.

The bursting of the economic bubble of seemingly ever-increasing stock and land prices has contributed to a waning in confidence.

The stock market has been unstable for a long time, a result of the economic downturn and the pricking of the property bubble.

on the bubble

If someone is **on the bubble**, they are in a difficult situation, and are very likely to fail. This expression is used in American English.

I'm always on the bubble, so I'm probably one of the best scoreboard readers you'll ever meet. If I make it, it'll be by one or two shots. If I miss, it'll be by one or two shots.

buck

the buck stops here
the buck stops with someone ◄◄

If you say **'the buck stops here'** or **'the buck stops with me'**, you are emphasizing that a problem is your responsibility, and that you are not expecting anyone else to deal with it.

I don't want anyone to blame the players. If you are going to point the finger at anyone, it must be at the man in charge and that's me. The buck stops here.

I approved the plan. I advised the President, but I did not advise him of the details. The buck stops with me.

□ You can also say that **the buck stops with** someone else.

Only now has Taylor accepted that the buck stops with him.

It's easy to depend on others to tell you when there are problems with your car, your health, your house or whatever. But ultimately the buck stops with you.

pass the buck ◄◄◄

If you accuse someone of **passing the buck**, you are accusing them of failing to take responsibility for a problem, and of expecting someone else to deal with it instead.

In the old days he would have resented having to hand over a case. Now he was glad of regionalization – you could pass the buck.

The two sides also opted for an approach that's gaining favor among unions and some employers alike: seeking to pass the buck to taxpayers.

He is our responsibility. Canada is the only place he has ever known and to deport him is simply passing the buck because of a legal loophole.

□ This kind of behaviour is referred to as **buck-passing**.

However, his apology, in this age of buck-passing and dodging, was frank and honest.

bucket

kick the bucket

If you say that someone **has kicked the bucket**, you mean that they have died. This expression is used to refer to someone's death in a light-hearted or humorous way.

Moss Hanley said the old girl is about to kick the bucket anyway – got some sort of kidney infection.

All the money goes to her when the old man kicks the bucket.

bud

nip something in the bud ◄◄◄

If you **nip** a bad situation or bad behaviour **in the bud**, you stop it at an early stage, before it can develop and become worse.

Unless the problem is nipped in the bud it could develop into the kind of intractable conflict that already exists between Armenia and Azerbaijan.

It is important to recognize jealousy as soon as possible and to nip it in the bud before it gets out of hand.

□ Occasionally this expression is used to say that something good is stopped before it can develop.

The higher prices would fuel inflation and nip the consumer recovery in the bud.

buffers

hit the buffers

If something such as an idea, plan, or project **hits the buffers**, it experiences difficulties which cause it to fail. This expression is used in British English, mainly in journalism.

Their plans may not get very far before they hit the buffers.

One leading Communist told me it was very difficult for a party with a seventy-year history to admit that it had hit the buffers.

bug

bitten by the bug ◄◄

If you **are bitten by the** gardening **bug**, for example, or **are bitten by the** acting **bug**, you become very enthusiastic about gardening or acting, and you start doing it a lot.

Before we bought our cottage I viewed gardens as merely places to sit during warm weather. But after watching all these changes take place, I've definitely been bitten by the gardening bug, and now I love the weeding and digging as much as the sitting.

Bitten by the travel bug, he then set off for a working holiday in Australia.

She also provides a guide to Britain's antiques markets and a very useful reference list for those seriously bitten by the bug.

bull

a bull in a china shop ◄

If you describe someone as **a bull in a china shop**, you mean that they say or do things which offend or upset people, or which cause trouble, in situations where they ought to act carefully and tactfully.

Unfortunately, Haig, the proverbial bull in a china shop, did not make the best negotiator, being impatient with contrary opinions, and ironically, intolerant of traditionalist views.

In confrontational situations I am like a bull in a china shop.

a red rag to a bull
a red flag before a bull ◄

If something always makes a particular person very angry, you can say that it is like **a red rag to a bull** or **a red flag before a bull**. 'Rag' is used more commonly in British English and 'flag' is used more commonly in American English. Compare **a red flag**; see **flag**.

This sort of information is like a red rag to a bull for the tobacco companies but it really needs to be exposed.

It's a red rag to a bull when my son won't admit that he's wrong.

☐ People sometimes vary these expressions.

To hit back at the authorities is to hold up a red rag in front of an already enraged bull.

The very idea that there is something special about the individual is likely to be taken as a red flag by progressive academics for whom individualism is tantamount to racism.

take the bull by the horns ◄

If you **take the bull by the horns**, you act decisively and with determination in order to deal with a difficult situation or problem. Other verbs are sometimes used instead of 'take'.

This is the time to take the bull by the horns and tackle the complex issues of finance.

So there will be further tinkering with the system, to try to improve efficiency, distribution and management, without any real effort to grasp the bull by the horns by allowing more radical reforms including a genuine freedom of the market.

bullet

bite the bullet ◄◄◄

If you **bite the bullet**, you accept a difficult or unpleasant situation.

There is a last option, known in the trade as 'self insurance'. Put simply it means that you do everything you can to protect your property, and if something gets lost, damaged or stolen, you bite the bullet and cover the cost yourself.

The same stressful event might make one person utterly miserable, while another will bite the bullet and make the best of it.

get the bullet
give someone the bullet

If someone **gets the bullet** or **is given the bullet**, they lose their job. This is an informal expression, which is used in British English.

The banks are still making money but they only have to have one bad year and everybody gets the bullet.

Six more Eldorado actors have been given the bullet. The stars were told the dramatic sack-

ing news during a break in filming yesterday afternoon.

bum

a bum steer

If you describe information that you are given as **a bum steer**, you mean that it is wrong and misleading. This expression is used mainly in American English.

Did you give me a bum steer about your name and address?

get the bum's rush
give someone the bum's rush ◄

If someone **gets the bum's rush** or **is given the bum's rush**, they are completely ignored or rejected in an unexpected and upsetting way. This is an informal expression, which is used mainly in American English.

He turned up there at 2.45 and sat down to lunch with European royalty, so we got the bum's rush.

bums

bums on seats ◄

If you say that a performer or performance puts **bums on seats**, you mean that they are very popular and succeed in attracting large audiences. This is an informal expression, which is used in British English.

He's always been like that and will never change. That's why he gets bums on seats – he's a showman.

This week, an original version of a Cervantes play is putting Catalan bums on seats at the Mercat de les Flors, Barcelona's showpiece modern theatre.

bundle

drop your bundle

If you are failing at something and you **drop your bundle**, you give up and stop trying to win or succeed. This expression is used mainly in Australian English.

At 25-6 University were losing badly, but to their credit they did not drop their bundle.

burn

burn your bridges
burn your boats ◄◄

If you **burn your bridges**, you do something which forces you to continue with a particular course of action, and makes it impossible for you to return to an earlier situation. In British English, you can also say that you **burn your boats**.

I didn't sell it because I didn't know how long I would be here. I didn't want to burn all my bridges.

She had burned her bridges behind her; she had called Mimi to tell her she couldn't take the job at the Foundation – she had accepted another job offer.

She didn't take his advice and decided to go to Glasgow to study for a degree in astronomy. Then, just before she started, she thought she might be burning her boats and so she did physics after all.

burner

on the back burner
on the front burner ◄◄◄

If you put a project or issue **on the back burner**, you decide not to do anything about it until a later date, because you do not consider it to be very urgent or important.

She put her career on the back burner after marrying co-star Paul Hogan two years ago while she made a home for them in Australia.

While the Bush administration appeared to have put the issue on the back burner, the Clinton administration has stressed the need for a rapid solution.

☐ If you put a project or issue **on the front burner**, you start to give it a lot of attention, because you think it is very urgent or important.

By putting tourism on the front burner, the government has opened up the opportunity for a substantial growth in visitors long-term.

☐ **Back burner** and **front burner** are used in many other structures and expressions with similar meanings.

Long-term health care advocates worry that the expense will push this issue onto a back burner, and that, they say, would be a mistake.

He has said that he will put into law the Freedom of Choice Act. That would be certainly the front-burner issue with me.

bush

the bush telegraph

If you talk about **the bush telegraph**, you are talking about the way in which information or news can be passed on from person to person in conversation. This expression is used in British English.

No, you didn't tell me, but I heard it on the bush telegraph.

Jean-Michel had heard of our impending arrival in Conflans long before we got there. The bush telegraph on the waterways is extremely effective.

not beat around the bush
not beat about the bush ◄

If you **don't beat around the bush**, you say what you want to say clearly and directly, without avoiding its unpleasant aspects. In British English, you can also say that you **don't beat about the bush**.

I decided not to beat around the bush. 'I'm at

Sam's,' I told her. 'Eddie didn't come back from his paper route yet. Nobody knows where he is.'

Let's not beat about the bush – they rejected it. The Review Group said it was their most important single recommendation and the Government rejected it.

bushel

hide your light under a bushel ◄

If someone tells you not to **hide** your **light under a bushel**, they mean that you should not be modest about your skills and good features, and instead you should be confident and willing to let people know that you have them.

If you have knowledge your superiors don't, or if you can do something they can't, don't be tempted to hide your light under a bushel for fear of upsetting them or making them look small. Be confident enough to promote yourself.

In these challenging times, it is essential we must go out there and tell the world what we have to offer. We are proud of the facilities in Newmarket and this is not the time to hide our light under a bushel.

☐ If you say that someone **does not hide** their **light under a bushel**, you mean that they are very confident about their skills and good features, and not at all modest.

There are those who find his vanity off-putting. He does not hide his light under a bushel.

☐ People often vary this expression, for example by replacing 'light' with another word such as 'talent'.

Never one to hide her talent under a bushel, she is all set to set up a legal practice with her solicitor husband.

bushes

beat the bushes

If you say that someone **is beating the bushes**, you mean that they are trying very hard to get or achieve something. This expression is used mainly in American English.

Maybe Democratic leaders should be beating the bushes to register voters to support their nominee.

He was tired of beating the bushes for work, and he did not want to ask for help or accept charity.

business

business as usual ◄

'Business as usual' is used to say that everything is continuing in the normal way, even though something unpleasant or unexpected has happened.

Base spokesman Mike Todd says it's been

business as usual there today despite the bombs.

If these guys are convicted, it could be the beginning of a real change. If they're not, it's business as usual.

in business

If you say that you are **in business**, you mean that you can start doing something because you have got everything ready for it. This expression is used in spoken English.

It plugs in here, right? Okay, we're in business. Let's see how it works, guys.

It'll be all right, Tony. With your man keeping tabs on her, we'll be in business the moment she makes a move.

like nobody's business

If you say that someone is doing something **like nobody's business**, you are emphasizing how well they are doing it or how much of it they are doing.

He sings like Sinatra, dances like Sammy Davis, plays piano like nobody's business, and lays on the charm like an old pro.

I mean Geoffrey can chat like nobody's business.

mean business ◄◄◄

If someone shows that they **mean business**, they show that they are serious and determined about what they are doing.

One of them poked a shotgun at me. I could see he meant business. I gave them what they wanted and that's the advice I'd give to anyone in the same situation.

Now, in the wake of the student-led demonstrations, the party is trying to convince people it means business.

Once the banker realizes that you mean business he or she will find a way to help.

busman

a busman's holiday ◄

If someone spends part of their holiday doing or experiencing something that forms part of their normal job or everyday life, you can say that they are having **a busman's holiday**. This expression is used mainly in British English.

This is probably the best fish restaurant in the country – at least one admiring chef a week passes through the cheery dining room on a busman's holiday.

A fire crew's Christmas outing turned into a busman's holiday when their coach caught fire.

busy

a busy bee
busy as a bee

If you describe someone as **a busy bee** or say that they are **busy as a bee**, you mean

that they enjoy doing a lot of things and always keep themselves busy.

'I enjoyed being a busy bee, getting things done,' she says in her confident way.

He is busy as a bee designing every production in London.

butter

butter wouldn't melt in your mouth ◄

If you say that someone looks as though **butter wouldn't melt in** their **mouth**, you mean that although they look completely innocent, they are capable of doing something unpleasant or horrible.

He may look as though butter wouldn't melt in his mouth, but I wouldn't trust him.

They looked as though butter wouldn't melt in their mouths. They were quite smartly dressed and looked like respectable executives.

butterflies

butterflies in your stomach
have butterflies
get butterflies ◄

If you say that you have **butterflies in** your **stomach**, you mean that you feel very nervous about something that you have to do.

He seemed so full of enthusiasm that I felt foolish still having butterflies in my stomach.

Now I can go there as a competitor, I'm starting to feel the butterflies in my stomach already.

□ You can also say that you **have butterflies** or **get butterflies**.

Any jockey who says he doesn't get butterflies down at the start is telling lies.

butterfly

break a butterfly on a wheel

If you talk about **breaking a butterfly on a wheel**, you mean that someone is using far more force than is necessary to do something. This expression is used in British English.

The Huglets have had their ideology combed over, examined, misinterpreted and rewritten. Talk about breaking a butterfly on a wheel.

button

at the touch of a button ◄◄◄

If you say that you can do something **at the touch of a button**, you are emphasizing that you can do it very easily and quickly, usually because of new technology. The nouns 'push' and 'press' are sometimes used instead of 'touch'.

Specially trained staff will be able to trace obscene and threatening calls at the touch of a button, and pass the information to police.

The Powerglyde will open and close your curtains for you at the mere touch of a button.

Within a few years picking an album, cassette or CD of your favourite artist will be done at the press of a button using a computerised music catalogue on a personal computer.

a hot button ◄◄

If you say that a subject or problem is **a hot button**, you mean that it is topical and controversial, and people have very strong feelings about it. This expression is used in American English.

If crime is the city's issue most known to outsiders, rent control is the city's hot button for its residents.

He portrays his accusers and his questioners as a lynch mob and that hits a hot button in the black community.

☐ **Hot-button** can be used before a noun.

He said he wanted a Constitutional amendment to ban abortion and spoke often about prayer in the classroom, but he never fought hard for those objectives. They are controversial, hot-button issues that create hazards for politicians.

on the button

If you talk about a time or amount being **on the button**, you mean that it is exactly that time or amount. This expression is used

mainly in American English.

He'd say he'd meet us at 10.00 on the button.

We double-counted it and it's 975,000 dollars on the button.

press the right button
push the right button

If you say that someone **presses the right button** or **pushes the right button**, you mean that they cleverly or skilfully do the things which are necessary to get what they want in a particular situation.

In what it describes as a well-judged performance, the newspaper says he pressed all the right buttons to please the representatives.

In later talks with the chairman, he helped his cause by pushing all the right buttons.

right on the button
on the button ◄

If someone says that you are **right on the button** or **on the button**, they mean that you have guessed correctly about something.

'Am I right?' 'Right on the button.'

The important thing is that the Treasury's forecast was right on the button.

The one who guesses on the button, picks up a big, mystery prize.

C

caboodle

the whole caboodle
the whole kit and caboodle ◄

If you refer to **the whole caboodle** or **the whole kit and caboodle**, you are referring to the whole of something. 'The whole caboodle' is used only in British English.

I would probably find that I could borrow the whole lot. I could borrow the whole caboodle.

No need, then, to throw away the whole kit and caboodle.

cackle

cut the cackle

If you tell someone to **cut the cackle**, you are telling them to stop chattering or talking in a meaningless way. This is an old-fashioned expression, which is used in British English.

'Right! Cut the cackle!' she snapped.

The programmes are still packed with speeches by party hacks, shouting wooden slogans from the platform. Cutting the cackle would be a great service to the party and to the nation.

cage

rattle someone's cage ◄

If you **rattle** someone's **cage**, you do or say something that upsets or annoys them.

If there's one thing I have learnt as an editor, it's that you can't create a truly superb magazine without rattling a few cages.

I don't rattle their cages and they don't rattle mine.

Cain

raise Cain

If someone **raises Cain**, they get very angry about something.

The opposition parties intend to use the budget debates to raise Cain over the relationship between politicians and gangsters revealed by the scandal.

I'm not sure she should come, but I figure she'd raise Cain if we tried to say no.

cake

have your cake and eat it ◄◄

If someone criticizes you for wanting to **have** your **cake and eat it**, they are criticizing you for trying to get all the benefits of two different situations or things, when you are only entitled to benefit from one of them.

What he wants is a switch to a market economy in a way which does not reduce people's standard of living. To many, of course, this sounds like wanting to have his cake and eat it.

The spokesman said Lithuanians wanted both independence and the privileges of belonging to the USSR, but they couldn't have their cake and eat it.

The fact that you have accepted his affairs over the years, when he tells you he can't help himself, has enabled him, to put it bluntly, to have his cake and eat it.

take the cake

If you say that someone or something **takes the cake**, you are expressing surprise or anger at their extreme behaviour or qualities. **Take the biscuit** means the same.

With his one good arm the driver tore off his oxygen mask and reached through the wreckage to answer his mobile phone. Officers say they get to see some pretty odd things at times but that one just about takes the cake.

cakes

cakes and ale

You can use **cakes and ale** to refer to a time or activity when you enjoy yourself greatly and have no troubles. This expression is used in British English.

Devotees of study holidays are quick to claim that being pale and acquiring poetic sensitivity does not necessarily mean stinting on the cakes and ale.

calf

kill the fatted calf

If you say that someone **kills the fatted calf**, you mean that they celebrate and do everything they can to welcome back a person who has been away for a period of time.

He went off to make movies, and rumour has it that, when he returned, his record company didn't exactly kill the fatted calf.

□ This expression comes from a story in the Bible about a father who celebrated the return of his son by killing a calf and preparing a feast.

call

a close call   ◄◄◄

If you say that something was **a close call**, you are indicating that someone very nearly had an accident or disaster, or very nearly suffered a defeat. You can replace 'call' with 'thing'.

'That was a close call,' Bess gasped, as the boat steadied and got under way.

It was a close call and looking back now I have no doubt that if my friend hadn't acted so promptly I would be dead.

The contest had shown that the gap between man and computer was narrowing. 'It was an extremely close thing. It shows that it can only be a matter of time before the computer wins.'

camp

a camp follower   ◄

You refer to someone as **a camp follower** when they follow or associate themselves with a particular person or group, either because they admire or support them, or because they hope to gain advantages from them. This expression is often used to show contempt. It is sometimes used to refer to women who are willing to have sex with the person or people that they want to be associated with.

Brecht was surrounded by 'groupies', by 'camp-followers' – hosts of imaginative and musical young and older women seemed to, or did, dote on him.

Even in my day as a player, we had our camp followers.

pitch camp

If you say that someone **pitches camp**, you mean that they temporarily settle somewhere or have control of a certain area.

As reporters pitched camp outside the Bennett home in Faversham, Kent, the family's political differences became public concern.

can

carry the can   ◄◄

If you **carry the can** for something that has gone wrong, you take the blame for it even though you are not the only person responsible for it. This expression is used in British English.

It annoys me that I was the only one who carried the can for that defeat.

Members of the Government decided to let Alan carry the can. They thought, 'Why not pick on him, he'll take the blame.'

in the can   ◄

If a film or piece of filming is **in the can**, it has been successfully completed.

We had to lie motionless for rehearsal after rehearsal, take after take, until the scene was in the can.

We've got the interview in the can.

candle

burn the candle at both ends   ◄

If you say that someone **is burning the candle at both ends**, you mean that they are going to have problems because they are trying to do too much and, for example, are regularly going to bed very late even though they have to get up early in the morning.

Most people need six or seven hours each night and you're burning the candle at both ends if you regularly sleep for less than five.

Frank delighted in burning the candle at both ends. No matter how much of a night-life he was living, he maintained our ritual of an early breakfast.

can't hold a candle to someone ◄

If you are comparing two people or things and you say that the first **can't hold a candle to** the second, you mean that the second is much better than the first.

There are football players now valued in the £2m bracket who can't hold a candle to Ian in terms of ability.

Surveys reveal that most people glean their knowledge of science from television. Newspapers, books and radio cannot hold a candle to television.

not worth the candle
the game is not worth the candle ◄

If you say that something is **not worth the candle**, you mean that it is not worth the trouble or effort which is needed in order to achieve or obtain it. This expression is used mainly in British English.

Sir David has described the democratic reforms proposed by the governor as 'not worth the candle'.

If it means falling into my present state afterwards, writing isn't worth the candle. If I can't do it without being in danger of drinking again, it's just not worthwhile.

☐ You can also say that **the game is not worth the candle**.

It is some kind of a success story to be able to boast you married the richest woman in the world. But he must sometimes wonder whether the game was worth the candle.

candy

like a kid in a candy store
like a child in a sweet shop

If you say that someone is **like a kid in a candy store**, you mean that they do whatever they want and do not restrict or moderate their behaviour. This expression is used mainly in American English. In British English, you can say 'sweet shop' instead of 'candy store'. Other words such as 'child' can be used instead of 'kid'.

He reacted to fame like the proverbial kid in a candy store and assumed that any woman who interested him would automatically be available.

Brett Brubaker, a money manager at Abraham and Sons in Chicago, went on a buy-

ing binge and 'felt like a kid in a candy store,' he recalls.

In Westminster the party of law and order seems to have become the party of deception and distortion. They showed all the monetary restraint of a child in a sweet shop.

like taking candy from a baby

If you say that doing something is **like taking candy from a baby**, you mean that it is very easy.

In the end it was like taking candy from a baby. For the second week in succession the Premier League leaders were offered three points on a plate and took maximum advantage to go four points clear at the top.

cannon

cannon fodder ◄◄

You refer to soldiers in a war as **cannon fodder** when they are considered unimportant by their officers and are sent to fight in the most dangerous areas, where they are likely to be killed.

The expendable 'useless mouths' – the fifty-five to sixty-five year-olds – would be sent to the front as cannon-fodder. Unarmed, they were to attack ahead of the regular troops in human waves, absorbing the enemy's fire.

If you're a squaddie, you're regarded as cannon fodder.

☐ In journalism, **cannon fodder** is sometimes used to refer to people in other kinds of situation where they are made to do difficult, unpleasant, or dangerous tasks.

The average member of parliament has little sense of commitment, changes parties at the drop of a hat, and is treated by his party leaders, not surprisingly, as cannon-fodder.

a loose cannon ◄◄

If you describe someone as **a loose cannon**, you mean that their behaviour is unpredictable and therefore could have unfortunate or dangerous consequences.

The current producer held nobody's respect. He was a loose cannon.

There is a widespread worry that the military command has turned into a loose cannon beyond the control of the government.

☐ You can also say that someone is **a loose cannon on the deck**.

Thomson can be a loose cannon on the deck. He's not easy to control.

canoe

paddle your own canoe

If you **paddle your own canoe**, you control what you want to do without anyone's help or interference.

You now have the self-knowledge and energy

to paddle your own canoe to a job that's perfect for you.

As far as the rest of Europe is concerned we've just got to paddle our own canoe.

cap

cap in hand ◄

If you go **cap in hand** to someone, you ask them very humbly and respectfully for money or help. This expression is used mainly in British English; the usual American expression is **hat in hand**.

Separated from Russia and Central Asia, Ukraine has to go cap in hand to its neighbours for oil and gas.

On holiday, if you rely on cash and lose the lot you could end up going cap in hand to the nearest British consulate.

if the cap fits

You can say **'if the cap fits'** when you are telling someone that unpleasant or critical remarks which have been made about them are probably true or fair. This expression is used in British English; the American expression is **if the shoe fits**.

Promotional and activity have become their unwieldy middle names, but does the corporate cap fit?

□ This expression is often varied, for example by saying 'does the cap fit?' or 'the cap no longer fits'.

put your thinking cap on
get your thinking cap on ◄

If you **put** your **thinking cap on** or **get** your **thinking cap on**, you try hard to solve a problem by thinking about it.

In Cairo, Eden, Wavell, Dill, Cunningham, and Longmore put on their thinking caps and tried to decide where the fleeing British armies could make a successful stand.

We've got five pairs of boots to give away, so get your thinking caps on and answer the question.

□ This expression is very variable. For example, you can use other verbs instead of 'put' and 'get', or just say **thinking caps are on**.

I applied my thinking cap and came up with the idea shown which is simplicity itself.

Thinking caps are on at Sotheby's. After recent claims that the country's oldest auction house may have lost market share to its archrival, Christie's, Sotheby's marketing and strategy departments have been working overtime to plot a comeback.

set your cap at someone

If a woman **sets** her **cap at** a man, she tries to make him notice her, usually because she wants to marry him. This is an old-fashioned British expression, which is used mainly in novels.

Now she wanted a big man and she set her cap at the biggest star of them all.

She set her cap at this financially secure and rather vague young man who scarcely seemed to regard her.

capital

Life with a capital L
Art with a capital A ◄◄

You say, for example, 'Life **with a capital** L' or 'Art **with a capital** A' to draw attention to the word 'life' or 'art' and emphasize its significance. You often do this to suggest that someone is taking something too seriously.

Students thought studying psychology would tell them something about Life with a capital L.

The British tend to see things in terms of principles with a capital P.

□ You also use this expression to suggest that someone or something is a very good example of the kind of thing mentioned, or has a particular quality to a great extent.

Here it comes folks, the biggest, most rip-roaring, full-throttle movie yarn of the year, and resplendent movie with a capital M it most certainly is.

By many standards of measure, Peter was indeed Great with a capital G.

carbon

a carbon copy ◄◄

If you say that one person or thing is **a carbon copy** of another, you mean that the two people or things seem to be identical, or very similar.

She's always been quiet. She's a carbon copy of her mother – her mother always hated making a fuss.

For decades, the organization has been a carbon copy of the Communist Party, mouthing its rhetoric and blindly obeying its commands.

card

a calling card ◄

If you describe what someone possesses or has achieved as **a calling card**, you mean that it gives them a lot of opportunities which they would not otherwise have had.

Some cabinet ministers, comparing their likely pension with their lifestyle, are tempted to look for jobs in the City while their present status remains a calling card.

Gary Roger says Mr. Trupin used the New York magazine cover story about him as 'his calling card'.

Despite the temptation to make low-budget films only as Hollywood calling cards, one director has remained true to the independent spirit, that is to making the film he wants to make.

☐ In American English, **a calling card** is a small card printed with your name and other personal information, which you give to people when you visit or meet them.

a wild card ◄

You describe someone or something as **a wild card** when they cause uncertainty, because nobody knows how they will behave or what effects they will have.

The Cossacks are the wild card in Kazakhstan. Armed and anarchic, they claim a million supporters and demand official recognition as a paramilitary force.

One wild card in the situation is the recent election of Jean Chrétien as the leader of the opposition Liberal Party.

cards

in the cards ◄◄

If you say that something is **in the cards**, you mean that it is very likely to happen. This expression is used in American English; the British expression is **on the cards**.

Reform of the way hospitals, schools and universities are funded is in the cards.

He believes an invasion was never in the cards.

lay your cards on the table
put your cards on the table ◄

If you **lay your cards on the table** or **put your cards on the table**, you tell someone the truth about your feelings and plans.

I will lay my cards on the table. I am an atheist.

We were shy of talking about the future because we hadn't laid our cards on the table.

Put your cards on the table and be very clear about your complaints. This should clear the air.

on the cards ◄◄◄

If you say that something is **on the cards**, you mean that it is very likely to happen. This expression is used in British English; the American expression is **in the cards**.

If he demands too much, the unions will vote him down. So a compromise is on the cards.

A political turn to the right was on the cards.

I think he'd like us to become engaged. There's no need to look so surprised. It's been on the cards, as they say, for a long time.

play your cards right ◄

If you **play your cards right**, you use your skills to do all the things that are necessary in order to succeed or gain an advantage. This expression is used mainly in British English.

Soon, if she played her cards right, she would be head of the London office.

The idea took root in his imagination that he could actually win an election provided that he played his cards right.

carpet

on the carpet
call someone on the carpet

In British English, if someone is **on the carpet**, they are in trouble for doing something wrong. In American English, you say that they **are called on the carpet**.

The 22-year-old bad boy of English cricket was on the carpet again this week for storming out of the ground when told to wear one of the club's sponsored shirts.

In my hospital, if I ever allowed a nurse or a technician to work alongside me without wearing gloves, I'd be called on the carpet immediately for not protecting our staff.

roll out the red carpet ◄

If you **roll out the red carpet** for someone, especially someone famous or important, you give them a special welcome and treat them as an honoured guest.

The red carpet was rolled out for Mr Honecker during his visit to Bonn in 1987.

The museum staff rolled out the red carpet; although it was a Sunday, the deputy director came in especially to show us round.

☐ You can also say that someone receives **red carpet** treatment or a **red carpet** welcome.

Castro says he's open to any business proposition from abroad, and last week he gave the red carpet treatment to some of Spain's most right-wing business people.

Yeltsin arrived in Rome this morning to a red carpet welcome by Italian officials.

sweep something under the carpet
◄◄◄

If you **sweep** something **under the carpet**, you try to hide it and forget about it because you find it embarrassing or shameful. Other verbs such as 'brush' and 'push' are sometimes used instead of 'sweep'. This expression is used mainly in British English; the usual American expression is **sweep** something **under the rug**.

People often assume if you sweep something under the carpet the problem will go away, but that is not the case.

The problem has been brushed under the carpet for decades.

carrot

carrot and stick ◄◄

If someone uses a **carrot and stick** method to make you do something, they try to make you do it, first by offering you rewards and then by threatening you. Compare **carry a big stick**; see **stick**.

But Congress also wants to use a carrot and stick approach to force both sides to negotiate an end to the war.

With the announcement that the hostages are to be released, it appears that Washington's new carrot-and-stick policy may have already brought results.

□ 'Carrot' and 'stick' are also used in many other structures with a similar meaning.

Protests continued, however, so the authorities substituted the carrot for the stick.

When the Security Council waves a stick at an offending country, the secretary-general can also offer a carrot as encouragement.

dangle a carrot in front of someone
offer someone a carrot ◄◄

If someone **dangles a carrot in front of** you or **offers** you **a carrot**, they try to persuade you to do something by offering you a reward if you do it.

She was very concerned about the speeches he was making and dangled carrots in front of his nose to try to shut him up.

An additional carrot being dangled in front of the Spanish is to move the headquarters of the company running the project from Munich to Madrid.

He is to offer the public a new carrot by reversing this week's doubling of petrol prices and rent increases on state flats.

□ This expression is often varied.

The money's dangling there like a huge carrot, and you want to grab it.

Tax cuts may be offered as a carrot to voters ahead of the next election.

carry

carry all before you ◄

If someone **carries all before** them, they are successful in a task or activity, and defeat all their rivals. This expression is used in British English.

He had clearly won the popular vote, and his supporters thought he had carried all before him.

Newcastle United under Keegan were carrying all before them, winning their matches and opening up an enviable lead at the top of the First Division.

cart

put the cart before the horse ◄

If you criticize someone for **putting the cart before the horse**, you think that they are making a mistake by doing things in the wrong order.

Creating large numbers of schools before im-

proving school management is putting the cart before the horse.

The old way of running public spending put the cart before the horse, by inviting ministers to make spending bids before the government determined the overall level of public spending which it could afford.

□ This expression is very variable.

They want to go down the road with the cart before the horse and spend the money before they have made it.

We put them in a situation where they are encouraged to win at all costs before we've actually taught them the skills. We've got ourselves a cart-before-the-horse situation.

case

be on someone's case
get on someone's case
get off someone's case ◄

If you say that someone **is on** your **case**, you mean that they keep criticizing you in an annoying way, because they think that you have behaved badly. You can also say that someone **is getting on** your **case**.

'My sister was on my case about that joke all night,' he continued. 'She told me it was completely sick and creepy and that you could have been really scared.'

Joanie's my best friend, but she can be kind of a pain sometimes. I just didn't want her getting on my case about something that didn't mean anything.

□ If someone tells you to **get off** their **case**, they are telling you in an impolite way to stop criticizing them.

Get off my case, will you? I'll tell them.

on the case ◄

If you say that you are **on the case**, you mean that you are dealing with a particular problem or situation.

All I know so far is that you dip the pasta sheets in olive oil before cooking. I am, however, on the case, and as soon as I have the recipe, I'll let you know.

Often the missions seem designed only as photo opportunities, a chance for politicians to show the folks at home they're on the case.

cash

a cash cow ◄

If you refer to a source of money as **a cash cow**, you mean that it continues to produce a large amount of money and profit over a long period, without needing a lot of funding.

The park has been a cash cow for the city. Property and sales taxes there account for approximately 15 per cent of the city's general fund.

The company wanted the transition to be so

gradual that it could milk its cash cow to the last drop.

castles

castles in the air
castles in Spain

If you say that someone is building **castles in the air**, you mean that they have unrealistic plans or hopes for the future. In British English, you can also say that they are building **castles in Spain**.

'Along the way I have to become very very rich.' He shook his head in wonder at her. 'You're building castles in the air, Anne.'

However, I also have a rich imaginary life, my equivalent of castles in Spain.

cat

cat and mouse
a game of cat and mouse ◄◄◄

In a contest or dispute, if one person plays **cat and mouse** with another, the first person tries to confuse or deceive the second in order to defeat them. You can also say that they play **a game of cat and mouse**.

He would play cat-and-mouse with other riders, sometimes waiting until the fourth lap to come from behind and win.

A diplomatic game of cat and mouse is continuing between the United Nations and the warring factions in the Yugoslav crisis.

□ **Cat and mouse** is also used before 'game' or another noun.

He was forced to drive around and use his car telephone to tell police what was going on as Amos played a cat and mouse game with officers.

They were arrested after a cat-and-mouse chase through the fields.

a cat on hot bricks
a cat on a hot tin roof

If you say that someone is as nervous or restless as **a cat on hot bricks**, you mean that they are very nervous or restless.

Why are you shifting from one foot to the other like a cat on hot bricks?

□ The expression **a cat on a hot tin roof** is sometimes used. This is also the title of a play by Tennessee Williams.

The company has unbalanced inventories and executives who are as nervous as a cat on a hot tin roof.

the cat's whiskers

If you describe someone or something as **the cat's whiskers**, you are saying in a lighthearted way that they are the best person or thing of their kind. This is an old-fashioned expression, which is used in British English.

As far as knowing the market and supplying it are concerned, she's the cat's whiskers.

Loose Ends release a long, long awaited new single on August 16. A new album will follow in October. Both are reliably tipped as the cat's whiskers.

□ If someone thinks that they are **the cat's whiskers**, they are very pleased with themselves or very proud of themselves.

She had this great dress on with huge skirts, and she thought she was the cat's whiskers as she came out along the gallery.

a fat cat ◄◄◄

You can refer to a businessman or politician as **a fat cat** when you disapprove of the way they use their wealth, power, and privileges, for example because it seems unfair or wrong to you.

The Government should launch an inquiry into the fat cats of commerce making huge profits out of the public.

Yet again privatisation is seen to line the pockets of City fat cats at the expense of the customer.

□ You can also use **fat cat** before a noun.

The taxpayer will be left to pay while the fat cat businessmen get the cream of Britain's rail services.

In a populist style, he promised to eliminate fat-cat salaries for union bosses and increase worker wages and job security.

fight like cat and dog ◄

If you say that two people **fight like cat and dog**, you mean that they frequently have violent arguments with each other.

'We used to fight like cat and dog,' she says. 'He was unfaithful, dishonest and chauvinistic. But whenever I looked at him my heart melted.'

They had fought like cat and dog ever since he could remember, and he wondered how they'd got together in the first place.

grin like a Cheshire cat ◄

If you say that someone **is grinning like a Cheshire cat**, you mean that they are grinning broadly, usually in a foolish way. Other verbs are sometimes used instead of 'grin'.

Standing on the door step and grinning like a Cheshire Cat was Bertie Owen.

Finally he'd come indoors smiling like a Cheshire cat, and I'd help him undress and get him into bed.

Charles was sitting in his place, looking like a Cheshire cat, when I joined him.

□ You can also say that someone has a **Cheshire cat** grin or a **Cheshire cat** smile.

I complained, but Jennifer stood there with her Cheshire cat grin.

A beaming Steve stood in the background,

nodding his head up and down and wearing a Cheshire Cat smile on his face.

let the cat out of the bag ◄

If someone **lets the cat out of the bag**, they reveal something secret or private, often without meaning to.

She'd known she was taking a real, if relatively small, risk in letting the cat out of the bag about Jacobs.

'The Mosses didn't tell the cops my name, did they?' 'Of course not,' she said. 'They wouldn't want to let the cat out of the bag.'

□ You can say that **the cat is out of the bag** when a secret has been revealed.

The cat was well and truly out of the bag. The biggest sex scandal for years was about to overtake the government.

like a scalded cat

If a person or animal moves **like a scalded cat**, they move very fast, as though they have been suddenly frightened or shocked. This expression is used in British English.

Scrambling around to recover his glasses, the scientist darted to his car like a scalded cat and clambered quickly in.

The Derby winner of that year set off like a scalded cat, and was never caught.

like the cat that got the cream
like the cat that ate the canary

If you say that someone looks **like the cat that got the cream** or **like the cat that ate the canary**, you mean that they look satisfied and happy with themselves, for example because they have been successful or done something they are proud of. 'Like the cat that got the cream' is used mainly in British English.

'Thanks a million,' he repeats, grinning like the cat that nearly got the cream.

I dare say you've noticed that Hugh's acting much like a cat that got into the cream.

Jule stands at one end, and on his face, more clearly than on those of his colleagues, is the look of the cat that ate the canary.

look like something the cat dragged in

If you say that someone or something **looks like something the cat dragged in**, you are saying in an unkind way that they look very unpleasant or unappealing. Instead of 'dragged in', you can use, for example, 'left'.

It is still possible to be an intelligent and successful lady and look like something the cat has dragged in. What money cannot buy is dress sense.

Although the dish 'tasted great', he advises serving it in the dark, 'since the topping looks like something the cat left'.

look what the cat's dragged in

You can say **'look what the cat's dragged in'** when someone arrives to express your dislike or disapproval of them, or as a lighthearted way of greeting them.

In strolls Babs. 'Now look what the cat's dragged in,' says Jeanie, with a nod.

no room to swing a cat

If you say that there is **no room to swing a cat** in a place, you are emphasizing that it is very small and there is very little space. This expression is very variable. It is used mainly in British English.

Inside, there is no room to swing a cat, and everything you see and touch is the most basic junk.

It was billed as a large, luxury mobile home, but there was barely room to swing a cat.

We went into the ward, and my first thought was, how is she going to sleep. You couldn't swing a cat.

put the cat among the pigeons
set the cat among the pigeons ◄

If a remark or action **puts the cat among the pigeons** or **sets the cat among the pigeons**, it causes trouble or upset. Other verbs can be used instead of 'put' or 'set'. This expression is used in British English.

The bank is poised to put the cat among the pigeons this morning by slashing the cost of borrowing.

Once again she set the cat among the pigeons, claiming that Michael was lying.

This whole thing has thrown the cat amongst the pigeons. There are people in the area at the moment apparently trying to establish whether there is any more land that can be claimed.

see which way the cat jumps

If someone waits to **see which way the cat jumps**, they delay making a decision or taking action on something until they are more confident about how the situation will develop. This expression is used mainly in British English.

I'm going to sit tight and see which way the cat jumps.

there's more than one way to skin a cat ◄

People say **'there's more than one way to skin a cat'** when they want to point out that there are several ways to achieve something, not just the conventional way. This expression is very variable.

Ministers who previously insisted there was no alternative to Britain's ERM policy were last night saying: 'There is more than one way to skin a cat.'

Major, in the words of one minister, had discovered 'there are more ways to skin a cat'. He had at last found a way to bring down interest rates.

when the cat's away, the mice will play

If you say **'when the cat's away, the mice will play'** or **'while the cat's away, the mice will play'**, you mean that people do what they want or misbehave when their boss or another person in authority is away.

'What's the hurry?' he croaked. 'While the cat's away the mice will play.'

□ People sometimes just say **'when the cat's away'** or **'while the cat's away'**.

While the cat's away – when a supervisor was out, some employees began straggling in late.

catbird

in the catbird seat

If someone is sitting **in the catbird seat**, they are in an important or powerful position. This is an old-fashioned expression, which is used in American English.

'The sonofabitch couldn't get along without me.' 'Yeah, he'd go broke tomorrow if you left him, right? And you, you'd be sitting in the catbird seat, right?'

If I can run around the world and buy that particular group, then I'll be in the catbird's seat.

Catch

a Catch 22 ◄

A **Catch 22** is an extremely frustrating situation in which one thing cannot happen until another thing has happened, but the other thing cannot happen until the first thing has happened.

There's a Catch 22 in social work. You need experience to get work and you need work to get experience.

□ You can also say that you are in a **Catch 22** situation or position.

It's a Catch 22 situation here. Nobody wants to support you until you're successful, particularly if you're a woman. But without the support how can you ever be successful?

□ This expression comes from **Catch 22**, the title of a novel by Joseph Heller.

cats

it's raining cats and dogs

You say **'it's raining cats and dogs'** to emphasize that it is raining very heavily. This expression is considered old-fashioned in British English.

'Could you see how he looked?' 'Not really. It was raining cats and dogs by then.'

'You mean she wasn't wearing a coat, even though it was raining cats and dogs?'

caution

throw caution to the wind ◄◄

If you **throw caution to the wind** or **throw caution to the winds,** you do something without worrying about the risks and danger involved.

If he seems mad about you too, do you still play it cool or just throw caution to the wind and enjoy?

This was no time to think, he decided. He threw caution to the winds and rang the bell of the ground-floor flat.

cent

not one red cent
not a red cent

If you complain that you get **not one red cent** from someone or that they do **not** give you **a red cent**, you mean that you do not get any money from them at all, even though you feel you ought to. This expression is used mainly in American English.

At an average return to the bank of 13 per cent over ten years, the bank made £12,480 of interest using the couple's money. The couple, of course, received not one red cent!

But investors have to remember that with many shows they won't get a red cent back.'

centre

centre stage ◄◄◄

If someone or something takes **centre stage**, they become the most significant or noticeable person or item in a situation. If they hold **centre stage**, they are the most significant or noticeable person or item.

In his fiction, drugs don't take center stage very often, but they are a persistent theme.

She has held centre stage for a decade now and has just enjoyed her biggest US hit in years.

The summit is the first time he has occupied centre stage at an important international gathering since coming to power last year.

□ 'Centre' is spelled 'center' in American English.

cents

your two cents' worth

If you have or you put in your **two cents' worth**, you give your opinion about something, even if nobody has asked you for it. People occasionally replace 'two' with another number. This expression is used mainly in American English, but is becoming more common in British English. Your **two penn'orth** means the same.

Your father kept telling me to hush up and don't be a damn fool, but you know me, I had to put in my two cents' worth.

chaff

separate the wheat from the chaff
separate the grain from the chaff
sort the wheat from the chaff ◀

If you **separate the wheat from the chaff** or **separate the grain from the chaff**, you decide which things or people in a group are good or necessary, and which are not. You can use 'sort' or 'sort out' instead of 'separate'.

The reality is often blurred by an overdose of propaganda. It is becoming more and more difficult to separate the wheat from the chaff.

It's up to Wilkinson to sort out the wheat from the chaff and get the team back to the top of the table before it's too late.

□ You can refer to the good or necessary things or people in a group as 'wheat' or 'grain', and to the others as 'chaff'.

Very little wheat in all this chaff.

Was there rather less grain than chaff?

chain

pull someone's chain
yank someone's chain

If you **pull** someone's **chain** or **yank** their **chain**, you tease them about something, for example by telling them something which is not true. These expressions are used mainly in American English.

He sat next to Wade's car, and he decided to take it: what the hell, why not? Let the man show him just how far he could go. Pull his chain, rattle his cage, and shake the man up a little.

I glared at her, and she smiled. When would I learn to smarten up and ignore her when she yanked my chain?

chalice

a poisoned chalice ◀

If you refer to a job or an opportunity as **a poisoned chalice**, you mean that it seems to be very attractive but you believe that it will, in fact, lead to failure or a very unpleasant situation. This expression is used mainly in British English.

Some people even claimed that the president appointed his former rival only in the belief that he was giving him a poisoned chalice and that he would not last more than a year.

The contract may yet prove to be a poisoned chalice.

chalk

by a long chalk ◀

You can use **by a long chalk** to add emphasis to a statement you are making, especially a negative statement or one that contains a superlative. This expression is used in British English.

The rest of us hadn't finished our drinks, not by a long chalk, but Finn seemed to want more.

Where do you think you're going, Kershaw? You haven't finished by a long chalk.

In fact this book is by a long chalk the best life of Sayers so far published.

chalk and cheese ◀

If you say that two people or two things are like **chalk and cheese**, you are emphasizing that they are completely different from each other. This expression is used in British English.

Marianne and Ellis just aren't compatible, they are like chalk and cheese. She is a serious, conscientious type while he is erratic and carefree.

Our relationship works because we are very aware of our differences, we accept that we are chalk and cheese.

She was 16, idyllically pretty and socially successful. As different from me as chalk from cheese.

chance

an eye for the main chance
the main chance ◀

You can say that someone has **an eye for the main chance** or **an eye on the main chance** when you believe that they are always looking for an easy opportunity to make money or to improve their situation. This expression is used in British English.

Are these the words of a genuine football reformer, or an opportunist with an eye for the main chance?

You make your own money and luck by being out in the world with your eye on the main chance and doing nothing risky.

□ You can also use **the main chance** with a verb such as 'look for' or 'take'.

He was just an idle boaster looking for the main chance.

She longs for them to succeed, to take the main chance, and she grieves with them for their failures.

not a cat in hell's chance
not a snowball's chance in hell
not have a chance in hell ◀◀

If you say that there is **not a cat in hell's chance** or **not a snowball's chance in hell** of someone doing something, you are emphasizing that there is no chance at all of them being able to do it. You can also say that someone does **not have a chance in hell** of doing something. These expressions are used in spoken British English.

The chairman of the finance committee said

£44 was totally unrealistic. 'There's not a cat in hell's chance of setting such a low figure,' he said.

The probability of being caught was horrendously high. If I was caught with all the film on me I had not a snowball's chance in hell of talking my way out of it.

They have not a chance in hell of privatising the economy. They have no idea how a free market works.

□ This expression is very variable. For example, you can also say that there is **not a cat's chance in hell** or **not a snowflake's chance in hell** of someone doing something.

None of these three conditions makes any sense, nor is there a cat's chance in hell of any of them being accepted.

Radio listeners heard him discussing Aids and saying there was hardly 'a snowflake's chance in hell' of catching it.

He told me the proposal had as much chance as a snowball in the Arizona desert.

change

a change of heart ◄◄◄

If someone has **a change of heart**, their attitude towards something changes.

At the last minute, she had a change of heart about selling it. It had been in her family for generations.

The government's change of heart on debt relief for the poorest countries is very good news.

It wasn't always immediately clear whether their change of heart was genuine or a cover.

get no change out of someone

If you **get no change out of** someone, you get no help from them at all. Other words can be used instead of 'no'. This expression is used in British English.

You won't get any change out of him, so don't expect it. And no promotion, either.

We didn't seem to get a lot of change out of them when we had problems.

changes

ring the changes ◄◄

If you **ring the changes**, you make alterations in the way something is organized or done in order to vary or improve it. This expression is used in British English.

I like to ring the changes with dark curtains in the winter, and light Indian ones in the summer.

The different varieties within each brand enable you to ring the changes to ensure that your dog never gets bored with his food.

chapter

chapter and verse ◄

If you say that someone gives you **chapter and verse** on a subject, you mean that they give you all the details of it, without missing anything out.

It gives chapter and verse on how to select a product, advertising, distribution and finances.

But I'm going to need chapter and verse on all this before I can tackle the Home Office.

When we expressed doubts they handed us the proof, chapter and verse.

a chapter of accidents

If a series of unlucky events happens in a short time, you can describe it as **a chapter of accidents**. This expression is used in British English.

Luckily for him, few people were witness to this chapter of accidents.

In fiction, however, such a chapter of accidents can end up seeming comic.

charity

charity begins at home ◄

If you say **'charity begins at home'**, you mean that you should deal with the needs of people close to you before you think about helping others. You can use 'start' instead of 'begin'.

Charity begins at home. There are many tasks right on campus that need volunteers as well.

There are other cases in other countries but I think that charity should start at home.

chase

cut to the chase

If someone **cuts to the chase**, they start talking about or dealing with what is really important, instead of less important things. This expression is used in American English.

Solo came to our room. He talked about the need to see all points of view, then he cut to the chase: 'Well, it looks like there is nothing here for me. I'm planning to fly back.'

The Council ought to cut to the chase and make a political decision based on what Council members feel is the best use for the house.

cheek

cheek by jowl ◄◄

If you say that people or things are **cheek by jowl**, you mean that they are very close together, especially in a way that seems undesirable or inconvenient.

You'd think living so close would make people friendlier, but it didn't. After about seven years, all this living cheek-by-jowl began to irritate people.

You had great unemployment, and you had an isolated population that lived cheek by jowl with some of the richest and most showy people in the country. It's just the most explosive situation you could think of.

In the drawing room, fine Coalport and Dresden china is placed cheek by jowl with wooden candle-sconces that probably once graced a merry-go-round.

turn the other cheek ◄◄

If you **turn the other cheek** when someone harms or insults you, you decide not to take any action against them in return.

Ian must learn to turn the other cheek, no matter what the provocation.

If they are unwilling to deal with the racists, we will take matters into our own hands by any means necessary. The days of turning the other cheek are long over.

cheese

a big cheese ◄

If you describe someone as **a big cheese**, you mean that they have an important and powerful position in an organization. This is an informal expression.

Henri Maire is undoubtedly the big cheese of the Jura wine producers, dominating the industry not only locally but also nationally and internationally.

During the conference big cheeses from the State Department were dropping in and out all the time.

□ **Big cheese** can also be used before a noun.

He was a big-cheese divorce lawyer.

cheque

a blank cheque ◄◄

If you give someone **a blank cheque** to do something, you give them complete authority to do what they think is best in a difficult situation. This expression is used mainly in talking about politics.

De Klerk had, in a sense, been given a blank cheque to negotiate the new South Africa.

He says he doesn't support a resolution giving the president a blank check to commit the nation to war at an unspecified time and under unspecified circumstances.

The resolution was later viewed as the blank cheque for US involvement in Vietnam.

□ If you write **a blank cheque** for someone, you promise them an unlimited amount of money.

We are not prepared to write a blank cheque for companies that have run into trouble through indifferent management.

□ This expression is often used literally to mean that someone gives another person a cheque without an amount of money written on it. 'Cheque' is spelled 'check' in American English.

chest

get something off your chest ◄◄

If you **get** something **off** your **chest**, you talk about a problem that has been worrying you for a long time, and you feel better because of this.

My doctor gave me the opportunity to talk and get things off my chest.

Sarah certainly seemed as though she had to get a lot off her chest.

play your cards close to your chest
keep your cards close to your chest ◄

If you **play** your **cards close to** your **chest** or **keep** your **cards close to** your **chest**, you do not tell anyone about your plans or thoughts. **Play** your **cards close to the vest** means the same.

Williams is playing his cards close to his chest, especially in terms of his driver line-up for next season.

The Prime Minister was said yesterday to be keeping his cards close to his chest after an informal discussion at cabinet on Thursday.

□ 'Cards' is often replaced with other nouns.

Taylor kept his thoughts close to his chest, saying only: 'I'm not prepared to comment.'

She looked up, meeting her friend's eye. 'Have you inside information?' 'Afraid not. Dave's playing this one close to his chest.'

chestnut

an old chestnut
a hoary old chestnut ◄◄

If you refer to a statement, story, or idea as **an old chestnut** or **a hoary old chestnut**, you mean that it has been repeated so often that it is no longer interesting. This expression is used mainly in British English.

But above all, the feminist struggle is too important to become an old chestnut over which people groan.

The film is based on the hoary old chestnut of good twin/bad twin, separated at birth, final fatal meeting – you get the idea.

chestnuts

pull someone's chestnuts out of the fire

If you **pull** someone's **chestnuts out of the fire**, you save that person from a very difficult situation which they have got themselves into, or you solve their problems for them. This is an old-fashioned expression.

Presidents frequently try to use the CIA to pull their chestnuts out of the fire.

It's not our business, pulling their chestnuts out of the fire.

chicken

chicken and egg: 1 ◄

If you describe something as a **chicken and egg** situation, you mean that you cannot decide which of two related things happened first and caused the other.

First of all, the link between current global temperature and carbon-dioxide emissions is not a chicken and egg situation. Cause and effect are quite clear.

It's a chicken-and-egg argument about which comes first: Do people create a neighborhood lifestyle? Or does a neighborhood environment influence how residents live?

chicken and egg: 2

If you say that something is a **chicken and egg** situation, you mean that it is impossible to deal with a problem because the solution is also the cause of the problem.

Until we get promotion, we won't get the top players. But until we get top players, we won't win promotion. It's a chicken and egg situation.

The Zoo may close for lack of public support. It is a chicken-and-egg situation in which the high cost of entry keeps people away.

chicken feed: 1 ◄

If you refer to an amount, usually of money, as **chicken feed**, you mean that it is very small. This expression is often used to emphasize that one amount is very small in comparison with another.

The £70,000-a-year backing received from sponsors is chicken feed compared to the £20m budgets available to some of his rivals.

If the shipyard, which employs 4,000, does not get the long-awaited government order, the Renfrew job losses will look like chicken-feed.

chicken feed: 2

If you say that someone or something is **chicken feed**, you mean that they are insignificant, especially in comparison to another person or thing.

There's Masters, too. He's the biggest threat. We're just chickenfeed.

like a headless chicken
like a chicken with its head cut off ◄◄

If you say that someone is running around **like a headless chicken** or **like a chicken with its head cut off**, you are criticizing them for behaving in an uncontrolled or disorganized way, and not thinking calmly or logically. 'Like a headless chicken' is used only in British English.

Instead of running round like a headless chicken you're using your efforts in a more productive way, more efficiently.

A dejected German coach Bertie Vogts said:

'We threw away our early chances, and after they scored we played like headless chickens.'

They were all running around like chickens with their heads cut off – they didn't know where to go, where to sit, who to talk to.

□ This expression is very variable.

The Tories, who have been in much of a shambles throughout the campaign anyway, collapsed into total farce. Never have so many chickens been seen running around without their heads.

chickens

not count your chickens
don't count your chickens before they're hatched ◄

If you say that you **are not counting** your **chickens**, you mean that you are not going to make plans for the future because you do not know for certain how a particular situation will develop.

If we get through, Real Madrid and the Italian side Genoa will be massive hurdles to overcome. Most of the top sides are better now than they were in the early eighties so I'm not counting my chickens. There are no walkovers like there were years ago.

The February housing figures are still way below a year ago, and that's why economists aren't yet counting their chickens.

□ This expression comes from the proverb **don't count your chickens before they're hatched**.

When dealing with important financial arrangements, it is imperative that you ensure that you are not counting your chickens before they are hatched.

chiefs

too many chiefs and not enough Indians
too many chiefs

People say **'too many chiefs and not enough Indians'** when they want to criticize an organization for having too many people in charge and not enough people to actually do the work. Many people consider this expression offensive.

Americans should also come to recognize that many of their organizations have too many chiefs and not enough Indians.

Another disadvantage was the overstaffing of headquarters and support personnel. It is the typical but highly relevant complaint of too many Chiefs and not enough Indians.

□ People sometimes just say **'too many chiefs'**.

If he chose to counter-attack against the criticism, he might point to the bank's structure. It includes 21 executive directors. No surprise, then, that some insiders say there are too many chiefs.

child

child's play ◄◄

If you say that something is **child's play**, you are emphasizing that it is very easy to deal with. This expression is often used in comparisons where you are mentioning something that is very difficult.

He thought the work would be child's play.

The problem in Western Europe was described by one EU energy expert as child's play compared to that in Eastern Europe.

After the tension in Osborne House, the rush and clamour of her office had seemed like mere child's play.

chin

keep your chin up ◄

If you **keep** your **chin up**, you stay calm or cheerful in a difficult or unpleasant situation.

Richards was keeping his chin up yesterday despite the continued setbacks.

Keep your chin up: they won't get away with it.

Mark was absolutely devastated at having to leave. He kept his chin up, and never lost faith in his ability, but he was still desperately disappointed.

lead with your chin

If you say that someone **is leading with** their **chin**, you mean that they are behaving very aggressively, and, for example, are starting a conflict.

This game is no place for a player who cannot lead with his chin.

We don't plan to attack the administration for not spending more on education. There's nothing to be gained from leading with our chins.

take it on the chin ◄◄

If someone **takes it on the chin**, they bravely accept criticism or a difficult situation and do not make a fuss about it. 'It' is sometimes replaced with nouns such as 'criticism' and 'defeat'.

When the police arrived, he took it on the chin, apologising for the trouble he'd caused them.

We've taken a big loss. We've taken it on the chin. But we're out there and we're going to stay in business.

Andrew is intelligent, wants to learn, and is therefore very coachable. He is also prepared to take criticism on the chin.

chink

a chink in someone's armour ◄

If you say that someone or something has **a chink in** their **armour**, you mean that they have a weakness that can be taken advantage of, although they appear outwardly to be very strong and successful.

There was always the chance that, with their superior knowledge, they might find the chinks in his armour.

Labour leaders hope to use their annual conference to attack what they currently see as the most vulnerable chink in the government's armour.

The HIV virus has a chink in its armour which could lead to a protective vaccine and make Aids as rare as polio, a researcher announced this weekend.

□ 'Armour' is spelled 'armor' in American English.

chip

a chip off the old block ◄

If you describe someone as **a chip off the old block**, you mean that they are very similar to one of their parents in appearance, character, or behaviour.

I've known Damon since he was a boy and he's a chip off the old block. He has the same dry sense of humour, and the same dedication and total commitment.

Lewis's lawyer James Crummet tells me 'He is a chip off the old block – a hothead and a bully just like his dad.'

a chip on your shoulder ◄◄◄

If you say that someone has **a chip on** their **shoulder**, you mean that they feel angry and resentful because they think that they have been treated unfairly, especially because of their race, sex, or background.

My father wasn't always easy to get along with; he had a chip on his shoulder and thought people didn't like him because of his colour.

I've never really had a chip on my shoulder but I suppose you could say that having come from a rather poor background I found it difficult to cope with the arrogance of some of the teaching staff.

A lot of gay people walk around with a chip on their shoulder. What you have to do is believe in yourself, because when you believe in yourself, other people will believe in you.

□ You can use **chip-on-shoulder** or **chip-on-the-shoulder** before a noun.

Its leaders have lately seemed to revert to the sort of chip-on-shoulder nationalism that naturally makes neighbouring countries nervous.

They all had that chip-on-the-shoulder look.

chips

call in your chips

If you **call in** your **chips**, you decide to use your influence or social connections in order to gain an advantage over other people. This expression is used mainly in British English.

That point needs making, before Mr Clinton's friends in the labour unions and the steel and textile industries try to call in their chips.

And the other thing is that China can lobby very hard to call in all its chips from, for example, the African bloc.

cash in your chips

If someone **cashes in** their **chips**, they sell something such as their investments, in order to raise money.

Many skittish mutual fund investors picked up the phone yesterday, but decided not to cash in their chips after all.

ICI was small in over-the-counter drugs in the States. It decided to cash in its chips at a surprisingly good price.

have had your chips

In British English, if you say that someone or something **has had** their **chips**, you mean that they have completely failed in something they were trying to do.

After the 4-1 defeat by Wimbledon which all but scuppered their title ambitions, most of the 10,000 crowd were convinced they'd already had their chips.

when the chips are down
the chips are down ◄◄

If you refer to people's behaviour **when the chips are down**, you are referring to their behaviour in a difficult or dangerous situation.

There will be no panic. We are at our best when the chips are down.

'How could you do that, knowing you might be rushing to your death?' And he smiled and he said, 'When the chips are down, you do what you have to do.'

□ If you say that **the chips are down**, you mean that a situation has become difficult or dangerous.

Manchester City face table-topping Newcastle today and the manager said: 'The chips are down and it's time to show a bit of character.'

chop

chop and change ◄◄

If you say that someone **is chopping and changing**, you mean that they keep changing their plans, often when you think that this is unnecessary. This expression is used in British English.

After chopping and changing for the first

year, Paul and Jamie have settled down to a stable system of management.

Chopping and changing around does not always pay and tends to get confusing.

for the chop: 1
get the chop ◄◄

If someone is **for the chop**, they are about to lose their job. If they **get the chop**, they lose their job. These are informal expressions, which are used in British English.

There are rumours that he is for the chop.

He had hardly settled into his new job when he got the chop due to cutbacks.

□ You can say that someone is trying to avoid **the chop** when they are trying to avoid losing their job, or that they face **the chop** when they are likely to lose their job.

They are turning up to work earlier, and leaving later, in a bid to avoid the chop.

He must play by next week or face the chop for the Challenge Cup final.

for the chop: 2
get the chop

If something is **for the chop**, it is not going to be allowed to continue or remain. If it **gets the chop**, it is not allowed to continue or remain. These expressions are used in British English.

He won't say which programmes are for the chop.

Some of the steamier scenes that got the chop in America will be put back in for the Australian release.

□ You can say that something is threatened with **the chop** when it is likely that it will not be allowed to continue or remain.

Weekly broadcasts are now threatened with the chop.

These were known to be loss-making factories that deserved the chop.

chord

strike a chord
touch a chord ◄◄◄

If something **strikes a chord** with you, it makes you respond in an emotional way, for example by feeling sympathy or pleasure. You can also say that something **touches a chord** with you.

It is a case which has shocked America – and one which has struck a chord with every family which has agonised over how much freedom teenagers should be allowed.

Little wonder that the play struck such a responsive chord in the hearts of both the young and the old.

His public criticisms at a critical political juncture have touched a sensitive chord here.

□ Some people use the word 'cord' instead of

'chord' in this expression, but it is generally considered incorrect.

church

a broad church ◄

You can refer to an organization, group, or area of activity as **a broad church** when it includes a wide range of opinions, beliefs, or styles. This expression is used in British English.

The movement is presently a very broad church, comprising trade unions, workers, the church, students, the business community and a ragbag of once prominent politicians.

Rock music in France is a very broad church indeed.

cigar

close but no cigar
nice try but no cigar

You use expressions such as '**close but no cigar**' or '**nice try but no cigar**' to point out to someone that they have failed in what they were trying to achieve or make you believe.

'I detest guards and burglar alarms. They're so vulgar. That's why I carry that dreadful gun in my purse, though I hardly know how to use it.' 'Nice try, Laura baby, but no cigar,' said Frank.

circle

come full circle
turn full circle
the wheel has come full circle ◄◄◄

If you say that something **has come full circle** or **has turned full circle**, you mean that it is now exactly the same as it used to be, although there has been a long period of changes. Other verbs are sometimes used instead of 'come' or 'turn'.

Looking at the current product, I am tempted to say the design has come full circle.

Her life had now come full circle and she was back where she started, in misery, alone.

Michael Crawford's current success as a singer has brought his career full circle.

□ People also say that **the wheel has come full circle** or that **the wheel has turned full circle**.

The wheel has turned full circle, we are back where we began.

square the circle ◄◄

If you try to **square the circle**, you try to solve a problem that seems to be impossible to solve.

Chile is trying to square the circle of knowing what poor people ought to have, but not yet being able to afford it.

All have the same hope: that foreign markets and, especially, foreign investment will somehow provide enough jobs to square the circle.

a vicious circle ◄◄◄

If you describe a difficult situation as **a vicious circle**, you are talking about how one problem has caused other problems which, in turn, have made the original problem even worse.

Patients discharged from the old 'mental hospitals' are being thrust into a vicious circle of poverty and illnesses, according to a report published by the national mental health charity MIND.

Kimelman believes the American economy has been caught in a vicious circle during the past two years. 'The economy couldn't create large numbers of jobs because consumers weren't spending. Consumers weren't spending because the economy wasn't creating jobs.'

circles

go around in circles
go round in circles ◄

If you say that someone **is going around in circles**, you mean that they are not achieving very much because they keep coming back to the same point or problem over and over again. In British English, you can also say that someone **is going round in circles**.

My mind was going around in circles.

They have been going round and round in circles about treatment methods. And their solution, in the end, was perfectly straightforward.

This was one of those debates which simply went round in circles with motions and countermotions being amended, withdrawn and re-submitted.

run around in circles
run round in circles

If you say that someone **is running around in circles**, you mean that they are having very little success in achieving something although they are trying hard, because they are disorganized. In British English, you can also say that someone **is running round in circles**.

She may waste a lot of energy running around in circles, whereas more careful planning could save a lot of effort and achieve a great deal.

Some kid's gone missing, and everyone's running round in circles.

circus

a three-ring circus ◄

If you describe a situation as **a three-ring circus**, you mean that there is a lot of noisy or very chaotic activity going on. This expression is used more commonly in American English than in British.

They might fight among themselves, but grief was a private thing, not something to be turned into a three-ring circus by over-eager reporters.

clam

shut up like a clam

If someone **shuts up like a clam**, they become very quiet and withdrawn because they are upset or worried.

When they are worried, they may well shut up like a clam, definitely not wanting to tell you what is wrong.

Later, when I found I wasn't his only love, I shut like a clam and let no one close. The hurt engulfed me as love once had.

clanger

drop a clanger ◄

If someone **drops a clanger**, they make a very embarrassing mistake. This expression is used in British English.

'You wouldn't have thought that Jimmy of all people would drop such a clanger.' Last night the show's producer admitted: 'It was an unfortunate oversight in the pressure of filming before Christmas.'

Tories in Eastleigh dropped a clanger in their election leaflet by admitting that few people will be voting Conservative tomorrow.

clappers

like the clappers

If you say that someone does something **like the clappers**, you are emphasizing that they do it very quickly. This expression is used in British English.

What is it that makes people run like the clappers for a train?

claws

get your claws into someone: 1

If someone **gets** their **claws into** you, they control or influence you in a selfish way for their own advantage. Other verbs can be used instead of 'get'.

These people had their claws into him and he didn't know how to get clear of them.

The Tigers want to get their claws into 20-year old striker Martin Carruthers from Aston Villa.

get your claws into someone: 2

If you say that a woman **has got** her **claws into** a man, you disapprove of her relationship with him, for example because you think that she is selfish and uncaring, or that she is not good enough for him. Other verbs can be used instead of 'get'.

Sadly for Jackie, Amanda got her claws into Gavin first.

She wasted no time in hooking her claws into Des.

clean

clean as a whistle: 1 ◄

If you describe someone as **clean as a whistle**, you do not think they have done anything wrong, or you have no evidence that they have done anything wrong.

'There is no sex, drugs or rock 'n' roll. His private life is as clean as a whistle,' says McSmith.

This is the man who oversaw a dirty, trivial campaign, and yet emerged from it with his reputation as clean as a whistle.

clean as a whistle: 2

If you say that something is as **clean as a whistle**, you mean that it is completely free from dirt.

It leaves your face feeling clean as a whistle but not bone-dry.

The launch team has spent six days vacuuming debris away and has inspected all joints with a fibre-optic microscope. 'It's as clean as a whistle,' says Gauss.

come clean ◄◄◄

If someone **comes clean** about something, they tell the truth about it.

I had expected her to come clean and confess that she only wrote these books for the money. But, no, she insists that she takes them all very seriously.

He says it is now essential for the Government to come clean, tell the world exactly how the recent tragedy happened and announce an investigation.

squeaky clean ◄◄◄

If you say that someone is **squeaky clean**, you mean that they live a very moral life and do not appear to have any vices. This expression is often used to suggest that this way of life is unnatural or uninteresting, or that someone is not as virtuous as they seem.

Our image has been a little over-exaggerated, saying that we're wholesome and squeaky clean. We're not all that, we're just very positive-minded people.

As a country-dweller myself, I can truthfully say that not all people living in the countryside are as squeaky clean as they like to think.

□ You can also use **squeaky-clean** before a noun.

Claudia's massive earnings and squeaky-clean image make her the perfect partner for royal marriage.

He has a squeaky-clean reputation and would be a tough target for the attacks about family values.

cleaners

take someone to the cleaners ◄

If someone **is taking** you **to the cleaners**, they are making you lose a lot of money in an unfair or dishonest way.

The feeling among many experts on the commercial side is that the price paid at the time was excessive. It sounds like he got absolutely taken to the cleaners.

Just for a change, the insurers discovered that they had been taken to the cleaners.

clear

clear as a bell ◄

If you say that something is as **clear as a bell**, you mean that it is very clear indeed.

Suddenly there is an unmistakable sound. It's as clear as a bell.

If the whole image isn't as clear as a bell, take it a bit further back.

clear as crystal

If you say that something is as **clear as crystal**, you mean that it is very clear indeed.

It was a brilliant blue day, as clear as crystal, with a sun that was just comfortably hot.

□ People also use the much more frequent adjective **crystal clear** to mean the same thing.

The water is crystal clear.

Let me make certain things crystal clear. This government has no intention of letting its authority be undermined.

clear as day ◄

If you say that something is as **clear as day**, you mean that it is very easy to see, or that it is very obvious and easy to understand. **Plain as day** means the same.

Suddenly she stepped out from behind a tree less than ten yards from me. I saw her face as clear as day.

If his drawbacks are clear as day to the rest of us, why is Nicole going ahead and getting married?

clear as mud

If you say that something is as **clear as mud**, you are saying in a light-hearted or sarcastic way that it is confusing and difficult to understand.

'It's all written down there! Self-explanatory! Clearly.' 'Clear as mud. Even I can't understand it, and I'm pretty smart.'

in the clear: 1 ◄

If someone is **in the clear**, they are free from blame or suspicion.

Rickmore was silent for a while, then he said: 'If your chief clerk confesses to the police what really happened, I'll be in the clear.'

Their possessions had not been searched so they were not officially in the clear.

in the clear: 2 ◄

If someone is **in the clear**, they are no longer in danger or trouble.

Doctors told Jenny her unborn child was at risk and she and her husband underwent an agonising 48-hour wait for the results of tests before discovering he was in the clear.

Nor is the Government in the clear yet over the composition of the committee, an issue that is likely to dog ministers in the weeks ahead.

in the clear: 3

If someone is **in the clear** in a competition or contest, they are ahead of other people.

There was more gloomy news for the Prime Minister in an opinion poll yesterday which showed Labour five points in the clear.

steer clear
steer someone clear of something ◄◄◄

If you **steer clear** of something or someone, you deliberately avoid them. If you **steer** someone **clear** of something, you help them to avoid it.

The Princess appealed to young people to steer clear of the dangers of drugs.

Steer clear of men you know are dodgy.

Friends look out for your welfare. They listen to your problems. They steer you clear of damaging situations.

clever

box clever ◄

If you say that someone is **boxing clever**, you mean that they are being very careful and cunning in the way they behave in a difficult situation, so that they can get an advantage over other people. This expression is used in British English.

They have boxed clever shaping the market to themselves, and themselves to the market.

He was not displeased at the way he had handled the meeting. You boxed cleverly, he told himself.

cloak

cloak-and-dagger ◄◄

You use **cloak-and-dagger** to describe activities, especially dangerous ones, which are done in secret. You sometimes use this expression to suggest that people are treating these activities in an unnecessarily dramatic way.

They met in classic cloak-and-dagger style beside the lake in St James's Park, both tossing snacks to the listless waterfowl.

Why all the cloak and dagger stuff?

Now that the Berlin Wall has come down, the cloak-and-dagger world of East-West espionage, immortalised by John Le Carré and other novelists, might appear to be outdated.

□ You can refer to such activities as **cloaks and daggers**.

Intelligence has very little to do with cloaks and daggers, being mostly about boring reports and endless statistics.

clock

round the clock
around the clock ◄◄◄

If people are working **round the clock** or **around the clock**, the work is being done continuously, throughout the day and night, often so that a particular task can be completed as quickly as possible.

Fire crews were working round the clock to bring the huge blazes under control.

'You looked tired, Leonard.' 'I've been working round the clock.'

She will no longer be guarded round the clock.

□ **Round-the-clock** and **around-the-clock** can be used before a noun to describe work that is being done continuously, throughout the day and night.

Staff alerted police and a round-the-clock surveillance of the four men began.

We can't afford to give you around-the-clock protection.

turn the clock back ◄◄◄

If you would like to **turn the clock back** or to **turn back the clock**, you would like to return to an earlier period, for example because you think it was a very good time or because you would like the chance to live your life differently. You can use 'put' instead of 'turn'.

The club wanted to turn the clock back to a happier era.

He said if he could turn back the clock, he would act differently.

No amount of money – not even millions like this – can put back the clock and change what happened.

clockwork

like clockwork: 1 ◄◄

If something goes or runs **like clockwork**, it works very well and happens in exactly the way it is expected to.

The journey there went like clockwork – flying out on Friday from Gatwick it took seven hours door-to-door.

He soon had the household running like clockwork.

like clockwork: 2
regular as clockwork ◄

If someone does something **like clockwork**, they do it regularly, always at the same time.

They would arrive like clockwork just before dawn.

Finally, toward evening, like clockwork, he would begin to reminisce about his past.

□ You can also say that someone does something, or that something happens, **regular as clockwork**.

Every three years, regular as clockwork, the great Anne Tyler produces a new novel.

clogs

pop your clogs

In British English, if you say that someone **has popped** their **clogs**, you mean that they have died. This expression is used to refer to someone's death in a light-hearted or humorous way.

Comedians are getting younger and pop stars older and the kids want their heroes young. They want to know that the person they're paying to see isn't going to pop their clogs during the performance.

close

too close to call ◄◄

If a contest is **too close to call**, it is impossible to say who will win, because the opponents seem equally good or equally popular.

The presidential race is too close to call.

Policy analysts say the Senate vote, now expected to take place tomorrow night, is too close to call.

Exit polls in Britain say that today's parliamentary election was too close to call, but it appears that no party will win a majority in the House of Commons.

closet

come out of the closet: 1 ◄◄

If someone **comes out of the closet**, they talk openly for the first time about beliefs, feelings, or habits which they have kept hidden until now. This expression is usually used to talk about homosexuals revealing their homosexuality for the first time to the public or to their families.

They feel if they come out of the closet as lesbians they will somehow lose their leadership.

This new law doesn't help people to come out of the closet.

I suppose it's time I came out of the closet and admit I am a Labour supporter.

□ This expression is sometimes varied. For example, if you talk about someone being forced back **into the closet**, you mean that they are being forced to hide their beliefs, feelings, or habits again.

The HIV Aids crisis threatened to push us all back into the closet.

□ You can also use **closet** before a noun in order to describe a person who hides their beliefs, feelings, or habits.

He is about to be exposed in a biography as a closet homosexual.

I'm really a closet greenie who likes to live close to nature.

□ People often just talk about homosexuals **coming out**, rather than 'coming out of the closet'.

I came out as a lesbian when I was still in my teens.

come out of the closet: 2
bring something out of the closet ◄

When a subject becomes widely known or openly discussed for the first time, you can say that it **comes out of the closet** or is **brought out of the closet**.

'Prostate cancer came out of the closet,' he adds, 'and men started to join self-help groups to talk openly about prostate problems and the issue of screening.'

The subject needs to be brought out of the closet and dealt with honestly.

cloth

cloth ears

If you accuse someone of having **cloth ears**, you mean that they are not paying attention to something which is important or that they do not understand it properly. This expression is used in British English.

The audience had been sitting there for two hours with cloth ears and they weren't attentive.

□ You can also describe someone as **cloth-eared**.

If they weren't quite so cloth-eared, they'd also discover a good old-fashioned hard-driving rock band somewhere within The Walkabouts' extensive repertoire.

cut from the same cloth

If two or more people **are cut from the same cloth**, they are very similar in their character, attitudes, or behaviour. If they **are cut from a different cloth**, they are very different. You can use other adjectives instead of 'same' and 'different'. This expression is used mainly in British English.

The charge I most frequently encounter today is that London critics are all cut from the same cloth: that they are predominantly white, male, middle-aged, middle-class and university-educated.

He was cut from a different cloth and you'd do well to respect him.

McCrickard was a marketing man to the cuffs of his Italian designer suits, but Ellwood is cut from more traditional cloth.

cut your cloth
cut your coat according to your cloth

If you **cut** your **cloth** according to your situation, you take account of the available resources when you are making plans and decisions. You can also say that you **cut** your **coat according to** your **cloth**. These expressions are used mainly in British English.

Ford would be forced to cut its cloth according to the demands of the market.

The Government would have to cut its cloth and eliminate programmes which were not used.

He had already made it very plain that it was up to organisations which were supported by the taxpayer to cut their coats according to the cloth available.

whole cloth

If you say that a story or statement is made out of **whole cloth**, you mean that it is completely untrue and is not based on fact. This expression is used in American English.

According to legend, the flag Old Glory was the result of a collaboration between a well-known Philadelphia seamstress and George Washington. But there are those who say that story was made of whole cloth.

When such mind-sets did not actually exist in the past, we sometimes take the additional step of creating them out of whole cloth and treating them as if they had been there all along.

clothes

steal someone's clothes ◄

If one politician or political party **steals** another's **clothes**, they take the second's ideas or policies and pretend that these ideas or policies are their own. This expression is used in British journalism.

Here lies Labour's chance. They could steal the Tories' neglected clothes, by making Labour the party of lower taxes.

It is some measure of Strathclyde's success that the Scottish Office appears to have stolen the region's clothes on the devolved management front.

cloud

on cloud nine ◄◄

If you are **on cloud nine**, you are very happy because something very good has happened to you.

I never expected to win, so I'm on cloud nine.

When Michael was born I was on cloud nine. I couldn't believe this beautiful little boy was ours.

□ If someone comes **off cloud nine**, they stop being so happy because they have to consider other things.

For most, however, it will take some time to come off cloud nine.

under a cloud ◄◄

If you are **under a cloud**, people disapprove or are critical of you, because of something that you have done or are believed to have done.

The president of Tennessee's biggest bank re-signed under a cloud several weeks ago.

He was under a cloud after his men failed to find who had placed the bomb in the office.

clover

in clover ◄

If you are **in clover**, you are happy or secure because you have a lot of money or are enjoying a luxurious lifestyle.

Developers and bankers were in clover until Congress abruptly changed the rules again, with the 1986 Tax Reform Act.

For the next ten days I was in clover at Vicky and Allen's house. They took me to all the town's attractions and its restaurants.

club

join the club

When someone has been telling you about their problems or about their feelings, you can say **'join the club'** to indicate that you have had the same experiences or feelings.

Confused? Then join the club.

The Tory MP Geoffrey Dickens gave the game away. 'I am having difficulty knowing what today's debate is about,' he said. Join the club, Geoffrey.

coach

drive a coach and horses through something

If someone **drives a coach and horses through** an agreement or an established way of doing something, their actions severely weaken or destroy it. This expression is used mainly in British English.

The judgment appeared to drive a coach and horses through the Hague agreement.

Managers are driving a coach and horses through what has been standard practice in the NHS since it began.

coalface

at the coalface

When people talk about what is happening **at the coalface** of a particular profession, they are talking about the thoughts, feelings, and actions of the people who are actually doing the job. This expression is used to suggest that these are the people who really know about the profession. This expression is used mainly in British English.

The only people who extol the newcomer are politicians and air marshals who are far removed from the feelings 'at the coalface'.

We were a bridge between the central admin-istration – the rules, the regulations, the university legislation – and the academic coalface.

coals

coals to Newcastle ◄

If you say that supplying something to someone is like taking **coals to Newcastle**, you mean that it is pointless and silly because they already have plenty of it.

Sending food to the former Soviet Union is like sending coals to Newcastle. There is plenty of food, the problem is the breakdown of the distribution system.

Taking a gun to the United States would be like taking coals to Newcastle.

□ You can also talk about a **coals-to-Newcastle** situation.

Travelling to Holland to test a British-built boat might seem a coals-to-Newcastle affair.

That Moscow with its dilapidated economic machine would try to sell high technology to Japan, one of the world's high-tech leaders, sounds like a coals-to-Newcastle notion.

□ 'Coals' and 'Newcastle' can be replaced with other nouns.

Taking our music to your country would be like selling sand to the Arabs.

It's like selling ice to the Eskimos.

haul someone over the coals
rake someone over the coals ◄

If you **are hauled over the coals** or are **raked over the coals** by someone, especially someone in authority, they speak to you very severely about something foolish or wrong that you have done. 'Haul someone over the coals' is used only in British English. Compare **rake over the coals**.

I heard later that Uncle Jim had been hauled over the coals for not letting anyone know where we were.

There's every reason for going along and hauling her over the coals for wasting police time.

She was raked over the coals by an opponent who compared her to a convicted tax evader.

rake over the coals
rake over the ashes

If you say that someone **is raking over the coals** or is **raking over the ashes**, you mean that they are talking about something that happened in the past which you think should now be forgotten or ignored. These expressions are used mainly in British English. Compare **rake** someone **over the coals**.

She is firmly in the camp that says, yes, we made mistakes in the past, but let us not waste time raking over the coals when there is hard work to be done.

Why must we keep raking over the ashes,

causing distress to so many people who should have been feeling only relief?

coast

the coast is clear ◄

If you say that **the coast is clear**, you mean that you are able to do something which someone does not want you to do, because they are not there to see you or catch you doing it.

She signals to them from the window when the coast is clear because her husband does not like to encounter them.

Midge stepped aside, nodding that the coast was clear, and Lettie ran through the lobby and up the main staircase.

coat

trail your coat

If you **trail** your **coat**, you risk starting an argument or disagreement. This expression is used in British English.

Never lose your temper, and if you do, apologise for it afterwards. I realise I am trailing my coat; someone will no doubt remember an incident when I myself fell far short of these ideals.

We made him a test case, trailing our coats by breaking all the rules in an attempt to discover their procedure in such circumstances.

coat-tails

on the coat-tails of someone ◄◄

If someone does something **on the coat-tails of** another person or a trend, they are able to do it because of the success or popularity of that person or trend, and not because of their own efforts.

She was looking for fame and glory on the coat-tails of her husband.

Campbell is running for the Senate as a Democrat in Colorado, and he wants to hitch a ride on Clinton's coattails.

He said Australia was set to ride the coat tails of economic recovery in the US.

□ 'Coat-tails' is usually written as 'coattails' in American English.

cobwebs

blow away the cobwebs ◄

If something **blows away the cobwebs**, it makes you feel more alert and lively, when you have previously felt tired or dull.

My boyfriend and I have a cottage in the Cotswolds, and getting back there after a few days in London really blows the cobwebs away.

The pattern of life was soon established. Breakfast in the garden, perhaps a National Trust visit, a pub lunch, or a walk to blow away the cobwebs.

□ Other verbs with a similar meaning are often used instead of 'blow away'.

Her election has dusted away the cobwebs that normally surround the presidency, a role that is limited and notably low-profile.

Once the quarterback Troy Aikman shook off the cobwebs after a week's rest and found his rhythm, the Dallas offence scored at will.

cock

a cock and bull story
a cock and bull tale

If you describe an explanation or excuse as **a cock and bull story**, you mean that you do not believe it. You can also say that something is **a cock and bull tale**.

They'll be believed, no matter what kind of a cock and bull story they tell.

I wasn't the one who fed her some cock-and-bull story about taking care of you.

Prosecutor Kevan Townsley told the jury they should look beyond the airy, fairy, cock and bull tales the defence was trying to advance.

cockles

warm the cockles of your heart

If something **warms the cockles of** your **heart**, it makes you feel happy and contented. This is a fairly old-fashioned expression.

In the bold black and white setting, the sunny yellow color of the house warmed the cockles of my heart.

Running on Tuesday evenings, this year's series of talks is sure to warm the cockles of the cultured heart on the bleakest of winter days.

coffee

wake up and smell the coffee

If you tell someone to **wake up and smell the coffee**, you are telling them to be more realistic and more aware of what is happening around them. This expression is used mainly in American English.

It's time Lewis woke up and smelt the coffee and contacted me.

It would really serve you well to wake up and smell the damned coffee and quit acting like a teenager.

coin

the other side of the coin ◄◄◄

If you are discussing a subject or situation and you want to mention a completely different and perhaps contradictory aspect of it or attitude towards it, you can refer to this as **the other side of the coin**. Adjectives such as 'opposite', 'reverse', and 'flip' are sometimes used instead of 'other'. Compare **two sides of the same coin**.

Of course the advertisement doesn't mention the other side of the coin.

Of course, I get lonely at times. But my husband was often away on business when I was married, so being lonely is nothing new. And the other side of the coin is the amazing freedom you have knowing you don't have to please anybody about anything, except yourself.

Hate is the opposite side of the coin to love, and often co-exists with love in a relationship.

pay someone back in their own coin

If someone has treated you badly or unfairly and you **pay** them **back in** their **own coin** or **in the same coin**, you treat them in exactly the same way that they have treated you.

The European Community has even released lists of American unfair trade practices, paying us back in our own coin.

two sides of the same coin
opposite sides of the same coin ◄

If you say that two things are **two sides of the same coin** or **opposite sides of the same coin**, you mean that they are closely related to each other and cannot be separated, even though they seem to be completely different. Compare **the other side of the coin**.

He says he draws no line between tragedy and comedy. 'I've always felt that they are inseparable, that they are two sides of the same coin.'

Love and hate are the opposite sides of the same coin.

We now know that learning and teaching are not two sides of the same coin. They are different processes.

cold

catch someone cold

In sport, if you **are caught cold**, you are not prepared for an attack by your opponent, and you suffer because of it. This expression is used mainly in British journalism.

Northern, seeking their eighth successive League win, were caught cold by Castleford.

Dewsbury maintained their two-point lead at the top of the Third Division with a 29-14 win after Barrow had caught them cold to lead 8-4 at the interval.

cold as ice ◄

If you say that someone or something is as **cold as ice**, you are emphasizing that they are very cold.

A hand that felt as cold as ice touched her forehead.

The next morning, Snoot sat cold as ice through breakfast, unyielding to Claire's hand on his shoulder as she passed his chair.

☐ People also use the much more frequent adjective **ice-cold** to mean the same thing.

He took a mouthful of the ice cold beer.

He felt a lash of fear, running ice-cold down his spine.

come in from the cold
bring someone in from the cold ◄◄

If someone or something **comes in from the cold**, they become popular, accepted, or active again after a period of unpopularity or lack of involvement. You can also say that they **are brought in from the cold**.

The terrorists have been looking to come in from the cold for five years. Their gun in one hand and ballot box in the other strategy has stagnated.

Over the past two years, Swedish investors have come in from the cold.

Grenada's former Health Minister who was fired from office two months ago has been brought in from the cold by the Prime Minister.

leave someone cold ◄◄

If something **leaves** you **cold**, it does not excite or interest you at all.

Given the world situation, chit-chat about shopping and hairdos leaves you cold.

I am not proud that modern 'classical' music leaves me cold: just honest.

out in the cold ◄◄◄

If a person or organization is left **out in the cold**, they are ignored by other people and are not asked to take part in activities with them.

The Association of South-East Asian Nations has expressed concern that developing countries might be left out in the cold in current world trade talks.

This is why Burma still finds itself partly out in the cold.

She has complained in public that her husband doesn't pay her enough attention. 'He's leaving me out in the cold,' she told guests.

when one person sneezes, another catches cold

If you say that **when** one country or person **sneezes**, another **catches cold**, you mean that the things that happen to one country or person have a great effect or influence on other countries or people. This expression is used mainly in British English.

When America sneezes the rest of the world catches a cold. Applying this adage to financial markets, some onlookers fear that this week's necessary increase in American interest rates may hinder equally necessary interest-rate cuts in Europe and Japan.

collar

hot under the collar ◄

If you get **hot under the collar**, you get annoyed about something.

Biographers tend to get a little hot under the collar when conversation turns to the invasion of privacy.

Judges are hot under the collar about proposals to alter their pension arrangements.

colour

the colour of someone's money

If you say that you want to see **the colour of** someone's **money**, you are expressing your doubts about their ability or willingness to pay for something.

He made a mental note never to enter into conversation with a customer until he'd at least seen the colour of his money.

Today, to be taken seriously by a target company, you have to show the color of your money by paying very substantial commitment fees.

□ 'Colour' is spelled 'color' in American English.

colours

nail your colours to the mast: 1

If you **nail** your **colours to the mast**, you state your opinions or beliefs about something clearly and publicly. This expression is used in British English, especially in journalism.

Let me nail my colours to the mast straightaway. I both like and admire him immensely.

nail your colours to the mast: 2

If you **nail** your **colours to the mast** of a particular person, idea, or theory, you say clearly and publicly that you support them. This expression is used in British English, especially in journalism.

In the Thatcher years, the young MP nailed his colours to Mrs T's mast more firmly than many.

If the man is so committed to evangelism, why doesn't he come out and firmly nail his colours to the mast of the group?

sail under false colours

If you say that someone **is sailing under false colours**, you mean that they are deliberately deceiving people.

This report sails under false colours. It purports to be a fair and rigorous examination of press regulation. But clearly the author had reached his basic conclusions long before he even began gathering any fresh evidence.

□ Sometimes people just use **false colours** to mean the same thing.

For too long the left has allowed itself to be painted by the right in false colours.

□ 'Colours' is spelled 'colors' in American English.

show your true colours
see someone in their true colours ◄◄

If someone **shows** their **true colours** or if you **see** them in their **true colours**, you become aware that they are not as nice, decent, or honest as you thought they were, because they show some unpleasant aspects of their character. Verbs such as 'declare' and 'reveal' are sometimes used instead of 'show'.

Seeking support, you'll turn to friends but beware, someone you trusted may now show their true colours.

I couldn't take his violence and bullying any longer. The children are seeing him in his true colours for the first time now, as they are now on the receiving end of his moods.

These men began to reveal the true colours of their personalities: some shouted, others grew insolent to the point of menacing us, others seemed quite mad.

□ 'Colours' is spelled 'colors' in American English.

with flying colours ◄◄

If you achieve something, such as passing an examination, **with flying colours**, you achieve it easily and are very successful.

She thought she was on a fast track to a good job as a medical assistant, especially when she passed the entrance exam with flying colors.

I had a medical in April and passed with flying colours.

□ 'Colours' is spelled 'colors' in American English.

comb

with a fine-tooth comb
with a fine-toothed comb ◄

If you go through something **with a fine-tooth comb** or **with a fine-toothed comb**, you go through it very carefully and with great attention to detail.

I have taken the responsibility of going through Ed's personal papers and letters with a fine-tooth comb.

Ms Hankin said neighborhoods where resisters were suspected of living were gone over with a fine-toothed comb.

We will scrutinise our mistakes with a fine tooth comb.

come

come out fighting
come out swinging ◄◄

In a conflict, if someone **comes out fighting** or **comes out swinging**, they show by their behaviour that they are prepared to do everything they can in order to win.

Saudi Arabia and other crude oil producers have come out fighting, claiming the West is using environmental issues as a way of cutting back on oil and developing alternative energy sources.

Several times during his presidency and during the campaign, when he has been attacked or criticized, he feels obliged to come out swinging, and he has certainly done so on this issue.

comfort

cold comfort ◄◄

If someone tells you something encouraging and you describe it as **cold comfort**, you mean that it does not make it any easier to bear a difficult or unpleasant situation.

'Three years in higher education is a long-term investment,' he says. But that is cold comfort to graduates who have worked so hard to get a degree only to find that no one seems to want them to work now.

Every year a diagnosis of multiple sclerosis comes as a life sentence to thousands of young, vigorous men and women in Britain. Finding out more about the disease can be cold comfort, as no cure and virtually no treatment are available.

commas

in inverted commas ◄◄

If you use a word and say that you are using it **in inverted commas**, you are drawing attention to the word, and showing that it is not an accurate or precise way to describe the situation you are referring to. You sometimes use this expression to suggest that a word is being used with almost the opposite meaning to its normal meaning. This expression is used in spoken British English. Compare **quote, unquote**; see **quote**.

John Walters has just retired, in inverted commas, after twenty years as a Radio One producer.

I think that the assumptions of some people were that we would take democratic decisions, well, democratic in inverted commas.

common

common as muck

In British English, if you say that someone is as **common as muck**, you mean that they are lower-class and not sophisticated. This expression is usually considered offensive, but is sometimes used ironically.

Leary guessed correctly that his guests were as common as muck and planned the menu accordingly.

concrete

set in concrete ◄

If you describe an idea, plan, or action as **set in concrete**, you mean that it is fixed and cannot be changed. Verbs such as 'embed' and 'cast' can be used instead of 'set'.

The appointment of Commander Ahmad

Shah Massoud as defense minister seems to be pretty set in concrete at the moment.

There'll be more meetings among the Europeans but at the moment it seems that the negotiating positions are embedded in concrete.

converted

preach to the converted ◄

If you say that someone **is preaching to the converted**, you mean that they are presenting an opinion or argument to people who already agree with them. You usually use this expression to criticize someone for wasting time or effort. Verbs such as 'talk' and 'speak' are sometimes used instead of 'preach'.

In any case the film was, by and large, preaching to the converted.

While cheered by the positive receptions we had received in August I was essentially preaching to the converted then.

This morning when he met the Emir of Kuwait he was talking to the converted.

cookie

caught with your hand in the cookie jar

If you say that someone **has been caught with** their **hand in the cookie jar**, you mean that they have been caught stealing or doing something wrong. This expression is used mainly in American English; the usual British expression is **have** your **hand in the till**.

She left me. I got caught with my hand in the cookie jar one time too many, I guess.

The banker had been caught with his hand in the cookie jar. Had my client not been aggressive he would have lost 35,000 dollars.

a smart cookie

If you describe someone as **a smart cookie**, you mean that they are clever and have good ideas.

She is too much of a smart cookie to join the fashion circuit which still entices most of her fellow supermodels.

As soon as movie film had been invented, around 1890, smart cookies started thinking about how to accompany pictures with sound.

that's the way the cookie crumbles

People say **'that's the way the cookie crumbles'** when they want to say that you should accept the way that things happen or turn out, even if they turn out badly.

'I thought you said you've been here for three years.' 'Just the way the cookie crumbled,' she said and went off to make her class.

Sometimes the cookie crumbles against all sense of what is just.

a tough cookie ◄

If you describe someone as **a tough cookie,**

you are admiring their qualities of courage, endurance, and independence.

One member of her local hunt said she was 'brave – a tough cookie'.

He has a reputation as one tough cookie.

A pushover is not how her bosses would describe her. They would say that, behind that sweet smile, there lies one tough cookie.

cooks

too many cooks
too many cooks spoil the broth
too many cooks in the kitchen

If you say that there are **too many cooks**, you mean that a plan or project goes wrong because there are too many people trying to do it at the same time.

So far nothing had worked. One problem was that there were simply too many cooks.

☐ This expression comes from the proverb **too many cooks spoil the broth**.

He is a great believer in the saying that too many cooks spoil the broth. So am I normally, but in this particular affair teamwork seemed to be producing far better results than solitary endeavour.

☐ In American English, you can also say that there are **too many cooks in the kitchen** to mean the same thing.

Declaring that 'there are simply too many cooks in the kitchen', Senator Robert Dole has proposed remedying the problems by creating a single committee to handle this year's legislation.

cool

cool as a cucumber ◄

If you say that someone is as **cool as a cucumber**, you mean that they are very relaxed, calm, and unemotional.

Lynda Bryans is usually as cool as a cucumber when she appears on television. But if a spider crosses her path during the BBC's week of programmes from an animal hospital, her poise could vanish in an instant.

Never once did she gasp for air or mop her brow. She was as cool as a cucumber.

keep your cool ◄◄

If you **keep** your **cool**, you control your temper and stay calm in a difficult situation. Compare **lose** your **cool**.

The manager has kept the pressure off the players by keeping his cool and it has paid off.

He is renowned for keeping his cool. Nobody can tell when he is feeling vulnerable, so nobody knows when to attack him.

lose your cool ◄◄

If you **lose** your **cool**, you get angry and behave in a bad-tempered or uncontrolled way. Compare **keep** your **cool**.

'Why don't you sit down and have a drink?' 'I don't want a drink,' Anne replied, losing her cool.

At this I lost my cool and shouted 'for goodness sake, stop!'

coop

fly the coop ◄

If someone **flies the coop**, they leave the situation that they are in, for example because they do not like it or because they want to have more freedom to live or work as they please. Compare **fly the nest**; see **nest**.

His wife is so fed up with his coldness she is about to fly the coop.

It should be a proud moment, junior hairwasher grows up, graduates to senior stylist and then flies the coop to set up in a salon of his or her own.

cop

not much cop

If you say that someone or something is **not much cop**, you mean that they are not very good. This expression is used in British English.

I'm not making excuses for him, because he's not much cop as far as I'm concerned.

She looked round the big room: 'there's no one here but us, this place can't be much cop.'

copybook

blot your copybook ◄

If you **blot** your **copybook**, you damage your reputation by doing something wrong. This expression is used in British English.

It was just that their relationship had been so perfect. Until he'd blotted his copybook over Susan.

I'm proud of my family heritage and I don't want to blot the copy book.

☐ You can also say that there is **a blot on** your **copybook**.

Alan's blot on his copy book was to take the new Rubik cube puzzle that William had been given for Christmas and start playing with it before William had a chance.

cord

cut the umbilical cord
cut the cord

If you say that someone **cuts the umbilical cord** or **cuts the cord**, you mean that they start acting independently rather than continuing to rely on the person or thing that they have always relied on.

I love you. I'll never forget all you've done for me, but it's time to cut the umbilical cord. I want you to go away. I need time alone to think things out and decide what to do.

core

to the core ◄◄◄

You use **to the core** to emphasize the extent of someone's feelings, beliefs, or characteristics. For example, if you are shocked **to the core** by something, it shocks you very much. If someone is conservative **to the core**, they are very conservative.

Father Godfrey Carney said the community was shocked to the core.

The insurance industry is rotten to the core.

Margaret Loxton, the artist, English to the core yet inspired by France, began painting seriously ten years ago after her family had grown up.

corn

earn your corn

If someone **earns** their **corn**, they are successful and therefore justify the money that has been spent, for example on training them or hiring them. This expression is used in British English.

Recording contracts tend to follow conductors and soloists rather than orchestras. Walter Weller, the new principal conductor, is already earning his corn in that respect.

The back four got us through the match. They earned their corn against Middlesbrough and that's why we came off with a win.

corner

fight your corner ◄◄

If you **fight** your **corner**, you state your opinion openly and you defend it vigorously. Verbs such as 'argue', 'defend', and 'stand' are sometimes used instead of 'fight'. This expression is used in British English.

The future of Britain lies in the EU and we must fight our corner from within using honest and intelligent arguments.

At any rate, he quickly showed that his courage to stand his corner, his enthusiasm and his friendliness made up for any lack of stature.

I always defend my corner and I often disagree with what gets included.

in a corner
in a tight corner
out of a corner ◄◄◄

If you are **in a corner** or **in a tight corner**, you are in a situation which is difficult to deal with or escape from.

The government is in a corner on interest rates and the same could well happen on fiscal policy.

Herb was a big, muscular man on the edge of 50: a guy who could obviously fend for himself if placed in a tight corner.

When he had been in a tight corner before,

Mr Gorbachev had been able to use his own powers of persuasion to produce a compromise.

☐ If someone **backs** you **into a corner**, they put you in a situation which is difficult to deal with or escape from. You can replace 'back' with other verbs such as 'force' or 'drive'.

As Atwater told the story, his own mother backed him into a corner and asked, 'Lee, did you do that?' 'No, Mama,' he replied.

He appears to have backed himself into a tight corner and his only escape appears to be promotion.

☐ If something gets you **out of a corner** or **out of a tight corner**, it helps you to escape from or deal with a difficult situation.

The South African move has got English cricket officials out of a tight corner.

in your corner ◄

If you say that someone is **in** your **corner** or that you have them **in** your **corner**, you mean that they are supporting you and helping you.

Harry and I were encouraged. We felt we had made a pretty good pitch. From words spoken after our meeting, we felt we already had Bob Uhlein in our corner.

I remember Jackie saying years ago that Red was a gentleman and he always was in his corner, he could always depend on Red to give him the necessary backup he needed.

just around the corner ◄◄◄

If you say that something is **just around the corner**, you mean that it is about to happen. You can vary this expression, for example by saying 'just around the next corner', or, in American English, by saying 'right around the corner'.

With summer just around the corner, there couldn't be a better time to treat your home to a bright new look.

He said the strike would adversely affect democracy when general elections were just round the corner.

Fearful that war was right around the corner, they promptly began to lay in extensive stores of food supplies.

The worry is about what may lie around the next corner.

paint someone into a corner
box someone into a corner ◄

If someone **paints** you **into a corner** or **boxes** you **into a corner**, they force you into a difficult situation where you have to act in a certain way. If you **paint** yourself **into a corner** or **box** yourself **into a corner**, you put yourself in a difficult situation by your own actions.

The big banks have allowed themselves to be painted into a corner. They need deregulation in order to turn things around, but won't be able to get it unless they can reassure the public that deregulation won't result in another financial disaster.

You'll fight to the death when you're boxed into a corner unless you're provided with a reasonable way out.

The Government has painted itself into a corner on the issue of equalising the State pension age.

turn the corner ◄

If someone or something **turns the corner**, they begin to recover from a serious illness or a difficult situation.

Joe turned the corner, medically.

Has California's economy finally turned the corner? In April the official figure for the state's unemployment rate dropped for the second month running.

corners

cut corners ◄◄◄

If you **cut corners**, you save time, money, or effort by not following the correct procedure or rules for doing something.

Don't try to cut any corners as you'll only be making work for yourself later on.

We sometimes have to cut corners in order to keep the discussion reasonably clear.

He accused the Home Office of trying to save money by cutting corners on security.

□ You can refer to this activity as **corner cutting**.

It was the Chief Inspector for Police who said that the present working culture was 'shot through with corner cutting and expediency'.

Corner-cutting contractors build tiny classrooms and narrow corridors.

the four corners of the world
the four corners of the earth ◄

You can use **the four corners of the world** or **the four corners of the earth** to refer to all the different parts of the world, especially the parts that are the furthest away from you. Other nouns referring to areas of land can be used instead of 'world' or 'earth'.

A foreign correspondent makes his friends in all four corners of the world.

Italy has sent 5,000 soldiers to the four corners of the earth to play their part in peacekeeping and crisis-management operations.

Young people came from the four corners of the nation in search of new ideas.

cost

count the cost ◄◄◄

If you **count the cost** of something damaging or harmful, you consider the extent of the damage or harm that has been done. This expression is used mainly in British English.

Meanwhile, the government counted the cost of an action that humiliated it at home and abroad.

Many people have gone in hot pursuit of someone who physically fulfils their fantasies only to count the cost later when things go wrong.

The central government in Delhi is today counting the political cost of the escalating dispute which has already prompted the resignation of one government minister.

couch

a couch potato ◄◄◄

If you describe someone as **a couch potato**, you are criticizing them for spending most of their time sitting around watching television, in a very lazy way.

In fact, we sit, like a pair of couch potatoes in front of television, and watch her eat.

Even a couch potato will be inspired to go walking in this perfect resort in the Bahamas.

count

down for the count ◄

If someone is **down for the count**, they have failed in something that they are doing. This expression is used mainly in American English.

The conservatives appeared to be down for the count. Yesterday morning they failed to win a vote of no confidence in the Yeltsin government.

Japan will have to do a lot more if it is to pull the sick economy round but the market is not down for the count just yet.

out for the count ◄

If someone is **out for the count**, they are temporarily unconscious. You can also use this expression humorously to say that someone is very deeply asleep.

He had had to do all the school runs and all the school picnics for two days 'cos his wife was out for the count for forty-eight hours.

At 10.30am he was still out for the count after another night disturbed by bawling and wailing.

counter

under the counter ◄

If you do something **under the counter**, you do it secretly because it is dishonest or illegal. This expression is used mainly in British English; the usual American expression is **under the table**.

The shirts disappeared from the displays but could still be purchased under the counter or in discreet back rooms as recently as last Friday.

Most of the trading was done under the counter, through some form of black-market barter.

□ An **under-the-counter** payment or deal is one that is secret and dishonest or illegal.

It was becoming common practice for athletes to receive under-the-counter payments from organizers to attend meetings.

Lionel Smart, a member of the Football Association Council, told Winchester Crown Court that any under-the-counter money deals would have been against board policy.

country

go to the country ◄◄

If a head of government or a government **goes to the country**, they hold a general election. This expression is used in British English.

The Prime Minister is about to call snap elections even though he doesn't have to go to the country for another year.

courage

Dutch courage ◄

When someone drinks alcohol so that they feel less frightened or nervous of a task they have to do, you can describe the drinks or their effect as **Dutch courage**. This expression is used mainly in British English.

The survey also noted how some performers used a little Dutch courage to overcome inhibitions.

Sometimes before leaving I would drink a glass of vodka on the stairs for Dutch courage and then go out.

course

on course for ◄◄◄

If you are **on course for** something, you are likely to achieve it.

Hungary's Krisztina Egerszegi is on course for a third gold medal at the European Championships.

We're well on course for a Labour victory in a general election.

City experts believe the club is on course for a £5 million profit this year.

run its course
take its course ◄◄◄

If something **runs** its **course** or **takes** its **course**, it develops gradually and comes to a natural end of its own accord.

If you allow such behavior to run its course without reacting, eventually the behavior will disappear on its own.

The real recovery for the auto industry won't come until the recession runs its course.

The Conservatives can be criticised as the party that prefers to let the market take its course.

stay the course ◄◄

If you **stay the course**, you finish a difficult or unpleasant task, even though you have been discouraged from doing so or have found it hard.

In Canada, where the infantry opened to women five years ago, very few have stayed the course.

Nevertheless, in her career she had seen a good many people come and go. Some had more talent than others and stayed the course better.

court

hold court ◄◄◄

If you **hold court**, you are surrounded by people who pay you a lot of attention because they consider you interesting or important. This expression is often used to suggest that the person holding court is rather self-important and does not deserve this attention and admiration.

Ray is holding court, speculating on the hits and misses of the current theatre season.

She used to hold court in the college canteen with a host of admirers who hung on her every utterance.

He used to hold court at Cole's Restaurant. He was the greatest raconteur I've ever encountered in my life.

laughed out of court ◄

If you or your ideas **are laughed out of court**, people dismiss your ideas and do not take you seriously.

Only a decade ago the idea of an Equal Opportunities Commission championing and strengthening the rights of women would have been laughed out of court as preposterous and ludicrous.

The whole exercise is a farce, and would be laughed out of court in any country where 'open government' was anything more than an empty election slogan.

ruled out of court
put out of court

If something that you want to do **is ruled out of court** or **is put out of court**, circumstances make it impossible for you to do it. This expression is used mainly in British English.

It seemed at one stage that I would be able to go into the medical course in September but then in August I caught polio which clearly put it out of court.

Coventry

send someone to Coventry ◄

If you **are sent to Coventry**, other people ignore you and refuse to talk to you because they disapprove of something you have done. This expression is used in British English.

There is a strong feeling of hostility towards his decision. He has been sent to Coventry. Maybe that sounds childish but the consensus is he has been selfish.

When she complained to bosses of sexual harassment she was sent to Coventry by staff.

cover

cover your back
cover your rear
cover your ass   ◄

If you do something in order to **cover** your **back** or to **cover** your **rear**, you do it in order to protect yourself, for example against criticism or against accusations of doing something wrong.

He had covered his back by persuading Moustafa Zohdi, chairman of Lafico's finance committee, to provide a written approval for the contract.

Don't try to use the FBI to cover your rear when your staff gets into trouble in the travel office.

☐ You can also say that you do something in order to **cover** your **ass**. This is a very informal expression, which many people consider offensive.

You had to have an answer for everything – you had to cover your ass all the time.

cow

have a cow

If you **have a cow**, you become very upset or angry. This is an informal expression, which is used in American English.

I won't be bullied into having a cow, understand. I'm going to put my foot down on this one.

a sacred cow   ◄

If you describe a belief, opinion, or tradition as **a sacred cow**, you disapprove of the fact that people are not willing to criticize or question it or to do anything to change it.

That would have meant leaving the Exchange Rate Mechanism – and the ERM is the sacred cow of British politics.

Many critics think reservation policies have become a sacred cow and should be abolished.

cows

until the cows come home   ◄

If you say that you could do something **until the cows come home**, you mean that you could do it for a very long time.

You can initiate policies until the cows come home, but unless they're monitored at a senior level, you won't get results.

Your child will enjoy this lively tape till the cows come home!

crack

at the crack of dawn   ◄

If you wake up **at the crack of dawn**, you wake up very early.

He was scheduled to get up at the crack of dawn for an interview on 'Good Morning America'.

On Monday at the crack of dawn I was rung up by somebody in the Law Faculty.

have a crack at something
take a crack at something   ◄◄

If you **have a crack at** doing something difficult or challenging, you try to do it. You can also say that you **take a crack at** something.

I've decided now to have a crack at the world cross country race.

She has no special ambitions, but would nonetheless like to have a crack at Hollywood.

He says if he had a chance he'd like to take a crack at writing the screenplay.

cracked

not all it's cracked up to be   ◄◄

If you say that something **is not all it's cracked up to be**, you mean that it is not as good as people say it is.

Alexander is finding life as a manager not all it's cracked up to be.

One of life's little luxuries is an annual holiday in the sun. But package holidays are not always all they're cracked up to be.

☐ This expression is very variable.

But are these islands in the sun everything they are cracked up to be?

It's one of those places you hear so much about that you wonder if it really is as good as it's cracked up to be.

cracking

get cracking   ◄

If you **get cracking**, you start doing something immediately and quickly. This is an informal expression.

I realised that if we got cracking, we could make the last 700 miles to St Lucia within our deadline.

I promised to get cracking on the deal.

cracks

fall through the cracks
slip through the cracks   ◄

If people **fall through the cracks** or **slip through the cracks**, the system which is supposed to help or deal with them does not do it properly. These expressions are used in

American English; the British expression is **slip through the net**.

Patients who are misdiagnosed are falling through the cracks of the new law.

This family slipped through the cracks in the system, they are not eligible for aid.

paper over the cracks ◄◄

If you say that someone **papers over the cracks**, you mean that they try to conceal the fact that something has gone badly wrong rather than deal with it effectively and honestly. 'Gloss over' and 'cover' are sometimes used instead of 'paper over'. This expression is used mainly in British English.

David Powers says accepting the minister's resignation will only serve to paper over the cracks of a much more serious rift.

I think the cracks have been papered over. But I think they've been papered over at a very high price.

The film is rather disjointed at times but the performances help gloss over the cracks.

cradle

cradle-snatching

If someone has a sexual relationship with a person who is much younger than them, you can say that they are **cradle-snatching**. This expression is usually used ironically or to show disapproval. This expression is used in British English; the American expression is **robbing the cradle**.

He was young enough to cause a first reaction of 'My God but she's cradle-snatching now'.

His uncle said: 'His dad and I just can't believe it. The woman is even older than his mother. It's cradle snatching.'

□ You can describe someone who does this as **a cradle-snatcher**.

The ageing actress is a cradle snatcher, says her toyboy's family.

from the cradle to the grave ◄

If you say that something happens **from the cradle to the grave** or **from cradle to grave**, you are emphasizing that it happens throughout a person's life.

He had few illusions about John, knew what John had done and what he was capable of doing, but the bond of brotherhood was one to last from the cradle to the grave.

I think she'll be remembered for her attack on the whole idea that the state is ultimately responsible for the individual and should, in effect, look after him from cradle to grave.

rob the cradle

If someone has a sexual relationship with a person who is much younger than them, you can say that they **are robbing the cradle**. This expression is usually used ironically or

to show disapproval. This expression is used in American English; the British expression is **cradle-snatching**.

'I'll always be younger,' he said, 'and there'll always be those who might accuse you of robbing the cradle.'

□ You can describe someone who does this as **a cradle robber**.

Women who make off with men 15 to 30 years younger are viewed as neurotic cradle robbers. But, in fact, there is evidence that nature may have intended 20-year-old boys as the lovers of 40-year-old women.

crash

crash and burn

To **crash and burn** means to fail badly, for example because of a careless mistake or an unfortunate action. This expression is used mainly in American English.

The UN's Rio Earth Summit clearly ranks as one of the most ambitious summit meetings ever held. Some say a meeting this big can only crash and burn.

When unacknowledged stress builds up, it can cause over-achievers to crash and burn, and they can end up suffering from emotional disorders and stress-related illnesses.

crazy

crazy as a bedbug

If you say that someone is as **crazy as a bedbug**, you are emphasizing that their behaviour is illogical. This expression is used mainly in American English.

By now she'd concluded that Skolnick was crazy as a bedbug.

cream

the cream of the crop ◄

You can refer to the best people or things in a particular set or group as **the cream of the crop**.

The first Midlands media degree show features the cream of the crop of this year's graduates in photography, film, and video.

The cream of the British crop, the literary dramas that are shown on U.S. public television as 'Masterpiece Theater', make up a relatively small part of British air time.

creature

creature comforts ◄

Creature comforts are modern sleeping, eating, and washing facilities that most people enjoy but which are not regarded as particularly extravagant or luxurious.

Each room has its own patio or balcony and provides guests with all modern creature comforts.

Obviously the camping lifestyle suits him? 'I like my creature comforts. But here I don't seem to need them,' he replies.

creek

up the creek
up the creek without a paddle
up shit creek ◄

If you say that someone or something is **up the creek**, you mean that they are in a very difficult situation.

We're up the creek because we don't know where to go from here.

The Chancellor of the Exchequer believes his critics are 'up the creek'. His tormentors think much the same about the Chancellor.

□ You can also say that someone or something is **up the creek without a paddle**.

It is now becoming increasingly obvious there won't be any boom. That leaves Australia up the creek without a paddle.

□ People sometimes say **up shit creek** to emphasize that the situation is extremely difficult. This is a very informal expression, which many people find offensive.

The economy's up shit creek, the recession has become a slump, everyone's unemployed.

crest

on the crest of a wave
ride the crest of the wave ◄

If you are **on the crest of a wave**, you are being very successful with something you are doing.

Founded in 1972, the Front has often been dismissed as a cranky fringe group. But now its members are confident they're on the crest of a wave.

Hippy rappers PM Dawn are riding on the crest of a wave with the worldwide success of their number one selling single 'Set Adrift On Memory Bliss'.

□ This expression is very variable. For example, you can say that someone **is riding the crest of the wave**.

Both men have chosen to make foreign tours at a time when they are riding the crest of the wave politically.

The Barnsleys had prospered on the crest of the wave of industrialisation but had maintained a strong social conscience.

□ You can replace 'wave' with words such as 'success', 'popularity' or 'confidence'.

He is riding a crest of rare confidence.

cricket

it's just not cricket ◄

In British English, people say **'it's just not cricket'** or **'it's not cricket'** when they are complaining that someone's behaviour is un-

fair or unreasonable. This is an old-fashioned expression, which is now used mainly in journalism.

His belligerent attitude to opposition batsmen is nothing short of rudeness. Younger players are set a bad example by such behaviour which is just not cricket, and I would hope not Australian.

The bank puts thousands of pounds a year into cricket – yet their treatment of staff is definitely not cricket.

crisp

burned to a crisp

If you say that something **is burned to a crisp**, you are emphasizing that it is badly burned. 'Burn' is sometimes replaced with other verbs with a similar meaning.

Customers who insist on having their food burnt to a crisp should get it that way.

Any spacecraft which approaches too close to the 6,000 degree inferno of the visible surface would fry to a crisp, so useful data can be obtained only from a respectful distance.

□ People sometimes use this expression to say that someone is very sunburned.

The white streaks on his nose and forehead were sunburn lotion (he had burned to a crisp that summer).

critical

go critical

If a project or organization **goes critical**, it reaches a stage of development where it can operate smoothly and successfully.

The programme confirmed its initial impact in week two, and really 'went critical' with the third edition on 8 December.

Bristol airport is about to 'go critical'. That will come when more than a million passengers a year pass through the terminal.

□ This expression is more commonly used in talking about nuclear power. When a nuclear power station **goes critical**, it reaches a state in which a nuclear fission chain reaction can sustain itself.

crock

a crock of shit ◄

You can describe what someone has said as **a crock of shit** when you consider that it is nonsense or completely wrong or worthless. This is a very informal expression, which many people consider offensive. It is used more commonly in American English than British.

'McAllister? Let's hear from you. Tell us what you think of the poem.' 'Frankly, Dr K, I think it's a crock of shit.'

All that stuff about us splitting up, it's such a crock of shit.

crocodile

shed crocodile tears ◄

If you accuse someone of **shedding crocodile tears**, you are accusing them of being insincere because they are pretending to sympathize with someone who they do not really care about. Verbs such as 'weep' and 'cry' are sometimes used instead of 'shed'.

He shed a lot of crocodile tears. He described the wrecking of the coal industry as 'the toughest decision I have ever had to take' and 'a dreadful thing to have to do'.

Labour MPs who weep crocodile tears over the plight of those who earn £10,000 a year insist that they cannot get by on ten times that amount.

□ You can refer to a display of sympathy or grief that is insincere as **crocodile tears**.

If ever I've seen crocodile tears, those are them. It was a con job. Who does she think she's kidding?

cropper

come a cropper: 1 ◄◄

If you say that someone **has come a cropper**, you mean that they have suffered a sudden and embarrassing failure. This expression is used mainly in British English.

The East London entrepreneur who began selling radio aerials from the back of a mini van, has come a cropper. The recession has finally caught up with him.

Scott must concentrate exclusively on learning his new trade. He will come a cropper if he thinks he knows it all before he starts.

Banks dabbling in industry can easily come a cropper.

come a cropper: 2

If you **come a cropper**, you accidentally fall and hurt yourself. This expression is used mainly in British English.

There are some well-known tricks in the business, like putting Sellotape on your rival's blades, so that as soon as he glides on to the ice he comes a cropper.

Bruised Premier's daughter Elizabeth Major had the day off work on doctor's orders yesterday after coming a cropper on her horseracing debut.

cross

a cross to bear ◄

If you have **a cross to bear**, you have a responsibility or an unpleasant or inconvenient situation which you must tolerate, because you can do nothing about it.

'My wife is much cleverer than me, it is a

cross I have to bear,' he quips at one point in the interview.

'One day,' Mary Pierce's father said a few years ago, 'she'll be better than any of them.' That sort of remark is not an easy cross to bear.

Healy believes broken fingers are crosses every keeper must bear and he is determined not to let the side down.

crossed

get your wires crossed
get your lines crossed ◄

If you **get** your **wires crossed** or **get** your **lines crossed**, you are mistaken about what someone else means or thinks. 'Get your lines crossed' is used only in British English.

Despite her tone of voice, she still looked vaguely confused. He began to wonder if he'd gotten his wires crossed.

He appeared to get his lines crossed. 'What part of America are you from?' he asked. 'Sweden,' came the reply.

□ You can refer to this type of misunderstanding as **crossed wires** or, in British English, **crossed lines**.

In a month where crossed wires abound for many people, it is essential to keep things in proportion.

crossfire

caught in the crossfire ◄

If you say that someone or something **is caught in the crossfire**, you mean that they suffer the unpleasant effects of a disagreement between other people even though they are not involved in it themselves.

Plans for the National Gallery's much-needed extension were caught in the crossfire of the architectural debate on the merits of modernism.

Britain is only one of the victims caught in the crossfire as the German mark continues to gain strength and the US dollar to fall.

Teachers say they are caught in the crossfire between the education establishment and the Government.

□ This expression is more commonly used literally to talk about a situation where someone is in the way of two sets of people who are firing guns, and so is likely to be shot by mistake.

crow

as the crow flies ◄

If you say that one place is a particular distance from another **as the crow flies**, you mean that the two places are that distance apart if you measure them in a straight line, although the actual distance when travelled by road would be much greater.

My name is Betty Perkes, and I live at Mesa, Washington, about 10 miles as the crow flies from Hanford.

Although not distant as the crow flies from Tehran, this mountainous area has always been and still is remote.

□ People occasionally replace 'crow' with another word which is relevant to the subject they are writing about.

They must travel 44 kilometres to visit relatives on the other side of the canal, one kilometre as the gull flies, unless they can catch the ferry.

eat crow

If someone **eats crow**, they admit that they have been wrong and apologize, especially in situations where this is humiliating or embarrassing for them. This expression is used mainly in American English.

But by the end of the year, Safire showed he was willing to eat crow. His first judgments of Watergate, he wrote, had been 'really wrong'.

crunch

when it comes to the crunch
the crunch comes
crunch time   ◄◄◄

If you talk about what you will do **when it comes to the crunch** or **if it comes to the crunch**, you are talking about what you will do when a situation reaches a critical point and you must make a decision on how to progress.

It may be, therefore, that when it came to the crunch last night, that certain people simply lost their nerve.

If it comes to the crunch, I'll resign over this.

□ You can also say **the crunch comes** when a situation reaches a critical point.

The crunch came when we discovered newly promoted white managers were getting more money than we were. We were training chaps who were earning more than we were. I thought this cannot be right.

□ You can refer to the time when an important decision has to be made as **crunch time**.

On the same day, the hospital will also be visited by a Department of Health official in a move which everyone regards as a crunch time in the campaign to save the 870-year-old hospital.

crust

earn a crust   ◄

If you **earn a crust** or **earn** your **crust**, you earn enough money to live on, especially by doing work you would prefer not to do. This expression is used in British English.

In his early days, he would do almost anything to earn a crust from the sport.

Mr Miller, a struck-off doctor, is now earning his crust as a bookmaker.

cry

a far cry from something   ◄◄◄

If you say that one thing is **a far cry from** another, you mean that the two things are very different from each other. You usually use this expression when you are contrasting an earlier situation with the current one.

It isn't a perfect democracy, but it's a far cry from the authoritarian rule of only a few years ago.

The level of interest in stock car racing is a far cry from what it was when Richard Petty first hit the circuit.

in full cry   ◄

You use the expression **in full cry** to emphasize that someone is doing something very actively or that something is happening very intensely. This expression is used mainly in British English.

We had left four or five people back in the bar where a Sunday lunchtime jazz band was in full cry.

Confronted by a press pack in full cry, her mother resorted to using the house intercom to communicate with them.

Her comic timing is impeccable, her gift for mimicry brilliant. There is no better entertainment than La Plante in full cry.

cudgels

take up the cudgels

If you **take up the cudgels** for someone or **take up the cudgel** for them, you speak up or fight in support of them.

The trade unions took up the cudgels for the 367 staff who were made redundant.

If you have any gripes or questions, let's hear from you. We'll take up the cudgels on your behalf.

The teachers' union has its own position to protect in taking up that cudgel.

cuff

off-the-cuff   ◄◄◄

An **off-the-cuff** remark, opinion, or comment is one that has not been prepared or carefully thought out.

Gascoigne offered an apology last night, saying: 'I'm sorry. I didn't mean any offence. It was a flippant, off-the-cuff remark.'

The immediacy of television news reporting, thrusting emotive pictures simultaneously under the noses of world leaders and into the living rooms of their electorate, encourages off-the-cuff decision-making.

□ If you say something **off the cuff**, you say it spontaneously without really preparing it or thinking about it very much.

Eisenman was speaking off the cuff, and it's possible that my tape recorder did not catch every last word.

His remarks – apparently made off-the-cuff at a meeting with an Indian diplomat – have raised a storm of protest.

cup

not your cup of tea ◄◄

If you say that something is **not** your **cup of tea**, you mean that you do not feel very enthusiastic about it or interested in it.

It's no secret that I've never been the greatest traveller. Sitting for hours on motorways is not my cup of tea.

'How well do you know the Parbolds, Maisie?' 'Not my cup of tea, and I'm not theirs.'

□ You can say that something **is** your **cup of tea** when you do feel enthusiastic about it or interested in it.

I don't have much time for modern literature. Chaucer's my cup of tea.

cupboard

cupboard love

In British English, you use **cupboard love** to refer to the insincere affection shown by children or animals towards someone who they think will give them something that they want.

The cat twined himself around her ankles, assuring her of complete agreement. 'Cupboard love,' she accused, freeing her ankles. 'You'd agree with anyone who could open the fridge or cooker.'

curate

a curate's egg

In British English, if you describe something as **a curate's egg**, you think that parts of it are good and parts of it are bad. You can also say that something is **like the curate's egg**.

Wasserman's collection of duets with famous friends is something of a curate's egg.

Like the curate's egg, the text is good in parts, but suffers from discontinuity.

Wooldridge goes out with a real curate's egg of a production; intermittently brilliant in the first half, but completely out of its depth in the second.

curiosity

curiosity killed the cat

You say **'curiosity killed the cat'** when you are warning someone that they will suffer

harm or damage themselves if they try to find out about other people's private affairs.

'Where are we going?' Calder asked. 'Curiosity killed the cat, dear. You'll find out soon enough.'

In his experience, curiosity had killed more than one cat.

curtain

bring the curtain down on something
the curtain comes down ◄◄◄

If someone or something **brings down the curtain on** an event, process, or state of affairs, they cause or mark its end. You can also say that **the curtain comes down** on something.

Today's simple but moving ceremonies bring down the curtain on that long and historic period in Philippine history marked by the presence of American troops in our territory.

Brian Clough brings the curtain down on one of the most amazing managerial careers of all-time this weekend.

Now the curtain ought to be coming down on one of the most appalling financial scandals in British history.

curtains

it's curtains
mean curtains
spell curtains ◄

If you say that **it's curtains** for someone, you mean that their career, their period of success, or their life is coming to an end. If you say that **it's curtains** for something, you mean that it will be destroyed or is likely to fail. You can also say that something **means curtains** or **spells curtains** for someone or something.

If the vote is yes, it's curtains for us. A way of life will disappear.

The fight with Wharton on December 10 is now of monumental importance because, if he fights like that, it could be curtains for his unbeaten record.

I would like what happened to Bryan to give hope to people in a similar position. A diagnosis like that doesn't always mean curtains.

curve

throw someone a curve
throw someone a curve ball
curve balls ◄

If someone **throws** you **a curve** or if they **throw** you **a curve ball**, they surprise you by doing something unexpected and perhaps putting you at a disadvantage. These expressions are used mainly in American English.

Just when they thought they might have the

boss figured out, Knight would throw them a curve. No-one could ever put him all together.

□ You can refer to unexpected problems as **curve balls**.

Once you learn the person's habits and idiosyncrasies, there will be few curve balls.

cut

cannot cut it
does not cut it

If you say that someone **cannot cut it** or **does not cut it**, you mean that they are not talented or ambitious enough to succeed in a particular job.

Most pop stars leave a wake of bitterness in their trail: musicians or managers who can't cut it at the highest level, or old friends whose telephone numbers have been forgotten.

'The money is a huge attraction,' said Jonathan Christie, a market maker in engineering and manufacturing. 'But it's a cut-throat business. If you don't cut it then you are out.'

a cut above the rest
a cut above ◀◀◀

If you say that someone or something is **a cut above the rest**, you think they are much better than other people or things they are being compared to. You can also describe someone or something as **a cut above**.

Crime fiction now basks in literary respectability, and Joan Smith's detective stories are a cut above the rest.

Near the top of the list is the Forte Crest which, whatever one's views of hotels owned by large chains, is distinctly a cut above the average of its kind.

I hate to be predictable, but like the last 18 R.E.M. singles, it's a cut above.

cut and dried ◀◀◀

If you say that a situation or discussion is **cut and dried**, you mean that it is clear and definite, and does not raise any questions or problems.

I like things planned and neat, cut and dried and precise.

Now, this situation is not as cut-and-dried as it may seem.

The link between stress and heart attacks is by no means cut and dried, although most people feel intuitively that it exists.

□ A **cut-and-dried** solution, answer, or matter is one that is very straightforward and does not raise any questions or problems.

There are no cut-and-dried answers as to why a mother or father kills their baby.

What appeared to be a cut-and-dried issue is now showing signs of life once again.

cut and run ◀

If you say that someone has decided to **cut and run** from a difficult situation, you are criticizing them for trying to escape from it quickly, rather than dealing with the situation in a responsible way.

When foreigners own property and corporations in the U.S., they are less likely to cut and run in bad times, and more likely to invest extra capital.

He had an unfortunate tendency to cut and run when things didn't go his way.

□ **Cut-and-run** can also be used before a noun.

Some people have been predicting a cut-and-run election much earlier than that, when the recovery has got moving and before it runs out of steam.

the cut and thrust ◀◀

If you talk about **the cut and thrust** of a particular activity or society, you are talking about the aspects of it that make it exciting and challenging. This expression is used in British English.

Why then does he want to go back into the harrowing cut and thrust of the airline business at an age when most men are happily retired?

You seem to enjoy the cut and thrust of historical debate.

□ A **cut-and-thrust** society or contest is one that is very exciting, although it is also competitive and stressful.

She has spent the past two years carving out a career as a production assistant in the cut-and-thrust world of advertising.

The entire match was a cut and thrust battle between the two evenly matched teams.

not cut out for something ◀

If you say that someone is **not cut out for** a particular lifestyle or job, you mean that it is not the sort of thing that they would enjoy or succeed in.

As you'll have gathered, I left medicine anyway. I wasn't really cut out for it.

Sometimes I think I'm not cut out for a steady relationship.

□ You can say that someone **is cut out for** a particular lifestyle or job when you think that they would enjoy it and succeed in it.

Unlike some distinguished players, he was cut out for management because underneath the affable, jocular exterior lies the prized quality of judgement.

cylinders

fire on all cylinders ◀◀

If someone **is firing on all cylinders**, they are doing a task with great enthusiasm and energy. 'Fire' is occasionally replaced with other verbs such as 'operate'.

I saw her a few weeks ago and she was firing

*on all cylinders. I don't think she would know
what to do with herself if she did not work.*

*When Wales are firing on all cylinders, they
can beat any country in the world at football,
as Germany and Brazil could tell you.*

*Boy, you two guys are operating on all cylin-
ders this morning.*

□ If someone is not doing a task as well as
they should be, you can say that they **are not
firing on all cylinders** or are only **firing on
two cylinders**.

*We were only firing on two cylinders instead
of four. But people have been told, and you
won't see a bad performance like that again.*

D

dab

a dab hand ◄◄

If you are **a dab hand** at something, you are
very good at doing it. This expression is used
in British English.

*She was an avid reader and a dab hand at
solving difficult crossword puzzles.*

*We gave big lunches every weekend and I be-
came a dab hand at roasts.*

daft

daft as a brush ◄

If you say that someone is as **daft as a
brush**, you are emphasizing that they are
very silly or stupid. This expression is used
in British English.

*She was as daft as a brush. Couldn't say
anything with any sense in it.*

*I've said before that he's as daft as a brush
and he is. I have never, ever come across anyone like him.*

daggers

at daggers drawn ◄

If two people or groups are **at daggers
drawn**, they are having a serious disagreement and are very angry with each other.
This expression is used in British English.

*It is rumoured that the publishing and record
divisions of the company were at daggers
drawn over the simultaneous release of the
book and the album.*

*The government now finds itself at daggers
drawn with the same press it had gone to such
great lengths to give freedom of expression to.*

look daggers at someone
shoot daggers at someone

If someone **looks daggers** at you or **shoots
daggers** at you, they stare at you in a very
angry way. Verbs such as 'stare' and 'glare'
are sometimes used instead of 'look' or
'shoot'. These expressions are used mainly in
novels.

*Christabel stopped caressing her hair and
looked daggers at Ron. Watching them glare
angrily at each other reminded me of some-*

*thing I'd read once; that hate was the reverse
side of the coin called love.*

*Dede shot daggers at her adversary until she
was out of sight.*

*Jon glared daggers at Michael and grabbed
the back of his belt, bringing him to a stand-
still.*

daisies

push up the daisies

If you say that someone is **pushing up the
daisies**, you mean that they are dead. This
expression is used to refer to someone's death
in a light-hearted or humorous way.

*'I hope I die before I get old,' sang Pete
Townshend in 'My Generation'. Instead of
pushing up daisies, Townshend is still among
the living, grey whiskers and all.*

damper

put a damper on something
put a dampener on something ◄◄

If someone or something **puts a damper on**
a situation, they stop it being as successful or
as enjoyable as it might be. In British English
you can also say that they **put a dampener
on** it.

*Fear of terrorism and war has put a damper
on bookings at Mike Dorman's Vacation
Hotline in Chicago.*

*Peggy was happy with her daughter's choice
of husband. The only thing that put a bit of a
damper on the whole thing was the fact that
her daughter would be moving to another town
to be near her husband's work.*

*Unemployment will be a central theme of the
Labour attack. It will highlight not only the
tragic human problems, but its effect as a
dampener on economic confidence and investment.*

dance

lead you a merry dance
lead you a merry chase ◄

If you say that someone **leads** you **a merry
dance** while you are trying to achieve something, you mean that they make a lot of difficulties for you, so that you do not achieve it

quickly or easily. You can also say that someone **leads** you **a merry chase**. These expressions are used in British English.

They had led the Irish Government a merry dance for the last seven months.

I began to court the lady who last year became my second wife. She led me quite a dance, but I never gave up.

He led Vincent Korda a merry chase across Italy before agreeing to take the part.

dander

get someone's dander up

If someone **gets** your **dander up**, they make you feel very annoyed and angry. This is an old-fashioned expression.

We came to try and solve things and now that's being undermined, and I, for one, am frankly outraged. That gets my dander up.

She was almost speechless with rage and despair. My God, Max thought, once she gets her dander up she catches fire!

dark

in the dark ◄◄◄

If you are **in the dark** about something, you know nothing about it. If you are kept or are left **in the dark** about something, people keep it secret from you, because they do not want you to know about it.

The sooner we can clear up the case, the better for you and everyone. But at the moment I'm in the dark.

Congress and the public were kept in the dark about the decision to cross the line from defense to preparation for war.

The officers who spoke to us were not obliged to give us any of this information. We could have been left in the dark until the inquest nine months later.

keep something dark

If you **keep** something **dark**, you keep it a secret.

She took pleasure in keeping dark the identity of the man who was coming.

a leap in the dark ◄

If you take **a leap in the dark**, you do something without knowing what the consequences will be, usually because you feel you have no other choice but to take this course of action. This expression is used in British English.

In the last five months, voters in both Brazil and Nicaragua have rejected old campaigners, preferring to take a leap in the dark by electing outsiders with little or no political experience to the highest office.

What I had before me wasn't a rational choice: it was a leap in the dark.

a shot in the dark
a stab in the dark ◄

If you refer to a guess as **a shot in the dark**, you mean that it is a complete guess, although there is a small chance that it will be right. You can also say that it is **a stab in the dark**.

The Japanese go about their business much as other nations do – with a pretty standard mixture of good judgment, luck, mistakes and shots in the dark.

It is impossible to undertake a wild stab in the dark and take a guess at their roots.

whistle in the dark ◄

If you say that someone **is whistling in the dark**, you mean that they are trying not to show that they are afraid, or that they are trying to convince themselves that a situation is not as bad as it seems.

Then I waited, trying not to feel as if I were whistling in the dark, but I experienced no easing of my fear and anxiety.

Boris is a careful pilot and he would never have run the tanks so low. Therefore the gauge must be giving a faulty reading. That was logic. Or maybe it was whistling in the dark.

dash

cut a dash ◄

If someone **cuts a dash**, they impress other people with their stylish appearance. This expression is used mainly in British English.

Then Mr Marsh's lawyer, a ruddy-cheeked Irishman who looks as though he would cut a dash on the hunting field, started his cross-examination.

Tania cut a daring dash with a dress slashed almost to the waist.

date

past your sell-by date
pass your sell-by date ◄◄

If you say that someone or something **is past** their **sell-by date** or **has passed** their **sell-by date**, you are saying that they are no longer useful, successful, or relevant. These expressions are used in British English. Other verbs can be used instead of 'pass'.

One critic said that when a black artist's audience is mainly white, he's past his sell-by date.

The feeling is that the broad-shouldered 'power dressing' of the Eighties has passed its sell-by date.

Critics of the monarchy say it has reached its sell-by date.

dawn

a false dawn ◄◄

If you refer to an event as **a false dawn**,

you mean that although it seems to mark an improvement in a bad situation, there is in fact no improvement. This expression is used mainly in British journalism.

The new age of enterprise which the Government hoped would revitalise Britain in the Eighties turned out to be a false dawn.

It may be another false dawn for the carmakers – there have been several in the past decade – or it may be something more lasting.

Elections are scheduled for next year. But Angolans have seen many false dawns before. Is the country really heading for democracy and a durable peace?

day

all in a day's work ◄

If you say that something difficult, unusual, or exciting is **all in a day's work** for someone, you mean that they find it easy or normal because it is part of their job or because they often experience this kind of thing.

For war reporters, dodging snipers' bullets is all in a day's work.

Performing live can prove tricky for essentially studio-based bands, but Elton reckons it's all in a day's work for rising starlets.

at the end of the day ◄

You can use **at the end of the day** to summarize several points you have made and to introduce your main conclusion. This expression is used mainly in journalism and in spoken English.

At the end of the day, it's the Germans who will decide.

At the end of the day, the Dolls seemed destined to be a minority taste, despite the growing fascination for glam brought on by David Bowie's transvestism.

call it a day: 1
call it a night ◄◄◄

If you decide to **call it a day**, you decide to stop doing something, usually because you are tired or are bored with it.

Jane was part of a team that has struggled hard to finish a difficult assignment. 'I wanted to call it a day and get home as much as anyone,' she recalls.

It was late afternoon and I searched for hours but I had to call it a day when darkness fell.

☐ In the evening, people sometimes say that they are going to **call it a night**.

Tomorrow is going to be busy, so let's call it a night.

call it a day: 2

If someone **calls it a day**, they retire.

It's no secret I want his job when he calls it a day. That's my great ambition.

He's finally decided to call it a day and retire as manager.

carry the day ◄◄

If a person or their opinion **carries the day** in a contest or debate, they win it. This expression is used mainly in journalism.

For the time being, those in favour of the liberalisation measures seem to have carried the day.

Mr Murphy's pessimistic analysis did not carry the day unchallenged.

Many here expect this radical plan to carry the day when the vote finally comes.

the day of reckoning ◄

If you talk about **the day of reckoning**, you are referring to the time when people are forced to deal with an unpleasant situation which they have avoided until now.

The day of reckoning has arrived. You can't keep writing checks on a bank account that doesn't have any money in it, and that's what's been going on in Michigan.

We consulted a sympathetic attorney, and prepared for our day of reckoning. As the date for the hearing approached Sara and I grew increasingly anxious.

don't give up the day job

If someone says to you '**don't give up the day job**', they are telling you in a humorous way that you should continue to do your normal job rather than trying something new which is not as secure and which you might fail at.

Her debut was followed by some harsh advice from more experienced colleagues: 'Don't give up the day job, Norma.'

I started business in 1973 in the teeth of a recession. People thought I was mad and said: 'Don't give up the day job.'

have had your day ◄◄

If you say that someone or something **has had** their **day**, you mean that the period during which they were most successful has now passed.

In Hollywood, there were still loyal supporters, but the general feeling was that Sturges had had his day.

Has radio had its day or is the golden age still to come?

After a century's domination, American popular music may finally have had its day.

late in the day ◄◄◄

If someone has done something **late in the day**, they have done it at the last moment or in the final stages of a situation. This expression is often used to criticize people for waiting too long before taking action.

It was, she screamed, too late in the day for him to start behaving like a loving husband.

Chief Superintendent John has admitted, rather late in the day, that detectives are handling a 'very sensitive' investigation.

It is good news that the department is now tentatively drawing up a strategy for the aerospace industry. It is just a shame such a move has come so late in the day.

make someone's day: 1 ◄◄

If someone or something makes you feel very happy, you can say that they **make** your **day**.

There was such a sincere expression of friendliness on both their faces that it was a joy to see. It really made my day.

They forget you are a person, sometimes. When you have a customer who turns round and thanks you, it makes your day.

make my day: 2 ◄

People sometimes say **'make my day'** when they want to challenge another person to compete or argue with them, in order to have the opportunity to prove that they are stronger and better than the other person.

They threaten dire reprisals to any journalist who dares to write 'propaganda' for the fur trade. All I can say is, go ahead boys, make my day. The only reason I don't have a fur coat yet is that I can't quite afford the one I want.

save for a rainy day ◄

If you **are saving for a rainy day**, you are saving some of your money in case there are emergencies or problems in the future. You can use 'put by', 'put aside', and 'put away' instead of 'save'.

Saving for a rainy day and paying off debts is now a top priority for families.

Job loss fears are forcing millions of consumers to save for a rainy day rather than borrow.

These people spent the money when they had it. They did not put it by for a rainy day!

seize the day ◄

If you tell someone to **seize the day**, you are advising them to do what they want straight away, and not to worry about the future.

I can't wait ten years. Life has taught me to seize the day, if not the hour.

The New Zealanders have seized the day. And good on them for their perspicacity and energy.

daylight

in broad daylight ◄◄◄

If someone does something illegal or daring **in broad daylight**, they do it openly in the daytime when people can see it. You often use this expression to emphasize that their behaviour is surprising or shocking.

Six gunmen attacked his car with automatic rifles in broad daylight.

I have recently spotted three women wearing Catwoman outfits in broad daylight.

daylights

beat the living daylights out of someone: 1

If someone **beats the living daylights out of** you or **beats the daylights out of** you, they attack you physically, hitting you many times. Verbs such as 'knock' and 'thump' can be used instead of 'beat'.

Steve beat the daylights out of him with a hefty length of bike chain.

Hardly an earth-shattering storyline, but then this type of game is essentially about whacking the living daylights out of the villains.

beat the living daylights out of someone: 2

If you **beat the living daylights out of** someone or **beat the daylights out of** them, you defeat them totally in a competition or contest. Verbs such as 'knock' can be used instead of 'beat'.

Sure, they enjoy the money, the endorsements, the fame. But their true pleasure comes from walking on to a golf course and beating the living daylights out of everyone else.

scare the living daylights out of someone ◄

If someone or something **scares the living daylights out of** you or **scares the daylights out of** you, they frighten you very much. The verb 'frighten' is sometimes used instead of 'scare'.

You scared the living daylights out of me last night. All that screaming.

A tremendous wind swept off the land and frightened the living daylights out of us.

days

have seen better days ◄

If you say that something **has seen better days**, you mean that it is old and in poor condition.

The houses had seen better days and their crumbling plaster was now dirty grey and moist.

There was an old brass double bed with a mattress that had seen better days.

it's early days
it's early in the day ◄◄◄

If you say that **it's early days** in a situation, you mean that it is too soon to be sure about what will happen in the future. You can also say that **it's early in the day**. These expressions are used in British English.

The British Embassy cannot recall when he

last paid a visit. However, it is early days yet and this could swiftly change.

Maybe in time we can find some common ground but it's very early days.

The spokesman did not expect any immediate moves on new competition or pricing policy. 'It is very early in the day yet.'

someone's days are numbered ◀◀◀

If you say that someone's **days are numbered**, you mean that they are not likely to survive or be successful for much longer.

His days are numbered. He seems mortally ill, is terribly thin, coughs all the time, gasps for breath at the slightest movement, and is running a high temperature.

As rebels advanced on the capital it became clear that the President's days in power were numbered.

dead

come back from the dead
rise from the dead
raise something from the dead

If you say that someone or something **comes back from the dead** or **rises from the dead**, you mean that they become active or successful again after a period of being inactive or unsuccessful.

I could not believe I had done it. I had come back from the dead and my career had survived the ultimate test.

After all, this was a company that, by all appearances, had risen from the dead.

☐ You can also say that someone **raises** something **from the dead** when they make it active or successful again after a period of being inactive or unsuccessful.

The company has been working on the scheme to raise this inner-city area from the dead since 1982.

cut someone dead

If someone you know **cuts** you **dead**, they deliberately ignore you or refuse to speak to you, for example because they are angry with you. This expression is used in British English.

You can only slag off people behind their backs for so long. I cut her dead when I realised what she was doing. She doesn't have many friends here.

Dyer cut me dead on the stairs.

dead as a dodo

If you say that something is as **dead as a dodo** or as **dead as the dodo**, you mean that it is no longer active or popular. This expression is used in British English.

The foreign exchange market was as dead as a dodo.

This lugubrious Mozart style is as dead as

the dodo everywhere in the world except Vienna and Salzburg.

dead as a doornail

If you say that someone is as **dead as a doornail**, you are emphasizing that they are dead. If you say that something is as **dead as a doornail**, you mean that it is no longer active or popular.

Samples under an electron microscope normally have to be covered with heavy metals, kept in a vacuum and then bombarded with high-energy particles. They end up dead as doornails.

When Senator Goldwater went down to that thrashing defeat in 1964, people said the Republican Party was deader than a doornail.

dead as mutton

If you say that someone is as **dead as mutton**, you are emphasizing that they are dead. If you say that something is as **dead as mutton**, you mean that it is no longer active or popular. This expression is used in British English.

We saw a viper. It was 4 feet long and was as dead as mutton.

He advised him that radio was just about to become as dead as mutton because of the advent of television.

dead in the water ◀◀

If you say that something or someone is **dead in the water**, you mean that they have failed and there seems to be little hope that they will be successful in the future. This expression is used mainly in journalism.

People are not going into auto showrooms; they're not buying houses; they're not going into stores. This economy is dead in the water.

I think for all practical purposes, the talks are now dead in the water.

One backbench Tory MP said last night: 'It looks as if he is dead in the water now.'

drop-dead: 1 ◀◀

You can use **drop-dead** to emphasize that someone or something is very attractive or beautiful.

She's drop-dead gorgeous.

His office had a drop-dead view of Central Park.

drop dead: 2

If you tell someone to **drop dead**, you are telling them to go away and leave you alone because you are very angry or annoyed with them.

Richard told me to drop dead.

Seventy-five percent of the firms he called for data were hostile and told him to drop dead.

knock 'em dead
knock someone dead

If you say that something will **knock 'em**

dead, you mean that it will impress people a great deal. You can also say that something **knocks** you **dead**.

Glamorous make-up is best reserved for evenings, or days when you want to go all out to knock 'em dead.

Just look 'em in the eye and knock 'em dead.

Their debut album is going to knock you dead.

□ **Knock 'em dead** can also be used before a noun.

What we needed was a bout of knock 'em dead rabble-rousing, and Guy duly obliged.

□ The word **'em** is a form of 'them' which is used in informal or non-standard English.

wouldn't be seen dead
wouldn't be caught dead ◄◄

If you say that you **wouldn't be seen dead** or **wouldn't be caught dead** in particular clothes, places, or situations, you are emphasizing that you strongly dislike or disapprove of them.

I wouldn't be seen dead in a black straw hat.

In past centuries, no true aristocrat would have been caught dead with a tan, which was the mark of a peasant forced to toil for a living in the open fields.

There's many a dad who wouldn't be seen dead wheeling a baby in a frilly-hooded pram through the park.

deaf

deaf as a post

If you say that someone is as **deaf as a post**, you are emphasizing that they are very deaf. This is an old-fashioned expression.

He must be as deaf as a post, half-blind and verging on the paralytic.

deal

a done deal ◄

If something such as a plan or project is a **done deal**, it has been completed or arranged and it cannot be changed. This expression is used mainly in American English.

We're rushing it as fast as we can, and it ought to be a done deal by the middle of next week.

The pact is far from being a done deal. It must be ratified by the legislative bodies of all three countries.

get a raw deal ◄◄◄

You can say that someone **gets a raw deal** when you feel that they have been treated unfairly or badly. Verbs such as 'have' and 'give' are often used instead of 'get'.

We must ask why bank customers get such a raw deal. And then find ways to make sure they get treated fairly in future.

White people were gloomy about prospects for racial harmony, with 53 per cent seeing no end to racial tension and 30 per cent thinking Blacks got a raw deal in the job market.

I have seen numerous cases where the foreign-born minority were given a raw deal and were treated as second-class or third-class citizens.

death

at death's door ◄

If someone is **at death's door**, they are seriously ill and are likely to die.

He has won five golf competitions in three months, a year after being at death's door.

□ You can say that someone comes back **from death's door** when they have recovered from a very serious illness.

The patient has been brought back from death's door by the radical treatment, say his doctors.

a death blow ◄

To deal **a death blow** to a process, situation, or organization means to cause it to come to an end.

This could deal a death blow to the collapsing national economy.

They warned that the deportations would be a death blow to the Middle East peace process.

dice with death

If someone **is dicing with death**, they are taking risks that endanger their life. This expression is used in British English.

In the daily routine of their toil, fishermen are constantly dicing with death.

I dice with death almost every night crossing the road outside Maidstone Barracks station.

fight to the death ◄◄

If someone **fights to the death** to achieve something or keep hold of something, they try very hard to achieve it or keep hold of it, and they will not give up easily.

I have been teaching home economics for 18 years and I will fight to the death to keep my place in the curriculum.

What drove them was a corporate culture that made them fight to the death for their firms, just as warriors of old did for their warlords.

□ You can also talk about **a fight to the death**.

Jimmy White now faces a fight to the death to reach the quarter-finals of the Embassy World Snooker Championship.

like death warmed up
like death warmed over

If you say that someone looks **like death warmed up** or **like death warmed over**, you mean that they look very ill, pale, and tired.

'Like death warmed up' is used in British English and 'like death warmed over' is used in American English.

You were looking like death warmed up, but you seem a lot better now.

He dragged in just after the funeral, sneezing and sniffing and looking like death warmed over.

like grim death

If you hold onto something **like grim death**, you hold onto it very tightly. This expression is used mainly in British English.

I clung to the chain like grim death.

a living death ◄

If someone's life is described as **a living death**, their quality of life is very poor indeed, for example because they are ill and unlikely to recover.

For nearly four years he has lain in a coma, sustained by a feeding tube but trapped in what one doctor described as a 'living death'.

Tens of thousands of workers, party officials, intellectuals, and students had been arrested and either shot or sentenced to a living death in the hell of the Siberian labor camps.

sign someone's death warrant
sign your own death warrant ◄◄

If one person **signs** another's **death warrant**, the first causes the second's ruin or death.

The summit in Moscow this week virtually signed the organisation's death warrant.

It was not too extreme to say that to identify her might even be tantamount to signing her death warrant.

□ If someone **signs** their **own death warrant**, they behave in a way which brings about their own ruin or death.

The president persuaded Congress to sign its own death warrant by agreeing to a referendum.

The day that he accused the King of murder was the day he signed his own death warrant, and he knew it.

□ A **death warrant** is used in many other structures with a similar meaning.

The plan is seen by all sides as a death warrant for the Bosnian state.

His signal had been innocuous enough, but it would become his death warrant as soon as Pemberton was interrogated.

to death ◄◄◄

You can use **to death** after adjectives such as 'scared', 'worried', and 'bored' to emphasize that someone is very frightened, very worried, or very bored.

'I am worried to death,' she wrote her husband. 'Even if something is wrong, why don't

you let me know? I'd always rather know than worry.'

She may have been scared to death he would leave her.

I've been bored to death since I left the army.

□ You can also say, for example, that something scares or bores you **to death**.

One woman described how she woke up in the morning and the hotel she was staying in was empty, which scared her to death.

Meetings bored me to death, legal cases, things that went on and on.

□ If you say that you love someone **to death**, you are emphasizing that you love them very much.

He loves me to death and I feel the same way.

deck

all hands on deck

If a situation requires **all hands on deck**, it requires everyone to work hard to achieve an aim or carry out a task. This expression is used mainly in British English.

The agency was given less than three weeks to put together the launch of radical plans to shake up Scottish football. It was all hands on deck, but it was a good test of our ability, and proved we could handle such a large project.

hit the deck

If someone or something **hits the deck**, they suddenly fall to the ground.

'We'll have to get a doctor!' I hit the deck yowling. My hands were wrapped round my knees.

Instead of pulling up, the plane seemed to go faster and faster before it hit the deck.

not play with a full deck
play with a loaded deck
play with a stacked deck

If someone **is not playing with a full deck**, they are not being completely honest in a contest or negotiation, and therefore have an unfair advantage over other people. Compare **stack the deck**; see **stack**.

This guy is either very good or he's not playing with a full deck.

□ You can also say that they **are playing with a loaded deck** or **are playing with a stacked deck** to mean the same.

Canadian trade officials say Washington is playing the free trade game with a stacked deck.

decks

clear the decks
clear the deck ◄◄

If someone **clears the decks**, they make sure that everything that they have been doing is completely finished, so that they are ready to start a more important task. You can also say that they **clear the deck**.

The British commanders had wanted to clear the decks for possible large-scale military operations.

Clear the decks before you think of taking on any more responsibilities.

The Chancellor has cleared the deck for an early entry into the Exchange Rate Mechanism of the European Monetary System.

deep

run deep
go deep   ◄◄◄

If you say that something such as a feeling, emotion, or problem **runs deep** or **goes deep**, you mean that it is very serious or strong, often because it has existed for a long time.

My allegiance to Kendall and his company ran deep.

Hatred of the army runs deep, and most here have come to side with the rebels.

His anger and anguish clearly went deep.

degree

give someone the third degree

If someone, especially a policeman or person in authority, **gives** you **the third degree**, they ask you a lot of questions in an aggressive manner in order to make you confess to something.

He gives me the third degree and wants me to account for where all the money is.

Surely, she thought, they were supposed to read you your rights before they gave you the third degree.

dent

make a dent in something
put a dent in something   ◄◄◄

If you **make a dent in** something or **put a dent in** it, you reduce its amount or level.

The savings from these cuts make only a small dent in the federal deficit.

The average family in Britain spends £100 a week on food, which makes a big dent in the household budget.

I hated to put any dents in his enthusiasm, but I was trying to be realistic.

department

not your department
be your department

If you say that a task or area of knowledge is **not** your **department**, you mean that you are not responsible for it or do not know much about it.

The political issues are something else, but that's not really my department.

'If you identify him, then what?' 'Not my department.'

□ If you say that something **is** your **department**, you mean that you are responsible for it or that you know a lot about it.

'So what do we do with him?' Admiral Polaski asked. 'That, gentlemen, is our department,' Rintner said.

Bill spoke expertly. This had been his department.

depth

out of your depth   ◄◄◄

If you are **out of** your **depth**, you feel anxious and inadequate because you have to deal with a situation or subject which you know very little about.

You may feel out of your depth on an honours degree course, in which case a change to a diploma course may be a good idea.

Faced with the latest in medical high-tech, the baffled prince admitted being out of his depth.

Lewis, who struggled for 90 embarrassing minutes, hopelessly out of his depth, managed to come up with the most honest assessment – 'We just didn't play that well.'

depths

plumb the depths: 1   ◄

If you say that someone's behaviour **plumbs the depths**, you mean that it is extremely bad.

'This crime plumbs the very depths of the abyss into which it is possible for the human spirit to sink,' the judge said.

Critics and the public both expected Ken Russell, the director of 'Princess Ida', to plumb new depths of tastelessness.

plumb the depths: 2   ◄

If you **plumb the depths** of something, you find out everything you can about it, including things that are normally secret or hidden.

He doesn't plumb the depths of a text in the way of his contemporaries Deborah Warner and Declan Donnellan.

When Weddington does see friends, she is more likely to discuss politics than to plumb the depths of her own soul.

plumb the depths: 3

If someone **plumbs the depths** of an unpleasant or difficult situation, they experience it to an extreme degree.

They frequently plumb the depths of loneliness, humiliation and despair.

The banks' popularity is plumbing new depths.

deserts

just deserts ◄◄

If you say that someone has got their **just deserts**, you mean that they deserve the unpleasant things that have happened to them, because they did something bad.

Some people felt sympathy for the humbled superstar. Others felt she was getting the just deserts of an actress with a reputation for being difficult.

Many in Australia's business world were stunned, but others said the man who once headed a £4 billion empire had received his just deserts.

□ The noun 'deserts' is related to the verb 'deserve', and it is pronounced with stress on its second syllable. Some people use the word 'desserts' instead of 'deserts' in this expression, but it is generally considered incorrect.

designs

have designs on something: 1 ◄

If someone **has designs on** something, they want it and are planning to get it, sometimes in a dishonest way.

When asked how long US troops will remain in Iraq itself, the Secretary of State said the United States has no designs on Iraqi territory.

They are particularly worried that the Italian Mafia has designs on the island.

have designs on someone: 2

If one person **has designs on** another, the first person wants to have a sexual relationship with the second, although the second person is not interested, or is already involved with someone else.

He had been demoted from sergeant to private because, so it was said, his colonel had had designs on his wife and she had spurned him.

devices

left to your own devices ◄◄◄

If someone **is left to** their **own devices**, they are left to do what they want, or to look after themselves without any help.

If left to my own devices, I would eat a chocolate dessert every night.

After tea we were left to our own devices, so we decided to take a walk in the neighbouring village.

The millions of Americans who do not have health insurance are often left to their own devices when they become ill.

devil

better the devil you know
better the devil you know than the devil you don't

If you say **'better the devil you know'**, you

mean that you would rather deal with someone you already know, even if you do not like them, than deal with someone that you know nothing about, because they may be even worse. This expression is used mainly in British English.

People concluded that he had improved his electoral chances as a result of the speech. And one told me this reflected the old adage, 'Better the devil you know.' His challenger remains an unknown quantity.

□ This expression comes from the proverb **better the devil you know than the devil you don't**.

It is becoming clearer to them that he is no angel; but better the devil you know than the devil you don't know.

between the devil and the deep blue sea

If you are **between the devil and the deep blue sea**, you are in a difficult situation where the two possible courses of action or choices that you can take are equally bad. This expression is used mainly in British English.

Now exactly what do we really want? You see we are between the devil and the deep blue sea on this issue and people just do not know exactly what to do.

I wouldn't contemplate getting on a bus without something to read, to the point, once, of spending my bus fare on a second-hand book, preferring the devil of hitchhiking to the deep blue sea of enduring half an hour bookless.

a devil of a job
the devil's own job ◄

If you say that you had **a devil of a job** doing something, or that you had **the devil's own job** to do it, you are emphasizing that it was difficult to do it.

We got there just in time, but we had a devil of a job finding you in that place.

I had to literally drag him out of there. I had a devil of a job to get him to the van and home for a hot bath as he could barely move, much less talk.

Michael was having the devil's own job to make himself heard next to the roadworks outside the Berkeley Square headquarters.

the devil take the hindmost
every man for himself and the devil take the hindmost

If someone says **'the devil take the hindmost'**, they mean that you should protect your own interests or safety without considering anyone else's interests. This is an old-fashioned expression.

Just get your laughs any way you can and the devil take the hindmost.

□ This expression comes from the saying

every man for himself and the devil take the hindmost.

We do not believe in the theory of every one for himself and the devil take the hindmost.

speak of the devil
talk of the devil

People say **'speak of the devil'** or **'talk of the devil'** if someone they have just been talking about arrives unexpectedly. This expression is used in spoken English.

'Speak of the devil,' she greeted him, smiling.

'Well, talk of the devil.' Duncan had wandered up from the beach in red wellies and a duffel coat.

diamond

a rough diamond: 1
a diamond in the rough ◀

If you refer to someone, especially a man, as **a rough diamond**, you like and admire them because of the good qualities they have, even though they are not very sophisticated or well-mannered. This form of the expression is used mainly in British English; in American English, the usual form is **a diamond in the rough**.

Marden was the rough diamond of the three, feared for his sardonic ruthlessness but respected for his First World War Military Cross.

'The character I'd like to have met,' Stanley Marric said, 'was Arthur Crook. I could really identify with a rough-diamond kind of lawyer like him.'

I liked Neil Murphy, who is somewhat of a diamond in the rough.

a rough diamond: 2
a diamond in the rough

If you refer to someone or something as **a rough diamond**, you mean that they have a lot of talent or potential which needs hard work before it can be revealed. This form of the expression is used mainly in British English; in American English, the usual form is **a diamond in the rough**.

British first novels are more likely to be rough diamonds, with flashes of inspiration in an imperfect whole.

When I heard this lady sing, I said 'Oh, my goodness.' So I ran to the theater, and I said, 'Chick, I found myself a diamond in the rough.'

dice

load the dice against someone ◀

If you are in a situation where everything seems to work to your disadvantage so that you are unlikely ever to have success, you can say that **the dice are loaded against** you.

The dice are loaded against black people and

sometimes the institutions of Britain, seemingly dedicated to ensuring equality, like the law, are the very citadels of racism.

I had emerged unscathed from skirmishes where others had lost their lives, and had survived that night on the mountain when all the dice were loaded against me.

no dice: 1

If you are trying to achieve something and you say there's **no dice**, you mean that you are having no luck or success with it.

I tried calling her and I tried one or two of her old friends in Hampstead, which is where I originally met her at a party of Geoffrey's, but there was no dice.

I spent part of that time calling everyone I knew to see if I could find another job for him. No dice.

no dice: 2

If someone asks you for something and you reply **'no dice'**, you are refusing to do what they ask.

Nope, sorry, we're not interested, no dice.

die

the die is cast ◀

If you say that **the die is cast**, you mean that you have made an important decision about the future and that it is impossible to change it, even if things go wrong.

Therese is regarded by them as having been singled out by God. The die is cast for her: she goes off to a convent and stays there for 20 years.

The die was cast and James was now part of the Hollywood drug scene.

dime

a dime a dozen ◀

If you say that things or people are **a dime a dozen**, you mean that there are a lot of them, and so they are not especially valuable or interesting. This expression is used mainly in American English; the usual British expression is **two a penny**.

Writers are a dime a dozen, a new one will be easy enough to find.

Films about primitive people are a dime a dozen right now.

dinner

done like a dinner

If you are **done like a dinner** in a contest or competitive situation, your opponents defeat you completely, often in an unfair way. This expression is used mainly in Australian English.

Aviation consultant Peter Harbison said US carriers had virtual carte blanche to fly in and out of Tokyo as they pleased. 'The Japanese get done like a dinner,' Mr Harbison said.

dinners

do something more than someone has had hot dinners

If you say that you **have done** something **more than** someone **has had hot dinners**, you are emphasizing that you have done it a great number of times. This expression is used in British English.

Bowe's trainer Eddie Futch, who's probably seen more fights than even most men of his age have had hot dinners, expects it to be one of the best he's been involved with.

Robin and Lizzie Hamer of First Ascent activity holidays have climbed more mountains than you and I have had hot dinners.

dirt

dig up dirt
dig for dirt
dig the dirt   ◄◄

If you say that one person **is digging up dirt** on another, you mean that the first is trying to find out something that may cause harm to the second. You can also say that someone **is digging for dirt**, or, in British English, that they **are digging the dirt**.

They hired a detective firm to dig up dirt on their rival.

Scoop-hungry reporters have done everything from going through trash cans digging for dirt on celebrities to paying prostitutes to lure Members of Parliament into compromising positions.

□ You can describe this activity as **dirt-digging**.

In the movie, a dirt-digging reporter is framed by a corrupt district attorney and sentenced for manslaughter.

dish the dirt   ◄

If you say that one person **dishes the dirt** on another, you disapprove of the way that the first person spreads stories about the second, especially when they say things that may embarrass or upset that person, or damage their reputation.

Many politicians who maintain that their private lives are their own, are not above dishing the dirt on a fellow politician, if it suits their own political or personal purposes.

In his autobiography Life Is Too Short, the singer, dancer, comedian, and actor holds nothing back. He dishes the dirt on his buddies and smudges his own shoes with admissions of womanising, gambling, and drugs.

□ People sometimes describe this activity as **dirt-dishing**.

Some publishers believe that by speaking out

as he did, he has pushed up the potential value of any dirt-dishing memoirs he cares to write.

do someone dirt
do the dirt on someone

If someone **has done** you **dirt** or **has done the dirt on** you, they have betrayed you or treated you very badly. This expression is used in American English; the British expression is **do the dirty on** someone.

They tell me you have done me dirt. Tell me it ain't true.

There is an unofficial biography out of Nancy Reagan which is doing the dirt on her all over the place.

dirty

do the dirty on someone

If someone **has done the dirty on** you, they have betrayed you or treated you very badly. You can also just say that they **have done the dirty**. These expressions are used in British English; the American expression is **do** someone **dirt**.

There are plenty of people only too ready to make use of a situation like this to do the dirty on somebody they don't like.

Apparently, Scott and the rest had been wanting to sack Joey since 1988. They even knew they wanted John as a replacement. It was only misplaced loyalty that prevented them from doing the dirty there and then.

wash your dirty linen in public
air your dirty laundry in public
do your dirty washing in public   ◄◄

If you say that someone **is washing** their **dirty linen in public** or **is washing** their **dirty laundry in public**, you are criticizing them for talking about unpleasant or personal matters in front of other people, when you consider that such things should be kept private. These forms of the expression are used mainly in British English; in American English, the usual forms are **air** your **dirty linen in public** or **air** your **dirty laundry in public**.

We shouldn't wash our dirty laundry in public and if I was in his position, I'd say nothing at all.

Public mud-slinging reflects no credit on sport. It brings football into disrepute, and washing dirty linen in public does nothing for the game.

It looks much more like the action of a bitter, lonely and selfish woman who thinks she can score points by airing the family's dirty linen in public.

□ In British English, you can also say that someone **is doing** their **dirty washing in public**.

We don't want any more to come out in pub-

lic. We want to stop doing our dirty washing in public.

☐ There are many other variations of this expression. For example, you can leave out 'in public' or 'dirty'.

In Spain, it seems, airing dirty linen is considered more serious than any offence itself.

He felt that my brother had embarrassed him, because he felt that my brother has washed that linen in public.

☐ You can also just talk about **dirty linen** or **dirty laundry**.

We know much more than we ever did before about the doings of Congressmen. So, we're seeing more dirty laundry.

It is certainly a huge disadvantage of being famous that everyone wants to see your dirty linen.

distance

go the distance
go the full distance ◄◄

If you **go the distance** or **go the full distance**, you complete what you are doing and reach your goal.

He wasn't supposed to be able to go the distance, you know, but in the end, he won the 12th round.

She's unlike anyone else, and has really worked her way up from someone who was kind of an ingenue to someone who is a true movie star. Geena Davis will go the distance in the nineties.

within spitting distance: 1 ◄

If someone or something is **within spitting distance** of a place, they are very close to it.

Most of the world's biggest financial firms are already established within spitting distance of the Bank of England.

Logan Airport is built out into the bay, within spitting distance of Boston's thoroughly fetching skyline.

☐ People sometimes vary this expression.

Kim and Thurston Moore live in an apartment block fashionably situated in the middle of Manhattan, with Broadway only spitting distance away.

within spitting distance: 2

If someone or something is **within spitting distance** of an amount, level, or goal, they are very close to achieving it.

Its share of world trade was within spitting distance of Britain's.

Economic recovery was not what got the Wilson government back to within spitting distance of success.

within striking distance: 1 ◄◄

If someone or something is **within striking distance** of a place, they are very close to it.

The cinema is within striking distance of ample car parking and gleaming new shops and restaurants.

Ironbridge is well signposted from the motorway and within easy striking distance of both Birmingham and Manchester.

within striking distance: 2 ◄

If someone or something is **within striking distance** of an amount, level, or goal, they are very close to achieving it.

We are surprised that we seem to be within striking distance of achieving 100 per cent of our objectives.

He is in striking distance of victory in the first round vote.

distraction

drive someone to distraction ◄

If you say that something or someone **drives** you **to distraction**, you mean that they annoy you a great deal.

Nothing I said or did would get them to tidy up. It drove me to distraction.

His obsessive attention to detail drove to distraction the artists and workers with whom he collaborated.

ditch

last ditch ◄◄◄

You can describe an action as a **last ditch** attempt or effort to do something when everything else has failed and this action is the only way left of avoiding disaster, although it too seems likely to fail.

The President has been making a last ditch attempt to prevent the rebels taking over the city.

Republican critics dismiss the report as a last ditch effort to justify an investigation that lasted nearly six years.

Knowing that power could be slipping from his grasp, Mr Major made a desperate last-ditch appeal to voters.

divide

divide and conquer
divide and rule ◄◄

If someone in power follows a policy of **divide and conquer** or **divide and rule**, they stay in power by making sure that the people under their control quarrel among themselves and so cannot unite to achieve their aims and overthrow their leader. 'Divide and rule' is used only in British English.

The same principle of divide and conquer that the Roman Empire used so effectively was applied once again by Yugoslavia's occupiers in 1941.

Trade unions are concerned that management

may be tempted into a policy of divide and rule by cultural divisions.

Part of the ruling class's divide and rule policy is promoting barriers between sexes, races, sexualities, nations.

□ When someone is following one of these policies, you can say that they are **dividing and conquering** or **dividing and ruling**.

The Summit sends a very strong message to him that he's not going to divide and conquer.

dividends

pay dividends ◄◄◄

If something **pays dividends**, it brings advantages at a later date.

Taking time out to get fit is time well spent and will pay you dividends in the long run.

Martin went out of his way to lavish attention on Mrs. Eaton, a move which later paid big dividends.

Dixie

whistle Dixie

If you say that you **are not whistling Dixie** or **are not just whistling Dixie**, you mean that you are being honest or realistic in what you are saying and you should not be ignored. This expression is used mainly in American English.

'Is that a threat?' 'I'm not just whistling Dixie.'

I don't think anyone left the meeting whistling Dixie. It gave credence to the declaration that Friday's market debacle was an abnormal condition, and not a disaster.

doctor

just what the doctor ordered ◄

If you say that something is **just what the doctor ordered**, you mean that it is extremely pleasant or useful, and that it helps to make you feel better or to improve a situation.

His creative power is what we need for games like this. He is just what the doctor ordered.

'Meatballs in tomato sauce!' Max exclaimed happily. 'Just what the doctor ordered.'

□ Sometimes people replace 'doctor' with a word or expression that is more relevant to the subject they are talking about.

Another football match would appear to be just what the bank manager ordered. Only last October Brighton made £100,000 from their visit to Old Trafford.

dog

die like a dog

If someone **dies like a dog**, they die in a painful and undignified way, usually after

they have been shot or injured in a violent fight. This is an old-fashioned expression.

The film begins with our chic hero stealing cars and ends with him dying like a dog in the street.

a dog and pony show ◄

If you refer to an event as **a dog and pony show**, you mean that it is very showy because it has been organized in order to impress someone. This expression is used mainly in American English.

I'm bombarding him and the others with charts, graphs, facts, and figures. The boss responds by dozing off during most of our dog and pony show.

The first step in Florida, as in most states, is the governor's office applying for a share of federal grant money. If, months later, the money is granted, state agencies spend more months putting on 'dog and pony shows' in hopes of getting a share.

dog-eat-dog ◄

You use **dog-eat-dog** to describe a situation in which everyone wants to succeed and is willing to harm other people or to use dishonest methods in order to do this.

In the 1992 campaign, he said that if it was going to be 'dog eat dog' he would do anything it took to get himself re-elected.

The TV business today is a dog-eat-dog business.

dog-in-the-manger

If you say that someone has a **dog-in-the-manger** attitude, you are criticizing them for selfishly wanting to prevent other people from using or enjoying something that they cannot use or enjoy themselves.

I think there'll be a certain group of intransigent Republicans who'll take a dog-in-the-manger kind of attitude and try to frustrate anything the president wants to achieve.

The council has an ambivalent attitude to the Carnival. On the one hand it has a high regard for its tourist benefits, but on the other it does not want it to have too high a profile. It's a dog-in-the-manger attitude which has taken the fun out of a great event.

a dog's breakfast
a dog's dinner ◄

If you refer to a situation, event, or piece of work as **a dog's breakfast** or **a dog's dinner**, you mean that it is chaotic, badly organized, or very untidy. These expressions are used in British English.

The act created what many admitted was an over-complex but inadequate system. One senior regulator described it as a dog's breakfast.

Now she's having to watch as those whom she grew up with in politics are in Cabinet and making a dog's breakfast of it.

The whole place was a bit of a dog's dinner, really.

every dog has its day

If you say **'every dog has** its **day'**, you mean that everyone will be successful or lucky at some time in their life. This expression is sometimes used to encourage someone at a time when they are not having any success or luck.

Former England player Davies said: 'Every dog has his day, although the way I kicked throughout the game, who would have thought that drop goal would even reach the posts?'

'I don't have any money to fight him. These people are all the time in court, anyway,' Cecchini says. 'But every dog has its day and I have lots of patience.'

it's a dog's life

People say **'it's a dog's life'** when they are complaining that their job or situation is unpleasant or boring.

It's a dog's life being a football manager.

you can't teach an old dog new tricks

If you say **'you can't teach an old dog new tricks'**, you mean that it is often difficult to get people to try new ways of doing things, especially if these people have been doing something in a particular way for a long time.

It is a convenient myth that a person cannot change their personality. Or as the saying goes: 'You can't teach an old dog new tricks'.

□ This expression is often varied. For example, if you say **'you can teach an old dog new tricks'**, you mean that it is possible to get people to try new ways of doing something.

Our work shows that you can teach an old dog new tricks.

An old dog can learn new tricks if he has both the will and the opportunity.

doghouse

in the doghouse   ◄

If you are **in the doghouse**, people are very annoyed with you because of something you have done.

Insurance companies are already in the doghouse over poor advice on pensions which has left hundreds of thousands of people worse off.

Four Caribbean prime ministers have landed themselves in the dog house after failing to turn up to a top-level meeting at the White House.

dogs

call off the dogs

If you tell someone to **call off the dogs** or to **call off** their **dogs**, you are telling them to stop challenging, attacking, or damaging you or another person.

Lenders will be ordered to call off the dogs, especially for families struggling to pay their mortgage through unemployment.

I'm hoping Mr Lewis will either take a look at these judgments and say enough is enough and call off his dogs, or he will at least explain to us what the hell is going on.

go to the dogs   ◄

If you say that a country, organization, or business **is going to the dogs**, you mean that it is becoming less powerful, efficient, or successful than it has been in the past.

In the 1960s the country was fast going to the dogs.

Television, we warned, would go to the dogs under the Government's crazy franchising system.

let sleeping dogs lie
a sleeping dog   ◄

If someone tells you to **let sleeping dogs lie**, they are warning you not to disturb or interfere with a situation, because you are likely to cause trouble and problems.

Mr. Dambar had been wondering if he should come right out and ask his wife when Henry was planning to leave. But this interruption gave him time to reconsider. Perhaps it was better to let sleeping dogs lie.

Why does she come over here stirring everything up? Why can't she let sleeping dogs lie?

□ You can refer to a situation that it would be better not to disturb as **a sleeping dog**.

The crux of the film is that his inquisitive son, by arousing the sleeping dog of the past, finds himself in danger.

Since the election, it has suited ministers to treat local government finance as the sleeping dog of British politics.

throw someone to the dogs

If someone **throws** you **to the dogs**, they allow you to be criticized severely or treated roughly, for example in order to protect themselves from criticism or harm, or because they no longer need you.

In all honesty he will trick you, cheat you, use you, drop you, throw you to the dogs, provided the security of France dictates it.

He told the judges he felt abandoned by his former commanders and that he had been, as he put it, thrown to the dogs.

doldrums

in the doldrums: 1   ◄◄◄

If an economy or business is **in the doldrums**, nothing new is happening and it is not doing very well.

After months in the doldrums, the lira strengthened.

The restaurant business, like many other businesses, is in the doldrums.

Property prices remain in the doldrums with rental a better option in the short term for people seeking a home.

in the doldrums: 2

If someone is **in the doldrums**, they are very depressed and inactive.

After what feels like a long time out in the doldrums of depression, I am now, at the age of 27, just learning how to overcome my weaknesses and build on my strengths.

out of the doldrums: 1   ◄

If an economy or business comes **out of the doldrums**, it improves and becomes stronger after a period of inactivity.

Still, today's estimate and several other positive economic reports in recent days provide hope the economy may finally be coming out of the doldrums.

We were hoping that the housing market was, in fact, going to come out of the doldrums that it's been in for the last few years.

out of the doldrums: 2

If someone comes **out of the doldrums**, they stop being depressed and feel happier.

With her humour and upbeat spirit, Jane got me right out of the doldrums I'd been in for three years.

dollar

bet your bottom dollar

If you say that you **bet** your **bottom dollar** that something will happen or is true, you are emphasizing that you are absolutely certain that it will happen or that it is true.

American designer Donna Karan may not be as internationally famous yet as her compatriots Calvin Klein and Ralph Lauren, but you can bet your bottom dollar that it won't be long before she is.

He's not ahead of us on this road, and I can't see him behind us. He hasn't passed us and we haven't passed him, but I'd bet my bottom dollar he's around somewhere.

the 64,000 dollar question   ◄

If you describe a question as **the 64,000 dollar question**, you mean that it is very important but very difficult to answer. You can also use other large amounts instead of '64,000' to mean the same thing.

Why should I, young, healthy and female, suddenly lose my hair? The sixty-four thousand dollar question remained unanswered.

They asked the million-dollar question: 'So what makes a good marriage?' Faithfulness comes out top of the list on that.

The billion-dollar question is: how much are those benefits worth?

dollars

dollars to doughnuts

If you say that it is **dollars to doughnuts** that something will happen, you are emphasizing that you are certain it will happen. This expression is used mainly in American English.

It's dollars to doughnuts that the bank of the future will charge more for its services.

Well, I'll bet you, Alex, almost dollars to donuts that I'll wake up at 3am, as I do every morning now.

□ 'Doughnuts' is sometimes spelled 'donuts' in informal American English.

look a million dollars
feel like a million dollars   ◄

If someone **looks a million dollars**, they look extremely attractive and well-dressed. If someone **feels like a million dollars**, they feel very healthy and happy.

She looked a million dollars when she got off the plane.

Casual trousers, comfortable shoes, immaculate hair. He looks a million dollars.

After all my injury problems I now feel a million dollars.

It was the most relaxed I've felt in ages. I felt like a million dollars.

domino

a domino effect   ◄◄

If one event causes another similar event, which in turn causes a further event, and so on, you can refer to this as **a domino effect**.

But if the Slovenes won independence, what about Slovakia, Moldavia, the Basques, a host of other people across Europe? Many feared a domino effect creating instability.

We have seen how bad the housing problem can become. Unused houses deteriorate rapidly, affecting the value of nearby homes; in a domino effect, the entire neighborhood can easily fall victim.

done

done and dusted

If you say that something is **done and dusted**, you mean that it is finished or decided and there is nothing more to be said or done about it. This expression is used mainly in British and Australian English.

'The deal is done and dusted,' Dorahy told The Sunday Mail. 'It's a matter of Wigan coming to an arrangement with the Broncos and Chris will be here full-time at the end of the season in Australia.'

'It's all done and dusted. There is nothing that remains to be said about what has happened,' he said.

donkey

donkey's years ◄

If you say that something lasts or has been happening for **donkey's years**, you are emphasizing that it lasts or has been happening for a very long time. This expression is used in British English.

I've been a vegetarian for donkey's years.

He owns some old iron mines that haven't been used in donkey's years.

do the donkey work ◄

If someone **does the donkey work**, they do all the most physically tiring or boring parts of a job or piece of work. This expression is used in British English.

Send for Andy Graham, get him to do the donkey work, tell him to search that roof and the one next door to it for any cartridge cases.

The bottom lot, and I was one of the bottom lot, were the engine corps who did the sheer physical donkey work.

We've been very fortunate getting a succession of secretaries who've managed to do the donkey work.

door

as one door closes, another one opens

If you say **'as one door closes, another one opens'**, you mean that if one thing you do fails, you will soon have an opportunity to try to succeed at something else. This expression is often used to encourage someone to keep trying after they have had a disappointment or failure.

Earlier in the week, Roberts was philosophical after losing his job. 'Obviously, I am a little disappointed,' he explained, 'But one door closes and another one opens. You can't dwell on these things and I will just put my head down and work a bit harder.'

beat a path to someone's door ◄

If people **are beating a path to** your **door**, they are eager to talk to you or do business with you.

Gone are the days when the man who made a better mousetrap than his neighbour could expect the world to beat a path to his door.

Business leaders should be beating a path to Mr Eggar's door demanding that tough environmental laws be passed.

Fashion editors now beat a path to Mugler's door and thousands of followers flock to get into one of his events.

by the back door
through the back door ◄◄◄

If someone gets or does something **by the back door** or **through the back door**, they do it secretly and unofficially. This expression is used mainly in British English.

He said the government would not allow any-
one to sneak in by the back door and seize power by force.

There will be no more increases for top officials through the back door.

□ **Back door** can be used before a noun.

David Hinchliffe, for Labour, accused the Government of introducing a back door method of closing council homes.

close the stable door after the horse has bolted
close the barn door after the horse has gone ◄

In British English, if you say that an action is like **closing the stable door after the horse has bolted**, you mean that it is too late to take this action now, because the problem which it would have prevented has already occurred. This expression is often varied. For example, you can use other verbs with similar meanings to 'close' and 'bolt', and you can use 'door' instead of 'stable door'.

It is nice to see Severn Trent taking positive action, even though it might look like closing the stable door after the horse has bolted.

Ever heard of shutting the stable door after the horse has run away?

At best, say critics, this strategy is like shutting the door after the horse has bolted.

□ In American English, you say that an action is like **closing the barn door after the horse has gone**. This expression can also be varied.

This all has the feeling of closing the barn door after the horse has gone.

Like the guy who closes the barn door after the proverbial horse has run off, I suddenly became very diet conscious.

knock at your door
come knocking at your door

If something such as a problem or opportunity **is knocking at** your **door** or **comes knocking at** your **door**, it is likely to happen soon or is starting to happen.

During these tough economic times, feeling the spirit of happiness can be difficult, especially when the recession has come knocking at your door.

All of his life he had been hankering after his personal freedom, and now freedom was knocking at his door, begging him to come in.

knock on the door ◄

If someone **is knocking on the door** of a club or group, they are trying to join it or become part of it.

They are two players I'm sure will be knocking on the England door soon.

Until recently women were knocking on the door of a man's world asking to be let in.

lay something at someone's door ◄◄

If you **lay** something **at** someone's **door**, you blame them for something unpleasant that has happened.

The Morning Star has no doubt about who is responsible for the riot. Its editorial says the blame must be laid at the door of the government.

The robberies were now laid at Brady's door.

not darken somewhere's door
never darken someone's door

If someone never goes to a place, you can say that they **do not darken** its **door**. If someone tells you **never to darken** their **door** again, they are ordering you never to visit them again because you have done something to make them very angry or upset. You can use 'doorstep' instead of 'door'. This is an old-fashioned expression.

He had not darkened the door of a church for a long time.

The law firm told them to destroy all dossiers and never darken their doorstep again.

push at an open door

If you say that someone **is pushing at an open door** or **is pushing against an open door**, you mean that they are finding it very easy to achieve their aims. These expressions are used in British English.

'Most departments were helpful,' she says, 'although enthusiasm was a bit muted in a few cases. In the main we now seem to be pushing at an open door.'

There is not much effort required, when you are pushing against an open door.

the revolving door: 1 ◄

If you talk about **the revolving door** of an organization or institution, you are referring to the fact that the people working in it do not stay there for very long, and so, for example, it is difficult for anything effective to be achieved.

The revolving door at Wests has only just stopped spinning. A huge turnover of players is usually not the ideal basis for success.

For the next 25 years, Caramoo had a revolving door of executives.

☐ You can also use **revolving-door** before a noun.

High spending in the '80s by Italy's revolving-door governments swelled the public sector debt.

the revolving door: 2 ◄

In politics, **the revolving door** is used to refer to a situation in which someone moves from an influential position in government to a position in a private company, especially where this may give them an unfair advantage. Sometimes this expression is used to refer to a situation where someone moves from the private sector to government, and then back again.

Mr Smith also spoke of the revolving door for senior civil servants getting jobs in industry connected with their former department.

Bill Clinton ran a campaign that included a strong pledge to stop the revolving door between public service and the private sector.

the revolving door: 3

You can use **the revolving door** to refer to a situation where solutions to problems only last for a short time, and then the same problems occur again.

East Palo Alto juveniles, like others nationwide, are caught in the revolving door of the justice system, ending up back on the streets after serving time, faced with their old life.

☐ You can also use **revolving-door** before a noun.

This is the revolving-door syndrome: no home, no job, no money; hence crime, increasing isolation from society, imprisonment; hence no home on release, and back again to prison.

doors

behind closed doors ◄◄◄

If people have talks or discussions **behind closed doors**, they have them in private because they want them to be kept secret. This expression is used mainly in journalism.

The summer I was fourteen and Rita was twelve, our parents started having long talks behind closed doors. They'd had a few arguments before, but this was different.

While there are many examples of decisions being publicly discussed, there are many other examples of the old approach, with decisions taken in secret behind closed doors.

☐ **Behind-closed-doors** can be used before a noun.

Political analysts say that the three factions have been mulling over the idea in a series of behind-closed-doors meetings.

His name was reportedly mentioned in relation to arms during a behind-closed-doors court case.

dos

the dos and don'ts ◄◄

The dos and don'ts of a particular situation are the things you should and should not do in that situation.

Disasters can be avoided if a few general dos and don'ts are considered.

Mills and Boon produces a detailed booklet and cassette tape full of dos and don'ts for aspiring authors, stressing that the heroine should be lovable, and the hero charismatic, and their relationship must always have a happy ending.

dot

on the dot ◄

If you do something **on the dot**, you do it punctually or at exactly the time you are supposed to.

At nine o'clock on the dot, they have breakfast.

He arrived right on the dot, as Brian had expected.

I sat on the front steps to wait for her, figuring that if she was anything like her father, she'd arrive on the dot of ten.

since the year dot
from the year dot

If you say that something has been the way it is **since the year dot** or **from the year dot**, you mean it has been like that for a very long time. This expression is used in British English.

Most of these folks have been here since the year dot.

The two-bedroomed apartment had been lived and worked in since the year dot by a psychiatrist, his wife, their two sons and the grandparents.

double

at the double
on the double ◄

If you do something **at the double** or **on the double**, you do it very quickly or immediately. 'At the double' is used only in British English.

At his desk across the town, Michael reached for the internal phone. 'Jill? My office, please, at the double.'

He said there was a report of a prowler at this address. I knew it was your place so I came over on the double.

down

down and dirty: 1 ◄

If you describe a person or their behaviour as **down and dirty**, you mean that they behave in an unfair or dishonest way in order to gain an advantage. This expression is used mainly in American English.

If the president gets deep down and dirty, the Governor will give as good as he gets.

Did this campaign get down and dirty?

□ You can also talk about a **down and dirty** person or act.

This isn't a guy who teaches comparative literature at Amherst. This is a down and dirty cop.

down and dirty: 2

Journalists sometimes refer to a performer or their performance as **down and dirty** when they like them because they are bold, direct, and perhaps vulgar. This expression is used mainly in American English.

Get down and dirty with Sandra Bernhard who comes to Britain with her one-woman show, Giving Till It Hurts.

People like Adam and his dad turned me onto the real down-and-dirty stuff like Otis Clay, William Bell and Albert King.

down and out: 1 ◄◄◄

If you describe someone as **down and out**, you mean that they have nowhere to live, usually have no job, and have no real hope of improving their situation.

Having been down and out himself, Vern Barry has insights into others who are down and out, and he's helped many get started and then move on to permanent jobs.

I know what it is to be down and out. One time back in the thirties, I was working in New York and I didn't have enough to rent a room.

□ You can refer to a person in this situation as **a down-and-out**.

In the glow of the side lights, he looked unshaven, shabby, a down-and-out.

There are hundreds of down and outs living just a few yards from his palace.

down and out: 2 ◄

In a competition or contest, if someone is **down and out**, they have been beaten, or they are losing and have no hope of winning.

I am sending you clippings from which you will see that Ted appears to be down and out as candidate for governor.

Leicester had looked down and out when they trailed 12-3 with only 12 minutes left.

□ You can say that someone is **down but not out** when they are losing but still have some hope of winning.

Rangers manager Walter Smith last night declared his side down but not out of the European Cup after their defeat by AEK in Athens.

The Democrats are down, but not out.

down-at-heel
down-at-the-heels ◄◄

A **down-at-heel** or **down-at-the-heels** person or place looks uncared for and untidy. 'Down-at-heel' is used mainly in British English and 'down-at-the-heels' is used mainly in American English.

The flight to Kathmandu is always full of scruffy, down-at-heel people like Hyde.

He had two rooms above a down-at-heel shop that sold electrical appliances.

When I was a down-at-the-heels private eye, I couldn't afford to eat here.

down the drain: 1
down the tubes
down the pan ◀◀◀

If you say that something is going **down the drain**, you mean that it is getting worse or being destroyed and that it is unlikely to recover. You can also say that something is going **down the tubes** or **down the pan**. Words such as 'plughole', 'tube', and 'toilet' are sometimes used instead of 'drain', 'tubes', or 'pan'.

They were forced to do something, because they were aware that their public image was rapidly going down the drain.

Small businesses are going down the drain because of the failed economic policies of this Government.

People don't like to see marriages going down the tubes.

down the drain: 2
down the tubes
down the pan ◀◀◀

If you say that your money, work, or time has gone **down the drain**, you mean that it has been lost or wasted. You can also say that it has gone **down the tubes** or **down the pan**. Words such as 'plughole', 'tube', and 'toilet' are sometimes used instead of 'drain', 'tubes', or 'pan'.

Over the years, the government has poured billions of dollars down the drain propping up its national airlines and other firms.

You have ruined everything – my perfect plans, my great organization. All those years of work are down the drain.

Millions have gone down the plughole after the finance director decided to deposit a hefty chunk of the station's cash with a dubious bank.

have a down on someone
have a downer on someone

If you **have a down on** someone or something or you **have a downer on** them, you do not like them or you disapprove of them. These expressions are used in British English.

Snobs would have a down on a man with a south London accent.

His fans manage to persuade him to return for an encore, at which point he starts mumbling incoherently about how the people reading a magazine at the front of the stage must really have a downer on him.

drag

drag someone through the mud ◀

If you say that someone **is dragged through the mud**, you mean that they are accused of behaving in an immoral or unacceptable way. This expression has several variations. For example, you can also say that

someone's reputation or name **is dragged through the mud**. Nouns such as 'mire', 'dirt', or 'filth' can be used instead of 'mud'.

One doesn't like to see an admired institution dragged through the mud like this.

He was furious when he heard what I'd done. Accused me of betrayal, of wanting to drag Guy's name through the mud.

'Can't you give us a name, Dr Denny?' 'Why drag someone else into the dirt?'

drag your feet
drag your heels ◀◀◀

If you say that someone **is dragging** their **feet** or **dragging** their **heels** on something, you are criticizing them for deliberately delaying making a decision about something that is important to you.

But there's been more substantial criticism of the United States for dragging its feet on measures to protect the environment.

The tobacco companies have always dragged their feet on health issues.

A spokesman strongly denied that the Government was dragging its heels on the issue.

drain

laugh like a drain

If you say that someone **laughs like a drain**, you mean that they laugh noisily and vigorously. This expression is used in British English.

I read my tattered copies of P.G. Wodehouse and laughed like a drain.

We glanced across at each other and I saw he was laughing like a drain!

drawer

the top drawer: 1 ◀◀

If you describe someone or something as from or out of **the top drawer**, you mean that they are among the best of their kind. This expression is used mainly in British English.

Horton insisted last night that money is no object, with quality being the priority. 'The player I am looking for will be right out of the top drawer.'

The Grange Hotel may be top drawer, but it's not pretentious.

Castleford produced a performance right out of the top drawer to thrash Wigan 33-2.

☐ You can use **top drawer** before a noun to say that someone or something is of a very high quality.

The dramatisation is wonderfully inventive and superbly played by a top-drawer cast including Maria Aitken and Tim Piggot-Smith.

Gooch described his team's fightback as 'a top drawer performance'.

the top drawer: 2

If you describe someone as from or out of **the top drawer**, you mean that they are from a privileged social background. This expression is used mainly in British English.

His companion came from right out of the top drawer of the Irish landed gentry, had been schooled in England and had held the Queen's commission in the exclusive Guards' Division.

Some attenders this year seemed – how should one say it – not exactly out of the top drawer.

dream

a dream ticket ◄◄

If two people are considered **a dream ticket**, they are expected to work well together and have a great deal of success. This expression is usually used to refer to people who are well known, for example politicians or actors. It is used mainly in British journalism.

The move raised the prospect of a 'dream ticket' of Tony Blair as leader and John Prescott as his deputy.

It should have been Hollywood's dream ticket: husband and wife Tom Cruise and Nicole Kidman starring together in a romantic blockbuster movie.

like a dream ◄◄

If you do something **like a dream**, you do it very well. If something happens **like a dream**, it happens successfully and without any problems.

She had noticed, from across the dance floor, that he danced like a dream.

Wilson, an eminent American biologist who has done more than anyone else to popularise the notion of biodiversity, writes like a dream.

The first stages of installation worked like a dream. Then the procedure threw up an error message.

dreams

beyond your wildest dreams ◄◄

If you describe something such as an achievement or some good news as **beyond your wildest dreams**, you are emphasizing that it is better than you could have imagined or hoped for.

We succeeded beyond our wildest dreams of focusing both governments on the issue.

It was an incredible effort. The response of viewers was beyond our wildest dreams. The money just kept pouring in.

never in your wildest dreams
not in your wildest dreams ◄

If you say that **never in your wildest dreams** or **not in your wildest dreams** could you imagine a particular thing, you are em-

phasizing that you think it is extremely strange or unlikely.

We were told we could expect a substantial win but never in my wildest dreams could I have thought it would be more than £1 million.

Not even in our wildest dreams did we think we would sell every seat for the entire season.

I never in my wildest dreams believed I would have to apologize for, or be required to justify, my bank's business ethics.

the person of your dreams
the thing of your dreams ◄◄◄

If you refer to someone or something as **the person or thing of your dreams**, you mean that you prefer them to all others.

Maybe, just maybe, the man of your dreams will walk through that door and into your life tonight.

It was in Tunisia that one day they saw the house of their dreams, the most beautiful dwelling imaginable.

In this chapter you'll learn the inside secrets of landing the job of your dreams.

dressed

all dressed up with nowhere to go

If you say that someone or something is **all dressed up with nowhere to go**, you mean that although they are prepared for something, they do not have the opportunity to do it.

There must remain the suspicion that the Labour leadership is still stuck in the position of being all dressed up with nowhere to go.

If funding dries up, the opera houses will be all dressed up, but with nowhere to go.

□ This expression is very variable. For example, you can say that someone or something is **all dressed up with no place to go** or **all dressed up and nowhere to go**.

She sat there, not knowing what to do with herself. 'I'm all dressed up,' she thought, 'with no place to go.'

With her expensive watch, silk scarf and cashmere sweater, Nuria seems an apt symbol for Andorra: all dressed up but unsure where to go next.

dressed to kill ◄

If you describe someone, especially a woman, as **dressed to kill**, you mean that they are wearing very smart or glamorous clothes which are intended to attract attention and impress people.

We're all familiar with the images – the gorgeous, pouting model, dressed to kill, with cigarette dangling from kissable lips.

She watched his plane come into Mascot airport, dressed to kill, her hand shielding her eyes.

drop

at the drop of a hat ◄◄

If you do something **at the drop of a hat**, you do it willingly and without hesitation. This expression is often used to suggest that someone does not think carefully enough about their actions.

Part of the answer is having more people sorting out their own minor problems and not calling the police at the drop of a hat.

There is a myth that we are a uniquely uncaring generation, shoving our old folk into institutions at the drop of a hat.

a drop in the ocean
a drop in the bucket ◄◄

If you say that something, especially an amount of money, is **a drop in the ocean** or **a drop in the bucket**, you mean that it is very small in comparison with the amount which is needed or expected, so that its effect is insignificant. 'A drop in the bucket' is used mainly in American English.

The size of the grants have been attacked by welfare groups as merely a drop in the ocean.

For West Germany, the Albanian refugees are a drop in the ocean compared to the three thousand East Germans who used to arrive here every day.

It's a tax on what's considered unhealthy habits, like cigarettes and alcohol, but unfortunately it wouldn't raise a lot of money. It would be a drop in the bucket, really.

drum

bang the drum
beat the drum ◄

If you **bang the drum** or **beat the drum** for something or someone, you support them strongly and publicly.

The trade secretary disagreed but promised to 'bang the drum for industry'.

If the French want to beat the drum on behalf of French culture, good luck to them.

□ You can say who or what is being supported by putting an adjective or noun before 'drum'.

Some in the media have been beating the environmental drums for a while.

drunk

drunk as a skunk

If you say that someone is as **drunk as a skunk**, you are emphasizing that they are very drunk. Nouns such as 'lord' or 'coot' are sometimes used instead of 'skunk'.

I'm sorry, honey. I put you through all this. It was my fault. I was drunk as a skunk.

She was drunk as a lord for seventeen days. She could do nothing.

I heard he was drunk as a coot last night and got into a big fight at Toby's.

dry

dry as a bone

If you say that something is as **dry as a bone**, you are emphasizing that it is very dry.

By the end of June the pond is as dry as a bone.

□ People also use the much more frequent adjective **bone-dry** to mean the same thing.

Firefighters battled blazes on Sunday that have ravaged more than 200,000 acres of bone-dry brushland and forests.

His throat was bone dry.

dry as dust: 1

If you say that something is **dry as dust**, you are emphasizing that it is very dry.

The hard-packed dirt of the floor was smooth and solid as cement, and the stone walls were dry as dust and hadn't been disturbed in a century.

The cold front now was again producing intermittent snow, flurries of small, feathery flakes which seemed as cold and dry as dust.

dry as dust: 2

If you describe something as **dry as dust**, you mean that it is very dull and uninteresting.

When you see the law in action, you realise how exciting it can be and what a buzz it gives people. It's so different from the dry-as-dust stuff we study at college.

It is not, however, dry-as-dust history, but an enthralling story full of insight and incident.

duck

a dead duck ◄

If you refer to someone or something as **a dead duck**, you mean that they are a failure.

The government is a dead duck; and the Supreme National Council does not have the means to govern.

Chelsea Harbour is known to be something of a dead duck. People have failed to move there in the quantities expected, shops have closed, flats and penthouses are still empty.

a lame duck: 1 ◄◄

If you refer to a politician or a government as **a lame duck**, you mean that they have little real power, for example because their period of office is coming to an end.

The credibility of both government and parliament is at a low ebb. The government is headed by a president who looks like a lame duck.

He said in this transitional period the last thing people needed was to feel that the government was a lame duck.

□ You can also use **lame duck** before a noun.

If he loses it's hard to see how he can ever regain his authority. He's already seen widely as a lame duck Prime Minister.

He could have lost so much political impetus that he would have found himself leading a lame-duck administration to near-certain defeat.

a lame duck: 2 ◄◄

If you say that someone or something is **a lame duck**, you are criticizing them for being in a very weak position and in need of support.

Rover intends to complete the transformation from the lame duck of the motor industry into a quality car maker with a series of 'high image' models.

'Moira's hardly going to regard you as a lame duck.' 'Moira considers all single people lame ducks.'

□ You can also use **lame duck** before a noun.

It is not proper to use British taxpayers' money to support lame-duck industries.

a sitting duck ◄

If you refer to someone as **a sitting duck**, you mean that they are an obvious target, and that it is very easy to attack them or criticize them.

If the Chinese authorities were on to me, I was a sitting duck at the airport.

A pilot performing this manoeuvre might keep his opponent in his sights but would be a sitting duck for a second enemy aircraft.

□ You can also use **sitting-duck** before a noun.

Labour is going to field another sitting-duck candidate for the forthcoming by-election. The Labour leadership must acknowledge the fact that the party has to stop wasting time and money fighting parliamentary seats it is never going to win.

take to something like a duck to water ◄

If you **take to** something **like a duck to water**, you discover that you are naturally good at it and find it very easy to do.

Some mothers take to breastfeeding like a duck to water, while others find they need some help to get started.

Gilbey decided that farming wasn't for him, and moved up to London, where he became a salesman for BMW. He took to it like a duck to water, quickly becoming Car Salesman of the Year.

ducks

get your ducks in a row

If you say that someone **has got** their **ducks in a row**, you mean they have got everything properly organized and under control. This

expression is used mainly in American English.

There is going to always be some disarray when you have a Republican White House and a Democratic Congress, but they do seem to have some trouble getting their ducks in a row.

play ducks and drakes with someone

If you accuse someone of **playing ducks and drakes with** people, you are accusing them of treating those people badly, by being dishonest with them or not taking them seriously. This expression is used in British English.

You are talking about the poorest and most disadvantaged people in the country. To play ducks and drakes with their service is reprehensible.

He accepted the ceasefire conditions, but since then has been playing ducks and drakes with the United Nations.

dudgeon

in high dudgeon ◄

If you say that someone is **in high dudgeon**, you are criticizing them for being unreasonably angry or annoyed about something. This is a literary expression.

She had left in high dudgeon after learning that the only perk was free coffee.

Washington businesses are in high dudgeon over the plan, especially the requirement that small businesses should insure their workers.

dull

dull as ditchwater
dull as dishwater

If you say that someone or something is as **dull as ditchwater** or as **dull as dishwater**, you are emphasizing that they are very boring.

Angus Wilson is a dull writer and that's a fact. Dull as ditchwater.

Sherry has an image of being as dull as ditchwater but the reality is that it's a subtle and stylish drink.

dummy

spit the dummy
spit out the dummy

If you accuse someone of **spitting the dummy** or **spitting out the dummy**, you are accusing them of behaving in a bad-tempered and childish way. This expression is used mainly in Australian English.

He spat the dummy when his wife decided to go back to work.

They are taking the money but not talking to us. If they want to spit out the dummy, that's their affair.

dumps

down in the dumps: 1
in the dumps   ◄

If you are **down in the dumps** or **in the dumps**, you feel depressed.

Try to be sources of support for each other when one of you is feeling down in the dumps.

Tommy has been a bit down in the dumps and he needs a change.

I was in the dumps when I met Jayne. I was self-destructive. I was drinking. And I was clearly not living the kind of life I should live.

in the dumps: 2
down in the dumps

If a business or economy is **in the dumps** or **down in the dumps**, it is doing badly.

With their economy in the dumps and the Americans demanding access to their markets, the Japanese want more decisive government.

California's economy is unlikely to stay in the dumps for more than two years, which gives the Governor plenty of time to take credit for the recovery.

dust

bite the dust: 1   ◄◄

If you say that something **bites the dust**, you mean that it fails or ceases to exist.

With the news that milk chocolate can help cut cholesterol, yet another healthy eating fad bites the dust.

There are over 4,000 such restaurants in and around London. Some make big money. Most break even, and quite a few have bitten the dust.

bite the dust: 2

If you say that someone **has bitten the dust**, you mean that they have died. This expression is used to refer to someone's death in a light-hearted or humorous way.

A Wild West showman nearly bit the dust when he blew himself up making blank bullets in his garden shed.

the dust settles
the dust clears   ◄◄◄

If you say that **the dust has settled** in a situation, you mean that it has become calmer and steadier after a series of confusing or chaotic events. You can also say that **the dust has cleared**.

Now that the dust has settled, it is clear that nothing much has changed.

I think we need to let the dust settle and see what's going to happen after that before we can get a really clear picture of what the prospects are.

When the dust cleared from Tuesday's election, Washington state found itself leading the

nation in the number of women elected to state executive positions.

eat someone's dust

In a competitive situation, if you **are eating** someone's **dust**, they are doing much better than you.

Aladdin has proved to be the most successful animated film of all time, leaving blockbusters like Home Alone 2 eating its dust.

gather dust   ◄◄

If something such as a project or problem **gathers dust**, it is not dealt with for a very long time.

A report written in 1951, which has been gathering dust on a shelf at the Institution of Civil Engineers in London, advocates a number of the building projects.

Certainly the government's cuts in the budget suggest that the fate of the report will be to gather dust rather than to animate policy.

not see someone for dust

If you say that you **can't see** someone **for dust**, you mean that they have left somewhere very quickly and run away. This expression is used in British English.

Come the dawn, I couldn't see him for dust.

shake the dust of somewhere from your feet

If you **shake the dust of** a place or situation **from** your **feet**, you leave it with the intention that you will never return to it. This expression is used in British English.

The Princess can never be free until she can shake the dust of Kensington Palace from her feet.

He insisted that the bank shake the dust of third-world debt from its feet.

dusty

a dusty answer
a dusty reply

If you ask or suggest something and you get **a dusty answer** or **a dusty reply**, you get a sharp and unpleasant response, for example a rejection of what you have asked for. These expressions are used in British English.

Plans to allow children into pubs received a dusty answer at the bar.

Her accusations after she came fourth that two of the three medal-winners had taken drugs have brought some dusty replies from her rivals.

Dutch

go Dutch
a Dutch treat

If two or more people **go Dutch**, they share the cost of the bill for something such as a meal or an evening out. This is a fairly old-fashioned expression.

We went Dutch on a cheap Chinese in Shaftesbury Avenue.

Many women are happy to go Dutch with a new boyfriend on the first date.

□ You can also say that you have **a Dutch treat**.

He wanted to pay the bill, but I objected and we settled on Dutch treat.

in Dutch

If you are **in Dutch**, you are in trouble. This is a fairly old-fashioned expression, which is used in American English.

Maybe he was in Dutch again and this time they offered him the chance of paying his debt by chasing me out of town.

Doug wants to get Manatelli in Dutch with his boss.

E

eagle

an eagle eye: 1   ◄

If you say that someone is keeping **an eagle eye** on a person or thing, you mean that they are watching that person or thing very carefully.

Managers of Europe's top clubs are keeping an eagle eye on the World Championships hoping to snap up new talent.

Phil's played first-class cricket for five years in England under the eagle eye of our umpires.

You must watch the builders with an eagle eye because some will cheat the minute you turn your back.

an eagle eye: 2

You can say that someone has **an eagle eye** when they are very good at finding or noticing things.

No antiques shop, market or junk shop escapes her eagle eye.

Mr Gould went to his hotel room, wrote a letter to Mr Smith, and came down to the foyer to post it. A few eagle eyes had seen the envelope; the word inevitably reached Mr Smith.

ear

bend someone's ear   ◄

If you say that someone is **bending** your ear, you mean that they keep talking to you about something, often in an annoying way.

He was fed up with people bending his ear about staying on at school or what he should do afterwards. He wanted to think it out himself.

You can't go on bending everyone's ear with this problem.

go in one ear and out the other

If you say that something **goes in one ear and out the other**, you mean that someone pays no attention to it, or forgets about it immediately.

I'd said it so many times before that it just went in one ear and out the other as far as he

was concerned.

The words went in one ear and out the other. They hardly registered.

grin from ear to ear
smile from ear to ear   ◄◄

If you say that someone **is grinning from ear to ear**, you are emphasizing that they look very happy. Verbs such as 'smile' and 'beam' can be used instead of 'grin'.

Brimming with confidence and grinning from ear to ear, China's leaders celebrated last night the end of the Asian Games, an event that has been as much a political as a sporting triumph.

McCarthy was beaming from ear to ear. His eyes were aglow. He absolutely radiated warmth and pride.

□ You can also say that someone has **a grin from ear to ear** or **a smile from ear to ear**.

I hadn't smiled so much in years. I had this grin from ear to ear.

□ You can use **ear-to-ear** before nouns such as 'grin' and 'smile'.

All around him were more ear-to-ear grins than I have seen before.

half an ear   ◄

If you listen to someone or something with **half an ear**, you do not give your full attention to them.

She is listening to the news of the siege with half an ear.

Shikanai worked harder than any other Japanese businessman to persuade the Western world that Japan was a mature and cultured nation whose views demanded serious attention. If the West gave him only half an ear most of the time, it was not for want of effort on his part.

have an ear for something   ◄

If you **have an ear for** something, such as music or language, you have the ability to learn quickly how it works or is structured, by listening to the various sounds and being able to reproduce them. Compare **have a tin ear for** something; see **tin**.

Allison has a great ear for dialogue and a remarkable ability to draw the readers into the tensions and conflicts of an intense and diverse family.

He had an ear for languages, which he enjoyed, and by this time he spoke five fluently.

have someone's ear ◄

If you **have the ear of** someone in a position of power, they pay great attention to what you think and say, and often follow your opinion on important issues.

He has been one of Italy's most influential figures, a man who is said to have had the ear of any Italian prime minister.

He has the President's ear, and it seems that his main sway may be over international environmental policy.

keep your ear to the ground
have your ear to the ground ◄

If you **keep** your **ear to the ground**, you make sure that you find out about the things that people are doing or saying. You can also say that you **have** your **ear to the ground**. These expressions are used mainly in British English.

Watch and learn. While you do this, keep your ear to the ground. Know who is coming, who is going: a new vacancy could be an opportunity for you.

I have a company which deals in arms. In that business, we have our ear very close to the ground.

Our man on the inside, with his ears to the ground around the clubs and venues of London, gives readers a sneak preview of some of the up-and-coming talent on the rock circuit.

lend an ear to someone ◄

If you **lend an ear to** someone or their problems, you listen to them carefully and sympathetically. Adjectives such as 'sympathetic', 'attentive', and 'serious' are often used in front of 'ear'.

They are always willing to lend an ear and offer what advice they can.

Proposals for preventing the next wages spiral before it starts are being studied by Labour – and are being lent a sympathetic ear in Downing Street, too.

out on your ear ◄

If you are **out on** your **ear**, you have been suddenly told to leave or dismissed from a course, job, or group. This is an informal expression.

I'd failed the first year exam in the History of Art. I had to pass the re-sit or I'd be out on my ear.

We never objected. Well, we couldn't, could

we? We'd have been out on our ears looking for another job if we had.

play it by ear ◄

If you **play** it **by ear**, you deal with things as they happen, rather than following a plan or previous arrangement.

'Where will we stay in Gloucestershire?' 'Oh, I guess a bed-and-breakfast place. We'll have to play it by ear.'

I can't give her the conclusions she wants. I don't know what will happen next. I'm playing it by ear.

'They could turn up tomorrow morning, couldn't they.' 'Well, we'll just have to play that one by ear as well.'

turn a deaf ear to something ◄

If you **turn a deaf ear to** something such as a request or argument, you refuse to consider it and do not pay any attention to it.

The Mayor of Paris, owner of two dogs, has long turned a deaf ear to Parisians who want tougher laws to protect the cleanliness of their pavements.

At the top are a bunch of people who have no idea what the real world is about, and when you try to tell them they turn a deaf ear.

ears

be all ears ◄

If you **are all ears**, you are ready and eager to listen to what someone is saying.

He is in the perfect position to speak out constructively to his audience, and certainly, this one was all ears.

'That's a large question, if not necessarily good. May I answer it frankly?' 'I'm all ears.'

between your ears ◄

If you say that someone has got nothing **between** their **ears**, you mean that they are stupid. If you say that someone has got a lot **between** their **ears**, you mean that they are intelligent. This expression is used in many other structures. It is usually used lightheartedly.

Some writers go to public school, then to Oxford or Cambridge, and end up in publishing or television and that's their life. It's a very class-limited existence; you end up with nothing between your ears.

He may be quick with his feet, but he is even quicker between the ears.

Haven't the people who run the banks anything between the ears besides dollar signs?

fall on deaf ears ◄◄◄

If something you say to someone **falls on deaf ears**, they take no notice of what you have said.

The charity suggests that if the human rights situation does not improve, foreign aid should be suspended. But privately, they admit that this appeal is likely to fall on deaf ears.

The mayor spoke privately to Gibson yesterday and asked him to resign, but said that his plea fell on deaf ears.

have something coming out of your ears ◄

If you say that you **have** something **coming out of** your **ears**, you are emphasizing that you have a great amount of it, often so much that you do not want any more.

I absolutely despise football. I've had football coming out of my ears. Everyone who wants to talk to me is talking about football. I can't get away from it.

Champagne is coming out of everybody's ears, the market is over-supplied.

I ate so much baked aubergine with ham, cheese, and tomatoes it almost came out of my ears.

have steam coming out of your ears

If you **have steam coming out of** your **ears**, you are very angry or irritated about something.

Not that Labour's front-benchers quite see it that way; indeed, steam comes out of their ears at the suggestion.

pin back your ears: 1

If you **pin back** your **ears**, you listen carefully to what someone is saying. This is an old-fashioned expression, which is used in British English.

Right, pin back your ears and listen.

The men ate a hearty breakfast while they discussed the dead man. Mrs Mason listened with both ears pinned back, but kept busy at her stove and sink.

pin someone's ears back: 2

If you **pin** someone's **ears back**, you tell them off for having done something wrong. This expression is used in American English.

Charles Drake of the Child Support Collection Association doesn't shy away from contacting a grandparent. 'Oh, absolutely. If the absent parent fails to cooperate, that's one of the first places I'm going to go to. I've had some grandparents pin their 40-year-old son's ears back.'

pin back your ears: 3

In sport, if someone **pins back** their **ears**, they run very quickly in an attempt to score and help their team win. This expression is used mainly in British English.

The Newport back division dropped the ball 30 metres out and Hughes pinned back his ears and raced to the line.

prick up your ears ◄

If someone **pricks up** their **ears**, they start listening eagerly, because they suddenly hear an interesting sound or piece of information.

She stopped talking to prick up her ears – and Kenworthy had heard the same sound.

Ears pricked up this week when Jesse Jackson, who four years ago won more votes as a candidate for the White House than any black politician in US history, sent a clear signal that he would run again next year.

someone's ears are burning

If you have a conversation about someone who is not present and then you meet them, you can ask them if their **ears were burning** in order to let them know that you were talking about them.

He decided to give Chris a call as promised. 'Dave! Talk about coincidence! Were your ears burning?' 'No, why?' 'I was just wondering if I could justify getting in touch with you.'

Pamela said 'He's been in my mind in recent weeks.' 'I must ask him if his ears have been burning,' the man said, 'I'm sure he'd be flattered.'

up to your ears ◄

If you say that you are **up to** your **ears** in work or in an unpleasant situation, you mean that you are very busy with it or are deeply involved in it.

'Why don't you come with me? It will do you good to get away from all this boring stuff for an evening.' He looked down at his desk and shook his head. 'I can't. I'm up to my ears in reports.'

He told her openly he had only married her for her money. It seems he is in debt up to the ears.

wet behind the ears ◄

If you say that someone is **wet behind the ears**, you mean that they are new to a situation and are therefore inexperienced or naive.

Hawking was a research student, still wet behind the ears by scientific standards.

Terry, it turned out, was just out of university, well-groomed but amiable, with a shapely haircut of medium length that failed to hide the fact that he was wet behind the ears.

□ You can also use **wet-behind-the-ears** before a noun.

The song is all about how he felt as a small-town, wet-behind-the-ears kid coming to LA for the first time.

earth

come down to earth
come down to earth with a bump
bring someone back to earth ◄◄◄

If you **come down to earth** or are **brought down to earth**, you have to face the reality of everyday life after a period of great excitement. You can also say that someone **comes back to earth** or is **brought back to earth**.

I was thrilled by the mountains and the

snow, by the magically fresh air, and then quickly came down to earth and started to spend money in the shops.

Jenny was quickly brought down to earth when she tried to claim benefit and was refused because she was a married woman.

When something good does happen, it's important that it is celebrated. Next day something will happen to bring you back to earth.

☐ You can say that you **have come down to earth with a bump** or **been brought down to earth with a bump**. Nouns such as 'bang', 'thump', and 'thud' can be used instead of 'bump'.

She was a household name, swanning around in fine clothes and an Italian sports car. She thought the whole world would sit up and take notice when she came to Britain. She came down to earth with a bump.

Circumstances beyond their control could yet bring them down to earth with a bang.

down to earth ◄◄◄

If you say that someone is **down to earth**, you approve of them because they are very realistic and practical.

They think she's too glamorous and won't want to speak to them. But that's just not Michelle at all. She's very friendly and very down to earth.

He is blunt, outspoken, practical and down to earth.

☐ You can use **down-to-earth** before a noun.

Everyone liked her down-to-earth approach to life.

They came across as natural, down-to-earth people, just as they do on TV.

go to earth

If you **go to earth**, you hide from someone or something. This expression is used in British English. **Go to ground** means the same.

The girl who had supplied the gun and plastic explosive device stayed put for a couple of weeks before she, too, went to earth.

promise the earth

If someone **promises the earth**, they promise to give people things that they cannot in fact possibly give them.

One voter summed up the mood: 'Politicians have lost credibility,' he complained, 'they promise the earth and don't deliver.'

In the past there have been numerous futuristic designs of planes and supersonic transports that promised the earth but got no further than the drawing-board.

run someone to earth

If you **run** someone or something **to earth**, you find them after a long search. This expression is used in British English. **Run to ground** means the same.

I must admit I thought I had run my man to earth, for although a great many people live there now, there could not be many that would match my description.

easier

easier said than done ◄◄◄

If you say that something is **easier said than done**, you mean that although it sounds like a good idea in theory, you think it would be difficult to actually do it.

'If you're not happy with yourself, then change.' Easier said than done, Alex thought.

The alternative option is to scrap the unwanted machines, and use the metal for some other purpose. But this, too, is easier said than done.

easy

easy as pie
easy as ABC ◄

If you say that something is **easy as pie** or **easy as ABC**, you are emphasizing that it is very easy to do.

Dave could not make head or tail of this, but Michael understood at once. 'What is the solution?' 'Why, that's easy as pie,' he said as the rest of us scratched our heads.

With our guide, planning your US fly-drive holiday will be as easy as ABC.

☐ **ABC** is pronounced 'a b c', as if you are spelling it out.

easy come, easy go

People say **easy come, easy go** to indicate that the thing they are talking about, for example earning money, does not need a lot of effort and is therefore not worth worrying about.

My attitude to money is easy come, easy go. That is to say, I earn a lot, but I also give quite a lot away in different ways.

I'm only used to getting a bit of praise from the local papers so all this national stuff is a big surprise. But I'm easy come, easy go, and it doesn't affect me.

go easy on someone: 1 ◄

If you tell someone to **go easy on** another person, you are telling them not to punish or treat that person severely.

Go easy on her, Michael. She might be in some sort of trouble.

They had to go easy on him because he was only thirteen and it was a first offense on top of that.

go easy on something: 2 ◄

If you tell someone to **go easy on** something, you are warning them not to have or use too much of it, because you think that it is bad for them.

Small meals at regular times are important. Go easy on the salt. Don't add extra sugar.

More of us than ever are going easy on the sun.

I made a mental note to go easy on the whisky before bedtime!

take it easy: 1
take things easy ◄◄◄

If you tell someone to **take it easy**, you are telling them to relax and not to worry, hurry, or do anything that needs a lot of energy. In British English, you can also tell someone to **take things easy**.

Take it easy, Bob. I'll explain everything.

The seven astronauts aboard the space shuttle Columbia are taking it easy today, following six full days of medical research.

There's about a five mile queue at present so take it easy on the roads today.

She has been advised to take things easy but is not thought to have been confined to bed.

take it easy: 2

In American English, **take it easy** is used as an informal way of saying 'goodbye'.

'Thanks. See you later.' 'Take it easy. Don't do anything I wouldn't do.'

ebb

at a low ebb
at your lowest ebb ◄◄◄

If someone or something is **at a low ebb**, they are very depressed or unsuccessful. You can also say that they are **at their lowest ebb**.

When I have been at a low ebb I have found the friendship and Christian love of my fellow churchgoers to be a great strength.

The increasingly bitter division within the Conservative Party over Hong Kong comes as the party's fortunes are at a low ebb.

It happened midway through the first summer of my suspension, when I was mentally and physically at my lowest ebb.

echo

cheer someone to the echo

If someone **is cheered to the echo**, they are loudly applauded for a long time. This is a fairly old-fashioned expression, which is used in British English.

Supporters turned out in their thousands to watch some of the best squash played in their country. They cheered Jansher's victory to the echo.

They cheered him to the echo, as they did every member of the cast.

eclipse

in eclipse

If something is **in eclipse**, it is much less successful and important than it used to be. This is a fairly formal expression.

He'd spent two decades nurtured by a system that, even in eclipse, seemed preferable to the uncertain alternatives.

Even when her career was temporarily in eclipse she 'had enough money to swing it'.

edge

the cutting edge: 1 ◄◄◄

To be at or on **the cutting edge** of a particular field of activity means to be involved in its most important, exciting, or advanced developments.

It is unrealistic for any designer to expect to be at the cutting edge of the fashion industry for anything longer than 15 years.

President Clinton unveiled a programme intended to keep the United States on the cutting edge of change.

This is hardly the cutting edge of theological debate.

□ You can use **cutting-edge** before a noun referring to people or activities that are at the cutting edge.

These were the men and women doing the cutting-edge research.

a cutting edge: 2 ◄

If someone or something gives you a **cutting edge**, they provide you with the ability to be more successful than your opponents.

We need a cutting edge and hopefully they can provide it.

With five goals so far Jurgen Klinsmann has given a cutting edge to what has so far looked a distinctly blunt German team.

lose your edge ◄◄

If someone or something **loses** their **edge**, they no longer have all the advantages and special skills or talents that they used to have.

When countries lose their competitive edge, manufacturing is hit hardest because it is the part of the economy most vulnerable to international competition.

Its staff disagrees with criticisms that their magazine is out of date or has lost its edge.

on edge ◄◄◄

If someone is **on edge**, they are nervous, anxious, and unable to relax.

She was on edge and wouldn't talk about it. I've been married and I recognized the signs. She was upset and I was the cause.

Brenda had every right to be on edge. Ever since I had left on the Saturday morning, she had been bombarded with telephone calls.

I was pathetic. I was a bit on edge at the start but that's no excuse for playing as badly as that.

on the edge of your seat
on the edge of your chair ◄

If something keeps you **on the edge of** your seat, it keeps you very interested and eager to know what happens next. In American English, you can also say that something keeps you **on the edge of** your **chair**. You use these expressions especially when talking about things such as plays, films, or books.

Based on the Stephen King book, the film has great special effects and the kind of story that keeps you on the edge of your seat throughout.

Saturday night's final had the spectators on the edge of their seats.

He seemed quite composed, but, obviously, nervous, kind of sitting on the edge of his chair and not knowing what to expect.

□ You can use **edge-of-the-seat** before a noun to say that the thing you are talking about has that effect on people.

It's a real action-packed edge-of-the-seat thriller about a cop on the trail of the only man who can prove his innocence in a murder rap.

take the edge off something ◄◄

If something **takes the edge off** a situation, especially an unpleasant one, it weakens its effect, intensity, or unpleasantness.

My head never seemed to clear completely, and the painkillers only took the edge off the pain.

If I don't feel happy, at least I'll pretend to be, and maybe that will take the edge off my misery.

edges

fray at the edges ◄

If you say that something or someone is **fraying at the edges** or is **fraying around the edges**, you mean that they are becoming weaker or less certain or stable, and that they are gradually being damaged or destroyed.

The government's army has begun to fray at the edges.

Married couples whose marriage is getting a little frayed around the edges go on second honeymoons, or move house, or have another child, all of which inject some new vigour into their joint life.

rough edges: 1 ◄

If you say that a person has **rough edges**, you mean that there are small faults in their behaviour towards other people. You use this expression when you generally approve of the person you are talking about.

He had the reputation of sometimes taking himself a little seriously. Those rough edges have long since worn off.

The school has a reputation for smoothing the rough edges of its pupils and no doubt they

will encourage Harry to assume a sense of humility.

□ You can also talk about a **rough-edged** person.

He is demanding and sometimes strident, exactly the sort of rough-edged entrepreneur who doesn't fit into a bureaucracy such as Stanford's.

rough edges: 2 ◄

If you say that a performance or piece of entertainment has **rough edges**, you mean that it is not technically perfect, although you generally approve of it.

The show, despite some rough edges, was an instant success.

Weller's voice may have a few rough edges but his fans say that's part of the attraction.

Kovacic appeared to be one of those players for whom all of Mozart's rough edges must be smoothed off.

□ You can also talk about a **rough-edged** performer, performance, or piece of entertainment.

She was untutored, rough-edged, but the audiences adored her.

Their rough-edged guitar music has become a regular fixture on the college circuit.

egg

egg on your face
egg all over your face ◄◄

If you get **egg on** your **face**, you feel embarrassed or humiliated by something you have done or said. You can also say that you get **egg all over** your **face**.

Steve didn't expect to win. He just didn't want to get egg on his face.

Wimpey, which builds up to 10,000 homes in a good year, sticks to what its customers want. 'Try anything new and we run the risk of ending up with egg on our face.'

I started showing off, talking indiscreetly. When I asked the host 'When does this show start?' he said 'When you shut your mouth', which got a huge laugh and left me with egg all over the face.

lay an egg

If something **lays an egg**, it fails because people are not interested in it or do not want it. This expression is used in American English.

Independent studies showed the ad laid an egg.

That 5.2 percent drop in revenues was fairly modest, considering that the stock market laid an egg in the interim.

eggs

put all your eggs in one basket ◄◄

If you say that someone is **putting all** their

eggs in one basket, you are pointing out that they are putting all their efforts or resources into one course of action and this means that they will have no alternatives left if it fails.

It was not as though the banks were unaware of the dangers of putting all their eggs in one basket. Just a few years before, they had lost billions on loans to the Third World.

Don't put your eggs in one basket; study hard at school and always keep an alternative job in mind.

☐ This expression is often varied.

How could the BBC have put so many eggs in one basket? Why didn't they test the show with a pilot episode or a limited-run series?

Countries such as Puerto Rico and Mexico have put their development eggs in the tourism basket, spending millions of dollars from public funds to build the sorts of facilities that foreign tourists demand.

eggshells

walk on eggshells
walk on eggs ◀

If you **are walking on eggshells** or **are walking on eggs**, you are very careful about what you say or do because you do not want to upset or offend someone, even though you think they are being over-sensitive. The verb 'tread' is sometimes used instead of 'walk'.

Healthy or sick, good days or bad, I felt I was always walking on eggshells around him.

Mike says, 'Living with you is like treading on eggs,' and I believe that living with someone like me must put an enormous strain on any second loving husband of a once battered wife.

elbow

elbow grease ◀

You can use **elbow grease** to refer to the energy and strength you need for doing physical work such as cleaning or polishing something.

Plenty of elbow grease soon moves all the dirt.

It took a considerable amount of polish and elbow grease before the brass shone like new.

elbow room: 1 ◀

If someone gives you **elbow room**, they give you the freedom to do what you need or want to do in a particular situation.

His overall message to governors, though, was that he intends to give them more elbow room to encourage innovation at the state level.

The republics are asserting their autonomy and making their own elbow-room, often in direct defiance of the president's centralising decrees.

elbow room: 2

If you have enough **elbow room**, you have enough space to move freely or feel comfortable, without feeling crowded or cramped.

There was not much elbow room in the cockpit.

not know your arse from your elbow
not know your ass from your elbow

If you say that someone **doesn't know** their **arse from** their **elbow** or **doesn't know** their **ass from** their **elbow**, you are saying in a very rude way that they have no common sense or that they are ignorant and stupid. These are very informal expressions, which many people find offensive. The form with 'arse' is used in British English and the form with 'ass' is used mainly in American English.

He's just a boy. A big, enthusiastic kid without an ounce of subtlety in him, who doesn't know his arse from his elbow.

☐ Sometimes people use this expression in a very humorous way, by replacing 'arse', 'ass', or 'elbow' with a different word.

Must we be governed by people who don't know their arias from their elbow?

Look, Preston Sturges, who doesn't know his ass from a hot rock, is making a picture. You have to stay with him all the time.

elbows

rub elbows with someone ◀

If you **rub elbows with** someone important or famous, you associate with them for a while. This expression is used mainly in American English; the usual British expression is **rub shoulders with** someone.

At the famous parties that he threw several times a month in his Park Avenue penthouse, where writers, artists, and celebrities rubbed elbows with the ultra-rich and the socially élite, his shyness was legendary.

He was a disc jockey at Studio 54, Kamikaze, Limelight and other trendy Manhattan clubs. In the 10 years prior to that job, he rubbed elbows with dozens of political super-celebrities, including Richard Nixon, Imelda Marcos, and Gerald Ford.

element

in your element
out of your element ◀◀◀

If you say that someone is **in** their **element**, you mean that they are doing something that they enjoy or do well.

'The sale will now commence. We will proceed in steps of two hundred thousand,' declared Bunbury, who was in his element.

My stepmother was in her element, organizing everything.

☐ You can say that someone is **out of** their

element when they are doing something that they do not enjoy or do not do well.

He stayed in the trade eight years, but was bored by the work and felt out of his element.

As I hadn't done much cooking recently I felt a bit out of my element in the kitchen.

elephant

a white elephant ◄◄

If you describe something such as a new building, plan, or project as **a white elephant**, you mean that it is a waste of money and completely useless.

Will the complex, constructed at some expense but never used, be regarded as a monumental folly, a great white elephant?

I don't see any train line turning into a white elephant unless we made some stupid decision to build a train line in some remote rural location where it wasn't needed in the first place.

embarrassment

an embarrassment of riches ◄

If someone has **an embarrassment of riches**, they have so many good things that these things have become a problem. This is a literary expression.

Football fans have an embarrassment of riches to choose from a week today when, for the first time in British television history, three matches will be screened live simultaneously.

empty

run on empty: 1

If a person or organization **is running on empty**, they are no longer as exciting or successful as they once were because they have run out of new ideas or resources.

The band's 1990 Reading appearance is widely agreed to be their finest two hours. Certainly, events after this suggest a band running on empty, delaying the inevitable.

A lot of societies are running on empty – muddling through without any clear sense of direction.

run on empty: 2

If you **are running on empty**, you feel tired, confused, and unable to think or work properly because you have not eaten for a long time.

If you don't feed your body daily nutrients you are running on empty – something you can only do for a short time.

Running on empty increases the stickiness of blood and raises the chance of clotting, say American researchers.

□ If a vehicle **is running on empty**, it has almost no fuel in its tank.

end

at a loose end
at loose ends ◄

If you are **at a loose end** or **at loose ends**, you have some spare time and you feel rather bored because you do not have anything particular to do. 'At a loose end' is used in British English and 'at loose ends' is used in American English. Compare **loose ends**; see **ends**.

After my return home I was at a loose end. I read the typescript over and over until I knew it by heart.

I assume you are both at a loose end after a rather dull day.

Brenda had agreed to see her at four-thirty, which left Mrs. Dambar at loose ends for two and a half hours.

come to a sticky end
come to a bad end ◄

If someone **comes to a sticky end** or **comes to a bad end**, they die in an unpleasant or violent way.

Defeated seven years later by a punitive expedition under Germanicus, Arminius also came to a sticky end, murdered by his own troops.

Hassan comes to a bad end, but so does almost everyone else in the book.

a dead end: 1 ◄◄◄

If a plan, project, or course of action leads to **a dead end**, there is no future in it and it will never develop any further.

There has never been a more successful economic policy than the one Japan has followed since 1960. But it is nearing a dead end.

The investigations into the sensational murder of former Prime Minister Rajiv Gandhi seem to have reached a dead end.

dead-end: 2 ◄◄◄

You can use **dead-end** to describe a job or situation when you dislike it or are scornful of it because you think it is boring and will never lead to anything more interesting or successful.

He was a dull, nondescript man in a dull, dead-end job.

Counseling a student in this dead-end situation is like trying to get a condemned man to plan for the future.

end it all ◄

If someone **ends it all**, they kill themselves.

I desperately wanted to end it all, but I had an adorable little boy who was totally dependent upon me.

Thoughts about ending it all are common among bewildered undergraduates.

the end of the road: 1
the end of the line ◄◄◄

If someone or something is at **the end of the road** or **the end of the line**, they are at a point where they can no longer continue or survive in a situation.

The administration realises now that they've come to the end of the road of their policy.

For Mr Kaparti it's the end of the road. The former political boss of the Army now retires, to spend his days fishing and playing with his grandchildren in the new Hungary.

Failure to beat Poland at Wembley in the next match almost certainly will spell the end of the line for the England manager.

the end of the road: 2
the end of the line ◄◄

If you refer to **the end of the road** or **the end of the line**, you are referring to what will eventually happen as a result of someone's actions.

There are many of us who tell kids who don't want to go to school that if drugs don't kill them, there's only jail at the end of the road.

We believe the sums do not add up. At the end of the line there will be bankruptcy for some.

go off the deep end: 1 ◄

If you say that someone **has gone off the deep end**, you mean that they have gone mad, or that their behaviour has become strange or extreme. This expression is used mainly in American English.

Ray gives a chilling performance as the seemingly nice cop who goes off the deep end and terrorises a couple he once rescued from villainy.

At first they thought that I'd gone off the deep end and had lost my mind.

His Aunt Ellen raised him after his mother went off the deep end.

go off the deep end: 2

If someone **goes off the deep end**, they become very angry. This expression is used in British English.

I thought that the real trouble would begin when my father got home. In fact, he didn't go off the deep end at all. He just said it wasn't fair to make my mother worry like that.

in at the deep end ◄◄

If you jump **in at the deep end** or are thrown **in at the deep end**, you start by doing the most difficult part of a job or task, before you have tried to do the easier parts or without any preparation.

It takes most TV hosts years to work up to live television, but Sunday Mail columnist Susan Hocking is jumping straight in the deep end when she anchors the evening news next week.

I started out with little self-confidence and built it up in the job. I believe you gain confidence by being thrown in at the deep end. Then there's no way out. You have to get on with it and produce the goods.

keep your end up
hold your end up ◄

If you **keep** your **end up** or **hold** your **end up** in a particular situation, you do what you have said you will do or what you are expected to do. You can also say that you **hold up** your **end of** something or **keep up** your **end of** something.

But David, despite being uncharacteristically nervous, holds his end up brilliantly, making his points and still managing to play it for laughs.

The pure fact of the matter is that we signed a contract and we've worked hard to keep up our end, and they must keep up their end.

on the wrong end of something ◄

If you **are on the wrong end of** an activity or situation, you are unsuccessful in it or suffer because of it. For example, if you **are on the wrong end of** a game, you lose it.

This is a year for change, that's clear. And we're on the wrong end of change this year.

A goal from Shaun Goater, a Bermudan international, left Howard Kendall's team on the wrong end of a 1-0 scoreline.

After last week's extraordinary events, they are once again on the wrong end of a publicity campaign.

the sharp end ◄◄◄

If someone is at **the sharp end** of an activity or type of work, they are the people who are actually involved in it and so know about the reality of the situation. This expression is used mainly in British English.

These men are at the sharp end of law enforcement and when a man is waving a gun, they have to act decisively to protect the public and colleagues.

We don't pretend to be at the sharp end of fashion. But we do try to produce items that are the basics of a stylish wardrobe.

The young are at the sharp end of violent changes now shaking America to its core.

to the bitter end ◄◄

If you do something **to the bitter end**, you are determined to continue doing it and finish it, even though it is becoming increasingly difficult.

Despite another crushing defeat, he is determined to see the job through to the bitter end.

They must carry on their battle to the bitter end not only to get a fair deal for themselves, but for the sake of all British business.

ends

loose ends ◄◄◄

If there are **loose ends** in something, small details or parts of it have not yet been sorted out satisfactorily. Compare **at loose ends**; see **end**.

She spent the rest of the afternoon tying up loose ends: editing footage for a feature on California Cuisine, making phone calls, answering memos that had languished on her desk for weeks.

The overall impact of the story is weakened by too many loose ends being left inadequately resolved.

make ends meet ◄◄◄

If you find it difficult to **make ends meet**, you find it difficult to pay for the things you need in life, because you have very little money.

Many people are struggling to make ends meet because wages are failing to keep pace with rising prices under the government's economic reform programme.

He says he has trouble making ends meet because he can't find work and his government check is barely enough to cover the rent.

play both ends against the middle

If someone **plays both ends against the middle**, they pretend to support or favour two opposing people or ideas in order to gain an advantage, or to try to get all the benefits that they can from a situation. You usually use this expression to show that you disapprove of this behaviour.

She plays both ends against the middle by deciding to marry the boy and still sleep with the man.

Englishman

an Englishman's home is his castle ◄

When people say **'an Englishman's home is his castle'**, they are referring to the belief that people have the right to do what they want in their own home, and that other people or the state have no right to interfere in people's private lives. This expression is used in British English.

An Englishman's home is his castle, and only recently courts have upheld the right of Englishmen to act in self-defence.

If an Englishman's home is his castle, his garden is his private estate.

☐ Journalists often vary this expression, for example by saying that an Englishman's home is a particular thing.

Far from being his castle, an Englishman's home is rapidly becoming a financial millstone.

Rightly or wrongly, and probably wrongly, an Englishman's home will remain his best investment.

error

the error of your ways ◄◄

If someone sees **the error of** their **ways**, they realize or admit that they have made a mistake or behaved badly.

I wanted an opportunity to talk some sense into him and try to make him see the error of his ways.

It took him a long time, he says, to realise the error of his ways.

The court is making the punishment fit the crime. If they are shown the error of their ways, it's better than locking them up.

even

don't get mad, get even

If someone says **'don't get mad, get even'**, they mean that if someone harms you, you should not waste your energy on being angry, but concentrate on harming them in return. Compare **get even**.

It's a case of don't get mad, get even. Mark Leavis wasn't too happy after Judge Carol Shapiro didn't give him what he wanted in his divorce. So a few hours after the ruling, the Seattle lawyer filed to run against the judge in her bid for a second term on the bench.

get even ◄◄◄

If you **get even** with someone who has hurt or insulted you, you get your revenge on them. Compare **don't get mad, get even**.

He is so incensed by what he considers shabby treatment that he's determined to get even.

He'd leapt at this chance to get even with the scum who had killed his sister.

He hasn't kept his side of their agreement, and she means to get even with him.

evil

put off the evil day

In British English, if you say that someone **is putting off the evil day**, you mean that they have to do something unpleasant but they are trying to avoid doing it for as long as possible. This expression is very variable.

Some people find it helps to cut down on the number of cigarettes they smoke before they actually give up. But the danger of doing this is that you can simply go on putting off the evil day and eventually find yourself smoking as much as ever.

The government has been putting off the evil hour about introducing the tough measures required to save Bulgaria's shattered economy.

evils

the lesser of two evils
the lesser evil ◄◄

If you have to choose between two bad

things, you can refer to the one which is less bad as **the lesser of two evils** or **the lesser evil**.

Should she choose the isolation of life on the streets or the constant abuse of her father? In the end it seemed the street was the lesser of two evils.

In a continent where economic successes are rare, authoritarianism may seem a lesser evil than abject poverty.

☐ People occasionally vary this phrase to refer to a choice between more than two bad things.

At the Whitechapel, the option of a temporary closure – with the possibility of hiring the gallery out – represented the lesser of several evils.

This has been an exercise in choosing between lesser evils to limit the damage such cuts inevitably cause.

exception

the exception that proves the rule ◄

If you are making a general statement and you say that something is **the exception that proves the rule**, you mean that although it seems to contradict your statement, in most other cases your statement will be true. People sometimes use this expression to avoid having to justify their statement in detail.

Towers should generally be arranged in clusters, but the Post Office Tower was the exception that proved the rule – it needs to stand alone so that its signals are not interrupted.

I have this theory that, apart from one or two exceptions that prove the rule, very attractive men do not fall in love.

expense

at someone's expense ◄◄◄

If someone laughs or makes a joke **at** your **expense**, they do it by making you seem foolish.

They can make him believe anything and are always ready to get a cheap laugh at his expense.

Being fat and bald has ruined my life. I'll never forget the people who made remarks at my expense.

Members of the studio audience, both male and female, love hearing women take the mickey out of men. But should the men retaliate and make jokes at the expense of the women, boos and jeers are guaranteed.

eye

cast an eye on something ◄

If you **cast an eye on** something, you examine it carefully and give your opinion about it. Adjectives such as 'cold' or 'critical' are often used before 'eye' to describe the way in which you examine something.

The Independent also casts an eye on the start of the Conservative Party conference in Bournemouth today.

Liz, the psychotherapist, appears on a television panel, provoking controversy merely by casting a cool eye on the hot topic of child abuse.

'Before the elections I was pessimistic,' says Jassem Saddoun, a leading economist who casts a critical eye on domestic affairs.

cast your eye over something
run your eye over something ◄◄◄

If you **cast** your **eye** or **run** your **eye** over something, you look at, consider, or read it quickly.

He cast his eyes over the bookcases. She had obviously been an avid reader.

Mr Barnes said the company often cast its eyes over projects and was always looking at new prospects.

Leonard ran his eye along the bottom of the chart to the exact month, day and time of day she had given.

cast your eyes on something
cast your eye on something ◄

If someone **casts** their **eyes on** something or someone, they want to have or possess them. You can also say that they **cast** their **eye on** them.

When Hitler cast his eyes on Czechoslovakia, Russia and France were prepared to go to war to defend that country.

To our amazement, another developer has cast greedy eyes on the field next door.

Air France is casting an acquisitive eye on some of the shares of domestic Air Inter that it doesn't already own.

catch someone's eye
catch the eye ◄◄◄

If something or someone **catches** your **eye** or **catches the eye**, you notice them because they are very striking, vivid, or remarkable.

When I walked into the coffee shop, a flower arrangement caught my eye.

She made sure she caught the eye of 49-year-old Frank Sinatra on the set one day and promptly flew on his jet to Palm Springs for the weekend.

A motion must have caught my mother's eye; she rose and moved to the windows, and Father and I followed.

He turned the page. The picture caught his eye instantly.

☐ You can also say that something is **eye-catching** when it is very striking, vivid, or remarkable.

My mother and my sister love stylish, eye-catching designer hats but cannot afford to buy them.

There's an eye-catching headline on the front page of the Sunday Times.

an eye for an eye
an eye for an eye, a tooth for a tooth

◄◄

People use **an eye for an eye** to refer to a system of justice where the punishment for a crime is either the same as the crime or equivalent to it.

They should bring back the death penalty. A lot of people are getting away with things like this, thinking 'So what, they cannot kill me'. I believe in an eye for an eye.

☐ You can use **an eye for an eye** before a noun.

The solution to our problems is about feeling our divisions and our differences and about building together, not the eye for an eye doctrine which is now being pursued.

☐ People sometimes say **'an eye for an eye, a tooth for a tooth'** with the same meaning.

It is practically impossible to remain rational and forgiving when reading of child abuse, rape and other terrible, unlawful acts. The immediate response is 'An eye for an eye, a tooth for a tooth'.

the eye of the storm ◄

If you are in **the eye of the storm**, you are deeply involved in a difficult or controversial situation which affects or interests a lot of people.

He was often in the eye of the storm of congressional debates related to U.S. troop withdrawals from Vietnam.

On a national level, there is an emergency in child abuse neglect across the country. California and Los Angeles County, in particular, seem to be at the eye of the storm.

get your eye in

If you **get** your **eye in** when you are doing a particular thing, you become more skilful or experienced in it, because you have been practising it or doing it for a long time. This expression is used in British English.

She bought the bulk of the chairs from the salerooms. She had this marvellous knack for wheeling and dealing. I helped her get her eye in, but the instinct was there.

We're going to shoot some clay pigeons later. Sort of getting our eye in for the grouse.

give someone a black eye

If you **give** someone **a black eye**, you punish them severely for something they have done, but without causing them permanent harm.

Whenever the Liberal Democratic Party gets too cocky or corrupt, voters tend to give it a black eye.

Becoming a republic is not about insulting the British or about Irish desires to 'give Brit-

ain a black eye'. It is about recognising Australia's political, social and economic reality.

☐ **Black eye** is more commonly used to refer to a dark-coloured bruise around a person's eye.

a gleam in your eye ◄

If you say that a plan or project is only **a gleam in** someone's **eye** at present, you mean that it is being planned or considered, but has not yet been properly started. You can replace 'gleam' with 'glint' or 'twinkle'.

The space-launched weapons that Mr Reagan wanted are still only a gleam in a few hopeful eyes.

The European central bank is still no more than a glint in its creators' eyes.

There are rumours of plans to upgrade Perugia's airport to receive international flights. At present, however, they seem to be no more than a twinkle in a developer's eye.

in the public eye
out of the public eye ◄◄◄

If someone is **in the public eye**, many people know who they are and are aware of what they are doing, because they are famous or because they are often mentioned on television or in the newspapers.

Increasingly, top executives, senior politicians and many other prominent people in the public eye are voicing concern about the effects of their lifestyle on their family life.

With the state of the British motor industry at the moment we need all the help we can get. The princess is very much in the public eye and anything she can do to promote UK products will be welcome.

No stunt is too outrageous, no pose too shocking so long as it keeps her in the public eye.

☐ If something such as an issue is **in the public eye**, people are aware of it and are discussing it.

They have won a great victory in turning public opinion and putting Aids in the public eye in such a positive way.

☐ You can say that someone **is out of the public eye** if they are normally in the news but are temporarily out of it.

Boris Yeltsin has been out of the public eye for two weeks, recuperating on the Black Sea from heart trouble.

keep your eye on the ball

If you say that someone **keeps** their **eye on the ball**, you mean that they continue to pay close attention to what they are doing. Compare **take** your **eye off the ball**.

She won widespread praise for her innovation, her tough negotiating skills and her ability to keep things moving, keep her eye on the ball.

look someone in the eye
look someone in the eyes ◄◄◄

If you **look** someone **in the eye** or **look** them **in the eyes**, you look at them directly in order to convince them that what you are saying is true, even though you may be lying. **Look** someone **in the face** means the same.

He looked me straight in the eye and said 'Paul, I will never lie to you.'

You can't look me in the eye and tell me I didn't play a good match out there.

'Now look me straight in the eyes,' Stephen continued. 'If I find you are lying, I shall never speak to you again.'

☐ If you **cannot look** someone **in the eye**, you are too ashamed or embarrassed by something that you have done to look at them directly.

He was terribly shy. He shuffled around staring at the ground and stumbling over mumbled words. He couldn't look me in the eye.

'What's your name?' she asked him softly. 'Damon Cross,' he answered, but he could not look her in the eye. 'Why didn't you tell me this before?' 'I was afraid to, and I was ashamed.'

the naked eye ◄◄◄

If something is big enough or bright enough to be seen with **the naked eye**, you can see it without the help of equipment such as a telescope or microscope.

These pests are often more green than red, are just visible to the naked eye and feed mainly under the leaves and on the younger growths.

Enough light gets through space for us to see thousands of stars with the naked eye, and millions with an optical telescope.

There could be some internal problem with the tires that isn't visible to the naked eye.

not bat an eye: 1

If you say that someone does something and nobody **bats an eye**, you mean that nobody seems to be shocked or offended by it, and that this is surprising. This expression is used mainly in American English; the usual British expression is **not bat an eyelid**.

When the company duly revealed that its profits for 1990 had fallen 43 per cent from a year earlier, the markets barely batted an eye.

People don't bat an eye when they pay 16 dollars a pound for cheese. They walk in and peel off 50 dollar bills like it's change.

You didn't bat your eye when I told you that your mother was dead.

not bat an eye: 2

If you say that someone does something **without batting an eye**, you are expressing your surprise that they are not nervous or worried about it. This expression is used mainly in American English; the usual British expression is **not bat an eyelid**.

Would you believe he ordered them to fill half a tin mug with that stuff and guzzled it without batting an eye, as if it was water?

one in the eye for someone

If you say that something you do is **one in the eye for** someone, you mean that it will annoy them. This expression is used in British English.

I want to show Arsenal they were wrong to let me go. Every goal I score now is one in the eye for them.

His Nobel prize will be seen in Mexico as one in the eye for the novelist, Carlos Fuentes, who is regarded as his great left-wing rival.

see eye to eye with someone ◄◄◄

If you do not **see eye to eye** with someone, you do not agree with them about something.

The Prime Minister did not see eye to eye with him on this issue.

She has a boyfriend, too, but they don't see eye to eye on much.

There were a number of points on which we did not see eye to eye completely.

☐ If you **see eye to eye** with someone, you agree with them completely.

We saw eye to eye on the essentials, and I'd even venture to say that we're now in perfect harmony.

spit in someone's eye

If you say that someone **spits in** your **eye**, you mean that they deliberately upset or annoy you.

Small businessmen, all typical Tory voters, have seen their companies destroyed by the recession. The minister for Trade and Industry spat in their eye yesterday when he said: 'I won't rescue bankrupt companies. I won't support the weak at the expense of the strong.'

take your eye off the ball ◄

If you say that someone **takes** their **eye off the ball**, you mean that they stop paying attention for a moment to something they are doing, and as a result they suffer some harm or things go wrong for them. Compare **keep** your **eye on the ball**.

His greatest disappointment must have been the coal dispute, which revealed that he had misjudged the mood of the public. He told friends later that the decision had been right, but he took his eye off the ball over the presentation.

Any reorganization is disruptive. It makes key management take their eye off the only ball that should ever be in play – the satisfaction of the customer.

there's more to something than meets the eye
there's less to something than meets the eye ◄◄

If you say that **there is more to** something or someone **than meets the eye**, you mean that they are more complicated or more involved than they appear to be at first.

Detective Superintendent Bill Scholes, who is leading the murder inquiry, said last night he believed Mr Urquhart had been the victim of a professional hit. Police were investigating the possibility of a drugs, arms, or cash laundering connection. 'There is a lot more to it than meets the eye,' he said.

'She was convinced there was more to your friendship than met the eye.' 'Well there isn't.'

☐ You can say that **there is less to** something or someone **than meets the eye** to mean that they are less complicated or less involved than they appear to be at first.

Though there's currently a construction boom in luxury apartments, there's much less to this than meets the eye. Since the war ended, little has been done to rebuild the country as a whole, and the economy is in ruins.

turn a blind eye to something ◄◄◄

If you **turn a blind eye to** something, you deliberately ignore it because you do not want to take any action over it, even though you know you should.

The authorities were turning a blind eye to human rights abuses.

Police usually turn a blind eye to topless sunbathing unless there are complaints.

She didn't act upon her suspicions. She chose to turn a blind eye to what she suspected was going on.

It is up to all of us to take notice when we hear these alarms. There are too many cases of people turning a blind eye when someone could be in difficulty.

with an eye for something
have an eye for something ◄◄◄

Someone **with an eye for** something is very skilful at dealing with that thing and has a good understanding of it. You can also say that they **have an eye for** something.

Mr Fromkin is a storyteller with an eye for detail and irony.

With his unerring eye for light, line and colour, Greenaway has mounted one of the most beautiful drawing exhibitions ever seen.

He has a good eye for companies that are about to become takeover targets.

would give your eye teeth for something ◄

If you say that you **would give** your **eye teeth** for something or **give** your **eye teeth** to do something, you are emphasizing that you

really want it and that you would do almost anything to get it.

He's the most exciting man I've ever worked with, and I'd give my eye teeth to do something with him again.

Is your son really up to the job or are you kidding yourself, because maybe you would have given your eye-teeth for such a chance at his age?

eyeball

eyeball to eyeball ◄

If you say that two people are **eyeball to eyeball**, you mean that they are disagreeing with each other, and may argue or fight as a result.

Miss Wynne sent everyone out and the two of us sat eyeball to eyeball. 'Why do you hate me?' she asked, quite without any apparent emotion.

The vision that informed these foreign-policy choices was of a world in which two superpowers were eyeball-to-eyeball, where small risks were justified in the name of staving off bigger risks.

☐ **Eyeball-to-eyeball** can also be used before a noun.

It was an immensely tough negotiation that led to eyeball-to-eyeball confrontations with union leaders.

eyeballs

up to the eyeballs: 1

If you say that someone is drugged **up to the eyeballs**, you mean that they have taken a lot of drugs which have strongly affected them.

Often you can tell that the women taking part are almost completely out of it – drugged up to the eyeballs.

We won't be able to speak to him today because he will be drugged up to the eyeballs. I don't even know the phone number of the hospital he's in.

up to the eyeballs: 2

If you say that someone is **up to the eyeballs** in an unpleasant situation, you mean that they are very deeply involved in it.

The one-time media tycoon is down on his luck, out of a job, and up to his eyeballs in debt.

The relationship didn't start for six months and didn't really take off for another six months after that. By the next year I was up to my eyeballs in it.

eyebrows

raise eyebrows ◄◄◄

If something that you do **raises eyebrows**, it surprises, shocks, or offends people.

The Princess of Wales has raised eyebrows

among older members of the British community in Cairo, as well as in Britain, by appearing in public with bare legs.

What she explains as the free manner of speech which would probably go down quite well in the United States has raised Canadian eyebrows.

President Clinton raised a few eyebrows when he chose Laura Tyson as the first woman to chair the Council of Economic Advisers.

☐ You can also say that what you do causes **raised eyebrows**.

Black has a recent history of shuffling loans between his two companies in a manner that provokes raised eyebrows in the City.

eyelid

not bat an eyelid: 1
not bat an eyelash   ◄◄

If you say that someone does something and nobody **bats an eyelid**, you mean that nobody seems to be shocked or offended by it, and that this is surprising. You can also say that nobody **bats an eyelash**. These expressions are used mainly in British English; the usual American expression is **not bat an eye**.

When it comes to naked women on the pages of a glossy magazine, no one seems to bat an eyelid.

I thought Sarah and David would be acutely embarrassed. But they didn't bat an eyelid.

This place could have burned to the ground, and he wouldn't have batted an eyelash.

not bat an eyelid: 2
not bat an eyelash

If you say that someone does something **without batting an eyelid**, you are expressing your surprise that they are not nervous or worried about it. You can also say that they **do not bat an eyelash**. These expressions are used mainly in British English; the usual American expression is **not bat an eye**.

Without batting an eyelid he launched into a set of instructions of the most breathtaking complexity.

Mr Yeltsin said the conspirators would have killed thousands of people without batting an eyelid.

eyes

all eyes are on someone   ◄◄◄

If **all eyes are on** someone or something, everyone is carefully watching that person or thing, often because they are expecting something to happen or develop. You can also say that **all eyes turn** or **focus on** someone or something.

All eyes will be on the new British Prime Minister to see whether he will take a more conciliatory approach to a united Europe than did his predecessor.

Harry swaggers around the tables, confidently aware that all eyes are on him.

It made me nervous to think that the moment we entered the restaurant for my birthday dinner, all eyes would be turned our way.

before your eyes
in front of your eyes   ◄◄◄

If you say that something happens **before your eyes** or **before** your **very eyes**, you mean that it happens directly in front of you, and that you cannot do anything to stop it or change it. You can also say it happens **in front of** your **eyes**.

With a wrenching crack the stone statue collapsed before my eyes and crumbled to pieces at the bottom of the fountain.

Marceline saw him falling apart before her very eyes and realized that something had to be done.

It was a particularly nasty crime, picking on a woman in distress. This pair are real cowards and the poor lady was left in tears. She saw her car driven off in front of her eyes.

can't take your eyes off someone
can't keep your eyes off someone   ◄◄◄

If you **can't take** your **eyes off** someone or something, or **can't keep** your **eyes off** them, you find it hard to look at anything else.

Anne looked so beautiful no one could take their eyes off her.

Desmond did not believe the diamond was real. He could not take his eyes off it.

We just couldn't keep our eyes off each other from the first time we met.

feast your eyes on something   ◄

If you **feast** your **eyes on** something, you look at it with a great deal of enjoyment and anticipation.

If family food means more to you than simply satisfying hungry mouths, then feast your eyes on our delicious dishes.

An exquisite Edinburgh Skye crystal goblet is only one of the beautiful things you can feast your eyes on at Harrods.

Billy pursed his lips and feasted his eyes on the toffee-apples.

have eyes in the back of your head   ◄

If you say that someone **has eyes in the back of** their **head**, you mean that they are very observant and seem to be aware of everything that is happening around them.

She has eyes in the back of her head and is always alert to the slightest trouble or sign of trouble.

Our daughter is at the stage where you need eyes in the back of your head.

'All sorts of things were going on off the

ball,' complained the Oldham skipper. He didn't expect referees to have eyes in the back of their heads but 'a good referee should sense what's happening around him.'

keep your eyes peeled
keep your eyes skinned   ◄

If someone tells you to **keep** your **eyes peeled**, they are telling you to watch very carefully for something. They can also tell you to **keep** your **eyes skinned**.

Keep your eyes peeled so you're not followed.

They drove there in Charlie's car, so Michael kept his eyes peeled for parking places.

She's on the loose. I doubt if she'll come back here, but keep your eyes skinned.

make eyes at someone

If someone **is making eyes at** you, they are trying to get you to notice them because they are sexually attracted to you. This is a fairly old-fashioned expression.

He's making eyes at one of the nurses.

When Naomi first noticed that the seemingly bashful boxer was making eyes at her across the room, she was impressed.

meet someone's eyes
meet someone's eye   ◄◄◄

If you **meet** someone's **eyes** or **meet** their **eye**, you look directly into each other's eyes. You can also say that two people's **eyes meet**. These expressions are used mainly in novels.

An uneasy moment of frozen silence passed as Steve looked down and then finally up at me, meeting my eyes with an intense glare.

Bella watched her with a stare of curiosity that was so blatant Mary felt herself blushing and unable to meet her eyes.

Laura stood her ground and met his eye unflinchingly.

She helped him out of his limousine, their eyes met and he asked her to marry him.

only have eyes for someone: 1   ◄

If you **only have eyes for** one person, they are the only person that you are interested in sexually.

The 26 year-old model is adored by thousands but has eyes for only one man – her husband.

They attracted lots of attention but they had eyes only for each other.

I love to look good and when I dress up, I want my man to have eyes for no-one else but me.

only have eyes for something: 2

You can say that someone **only has eyes for** a particular thing when they are determined to have it.

Given a choice between Cup success and promotion, Corfe has eyes only for the Premier League.

The president came seeking investment in Mexico, but found Western Europe had eyes only for the new democracies to its east.

open the eyes of someone: 1
open someone's eyes   ◄◄◄

If something **opens the eyes of** someone or **opens** their **eyes**, it causes them to become aware of things for the first time.

The need for female labour created during two world wars opened the eyes of many women to better paid lives in factories and offices.

Did being in prison open your eyes to things in modern America you weren't aware of before?

open your eyes: 2
keep your eyes open   ◄◄

If someone tells you to **open** your **eyes** or **keep** your **eyes open**, they are telling you to become aware of things that you can do in a particular situation.

Wake up, open your eyes and minds and get angry, because political debate is back on the agenda.

Take up any opportunity to increase your knowledge and broaden your horizons. Keep your eyes open for any likely study courses starting in February.

up to your eyes   ◄

If you say that you are **up to** your **eyes** in work or in an unpleasant situation, you mean that you are very busy with it or are deeply involved in it.

I'm afraid I shall be late getting back. I am up to my eyes in work.

Sir Ranulph is up to his eyes preparing for the trip, so we had to use a model.

If you are up to your eyes in debt and already set to lose your home, get advice on bankruptcy. That way your debts may be written off after three years.

with your eyes closed
with your eyes shut

If you say that you can do something **with** your **eyes closed** or **with** your **eyes shut**, you are emphasizing that you can do it very easily.

He reassembled the gun quickly and expertly. It was something he could do with his eyes closed.

Prince is so good he could do a show like this on crutches with his eyes shut.

with your eyes glued to something   ◄

Someone with their **eyes glued to** something is watching it with all their attention. You can also say that their **eyes** are **glued on** something.

People who had dropped by just to get a cup of coffee suddenly found themselves lingering for hours, eyes glued to the TV set with a look usually reserved for a good suspense film.

Coral tried to distract me by pointing to a tractor and a load of firewood, and I just kept my eyes glued to the road.

Wearing ties and blazers, the boys sit politely on the wood gym floor, eyes glued on the special visitor.

F

face

at face value: 1 ◄◄◄

If you take what someone says **at face value**, you accept it and believe it without thinking about it very much, even though it may be incorrect or untrue.

Clients should know better than to take the advice of a wholesaler at face value.

It took some convincing, but I think she finally accepted my statement at face value.

Allegations of a plot from the federal government cannot be taken at face value. The talk of plots and the arrests could be seen as provocative and politically motivated.

at face value: 2 ◄

If you take someone **at face value**, you accept the impression that they give of themselves, even though this may be completely false.

For a time I took him at face value. At that time, I had no reason to suspect him.

We meet so many new people all the time that we're far more likely simply to accept them at face value than to waste time questioning the image they project.

blow up in your face
explode in your face ◄◄

If a situation **blows up in** your **face**, it unexpectedly goes wrong and destroys your plans or your chances of something. You can also say that a situation **explodes in** your **face**.

It is very hard to say what made him allege a Republican plot, but he must have known that having no evidence, this would blow up in his face.

His outburst yesterday could blow up in his face. Those that have supported his cause will certainly question his motives.

The scandal has exploded in the government's face, and once again brought into question the future of the Trade and Industry Secretary.

come face to face with someone: 1
meet someone face to face ◄◄◄

If you **come face to face** with someone or **meet** someone **face to face**, you meet them and can talk to them directly.

Following his meeting with Eden, Hopkins visited Number 10 Downing Street and came face to face with Churchill for the first time.

When I first heard of his death I didn't want to call her or meet her face to face. In spite of our closeness of forty years, I didn't know what to say or how to act.

Now that he was face to face with the estate agent, Arnold found it difficult to explain.

☐ A **face-to-face** meeting or encounter is one where the people meet and can talk to each other directly.

The first face-to-face meeting between the heads of the Trade Union Confederation and the Employers' Association got nowhere yesterday.

The three major vice-presidential candidates took the stage tonight in Atlanta in their only face-to-face confrontation of the campaign.

come face to face with something: 2
bring someone face to face with something ◄◄◄

If you **come face to face with** a problem or **with** reality, you are forced to experience it and have to deal with it or accept it. You can also say that you **are brought face to face with** something.

Before the deal was fully closed, however, Beaverbrook came face to face with a serious problem.

I had achieved some standing among my fellow workers, but was gradually being brought face to face with the fact that I had very little success in alleviating human misery.

a face like thunder

If you say that someone has **a face like thunder**, you mean that they look extremely angry. This expression is used in British English.

The kitchen had flooded and Mick was stalking around the house with a face like thunder.

Mr Clarke had a face like thunder after his assistant's mistake.

fly in the face of something ◄◄◄

If you say that something **flies in the face of** accepted ideas, rules, or practices, you mean that it conflicts with them or contradicts them.

The plan to sell rhino horn flies in the face of the international ban.

The reputable Washington-based George Marshall Institute flew in the face of accepted opinion and published research suggesting the world may not be getting hotter.

The decision flies in the face of an emotional

appeal by the President last week for Congress to deal quickly with the nomination.

get out of someone's face ◄

If someone tells you to **get out of** their **face**, they are telling you in a rude and aggressive way to leave them alone and to stop annoying them or interfering with them.

Get out of my face or else I'm going to slap you.

He whinged after the verdict went against him in our first fight. That irritated me. I told him to get out of my face.

in-your-face ◄◄

If you describe someone or something as **in-your-face**, you mean that they are unconventional and provocative, and may upset or offend some people. This is an informal expression.

Christina James plays Perry's widow, a vivacious, in-your-face woman who is sometimes too honest for her own good.

Von Preinheim is known in the gay community as both a film and mischief maker for his ferocious, often in-your-face movies.

Wry, witty, and downright rude, Lea's act combines stand-up with gutsy jazz and blues. Totally in-yer-face.

□ This expression is sometimes spelled 'in-yer-face', to represent an informal pronunciation of 'your'.

keep a straight face
with a straight face ◄◄◄

If you **keep a straight face**, or say or do something **with a straight face**, you manage to look serious, even though you really want to laugh or smile.

His laugh was hard for Nancy to resist, but she managed to keep a straight face.

'I don't see that there's anything funny about it,' he said, offended. 'Of course there isn't,' she said, trying to keep a straight face.

We've all been practicing trying to say we charge $1,000 an hour with a straight face. But so far we haven't been able to do it.

□ You can also say that someone or something is **straight-faced**.

It's the way he tells a joke. He is completely straight-faced and I just fall about laughing.

A book has been published in the US entitled 'What Bird Did That'. The blurb on the cover describes it as being 'a hilarious, straight-faced, full-colour guide to bird droppings'.

laugh on the other side of your face

If someone says **'you'll be laughing on the other side of your face'**, they are warning you that although you are happy or successful at the moment, things are likely to go wrong for you in the future. This expression is used in British English; the American expression is **laugh out of the other side of** your **mouth**.

You'll be laughing on the other side of your face when they get Paul Stewart back from Liverpool.

a long face ◄

If you say that someone has **a long face**, you mean that they look very serious or unhappy.

He came to me with a very long face and admitted there had been an error.

There were some long faces in Paris that day. Astoundingly, an American had won the Tour de France.

□ You can also say that someone is **long-faced**.

After a short ceremony we stood, long-faced, by the graveside.

look someone in the face ◄

If you **look** someone **in the face**, you look at them directly in order to convince them that what you are saying is true, even though you may be lying. **Look** someone **in the eye** means the same.

He looked me in the face again and repeated, 'I swear to you that it wasn't me.'

Look me in the face. Do I look like a liar?

□ If you say that you **cannot look** someone **in the face**, you are too ashamed or embarrassed by something that you have done to look at them directly.

Why did I do that? I can't ever look her in the face again.

If I took up their offer I couldn't look my friends in the face again.

lose face ◄◄◄

If you **lose face**, people think less well of you because you are made to look foolish or because you do something which damages your reputation. You can also say that something **loses** someone **face**. Compare **save face**.

It is inconceivable that the Communist Party would ever allow itself to lose face by losing an election.

The world's motor industry is giving an object lesson in how big business can co-operate with its competitors without losing face.

Political observers said the army chief had lost a lot of face because of the government's victory.

Opposition leaders said he should not go, as the circumstances in which his most senior colleague had resigned would lose him face with the Americans.

make a face
pull a face ◄◄◄

If you **make a face** or **pull a face**, you show a feeling such as dislike, disgust, or defiance by twisting your face into an ugly expression, or by sticking out your tongue. 'Pull a face' is used only in British English.

She made a face at the musty smell, and hurried to open the windows.

He was taught from an early age to address people as 'Mister' and not to poke his tongue out or pull faces.

□ If someone **makes** or **pulls a** particular kind of **face**, they show that feeling in their expression.

'Here I am,' Chee said. 'What can I do?' Janet made a wry face.

He pulled funny faces at her and cracked a few jokes.

not have the face

If you **don't have the face** to do something, you are too nervous or embarrassed to do it. This expression is used in British English.

You wouldn't lend me a couple of quid, would you? I mean, I'm dying for a smoke, and I haven't the face to borrow off Michael.

They were all placing their orders. They had not quite the face to view the Collection more than once without doing so.

put a brave face on something
put a good face on something
put a brave front on something ◀◀◀

If someone **puts a brave face on** a difficult situation or **puts on a brave face**, they try not to let anyone see how upset or disappointed they are. You can replace 'brave' with 'good' and 'face' with 'front'.

The news caused share prices to slump by around £5 billion and the pound to weaken. Mr Major put a brave face on the trade figures, saying they suggested recovery was on the way.

They don't like to see how grieved, how awful we're feeling. They'd much rather we put on a brave front and pretend nothing has happened because they can't cope with it.

The Prince's manners rarely fell below excellence and he would have gone to great pains to put a good face on his sufferings.

□ This expression is extremely variable. For example, you can say that someone **puts up a brave face** or **front** or **keeps up a brave face** or **front**. You can also just talk about **a brave face**.

Now the atmosphere in Sloane Street is more muted, although shopkeepers are keeping up a brave face. The shops are dominated by sales, with reductions of up to 70 per cent.

Colleagues said that despite his brave face, Mr Hutchinson was deeply hurt at his treatment.

save face ◀◀◀

If you **save face**, you do something so that people continue to respect you and your reputation is not damaged. If someone **saves** your

face, they do something to keep people's respect for you and save your reputation. Compare **lose face**.

Most children have an almost obsessive need to save face in front of their peers.

Last Wednesday Poland somehow allowed the United States to take a three-goal lead before slightly saving face by scoring two themselves.

The most important thing now to be done was to end the war before thousands more were killed or maimed to save the faces of a few politicians.

□ You can talk about a **face-saving** action.

The change of heart on aid seems to show that officials are looking for a face-saving way to back down.

This offer is being made subject to the same conditions as the president's previous attempt. No negotiations, no compromises, no attempts at face-saving, and no rewards for aggression.

□ Journalists sometimes refer to an action or excuse which enables someone to save face as **a face-saver**.

Nobody can object to a prisoner exchange between combatants. The hope is that this exchange will also give the kidnappers the face-saver they need to release the hostages.

set your face against something ◀

If you say that someone **has set** their **face against** something, you mean that they oppose it in a determined way. You often use this expression when you think the person is being stubborn or unreasonable. This expression is used mainly in British English.

Tricia wondered if he had ever considered moving, but heard that he had set his face against the idea.

Both the government and the major rebel groups appear to have set their faces against a negotiated settlement to the conflict.

show your face: 1 ◀

If you do not want to **show** your **face** somewhere, you do not want to go there, for example because you are embarrassed or ashamed about something you have done.

Louis skulked in his Harlem apartment for three days after his defeat, too ashamed to show his face. His ego was badly bruised.

If she shows her face again back in Massachusetts she'll find a warrant for her arrest waiting.

show your face: 2 ◀

If you **show** your **face** somewhere, you go there briefly, for example because you have been invited there and you feel obliged to go for a short time.

I'll probably just be going to show my face really and then come home and go to bed, because I'm absolutely exhausted.

I felt I ought to show my face at her father's funeral.

I was in America for the first time, and my agent thought it would be a good idea for me to show my face around the various studios.

stare something in the face: 1   ◄◄

If you **are staring** a bad situation **in the face**, the situation is very likely to occur, or is about to occur. You can also say that the bad situation **is staring** you **in the face**.

The Communists could be staring defeat in the face.

Some of my patients are actually staring death in the face. They've suffered a heart attack, maybe two.

After this defeat, relegation stares the club in the face as starkly as it did in 1972.

stare someone in the face: 2   ◄

If the facts about something **are staring** you **in the face**, they are very obvious, although you may not yet have realized this.

Even when the evidence is staring them in the face they deliberately misread it.

Tom had an insight, the kind of insight that you sometimes have when you're trying to solve a complex problem, and you suddenly realise that the answer has been staring you in the face all along.

throw something back in someone's face   ◄

If you say something or do something for someone and they **throw** it **back in** your **face**, they reject it completely in a way that seems very ungrateful or impolite to you.

Don't be surprised if your concern for their wellbeing is misunderstood and gets thrown back in your face.

We extended the hand of friendship and you have thrown it back in our faces.

to someone's face   ◄◄◄

If you say something, especially something critical or unpleasant, **to** a person's **face**, you say it openly in their presence.

He was too old, too rigid, too inflexible, he had to step aside. But who was going to say so to his face?

At school it was hard when people talked about me. No-one would ever say anything to my face because they were scared of me.

His most painful moment came when he told Mrs Thatcher to her face that she would be beaten if she fought on.

until you are blue in the face   ◄

If you say that someone can do something **until** they **are blue in the face**, you mean that however long they do it or however hard they try, they will still fail.

You can speculate till you're blue in the face, but you can't prove a thing.

The president can issue decrees until he is blue in the face, but they are ignored.

written all over your face

If an emotion such as relief or misery, for example, **is written all over** your **face**, it is very obvious to people that you are relieved or miserable, because of your expression.

My misery must have been written all over my face.

Utter jubilation and relief were written all over the faces of the freed hostages.

fair

all's fair in love and war

In a competition or contest, people say **'all's fair in love and war'** when they want to justify dishonest or unfair behaviour, by suggesting that under difficult circumstances any kind of behaviour is acceptable.

He appears to live by the boorish credo that all is fair in love and war. And being cruel to mistresses and wives isn't wrong.

'Why would someone in your own family try to get the U.S. government to brand you as a racketeer?' he asks. 'Basically,' says William, 'because all is fair in brotherly love and war.'

☐ Sometimes people use other words instead of 'war' depending on the situation they are in.

It seems women are at last realising what men have known for years: All is fair in love and divorce.

fair and square   ◄

If you say that someone won a competition or did something **fair and square**, you mean that they did it honestly and without cheating or lying.

This might start further accusations, but we don't care any more. We won fair and square.

I was beaten fair and square.

My father bought them fair and square. Fifty years ago. We've still got the receipts.

fall

be heading for a fall
be riding for a fall
be headed for a fall   ◄

If you say that someone **is heading for a fall** or **is riding for a fall**, you mean that they are doing something which is likely to have unpleasant consequences for them. You can also say that someone **is headed for a fall**.

The Tory Party is heading for a great fall.

Here was a company that seemed to be riding for a fall. Now, things look completely different. It has become the sixth-biggest firm in the market.

There were some who wondered whether

Black's vanity and military turn of mind indicated that he was headed for a fall.

familiarity

familiarity breeds contempt
familiarity breeds content ◄

If you say that **familiarity breeds contempt**, you mean that if you know someone or something very well, you can easily become bored with them and stop treating them with respect or stop paying attention to them. Other nouns are sometimes used instead of 'contempt'.

It is the old case of familiarity breeding contempt. The more people read about the political turmoil, the more it drags on, the more they feel comfortable about the problem being there in the background.

Familiarity breeds inattention. Typically, family members are so convinced they know what another family member is going to say that they don't bother to listen.

□ Sometimes this expression is varied, for example as **familiarity breeds content**, to say that when you know someone or something very well, you grow to like them more or have more respect for them, rather than less.

Through carefully maintaining a less grand image, the Queen has become as familiar to her people as a member of their own family – a familiarity that has bred content.

farm

buy the farm

If someone **buys the farm**, they die. This is an informal expression.

The plane spun down and never came out of it; it nosedived into the ground and exploded. He bought the farm.

fashion

after a fashion ◄

If you say that something was done **after a fashion**, you mean that it was done, but not very well. If you say that something is true **after a fashion**, you mean that it is mostly true, but not entirely true.

She was educated, after a fashion, by a governess at home.

We were friends, after a fashion.

It all works after a fashion, possibly better than it should.

fast

play fast and loose ◄

If you accuse someone of **playing fast and loose** with something important, you are accusing them of treating it without proper care or respect.

The banks claim high interest rates are neces-

sary because the government is playing fast and loose with public spending.

This kind of talk not only confuses the public but actually encourages them to play fast-and-loose with their own future and – more importantly – the future of their children.

pull a fast one ◄

If someone **pulls a fast one** or **pulls a fast one on** you, they succeed in tricking you in order to get an advantage.

Management recently tried to pull a fast one. Behind the backs of workers, the directors arranged to buy up the majority of shares to be issued. This meant that the number of shares issued to the workers would be far fewer.

Someone had pulled a fast one on her over a procedural matter and she was not going to let them get away with it.

fat

chew the fat ◄

If you **chew the fat** with someone, you chat with them in an informal and friendly way about things that interest you.

We'd been lounging around, chewing the fat for a couple of hours.

It's a chat show which gives her the chance to chew the fat with the likes of Tony Curtis, Diana Ross and Sir Peter Ustinov.

the fat is in the fire

If you say that **the fat is in the fire**, you mean that someone has said or done something which is going to upset other people and cause a lot of trouble.

Immediately the fat was in the fire, for in making an accusation directly and in the open, the minister for education and science had broken all the rules.

□ You can say that someone **pulls the fat out of the fire** when they prevent or stop trouble by taking acting at a very late stage.

Don't rely on pulling the fat out of the fire by launching a late, last-ditch negative campaign against Clinton.

the fat of the land

If you say that someone is living off **the fat of the land**, you mean that they have a rich and comfortable lifestyle without having to work hard for it. You often use this expression to criticize someone who is rich because they are exploiting people.

He was pretty fed up with these bloated royalists who were living off the fat of the land and off American aid while the rest of the country was starving, literally.

fate

seal someone's fate ◄◄◄

If something **seals the fate** of a person or thing, it makes it certain that they will fail or that something unpleasant will happen to them.

The plan removes power from the government, sealing the fate of the unpopular Prime Minister, and transfers it to the President.

The women's marital fate is sealed by their parents, sometimes when they are as young as three years old.

The parliament's decision today could seal the Republic's fate.

tempt fate
tempt providence ◄◄

If you say that someone **is tempting fate**, you mean that they are taking unnecessary risks when doing something, or acting in a way that may bring them bad luck. You can also say that someone **is tempting providence**.

Indeed, many experienced yachtsmen charge the organisers with tempting fate in sending so many ill-prepared crews into such dangerous waters.

I can't see any farther than the next six months – it's like tempting fate to think of the future.

I used to take the most appalling risks because it was in my nature to push everything to the extreme. I was tempting providence all the time.

fault

to a fault ◄◄

If you say that someone has a good quality **to a fault**, you are emphasizing that they have more of this quality than is usual or necessary.

She was generous to a fault and tried to see that we had everything we needed.

He's honest to a fault, brave, dedicated, and fiercely proud of the New York Police Department.

feast

enough is as good as a feast

If you say **'enough is as good as a feast'**, you mean that there is no point in having more of something than you need or want. This is an old-fashioned expression, which is used in British English.

'Enough is as good as a feast,' my great aunt Daisy was wont to say to me, as I reached an ever-chubbier hand towards the chocolate biscuits.

I too am very fond of music; nobody loves a tune better than I do. But I always say enough is as good as a feast; do you not agree?

feast or famine

If someone says 'it's **feast or famine**', they mean that sometimes they have too much of something such as money, while at other times they do not have enough.

While her life is rich in memories, funds are a problem. 'It's feast or famine with me,' she says.

□ People often vary this expression.

Shadow Consumer Minister Nigel Griffiths last night demanded an investigation into the scandal. He said, 'It is a case of feast for the chosen few and famine for the rest of us.'

After a long famine, a mini-feast: investors are once again providing banks with the capital they need.

the spectre at the feast
the ghost at the feast
the skeleton at the feast ◄

If you describe a person or event as **the spectre at the feast**, **the ghost at the feast**, or **the skeleton at the feast**, you mean that they spoil other people's enjoyment, for example because they remind them of an unhappy event or situation. These expressions are used in British English.

The party that broke out that night, the sense of liberation and the euphoria that gripped the town was amazing. The only skeletons at the feast were the Russian military.

Mairie Hastings makes her entrance as the widow Tancred, spectre at the feast where the Boyles celebrate the inheritance they will never have.

feather

a feather in your cap ◄

If you describe someone's achievement as **a feather in** their **cap**, you mean that they have done very well and you admire them.

Hauptmann's arrest and conviction had been hailed as a triumph for justice and a feather in the cap of the New Jersey police.

An overwhelming 4-1 victory over the champions, Leeds, last weekend was another feather in the cap of Middlesbrough manager, Lennie Lawrence.

you could have knocked me down with a feather

If you are telling someone about something that happened and you say **'you could have knocked me down with a feather'**, you are emphasizing that you were extremely surprised or shocked by it. This is an old-fashioned expression.

I won 54 votes to 48. I was completely overwhelmed; you could have knocked me down with a feather.

feathers

ruffle someone's feathers ◄◄

If someone **ruffles** your **feathers**, they say or do something which upsets or annoys you.

The country has, for example, ruffled a few feathers by breaking with the Western consensus on trade with China.

The tall Texan ruffled some English feathers by remarking: 'To get on you must do the best you can with whatever fate has given you, or be really English and sit around moaning a lot about everyone else.'

No one doubts his ability to make sound judgments and to prevent feathers from getting ruffled.

smooth ruffled feathers ◀

If someone **smooths ruffled feathers**, they calm things down when an argument or disagreement gets intense and they attempt to solve the problem. You can replace 'smooth' with 'soothe'.

His function was to smooth ruffled feathers. That was always Marcus's function. He would go around trying to convince people that they were making a lot of fuss about nothing.

Members of the exchange objected to Mr Rawlins's confrontational style. Mindful of this, Mr Lawrence has been soothing ruffled feathers.

feelers

put out feelers ◀

In a difficult situation, if you **put out feelers**, you carefully try to find out about other people's feelings or plans, so that you will know what to do next. You can replace 'put' with other verbs such as 'send', 'have', or 'throw'.

We're going to the United States in mid-May to put some feelers out and have a bit of a break, but we've really got more than enough work locally.

'I'm looking to play in Britain at the end of the next Australian season,' he said last night. 'I've had some feelers out for one or two clubs already.'

feet

dead on your feet

If you are **dead on** your **feet**, you are completely exhausted.

When we arrived, the police there were exhausted. They were stumbling around, dead on their feet.

I'm usually dead on my feet at the end of the game.

feet on the ground ◀◀◀

If someone keeps their **feet on the ground**, they continue to act in a sensible and practical way even when new or exciting things are happening or even when they become successful or powerful. Compare **get** your **feet on the ground**.

He says he keeps his feet on the ground by keeping childhood friends around him.

A year on from winning the world junior cross-country title, Radcliffe still has her feet firmly on the ground.

Kevin was always level-headed with both feet on the ground.

find your feet ◀◀◀

If you say that someone in a new situation **is finding** their **feet**, you mean that they are becoming more confident and learning what to do.

Robert is looking a lot sharper. He's finding his feet after doing a couple of extra afternoon sessions with our coach Don Howe and I know he's really looking forward to the game.

It takes a while for people to find their feet at this level and gain the necessary confidence.

get cold feet
have cold feet ◀◀

If you **get cold feet** or **have cold feet** about something, you are not sure whether you want to do it, or you become too nervous and worried to do it.

I feel your boyfriend got cold feet about being in a committed relationship. He may even have fallen out of love.

After the Government's defeat in Newbury and the local government elections, it is hardly surprising the Tories now have cold feet over tackling such a politically sensitive issue.

get your feet on the ground

If you **get** your **feet on the ground**, you become established in a new situation, or become re-established in an old one. This expression is used mainly in American English. Compare **feet on the ground**.

They have modest two-room apartments, and until they get their feet on the ground, they take most meals at the institute's cafeteria.

We are the new boys and we have it all to do. We need to get our feet on the ground first.

get your feet under the table ◀

If someone **gets** their **feet under the table**, they establish themselves firmly in a new job or situation. You can replace 'table' with 'desk' when talking about someone's new job. This expression is used in British English.

Mr MacGregor will wait for the new Transportation Secretary in the incoming administration to get his feet under the table, but hopes to have an initial meeting in March or April.

I think I shall be able to do something about that next year. But let me get my feet under the table.

He was acting like a man with his feet very firmly under his desk.

get your feet wet
have your feet wet

If you **get** your **feet wet**, you get involved in something or experience something for the first time. You can also say that you **have** your **feet wet**. These expressions are used mainly in American English.

Charlton thinks it's time for me to get my feet wet. He says I'll be able to help the department a lot more if I learn how police actually solve crimes.

Well, the Secretary of State now has his feet wet in the Middle East again. Do you think that the president is going to wade in soon and join him?

have feet of clay
clay feet ◄

You say that someone who is greatly admired or respected **has feet of clay** to point out that they have serious faults or weaknesses which people generally do not know about.

When those idols are found to have feet of clay the pain of disenchantment can be profound.

For all his right-on posturing about how much he cares for his fans, Bruce is just another corporate rock star with feet of clay.

☐ You can also say that someone has **clay feet**. This form is used mainly in American English.

So do you think he was familiar with the clay feet of the justices and therefore didn't have great heroes among them?

itchy feet ◄

If you say that you have got **itchy feet**, you mean that you have become bored with the place or situation that you are in, and you want to move somewhere new or start doing something new.

I hated living in London, and I started getting itchy feet. Last year, I decided I really wanted to come out to the States.

I could either wait until I was promoted or I could change what I was doing. The thought gave me really itchy feet so within a couple of months I decided to leave.

land on your feet
fall on your feet ◄◄

If you say that someone **lands on** their **feet** or **falls on** their **feet**, you mean that they find themselves in a good situation, which you think is the result of luck and not their own efforts. 'Fall on your feet' is used only in British English.

Everything I want, she's got: good marriage, good home, nice children. While I struggle through life, she lands on her feet.

He has fallen on his feet with a new career set to earn him a fortune.

put your feet up ◄◄◄

If you **put** your **feet up**, you have a rest from your work and relax, for example by lying down or sitting in a comfortable chair.

All these dishes can be oven-baked from frozen, while you put your feet up and relax.

If I'm early and you're not here I can put my feet up for a moment and have a rest.

rushed off your feet ◄

If you complain that you **are rushed off** your **feet**, you are complaining that you are very busy, often because you are not getting any help or support in your work. This expression is used in British English.

Now we have a cut-back in staff in this department, and I'm rushed off my feet.

You've been rushed off your feet all day, dashing from place to place, making telephone calls and willing the kettle to boil quicker. But what have you actually achieved – and where did the time go?

stand on your own two feet
stand on your own feet ◄◄

If you **stand on** your **own two feet** or **stand on** your **own feet**, you show that you are independent and do not need anyone to help you or support you.

It now seems clear that foreign aid levels of the 1980s will never be seen again and that the Caribbean will have to stand on its own two feet if it hopes to survive in a world dominated by massive trading blocks.

Having spent the past decade learning to stand on their own feet, Japan's drug makers now hope to take on the world.

sweep someone off their feet: 1 ◄◄

If someone **sweeps** you **off** your **feet**, you fall in love with them almost as soon as you meet them because they are so attractive and exciting, and they behave very romantically towards you. This expression is used mainly in written English.

By the end of the date he said he was going to marry me in two weeks' time. I was swept off my feet. I had always dreamed of being an officer's wife.

He is a good fifteen years older than Felicity. He swept her off her feet, though. And I suppose it seemed very romantic.

sweep someone off their feet: 2

If you say that something **sweeps** you **off** your **feet**, you mean that it extremely attractive or appealing to you. This expression is used in written English.

When she first spotted a photograph of a romantic-looking house dating back to 1770, in an estate agent's window in Cheshire, she was swept off her feet by its charm.

Ten British chefs plan to cook a feast they hope will sweep the French off their feet.

think on your feet ◄

If you **think on** your **feet**, you make good decisions and achieve things without having to think about them or plan them first.

We always have room for a guy who can think on his feet. The boy's smart.

You have to make decisions on the spot. I enjoy thinking on my feet and seeing the end product of my work immediately.

Being a parent means thinking on your feet and adapting as you go along.

under someone's feet ◄

If you complain that someone is **under** your **feet**, you are annoyed because they are always around you and keep getting in your way when you are trying to do something.

There really is no pleasing parents. When you're in the house they moan about you always being under their feet. When you're out of the house they moan because you're never around when they want you.

The conservatory is good for children to play in as you can keep an eye on them while they and their toys are out from under your feet.

vote with your feet ◄◄

If people **vote with** their **feet**, they indicate what they want through their actions, for example showing their dislike of a place or situation by leaving it.

It seems thousands of people are already voting with their feet, and leaving the country for the hope of a better life.

If Philadelphia's economic future deteriorates, rich people will vote with their feet. They have the ability and wherewithal to move out of this city, as businesses and corporations do.

In spite of continuing intense pressure to become a couple, the latest statistics show we are voting with our feet and increasingly opting for the single life.

fence

sit on the fence
come off the fence ◄◄◄

You say that someone is **sitting on the fence** to express your disapproval of them for refusing to state a definite opinion about something or to say who they support in a conflict. Verbs such as 'stay' and 'be' can be used instead of 'sit'.

The commission has chosen, extraordinarily, to sit on the fence, murmuring that schools must decide for themselves.

Democrats who'd been on the fence about the nomination trooped to the floor one after another to decry what they called the rush to judgment.

☐ You can refer to this kind of behaviour as **fence-sitting**, and to someone who behaves like this as **a fence-sitter**.

At his first press conference there was much fence-sitting.

I have a sense, just from what I've read and from talking to people, that there are a lot of fence sitters out there.

☐ If you say that someone **comes off the fence**, you mean that they at last state their opinion about something or show who they support. Verbs such as 'climb' and 'get' can be used instead of 'come'.

The defeat of the government in a confidence vote on Friday appears to have forced the President to come off the fence and support the market reformers.

It is time for us to get off the fence, to speak up, and to vote.

fences

mend fences ◄◄

If you have a difficult relationship with someone and you do something to try and improve it, you can say that you are trying to **mend fences** with them or **mend** your **fences** with them.

Yesterday he was publicly criticised for not doing enough to mend fences with his big political rival.

The US, sensing the time is right for a reconciliation between Argentina and Britain, is nudging them to try to mend their fences.

☐ You can refer to this process as **fence-mending**.

King Hussein made numerous diplomatic missions. He's even now out of the country on a fence-mending mission to the European Community.

fever

fever pitch ◄◄◄

If a situation or a feeling reaches **fever pitch**, it becomes very intense and exciting, or very desperate.

Rumors of the love affair hit fever pitch in the past few days after the pair were seen around Sydney.

The grief and outrage provoked by his assassination have heightened tensions in the area to fever pitch.

In the past year, the civil conflict has reached a fever pitch.

fiddle

on the fiddle

If someone is **on the fiddle**, they are getting money dishonestly, for example by cheating with the accounts at work. This expression is used in British English.

A postman earning only £136 a week drove around in a Porsche for six months before his bosses realised he was on the fiddle.

The belief in many countries that politicians, officials, and businessmen are likely to be on the fiddle, whether they are or not, is part of the crisis of the system.

play second fiddle ◄◄

If you have to **play second fiddle** to someone, you have to accept that you are less important than they are and do not have the same status, even though you may resent this.

The 44-year-old senator will play second fiddle to a man who, although of the same political generation, has been his clear junior in the Democrat hierarchy.

There is, quite evidently, some resentment among health professionals at having to play second fiddle in the new structure.

Both of these cities play second fiddle to London on the international stage.

□ You can also just say that someone is **second fiddle**.

I think Caryl would have to admit that we're no longer second fiddle to our American cousins.

field

have a field day ◄◄◄

If you say that someone **is having a field day**, you mean that they are taking advantage of a situation, especially one which other people find upsetting or difficult.

When the news first broke that the Hubble Space Telescope was not working as expected, the newspapers had a field day.

Debt collectors are having a field day in the recession.

Our closeness is observed, of course, but not commented upon, at least never to us. In our absence the office gossips are probably having a field day.

□ **Field day** is used in other structures with a similar meaning.

Conservative sections of the British media enjoyed a field day in the aftermath of the incident.

The Act will undoubtedly provide a field-day for lawyers keen to offer advice to agents, with members of the public having to bear the brunt of the costs of tighter regulation.

lead the field ◄◄◄

If you **lead the field** in an activity or competition, you are the best or most successful person at it, or the most likely to win.

US and European cyclists predominate and usually lead the field. This could be due to their hi-tech equipment.

The Americans continue to lead the field when it comes to child actors.

Sam Torrance led the field after two rounds of the Kronenbourg Open at Salò, Italy, and

his immediate reward was to win his own weight in champagne.

left-field

People use **left-field** to describe an unusual and unconventional performer or piece of entertainment. This expression is used mainly in British journalism.

Over the last few years, the most left-field films in world cinema have come from Japan.

Jagged political bite and left-field humour are stirred into this unique social commentary.

out in left field
out of left field

If you say that someone or something is **out in left field** or comes **out of left field**, you mean that they are unusual and unconventional. These expressions are used mainly in American English.

If the adoption referral needs to be prepared, it's not going to be prepared by someone out in left field. It's done by the social worker who's carrying that case.

Most of the business tips are common sense, but others are right out of left field.

out of left field

A question, statement, or event which comes **out of left field** is completely unexpected. This expression is used mainly in American English.

'You and Brian got married, didn't you?' The question came out of left field, but Mary Ann wasn't really surprised.

All the firms we've talked to have indicated that they don't know. This has really come out of left field to most people.

play the field ◄

If someone **plays the field**, they have many different romantic or sexual relationships rather than staying with one person.

I'm just playing the field, Dad. Don't worry, I'm not thinking of settling down.

He gave up playing the field and married a year ago.

Kristin stars as a sexy career girl who plays the field before setting out to get a handsome American in the new BBC1 drama series 'Look At It This Way'.

fig

a fig leaf ◄

Something which is intended to hide an embarrassing or awkward situation can be referred to as **a fig leaf**.

My interpretation is that the pledge to rejoin the ERM was a fig leaf, designed to indicate that the government's economic strategy was not dead but merely sleeping.

The western world was swift to praise Ameri-

ca's intervention, behind the fig-leaf of the United Nations in Somalia.

fight

a knock-down drag-out fight

If you describe a debate, argument, or fight as **a knock-down drag-out fight**, you mean that it is very serious, emotional, and angry or even violent. This expression is used in American English.

Nobody had much of a stomach this year for another knock-down, drag-out fight over the state budget.

Adolescents need to know that it is normal for people to argue, even if they love one another. This doesn't mean that you should engage in knock-down, drag-out fights in front of your children, any more than you would in front of your friends and neighbors.

fill

have had your fill of something ◄◄

If you **have had** your **fill** of something, you have had as much of it as you can bear, and do not want any more.

By the time she was 29, Sarah had had her fill of Peter and married life.

They have had their fill of war, poverty, and repression.

finders

finders keepers

If someone, especially a child, says **'finders keepers'** when they find something, they mean that they have a right to keep it.

Although I phoned the club immediately I got home and checked again on Saturday, my umbrella has not been returned. Obviously, someone picked it up and has made no effort to find the owner. Finders, keepers.

fine

cut it fine
cut it close
cut things fine ◄

If you **cut it fine**, **cut it close**, or **cut things fine** when you go somewhere or do something, you do not leave much time to get there or do it and so you are nearly late.

'This may take a little while, but I'll be right behind you.'. 'Okay,' said Bunbury. 'But don't cut it too fine.'

They didn't plan to get it to us until six o' clock, and that's cutting it a little close.

They would be cutting things fine, unless they had decided to stay for the night on the island.

finger

give someone the finger

If someone **gives** you **the finger**, they do something which shows their contempt, anger, or defiance of you. This is an informal expression, which many people consider offensive.

Barker's personal worth has been put at around £30 million, but it could be greater by a factor of as much as five if he didn't give the finger to most of the commercial opportunities that come his way.

□ 'To give someone the finger' also means to make a rude and offensive gesture with one hand, with the middle finger pointing up and the other fingers bent over in a fist.

have a finger in every pie
have a finger in the pie ◄

If you say that someone **has a finger in every pie**, you mean that they are involved in many different activities, often in a way that you disapprove of. This expression is very variable.

He has a finger in every pie and is never short of ideas for making the next buck.

He was an economist called Clarkson who had a finger in a good many pies.

□ If you say that someone **has a finger in the pie**, you mean that they are involved in the activity you are talking about.

Foreign policy is farmed out to a number of other departments of the government. Each one has its finger in the pie, and the Secretary of State simply does not have the authority to pull things together.

They describe 45 governmental and non-governmental organisations with fingers in the environmental pie.

have your finger on the pulse
keep your finger on the pulse
have your finger on the button ◄◄

If you **have** your **finger on the pulse** or **keep** your **finger on the pulse**, you know all the latest information about something or have a good understanding of how it works. You can also say that you **have** your **finger on the button**.

Although I'm Scottish, after all these years in America I think myself and my editors have our finger on the pulse of America.

Experience in the different fields of angling helps greatly with the business, as keeping your finger on the pulse you can gauge what to stock and what will sell.

Hart is a businessman with his finger on the button.

not lay a finger on someone ◄

If you say that someone **has not laid a finger on** another person, you mean that they have never hurt that person in any way. If you say that someone has **not laid a finger**

on something, you mean that they have never touched it.

One of the men accused of attacking trucker Reginald Denny at the start of the Los Angeles riots says he never laid a finger on him.

'If,' Meg told her quietly, 'you ever lay a finger on me again, I promise you faithfully I'll kill you.'

Diana's son now knows how to use the washing machine and refuses to let anyone else lay a finger on his rugby shirts and underwear.

not lift a finger
not raise a finger ◄◄

If you accuse someone of **not lifting a finger** or **not raising a finger** to do something or to help someone, you are criticizing them for not doing it or not helping them.

Courage is what is shown by the men and women who are fighting to save their companies and jobs, not by a Chancellor who refuses to lift a finger to help them.

I'm the one who has to clean it all up. She wouldn't lift a finger if I didn't beg her.

This is a man who never ever raised a finger during the Communist years to protest what was going on.

point the finger at someone ◄◄◄

If you **point the finger at** someone, you blame them for a mistake they have made or accuse them of doing something wrong.

I think you have to point the finger at successive governments, which have really underfunded British Rail for years and years and years now.

One socialist blamed the press for his suicide, but some commentators pointed a finger at the political establishment.

□ You can also say, for example, that you **point the finger of blame** or **the finger of suspicion** at someone.

It would be easy to point the finger of blame at individuals, and dismiss the problem by calling them irresponsible and naive.

□ When people blame or accuse each other in this way, you can refer to this as **finger-pointing**.

Whether or not the investigation succeeds, it is bound to lead to finger-pointing and backbiting.

Initially there was considerable finger-pointing at the government and the police for what was assumed to have been a terrible breach of security.

pull your finger out
get your finger out ◄

If you tell someone to **pull** their **finger out** or **get** their **finger out**, you are telling them rudely to start working harder or to start dealing with something. This expression is used in British English.

If anything violent happens, it happens here first. If Bexley Council had any sense they would pull their finger out and shut the place down.

I have told them to get their fingers out and start winning games. We haven't had a victory for eight matches and it's not good enough.

put the finger on someone

If you **put the finger on** a particular person, you tell someone in authority that the person has done something wrong or illegal. This expression is used mainly in novels.

It's not like we put the finger on someone real, Janie. Nobody is suffering because of what we told that detective.

put your finger on something ◄◄◄

If you **put** your **finger on** something, for example the cause of a problem or the answer to a question, you realize what it is and identify it. If you cannot see the cause of a problem or the answer to a question, you can say that you **can't put** your **finger on** it.

He put his finger on a major weakness of its education policy when he said that the country needed improved education, not perpetual experimentation.

He had thought that Houston would have arrived at that solution first; but, no, it was Dr. Stockton who had put his finger on the truth.

Had they known each other as children? At school? She couldn't put her finger on it.

twist someone around your little finger
wrap someone around your little finger

If you say that you can **twist** someone **around** your **little finger** or **wrap** them **around** your **little finger**, you mean that you can make them do anything you want them to. Other verbs are sometimes used instead of 'twist' or 'wrap'.

Anna is not the brightest person in the world, but she would know exactly how to twist him around her little finger.

A child who is spoilt is able to wrap her parents around her little finger.

I didn't think there was a man in the world you were afraid of, Christabel, or one you couldn't wind around your finger.

fingers

count something on the fingers of one hand
count something on your fingers ◄

You say that you can **count** things **on the fingers of one hand** or **count** them **on** your **fingers** to emphasize that there are surprisingly few of them.

The jobs advertised each year could be counted on the fingers of one hand.

She was a really nice woman but hardly ever

spoke to anyone. In the six years I have known her I could count on my fingers the number of times we have spoken.

get your fingers burned
burn your fingers   ◄◄

If you **get** your **fingers burned** or **burn** your **fingers** when you try do something, it goes wrong, and there are very unpleasant consequences for you, so that you feel nervous about trying again.

The government, after getting its fingers burned so badly, will surely not want to make the same mistake again.

In St Petersburg, several hundred thousand people recently burned their fingers when two investment funds turned out to be run by crooks.

have green fingers   ◄◄

If you say that someone **has green fingers**, you mean that they are very good at gardening. This expression is used in British English; the American expression is **have a green thumb**.

Part of a splendid 1837 house, their home is just a mile or so from Toxteth with a pretty garden. 'My husband has green fingers,' says Mrs Andrews.

Propagating is a skill as well as an art, so even if you were not born with green fingers you can easily learn a few simple techniques to help you achieve success.

□ You can describe someone who is good at gardening as **green-fingered**.

Even if you're not green-fingered you can put on a stunning show of flowers right through summer and beyond.

itchy fingers

If you have **itchy fingers**, you are very keen to get involved in a particular activity. This expression is used mainly in British English.

I went into town to watch people playing chess. After a few days of this I started getting itchy fingers. I didn't dare ask my family for money, but I made a chess set for myself out of cardboard and took it to school to play with.

keep your fingers crossed
cross your fingers
fingers crossed   ◄◄◄

If you say that you **are keeping** your **fingers crossed** or **are crossing** your **fingers**, you mean that you are hoping for luck or success in something.

I will be keeping my fingers crossed that everything goes well.

We all cross our fingers and hope it never happens. But if long-term illness struck tomorrow, could you keep paying the bills?

□ People say **'fingers crossed'** when they are wishing someone good luck.

You can take your chance and turn up on the

night. Fingers crossed you might be able to get in.

□ People sometimes actually cross their middle finger over their index finger when they use this expression or are wishing someone good luck.

slip through your fingers   ◄◄

If you let something **slip through** your **fingers**, especially something good, you fail to get it or keep it.

If your income is greater than your expenses, count yourself lucky – and don't let it slip through your fingers! Hire a good investment counselor and keep your money safe.

You mustn't allow a golden opportunity to slip through your fingers or you will regret it later.

work your fingers to the bone

If you talk about someone having to **work** their **fingers to the bone**, you mean that they have to work extremely hard.

What sort of life is this if, like a miner, you work your fingers to the bone?

I married him when I was fifteen and have borne him sons. I have washed, cooked, fetched and carried all my life. I worked my fingers to the bone in his house.

fingertips

at your fingertips: 1   ◄◄

If you have something **at** your **fingertips**, it is readily available for you to use or reach.

All basic controls are at your fingertips for straightforward, no fuss operation.

Far from being tied, Anita Roddick has the kind of freedom at her fingertips that would drive most of us into a lather of anticipation.

at your fingertips: 2   ◄

If you have facts or information **at** your **fingertips**, you know them thoroughly and can refer to them quickly.

She is well-trained, having attended courses in Moscow, she has figures about the performance of her business at her fingertips, and she has no desire to see her enterprise privatised.

He wanted to know all about his latest projects, so that the correct answers were at his fingertips when he was questioned by the right people.

hang on by your fingertips
hang on by your fingernails   ◄

In a difficult situation, if you **are hanging on by** your **fingertips** or **hanging on by** your **fingernails**, you are managing to survive or to stay in the position you want to, but you are always in danger of failing. You can replace 'hang' with 'cling'.

This will cost the business community one bil-

lion pounds a year in interest payments alone. There are firms already hanging on by their fingertips who will not be able to take this.

Real Madrid's poor start to the season has left coach Benito Floro hanging on to his job by his fingernails.

Every so often, a minister teeters on the edge of resignation. Some jump, some are kicked and some cling on by their fingernails.

□ You can also say that someone has a **fingertip hold** on something.

A Bolton own goal early in the second half gave Liverpool, who were two goals behind at half-time, the fingertip hold they needed to retain their grasp of the FA Cup.

fire

breathe fire ◄

If you say that someone **is breathing fire** about something, you are emphasizing that they are very angry about it.

Senators, who for months have breathed fire about the need for tougher American trade policies, have meekly endorsed the president's request.

One Democratic legislator who was breathing fire over the Weinberger indictment yesterday was Brooks.

catch fire

If something such as an event or performance **catches fire**, it becomes exciting, entertaining, and enjoyable.

Some fans of the book may feel Streisand has done it justice, but the film never quite catches fire.

The play only really catches fire once Aschenbach falls in love.

come under fire
be under fire ◄◄◄

If someone or something **has come under fire** or **is under fire**, they are being strongly criticized.

The president's plan first came under fire from critics who said he didn't include enough spending cuts.

Britain's prisons are under fire from an international human rights group.

□ This expression is more commonly used literally to talk about a situation where someone is actually being fired at.

draw someone's fire ◄

If you **draw** someone's **fire**, you do or say something which makes them strongly criticize you.

Their first substantial work was the flats at Ham Common in 1957. This immediately drew the fire of the architectural establishment.

Moynihan's plan to cut the Social Security payroll tax has already drawn fire from the

administration, which says it will bankrupt the Social Security system by the year 2005.

fight fire with fire ◄

If you **fight fire with fire**, you use the same methods of fighting and the same amount of force as your opponent. Other verbs such as 'meet' or 'match' are sometimes used instead of 'fight'.

The chancellor answered by fighting fire with fire. In a letter he attacked Mr Brown for 'wasting so much time and energy on an issue which is totally irrelevant to the concerns of the British people'.

Down here it is essential to adapt to conditions and meet fire with fire. We have the ability to play any style when required.

fire in your belly ◄

If you say that someone does something with **fire in** their **belly** or with **fire in the belly**, you mean that they do it in a very enthusiastic, energetic, and passionate way.

Some people claim he has changed his style, but Ian has played with fire in his belly throughout his career. He would not be the same without the aggressive streak.

The trouble with Jack, Ann says, is also what attracted her to him: the absence of a 'fire in the belly' about his work.

hang fire

If someone **hangs fire**, they wait and do not do anything for a while. If something **hangs fire**, nothing is done about it for a while.

Banks and building societies are hanging fire on interest rates to see how the French vote in their referendum.

It is now imperative that a number of policy initiatives, which have been hanging fire for some time, should be implemented.

hold your fire
hold fire ◄

If you **hold** your **fire** or **hold fire**, you delay doing something, for example attacking or criticizing someone, because you are waiting to see what will happen.

The administration will hold its fire until it sees the detail of the bill, but is likely then to oppose it.

We are holding fire on our assessment of the situation until a detailed analysis can be made after a longer period.

□ This expression is more commonly used literally to talk about a situation where soldiers stop shooting, or wait before they start shooting.

light a fire under someone ◄

If you **light a fire under** someone, you force them to take action or to start behaving in the way you want. This expression is used mainly in American English.

They need to crank up their technical research and light a fire under their marketing force because their stream of new products is too slow.

Johnson told Sage to call Shearson and light a fire under Project Stretch.

play with fire ◄◄

If you accuse someone of **playing with fire**, you are warning that they are behaving in a very risky way and are likely to have problems.

It is the Government that is playing with fire. If it carries on in this way, it will cause civil war within the Conservative Party.

Schulte warned government and industrial leaders that those who even venture to think about mass layoffs are playing with fire.

fish

a big fish ◄◄

If you refer to someone as **a big fish**, you mean that they are important or powerful.

In the Seventies three MPs became embroiled in a scandal surrounding the corrupt activities of a Pontefract architect called John Poulson. Two of them were nonentities, the third was a very big fish indeed.

The four who were arrested here last September were described as really big fish by the U.S. Drug Enforcement Agency.

a big fish in a small pond
a big frog in a small pond ◄

If you refer to someone as **a big fish in a small pond**, you mean that they are one of the most important and influential people in a small organization or social group. You often use this expression to suggest that they would be less important or interesting if they were part of a larger organization or group. This expression is very variable. In American English, you can also talk about **a big frog in a small pond**, with the same meaning.

In Rhodesia I was a big fish in a small pond. But here there'd be many lean years before I built up a reputation.

As a large fish in a small pond, Smith found it easy to dominate fashion photography in Australia.

Being a big fish in a tiny, stagnant pool clearly gives controversial columnists ideas way above their station.

□ You can refer to someone as **a small fish in a big pond** if they are not very important or influential because they are part of a much larger organization or social group.

I was used to being a big fish in a small pond. Now I'm the smallest fish in a very big pond. But that has its own advantages because it stretches you as a designer to try to achieve more.

a cold fish ◄

If you refer to someone as **a cold fish**, you mean that they seem unemotional, and this makes them appear unfriendly or unsympathetic.

Since the President is generally seen as a cold fish, it is all the more impressive when he does show his feelings.

He didn't really show much emotion – he is a bit of a cold fish.

drink like a fish

If you say that someone **drinks like a fish**, you mean that they regularly drink a lot of alcohol.

When I was younger I could drink like a fish and eat like a pig.

The father was not too bad but the mother drank like a fish.

a fish out of water ◄

If you feel like **a fish out of water**, you feel awkward or ill at ease because you are in an unfamiliar situation or surroundings.

I think he thought of himself as a country gentleman and was like a fish out of water in Birmingham.

It's not as if I had any obvious trauma in my life; I just felt like a fish out of water.

□ You can use **fish-out-of-water** before a noun, to describe a situation where someone feels awkward or uncomfortable.

The fish-out-of-water feeling continued when she went to study in Cambridge, having already spent two years working in Africa.

have other fish to fry
have bigger fish to fry ◄

If you say that someone is not interested in something because they **have other fish to fry** or **have bigger fish to fry**, you mean that they are not interested because they have more important, interesting, or profitable things to do.

I didn't pursue it in detail because I'm afraid I had other fish to fry at the time.

Although she nearly lost her temper with Baker, Linda Robinson tried to avoid wasting time on bureaucratic squabbling. She had bigger fish to fry.

□ This phrase is often varied. For example, if someone **has** their **own fish to fry**, they are not interested in doing something because they have business of their own to attend to.

Tony comes and goes. He's got his own fish to fry, as they say.

like shooting fish in a barrel

If you say that a battle or contest is **like shooting fish in a barrel**, you mean that one side is so much stronger than the other that the weaker side has no chance at all of winning.

I heard one case where some of the enemy soldiers had come out and they were saying it was like shooting fish in a barrel.

While Taylor insists that he is not treating this game as a one-off opportunity to shoot fish in a barrel, he is well aware of the necessity for his players to take a high proportion of the chances that are bound to arise.

neither fish nor fowl ◄

If you say that something or someone is **neither fish nor fowl**, you mean that they are difficult to identify, classify, or understand, because they seem partly one thing and partly another. People occasionally replace 'fish' with 'flesh'.

Brunel's vessel was neither fish nor fowl: a passenger liner too ugly and dirty to offer much beyond novelty value.

By the mid-1980s, Canada had a constitution that was neither fish nor fowl in terms of political philosophy.

He thought of that young man Corsari, neither flesh nor fowl, who had made a friend of both girls.

there are plenty more fish in the sea
there are other fish in the sea

If your romance or love affair has ended and someone says to you **'there are plenty more fish in the sea'** or **'there are other fish in the sea'**, they are trying to comfort you by pointing out that there are still many other people who you might have a successful relationship with in the future.

If your daughter is upset because her boyfriend left her, declaring cheerfully 'There are other fish in the sea' won't help.

Never mind, he says, there are plenty more fish in the sea.

fishing

a fishing expedition ◄

If you are on **a fishing expedition**, you are trying to find out the truth or the facts about something, often in a secretive way. This expression is used mainly in American English.

You know why you're here. You're on a fishing expedition. You're hunting for material.

He was asked whether Wilkey was engaged in a fishing expedition aimed at politically embarrassing the House.

fist

an iron fist
an iron fist in a velvet glove ◄◄

If you say that someone controls a situation with **an iron fist**, you mean that they do it with great force, often without regard to other people's welfare.

The Generals have ruled the nation with an

iron fist for more than half of its independent existence.

The symbol of their rule was not so much the iron fist of repression as the queues and empty shelves of a pathetically failing economy.

□ You can talk about **an iron fist in a velvet glove** when someone actually uses a lot of force although they give the appearance of being caring or gentle.

If a kid isn't paying attention then he probably has more pressing things to think about. While the team is inherently sympathetic, the iron fist in the velvet glove approach is occasionally employed.

fit

fighting fit ◄

If someone is **fighting fit**, they are very healthy and feel very well and in the right condition to deal with a difficult task. This expression is used in British English.

Nathan is now fighting fit and ready to tackle school again after his three-month battle for life.

For most of us the balance is not perfect; one day we feel fighting fit, the next a bit under the weather.

fit as a fiddle
fit as a flea ◄

If you say that someone is **fit as a fiddle** or **fit as a flea**, you mean that they are very fit and healthy. 'Fit as a flea' is used only in British English.

He was nearly 80 and fit as a fiddle. His death was out of the blue, and I felt devastated.

I'm as fit as a fiddle, I'm never ill, I have an iron constitution.

He will want to make up for time lost. He is young enough at 33 and fit as a flea. He's a brilliant goalkeeper, no different from when I signed him as a teenager for Aberdeen, just more experienced.

fit to be tied

If you are **fit to be tied**, you are very angry. This expression is used mainly in American English.

After the Christmas holidays, one patient was fit to be tied. She was angry at having to cook all the foods she couldn't eat.

Douglas was fit to be tied. He almost killed Harry. He made Harry pay back every last penny.

fits

in fits and starts ◄◄

If something happens or is done **in fits and starts**, it does not happen continuously, but regularly stops and then starts again.

The employment picture had been improving in fits and starts during the past several months, and most economists had been predicting more improvement for June. But that didn't happen.

Denise's career plans can only proceed in fits and starts.

At dawn, after a number of fits and starts, the convoy finally approaches Baidoa.

fix

no quick fix ◄◄◄

If you say that there is **no quick fix** to a problem, you mean there are no simple ways of solving it.

There can be no quick fix for public spending. If the recovery fails to cut the deficit sharply, a rise in taxes will be needed.

Any tax measures enacted now as a quick fix would only be reversed in a few years when the economy picks up.

☐ You can also use **quick-fix** before a noun.

The fight against crime is not a quick-fix operation. It has to be total and relentless. We are pursuing a combination of short, long and medium term measures.

He warned Congress against any quick fix solutions to get the economy moving.

flag

fly the flag ◄◄◄

If you **fly the flag** for your country or a group to which you belong, you represent it at a sporting event or at some other special occasion, or you do something to show your support for it. Verbs such as 'carry' and 'show' are sometimes used instead of 'fly'.

It doesn't matter whether you are flying the flag for your country, or the Horse Trials Group, or your sponsor, the image you present is all-important.

The Kuwaiti team however have made many friends. They won no medals, but said they were only in Peking to show the flag.

He believed in the sacred power of great music: he felt that he was carrying the flag of high culture, speaking of lofty truths to an educated elite.

keep the flag flying

If you **keep the flag flying**, you do something to show your support for a group to which you belong, or to show your support for something that you agree with.

I would ask members to keep the flag flying by entering some of their plants in both shows.

It's important that artists say that they have an entirely different opinion and that they will keep the flag of tolerance flying.

a red flag ◄

You can refer to something that gives a warning of a bad or dangerous situation or event as **a red flag**. This expression is more commonly used in American English than British. Compare **a red flag before a bull**; see **bull**.

These are devices that are necessary components of nuclear weapons, and clearly that has raised a red flag in the minds of a lot of people.

I have never seen a set of financial statements that showed more red flags and raised more questions in my life.

Cholesterol was the red flag that alerted millions of Americans to the fact that diet really does matter.

wrap yourself in the flag
drape yourself in the flag ◄

If you say that someone, especially a politician, **is wrapping** themselves **in the flag** or **is draping** themselves **in the flag** of their country, you are criticizing them for trying to do something for their own advantage while pretending to do it for the good of their country. These expressions are used mainly in American English.

Politicians always try to wrap themselves in the flag on Independence Day, but I think most people can see through that.

Mr. Doherty also chastised advertisers for fighting proposed cigarette ad restrictions by draping themselves in the flag and lecturing about their First Amendment freedoms of speech.

flagpole

run something up the flagpole

If you **run** a new idea **up the flagpole**, you suggest it to people in order to find out what they think of it.

The President should consider running the capital-gains cut back up the flagpole.

flags

put the flags out

If you **put the flags out** or **put out the flags**, you celebrate something special that has happened. This expression is used in British English.

Even now, they must be putting the flags out in beleaguered British holiday resorts like Bognor and Blackpool.

Birthdays and christenings, or just a spell of good weather, are all the excuse you need to put out the flags and celebrate summer in the garden.

flame

an old flame ◄◄◄

An old flame is someone who you had a romantic relationship with in the past.

Last week Alec was seen dining with his old flame Janine Turner in New York.

Julia Samuel was one of Prince Andrew's old flames but went on to marry a businessman.

What do you do when he continues to nurse a passion for an old flame from his past?

flames

fan the flames   ◄◄

If something that someone says or does **fans the flames**, it makes a bad situation worse. **Add fuel to the fire** means the same.

The mayor's creation of a commission to investigate police corruption further fanned the flames of resentment that finally exploded into race hatred.

Extremist organisations in the west were actively fanning the flames in the east, he said.

go up in flames
go down in flames   ◄

If something **goes up in flames** or **goes down in flames**, it fails or comes to an end, or is destroyed completely.

The Hollywood she'd known had gone up in flames the day she left. A new Hollywood and a new Washington had grown up.

Lineker, Taylor and the whole of England will be hoping England's Championship dream does not go up in flames, too.

On May 1st, the proposal went down in flames.

□ The expression **go up in flames** is more commonly used literally to talk about something being destroyed by fire.

The building went up in flames.

shoot down in flames   ◄

If an idea or plan **is shot down in flames**, it is criticized strongly or rejected completely.

Just six months ago his idea would have been shot down in flames for its sheer lunacy.

Let me shoot down in flames this concept that some bureaucracy in our government will block this initiative.

□ If you **are shot down in flames**, you are severely criticized or made to look foolish for something that you have done or suggested.

Weren't this band the band of the month last month? And now they're just shot down in flames.

I know damn well they'll probably shoot me down in flames and come out with a load of excuses.

flash

flash in the pan   ◄◄

If you say that an achievement or success is **a flash in the pan**, you mean that it is unlikely to be repeated or to last. If you say that someone who has had a success is **a flash in the pan**, you mean that their success is unlikely to be repeated.

In the days following Beckon's victory, the British establishment has gone out of its way to try and dismiss the result as a flash in the pan.

Hopefully now I'll be taken seriously, I'm not a flash in the pan.

□ You can use **flash-in-the-pan** before a noun.

It's a marvellous follow-up to Cole's promising debut play, and one so different in conception, style and tone that it suggests hers is no flash-in-the-pan talent, but a major and mature new voice.

flat

fall flat: 1   ◄◄◄

If an event or an attempt to do something **falls flat**, it is completely unsuccessful.

Murray warns that if the efforts fall flat and the economic situation does not change, this city can expect another riot 25 years from now.

The champagne opening of a new art gallery fell flat when the boss's wife fired a cork straight through the most expensive painting on show.

fall flat: 2

If a joke **falls flat**, nobody thinks it is funny.

He then started trying to tell jokes to the assembled gathering. These too fell flat.

fall flat on your face   ◄

If you say that someone **falls flat on** their **face** when they try to do something, you mean that they fail or make an embarrassing mistake.

I may fall flat on my face or it may be a glorious end to my career.

Every so often the film trips over itself and falls flat on its face.

flat as a pancake   ◄

If you say that something is as **flat as a pancake**, you are emphasizing that it is very flat.

There was barely a breeze and the water was as flat as a pancake.

Could he really put up interest rates now? With the economy flat as a pancake and the housing market in crisis?

flat-footed

catch someone flat-footed   ◄

If someone **is caught** or **left flat-footed**, they are put at a disadvantage when something happens which they do not expect, with the result that they do not know what to do next and often look clumsy or foolish.

'The people around were caught flat-footed,' said Mr. Enko. 'Nobody expected floods of such magnitude.'

Pentland had agreed to buy Adidas but pulled out of the deal suddenly last week leaving the French millionaire flat-footed.

flavour

flavour of the month ◄◄◄

If you say that someone or something is **flavour of the month**, you mean that they are currently very popular. This expression is often used to suggest in a critical way that people change their opinions very frequently, so that the people or things that are popular now are unlikely to stay popular for very long. This expression is used mainly in British English.

I've been around long enough to know you can be flavour of the month and then out of fashion.

At the moment the flavour of the month is the fixed-rate loan.

Talk to film stars these days, and the odds are they'll be declaring an unprecedented interest in the destruction of the rainforests, in animal rights, in AIDS awareness, or whatever cause is the latest flavour of the month in celebrity circles.

□ Instead of 'month', you can mention other periods of time such as 'year', 'week', or 'moment'.

Monetarism was the flavour of the year.

Suddenly, he was flavour of the moment on both sides of the Atlantic.

□ 'Flavour' is spelled 'flavor' in American English.

flea

a flea in your ear ◄

If someone sends you away with **a flea in your ear**, they angrily reject your suggestions or attempts to do something. This expression is used in British English.

I was prepared to be met with hostility as another nosy outsider, even to be sent off with a flea in my ear. But Moira was happy to chat.

The clerk refused to serve her, saying that for all he knew she could be the maid. She was forced to return later with her husband, who gave the clerk a large flea in his ear.

flesh

flesh and blood: 1 ◄◄

If you say that someone is your own **flesh and blood**, you are emphasizing that they are a member of your family, and so you must help them when they are in trouble.

The kid, after all, was his own flesh and blood. He deserved a second chance.

You can't just let your own flesh and blood go to prison if there's any way you can help.

He's my flesh and blood, I'll stick by him whatever he does.

flesh and blood: 2 ◄

If you say that someone is **flesh and blood**, you are emphasizing that they have human feelings or weaknesses, and that they are not perfect.

I'm flesh and blood like everyone else and I, too, can be damaged.

We priests are mere flesh and blood. In fact we're often even weaker than others.

flesh and blood: 3 ◄

If you describe someone as a **flesh and blood** person, you are emphasizing that they are real and actually exist, rather than being part of someone's imagination.

His absence ever since her second birthday made her think of him as a picture rather than a flesh-and-blood father.

He was the first writer since Shakespeare to make history live, to show his readers that the past was peopled by flesh and blood human beings very like themselves.

in the flesh ◄◄◄

If you meet or see someone famous **in the flesh**, you actually meet or see them, rather than, for example, seeing them in a film or on television.

But what does Jamie think of his hero now, having met him in the flesh?

He was hurrying though he wasn't late for our meeting. I was early. I'd been impatient to see him in the flesh.

It was strange to see in the flesh a man whose name and face had been almost as familiar to me as that of Churchill or Hitler.

make your flesh creep
make your flesh crawl ◄

If you say that something **makes** your **flesh creep** or **makes** your **flesh crawl**, you mean that you find it unpleasant and it makes you frightened, distressed, or uncomfortable. **Make** your **skin crawl** means the same.

I didn't like him the first time I set eyes on him and now I know why. He made my flesh creep.

This novel has moments to make the flesh creep.

I could see nobody. But they could see me. It made my flesh crawl. They were watching, perhaps through rifle sights.

put flesh on something
put flesh on the bones of something ◄

If you **put flesh on** something or **put flesh on the bones of** something, you add more detailed information or more substance to it.

The central bankers' blueprint is nevertheless the first clear picture of what a central bank-

ing system would look like and puts flesh on the European vision of monetary integration.

What would a Middle East at peace actually look like? Somebody needs to start putting flesh on those bones.

flick

give someone the flick
give someone the flick pass

If you **give** someone or something **the flick** or if you **give** them **the flick pass**, you reject them or get rid of them. These expressions are used mainly in Australian English.

Nikki has given Brandon the flick.

Adrian Brunker plans to give work the flick pass by the time he hits 30. He reckons that will give him more time to play golf.

flies

drop like flies: 1

If you say that people **are dropping like flies**, you mean that large numbers of them are dying within a short period of time, usually for the same reason.

Relief officials say two-thirds of the seven million population are at risk. 'What we are seeing is the complete elimination of a nation. They are dropping like flies.'

Meanwhile Burketown was left without a police officer while people dropped like flies.

drop like flies: 2

If you say that large numbers of similar things **are dropping like flies**, you mean that they are all failing, within a short period of time.

While other retailers are dropping like flies, supermarkets are making fat profits.

We will see interest payments on the national debt greater than total income taxes collected, our nation in a steady state of stagnation, and cities dropping like flies into bankruptcy.

there are no flies on someone

If you say **there are no flies on** someone, you mean that they are quick to understand a situation and are not easily deceived.

You have to establish that you are an officer with good and tried soldiers: there are no flies on them.

flight

a flight of fancy ◀◀◀

If you refer to an idea, statement, or plan as **a flight of fancy**, you mean that it is imaginative and pleasant to think about but not at all practical.

But their claim to be best-placed to co-ordinate such research will be credible only if they avoid the flights of fancy that have marked the past few years.

Completely restored steam trains run a service to Wootton, allowing transport enthusiasts to indulge in flights of fancy about the Victorian era of steam.

This is no flight of fancy. The prototype is already flying, and production is to begin next year.

flip

flip your lid
flip your wig ◀

If someone **flips** their **lid** or **flips** their **wig**, they become extremely angry or upset about something, and lose control of themselves.

'Boy, you are brave,' she said, stroking the bleeding cut. 'A lot of grownups flip their lids when you clean a cut like this.'

There were always ominous undercurrents underlying Greg Ackell's pop songs, but never before have they seemed quite this sinister. Maybe it was the break-up of the old group that finally made him flip his wig.

floodgates

open the floodgates
the floodgates open ◀◀◀

If an event, action, or decision **opens the floodgates** to something, it makes it possible or likely that a particular thing will be done by many people, perhaps in a way that seems undesirable. You can also say that **the floodgates open**.

Giving in to the strikers' demands, government ministers said, would open the floodgates to demands by workers in other large state-owned industries like textiles and mining.

The floodgates were opened yesterday for cheaper new cars for thousands of motorists. Laws preventing drivers from buying vehicles from abroad at knockdown prices without severe tax penalties were swept aside.

Chinese factories, office blocks and power stations are rising as fast as UK firms are going bust and when the trade floodgates open, the Chinese will be hot-foot to their airports.

floor

through the floor ◀

If prices or values have fallen **through the floor**, they have suddenly decreased to a very low level.

Property prices have dropped through the floor.

On the fateful day, Oct. 19, the value of those stocks fell through the floor.

wipe the floor with someone ◀

If you **wipe the floor with** someone, you prove that you are much better than they are at doing something, or you defeat them totally in a competition, fight, or discussion.

When you play against people whose technique is superior and who can match your courage and commitment, they're going to wipe the floor with you.

If he could wipe the floor with the Prime Minister on his first outing as opposition leader, just imagine what he will be able to do with a bit of practice.

flow

go with the flow   ◄◄

If you **go with the flow**, you let things happen to you or let other people tell you what to do, rather than trying to control what happens yourself.

I didn't choose to become president. It was just the natural flow of things. I went along with the flow and accepted the decision of the others.

This year I'm going to take a deep breath, leave my troubles and tension in the departure lounge and go with the flow.

in full flow: 1
in full flood
in full spate   ◄◄

If you say that an activity, or the person who is performing the activity, is **in full flow**, you mean that the activity has started and is being carried out with a great deal of energy and enthusiasm. You can also say that someone or something is **in full flood** or **in full spate**. 'In full flood' is the only form which is used in American English.

When she's in full flow, she usually starts around 7pm, breaks for dinner, then works late, sometimes right through the night till 6am.

The rhythm is always crucial, so to hear the drum and bass of the Barrett brothers in full flow is a real treat for long-time fans.

By 1944-45 he was in full flow, scoring in twelve successive matches and totalling twenty-seven goals in this sequence.

The military have been taking the lead in the reactionary right-wing offensive, which has been in full flood now for about three months.

With family life in full spate, there were nevertheless some times of quiet domesticity.

in full flow: 2

If someone is **in full flow**, they are talking fluently and easily, and seem likely to continue for some time. This expression is used in British English.

Jarvis parked in his usual place and came through the main door. A male voice was in full flow in the lounge.

As he jumped out of his pick-up, Mark Mueller was already in full flow, telling me how he had been the first to know the movie men were back in town.

fly

the fly in the ointment   ◄

If you refer to someone or something as **the fly in the ointment**, you mean that they are the person or thing that prevents a situation from being as successful or happy as it otherwise would be.

The only flies in the ointment were the older boys, who objected to the character of their school changing. They did not care much for Mr Cope's new rules.

The only fly in the ointment is the enormous debt portfolios of Marine Midland in Latin America.

If he was aware of Roger Denny as a fly in the domestic ointment, he showed no sign.

a fly on the wall   ◄◄

If you say that you would like to be **a fly on the wall** when a particular thing happens, you mean that you would like to hear what is said or to see what happens, although this is actually impossible because it will take place in private and you cannot be there.

I'd love to be a fly on the wall at their team meetings.

What I'd give to be a fly on the wall when Draper finds out what's happened to his precious cargo!

☐ You can use **fly-on-the-wall** to describe something such as a documentary film, where the makers of the film record everything that happens in an unobtrusive way, so that the film seems as accurate and natural as possible.

Thursday night should mean compulsory viewing of Sylvania Waters, which if anyone doesn't already know, is the BBC's fly-on-the-wall real life family documentary.

I'd love to work as the personal photographer of a rock star for a year, documenting their life on the road from a fly-on-the-wall perspective.

like a blue-arsed fly

If you do something **like a blue-arsed fly**, you do it very quickly and without having much control. This is a very informal expression, which is used in British English. Some people find it offensive.

I ran around like a blue-arsed fly, packed two suitcases and a trunk, and left everything else.

on the fly   ◄

If you do something **on the fly**, you do it quickly and automatically, without thinking about it or planning it in advance.

The negotiation has been passed out of the hands of the diplomats into the hands of the politicians, people who can make decisions on the fly and don't have to phone home to their boss.

This gives architects and designers the power

to build an environment, explore it and maybe do some designing on the fly.

wouldn't hurt a fly
wouldn't harm a fly ◄

If you say that someone **wouldn't hurt a fly** or **wouldn't harm a fly**, you mean that they are very kind and gentle.

He is, he insists, a pacifist, who would not hurt a fly.

She was such a lovely girl, who would not have harmed a fly.

food

food for thought ◄◄◄

If something gives you **food for thought**, it makes you think very hard about an issue.

I am not a religious person, but knowing what a good and faithful servant my friend has been, it has certainly given me food for thought.

This event also provided the international selection committee with encouragement and some food for thought when it meets to discuss the team.

fool

a fool and his money are soon parted

People say **'a fool and his money are soon parted'** to point out that it is easy to persuade someone who is not sensible to spend their money on worthless things. This expression is very variable.

They can be charming – no one is better at parting a fool from his money – but as the picture opens, they're a little desperate.

fool's gold ◄◄

If you say that a plan for making money is **fool's gold**, you mean that it would be foolish to carry it out because you are sure that it will fail.

The Chancellor dismissed as 'pure fool's gold' the idea that devaluing the pound could assist the British economy.

All we wanted was an honourable settlement. He chose to go after fool's gold and lost.

□ **Fool's gold** is a gold-coloured mineral that is found in rock and that people sometimes mistake for gold.

live in a fool's paradise ◄

If you say that someone **is living in a fool's paradise**, you are criticizing them for believing wrongly and stupidly that their situation is good, when really it is not.

But anyone who believes that this deal heralds a golden new era for the long-suffering European air traveller is living in a fool's paradise. The struggle has only just begun.

Parents live in a fool's paradise when it comes to drugs. More than 90 per cent refuse to

accept that their child would take drugs, but a third think their children's friends do.

fools

fools rush in where angels fear to tread
fools rush in

People say **'fools rush in where angels fear to tread'** or **'fools rush in'** to comment on or criticize a person who did something hastily without thinking clearly about the likely consequences. This expression is very variable.

Even with such a crowded schedule, she still finds time to read the 2000 or so letters she receives every year. 'Sometimes I stop and think, Good God, how did I get into this,' she says with a laugh. 'Fools rush in where angels fear to tread.'

That was something none of the three of us would have dared to say. Fools rush in...

foot

the boot is on the other foot
the shoe is on the other foot ◄

If you say that **the boot is on the other foot**, you mean that a situation has been reversed completely, so that the people who were previously in a better position are now in a worse one, while the people who were previously in a worse position are now in a better one. This form of the expression is used in British English; in American English, the form is **the shoe is on the other foot**.

Comments like that from a manager are better made in private. If the boot was on the other foot and a player went public like that after a game, his club would quickly be looking to slap a fine on him.

The fact is, I'm in the job. You may have assisted along the way, but as far as I know you're not in a position to remove me. The boot is now on the other foot.

That's a view conservatives have espoused for years, but they said it when they thought the courts were working against majority opinion. Now the shoe's on the other foot, and liberals are going to the people to overturn the courts.

caught on the wrong foot

If you **are caught on the wrong foot**, something happens quickly and unexpectedly, and surprises you because you are not ready for it. Compare **get off on the wrong foot** and **start off on the right foot**.

The supermarket chain seems to have been caught on the wrong foot, still trying to escape its 'cheap' past just as it should be capitalising on that record.

The recent change of public mood has caught the government clumsily on the wrong foot.

☐ The verb **wrong-foot** is also used, and is much more common.

Again and again European and UN diplomacy has been wrong-footed by events in the Balkans.

Newspapers, radio and television wrong-footed ministers by highlighting one emotive aspect of the speech at the expense of the broader, gentler, message.

a foot in both camps
a foot in each camp

If someone has **a foot in both camps**, they support or belong to two different groups, without making a firm commitment to either of them. You can also say that someone has **a foot in each camp**.

With an Indian father and an English mother, she had a foot in both camps – or perhaps in neither.

Sagdeev is trying to promote a compromise because he has one foot in each camp.

a foot in the door: 1   ◄◄

If someone is trying to get involved in something, for example to start doing business in a new area, and you say that they have got **a foot in the door**, you mean that they have made a small but successful start and are likely to do well in the future.

China is opening its state owned airlines to foreign investors and if British Airways gets a foot in the door, the profits will be enormous.

He's now trying to capitalise on his connections in the region. He wants to get his foot in the door ahead of his long time rival.

The company said it issued the low bid because it wanted a foot in the door of a potentially lucrative market.

foot-in-the-door: 2

If you describe a way of doing something as **foot-in-the-door**, you mean that it is done in an aggressive or forceful way, in order to persuade someone to agree to do something which they probably do not want to do.

Double glazing salesmen have become a bit of a national joke, what with their foot-in-the-door methods.

get off on the wrong foot   ◄

If you start doing something and you **get off on the wrong foot**, you start badly or in an unfortunate way. Compare **caught on the wrong foot** and **start off on the right foot**.

The last few times I've been at home on leave everything seems to have gone wrong. We seem to get off on the wrong foot from the start. We row a lot.

Even though they called the election and had been preparing for it for some time, they got off on the wrong foot.

not put a foot wrong   ◄◄

If you **don't put a foot wrong**, you do not make any mistakes. This expression is used in British English.

John Walker has said that all great athletes have a season in which they don't put a foot wrong.

He glided smoothly through his news conference, never putting a foot wrong and giving a strong impression of a man who is recapturing the political initiative from his more radical opponents.

He hardly put a foot wrong in defence and was fine in attack, except for one misdirected pass.

one foot in the grave

If you say that someone has **one foot in the grave**, you mean that they are very ill or very old and are likely to die soon. You use this expression when you are talking about illness and death in a light-hearted way.

The guard and warder are taken in, they're convinced De Fiore's got one foot in the grave.

Richard is far from having one foot in the grave – and he never means to get to that point.

put your best foot forward   ◄◄

If you are doing something and you **put your best foot forward**, you work hard and energetically to make sure it is a success.

We remember our mother's stern instructions not to boast, but completely forget her advice to put our best foot forward.

Sir David said that having been faced with a warning of one last chance, the commission should have put its best foot forward and produced something independent.

put your foot down: 1   ◄◄

If you **put your foot down**, you use your authority in order to stop something from happening.

Annabel went through a spell of saying: 'I can do my homework and watch TV.' Naturally I put my foot down.

He had planned to go skiing on his own, but his wife had decided to put her foot down.

put your foot down: 2   ◄

If you **put your foot down** when you are driving, you start to drive as fast as you can. This expression is used in British English.

Once out of the park and finding a clear stretch of the Bayswater Road, he put his foot down.

She gives this advice to those setting off on car journeys from London to Scotland: 'Just stick in the fast lane and put your foot down.'

put your foot in it
put your foot in your mouth   ◄◄

If you **put** your **foot in it** or **put** your **foot**

in your **mouth**, you say something which embarrasses or offends the person you are with, and embarrasses you as a result.

I put my foot in it straight away, referring to folk music. Tom sat forward and glared. 'It's not folk music, man. It's heritage music.'

To the majority of voters, he is hopelessly unpresidential, a lightweight, forever putting his foot in his mouth.

☐ Journalists sometimes refer humorously to someone's **foot-in-mouth** tendencies.

I loved Prince Philip's latest attack of foot-in-mouth disease when he asked a Cayman Islander: 'Aren't most of you descended from pirates?'

shoot yourself in the foot ◄◄◄

If you **shoot** yourself **in the foot**, you do or say something stupid which causes problems for yourself or harms your chances of success.

If I was to insult the contestants I would be shooting myself in the foot.

The shop ran a 25 per cent off sale early in December. It now looks as if it shot itself in the foot, attracting people who meant to shop there anyway to do so during the promotion instead.

Unless he shoots himself in the foot, in all probability he will become President.

start off on the right foot

If you **start off on the right foot**, you immediately have success when you begin to do something. Compare **caught on the wrong foot** and **get off on the wrong foot**.

Share your feelings, both positive and negative. If you decide to go ahead, you will be starting off on the right foot.

To me this was a man who was prepared to start off on the right foot; he was mature with some common sense, and the type who would not expect to become an expert in a very short time.

footloose

footloose and fancy-free

If someone is **footloose and fancy-free**, they are not married or in a long-term relationship, and they have very few responsibilities or commitments. This is an old-fashioned expression.

A divorced man is footloose and fancy-free. He can go to parties and pubs on his own, and come and go as he pleases.

footsteps

follow in someone's footsteps ◄◄◄

If you **follow in** someone's **footsteps**, you do the same thing that they did.

Rudolph Garvin was a college student, the son of a physician, who wanted to follow in his

father's footsteps. His prospects were dim because of his failing grades.

He has developed and flourished on the pitch into a highly talented player, poised to follow in the footsteps of such Portuguese greats as Eusebio.

forelock

tug your forelock
touch your forelock ◄

In British English, if you think that someone is showing an excessive amount of respect to another person and making themselves seem very humble and inferior, you can say that they **are tugging** their **forelock** or **touching** their **forelock** in order to express your criticism of their behaviour.

Last night the Prime Minister accused the Labour leader of being prepared to tug his forelock to Brussels over whether Britain should join a single European currency.

These are the same old fogeys who tug the forelock to the British establishment.

A lot of people seem to think we're supposed to go round touching our forelock and scraping our heads against the floor. We're not.

☐ You can refer to this kind of behaviour as **forelock-tugging** or **forelock-touching**.

The idea of forelock-tugging is totally alien to us, as is the idea that some people can be bred to rule.

forewarned

forewarned is forearmed

People say **'forewarned is forearmed'** to mean that if you know about something which is going to happen in the future, you can be ready to deal with it.

The authors' idea is that to be forewarned is to be forearmed: if we know how persuasion works, perhaps we can resist some of it.

A Maryborough principal decided forewarned was forearmed recently. When he heard Pat would be in town, he warned his pupils that if they came upon a man with a beard in the school grounds, they were to be nice to him and then go and tell the principal.

fort

hold the fort
hold down the fort ◄

If you **hold the fort** for someone, you look after things for them while they are somewhere else or while they are busy doing something else. In American English, you can also say that you **hold down the fort**.

Since she entered Parliament five years ago, he has held the fort at their Norfolk home during the week.

Her 13-year-old daughter is holding the fami-

ly together. 'She's doing fine. She's the one that's cool, calm and collected. She's the one that's kind of holding down the fort.'

fortune

a small fortune ◄◄◄

You describe a sum of money as **a small fortune** to emphasize that it is a very large amount.

This was the first of hundreds of visits I made to psychiatrists in the course of the next twenty-five years, and which altogether cost a small fortune.

For almost two years, Hawkins made a small fortune running a drugstore.

You can spend a small fortune on locks and alarms and still become a target for the housebreaker.

Sharon didn't know much about antiques, but the lamps alone were probably worth a small fortune.

foundations

shake the foundations of something ◄

If someone or something **shakes the foundations of** a society or a system of beliefs, or **shakes** it **to** its **foundations**, they cause great uncertainty and make people question their most deeply held beliefs. Other verbs with a similar meaning can be used instead of 'shake'.

The new era is shaking the foundations of all Russia's cultural landmarks.

When an American president is forced to resign, the country is shaken to its foundations.

The music industry was rocked to its foundations last night when it was revealed that the Midlands' top live music venue was to close.

frame

in the frame: 1
the name in the frame ◄◄◄

If you are **in the frame** for promotion or success, you are very likely to get a promotion or to be successful. This expression is used in British English.

Steve has done well. He's close to being back in the frame and I will have a good look at him in training this week.

Darren Bicknell put himself firmly in the frame for an England call-up at Lord's yesterday.

□ You can talk about someone being **the name in the frame** when they are very likely to get a promotion or be successful.

Speculation about potential replacements is already rife, with Sir David Scholey of Warburgs and Sir Nigel Wicks at the Treasury and Lord Lawson among the names in the frame.

in the frame: 2

If someone is **in the frame** for something, people think that they are responsible for a crime or an unpleasant situation, even though this might be untrue. This expression is used in British English.

The fact is, there's only ever been one guy in the frame for this killing, and that's the husband.

After all, wasn't it the Chancellor who originally put Germany in the frame for the pound's failure?

frazzle

wear yourself to a frazzle

If you **wear** yourself **to a frazzle** or if you **are worn to a frazzle**, you feel mentally and physically exhausted because you have been working too hard or because you have been constantly worrying about something.

Why should I wear myself to a frazzle, trying to save your skin for you?

His mother had been worn to a frazzle. Guy helped by looking after his sister.

free

free as the air
free as a bird ◄

If you say that someone is **free as the air** or **free as a bird**, you mean that they are completely free and have no worries or troubles. 'Free as the air' is used only in British English.

They think of us as favoured beings, going where we like, working when we feel like it, free as the air.

I have been island-hopping in the Pacific for the past two and a half years, free as a bird.

freefall

go into freefall
in freefall ◄◄◄

If the value or level of something **goes into freefall**, it starts to fall very quickly. If it is **in freefall**, it is falling very quickly. These expressions are used mainly in journalism.

John Major cancelled a trip to Spain yesterday as the pound went into freefall. The crisis worsened when it was revealed Mr Major had refused German demands to devalue the pound.

Fears are now widespread that shares could go into freefall before Christmas.

Perot's ratings were in freefall; the inner circle of campaign advisers had been unable to persuade the egocentric and stubborn Texas billionaire to produce any policies or to devise a professional election campaign.

□ **A freefall** is a situation in which the value or level of something is falling very rapidly.

You can also say that the value or level of something **freefalls**.

Others underlined the potential for monetary chaos unleashed by the free fall of sterling.

His career seemed about to freefall into oblivion and retirement after a series of drug-related scandals.

frenzy

a feeding frenzy ◄◄

When people refer to **a feeding frenzy**, they are referring to a situation in which a lot of people become very excited about something, often in a destructive or negative way. This expression is often used to refer to journalists writing about a famous person or an exciting or scandalous event.

Parents and other concerned citizens are meeting to discuss the scandal. Lakewood mayor Mark Title says the media feeding frenzy is taking bites out of what he calls an outstanding community.

Stan and Debbie exemplify two different critiques of the financial feeding frenzy of the 1980s; the school of thought that says 'Why did it ever end?' and the other school that asks 'Why did it ever begin?'

fresh

fresh as a daisy
fresh as paint ◄

If you say that someone or something is as **fresh as a daisy**, you are emphasizing that they are very fresh, bright, or alert. In British English, you can also say that they are as **fresh as paint**.

Once you've done some stretching, breathing and toning exercises in this revitalizing bath, you will be as fresh as a daisy again.

She can sleep through anything and emerge fresh as a daisy at the end of it.

Young Hustler looked as fresh as paint despite this being his 14th race of the season.

frighteners

put the frighteners on someone ◄

If someone **puts the frighteners on** you, they threaten you and try to scare you into doing what they want. This expression is used in British English.

He and his chums tried to put the frighteners on Kelley before she had written a single word.

Glenn Close put the frighteners on Michael Douglas and his family in 'Fatal Attraction'.

fritz

on the fritz

A piece of machinery that is **on the fritz** is not working properly. This expression is used in American English.

My mother's toaster went on the fritz.

'They're setting up communications,' Rizzuto said. 'But the goddamned mobile command post has gone on the fritz.'

frog

a frog in your throat

If someone has **a frog in** their **throat**, they find it difficult to speak clearly because they have a cough or a sore throat. Compare **a lump in** your **throat**; see **lump**.

I've got a bit of a cough, excuse me, a frog in my throat.

Oh excuse me, I nearly choked then. Little frog in the back of the throat.

fruit

bear fruit ◄◄◄

If an action **bears fruit**, it produces good results.

Mr Buckland was radiating optimism yesterday, suggesting that the strategy put in place two years ago of concentrating the company's efforts on a smaller range of businesses is now beginning to bear fruit.

People see material conditions getting worse. They don't see the economic reforms championed by the President as bearing fruit.

forbidden fruit ◄

If you describe something as **forbidden fruit**, you mean that you want it very much but are not allowed to have it, or you are not supposed to have it.

Knowing that from now on you can't drink alcohol or have sugar in your tea can make you want those forbidden fruits even more.

In the days of Maoism, auctions were barred. Now Peking's first auction house, which is highly successful, gives a taste of the forbidden fruit.

☐ This expression refers to the story in the Bible in which Eve tempts Adam to eat the fruit of the tree of knowledge, which God had forbidden them to touch.

frying pan

out of the frying pan into the fire ◄

If you say that someone has gone or jumped **out of the frying pan into the fire**, you mean that they have moved from a bad situation to an even worse one. This expression is very variable.

If you do decide to take such a drastic step, first take every possible precaution that you do not go from the frying pan into the fire.

They should try to develop the ability to consider problems in real detail and avoid the tendency to jump from the frying pan into the fire.

This week John Major steps from the Tory

conference frying pan into the fire of the real world.

fuel

add fuel to the fire
add fuel to the flames ◄◄

If something that someone says or does **adds fuel to the fire** or **adds fuel to the flames**, it makes a bad situation worse. **Fan the flames** means the same.

You must not take the route of trying to borrow your way out of trouble when over-borrowing got you into this state in the first place. This really would be adding fuel to the fire.

The government is warning that a return to the traditional system of wage indexation will only add fuel to the inflationary fires.

□ These expressions are very variable. For example, you can say that something **fuels the fire** or **fuels the flames**, or just that it **adds fuel**.

I'm not going to fuel the fire here: people are perfectly entitled to their own opinion. I would just hope that we might see a little more reason and a lot more understanding in the debate.

These are both recognised as factors which have fuelled the flames of conflict.

His comments are bound to add fuel to the debate already taking place within the party about the Greens' public image.

funeral

it's your funeral

If you are insisting on doing something in a particular way and someone says **'it's your funeral'**, they are pointing out that they think you are wrong but that you will be affected by the bad consequences resulting from it, and they will not.

Have it your own way. You'll be sorry. It's your funeral.

Brand shook his head. 'I'll pass, thanks.' He didn't add, 'It's your funeral, not mine,' although it was the truth.

fur

the fur is flying

If you say that **the fur is flying** over something, you mean that people are arguing very fiercely and angrily about it.

He was one of the churchwardens at St Edward the Confessor's. Where, as I suspect you have already heard, there's been a lot of fur flying these last few months.

A blazing row between Euro factions at last week's meeting of the 1922 Committee set the fur flying again on the Tory backbenches.

furniture

part of the furniture ◄

If you say that someone or something is **part of the furniture**, you mean that they have been present somewhere for such a long time that everyone accepts their presence without questioning it or noticing them.

In ten years he has become part of the furniture of English life, his place on the stage firmly fixed and universally respected.

Once cameras in courts have become part of the furniture, witnesses are so absorbed in answering questions that they forget the cameras are there.

furrow

plough a lonely furrow
plough a lone furrow ◄

If someone **ploughs a lonely furrow** or **ploughs a lone furrow**, they do something by themselves and in their own way, without any help or support from other people. This is a literary expression, which is used in British English.

It seems that Shattock was something of an original thinker, ploughing a lonely furrow.

Amokachi willingly ploughed a lone furrow in his team's cause, but said afterwards that he would find the peculiar physical demands of the English game difficult to master without help.

□ This expression is very variable.

Richardson could have protected himself by seeking the backing of the old guard, but chose not to. He ploughed his own furrow instead.

The Syrian government is more than adept at ploughing its own diplomatic furrow.

After the war I should think he must have had a very difficult furrow to plough because every university was in turmoil.

fuse

blow a fuse

If you **blow a fuse**, you suddenly lose your temper and cannot control your anger.

For all my experience, I blew a fuse in the quarter-final and could have been sent off.

The more adept you become at switching off and letting your toddler blow a fuse without giving in or getting angry, then the sooner he will understand that tantrums don't work.

light the fuse ◄

If you say that someone **lights the fuse**, you mean that they do something which starts off a new and exciting development, or which makes a situation become dangerous.

Ghana's independence in 1957 lit the fuse which led to the rapid freeing of colonial Africa.

MP Bernie Grant has lit a fuse under the im-

migration issue by suggesting that the government should consider paying black people to leave Britain permanently.

on a short fuse
have a short fuse ◄

If you say that someone is **on a short fuse** or **has a short fuse**, you mean that they lose their temper very easily and are quick to re-act angrily when something goes wrong.

In the office he tended to work on a short fuse; but explosive though he was at times, there was always a tremendous compassion ever-ready to be shown to strangers, friends and colleagues alike.

Perhaps he's irritable and has a short fuse, letting you know when he's not pleased.

G

gaff
blow the gaff

If you **blow the gaff**, you tell people something which was supposed to be kept secret. This expression is used in British English.

Scottish Nuclear Ltd has now blown the gaff by saying that it may decide to do without reprocessing altogether.

On being hauled up before Captain Douglas, he had blown the gaff. While utterly denying his part in the crime, he had nevertheless turned informer.

gallery
play to the gallery ◄

If you say that someone such as a politician is **playing to the gallery**, you are criticizing them for trying to impress the public and make themselves popular, instead of dealing seriously with important matters.

It took more than 20 years for the House of Commons to allow TV cameras there, because some members were frightened that others would play to the gallery.

Her obstinate refusal to play to the gallery had eventually won her the reverent respect of all but a tiny minority among her people.

game
ahead of the game ◄◄

If someone is **ahead of the game**, they are well prepared to deal with any change that happens in the activity which they are involved in.

We're always looking at new technologies to keep ahead of the game.

The way scientists keep ahead of the game is to use a combination of molecular analysis and careful judgement to predict what strain, or strains, of virus will cause the next outbreak.

beat someone at their own game ◄◄

If you **beat** someone **at** their **own game**, you do something more successfully than they do, although they have a reputation for doing it better than anyone else.

The East is said to be beating the West at its own game. Its business conglomerates, which lay in ruins only a few decades ago, now out-perform those of Europe and America.

Who do these New Yorkers think they are, coming out here and beating us at our own game?

the game is up ◄◄

If you say that **the game is up** for someone, you mean that they can no longer continue to do something wrong or illegal, because people have found out what they are doing.

Both runners, once the game was up, freely admitted using steroids, human growth hormone and testosterone.

He narrowed his eyes as the blue lights of the police car filled the cab. Sensing the game was up, he pulled over.

Michael's game is up when Kimberly catches him in bed with Sarah.

a game plan ◄◄

Someone's **game plan** is the things that they intend to do in order to achieve a particular aim.

So few people stick to their game plan. I stuck to mine. I had always wanted to be a millionaire from a very early age.

There was and still remains no overall game plan, and no agreed objective for any Western policy.

Couples often have different game plans when they enter relationships.

give the game away ◄◄

If someone or something **gives the game away**, they reveal something which someone had been trying to keep secret.

Johnson had intended to make his announcement in a forthcoming feature in The Times but the paper gave the game away by advertising the feature a week before publishing.

Twelve stowaways have been caught on board a boat bound for Italy. They were detected inside two sealed containers when they gave the game away by screaming for help after being cooped up for seven days.

She looks every inch a Beverly Hills native as

she leans against a palm tree. Only the English accent gives the game away.

new to the game ◄

If you say that someone is **new to the game**, you mean that they have no previous experience of the activity that they are taking part in.

We remember thinking at the time we were getting far too much exposure in the press and trying to do too much. But we didn't do anything about it because we were fairly new to the game and just did what our record company said.

Don't forget that she's new to this game and will take a while to complete the task, so you need to be very patient.

not play the game

If you accuse someone of **not playing the game**, you are accusing them of behaving in an unfair and unacceptable way. This is an old-fashioned expression, which is used mainly in British English. Compare **play the game**.

She said that research grants should all be the same level, and yet some students got more than others. She said this was unfair and wrote to Sir Montague, who then called us all together and berated us for not playing the game.

the numbers game ◄◄

If you say that someone is playing **the numbers game**, you mean that they are using amounts, figures, or statistics to support their argument, often in a way that confuses or misleads people.

He'd noticed before now how rarely statistics in support of an argument were ever countered by statistics demolishing it. If one side started playing the numbers game, the other insisted on arguing in human terms.

The document derides the numbers game which automatically argues that an exhibition receiving 5,000 visitors each day is better than one receiving 3,000.

the only game in town ◄

If you say that someone or something is **the only game in town**, you mean that they are the best or most important of their kind, or the only one worth considering. Other adjectives can be used instead of 'only'.

He's the only game in town, and I am hoping that he can show some real leadership strength.

This plan is the only game in town that may lead to a durable and viable peace, for the alternatives are too awful to think about.

on the game ◄

If a woman is **on the game**, she is working as a prostitute. This is an informal expression, which is used in British English.

How can anyone with kids think of going on the game?

play someone at their own game

If you **play** someone **at** their **own game**, you behave towards them in the same unfair or unpleasant way that they have been behaving towards you.

It used to bug me when men used to come in the office and I never used to get introduced. So I've started playing them at their own game. When I had clients to come and see me, I'd never introduce the men either.

play the game ◄◄

If you have to **play the game**, you have to do things in the accepted way or in the way that you are told to by your superiors, in order to keep your job or to achieve success. Compare **not play the game**.

In order to survive and to prosper in the political system, they have to play the game.

The two official opposition parties must also play the game by the President's rules.

a waiting game ◄◄

If you play **a waiting game**, you delay making any decisions or taking any action, because you think that it is better to wait and see how things develop.

I propose to play a waiting game, and hope that a few of the pieces of this puzzle will soon begin to fit together.

The government seems more inclined to lay aside the contingency plans for air attack and play the waiting game.

games

play games ◄◄

If you accuse someone of **playing games**, you mean that they are not being serious enough about a difficult situation, or that they are deliberately misleading you or making you do unnecessary things.

The company says it needs about a week to decide how many employees will be called back. One turned-away union employee says he thinks the company is playing games with them.

To most Americans, there seems something simply immature about playing games with the fate of a nation already in trouble.

Don't play games, Mona. I know about the theft, and I know that you know about it. I repeat: why are you here?

garbage

garbage in, garbage out

Garbage in, garbage out is a way of saying that if you produce something using poor quality materials, the thing you produce will also be of poor quality.

A computer expert, he said he'd learned from

computer programming that if you put garbage in, you get garbage out.

*Hi-fi has hi-jacked the computer industry
maxim 'Garbage in equals garbage out', to reinforce the concept that a terrific pair of speakers will show up a shoddy CD player for the
piece of junk it is.*

garden

common-or-garden
garden-variety   ◄◄

You can use **common-or-garden** to say that
something is of a very ordinary kind and has
no special features. This form of the expression is used in British English; in American
English, the form is **garden-variety**.

*Moreover, it will not be long before common-
or-garden computer programs can vary the
weight and shape of letters instantaneously, as
well as setting them on the page.*

*She didn't look remotely like a woman going
down with a common or garden head cold.*

*The experiment itself is garden-variety science
that normally would attract scant public attention.*

lead someone up the garden path
lead someone down the garden path   ◄

If someone **leads** you **up the garden path**,
they deceive you by making you believe something which is not true. Other verbs are
sometimes used instead of 'lead'. This form of
the expression is used mainly in British English; in American English, the usual form is
lead someone **down the garden path**.

*He may have led me up the garden path. He
said everything was over with Penny but now
he seems to be seeing her again.*

*She said warningly, 'Be careful not to be
lured up the garden path.'*

*The company spends a lot of time keeping
other software houses up-to-date with its plans.
Some have grown very rich indeed following its
advice. Yet others complain that they have been
led down the garden path as the company's
strategy has changed over the years.*

gas

run out of gas   ◄

If you **run out of gas**, you suddenly feel
very tired or lose interest in what you are doing, and so you stop completely or fail. This
expression is used mainly in American English.

*She ran out of gas. Suddenly. She stopped
talking, came over and slumped next to him on
the couch.*

*Jimmy Connors won in two matches during
the week, but it sounds like he just ran out of
gas against Chang.*

*He ran out of gas, artistically speaking, and
retired for roughly a decade.*

*The production runs out of gas long before
the end.*

gasp

last gasp: 1   ◄◄

You can use **last gasp** before a noun to say
that something is achieved at the last possible
moment. This expression is used mainly in
journalism.

*Sachin Tendulkar's explosive talents inspired
Yorkshire to a thrilling last gasp victory over
Lancashire at Headingley.*

*Last gasp negotiations by the National Mu-
seum of Photography could ensure major new
shows by legendary photographers Richard
Avedon and Sebastião Salgado.*

the last gasp: 2   ◄

The very last stage of a long process or period of time can be referred to as **the last gasp**
of it.

*The summer of '92 may be looked upon with
nostalgia as the last gasp of the live rock concert era.*

*Eleven thousand years ago, at the last gasp of
the ice age, the area was covered with rich,
semi-deciduous forest, not dry grassland.*

gauntlet

run the gauntlet: 1   ◄◄

If you have to **run the gauntlet**, you have
to go through a place where people are trying
to harm or humiliate you, for example by attacking you or shouting insults at you.

*The trucks tried to drive the five miles to the
British base at Vitez, running the gauntlet of
marauding bands of gunmen.*

*President-elect Chamorro also had to run the
gauntlet as bags of water rained down from
the Sandinista section of the stadium.*

*She was forced to run a gauntlet of some 300
jeering demonstrators, waving placards denouncing her as a 'witch'.*

run the gauntlet: 2

If you have to **run the gauntlet** of some
kind of unpleasant behaviour, you have to
suffer it because of something you are trying
to achieve.

*He has decided to run the gauntlet of Tory
jibes that Labour stands for nothing.*

*Edward Said has run a gauntlet of vitriolic
criticism on the way to the Reith Lectures
which start tonight.*

take up the gauntlet
pick up the gauntlet   ◄

If you **take up the gauntlet** or **pick up the
gauntlet**, you respond to something which
seems like a challenge by showing that you

accept the challenge. Compare **throw down the gauntlet**.

We received many letters on the subject, and several said we should ask our readers for nominations. We are taking up the gauntlet. Write to us with suggestions of women who would make stimulating panellists in television discussions.

throw down the gauntlet   ◄◄

If you **throw down the gauntlet**, you do or say something that challenges someone to take action or to compete against you. 'Lay down' and 'fling down' are sometimes used instead of 'throw down'. Compare **take up the gauntlet**.

The truckers threw down their gauntlet to the government after an all-night meeting of their strike committee. They say they will now keep up their action indefinitely until their demands are met.

He has laid down the gauntlet and presented us with two options which appear to be non-negotiable.

Boris Yeltsin flung down the gauntlet to his conservative opponents yesterday, summoning regional leaders to join him in drafting a new Constitution over the heads of Parliament.

gear

get into gear
get in gear
in gear   ◄◄◄

If you **get into gear** or **get in gear**, you start to deal with something in an effective way. When you are dealing with something effectively, you can say that you are **in gear**. You can also **get** someone or something else **into gear**. When a process begins to operate effectively, you can say that it **gets into gear**. Other verbs can be used instead of 'get'.

The town itself has got into gear with a campaign to improve the environment.

I have fallen back into my rhythm and stride quickly. I am pretty much in gear now.

Ultimately, he does help her to get her life into gear again.

Even as the publicity machine moves into gear, Mbongeni has another project in the pipeline.

get your arse in gear
get your ass in gear

If you **get your arse in gear** or **get** your **arse into gear**, you quickly start doing something. This is a very informal expression, which some people find offensive. This form of the expression is used in British English; in American English, the form is **get** your **ass in gear**.

If we can't buy the sort of stuff we're interest-

ed in, we'll get our arses in gear and make it ourselves.*

□ 'Bum' is sometimes used instead of 'arse', and 'butt' is sometimes used instead of 'ass'.

Get your bum in gear and do it.

get your brain into gear
have your brain in gear

In informal English, if you **get** your **brain into gear** or **get** your **brain in gear**, you start thinking clearly about something, so that you can achieve what needs to be done. You can use other verbs instead of 'get', and you can use 'mind' instead of 'brain'.

All I want is to get my brain in gear and get back to the top.

It gives you a chance to think, plan and generally get your mind into gear.

□ If you **have** your **brain in gear**, you are thinking clearly and can act appropriately.

I don't have my brain in gear yet.

genie

the genie is out of the bottle
let the genie out of the bottle
put the genie back in the bottle   ◄

If something has been done or created which has made a great and permanent change in people's lives, especially a change which people regret, you can say that **the genie is out of the bottle** or that someone **has let the genie out of the bottle**.

I would say get the criminals off the street rather than get the guns off the street because I think the genie's out of the bottle. You can't get all the guns off the street.

If the President came to believe that parliament was too disruptive, he might dissolve it and call new elections. But having let the democratic genie out of the bottle, he has to be careful.

□ People often vary this expression, for example by saying that you cannot **put the genie back in the bottle**.

We cannot unlearn what we know. We cannot put the genie of knowledge back in its bottle of secrecy and mystery.

For a generation, the world's nuclear powers have talked about restraining the nuclear 'genie' in its bottle.

gentle

gentle as a lamb

If you say that someone is as **gentle as a lamb**, you mean that they are kind and mild.

Brian was as gentle as a lamb and wouldn't hurt anyone.

Verdy was as gentle as a lamb off the field but a raging lion on it.

ghost

give up the ghost: 1 ◄

If you **give up the ghost**, you stop trying to do something, because you no longer believe that you can succeed.

In Manhattan there was no Memorial Day parade this year. The organizers said they've given up the ghost after so few people turned out to see last year's parade.

Having taken a convincing 29-0 lead, their forwards seemed to give up the ghost and to tire rapidly, allowing the Italians to mount a counter offensive which brought two good tries.

give up the ghost: 2

If you say that a machine **has given up the ghost**, you are saying in a humorous way that it has stopped working.

A short way off the return ferry, Danny's car gave up the ghost again.

He uses manual cameras supported on heavy tripods because batteries can give up the ghost in extreme weather.

□ This expression originally meant 'to die', and people still occasionally use it with this meaning.

lay the ghost of something
lay to rest the ghost of something

If you **lay the ghost of** something bad in your past, you do something which stops you being upset or affected by it. You can also **lay to rest the ghost of** something.

Jockey Adrian Maguire laid the ghost of a ghastly week with a comprehensive win in the Irish Champion Hurdle yesterday.

Timmis seems to have laid to rest the ghost of her unhappy 1992 campaign when she failed to make the Olympic team.

gift

the gift of the gab
the gift of gab ◄

If you say that someone has **the gift of the gab**, you mean that they are able to speak confidently, clearly, and in a persuasive way. In American English, you can also say that someone has **the gift of gab**.

He was entertaining company and certainly had the gift of the gab.

Paulo knows that the gift of the gab is one of the requisite skills for working as a barman.

He was a pleasant little man with spiked hair, a black pipe, and a great gift of gab.

God's gift: 1
God's gift to women

If you say that a man thinks he is **God's gift** or **God's gift to women**, you mean that he behaves as if all women find him attractive, and you find this very irritating.

He thinks he's God's gift and is more interested in conquests than in love.

They strut the earth like God's gift to womanhood.

God's gift to someone: 2

If you say that someone or something is **God's gift to** a group of people, you mean that they are exactly what those people like or need.

This woman is God's gift to romantics.

The telephone is still seen by many people as God's gift to gossips.

gift horse

look a gift horse in the mouth ◄

If someone tells you not to **look a gift horse in the mouth**, they mean that you should accept something that is being offered to you, or take advantage of an opportunity, and not try to find faults or difficulties.

When you're an entrepreneur, you don't look a gift horse in the mouth.

The opportunity is there to sign a player with massive know-how. I'm simply amazed that some teams seem to feel they can look a gift horse in the mouth.

gills

green around the gills

If you say that someone looks **green around the gills**, you mean that they look as if they are going to be sick.

One year, the delegates turned up at the civic reception looking distinctly green about the gills, having just returned from an outing to the local crematorium.

Kenny stumbled out from the washroom. 'I'm all right now.' He still looked quite green around the gills.

gilt

take the gilt off the gingerbread

In British English, if someone or something **takes the gilt off the gingerbread**, they spoil something or make it seem less good. This expression can be varied. For example, if something is beginning to seem less good, you can say 'the gilt is wearing off the gingerbread'.

Much of the gilt is off the gingerbread already.

The film has some good jokes, but Martin plays cute and Hawn plays kooky. They've been doing it for years and the gilt is wearing off the gingerbread.

girl

a big girl's blouse

If someone describes a man as **a big girl's blouse**, they are showing that they disapprove of him, because they think that his behaviour is not manly enough. This expression is used in British English.

We'll get that soppy big girl's blouse with the dodgy knee who cries all the time.

give

give and take ◄◄◄

If you say that something needs **give and take**, you mean that the people involved must compromise or co-operate with each other, in order for it to be successful.

I'm in a happy relationship where there's a lot of give and take.

These are all questions that are going to be resolved through a political give-and-take over the next year or year and a half.

□ You can use **give-and-take** before a noun.

In many ways, working with Godfrey resembled the give-and-take process to which I had become accustomed in the theater.

give or take: 1 ◄◄

Give or take is used to indicate that a number, especially a large number, is approximate. For example, if you say that something is a thousand years old, **give or take** a few years, you mean that it is approximately a thousand years old.

There is a buried crater 35 kilometres across, in North America. It dates back 66 million years, give or take a million.

Add up the number of people watching them on TV each week and it comes to an amazing 46 million, give or take a few hundred thousand.

give or take: 2 ◄

Give or take is also used to mean 'apart from'. It is often used humorously or ironically. For example, if you say two things are the same **give or take** particular features, you are really emphasizing that the two things are very different.

We are not in Sydney; this is Manchester. With the wind in the right direction and the weather just so, the two do have a similar feel to them, give or take the odd beach, bridge, harbour and opera house.

Give or take the odd servant and lots of sun and space, the life of a middle class white child in rural South Africa is not much different from that of its British counterpart.

glance

at first glance ◄◄◄

You can say **at first glance** when you are describing your first impression of someone or something. You usually use this expression to indicate that this first impression was wrong or incomplete. **At first sight** means the same.

At first glance the yard looks chaotic, but it soon becomes apparent that it's quite the opposite.

The difficulty comes when two people, who appeared at first glance to have so much in common, discover that they have simply grown apart.

At first glance he gave the impression of being quiet and unobtrusive, not a man who would stand out in a crowd.

glass

the glass ceiling ◄◄

When people talk about **the glass ceiling**, they are referring to the invisible barrier formed by such things as attitudes and traditions, which can prevent women, or people from ethnic or religious minorities, from being promoted to the most important jobs.

At the age of 43 she became Assistant Chief Constable in Merseyside and the highest ranking woman officer in the country, only to find she'd hit the glass ceiling.

A woman judge has at last succeeded in breaking through the glass ceiling into the Court of Appeal, the second highest court in the land.

The programme offers minority ethnic staff an opportunity to break through the glass ceilings which so often limit progress up the corporate ladder.

people who live in glass houses shouldn't throw stones ◄

If you are told **'people who live in glass houses shouldn't throw stones'**, you are being reminded that you have faults and so you should not criticize other people for their faults. This expression is often varied.

When will they learn? People in glass houses really shouldn't throw stones.

There are arguments to be made on both sides, but I would say people who live in glass houses should be careful about their stones.

gloss

put a gloss on something

If you **put a gloss on** something or **put an** optimistic or positive **gloss on** it, you try to convince people that things are better than they really are. Other verbs are sometimes used instead of 'put'.

The clash came when the smaller auction house attempted to put a gloss on poor figures resulting from the art market slump.

Garland could see no harm in putting an optimistic gloss on what the specialist had actually said.

The gloss put on this most recent setback by Mr Yeltsin's advisers is that it is a wise tactical retreat.

glove

fit like a glove

If you say that something **fits like a glove**, you mean that it is exactly the right shape or size, or that it is exactly right or appropriate in some other way.

She let me try on her wedding dress. Black velvet, and you know it fits me like a glove?

Surprisingly, she has not sung Leonora for a long time, yet, as I reminded her, she used to say the part fitted her voice like a glove.

Mr Grunow said the marine products business of the two companies were a perfect match: 'They fit like a glove. For example, we make rigging and they make masts.'

gloves

the gloves are off
take the gloves off ◄

If you are talking about a situation in which people have decided to fight or compete aggressively with each other, you can say **the gloves are off**. If someone **takes the gloves off**, they get ready to fight or compete with someone else. These expressions are used mainly in journalism.

The gloves are off in the war against anti-anglers as organisations get serious about the threat to their sport.

In the software price war, the gloves are coming off.

The president had said that he'd wait until after the convention to take the gloves off and really begin the campaign.

glutton

a glutton for punishment

If you say that someone is **a glutton for punishment**, you are showing surprise that they keep on doing something which is uncomfortable, unpleasant, or embarrassing for them.

What I want to know is why on earth you want anything to do with this wretchedly confused and angry man. Obviously you're a glutton for punishment.

A dozen hardy nudists proved they were also gluttons for punishment when, undeterred by biting winds and constant showers, they huddled together on the naturist beach at Studland Bay.

gnat

strain at a gnat
strain at a gnat and swallow a camel

If you say that someone is **straining at a gnat**, you mean that they are concerning themselves with something minor or trivial, and perhaps neglecting something important. You can also say that they **are straining at a gnat and swallowing a camel**. These are literary expressions.

When it comes down to distinguishing 1 percent growth from a mild recession, you'd be straining at gnats to tell the difference.

One must beware of straining at a gnat and swallowing a camel in the name of correct spelling. To spell badly is a social rather than a moral or intellectual fault.

go

have a go at someone: 1 ◄◄◄

If you **have a go at** someone or something, you criticize them strongly, often without good reason. This expression is used mainly in British English.

Finally I felt angry, because I figured she was just having a go at me for the sake of it.

One of France's leading newspapers Le Monde is having a go at Britain's second city, describing it as a mixture of slum housing, unemployment, crime, drugs and garbage.

Predictably, Mr Harkin had a go at foreigners in his Iowa speech.

have a go at someone: 2 ◄

If you **have a go at** someone, you attack them physically.

My dad hit my mum. He was drunk, so she knocked him down and put her shoe on his face but he got up and had a go at her.

A mob had a go at him with a hatchet.

what goes around comes around

If you say **what goes around comes around**, you mean that people's actions will eventually have consequences which they will have to deal with, even though this may not happen for a long time. You use this expression especially when you are talking about bad or unpleasant things which people do.

He still wasn't completely beyond feeling things like guilt and shame. Besides, he thought, what goes around comes around. You ignore the other guy when he asks for help, you might just be setting yourself up for a little of the same later on.

goal

an own goal ◄◄

If someone takes a course of action which fails to achieve the effect that they want and instead harms their own interests, you can say that they score **an own goal**. This expression is used in British English.

Although the Labour Party supported the plans to allow expatriates the vote, it was swiftly seen by some Labour MPs as an own goal, with estimates suggesting that four out of five voters would use their vote to keep the Conservatives in power.

He said that the Government must get its act together and stop scoring economic own goals.

The terrorists knew almost immediately that the operation was yet another own goal.

goalposts

move the goalposts ◄

If you accuse someone of **moving the goalposts**, you mean that they have changed the rules, policies, or aims in a situation or activity, in order to gain an advantage for themselves and to make things more difficult for the other people involved. Other verbs are sometimes used instead of 'move'.

He was always moving the goalposts so that we could never anticipate what he wanted.

They seem to move the goalposts every time I meet the conditions which are required.

It is apparent that the administration is shifting the goalposts and changing its demands.

goat

act the goat

If someone **acts the goat**, they behave in a silly way. This expression is used in British English.

It was coming on to rain. I left them there, crossing among the traffic. They stood side by side. Betty had a little yellow umbrella up. I acted the goat a bit, turning and waving umpteen times till she was laughing.

get someone's goat ◄

If you say that someone or something **gets** your **goat**, you mean that they annoy you intensely.

It was a bad result and a bad performance, but what really got the media's goat was the manager's refusal to take all the blame.

'He was just so provocative,' says White. 'He liked to get someone's goat, to make trouble for even the most well-intentioned people.'

God

play God ◄◄

If you say that someone **is playing God**, you are criticizing them for behaving as if they have unlimited power and can do anything that they want.

He insisted that the government should not play God: the market alone should decide what industries should be set up.

These are intelligent people whose response to physicians who tried to play God was to walk out on treatment.

gold

all that glitters is not gold
all that glisters is not gold

People say **'all that glitters is not gold'** to warn you that someone or something may not be as good or as valuable as they first appear. In British English, people also say **'all that glisters is not gold'**. The verb 'glisten' is sometimes used instead of 'glitter' or 'glister'.

All that glitters is not gold and it's a good idea to delay finalising any important agreements, otherwise you may jeopardise a valuable relationship.

□ Journalists sometimes change 'gold' to a word that is relevant to the subject that they are talking about.

Faldo has adopted the refreshing philosophy of accepting that all that glitters is not golf. 'There are other things in life,' he said.

gold dust ◄

In British English, if you say that particular things, especially tickets for a sporting event or show, are like **gold dust** or are **gold dust**, you mean that they are very difficult to obtain, usually because so many people want them.

Leg make-up was essential during the War when stockings were like gold dust.

Tickets for this match are gold dust on the south coast.

a pot of gold
a crock of gold ◄◄◄

You can refer to a lot of money that someone hopes to get in the future as **a pot of gold** or **a crock of gold**. Compare **the pot of gold at the end of the rainbow**; see **rainbow**.

There are already 11,000 laser disc titles available in Japan and 6,000 in America. That could mean a pot of gold for music companies.

When he went to Hamburg, he should have said he was going to make his pot of gold. Instead, he said he was going to improve his football.

□ You can refer to something else that someone wants very much as **a pot of gold** or **a crock of gold**.

There was one particularly wonderful man but I didn't feel that he was right. I do try not to let things get me down. I'm always looking for that crock of gold.

strike gold ◄

If you **strike gold**, you find, do, or produce something that brings you a lot of money or success.

Australia finally struck gold with a world-record performance to beat defending champions Germany.

A California nurse has struck gold on a slot machine. She's hit the jackpot, which added up to 9.3 million dollars.

The company has struck gold with its new holiday development.

good

give as good as you get ◄◄
In an argument, fight, or contest, if someone **gives as good as** they **get**, they argue, fight, or compete as strongly and fiercely as their opponent.

He's finally found himself a woman who stands up to him and gives as good as she gets.

Always give as good as you get in discussions and meetings.

Arsenal are a tough side, but we can give as good as we get and we don't fear anyone.

good as gold ◄
If you say that someone, especially a child, is as **good as gold**, you are emphasizing that they are behaving very well.

The children settled for their sleep as good as gold at 9.45.

They were both in the playroom as good as gold.

good as new ◄◄
If you say that something is as **good as new**, you mean that it is in as good a condition as it was when it was new. If you say that a person who has been ill is as **good as new**, you mean that they have recovered and are just as well as they were before their illness.

Manufacturers recommend that carpets should be washed regularly to prolong their life and keep their colour and texture looking as good as new.

I'd worked myself into near exhaustion, but after a week's vacation I was as good as new.

□ A **good-as-new** thing is in nearly as good a condition as it was when it was new.

These upmarket second-hand shops deal in good-as-new clothes with prestige labels.

good-for-nothing ◄
If you describe someone as **good-for-nothing**, you mean that they are lazy or irresponsible or behave in a way which is likely to harm or upset other people.

Ruth's father was a rich, charming, but good-for-nothing man.

You, Jeremy, are a conniving, cunning, devious, good-for-nothing so-and-so.

□ You can also refer to a person as **a good-for-nothing**.

He attacked teachers as idle, politically motivated good-for-nothings.

you can't keep a good man down
you can't keep a good woman down
If you say that **you can't keep a good man down**, you mean that if people are able and determined, they will recover from any difficulties or setbacks and be successful. You can replace 'man' with 'woman' or with another word referring to a person.

Frank Bruno is living proof that you can't keep a good man down. After his defeat by Mike Tyson, Britain's best-loved boxer is in training again.

He will come through. You can't keep a good 'un down for long.

□ You sometimes use this expression to talk about things rather than people, when you want to say that something continues to be popular or successful despite difficulties.

It would seem you cannot keep a good boat down. In the second race, Sunstone, the 27-year-old Sparkman and Stevens design, beat the purpose-built Argentinian boat, Bwana, by more than four and a half minutes.

goodbye

kiss goodbye to something
say goodbye to something ◄◄
If you have to **kiss goodbye to** something or **say goodbye to** something, you have to accept the fact that you are going to lose it or that you will not be able to have it.

Obviously if the radical faction wins out, we may have to kiss goodbye to billions invested in that region.

I felt sure I'd have to kiss my dancing career goodbye.

Britain depends on tourism and the greatest attractions are the royal palaces. If the Royal Family disappeared, we could say goodbye to tourism.

goods

deliver the goods ◄◄◄
If someone or something **delivers the goods**, they achieve what is expected or required of them. 'Come up with' and 'produce' are sometimes used instead of 'deliver'.

Is the leadership in a position to deliver the goods in two years?

If he fails to deliver the goods, they could well be looking for a new prime minister by next summer.

Probably the least funny thing about being known as a funny novelist is having to come up with the goods, time and time again.

Once more the Royal National Theatre has produced the goods.

have the goods on someone
get the goods on someone
If you **have the goods on** someone, you know things about them which could harm them if these things were made public. If you **get the goods on** someone, you obtain information of this kind. These expressions are used in American English.

The Republicans keep saying that they've got the goods on Bill Clinton.

His compulsive need to control his environ-

ment, get the goods on his enemies, led to the Watergate scandal.

goose

cook your goose
your goose is cooked ◄

If you **cook** your **goose**, you do something which gets you into trouble or spoils your chances of success. You can also **cook** someone else's **goose**.

By trying to nick my girlfriend he cooked his goose. After that I just had to sack him.

There was another possibility; that somehow they had been able to check up on me and had discovered my false history. That, I was sure, would cook my goose.

□ If you are in trouble or will certainly fail at something, you can say that your **goose is cooked**.

I fully expected we would be attacked by ground forces. We all felt that our goose was cooked. There was absolutely no way to retreat.

kill the goose that lays the golden egg
kill the golden goose ◄

If something **kills the goose that lays the golden egg** or **kills the golden goose**, it results in an important source of income being destroyed or seriously reduced.

Most professionals in the travel and tourism industry know that unregulated tourism can kill the goose that laid their golden egg.

Few councils would today risk killing the golden goose by levying too onerous a local tax.

□ You can refer to an important source of income as **a golden goose**, especially when it is in danger of being destroyed or seriously reduced.

It was alleged in court that Hewitt treated Whittaker as a 'golden goose'.

No one can be sure that the golden goose of the manufacturing industry hasn't been so badly battered during the past decade that it is incapable of delivering the revenues to which we have become accustomed.

a wild goose chase ◄

If you complain that you have been sent on **a wild goose chase**, you are complaining that you have wasted a lot of time searching for something that you have little chance of finding, because you have been given misleading information.

If he wasted police time, and thus police money, on a wild goose chase, his superiors would take a dim view.

Every time I've gone to Rome to try to find out if the story could be true, it has turned out to be a wild-goose chase.

wouldn't say boo to a goose

If you say that someone **wouldn't say boo**

to a goose, you mean that they are very timid, gentle, and shy.

'If you remember, at college I wouldn't say boo to a goose.' 'That's right, you were very quiet.'

She would fall into that category of people who tend the sick and visit the old, never saying boo to a goose.

gooseberry

play gooseberry

If you say that someone **is playing gooseberry**, you mean that they are joining or accompanying two people who are having a romantic relationship and who want to be alone together. This expression is used in British English.

Come off it, Mum! He knows you've got a boyfriend and far be it from him to play gooseberry.

gospel

take something as gospel
accept something as gospel
the gospel truth ◄

If you **take** something **as gospel** or **accept** it **as gospel**, you accept it as being completely true. You can also **take** or **accept** something **as the gospel truth**.

You will read much advice in books and magazines but you should not take it all as gospel.

While Carter was still trying to unravel the truth of the woman's story, Tench had accepted it as gospel.

Only once did Gill show unwillingness to accept the voice of authority as gospel truth.

□ If you say that something is **the gospel truth**, you are emphasizing that it is completely true.

When people have asked me how old I am, and I say I don't know, they think I'm coy. But it's the gospel truth.

grabs

up for grabs ◄◄◄

If you say that something is **up for grabs**, you mean that it is available for anyone who is willing or able to compete for it.

Thirty-five Senate seats are up for grabs in tomorrow's election.

Writers have until September 17 to enter Suncorp's 1993 Literary Awards, with $15,000 in prizes up for grabs.

Despite the fact that neither Japan nor Saudi Arabia has ever been to a World Cup Finals before, they are expected to take the two places up for grabs.

grace

fall from grace ◄◄◄

If you talk about someone's **fall from grace** or say that they **have fallen from grace**, you are referring to the fact that they have made a mistake or done something wrong or immoral, and as a result have lost their power or influence and spoiled their good reputation.

The cause of Ms Wood's fall from grace was the same as Ms Baird's: she had once hired an illegal immigrant to look after her son.

Rock Hudson's story represents one of the most spectacular falls from grace in film history.

The band later fell from grace when it was discovered that they never sang on their own records.

☐ Journalists sometimes talk about **the fall from grace** of a company, organization, or institution when people no longer approve of it or trust it.

The increasing number of complaints and the banks' fall from grace in the eyes of the public have also taken effect.

GPA's dramatic fall from grace was precipitated by the collapse of the share sale, which deprived it of hundreds of millions in cash.

a saving grace ◄◄◄

A **saving grace** is a good quality or feature in someone or something that prevents them from being completely bad or worthless.

Albert Coombs Barnes was a cranky, boorishly opinionated doctor. But he had one saving grace: he assembled one of the greatest private art collections of this century.

She definitely outshone the so-called 'stars' and is one of the film's few saving graces.

grade

make the grade ◄◄◄

If you **make the grade**, you succeed at something, usually by reaching a particular standard.

She beat the men's professional record for the course by two shots. 'That one round gave me tremendous hope and convinced me I could make the grade,' she says.

Top public schools failed to make the grade in a new league table of academic results.

grain

go against the grain ◄◄◄

If you say that an idea or action **goes against the grain**, you mean that it is very difficult for you to accept or do, because it conflicts with your ideas, beliefs, or principles. 'Run' is sometimes used instead of 'go'.

The way he had violated our agreement without so much as an apology went against the grain. That's why I never dealt with him again.

Heaping such lavish praise on an 18-year-old goes against the grain.

This production runs against the grain of what Americans perceive opera to be all about.

grandmother

teach your grandmother to suck eggs

In British English, if you tell someone that they **are teaching** their **grandmother to suck eggs**, you are criticizing them for giving advice about something to someone who actually knows more about it than they do. 'Granny' is often used instead of 'grandmother'.

'It's a sarcophagus. Dig it good and wide,' he said. 'Go teach your grandmother to suck eggs,' said Leshka, and waved him away with a show of irritation.

grapes

sour grapes ◄◄◄

If you describe someone's attitude as **sour grapes**, you mean that they are jealous of another person's success and show this by criticizing the other person or by accusing them of using unfair methods.

These accusations have been going on for some time now, but it is just sour grapes.

The government retorts that Mr Fedorov's criticisms are mere sour grapes.

One source said that any complaints were sour grapes by banks which had lost money in dealings just before the announcement.

grapevine

hear something through the grapevine
hear something on the grapevine ◄◄◄

If you say that you **heard** something **through the grapevine**, you mean that you heard about it informally from your friends, colleagues, or acquaintances. In British English you can also say that you **heard** something **on the grapevine**.

I hear through the grapevine that you are getting ready to sue us. If that's true, I want to hear it from you.

At 25, she became the editor of the fashion and beauty magazine 'Looks' and at 26, the editor of 'Company' magazine, a job she heard about on the grapevine.

☐ **The grapevine** is the way news or gossip spreads among a group of people who know each other.

Spread the word that you are very keen for your guests to choose gifts from your wedding list: tell a few close friends and your family and you will be surprised how effective the grapevine can be.

grass

the grass is always greener on the other side of the fence
the other man's grass is always greener   ◄

If someone says **'the grass is always greener on the other side of the fence'**, they are pointing out that other people may appear to be in a better or more attractive situation than you, but in reality their situation may not be as good as it seems. This expression is often varied: for example, you can use another word instead of 'fence'. You can also say **'the other man's grass is always greener'**.

The old saying goes that, to many people, the grass is always greener on the other side of the fence, and the majority of Britain's young people are no exception.

Diana should beware. The grass may not be greener on the other side of the Atlantic.

A lot of players who have left in the past have found that the grass isn't always greener elsewhere.

He had learned the other man's grass was indeed greener.

the grass roots   ◄◄◄

The grass roots of an organization or movement are the ordinary people who form the main part of it, rather than its leaders.

No decision had been taken because the matter had been referred back to the party's grass roots inside South Africa.

The revolution is actually coming from the grass roots and I think eventually the authorities will follow.

□ **Grass-roots** can be used before a noun.

It was a grass-roots campaign and that's how the country's newest president won the election.

The leadership has become detached from what's going on at grassroots level.

put someone out to grass   ◄

If someone **is put out to grass**, they are made to retire from their job, or they are moved to an unimportant job, usually because people think that they are too old to be useful. **Put** someone **out to pasture** means the same.

Members of the House of Lords are either political time-servers who have been put out to grass or the heirs of aristocrats rewarded for some long-forgotten favour.

The Prime Minister refused to be put out to grass. Asked if he would quit, he replied 'The answer is no.'

watch grass grow

If you say that watching something is like **watching grass grow**, you mean that it is extremely boring.

Some people say that watching a cricket match is like watching grass grow.

Those who still feel that watching England play football is marginally more interesting than watching grass grow may be about to have another illusion shattered.

grave

dig your own grave   ◄

If you **dig** your **own grave**, you put yourself in a difficult situation by doing something wrong or making foolish mistakes.

United States prosecutors and other law enforcement officials were more than happy to let Pollard dig his own grave.

If you go ahead with what you seem to imagine can be a private investigation, you'll be digging your own grave professionally.

turn in your grave
turn over in your grave   ◄◄

If you say that someone who is dead would **turn in** their **grave**, you mean that they would be very angry or upset about something which is happening now, if they knew about it. Verbs such as 'spin' and 'roll' are sometimes used instead of 'turn'. This form of the expression is used in British English; in American English, the form is **turn over in** your **grave**.

Churchill and Bevan would turn in their graves if they could hear the pathetic attempts at public speaking made by members of all parties in the past three weeks.

If the guy who wrote that song could hear that fellow sing it, he'd turn over in his grave.

By selling off the art, my father may have derived pleasure in the knowledge that his own father would be spinning in his grave.

gravy

a gravy train   ◄◄◄

If you talk about **a gravy train**, you are referring to a secure and easy way of earning money over a long period, especially by having a job that is easy and well-paid.

Software companies realise that the gravy train can't go on for much longer. Cut-throat competition in the recession is sending computer prices tumbling.

The boardroom gravy train continued to roll happily along yesterday, with news of pay-offs and awards to three executives totalling nearly 1.4 million pounds.

I keep his salary down because I don't want anyone to think he's riding into work on a gravy train.

Greek

be Greek to someone
be all Greek to someone

If you say that something **is Greek to** you, you mean that you do not understand it at all.

In British English, you can also say that something **is all Greek to** you.

'Great heavens!' he cried. 'Haven't you heard of figures of speech?' And he threw the newspaper at our heads. Figures of speech were Greek to us, and we were left with the suspicion that we still had a lot to learn.

Soccer is, frankly, all Greek to me.

green

green as grass

In British English, if you say that someone is as **green as grass**, you mean that they are inexperienced or naive.

I was a newcomer to the sport, green as grass, but now I've had a chance to evaluate the costs for a season.

My brother's a joiner and he said 'You don't want to be a bricklayer.' I was still green as grass so I said 'Oh well, I'll be a painter then.'

□ It is much more common just to say that someone is **green**.

They admit they were very green when they arrived in Afghanistan.

green with envy   ◄

If you say that someone is **green with envy**, you mean that they are extremely envious of something that another person has or does. This expression is usually used light-heartedly rather than disapprovingly.

She told us all she was planning a weekend in Paris, where she could whirl around the boutiques, linger at outdoor cafes and dine by candlelight. Not surprisingly, we were all green with envy.

This is the most unexpected discovery I have made in 20 years of digging. Archaeologists in other parts of the world will be green with envy.

grin

grin and bear it   ◄

If you are talking about a difficult situation and you say that someone will have to **grin and bear it**, you mean that they will have to accept it, because there is nothing they can do about it.

Women suffer in silence because they think male doctors will feel they are 'making a fuss over nothing'. If they can't see a woman doctor, they'd rather grin and bear it.

In the past, a royal trapped in a loveless marriage would have been obliged to grin and bear it.

Severe or recurrent abdominal pain should always be checked. Don't just grin and bear it.

grip

get a grip on something: 1
take a grip on something
keep a grip on something   ◄◄◄

If you **get a grip on** a situation or **take a grip on** it, you take control of it so that you can deal with it successfully. If you continue to control it, you can say that you **keep a grip on** it. Other verbs can be used instead of 'keep'.

So far the country has failed to get a grip on its inflation rate.

It is clear that the new leader has taken a grip on the party machine.

This is a victory for the powerful and corrupt clique of politicians who have managed to keep a grip on power here.

get a grip on yourself: 2
get a grip
keep a grip on yourself   ◄

If you **get a grip on** yourself or **get a grip**, you make an effort to control yourself, so that you can deal with things successfully. You can also say that you **keep a grip on** yourself.

A bit of me was very frightened and I consciously had to get a grip on myself.

He told himself to get a grip: he was merely being paranoid.

He was trying his best to keep a grip on himself.

lose your grip: 1   ◄◄

If you **lose** your **grip** on a situation, you lose control over it.

The central bank is losing its grip on monetary policy.

The opposition feel that the president has lost his grip on the country, and that if support for the strikes this week remains solid, they can oust him from office.

lose your grip: 2

If you say that someone is **losing** their **grip**, you mean that they are becoming less efficient and less confident, and less able to deal with things.

He wondered if perhaps he was getting old and losing his grip.

What had happened to her? Why was she losing her grip?

grips

get to grips with something
come to grips with something   ◄◄◄

If you **get to grips with** a problem or **come to grips with** it, you start dealing with it seriously, for example by getting a proper understanding of it.

The stop-go nature of economic policy is a

*worrying sign of the country's inability to get
to grips with the real problems.*

*I felt near to tears and attempted to come to
grips with the situation by firing off a lot of
questions which the doctor tried to answer.*

grist

grist for the mill
grist to the mill ◄◄

If you say that something is **grist for the
mill**, you mean that it can be put to good use
in a particular situation, or that it can be
used to support someone's point of view. In
British English, you can also say that something is **grist to the mill**.

*You are, of course, much better at writing
songs when you are completely miserable – it
gives you so much more grist for the mill.*

*Mr Kinkel and his senior aides had warned
that changes to the nationality laws would be
grist to the mill of right wing extremists.*

*It is sad to see great art viewed solely as grist
for contemporary propaganda mills.*

groove

in the groove
in a groove ◄◄

If you say that a sports person or a sports
team is **in the groove** or **in a groove**, you
mean that they are having a continuous series of successes.

*Nick is in the groove, as he showed with sev-
en goals last weekend.*

*Agassi said: 'I was in such a groove, I was
able to put the ball exactly where I wanted.'*

ground

break ground ◄

If someone **breaks ground on** a new building, they start building it. You can also say
that the building **breaks ground**. This expression is used in American English.

*Simpson and Hurt hope to break ground on a
planned outdoor theater at Ten Chimneys next
August.*

*The first co-housing project in America, in
Washington state, will break ground soon.*

☐ When something else new is being established, you can say that it **breaks ground**.
You can also say that the people establishing
it **break ground**.

*Perhaps I am lucky to have been in there at
the start, when this music was breaking
ground for the first time.*

*Health law professor Jeff Havers says Hol-
land still has to proceed cautiously as it breaks
ground in the law concerning euthanasia.*

break new ground ◄◄◄

If someone **breaks new ground**, they do
something completely different, or they do

something in a completely different way. You
use this expression to show approval of what
is being done.

*The programme broke new ground, in giving
to women roles traditionally assigned to men.*

*She hopes to break new legal ground by con-
vincing the court that verbal harassment con-
stitutes a wrongful act under Japanese civil
law.*

☐ You can talk about **ground-breaking** work.

*These three and others have done ground-
breaking work in identifying certain ways of
thinking and acting as characteristically femi-
nine.*

*The impact of Professor Jonker's declaration
at this ground-breaking conference has already
been substantial.*

cut the ground from under someone
cut the ground from under someone's
feet ◄

If you **cut the ground from under** someone
or **cut the ground from under** their **feet**,
you seriously weaken their argument or position, often by doing something unexpected.

*On February 9th, he departed from Labour
tradition and cut the ground from under the
opposition by promising a cut in corporate-tax
rates.*

*The scenario is this – you overspend on credit
cards or take on too big a mortgage; and then
an interest-rate hike, the loss of a job or a
downturn in business cuts the ground from under your feet.*

fall on stony ground ◄

If something such as a warning or piece of
advice **falls on stony ground**, it is ignored.
This expression is used in British English.

*The reforms proposed three years ago by the
Lord Chancellor fell on stony ground, largely
through the opposition of senior members of
his profession.*

*Dire warnings about the effects on public ser-
vices fell on stony ground.*

find common ground
on common ground ◄◄◄

When people or organizations come to an
agreement on something, you can say that
they **find common ground**. When they have
the same aims, you can say that they are **on
common ground**.

*The participants seem unable to find common
ground on the issue of agriculture.*

*Mike and I were on common ground. We both
wanted what was in the best interests of the
company.*

gain ground ◄◄◄

If something or someone **gains ground**, they
make progress and become more important or
more powerful. Compare **lose ground**.

The idea that Britain ought to change its constitution has been gaining ground for years.

The pound has gained ground on the foreign exchanges this morning.

Proponents of tougher auto standards gained some ground yesterday when eight Northeastern states agreed to adopt tougher auto emissions rules.

get in on the ground floor ◄

If you **get in on the ground floor**, you get involved from the very beginning with something, especially something that is likely to be profitable for you.

These smaller companies are getting in on the ground floor of what will be a gigantic industry.

I did get you in on the ground floor of some very worthwhile enterprises.

get something off the ground
get off the ground ◄

If you **get** something **off the ground**, you put it into operation, often after a lot of hard work getting it organized. If something **gets off the ground**, it starts operating or functioning.

You should not underestimate the amount of work and attention to detail required to set up a new business if you are going to get it off the ground successfully.

Councillor Riley spoke of the dedication and enthusiasm of staff and volunteers in getting the schemes off the ground.

If the proposed talks can get off the ground, the chances of peace between South Africa's leading black political organisations must improve.

go to ground ◄

If you **go to ground**, you hide from someone or something. This expression is used in British English. **Go to earth** means the same.

For the first time since May, citizens of East Beirut went to ground in basements and shelters as the rival forces traded tank and rocket fire.

He left the hotel and went to ground in the station waiting-room. It was a safe place.

hit the ground running

If you **hit the ground running**, you start a new activity with a lot of energy and enthusiasm, and do not waste any time.

The last thing we want is to have someone who really does not have experience in that field, someone who needs on-the-job training. Instead, we need someone who can hit the ground running, who has background and experience.

She is in excellent shape and in good spirits. She will hit the ground running when she gets back.

lose ground
make up lost ground ◄◄◄

If someone or something **loses ground**, they lose some of the power or advantage that they had previously. Compare **gain ground**.

The prime minister hoped to give a new look to his Conservative government, which is losing ground in the opinion polls after just over a year in power.

The United States lost more ground in its trade balance with other countries during the third quarter, running up the biggest trade deficit so far this year.

☐ If someone or something **makes up lost ground**, they recover some of the power or advantage which they had previously lost. Verbs such as 'recover' and 'regain' are sometimes used instead of 'make up'.

The President's inability to make up lost ground in the polls increasingly suggests he may lose.

The U.S. currency recovered much of the lost ground from its collapse on Friday.

the moral high ground
the high ground ◄◄◄

If you say that a person or organization has taken **the moral high ground**, you mean that they consider that their policies and actions are morally superior to the policies and actions of their rivals.

The US has taken a moral high ground in telling others what their problems are, while not devoting enough time to its own domestic problems.

The party now held the moral high ground and he, as President, could defend it in every country in the world.

☐ You can say that a person or organization has taken **the high ground** when they have gained an advantage over their rivals, especially by having policies and actions that they consider to be morally superior.

The document is an attempt to win back the political high ground on citizens' rights, which is likely to be one of the main themes of the next general election.

The party was determined to take the high ground on environmental issues.

prepare the ground ◄◄◄

If you **prepare the ground** for a future event, course of action, or development, you do things which will make it easier for that thing to happen.

They are carefully preparing the ground for staying in power or for minimising the effects of an electoral defeat.

The talks prepared the ground for the meeting of finance ministers and central bankers in Washington on September 19.

I like whenever possible to prepare the

ground beforehand. If it is a certain district I am going to photograph, I try to visit it first – wandering round, looking at the houses, watching the people.

run someone into the ground: 1
run yourself into the ground ◄

If you **run** someone **into the ground**, you make them work so hard and continuously at something that they become exhausted. If you **run** yourself **into the ground**, you work so hard and continuously at something that you become exhausted. Other verbs are sometimes used instead of 'run'.

Well-trained horses had been starved to death or run into the ground.

Liverpool's young players in particular ran themselves into the ground.

Workers were driven into the ground. They died from exhaustion, once their strength was spent.

run something into the ground: 2

If you **run** something **into the ground**, you use it continuously without repairing or replacing it, so that eventually it is destroyed or useless.

Britain's public housing has been virtually run into the ground and the Government shows absolutely no desire to revive it.

They're quite good bikes, you can run them into the ground for quite a long time, then just get a new one.

He let the economy run into the ground, sinking deeper into debt and deficits, with almost no growth and falling real wages.

run someone to ground

If you **run** someone or something **to ground**, you find them after a long search. This expression is used in British English. **Run to earth** means the same.

Truman eventually ran him to ground, asleep and rather the worse for wear in a hotel.

Running this source to ground is made no easier by the fact that Yeats's sole published reference to the volume is in a letter to George Russell.

stamping ground
stomping ground ◄

If you describe a place as someone's **stamping ground**, you mean that they work there or go there regularly. If you say that someone returns to their **old stamping ground**, you mean that they return to a place where they used to work or where they used to go regularly. You can also talk about someone's **stomping ground** or **old stomping ground**.

I'm not fond of the City of London because I'm a West End man, myself. Park Lane, Knightsbridge, Piccadilly and Bond Street are my favourite stamping grounds.

Former pals also found her much changed at Christmas, when she made a fleeting return to her old stamping ground, the Blue Anchor pub in Croydon, South London.

Her scandalous parties were the stomping-ground for such infamous people as Man Ray, André Gide and Isadora Duncan.

suit someone down to the ground ◄

If something **suits** you **down to the ground**, it completely meets your needs or requirements. This expression is used in British English.

Helen has finally found a method of exercise that suits her outgoing character down to the ground.

I was attracted by the modular programme at London Guildhall University which suited me down to the ground.

thick on the ground

If people or things are **thick on the ground**, there are a lot of them. This expression is used in British English. Compare **thin on the ground**.

Since the man's enemies were thick on the ground, twenty-four-hour protection had been provided at the public expense.

Jobs are not exactly thick on the ground.

thin on the ground ◄◄◄

If people or things are **thin on the ground**, there are very few of them. This expression is used in British English. Compare **thick on the ground**.

Good players are so thin on the ground that the clubs are recruiting abroad, signing Poles, Dutchmen, Scandinavians and, of course, Englishmen.

Clergymen remained very thin on the ground in Andalucia throughout the whole of the nineteenth century.

Ideas are thin on the ground in the British film industry.

Yacht facilities are a bit thin on the ground in the remote Falkland Islands.

guard

catch someone off guard
take someone off guard ◄◄◄

If something happens and **catches** you **off guard** or **takes** you **off guard**, it happens unexpectedly and completely surprises you.

The noise caught the trespasser off guard. The torch clattered to the floor, its light shooting a frail beam that fanned out eerily across the carpet.

When you are caught off guard by a blatantly sexist remark, whether intentional or otherwise, it is sometimes difficult to think of the right answer.

There was a bright flash, a brief sensation of heat, followed a few moments later by a thunderous roar that took us all off guard.

lower your guard
drop your guard
let your guard down ◄◄

If you **lower** your **guard**, **drop** your **guard**, or **let** your **guard down**, you relax when you should be careful or alert, often with unpleasant consequences.

The U-boat's crew had made the mistake of relaxing, of lowering their guard at the precise moment when their alertness and sense of danger should have been honed to its keenest edge.

It takes me a long time to drop my guard and get close to people.

Many men work in extremely competitive atmospheres where letting down their guard could leave them vulnerable.

off your guard
off guard

If you are **off** your **guard** or **off guard**, you are not prepared for something when it happens, and so you do not react normally. Compare **on** your **guard**.

Miss Marple is not perceived to be a threat in any way. And, therefore, the criminal is off his guard.

He had been so polite and amicable during the interview and the lunch which followed that Mary was quite off guard when she entered his office for the second time.

the old guard ◄◄◄

You can refer to a group of people as **the old guard** when they have worked in an organization or system for a very long time. You often use this expression to show disapproval of such people when they are unwilling to accept new ideas or practices.

France must move its support away from the old guard of African leaders if it is to maintain its influence on the continent.

When in 1990 he merged his party with the then ruling party under a deal that has since led him to the presidency, he was bitterly opposed by many in the ruling party's old guard.

The company's old guard is stepping aside, making way for a new, more youthful team.

on your guard
on guard ◄◄◄

If you are **on** your **guard** or **on guard**, you are alert and prepared for any attack against you. Compare **off** your **guard**.

When Hilton came, he would have to be on his guard each second, for the man was dangerous.

No-one ever locked their doors here: no-one had any surplus belongings to steal so there wasn't any need to be on your guard.

He is constantly on guard against any threat of humiliation and will take offence quickly.

guest
be my guest

You say **'be my guest'** to someone when you are giving them permission to do something, or inviting them to do something. This expression is sometimes used in a sarcastic way. For example, you might use it to invite someone to do something difficult or unpleasant.

'Dad,' she said. 'Tomorrow, I want to go swimming.' I indicated the cool, clear water before us. 'Be my guest,' I said.

'Taking care of Pop, eh?' 'You want to take care of him? Be my guest.'

guinea pig
a guinea pig ◄◄◄

If someone is used as **a guinea pig**, new ideas, methods, or medical treatments are tested on them.

Parents said they were not prepared to see their children used as guinea pigs for the Government's latest attempts to push up classroom standards.

The Government faces another scandal over sick ex-servicemen who were used as human guinea-pigs in chemical weapons tests.

gum tree
up a gum tree

If someone is **up a gum tree**, they are in a very difficult situation. This is an old-fashioned expression, which is used in British English.

If you look at any problem like this in terms of right and wrong you'll find yourself nowhere but up a gum tree.

gun
jump the gun ◄◄

If someone **jumps the gun**, they do something before the right, proper, or expected time. You usually use this expression when you disapprove of this behaviour.

If inflation continues to fall, then prices will be reduced later this year. We do not want to jump the gun and then put prices back up again.

Spain has already jumped the gun on diplomatic contacts by announcing earlier this month that its foreign minister would soon visit China.

The book wasn't due to be released until September 10, three days after the tour squad is named, but some booksellers have jumped the gun and decided to sell it early.

a smoking gun ◄◄

If you talk about **a smoking gun**, you are referring to a piece of evidence which proves that a particular person is responsible for a crime. This expression is used mainly in American English.

He says the search for other kinds of evidence, for compelling documents tying them to trafficking, has not produced a smoking gun.

Remember that the smoking gun that drove President Nixon from office was the taped evidence that he tried to get the CIA to take the rap for Watergate.

First of all, there's no smoking gun. In the course of our investigation we did not find a single piece of evidence.

under the gun ◄

If you are **under the gun**, you are under great pressure and your future success is being threatened. This expression is used mainly in American English.

We were under the gun. We were fighting for the very support that would ensure our ultimate survival.

Society, in many ways, is under the gun. We have a multitude of problems – medical, health problems, drug problems, crime problems, educational, literacy.

guns

the big guns
a big gun ◄◄

If you talk about **the big guns**, you are referring to the most important and powerful people in an organization. You can refer to an individual person as **a big gun**.

She has been much sought after by the film industry's big guns.

Back in the early '70s Arsenal and Leeds were the two big guns in the First Division.

It is about ideas. To win these days, to be the big gun, you have to have new ideas.

go great guns ◄

If you say that someone or something **is going great guns**, you mean that they are being very successful at something.

It must have eaten into his confidence when, while his troubles piled up, he heard that Nick Faldo was going great guns.

I called Gray's merchandise manager Robert Meachum. I said, 'Mr. Meachum, I have a product called Ayer Magic. It's going great guns throughout the region.'

spike someone's guns

If you **spike** someone's **guns**, you prevent them from carrying out their plans, or you do something to make their actions ineffective. This expression is used in British English.

Hitler may even have contemplated a rapprochement between Germany and Soviet Russia, or between Germany and White Russia should there be a successful counter-revolution, in order to spike the guns of the western powers.

Jubilant Tories poured out of the Commons hailing the Chancellor as a genius for spiking Labour's guns with his giveaways for the lower paid.

stick to your guns ◄◄◄

If you **stick to** your **guns**, you refuse to change your decision or opinion about something, even though other people are trying to tell you that you are wrong.

We believe that if we stick to our guns, the people who are holding these hostages will understand that no way will we budge without our prisoners being included in the deal.

He should have stuck to his guns, refused to meet her. But beneath the familiar churning of his stomach was a rising tide of excitement.

with all guns blazing ◄

If you do something **with all guns blazing**, you do it with a lot of enthusiasm and energy.

Manchester United stormed into the European Cup with all guns blazing.

Kasparov tends to come out with all guns blazing, take the lead, suffer a collapse caused by over-confidence, then return with a perfect final game.

gut

bust a gut ◄

If you **bust a gut** doing something, you work very hard at it. This is an informal expression.

I was busting a gut doing horrible jobs – toilet cleaning among other things – to support us.

I've done quite well financially without busting a gut, and at last I have a decent place to live.

□ A **gut-busting** job or task requires a lot of hard work.

guts

spill your guts

If someone **spills** their **guts**, they tell you everything about something secret or private. This is an informal expression.

Vincent has spilled his guts. Everything. We got a signed confession from him.

People call in and just spill their guts about whatever's bothering them on the job or in a relationship.

work your guts out ◄

If you **work** your **guts out**, you work very hard. Verbs such as 'slog' and 'flog' can be used instead of 'work'. This is an informal expression.

These women were amazing. They worked their guts out from 7.30 to 4.30 every day, often all evening and weekend too if they had families.

I have children, several finishing studies at university, but will they find a job? They have

been slogging their guts out for years. But what is at the end of it?

H

hackles
raise someone's hackles
someone's hackles rise ◄◄

If something **raises** your **hackles**, it makes you angry or annoyed. When something makes you angry or annoyed, you can say that your **hackles rise**.

The taxes will presumably be designed not to raise voters' hackles too much.

The United deal is going to raise a lot of hackles.

My hackles rose when I read your report. Media coverage of women's football is woefully inadequate but I would rather read nothing about the game at all than the sneering comments made by your reporter.

hair
curl your hair
make your hair curl

If something **curls** your **hair** or **makes** your **hair curl**, it makes you very shocked or worried.

She's been leading a 'family values' crusade against the lyrics of several artists. 'I'm a fairly with-it person,' she says, 'but this stuff curls my hair.'

I could tell you stories that would make your hair curl.

a hair of the dog
a hair of the dog that bit you

Some people believe that you can cure a hangover by having another alcoholic drink. This extra drink is called **a hair of the dog**. This expression is used in spoken English.

I need a drink, chum. A large hair of the dog.

I'm hoping some of the lads'll be there, lend me enough for a hair of the dog.

□ You can also talk about **a hair of the dog that bit** you.

Now he was feeling the worse for it and wondering if a hair of the dog that bit him might not set him up for the day.

a hair's breadth: 1 ◄

You use **a hair's breadth** when you are talking about something almost happening or almost being achieved. For example, if you say someone came **within a hair's breadth of** doing something, you mean that they very nearly did it.

The parliament came within a hair's breadth of forcing immediate political union between the two countries.

The town suffered heavy shell-fire, coming within a hair's breadth of being destroyed altogether.

His startling assertion brought Mr Cossiga within a hair's breadth of provoking a constitutional crisis.

□ If you avoid something unpleasant **by a hair's breadth**, it very nearly happens to you. If you fail to achieve something **by a hair's breadth**, you very nearly achieve it.

He literally missed death by a hair's breadth, surviving with a dozen stitches in his head.

He missed the two-minute barrier by a hair's breadth, finishing in 2.00.04 and setting a new British record.

□ If you say a serious situation is only **a hair's breadth away**, you mean that it is likely to happen very soon. You can also say people are only **a hair's breadth away** from a serious situation.

Conflict is only a hair's breadth away.

The Middle East is just a hair's breadth away from war.

a hair's breadth: 2

You use **a hair's breadth** when you are emphasizing that one thing is very close to another. For example, you say that one thing is **within a hair's breadth** of another.

Sumpa allowed the van to slip to within a hair's breadth of the precipice, then gave the engine full throttle.

It took some experimenting before he could get comfortable and even then he found that his head was a hair's breadth away from the car roof.

a hair shirt ◄

If you say that someone is wearing **a hair shirt**, you mean that they are deliberately making their own life unnecessarily unpleasant or uncomfortable, especially by not allowing themselves any luxuries.

No one is asking you to wear a hair shirt and give up all your luxuries.

If you are used to eating in restaurants, or flying down to see friends in the South of France for the weekend, it seems a bit of a hair shirt to have to do without these things.

□ **Hair-shirt** can also be used before a noun.

He has lived a life of almost hair-shirt austerity.

They imposed upon themselves hair-shirt penances.

in your hair

If you say that someone gets **in** your **hair**, you mean that they annoy you and are a nuisance to you. Compare **out of** someone's **hair**.

The General's unfortunate tendency to get in other people's hair hindered his recruiting efforts.

They were very busy and had little time to get into one another's hair.

keep your hair on

If someone tells you to **keep** your **hair on**, they are telling you in a forceful way to calm down and not be angry or impatient. This expression is used mainly in British English; the usual American expression is **keep** your **shirt on**.

His annoyance evaporated in a grin. 'You're right. She's got a tough job. I'll try to keep my hair on in future.'

let your hair down ◄◄

If you **let** your **hair down**, you relax and enjoy yourself, and do not worry about being dignified or behaving correctly.

It is only with friends that most people feel they can let their hair down and be themselves.

He enjoyed all the jokes, and laughed as much as anybody, but you got the impression he couldn't really join in the fun – he couldn't let his hair down.

make your hair stand on end
someone's hair stands on end

If something **makes** your **hair stand on end**, it makes you very frightened or shocked. When someone is very frightened, you can say that their **hair stands on end**.

The first ten minutes of the film made my hair stand on end.

'What's that?' Chet's hair stood on end as an eerie howling came to his ears.

□ If you are telling someone about something and you say that it **would make** their **hair stand on end** or that it **would stand** their **hair on end**, you are suggesting that there are many things about it which would shock or surprise them.

I received hate mail and cassettes that carried death threats. I was spat on, and so-called supporters tried to hit me. Things happened that would make your hair stand on end.

There were plenty of tales about the gunfighter that would stand a man's hair on end.

not a hair out of place ◄

You say that someone **does not have a hair out of place** to emphasize that their appearance is very neat and tidy.

Not a hair out of place, dressed in navy and white for our photograph, she is clearly a perfectionist.

I've never seen Jimmy with a hair out of place.

not turn a hair ◄

If you say that someone **did not turn a hair** in an unpleasant or difficult situation, you mean that they were very calm, and did not show any sign of being afraid or anxious.

His men were so accustomed to his rages that they never turned a hair.

She started off by accusing him of blackmail but he didn't turn a hair: in fact he more or less ignored her.

The girl playing Myra was ordered to bed by her doctor. We were lucky that Jeanne Lee, who came down to the theatre to help backstage, took on the part without turning a hair.

out of someone's hair: 1

If you get **out of** someone's **hair**, you stop being a nuisance to them, for example by leaving the place where they are and going somewhere else. Compare **in** your **hair**.

Would you like me to get out of your hair and leave you alone?

Right now I could be out of your hair, and home in peace.

out of someone's hair: 2

If you get someone who is a nuisance **out of** your **hair**, you succeed in arranging things so that you are no longer involved with them.

Initially, the point of privatising these companies was to get them out of the state's hair.

Just do me a favor, will you? Keep her out of my hair from now on.

tear your hair out
pull your hair out ◄

If you say that someone **is tearing** their **hair out** or **pulling** their **hair out**, you mean that they are very angry, upset, or anxious about something. You can also say that they **are tearing** their **hair**.

The nation is tearing its hair out over what to do with these child criminals.

They must have been pulling their hair out by the time they reached home.

Bureaucratic confusion and a lack of initiative at local factories has him tearing his hair.

hairs

by the short hairs

If someone has you **by the short hairs**, they have you completely in their power. **By the short and curlies** means the same.

'Once we stepped forward with a bid,' Hill recalled months later, 'the board knew they had us by the short hairs.'

The hard fact is that they have got us by the

short hairs. We can't do anything without material support from them.

put hairs on your chest
put hair on the chest

If you say that an alcoholic drink will **put hairs on** someone's **chest** or will **put hair on the chest**, you mean that it is very strong. You can also use this expression to suggest that food is very filling or nourishing.

Some of the concoctions would put hairs on your chest and indeed those brave enough to sample some left with distinct smiles on their faces.

Then there's the food, which is alleged to consist entirely of eggs and chips and various varieties of gruel designed to create big brawny arms and put hair on the chest.

split hairs ◄

If you accuse someone of **splitting hairs**, you are accusing them of making distinctions in a situation where the differences between things are actually very small and unimportant.

But once you start splitting hairs like that, where are you going to stop?

Don't split hairs. You know what I'm getting at.

□ You can also accuse someone of **hairsplitting**.

This, to those interested in the purpose of the insider-trading law, is lawyers' hair-splitting.

On BBC Radio she accused her critics of hair-splitting.

halcyon

halcyon days ◄

If you talk about the **halcyon days** of something, you are talking about a time in the past when it was especially successful. This is a literary expression.

When we ask him whether the wool industry will ever see those halcyon days again, he turns back to his beer and shakes his head.

If there is an economist in the land who believes that Britain will return speedily to those halcyon days when unemployment was under 500,000, he or she is keeping pretty quiet about it.

□ You also use **halcyon days** to talk about a time in the past when your life was especially peaceful and happy.

I experienced again the sense of peace and lightness that I associated with the halcyon days at La Chorrera.

I had a sudden memory of those halcyon days when love had meant sharing a bag of boiled sweets in St Saviour's dusty church hall.

half

go off half-cocked
go off at half cock ◄

If someone **goes off half-cocked**, they are unsuccessful in what they are trying to do, because they have not taken enough care or prepared properly.

Remember, don't go off half-cocked when we get there. Stick to the plan.

This is only the start of the debate and it is no time for anybody or any interested group to go off half-cocked.

□ In British English, you can also say that actions or people **go off at half cock** when they are unsuccessful.

In the hands of a lesser chef many of these dishes would go off at half cock, but she turns them out with apparent ease and skill.

The affair was worrying. He couldn't have the Pole going off at half-cock; not now.

□ **Half-cocked** and **half-cock** can also be used before a noun.

In-store guest appearances are usually embarrassing, half-cocked events.

Three basic issues have been raised by America's half-cock deregulation of financial services over the past 15 years.

how the other half lives ◄

If you refer to **how the other half lives**, you are referring to the lives of people who are very different from you, for example very rich or very poor, or living in a different country.

He clearly has little idea how the other half lives, though, carrying a 1,000-dollar note in his pocket to flourish in small shops which cannot give him change.

your other half
your better half ◄◄

If you refer to your **other half** or your **better half**, you mean your husband, wife, or partner. These expressions are often used humorously.

They invited us out to dinner after the election because they said it was high time they met my other half.

His better half has told him that making love is good for the heart.

halfway

meet someone halfway ◄◄

If you **meet** someone **halfway**, you accept some of their opinions or wishes, so that you can come to an agreement with them or have a better relationship with them.

Senator Gray said Democrats are willing to meet the president halfway on measures to stimulate the economy.

It has always been part of my teaching phi-

losophy to make young people develop skills at forming relationships with adults by meeting them half-way.

halves

not do things by halves
not do anything by halves ◄

If you say that someone **does not do things by halves**, you mean that they always do everything very well and very thoroughly. You can also say that they **do not do anything by halves**.

In Italy they rarely do things by halves.

When designers latch on to a theme, they work it through thoroughly, producing the world's most wearable clothes in the most beautiful fabrics.

Jimmy never did anything by halves. His cruise was planned like a polar expedition, the boat prepared to withstand whatever the elements could toss her way.

Anything you do, or feel, you set about with expertise, with total commitment. You do nothing by halves.

hammer

go at it hammer and tongs: 1
hammer and tongs

If you **go at it hammer and tongs**, you do something very energetically, vigorously, and enthusiastically. This expression is used in British English.

'He loved gardening,' sniffed Mrs Gascoigne. 'He went at it hammer and tongs as soon as he got back from work.'

□ You can use **hammer and tongs** in other structures with a similar meaning.

She will go hammer and tongs to get what she wants.

They'll come at us from all angles, hammer and tongs, but when we get the ball we'll go at them. It should be a good game.

go at it hammer and tongs: 2
go at someone hammer and tongs

If you say that two people **are going at it hammer and tongs**, you mean that they are having a noisy argument. You can also say that one person **is going at** the other **hammer and tongs**. These expressions are used mainly in British English.

'They were going at it hammer and tongs.' 'What about?' 'I'm not very sure, but they were arguing.'

Goodness knows how long she had been going hammer and tongs at the child like this.

under the hammer ◄◄◄

If something goes **under the hammer**, it is offered for sale at auction. This expression is used in British English; the American expression is **on the block**.

The first half of the collection goes under the hammer on Friday and there are some real treasures.

A portrait by Dutch master Rembrandt went under the hammer for £4.18 million at Sotheby's yesterday.

Nine out of ten properties that come under the hammer are sold for less then their market value, and often the savings can be very marked.

hand

bite the hand that feeds you ◄◄

If you talk about someone **biting the hand that feeds** them, you mean that they are ungrateful and behave badly towards the person who has helped them or supported them.

She may be cynical about the film industry, but ultimately she has no intention of biting the hand that feeds her.

Talk about biting the hand that fed him! Leyland was a generous patron and Whistler insulted him unforgivably.

□ This expression is sometimes varied.

The world of the arts has turned to bite the hand that quadrupled the arts budget and underwrote the French cinema.

bound hand and foot

If you say that someone **is bound hand and foot** by something, you mean that they cannot act freely or do what they want because it prevents them, usually in a way that you consider unnecessary and harmful.

'Within his own tribal laws,' she wrote, 'the aboriginal is bound hand and foot by tradition.'

In a land bound hand and foot by petty regulations and bureaucracy, Sterligov saw that there were thousands of deals just waiting to be done if only the buyers and sellers could be brought together.

the dead hand ◄

If you talk about **the dead hand** of someone or something, you are criticizing them for having a very negative influence on a situation, for example by preventing change or progress. This expression is used mainly in British English.

The North Korean economy had started to shrink under the dead hand of central planning.

Serious-minded, analytical academics were among those he most despised. They laid, he thought, a dead hand upon literature.

force someone's hand ◄◄◄

If someone **forces your hand**, they force you to do something that you are not ready to do or do not want to do.

He blamed the press for forcing his hand. He claimed he hadn't wanted to talk about the *planned campaign against his daughter but had no choice when reporters told him they knew about it.*

Today's move may be a tactical manoeuvre designed to force the hand of the Prime Minister.

The Government is very reluctant to make such a move. But the exchange markets may force its hand, keeping up pressure on the pound until interest rates are raised.

a free hand ◄◄◄

If you have or are given **a free hand** to do something, you have the freedom to make your own decisions on how it should be done.

I shall have a free hand and be able to train the squadron as I like.

The South West African People's Party had to win a two-thirds majority in order to have a free hand in writing the constitution.

She was given a totally free hand by her clients to do exactly as she pleased.

get out of hand ◄◄◄

If a situation or person **gets out of hand**, they cannot be controlled any longer. Compare **out of hand**.

At the time of the strike in the Gdansk shipyards in the summer of 1980, the Kremlin felt things were rapidly getting out of hand.

Kenneth's aggressive nature has gotten a bit out of hand.

give someone a big hand
a big hand for someone

If you ask an audience to **give a big hand** to a performer, you are asking them to clap him or her. You can also ask for **a big hand for** the performer.

I'm Hal Morgan and these are the Praise Him Singers from Muncie, Indiana, so let's give 'em a big hand.

give with one hand and take away with the other

If you accuse someone of **giving with one hand and taking away with the other**, you mean that they seem to be helping you in one way, but are also doing something which has the opposite effect, for example harming you or preventing you from achieving what you want.

The countries of the European Union alone spend more than $9 billion helping Africans build roads, plant saplings and fill bellies. Yet Africa stays poor. One reason is that the rich world gives with one hand and it takes away with the other.

Although my parents were very supportive, in a way they gave with one hand and took back with the other, because I never really learned what it was to be independent.

hand in glove ◄

If one person or organization is working **hand in glove** with another person or organization, they are working very closely together. You usually use this expression to suggest that the people you are talking about are doing something dishonest or immoral.

Many of the city's politicians are hand in glove with smugglers.

Employment on the building sites is controlled by more than 40 gangs, who are believed to be hand-in-glove with the police.

hand in hand: 1 ◄◄◄

If two things go **hand in hand**, they are closely connected and cannot be considered separately from each other. You can also say that one thing goes **hand in hand** with another thing.

The principle of the playgroup movement is that play and learning go hand in hand: your child masters new skills and absorbs knowledge while having fun.

Poland alone will need around 25,000 million dollars just to stop air, water and land pollution getting any worse. At that price, environmental reforms must go hand in hand with economic reforms.

hand in hand: 2 ◄

If two people or organizations work **hand in hand**, they work closely together, often with a single aim. You can also say that one person or organization works **hand in hand** with another.

Gooch and Stewart have worked hand in hand together for three years.

Steelmakers are working hand-in-hand with auto makers to slash the cost of producing automotive parts.

hand over fist ◄

If someone is making money **hand over fist**, they are making a lot of money very quickly. If they are losing money **hand over fist**, they are losing it very quickly.

North Carolina National Bank in its North Carolina operations is barely making money. But it's making money hand over fist in Texas.

The companies had no skills and almost all were losing money hand over fist.

hand-to-mouth

You can say that someone is acting in a **hand-to-mouth** way when they do not plan ahead, but decide what to do from day to day. You usually use this expression critically or disapprovingly. This expression is used mainly in journalism. Compare **live from hand to mouth**.

Unless a government sets its course from the start, it is doomed to spend the rest of its term in hand-to-mouth improvising.

The loyalists cannot conceal their worries

about what are seen to be the Prime Minister's hand-to-mouth responses.

have a hand in something
take a hand in something ◄◄◄

If you **have a hand in** something, you are one of the people involved in doing it or creating it. If you **take a hand in** something, you become involved in doing it or creating it.

The second wave of appointments yesterday included people who will have a hand in shaping his policy.

Peter is a very experienced yachtsman, and had a hand in the design himself.

Perhaps it is time for ministers to step in and take a hand in deciding what services the BBC should provide now that the BBC is no longer the sole provider of national programmes.

□ You can talk about the extent to which someone is involved by putting an adjective such as 'strong', 'big', or 'small' before 'hand'.

Browner was a former legislative director to Senator Al Gore, who had a strong hand in her selection.

have someone eating out of your hand
have someone eating out of the palm of your hand ◄

If you **have** someone **eating out of** your **hand** or **have** them **eating out of the palm of** your **hand**, they will do whatever you want because they admire you so much. These expressions are often used to refer to situations where someone is suspicious or uncooperative at first, but then starts to like you and agree to anything you say.

No one can handle the press as she can and she usually has them eating out of her hand by the time they leave.

He is a silver-tongued lawyer famed for having juries eat out of the palm of his hand.

The Governor was rather unhelpful to start with, but ended up eating out of our hands.

have to hand it to someone ◄

In spoken English, people use expressions such as **'I have to hand it to you'** or **'you've got to hand it to him'** in order to acknowledge how well someone has done something or how good they are at it. People use these expressions even when they do not like the person or do not approve of their actions.

I have to hand it to you, though. You came pretty close to making a getaway.

Whatever you thought of his act, you had to hand it to him – he knew how to make money.

I've got to hand it to Yvonne; when she does something, she does it in a big way.

a heavy hand ◄

If you say that someone in a position of power uses **a heavy hand** in dealing with

people, you mean that they treat people very harshly or severely and often unfairly.

The Communists imposed a heavy hand on Eastern Europe and offered little room for political freedom.

The heavy hand of the military has not prevented their economies from doing very well.

hold someone's hand ◄

If someone **holds** your **hand** in an unfamiliar or difficult situation, they help and support you, for example by being with you.

Tony will hold your hand through the sale, check agents, suggest ways to make your home easier to sell, deal with offers and advise on particulars.

The staff were wonderful at holding our hands – taking us to ski hire and ski school and organising lift passes.

I will support him up to a point but I can't hold his hand forever and there comes a time when John has to take responsibility himself.

□ People sometimes use the expression **hand-holding** to refer to the technical support which a company gives its customers.

Customers are less willing to pay for service and hand-holding, especially if they already own lots of machines.

Several firms of stockbrokers are offering a hand-holding service for investors who find form filling complicated.

in the palm of your hand: 1

If you have a group of people, especially an audience, **in the palm of** your **hand**, they are giving you their full attention and are responding enthusiastically to everything you say or do.

A cursory look at the audience shows that she's got them in the palm of her hand.

Then, with the audience in the palm of his hand, he drew a deliberate link between the welfare of the 'kids' and next Tuesday's vote.

in the palm of your hand: 2
in the hollow of your hand

If you have someone **in the palm of** your **hand**, you have complete control over them and they will do whatever you want. You can also say that you have them **in the hollow of** your **hand**.

Boris shrugged off a warning that he is 'playing with fire'. Barbara's ex-boyfriend said: 'She has Boris in the palm of her hand.'

I reckoned I'd got Cheryl in the hollow of my hand.

keep your hand in ◄

If you do something to **keep** your **hand in**, you do it in order to use the skills which you have developed in the past, so that you do not lose them.

I had to wait two years before I was offered another part, and just to keep my hand in, I went on tour with a play that wasn't very good.

Words – written words – were what mattered to him, and he kept his hand in writing books and magazine articles.

know something like the back of your hand

If you say that you **know** something **like the back of** your **hand**, you are emphasizing that you know it very well.

He knows the city like the back of his hand.

He was an amazing navigator. He could predict hurricanes and knew the sea like the back of his hand.

They were born in the county, knew it like the backs of their hands and wanted to get home before the snowstorm made the roads impassable.

lend a hand
lend someone a hand ◄◄◄

If you **lend a hand**, you help someone to do something. You can also say that you **lend someone a hand**.

If I'd known, I'd have been glad to lend a hand – you should have rung me up.

I do the cooking and Bryan lends a hand with the washing-up.

From the first day of your job search, the Employment Service will lend you a hand.

Encourage him to lend a helping hand at such occasions as the school play or concert.

□ **A hand** is used in many other structures with a similar meaning.

I used to give Mary a hand with the catering.

Need a hand with those?

I could see you'd want a hand with the children.

live from hand to mouth
live hand to mouth ◄◄

Someone who **lives from hand to mouth** or **lives hand to mouth** does not have enough money to live comfortably, and has no money left after they have paid for basic necessities. You can also say that someone like this **is hand to mouth**. Compare **hand-to-mouth**.

I have a wife and two children and we live from hand to mouth on what I earn.

I just can't live hand-to-mouth, it's too frightening.

I do look after the family finances, but we're always hand-to-mouth.

□ You can also talk about a **hand-to-mouth** existence or a **hand-to-mouth** economy.

Unloved and uncared-for, they live a meaningless hand to mouth existence.

The village of Cuestecita is typical of the desperate hand-to-mouth economy that exists on the fringes of Cerrejon.

an old hand ◄◄◄

If someone is **an old hand** at something, they are very skilled at it because they have been doing it for a long time.

Being faced with decorating a flat like this from scratch would have put a lot of people off, but Bryce relished the challenge. He is, after all, an old hand at this kind of project, having moved house six times in ten years.

An old hand at photography, 34-year-old Tim has been shooting British landscapes and wildlife as a hobby for the last 13 years.

Whether you're a beginner or an old hand, these two new books will help you enjoy this satisfying craft.

□ You can describe someone as **an older hand** when you are comparing them with someone who is less experienced.

The original director left the project just days after filming began, to be replaced by Waris Hussein, an older hand in the art of dealing with strong female stars.

Although candidates might safely talk at job interviews of commitment to serve the public, older hands find that such sentiments no longer command the respect in the outside world that they once did.

out of hand ◄◄◄

If you reject an idea or suggestion **out of hand**, you reject it without hesitating and without discussing it or considering it first. Compare **get out of hand**.

He has rejected out of hand any suggestion that there can be any compromise over the proposals.

He said he hadn't rejected the idea out of hand.

The Russian Federation leader did not dismiss the proposals out of hand.

overplay your hand ◄

If someone **overplays** their **hand**, they act more confidently that they should, because they believe they are in a stronger position than they really are.

US officials tried to persuade Nazarbayev he had overplayed his hand, that he would lose any prospects for economic and technical assistance by holding onto the weapons.

the right hand doesn't know what the left hand is doing

If you say that an organization's **right hand doesn't know what** its **left hand is doing**, you mean that the people in one part of the organization do not know what the people in another part are doing and this is leading to confusion or difficulties. You use this expression when you want to criticize people or organizations for not communicating or cooperating properly.

The great service industries of Britain are

still in the situation where their right hand doesn't know what the left is doing. Usually they dig up roads, fill them in and then another service does the same a few days later.

□ People sometimes vary this expression.

At the moment it does seem a case of the right and left hand not working in tandem.

The government's left hand discovered what its right hand was doing only at the end of the first week.

show your hand ◄

In a competitive situation, if you **show** your **hand**, you let other people see what your position is and what you intend to do. You can replace 'show' with 'reveal'.

On domestic politics he seemed unwilling to show his hand too clearly.

It may be no accident that Manchester United have shown their hand in their attempt to lure David Hirst to Old Trafford.

Whatever flexibility the European Commission thinks it has on agriculture, it is unlikely to reveal its hand before November 1st.

a steady hand on the tiller ◄

If you describe someone as having **a steady hand on the tiller**, you are showing admiration for the way that they are keeping control of a situation. Adjectives such as 'firm' can be used instead of 'steady'.

'If ever there was an urgent need for a steady hand on the tiller, it is now,' said one European diplomat.

He was convinced that the job of those in power was to keep a firm hand on the tiller guiding the course of national development.

take someone in hand ◄◄

If you **take** someone or something **in hand**, you take control of them, in order to improve them.

'This woman makes me strong,' he has said of his girlfriend of more than two years. She took him in hand and told him that she wanted to see him win again.

I took myself in hand about a year ago and lost weight.

The feeling is growing that the present government is incapable of managing, is drifting and only reacts to events rather than taking the situation in hand.

Millions of pounds have been spent since 1978 when the problem was first taken in hand, but millions more are still needed.

throw in your hand

If you **throw in** your **hand**, you give up trying to do something.

Defeat on this embarrassing issue might just tip Mr Major into throwing in his hand.

try your hand at something ◄◄◄

If you **try** your **hand at** something, you try

doing it in order to see whether you like it or whether you are good at it.

In his latest book, he tries his hand at fiction.

After he left school, he tried his hand at a variety of jobs – bricklayer, cinema usher, coal man.

Several local people tried their hands at fish farming, only to discover the snags once their money had been invested.

He tried his hand as a writer.

Try your hand using some of the recipes on this page.

turn your hand to something ◄◄◄

If you **turn** your **hand to** something, you start doing it and do it well, even though you may not be trained to do it.

Judy is one of those women who can turn her hand to most things.

Although he maintains he's first and foremost an actor, he has turned his hand to writing a short film which he's hoping to get off the ground soon.

the upper hand ◄◄◄

If one side has **the upper hand** in a competitive situation, it has more power than the other side and can control things. If one side gains **the upper hand**, it gets more power and becomes able to control things.

The changes are by no means revolutionary, but they do suggest that for the first time economic reformers now have the upper hand in the party hierarchy.

Whenever conflict arose between her and her son, she held the upper hand, for she alone controlled the bulk of the family fortune.

Diplomats believe it is still far from clear which side is gaining the upper hand in the economic debate.

He seems to have taken the upper hand by making a far bolder proposition.

wait on someone hand and foot

If someone **is waited on hand and foot**, another person looks after them, taking care of them in every way and making them very comfortable. This expression is usually used to suggest that it is unreasonable for someone to be looked after in this way.

Many men expect to be waited on hand and foot because they've been spoiled rotten by their mothers.

If you are incapable of lying on a beach and being waited on hand and foot, then La Samanna, on the Caribbean island of St Martin, is not for you.

with one hand tied behind your back:1

If you say that you can do something **with one hand tied behind** your **back**, you are emphasizing that you can do it very easily.

The Explorer camcorder is so neat and nifty

you can operate it with one hand tied behind your back.

I was just thinking, the average housewife could run Derby County with one hand tied behind her back, couldn't she?

with one hand tied behind your back: 2
with your hands tied behind your back

If you complain that you have to do something **with one hand tied behind** your **back** or **with** your **hands tied behind** your **back**, you mean that you have a disadvantage which makes it difficult for you to succeed.

David Pleat is trying to steer us back towards the good old days, but he's having to do it with his one hand tied behind his back because he's had no money to spend on new players.

We'd like to open when our customers want us to and not only when the law says we can. Basically we're competing with both our hands tied behind our back.

They insist they would have won if the politicians had not tied their hands behind their backs.

handle

fly off the handle ◄

If you **fly off the handle**, you suddenly become very angry about something and behave in an uncontrolled and irrational way.

When I finally managed to get in touch with him, he flew off the handle. He shouted down the phone. How dare I question him? He was supposed to be doing me a favour.

Unless some decision was reached they might fly off the handle and do something foolish.

hands

at the hands of someone ◄◄◄

If someone experiences a particular kind of treatment, especially unpleasant treatment, **at the hands of** a person or organization, they receive it from them.

After their 4-0 home defeat at the hands of Vitesse Arnhem, United may find morale a problem.

She spoke of the humiliation she endured at the hands of the police.

All the children suffered at her hands.

change hands ◄◄◄

If something **changes hands**, one person or organization gets it from another, usually by buying it.

As an example, a bottle of this wine cost around £2 in 1962. Today, the same bottle would change hands for anything up to four hundred pounds.

By the close of business, only 383 million shares had changed hands.

The property has changed hands several times recently.

It was a very confusing race, with the lead changing hands several times.

□ When something is sold for a particular amount of money, you say that amount of money **changes hands**.

Record sums of money changed hands at Christie's in New York, where a portrait by Vincent Van Gogh has been sold for more than eighty million dollars.

dirty your hands

If you say that someone does not **dirty** their **hands**, you mean that they avoid doing physical work or the parts of a job that they consider unpleasant or distasteful. This expression is often used in criticizing someone for not getting involved in things. Compare **get** your **hands dirty**.

These are people who live in the commuter belt around the capital with more secure jobs and who have never had to dirty their hands to earn a living.

Very few academics of his distinction are willing to dirty their hands with political activity to the extent that he does.

fall into someone's hands
fall into the wrong hands ◄◄◄

If someone or something **falls into the hands** of an opponent or enemy, they are taken or caught by that person. You can also say that they **fall into the wrong hands**.

There is a real fear that food supplies could fall into the hands of the Mafia, thus increasing the misery of ordinary citizens.

On their release, the captain and officers were reprimanded for allowing their ship to fall into enemy hands.

The proposal is regarded as risky, with the possibility of weapons falling into the wrong hands.

get your hands dirty ◄◄

If you **get** your **hands dirty** in your job, you get involved with all aspects of it, including routine, practical, or more junior work, or dealing with people directly. This expression is usually used showing approval. Compare **dirty** your **hands**.

Getting their hands dirty keeps top managers in touch with the problems of customers and the experience of the front line, and it shows everybody that serving customers is important.

The second lesson is that the business schools need to get their hands dirty, forging closer links with the businesses that are their ultimate customers.

The guys at the top make all the money, while the people actually getting their hands dirty get exploited.

get your hands on: 1
lay your hands on ◄◄◄

If you **get** your **hands on** something you

want or need, or **lay** your **hands on** it, you succeed in obtaining it.

'If people have decided to buy up everything they can lay their hands on,' he said, 'what can I do about it?'

First of all, how was he able to get his hands on that money so easily?

The police are also worried about the determination of some right-wingers to get their hands on weapons.

While the house was in the process of being decorated, they read all the books and magazines they could lay hands on to get ideas.

get your hands on: 2
lay your hands on   ◄◄◄

If you **get** your **hands on** someone who has done something wrong or **lay** your **hands on** them, you catch them and usually punish them.

She declared that if she could get her hands on him she would know what to do.

That's the most likely explanation, they say, but we can't be sure until we lay our hands on the culprits.

If they do lay their hands on you, tell them I forced you to help me.

Two policemen managed to lay hands on one of the gunmen who'd commandeered a taxi but then allowed him to get away.

have your hands full
your hands are full   ◄◄◄

If you **have** your **hands full** or if your **hands are full**, you are very busy. You often use these expressions to indicate that you have many responsibilities or jobs, and do not have enough time for any more.

The federal government will obviously have its hands full trying to enforce environmental laws while keeping residents happy.

She's doing fine. Got her hands full with the kids, of course.

His hands are quite full enough without having me around.

in safe hands   ◄◄◄

If you say that someone or something is **in safe hands**, you mean that they are being cared for by a competent person or organization and are therefore not likely to be harmed or damaged. Compare **a safe pair of hands**.

They could get on with their own lives, knowing their girls were in safe hands.

All the time at the back of your mind you're aware that you're in the safe hands of a highly trained pilot.

Senior military figures have been assuring the outside world that control of the weapons remains in safe hands.

☐ You can replace 'safe' with 'good' or another adjective.

Although I knew the children would be in

good hands, and they'd have a great time, I still felt anxious.

He was also forced to relinquish his business, which is now in the capable hands of his only son.

in your hands   ◄◄◄

If something is **in** your **hands**, it is in your possession or under your control.

Some delegates have criticised the move, saying it will leave too much power in the hands of the party leadership.

Seventy per cent of Azerbaijan's production came from the thirty per cent of the farmland still in private hands.

Her passport to is to remain in police hands and she has to live at an undisclosed address.

off your hands   ◄◄

If someone or something is **off** your **hands**, you are no longer responsible for them, because another person has taken responsibility for them instead of you. Compare **on** your **hands**.

I can always take the children off your hands for a while, if you've nothing much else for me to do.

He fervently hoped that all the girls would inherit their mother's beauty, and thus marry and be off his hands.

Mr Robinson, who lives next door to the cottage, says: 'I was just glad to get it off my hands.'

on your hands: 1   ◄◄◄

If you have a problem or task **on** your **hands**, you have to deal with it. Compare **off** your **hands**.

Mr Antall will have a tough fight on his hands to persuade a sceptical public of the virtues of a massive and instant dose of painful remedies.

What is already clear though is that the Colombian police now have yet another drug problem on their hands.

'Go and worry Inspector Upshire if you must,' he finished plaintively, 'I've got enough on my hands.'

☐ This expression is generally used to refer to bad or difficult situations. However, it is sometimes used to refer to good situations, for example when you say that someone has a hit or a success **on** their **hands**.

Greensleeves Records had a monster hit on its hands with Tippa Irie's 'Hello Darling'.

Now, a few years on, the Barrys have a success story on their hands. They've transformed the whole of the house to create a comfortable home that they love.

on your hands: 2   ◄

If you have a person **on** your **hands**, you are responsible for caring for them or dealing with them. You use this expression when this responsibility is likely to be difficult or demanding for you. Compare **off** your **hands**.

Graham said: 'I have got tired players on my hands and we are only five weeks into the season.'

Those parents who took a lax attitude to family discipline now have hooligan children on their hands.

out of your hands ◄◄◄

If something is **out of** your **hands**, you are no longer responsible for it. Compare **on** your **hands**.

The matter has been taken out of our hands. We are referring all enquiries on the disposal of County Hall to the Department of the Environment.

Things were out of our hands now. We could only wait.

Everyone seems to forget that it's out of my hands – I can't control anything that people say.

play into someone's hands ◄◄◄

If you **play into** someone's **hands**, you make a foolish mistake or act in the way that they want you to act, so that they gain an advantage over you or defeat you.

Trying to prevent an investigation not only plays right into the hands of our critics but will severely damage shoppers' confidence in their supermarkets.

The main opposition parties played into his hands by boycotting the election.

Iran's spiritual leader has called for unity between the two government factions and said differences of opinion over policy could play into the hands of Iran's enemies.

In each case it would be easy to react angrily – this will only play into the hands of your critic.

rub your hands ◄◄

If you say that someone **is rubbing** their **hands**, you mean that they are very pleased about something, often something bad which has happened to an enemy or opponent. This expression is used mainly in British English.

Leaders of the Windward Islands opposition parties are rubbing their hands in glee at the news that British banana magnates have suffered a cut in profits.

By the turn of the century, there will be 20 million mobile-phone subscribers in Japan. Compare that with the 55 million conventional phone subscribers and you see why Japan's electronics firms are rubbing their hands.

Hank Steinbrecher, General Secretary of the US Soccer Federation, used to sell breakfast cereal. Now he's rubbing his hands together at the prospect of selling the World Cup to the USA.

a safe pair of hands
safe hands ◄

If you refer to someone, especially a politician, as **a safe pair of hands**, you mean that they are good at their job and unlikely to make any serious mistakes. This expression is used mainly in British English. Compare **in safe hands**.

Douglas Hurd is widely regarded within the party as being what's known as a safe pair of hands.

□ You can also refer to someone who is thought of in this way as **safe hands**.

In front of Munich's city hall, Max Streibl and Theo Waigel urge people to vote again for safe hands.

shake hands on something

You can say that two people or groups **shake hands on** a deal or an agreement when they conclude it successfully.

So keen were the Russians to shake hands on the deal that they offered to accept palm oil in part payment.

There is hope of better behaviour; and it is heartening that these representatives of the three great faiths, Christianity, Judaism and Islam, should seem to shake hands on that.

sit on your hands ◄◄

If you say that someone **is sitting on** their **hands**, you are criticizing them for not doing something which they ought to be doing.

I think the US troops there are beginning to feel quite embarrassed about sitting on their hands while refugees stream through the lines with tales of horror.

The pace of development in Formula One is so fast that if you sit on your hands you quickly regret it.

☑ In American English, you can also use this expression to show your approval of someone for restraining themselves and waiting for the best time to take action.

Force yourself to read the draft in its entirety. Sit on your hands. Give the draft a chance before you begin reworking it.

sully your hands

If you talk about someone **sullying** their **hands** by doing something, you mean that they would find it unpleasant or distasteful to do it. This is a formal expression, which is often used to criticize people's attitudes towards an activity.

He had no intention of sullying his hands by playing politics: he wished to be, as he so frequently declared, 'above politics'.

As the moral fabric of the isles goes from strength to strength, with some islanders barely sullying their hands with toil for fear of corruption, the economic fabric is likely to deteriorate severely.

wash your hands of something ◄◄◄

If you **wash** your **hands** of a problem or of a person who causes problems, you refuse to be involved with them or to take responsibility for them any longer.

In a sense the government has been washing its hands of the army's actions, especially its more destructive provocative actions.

The Macclesfield MP said: 'We cannot wash our hands of responsibility for the state of the economy.'

'If Charles was my patient I would wash my hands of him,' said specialist Dr George Raine at the time.

The government has got to do something about this. It cannot continue to sit back and wash its hands.

win hands down: 1
beat someone hands down ◄◄

If you say that someone **wins** a contest **hands down**, you are emphasizing that they win it easily. You can also say that they **beat** someone else **hands down**.

They predict that if a general election was held now, the Conservative Party would win hands down.

When he said he would beat me hands down, I didn't expect him to run like that.

win hands down: 2
beat something hands down ◄◄

When you are comparing things to see which is best, you can say that the thing which is clearly best **wins hands down** or **beats** the others **hands down**.

The New Winter Palace Hotel wins hands down for both comfort and evocative location, situated a few steps away from the banks of the Nile and opposite the mountains on the West Bank.

I had always enjoyed driving through the New Forest, but two-wheeled travel beats the car hands down.

□ You can also talk about a **hands-down** winner. This expression is used mainly in journalism.

Foliage that looks presentable all season is a vital consideration in choosing plants for the border. Sedum 'Autumn Joy' is a hands-down winner in the foliage department.

□ **Hands down** is used in other structures where you are saying that something is clearly the best.

We are hands-down, flat-out the leaders of the world in this.

Grant Lee Buffalo have made 1993's finest album, hands down.

with your bare hands ◄◄◄

If someone does something **with** their **bare hands**, they do it without using any weapons or tools.

If I thought that, I'd kill you now with my bare hands.

The protesters fought with bare hands, stones and knives.

Rescue workers and residents were digging through tonnes of mud with shovels and their bare hands yesterday in search of survivors.

□ You can also say that someone does something **bare-handed**.

You see, nobody wants to die, nobody faces tanks bare-handed just out of fanaticism.

wring your hands ◄◄◄

If you say that someone **is wringing** their **hands**, you mean that they are expressing sadness or regret about a bad situation, but are not taking any action to deal with it. You usually use this expression to show your disapproval of them for behaving like this.

Yet while Europe faces its most barbaric conflict since the end of World War Two, the UN stands hopelessly on the sidelines, wringing its hands piously.

Mr Ashdown had accused the Government of wringing its hands and doing nothing as the country's jobless figures spiralled.

□ When someone behaves like this, you can refer to **hand-wringing** or **wringing of hands**.

Condolences and hand-wringing are not enough.

I expect there'll be shock, horror and wringing of hands.

your hands are tied
have your hands tied
something ties your hands ◄◄◄

If your **hands are tied**, something such as a law is preventing you from acting in the way that you want to. You can also say that you **have** your **hands tied** or that something **ties** your **hands**.

He would like to help but he is powerless because his hands are tied by regulations approved by the council of ministers.

The Americans, however, know they cannot control the Security Council and prefer not to have their hands tied when they think action is needed.

The present rule ties jockeys' hands and I don't feel it is fair. It should be changed.

She would not admit to being angry, only frustrated by it all. 'We feel as though our hands have been tied because we have no power at all.'

handsome

handsome is as handsome does
pretty is as pretty does

When people say **handsome is as handsome does** or **pretty is as pretty does**, they mean that you should judge someone by their actions and not by their appearance. These are old-fashioned expressions.

Handsome is as handsome does, my mother and grandmother always said in order to counter self-admiration.

Instead of worrying about making a fool of yourself, forget about how your swing may look and concentrate instead on where you want the ball to go. Pretty is as pretty does.

hang

get the hang of something   ◄◄◄
If you **get the hang** of an activity, you learn how to do it competently.

Once one gets the hang of it, reading a good play can be a delightful and challenging experience.

'After a few months', he says, 'you think you are getting the hang of the language and expressing yourself quite well.'

I was exhausted at first, but now that I've got the hang of it, I wouldn't know how to sit down and relax.

hang someone out to dry   ◄
If you say that someone **has been hung out to dry**, you mean that they are in a very difficult situation and have been abandoned by the people who previously supported them.

Once again, the CIA – apparently unable to resist political manipulation by the administration – is in danger of being hung out to dry.

Anything happens to you in there and, believe me, we'll hang you out to dry.

hang up your boots   ◄
If a sports player, especially a footballer, **hangs up** their **boots**, they stop playing and retire.

I want a few triumphs and medals to reflect on when I eventually hang up my boots.

I'm slower now and the time has come to hang up my boots.

☐ People often replace 'boots' with another word which relates to a person's job, to mean that they stop doing that job.

Superstar Clint Eastwood wants to hang up his cowboy hat, even though his latest western has received rave reviews.

Nurse Christine Soutar hung up her uniform to look after her four young sons.

As for the future of his boxing career, Taylor continues to maintain that he has hung up his gloves for good.

☐ 'Hang up your boots' is used in British English. The other forms are used in both British and American English.

let it all hang out   ◄
If someone **lets it all hang out**, they behave in a very informal and relaxed way, without worrying about hiding their emotions or behaving politely.

The defence most frequently claimed for the baring of the more dreadful revelations is that of 'unburdening': let it all hang out and you will feel better.

☐ You can use **let-it-all-hang-out** before a noun to describe a situation in which people behave in this way.

In Hollywood, drugs have always been plentiful, but they began a spectacular ascent during the let-it-all-hang-out Sixties.

happy

happy as a clam
If you are **happy as a clam**, you are very happy. This expression is used in American English.

Join the other kids. Do that, and before you know it you'll be happy as a clam.

happy as a lark
If you are **happy as a lark**, you are very happy.

Look at me – eighty-two years old and happy as a lark!

happy as a pig in muck
If you are **happy as a pig in muck**, you are very happy. This is an informal expression, which is used in British English.

From day one I adored it. I was as happy as a pig in muck.

☐ This expression has several variations. For example, some people talk about being **happy as a pig in shit**. Many people find this offensive.

I'd much rather be as I am, I couldn't imagine being any different. Happy as a pig in shit.

Frankly, I was like a pig in shit – oh, how I revelled in the opportunity of standing next to famous people!

happy as a sandboy
If you are **happy as a sandboy**, you are very happy. This expression is used in British English.

He's all smiles and happy as a sandboy.

happy as Larry
If you are as **happy as Larry**, you are very happy. This is an informal expression, which is used in British English.

I gave her a police badge to wear on her sleeve and she's as happy as Larry.

I'd strapped him in his chair in the back and he'd sat there, happy as Larry.

hard

hard as nails   ◄
If you say that someone is as **hard as nails**, you mean that they are very unsympathetic towards other people, or do not seem to care about them.

He's a shrewd businessman and hard as nails.

When necessary she could be as hard as nails.

□ You can use **hard-as-nails** before a noun.

That was his hard-as-nails trade representative, Carla Hills.

hard done by ◄◄

If someone feels **hard done by**, they feel that they have been treated unfairly. This expression is used in British English.

Those who felt hard done by made their dissatisfaction clear.

He really felt they'd been hard done by, and he would have liked to right it.

□ You can use **hard-done-by** before a noun to describe someone who is thought to have been treated unfairly.

I'm the hard-done-by husband.

old habits die hard ◄◄◄

If you say **'old habits die hard'**, you mean that people are often reluctant to change their way of doing something, especially something which they have been doing for a long time.

Despite ideas of equality, old habits die hard and women still carry the main burden of looking after home and family.

The Council had introduced some changes, but old habits die hard. The Management Committee was made up mostly of the former members of the old Board of Guardians, which had run the place for decades.

□ You can use other words instead of 'habit'. For example, if people are reluctant to change their opinions about something, you can say **'old ideas die hard'**.

I don't believe we'll ever attain true equality until we have socialism, although I know women are still unequal in socialist countries and old attitudes die hard.

The Germans are the first to admit that old national prejudices die hard.

□ **Die-hard** is used to describe people who continue to support a person or an ideology that is no longer popular with most people.

The band broke up in 1970 and die-hard fans have been waiting for a reunion ever since.

The party congress is dominated by diehard conservatives clinging to traditional ideology.

play hard to get ◄

If you say that someone **is playing hard to get**, you mean that they are deliberately making it difficult for you to obtain something that you need from them, such as their agreement or permission.

Only a few days ago, the Social Democrats were playing hard to get as the CDU tried to woo them into coalition talks.

Dozens of newspaper articles tried to push the

case for a 'yes' vote. But the French, ever suspicious of those in power, played hard to get.*

□ If you say that a woman **is playing hard to get**, you mean that she is discouraging a man from making sexual advances to her, as a way of making herself more attractive and interesting to him.

She would also play hard to get with her admirers. She gleefully told a friend: 'I don't answer the telephone when he rings me. In fact he called me four times last night and I didn't pick it up.'

'Why don't you leave me alone?' she said. Larry grinned again. 'Ah, you're just playing hard to get.'

hardball

play hardball ◄

If someone **plays hardball**, they will do anything that is necessary to achieve or obtain what they want, even if this involves being harsh or unfair. This expression is used mainly in American English. Compare **play ball**; see **ball**.

He's going to play hardball, with money and with political favors.

Playing hardball, Kodak has decided to cancel business with distributors that also sell Fuji products.

The White House decided to retaliate by taking jobs away from his state, showing they were tough guys who could play hard ball.

hare

run with the hare and hunt with the hounds

If you say that someone **runs with the hare and hunts with the hounds**, you mean that they try to support both sides in an argument or conflict, in order to make their own life easier. This expression is used in British English.

They want to keep the peace and have everybody happy. For this reason they learn very quickly to run with the hares and hunt with the hounds; to side with whoever is nearest in a relentless quest to avoid rows.

start a hare

If someone **starts a hare**, they introduce a new idea or topic which other people become interested in. This expression is used in British English.

Some work needs to be done before the connection between aluminium and heart disease is proved to everyone's satisfaction. But Mr Birchall has started a hare that many researchers will be watching.

harness

in harness: 1 ◄

You say someone is **in harness** when they are actually doing a job which they have been appointed to do. This expression is used mainly in British English.

He was with the labour battalion only a few weeks but he could at least feel himself to be properly in harness.

They hope to have the Australian Test forward Troy Coker back in harness before the end of the season.

in harness: 2 ◄

If two or more people work **in harness**, they work together or produce something together. This expression is used mainly in British English.

Experts in production statistics and computing may work in harness on a single project.

At Opera North he will be in harness with Paul Daniel, the 34-year-old conductor appointed music director last year.

hat

eat your hat

You say that you will **eat** your **hat** if a particular thing happens in order to emphasize that you do not believe that it will happen. This is an old-fashioned expression.

I will eat my hat if the Liberal Democrats improve their parliamentary representation at the next general election.

He has promised to eat his hat if he is wrong.

hat in hand ◄

If you go **hat in hand** to someone, you ask them very humbly and respectfully for money or help. This expression is used mainly in American English; the usual British expression is **cap in hand**.

The damage wrought by one such venture forced Illinois to go hat in hand to financiers in New York, London, and Boston to salvage its finances.

He won't go hat-in-hand to the White House to ask that sanctions be lifted against his country.

keep something under your hat ◄

If someone tells you something and then asks you to **keep** it **under** your **hat**, they are asking you not to mention it to anyone else.

Hardly anyone's been told except the families concerned and you, darling. So keep it under your hat.

Look, if I tell you something will you promise to keep it under your hat. Promise now, not a word to anyone?

knock something into a cocked hat ◄

If you say one thing **knocks** another **into a cocked hat**, you are emphasizing that the

first thing is much better or more successful than the second. This expression is used mainly in British English.

I am writing a novel which is going to knock Proust into a cocked hat.

As for being the most beautiful women in the world, Catherine Zeta Jones and the Princess of Wales could knock them all into a cocked hat.

old hat ◄◄◄

If you describe something as **old hat**, you are being scornful of it, because you think it is unoriginal or out of date.

The younger generation tell me that religion is old hat and science has proved this, but has it? The more I read of scientific discoveries, the more credible I find some parts of the Bible.

It is to the credit of many British companies, dismissed as fuddy-duddy and old-hat, that they kept the flame of British quality alive.

I think that's a bit old hat now, isn't it? I wanted to do something quite different.

pass the hat
pass the hat around ◄

If people **pass the hat** or **pass the hat around**, they collect money for someone or something.

The United States is also passing the hat among rich countries to help to pay for our military effort.

Airbus will soon be passing the hat around again for an enormous 700-seat aeroplane.

☐ You can refer to an instance of this as **a passing of the hat** or **a passing round of the hat**.

He explains the Somali custom of Qaaraan – a kind of passing round of the hat for someone in dire need.

pull a rabbit out of the hat
pull something out of the hat ◄◄

If someone **pulls a rabbit out of the hat**, they unexpectedly do something which solves a problem or helps them to achieve something. This expression is used mainly in journalism.

'We pulled a rabbit out of the hat tonight,' said Toronto's coach Pat Burns.

I cannot pull a rabbit out of a hat every time I go into the boxing ring. All I can do is do my best.

☐ This expression is often varied.

It looks as though I will have to pull a few rabbits from the hat.

Almost every politician with whom they had dealings appeared to act as if rabbits could pop out of any hat.

☐ You can also say that someone **pulls** something good or successful **out of the hat**.

The Chancellor failed to pull any economic

*miracles out of the hat last night when he un-
veiled his latest strategy for recovery.*

*It's hard to identify anything he could pull
out of his hat that would really affect US
forces.*

*He might still be able to pull something out
of his hat, but I'd be kind of surprised at this
point.*

□ This expression refers to a traditional ma-
gician's trick, in which a rabbit is produced
mysteriously out of an apparently empty hat.

take your hat off to someone
hats off to someone ◄◄

If you say you **take** your **hat off to** someone, you are expressing admiration for something that they have done.

*I take my hat off to them. They've done very
well.*

*You have to take your hat off to whoever
thought this one up.*

*The chances are that we'll all be taking our
hats off to Richardson's achievements by the
autumn.*

□ You can also say **hats off to** someone.

Hats off to them for supporting the homeless.

*Hats off to the journalists and to the camera-
men who have shown the pictures on television.*

talk through your hat

If you say that someone **is talking through**
their **hat**, you are saying rudely or scornfully
that what they are saying is ridiculous or totally incorrect.

*Mrs Smith had told Adam he was talking
through his hat if he thought economic ration-
alism would work.*

*He is talking through his hat when he attrib-
utes the overcrowding and over-use of parts of
the Lake District to its designation as a national park.*

throw your hat into the ring
throw your cap into the ring ◄

If you **throw** your **hat into the ring** or
throw your **cap into the ring**, you become
one of the people taking part in a competition
or contest. Other verbs are sometimes used
instead of 'throw'.

*She would have been the first woman to serve
as Germany's top diplomat, but she lost the
nomination after Kinkel threw his hat into the
ring at the last moment.*

*He said straightaway that he would play. I
am delighted that he has decided to throw his
cap into the ring.*

*Last night the senior backbencher, Cyril
Townsend, who was originally opposed to a
contest, called for Mr Heseltine to put his hat
into the ring.*

hatch

down the hatch

If you say some food or drink goes **down
the hatch**, you mean someone eats or drinks
it, usually quickly or greedily.

*A record £4.4 billion worth of confectionery
went down the hatch last year.*

*My daughter raised the shell to her lips,
closed her eyes and down the hatch went the
oyster.*

□ People sometimes say **'down the hatch!'**
just before drinking an alcoholic drink.

*She said 'Down the hatch!' and drank the
whole lot in one gulp.*

hatches

batten down the hatches ◄

If you **batten down the hatches**, you prepare for a difficult situation by doing everything you can to protect yourself.

*While most companies are battening down the
hatches, fearing recession, Blenheim is leading
an assault on the US market.*

*They are obviously battening down the
hatches in order to prepare a plan.*

hatchet

bury the hatchet ◄

When people who have quarrelled **bury the
hatchet**, they agree to forget their quarrel
and become friends again.

*One employee said Viscount Althorp had been
to see his father before his death and this
showed the two had finally buried the hatchet
after their falling-out.*

I want to bury the hatchet. I still love her.

a hatchet job ◄

To do **a hatchet job** on someone or something means to say or write a lot of bad
things about them in order to harm their
reputation.

*Tories fear the Shadow Home Secretary can
do the same hatchet job on Mr Major as he
has on Home Secretary Michael Howard.*

*His review of the Manics' Marquee gig was
the most heavily poisoned hatchet-job I have
read in this paper.*

a hatchet man ◄

You describe a man as **a hatchet man** when
his job is to destroy things or do unpleasant
tasks, often on behalf of someone else. This
expression is usually used showing disapproval.

*But Hall, they reckoned, was a hatchet man,
out to shred the workforce and totally crush
the union.*

*He had to play the hatchet man and it was
not pleasant for the many he laid off.*

haul

a long haul
in something for the long haul ◄◄
If you say a task or course of action will be **a long haul**, you mean that it will be very difficult to deal with and will need a great deal of effort and time.

Revitalising the economy will be a long haul.

The American Defence Secretary, Mr Dick Cheney, said the United States was prepared for a long haul.

International banking sources suggest that the bank and its president face a long haul to rebuild credibility.

□ In American English, if you say that you are **in** something **for the long haul**, you mean that you intend to continue doing it until it is finished, even if it is difficult or unpleasant.

Impatience is not our problem. We're in it for the long haul. Five years is the minimum.

over the long haul ◄◄
If you talk about the effect that something will have **over the long haul**, you are talking about its effect over a long period of time in the future. This expression is used mainly in American English.

The fact is that over the long haul, most investors would be pleasantly surprised at just how much can be earned by putting their money into good, sound, safe investments.

The smart economic message for the nation is that prudent leadership, coupled with patience, will accomplish more over the long haul.

hawk

watch someone like a hawk
If you **watch** someone **like a hawk**, you pay close attention to everything they do, usually to make sure that they do not do anything wrong.

Some guys just sit there and watch her like a hawk, dead sure she's trying to cheat.

If we hadn't watched him like a hawk, he would have gone back to London.

hay

make hay while the sun shines
make hay ◄
If you **make hay while the sun shines**, you take advantage of a good situation which is not likely to last.

Making hay while the sun shines, the Egyptian government has taken radical measures to liberalise the economy.

You've got to make hay while the sun shines and it doesn't shine long in a sporting life.

□ This expression is often varied.

We were determined to make hay while we could.

□ You can say that someone **makes hay** out of any situation that they take advantage of, especially if you disapprove of their behaviour.

There are unscrupulous therapists who will try to make hay out of the government's new-found interest in alternative medicine.

The New Zealand media made hay with the issue.

head

bite someone's head off
snap someone's head off
If someone **bites** your **head off**, they speak to you in an unpleasant, angry way, because they are annoyed about something. You can also say that they **snap** your **head off**.

Whenever possible, suggest she talks about it but be aware she may bite your head off for your trouble.

And don't bite my head off just because you're bad tempered.

I snapped her head off on the phone.

bury your head in the sand ◄◄
If you say that someone **is burying** their **head in the sand**, you mean that they are deliberately refusing to accept the truth about something unpleasant. Verbs such as 'stick', 'hide', and 'keep' are sometimes used instead of 'bury'.

Don't be an ostrich and bury your head in the sand, hoping your problems will disappear.

No one has the luxury of sticking their head in the sand when it comes to standing up for basic civil rights.

□ You can also say that someone has a **head in the sand** approach or a **head in the sand** attitude. This form is used mainly in journalism.

I oppose it because it's a stupid, head-in-the-sand approach to the global problem of nuclear waste disposal.

□ People used to think that ostriches buried their heads in the sand when they were in danger.

can do something standing on your head
If you say that you **can do** something **standing on** your **head**, you are emphasizing that you can do it very easily.

'Guess I can leave that to you and Tom, huh?' Since Tom, the cameraman, had won five Oscars during his long working life, and could have directed the whole picture standing on his head while playing a game of cards, Joanna didn't need to answer this one.

cannot make head or tail of something

◄

If you **cannot make head or tail of** something or **cannot make head nor tail of** it, you cannot understand it at all.

I couldn't make head or tail of it myself, but it sounded like part of some sort of hymn or prayer.

I did understand the recent fury of the railroad clerks, who went on strike because they couldn't make head nor tail of a new American ticket-writing computer called 'Socrates'.

come to a head
bring something to a head

◄◄◄

If a problem or disagreement **comes to a head**, it reaches a state where you have to take action to deal with it. You can also say that a particular event or factor **brings** a problem or disagreement **to a head**.

Matters came to a head on Monday when he implicitly threatened to dissolve Parliament after a committee of MPs threw out the government's political reform program.

These problems came to a head in September when five of the station's journalists were sacked.

It was Mrs Thatcher's attitude and style of leadership over Europe that really brought things to a head.

a cool head

◄◄

If someone keeps **a cool head**, they remain calm in a difficult situation.

I have to keep a cool head and try not to let my anger show.

Planning and cool heads are needed above all to repair the damage the storm has wrought.

I value her cool head when I'm trying to come to a decision.

do your head in

◄

If something or someone **does** your **head in**, they make you very unhappy, upset, confused, or ill, and make you feel as if you cannot cope or are going mad. This expression is used mainly in spoken British English.

During her year off she worked at a boutique in Bromley, doing things like cleaning coat hangers. 'It did my head in,' she laughs.

A man who has lost his memory made an emotional appeal for help yesterday. 'Somebody out there must know who I am – this is doing my head in.'

fall head over heels
be head over heels

◄◄

If you **fall head over heels** in love with someone, you fall suddenly and deeply in love with them. If you **are head over heels** in love, you are very deeply in love.

It was obvious that Alan had fallen head over heels in love with Veronica.

When I was 18, I fell head over heels for my first 'proper' boyfriend, Alex.

It's plain from the sheepish tone in Colin's voice that he's head over heels.

from head to toe
from head to foot

◄◄◄

You can use **from head to toe** or **from head to foot** to emphasize that you are talking about the whole of someone's body. **From top to toe** means the same.

She was covered from head to toe with black and blue marks.

She was trembling from head to foot.

Mrs Smith's daughter came, dressed head to toe in black.

The boy is wrapped head to foot in a green blanket.

□ You can use **head-to-toe** or **head-to-foot** before a noun.

He turned up clad in head-to-toe black.

Standing against the wall was this man in head to foot leather.

get in over your head
be in over your head

◄

If you say that someone **gets in over** their **head**, you mean that they become deeply involved in a situation which is too difficult for them to deal with. You can also say that someone **is in over** their **head**.

Five years ago the Dutch director George Sluizer made a quietly horrifying film, The Vanishing, about a man who gets in over his head as he searches obsessively for his missing girlfriend.

He realized that he was in over his head, and that only his family could help him.

get your head around something
get your mind around something

◄

If you **get** your **head around** something such as a new or unfamiliar idea, you succeed in understanding it or accepting it.

He can't get his head around the fact that the children born in this country are not 'immigrants'.

I haven't quite got my head round it yet but it's brilliant. This is the first money we've ever been given to do our thing.

□ You can also say that you **get** your **mind around** something.

MacGregor took the job with integrity and got his mind round complicated issues.

give someone their head

◄◄

If you **give** someone their **head**, you allow them to do what they want to do, without trying to advise them or stop them.

He was a nice, decent man who treated people properly and he recognised ability and gave people their heads.

By giving nationalism its head, the communists unleashed forces they could not control.

go over someone's head: 1 ◄◄

If you **go over the head of** someone who is in authority or who has responsibility for something, you appeal to a higher authority than them in an attempt to get what you want.

Don't break office protocol by going over your boss's head. But make sure that your seniors know what suggestions came from you.

He was reprimanded for trying to go over the heads of senior officers.

What if he follows through on his threats to go over the heads of the Congress to the people?

go over someone's head: 2
be over someone's head
talk over someone's head ◄◄

If something that someone says or writes **goes over** your **head**, you do not understand it because it is too difficult for you. You can also say that something **is over** your **head** or that someone **talks over** your **head**.

The few books that exist today either come from abroad, having been written for preschool native speakers, or introduce grammar that goes over young heads.

I bought a handful of photographic magazines last month and when I got home to read them, I found they were completely over my head.

The nurses were brilliant at explaining everything. However, the doctors talked over my head and did not involve me in decisions.

go to your head: 1 ◄◄

If you say that someone lets success **go to** their **head**, you mean that they start to think that they are better or cleverer than other people, and they begin to behave in an arrogant or silly way.

Ford is definitely not a man to let a little success go to his head. He knows he still has a lot to learn.

I think Jenny's salary rise went to her head. She felt that because she had so much more money than I did, she could speak her mind and I'd just have to listen.

go to your head: 2

If alcohol **goes to** your **head**, it makes you slightly drunk and perhaps affects your judgement so that you do silly things.

He was not accustomed to strong liquor and it went to his head.

hang over your head ◄◄

If you say that something difficult or unpleasant **is hanging over** your **head**, you mean that it worries you because it may cause something bad to happen to you in the future.

If the post fell vacant, it is unlikely that the Home Office would want to appoint him if an inquiry was hanging over his head.

Now that thousands of nuclear weapons were hanging over everyone's head, modern technology no longer sounded entirely wonderful.

And with the threat of American trade sanctions hanging over its head, the Japanese government decided to reach a compromise with the United States.

have your head in the clouds
with your head in the clouds ◄

If you say that someone **has** their **head in the clouds**, you mean that they are out of touch with reality and perhaps have impractical ideas about achieving success. You can also say that someone does something **with** their **head in the clouds**.

Whether some of them still have their heads in the clouds after our FA Cup win over Spurs, I don't know.

When we were leaving school, Rosemary used to say she was going to be a very rich lady one day. We all thought it was typical of her, she seemed to live with her head in the clouds.

☐ You can also use **head-in-the-clouds** before a noun.

He was a classics man, from Oxford I think. A rather head-in-the-clouds man.

have your head screwed on

If you say that someone **has** their **head screwed on**, you mean that they are sensible and realistic.

Good girl! I always knew you had your head screwed on properly.

The only one with her head screwed on was granny.

have your head up your arse
have your head up your ass

If someone accuses you of **having** your **head up** your **arse** or of **having** your **head up** your **ass**, they are criticizing you for deliberately refusing to accept the truth about something, or for thinking more about yourself than about other people or things that are happening around you. This is a very informal expression, which many people consider offensive. The form with 'arse' is used in British English and the form with 'ass' is used in American English.

head and shoulders above someone ◄◄◄

If you say that one person or thing is **head and shoulders above** others of their kind, you mean that they are clearly better than them. People occasionally use other prepositions instead of 'above'.

In the world of newspaper publishing, there is one success story that stands head and shoulders above the rest.

Richards, according to Imran Khan, was head and shoulders above any other player at his peak.

So wrote the Negro author, Louis Lomax, catching the crucial spark that made Martin Luther King Jr stand out head and shoulders from his fellow ministers in the South.

a head of steam: 1 ◄

If someone builds up **a head of steam**, they gradually become more and more angry, anxious, or emotional about something until they can no longer hide their feelings.

Bob was the most angry, as if in waiting for the other items to be cleared he had built up a greater head of steam.

a head of steam: 2

If someone gets **a head of steam** for something such as a plan or cause, they gain a lot of support for it.

While most senior Conservative MPs still believe an election next year is more likely, there's an increasing head of steam behind November.

Hitherto, the only remedy for the victims of judicial mistreatment has been to get friends and relatives to campaign for public support and to get a sufficient head of steam to force the Foreign Office to act on their behalf.

head-to-head: 1 ◄◄◄

If two people or organizations go **head-to-head**, they compete directly with each other. This expression is used mainly in talking about business and sport.

General Motors and Ford are expected to go head to head in the markets to buy up rival 15% stakes in Jaguar.

Some Mexican businessmen and farmers fear they will lose out when they compete head to head with their US counterparts.

Radio 1 is our main competitor and we will primarily be head-to-head with them.

☐ You can also talk about a **head-to-head** battle or competition.

American Airlines, which is in a desperate head-to-head battle for custom with British Airways, was quick to point out that they have been offering such cheap fares since April.

As top athletes, we should be running against each other whenever possible. Head-to-head competition makes our sport what it is.

head-to-head: 2 ◄

If two people or groups who are in conflict have **head-to-head** talks, they meet to discuss the subjects they disagree about.

They have just begun a third session of head to head talks which are expected to last until late afternoon.

It is not worth arguing head-to-head with this person but better to listen to them and offer your opinion.

☐ **A head-to-head** is a discussion, disagreement, or confrontation.

Next time you have a head-to-head with someone in authority, watch your language.

hold a gun to someone's head
put a gun to someone's head ◄

If someone **holds a gun to** your **head** or **puts a gun to** your **head**, they force you to do something by threatening to take extreme action against you if you do not do it. People sometimes use 'pistol' instead of 'gun'.

The problem with this process is that it's been undertaken with the reality and threat of continuing genocide held as a gun to our heads.

Not a man to have a gun put to his head, Mr Riordan was soon tearing up the offer and cancelling future meetings with the union.

The banks' insistence on action has put a pistol to their heads.

keep your head ◄◄

If you **keep** your **head**, you remain calm in a difficult situation. Compare **lose** your **head**.

Keep your head. A calm presence is an invaluable asset.

The most important thing is to keep your head and look to the future.

keep your head above water ◄◄

If you are trying to **keep** your **head above water**, you are struggling to survive, for example by keeping out of debt.

Thousands of other small businesses like mine are, at best, struggling to keep their heads above water or, at worst, have gone bust.

He wrote his first novel at fourteen, his second at sixteen and his third at nineteen. 'I felt I was sinking, and the writing was a way of keeping my head above water.'

keep your head down: 1
get your head down ◄◄

In a difficult or dangerous situation, if you **keep** your **head down**, you try to avoid trouble or involvement by behaving in a quiet way, so that people will not notice you. You can also say that you **get** your **head down**.

I just decided to keep my head down and do my job and eventually I was accepted by the male pilots and everything was going well.

After unity, he had little time for Christian Democrats who had kept their heads down under the old regime.

Many have spent the last two years with their heads down, surviving as best they could throughout the economic hardships.

If I'd got Noll back and there'd been no sign of Oliver, I'd have got my head down somewhere, changed my name, asked for police protection, done anything to keep him safe.

keep your head down: 2
get your head down ◄◄

If you **keep** your **head down**, you continue to concentrate and work hard at something. If you **get** your **head down**, you start to concentrate and work hard at something.

When he gets a chance of winning he keeps his head down and really goes for it.

It's obviously difficult to play when this sort of thing is going on around you, but they have to get their heads down and battle on.

knock something on the head: 1 ◄

If you **knock** a story or idea **on the head**, you show that it is not true or correct. This expression is used in British English.

It's time to knock on the head the idea that we are not fully human, not fully alive, unless we have that special somebody in our lives.

I think this is another fallacy that needs to be knocked on the head, the idea that women never went out to work till the First World War.

knock something on the head: 2

If you **knock** an activity **on the head**, you decide to stop it, or not to go ahead with it. This expression is used in British English.

I remember us in the early days saying: 'We'll never be like The Rolling Stones. When we stop enjoying ourselves, we'll knock it on the head.'

laugh your head off
shout your head off ◄◄

If you **are laughing** your **head off**, you are laughing a great deal. If you **are shouting** your **head off**, you are shouting a great deal. You can use other verbs with similar meanings to 'laugh' and 'shout' in this way.

They were probably laughing their heads off.

Laura was sitting inside, giggling her head off.

There was one bloke in the box shouting his head off.

They were yelling their heads off.

lose your head ◄◄◄

If you **lose** your **head**, you panic and do not remain calm in a difficult situation. Compare **keep** your **head**.

Michael Heseltine warned the party not to lose its head, saying that it was not a 'time for panic'.

He said that he had never used the green flag before for an express train, but on this occasion he lost his head.

When he was questioned by the police, he completely lost his head, told a number of lies and omitted to mention one or two things that might have helped him.

not right in the head ◄

If you say that someone is **not right in the head**, you mean that they are strange, foolish, or crazy. This expression is used mainly in spoken English.

'According to Great-aunt Luise,' I said, 'the grandmother wasn't quite right in the head. Maybe Mrs Issler was ashamed of that too.'

off the top of your head: 1 ◄

If you say that you are commenting on something **off the top of** your **head**, you mean that what you are about to say is an immediate reaction and is not a carefully considered opinion, and so it might not be correct. This expression is used mainly in spoken English.

I can't remember off the top of my head which plan they used, but it certainly wasn't the Ordnance Survey plan.

Last year the amount of money we put into curriculum initiatives development and support was, off the top of my head, I think about twenty-eight thousand pounds.

I am thinking off the top of my head here.

off the top of your head: 2 ◄

If you know something **off the top of** your **head**, you know it well and can remember it easily.

He doesn't draw a breath when he responds to those questions; he just knows the answers off the top of his head.

OK, off the top of your head, do you know the capital of South Korea?

He couldn't give a list off the top of his head of what he considers to be the most important cases decided by the Supreme Court over the past 20 years.

off your head: 1 ◄

If you say that someone is **off** their **head**, you mean that they are very strange, foolish, or dangerous. This is an informal expression, which is used mainly in British English.

It's like working in a war zone. You must be off your head to live in that area.

It's Ian Trimmer. He's gone completely off his head. He's holding my wife hostage at the Arrigo Hall. He's threatening to kill her.

off your head: 2 ◄

If someone is **off** their **head**, they have taken so many drugs or drunk so much alcohol that they do not know what they are doing. This is an informal expression, which is used in British English.

I find it really annoying the way people come up to you and say 'Hey, I just smoked a couple of joints and I'm really off my head.'

Basically, this song sounds great when you're off your head on Ecstasy.

on your head

You can use expressions such as **on** your **own head** and **on** your **head be it** to warn someone that they are responsible for something that they intend to do or something that happens as a consequence. These expressions are used more commonly in British English than American.

If you choose to ignore my generous offer, then on your own heads be it.

out of your head: 1 ◄

If you say that someone is **out of** their **head**, you mean that they are very strange, foolish, or dangerous. This is a fairly informal expression.

If he didn't kill anybody it was only by luck because he was out of his head and screaming like a maniac.

'I can't ever see us doing anything else,' states Brian pragmatically. 'We're going to be 70 years old, out of our heads and still moaning about it.'

out of your head: 2
out of your skull ◄

If you say that someone is **out of** their **head** or **out of** their **skull**, you mean that they have drunk so much alcohol or taken so many drugs that they do not know what they are doing. These are informal expressions.

Did she take a great deal of drugs herself? 'Good God, no. I get out of my head on one glass of wine,' she says.

Everybody was totally out of their skull on smack.

put your head above the parapet
keep your head below the parapet ◄

If someone **puts** their **head above the parapet**, they do or say something in public that has previously been kept private, and risk being criticized or attacked. Verbs such as 'raise', 'stick', or 'lift' can be used instead of 'put'. This expression is used in British English.

In private, however, some now acknowledge this is a policy option which cannot be ignored – although they are not prepared to put their heads above the parapet to say so.

Communicating with the public was seen by many scientists to be necessary, so that the case for using animals in medical experiments could be made: 'We've got to stick our heads above the parapets to show we are actually ordinary people trying to do a good job for humankind.'

People have become more and more reluctant to raise their head above the parapet – people are frightened to address these issues.

□ If someone **keeps** their **head below the parapet**, they do not risk saying or doing something in public that has previously been kept private, even though they may feel that they ought to.

We are not very good at publicity stunts, at drawing attention to ourselves. We like to keep our heads below the parapet.

put your head in a noose
stick your head in a noose

If you **put** your **head in a noose** or **stick** your **head in a noose**, you deliberately do something which will put you in danger or in a difficult situation.

If I have to be caught, OK, but I am damned if I will put my head in a noose and walk into that hotel!

He is saying things no one else dares to. He is sticking his head in the noose for you and he's probably gonna die for it.

rear its head
raise its head
rear its ugly head ◄◄◄

If you say that something undesirable **rears** its **head** or **raises** its **head**, you mean that it starts to appear or be active. You often use this expression when the thing you are talking about appears again after being hidden or absent for a period of time.

When a problem rears its head there is a tendency to get bound up in it and lose your confidence.

Now the same ugly forces of racial hatred are beginning to rear their heads again.

The familiar pattern of violence is raising its head once again in Punjab.

□ People often say that something undesirable **rears** or **raises** its **ugly head**.

Any club where there is a pitch invasion will find itself with questions to answer. We will not allow hooliganism to rear its ugly head again.

Igor Reichlin, who writes for 'Business Week', looks at fears that inflation may yet raise its ugly head again, affecting both Germany and its eastern neighbours.

scratch your head ◄◄◄

If you **are scratching** your **head** about a problem or question, you are puzzled and unsure about what to do or what the solution is.

Councillors in the Shetlands are still scratching their heads over how the arrival of a firm of consultants to advise on streamlining the authority resulted in 75 additional jobs and extra costs of £1.2m a year.

Even as the troops mingled with the children inside the orphanage, relief workers outside were scratching their heads about what to do next.

A lot of people are scratching their heads and saying, 'What are we doing? Are we getting our money's worth?'

□ You can also talk about **head-scratching**.

That caused a lot of head scratching and another hour and a half delay, but finally things seemed to work all right.

turn something on its head
stand something on its head ◄◄◄

If you **turn** something such as an argument or theory **on** its **head** or **stand** it **on** its **head**, you use the same facts to produce a different or opposite conclusion.

Instead of pleading for women's rights, the Equal Opportunities Commission should turn the argument on its head and point out the cost of denying women the right to earn.

Across the country the communists built up a network of party cells in every factory and farm. But the theory of workers' control was stood on its head: they obeyed the diktats of the party, and its local bosses behaved like petty tyrants.

headlights

like a rabbit caught in the headlights
like a deer caught in the headlights ◄

If you say that someone is **like a rabbit caught in the headlights** or **like a deer caught in the headlights**, you mean that they are so frightened or nervous that they do not know what to do.

He just sat there, like a rabbit caught in the headlights.

Gore claimed that President Bush and Quayle were like deer caught in the glare of headlights when the recession hit.

☐ This expression is very variable. For example, you can just say that someone is caught or frozen **in the headlights**.

That's a bad place to be. They're sort of frozen in the headlights and they don't know what to do, so they're going to stand there and do nothing.

It often seems, from the outside, that the optimum strategy for a writer caught in the headlights of unexpected celebrity is simply to keep bashing on, to keep writing and publishing.

heads

heads roll ◄◄

If **heads roll** when something goes wrong, the people responsible or in positions of power are punished, usually by losing their job or position.

This week one senior government official hinted that some undesirable heads will almost certainly roll.

The widely-held view is that heads should roll over the losses.

In the old days one might have expected a prompt resignation in the wake of so serious a fiasco. Even now, at least one senior head ought surely to roll.

knock people's heads together
bang people's heads together ◄

When people disagree and someone in authority **knocks** their **heads together** or **bangs** their **heads together**, they force them to reach an agreement. These expressions are used mainly in British English.

If he's unable to knock everybody's heads together, then questions are going to be raised about his own ability to continue in office.

'John believes that you usually get what you want by talking to people rather than banging heads together,' said an aide.

put your heads together ◄

If people **put** their **heads together** to solve a problem, they try to solve it together.

If there's a problem, there's no sense of floundering around. We all just sit down, put our heads together and figure it out.

turn heads ◄◄◄

If someone or something **turns heads**, they are so beautiful, unusual, or impressive that people are attracted to them and cannot help looking at them or paying attention to them.

At the age of 20, the dark-haired actress was already turning heads in the right places.

The Aston sits squarely and surely on the road: it's a handsome car that turns heads wherever it goes.

The Flying Elephants, who sing original material in English, are already big in their own country and are currently turning heads in America.

☐ Journalists sometimes describe someone or something as **head-turning**, or refer to them as **a head-turner**.

Gardams' designers have created a range of head-turning evening wear in their latest collection.

The car is solid, fun to drive, quick off the blocks and a real head-turner.

headway

make headway ◄◄◄

If you **make headway**, you make progress in the thing that you are trying to achieve.

A spokesman said the two sides have agreed on a timetable for the rest of the talks and have also made headway on some security issues.

This has enabled a number of developing countries to make some headway in fighting hunger and poverty.

There was concern in the city that police were making little headway in the investigation.

heap

the bottom of the heap
the top of the heap ◄

Someone who is at **the bottom of the heap** is low down in society or in an organization. Someone who is at **the top of the heap** is high up in society or in an organization. The expressions **the bottom of the pile** and **the top of the pile** mean the same.

At the bottom of the heap live at least 1 million people – the rural poor.

Why do we want to find progress in evolution? He wonders whether it is a device 'to justify our position on the top of the biological heap'.

heart

a bleeding heart ◄◄

If you refer to someone as **a bleeding heart**, you are criticizing them for being too sympathetic towards people who claim to be poor or suffering, either because you think the people do not deserve sympathy, or because you think that the person you are criticizing is not sincere. Compare **your heart bleeds for** someone.

I know how the lawmakers and the judges and the bleeding hearts screw things up for the police. Hell, I've been a cop as long as you have.

□ You can also say that someone has **a bleeding heart**.

You need neither a bleeding heart nor a blindness to horrors elsewhere to ask what more should be done to stop the war in former Yugoslavia.

□ **Bleeding heart** is often used before a noun.

This was precisely the sort of bleeding-heart sentimentality that Charles Lindbergh deplored. We must not permit our sentiment, our pity, our personal feelings of sympathy to obscure the issue.

This could have been the old bleeding heart rhetoric, but he skillfully modernized it to show how public help today can again give ambitious people a chance.

break your heart: 1
a broken heart ◄◄◄

If someone **breaks** your **heart**, they make you feel extremely upset and unhappy, because they end a love affair or close relationship with you.

When he left his wife for me I was appalled. What I'd wanted was a good time, but in the end I broke his heart.

□ You can also say that someone has **a broken heart** when they feel very sad because a love affair or close relationship has ended.

We have all read in fiction of people dying of a broken heart, but in reality this seems close to the truth, with the death rate among newly-bereaved spouses several times higher than that of non-bereaved people of a similar age.

□ You can also say that someone is **heartbroken** or is **broken-hearted**.

Mary is broken-hearted and has spent many nights crying.

break your heart: 2 ◄◄◄

You can say that something **breaks** your **heart** when the fact that it is happening makes you feel sad and depressed, because you believe that it is bad or wrong.

Walker John Rich is sad that he has been barred from paths he has used for 50 years. 'It breaks my heart to think we could lose our rights.'

It broke my heart to see this woman break down the way she did.

close to your heart
dear to your heart
near and dear to your heart ◄◄◄

If you describe a subject as **close to** your **heart** or **dear to** your **heart**, you mean that it is very important to you and that you are concerned about it or interested in it.

For presenter Manjeet K. Sandhu the position of Asian women in society is an issue very close to her heart.

The WBC treads a fine line between trying to make money and trying to support the things dear to the heart of the Left.

□ In American English, you can also say that a subject is **near and dear to** your **heart**.

She has impressed Senators with her knowledge of subjects near and dear to their hearts, and with her political acumen.

cross my heart ◄

You can say **'cross my heart'** when you want to assure someone that you are telling the truth. This expression is used in spoken English, mainly by children.

And I won't tell any of the other girls anything you tell me about it. I promise, cross my heart.

□ **Cross my heart and hope to die** means the same.

Sam grinned and held out his hand toward her. 'You don't have to worry, okay.' 'Are you sure?' Erin asked. 'Cross my heart and hope to die.'

cry your heart out
work your heart out ◄◄

If you **cry** your **heart out** or **work** your **heart out**, for example, you cry a great deal or work very hard. You can use this expression with other verbs instead of 'cry' or 'work' when you want to say that someone does something with great enthusiasm or to a great extent.

I threw myself on to the bed and cried my heart out. It took me a good while to get over the emotional damage of that encounter.

I know the woman will work her heart out to prove herself.

Everyone danced their hearts out.

eat your heart out   ◄◄

When you want to draw attention to something you have done, you can say '**eat your heart out**' and mention the name of a person who is famous for doing the same kind of thing.

My worst driving fault is speeding. Eat your heart out, Nigel Mansell!

I think I have the makings of a novel here. Marcel Proust, eat your heart out.

□ In these examples, Nigel Mansell is a British racing driver, and Marcel Proust was a French novelist.

from the bottom of your heart
at the bottom of your heart   ◄

If you say that you mean something **from the bottom of** your **heart**, you are saying that you mean it very sincerely.

I want to thank everyone from the bottom of my heart. So many people have helped me.

It was an apology from the bottom of my heart and I hope that the rest of the nation will accept it from me.

□ You can also talk about the feelings that someone has **at the bottom of** their **heart**.

At the bottom of our hearts we still believe you can have anything you want if you need it badly enough and if you are prepared to slog your way through the barriers to get it.

a heart of gold   ◄◄

If you say that someone has **a heart of gold**, you mean they are kind and generous, and enjoy helping other people.

He is a tough guy, but with a heart of gold.

He helped all the local sporting organisations – bowls, hockey, rugby and tennis. He had a heart of gold.

in your heart of hearts   ◄◄

If you say that you believe, know, or feel something **in** your **heart of hearts**, you mean that you believe, know, or feel that it is true, even though you are very reluctant to accept it.

I suppose in his heart of hearts, he doesn't believe he's doing it.

But in your heart of hearts, you must know that you're not going to save some of these children?

lose heart   ◄◄

If you **lose heart**, you start to feel discouraged or to lose interest in something, usually because things are not progressing in the way that you hoped.

I suppose I'm less optimistic than I was at first. This disease seems to recur so often you begin to lose heart.

President Aristide fled to Venezuela after the coup and from there appealed to his countrymen not to lose heart.

lose your heart   ◄

If you **lose** your **heart** to someone, you fall in love with them. This is a literary expression.

She falls in love with Raul, who in turn has lost his heart to Silvia.

Don't lose your heart to him too soon because he could just be filling in time with you.

open your heart
pour out your heart   ◄◄◄

If you **open** your **heart** or **pour out** your **heart** to someone, you tell them your most private thoughts or feelings.

A vicar has opened his heart to parishioners and admitted his marriage is on the rocks.

Chris Eubank last night opened his heart for the first time about the tragedy.

At first my boyfriend was incredibly supportive. I'd phone him up and pour out my heart in a way I couldn't to anyone else.

She poured her heart out about her separation and pending divorce.

set your heart on something   ◄◄

If you **set** your **heart on** something, you decide that you want it very much and aim to achieve or obtain it.

She decided not to try for university. Instead she set her heart on a career in catering.

She admits that when she saw the flat Jeremy had set his heart on, her first reaction was horror. 'I couldn't believe Jeremy was serious about buying this place.'

take something to heart   ◄◄◄

If you **take** someone's advice or criticism **to heart**, you pay a lot of attention to it, and are greatly influenced or upset by it.

Few people take this advice to heart, and their continuing overweight and resultant diabetes place them at significantly increased risk of heart disease.

He could have taken this criticism to heart since he built his reputation on being a good manager.

I hope her words are taken to heart.

wear your heart on your sleeve   ◄

If you **wear** your **heart on** your **sleeve**, you allow your feelings to be obvious to everyone around you.

She simply doesn't wear her heart on her sleeve so it's sometimes difficult to know what she's feeling.

□ This expression is often varied.

Everybody who knows me knows that I play with my heart on my sleeve, and I'm the same off the pitch.

You would have thought the heart-on-the-sleeve atmosphere would have suited his nature.

your heart bleeds for someone ◄

If you say that your **heart bleeds for** someone, you mean that you feel a lot of sympathy for them because they are suffering. Compare **a bleeding heart**.

You looked so sad when you walked up the aisle at the funeral. My heart bled for you when I watched it.

European peace negotiator Lord Owen also made an emotional plea for an end to the carnage. 'My heart bleeds for the people of Gorazde,' he said. 'We have to get a food convoy in there.'

□ This expression is often used ironically to show that you think someone does not deserve any sympathy, because you do not believe that they are genuinely suffering.

I must say my heart bleeds for the poor BT share issue investors who made a mere 15 per cent on their investment in one day.

My heart bleeds for those MPs who want a cut in hours because they say overwork puts their marriages at risk.

your heart hardens
harden your heart ◄

If your **heart hardens** against someone or something, you start to feel unfriendly or unsympathetic towards them. If you **harden** your **heart** against them, you force yourself to feel this way, even if you do not want to.

All of a sudden my heart hardened against my beautiful mother and her desire for fun and a rich, handsome husband. I wouldn't speak to her any more.

The most important things for Nicholas now are mobility and Braille lessons. You will have to harden your heart against doing everything for him.

your heart is in the right place ◄

If you say that someone's **heart is in the right place**, you mean that they are kind, considerate, and generous, although they may lack other qualities which you consider to be important.

Whether Johnson's professional judgement was good or not, I decided that his heart was in the right place.

They've probably got their hearts in the right place but they just haven't got any common sense.

your heart is in your mouth ◄

If you say that your **heart is in** your **mouth**, you mean that you feel extremely anxious or nervous, because you think something unpleasant or unfortunate may be about to happen.

My heart was in my mouth when I walked into her office.

'Wait!' a rough voice commanded. Nancy stopped, then turned, her heart in her mouth.

your heart isn't in something ◄

If you are doing something that you are unenthusiastic about and which you are not enjoying, you can say that your **heart isn't in** it.

Playing was no longer fun. I lost my competitiveness and my heart wasn't in it.

She had been a successful teacher, popular with her pupils and her colleagues, but her heart had never been in her work.

heartstrings
tug at the heartstrings ◄◄

If you say that someone or something **tugs at the heartstrings**, you mean that they cause you to feel a great deal of pity or sadness for them. You can use the verbs 'pull' and 'pluck' instead of 'tug'. You can also omit the word 'at'.

Miss Cookson knows exactly how to tug at readers' heartstrings.

There is a resistance in our organisation's culture to sentimentality, to betraying our cause by pulling heart strings rather than getting messages across about certain issues.

□ **Heartstrings** is used in several other structures and expressions with similar meanings.

This is not a movie that aims for the heartstrings.

heat
the heat is on ◄

If you say **the heat is on**, you mean that you are under a lot of pressure to do or achieve something.

To perform well when the heat is on, all you have to do is let it happen.

Events will show that we kept going just that little bit better than our rivals when the heat was on.

if you can't stand the heat, get out of the kitchen

If someone is involved in a difficult or unpleasant activity and they start complaining, you can say to them **'if you can't stand the heat, get out of the kitchen'**. This is a way of telling them that they should either learn to tolerate the difficulty or unpleasantness, or give up their involvement in that activity.

Submitting questions 24 hours in advance makes it a stage-managed performance by the Prime Minister. If he can't stand the heat he must get out of the kitchen.

If you are a manager of a top football club and you don't like the heat you should get out of the kitchen.

in the heat of the moment ◄◄

If you do or say something **in the heat of the moment**, you do it without stopping to think about what you are doing or saying, because you are angry or excited.

We all do things in the heat of the moment, but out on the pitch you have to show the right type of discipline.

He said that his comments were made in the heat of the moment and were not supposed to be a personal attack.

turn up the heat on someone
turn the heat on someone ◄◄

If someone **turns up the heat on** a person or situation, they put pressure on them in order to get what they want.

The firm will be turning up the heat on its rivals in a highly competitive industry now scrapping for a share of the domestic market.

Welsh rugby has been rocked by news that the Inland Revenue have turned up the heat in the illegal payments controversy.

□ You can also say that one person **turns the heat on** another.

Progress in Somalia now depends, I believe, on the UN turning the heat on the other major militia leaders and persuading them to surrender their heavy weapons.

In recent years it has come to light that, in all probability, someone had indeed neutralised J. Edgar Hoover and kept him from turning the heat on some of his friends.

heather
set the heather on fire

If you say that something **sets the heather on fire**, you mean that it is very exciting and successful. This expression is used mainly in Scottish English.

Their results have not set the heather on fire.

heaven
in seventh heaven ◄

If you say that you are **in seventh heaven**, you are emphasizing that you are extremely happy.

After I was given my first camera I was in seventh heaven.

Actor Siddig El Fadil is in seventh heaven after being picked for the new Star Trek series.

move heaven and earth ◄

If you **move heaven and earth** in order to do something, you do everything you possibly can to make sure that you do it.

When you know the pressure is getting to you, it's worth moving heaven and earth to get away for a day or two.

Look how you loved that little dog. You moved heaven and earth to see it got a good home when the landlord would not let you keep it here.

He had been moving heaven and earth for six

weeks in order to prevent the film being made; and he had failed.

heavens
the heavens open ◄

If you say that **the heavens opened**, you mean that it began to rain very heavily. This is a literary expression, which is used mainly in British English.

The sky was overcast and the mountains shrouded in mist. Then the heavens opened and it poured.

As we sat down to eat, the heavens opened for a few minutes and we all crouched under our blue awning holding our plates.

heel
bring someone to heel
call someone to heel ◄◄

If you **bring** someone **to heel** or **call** them **to heel**, you force or order them to obey you.

In practice it's still not clear how the president will use his power to bring the republics to heel.

But on this issue, the government appears to be unwilling to be brought completely to heel by international pressure.

Peter is playing the male trick – pull the purse strings and it will bring me to heel. But it won't.

They have a naive belief that he will call to heel the guerrilla gangs who are now plundering the region.

heels
at your heels: 1 ◄◄

If a person or animal is **at** your **heels**, they are following close behind you, for example because they are chasing you. This expression is used mainly in written English, especially novels.

She then strode off down the restaurant with Cavendish following close at her heels.

Children ran, calling, along the narrow path towards them, a small dog yapping at their heels.

Then, with the three boys at their heels, he and the other man hurried out of the house to a waiting jeep.

at your heels: 2 ◄◄

In a competitive situation, if you say that a person or organization is **at** your **heels**, you mean that they are threatening or challenging you in some way. This expression is used mainly in written English, especially journalism.

Intel and Motorola may dominate the market for microprocessors but scores of firms are snapping at their heels.

With the world's finest golfers at his heels, Norman produced an almost flawless 64.

Five years ago Cathy Dennis was singing The Birdy Song at holiday camps. Today she is notching up Top Ten hits and snapping at the heels of Madonna.

dig in your heels ◄◄

If you **dig in** your **heels** or **dig** your **heels in**, you refuse to do something such as change your opinions or plans, especially when someone is trying very hard to make you do so.

He could dig in his heels and fight stubbornly for what he believed to be right.

It was really the British who, by digging their heels in, prevented any last-minute deal.

I begged her to come home but she dug her heels in.

hard on the heels of something: 1
hot on the heels of something
close on the heels of something ◄◄◄

If you say that one event follows **hard on the heels of** another or **hot on the heels of** another, you are emphasizing that one happens very quickly or immediately after another. You can also say that one thing happens **close on the heels of** another.

The news comes hard on the heels of the appointment of new chief executive Cedric Scroggs.

The visit follows hot on the heels of their season at the Edinburgh International Festival.

The Prime Minister's statement comes close on the heels of the recent American moves to defuse tension in the Indian sub-continent.

hard on your heels: 2
hot on your heels
close on your heels ◄◄◄

In a competitive situation, if someone is **hard on** your **heels** or **hot on** your **heels**, they are doing nearly as well as you, and it is likely that they will soon be doing better than you. You can also say that someone is **close on** your **heels**.

The next generation of British athletes is pressing hard on the heels of today's champions.

This step began three thousand years ago and was taken first by the Polynesians, with the Europeans following hard on their heels.

hard on your heels: 3
hot on your heels
close on your heels ◄

If someone is **hard on** your **heels**, they are close behind you, for example because they are chasing you. You can also say that someone is **hot on** your **heels** or **close on** your **heels**.

But the law was hard on their heels. Within

two weeks gang leader Michael McAvoy and Brian Robinson were behind bars.

Our pilot followed close on the heels of the departing inspector.

kick up your heels

If someone **is kicking up** their **heels**, they are enjoying themselves a lot, for example at a party.

Proof that the composer was capable of kicking up his heels in the privacy of the recording studio comes from a riotous version of a Russian folksong, 'Powder and Paint'.

Combine music, culture and good food in Jersey this month. Kick up your heels at the annual Jersey Jazz Festival.

kick your heels
cool your heels ◄◄

If you **are kicking** your **heels** or **are cooling** your **heels**, you are waiting somewhere and feel bored or impatient because you have nothing to do, or because someone is deliberately keeping you waiting. The form with 'kick' is used more commonly in British English and the form with 'cool' is used more commonly in American English.

The Tunisian authorities wouldn't grant us permission to fly all the way down to Sfax, so I had to kick my heels at Tunis Airport.

A team of 60 UN weapons inspectors and aides have been cooling their heels in Bahrain for almost a week.

set you back on your heels
rock you back on your heels

If something **sets** you **back on** your **heels** or **rocks** you **back on** your **heels**, it surprises or shocks you, and often puts you at a disadvantage.

Someday I'm going to build Aunt Molly a house beside the river that is so grand it will set Turtle Ridge back on its heels.

Ireland started brightly, only to be rocked back on their heels by the first error just 10 minutes into the match.

show a clean pair of heels: 1

In a sporting contest, if one competitor **shows** the others **a clean pair of heels**, he or she wins clearly and decisively. This expression is used mainly in British English.

Another working-class hero with whom I identified was Alf Tupper, who trained on fish and chips, ran in a borrowed vest and showed the world's best runners a clean pair of heels.

show a clean pair of heels: 2

When journalists are talking about a competitive situation in which one person or organization is clearly better than the rest, they sometimes say that person or organization **shows** the others **a clean pair of heels**. This expression is used mainly in British English.

Only one point stands: Japan has shown all the other rich countries a clean pair of heels.

take to your heels

If you **take to** your **heels**, you run away. This is a literary expression.

He took to his heels and rushed out of the room.

heights

the dizzy heights
dizzying heights ◄◄

If you say that someone has reached **the dizzy heights** of something or has reached **dizzying heights**, you mean that they have reached a very high level of success in a particular field. This expression is sometimes used ironically to say that someone has not achieved very much at all. In American English, only 'dizzying heights' is used.

She had first known such dizzy heights in the 1960's when, with her husband Ike, she became one of the top exponents of black American music.

After three and a half years, I had reached the dizzy heights of assistant account handler.

Due perhaps to the influence of Haig's cautious staff, confidence did not stray to dizzying heights.

hell

all hell breaks loose
all hell breaks out ◄◄

If you say that **all hell breaks loose**, you mean that there is a lot of fuss, arguing, or fighting. You can also say that **all hell breaks out**.

In 'Jungle Fever', a happily-married black architect (Wesley Snipes) begins an affair with his Italian-American secretary, but all hell breaks loose when his wife finds out.

We were just having a good time when they broke into the square and then suddenly all hell broke loose.

come hell or high water
through hell and high water ◄

If you say that you will do something **come hell or high water**, you are emphasizing that you are determined to do it, in spite of the difficulties involved. You can also say that you will do something **through hell and high water**.

The chairman of the Senate Judiciary Committee, Senator Joseph Biden, says the all-male panel will have two female members this year, come hell or high water.

The Prime Minister has another great chum whom he is also standing by through hell and high water.

He rises at 7.15, or whenever he rises, because

the alarm clock tells him to, winter or summer, hell or high water, dark or light.

from hell ◄◄◄

You can use **from hell** after a noun to refer humorously to something or someone extremely unpleasant, or as bad as they can possibly be. For example, if you describe someone as 'the guest from hell', you mean that they behave as badly as it is possible for a guest to behave.

If you want to preserve all that's wonderful in your relationship and avoid the longed-for break turning into the holiday from hell, think ahead and follow the seven cardinal rules.

A cute family puppy turns into the pet from hell in this comedy starring Charles Grodin.

Now, Secretary of State Warren Christopher is saying it's a problem from hell, it's centuries old, there's little that can be done about it.

give someone hell: 1 ◄

If someone **gives** you **hell**, they make your life very unpleasant by behaving badly towards you.

She gets teased at school. The children give her hell, particularly the older boys.

He's spiteful, jealous, and gives her hell. Only a saint would put up with it.

give someone hell: 2 ◄

If you say that someone **gives** you **hell**, you mean that they shout at you or speak to you angrily because you have done something wrong.

When she didn't get off the train at Euston, I phoned the police in tears and they found her in a sleeping compartment. She gave me hell for embarrassing her!

give someone hell: 3

If you say that a part of your body **is giving** you **hell**, you are emphasizing that it is very painful.

My back's giving me hell, let me tell you! But I'm going to dig the garden up.

go through hell
put someone through hell ◄◄◄

If you **go through hell** or if someone **puts** you **through hell**, you have a very difficult or unpleasant time.

I have been going through hell but I hope that we can now settle this matter.

After the case he made no comment, but his solicitor said that he had been through 10 months of hell.

Her family say the girl has put them through hell since the incident.

go to hell
shot to hell
go to hell in a handbasket ◄

If you say that something **is going to hell,**

you mean that it is being destroyed. You can also say that something **is being shot to hell**.

This government has to wake up. The country is going to hell and they're just sitting on their backsides.

After seeing an average of five films a day recently, I have a strong suspicion that my judgement is shot to hell as I actually quite liked lumbering Hulk Hogan as Suburban Commando.

☐ People sometimes say that things **are going to hell in a handbasket** to emphasize that they are being destroyed very quickly. The nouns 'bucket', 'basket', and 'handcart' are sometimes used instead of 'handbasket'.

If we don't do something to de-escalate this tension, either another police officer or some black youth is going to be shot. And then this city is going to go to hell in a handbasket.

'Delicatessen' is set in some undefined future world where the human race is going to hell in a bucket, the shops are back to rationing and unemployment has reached epidemic proportions.

hell for leather ◄

If you say that someone is going **hell for leather**, you are emphasizing that they are moving or doing something very quickly, and often recklessly.

The Dutch boys are confident from all their skating and go hell for leather.

Once I decide to write a play, I have to go for it hell for leather.

☐ You can also use **hell-for-leather** before a noun.

The only way to recovery lies in a hell-for-leather drive for investment and exports.

hell freezes over

If you say that something will not happen until **hell freezes over**, you mean that you are certain that it will never happen.

We will bargain with it because the law says so. We will bargain until Hell freezes over, but they won't get anything.

'Tell them you'll get married when hell freezes over,' she says.

hell hath no fury like a woman scorned ◄

People say **'hell hath no fury like a woman scorned'** to suggest that women often react to something which hurts or upsets them by behaving very angrily and viciously. This expression is often used to refer to cases where a woman has an unfaithful partner and takes revenge.

Faithless husbands who doubt that hell hath no fury like a woman scorned should read Tolleck Winner's novel 'Love With Vengeance' and beware.

☐ This expression is often exploited, especial-

ly by journalists, to make it appropriate to the subject which they are writing about.

Hell hath no fury like a rock fan scorned. Last Saturday, Michael Jackson scorned 72,000 of them in one go and left them in Wembley Stadium feeling out of luck, out of sorts and considerably out of pocket.

Ian Woosnam, having decided to absent himself from next week's International Golf Open competition, has discovered that hell hath no fury like a sponsor spurned.

hell on earth ◄

If you say that a place or a situation is **hell on earth**, you are emphasizing that it is extremely unpleasant or that it causes great suffering. You can also say that it is **a hell on earth**.

Cannes, magnificent in good weather and hell on earth in bad, is capable of showing the best, and the worst, films in the world.

Organising it all has been hell on earth, but it's worked absolutely brilliantly.

Cholera, cerebral malaria and dysentery made building the railway a hell on earth for the labourers.

just for the hell of it ◄◄

If someone does something **just for the hell of it** or **for the hell of it**, they do it for fun or for no particular reason. You can also say that they do something **for the sheer hell of it**.

On the same street, David, aged 10, has been arrested for burglary. Another boy has been caught putting sugar in petrol tanks, just for the hell of it.

I would never read someone's diary for the hell of it, but now I can't say I would never do it again.

Many of the 2,000 athletes gathered here are running for medals. Some for money. Some for glory. Some even for the sheer hell of it.

a living hell ◄◄

If you describe a situation or a place as a **living hell**, you are emphasizing that it is extremely unpleasant or that it causes great suffering.

School is a living hell for some children.

Their marriage had become a living hell.

This pain is a living hell for me. It's like walking on hot coals all the time.

play hell
play merry hell

If you say that someone **plays hell** or **plays merry hell**, you mean that they cause trouble by behaving badly or that they protest strongly or angrily about something.

She played merry hell and stormed out in a rage.

play hell with something
play merry hell with something

If you say that one thing **plays hell with** another, you mean that the first thing has a bad effect on the second one or causes great confusion. In British English, you can also say that one thing **plays merry hell with** another.

Divorce and remarriage play hell with property and inheritance law.

Slugs play merry hell with emerging shoots; earwigs and woodlice gobble the leaves.

raise hell: 1 ◄◄

If you say that someone **raises hell**, you mean that they cause trouble by behaving badly in public, for example by getting drunk and breaking things or upsetting other people.

If it was between me and them, I'd say, 'OK, you guys destroyed things and raised hell – now you're going to fix everything.'

Are they the type that first thing they want to do is go out and raise hell, or are they here to play football?

□ A **hell-raiser** is someone who frequently causes trouble by behaving badly in public.

He has had a reputation as a hell-raiser but claims to have now settled down.

□ You can also talk about a **hell-raising** person or **hell-raising** behaviour.

Once notorious for his hell-raising and heavy drinking, Hughes has controlled the side of his character which once threatened to wreck his career.

The hell-raising actor was fined £63 with £20 costs yesterday for driving at 91mph through a police speed trap.

raise hell: 2 ◄

If someone **raises hell** about a situation, they protest strongly and angrily about it in order to persuade other people to correct it or improve it.

'There is nothing left,' said Mr Fyodorov. 'I am raising hell about that at the moment.'

She came in and raised hell. Her son's sports bag was missing. It had everything in it – trainers, track suit, hundreds of pounds' worth.

the road to hell is paved with good intentions

You say **'the road to hell is paved with good intentions'** when you are pointing out to someone that it is not enough for them to make plans or promises, but they must also carry them out. Nouns such as 'path' are sometimes used instead of 'road'.

The road to hell is paved with good intentions, or maybe the country's new constitution. Adopted in 1988, it is littered with well-meaning provisions that have been tripping up the economy ever since.

The path to hell is paved with good inten-

tions, and there are many, many pots of vitamin tablets which have been started but never finished.

there'll be hell to pay
there'll be merry hell to pay ◄

You can say that **there'll be hell to pay** to warn someone that there will be serious trouble if a particular thing happens or if it does not happen. You can also say that **there'll be merry hell to pay**.

If I try to get through the kitchen with these, there'll be hell to pay. You know what she's like.

A child doesn't decide for himself that he's stupid. He has to hear it and learn it in some way every day. And there's hell to pay when that child learns what he's taught.

'Drop that!' she snarled at Kenny. 'If the girls see it, there'll be merry hell to pay!'

to hell and back
through hell and back ◄

If you say that someone has been **to hell and back**, you mean that they have had a terrible experience, although it is now over. You can also say that someone has been **through hell and back**.

We have been to hell and back but the love of this little boy has kept us going.

But after his journey to hell and back, he's philosophical about the whole nightmare.

I've been through hell and back but this is the best day of my life. All the heartache was worth it in the end.

hen

rare as hen's teeth
scarce as hen's teeth

If you say that something is as **rare as hen's teeth** or as **scarce as hen's teeth**, you are emphasizing that it is extremely rare. These are fairly old-fashioned expressions.

Record companies are becoming as rare as hen's teeth, and by the end of the decade there probably won't be anybody left except the five international distributors.

herd

ride herd on someone ◄

If someone **rides herd on** other people or their actions, they supervise them or watch them closely. This expression is used in American English.

In his speeches recently, he's been talking more about the economy and about how he plans to ride herd on Congress in his second term.

His departure would undermine state efforts to ride herd on the oil companies.

It became apparent that I would have a choice: I could ride herd over every little detail of this movie's release or have some kind of life. I chose having a life.

here

neither here nor there ◄◄

If you say that something is **neither here nor there**, you mean that it is completely unimportant or irrelevant, and does not affect the situation in any way. This expression is used mainly in spoken English.

That the Vikings may have got to America 500 years earlier is simply neither here nor there. The critical factor in the development of the modern world was the arrival of Europeans in the Americas exactly at a time when they were best prepared to make the most of it.

You know, five hundred pounds is neither here nor there to most of them.

herring

a red herring ◄◄◄

If you describe a piece of information, a suggestion, or an action as **a red herring**, you mean that it is irrelevant and, often deliberately, is taking people's attention away from the main subject, problem, or situation that they should be considering.

This is a total political red herring and an attempt to divert from the main issues in the campaign.

All the fuss about high pay for former nationalised industry chairmen is a bit of a red herring. The really serious money is to be found in private companies, where huge salaries and dividends can be awarded without a murmur from the City and Westminster.

The plot is as complex as you'd expect from the author of The Woman in White and The Moonstone, with false names, red herrings and such memorable characters as the manic Miserrimus Dexter.

hide

haven't seen hide nor hair of someone

If you **haven't seen hide nor hair of** someone or something, you have not seen them, although you expected to.

They never found her. It was a bad business. The wrong she did, it's never left me, but I haven't seen hide nor hair of her since.

☐ You can also say that you **haven't seen hair nor hide of** someone or something.

After nearly two weeks in Australia I had seen neither hair nor hide of a kangaroo.

hiding

on a hiding to nothing ◄

If you say that someone is **on a hiding to nothing**, you mean that they have absolutely no chance of being successful at what they are trying to do. This expression is used in British English.

A car manufacturer capable of making only 50,000 cars a year is on a hiding to nothing.

The amateurs are paying entry fees to subsidise the prize list for the professionals, and they are on a hiding to nothing.

high

high as a kite ◄

If someone is as **high as a kite**, they feel very excited, or they are strongly affected by alcohol or drugs.

When I had finished the course I felt as high as a kite. But when my wife asked me what I had learnt I could not be specific.

He's going to be high as a kite because he was able to get me here when he knew I didn't want to come.

I felt so strange on the steroid injections. I was as high as a kite some of the time.

leave someone high and dry ◄◄

If someone **leaves** you **high and dry**, they leave you in a difficult situation which you are unable to do anything about.

The surrender of General Aoun a week ago left the Chamoun family high and dry, without military power and surrounded by enemies.

By introducing an element of competition, schools with better reputations will be flooded with applications while poorer schools will be left high and dry.

ride high ◄◄◄

If you say that someone or something **is riding high**, you mean that they are very popular or successful at the present time.

The elections have come at a time when Labour is riding high in the opinion polls, while support for the Conservatives and the Liberal Democrats has slumped.

Armistead Maupin read from his latest novel, 'Maybe The Moon', which is currently riding high in the booksellers' charts.

From the 1960s through to the early 1980s, the James Bond films rode high and were easily the most successful series of movies ever made.

search high and low for something
hunt high and low for something ◄

If you **search high and low for** something or **hunt high and low for** it, you search for it very carefully and thoroughly, looking in every possible place that it could be.

The babysitter searched high and low for them through the cluttered old farmhouse, but she couldn't find them.

I've hunted high and low for the photos, but I've moved since then and I can't find them.

hill

over the hill ◄◄

If you say that someone is **over the hill**, you mean that they are no longer young, and are too old to do a particular thing.

It's true some people regard you as probably over the hill at fifty.

If you're a typist or interpreter you might be over the hill at the age of 35, especially if you want to work for the EU in Brussels.

He looked like an over-the-hill heavyweight just back from a training run.

hilt

to the hilt
up to the hilt ◄◄◄

You use **to the hilt** or **up to the hilt** to emphasize that someone does something to the greatest possible extent.

He'll be a good candidate. We'll back him up to the hilt.

If Fred raises this issue when we meet tomorrow, I will defend my actions to the hilt.

She revelled in her stardom, playing her sexgoddess image to the hilt.

Many unemployed people are highly skilled, highly motivated and trained up to the hilt. They do not need non-stop training.

hip

joined at the hip

If you say that two people are **joined at the hip**, you mean that they are very close to each other emotionally and that they spend a great deal of time together. People often use this expression when they disapprove of this degree of closeness.

The couple who are almost joined at the hip in their 20s may have become quite different and distant in their 40s.

Though we often work together, we're not joined at the hip, so we see things differently.

□ If you say that two problems or factors are **joined at the hip**, you mean that they are very closely linked and cannot be considered or resolved separately.

Trends in world trade and trends in the environment are supposed to be joined together at the hip.

shoot from the hip
fire from the hip ◄

If you say that someone **shoots from the hip**, you mean that they give their opinion or react to situations very quickly, without stopping to think it through properly. You can also say that someone **fires from the hip**.

Both men shoot from the hip, talk without self-censure, and speak clearly and feelingly without jargon or cant.

She specifically declared that she did not shoot from the hip. She liked to think hard and long before taking decisions.

He certainly has a tendency to fire from the hip – to be impulsive. On the other hand, over the years he's shown considerable delicacy and tact in feeling the public mood.

history

be history ◄◄◄

If you say that an event, thing, or person is **history**, you mean that they are no longer important, relevant, or interesting. This expression is used mainly in spoken English.

He sometimes wonders if he made the right choice when he decided to give up football. 'I might have made it in football, but that's all history now.'

If you forget to do your homework, you're out – fail to pay attention, you're history.

The Charlottetown agreement is history.

the rest is history ◄◄◄

If you are telling someone about an event and you say **the rest is history**, you mean that you do not need to say any more because you are sure that everyone is familiar with what happened next.

A job with the company was advertised in The Daily Telegraph. I applied and the rest is history.

After Saint Laurent left hospital, he was persuaded to start his own fashion house, which he did in 1961. The rest is history.

After a few more secretarial jobs, she wrote to the editor of Tatler. She wrote one piece for them, was offered a staff job and the rest, as they say, is history.

hit

hit and miss
hit or miss ◄◄◄

If you describe something as **hit and miss** or **hit or miss**, you mean that it is done carelessly or without proper planning, so that it is equally likely to fail or succeed.

His studies did much to make wine making a science, not a hit and miss affair based on country and folk remedies and superstition.

The acting, however, is hit and miss: it ranges from the highly stylish to the appallingly gauche.

This new sort of newspaper publishing – rich in technology and aggressively professional – is a far cry from the hit-or-miss style that ruled in the fifties.

hit it off ◄◄◄

If two people **hit it off** when they first meet, they find that they like each other or get on well together and have many things in common.

Al met Mike three years ago, when he went to work for a new company. They hit it off straight away and often went out for drinks together.

After their extended two hour talk yesterday, the two leaders actually seem to have hit it off.

I couldn't stand the new boss, never hit it off with him, so I got out while the going was good.

a hit list: 1 ◄◄◄

If someone has **a hit list** of people or things, they are intending to take action concerning those people or things, for example by getting rid of them or refusing to deal with them.

Washington published a hit list of countries guilty of unfair trade practices, and called for bilateral negotiations with the offending countries.

The report said that none of the 31 pits on the hit-list should close until the consequences for employment had been fully assessed.

a hit list: 2 ◄◄◄

If a terrorist or criminal organization has **a hit list**, they have a list containing the names of important people who they intend to kill.

It was confirmed by the police today that he had been on an IRA hit list of a hundred prominent people discovered when police raided a house in London last year.

The name below his on the hit list is almost certainly Leoluca Orlando, the outspoken leader of La Rete, the anti-Mafia party that is the second biggest party in Sicily.

hit the sack
hit the hay

If someone **hits the sack** or **hits the hay**, they go to bed.

It was raining and we were tired, so we only half-unpacked the car and then hit the sack.

Are you tired? Do you want me to take you up to your bed? Are you ready to hit the hay?

make a hit

If you **make a hit** with someone, they like you or are impressed by you when they meet you.

Eleanor and Sara made a hit with the whole delegation.

She sends her best – you've obviously made a hit there.

Hobson

Hobson's choice

You can refer to a decision as **Hobson's choice** when it forces you to choose between two things which are both unsatisfactory, and so you cannot possibly be happy. This expression is used mainly in British English.

They want rid of him, but he won't go. And if he did go, he leaves such a gap in the house

that he is virtually irreplaceable. It really is Hobson's choice for them. Hell with him, or Hell without him.

Now employers face a Hobson's choice. If they decide not to settle the initial discrimination claim and lose, they pay; if they settle, they're still open to years of litigation brought by white employees.

hog

go hog wild

If you **go hog wild**, you behave in an uncontrolled and excited way. This expression is used in American English.

That doesn't mean you should go hog-wild and double the recipe's sugar content. Just keep the word 'moderation' in mind.

go the whole hog
go whole hog ◄◄

If someone **goes the whole hog**, they do something to the fullest extent possible. This expression is often used ironically to suggest that someone is being too extreme in their behaviour or actions.

Dixons sells a range of hi-fi speakers costing from £10.99 to £72.99. Or you can go the whole hog and buy a dedicated sound output system for £299.00.

Curious, isn't it, that when children are tiny and unable to appreciate all the glitzy bits of Christmas, we nevertheless insist on going the whole hog, but by the time they get interested in it, we rapidly begin to lose interest ourselves.

☐ In American English, you can also say that someone **goes whole hog**.

The thing to do in life is to find out what gives you pleasure and go for it whole hog.

live high on the hog

If someone **is living high on the hog**, they have a good life, with plenty of money. This expression is used mainly in American English.

He and Austen were living high on the hog in a flat with three servants.

From the looks of his home he lived alone and probably not very high on the hog.

hold

on hold ◄◄◄

If you put something **on hold**, you decide not to do it, change it, or deal with it now, but to leave it till later.

Some observers suggest that, as a result of this, he'll just put the project on hold until the political climate changes.

In August his plans were put on hold when city officials required that an environmental review be completed before he could alter the ornately detailed interior.

Everything was on hold, as if the clock stopped until the Supreme Court decided what to do.

holds

no-holds-barred ◄◄◄

You use **no-holds-barred** when describing a way of behaving when people act very forcefully or enthusiastically, without paying attention to any restraints, limits, or restrictions that may exist.

At left-back, Jones became something of a cult figure with his no-holds-barred approach to the game.

This is no surprise at all, given the no-holds-barred campaign the president has already launched for his economic plan.

We are in a state of war. It is a war with no holds barred and we must prepare to resist.

hole

blow a hole in something: 1 ◄

To **blow a hole in** something such as a plan means to spoil it or reduce its effectiveness.

If schools opted out of local authority control, would it blow a hole in the new system?

Fears are growing that the widespread Caribbean trend of deporting thousands of illegal immigrants could blow a hole in the area's plans for regional integration.

blow a hole in something: 2

To **blow a hole in** an amount of money means to reduce it considerably.

A major natural disaster such as an earthquake or hurricane could blow a hole in the fund.

The property slump and bad debts have blown a gaping hole in profits.

burn a hole in your pocket ◄

If money **is burning a hole in** your **pocket**, you are very eager to spend it as soon as possible, especially on something you do not really need but would like to have.

Money always tends to burn a hole in my pocket.

After a while Andrew's cheque book began to burn a hole in his pocket. He decided to sell his boat, and purchase a larger one for use in the Med.

a hole card

A hole card is something that you keep secret or hidden until you are ready to use it to gain an advantage over other people. This expression is used mainly in American English.

The fact that I knew where she was and had in my possession a boxful of evidence were my only two remaining hole cards.

hole-in-the-corner
hole-and-corner

If you describe something as **hole-in-the-corner** or **hole-and-corner**, you disapprove of the fact that it is secretive and possibly dishonest. These are fairly old-fashioned expressions, which are used in British English.

I won't countenance any hole-in-the-corner stuff. I won't let anyone think we don't wholly approve of this marriage.

I think we were treated in a rather hole-and-corner fashion.

in a hole
out of a hole ◄

If you are **in a hole**, you are in a difficult or embarrassing situation. This expression is used mainly in British English.

One unfortunate minister found himself in a hole and had to go.

The Tories are now in a dreadful hole after last Thursday's election results.

□ If someone or something gets you **out of a hole**, they get you out of a difficult or embarrassing situation.

The Mayor has had a lot of civil unrest on the streets, and he's taken these measures to try and dig himself out of a hole.

What finally pulled me out of the hole I was in was God.

in the hole ◄

If a person or organization is **in the hole**, they owe money to someone else. This expression is used in American English.

The Federal Housing Administration has just been discovered to be $4 billion in the hole.

By then they're so deep in the hole, it's a little late.

need something like a hole in the head ◄

If you say that you **need** something or someone **like a hole in the head**, you are emphasizing that you do not want them at all, and that they would only add to the problems that you already have.

We need an interest rate rise like we need a hole in the head.

Campaigners admitted privately yesterday that the row over Mr Flynn's remarks had damaged their candidate's chances. 'We needed this like a hole in the head,' one said.

He needs her like a hole in the head.

holes

pick holes in something ◄

If you **pick holes in** something such as an argument or theory, you find weak points in it which disprove it or show that it is wrong. Verbs such as 'poke' and 'shoot' can be used instead of 'pick'.

They say that the great science of the 21st century will be biology. Thus we do not need so many physicists as in the past. It is easy to pick holes in this argument.

For him, a winning start to the European Championship campaign was not enough and yesterday he picked holes in the team's performance against Poland.

The defense lawyers attempted to poke holes in the testimony of a prosecution witness.

hollow

beat someone hollow

If you **beat** someone **hollow**, you defeat them completely. This expression is used in British English.

Waterman was the first independent operator to take on the big boys at the pop game and beat them hollow.

ring hollow
sound hollow
have a hollow ring ◄◄◄

If a statement or promise **rings hollow** or **sounds hollow**, it seems worthless, false, or insincere. Compare **ring true**; see **true**.

Without any impartial scrutiny of polling and counting, the authorities' claim that the elections will be free and fair rings hollow.

Words of sympathy and understanding from the terrorists, no matter how sincerely offered to these families, ring hollow at this moment.

Official assertions that the two countries are close friends sound increasingly hollow.

□ You can also say that a statement or promise **has a hollow ring**.

The Government's claim to be making record investments in railways has a very hollow ring. The reality is that investment is totally inadequate.

holy

the holy of holies

If you describe something as **the holy of holies**, you mean that people think it is the most special or important thing of its kind. This expression is sometimes used ironically, to suggest that you do not agree with them.

Last year, his work was performed for the first time at the Aldeburgh Festival, the holy of holies in the contemporary British music scene.

home

at home: 1 ◄◄◄

If you feel **at home** in a particular situation, you feel relaxed, comfortable, and happy.

Suddenly Alice's doubts left her. She felt relaxed and at home. She went over to the bookcase and started looking at the titles.

Four Croatian girls began school in Berkshire yesterday after being brought to Britain from a Bosnian refugee camp. The head teacher said, 'They seem to be quite at home and I'm sure they will settle in very well after all the excitement dies down.'

Melanie is equally at home singing oratorio, spirituals, jazz or performing in musical theatre.

Whatever scenes he had to play were always shot with the minimum number of takes. From the day we arrived he was completely at home with the camera.

at home: 2 ◄◄

If someone or something looks **at home** somewhere, they look as if it is normal, natural, or appropriate for them to be there.

Bulging muscles are packed into every inch of her frame. The 16-year-old's huge shoulder and arm muscles would look more at home on a male hammer thrower.

Le Moulin's painted chairs with cane or rush seats are typically French, but would look quite at home in an English country kitchen.

bring home the bacon: 1

The person in a family who **brings home the bacon** is the person who goes out to work and earns enough money for the family to live on.

The question 'Who brings up the baby and who brings home the bacon?' will, increasingly in coming years, be the most important of all political questions.

If divorces were rare in the past, it wasn't because husbands and wives loved each other more in the old times, but because husbands needed someone to cook and keep house, wives needed someone to bring home the bacon, and children needed both parents in order to eat, sleep, and get a start in the world.

bring home the bacon: 2

In sport, if someone **brings home the bacon**, they win or do very well. This expression is used mainly in journalism.

But Reid and Duffield showed that, given the right horsepower, they and many more less fashionable jockeys like them are equally capable of bringing home the bacon in style.

The fact is, Mansell continues to bring home the bacon.

bring something home to someone ◄◄◄

If you **bring** something such as a problem, danger, or situation **home to** someone, you make them fully aware of how serious or important it is. Verbs such as 'drive', 'press', and 'hammer' are often used instead of 'bring'.

I think it is grossly irresponsible that a bar such as this should serve people with alcohol when they are clearly intoxicated. This tragic *death brings it home to people in the drinks trade just how dangerous alcohol can be.*

It was beginning to be brought home to me how very rash I had been.

He will drive home the message that heterosexuals cannot continue to dismiss AIDS as a disease of the poor, the gay and the drug-addicted.

The current drought has hammered home the point that trying to raise cattle in a fragile habitat with low rainfall is not viable.

close to home ◄

If you say that a remark is **close to home**, you mean that it makes people feel uncomfortable or upset because it is about a sensitive or very personal subject.

I just finished listening to Susan Stamberg's piece on young, fat people attending camp near New York. The message it conveyed struck so hard and so close to home that it moved me to tears.

The spectacle touched too close to home for a man whose grandparents had died in the Holocaust.

hit a home run

If someone **hits a home run**, they do something that is very successful. This expression is used in American English.

On Wall Street, Simon was considered a minor leaguer whose client list occasionally enabled him to hit a home run.

Bartlett Giamatti, Professor of English at Yale, hits a home run here with his memoir of encounters with W.H. Auden over many years.

hit home
strike home ◄◄◄

If a situation or what someone says **hits home** or **strikes home**, people realize that it is real or true, even though it may be painful for them to accept it.

In many cases the reality of war doesn't hit home with reservists until they're actually called upon to fight.

Whether we all agreed with the feminist movement or not, some of the messages it preached hit home.

The severity of the situation struck home last week when hundreds of troops mutinied because they had received no pay for nine months and no food for two.

home and dry
home and hosed ◄◄

If you say that someone is **home and dry** in a contest or other activity, you mean that they have achieved victory or success, or that you are certain that they will achieve it. This expression is used mainly in British English.

I was watching the competition with Mark and he said, 'Look at that, she's nine seconds

up on anyone else – she has to be home and dry.'

There are still three weeks to polling day and the Labour candidate is not yet home and dry.

□ You can also say that someone is **home and hosed**. This form of the expression is used mainly in Australian English.

Queensland almost snatched a draw in the final 90 seconds when Meninga made a 60m sideline run. I thought he was home and hosed.

the home stretch
the home straight ◄

If you are in **the home stretch** or **the home straight** of a long or difficult activity, you are on the last part or stage of it.

As the campaign hits the home stretch, opinion polls show that the Labor Party and a conservative alliance, called the Liberal National Coalition, are running head and head.

Club football will take second place to World Cup fever this month, when Wales take on the Czech Republic in the home straight of the qualifying competition.

make yourself at home ◄◄

If you **make** yourself **at home** somewhere, you relax and feel comfortable as if you were in your own home or in a very familiar situation.

Arnold and Gwen had found the hidden key just where it was supposed to be and made themselves at home.

Once the boat left, the passengers all made themselves at home.

□ You say **'make yourself at home'** to a guest to make them feel welcome and to invite them to behave in an informal, relaxed way.

'Sit down,' Anne said. 'Make yourself at home.'

Please make yourself at home. Maria has put a quiche and salad and fruit and cheese in the refrigerator for your tea. Help yourself to anything you want.

nothing to write home about
something to write home about ◄

If you say that something is **nothing to write home about** or **not much to write home about**, you mean that it is not very interesting, exciting, or special.

Yes, there is cheese, bread and meat in Brighton market and the surrounding shops, but it's nothing to write home about, whereas in Dieppe the quality is quite simply dazzling.

The nightlife is not much to write home about but untracked snow lasts longer than at fashionable resorts like Val d'Isère and Chamonix.

□ If you say that a thing is **something to write home about**, you mean that it is interesting, exciting, or special.

And you're giving that poor man a new start in life. That's something to be proud of and, incidentally, something to write home about.

on home ground ◄◄◄

If someone is **on home ground**, they feel confident and secure because they are in the area where they work or live, or are doing something that is very familiar to them. The nouns 'turf' and 'patch' are sometimes used instead of 'ground'.

Students benefit by experiencing interviews with prospective employers on their own home ground, without too much of a disruption to their studies.

Compared with the flashy triviality of 'The Office Party' and 'On The Piste', this is a play where Godber is on home ground, writing with cold-eyed affection about the Yorkshire mining communities of his formative years.

Communications Minister David Beddall was back on home turf in Brisbane yesterday vigorously defending his performance in the pay TV fiasco.

honest

honest as the day is long

If you say that someone is as **honest as the day is long**, you are emphasizing that they are very honest. This is a fairly old-fashioned expression.

This boy's hard-working, ambitious, smart, and honest as the day is long. They don't come any better than Russell here.

hoof

on the hoof: 1 ◄◄

If you say that someone does something **on the hoof**, you mean that they do it in response to things that happen, rather than as part of a carefully considered plan. This expression is used in British English.

They expressed their disquiet at the disarray over the government's handling of its economic policy and their fears that policy was being made on the hoof.

There is nothing more dangerous than policy-making on the hoof. All ministers are prone to it, particularly during a parliamentary recess.

on the hoof: 2

If someone does something **on the hoof**, they do it while they are doing something else, or without stopping to sit down.

We know the character: his shirt is always undone, he is rude, consumes junk food on the hoof and is always complaining.

Presumably, like everybody else, you learnt the job on the hoof.

hook

by hook or by crook ◄

If someone says they will do something **by hook or by crook**, they mean that they are determined to do it even if it is very difficult for them, or they have to use dishonest means.

These are the 'strike force', the men whose job it is to make sure records get into shops and ultimately into the charts by hook or by crook.

If a man took Antonia's fancy, she would go out of her way to get him by hook or by crook.

hook, line, and sinker: 1 ◄

If you say that someone has swallowed something **hook, line, and sinker**, you are criticizing them for being fooled into believing something completely and being deceived by it.

The Major had swallowed hook, line and sinker the notions of manhood that had been drummed into him at Eton, Sandhurst and during his 20 years in the Household Cavalry.

Our president is one heck of a salesman, and people are just swallowing this thing hook, line, and sinker, without knowing what it's all about.

hook, line, and sinker: 2

You use **hook, line, and sinker** to emphasize that someone does something very intensely, deeply, or fully.

I fell for her hook, line and sinker.

I was all against nationalization. I resisted it hook, line and sinker and became quite unpopular in the process.

off the hook ◄◄◄

If someone who has done something wrong gets **off the hook**, they manage to get out of the awkward situation they are in without being punished or blamed.

We cannot let the government get off the hook for what it has done.

He suggested I tricked Jack into believing that I'd got him off the hook where the girl's murder was concerned.

The American people are going to resent any hint that he will be let off the hook because of his privileged position.

on your own hook

If you do something **on your own hook**, you do it alone, without any help. This expression is used in American English.

St. Mary's Hospital does not meet incoming flights with its own vehicle. Patients come on their own hook.

ring off the hook ◄

If your telephone **is ringing off the hook**, so many people are trying to call you that it is ringing all the time. This expression is used in American English.

His phone was ringing off the hook, and he was getting phone calls from Hollywood studios and executives and very major documentary filmmakers.

Since war broke out in the Middle East, the phones at donation centers have been ringing off the hook.

□ If you take a telephone **off the hook**, you take the receiver off the part that it normally rests on, so that the telephone will not ring.

sling your hook

If someone tells you to **sling** your **hook**, they are telling you to go away. This expression is used in British English.

I've always said that there's no point in keeping unsettled players at a football club. Spurs are entering a new era and if Ruddock doesn't want to be part of it then he should sling his hook.

hooks

get your hooks into someone

If you say that someone or something **has got** their **hooks into** you, you mean that they are controlling or influencing you very strongly, often in a way that is not good for you.

Spielberg has gotten his hooks into 'Peter Pan' and the result is an unseemly desecration of a classic the world loves.

But 8mm video faces problems and tough competition. For instance, the rival VHS format has really got its hooks into the American consumer.

hoops

jump through hoops
go through the hoops ◄

If someone makes you **jump through hoops** or **jump through the hoops** to obtain something that you want, they make you prove your ability and willingness by forcing you to do a lot of difficult things first. You can also say that they make you **go through the hoops**.

Eventually, if they jump through enough hoops, illegal workers can get work visas.

The academic staff still wanted the rigour so they basically put a four-year course into three years and made us jump through hoops.

When vacancies occur, the office puts out feelers to the universities but likely candidates must still go through the hoops.

hoot

not give a hoot
not give two hoots ◄

If you say that you **don't give a hoot** or **don't give two hoots** about something, you mean that you do not care about it at all.

Too many tabloid hacks have pursued this case and many other lurid murder stories motivated solely by profit for their papers and themselves, whilst not giving a hoot about the feelings of victims.

I'm really disgusted with our politicians in Washington. All they're doing is looking out for their own little selves. They don't give two hoots about their constituents.

hop

catch someone on the hop
keep someone on the hop
have someone on the hop ◄◄

If someone **is caught on the hop**, they are unprepared for something that happens and so are unable to respond quickly or appropriately. You can also **keep** someone **on the hop** or **have** someone **on the hop**. These expressions are used in British English.

In both cases the West was caught on the hop when a brutal dictator decided that it was safe to use force to resolve a long-standing territorial dispute.

Adam took the fourth qualifying place in his semi-final in 20.63 seconds and admitted his success had caught him on the hop.

Better policing by American-trained enforcers is keeping the drug traffickers on the hop and driving down prices paid to growers.

a hop, skip, and a jump
a hop and a skip

If one thing is only **a hop, skip, and a jump** away from another, they are very close together or very closely linked. You can also say that one thing is only **a hop and a skip** away from another.

Wells, Maine, is just a hop and skip from George Bush's place in Kennebunkport.

Of course, the Romanian language is just a hop, skip and a jump from Italian.

horizon

on the horizon ◄◄◄

If something is **on the horizon**, it is almost certainly going to happen or be done quite soon.

With no solution to the problem in sight, the threat of even more violent confrontation looms on the horizon.

But there is hope on the horizon. New enterprise zones in the industrial areas have created thousands of new jobs.

With breast cancer, as with many common diseases, there is no obvious breakthrough on the horizon.

horn

blow your own horn

If you accuse someone of **blowing** their

own **horn**, you are criticizing them for boasting about themselves. This expression is used in American English; the British expression is **blow** your **own trumpet**.

Maybe I am a superstar right now, but I don't go around blowing my own horn; this is a game which kicks you right back in the face.

hornet

stir up a hornet's nest ◄

If you say that someone **has stirred up a hornet's nest**, you mean that they have done something which has caused a lot of controversy or has produced a situation which is extremely difficult to deal with.

According to my brother Paul, this Lonnie Norton was asking a lot of questions and stirring up a hornet's nest around town.

I seem to have stirred up a hornet's nest. Three weeks ago I wrote a column about the teaching of Shakespeare in schools. Letters, from Beijing to Borehamwood, have poured in ever since.

□ Sometimes people just talk about **a hornet's nest**.

From that time on a hornet's nest was let loose, though it had little impact on the general public.

Wasserman had no idea what a hornet's nest he was stepping into.

horns

the horns of a dilemma ◄

If you are on **the horns of a dilemma**, you have to choose between two or more alternatives, which seem to be equally good or equally bad.

I was often caught on the horns of a dilemma. Do I work late in the air-conditioned cool darkness of the office, or retreat to the bar for cold beer?

'We're caught on the horns of a dilemma,' says Nicholas Hinton of the Save the Children Fund. Fund raising and grants brought in £52m this year. But the problem facing him is how best to spend the money.

lock horns ◄

If you **lock horns** with someone, you argue or fight with them.

During his six years in office, Seidman has often locked horns with lawmakers as well as the administration.

In midtown Manhattan's densely built real estate market, developers and preservationists often lock horns.

I remember a harrowing few days in the October of 1962 when Mr Khrushchev and President Kennedy locked horns over Russian missiles based in Cuba.

□ You can also talk about a **locked-horns** situation.

In personal relationships, differences could be building up slowly towards a locked-horns situation.

pull in your horns
draw in your horns ◄

If you **pull in** your **horns** or **draw in** your **horns**, you start behaving more cautiously than you did before, especially by spending less money.

The world's big spenders have pulled in their horns during the recession and the top designers – such as Yves Saint Laurent – have felt the pinch.

Customers are drawing in their horns at a time of high interest rates, and delaying payment to suppliers. Among small businesses the knock-on effect can produce an avalanche of failures.

horse

back the wrong horse ◄

If someone **backs the wrong horse**, they support the wrong person, for example the loser in a contest or election. Verbs such as 'bet' or 'pick' can be used instead of 'back'.

We think they're backing the wrong horse if they support the Mengistu government.

Mr Yanagitani had a wide following among ambitious younger employees, who now fear they have ruined their prospects by backing the wrong horse.

Many companies have lost millions of dollars placing bets on the wrong horses.

a dark horse ◄◄◄

If you describe someone as **a dark horse**, you mean that very little is known about them, although they may have recently had success or may be about to have success.

To many people, Robert Ayling is an unknown quantity, a dark horse who worked away behind the scenes at BA, only to be thrust into the limelight last February.

A television debate between Poland's two presidential candidates Lech Walesa and the dark horse of the campaign, the expatriate businessman Mr. Stanislaw Tyminski, was called off today when Mr. Tyminski failed to appear in the studio.

□ You can also use **dark horse** before a noun.

William Randolph Hearst had briefly been a dark horse candidate for President in 1908.

eat like a horse

If you say that someone **eats like a horse**, you mean that they eat a lot because they have a large appetite.

When Kelly is on medication, he eats like a

horse and when he is off, he has almost no appetite at all.

flog a dead horse
beat a dead horse

If you say that someone **is flogging a dead horse**, you mean that they are wasting their time trying to achieve something that cannot be done. This form of the expression is used in British English; in American English the form is **beat a dead horse**.

You can see it in the players' eyes and faces. They've had enough. They're shattered, exhausted, they're totally fed up with playing. You're flogging a dead horse. You have some talented boys but they're playing like run-down machines.

If bad grades have any coercive value at all, it disappears when the high and low groups divide. For students who get them after elementary school, they are like beating a dead horse.

from the horse's mouth ◄

If you get a piece of information **from the horse's mouth**, you get it directly from the person who knows best or knows most about it, and so you are sure it is true.

He wanted the guidelines crystal clear, and from the horse's mouth.

Most of the book is completely true; it comes from the horse's mouth.

get on your high horse
come down off your high horse ◄

If you say that someone **is getting on** their **high horse**, you are showing disapproval of them for behaving as if they are superior to other people, and for refusing to accept any criticism of themselves. Other verbs can be used instead of 'get'.

When Kuwait was occupied, President Bush and Prime Minister John Major lost no time in getting on their high horses.

Understandably, they have climbed a high horse because they have been called cheats.

The time has come for the police to join forces with residents to prevent crime. As long as the police stay on a high horse, communications between citizens and police will continue to remain weak.

☐ If someone **comes down off** their **high horse** or **gets down off** their **high horse**, they stop acting in a superior way.

Prudence, the older girl, starting law school with an eventual judgeship in mind, often came down off her high horse and was even heard occasionally to tell a risqué joke.

It is time for the intellectuals to get off their high horses and to really take the struggle into the ghettoes.

a one-horse race ◄

If you say that a contest is **a one-horse race**, you mean that it is obvious even before it starts that one person or team is much better than the others and will win. This expression is used mainly in British English.

Marseilles are threatening to turn the French championship into a one-horse race.

He describes it as a one-horse race. He expects that the president will win a landslide vote of approval.

a one-horse town ◄

If you describe a town as **a one-horse town**, you mean that it is very small, dull, and uninteresting.

Lumut is something of a one-horse town, but you can always take a boat across to Pangkor island and look at Dutch ruins.

I mean, would you want to live in a small one horse town for your whole life?

a stalking horse: 1 ◄

If you describe something as **a stalking horse**, you mean that it is being used to obtain a temporary advantage so that someone can get what they really want at a later date. This expression is usually used to show disapproval.

The development will act as a stalking horse for further exploitation of the surrounding countryside.

These are big players with deep pockets. And although the struggle is centred on London, it has a wider significance for commercial radio. The successful applicants will almost certainly use victory as a stalking horse for an altogether more lucrative prize: the third national commercial licence.

a stalking horse: 2 ◄

In politics, **a stalking horse** is someone who stands against the leader of a party to test the strength of any opposition to the leader. They then withdraw in favour of a stronger challenger, if it looks likely that the leader can be defeated.

These days, she is often touted as a stalking horse in a leadership contest if John Major is forced to quit.

The newspaper is taking Mr Heseltine's challenge very seriously. He is no stalking horse for a possible later challenger.

☐ You can also use **stalking horse** before a noun.

The notion of a stalking horse challenge at the autumn party conference seemed highly unlikely.

a Trojan horse ◄◄

If you describe a policy or activity as **a Trojan horse**, you mean that it seems harmless, but is likely to damage or destroy something important.

Socialist politicians have used the Trojan horse of 'urgent need' to conceal their hidden ambitions for general income redistribution.

Nor is the landscape safe from further tourist and leisure intrusions. Speculative golf course proposals are now seen as a Trojan Horse for hotel and conference centres.

☐ In Greek mythology, the **Trojan horse** was a hollow wooden horse which the Greeks used to get soldiers into the city of Troy and destroy it.

you can lead a horse to water but you can't make him drink

If someone says '**you can lead a horse to water, but you can't make him drink**', they mean that you can give someone the opportunity to do something, but you cannot force them to do it if they do not want to. This expression is often varied.

Father Whittaker exploded. 'You are the limit. Obviously you have not listened to a word of what has been said. You were brought to Pontywen for training. However, as the old proverb says, you can bring a horse to the water but you can't make him drink.'

You can lead a boy to books, but can you make him read?

That is the trouble with llamas. You can take them up a mountain, but you can never make them enjoy the view.

horses

hold your horses

If you say to someone '**hold your horses**', you are telling them to wait, slow down, or stop for a moment, often when you think that they are going to do something hasty. This expression is used in spoken English.

Hold your horses a minute, will you, and just take another look at this badge.

horses for courses ◄

If you say that something is a matter of **horses for courses**, you mean that different people are suitable for different things or kinds of situation, and this ought to be taken into account when making choices in particular cases. This expression is used in British English.

We know the selection for the matches will be a case of horses for courses, and so, like anyone else, I'll just be happy to be playing, whatever position.

Companies started practising horses for courses, hiring law firms for their specialities rather than sticking with long-term relationships.

☐ A **horses for courses** policy or method takes account of the differences between people or things.

Leeds usually required a horses for courses policy, and early evidence suggested that they did not choose a side that would give them the long periods of control they needed in the field.

ride two horses at the same time
ride two horses at once

If you say that someone **is riding two horses at the same time** or **is riding two horses at once**, you are criticizing them for trying to follow two conflicting sets of ideas at the same time. These expressions are used in British English, mainly in journalism.

He is not doing his popular appeal much good by continuing to ride two horses at the same time.

I have to tell you that you're riding two horses at once and no man can do that successfully. You are trying to have a free economy, but you still want to plan and have rigidities within your economic system.

wild horses

You can use **wild horses** in expressions such as 'wild horses would not drag me to something' or 'wild horses would not make me do something' to emphasize that you will not do something even if other people try to force you to.

I would not confess. Wild horses wouldn't drag this secret out of me.

Wild horses wouldn't make Nicola sell the yard if she found out it would make me rich.

hostage

a hostage to fortune ◄

If you are **a hostage to fortune**, you cannot control how a situation develops, and so you have to accept any bad things that happen. This expression is used mainly in British English.

Charles, then nearly 33, had already made himself a hostage to fortune by declaring that 30 was a suitable age to settle down.

He was a bachelor and housekeepers were not in plentiful supply. As a hostage to fortune he had no alternative but to ignore her laziness.

☐ If you say that you do not want to give any **hostages to fortune**, you mean that you do not want to say or do something which could cause problems for you in the future, because you will have no control over how the situation develops.

Despite persistent questioning, he gave no hostages to fortune in the form of a timetable.

By opting for the best rather than the mediocre, the council recognises that it may have handed a hostage to fortune. Many departments may be hard pressed to achieve the new standards that have been set for them.

hot

blow hot and cold: 1 ◄

If you say that someone **blows hot and cold** on something, you mean that their attitude to it keeps changing, so that sometimes they

seem enthusiastic or interested, and sometimes they do not. This expression is often
used to show disapproval.

*The media, meanwhile, has blown hot and
cold on the affair.*

*For years Prince Sihanouk has blown hot
and cold with those trying to bring peace to
Cambodia.*

□ In British English, you can also say that
someone **is blowing hot** to mean that they
are enthusiastic about something or interested in it at the moment, but that you are sure
their attitude will soon change.

*He was capricious, indeed some would say
treacherous, on the issue of mine closures,
blowing hot one day in defence of the miners,
and backing down a few days later.*

blow hot and cold: 2

If you say that someone **blows hot and
cold**, you mean that sometimes their work or
performance is good, and sometimes it is not.

*They seem to have blown hot and cold in
their early matches.*

hot and bothered ◄

If you say that someone gets **hot and bothered** about something, you mean that they become very upset or worried about it. You
usually use this expression when you want to
suggest that they are getting upset about
something unimportant.

*Sir Terence was astonished that everybody
had got so hot and bothered about the affair.*

*The boss was asking for you earlier. He
sounded hot and bothered.*

hot and cold

If you say that someone or something makes
you feel **hot and cold**, you mean that they
make you feel extremely worried or nervous,
and this causes you to feel as if your body is
both hot and cold at the same time. This expression is used in British English.

*Neither of them had ever made her feel hot
and cold at the same time, as Gordon Hardie
was doing.*

*When she realized what she was reading she
grew hot and cold all over.*

hot as hell
hot as Hades

If you say that it is as **hot as hell**, you are
emphasizing that it is extremely hot.

*In the summer it is hot as hell. The heat
lands like a blanket thrown over you as soon
as you step off the plane.*

□ You can also say that it is as **hot as Hades**. This is a fairly literary expression.

*The shafts were dug straight down, hundreds
of feet into rock and blackness. It was always
bone-cold at the top, and hot as Hades as you
descended.*

too hot to handle ◄

If you say that someone or something is **too
hot to handle**, you mean that they are so
dangerous, difficult, or extreme that people do
not want to be involved with them.

*Even for someone of Mr Hurd's skill and ex-
perience, the situation proved too hot to handle.*

*Wherever he has been based, his host country
has eventually found him too hot to handle.*

*To do so would require changing the constitu-
tion, and that is too hot for any politician to
handle.*

hot cakes

sell like hot cakes
go like hot cakes
sell like hotcakes ◄

If you say that things **sell like hot cakes** or
go like hot cakes, you mean that they are
very popular and people buy large quantities
of them in a short time.

Their whisky was selling like hot cakes.

Her products sold like hotcakes.

*The salesman says they've been going like
hotcakes.*

□ 'Hotcakes' is the usual form in American
English, and it is also occasionally used in
British English. In American English,
'hotcakes' are pancakes, while in British English 'hot cakes' are cakes which have just
been baked.

hots

have the hots for someone
get the hots for someone ◄

If someone **has the hots for** you or **gets the
hots for** you, they are very strongly attracted
to you sexually. These are informal expressions.

*But it's obvious Catherine has the hots for
Curran too and soon the two are locked in
each other's arms.*

*Just as I suspected, Angie. You're starting to
get the hots for James. Poor guy, he doesn't
stand a chance now.*

hour

the eleventh hour ◄◄◄

If something happens at **the eleventh hour**,
it happens very late or at the last possible
moment.

*The cause seemed lost until, at the eleventh
hour, a telegram arrived at the Fund from an
unknown English lady living abroad, offering
to make up the balance.*

*The concert, scheduled for last Saturday, was
cancelled at the eleventh hour, after the star
Peter Gabriel pulled out on Thursday.*

*Labour clung on to fading hopes of victory
until the eleventh hour.*

□ An **eleventh hour** decision or action is one that occurs at the last possible moment.

The eleventh hour decision came as the President made it clear he was prepared to gamble his political career if it came to conflict.

The company has sold off 31 social clubs to Mansfield Brewery in an eleventh hour deal.

house

bring the house down ◄

If a person or their performance **brings the house down**, the audience claps and cheers loudly for a long time because they liked the performance so much.

Juliet Stevenson, used to bringing the house down when she appears on stage, was particularly pleased at the enthusiastic reception for her latest performance.

We had just one rehearsal and I was petrified but, as Lenny predicted, the sketch brought the house down.

eat someone out of house and home

If you say that someone **is eating** you **out of house and home**, you are complaining that they eat so much food that it costs you a lot of money to feed them.

Now all her remaining savings were under threat, because Cissie had let her down. Not to mention Dot and Meg, who were eating her out of house and home.

They eat everybody out of house and home but nobody minds because they provide such first-rate entertainment.

get on like a house on fire ◄

If two people **get on like a house on fire**, they quickly become close friends, for example because they have similar interests.

I went over and struck up a conversation, and we got on like a house on fire.

When I introduced Nicky to my old school friend Alex, the pair of them got on like a house on fire.

a halfway house ◄

A **halfway house** is a compromise between two things, or a combination of two things. This expression is used in British English.

A halfway house between the theatre and cinema is possible.

In any case, the closer some countries have come to Brussels, the less attractive has appeared the halfway-house option and the more appealing full membership of the Community.

a house of cards ◄◄

If you say that a system, organization, or plan is like **a house of cards**, you mean that it is likely to fail or collapse.

This government could fall apart like a house of cards during the first policy discussion.

The banking and monetary system, which

was at best a fragile house of cards under the Communists, is already in collapse.

not give someone house room ◄

You can say that you would **not give** someone or something **house room** when you strongly dislike or disapprove of them and you want to have nothing to do with them. This expression is used in British English.

Conservatives should not give house room to those arguing we can trade a little more inflation for a little more growth.

Personally, I feel that some of the paintings that people pay thousands and thousands of pounds for are absolute rubbish. You know, I wouldn't give them house-room.

I've talked to no-one who gives this malicious slur an inch of house-room.

put your house in order
get your house in order ◄◄◄

If you **put** your **house in order** or **get** your **house in order**, you make sure that all your affairs are arranged properly and there is nothing wrong with them. Verbs such as 'keep' or 'set' can be used instead of 'put' or 'get'.

The government gives the newspaper industry a twelve-month deadline to put its house in order or face tough statutory controls.

The government is also trying to put its own house in order and trim its deficit by cracking down on tax evasion.

The President said the United States remains the world's 'engine of prosperity', but must get its economic house in order by adopting his plan for deficit reduction and investment.

She claimed the high street banks were incapable of keeping their house in order and called for the Government to introduce regulation through the Bank of England.

houses

round the houses

If you say that someone is going **round the houses**, you mean that they keep talking about unimportant things, rather than concentrating on what they are supposed to be discussing. This expression is used in British English.

What certainly came into my notes at the last meeting is that although in many cases we talk round the houses, we get to the important issues as well.

hue

a hue and cry ◄

If there is **a hue and cry** about something, there is a loud protest about it or opposition to it.

There probably will be a hue and cry about my suggestion of more power to the police, but until the criminals realise someone will take them in hand, they will do exactly what they want.

Your officers know what's expected of them. They prepare, take a test, and accept the results without any hue and cry.

huff

in a huff ◄◄

If you say that someone is **in a huff**, you mean that they are behaving in an irritable, bad-tempered, and childish way, because they could not get something they wanted.

He stormed off in a huff because he didn't win.

He was an officer in the Guards, from which he had resigned in a huff when he was passed over for promotion.

hump

get the hump

If you **get the hump**, you get annoyed or irritated by something. This expression is used in British English.

Dad used to coach me in the back garden when I was about 10 or 11 – but he tried to drum too much into me and I used to get the hump with him.

over the hump

If you are **over the hump** in an unpleasant or difficult situation, you are past the worst part of it.

I think we're basically over the hump in this instance. We've got an economy now that's likely to grow.

I

i

dot the i's and cross the t's

If someone **dots the i's and crosses the t's**, they add the final minor details to a piece of work, plan, or arrangement.

The two sides went into these talks with positions that were not very far apart in terms of their political demands. Dotting all the i's and crossing all the t's may take some time, however.

Unless all the i's are dotted and the t's are crossed, a contract is not likely to be enforced.

ice

break the ice ◄◄◄

If you **break the ice** at a party or meeting, or in a new situation, you say or do something to make people feel relaxed and comfortable.

Break the ice with tea or coffee and get to know your client a little better.

I started off by grinning at the audience and remarking that it seemed natural to be back in Madison Square Garden again. That broke the ice and from then on all was smooth sailing.

The first half hour or so passed with many suffering from extreme self-consciousness, until the ice was broken by excellent beer from the local brewery.

☐ An **ice-breaker** is something that you say or do to break the ice.

This presentation was a good ice-breaker. A few laughs go a long way toward making a potential client comfortable.

☐ An **ice-breaking** comment or action is one that breaks the ice.

Graham's breakfast-time phone call to David was an ice-breaking exercise.

cut no ice ◄◄◄

If you say that something **cuts no ice** with you, you mean that you are not impressed or influenced by it. Words such as 'little', 'much', or 'any' can be used instead of 'no'.

Flying is dreadful. Statistics cut no ice with anyone scared of going up in the air in a plane.

Mikhail Gorbachev won the Nobel Peace Prize, but this cut little ice at home.

In the centre stands Alberto Michelini, an outgoing member of parliament, and once a popular television journalist with strong church backing. Such credentials may no longer cut much ice in Italian politics.

put something on ice
on ice ◄◄◄

If something such as a plan or project **is put on ice**, it is postponed. If a plan or project stays **on ice** or is **on ice**, no action is taken to put it into operation.

The exchange of prisoners, the top priority on the list of issues to be resolved, has been halted, and further high-level meetings have been put on ice.

Plans have been put on ice for a meeting in London of the five permanent members of the United Nations Security Council to discuss the issue.

A further cut in base rates to 6% is now likely to stay on ice till next year.

skate on thin ice ◄◄

If you say that someone **is skating on thin ice,** you mean that they have got themselves into a difficult situation which may have serious or unpleasant consequences for them. Other verbs such as 'tread', 'walk', 'stand', or 'be' can be used instead of 'skate'.

All through my career I had skated on thin ice on many assignments and somehow had, so far, got away with it.

Watch it Max, Christopher thought gleefully, you're treading on very thin ice.

I could see I was on thin ice. His professional pride was injured.

icing

the icing on the cake
the frosting on the cake ◄◄◄

If you describe something as **the icing on the cake,** you mean that it is an extra good thing that happens and makes a situation or activity even better. In American English, you can also talk about **the frosting on the cake.**

I was proud to be a member of the Mercedes-Benz Grand Prix team, but to drive their fantastic sports cars as well really was the icing on the cake.

To ride for one's country is the ultimate accolade. To be in a winning team is the icing on the cake.

If it works out that he or she becomes a friend after you have enjoyed a good professional relationship, that is frosting on the cake.

□ You can also use these expressions to refer to something which is only a minor part of the main thing you are talking about.

Consumer electronics in Japan is now a 35 billion dollars a year business. This is just the icing on the cake. Counting all the industrial equipment that Japanese electronics companies make as well, they are now generating between them an annual 200 billion dollars of sales.

Finance Minister Vaclav Klaus has dismissed environmental issues as the frosting on the cake.

inch

come within an inch of doing something ◄

If you **come within an inch of** doing something, you very nearly do it. You can also say that you **are within an inch of** doing something.

A driver who nearly sideswipes a truck and comes within an inch of smashing into a tree will nonetheless grandly proclaim that there is nothing wrong with his eyesight.

It was against everything she had always believed in. She had been within an inch of discarding the idea altogether. Now she looked

into his soft brown eyes and wondered, why not?

give someone an inch and they'll take a mile

If you say **'give** someone **an inch and they'll take a mile'**, you mean that if you do a small favour for someone, they will become greedy and ask you to do bigger and bigger favours for them and make you regret doing the first favour.

Gorbachev hoped to promote reform, not so as to lead on to revolution, but precisely to prevent it. He meant to give the GDR socialism with a human face, not to get rid of the GDR altogether. But when the leaders gave an inch the people took a mile.

□ Sometimes people just say **'give them an inch'**, or use another word instead of 'mile'.

You need to keep the leading rein taut if you want to be seen as a macho manager. Besides, everyone knows what happens when you give them an inch.

The problem with him was that if you gave him an inch he'd take six.

to within an inch of your life

If someone beats another person **to within an inch of** their **life,** they beat them very severely.

His fists were clenched as if he were going to beat Smythe to within an inch of his life.

□ You can use **to within an inch of** their **life** or **within an inch of** their **life** after other verbs to say that someone does something to an extreme degree.

Number 20 was seen not as decorated, but decorated to within an inch of its life. To the buyer's eye, it was horribly overdone.

Poor old PK is bullied within an inch of his life.

ink

bleed red ink

If a company **is bleeding red ink,** it has severe financial problems. This expression is used mainly in journalism.

Even large companies are bleeding red ink. But they are quickly closing plants and axing thousands of jobs to boost performance.

In 1991, although growth was at a solid 4.4%, annual inflation was 50% and government-owned businesses continued to bleed red ink.

innings

have a good innings: 1

You can say that someone **has had a good innings** or **has had a long innings** when they have just stopped doing something, for example a job, that they have been doing successfully for a long time. This is an old-fashioned expression, which is used mainly in British English.

His career ended when his horse fell and hoof kicks in the face left him with injuries to his cheekbone and the permanent loss of 90 per cent vision in his left eye. 'I had a good innings,' he says in that incredibly modest way of jump jockeys.

have a good innings: 2

When someone has just died or is about to die, if you say that they **have had a good innings**, you mean that they have lived for a long time and have had a fulfilling and rewarding life. This is an old-fashioned expression, which is used in British English.

His mental attitude towards his Aids was stoical: he himself had had a good innings, he said, but he was smitten with pity for younger victims in desolate circumstances.

ins

the ins and outs ◄◄

If you refer to **the ins and outs** of a situation or system, you mean all the complicated details or facts about it.

Without medical qualifications it is impossible to understand the ins and outs of heart remedies.

There are many helpful books now available written by cookery and dietary experts who can advise on the ins and outs of dieting in great detail.

insult

add insult to injury ◄◄◄

If you **add insult to injury**, you make a bad situation worse by doing something that upsets or harms someone, after you have already done something bad to them.

The Council of State opposed the president's unconstitutional referenda and added insult to injury by leaking its hostile and secret comments to the press.

The absence of District Council representatives at the meeting, who could have answered the criticism, added insult to the injury and led the critics to believe that the Council attached no importance to the race relations of the community.

☐ You can use **to add insult to injury** or **adding insult to injury** to introduce a further unpleasant thing that has happened and that you are reporting.

The driver of the car that killed Simon Collins got a £250 fine and five penalty points on his licence. To add insult to injury, he drove away from court in his own car.

iron

cast iron ◄

A **cast iron** guarantee or alibi is one that is absolutely certain and can definitely be believed.

They are demanding cast iron guarantees of a fair hearing and a promise they will not be handed over to Western intelligence services.

Even if one could visualize her as a murderer, she has a cast-iron alibi.

They come down hard on unpunctuality, unless you've a cast-iron excuse.

☐ 'Cast iron' is often written as 'cast-iron' in British English.

strike while the iron is hot

If you say that someone should **strike while the iron is hot**, you mean that they should act immediately, while they have the best chance of succeeding at something.

This is the week to get plans off the ground. It's time to strike while the iron is hot.

After the ordeals of the past few months, governments will be looking over their shoulders at unpredictable markets and volatile voters. They may decide to strike while the iron is hot.

irons

have a lot of irons in the fire ◄

If someone **has a lot of irons in the fire**, they are involved in several different activities or have several different plans at the same time, so that there is likely to be something which succeeds even if others fail. This expression is very variable.

'I will be earning a lot more money,' he says, declining to say how much more. 'I also have a number of other irons in the fire.'

Be realistic about your goals. Too many irons in the fire can sap your energy and prevent you from seeing which path to take in your career.

ivory

an ivory tower ◄◄◄

If you accuse someone of living in **an ivory tower**, you mean that their lifestyle or their work prevents them from experiencing the problems experienced by other ordinary people, and so they remain generally unaware of these problems.

They're all out of touch – they live up in a little ivory tower, and they don't see what's going on down here.

This won't happen until strategists come down from their ivory tower and learn to work in the real world of limited budgets and uncertain futures.

If you just want to discuss pretty little theories in your ivory towers, that's no good.

J

jack

a jack of all trades: 1 ◄
If you describe someone as **a jack of all trades**, you mean that they have many different skills.

He soon caught the theatre bug, and became a jack of all trades at the local amateur theatre.

a jack of all trades: 2 ◄
If you say that someone is **a jack of all trades**, or **a jack of all trades but master of none**, you mean that they can do a large number of different things but that they are not very good at doing any of them.

His critics sometimes described him as a jack-of-all-trades.

I believe in specialisation. Too many photographers are jacks of all trades and masters of none.

jackpot

hit the jackpot: 1 ◄◄
If someone **hits the jackpot** with something, it is very successful and they earn a lot of money from it.

The National Theatre hit the jackpot with its first musical, Guys And Dolls.

Sylvester Stallone, Arnold Schwarzenegger and Bruce Willis hit the jackpot when they opened a restaurant in New York.

hit the jackpot: 2
You can say that someone **hits the jackpot** when they succeed in getting or finding something which they have been trying to get or find.

I went through all the people called Lasalles in the Sydney phone book until I hit the jackpot.

jam

jam tomorrow
jam today ◄
If someone says **'jam tomorrow'**, they mean that people are being promised that they will have something in the future, although they cannot have it now. This expression is often used to suggest that people are in fact unlikely to receive what they have been promised. It is used mainly in British English.

The City simply does not believe it. It has been promised jam tomorrow too many times before by the company.

There is also an element of 'jam tomorrow' about some of Mr Lamont's measures.

□ **Jam today** is used to refer to the idea that people can have or get something immediately, rather than having to wait.

Economists generally assume that most people value jam today more highly than the same quantity of jam tomorrow.

□ This expression comes from the children's story 'Through the Looking Glass', by Lewis Carroll, where the Red Queen says, 'The rule is jam tomorrow and jam yesterday, but never jam today.'

Jell-O

like trying to nail Jell-O to the wall
If you say that something is **like trying to nail Jell-O to the wall**, you are emphasizing that it is extremely difficult or impossible. This expression is used in American English.

He also complained that pinning down PCC's cost formula 'was like trying to nail Jell-O to the wall'.

Right now, it's just about like trying to nail five pounds of Jell-O to the wall with a 16-penny nail.

□ **Jell-O** is a trademark.

jewel

the jewel in someone's crown ◄◄◄
If you describe something as **the jewel in someone's crown**, you consider it to be the best thing they have, or the achievement that they can be most proud of.

His achievement is astonishing and this book is the jewel in his crown.

But probably the jewel in the architectural crown of North Yorkshire is Castle Howard.

Full employment should again become the jewel in the crown of political ambition.

job

do a job on someone
If one person **does a job on** another, the first person defeats the second or harms them in some way. This is an informal expression.

Coetzer is a difficult opponent. But I'm equally sure I can do a job on him.

They sure did a job on you. With a stout stick, I'd say.

a full-time job ◄
If you say that doing something, for example looking after someone, is **a full-time job**, you are emphasizing that it takes a great deal of time and effort.

Maintaining a happy home in which a family

can thrive is a full-time job, and for many women it becomes their career for life.

jobs

jobs for the boys
jobs for the girls ◄

If you refer to a situation as **jobs for the boys**, you are pointing out disapprovingly that well-paid or prestigious jobs in a particular organization are being given to people who are the friends, relatives, or supporters of someone in that organization, rather than to the people who are best qualified to do the job. This expression is used in British English.

The council has faced a string of allegations over 'jobs for the boys'.

By backing him through all this turmoil he's proving that it's jobs for the boys.

□ **Jobs for the girls** is used to indicate that work is given to women.

The customary Eighties insistence on jobs for the girls may fall upon deaf ears.

Johnny

Johnny-come-lately ◄

You use **Johnny-come-lately** to refer to someone who becomes involved in an activity or organization after it has already started, when you think that they are less reliable or experienced than the people who have been involved since the beginning.

The basic trouble was that, in the eyes of the left, Benn was always something of a Johnny-come-lately.

He is regarded by many other managers as a Johnny-come-lately. But if they believe he is inexperienced, he knows much more than the vast majority of them about foreign coaching methods.

□ **Johnny-come-lately** can also be used before a noun.

We advise members who want to rent cars to ensure that they are dealing with a reliable and long-established company – not the Johnny-come-lately firm that's just set up round the corner.

□ 'Johnny' is sometimes replaced by another name, to refer more directly to the person being discussed.

This ex-Republican David-come-lately is still mistrusted by the left-leaning young veterans of the campaign.

joker

the joker in the pack ◄

If you describe something or someone as **the joker in the pack**, you mean that they are different from the other things or people in a situation and do not seem to fit in, or may

cause problems. This expression is used mainly in British English.

The Nova, for a long time the joker in Vauxhall's pack, is due for replacement by a new model, to be called the Corsa.

Franco Moschino is described as the joker in the pack of Italian fashion.

Joneses

keep up with the Joneses ◄

If you say that someone is trying to **keep up with the Joneses**, you mean that they are trying to have or do the same things as other people that they know, even if they do not really have enough money to do this, or are not really interested in these things.

Her mother, Louise, was very keen on keeping up with the Joneses, and through much of her teens Linda accepted what she now calls 'these false values'.

Of course, in this desperate attempt to keep up with the Jones's, they are all the more likely to end up poor.

judgment

sit in judgment ◄

If you say that someone should not **sit in judgment** on other people, you mean that they do not have the right to criticize them or give opinions about their achievements.

I think people should work hard to keep a marriage alive. I don't want to sit in judgment on other people, but if there's anything that's good you should try to hold on to it.

I was too junior in government to have political dealing with him so I never had any reason not to trust him. It would be presumptuous of me to sit in judgement on him.

□ 'Judgment' is often spelled 'judgement' in British English.

jugular

go for the jugular
go for the throat ◄◄

If you say that someone **goes for the jugular**, you mean that they attack their opponent or enemy very decisively at the point where they can cause the greatest damage. You can also say that they **go for the throat**.

If England go for the jugular in tonight's game and play anything like they did against the Poles at Wembley, we won't have to worry about scraping a draw.

Why is it so difficult for the Democrats to go for the jugular on the issue of mismanaging the economy?

When you can win, you go for the throat. When you're going to lose, you go for the compromise.

□ You can also use 'jugular' in many other

expressions and structures with a similar meaning.

Smith didn't have the instinct for the jugular that his successor Ed Meese had.

This old guard worries that go-for-the-jugular journalism oversimplifies the world – reporting as black and white what should be grey.

jump

for the high jump

If you say that someone is **for the high jump**, you mean that it is certain that they will be punished for something they have done wrong. This expression is used in British English.

God help anyone who was sneaking a cup of tea when they shouldn't have been. They'll be for the high jump.

get a jump on someone ◄◄

If you **get a jump on** someone or something, or **get the jump on** them, you do something before they do and so gain an advantage over them. Other verbs such as 'have' are sometimes used instead of 'get'. This expression is used mainly in American English.

This year, many stores did try to get a jump on the shopping season by holding promotional sales even before Thanksgiving.

Fittipaldi got the jump on him and with two laps to go led by 1.8 seconds.

Schools in the upper part of Florida are playing games now while we haven't even been practicing lately, so they're going to have a jump on us.

jump up and down ◄◄

If you say that someone is **jumping up and down** about something, you mean that they are very excited, angry, or upset about it.

They're jumping up and down and saying: 'We will do something about this.'

take a running jump

If someone tells you to **take a running jump**, they are telling you in a rude way to mind your own business and not interfere because they do not care what you think. This expression is used mainly in British English.

'My dad reckons your letters are all made up.' 'Well you can tell your dad to take a running jump because we don't make up the letters – ever.'

That's final then. He's staying and public opinion can take a running jump.

'I hope Mr Perry doesn't see this.' 'Mr Perry,' Ed said, 'can go take a running jump at himself.'

jury

the jury is still out ◄◄

If you say that **the jury is still out** on a particular subject, you mean that people have not yet formed an opinion about it or reached a decision. You can also just say that **the jury is out**.

The jury's still out on what are the long-term effects of air pollution.

Specialists haven't been able to make up their minds whether hair dye is safe or not. 'The jury is still out,' says Dr Venitt firmly. 'There are niggling doubts.'

K

kangaroos

kangaroos in your top paddock

If you say that someone has **kangaroos in their top paddock**, you mean that they have peculiar ideas or are crazy. 'Roos' can be used instead of 'kangaroos'. This is an informal expression, which is used mainly in Australian English.

I have this passion for life, a desperate desire to drink it by the bucketful while others sip it delicately by the spoonful. Some attribute it to a low boredom threshold, while others simply put it down to having a few kangaroos loose in the top paddock.

A woman's a dangerous and unpredictable creature. A guy who pretends to understand the sheilas has got roos in his top paddock.

keel

on an even keel ◄◄

If someone or something is **on an even keel**, they are calm or are progressing steadily, especially during or after a period of troubles or difficulties.

She sees it as her role to keep the family on an even keel through its time of hardship.

You may begin to wonder if having a baby was the right thing to do and whether you'll ever get back on an even keel.

keen

keen as mustard

You say that someone is **keen as mustard** to emphasize that they are very eager or alert. This is an old-fashioned expression, which is used mainly in British English.

I have an adult pupil who scored very low in assessments but is keen as mustard. He's made staggering progress and loves every minute of it.

☐ You can also describe someone as **mustard-keen**.

Sir Richard was mustard-keen to say his bit.

Chapple took two wickets largely through being mustard keen.

keep

earn its keep ◄

If you say that something **earns** its **keep**, you mean that it is good value and justifies the amount of money that it costs or the space that it takes up.

In Bob's garden everything must earn its keep, with fruits and vegetables given priority over flowers.

If you're short of storage space in your kitchen, whatever appliances you do have really need to earn their keep.

keeper

not someone's keeper

If you are asked where someone is and you answer that you are **not** their **keeper**, you are saying in quite a rude way that you do not know where they are and you cannot be expected to know.

'I don't know where he is,' Hughes replied, 'I'm not his keeper.' 'No, simply his employer.' Aubrey sighed once more. 'We know that you must have a precise idea as to his whereabouts.'

not your brother's keeper

You can say that you are **not** your **brother's keeper** to indicate that you do not accept responsibility for other people in any way.

Part of me wants to help him, but part of me realizes I can't be my brother's keeper.

ken

beyond your ken ◄

If you say that something is **beyond** your **ken**, you mean that you do not have much knowledge, understanding, or experience of it.

For the millions under the age of 40 who will be voting in the next general election, Labour governments are beyond their ken.

Much art in Soviet museums has remained beyond the ken of Western connoisseurs.

kettle

a different kettle of fish
another kettle of fish ◄◄

You can say that something is **a different kettle of fish** or **another kettle of fish** to emphasize that it is completely unlike another thing that you are mentioning.

Artistic integrity? Who needs it? Money? Now that's a completely different kettle of fish.

Car hi-fi is another kettle of fish altogether, since it's not just a matter of buying the gear, but having it installed as well.

☐ In journalism, people sometimes replace 'fish' with a more specific word for a fish, or with another word which is relevant to the situation that they are talking about.

This is another kettle of herring altogether.

Like it or hate it, no one could possibly ask what the Attlee government stood for. Harold Wilson, though, was a different kettle of fudge.

a pretty kettle of fish
a fine kettle of fish

If someone describes a situation as **a pretty kettle of fish** or **a fine kettle of fish**, they are being ironic and criticizing it because it is confused and unsatisfactory. These are old-fashioned expressions.

Well, this is a pretty kettle of fish, as Queen Mary said.

kibosh

put the kibosh on something

If someone **puts the kibosh on** something, they prevent it from happening, continuing, or being successful.

The export boom has also put the kibosh, once and for all, on the old belief that the American economy is relatively self-sufficient.

kick

kick ass
kick butt ◄◄

If a person in authority **kicks ass**, they behave in an unpleasant and aggressive way towards people, giving them strict orders to carry out, and punishing them if they refuse. You can also say that they **kick butt**. These are very informal expressions, which many people find offensive. They are used mainly in American English, but are becoming more common in British English.

A whole society is based upon the premise that the man or woman with the power and the money can kick ass whenever or wherever he or she likes.

Everybody says they've really been kicking ass lately. Busting places up, harassing everybody.

kick someone in the teeth
a kick in the teeth ◄◄

If you say that you **have been kicked in the teeth**, you mean that someone has unexpectedly treated you very badly and unfairly.

The union had been led to expect that the

coalfield would be given favourable treatment: 'Instead we have been kicked in the teeth.'

This is not about vengeance, it's about fair play. As it is, 51 people have died in vain and the survivors have been kicked in the teeth.

We have had ministers round before saying you are doing a wonderful job, and then kicking you in the teeth.

☐ You can also say that you get **a kick in the teeth**.

Pendry described the letter as a 'kick in the teeth' and an 'insult'.

I laid my life on the line for the company and they repaid me with a kick in the teeth.

kick someone when they are down ◄

If you say that you should not **kick** someone **when** they're **down**, you mean that when someone is in a weak position and at a disadvantage, it is wrong to hurt, upset, or criticize them further.

It's time to let Kinnock bow out gracefully if he wants to. He has done an awful lot for the Labour party, so don't kick a man when he's down.

He must be monitored rigorously to ensure that the poor are not kicked while they're down by a reform which otherwise has a lot going for it.

I'm afraid that is human nature. You always get kicked when you're down.

a kick up the backside
a kick in the butt
a boot up the backside ◄◄

You say that someone needs **a kick up the backside** or **a kick up the arse** when you disapprove of their behaviour and attitudes and you think that they should start acting in a more reasonable, modest, and acceptable way. These forms of the expression are used in British English, and there are many variations. In American English, people talk about **a kick in the butt** or **a kick in the ass**. These are all very informal expressions and many people consider them offensive.

I hope this gives him the kick up the backside he needs. Maybe he'll knuckle down and still do a job for the club. If not he'll have to go.

He got four goals. But he needed a kick up the arse before he started to play properly.

They deserve a kick up the rear end then, don't they, for that.

He was going to have to give this unit a real kick in the ass, shake things up.

☐ You can also say, for example, that someone **is kicked up the backside**.

Why would you have preferred students to be more stroppy on committees? Did you think universities need in fact kicking up the backside a little bit?

It hurts like hell, but that's racing. One minute on top of the world, the next getting kicked in the butt.

☐ In British English, people occasionally replace 'kick' with 'boot'.

There are certain players in need of an extra boot up the bum, particularly those on the fringe of selection.

kick-off

for a kick-off

You use **for a kick-off** to indicate that you are mentioning just one of a number of things, points, or reasons which you could list or mention if you wanted to.

Is it not in fact the opinion of the public that most dentists earn far too much for a kick-off?

kid

treat someone with kid gloves
handle someone with kid gloves ◄

If you **treat** someone **with kid gloves** or **handle** them **with kid gloves**, you treat them very carefully, for example because they are very important or because they are easily upset. People sometimes use this expression when they want to suggest that they do not think this kind of treatment is right or necessary.

To a large degree Mr Sarbutts was treated as a VIP. He was very much our guest at the police station, which I was not too happy about, and everybody was treating him with kid gloves.

I'm not suggesting that you all begin handling Bessie with kid gloves.

Even in presidential campaigns, foreign policy is treated with kid gloves.

☐ **Kid gloves** is used in other structures and expressions where you are describing how carefully someone is being treated.

The oddest aspect of the film, however, was the kid-glove treatment of Captain Jo Hazlewood, the man actually in charge of the doomed tanker.

We must take off the kid gloves and smash these evil monsters once and for all.

Kilkenny

fight like Kilkenny cats

If you say that people **fight like Kilkenny cats**, you mean that they fight or disagree very violently and destructively. This is an old-fashioned expression, which is used in British English.

For six years Mr Wilder and Mr Robb have been fighting like Kilkenny cats.

kill

in at the kill
in on the kill

If someone is **in at the kill** or is **in on the kill**, they are present and either watching or taking part when a contest or struggle comes to an end and one side is decisively defeated. 'In at the kill' is used only in British English.

Burns was one of the happiest men at the finish. He had sparked the action after only five miles and was in at the kill 106 miles and four-and-a-quarter hours later.

move in for the kill
go for the kill ◄◄

In a fight or contest, if someone **moves in for the kill** or **goes for the kill**, they act decisively to defeat their enemy or opponent. Other verbs are sometimes used instead of 'move' or 'go'.

Manager Graeme Souness had urged his players to go for the kill and that vital breakthrough almost came after 14 minutes.

Efforts to paint the princess's circle as unsuitable will increase, as cynical newspapers move in for the kill.

killing

make a killing ◄◄◄

If someone **makes a killing**, they make a large profit very quickly and easily.

The boss of Britain's top pizza concern made a killing on the market yesterday by selling off a parcel of his shares.

Officials will crack down on speculators who try to make a killing on the Stock Exchange by exploiting advance knowledge of poll results.

kindness

kill someone with kindness

If you **kill** someone **with kindness**, you treat them very kindly even though this is not what they need or want.

'He is killing me with kindness,' Sallie says. 'He's just too attentive.'

king

live like a king

If you say that someone **lives like a king**, you mean that they have a luxurious and very comfortable lifestyle.

Although he lives like a king, he manages it without provoking resentment.

It was no lie. Company executives lived like kings. The top thirty-one executives were paid a total of 14.2 million dollars, or an average of 458,000 dollars.

kingdom

blow someone to kingdom come

To **blow** someone or something **to kingdom come** means to destroy them, especially in a very violent way. Verbs such as 'blast' and 'shoot' are sometimes used instead of 'blow'.

There was tremendous damage in these industrial towns down to the South – homes flattened, trailers blown to kingdom come.

No one knows what that guy is doing – or what he's gonna do. He could blow 'em all to kingdom come.

kiss

kiss and make up ◄

If two people or groups have been in conflict with each other and you say that they **have kissed and made up**, you mean that they have sorted out their disagreements and ended their conflict.

All parties appeared to have kissed and made up and all were at pains to emphasise that the event had been a resounding success despite the misunderstandings.

They bicker constantly and publicly but always manage to kiss and make up.

kiss-and-tell ◄◄

If someone who has had a love affair with a famous person tells the story of their affair in public, for example in a newspaper or book, you can refer to what they say as a **kiss-and-tell** story.

On many occasions we discussed selling details of kiss-and-tell stories.

It looks unlikely that there will be a kiss and tell book.

□ If someone tells their story in this way, you can say that they **kiss and tell**. You can also refer to their behaviour as **kissing and telling**.

In no circumstances will I kiss and tell.

The girl he picked was a publicity-seeking actress who kissed and told her friends, who told the papers every sordid detail.

Kissing and telling is not ladylike.

kiss ass
kiss someone's ass ◄

If you accuse someone of **kissing ass** or of **kissing** a person's **ass**, you are criticizing them in a very rude way for deliberately flattering that person in order to gain an advantage for themselves. Other words are sometimes used instead of 'ass', for example 'butt' in American English and 'arse' in British English. These are very informal expressions, which many people consider offensive.

I'm just tired of kissing ass in here. I'm tired of talking to these people.

How do you know if the people really like you or if they're just kissing your ass?

People are not kissing my arse, but just being very friendly.

□ If you say to someone **'kiss my ass'**, you are telling them rudely that what they are suggesting is foolish and you do not agree or are unwilling to do it. This is a very informal expression, which many people consider offensive.

'I'm not telling you anything. Why should I?' 'Because I've bought you forty dollars worth of beer.' 'Kiss my ass.'

the kiss of death　◄◄

If you say that a particular event is **the kiss of death** for something, you mean that it is certain to cause that thing to fail or be ruined.

The conventional view of timber extraction is that it is the kiss of death for a rainforest.

He loathes the idea of being thought of as conventional. That is the kiss of death to him.

kitchen

everything but the kitchen sink

You use expressions such as **everything but the kitchen sink** to say in a light-hearted way that there are very many things in a place and that many of them are unnecessary.

They love being surrounded by familiar possessions and tend to pack everything but the kitchen sink in rather too many suitcases.

They want 10 per cent of everything, including the kitchen sink, but they are not going to get it.

kite

fly a kite　◄

If you say that someone **is flying a kite**, you mean that they are suggesting ideas or possibilities in order to see how people react to them before deciding whether or not to put them into practice. This expression is often used to suggest that the ideas that are being put forward are stupid or unrealistic. It is used mainly in British English.

The committee has paid a good deal of attention to what might be politically possible. It is consciously flying a kite.

The Government flies these kites of disinformation then people feel grateful when they don't happen.

□ You can also talk about **kite-flying**.

Recent kite-flying exercises outlined in your paper concerning health service cuts should not deflect, as they are intended to, the attention of the electorate from the underlying problems facing the Government.

kittens

have kittens

If someone **has kittens**, they are extremely worried or upset by something. This expression is used mainly in British English.

The boss will have kittens if I don't get that dress back inside the hour.

The Government was having kittens over the Maastricht treaty.

knee

knee-high to a grasshopper

If you say that you have done something since you were **knee-high to a grasshopper**, you mean that you have done it since you were a very young child. This is a fairly old-fashioned expression.

I've lived here since I was knee-high to a grasshopper.

□ People sometimes change 'grasshopper' to a word or expression that is relevant to the subject they are talking about. In the example below, the people mentioned were all famous songwriters.

She had met Irving Berlin, Rodgers and Hammerstein and the Gershwins when only knee-high to a piano stool.

knees

bring something to its knees: 1
be on its knees　◄◄◄

If you say that something **has brought** a country or organization **to** its **knees**, you are emphasizing that it has caused the country or organization to be in an extremely weak condition. You can also say that the country or organization **is on** its **knees**.

Britain was brought to its knees after a wave of paralysing strikes.

Its old protectionist ways stifled initiative and brought the economy to its knees.

The Government was on its knees, the Tory party divided.

bring someone to their knees: 2
be on your knees

If you say that something **has brought** you **to** your **knees**, you are emphasizing that it has made you extremely weak or tired. You can also say that you **are on** your **knees**.

The sheer weight of other people's great expectations brought me almost to my knees.

Several times this afternoon he had sounded as if he were on his knees.

down on your knees
on bended knee

If you say that someone goes **down on** their **knees** or goes down **on bended knee** to beg for something, you mean that they beg desperately for it, in a way which makes them look foolish.

He would be looking for mutually advantageous co-operation, not charity. He would not be going down on his knees to beg.

At a time when film-makers, especially English film-makers, are going on bended knee to funders anywhere, Mike Leigh refuses to compromise on the way he makes movies.

knell

sound the death knell
the death knell sounds ◄◄◄

If you say that something **sounds the death knell** for an activity or organization, you mean that it is likely to cause the activity or organization to end or fail. This expression has many variations. For example, you can also say that **the death knell sounds** for the activity or organization.

The announcement that the mine would close in March with the loss of more than 980 jobs sounded the death knell for the village.

There are those who fear that the decision to allow women to become priests sounds the death knell of the Church of England.

The death-knell of the German Left has not yet sounded.

Ministers believe a 'no' vote would be the death knell for plans for a single European currency.

knickers

get your knickers in a twist
have your knickers in a twist ◄

In British English, if you say that someone **gets** their **knickers in a twist**, you are emphasizing that they become extremely upset or worried about something. You can also say that someone **has** their **knickers in a twist**.

We seem to be getting our knickers in a twist, if you don't mind me saying so.

The Co-op has its knickers in a twist about Sunday trading.

Let's not get our knickers in a twist until we see the outcome of those games.

□ You can use 'knot' instead of 'twist'.

It was the restrictive system that had reporters' knickers in a knot.

□ People sometimes change **knickers** to another word or expression which refers to underpants, or to another word or expression which has some relevance to the person or thing they are talking about.

The government got its Y-fronts in a fine old twist over the Maastricht treaty.

One of the reasons Hilton Kramer got his bow tie in a twist over Sontag was that she said she liked the Supremes.

knife

like a hot knife through butter
like a knife through butter

If you manage to overcome a difficulty quickly and without any problems, you can say that you cut through it **like a hot knife through butter** or **like a knife through butter**. 'Like a knife through butter' is used only in British English.

They will be cutting through the competition like a hot knife through butter.

Think about the women who have gone through life like a knife through butter, slicing through every kind of setback and discouragement.

on a knife-edge
walk a knife-edge ◄◄◄

If someone or something is **on a knife-edge**, they are in a situation in which nobody knows what is going to happen next. This expression is used mainly in British English.

I thrive on being on a knife-edge of uncertainty and excitement every day, not knowing whether I'm going to ride a winner or get hurt.

No further incidents have been reported today, but this remains a town on the knife-edge of conflict.

With recovery poised on a knife edge the country needs a leader with vision and stature.

□ You can also say that someone **walks a knife-edge**.

She walks an emotional knife-edge.

□ You can also use **knife-edge** before a noun.

The government faces a knife-edge vote on its plans for the coal industry.

put the knife in
stick the knife in

If someone **puts the knife in** or **sticks the knife in**, they deliberately do or say things which will upset another person or cause problems for them.

It is also an attempt to make those who have put the knife in look bad before the world.

She knows exactly where to stick the knife to do the most damage.

twist the knife
twist the knife in the wound ◄

If someone **twists the knife** or **twists the knife in the wound**, they deliberately do or say things which make a situation even worse for someone who is already upset or experiencing problems. You can replace 'twist' with 'turn'.

Her daughter manages to twist the knife still further by claiming Nancy never loved her.

The paper chose to turn the knife in the wound by writing that the story about the alleged affair only 'echoed the worries of the queen, the prime minister and the whole government'.

□ You can also talk about **a twist of the knife**.

It gave them the confidence to make the final twist of the knife in England's gut.

you could cut the atmosphere with a knife

If you say that you **could cut the atmosphere with a knife**, you are complaining that the atmosphere in a place is extremely tense or unfriendly. You can use 'air', or a word such as 'tension' that refers to an unpleasant feeling, instead of 'atmosphere'.

There have been some embarrassing silences at meal times. You could cut the atmosphere with a knife.

As soon as we entered the church, you could cut the air with a knife.

At secondary school, when the stakes are higher, the tension on parents' nights can be cut with a knife.

knight

a knight in shining armour   ◄

If a man is kind and brave, and rescues you from a difficult situation, you can describe him as **a knight in shining armour**.

Detective Constable Paul Sexton said: 'It was a cowardly attack on a man defending a lady. He was like a knight in shining armour.'

I just felt dizzy and then I collapsed. The next thing I woke up in intensive care. I am very, very grateful to Tom and I always will be – he really was my knight in shining armour.

□ 'Armour' is spelled 'armor' in American English.

knitting

stick to your knitting

If someone, especially a company or organization, **sticks to** their **knitting**, they continue to do something that they are experienced at and do not try to do something different about which they know very little.

It failed because we did not understand the plumbing business, and it taught us a lesson about sticking to our knitting!

He stuck to his knitting. He stuck to that populist, economic message that worked well when he was running against Tsongas.

knives

the knives are out
have the knives out   ◄◄

If you say that **the knives are out** for you, or that people **have** their **knives out** for you, you mean that other people are feeling very angry or resentful towards you, and are try-

ing to cause problems for you. These expressions are used mainly in British English.

The knives are out for me at the moment.

With the knives out for Sikorski in various quarters, sabotage looked a strong possibility.

Arendt and Huber had their knives out, and they were being encouraged to stick them in me.

Richard will have his knife out for me with a vengeance from now on.

knock

knock someone sideways: 1

If something **knocks** you **sideways**, it makes you feel amazed, confused, or very upset. This expression is used in British English.

There is more to Bologna than mouthwatering meals. What's barely mentioned but knocks most visitors sideways is the sheer power and beauty of the place.

I was very near to killing myself. Something like this, a huge shock, completely knocks you sideways.

knock something sideways: 2

If you say that something **has been knocked sideways**, you mean that it has been severely damaged, and may not recover. This expression is used in British English.

Most of the country's trade unions have been knocked sideways in the past decade.

Confidence in the British legal system has been knocked sideways, hasn't it?

knot

a Gordian knot
cut the Gordian knot   ◄

If you describe a situation or problem as **a Gordian knot**, you mean that it is very complicated and difficult to resolve. If someone succeeds in resolving it, you can say that they **cut the Gordian knot**. These are literary expressions.

The federal deficit has become the Gordian knot of Washington.

On Monday one of the Tories' leading thinkers will argue in a pamphlet that the Government can cut the Gordian knot by raising the pension age.

tie the knot   ◄◄◄

If two people **tie the knot**, they get married. This is an informal expression.

The couple tied the knot last year after a 13-year romance.

It was two years before they actually tied the knot.

Len tied the knot with Kate five years ago.

knots

tie someone in knots: 1 ◄

In a discussion or argument, if someone **ties** you **in knots**, they confuse you by using clever arguments, so that you cannot argue or think clearly any longer. You can also say that they **tie** you **up in knots**.

He could tie her in knots in an argument and never once missed an opportunity to prove his intellectual superiority.

He had easily tied her up in knots, cunningly casting serious doubt on her mental faculties.

tie yourself in knots: 2 ◄

If you **tie** yourself **in knots**, you make yourself confused or anxious, and so you are not able to think clearly about things. You can also say that you **tie** yourself **up in knots**.

The week after Jordan's appointment the New York Times editorial page tied itself in knots trying to find the correct tone with which to treat him.

Catherine is tying herself up in knots with worry because nine-year-old Alice has school phobia.

know

know something inside out
know something inside and out ◄◄

If you **know** something or someone **inside out** or **know** them **inside and out**, you know them extremely well.

Liam has played for and against some of the greatest clubs in Europe and knows the game inside out.

I used to think I knew my daughter inside out, and I still find it hard to understand what she has done to me.

He knows the house inside and out, you know, having stayed there so often when Dolph's aunt and uncle were alive.

not know whether you are coming or going

If you **don't know whether** you **are coming or going**, you feel very confused and are unable to think clearly. This expression is used mainly in spoken English.

We worked 16 hours a day during the Gulf war and the Falklands. By the end of the week you didn't know whether you were coming or going.

You wanted to fire him from the minute you laid eyes on him. And he knew it. He's not dumb. You had him so scared he didn't know if he was coming or going.

The truth is I'm so excited that I hardly know whether I'm coming or going.

knuckle

near the knuckle

If you say that something someone says or writes is **near the knuckle**, you mean that it is close to the limits of what people find acceptable, for example because it is sexually explicit or offensive to particular groups. This expression is used in British English.

Decide for yourself whether stand-up comedian Frank Skinner is as near the knuckle on TV as in his own live show when he tours the UK in October.

There are important people who fear the public will be outraged. This kind of material is very near the knuckle.

□ You can use **near-the-knuckle** before a noun.

Comic Bernard Manning, who appeared on the show and has made a career out of near-the-knuckle routines, said, 'We need all the laughter we can get in this world.'

He was invited to speak at the Police Federation's annual get together but told organisers he would not attend if the near-the-knuckle comic turned up.

knuckles

rap someone on the knuckles
rap someone's knuckles ◄◄

If someone in authority **raps** you **on the knuckles** or **raps** your **knuckles**, they criticize you or blame you for doing something they consider to be wrong.

I was rapped on the knuckles for interfering in things that were not my concern.

The report raps teachers over the knuckles for not appearing to have any influence over children at all.

The commission said it had asked the state prosecutor to look into possible insider trading in Michelin shares. It also rapped the firm's knuckles for failing to provide the market promptly with information.

□ You can also say that you **have** your **knuckles rapped**, or that you get **a rap on the knuckles**.

Just two months earlier, the lawyer had had his knuckles rapped by a Delaware judge for his role in the buyout of a Wisconsin paper company.

Southampton yesterday received a rap on the knuckles from the Football Association, which fined the club £20,000 for its poor disciplinary record last season.

□ Some people use the word 'wrap' instead of 'rap' in this expression, but it is generally considered incorrect.

L

labour

a labour of love ◄◄◄

A **labour of love** is a job or task that you do for pleasure or out of duty without expecting a large reward or payment for it. Often other people may think that the job or task is not worth doing or is unpleasant.

There is no doubt that Agenugba's self-published debut novel is a labour of love, and obviously very close to his heart.

They concentrated on restoring outbuildings such as the Victorian greenhouse, an expensive labour of love.

There are still a few mills left that produce stone-ground flours and cornmeal as it was done in the past. It is a labor of love, and through them we may still get a taste of what bread was like one or two hundred years ago.

□ 'Labour' is spelled 'labor' in American English.

lads

one of the lads ◄

If you describe a man as being **one of the lads**, you mean that he is accepted as being part of a group of men who behave in ways which are considered typically masculine. This expression is used in British English. Compare **one of the boys**; see **boys**.

He likes being one of the lads, you know, having pints down the pub.

He is immensely popular, truly one of the lads.

lady

it isn't over until the fat lady sings ◄

If you say to someone, for example someone who is losing a contest, '**it isn't over until the fat lady sings**', you are encouraging them not to give up hope because nothing is certain and there is still time for the situation to change.

Injured jockey Eddery is not conceding defeat. 'There's still a long way to go and, who knows, Michael might fall off and break a leg,' he joked. 'As they say, it's not over until the fat lady sings.'

We can do this, we can do it all, it's not too late. The catastrophes are coming, but they're not upon us yet. The game, as they say, isn't over until the fat lady sings, and she hasn't started singing yet.

lam

on the lam ◄

If someone is **on the lam**, they are trying to escape or hide from someone, for example the police or an enemy. This expression is used mainly in American English.

He has a record of drug trafficking and assault, and is currently on the lam, wanted for the sale and trafficking of cocaine.

A Rhode Island banker accused of stealing millions has turned himself in after months on the lam.

lamb

like a lamb

If you say that someone is **like a lamb**, you mean that they are gentle, quiet, and obedient.

She'd followed him like a lamb. She hadn't asked him why he was taking her to a medical research laboratory in a university rather than to a normal hospital or clinic.

lambs

like lambs to the slaughter
like sheep to the slaughter ◄

If you say that people go somewhere **like lambs to the slaughter** or **like sheep to the slaughter**, you mean that they behave quietly and obediently without resisting because they have not realized that it will be dangerous or unpleasant, or because they realize that they are powerless.

The record companies have an easy life. We grovel and follow their every word like lambs to the slaughter.

We're just like sheep being led to slaughter. We're following right along.

land

the lay of the land
the lie of the land ◄

If you get **the lay of the land** or get **the lie of the land**, you learn or find out the details of a situation or problem.

I'm not sure what's going to happen. That's why I'm coming in early. I want to get the lay of the land.

The book is about looking at the lie of the land and making your move.

land-office

do a land-office business

If you say that a business **is doing a land-**

office business, you mean that they are very successful. This expression is used in old-fashioned American English.

The Paradiso, one of the capital's newest and most luxurious clubs, was doing a land-office business.

lane

the fast lane
the slow lane ◄◄◄

If you say that someone lives their life in **the fast lane**, you mean that they live in a way which seems full of activity and excitement but which often involves a lot of pressure as well.

Tired of life in the fast lane, Jack, a fifty-ish American businessman, decides to give it all up to fulfil a dream of becoming a painter.

Offscreen, Cooper moved quickly into the fast lane of Hollywood society, keeping company with actresses Clara Bow and Lupe Velez.

□ You can also use **fast lane** before a noun.

He had to quit, and not only did he have to quit, but he had to get away from this fast-lane, high-society lifestyle.

□ You can say that someone lives their life in **the slow lane** when their life is quiet and boring without any exciting incidents.

For your own sake, pull over and enjoy traveling in the slow lane of life for a while.

At the age of 31, Gullit, rather than moving over into the slow lane, has been having fun proving his critics wrong.

lap

fall into your lap
drop into your lap ◄

If something good happens to you without any effort on your part, you can say that it **falls into** your **lap** or **drops into** your **lap**.

Best-selling US author Terry McMillan has revealed in Ebony magazine that she is sometimes at a loss about what to with the 'embarrassingly' fat cheques that regularly fall in to her lap.

It would not be safe to assume that victory will drop into our lap at the next election.

in the lap of luxury ◄

If you say that someone lives **in the lap of luxury**, you mean that they live in conditions of great comfort and wealth.

We don't live in the lap of luxury, but we're comfortable.

They are heading for retirement and intend to spend it in the lap of luxury.

□ You can say that something is **the lap of luxury** when it is very comfortable.

It seemed like the lap of luxury.

in the lap of the gods ◄

If you say that something is **in the lap of the gods**, you mean that it will be decided or affected by luck or chance, rather than anything you can do.

Once they had repaired my lung they had to stop the operation. The liver is self-healing anyway, so at that stage, my life was in the lap of the gods.

land in your lap
be thrown into your lap ◄

If you are forced to deal with a problem which is not really your responsibility, you can say that it **has landed in** your **lap** or **has been thrown into** your **lap**. Other verbs are sometimes used instead of 'land' or 'throw'.

These problems have landed in the lap of Donald Jackson, an unassuming manager with little international experience whom Mr Degroote picked as his successor.

The solution of the funding crisis should not be thrown into the lap of students.

Yet few governments, least of all the Americans, seem ready to pay the bill for tossing the world's problems into the UN's lap.

large

large as life
big as life ◄

When you want to say that you have found someone in a place, especially a place where they are not supposed to be, you can say that you found them there **large as life** or, in American English, **big as life**. You often use these expressions to suggest that the person should have been embarrassed at being found there.

I called on him one Friday night on some pretext or other and there they all were, large as life.

That's what Amos thinks as he walks big as life into the diner and takes his time over the menu.

larger

larger than life
bigger than life ◄◄◄

If you describe someone as **larger than life**, you mean that they seem more interesting or exciting than other people, for example because they are very talented, or because they behave in an unusual or interesting way. In American English, you can also describe them as **bigger than life**.

It is well known that the Earl was larger than life and that, through sheer force of personality, there was a tendency for him to take over whenever he entered a room full of people.

John Huston was a larger-than-life character,

whose temperament was as dramatic as any of the fictional figures in his own films.

The music is fast losing its character. Today's musicians do not have nicknames. With a few exceptions – Rollins, Lionel Hampton – they are not bigger than life.

lark

up with the lark

If someone is **up with the lark**, they are up very early in the morning. This is an old-fashioned expression, which is used mainly in British English.

Most bakers are up with the lark, but Neville Wilkins is in action hours before the rest.

last

stick to your last
let the cobbler stick to his last

If you advise someone to **stick to** their **last**, you mean that they should continue doing what they know about and not try to do new things, at which they are likely to fail. This expression is fairly old-fashioned.

Looking back, I should have stuck to my last and gone on to get a research job in one of the studios.

□ This expression comes from the proverb **let the cobbler stick to his last**. A 'last' is a foot-shaped object which a cobbler uses as a model or mould to make shoes the right shape and size.

I was afraid they'd think, 'Why can't the cobbler stick to his last?'

lather

in a lather ◄

If someone gets **in a lather** or works themselves **into a lather**, they become very agitated about something.

The truth of the matter is that you have spent the past six months worrying and working yourself up into a lather over situations which are really none of your business.

'Brenda!' she shouted, in a great lather. 'It's happened again!'

laugh

have the last laugh ◄◄◄

If you **have the last laugh**, you make your critics or opponents look foolish or wrong, by becoming successful when they said that you would fail.

Singer Des O'Connor is expecting to have the last laugh on his critics by soaring to the top of the Christmas hit parade.

Instead of fading sadly into the background, she has had the last laugh, by going out in a spectacular blaze of scandal.

laundry

a laundry list ◄◄

If you have a large number or long list of things, you can say that you have **a laundry list** of them. This expression is used mainly in American English.

The president then went through a laundry list of proposals, some old, some new, which make up his agenda for American renewal.

This document is expected to set out a laundry list of reasons why shareholders should reject the bid.

laurels

look to your laurels

If you tell someone to **look to** their **laurels**, you are telling them to work hard or think seriously about what they are doing, in order to make sure that they continue to be successful and do not start to fail.

The City of London maintains a dominant role, but it must now look to its laurels.

The establishment of new technology across Europe (East as well as West) will force the Japanese to look to their laurels.

not rest on your laurels ◄◄

If you say that someone **is not resting on** their **laurels**, you mean that they do not rely on their previous successes and that they carry on working hard to make sure that they have continued success.

Earthwatch Europe is not resting on its laurels. As well as reacting to the proposals it receives from researchers, the organisation is also trying to stimulate research in areas it considers fruitful.

He never rested on his laurels. He continually evolved artistically because he had such an extremely open mind.

The trouble with all successful restaurants, however, is the tendency to rest on their laurels and stagnate.

law

the law of the jungle ◄

You use **the law of the jungle** to describe a situation where the normal rules or codes of civilized life do not exist, and so, for example, strength, power, and aggressiveness have more effect than moral codes and legal rights.

The question for the United Nations Security Council was whether to build civilised relations between states, or to live by the law of the jungle.

The streets are subject to the law of the jungle and policing has been entrusted to private law enforcement agencies.

a law unto yourself ◄◄

If you say that a person or organization is **a law unto** themselves, you mean that they behave in an independent way, ignoring laws, rules, or conventional ways of doing things.

When he goes about his work, he does it well but in an unconventional way. He is truly a law unto himself.

Most athletic departments are pretty much a law unto themselves – unaccountable in terms of where this money goes.

lay down the law ◄◄

If you say that a person in authority **lays down the law**, you mean that they tell people very forcefully and firmly what to do.

They were traditional parents, who believed in laying down the law for their children.

The Prime Minister laid down the law and said he would accept no weakening of the bill.

take the law into your own hands ◄◄◄

If you **take the law into** your **own hands**, you punish someone who you believe has done something wrong, even though you have no right to, and even if this means that you yourself break the law. You do this because you consider the person is not being punished properly by the usual authorities.

Ordinary people have apparently decided to take the law into their own hands, faced with what they see as the inability of law enforcement agencies to control a crime wave which has created unprecedented feelings of insecurity in the region.

He took the law into his own hands when his mother was mugged. He went out and attacked the man with a baseball bat.

lead

go down like a lead balloon
a lead balloon ◄

If you say that something **went down like a lead balloon**, you mean that it was completely unsuccessful and people did not like it at all.

A senior source said the memo had gone down like a lead balloon.

John Major's tub-thumping speech at the Guildhall on Monday night went down in the City like a lead balloon.

□ You can refer to something that is unsuccessful or unpopular as **a lead balloon**.

Truman knew that this cause was a lead balloon at the UN.

□ 'Lead' is pronounced with the same vowel sound as the word 'red'.

put lead in your pencil
have lead in your pencil

If someone says that something **will put lead in** a man's **pencil**, they are suggesting humorously that it will improve his sexual ability. If they say that he **has lead in** his **pencil**, they are praising his sexual ability.

These are informal and old-fashioned expressions, which are used in British English.

Steve worked his mouth around the tobacco and spat a brown spot into the snow. 'Puts lead in your pencil.'

Back then, he'd been blessed with amazing stamina and a lot of lead in his pencil.

□ 'Lead' is pronounced with the same vowel sound as the word 'red'.

swing the lead

If you accuse someone of **swinging the lead**, you are accusing them of pretending to be ill and not doing something they should be doing, such as going to work. This expression is used in British English.

There is no question of taking money away from those who are genuinely sick. It is a question of getting the right benefits to the right people, and we want to stop anyone swinging the lead.

□ 'Lead' is pronounced with the same vowel sound as the word 'red'.

leaf

take a leaf out of someone's book ◄◄

If you **take a leaf out of** someone's **book** or **take a leaf from** their **book**, you copy them and behave or do something in the same way as them, usually because they were successful when they acted in that way.

Some experts are now saying that we could usefully take a leaf out of the Americans' book. They take into consideration how well a shop is trading and fix the rent accordingly. This means there is more chance of keeping shops open in tough times.

If he wants a better rapport with the British public, it's high time he took a leaf out of Frank Bruno's book and started doing the media things – chat and game shows, even pantomimes.

New Zealand, taking a leaf from the German book, has pulled inflation down from 7.2 per cent in 1989 to 1 per cent last year.

turn over a new leaf ◄◄

If someone **has turned over a new leaf**, they have started to behave in a better or more acceptable way than previously. Compare **turn the page**; see **page**.

While Eddie has turned over a new leaf, his 31-year-old actor brother can still be spotted in the bars along Sunset Strip.

The military leader said he and the king have agreed to turn over a new leaf in their relations with one another.

leaps

in leaps and bounds
by leaps and bounds ◄◄

If something grows or progresses **in leaps**

and bounds or **by leaps and bounds**, it grows or progresses very rapidly. If someone improves **in leaps and bounds** or **by leaps and bounds**, they make rapid progress in something they are doing.

Once your child passes his second birthday, speech develops in leaps and bounds and the more you talk to him and involve him in what you do, the greater his vocabulary becomes.

The U.S. population grew by leaps and bounds.

He's improved as a player in leaps and bounds this season.

lease

a new lease of life
a new lease on life ◄◄◄

If someone or something is given **a new lease of life** or **a new lease on life**, something makes them successful once again or improves their condition. Words such as 'another', 'fresh', or 'second' are sometimes used instead of 'new'. The variations with 'of' are used only in British English; American English always uses 'on' instead.

The old oak table which is used for family breakfasts was another bargain, picked up for just £4 and subsequently given a new lease of life by Kim's mother.

After a career as a comedian, he found a new lease of life as an actor.

Although my weight hasn't changed much, swimming gave me a new lease on life.

T-shirts and hats can be given a fresh lease of life with glass beads.

leash

a longer leash

If someone is given **a longer leash**, another person allows them a lot of freedom to do what they want, rather than controlling them very strictly.

At the beginning of the 1992 campaign, Dan Quayle was given a longer leash than ever before.

If there is any sympathy in Congress for giving big banks a longer leash, that is only because letting them do more and different kinds of business is seen as one way of saving taxpayers from bailing many of them out of their current trouble.

on a short leash
on a tight leash ◄

If someone is kept **on a short leash**, another person controls them carefully and only allows them a small amount of freedom to do what they want. You can also say that someone is kept **on a tight leash**, or simply that they are kept **on a leash**.

Refusing to comment, the spokeswoman said: 'I am on a very short leash on this subject.'

The government strove to impress the country with its calm reasonableness and kept its troops on a tight leash.

He has demonstrated time and time again that he needs to be kept on a leash.

strain at the leash ◄

If you say that someone **is straining at the leash**, you are emphasizing that they are very eager to do things.

Most Labour delegates at Blackpool this week are straining at the leash, raring to go.

The players had better realise that we have enough youngsters straining at the leash to take their places if they don't do their jobs.

least

least said, soonest mended

If someone says **'least said, soonest mended'**, they mean that it is a good idea to say very little, because you might upset someone or make a situation worse if you say too much. This is an old-fashioned expression, which is used in British English.

'Say nothing. It's the only thing they can't hold against you.' 'Least said, soonest mended is what I always say,' nodded another. 'Especially in court.'

left

left, right, and centre
left and right ◄

You use **left, right, and centre** or **left and right** to emphasize that something is happening or being done a great deal. 'Left, right, and centre' is used in British English and 'left and right' is used in American English.

They're all expecting the state to pay out money left right and centre.

The Postal Service has been losing customers left and right to the alternative mail facilities.

Predictably, though, Taple is now threatening legal action left, right and centre.

leg

break a leg

People say **'break a leg'** to a performer who is about to go on stage as a way of wishing them good luck.

Jason sent Phillip a fax from the airport before Monday's show, with the greeting: 'Break a leg and enjoy yourself.'

get your leg over ◄

If someone **gets their leg over**, they have sex. This is a very informal expression, which is used in British English. Many people find it offensive.

They would say things like 'Have you got

your leg over yet?' or exclude me from the conversation saying it was 'men's talk'.

He told me how at least two ministers had, as he inelegantly put it, tried unsuccessfully to get a leg over.

☐ You can also refer to **a legover**.

Be your boyfriend? I can't be bothered to go through that caper. What I want's a legover, hello and goodbye.

give someone a leg up
get a leg up
have a leg up   ◄◄

If you **are given a leg up** or **get a leg up**, someone helps you to achieve something and become successful, especially by giving you an advantage that other people do not have. If you **have a leg up**, you have an advantage.

The mother seemed to think that her name had given her boy a leg up on the competition.

Two highly-favoured ministers, Peter Lloyd and Brian Mawhinney, get a leg up the political ladder with their appointment as Privy Counsellors.

I felt she had some kind of leg up on me – she had a firmer sense of purpose, a bouncier step, a more cheerful disposition.

not have a leg to stand on   ◄

If you say that someone **does not have a leg to stand on**, you are emphasizing that they are in a very weak position, for example because they are unable to prove a claim or statement they have made.

You'd never win. Our lawyers said you wouldn't have a leg to stand on.

I haven't got a leg to stand on. I had no witnesses.

pull someone's leg   ◄

If you **pull** someone's **leg**, you tease them about something, for example by telling them something which is not true.

Is he serious or just pulling our legs?

She was perpetually having her leg pulled over the frequency with which she went to the loo.

☐ You can refer to a joke like this as **a legpull**.

I never know what to say about this kind of painting anyway, still less how to explain its virtues to those who consider it a leg-pull.

talk the hind leg off a donkey

If you say that someone can **talk the hind leg off a donkey**, you are emphasizing that they are very talkative. This expression is used in British English.

He could talk the hind leg off a donkey. It took real perseverance to get through to him on the telephone.

legs
have legs

If you say that an idea, plan, or story **has legs**, you consider that it is likely to work or be true. This expression is used mainly in American English.

Mr Blucher was confident that his concept had legs, so he persisted and pressed Mr Cooper for a meeting.

In this instance the story might not have legs. But all media outlets would have been remiss if they had not followed the story through.

on your last legs   ◄

If you say that something or someone is **on** their **last legs**, you mean that they are no longer as useful, successful, or strong as they were and are about to fail altogether.

The long, heavy, dark-blue, striped towelling dressing-gown I've worn for years is on its last legs.

By the mid-1980s, the copper industry in the US was on its last legs.

leopard
a leopard does not change its spots   ◄

If you say that **a leopard does not change its spots** or **a leopard cannot change its spots**, you mean that it is not possible for someone bad or unpleasant to change and become good and pleasant. This expression is used mainly in British English.

Women who believe they have tamed a 'wild' man and announce their achievement to the world will always end up being publicly humiliated. The cliché that leopards don't change their spots still happens to be true.

It only goes to show how this racist leopard has in no way changed his spots.

letter
a dead letter   ◄

If you say that a law or agreement is **a dead letter**, you mean that people do not pay any attention to it, although it still exists.

In this conflict, international humanitarian law is a dead letter. Unacceptable practices are going on.

This treaty would be a dead letter in Britain, due to the opt-out clauses.

the letter of the law   ◄◄

If you say that someone keeps to **the letter of the law**, you mean that they act according to what is actually written in the law, rather than according to the moral principles on which it is based. You usually use this expression to show disapproval.

The Home Office stuck to the letter of the law over the definition of dependants.

Michael Brower says such transactions violate the spirit, if not the letter, of the law.

to the letter　　　◄◄

If you follow instructions, rules, or advice **to the letter**, you carry them out exactly in every detail.

Be very careful with this stuff, it can be dangerous if it isn't handled properly so follow the instructions to the letter.

Even if that international agreement is followed to the letter, the ozone layer won't recover fully until the year 2060.

level

on the level　　　◄

Someone who is **on the level** is honest and truthful. Something that is **on the level** is true or honest.

Wait a minute, is this guy on the level or not?

I can offer you something better than this, Trish. And all on the level.

licence

a licence to print money　　　◄

If you describe a commercial activity as **a licence to print money**, you disapprove of the fact that it allows people to get a lot of money with little effort or responsibility. This expression is used mainly in British English.

The Edinburgh Festival is something of a licence to print money for those renting their homes to groups of performers.

Under this Government the privatised utilities have become a licence to print money at the expense of the consumer.

But is owning a sporting goods store a license to print money?

□ The noun 'licence' is spelled 'license' in American English.

lid

blow the lid off　　　◄

To **blow the lid off** a difficult or dangerous situation or problem means to reveal its true nature which has previously been hidden. This expression is used mainly in journalism.

'The Knowledge' is a new documentary series blowing the lid off music business scandals.

You'll be terribly disappointed, however, if you think that Altman blows the lid off Hollywood.

keep the lid on something
put the lid on something　　　◄◄◄

To **keep the lid on** or **put the lid on** a particular situation or problem means to keep its true nature hidden, or to control it and stop it becoming worse.

But I understand that Murray was desperately trying to keep the lid on a potential scandal.

The question is whether Walesa can provide the goods in keeping the lid on a population which has still got to face very severe economic cutbacks.

We want the public to assist us in putting a lid on crime.

put the tin lid on something

You say that something **puts the tin lid** on a bad situation when it is a final unpleasant event in a series. This is an old-fashioned expression used in British English.

Next day, to put the tin lid on things, a hospital appointment letter for Jane was forwarded from the clinic.

take the lid off
lift the lid off　　　◄

To **take the lid off** or **lift the lid off** a situation or problem means to reveal its true nature which has previously been hidden. These expressions are used mainly in journalism.

His most recent novel, Brightness Falls, takes the lid off Manhattan in the dizzy days before Wall Street's Black Monday in 1987.

People often do feel worse initially, because therapy is taking the lid off problems.

He lifts the lid off Crystal Palace football club with a number of startling revelations.

lie

live a lie
a living lie　　　◄◄

If someone **is living a lie**, they are living in a way which they feel to be dishonest and false, for example because they are doing something which no longer seems meaningful to them.

But now Jackie, who had been so open with her husband, began to keep a large part of her life a secret from him. She started to live a lie.

My mother never told my father the truth about me. We've been living a lie all this time, and now she has taken me from him.

□ You can also talk about **a living lie**.

Juan Carlos is wide-eyed, as if realizing this ceremony was like his whole life now, a living lie.

nail a lie

If you **nail a lie**, you show that it is definitely not true. This expression is used in British English, especially in journalism.

Top designer Calvin Klein is one of those helping to finally nail the lie that young is best. He has just appointed 40-year-old Lisa Taylor as his new top model.

a white lie　　　◄

If you tell **a white lie**, you say something which is untrue, often in order to protect someone or to avoid hurting someone's feelings.

The issue here for me was whether doctors are justified in telling these little white lies in order to benefit the patient.

He was not adept at telling white lies. 'Gretchen has come down with a touch of the flu,' he had explained to Mrs. Keely.

I believe that this is a case where a little white lie is really more appropriate than the truth.

life

can't do something to save your life

If you say that you **can't do** something **to save** your **life**, you are emphasizing that you cannot do it at all. This expression is used mainly in spoken English.

I'm never nervous at exams but I can't study to save my life.

He can't sing to save his life but he is a good guitarist.

fight for your life
a fight for life   ◄◄◄

If someone is very seriously ill or injured and they are in danger of dying, you can say that they **are fighting for** their **life**. You can also say that an organization or country **is fighting for** its **life** when it is in danger of failing or being defeated.

A boy aged 15 was fighting for his life last night but two younger children were said to be out of danger.

A toddler is fighting for life after being run over by a boy who was playing in his father's car.

An ancient Scottish university institution is fighting for its life.

□ You can also talk about **a fight for life**.

Mary won a desperate fight for life but was left paralysed from the waist down.

□ If a politician is in serious difficulty and it seems likely that their career may end, journalists sometimes say that they **are fighting for** their political **life**.

Mr Major had hoped to spend this week celebrating his election victory but now he is fighting for his political life.

frighten the life out of someone
scare the life out of someone   ◄

If you say that someone or something **frightens the life out of** you or **scares the life out of** you, you are emphasizing that they frighten you a great deal.

Their only chance was to run alongside when the train was moving, throw their gear on and jump on when they could. It used to frighten the life out of me because so many of them fell and just missed going under the wheels.

Further tests revealed that three of my veins

had furred up and I needed triple bypass surgery. It scared the life out of me.

get a life   ◄

You tell someone to **get a life** to express scorn, criticism, or ridicule of them, for example because they never do anything interesting, or because they are being unrealistic and stupid, or because you want them to go away.

It seems that young people in Cheltenham would rather wallow in their pints than try and make their lives a touch more exciting. Wake up, Cheltenham, and get a life.

It was six o'clock in the evening. I was still in my pajamas. Nichole looked at me, said she thought I was deteriorating, and suggested I get a life.

This is silly, you've pursued this much too long. Get a life, Joan.

the life and soul of the party
the life of the party   ◄◄

If you refer to someone as **the life and soul of the party**, you mean that they are very lively and entertaining on social occasions, and are good at mixing with people. You can replace 'party' with other nouns. This form of the expression is used in British English; in American English, the form is **the life of the party**.

She was having a very enjoyable time and was clearly the life and soul of the party.

He gives the impression of having been the life and soul of the campus.

Murray's abilities to turn a wallflower into the life of the party began with himself. A tall and gawky teenager, Murray said he gained confidence after he learned to dance.

life is a bowl of cherries

If someone says '**life is a bowl of cherries**', they are saying that they think life is full of pleasure and enjoyment. This expression is often used negatively to comment on an unpleasant or difficult situation.

'He had an impish sense of fun and so much zest,' says one admirer. 'To him, life was a bowl of cherries.'

Life's not exactly a bowl of cherries when you're an international champ.

live the life of Riley

If you say that someone is **living the life of Riley**, you mean that they are having a very enjoyable time because they have no worries about money or work. This expression is sometimes used to show disapproval or envy.

He was living the life of Riley, enjoying holidays in Italy, weekend breaks in mid-Wales and trips to the theatre, while we had barely enough to eat.

It was like paradise. It was just like, you know, living the life of Riley.

put your life in someone's hands
your life is in someone's hands   ◄

If you **put** your **life in** someone's **hands**, you put yourself in a situation where they have complete control over what happens to you. You can also say that your **life is in** their **hands** or that they **hold** your **life in** their **hands**.

After all these years, do you take me for a fool? What makes you think I would put my life in your hands?

The realization that another woman's life may be in my hands is a frightening and humbling one.

You feel a responsibility to people because sometimes you're holding their life in your hands.

risk life and limb   ◄

If someone **risks life and limb,** they do something very dangerous that may cause them to die or be seriously injured.

He is not prepared to risk life and limb on this dangerous track to clinch the title.

Hang gliding no longer deserves its reputation as a sport for reckless idiots who get a thrill risking life and limb by leaping off cliffs and mountains.

take your life in your hands   ◄

If you **take** your **life in** your **hands** when you do something, you take a lot of risks when you do it.

Nationalised industries are set to be sold off solely for the benefit of the Prime Minister and his close cronies, and anyone who opposes this is taking his or her life in their hands if they dare speak up.

A rider who does not know the road takes his life in his hands by cycling in the dark.

light

give the green light   ◄◄◄

If a plan or action **is given the green light** or **is given a green light**, someone in authority says that it can be carried out. Verbs such as 'get' and 'receive' are sometimes used instead of 'give'.

Despite local planning opposition he has finally been given the green light to develop a terrace of 11 derelict houses he owns in South Kensington.

I've got a bunch more songs, and if I can get the green light from the powers that be, I'd like to go straight back in and record some more.

Is that a green light for interest-rate cuts or a red one?

in the cold light of day   ◄

If you think about a problem, feeling, or event **in the cold light of day**, you think about it some time later and in a calmer or more practical way than was possible at the

time it happened. Words such as 'dawn' and 'morning' are sometimes used instead of 'day'.

He has to sit down in the cold light of day and analyse what needs to be done to prevent the club from being relegated.

Because these things are said at a moment of heightened passion, we feel self-conscious about them in the cold light of calm reflection.

a leading light   ◄◄◄

If you say that someone is **a leading light** of an organization or campaign, you mean that they are considered to be one of the most important, active, and successful people in it. This expression is used mainly in British English.

He is a leading light in the just launched campaign to rid football of racism.

She was the leading light of all the nuclear protests in the area. She was a skilled campaigner, veteran of many a confrontation with the law.

light as a feather   ◄

You can say that someone or something is as **light as a feather** to emphasize that they weigh very little.

'Put me down,' I said. 'I'm too heavy.' 'Light as a feather,' he retorted, ignoring my request.

It was a monstrous machine as large as the Albert Hall and as light as a feather.

the light at the end of the tunnel   ◄◄◄

If you refer to **the light at the end of the tunnel,** you are referring to something which gives you hope about the future and for the end of a difficult or unpleasant situation.

After horrific times we are seeing light at the end of the tunnel.

People feel hopeless. They don't see any light at the end of the tunnel.

Suddenly there seemed to be light at the end of the recessionary tunnel.

light dawns   ◄

If you say that **light dawns** on someone, you mean that they suddenly realize or understand something that they should have realized or understood before.

'Oh!' she said, as if the light had finally dawned on her. 'I'm on the wrong floor, huh?'

'You know her last name?' 'Ramsey. Mona Ramsey.' The light dawned. Bobbi giggled at her own stupidity. 'Oh, gee,' she said, 'We never call her that!'

out like a light

If someone is **out like a light**, they are very deeply asleep. If someone goes **out like a light**, they fall asleep very quickly.

Dad gently closed the door again. 'She's out like a light,' I heard him whisper to my anxious mother.

When I had got him into the cab of my vehicle, he went out like a light.

see the light ◄◄◄

If someone **sees the light**, they come to understand or agree with something, especially after a long period when they have not understood or agreed with it. This expression is sometimes used about people who suddenly start believing in God.

'People these days realise that they don't have to put up with discrimination,' says Jill Chesworth. But male bosses have been slow to see the light.

Christianity taught him values which the West preached but largely ignored in practice. But he had seen the light and urged every one to share it with him.

see the light of day: 1
see the light ◄◄

If you say that something **sees the light of day**, you mean that it becomes known by or available to a large number of people. You often use this expression to suggest that difficulties have to be overcome before this can happen.

This book might never have seen the light of day without the enthusiasm, support, and friendship of my editor, Daniel Bial.

It's highly unlikely that any of this proof will ever see the light of day.

☐ You can also say that something **sees the light**.

All this may change with the news that Christopher Isherwood's diaries are now at last to see the light.

Mr Genscher's 'idea', it emerges, first saw the light and met with British approval at a meeting of the West European Union.

see the light of day: 2

People sometimes use **see the light of day** as a way of saying that someone is born.

The population in Africa is growing faster than anywhere else in the world, which means that tens of millions of new souls are seeing the light of day there each year.

lightning

lightning does not strike twice ◄

You say that **lightning does not strike twice** when you want to say that someone who has been exceptionally lucky or unlucky is unlikely to have the same good or bad luck again. You can also say that **lightning strikes twice** or that **lightning strikes again** when someone actually does have the same good or bad luck again.

Observers reckon he will be very lucky to repeat the performance. Lightning rarely strikes in the same place twice, particularly in big business.

Keith Curle reckons there's no reason why history can't repeat itself. Curle says 'Why shouldn't lightning strike twice?'

Then, several years later, lightning struck again. Her other son Stephen died suddenly at the age of 13.

a lightning rod for something ◄

If you say that someone is **a lightning rod for** something such as public anger or criticism, you mean that they are the person who is naturally blamed or criticized by people, although there are other people who are responsible. This expression is used mainly in American English.

Writer-director Spike Lee is a lightning rod for controversy.

His proposal contains no new money for education, and it's made the governor a lightning rod for parents' pent-up frustration.

He told the Palermo court he was an innocent lightning rod for Italy's many crime problems.

like lightning
like greased lightning ◄

You can use **like lightning** or **like greased lightning** to emphasize that something moves extremely quickly or happens very suddenly and unexpectedly.

I ran across that room like lightning and pushed back the curtain.

By comparison with the budget turmoils of the past few years, Washington has moved like greased lightning.

The idea struck like lightning.

lights

the lights are on but nobody is at home

If you say of someone that **the lights are on but nobody is at home**, you think that although they seem to be normal or satisfactory, they are in fact very stupid or useless.

According to Mark Harrington, many projects are insufficiently co-ordinated or thought through: 'You get the feeling that the lights are on but no one's at home.'

lily

gild the lily

If you say that someone is **gilding the lily**, you mean that they are trying to improve something which is already very good, and so what they are doing is unnecessary.

Here in Europe I'm gilding the lily. There they really need advice.

If Kate picked up higher than average claims, the Tax Office would knock on the door and audit 10 per cent of the tax agent's practice. Then if enough clients blamed the agent for 'gilding the lily', the agent could lose his or her licence.

limb

out on a limb
on a limb ◄◄◄

If you go **out on a limb**, you do something risky or extreme, which puts you in a position of weakness. If you are left **out on a limb** or are **on a limb**, you are left in a position of weakness without any help or support.

It seems to me that you fear change and would prefer to stay in your present situation even though it seems to be tiresome, rather than go out on a limb and try something completely new.

No company wants to be the first to put its rates up. The companies who have tried have found themselves out on a limb.

She felt on a limb at the ministry and quit the government in October 1990.

tear someone limb from limb

If someone threatens to **tear** you **limb from limb**, they are extremely angry with you and threaten you with violence.

Police were lucky they found him before I did because they would have been arresting me. I would have torn him limb from limb.

limits

off limits ◄◄◄

If an area is **off limits** to someone, they are not allowed to go there. If a thing is **off limits** to someone, they are not allowed to use it or do it.

The area was kept off-limits to foreign journalists until early this year.

The ideal is to have one room that's off-limits for the kids.

Many of the biggest and most desirable trees in those forests would soon be off limits to the timber industry.

line

all the way down the line
all along the line ◄

If you say that something happens **all the way down the line**, you mean that it happens at every stage of a situation or activity, or that it includes all the people or things involved in a situation or activity. This expression has several variations. For example, you can also say that something happens **right down the line** or **all along the line**. Compare **down the line**.

It is the British government that has fought for reform all the way down the line.

Republicans differed right down the line on what the proper responses were.

The survey shows support for the President's decision all along the line, including a willingness to commit American troops into battle.

along the line
down the line ◄◄◄

If something happens somewhere **along the line** or **down the line**, it happens during the course of a situation or activity, often at a point that cannot be exactly identified. Compare **down the line**.

And then somewhere along the line I looked at what was really happening.

Admittedly every parent makes mistakes along the line.

They feel that something was wrong somewhere down the line.

the bottom line ◄◄◄

In a discussion or argument, if you describe one particular point as **the bottom line**, you mean that it is the most important and fundamental part of what you are discussing.

The bottom line is that the great majority of our kids are physically unfit.

At times there is some fairly intense anger between us. But the bottom line is he's a real nice guy; he's sensitive and I don't want to hurt him.

□ You can use **bottom-line** before a noun.

This is a cracking good story, and that is the bottom-line criterion for any novel.

cross the line ◄◄

If you say that someone **has crossed the line**, you mean that they have started behaving in an unacceptable way, for example by getting involved in something extreme or anti-social.

Congress and the public were not informed about the decision to cross the line from defense to preparation for war.

The show's pretty outrageous, but I don't think it crosses the line.

down the line: 1 ◄◄

You can talk about something happening further **down the line** when it happens at a later date. You can talk about something happening a long way **down the line** when it happens at a much later date. Compare **all the way down the line** and **along the line**.

Whether that happens further down the line we cannot say.

He thought the resumption of military cooperation was still, as he put it, a long way down the line.

down the line: 2 ◄

If you talk about something happening a particular number of years or months **down the line**, you are talking about its happening after that amount of time. **Down the road** means the same.

About five to six months down the line I got a call from Steve saying he had something for me to work on.

So 25 years down the line, you look back and there's a sense that it was all better back then.

Two years down the line things have changed.

draw a line under something ◄

If you say that something **draws a line under** a bad situation which has now ended, you mean that it enables the situation to be considered as over, so that people can start again or continue with things more productively.

He said the document draws a line under the painful chapters of our past and clears the way for a new beginning.

Let's deal with these proposals so we can draw the line under the directives and go forward to the next phase.

draw the line ◄◄◄

If you talk about knowing where to **draw the line**, you are talking about knowing at what point an activity or situation stops being reasonable and starts to be unacceptable.

It is difficult for charities to know where to draw the line between acceptable and unacceptable sources of finance.

Where do you draw the line about who the press can and can't investigate? Can they still be allowed to say things about pop stars?

☐ If you say that you would **draw the line** at a particular activity, you mean that you would not do it, because you disapprove of it or because it is so extreme.

I'll do virtually anything – although I think I'd draw the line at running naked across the set!

I have to draw the line somewhere. I refuse to go in for spiritualism.

a fine line
a thin line
a narrow line ◄◄◄

If you say that there is **a fine line** between two different activities or situations, you mean that there is, in fact, a point at which it is difficult to distinguish between them. You often say this when one activity or situation is acceptable, and the other is not. You can also talk about **a thin line** or **a narrow line**.

There is a fine line between being nicely looked after and being fussed over too much – so don't overdo it.

A new exhibition explores the fine line between genius and insanity.

There is a thin line between being a good player and being one of the best.

It is a very narrow line between being over-intrusive and offering enough care and hospitality.

☐ If you say that someone is walking or treading **a fine line** between two activities or situations, you mean that their behaviour is acceptable, but that they are very close to the point at which it would become unacceptable. You can also talk about walking **a thin line** or **a narrow line**.

At present we are walking a very fine line between getting away with it and having a very serious incident.

He has made his fortune treading the thin line between art and porn.

get a line on someone
have a line on someone ◄

If you **get a line on** someone or something, you get some information about them. If you **have a line on** someone or something, you have some information about them. These expressions are used mainly in American English.

We've been trying to get a line on you, and the more we try, the less we find.

I really don't have a line on what's going to happen yet.

in the firing line
out of the firing line ◄◄◄

If you are **in the firing line**, you are in a position where you are likely to be criticized or attacked. **In the line of fire** means the same.

Governor-designate Eddie George is in the firing line of the committee's criticisms.

Even if your child seems to be very easy-going, there comes a time in his life when he begins to test the influence he has over others and, as parents, you are first in the firing line.

☐ If you are taken **out of the firing line**, you are removed from a position where you are likely to be criticized or attacked.

He was a caring man, concerned for his client. He wanted her to first leave home, to get her out of the firing line before applying for any court orders.

☐ **In the firing line** is often used literally to talk about the fact that someone is in the way of people who are firing guns, and therefore likely to be shot.

in the front line
on the front line ◄◄

If someone is **in the front line** or **on the front line**, they have a very important part to play in achieving or defending something.

Those in the front line of the British economy are united in believing that Britain must remain a full playing member of the EU.

Local authorities of course are in the front-line of providing help, but they're starved of resources due to the government's policy.

Record retailers are on the front line and if they don't feel comfortable selling our product, then we're in big trouble.

in the line of fire

If you are **in the line of fire**, you are in a position where you are likely to be criticized or attacked. **In the firing line** means the same.

All very well to say that, when you're not in the line of fire like me.

☐ This expression has several variations. For example, you can talk about removing someone **from the line of fire**.

Yeltsin took steps last week to remove them from the line of fire.

☐ **In the line of fire** is often used literally to talk about the fact that someone is in the way of people who are firing guns, and therefore likely to be shot.

not your line of country

If you say that something is **not your line of country**, you mean that it is not a subject that you know a great deal about, or one in which you are very interested. This is a fairly old-fashioned expression, which is used in British English.

I am rather ignorant on this matter – it is not quite my line of country.

At first sight, Buchan is straying out of his usual line of country.

on line   ◄◄

If a plan or a project comes **on line**, it begins to operate fully. If it is **on line**, it is operating fully. This expression is used mainly in American English; the usual British expression is **on stream**.

Boeing officials say the charter plane was the first 767 to be lost since the popular model came on line in 1982.

The Bulgarian Government, faced with a major energy crisis, is eagerly waiting for another reactor to go on line.

We expect to be on line as export numbers build up with a capacity to produce tens of thousands of tonnes of feed.

out of line
way out of line

If you tell someone that they are **out of line** or **way out of line**, you mean that they are completely wrong to say or do a particular thing. These expressions are used mainly in spoken American English. Compare **step out of line**.

Addressing a fellow officer like that is out of line, and I won't stand for it, hear me?

Do you think that I would be out of line to be wondering whether you were really gonna be a fair judge to me?

It was clear to all concerned that Cross was way out of line.

put something on the line: 1
lay something on the line
be on the line   ◄◄◄

If you **put** or **lay** something such as your reputation or your job **on the line**, you do something which causes you to risk losing it.

He had put his career on the line and I wasn't prepared to allow what he had done to be diminished in significance.

Don't put our friendship on the line like this, Martin.

Rob Reiner, the director, laid his reputation on the line when he cast her in the film. But he had no doubts about her right to the part.

☐ You can say that you **put** yourself **on the line** or **lay** yourself **on the line** when you risk something such as your reputation or your job.

Ferguson has to take the responsibility for everything, and in that sense, he did put himself on the line.

They admit they are laying themselves on the line.

☐ You can also say that something such as your reputation or your job **is on the line**.

Using a small, one-man business can also be a good idea. You are likely to get more care and attention because his reputation is on the line.

put something on the line: 2
lay it on the line   ◄

If someone **puts** or **lays** their heart or their emotions **on the line**, they speak truthfully and directly about their feelings. You can also say that someone **puts** or **lays** himself or herself **on the line**.

You have to put your emotions on the line with love, but he cannot do this.

There's incredible vulnerability in it. He's really laying himself on the line.

☐ If someone **lays** or **puts it on the line**, they say what needs to be said truthfully and directly. If someone **lays** or **puts everything on the line**, they say everything that needs to be said, without leaving anything out.

He said he was shattered at what he had to tell me and it shouldn't have happened to me. Then he laid it on the line and said without treatment I had only three months to live.

Mr. Dambar had planned to march straight over to the trailer and lay everything on the line.

put your neck on the line
put your ass on the line   ◄

If you **put** your **neck on the line**, you do something although it is risky and you may lose your reputation or money as a result. You can also say that your **neck is on the line**.

Gere put his neck on the line to make

Sommersby. It was a gamble, both in terms of his public image – would fans accept the American gigolo as a husband and a father in a costume drama and his wallet, as he served as one of the film's executive producers.

Our necks are on the line, but we don't care.

☐ In informal American English, you can say that someone **puts** their **ass on the line**. Many people consider this form of the expression offensive.

I appreciate your putting your ass on the line.

shoot a line

You say that someone **is shooting a line** when you think that what they are saying is exaggerated, untrue, or difficult to believe. This expression is used in British English.

He'd been looking for new blood for his office in Vienna. That was the line he shot, though knowing him as I did I'm sure he had a more personal, ulterior motive.

sign on the dotted line
sign on the line ◀◀

If you **sign on the dotted line**, you formally agree to something by signing an official document. This expression is often used to mean simply that you make a firm commitment about something.

Once you sign on the dotted line you are committed to that property.

I wanted to be on the safe side before I signed on the dotted line.

☐ You can also say that someone **signs on the line**.

He signed on the line and can only blame himself.

☐ If you say that someone's name is needed **on the dotted line** or **on the line**, you mean that you want them to formally agree to something by signing an official document.

He went to see Malcolm's widow, Betty, too; he needed her name on the dotted line.

step out of line ◀◀◀

If someone **steps out of line**, they do something that they should not do or they behave in an unacceptable way. Other verbs such as 'get' can be used instead of 'step'. Compare **out of line**.

The government should empower the Police Services Commission to be tougher with officers who step out of line.

Values and traditions were accepted and agreed by everyone. If you stepped out of line, you knew what to expect.

Very few people dared to step out of line – you never knew who was watching.

Boy, if you get out of line you're in trouble.

toe the line ◀◀◀

If you refuse to **toe the line**, you refuse to

behave in the way that people in authority expect you to behave. If you **toe the line**, you behave in the way they expect.

The new legislation could force them out of business if they don't toe the line.

Journalists who refuse to toe the line will have to be sacked.

☐ You often use a word before 'line' to indicate who the people in authority are.

He was sacked for not toeing the Party line.

During the early 1980s he toed the Government line with unseemly vigour in an attempt to regain favour.

☐ Some people use the verb 'tow' instead of 'toe' in this expression, but it is generally considered incorrect.

lines

on the right lines
along the right lines ◀

If someone is **on the right lines** or is proceeding **along the right lines**, they are behaving in a way which is likely to result in success. This expression is used in British English. **On the right track** means the same.

Sometimes all you really require is just a friendly voice to tell you that you are on the right lines.

We are, it seems, proceeding along roughly the right lines with government action encouraging more efficient engines, while keeping an eye on developing alternatives.

☐ You can also use this expression to suggest that someone is almost, but not completely, managing to achieve the required result.

The treatment offered so far has been along the right lines, but not successful in curing the condition completely.

read between the lines ◀◀◀

If you **read between the lines**, you understand what someone really means, or what is really happening in a situation, even though it is not stated openly.

If one reads between the lines of their public statements, one is left with the impression that they're just pretending to investigate and that the decision to go ahead with mining has already been made.

He was reluctant to go into details, but reading between the lines it appears that the Bank of England has vetoed any idea of a merger between British banks.

☐ You can also talk about the message **between the lines**.

He didn't give a reason, but I sensed something between the lines.

Mr Major's speech seemed hostile to the idea of a single currency. Yet, between the lines, there was much to suggest that he is not against it for ever.

link

a weak link
a weak link in the chain ◄◄◄

If you describe someone or something as **a weak link** or **a weak link in the chain**, you mean that they are an unreliable part of a system, and because of them the whole system may fail.

It was automatically assumed that Edward would be the weak link in the partnership.

The federally appointed auditors may have identified a weak link in the chain of rules governing bookkeeping by thrifts.

☐ People sometimes say that a system **is only as strong as** its **weakest link**.

A rail system is only as strong as its weakest link, as any commuter trapped behind a broken-down train can testify.

lion

fight like a lion

If you say that someone **fights like a lion**, you are emphasizing that they fight bravely. Verbs such as 'battle' and 'defend' are sometimes used instead of 'fight'.

She would have fought like a lion to protect her son.

To win, Scotland must score goals. To draw, they must defend like lions.

the lion's share ◄◄◄

If you get **the lion's share** of something, you get the largest part of it, leaving very little for others.

Not the least of the government's hopes for the coming competition is that Chinese athletes win the lion's share of the medals.

While Gladys absorbed the lion's share of their mother's attention, Mary and her two younger brothers revelled in unconditional freedom.

Defence has taken the lion's share of this year's budget.

put your head into the lion's mouth

If you **put** your **head into the lion's mouth**, you deliberately place yourself in a dangerous or difficult situation. **Walk into the lion's den** means the same.

Put your head in the lion's mouth and just say 'I don't know what the hell is going on.'

walk into the lion's den
Daniel in the lion's den ◄◄

If you **walk into the lion's den**, you deliberately place yourself in a dangerous or difficult situation. Other verbs can be used instead of 'walk'. **Put** your **head into the lion's mouth** means the same.

With the confidence of a man who believes that he has done no wrong, the Minister last night walked into the lion's den of his press ac-

cusers, *looked them in the eye, and fought back.*

The talking is finally over for Prime Minister John Major. At exactly 8.30 this morning he steps into the political lions' den to face the men who want to turn Europe into a super state run by the Brussels bureaucrats.

☐ People also say that they feel like **Daniel in the lion's den** when they are in a dangerous or difficult situation and feel very alone and nervous. This expression comes from a story in the Bible.

When I first went in the hostility from some sections of the newsroom was palpable. I felt rather like Daniel in the lion's den. Some people were really nice and really supportive. But a lot of the men were very hostile towards me as an openly gay man.

lions

throw someone to the lions

If someone **throws** you **to the lions**, they allow you to be criticized severely or treated roughly, and they do not try to protect you. **Throw** someone **to the wolves** means the same.

Tanya isn't sure exactly why she's been thrown to the lions. She traces it back to quotes she made about the business that were reproduced out of context.

The mystique of the film star has been steadily eroded over the years by an increasingly inquisitive press. And so Hollywood, in its desperate need to make money in a world which no longer worships the cinema, has thrown its stars to the lions.

lip

button your lip
button it

If you **button** your **lip**, you keep silent about something although you would really like to speak.

He had the grace and good sense to button his lip, even though this clearly caused him personal pain.

As I enter his sitting room I laugh involuntarily, and am met with an impatient glare. I hastily button my lip.

☐ If you tell someone to **button it** or **button** their **lip**, you are telling them rudely to be quiet.

'What have I done to deserve this?' 'Just button it, Park,' the Chief said.

One critic declared 'If anyone needs to get his attitude right, it is him. For a start, he should button his lip.'

pay lip service to something
give lip service to something ◄◄◄

If you say that someone **pays lip service** or

gives **lip service** to an idea, you are being critical of them because they appear to be in favour of it, but are not doing anything to support it.

Nearly all Western manufacturers now pay lip-service to Japanese management techniques.

These agreements give lip service to money going back to the people. But there are no specific amounts or shares or even a formula for how it would be determined.

☐ You can also just talk about **lip service**.

All the talk about nation-building is pure lip-service, because people who are selfish will never join with others to build the nation and preserve the good welfare of others.

a stiff upper lip ◄◄◄

If someone is keeping **a stiff upper lip**, they hide their emotions and do not let other people see what they are feeling. You can also say that someone is keeping their **upper lip stiff**.

I shared my feelings with no one because I had always believed in keeping a stiff upper lip, crying in private, and putting on my best face for family and friends.

His pathetic attempt to maintain a stiff upper lip failed.

Lady Spender, speaking from her house near Avignon, was keeping her upper lip commendably stiff.

☐ You can also refer to the attitude or behaviour of people who do not like to show their emotions as **the stiff upper lip**.

Another problem is the British stiff upper lip which prevents many patients from asking for painkillers for fear of appearing weak and cowardly.

lips

lick your lips
lick your chops ◄

If someone is looking forward eagerly to a future event, you can say that they **are licking** their **lips**.

His home supporters licked their lips in anticipation of the first Scottish-born winner since Tommy Armour in 1931.

Peter says the Government may collapse. It looks as if he's waiting to pounce. You can almost see him licking his lips.

☐ In informal English, you can say that someone **licks** their **chops**.

After hearing the president's plan for economic recovery, they were licking their chops.

on someone's lips: 1 ◄◄

If you say that something is **on** people's **lips**, you mean that a lot of people are talking about it and seem to be interested in it.

Unification was the word on everybody's lips.

The question on most people's lips was not whether there would be war but when it would it break out.

A new word was on the lips of foreign companies and governments: privatisation.

on someone's lips: 2 ◄◄

If a question or comment is **on** your **lips**, you want to ask or say it or you are in the process of asking or saying it.

The question had been on my lips the whole time. 'What has happened to her?' The priest smiled. He guessed it was Belinda I was asking about. 'She's safe,' he said.

He stopped in the dressing room beside their bedroom, hung his coat over the corner chair, his apology already on his lips.

read someone's lips ◄

If someone tells you to **read** their **lips**, they are telling you to believe and trust what they are saying.

Mr Bush won the White House in 1988 thanks, in large part, to his now infamous pledge 'read my lips: no new taxes'.

someone's lips are sealed
seal someone's lips ◄

If you say that your **lips are sealed**, you mean you will keep a secret that someone has told you.

As for anything told to me in confidence, well, my lips are sealed.

'The Player' is worth seeing for its deeply funny finale alone but my lips are firmly sealed on that.

☐ You can also say that someone has **sealed lips**.

The leading players in the story, like John Aspinall, refused point-blank to talk to him about the murder. Elsewhere he met sealed lips and a wall of silence.

☐ If someone or something **seals** your **lips**, they prevent you from talking about a particular subject.

'Did Nolan ever use a green van?' he asked, but the switch back to business and away from salacious gossip seemed to effectively seal the foreman's lips.

litmus

a litmus test ◄◄◄

If you say that something is **a litmus test** of the quality or success of a particular thing, you mean that it is an effective and conclusive way of proving it or measuring it. This expression is used mainly in journalism.

The election is a crucial litmus test of your policies of increased urban density and you will soon appreciate the political cost of experimenting with the legitimate housing expectations of Australians.

The success of wind power represents a litmus test for renewable energy.

live

live and breathe something ◄

If you say that someone **lives and breathes** a particular subject or activity, you are emphasizing that they are extremely enthusiastic about it.

'She might change her mind about what she wants to do.' 'I doubt it. She's fifteen now, and she's lived and breathed theatre since she was six.'

Williams lived and breathed motor racing.

☐ You can include other verbs in this expression.

When you play for Manchester United, you have to live, eat, and breathe football 24 hours a day.

As finals approached, I lived, breathed, and dreamed art and literature.

lives

have nine lives

If you say that someone **has nine lives,** you mean that they keep managing to get out of difficult or dangerous situations without being hurt or harmed. This expression is sometimes used to suggest surprise that they have survived so long.

But at the back of my mind I was certain that one day my nine lives would run out and I would be caught – or worse.

I think this is probably going to be the end, although he has shown he is a political cat with far more than nine lives.

☐ This expression comes from the saying **a cat has nine lives,** which people use to say that cats seem to survive a lot of very dangerous situations or events.

loaf

half a loaf is better than none

If you say that **half a loaf is better than none,** you mean that it is better to take what you can get, even if it is very little, than to risk having nothing at all. Other words can be used instead of 'loaf' and 'none'.

Leeds are now a point behind Manchester United, who have a game in hand. Their manager said: 'Half a loaf is better than none. We'll just have to get on with it.'

I'm very disappointed that all we have in the form of test matches is just one solitary test, but half a loaf is better than no loaf, and we are happy that at least we are getting this test.

'I hate it when they dry up after only half a story.' 'Let's get this lot signed before she changes her mind,' said Dave. 'Half a story's better than no story at all.'

lock

lock, stock, and barrel ◄◄

You use **lock, stock, and barrel** to emphasize that you do something completely or include every part of something.

It would have been much easier for us to have shut the business down lock, stock and barrel, and to have saved our cash and not paid a dividend.

He has moved down from the north-east, lock, stock and barrel.

log

easy as falling off a log
simple as falling off a log

If you say that something is as **easy as falling off a log,** you are emphasizing that it is very easy to do. You can also say it is as **simple as falling off a log** or **like falling off a log**.

She's just the sort of woman who could cook a four-course dinner for 12 while singing all of Fauré's Requiem, and making it look to the rest of the world as easy as falling off a log.

The band had only been together for a year when they got signed to Epic. 'Getting signed was like falling off a log,' they said.

loggerheads

at loggerheads ◄◄◄

If one person or group is **at loggerheads** with another, they strongly disagree about something.

The European Community has been at loggerheads with America and other farm-goods exporters, which want big cuts in farm subsidies.

Social workers and doctors are at loggerheads over how well the new system will work.

Trevor and his estranged wife Becky ended up at loggerheads – this time having a shouting match on the doorstep.

loins

gird your loins ◄

If you say that someone **is girding** their **loins** or **girding up** their **loins,** you mean that they are preparing themselves to deal with a difficult or stressful situation, especially by preparing themselves mentally or psychologically. This is a literary expression, which is now used mainly in journalism.

Conservation organisations are girding their loins to take on the European Community.

He is girding up his loins for another round of high-level meetings.

long

long as your arm ◄

If you say that something, such as a list, is

as **long as** your **arm**, you are emphasizing that it is very long.

The phone's been buzzing non-stop. I've a list of messages as long as my arm.

long on one thing and short on another ◄◄

If someone says that something is **long on** one thing **and short on** another, they mean that it has a lot of the first thing but not very much of the second. This expression is usually used to suggest that there is more of the first thing than you need and not enough of the second.

This performance is long on showmanship and short on worthwhile music.

The prime minister's speech was long on words but short on solid action.

☐ You can say that something is **short on** one thing **and long on** another. This expression is usually used to suggest that something has very little of a bad quality and plenty of a good one.

The script is blissfully short on polemic and long on situations which allow Murphy to employ his gift for accents.

look

a dirty look
a filthy look
a black look ◄

If someone gives you **a dirty look**, **a filthy look**, or **a black look**, they look at you in a way that shows that they are very angry about something.

Tony was being a real pain. Michael gave him a dirty look and walked out of the kitchen.

He caught the filthy look his daughter flashed him.

Passing my stall, she cast black looks at the amount of stuff still unsold.

looked

have never looked back ◄◄◄

When an event causes a permanent change in someone's life for the better, you can mention that event and say that they **have never looked back** or **have not looked back**.

He became a professional photographer in 1978, and has never looked back.

I quit my job as a bus driver, packed my bags, and never looked back! From that day forward, I vowed never to settle for a boring job again.

She was asked to write Sainsbury's first cookery book and hasn't looked back since. She is now cookery editor for The Sunday Telegraph.

loop

throw someone for a loop
knock someone for a loop ◄

If someone or something **throws** you **for a loop** or **knocks** you **for a loop**, they shock you or surprise you very much. These expressions are used mainly in American English.

The banker was surprised to find Johnson in his usual high spirits. If Kravis's offer had thrown him for a loop, Johnson wasn't letting it show.

Then the doorbell rings. The friend goes to the door. This young woman chimney sweep is there with her cleaning things. She's wearing a top hat, the sight of which knocked J.P. for a loop.

loose

cut loose ◄◄◄

If someone **cuts loose** or **is cut loose**, they become free from the influence or authority of other people.

He's cut loose from this business except, possibly, where James is concerned.

Italy has not cut loose from the ERM as determinedly as Britain.

The plant is struggling to find new markets. That would be tough enough, but it's also in the throes of privatization. It's about to be cut loose from the state on which it has so long depended.

hang loose ◄

If you tell someone to **hang loose**, you are telling them in an informal way to relax or not to be too serious about something, because you do not consider it to be very important.

Get something to eat and come back to the office. And hang loose.

Doesn't it make sense for you to hang loose with old friends.

on the loose: 1 ◄◄◄

If a dangerous person or animal is **on the loose**, they are free because they have escaped from somewhere.

You have to wake up every day knowing that whoever carried out those awful murders is still on the loose.

Everyone had to vacate the meeting as rapidly as possible because there was a lion on the loose in the building.

on the loose: 2

If you say that someone is **on the loose**, you mean that they are not being controlled or supervised by anyone and they are free to behave however they want.

Home Alone 2 is about the escapades of a mischievous young boy on the loose in New York.

The problem is high-spirited youngsters on the loose in the country's leafy lanes.

loss

at a loss ◄◄◄

If someone is **at a loss**, they do not know what to do or say in a particular situation.

These women also face language barriers and are at a loss to know where to go for help.

With over 190 different recipes for more than 100 varieties of pasta, Rosa is seldom at a loss for something to cook.

The Spanish authorities were at a total loss as to how to handle the situation.

a dead loss ◄

If you describe someone or something as **a dead loss**, you think that they are completely useless.

Politics is in crisis, and politicians are a dead loss.

The Keep Sunday Special Campaign claims the figures show Sunday trading is 'a dead loss'.

I have always been a dead loss at competitive sports and games. I always want the opposition to win.

losses

cut your losses ◄◄◄

If you **cut** your **losses**, you decide to stop spending time, energy, or money on an activity or situation on which you have already spent a lot without having any success.

Since the software market is already intensely competitive, and existing customers are fed up with the firm's high maintenance fees, creditors may well prefer to cut their losses and liquidate the firm.

Only you can decide if you should push on to the end of your degree or cut your losses and get out.

It may be men are just as capable of making a serious commitment but reserve the right to cut their losses, should a relationship begin to disintegrate.

lot

all over the lot ◄

If something is **all over the lot**, it is spread across a large area or over a wide range of things. This expression is used in American English; the British expression is **all over the shop**.

IBM's investments have been all over the lot – in fiber-optic technology, data-retrieval systems, computer networks and so on.

Estimates of Iraqi troops who died in the Persian Gulf range all over the lot.

throw in your lot with someone
cast your lot with someone ◄◄

If you **throw in** your **lot with** someone, or **cast** your **lot with** them, you decide to join them and to share whatever good or bad things happen to them.

That does not mean that France is ready to throw in its lot with other Community states on defence matters.

Later that year, Dali threw in his lot with Gala and left his family and Spain to be with her and paint in Paris.

I cast my lot with him through the long, difficult, comeback years of 1965 through 1968.

loud

loud and clear ◄◄◄

If someone says something **loud and clear**, they say it openly, unambiguously, and forcefully so that it cannot be misunderstood or ignored.

The message must come across loud and clear from the manager: No matter how hard I ask you to work, I work as hard or harder.

The message coming through loud and clear is that men expect much more of their women than they do of themselves.

In the past we didn't have an African Caribbean voice in the council. Now our views and our voices are being heard loud and clear in the town hall.

□ You can also use **loud and clear** before a noun.

The statement said the international community had transmitted a loud and clear message that all expressions of hatred and intolerance are unacceptable to enlightened nations.

love

for love nor money ◄

If you say that you cannot get something **for love nor money** or **for love or money**, you are emphasizing that it is very difficult to get.

You won't get a room here, not for love nor money.

Norman had created a fine vegetable garden that bulged with spinach and courgettes and French beans and little peas and all the things you couldn't buy in the local shops, for love or money.

no love lost
little love lost ◄◄

If you say that there is **no love lost** between two people or groups, or **little love lost** between them, you mean that they do not like each other at all.

There was no love lost between the country's two most powerful politicians.

There was little love lost between Mellor and

Isaacs, and the opera house was seen as not being big enough for both of them.

luck

down on your luck ◄

Someone who is **down on** their **luck** is suffering a period of bad luck.

Even when people are down on their luck and need the kind of services that an agency like HRA provides, they deserve the same human courtesy that any of us would expect when we're going to receive a service.

This is the poignant story of many-times married Buffy, an ageing actor down on his luck doing voice-overs for commercials.

□ You can use this expression before a noun.

Unless the couple do eventually produce a son, the earldom would pass to a down on his luck 60-year-old bachelor.

the luck of the draw

If something that happens depends on **the luck of the draw**, it depends on chance rather than on the efforts or merits of the people involved.

On better acquaintance, you may decide that there's no basis for a real friendship with a colleague or client or fellow-member of your evening class. That's just the luck of the draw.

lucky

strike lucky ◄◄

If someone **strikes lucky** or **strikes it lucky**, they suddenly have some good luck, for example by winning some money. This expression is used in British English.

I arrived at 12.30 to give myself time to find a parking meter, but struck lucky immediately.

US economists have criticised the draws as a way of raising state cash, because they mainly take money from the poorest people, who dream of striking it lucky.

lump

like it or lump it
have to lump it ◄

If you say that someone has to **like it or lump it**, you mean that they will have to accept a situation even though they do not like it, because they cannot do anything to change it. This is an informal expression.

Like it or lump it, Cannes is the place where the entire spectrum of world film has its annual meeting.

If you're a shareholder in the club then you have some sort of say in the way things are run. But as a paying customer you like it or lump it.

□ You can also say that someone will **have to lump it** when they have to accept a situation whether they want to or not.

When we pointed out they'd effectively taken part of our garden, they said they hadn't even noticed. We just had to lump it.

a lump in your throat
bring a lump to your throat ◄◄

If you say that you have **a lump in** your **throat**, you mean that you have a tight feeling in your throat because of a strong emotion such as sorrow, nostalgia, or gratitude. You can also say that something **brings a lump to** your **throat**. Compare **a frog in** your **throat**; see **frog**.

Meg felt a lump in her throat. She was going to miss Dot, even though the two of them had never been particularly close.

It brings a lump to my throat. We are so proud of her.

lunch

out to lunch ◄

If you say that someone is **out to lunch**, you mean that they do not seem aware of what is happening around them, or they do not seem intelligent or capable.

He has failed to fulfil his role as the mayor who could take charge. He is seen as a man who is out to lunch.

□ You can use **out-to-lunch** before a noun.

He concentrates on cracking endless waves of out-to-lunch jokes.

there's no such thing as a free lunch ◄◄

People say **'there's no such thing as a free lunch'** or **'there is no free lunch'** to mean you cannot expect to get things for nothing, since most things that are worth having need to be paid for or worked for.

The government has spent 14 years telling the nation that there is no such thing as a free lunch and lecturing us on the virtues of sound economics.

The book is simple homespun philosophy. It includes 25 Lessons for Life: Lesson 1: There is no free lunch. Don't feel entitled to anything you don't sweat and struggle for.

lurch

leave someone in the lurch ◄◄

If you say that someone **has left** you **in the lurch**, you are complaining that they have put you in a difficult situation by suddenly going away or abandoning you, without giving you very much notice of their plans.

My secretary left me in the lurch on Friday and I haven't found a replacement yet.

Chicago-based Midway Airlines has shut down, leaving thousands of ticket holders in the lurch.

lying

not take something lying down   ◄◄

If something bad is happening and you say that you **will** **not** **take** it **lying** **down**, you mean that you will complain about it or resist it.

It is clear that he means to push everyone out

if he can who does not agree with him, and I for one am not going to take it lying down.

They still say there's nothing wrong at all with their systems. So anyway, I don't take these things lying down, so I complained several times by letter.

M

mad

mad as a hatter

If you say that someone is as **mad as a hatter**, you think that they are very strange, foolish, or crazy. This expression is used mainly in British English.

Her sister's as mad as a hatter and if you ask me she's not much better herself.

mad as a hornet

If you say that someone is as **mad as a hornet**, you mean that they are extremely angry. This expression is used mainly in American English.

Bob grinned. 'I'll bet he's as mad as a hornet.' 'He did not sound at all pleased,' Jerry admitted.

map

on the map   ◄◄◄

If someone or something puts a person, place, or thing **on the map**, they cause them to become well-known or important.

Tim Mansel of the BBC looks at the career of the man who, in 13 years as Chancellor, put Austria back on the map.

The film which really put Ellen Barkin on the map was The Big Easy.

The Great Age of British Watercolours found a perfect venue at the National Gallery, Washington DC – the more so because Washington's great patron Paul Mellon helped to put watercolours on the map.

marbles

lose your marbles
have all your marbles   ◄

If you say that someone **has lost** their **marbles**, you mean that they are crazy, insane, or senile. This is an informal expression.

At 83 I have not lost my marbles and my memory is, thank God, as clear as it ever was.

People are talking about him as if he's lost his marbles. Makes you wonder what he's up to.

□ You can say that someone **has all** their **marbles** when it is obvious that they are completely sane and rational.

The producer Mirian Adhtar has found four particularly fearless old ladies; they have all their marbles, crystal clear recollections and, at ninety-odd, no false modesty.

pick up your marbles and go home

If you say that someone **picks up** their **marbles and goes home**, you mean that they leave a situation in which they are involved because they are dissatisfied with the way things are going. You can use this expression to suggest that you think they are wrong to do this. This expression is used in American English.

Many Asians regard a U.S. presence as a desirable counterweight to Japanese influence. No one wants the U.S. to pick up its marbles and go home.

march

march to a different drummer
march to the beat of a different drummer
march to a different tune   ◄

If you say that someone **marches to a different drummer** or **marches to the beat of a different drummer**, you mean that they act in accordance with beliefs or expectations which are different from those of their colleagues or associates. These expressions are used mainly in journalism.

Can't Congress see that this only compounds the problem? Or does Congress march to a different drummer?

The state-supported school marches to the beat of a different drummer, and I will permit it to continue to do so.

□ This expression is sometimes varied, for example by replacing 'drummer' with 'drum'.

As a player Lindner has always marched to the beat of a different drum.

□ In British English, you can also say that someone **marches to a different tune**.

Clough has always marched to a different tune, but this time his perversity may finally be his undoing.

mark

steal a march ◄◄

If you **steal a march** on someone, you do something before they do and so gain an advantage over them.

Investors from other countries will be annoyed that their Japanese competitors have once again stolen a march on them, and they are likely to press their governments harder to follow the Japanese example.

The bold move is designed to entice shoppers away from Tesco, which stole a march by opening more stores on the Sundays in the run-up to Christmas.

mark

a black mark ◄◄

If people form a low opinion of you as a result of something that you have done or that they think you have done, you can say that you get **a black mark**.

Any complaints, you got a black mark straight away, didn't matter whether there was anything in them or not.

I knew I had no history of bad debts and couldn't think why there should be a black mark against my name.

get off the mark ◄

In a sporting contest, when someone **gets off the mark**, they score or win for the first time. If you **get off the mark** in another activity, you start to do it quickly. This expression is used mainly in British English.

The goal was Atkinson's second of the season, having got off the mark against Ipswich Town on Saturday.

Don't waste time with small talk; you might have only five minutes to present your case. Get off the mark right away.

hit the mark ◄

If you say that something such as a film, a book, or a performance **hits the mark**, you mean that it is very good and succeeds in pleasing people.

Every Australian film that hits the mark for the next five years will probably be compared somewhere, in some way, to last year's megahit 'Strictly Ballroom'.

The band have really hit the mark. Already acclaimed as a Single Of The Week, 'Call It What You Want' is destined to be one of the successes of the year.

leave your mark
leave a mark ◄◄◄

If you **leave** your **mark** on someone or something, you do something important that has a lasting effect on them. If an event or experience **leaves** its **mark** on someone or something, it has a lasting effect on them.

He now has five more years in office and would still dearly like to leave his mark on the world.

I lived abroad, in Asia, for four years, and this is an experience that tends to leave its mark.

□ You can also say that you **leave a mark** on someone or something.

Chris Hani has left an indelible mark on the politics of South Africa.

make your mark
make a mark ◄◄◄

If you **make** your **mark**, you do something which causes you to become noticed or famous. If something **makes** its **mark**, it starts to be noticed or to have an effect.

Another highlight of this year's festival is Japan Focus, which looks at the new generation of Japanese directors making their mark in world cinema.

When I was younger it was a matter of getting on and competing and making your mark. I don't feel that need any longer.

□ You can also say that someone or something **makes a mark**.

One of the athletes who made a mark for himself at the 1964 Olympics was Kichogi Kano.

off the mark: 1
on the mark ◄

If something that you say or write is **off the mark**, it is incorrect or inaccurate.

While he does make some specific points regarding particular individuals and particular theoretical observations, I find much of his argument off the mark.

They're sometimes called 'Poor Man's Oyster', but I think that name is way off the mark. Mussels are every bit as good as the more expensive oyster.

off the mark: 2

If you describe someone's words or behaviour as **off the mark**, you are criticizing them for being unfair. This expression is used mainly in British English.

There are good and bad decisions in every Test Match you play in, even in England. Mistakes are being made, but to question the umpires' integrity is off the mark.

on the mark ◄

If something someone says or writes is **on the mark**, it is correct or accurate.

A thousand thanks for your interview with Michael Medved. He's right on the mark about movies being out of step with American culture.

overshoot the mark

If you **overshoot the mark**, you do something to a greater extent than is necessary or desirable.

I quite unwittingly overshot the mark, and I still feel embarrassed about it.

overstep the mark ◄

If someone **oversteps the mark**, they behave in a way that is considered unacceptable, for example by doing something which they are not allowed to do.

Sometimes newspapers overstep the mark but overall they do more good than harm.

He overstepped the mark and we had no option but to suspend him.

quick off the mark
first off the mark
slow off the mark ◄◄

If someone is **quick off the mark**, they are quick to understand or respond to something, or to take advantage of an opportunity. If they are **first off the mark**, they act more quickly than anyone else. These expressions are used mainly in British English.

These price cuts are great news for the holidaymaker who is quick off the mark.

Several agencies have been looking at the options but Merrett appears to have been quicker off the mark than its rivals.

The new fine art season moved into top gear yesterday with Christie's and Sotheby's announcing big collections for the autumn sales in London and New York. Christie's were first off the mark with a collection of seven paintings by Paul Cézanne.

□ If someone is **slow off the mark**, they are slow to act or to react to a situation or event.

International relief efforts on behalf of the refugees were slow off the mark, partly because of a belief that the refugees would soon be repatriated.

up to the mark ◄

If you say that something is **up to the mark**, you mean that it is of a satisfactory standard or quality.

Employers would then have to pour lots of money into the fund to bring it up to the mark.

They get rid of those whose work is not up to the mark and help those who are trying but have not yet learnt the best way to do things.

wide of the mark ◄◄

If something that you say or write is **wide of the mark**, it is incorrect or inaccurate.

The SIB said last night: 'Any suggestions that we are putting any pressure on Sir Gordon to step down are very wide of the mark.'

For once, it seems that the AA's figures might not be too wide of the mark.

Perhaps we are wide of the mark on what the origin of this condition really is.

market
a cattle market
a meat market

If you refer to a situation as **a cattle market** or **a meat market**, you mean that people are being treated in an undignified way which shows no respect for them as individuals. For example, you might refer to a beauty contest as **a cattle market** or **a meat market** if you disapprove of the fact that the contestants are being considered only in terms of their physical attractiveness. 'A cattle market' is used mainly in British English.

The parade of beautiful girls from every nation in the world was rightly called a cattle market.

'Is it a meat market?' 'Yes, of course, but no more than any other nightclub.'

in the market for something ◄◄

If you are **in the market for** something, you are interested in buying it or getting it.

If you're in the market for expensive skin care products, the following list includes some of the most well known.

There's no way you'd be in the market for buying a book like that.

marrow
chilled to the marrow
frozen to the marrow

If you say that you are **chilled to the marrow** or **frozen to the marrow**, you are emphasizing that you are very cold. These expressions are used in British English.

An icy wind murmured through the trees and shrubbery and passed over Lenny's back, but he didn't need that to feel a chill to the marrow of his bones.

When I got back from the forester's lodge at about ten a.m., I was frozen to the marrow.

to the marrow

You can use **to the marrow** to emphasize the intensity of someone's beliefs or feelings.

She hadn't heard the name de Gaulle till she picked it up listening illegally to the BBC, and from then on she was Gaulliste to the marrow.

I wasn't expecting to be thrilled to the marrow with it.

masters
not serve two masters

If you say that a person **cannot serve two masters**, you mean that it is impossible to be loyal to two opposing principles, beliefs, or organizations.

But there is something more fundamentally wrong: the inherent conflict of interest in Sir Nicholas's job. He is expected to serve two masters: politics and the law.

mat

go to the mat

If someone **goes to the mat**, they fight very fiercely about something. This expression is used mainly in American English.

To civil rights leaders, this talk is rank heresy. So they will go to the mat to destroy him.

Librarians have gone to the mat for us and I'm determined to do my bit to help them meet the demand for the books.

match

meet your match ◄◄

If you **meet** your **match**, you find that you are competing or fighting with someone who is as good as you or is better than you.

He met his match in Chris Dittmar of Australia at the European championships in West Germany.

When I got into the room with Wesley, it was almost like looking into a mirror for me. I had finally met my match in power and intellect.

a shouting match

If people or organizations have **a shouting match**, they have an angry debate about something.

We didn't want to get into a horrible shouting match with the university.

Four frustrating years of talks ended in a shouting match over farm subsidies between the European Community and America.

□ This expression is more commonly used to talk about a quarrel in which people shout at one another.

the whole shooting match

You can use **the whole shooting match** to refer to the whole of something.

The head of this division would run the whole shooting match. He would have to get products, write presentations, devise campaigns, hire, fire, and a hundred other things.

I filled in my donor card, ticking the whole shooting-match, from kidneys to liver.

McCoy

the real McCoy ◄

If you describe something as **the real McCoy**, you mean that it is genuine or the original, rather than a fake or copy, and is therefore often considered to be the best.

It is important not to confuse English wine with British. The former is the real McCoy, wine made from home-grown grapes; the latter is made from cheap, imported grape concentrate.

Unlike some other products which are promoted as the real McCoy, Cobra is a genuine Indian product.

meal

make a meal of something ◄

If you say that someone **is making a meal of** something or **is making a meal out of** it, you are criticizing them for spending more time or energy on it than is necessary. This expression is used mainly in British English.

Alexander has made such a meal out of a mildly mistaken newspaper report.

The Herald made a week-long meal of the story. So did the big national television networks.

'He's making a meal of this,' she said, 'a four-course one, to say the least. I think you had better have a word with him.'

a meal ticket ◄

If you describe something as **a meal ticket**, you mean that it is a way of getting money on a regular basis and securing a good lifestyle.

A degree has never been a meal ticket, but the recession is making life for graduates tougher than ever.

I just can't understand how anyone would want to do something just for money. I mean, one's job isn't just a meal ticket. It's an extension of one's whole personality.

Four out of ten men fear their partner may be after a life-long meal ticket.

a square meal ◄

If you have **a square meal**, you have a large, filling, nutritious meal.

Do you survive on yogurt at lunchtime while your partner wants a square meal?

The troops are very tired. They haven't had a square meal for four or five days.

meaning

not know the meaning of the word ◄

If you mention a quality or kind of experience and you say that someone **doesn't know the meaning of the word**, you are emphasizing that they do not have that quality or never have that kind of experience. People sometimes replace 'word' with 'phrase' or 'term'.

She is an optimist; Ruthie doesn't even know the meaning of the word depression.

Service? In Britain we don't know the meaning of the word.

means

by fair means or foul

If someone tries to achieve something **by fair means or foul**, they are prepared to use any possible method to achieve it, and they do not care if their behaviour is dishonest or unfair.

She never gave up trying to recover her property, by fair means or foul.

He accused the company of being hell bent on achieving its cuts by whatever means, fair means or foul, irrespective of the financial and emotional impact.

measure

for good measure ◄◄◄

If something is done **for good measure**, it is done in addition to other things in order to make certain that something is successful or complete.

This is a fairly conventional love story, with a murder mystery thrown in for good measure.

In the opening ceremonies for New England's newest Wal-Mart in Farmington, Maine, the mayor predicted good fortune for both the store and its shoppers, but a local minister offered a prayer for good measure.

He and the landlord gave us much precious information and the landlord threw in for good measure an invaluable local guide.

have the measure of someone ◄◄

If you **have the measure of** someone or something, you understand them or know what they are like. You can say that you **get the measure of** them or **take the measure of** them when you discover what they are like.

Lili was the only person I knew who had the measure of her brother.

He had the measure of Allen and his clique, and he treated them with polite contempt.

Amsterdam is that rare thing: a major city you can get the measure of in just four days.

Elizabeth was taking the measure of the opposition.

meat

dead meat: 1 ◄

If someone says that a person is **dead meat**, they mean that that person is in serious trouble which may result in them being injured or killed. This is an informal expression, which is often used in threats.

He's scum – and dead meat if he comes back here.

dead meat: 2

If someone says that a person is **dead meat**, they are saying in an unkind way that that person is in serious trouble which they think will have unpleasant consequences for them, such as losing their job.

Anyone who remembered her said she was dead meat.

meat and drink to someone

If something is **meat and drink to** you, it is something you find easy to cope with and enjoy doing. This expression is used mainly in British English.

What normal people considered pressure was meat and drink to Robert Maxwell.

He was attracted to heart surgery because it was a field in which you can often put things right. This is meat and drink to any doctor. In many other fields you can't cure things just like that.

one man's meat is another man's poison

If you say that **one man's meat is another man's poison**, you are pointing out that different people like different things.

Art is everywhere. Because it is a question of personal taste, the cliché of one man's meat being another's poison is in this case especially fitting.

medicine

give someone a taste of their own medicine
give someone a dose of their own medicine ◄

If someone has behaved badly and you **give** them **a taste of** their **own medicine** or **a dose of** their **own medicine**, you treat them badly in return.

The cowardly thugs who mug old people should be given a taste of their own medicine with the return of corporal punishment.

For the past few months, enemy guerrillas, bursting out of the enclaves, have given them a dose of their own medicine.

melting pot

in the melting pot ◄

If something is **in the melting pot**, it is constantly changing, so that you do not know what will finally happen to it. This expression is used mainly in British journalism.

Their fate is still in the melting-pot, and much suffering may lie ahead.

Australia had more spark and a little more finesse. These assets proved critical when the match was in the melting pot in the second half.

I am very disappointed. The whole business has been put into the melting pot again.

men

sort out the men from the boys
separate the men from the boys

If a difficult or challenging situation **sorts out the men from the boys** or **separates the men from the boys**, it tests people and shows who is strong and capable and who is not.

This is the game that will sort out the men from the boys. It is absolutely vital to win the replay and get to the final.

messenger

shoot the messenger ◄

If someone accuses you of **shooting the**

messenger, they are criticizing you for unfairly blaming a person who has given you unpleasant news or information, when you should instead be angry with the people who are really responsible for the situation.

Nobody enjoys paying tax, but at least be sure of your facts before you criticize the Inland Revenue, and remember the government makes the rules which the Revenue then has to enforce. If you don't like the message, don't shoot the messenger.

mickey
take the mickey
take the mick   ◄◄◄

If you **take the mickey** out of someone or something, you tease them or make jokes about them in a way that causes them to seem ridiculous. This expression is used in British English.

He started taking the mickey out of this poor man just because he is bald.

Kenworthy did not know whether Neville was taking the Mickey out of him or not.

□ You can also say that someone **takes the mick** out of someone or something.

He has created a very Californian comedy that takes the mick out of absentee fathers and selfish mothers.

□ When someone behaves like this, you can refer to their behaviour as **mickey-taking**. You can refer to an instance of it as **a mickey-take**.

Until puberty I was really quite plump and had to put up with all the mickey-taking that went with it.

It was actually a big mickey-take.

middle
in the middle of nowhere
out in the middle of nowhere   ◄◄◄

If you describe a place as being **in the middle of nowhere** or **out in the middle of nowhere**, you are emphasizing that it is a great distance from other places.

When I was 14, my family moved away from Glasgow to a village in the middle of nowhere.

It was impossible to understand why someone would rather live in the middle of nowhere than in a big city.

The island really is in the middle of nowhere.

middle-of-the-road: 1   ◄◄

If you describe a person or their political ideas as **middle-of-the-road**, you mean that they are neither very left-wing nor very right-wing.

He has represented himself as being a moderate, middle-of-the-road kind of person who understands and takes into consideration both sides of the issues.

The Labour Party metamorphosed during the '80s under Neil Kinnock's leadership into smartly dressed, articulate, middle of the road socialism.

middle-of-the-road: 2   ◄

If you describe someone or something as **middle-of-the-road**, you mean that they are very ordinary, rather than unusual, exciting, or extreme.

These are, for the most part, ordinary middle-of-the-road people who want the usual things out of life.

Delroy Pinnock's new single 'No Man' is a middle of the road soul song. This is bedtime music which will easily send me to sleep.

midnight
burn the midnight oil   ◄

If you **burn the midnight oil**, you stay up very late at night in order to finish a piece of work.

I wanted Heinze and Peterson to know I was burning the midnight oil.

Chris is asleep after burning the midnight oil trying to put together his article on the Bosnian situation.

□ You can use **midnight oil** in other contexts to suggest that someone has been staying up very late.

My speeches always smacked too much of midnight oil.

midstream
change horses in midstream
switch horses in midstream   ◄

If someone who is involved in an activity **changes horses in midstream** or **switches horses in midstream**, they stop using one method or thing and start using another one, or they stop supporting one person and start supporting someone else. These expressions are often used to advise someone against doing one of these things.

Treasury Secretary Nicholas Brady wrote a letter to Riegle in support of Clarke saying, in essence, this was no time to switch horses in midstream.

I think we were very wise not to change horses in mid-stream.

□ You can just say that someone **changes horses** or **switches horses**.

When Mr Poloskov failed to beat Mr Yeltsin, the Communist leadership plainly decided to switch horses again. Mr Poloskov withdrew and Mr Vlasov announced that he would, after all, stand against Mr Yeltsin.

□ Sometimes people replace 'horses' with another noun.

It would be stupid for Zambians to change their oxen in midstream.

They haven't hesitated to change the rules in midstream in order to try to thwart the President.

mile

go the extra mile   ◄

If you say that someone is willing to **go the extra mile**, you mean that they are willing to make a special effort to do or achieve something.

The President is determined to go the extra mile for peace.

I discovered that going the extra mile has always been the hallmark of successful people.

□ People sometimes replace 'go' with another verb and 'mile' with 'yard'.

We will travel the extra mile to arrive at peace.

He has enormous compassion for people and a willingness to go the extra yard to help them, which makes him a great loss for the club.

a mile off
a mile away   ◄

If you say that you can spot something or someone **a mile off** or **a mile away**, you are emphasizing that they are very obvious and easy to recognize.

You can spot undercover cops a mile off.

I thought the wig looked all right at the time but, looking back, I can see that people could tell I was wearing it a mile off.

He knew Ann could spot a lie a mile away.

□ This expression is often used to suggest that someone is especially good at recognizing a particular thing.

I can tell a crook a mile off.

run a mile   ◄

If you say that someone would **run a mile** if they were faced with a particular person, situation, or thing, you mean that they would do anything to avoid them or escape from them. This expression is used in British English.

They are tough, independent career girls who would run a mile from cosy domesticity.

These days most of us run a mile at the mention of plastic.

He likes the ladies but he'd run a mile if one chased him.

miles

miles away

If you say that someone is **miles away**, you mean that they are unaware of what is happening or of what someone is saying, because they are thinking deeply about something else.

She looked up at Siobhan. 'Sorry, I was miles away.' 'Thinking about all the money Mike could win?' Siobhan said with a grin.

Her mother was pacing up and down and seemed miles away. She hadn't noticed them at all.

□ **Miles away** is more commonly used literally to say that one person or thing is a very great distance away from another.

The nearest neighbors were miles away.

milk

it's no use crying over spilled milk   ◄

If you tell someone **'it's no use crying over spilled milk'**, you are telling them that it is pointless to worry or be upset about something that has happened and cannot be changed.

She couldn't help but wonder, though, if knowing the truth would have made Angela any more loving toward Charles, not that there was any point in crying over spilled milk.

I'm a man, I can take it. I ain't going to cry over spilt milk, I was beaten fair and square.

milk and honey
the land of milk and honey   ◄

You can describe a time or a situation in which you are very contented and have plenty of money as a time of **milk and honey**. This is a literary expression.

Many of the musicians working with him, including Charlie Parker, made the biggest money of their careers. It was an era of milk and honey for jazz.

The days of milk and honey are back – at least for US equity salesmen in the City.

□ You can use **milk and honey** before a noun.

In her best-selling guide to household management for today's woman, Shirley Conran urged her readers to ignore the 'impossible milk and honey standards of the impossible TV housewife.'

□ This expression is a shortened form of **the land of milk and honey** which describes a place where people will be happy and have plenty of food and wealth.

They represent the golden age, when we lived in the land of milk and honey.

milk and water

If you describe something or someone as **milk and water**, you mean that they are weak and ineffectual. This expression is used in British English.

Now, looking at the faces around her, Amy realized that her own groping ideas were as weak and vague as milk and water beside the ideals that flared here.

Fryer dismissed the Cadbury report as milk and water.

□ You can use **milk and water** before a noun.

The only time we have ever won an election, is when it was fought on principle; every other time we've put forward this milk and water liberalism, and we've lost.

mill

go through the mill
put through the mill ◄

If you **go through the mill** or are **put through the mill**, you experience a very difficult period or situation.

'Oh I've been through the mill,' said Shirley casually, waving her hand in dismissal. 'Single parent, no money, and a boyfriend who beat me up.'

Richard confesses he'll put a junior through the mill for the first few months, and work them hard to see if they can keep their temper.

run-of-the-mill ◄◄◄

You use **run-of-the-mill** to describe something or someone that you think is ordinary and unexciting.

They must organise their staff photographers to ensure that daily run-of-the-mill events are covered.

I was just a very average run-of-the-mill kind of student.

million

one in a million

If you say that someone or something is **one in a million**, you mean that they are very special or the best of their kind. You can replace 'one' with a noun.

At 25, Bernstein was a star. One in a million.

He'll be a horse in a million if he wins.

□ You can also use **one-in-a-million** before a noun.

We still want love and the unique experience of a close, lasting partnership with that one-in-a-million man.

a one in a million chance
a chance in a million ◄

If you say that something is **a one in a million chance** or that there is **a chance in a million** of it happening, you mean that it is very unlikely to happen, and that you would be either extremely lucky or extremely unlucky if it happened to you.

Martyn's accident occurred at the end of a tough practice session yesterday morning, and was described as being a one-in-a-million chance.

It is amazing really. He had a chance in a million of surviving. We are so relieved he is all right.

millstone

a millstone around your neck ◄◄

If you say that something is like **a millstone around** your **neck**, you mean that it is a very unpleasant problem or responsibility that you cannot escape from.

Argentina's notoriously inefficient telephone company, Entel, has been a millstone round the government's neck.

Long-term illness can make you feel like a complete waste of space, a millstone around your family's necks.

□ **Millstone** is often used on its own with this meaning.

There is the continuing millstone of the country's enormous foreign debt.

mincemeat

make mincemeat of someone ◄

If you **make mincemeat of** someone, you defeat them completely in a fight, argument, or competition.

I remember old Fiona made mincemeat of him at a dinner party without him even realizing.

He tries to make mincemeat of my arguments against drugs.

Naturally, Lord Goodman will make mincemeat of this absurd claim.

mind

bear something in mind
keep something in mind ◄◄◄

If you tell someone to **bear** something **in mind** or **keep** something **in mind**, you are reminding or warning them about something important which they should remember.

There are a few general rules to bear in mind when selecting plants.

Go where you like, but keep in mind that some places are more problematic than others for women traveling alone.

Add salt, pepper and spices to taste, bearing in mind that dishes served cold often need a little more seasoning.

blow your mind ◄◄◄

If you say that something **blows** your **mind**, you mean that you find it so exciting, amazing, or interesting that it is hard to believe it.

Oxford really blew his mind. He loved the feeling of the place, he loved the people.

After months of begging him to let her sing, she finally grabbed the mike one night during a break and blew his mind with her voice.

□ You can also say that you find something **mind-blowing**.

In the museum, the artist's impression of how Delphi must once have looked is mind-blowing in its majesty.

Prague is a mind-blowing blend of Czech, German and Jewish cultures. And it's all wrapped up in some fairly incredible baroque architecture.

cross your mind ◄◄◄

If something **crosses** your **mind**, you suddenly think of it.

Steve would rouse me from sleep at 2:00 a.m. with a phone call to chat about an idea that suddenly crossed his mind.

The thought instantly crossed my mind that she might be lying about her age.

☐ If you say that something **did not cross** your **mind** or **never crossed** your **mind**, you mean that it never occurred to you or you did not consider that it could happen.

It evidently never crossed his mind to enter politics.

It hasn't even crossed my mind that I won't win this fight.

give someone a piece of your mind ◄

If someone has annoyed or upset you and you **give** them **a piece of** your **mind**, you angrily tell them what you think of them.

You can't let people get away with that sort of thing. You should have given her a piece of your mind.

The more she thought about it, the more upset she became. She would like to go out and give him a piece of her mind.

have a one-track mind

If you say that someone **has a one-track mind**, you mean that they seem to only ever think or talk about one subject. This expression is often used light-heartedly to refer to people who think or talk about sex a lot.

In my view Saunders is the complete modern striker, busy, quick, and with a one-track mind for scoring goals.

in your mind's eye ◄◄◄

If you see something **in your mind's eye**, you have a clear picture of it in your imagination or memory.

I can often see you in my mind's eye, sitting in your flat alone.

Susie had a clear picture in her mind's eye of how she wanted the house to look.

in your right mind ◄◄◄

If you say that nobody **in their right mind** would do a particular thing, you mean that it is an irrational thing to do, and you do not expect anyone would ever do it.

Those places are so barren, dangerous and inhospitable that no one in their right mind would go there unless they had a contract to fulfil.

How are you going to persuade a jury that any man in his right mind is going to lay a trail that points directly at himself?

the mind boggles ◄◄◄

You say **'the mind boggles'** when you find something difficult to imagine or understand because it is so amazing, strange, or complicated.

There's so much myth and mystery and so many messages to sift through that the mind boggles at how much more he might have taught us had he survived.

The mind boggles to think what they could eventually achieve.

☐ You can also describe something amazing, strange, or complicated as **mind-boggling**.

Why does Dame Barbara Cartland keep on writing books? She's the author of a mind-boggling 553 works so far, and more are on the way.

Just the idea that this man may have prevented that war is mind-boggling.

☐ You can also say that something **boggles the mind** or that it **boggles** your **mind** when you find it difficult to imagine or understand because it is so strange, amazing, or complicated.

Such statements boggle the mind.

Talk about bizarre coincidences – this one absolutely boggled my mind.

mind over matter ◄

You can use the expression **mind over matter** to describe situations in which someone seems able to control events or solve a physical problem or difficulty by means of their attitude and by thinking in a focused way about it.

Good health is simply a case of mind over matter.

Once your mind has fully accepted the suggestion that you are well and fit, you immediately start to feel better. This mind over matter effect is very real.

out of your mind: 1 ◄◄

If you say that someone is **out of** their **mind**, you mean that they are crazy, foolish, or insane.

When her boss told her she would have to increase the models' salaries, she snapped, 'Are you out of your mind?'

Just before they reached the house something happened which made Rachel wonder for a moment if she might be going out of her mind.

out of your mind: 2 ◄◄

If you say that you have been **out of** your **mind** with worry, jealousy, or fear, you are emphasizing that you have been extremely worried, jealous, or afraid. You can also say, for example, that you were worried or scared **out of** your **mind**.

She's out of her mind with worry; apparently her husband left the hotel when she was out this morning, and hasn't been seen since.

I was out of my mind with fear, I didn't know what to do.

Charlie and the girl were younger by 25 years than anyone else at the party. He thought she looked bored out of her mind.

slip your mind ◄

If something **slips** your **mind**, you forget it.

Surprisingly, it soon slipped my mind that there were several people working only yards away on the other side of the door.

The reason for my visit had obviously slipped his mind.

a weight off your mind
a load off your mind

If something that has been worrying you is resolved, and so you no longer need to worry about it, you can say that it is **a weight off** your **mind** or **a load off** your **mind**.

Armstrong heaved a sigh of relief, 'That's a weight off my mind. Ella likes you.'

Her letter, she says, is in the post confirming my job, and she expects me Thursday. That's a load off my mind.

minds

in two minds
of two minds ◄◄

If you are **in two minds** about something, you are very hesitant and cannot reach a decision about it. In American English, you can also say that you are **of two minds**.

Like many parents, I am in two minds about school uniforms. Part of me can remember the deep loathing I had for my own; the greater part thinks it is a fine thing to see lots of children dressed neatly and identically.

Roche was in two minds whether to make the trip to Oslo.

Her family was of two minds about what was happening, proud that Miss Kim was being honored by the state and distressed that she had to leave home.

misery

put someone out of their misery: 1 ◄

If you **put** someone **out of** their **misery**, you put an end to a situation which is causing them to suffer, for example by telling them something they have been waiting anxiously to hear.

Manager Ossie Ardiles yesterday put young player Matty Appleby out of his misery by handing him a new contract.

As A-level students continued the long wait for their results last week, almost 1,000 British school leavers awaiting exam results were put out of their misery.

put someone out of their misery: 2 ◄

If someone deliberately kills a person who is suffering, for example because they have an incurable illness, people sometimes say that the first person **puts** the second person **out of** their **misery**. This expression is usually used to show that the speaker or writer approves of or is sympathetic towards this action.

His attorney today welcomed such a trial, predicting that no Michigan jury would ever convict the doctor for 'putting suffering people out of their misery'.

There were at least a dozen pills in the bottle, surely enough to put her out of her misery.

put something out of its misery: 3 ◄

If someone **puts** an animal **out of** its **misery**, they kill it because it is very old or sick, or because it is badly injured.

I carry medicines to relieve sick and injured animals. Some are in such pain that I'm forced to put them out of their misery.

miss

miss the boat
miss the bus ◄◄◄

If someone **misses the boat**, they fail to act in time to take advantage of an opportunity, with the result that they lose the chance to do something or to benefit from something. You can also say that someone **misses the bus**.

Critics would say that both Congress and the White House have seriously missed the boat on this set of issues over the last few years.

My mother and my grandmother were both married at 24 and at that age, I suddenly thought I'd missed the boat – but I have a wider world than they ever had.

Orders received by December 10 will be sent in time for Christmas. Too bad if you missed the bus.

□ You can put an adjective before 'boat' or 'bus' to say what kind of opportunity is being missed.

Rupert Bruce says those who bought in May missed the investment boat.

mockers

put the mockers on something

If someone **puts the mockers on** something, they prevent it from happening or from being successful. This expression is used in British English.

When it was first suggested that the group might tour with them back in 1990, the Happy Mondays themselves put the mockers on it.

money

have money to burn ◄

If you say that someone **has money to burn**, you mean that they are wasting so much money on something that they must have far more money than they need. People often use this expression to show disapproval of someone's behaviour.

Investment in football clubs is for rich men with money to burn. The rest of us should stick to watching them play.

It's certainly a ridiculous figure. I'd expected something like £30 or £40. They must have money to burn, these people.

money for old rope
money for jam ◄

If you say that someone is getting **money for old rope** or **money for jam,** you mean that they are getting money very easily and with very little or no effort on their part. These expressions are used in British English.

I had always believed that the fashion model's job was money for old rope.

Who on earth can afford five pounds per hour? This is robbery, money for jam.

☐ People sometimes use other nouns instead of 'rope' or 'jam', especially when they want to create a humorous effect.

You know it's rather sickening to say the least. He's got to earn ten weeks' wages to get as much as one week's pay rise for his boss. And he works very hard. I mean, it's money for old executives, isn't it?

money talks ◄◄

If you say that **money talks,** you mean that people with a lot of money have power and influence and they can get whatever they want.

As far as he is concerned, money talks and he can do what he likes.

Nowhere does money talk louder than in Las Vegas.

put your money where your mouth is ◄◄◄

If you **put** your **money where** your **mouth is,** you give practical support to causes or activities that you believe are right, especially by giving money.

If the minister is so keen on the school he should put his money where his mouth is and give us more resources.

Musicians can also put their money where their mouths are and play benefit gigs.

☐ Journalists sometimes replace 'money' or 'mouth' with other nouns in order to refer to a particular situation or to the type of support someone might give.

It seems reasonable to ask the public to put its money where its interests are.

He wants Sinead to put her commitment where her mouth is.

We'll be watching to see how many Members of the Rules Committee end up putting their votes where their rhetoric is.

right on the money ◄

If you say that someone is **right on the money,** you mean that they are completely right. This expression is used mainly in American English.

If you had used the market's trading information to predict the popular vote, you'd have been right on the money.

They say his analysis of what was wrong with General Motors was right on the money.

the smart money: 1 ◄

You say that **the smart money** is on a particular event when that event seems very likely to happen, or is expected to happen by the people who know a lot about it.

The smart money is on him losing his seat to the Labour challenger.

A lot of smart money in Washington says that peace is nearly at hand.

the smart money: 2 ◄

People who have a lot of experience and knowledge of investing money are sometimes referred to as **the smart money.** This expression is used mainly in journalism.

Today, a lot of the smart money is turning to bonds.

Smart money has been snapping up South African equities too, though it has steered clear of traditionally popular gold stocks.

☐ This expression is also used to refer to investments made by people like this.

The vast bulk of the smart money – several billion of it to date – has gone into some form of residential property.

☐ You can use **smart-money** before a noun.

It wasn't the well-heeled smart-money crowd that sent Harley-Davidson shares soaring.

spend money like water

If you say that someone **spends money like water,** you are critical of them for spending a lot of money unnecessarily.

She begins affairs with two men and spends money like water to create a luxurious home far beyond the means of her humble husband.

throw good money after bad ◄

If you say that someone **is throwing good money after bad,** you are criticizing them for spending a lot of money in an attempt to get back money which they have already lost, for example in a bad investment, even though this is unlikely to be successful. People sometimes use other verbs instead of 'throw'.

Germany is pledging trust and goodwill but no more cash. As one senior official put it, we don't want to throw good money after bad.

Some Western politicians believe that to provide more cash before fundamental reforms have been undertaken will simply be to pour good money after bad.

monkey

throw money at something: 1 ◄◄

If you say that a government or other organization **is throwing money at** a problem or a difficult situation, you are criticizing them for trying to solve or improve it by spending a lot of money on it, instead of thinking about it carefully or doing other things.

The government's answer to the problem has been to throw money at it.

The question today for policy makers is whether there is any point in throwing money at proposed solutions when the problem is so badly understood.

throw money at someone: 2

If you say that a person or organization **is throwing money at** someone, you are suggesting that this is wrong because the person receiving the money does not need it or deserve it.

We are not just throwing money at academic departments for reports that gather dust in the library.

We've put millions behind these guys. You don't think we'd throw our money at any old rubbish do you?

monkey

have a monkey on your back
get the monkey off your back ◄

If you **have a monkey on** your **back**, you have a serious problem that is making your life difficult or unpleasant. This expression is used mainly in American English.

That job has been foisted upon us actually. We've got a monkey on our backs of having to reveal the character of our candidates, because the parties are no longer screening them.

□ If you **get the monkey off** your **back**, you put an end to a serious problem that has been making your life difficult or unpleasant.

'This is a big monkey off my back,' said McEnroe. 'It's been so long since I had such a big win.'

make a monkey out of someone

If someone **makes a monkey out of** you, or **makes a monkey of** you, they make you seem ridiculous or stupid.

If it makes any difference, I'm not here to make monkeys out of the police, I'm a cop myself.

As you can gather, there are different strategies for every situation. If you follow the proper steps, you won't make a monkey of yourself in any of them.

monkey business ◄

If you refer to someone's activities as **monkey business**, you are suggesting that they are dishonest or unacceptable.

Senator Jose Maria Sala runs the party ma-

chine in Catalonia, where the monkey business is alleged to have gone on.

He declares that 'for better or worse, British spies taught the CIA most of what it knows about political monkey business in the Third World.'

not give a monkey's

If you say that you **don't give a monkey's** about something, you mean that you do not care about it at all. This is a very informal expression, which is used British English. Some people consider it offensive.

They constantly said they would not injure the maid or the child because they had children of their own, but they said they didn't give a monkey's about what they did to me.

□ People sometimes put a noun such as 'cuss' after 'monkey's'.

He seemed to breathe football, and didn't give a monkey's cuss for anything he thought was pompous or big-headed.

monkeys

a cartload of monkeys

If you say that someone is as cunning or as clever as **a cartload of monkeys**, you are emphasizing that they are extremely cunning or clever. You can use 'barrel load' or 'barrel' instead of 'cartload'. This is an old-fashioned expression, which is used in British English.

They are engaging creatures, cunning as a cartload of monkeys.

Madame doesn't have much time for clever women, which is queer seeing as she's as clever as a barrel load of monkeys herself.

month

a month of Sundays: 1

You say that a period of time seems to last for **a month of Sundays** to emphasize that it seems to be very long.

Torrential rain and jet-black skies can make each day seem like a month of Sundays.

a month of Sundays: 2

If you say that something will not happen in **a month of Sundays**, you are emphasizing that it is very unlikely to happen.

'I think I know what you're about,' he growled, 'but it'll never work – not in a month of Sundays.'

monty

the full monty
the full monte

If you say that something is **the full monty** or **the full monte**, you are emphasizing that it is as complete or extreme as possible. This expression is used in British English.

Ron choked back the tears and sang 'My

*Way' right through, from the simple piano in-
tro to the big orchestral finish, the full monty.*

*The band opened with two new songs.
They're promising the full monty at their two
Brixton Academy shows.*

moon

ask for the moon
cry for the moon ◄

If you say that someone **is asking for the
moon** or **is crying for the moon**, you mean
that they are asking for something that they
cannot possibly have.

*We're not asking for the moon, but we are
asking for some stability so that we can continue the progress that has been made and not
go backwards.*

*'What I'd like is for my grandson no longer
to have that need.' 'Then I'm afraid,' said
Moira, 'that you're crying for the moon.'*

bay at the moon
howl at the moon

If you say that someone **is baying at the
moon**, you mean that they are wasting their
time and energy trying to do something
which is impossible or to get something
which they cannot have. You can also say
that they **are howling at the moon**.

*Asking for improved childcare provision has
so far proved as fruitful as baying at the
moon.*

*The much-vaunted watchdog which was sup-
posed to stop the worst excesses of private ownership appears to be reduced to howling vainly
at the moon.*

once in a blue moon ◄

Something that happens **once in a blue
moon** is very rare and hardly ever happens.

*Only once in a blue moon do properties of
this quality, style and position become available.*

*I only get over to Cambridge once in a blue
moon and I'm never in London.*

over the moon ◄◄◄

If you are **over the moon** about something,
you are very happy about it. This expression
is used mainly in spoken British English.

*I'm over the moon about the way this album
turned out.*

*The couple flew off to Los Angeles last week
having told friends that they are expecting
their first baby. They are over the moon, I'm
told.*

promise the moon

If someone **promises the moon**, they promise to give people things that they cannot in
fact possibly give them.

*Such over-generosity provides no incentive for
depositors to choose their banks carefully and*

*every incentive for banks to lure customers by
promising the moon.*

moth

like a moth to a flame ◄

If you say that people are attracted to someone or something **like moths to a flame**, you
mean that the attraction is so powerful that
they cannot resist. This expression is very
variable. For example, you can talk about
'moths around a flame', or replace 'flame'
with 'candle'.

*The bright lights of west London drew
Kharin like a moth to a flame.*

*While the women and the priest prefer to lec-
ture her on the wages of sin, the menfolk hover
like moths around a flame, only to meet with
rejection.*

motions

go through the motions ◄◄◄

If you say that someone **is going through
the motions**, you mean that they are doing
something that they have to do or are expected to do, but without any real effort or enthusiasm.

*Many of the students who did attend classes
with any regularity were just going through
the motions.*

*By continuing to go through the motions of
diplomatic negotiations, we're avoiding really
dealing with the problem.*

mould

break the mould ◄◄◄

If someone or something **breaks the mould**,
they completely change the way something
has traditionally been done, and do it in a
new way. The verbs 'shatter' and 'crack' are
sometimes used instead of 'break'.

*One of the most dramatic chapters of recent
British politics was closed yesterday when Dr
David Owen and his remaining allies voted
overwhelmingly to wind up the SDP, the organisation founded nine years ago to break the
mould of the two-party system.*

*Mayall would shortly become associated with
the new vanguard of alternative, left-wing comics who were to break the British comedy
mould in the late Seventies.*

□ You can use **mould-breaking** to describe
someone or something that completely
changes the way something has traditionally
been done.

*Southwold, a sleepy fishing town on the ex-
treme eastern edge of England, might seem an
odd place from which to launch a mould-
breaking wine business.*

□ You can refer to someone who has done
something in a completely new way as **a
mould-breaker**.

She is frequently praised as a mould-breaker: in the words of Steve Rider, 'Julie Welch demonstrated that a woman's opinion on the game is as valid as a man's.'

□ 'Mould' is usually spelled 'mold' in American English.

they broke the mould when they made someone

If you say that **they broke the mould when they made** someone or something, you are emphasizing that the person or thing is special or unique, and that there is nobody else or nothing else quite like them.

He is a most remarkable man. They broke the mould when they made him.

□ You can also just say that **they broke the mould**.

But they don't make them like that any more – I think they broke the mold.

□ 'Mould' is usually spelled 'mold' in American English.

mountain

if Mohammed will not go to the mountain, the mountain must go to Mohammed

People use expressions such as **'the mountain must come to Mohammed'** or **'Mohammed comes to the mountain'** to say that if someone you want to see does not come to you, then you must go to them.

Another member of the RAF staff added that all the freed hostage's needs would be met on the base. The mountain would come to Mohammed, he said.

Fifteen minutes later, Napoleon Chotas was ushered into the office of the Prosecuting Attorney. 'Well,' Demonides said. 'Mohammed comes to the mountain. What can I do for you?'

□ People do not normally use the full expression, but refer to it partially or indirectly.

Rudge admits that the market is very quiet, and has decided, on the Mahomet and the Mountain principle, to go out and get the clients.

Alsop has definitely not gone to the mountain, the mountain has strolled over to him and given him the work.

□ These expressions are based on a story about the prophet Mohammed, who was asked to show his power by making Mount Safa come to him.

make a mountain out of a molehill

If you say that someone is **making a mountain out of a molehill**, you are criticizing them because you think that they are making a small, unimportant problem seem big and important.

The Kremlin's initial reaction to western re-

ports was an attempt to say the West was trying to make a mountain out of a molehill.

□ People often exploit this expression, for example by saying that someone **is making molehills out of mountains** if they are trying to make a big, important problem seem small and unimportant.

There has been a family feud going on for the last two years. It is so trivial, but it has grown from a molehill to a mountain.

a mountain to climb   ◄

If you say that someone has **a mountain to climb**, you mean that it will be difficult for them to achieve what they want to achieve. This expression is used mainly in British English.

We nearly beat Warrington in the Cup last season and although it's a mountain to climb we can do it.

His government has an economic mountain to climb. And it has to find a solution to the violence in this province.

mountains

move mountains   ◄

People sometimes say that something such as faith or love can **move mountains** in order to emphasize that it can be a very powerful force.

If faith can move mountains, achieving promotion to the Premier League will be a pushover for Kevin Keegan this season.

We should all repeat five times a day, 'It is possible to change!' With this belief, you can move mountains.

mouth

all mouth and trousers
all mouth and no trousers

If you say that someone is **all mouth and trousers**, you disapprove of the fact that they talk a lot about doing something but never actually do it. People also say **all mouth and no trousers**, or use other nouns instead of 'trousers'. This expression is used in British English.

He wants to write a play about two Scottish brothers, the one a none-too-successful West of Scotland man with vague criminal connections; the other a fast-talking, London media type, all mouth and trousers.

Sandra is all mouth and no talent.

□ Sometimes people just say that someone is **all mouth**.

They are all mouth in the name of the cause, and are always seen to be saying the right thing.

down in the mouth

If you feel **down in the mouth**, you feel unhappy or depressed. This expression is used in British English.

As for George, I hear he's rather down in the mouth.

Just in case you are feeling really down in the mouth, and are finding it hard to adopt a positive attitude, you must remember a fact of vital importance. You are unique!

foam at the mouth: 1
froth at the mouth

If you say that someone **is foaming at the mouth** or **is frothing at the mouth**, you mean that they are very angry.

Stewart was foaming at the mouth about an incident at Gooch's private hospital the previous afternoon.

It is now taken for granted that 'political correctness' is undesirable. Its mere mention is enough to cause journalists to froth at the mouth.

foam at the mouth: 2
froth at the mouth

If you say that someone **is foaming at the mouth** or **is frothing at the mouth**, you mean that they are very excited about something.

At that time the newspaper had foamed at the mouth in favour of agreement with Fascist countries.

The news that the team's top player might be up for sale at the end of the season has got Premier League bosses frothing at the mouth in excitement.

laugh out of the other side of your mouth

If someone says **'you'll be laughing out of the other side of your mouth'**, they are warning you that although you are happy or successful at the moment, things are likely to go wrong for you in the future. This expression is used in American English; the British expression is **laugh on the other side of your face**.

make your mouth water: 1

If food **makes** your **mouth water**, it looks or smells extremely delicious.

She was bent down getting the casserole from the oven. The fragrant steam made his mouth water.

□ People also use the much more frequent adjective **mouth-watering** to mean the same thing.

There are quite a number of cookbooks nowadays that give numerous mouth-watering recipes for meals that satisfy without putting on weight.

make your mouth water: 2

If you say that something **makes** your **mouth water**, you are emphasizing that it is

very attractive or appealing. This expression is used mainly in journalism.

London Zoo now has fewer visitors than its counterpart in Chester. Its site in Regent's Park would make any developer's mouth water.

The guitar solo is so luscious it makes my mouth water.

□ People also use the much more frequent adjective **mouth-watering** to mean the same thing.

The perks that go with the governorship are mouth-watering.

shoot your mouth off: 1 ◄

If you say that someone **is shooting** their **mouth off**, you are criticizing them for talking loudly and boastfully about themselves or their opinions.

He'd been shooting his mouth off saying he could sing, when of course, he couldn't.

He shot off his mouth about the Fascist government one Saturday night in his local. That weekend was the last time his family saw him.

shoot your mouth off: 2

If you say that someone **has been shooting** their **mouth off** about something, you are criticizing them for talking publicly about something which is secret.

'What if he decides to try for a little more money, or to shoot his mouth off around town?' 'I've thought of that. Without me to back him up with Lonnie's story about the mine explosion, the people would only laugh at him.'

speak out of both sides of your mouth
talk out of both sides of your mouth

If you accuse someone of **speaking** or **talking out of both sides of** their **mouth**, you are criticizing them because in different situations they give completely different advice or opinions, even though they are talking about the same thing. This expression is used in American English.

This whole thing shows one of Larry's problems, which is speaking out of both sides of his mouth. At Harvard he panders constantly to the students with his radical rhetoric. But then, in the outer world, he is Laurence Tribe, national figure, who has to pull back from these positions.

movers

the movers and shakers ◄◄

If you refer to people as **the movers and shakers** of a particular event, organization, or movement, you admire them because they are the people who take an active part in it and make things happen, or who bring in new developments. This expression is used mainly in journalism.

She and her husband, the millionaire author

Ken Follett, have become movers and shakers behind the scenes of the Labour Party.

Cochran was only 21, but in four short years had established himself as one of the movers and shakers of '50s rock'n'roll.

mud

mud sticks ◄

If you say that **mud sticks**, you mean that when something bad is said about someone, people will continue to believe it, although it may have been proved to be completely untrue. This expression is used mainly in British English.

Whether he's innocent or not, some of the mud has stuck.

Unfortunately for Johnson, whatever the outcome of the trial, he will never be able to walk away from this story without some of the mud sticking.

sling mud
throw mud ◄◄

If you say that one person **is slinging mud** or **is throwing mud** at another, you disapprove of the first person because you think that they are trying to spoil the second person's reputation by saying bad things about them or by telling lies.

The elections have been straight personality contests, with the candidates slinging as much mud at their opponents as they can muster.

The newspaper and magazine articles that followed were especially vicious, with supporters of both stars quick to throw mud.

☐ You can refer to this kind of behaviour as **mud-slinging**.

A fragile truce seemed to be holding last night as Labour and Tory chiefs ordered an end to political mud-slinging.

a stick-in-the-mud ◄

If you refer to someone as **a stick-in-the-mud**, you disapprove of them because they do not like doing new things or having fun.

I felt sorry for him because he obviously wanted to enjoy himself but was married to a real stick-in-the-mud.

It was such a shame many of the guests didn't bother to dress up. What stick-in-the-muds.

☐ You can use **stick-in-the-mud** before a noun.

For a brief, glorious period at the beginning of this century the Beauvais tapestry workshops were shaken from their stick-in-the-mud traditions and galvanised into producing new, revolutionary designs.

☐ You can also say that someone **sticks in the mud**.

Some people stick in the mud, they're satisfied with the way they are.

murder

get away with murder ◄◄

If you say that someone **gets away with murder**, you are complaining that they seem to be able to do whatever they like without anyone trying to control, punish, or criticize them.

His charm and the fact that he is so likeable often allows him to get away with murder.

British firms are being clobbered time and again by this power-hungry Commission when continental firms get away with economic murder.

It's hard for old women to travel. If you're a man you can get away with murder. Everywhere you go you're made welcome. But a single woman, no way!

scream blue murder
scream bloody murder ◄

If you say that someone **is screaming blue murder** or **screaming bloody murder**, you mean that they are making a lot of noise or fuss about something. Other verbs can be used instead of 'scream'. 'Scream blue murder' is used only in British English.

People are screaming blue murder about the amount of traffic going through their town.

On the one hand, the politicians want to be told what the policy is and the president to have a strong voice. On the other hand, they would scream bloody murder if they weren't consulted.

The lads push forward, shrieking blue murder, kicking down barriers, till they reach the high perspex wall that separates the gangs.

muscles

flex your muscles
flex your muscle ◄◄◄

If people or organizations **flex** their **muscles**, they behave in a way intended to show that they have power and are considering using it. You can also say that people or organizations **flex** their **muscle**.

The National Party is certainly flexing its muscles in the early days of this new Government.

It's time to flex your muscles and show the world what you are capable of.

The miners' actions last year seem to have encouraged workers in the oil industry to flex their industrial muscle.

music

face the music ◄◄

If you **face the music**, you accept responsibility for something that you have done wrong and you prepare yourself to be criticized or punished for it.

There was no need for an explanation. We

were foreigners in a forbidden area, the authorities had found out and we were about to face the music.

I know the police aren't likely to think of looking for me here in the Regency-Ritz, but I can't hole up here forever. Sooner or later, I'm going to have to face the music.

music to your ears ◄◄

If you say that something is **music to** your **ears**, you mean that it makes you feel very happy when you hear it, for example because you have been hoping or waiting to hear it for a long time.

Old Judge Lebrun's words were music to the ears of a twenty-nine-year-old lawyer who had just won the first important case she had ever pleaded as leading barrister.

'There'll be another big bonus in it for you.' 'Music to my ears.'

mustard

not cut the mustard ◄

If you say that someone **doesn't cut the mustard**, you mean that their work or performance is not as good as it should be.

Is it possible, I ask with some trepidation, that Potter may be a fine writer but as a director, certainly of his own material, he doesn't quite cut the mustard?

You have to be on form every week and people soon start noticing if you're not cutting the mustard.

☐ You say that someone can **cut the mustard** to emphasize that their work or performance is as good as or better than you expected it to be.

The first backstage reports are that Sarah is okay. She has great presence and can really cut the mustard.

muster

pass muster ◄◄

If someone or something **passes muster**, they are considered to be satisfactory for a particular purpose or job. This expression is used mainly in written English.

I had but one fellow traveller for a moment, a Frenchman who, finding that I could not pass muster in his language, mercifully left me in search of more congenial company.

Only Azerbaijan has yet to fulfill all the membership requirements, but it is expected to pass muster soon.

mutton

mutton dressed as lamb ◄

If someone describes a middle-aged or old woman as **mutton dressed as lamb** or **mutton dressed up as lamb**, they disapprove of her because she dresses in a style which they consider suitable only for younger women. This expression is used in British English.

You would never be able to describe her as mutton dressed up as lamb because she obviously still feels young and fresh in herself so she carries off the look extremely well.

☐ This expression is occasionally applied to things rather than people, in order to suggest that something old is being falsely made to look new.

Union leader, Jim Thomas described the move as 'mutton dressed up as lamb'. He said the jobs were not new but part of a relocation deal with Germany, in which the UK lost more jobs than were gained.

☐ People sometimes exploit this expression, for example by replacing 'lamb' with another noun.

This mutton dressed as lamentable science was sandwiched between the proceedings of a conference on chaos theory.

N

nail

another nail in the coffin
the last nail in the coffin
the final nail in the coffin ◄◄◄

If you say that an event is **another nail in the coffin** of something or someone, you mean that it is the latest in a series of events which are seriously harming that thing or person.

The vote is another nail in the coffin of the one-party system which the country has now largely renounced.

The President took the blame for the chaos

and it became another nail in the coffin of his regime.

☐ If you say that an event is **the last nail** or **the final nail in the coffin** of something, you mean that it finally destroys that thing. If you say that an event is **the last nail** or **the final nail in the coffin** for a person, you mean that it finally puts an end to that person's hopes or plans.

Historians may well record the past three days in Moscow as driving the final nail into the coffin of more than seventy years of Soviet communism.

Another rise in the already crippling interest

rates would be the final nail in the coffin for millions of home owners whose mortgage is already worth more than their home.

hit the nail on the head ◄

If someone makes a comment and you say that they **have hit the nail on the head**, you mean that they have described a situation or problem exactly.

'It really reflects badly on the state of our game when so many top clubs are queuing up to pay £3 million for an average player. Football clearly doesn't understand the value of money anymore.' 'You've hit the nail right on the head.'

I agree with Dr Carey, everything he says. I think he's hit the nail right on the head.

on the nail: 1

If you pay cash **on the nail** for something, you pay for it immediately and in cash. This expression is used in British English; the American expression is **on the barrelhead**.

You have to pay cash on the nail sometimes, and this was one of them.

☐ If you pay money **on the nail**, you pay it at exactly the time you are supposed to.

The Marwood family has subsequently said that the money was never repaid but Violet, who was handling Ford's affairs, said it was, and on the nail.

on the nail: 2
hit it on the nail

If you talk about a particular time or amount **on the nail**, you mean that time or amount exactly. If you say that someone **has hit it on the nail**, you mean that they have described a situation exactly.

'When did Captain Schmidt come to see you?' 'Six o'clock, just about on the nail.'

'It sounds as if he almost depended on you as much as you depended on him.' 'You just hit it on the nail.'

name

make a name for yourself ◄◄◄

If you say that someone **has made a name for** themselves by doing a particular thing, you mean that they have become famous or well-known as a result of doing that thing.

Diane Abbott has made a name for herself as a hardworking MP.

Mel Fisher has made a name for himself hunting for and finding underwater treasure off the Florida Keys.

In the early '70s, this cartoon strip made a name for itself by attacking the Nixon administration.

the name of the game ◄◄◄

If you say that something is **the name of the game**, you mean that it is the most im-

portant aspect of the activity that you are talking about.

In the current economic climate, survival is the name of the game.

The name of our game is to provide a quality product to the consumer at a fair price.

Having fun in the sun, and forgetting about tomorrow, is the name of this particular game. And a lot of people out there are playing it for all they are worth.

a name to conjure with ◄

If you say that someone or something is **a name to conjure with**, you mean that they are very important, influential, or memorable. This expression is used mainly in British English.

His partners are serious about his potential as a name to conjure with in the scent market.

Bugattis, Bentleys, Ferraris – motoring names to conjure with, and all part of a breath-taking display of classic cars.

not have a penny to your name
not have a cent to your name ◄

If you say that someone **hasn't a penny to** their **name** or **hasn't a cent to** their **name**, you are emphasizing that they have very little money.

He didn't have a penny to his name.

My baby will end up a helpless old man without a cent to his name.

☐ If someone has a certain amount of money **to** their **name**, that is the amount of money that they have.

In 1990, with only $500 to her name, she landed a $33,000-a-week contract.

take someone's name in vain

If someone says that another person **takes** God's **name in vain**, they mean that the person uses it disrespectfully, especially by swearing.

He persevered, and always gently corrected us when we took the Lord's name in vain.

☐ You can say that someone **is taking** another person's or a thing's **name in vain** when you think that they are using them for their own purposes in an inappropriate or disrespectful way.

The minister for science cited Green's work as an example of good British research. Green feels that his name was being taken in vain. 'There is a tremendous amount of bitterness at what has been done by the government,' he says. 'If there has been good research, it has been in spite of what the government has done.'

your name is mud

If you say that someone's **name is mud**, you mean that they have said or done something which has made them very unpopular with a particular group of people.

His name has been mud at the Telegraph since he left to work for a rival newspaper.

names

call someone names   ◄◄◄

If someone **calls** you **names**, they use insulting words or expressions to describe you when they are talking to you or about you.

At my last school they called me names because I was so slow.

Did anybody ever give you any trouble, yell at you, call you names?

They had, among other things, called her rude names and stuck lewd pictures on the fire station's walls.

☐ You can describe this behaviour as **name-calling**.

The newspaper's political stance at the moment consists of little more than name-calling.

It's a silly name that people like you call us. I grew out of name calling at school.

napping

catch someone napping   ◄

If someone **is caught napping**, they are not prepared for something that happens, and perhaps lose an advantage as a result.

The security services were clearly caught napping and their immediate reaction was to detain large numbers of people, many apparently with little or no connection with the actual plot.

European firms have been caught napping. As a result, they now control barely one-tenth of the world market for semiconductors, while fast-moving Japanese firms control nearly half of it.

nature

the nature of the beast   ◄

If you say that something is **the nature of the beast**, you mean that it is an essential part of the character of the person or thing that you are talking about.

Baker likes to say that negotiations always get tougher towards the end. That's the very nature of the beast.

☐ If you say that someone knows or understands **the nature of the beast**, you mean that they know or understand a particular person or thing very well.

Having served as Secretary of State for Education in Edward Heath's government, she knew the nature of the beast.

Why did he join the army in the first place, when he must have been aware of the nature of the beast?

navel

navel-gazing
navel-contemplation
gaze at your navel
contemplate your navel   ◄

If you accuse someone of **navel-gazing** or **navel-contemplation**, you are criticizing them for thinking only about themselves and their own problems or activities, rather than concerning themselves with the problems or activities of other people.

I'm very good at motivating people to do things, so I'm a doer rather than a thinker. I've never really done much navel-gazing!

Not even the cruellest critic of the British art world could accuse this autumn's exhibitions of insularity. Navel contemplation has been banished, and horizons extended to some of the most remote regions of the world.

☐ **Navel-gazing** can be used before a noun.

The film is a sort of navel-gazing look at Hollywood.

☐ You can also say that someone **gazes at** their **navel** or **contemplates** their **navel**.

The Institute has always been famous for contemplating its own navel.

near

so near and yet so far   ◄

You say **so near and yet so far** or **so near yet so far** to express regret or sadness when you have got very close to achieving what you wanted, but in the end you just failed.

Manager Jim Smith admitted that to have victory snatched away in such a desperate manner was a crushing experience. 'It's heartbreaking to be so near, yet so far,' he said.

neck

breathe down someone's neck: 1   ◄

In a race, contest, or other competitive situation, if someone **is breathing down** your **neck**, they are close behind you and may soon catch up with you or beat you.

I took the lead with Colin Chapman breathing down my neck in his Lotus Eleven.

No doubt Jones and Armstrong maintain a consistently high standard because both have talented rivals breathing down their necks.

breathe down someone's neck: 2   ◄

If you say that someone **is breathing down** your **neck**, you mean that they are closely watching and checking everything that you do.

Most farmers have bank managers breathing down their necks, so everything has to have an economic reason.

Lawyers have been working into the night to complete legal documents, with civil servants breathing down their necks.

dead from the neck up

In British English, if you say that someone is **dead from the neck up**, you are saying very rudely that they are stupid. If you say that something is **dead from the neck up**, you mean that it is not intellectually challenging or original in any way. 'Upwards' can be used instead of 'up'.

Your driver just sat there. He had never considered the prospect of kidnapping, of having to take evasive action. If you want my opinion, your driver was dead from the neck up.

The debate on Labour's future has been dead from the neck upwards. It has utterly failed to excite the party, let alone the country.

get it in the neck ◄

If someone **gets it in the neck**, they are punished or strongly criticized for something wrong that they have done. This expression is used in British English.

This film is an attack on the media, especially the television news media. It's quite nice to see them get it in the neck for once.

neck and neck ◄◄◄

In a race or contest, if two competitors are **neck and neck**, they are exactly level with each other, so that it is impossible to say who will win.

The latest opinion polls show both parties running neck and neck.

Leeds are currently neck-and-neck with Manchester United for the Championship.

□ You can use **neck and neck** before a noun.

Philippe Jeantot of France and the South African John Martin are involved in a neck and neck race to finish second across the line.

risk your neck ◄

If you do something dangerous which could result in your being killed or injured, you can say that you **risk your neck** doing it.

Drew even insisted on doing her own stunt riding. She risked her neck in one scene when she had to ride over a fence, guns blazing, before ducking under an arch.

I won't have him risking his neck on that motorcycle.

stick your neck out ◄◄

If you **stick your neck out**, you say or do something which other people are afraid to say or do, even though this may cause trouble or difficulty for you.

First of all, I'll stick my neck out here and I will say that Aston Villa won't go into the Second Division next season.

At the risk of sticking my neck out, I doubt whether the compensation fund will be needed.

up to your neck ◄◄

If you say that someone is **up to** their **neck** in something bad such as debt or corruption, you mean that they are very deeply involved in it.

The city appeared to be constantly either hovering on the brink of financial ruin or up to its neck in allegations of corruption.

The Prime Minister was up to his neck in scandal.

He is in the cocaine traffic right up to his neck.

wring someone's neck ◄

If you are very angry with someone, you can say that you would like to **wring** their **neck**.

That crazy Dot! He could wring her neck for this! She had no right to tell tales to his mother!

I still love you even though I'd like to wring your neck.

your neck of the woods ◄

You can refer to the place where you live as your **neck of the woods**.

I discovered, however, that stone troughs were pretty scarce in my neck of the woods and expensive as well.

□ You can refer to the place where you are at the moment as **this neck of the woods**.

Now, in this neck of the woods at least, well-supported new plays are to be seen from new and established companies.

What's there to do in this neck of the woods?

needle

like looking for a needle in a haystack ◄

If you say that trying to find something is **like looking for a needle in a haystack**, you mean that it is extremely difficult or even impossible to find it.

Police have told Mrs Barrow that searching for the dog will be like looking for a needle in a haystack. She agrees that once a greyhound has disappeared, the chances of recovering the animal are slim.

□ People often extend or vary this expression. For example, if you say that looking for something is **like looking for a needle in several haystacks**, you are emphasizing that you are very unlikely indeed to find it.

Finding a gene amongst the hundreds of thousands of genes contained on a chromosome is rather like looking for a needle in several haystacks.

Then of course we've got to find the antibody that we want, and that's the problem with the new technology. It's really like the needle in the haystack. We've got to go through the haystack, straw by straw, pulling out the needle.

nelly

not on your nelly

You can say **'not on your nelly'** to emphasize that there is no chance at all of something happening. This is a rather old-
fashioned expression, which is used in British
English.

*'If you've got something to say, then come out
with it, or, better still, come in and see me.'
'Not on your nelly. You've done nothing about
our Kev. You're as twisted as the other lot.'*

*They finally become adults, thanks to all your
hard work, and do they turn up for mum's
birthday? Not on your nellie.*

☐ 'Nelly' is sometimes spelled 'nellie'.

nerve

touch a nerve
strike a raw nerve
hit a nerve   ◄◄◄

If something that you say **touches a nerve**
or **touches a raw nerve**, it upsets someone,
because you have mentioned a subject that
they feel strongly about or are very sensitive
about. You can also say that it **strikes** or **hits
a nerve** or **a raw nerve**.

*Buchanan's speech touched a raw nerve here
at the Capitol.*

*She seemed to strike a nerve when she asked
Dr. Lowe about his past life.*

*Those remarks hit a raw nerve with congres-
sional Democrats, drawing an angry response
from Senate Majority Leader George Mitchell
of Maine.*

☐ You can also talk about a remark **finding**
or **exposing a raw nerve**.

*In making their call for a neutral inspection
team, the government have exercised their talent for finding a raw nerve, as doubts have
been raised about the neutrality of some of the
weapons inspectors.*

Every raw nerve had been exposed.

nerves

a bundle of nerves
a bag of nerves   ◄

If you say that someone is **a bundle of
nerves**, you mean that they are extremely
nervous, worried, or tense. In British English,
you can also say that they are **a bag of
nerves**.

What's the matter? You're a bundle of nerves.

*When we met, I was such a bag of nerves. I
had no confidence in myself at all.*

get on someone's nerves   ◄◄◄

If you say that someone or something **gets
on** your **nerves**, you mean that they annoy or
irritate you.

*It was so hot, and there we were, just cooped
up together, getting on each other's nerves.*

*The phone used to get on my nerves – people
ringing him at home as if it was an extension
of the office.*

live on your nerves
live on your nerve ends

If you say that someone **is living on** their
nerves or **living on** their **nerve ends**, you
mean that they are always worried and anxious, because they are in a difficult situation.
These expressions are used in British English.

*Once this is all over and done with I've told
her she's to go into the clinic for a complete
rest to get her strength back, because she's living on her nerves.*

*'There are times of such depression,' says Mrs
Velic, who lived on her nerves for two months
after escaping Sarajevo in October.*

a war of nerves
a battle of nerves   ◄◄

If two opposing people or groups are carrying on **a war of nerves** or **a battle of
nerves**, they are trying to weaken each other
psychologically, for example by frightening
each other, in order to get what they want
without taking any direct action.

*Iraqi officials insist they did not back down
in the latest war of nerves with the US and its
allies.*

*There may be a truce in the long war of
nerves between the White House and Congress
over how this country conducts secret intelligence operations abroad.*

*In what is increasingly becoming a battle of
nerves, the drug barons have increased pressure on the government.*

nest

feather your nest   ◄

If you accuse someone of **feathering** their
nest, you are accusing them of taking advantage of their position in order to get a lot of
money, so that they can lead a comfortable
life.

*The politicians seem anxious to feather their
nests at the expense of the people.*

*It wasn't done to feather his own nest, it was
for his son.*

fly the nest
leave the nest   ◄

When children **fly the nest** or **leave the
nest**, they leave their parents' home to live on
their own. Compare **fly the coop**; see **coop**.

*One day the children are going to fly the nest
and have their own lives.*

*When their children had flown the nest, he
and his wife moved to a thatched cottage in
Dorset.*

Catherine is soon to leave the nest: tired of

London life, she's off to the Sorbonne with a friend.

foul your own nest

If you say that someone **has fouled** their **own nest**, you mean that they have done something which damages their own interests or chances of success. This is a literary expression.

Man has invented a hundred brilliant ways of fouling his own nest – the grime, the pollution, the heat, the poisons in the air, the metals in the water.

a nest egg   ◄◄◄

A **nest egg** is a sum of money that you are saving for a particular purpose.

All he wanted was a few months decent money to help him retire. He thought this was his last chance to build a nest egg.

He collected about $450m as a retirement nest-egg when he sold most of his controlling stake to Canadian Pacific.

net

cast a wide net
cast the net wider   ◄◄

If you **cast a wide net**, you involve a large number of things or people in what you are doing. If you **cast the net wider**, you increase the number of things or people that are involved. These expressions can be varied; for example, you can use 'spread' instead of 'cast'.

The U.S. has cast a wide diplomatic net, asking a variety of other nations to deliver the same message to Iran and to Syria.

We will cast the net wider to look at many other factors too.

In 1952 and 1953 I made my first intelligence contacts with the British and French. Later, in London, I was able to spread my net wider.

This is an ambitious book that casts its net over a wide range of subjects.

slip through the net: 1
fall through the net   ◄◄

If people **slip through the net** or **fall through the net**, the system which is supposed to help or deal with them does not do it properly. These expressions are used in British English; the American expression is **fall through the cracks**.

It's hard to knock the selection process because the chances of any young talent slipping through the net are so minimal.

Ninety-one per cent of GPs believed patients would fall through the net under the system.

Vulnerable adults may be slipping through the social work net.

slip through the net: 2   ◄

If someone who is behaving illegally **slips**

through the net, they avoid being caught by the system or trap that is meant to catch them. This expression is used mainly in British English.

Government officials fear some of the thugs identified by British police may have slipped through the net.

□ If illegal goods **slip through the net**, the system which is meant to discover them does not find them.

A shipment of 44 kilos of cocaine slipped through the customs net at Gatwick.

□ You can use other verbs instead of 'slip'.

We have an exceptionally comprehensive drug detecting system. I would hope that there is nothing that would get through the net, but one can't be so confident that there isn't something that we would miss.

nettle

grasp the nettle   ◄◄

If someone **grasps the nettle**, they deal with a problem or unpleasant task quickly and in a determined way. This expression is used mainly in British English.

It's better to grasp the nettle, speak to your superior and make it clear you regret your mistake and are determined it will never happen again.

Some industrialists believe the government should grasp the nettle of devaluation before the referendum.

news

be news to someone   ◄◄

If someone says something and you say that it **is news to** you, you mean that you did not know about it previously. You usually use this expression to express surprise at what has been said, or to suggest that it may not be true.

When he was told about the story, the governor said it was news to him.

'I'm a very experienced babysitter,' she said quickly. 'I've had lots of child-care experience back home.' This was news to me. As far as I could tell, Pat hardly knew the difference between a baby and a bottle of ketchup.

no news is good news   ◄

If someone is waiting for information about a situation and they do not hear anything, you can say to them '**no news is good news**'. This is a way of saying that there is no need to worry, because people normally only send information when something bad has happened.

I had heard nothing all week. 'Oh well,' I thought. 'No news is good news.'

□ People often exploit this expression, for example by saying that **no news is bad news**.

This is a way of saying that a lack of information about something is worrying.

People always suspect that no news is bad news.

No news is not always good news.

nice

nice as pie

If you say that someone is as **nice as pie**, you mean that they are very kind, friendly, and charming. You usually say this when their behaviour is not what you expect, or when it contrasts with their behaviour at other times. Compare **sweet as pie**; see **sweet**.

He is nice as pie when you meet him, then you hear he is going around bad-mouthing you.

niche

carve a niche ◄◄

If you **carve a niche** for yourself or **carve out a niche**, you create a secure position for yourself, especially at work.

He has carved a niche for himself as an ABC television commentator and is certain to be retained provided the network continues to broadcast Saturday matches.

The firm is carving out what could be a lucrative niche in the market for microprocessors.

nick

in the nick of time ◄◄

If you say that something happens **in the nick of time**, you mean that it happens at the last possible moment, when it is almost too late.

She woke up in the nick of time and raised the alarm.

You were just in the nick of time. I was nearly suffocated.

nickel

nickel and dime: 1 ◄

If you describe someone or something as **nickel and dime**, you mean that they are not very important or only function on a small scale. 'Nickels and dimes' and 'nickel-dime' are also used with the same meaning. These expressions are used in American English.

The boss is dead and now every nickel and dime drug dealer and money launderer can come in here and ply his trade.

It's only a nickels and dimes business.

It's nickel-dime stuff, though, compared to what you and Michael have to deal with.

nickel and dime: 2 ◄

If you accuse a person of **nickel and diming** someone or something, you are criticizing that person for weakening or exhaust-

ing them, for example by continually taking small amounts of money away from them, or by continually making small changes or requests. This expression is used in American English.

Larger spending cuts are often easier to swallow than smaller ones. It's easier to carve out a chunk someplace and meet your target than it is to nickel and dime everyone and have everybody angry at you.

Oakland, like other cities, has been reeling from financial crisis and consequently has been nickel-and-diming essential services for years.

The price tag was becoming more than the budget could absorb. A fundamentally solid idea was about to be nickeled and dimed to death.

a wooden nickel

If you refer to something as **a wooden nickel**, you mean that it is completely false or worthless. This expression is used in American English.

He looked at the card as though it were a wooden nickel. 'That doesn't prove a thing,' he said.

night

a night owl ◄

If you describe someone as **a night owl**, you mean that they regularly stay up late at night, or prefer to work late at night.

Behind Madrid's historical facades is the vibrant, beating heart of a city which will test even the most energetic night owl.

The street noise and late-night parties make this hotel a haven for night owls.

ninepins

fall like ninepins ◄

If you say that things **are falling like ninepins**, you mean that they are rapidly being damaged or destroyed, one after another. 'Go down' and 'drop' can be used instead of 'fall'. This expression is used in British English.

Conservative council seats fell like ninepins.

There was a time when Liverpool players never seemed to get injured, but now they are going down like ninepins.

nines

dress to the nines ◄

If you say that someone is **dressed to the nines** or is **dressed up to the nines**, you mean that they are wearing very smart or glamorous clothes. This expression is often used to suggest that someone is dressed in an exaggerated or inappropriate way.

Everyone is dressed up to the nines. Huge hats, frills, tight dresses, sequins and high heels.

They dress to the nines when they go out on the town.

□ In British English, you can also say that someone **is done up to the nines** or **is togged up to the nines**.

You're more likely to find the genuine rogue done up to the nines in an Armani suit.

They're off to some night spot, all togged up to the nines.

nineteen

talk nineteen to the dozen

If you say that someone is talking **nineteen to the dozen**, you mean that they are talking very quickly, without pausing. This expression is used in British English.

Ms Wallace visited them on February 28th and found them 'vivacious and chatty and talking nineteen to the dozen'.

nip

nip and tuck ◄

In a competition or contest, if it is **nip and tuck**, it is impossible to say who will win because both sides are performing equally well.

It was nip and tuck throughout as the players struck the ball with equal venom.

It was nip-and-tuck from start to finish.

nits

pick nits

If you say that someone **is picking nits**, you mean that they are pointing out small problems or faults with something, often ones which seem relatively unimportant.

Like many people who have been in the field for decades, he has some nits to pick with some of the recent trends in waiting tables.

He then spent the second half of his intervention picking nits, particularly about the environmental impact for 'the beautiful' Bluebell Hill.

□ The verb 'nitpick' has a similar meaning, and there is also a much more frequent word 'nitpicking'. These words are generally used more disapprovingly than 'pick nits', to express criticism of someone who is deliberately trying to find faults.

nod

give someone the nod
get the nod ◄◄◄

If someone **gives** you **the nod**, they give you permission to go ahead with something, or they promise you their support. You can also say that you **get the nod** from them.

The summit will probably give the nod to the idea of a Community-wide strategy for economic growth.

We'll hold off interviewing Hythe any further until we get the nod from you.

□ This expression can be varied. For example, if you **are waiting for the nod** from someone, you are waiting for them to give you permission or to promise support. If you **have the nod**, you have been given permission or have been promised support.

We're waiting for the nod from the Secretary-General.

GK already holds 28.5 per cent that it bought from Whitbread Investment Company and has the nod from them for a further 14.9 per cent.

a nod and a wink ◄

If someone gives you **a nod and a wink**, they communicate something to you by saying it indirectly or by giving you some kind of signal. This expression is usually used to show disapproval, often because something illegal or dishonest is taking place. This expression is used in British English.

The newspaper report suggested that he had given a 'nod and wink' for machine tool makers to break the spirit of the arms embargo by emphasising that their equipment was for peaceful and not military purposes.

A nod and a wink from the chairman is all it takes to move share prices up or down.

□ You can say that someone uses a **nod and wink** approach.

There has been so-called 'nod and wink' diplomacy on the sidelines.

□ If you say **'a nod's as good as a wink'**, you mean that it is not necessary to explain something further, because you understand what someone has already signalled to you or told you indirectly.

on the nod

If a proposal goes through **on the nod**, it is accepted without being questioned or argued about. This expression is used in British English.

Once upon a time, the matter would have gone through on the nod, but no longer. After an hour and a half of reportedly angry discussion, the council's housing commission said no.

The party cannot be seen to let the treaty through on the nod.

noises

make noises ◄◄

If you say that someone **is making noises** about something, you mean that they are talking about it in a vague, indirect, or indefinite way.

John Major has been making noises about making government more open.

During his 18th year Paul's mother had started making noises about it being time for him to leave home, something which worried him a great deal.

□ You can show what kind of impression someone is trying to create by putting an adjective before 'noises'.

He made all sorts of encouraging noises that he would love Scotland to stage the European Championships.

He bought 20 per cent of Mr Rowland's international holding company Lonrho, and then made threatening noises about taking it over.

make the right noises ◄

If you say that someone **is making the right noises** about a problem or issue, you mean that their remarks suggest that they will deal with the situation in the way that you want them to.

The company is making the right noises about further cuts in costs and capital expenditure, and the disposal of non-core businesses.

The President was making all the right noises about multi-party democracy and human rights.

nooks

the nooks and crannies
every nook and cranny ◄◄◄

If you talk about **the nooks and crannies** of a place or object, you are talking about the smaller or less accessible parts which are not normally noticed. If you talk about **every nook and cranny**, you are emphasizing that you mean all parts of a place or object.

In the weeks before Christmas, we would scour the house, searching all the nooks and crannies trying to find our presents.

That would explain why all these guys are so eager to get hold of our boat. It's full of nooks and crannies where it would be easy for a smuggler to sneak stuff through customs.

I do love how he knows every nook and cranny of Venice and can speak such good Italian.

nose

cut off your nose to spite your face

If you say that someone **is cutting off** their **nose to spite** their **face**, you mean they are doing something in order to hurt another person, without realizing or caring that they will hurt themselves just as much or even more.

It is clear that while the manager would not be prepared to cut off his nose to spite his face by leaving out the centre-half, he is concerned that the player should realise the error of his ways.

follow your nose: 1

If you **follow** your **nose**, you make decisions and behave in a particular way because you feel instinctively that this is what you

should do, rather than because you are following any guidelines or rules.

I'd started a bit of journalism, so I had a source of income. And I've just followed my nose doing that ever since.

There was a feeling that people in the institutes were just following their noses and not doing anything that was relevant.

follow your nose: 2

If someone tells you to **follow** your **nose** when you are looking for a place, they are telling you to go straight ahead, or to follow the most obvious route.

More or less follow your nose till you come to Marks and Spencer's. Bear right there. And it's there.

get up someone's nose ◄◄

If you say that something or someone **gets up** your **nose**, you mean that they irritate you a great deal. This is an informal expression, which is used mainly in British English.

Imagine my surprise when I contacted the dealers and was told 'Sorry, it will not arrive until February 10.' What really gets up my nose is that all I want is a standard white car.

This producer looks as if he's going to get up everybody's nose. He has only been here for a few hours and already he has been babbling about 'discipline' to Annie.

give someone a bloody nose: 1
get a bloody nose
bloody someone's nose ◄

In a contest or competition, if one side **is given a bloody nose**, it is defeated in a way that does not cause permanent damage but makes it look foolish or inferior. You can also say that it **gets**, **receives**, or **has a bloody nose**. These expressions are mostly used in written English.

Most are so fed up with this current attack on the elderly they are threatening to give the Government more than a bloody nose in the forthcoming by-election.

□ You can also say that one side in a contest **bloodies the nose of** the other side.

A full-scale ambush is almost certainly beyond the Welsh team. But they'll be looking for a few opportunities to bloody English noses, all the same.

give someone a bloody nose: 2
get a bloody nose

In a war or conflict, if one side **is given a bloody nose**, it is damaged sufficiently to cause it to withdraw, at least for a time. You can also say that one side **gets, receives**, or **has a bloody nose**. These expressions are used mainly in written English.

Giving the national army a bloody nose is one thing. Taking on its full might is another.

□ You can also say that one side in a conflict **bloodies the nose of** the other side.

He never forgave the rebels for bloodying the nose of the army he sent against them in 1979.

keep your nose clean ◄

If you **keep** your **nose clean**, you behave well and avoid trouble.

Most of them have done nothing brave or remarkable. They have merely done their jobs properly, kept their noses clean and have already been amply rewarded by hefty salaries.

The best advice I can give is tell you to keep your nose clean.

keep your nose out of something

If someone tells you to **keep** your **nose out of** something, they are telling you rather rudely not to interfere in it, because it does not concern you. Compare **poke** your **nose into** something.

Nancy realized that this was his way of telling her to keep her nose out of his business.

The libertarians will try to argue that the government should keep its hand out of Americans' wallets and its nose out of their bedrooms.

keep your nose to the grindstone ◄

If you **keep** your **nose to the grindstone**, you concentrate on working hard at your job, and do not concern yourself with other things.

There is more to life than keeping one's nose to the grindstone and saving for a rainy day.

He told the accountants to get back to the grindstone and try to figure out a way to show a profit.

lead someone by the nose

If someone **leads** you **by the nose** or **leads** you **around by the nose**, they control you completely so that you do whatever they want. This expression is often used to suggest that the person being led is foolish or wrong to let this happen.

The Government has let itself be led by the nose by the timber trade into suppressing the report for the narrow commercial advantage of those involved.

look down your nose at something ◄◄

If you say that someone **looks down** their **nose at** a thing or person, you mean that they regard that thing or person as inferior and treat them with scorn or disrespect. You use this expression to show disapproval of this attitude.

If anyone leaves my shop feeling that we'd looked down our noses at them for not buying expensive cheese, I would be very ashamed.

The minister and his intellectual friends still look down their noses at Disneyland and the American soap operas such as Santa Barbara.

a nose for something ◄◄

If you say that someone has **a nose for** something, you mean that they have a natural talent for finding it.

He had a nose for trouble and a brilliant tactical mind.

Harry runs his own news agency in the north. He has a well-trained nose for a story.

How does he rate a good record over an indifferent one? 'You just feel it, somehow, if it's good,' he says. 'You develop a nose for it.'

not see beyond your nose
not see beyond the end of your nose

If you say that someone **can't see beyond** their **nose**, or **can't see beyond the end of** their **nose**, you are criticizing them for thinking only about themselves and their immediate needs, rather than about other people or wider and longer-term issues. You can replace 'beyond' with 'further than', and 'see' with other verbs.

We want our people to be able to see beyond their own noses and to keep things in perspective. We want them to understand that what is best for the whole organization might not be best for their own part in it.

It is high time that British industry started thinking beyond the end of its nose. The trouble is that what companies perceive to be in their own interest is not necessarily what the country needs.

on the nose: 1

If you talk about a time or amount being **on the nose**, you mean that it is exactly that time or amount.

This is Radio One FM. Precisely on the nose seven sixteen.

on the nose: 2

If you describe someone or something as **on the nose**, you mean that they are considered to be unpleasant or offensive. This expression is used mainly in Australian English.

North West Airlines might be on the nose here and in Japan but it's definitely flavour of the month in the United States.

His comments are really on the nose.

pay through the nose for something ◄

If you **pay through the nose** for something, you pay more for it than you consider fair or reasonable. This is a fairly informal expression.

Some restaurateurs have cottoned on to the fact that we do not like paying through the nose for our wines when eating out.

It looks as though those taking out new insurance policies on their houses, cars, boats and planes will be paying through the nose.

poke your nose into something
stick your nose into something   ◄◄

If you say that someone is **poking** their **nose into** something or **sticking** their **nose into** it, you mean that they are interfering in something that does not concern them. Compare **keep** your **nose out of** something.

We don't like foreigners who poke their noses into our affairs.

Newspapers are full of snide remarks about the European Commission's bureaucrats sticking their noses into every nook and cranny of our private lives.

If anyone should be apologizing, it should be me for poking my nose in where it doesn't belong.

put someone's nose out of joint   ◄

If something **puts** someone's **nose out of joint**, it offends or upsets them, because they think that they have not been treated with the respect that they deserve. You often use this expression to suggest that the person who is offended thinks that they are more important than they really are.

Gillian's sons, 17 and 15, were resentful of the female invasion. Barry, the youngest, had his nose put out of joint by Lucy's aloof sophistication, although she was his junior.

☐ You can also say that someone's **nose is out of joint** or that someone **has** their **nose out of joint**.

The old kind of Democrat has tried and failed miserably and there are some old kinds of Democrats around Washington who have their noses a little out of joint about that.

rub someone's nose in it
rub someone's nose in the dirt   ◄◄

If you **rub** someone's **nose in it** or **rub** their **nose in the dirt**, you embarrass or upset them by reminding them of something that they do not want to think about, such as a failure or a mistake that they have made.

You obviously delight in the defeat of a fellow performer! And proceed to rub his nose in it, don't you?

If he agrees to withdraw his forces, should there be some other arrangement which would be a let-out rather than rubbing his nose in the dirt?

☐ You can also say that someone's nose **is rubbed in** a particular thing.

America should have basked in triumph after the fall of communism, but instead found its nose rubbed in inadequacies at home.

thumb your nose at someone   ◄◄

If you **thumb** your **nose at** someone or something powerful or influential, you behave in a way that shows disrespect or contempt for them.

There is a hard-core of young persistent of-

fenders, and too many of them are simply laughing at authority and thumbing their noses at the court.*

Workers are laid off while bosses are given enormous pay increases and vast bonuses, thus thumbing their noses at both employees and consumers.

☐ You can describe this behaviour as **nose-thumbing**.

These women's lives, as portrayed by Hollywood, were a nose-thumbing at stuffy Victorian England.

turn up your nose at something   ◄◄

If you say that someone **turns up** their **nose at** something, you mean that they reject it because they think that it is not good enough for them. You use this expression to show disapproval of the person's behaviour, because you think that they are being foolish or too proud.

Even in the United States top-flight university graduates turned up their noses at business jobs and tried instead to get into government service or university teaching.

You should never turn your nose up at inexpensive plants.

He acted in about 30 commercials as a struggling young actor, happily taking them on while his former classmates at the Yale drama school turned up their noses and waited on tables instead.

under your nose
from under your nose   ◄◄◄

If something, especially a bad thing, happens **under** your **nose**, it happens in your presence or very near to you, and you do not or cannot do anything to stop it.

The destruction of cities and millions of lives right under our noses is greeted with shrugs.

I really don't care what people do, as long as it's not under my nose.

☐ If someone takes something **from under** your **nose**, they do not try to hide the fact that they are taking it, and you either do not notice or cannot stop them.

Two prisoners handcuffed together in the back of a police car stole it from under the noses of two red-faced traffic officers.

nowhere

from nowhere
out of nowhere   ◄◄◄

If you say that someone or something comes **from nowhere**, you mean that they appear suddenly or unexpectedly, without any previous indication that they would appear. You can also say that someone or something comes **out of nowhere**.

I remember looking both ways before crossing

and seeing nothing. The car came from nowhere and hit me.

The film appeared out of nowhere and looks likely to disappear just as quickly.

All of these diseases have appeared seemingly out of nowhere, causing much misery and death.

nuclear

go nuclear

If someone **goes nuclear**, they get extremely angry and start behaving in a forceful or irrational way as a result. This expression is used mainly in British English. **Go ballistic** means the same.

Labour's tabloids were ready to go nuclear against the Tories if personal smears were deployed against Neil Kinnock and his team during the general election campaign.

nudge

a nudge and a wink
nudge-nudge, wink-wink ◄

You use expressions such as **a nudge and a wink** or **nudge-nudge, wink-wink** to indicate that someone is talking about something in a sly, suggestive way, because the subject is embarrassing or because they may get into trouble if they say it openly.

We are now being sued for approaching in an open, adult way what papers such as yourselves have been alluding to via nudge-and-a-wink innuendo for the past two years.

I'm tired of all the nods, all the nudges and the winks. I'm tired of all conjecture.

The article then listed a series of nudge-nudge, wink-wink rumors that have appeared in broadsheet and tabloid newspapers over the last two years, insinuating the Prime Minister was having an affair.

number

a back number

If you refer to someone as **a back number**, you are saying in a rather unkind way that they are no longer useful or successful.

The film gives us a real sense of the way the Japanese still honour those who might in other societies be considered back numbers.

Lester is 55 in November, but I don't think that will make much difference. He's a great jockey and won't be a back number even at that age.

□ A **back number** of a magazine or newspaper is an edition of it that was published some time ago and is not the most recent.

do a number on someone

If someone **does a number on** you, they harm you in some way, for example by cheat-

ing you or by totally defeating you in a game or match. This is an informal expression.

I really did a number on him. I'm going to try and make it up to him, if he'll let me.

The Irish team are looking to do a number on England in Dublin tomorrow.

have someone's number

If you **have** someone's **number**, you understand what kind of person they are, and so you know how to treat them or deal with them.

Oh, they've got his number. Beryl and Russell show up at 7:59, make a big point of saying good morning to him, and then they disappear. On sales calls, they say.

If they have your number from the start, and it is a small hotel, you are bound to get extra attention.

look after number one
look out for number one ◄

If you say that someone **looks after number one** or **looks out for number one**, you mean that they selfishly put their own needs and interests before everyone else's.

This sums up the attitude of many greedy big earners – look after Number One and to hell with everyone else.

My priority is to look after number one – to create a lifestyle I am happy with.

someone's number is up

If you say that someone's **number is up**, you mean that something unpleasant is going to happen to them, and that there is nothing that they can do about it. This expression is sometimes used to say that someone is certain to fail at something, or that they are about to lose their job. It can also be used to say that someone is going to die.

When Michael Stich found himself two match points down to Marc Rosset of Switzerland last night, he thought his number was up.

'Oh, Nancy, we're safe!' breathed Bess. 'I thought for a while our number was up!'

nut

do your nut

If someone **does** their **nut**, they become very angry about something. This expression is used in British English.

I wanted to ask Lorraine out and I knew that Wendy would do her nut if she found out.

a sledgehammer to crack a nut ◄

If you say that someone is using **a sledgehammer to crack a nut**, you mean that the methods they are using to solve a problem are far stronger than is necessary. People sometimes replace 'sledgehammer' with 'hammer'. This expression is used in British English.

Morocco took a similar view, saying there

was no justification for sanctions. These immediate Arab reactions reflect a view across the region that the West is using a sledgehammer to crack a nut.

Bankers say that the proposed law is a sledgehammer to crack a nut.

Robbins's film takes a large hammer to crack a familiar nut.

a tough nut to crack
a tough nut ◄

If you say that a problem is **a tough nut to crack**, you mean that it is difficult to resolve. If you say that someone is **a tough nut to crack**, you mean that they are difficult to deal with or to defeat in an argument or competition. You can replace 'tough' with another adjective such as 'hard' or 'difficult'.

The toughest nut to crack is the rather profound philosophical question: what is life?

Despite not having won a title of note, Harrington has taken 17.5 points from a possible 20 in international singles, making him a tough nut to crack.

I am looking for victory, but they are an organised team and could be a hard nut to crack.

□ You can also just refer to a difficult problem as **a tough nut**.

But the tough nut is the economy and health care, those two issues that do cost money and that require some complex strategy and a lot of risk taking.

nuts

the nuts and bolts of something ◄◄◄

The **nuts and bolts of** something are the detailed facts about it and its practical aspects, as opposed to abstract ideas about it.

Surely you have to work out the nuts and bolts of something before you can commit yourself to it?

Tonight Margaret Atwood will discuss the nuts and bolts of the writer's craft.

□ You can also use **nuts and bolts** before a noun.

I'm a nuts and bolts politician. I always have been.

Nuts-and-bolts information on the island is covered in Cuba Official Guide by A. Gerald Gravette.

nutshell

in a nutshell ◄◄◄

You say **in a nutshell** when you are summarizing something in a concise or brief way.

She wants me to leave the company. I want to stay. That's it in a nutshell.

To put the outcome of the UN summit in a nutshell, governments came round to recognising the decline of the environment.

nutty

nutty as a fruitcake

If you say that someone is as **nutty as a fruitcake**, you think that they are very strange, foolish, or crazy. This expression is used in British English.

He sounds a trifle defensive, but there's no need for it. Despite his maddening fidgeting, the man is a charmer – intense, funny, and nutty as a fruitcake.

O

oaks

great oaks from little acorns grow

People say **'great oaks from little acorns grow'** when they want to point out that something large and successful began in a small and insignificant way. Other adjectives can be used instead of 'great' and 'little'.

Big oaks from little acorns grow. Osborne & Little, one of the most established and best-known names in British interior design, started when two young men set up business in a tiny shop that is now part of an Italian restaurant.

Henry Ford did not start his operations by hiring 330,000 employees and opening hundreds of factories in his first year. Remember, mighty oaks from tiny acorns grow.

oar

put your oar in

If someone **puts** their **oar in** during a discussion or argument, they give their opinion, even if other people have not asked them for it. Verbs such as 'stick' and 'get' can be used instead of 'put'. This expression is used mainly in British English.

The ex-party leader could not resist putting his oar in at the 1983 General Election. In a speech in Cardiff he dissociated himself from Labour's manifesto commitment to unilateral nuclear disarmament.

He is modest enough to let them say their piece without feeling the need to put his oar in; he is obviously a good listener.

oars

rest on your oars
lean on your oars

If you say that someone **is resting on** their **oars** or **is leaning on** their **oars**, you are criticizing them for not working hard, so that they are in danger of suffering harm or defeat. These expressions are used in British English.

In the absence of any other source of pressure, many boards take their time over making necessary changes, leaning on their oars while another study is done and another year goes by.

oats

sow your wild oats ◄

If you say that someone, especially a young man, **is sowing** their **wild oats**, you mean that they have many sexual relationships, without expecting or wanting any of them to become serious or permanent.

What this survey highlights is that while men definitely do eventually seek commitment in a relationship, they still see nothing wrong in sowing their wild oats with a multitude of one-night stands along the way.

I got all that sowing wild oats out of my system before I got married.

odds

at odds with someone: 1 ◄◄◄

If one person is **at odds with** another, or if two people are **at odds**, they disagree about something.

The region has reportedly been at odds with the central government both militarily and politically.

The Trade and Industry Secretary dismissed press reports that he and the Chancellor of the Exchequer had been at odds over the imposition of VAT on domestic fuel.

The authorities, the security forces and the politicians remain at odds over how to deal with the campaign by militants for a separate independent homeland.

at odds with something: 2 ◄◄

If you say that one thing is **at odds with** another, you mean that it does not match or correspond to that other thing.

His outlook on life was pessimistic, quite at odds with his wife's description of his normal out-going personality.

He was a good piano player, but slightly ashamed of it, as it seemed at odds with his macho image.

Close on the heels of the jobs data comes the purchasing agents' index. Last month the two statistics were at odds, since employment figures indicated strength and the index predicted a declining economy.

at odds with the world
at odds with yourself

If you say that someone is **at odds with the world** or **at odds with** themselves, you mean that they are confused or discontented, and unsure what they want to do or how they want to see things develop.

We are more inclined to blame a feeling of being generally out of sorts and at odds with the world on a headache or upset stomach, rather than the other way round.

He willingly confesses that he was still at odds with himself. 'I was all over the shop at the time. I didn't have a clue what was going on.'

pay over the odds ◄◄

If you **pay over the odds** for something, you pay more for it than it is really worth. This expression is used in British English.

London Clothesline was born in 1986 when Libby and Ricky discovered a shared belief that many customers were paying over the odds for top quality clothes.

Over the years, London's beer drinkers have got used to having to pay a little bit over the odds for their pint. It has been the price of living in a prosperous area where costs are higher.

In return for public works contracts, firms pay over the odds to the governing politicians, who then use the money to line their own pockets and those of their parties.

odour

in bad odour
in good odour

If you are **in bad odour** with someone, they disapprove of you because they think you have done something bad or wrong. This is a fairly old-fashioned expression.

The republic's policy of repression has put them in bad odour with Western human rights groups.

☐ You can say that you are **in good odour** with someone when they think you have done something good or right.

He became director of central intelligence in 1987. The agency has managed to keep out of trouble since then and he is keen to leave while it is still in good odour.

☐ 'Odour' is spelled 'odor' in American English.

off-chance

on the off-chance ◄◄

If you do something **on the off-chance** that something good or pleasant will happen, you do it because there is a small chance that the good or pleasant thing will happen.

There are a number of advantages in writing

*to potential employers and offering your services
on the off-chance that they have a suitable vacancy.*

*Jane and Cathy have come all the way from
Australia on the off-chance of watching
Navratilova play.*

I just thought I'd call on the off chance.

☐ If you say that there is **an off-chance** that
something good or pleasant will happen, you
mean that there is a small chance that it will
happen.

*An additional motivation of her attendance
was the off-chance that she might find Darren
there.*

oil

no oil painting

If you say that someone is **no oil painting**,
you mean that they are unattractive or ugly.
This expression is used in British English.

*I started seeing a guy who was no oil paint-
ing but wonderfully bright and interesting.*

oil and water

If you say that you cannot mix **oil and water**, you mean that if two people or things are
very different they cannot work together or
exist together successfully.

*'One might just as well try mixing oil and
water,' Marianne replied, 'as people from the
arts with those who have cash registers where
their hearts should be.'*

☐ You say that two people or things are **like
oil and water**, or that they **are oil and water**, to emphasize that they are very different.

*He had an instant falling out with General
Leslie Groves, who headed the Manhattan Project. The two were like oil and water together.*

*We got along well despite being oil and wa-
ter.*

pour oil on troubled waters ◄

If you **pour oil on troubled waters**, you do
or say something to make an angry or tense
situation calmer or more peaceful.

*He is an extremely experienced politician,
who some diplomats believe may be able to
pour oil on the troubled waters.*

*Friends are a blessing – they pour oil on
troubled waters, drag you to parties and make
you feel loved.*

☐ This expression is sometimes used in other
structures.

*I was the go-between, the pourer of juvenile
oil on oft-troubled waters.*

*I'm not good at getting angry, I'm an oil-on-
troubled-waters lady.*

strike oil

If you say that someone **has struck oil**, you
mean that they have suddenly become successful in finding or doing something.

*'It won't tell us where he was at the time of
the murder.' 'Work on it. The police aren't likely to strike oil in the King Edward. Not the
sort of pub where people take time to stand
and stare.'*

☐ This expression is more commonly used literally to say that someone discovers oil in the
ground as a result of drilling.

old

old as the hills

If you say that something is as **old as the
hills**, you mean that it is very old, and perhaps old-fashioned or very traditional.

*Their equipment may be modern, but the
techniques remain as old as the hills.*

olive

an olive branch ◄◄◄

If you hold out **an olive branch** to someone,
you say or do something to indicate that you
want to end a disagreement with them or stop
them feeling resentful, bitter, or angry with
you.

*He held out an olive branch to the 500,000-
strong Hungarian minority, some of whom feel
their future in an independent Slovakia may be
less than secure.*

*It's not difficult to see why the authorities
have offered an olive branch to the community.
They doubtless hope this will cool passions in
the run-up to the anniversary of the massacre.*

*It would be some time before he would accept
the olive branch extended to him.*

☐ You can use **olive branch** to mean an offer
of peace or friendship.

*I think the olive branch will have to come
from both sides.*

*He invited the world to choose between the
gun and the olive branch.*

omelette

you can't make an omelette without breaking eggs

If you say that you **can't make an omelette
without breaking eggs**, you mean that it is
impossible to achieve something without
there being bad or unpleasant side-effects.

*You can't make an omelette without breaking
eggs. If you want universal health care there's
just no way of getting it without us putting
more money into it.*

*He adds, 'You can't make an omelette without
breaking eggs – you just have to break as few
as possible.' Meanwhile, it seems astonishing
that anyone should think it acceptable to put a
major road through a landscape of such obvious sensitivity.*

☐ This expression is often varied or exploited.

The 'radiant future' promised in Lenin's

name simply failed to materialise. The eggs were broken, but with no omelette to show for the shells.

□ 'Omelette' is usually spelled 'omelet' in American English.

omnibus

the man on the Clapham omnibus ◄

When people talk about **the man on the Clapham omnibus**, they mean ordinary, average people. Other place names are sometimes used instead of 'Clapham'. This expression is used in British English.

The wealthy and powerful never liked the man on the Clapham omnibus knowing what they were about.

□ Clapham is an area of London, and 'omnibus' is an old-fashioned word for bus.

once-over

give someone the once-over ◄

If you **give** someone or something **the once-over**, you look at them or analyse them quickly to get a general impression of their appearance or character.

Penny gives me the once-over. I'm wearing a bright jacket that'll go down well with European viewers, she says. But if I were broadcasting to Asia, I'd have to wear something pale-coloured and lightweight.

Mary Ann gave the apartment a once-over.

□ You can also **give** something a **once-over with** a particular thing when you pay some attention to it for a short period of time.

When you're in the bath, give your feet a once-over with a pumice stone or loofah to remove rough or hard skin.

one

be one up on someone
get one up on someone ◄

If you **are one up on** someone, you have an advantage over them, because you have done something which they have not done or because you know something that they do not know. If you try to **get one up on** them, you try to get this kind of advantage over them.

You don't want the competitive kind who will see this as the opportunity to be one up on you.

Even the best of friends can be left with an unconscious desire to hurt or to get one up on the other.

got it in one

If someone guesses something and you say **'got it in one'** or **'you've got it in one'**, you mean that they have guessed correctly. These expressions are used in British English.

'My husband just broke my favourite piece of china,' said my friend. 'Guess whose fault it was.' 'Yours,' I said. 'Got it in one,' she said.

'Is that a Birmingham accent?' I asked, explaining that all my family were originally from that part of the world. 'You got it in one. I grew up in Birmingham.'

□ You can also use these expressions after asking a question, to indicate that the answer is obvious.

Guess who objected strongly to the scheme? You've got it in one!

put one over on someone
get one over on someone ◄

If you **put one over on** an opponent or rival, or **get one over on** them, you gain a victory or advantage over them.

Clark insisted: 'It's nice to put one over on your old boss but I don't hold any grudges.'

Managers wouldn't help each other. They were all trying to get one over on each other.

onions

know your onions

If you say that someone **knows** their **onions**, you mean that they know a great deal about a particular subject. This is an old-fashioned British expression.

It shows she really knows her onions in the historical field too.

open

open and shut ◄

If you say that something, especially a legal case, is **open and shut**, you mean that it is easily decided or solved because the facts are very clear.

The prosecution behaved as if they had an open-and-shut case.

We'll need to come back here and measure things for the report, but it seems open and shut to me.

order

the order of the day ◄◄◄

If you say that something is **the order of the day**, you mean that it is what is happening in a particular situation, or what someone considers should be happening then.

Terror is the order of the day for those refugees waiting to leave.

Wage cuts were the order of the day owing to the government's deflationary policy.

Informality is the order of the day among all the Princess Royal's household.

Rice pudding and shepherd's pie were the order of the day – Kate considered Greek food unsuitable for children.

a tall order ◄◄◄

If you describe a task as **a tall order**, you mean that it is going to be very difficult.

Financing your studies may seem like a tall

order, but there is plenty of help available as our guide reveals.

I've got to beat him by four shots tomorrow, and that's a very tall order.

It's a tall order for local residents to pay this huge bill. It's not fair that we have to pay for all of it.

orders

marching orders: 1 ◄◄

If you are given your **marching orders**, you are made to leave something such as a job or a relationship. If a player in a team sport is given their **marching orders**, they are ordered to leave the pitch because they have behaved in an unacceptable way. This expression is used in British English; the American expression is **walking papers**.

The journalists' own loyalties are under strain. Last week the political correspondent was given his marching orders.

What does it take for a woman to say 'that's enough' and give her man his marching orders?

He was given his marching orders after attacking the opposition goalkeeper twice. He has now been banned for two weeks.

marching orders: 2 ◄

Your **marching orders** are the instructions that you are given in order to carry out a plan or achieve an aim. This expression is used in American English.

As one mid-level White House official put it, 'We're still waiting for our marching orders.'

Now program executives have new marching orders for Hollywood producers: If the show is like 'Miami Vice,' we're not interested.

organ

the organ grinder's monkey

If you refer to someone as **the organ grinder's monkey**, you mean that they are closely associated with a powerful person and act on their behalf, but have no real power themselves. This expression is often used to show contempt or dislike for both of the people you are talking about, but especially for the 'monkey'. This expression is used in British English.

'Do you feel that you've been squeezed out?' 'Well, I feel more like the organ-grinder's monkey, actually.'

□ The wording of this expression is not very fixed, and people often refer to it partially or indirectly.

Why bother with monkeys when you can deal with the organ-grinder?

Some will reason that I focus too much attention on the monkey, whilst allowing the organ grinder to get off scot free.

out

out-and-out ◄◄◄

You use **out-and-out** before a noun in order to emphasize that someone or something is very clearly and definitely the kind of person or thing mentioned.

About six years ago it bought a little retail outfit called Early Learning Systems which specialises in toys for bright toddlers and the investment has emerged an out-and-out winner.

This was almost certainly an out-and-out lie.

overdrive

go into overdrive
be in overdrive ◄◄◄

If someone or something **goes into overdrive**, they begin to work very hard or to perform intensely or very well. You can also say that someone or something **is in overdrive**.

When the bodies were discovered, the media went into overdrive. Antena 3 devoted all but two minutes of its main news bulletin to the story.

My imagination went into overdrive. I tried to make new dishes, not from recipe books but from books about wild plants.

The campaign that began in the cold of New Hampshire is in overdrive now with the candidates crisscrossing the nation in a final push for votes.

overtime

work overtime

If you say that someone **is working overtime** to do something, you mean that they are working very hard in order to achieve it.

The team had been working overtime to improve the Labour image.

This might explain why people are prone to excessive sleep when the immune mechanisms are working overtime to fight off infections.

□ This expression is more commonly used to say that someone is spending extra time doing the job that they are employed to do.

own

hold your own ◄◄◄

If you **hold** your **own**, you are able to defend your position against someone who is attacking you or threatening you.

Some areas of heavy industry, such as shipbuilding, were able to hold their own in international markets.

If Fiat cannot hold its own against its European rivals then it is certain to get a drubbing once Japanese producers are allowed to increase their sales.

The most highly skilled members of the American workforce can hold their own with any in the world.

P

p

mind your p's and q's
watch your p's and q's

If you **mind** your **p's and q's** or **watch** your **p's and q's**, you try to speak and behave politely or to act in an acceptable way, so that you do not offend people.

She always put on her best act and minded her p's and q's in front of the queen, but their relationship wasn't that close.

Mayor Brown was interviewed not long ago about the fact that Bosco had moved to Livermore, and she did acknowledge that she was going to have to watch her p's and q's with a politician that popular moving into her area.

pace

can't stand the pace
can't take the pace ◄

If someone **can't stand the pace** or **can't take the pace**, they do not work or function effectively when they are under pressure, and so cannot compete or do things as well as other people.

Most journalists know of a colleague who abandoned journalism for advertising. We curl our lips at such a fellow. He is a sell-out, a loser, somebody who couldn't stand the pace in the real game.

They were constantly testing me, as if to prove I couldn't take the pace. For instance, if I was very tired at the end of the day, someone would always seem to materialise with a rush job.

set the pace ◄◄

If someone **sets the pace**, they do something which is regarded as a good example, and other people then do the same thing.

The consensus is that Versace has got it right this season and has set the pace for mainstream fashion.

In a deal that could set the pace in forthcoming pay rounds, the 700,000 chemical workers settled for a 2 percent increase in pay and promised to work more flexible hours.

paces

put someone through their paces ◄◄◄

If you **put** someone or something **through** their **paces**, you get them to show you how well they can do something. Other verbs can be used instead of 'put'.

The eleven boxers on the British team are in the hands of the British coach, Ian Irwin, who is putting them through their paces.

At St Barbara barracks dozens of tanks are being put through their paces to check that they're running correctly before they're subjected to the rigors of the Saudi Arabian desert.

The distributor was taken with the gadget and asked for a demonstration. After watching it go through its paces, he asked if the machine could be adapted to cook other foods.

pack

ahead of the pack ◄

If a person or organization is **ahead of the pack**, they are being more successful than their competitors or rivals.

Hoping to stay ahead of the pack, the company is emphasizing innovation with a new bike frame that weighs just 2.7 pounds – a pound less than the lightest mountain-bike frame on the market.

This decentralized management system has kept the company far ahead of the pack in terms of product development.

page

on the same page

If two or more people are **on the same page**, they are in agreement about what they are trying to achieve. This expression is used in American English.

I think everybody's on the same page, as they say, and that a ground war is only a matter of weeks away, if that.

We're all on about the same page in our careers, we all have the same professional needs.

turn the page

If someone **turns the page**, they make a fresh start after a period of difficulties and troubles. Compare **turn over a new leaf**; see **leaf**.

Shareholders at Fiat's annual meeting will be looking for signs that the troubled company really does mean to turn the page.

There is a sense that America has turned the page toward something new.

paid

put paid to something ◄◄◄

If an unexpected event **puts paid to** someone's hopes, chances, or plans, it completely ends or destroys them. This expression is used mainly in British English.

Great Britain gave a limp performance here last night that put paid to their chances of reaching the Olympic finals.

The past week has probably put paid to hopes that share prices in New York and London would rise strongly for the rest of the year.

pain

a pain in the arse
a pain in the ass ◄◄

If you think that someone or something is very annoying, you can say that they are **a pain in the arse** or **a pain in the ass**. Other words meaning 'bottom' can be used instead of 'arse' or 'ass'. The form with 'arse' is used in British English and the form with 'ass' is used in American English. These are very informal expressions, which many people consider offensive.

He'd dealt with the Hendersons of the world before. They always meant money, but they were an almighty pain in the arse to deal with just the same.

Leone could soon be following her uncle and cousin into film roles. 'Having the name Connery is a terrific advantage and a pain in the backside at the same time,' she said.

a pain in the neck ◄◄

If you think that someone or something is very annoying, you can say that they are **a pain in the neck**.

He was a pain in the neck. I was glad when he left my department.

'Sorry,' he said. 'They've forgotten to insure the plane. It's a pain in the neck, but what can I do?'

pains

growing pains ◄

If an organization or a relationship suffers from **growing pains**, it experiences temporary difficulties and problems as it develops and grows stronger.

He knew it was just a case of growing pains, the natural transition process from small-time local supplier to major distributor.

The country is now facing some troublesome growing pains. The economy is still expanding, but at a slower rate than in the recent past.

Their three year-old marriage has been going through some growing pains.

paint

watch paint dry

If you say that something is like **watching paint dry**, you mean that you find it extremely boring.

'We've done one shot since nine this morning,'

complains Donna, a student who has taken the day off to be an extra. 'It's like watching paint dry. And it's only 12 o'clock!'*

The village of Lefkara is about half-an-hour's drive away, and there you can see embroidery in the making (an activity I found marginally more exciting than watching paint dry) and purchase the cheap, handmade silver jewellery.

pale

beyond the pale ◄◄

If you say that someone's behaviour goes **beyond the pale**, you mean that it is completely unacceptable.

He is glorifying cheating and fighting and I'm appalled. It goes beyond the pale.

Tina, too, had outraged society. She had lived beyond the pale of its approval and died with another's death on her conscience.

There will be no more compromises with people whose views are beyond the pale.

palm

grease someone's palm

If you accuse someone of **greasing** an official's **palm**, you are accusing them of giving money to the official in order to gain an unfair advantage over other people or in order to get something that they want. You can replace the verb 'grease' with the verb 'oil'.

Italy's continuing corruption probe took a fresh turn with the confession by Carlo De Benedetti, Olivetti's chairman, that he, too, was forced to grease a few palms along the way.

She thought that files do not move in government offices unless you grease the palms of officials.

□ You can describe this activity as **palm-greasing**.

Palm-greasing for just about anything from entry to a favoured school to obtaining a bank loan has been considered a fact of life.

Pandora

a Pandora's box ◄◄◄

If someone opens **a Pandora's box**, they do something that unintentionally causes a lot of problems, which they did not know existed before.

This latest controversy has opened up a Pandora's box of intrigue amongst the coalition government's different factions.

Ministers acknowledge they are opening a Pandora's Box, and that in trying to undo some of the ills of 40 years of communism they will not be able to please everyone.

□ You can also describe a potentially difficult situation or thing as **a Pandora's box**, for example when you are warning that it must be dealt with carefully.

I have plenty of friends who are angry at their partners for not doing their share of childcare, with the baby providing a Pandora's Box of new possibilities for quarrels.

pants

beat the pants off someone

If you **beat the pants off** someone or if you **beat** their **pants off**, you defeat them decisively in a contest or competition.

Devlin indicated the chess table beside the sofa. 'Any excuse to get away from that. He was beating the pants off me.'

My opinion of Michael has gone down quite a bit since then and I want to beat his pants off. I know I can win at Suzuka and that's what I'm going to do.

bore the pants off someone
scare the pants off someone
charm the pants off someone ◄

If someone or something **bores, scares,** or **charms the pants off** you, they bore, scare, or charm you a lot.

When I was a kid, circuses bored the pants off me, but I'd always wanted to be a performer.

Stephen Daldry is the sort of person who loves rushing around, charming the pants off everyone he meets.

□ People occasionally replace 'bore', 'scare', or 'charm' with other verbs.

We all love to frighten the pants off ourselves by going on hair-raising rides at funfairs.

catch someone with their pants down
catch someone with their trousers down ◄

If someone **is caught with** their **pants down** or **is caught with** their **trousers down**, something happens that they are not prepared for and that reveals an embarrassing or shocking fact about them. 'Catch someone with their trousers down' is used only in British English.

In July 1991, the Department of Transport was caught with its pants down and took seven months to produce the consultative document needed to change legislation.

Resignations are for Prime Ministers and cabinets, and those caught with their trousers down. Not for me.

paper

can't fight your way out of a paper bag

If you say that someone **can't fight** their **way out of a paper bag**, you are saying in a contemptuous way that they are very bad at fighting.

We've already shown you that they are no use to you as allies. They couldn't fight their way out of a paper bag.

□ You can replace 'fight' with other verbs that state what someone is incapable of doing.

Certainly, too, the democratic parties that support Mr Yeltsin could not organise their way out of a paper bag.

not worth the paper it's written on ◄

If you say that a promise, agreement, or guarantee **is not worth the paper it's written on**, you mean that although it appears to be official or definite, it is in fact worthless. 'Printed' can be used instead of 'written'.

If consumers are unaware of their right to compensation when a service breaks down, guaranteed service standards will not be worth the paper they are written on.

The certificate is not worth the paper it is printed on.

on paper ◄◄

If you say that something looks or sounds good **on paper**, you mean that it seems to be a good idea, plan, or argument when you read or hear about it, but may not be good in reality.

This system looks good on paper but it is expensive and, in my view, still of very limited value.

These reforms are more impressive on paper than in reality.

a paper tiger ◄

If you say that a person, country, or organization is **a paper tiger**, you mean that although they seem to be powerful, they do not really have any power.

The Khmer Rouge has already managed to make the U.N. in Cambodia look like an expensive paper tiger, without the teeth to carry out what it was sent to do.

Russia's Asian forces are a paper tiger these days. Starved of fuel and spare parts, low on morale, they are barely in shape even for manoeuvres, let alone war.

a paper trail ◄

Written evidence of someone's activities can be referred to as **a paper trail**. This expression is used mainly in American English.

The criminal proceedings were raised after investigations found a paper trail of checks that were written on dummy bank accounts.

papers

walking papers

If you are given your **walking papers**, you are made to leave something such as a job or a relationship. This expression is used in American English; the British expression is **marching orders**.

Sol Siegel having been ousted several months earlier, it was Vogel's turn to get his walking papers from the board of directors.

par

below par: 1
under par
not up to par ◄◄◄

If you say that someone or something is **below par**, you are disappointed with them because they are below the standard you expected. You can also say that they are **under par** or **not up to par**.

The recession has left sales a little below par in the past two or three years.

Bad teachers could face pay freezes or the sack if their work is under par once the scheme starts in September.

The explosion caused a wave of panic in the area and raised concerns that safety standards were not up to par.

□ You can also use **below-par** before a noun.

The other time I saw her was onstage at a below-par Brighton concert last year.

below par: 2
under par ◄

If you feel **below par** or **under par**, you feel tired or ill and unable to perform or work as well as you usually do.

Women who feel below par are unlikely to perform at their best.

After the birth of her baby she felt generally under par.

par for the course ◄◄

If you say that something that happens is **par for the course**, you mean that you are not pleased with it but it is what you expected to happen.

We had 75 mile-per-hour gusts and there's leaves and branches all over the streets, and the power is out. But, I mean, that's all kind of par for the course in a hurricane.

He said long hours are par for the course. 'I'm up every morning at six, or even earlier.'

parade

rain on someone's parade

If someone **rains on** your **parade**, they do something which spoils a plan of yours, usually a plan that is very important to you. This expression is used mainly in journalism.

She was there to ask a favour of Mimi – she didn't want to rain on her parade.

Damon Hill is ready to rain on Nigel Mansell's comeback parade in Sunday's French Grand Prix.

parker

a nosey parker ◄

If you say that someone is **a nosey parker**, you are criticizing them for being interested in things that are nothing to do with them. This expression is used in British English.

The village's resident nosey parker, Olive, likes to spy on her neighbours with binoculars.

Supermarkets are a nosy parker's paradise. The contents of strangers' trollies amount to peep-holes on their lives.

□ 'Nosey' is sometimes spelled 'nosy'.

parrot

parrot fashion ◄

If a child learns something **parrot fashion**, they learn it by repeating it many times, but they do not really understand what it means. This expression is used in British English.

Under the old system pupils often had to stand to attention and repeat lessons parrot fashion.

There are no books, pens or chairs here, just a blackboard and a dirt floor where 150 dusty children sit in rows, learning their words parrot-fashion.

part

look the part: 1 ◄◄◄

If someone **looks the part**, they dress or behave in the way that is characteristic of a particular kind of person.

You look the part of an English gentleman, so he is half ready to believe you as soon as you meet.

He won't say which army but friends suspect it may have been the Foreign Legion. He certainly looks the part: his hair is crew cut and he has a raw gash above his left eye.

look the part: 2

If you want to say that someone or something seems impressive, you can say that they **look the part**. This expression is used mainly in British English.

Strachan believes that Cantona has always had the hallmark that distinguishes world-class players from the rest. 'When I played for Scotland in France, Eric scored against us, and even then I thought he looked the part,' he says.

The Alpha 5 CD player certainly looks the part with a stylish slimline design, moulded front panel and finely-textured paint finish.

part and parcel ◄◄◄

If one thing is **part and parcel** of another, it is involved or included in it and cannot be separated from it.

It was a house healthy – and noisy – with political argument and dissent; strong views and humour were part and parcel of home life.

There comes a time during every player's season when his form dips and the goals don't go in. It's part and parcel of being a professional.

He said it's all part and parcel, just a day's work really, you know, it's nothing serious.

take someone's part

If you **take** someone's **part**, you support them or defend them, especially in a dispute with other people. This is an old-fashioned expression, which is used in British English.

It seemed to me that she should have taken my part, should somehow have defended me from my father.

China, which in the past had taken North Korea's part, abstained.

take something in good part

If someone **takes** something such as criticism **in good part**, they are not offended or upset by it. This expression is used in British English.

I tried to eliminate from the critical comments the casual, the superficial and the trivial, but I nevertheless agonized over having to pass on to Pasternak even the sort of objections with which I could not myself agree. But he took it all, however unusual, in good part.

party

bring something to the party

If you talk about what someone **brings to the party**, you are talking about the contribution they make to a particular activity or situation.

Johnson asked, 'What do they bring to the party?' 'They bring a lot to the party,' Cohen replied, 'principally $3 billion in capital.'

They are far better than nearly every band in London, but they need to recover from a couple of misfired years and find something fresh to bring to the party.

pass

sell the pass

If you say that someone **has sold the pass**, you are accusing them of betraying their friends or allies by giving an enemy or opponent what they wanted. This is an old-fashioned expression, which is used in British English.

English Heritage has been notably inactive in defending ancient battlefields in the past, and was widely blamed for selling the pass at a public enquiry in 1985 which enabled a new motorway to be built over the site of the battle of Naseby.

past

be past it
be getting past it ◄

If you say that someone or something is **past it**, you are saying in a cruel or scornful way that they are no longer as good as they used to be. You can also say that they **are getting past it**. These expressions are used in British English.

In August 1991, after suffering an elbow injury to his throwing arm which kept him out all season, they said that at 25 years old, Joe Montana was past it.

My husband Eric could do with another second-hand car. The one we've got at the moment is getting a bit past it.

wouldn't put it past someone ◄

If you say that you **wouldn't put it past** someone to do something bad, you mean that you would not be surprised if they did it.

I wouldn't put it past him to double-cross Schrader, especially after the rumour I heard the other day.

pasture

put someone out to pasture

If someone **is put out to pasture**, they are made to retire from their job, or they are moved to an unimportant job, usually because people think that they are too old to be useful. **Put** someone **out to grass** means the same.

I'm retiring next month. They're putting me out to pasture.

He should not yet be put out to pasture. His ministerial experience is valuable.

At 28, I'm hardly ready to be put out to pasture and it's not so long ago I was England's No 1 strike bowler for 18 months.

pastures

greener pastures

If someone seeks **greener pastures**, they try to leave a situation which they do not like, in order to find a new and better one.

There are drawbacks for nurses seeking greener pastures overseas, and many are put off by the lengthy process involved in going to work in the US.

They moved around for years, sometimes even leaving the state for what they thought would be greener pastures.

□ Instead of 'greener', you can use an adjective which describes the new situation.

A defeatist might retreat to quieter pastures.

pastures new
fresh pastures ◄◄

If someone moves on to **pastures new**, they leave their current situation and enter a new one. This expression is used in British English.

Michael decided he wanted to move on to pastures new for financial reasons.

I found myself packing a suitcase and heading for pastures new.

If the job doesn't meet my ambitions I'll be off to pastures new. I want to go to the top.

□ You can also talk about moving on to **new pastures** or **fresh pastures**.

No matter how much we long for new pastures, when we reach them they can seem like a bad idea.

pat

a pat on the back
pat someone on the back　　◄◄◄

If you give someone **a pat on the back**, you congratulate them or show your appreciation for something they have done. If you give yourself **a pat on the back**, you feel pleased about something you have done.

Any mail order shop that gives such rapid response to a customer's complaint deserves a pat on the back.

The industry can give itself a little pat on the back for the constructive moves it has made to help towards its own recovery.

□ You can also say that one person **pats** another **on the back**, or that someone **pats** themselves **on the back**.

The editor of the newspaper asked to see me, and I thought he would pat me on the back and say, 'Well done!' Instead he fired me.

I decided if giving up smoking was going to be so hard, I'd need more pleasurable things in my life, so each day I kept patting myself on the back and treating myself.

stand pat　　◄

If someone **stands pat**, they do not change something or they refuse to change their mind about something. This expression is used mainly in American English.

The last time the Federal Bank cut short-term interest rates, long-term rates rose due to investor fears of inflation, all of which makes it hard for the bank to do anything but stand pat till the economy's direction becomes clearer.

Building society managers are willing to stand pat on mortgage rates for the moment.

There are certain issues on which Britain would stand pat and insist on unanimity.

patch

not a patch on someone　　◄◄

If you say that one person or thing **is not a patch on** another, you mean that the first is not nearly as good as the second. This expression is used in British English.

A decorative young man sat on a chair close at her side, springing to his feet at Susan's entrance. Handsome, she thought, but not a patch on Alex.

Of course, the facilities aren't a patch on those of richer schools, but the boys think they're terrific.

path

cross someone's path　　◄◄◄

If someone **crosses** your **path** or if your

paths cross, you meet them by chance.

The book is full of cutting criticisms of the celebrities who crossed her path.

Vicki and Lisa first crossed paths when they attended the Australian Ballet School in 1983 and became flatmates.

He made no mention of keeping in touch but hoped that sometime their paths would cross again.

path-breaking
break a new path　　◄

You describe someone's achievement as **path-breaking** when they have done something completely different and new which will affect the way in which things are done or considered in the future. This expression is used mainly in American English, but it is also used in British journalism.

Russia's Parliament today approved a path-breaking measure that gives individual farmers a right to buy and sell their own land.

Historian Carl Degler in a pathbreaking book points out that at times there were more groups opposed to slavery in the South than in the North.

Path-breaking work in computing is always risky.

□ You can refer to someone who achieves something path-breaking as **a path-breaker**.

Chung is a path-breaker. But she is a rather odd choice for the role.

□ You can also say that they **break a new path**.

While older students are extending their learning through a variety of flexible arrangements, traditional 18-to-22-year-olds are also breaking new paths.

pay dirt

hit pay dirt
strike pay dirt　　◄

If you **hit pay dirt** or **strike pay dirt**, you find or achieve something important and valuable. These expressions are used mainly in American English.

'Let's not give up on the courts,' Millard says. 'We still might hit pay dirt with one of the issues.'

The first two people with whom she spoke hung up on her. The third was not rude, but he refused to help her. With the fourth, she struck pay dirt.

□ 'Pay dirt' is often written as 'paydirt'.

peanuts

if you pay peanuts, you get monkeys

If you say '**if you pay peanuts, you get**

monkeys', you mean that if an employer pays very low wages, they cannot expect to find good staff. This expression is used in British English.

We are not against change designed to improve profitability, but there must be something in it for us. If you pay peanuts you get monkeys. Nobody wants a strike, but it is our last resort.

The present pay policy will inevitably have an adverse effect on quality. As Sir Roger put it, 'The truth of the matter is that if they pay peanuts, they will get monkeys.'

□ You can refer to a very small sum of money as **peanuts**.

I design the clothes. She takes all the credit, and she pays me peanuts.

pearls

cast pearls before swine ◄

If you say that someone **is casting pearls before swine**, you mean that they are wasting their time by offering something that is helpful or valuable to someone who does not appreciate or understand it. This is a literary expression.

I have wonderful costumes. I scour second-hand shops for interesting pieces like feathers and top hats, but it's like casting pearls before swine, they don't care what you wear.

□ You can vary this expression in several ways, for example by saying that something **is pearls before swine**.

The Musical Times, she tells me, is written by professionals for those with a genuine understanding of the finer points. I certainly hope so, or else my piece on some new Rossini editions, due to appear in the September issue of MT, will be pearls before swine.

pearls of wisdom ◄

If you describe something that someone has said or written as **pearls of wisdom**, you mean that it sounds very wise or helpful. You can also talk about **a pearl of wisdom**. People usually use this expression ironically, to suggest that in fact they think the person is saying something very obvious or boring.

While we here in Arkansas are always so grateful for all the pearls of wisdom that may fall from Mr. Greenberg's lips, I believe that your audience should know that when Mr. Greenberg speaks on Arkansas politics he's not speaking as an objective, unbiased journalist.

'Never be afraid of failure; just be afraid of not trying.' Another pearl of wisdom.

peas

like two peas in a pod
alike as two peas in a pod ◄

If you say that two people are **like two peas in a pod** or are **alike as two peas in a pod**, you mean that they are very alike in appearance or character.

She is convinced the men are brothers. She said: 'It was uncanny. They were like two peas in a pod.'

'I remember,' he replied almost wistfully, 'when you brought the twins to be baptized, Laura. Alike as two peas in a pod! I nearly mixed them up.'

□ People often vary this expression, for example by describing two people as **peas from the same pod**.

The two men are peas from the same pod. They can conceive of no system other than democratic pluralism; they know of no way of ordering economies other than capitalism.

pebble

not the only pebble on the beach

If you say that someone is **not the only pebble on the beach**, you mean that they are not the only person who is important or should be considered in a particular situation, although they may think they are. This expression is used mainly in British English.

You should encourage him to understand that he is very definitely not the only pebble on the beach.

As boarders at school, they have learnt that they are not the only pebbles on the beach much sooner than their non-boarding counterparts.

pecker

keep your pecker up

If someone tells you to **keep** your **pecker up**, they are encouraging you to remain cheerful in a difficult situation. This expression is used in British English.

'I'll give you a ring later because I must go now.' 'Fine. Well, keep your pecker up.' 'I'll try.'

□ If someone or something **keeps** your **pecker up**, they help you to remain cheerful.

Mintel, the market analyst, tries to keep the business's pecker up. The Mintel report reckons there will always be a demand for package trips of some sort.

pecking

the pecking order ◄◄◄

The pecking order in a group is the order of importance of the people or things within that group.

Offices came in 29 sizes, which varied in accordance with the occupant's place in the corporate pecking order.

As a player in category 12, he is way down the pecking order.

At its annual meeting in Nottingham, the British Medical Association issued a grim warning that doctors may be forced to draw up a pecking order of operations.

pedestal

knock someone off their pedestal ◄

If someone or something **knocks** you **off** your **pedestal**, they show that you are not as good or talented as people generally think, or make people realize that you are not perfect. Other verbs such as 'force' can be used instead of 'knock'.

The lowest point of my life was failing my surgery exams on one small part: a 15-minute oral exam. That failure knocked me off my pedestal.

The tabloids have been trying for several years now to knock Jackson from his pedestal.

Many film stars of that generation were forced off their pedestal by the arrival of sound.

□ If you say that someone should come **down from** their **pedestal**, you mean that they should stop behaving as though they think they are perfect.

She finds it difficult to come down from the pedestal where she had placed herself as the heroine of democracy.

My advice to Paula is to climb down off her pedestal and get in touch with reality.

put someone on a pedestal
be on a pedestal ◄◄◄

If someone **puts** you **on a pedestal**, they think you are extremely good or talented, or they seem not to realize that you are not perfect. Other verbs such as 'place' can be used instead of 'put'.

I put my own parents on a pedestal. I felt they could do no wrong.

Our toughest task is to resist the tendency to place the other person on a pedestal, expecting them to live out for us some hero or heroine role which they cannot possibly fulfil.

He had set her on a pedestal.

□ You can say that someone **is on a pedestal** or **sits on a pedestal** when people think of them in this way.

The Emperor is still safely on a pedestal.

How can you have a relationship with a perfect being who's way up on a pedestal?

She does not need to sit on a pedestal to support her own self-esteem.

peg

a peg on which to hang something

If you use something as **a peg on which to hang** your ideas or opinions, you use it to introduce or draw attention to these ideas or opinions. This expression can be used to indi-

cate that the ideas or opinions are not directly relevant to the main subject being discussed.

He rarely discusses the book, using it as a peg on which to hang his opinions – and not necessarily those related to the book.

In a purely political sense the detail is of little importance. It gives Opposition spokesmen a peg on which to try to hang accusations of government incompetence and mismanagement.

a square peg in a round hole ◄

If you say that someone is **a square peg in a round hole**, you mean that they are in a situation or are doing a task that does not suit them at all. You can also talk about a system forcing **a square peg into a round hole** to refer to this kind of situation.

Taylor is clearly the wrong man for the job – a square peg in a round hole.

The social conditioning factor has, in my opinion, caused more mental and physical illness than might be imagined. Too many square pegs have been forced into round holes.

This is an example of a square peg being driven mercilessly into a round hole.

□ People often vary this expression.

The system too often leads to round pegs being appointed to square holes.

Can the work place provide enough square holes for square pegs, or society round pegs for round holes? Should we even expect a perfect person-job fit?

take someone down a peg or two
bring someone down a peg or two ◄

If you say that someone needs **taking** or **bringing down a peg or two**, you mean that they are behaving in an arrogant and unpleasant way and they should be made to realize that they are not as important or talented as they think.

I do think he needed taking down a peg or two.

We thought it was time they were brought down a peg or two.

We'd have liked to see her taken down a peg, but not this way.

□ You can make this expression more emphatic by talking about **taking** someone **down a peg or three** or **taking** them **down several pegs**.

Perhaps it was just as well that my first contact with my relatives should take me down several pegs.

pegged

have someone pegged

If you say that you **have** someone **pegged**, you mean that you understand completely the way they are or who they are.

Those who have her pegged as fragile singer-

songwriter should hear her touring band at full tilt blasting out the Na Na Song.

I want you to know that the drinkers in the cocktail lounge have you pegged for a detective.

pennies

pinch pennies

If someone **pinches pennies**, they try to spend as little money as possible.

States and the federal government are pinching pennies everywhere they can and often cutting arts programs first.

Markets are shrinking and customers are pinching pennies.

□ The verb 'pennypinch' has a similar meaning, and there is also a much more frequent word 'pennypinching'. These words are generally used more disapprovingly than 'pinch pennies'.

penn'orth

your two penn'orth ◄

If you have or put in your **two penn'orth**, you give your opinion about something, even if nobody has asked you for it. People occasionally replace 'two' with another number. This expression is used in British English; the American expression is your **two cents' worth**.

I'm just putting my two penn'orth in, that's all. The same as you are.

The meeting dragged on for more than five hours to ensure that they all had their four penn'orth.

penny

in for a penny, in for a pound

You say **'in for a penny, in for a pound'** to indicate that you are firmly committed to a particular course of action, even though it will probably cost a lot of money or use a lot of resources if you continue. This expression is used in British English or in old-fashioned American English.

In for a penny, in for a pound. I took the wine to the counter.

□ This expression is sometimes varied. For example, if someone says **'in for several pounds'** instead of 'in for a pound', they are emphasizing that the cost of something is likely to be extremely high.

In for a penny, in for several pounds, I decided to top off my Versace leggings with a Donna Karan jacket.

In for a penny, in for a pound. And I suppose, what with inflation, it follows that it's in for several pennies, in for several hundred pounds.

the penny drops ◄◄

When someone finally understands or realizes something, you can say that **the penny has dropped**. This expression is used mainly in British English.

It seems the penny has finally dropped – house prices won't budge until first-time buyers are tempted into the market.

Eventually the penny dropped: when I got annoyed I succeeded, because of the extra force behind the shot.

Quite suddenly the penny began to drop among national governments that a great deal of this obsession with secrecy was quite unnecessary.

It took a while for the penny to drop.

penny-wise and pound-foolish

If you say that someone is **penny-wise and pound-foolish**, you are criticizing them for being careful in small matters but careless in more important ones. This is an old-fashioned expression, which is used mainly in British English.

If we had the right number of auditors to go out and check on this, we would have saved billions of dollars. In other words, we have been penny-wise and really pound-foolish here.

We are being penny wise and pound foolish, trying to save a few dollars and hastening the time when we are going to have another accident.

turn up like a bad penny

If you say that someone or something **turns up like a bad penny**, you mean that they appear again in a place where they are not welcome or wanted. You often use this expression to indicate that they keep doing this. This is an old-fashioned expression, which is used in British English.

Her husband was able to trace her, to turn up again on her doorstep like the proverbial bad penny.

Like a bad penny, the report has turned up again.

two a penny
ten a penny ◄

If you say that things or people are **two a penny** or **ten a penny**, you mean that there are a great deal of them, and so they are not especially valuable or interesting. This expression is used in British English; the American expression is **a dime a dozen**.

Books on golf are two a penny. There are ones on personalities; others on how to play the game; more on courses; and so on.

Leggy blondes are two-a-penny in Hollywood.

Gloomy economic forecasts are ten-a-penny in Europe.

perch

fall off the perch

If you say that someone **falls off the perch**

or **falls off** their **perch**, you are saying in a humorous or light-hearted way that they die. 'Drop' and 'topple' are sometimes used instead of 'fall'. This is an old-fashioned expression, which is used in British English.

He fell off the perch years ago.

He'll topple off his perch one morning. You know how it is.

knock you off your perch
fall off your perch ◄

If someone or something **knocks** you **off** your **perch**, they cause you to fail, or they damage your status or position. When this happens, you can say that you **fall off** your **perch**; instead of 'fall', you can use other verbs such as 'topple'. These expressions are used in British English.

For the leading regional firms this is an excellent time to knock London firms off their perch and seize the advantages of lower fees and local contacts.

There'll be no end of people ready to knock you down or grin with glee when you fall off your perch.

As one after another of the star companies of the 1980s fall on hard times, their high-flying executives are toppling from their perches.

petard

hoist by your own petard ◄

If someone **is hoist by** their **own petard**, their plan to benefit themselves or to harm someone else results instead in benefit to the other person or harm to themselves. 'By' can be replaced with 'with', and in American English you usually use 'on'. This is a formal expression.

When Japan and America were negotiating a bilateral commercial treaty, the Americans insisted on a provision that ensured American multinationals could put their own people into top positions in their Japanese subsidiaries. Now that Japanese multinationals are leading the way, America finds itself hoist by its own petard.

Peter

rob Peter to pay Paul

If someone **is robbing Peter to pay Paul**, they are using money meant for paying off one debt to pay off a different debt and so they are still in debt.

His mortgages ran into arrears and he borrowed from loan companies. He started robbing Peter to pay Paul.

I have not starved yet but I am very conscious of shelving debts, of robbing Peter to pay Paul.

phrase

to coin a phrase ◄

You say **'to coin a phrase'** when you are making a pun or using a cliché or colloquial expression, in order to show that you realize people might think that it is a silly or boring thing to say, but you think it is relevant in spite of this.

Being gay is what I am, not the easiest of roads to follow, but it wasn't a choice. To coin a phrase, 'I am what I am'.

To coin a phrase, I am gobsmacked at John Major's warning that we must not expect too much from the Earth Summit and that Britain is too broke to help.

picnic

be no picnic ◄

If you say that an experience, task, or activity **is no picnic**, you mean that it is difficult or unpleasant.

'Poor little mites,' she said of the evacuees. 'It's no picnic for them being taken away from their homes.'

Being in between jobs ain't no picnic.

picture

get the picture ◄◄

If someone **gets the picture**, they understand what another person is trying to explain or describe to them. This expression is often used in contexts where you are saying that someone does not understand something immediately.

Anna was giggling. She was beginning to get the picture.

They smoke, they play snooker, they do the pools. You get the picture, I'm sure.

in the picture: 1 ◄

If you say that someone is **in the picture**, you mean that they are involved in the situation you are talking about. Compare **out of the picture**.

Some people don't believe it will ever be safe to go home as long as the terrorists are still in the picture.

If there is a home-wrecker in the picture, it is not her.

in the picture: 2

If you are **in the picture** for promotion or success, you are very likely to get a promotion or be successful. Compare **out of the picture**.

I don't think Foreman is in the picture. The only way we would consider him is if he fought and beat someone like Lennox Lewis.

He told me that Annabella was back in the picture. She was the best one they could find.

pie

out of the picture: 1 ◄

If you say that someone is **out of the picture**, you mean that they are no longer involved in the situation you are talking about. Compare **in the picture**.

Once Derek was out of the picture, however, Malcolm's visits to the Swires became more frequent.

Maybe with Paula out of the picture, Mark would be willing to talk.

out of the picture: 2 ◄

If someone is **out of the picture**, they are not one of the people who is being considered for a promotion or place on a team. Compare **in the picture**.

But I've been told I'm fifth-choice striker, so I'm totally out of the picture.

put someone in the picture
keep someone in the picture ◄◄

If you **put** someone **in the picture**, you tell them about a situation which they need to know about. If you **keep** them **in the picture**, you keep them aware of any changes or developments in the situation. These expressions are used in British English.

I believe that I could now produce evidence to prove my case, if you are prepared to listen. I brought you here for that reason, to put you in the picture.

Has Inspector Fayard put you in the picture?

He's changed so many things – too many to mention. But he's always kept me in the picture.

pie

eat humble pie ◄

If someone **eats humble pie**, they admit that they have been wrong and apologize, especially in situations where this is humiliating or embarrassing for them.

The Queen's Press secretary offered his resignation over his personal attack on the duchess. He was forced to eat humble pie yesterday and publicly apologise to the duchess.

After their victory at Tottenham, Molby insisted, 'The critics were too quick to give their verdict on us. We hope they'll be eating humble pie before the end of the season.'

□ **Humble pie** is sometimes used in other structures with a similar meaning.

Nigel Mansell's critics may be helping themselves to a slice of humble pie this morning after his hard-won third place in yesterday's race.

pie in the sky ◄◄

If you describe an idea, plan, or promise as **pie in the sky**, you mean that it is very unlikely to happen.

Jimmy Knapp, the leader of the biggest

railwaymen's union, promptly claimed that privatisation was now even more pie in the sky.

Ideally what I would like to see would be free childcare, but I think that's a bit pie in the sky at the moment.

□ You can also use **pie-in-the-sky** before a noun.

Changes are a real possibility. This is not pie-in-the-sky stuff.

Is it all just a pie-in-the-sky idea? It is certainly a major job, and not cheap.

piece

all of a piece ◄

If something is **all of a piece**, each part or aspect of it is consistent with all the others. You can also say that one thing is **all of a piece** with another.

Thus the biosphere is all of a piece, an immense, integrated, living system.

The sudden familiarity when he got up and took her proffered hand was all of a piece with the gentle ease with which he inquired how she was.

a piece of cake ◄◄

If you say that something is **a piece of cake**, you mean that it is very easy to do.

'It's not exactly a stressful job is it?' 'If it's quiet, it's a piece of cake. It's just a bit boring.'

Fathoming the complexities of maternity benefits makes the actual process of childbirth look like a piece of cake.

a piece of piss

In British English, if you say that something is **a piece of piss**, you mean that it is very easy to do. This is a very informal expression, which some people find offensive.

The one thing people think is how difficult touring is, but really, it's a piece of piss.

say your piece ◄

If you **say** your **piece**, you give your opinion about a particular matter, although you are aware that other people may not agree with you, or be interested in what you have to say.

Each preacher stood for two minutes on a box, said his piece, and stepped down.

You've got to say your piece quickly before you get cut off.

pieces

go to pieces: 1 ◄◄

If you **go to pieces**, you are so upset or distressed by something that you cannot control your emotions or cope with the things that you have to do.

She's a strong woman, but she nearly went to pieces when Arnie died.

Every time he's faced with a problem he goes to pieces.

go to pieces: 2

If you say that something such as your work or a relationship **has gone to pieces**, you mean that it is no longer as good as it once was and you cannot stop it getting worse.

My work is all going to pieces.

She was one point away from a seemingly unassailable 5-1 lead over Steffi Graf, when her game went to pieces.

pick up the pieces ◄◄◄

If you **pick up the pieces** after something bad has happened, you do what you can to get the situation back to normal again.

Louie had sent his business manager into my life to help pick up the pieces of my shattered career and finances.

People in the high desert communities near Palm Springs, California, are picking up the pieces after last night's earthquake.

shot to pieces

If you say that something such as your confidence or a plan is **shot to pieces**, you mean that it is completely ruined.

When I came here my confidence was shot to pieces. What's happened since is all down to Kevin. He's worked wonders, just filling me with so much self-belief.

Bob's been gone two days, off with some new girlfriend, and the whole schedule's shot to pieces.

The economy is shot to pieces, thousands are losing their jobs every day, and the chances of economic recovery have receded for yet another year.

pig

eat like a pig

If you say that someone **eats like a pig**, you disapprove of the way that they eat a lot of food, usually in a greedy or disgusting manner.

She could hear the part of herself that was self-critical say, 'You eat like a pig. I can't stand looking at you. You're fat.'

In the Middle Ages everyone ate in the same manner – like pigs.

like a greased pig

If someone moves **like a greased pig**, they move very fast and nobody can catch them or stop them. This expression is used mainly in American English.

make a pig of yourself

If you say that someone is **making a pig of** themselves, you are criticizing them for eating a very large amount at one meal.

I'm afraid I made a pig of myself at dinner.

make a pig's ear of something

If you say that someone **makes a pig's ear of** something that they are doing, you are saying in a forceful way that they are doing it very badly. This expression is used in British English.

I made a pig's ear of it last time and I'm going to make sure that won't happen again.

Other countries, it is true, have also made a pig's ear out of their radioactive waste policy. But Britain's performance is the worst.

☐ People sometimes vary this expression, for example by saying that something **is a pig's ear**.

A decent producer was brought in to tidy up Steve's pig's ear of a production.

The current state of British sports politics represents an absolute pig's ear.

a pig in a poke

If you buy or accept **a pig in a poke**, you buy or accept something without examining it or thinking about it carefully first, with the result that you do not know what you are getting, or you get something that you do not want. This is a fairly old-fashioned expression.

The state was going to get a building that they could redevelop. But what's really happening here is that the state may be stuck with a pig in a poke.

Most of these people, I think, are more comfortable muddling along as they are than going with the kind of pig in a poke that these military coup plotters have promised.

squeal like a stuck pig

If you say that someone is **squealing like a stuck pig**, you mean that they are screaming very loudly, as though they are in a lot of pain. You can replace 'squeal' with 'scream' or 'sound'.

Alan tried to calm him while Miller continued to scream like a stuck pig.

sweat like a pig

If you say that someone is **sweating like a pig**, you are emphasizing that they are very hot and they are sweating a lot. This is an informal expression.

The two officers standing just out of camera shot were sweating like pigs in the studio lights.

To put it quite bluntly, my husband sweats like a pig.

pigeon

be someone's pigeon

If something is your **pigeon**, you have to deal with it. This is an old-fashioned expression, which is used in British English.

I'm sorry to load this on you, Harry, but I'm

selfishly glad it's your pigeon rather than mine.

piggy

the piggy in the middle

You can say that someone is **the piggy in the middle** when they are involved against their will in a conflict between two other people or groups, which leads to a very unpleasant situation for them. This expression is used in British English.

When the men in boiler suits arrive on Doug's cruiser it's not to service his engine. He finds himself piggy in the middle of a cannabis smuggling outfit and the Customs.

□ **Piggy in the middle** is a children's game in which two children throw a ball to each other over the head of a third child who tries to catch it.

pigs

pigs might fly
when pigs fly ◄

If you say **'pigs might fly'** or **'when pigs fly'** after someone has said that something might happen, you mean that you think it is very unlikely. These expressions are used mainly in spoken English.

'There's a chance he isn't involved in this, of course.' 'And pigs might fly.'

□ People often vary this expression, for example by saying they saw **a pig flying by**.

'Maybe one day we'll be seen as entertaining.' 'Oh look, I just saw a pig fly by my window.'

pike

come down the pike ◄

If something **is coming down the pike**, it is starting to happen or to become available. This expression is used in American English.

There may be some new treatments coming down the pike. There's a new medicine called tacrine or THA that was recently made available.

There's been threats out of the White House to veto any legislation that comes down the pike, like family leave or a civil rights bill.

pile

the bottom of the pile
the top of the pile ◄

Someone who is at **the bottom of the pile** is low down in society or in an organization. Someone who is at **the top of the pile** is high up in society or in an organization. The expressions **the bottom of the heap** and **the top of the heap** mean the same.

Tragically, organized labour has paid for its disregard of workers at the bottom of the pile.

Their position, at the bottom of the social pile, has resulted in them suffering from indifference at best, exploitation and oppression at worst.

You may not like to admit that you are ambitious but you must know deep down that you want to be on the top of the pile.

pill

sugar the pill
sweeten the pill
sugar-coat the pill ◄◄

If you **sugar the pill** or **sweeten the pill**, you try to make bad news or an unpleasant situation more acceptable for someone by giving them or telling them something good or pleasant at the same time. These forms of the expression are used in British English; in American English, the usual form is **sugar-coat the pill**.

Ministers may reprieve Harefield hospital, the world's leading heart transplant centre, to sugar the pill of a further round of hospital cuts and closures in London and the South-east.

Actors – even the most famous – are often insecure and, anyway, we all thrive on encouragement. A few words of praise help to sweeten the pill of criticism.

His bitter pill was sugar-coated with a promise of 'free and fair' elections.

□ These expressions are often varied.

The appalling timing of that vote has brought the game's followers to an anger rarely equalled. Now comes the sugared pill in the shape of the Conference, and not surprisingly Geoff Fletcher was not prepared to swallow it.

All that talk about our 'mutual' concerns was nothing, of course, but sugar-coating meant to ease the pill down his throat.

swallow a bitter pill
a bitter pill to swallow ◄◄

If someone has to **swallow a bitter pill**, they have to accept a difficult or unpleasant fact or situation.

Mr Major hopes that with Ministers taking a lead in the bid to keep down wages, the nation can be persuaded to swallow the bitter pill.

Gordon Hodgson, Cowie's chief executive, said the failure to win was 'a little bit of a bitter pill to swallow'.

New music is no longer a bitter pill that must be swallowed before we can wallow in old favourites.

□ You can also refer to a difficult or unpleasant fact or situation which you have to accept as **a bitter pill**.

I'm not going to tell you this is not a bitter pill for the armed forces, because clearly it is.

pillar

from pillar to post ◄

If someone is moved **from pillar to post**, they are moved repeatedly from one place or position to another, usually in a hurried or disorganized way so that they suffer as a result. This expression is used in British English and in old-fashioned American English.

A police spokesman said: 'Both sides are exhausted after a weekend of being shoved from pillar to post.'

I didn't want the children pushed from pillar to post.

pillar to post

In sport, especially horse racing, a **pillar to post** victory is one in which the winner was in the lead from the start of the race. This expression is used in British journalism.

Sally Prosser held off the best of the Far East to top the Asian circuit, thanks largely to a pillar to post victory in the JAL Malaysian Open.

pilot

on automatic pilot
on autopilot ◄◄

If you are **on automatic pilot** or **on autopilot**, you are acting without thinking about what you are doing, usually because you have done it many times before or because you are very tired.

Razzall has worked at number 28 Lincoln's Inn Fields since he joined the firm in 1966. 'I expect I'll turn up here on auto-pilot for the first few weeks before I find I'm in the wrong place,' he says.

Steve seemed to be on automatic pilot and able to go on driving without a word of complaint or apparent fatigue.

When the kids came home I just switched on to autopilot, making the tea, listening to them fight.

□ 'Autopilot' is often written as 'auto-pilot' in British English.

pinch

at a pinch
in a pinch ◄◄

If you say that it is possible to do something **at a pinch** or **in a pinch**, you mean that it can just be done if it is absolutely necessary. 'At a pinch' is used in British English and 'in a pinch' is used in American English.

Six people, and more at a pinch, could be seated comfortably at the table.

This dish is best served cold. Allow at least an hour of marinating time, but 10-15 minutes will do at a pinch.

The ballroom could easily handle two hundred chairs, more in a pinch.

feel the pinch ◄◄◄

If a person or company **is feeling the pinch**, they do not have as much money as they used to have, and so they cannot buy the things they would like to buy.

Poor households are still feeling the pinch and the imposition of VAT on fuel from next April will make matters worse.

Japanese car makers are feeling the pinch of an economic slowdown at home.

Economic problems are mounting to the point where ordinary voters are beginning to feel the pinch.

pink

in the pink

If you say that someone is **in the pink** or **in the pink of condition**, you mean that they are very fit and healthy. You can also say that they are **in the pink of health**. These are all old-fashioned expressions.

He insists that Mr Harris, a non-smoker, appeared in the pink of health.

tickled pink ◄

If you are **tickled pink** about something, you are extremely pleased about it.

'As a developer, I'm tickled pink by the dropping prices,' he said.

Her dressmaker, Nicole Marnier, would just be tickled pink if we put one of her outfits in the magazine.

pins

for two pins

People say **'for two pins'** to indicate that they would definitely do something if they were able to, but other factors or considerations make it impossible to do it. This is an old-fashioned expression, which is used mainly in British English.

Now his eyelids were smarting and heavy and he could feel that his face was flushed in the hot little room. For two pins he'd have fallen asleep there and then.

on pins and needles
sit on pins and needles

If you are **on pins and needles** or **are sitting on pins and needles**, you are very anxious or nervous because you are waiting to see if something happens the way you want it to. These expressions are used mainly in American English.

We were approaching Cape Horn, where we had almost lost our lives two years ago, and so until we would get around Cape Horn, I was definitely on pins and needles.

I think we all have been sitting on pins and needles and anxious for something to happen.

pipe

put that in your pipe and smoke it

People sometimes say **'put that in your pipe and smoke it'** to tell you that although you may dislike or disagree with something they have just said, you must accept that it is a fact or true.

As for rules, the only person who makes rules in this house is me. So you can tell Miss Underwood from me: she can put that in her pipe and smoke it.

pipeline

in the pipeline ◀◀◀

If something is **in the pipeline**, it is being planned or is in progress. **In the works** means the same.

New security measures are in the pipeline, including closed-circuit TV cameras in most stores plus secret tags on goods.

The worrying thing is that the Government denied there would be mine closures, even when they were already in the pipeline.

Over 350 major hospital schemes have been completed. There are nearly 300 more in the pipeline.

piper

he who pays the piper calls the tune ◀

When people say **'he who pays the piper calls the tune'**, they are referring to the idea that the person who pays for something has the right to decide how that thing operates or is organized. **Call the tune** is also used on its own as an expression: see **tune**.

Chairman John Elfred Jones, said: 'He who pays the piper should call the tune. It's important our customers have a real say on the balance between demands for improved services and increasing charges.'

The ancient law that he who pays the piper calls the tune has not been repealed even in this permissive democracy.

□ People often vary this expression.

If Europe and Japan are to pay the piper, they will expect at least some say in his choice of tune.

Britain's 35 million domestic policyholders have nothing to worry about yet, but eventually someone has to pay the piper.

He said there was a strong tendency to call the tune without paying the piper or providing the pipe.

piss

take the piss ◀◀◀

In British English, if someone **is taking the piss** out of another person or thing, they are teasing them or making jokes about them in a way that causes them to seem ridiculous. This

is an informal expression, which some people find offensive.

Men will not worry about how powerful their Hoover is, but they'll hit each other if one thinks the other is taking the piss out of his car.

□ You can refer to an instance of this behaviour as **a piss-take**.

In a long-overdue piss-take of the cop movie, Emilio Estevez and Samuel L Jackson crash through 83 minutes of slam-bam entertainment.

pitch

make a pitch: 1 ◀◀

If someone **makes a pitch** for something, they tell people how good that thing is and try to persuade them to support it or buy it.

The president also used his remarks to make a pitch for further space exploration.

She made her entire pitch without once mentioning where the merchandise was manufactured.

Bill Clinton made a final pitch to Wisconsin voters last night.

make a pitch: 2 ◀◀

If someone **makes a pitch** for something, they try to obtain that thing.

So far Federal Reserve Chairman Alan Greenspan hasn't made a pitch for the job.

When we first opened the restaurant, we made a pitch for Chinese diners.

queer someone's pitch

If someone **queers** your **pitch**, they make it very difficult for you to achieve what you are trying to do. This expression is used mainly in British English.

We did everything we could for you here, and you repay the school by doing your best to queer the pitch for us at a college to which we normally send a number of boys.

It could just be the poachers are trying to tell the government not to queer their pitch.

place

fall into place: 1 ◀◀◀

If you have been trying to understand something, and then everything **falls into place**, you suddenly understand it and everything becomes clear. Verbs such as 'click' and 'fit' can be used instead of 'fall'.

Bits of the puzzle fell into place. He knew now who had written the letter summoning Father Benjamin.

Suddenly, everything clicked into place. I could see now how to get the shot I wanted.

It was all fitting into place.

fall into place: 2 ◀◀◀

If things **fall into place**, events happen naturally to produce the situation you want.

Verbs such as 'click' and 'fit' can be used instead of 'fall'.

During February everything will start to fall into place, leaving you with a satisfied feeling that you're living life to the full.

As soon as I moved into midfield everything started falling into place. All my confidence came flooding back and I ended up winning a place with England.

a place in the sun ◄

If you say that someone has found their **place in the sun**, you mean that they are in a job or situation where they will be happy and well-off, and have everything that they want.

I've done what everybody's done. I've fought my way in. I think I've earned my place in the sun.

With the years of hardship and humiliation behind them, they were looking forward to a period of stability and the chance of a place in the sun.

put someone in their place ◄◄

If you **put** someone **in** their **place**, you show them that they are less important or clever than they think they are.

In a few words she had not only put him in his place, but delivered a precise and damning assessment of his movie.

take second place ◄◄◄

If one thing or person **takes second place** to another, the first thing or person is considered to be less important and is given less attention than the second.

My personal life has had to take second place to my career.

Stall holders appeared to be doing brisk business in the bright June sunshine. But business definitely took second place to entertainment.

She was for years married to Ben Nicholson, and nobody ever saw her as taking second place.

places

go places ◄◄

If you say that someone **is going places**, you mean that they are showing a lot of talent or ability and are likely to become very successful.

When we came out, one of the doctors said, 'You're a hell of a surgeon. You are going places.'

If we can play like that every week, then this club is going places.

in high places ◄◄◄

People **in high places** are people who have powerful and influential positions in a government, society, or organization.

You do not rise so high, so fast, without having a few friends in high places.

Last year's attempted coups had been motivated, the plotters said at the time, by the desire to end corruption in high places.

An opponent talked of his 'flawed pedigree'; a rival once spoke of 'low standards in high places'.

plague

avoid something like the plague ◄

If you say that you **avoid** someone or something **like the plague**, you are emphasizing that you deliberately avoid them because you dislike them so much.

I would avoid him like the plague when his wife and my parents were around.

I normally avoid cheap Chianti like the plague.

plain

plain as a pikestaff

If you say that something is as **plain as a pikestaff**, you are emphasizing that it is very obvious or easy to understand. This is an old-fashioned British expression.

The Inspector sat back, relaxed. 'You're on to a loser here, Lennox. Plain as a pikestaff, the whole thing.'

plain as day

If you say that something is as **plain as day**, you mean that it is very easy to see, or that it is very obvious and easy to understand. **Clear as day** means the same.

He was lying there plain as day, a starchy sheet covering the lower half of his hospital gown.

I think we're entitled to be optimistic because it's just as plain as day that Queensland has grown 13 percent since 1986.

plain as the nose on your face

If you say that something is as **plain as the nose on** your **face**, you are emphasizing that it is very obvious or easy to understand.

It's plain as the nose on your face that this company is wildly undervalued.

His humour can be as plain as the nose on your face.

plank

walk the plank
walk the gangplank ◄

If something goes wrong and someone in a position of authority **walks the plank**, they accept responsibility for what has happened and leave their position. You can also say that someone **walks the gangplank**. These expressions are used mainly in journalism.

If they think that the President is going to

plate   302   playing field

lose, they might decide, 'OK, why should I walk the plank for him?'

British Petroleum will unveil its second-quarter results on Thursday, only six weeks after the boardroom mutiny that saw Robert Horton walk the plank.

□ Many people believe that pirates used to kill their prisoners by forcing them to walk along a plank or gangplank sticking out from the edge of a ship until they fell into the sea.

plate
hand someone something on a plate
◄◄

If you say that someone **was handed** something desirable **on a plate**, you are showing disapproval of the fact that they were given it without having to work for it or make an effort to get it. Other verbs can be used instead of 'hand'. This expression is used mainly in British English.

He conveyed the unfortunate impression of never having had to fight for anything in his life: even the presidency was handed to him on a plate.

He had had everything, the whole world handed to him on a plate.

Why must our kids have everything served up on a plate? We had to make do with our own ingenuity and I'm sure we had more fun and satisfaction as a result.

have enough on your plate
have a lot on your plate
have your plate full
◄◄

If you **have enough on** your **plate** or **have a lot on** your **plate**, you have a lot of work to do or a lot of things to deal with.

I'm sorry to bother you with it, Mark, but John's got enough on his plate.

He's got enough on his plate without worrying about tactics and the performances of others.

Yeltsin's got a lot on his plate. He's got to sort out the future structure of power within his own republic.

□ You can also say that someone **has** their **plate full** or **has a full plate**.

I'm making no promises. My staff have their plate full at the present time.

platter
on a silver platter
on a platter
◄

If you are given something **on a silver platter** or **on a platter**, you are given it without having to work or make an effort to get it.

If someone offers you Paris, fashion, and the Louvre on a silver platter, how can you hesitate?

You act like a five-year-old. You expect me to

hand you everything on a silver platter, and when you don't get it, you stamp your little foot and cry.

The Opposition has been handed this issue on a platter.

play
make a play for: 1
◄

If someone **makes a play for** something that they want, they try to get it.

Analysts say the company could soon be making a play for properties around the world.

He wondered if Sheridan were capable of making a destructive play for control of the Society.

make a play for: 2

If someone **makes a play for** a person who they find sexually attractive, they try to win their attention or admiration.

All the girls made a play for him.

If a woman makes an obvious play for a man it can be immensely flattering.

make great play of something
make a big play of something
◄

If you say that someone **makes great play of** something, you mean that they put too much emphasis on it or exaggerate its importance. You can also say that someone **makes a great play of** something or **makes a big play of** it. These expressions are used in British English.

The Conservatives made great play of the defection to them of 20 former members of the SDP.

They're very nervous, very eager to show who's boss. They get us out of the car and make a big play of examining our papers.

Maria was there, making a great play with a duster, but apparently doing very little.

□ You can just say that someone **makes a play of** something.

Both men made a play of wiping the dirt from her coat.

play someone for a fool

If someone **plays** you **for a fool**, they deceive you and use you for their own advantage. Other nouns with a similar meaning can be used instead of 'fool'.

John, do not play me for a fool. You owe me better than that.

The time wore on, though, and she realized she was no closer to getting the money than before. Ken had probably played her for a sucker again.

playing field
a level playing field
level the playing field
◄◄◄

You use **a level playing field** to refer to a

situation that is fair. You usually use this expression when talking about the fact that a situation is not fair, or when saying that you think it should be fair. This expression can be varied, for example by using 'even' or 'uneven' instead of 'level'.

At the moment we are not competing on a level playing field.

We must insist that trade with the nations of Europe, Asia and elsewhere at the very least be conducted on a level playing field.

The playing field isn't quite level yet.

Back-door maneuvering is not the place where Great Lakes protection should be decided. It needs to be decided out in the public where we can all participate on an even playing field.

☐ If you say that you want to **level the playing field**, you mean that you want to make a situation fair, by ensuring that nobody has an advantage over other people.

That's another way of leveling the playing field.

Industry analysts say the agreement should help level the playing field, but won't end cutthroat competition for control of the world aircraft market.

plot

the plot thickens ◄

If you say '**the plot thickens**' when you are describing a complicated situation or series of events, you mean that it starts to become even more complicated or mysterious.

I rang my ever-useful neighbour, Farmer White, to ask his advice. Here the plot thickens; for he knows an engineer of the old school, ideal to carry out such a repair. But he is a retired man and will only work for a chosen few. Will he come or won't he?

At this point the plot thickened further. A link emerged between the attempt to kill the Pope and the kidnapping of the American.

plug

pull the plug on something ◄◄◄

If someone with power **pulls the plug** on a project or activity, they stop supporting it, so that the project or activity fails and has to stop. You usually use this expression to talk about financial support being withdrawn.

Theoretically, the banks have the power to pull the plug on the project if they do not like the companies' sums.

The Government has set out detailed conditions under which it would pull the plug on the sale.

Recovery brings an increase in asset values. That makes it more profitable for creditors (mainly banks) to pull the plug, because there is more chance of them getting their money

back once the assets they can sell are worth something.

plum

a plum in your mouth

In British English, if you say that someone speaks with **a plum in** their **mouth**, you are showing your disapproval of them for having an upper-class accent or for being upper-class.

I heard Mr Downer speaking on the radio on the previous day. I was not conscious of the 'plum in the mouth', but I was aware of his clear diction.

Where a Tory spokesman may speak with a plum in his mouth, it is fitting that Labour's man does it with ball-bearings.

plunge

take the plunge ◄◄◄

If you decide to **take the plunge**, you decide to do something that you have been thinking of doing for some time, even though it is difficult, risky, or unpleasant.

Helen decided to take the plunge and turned professional in 1991.

The problem is that no one government is prepared to take the plunge. Everyone is waiting for everyone else to go first.

Finally, Mona took the plunge. 'I have something to tell you,' she said.

poacher

poacher turned gamekeeper

If you say that someone is **poacher turned gamekeeper**, you mean that they have changed their job or opinion and now have one which seems the opposite of the one they had before. This expression is used in British English.

John Walters has just retired after twenty years as a Radio One producer but it's going to be a case of poacher turned gamekeeper for John because, this week on Greater London Radio, he'll become a DJ.

Gary Mason, boxing's poacher turned gamekeeper, will make his managerial debut tomorrow.

☐ You can also say that someone is **gamekeeper turned poacher**, especially when you think they have gone from a respectable position to a less respectable one.

Gamekeeper turned poacher: after two years with the Financial Times, energy reporter Jane Sayers resigned yesterday to join a public relations firm.

pocket

dip into your pocket
dig deep into your pocket
dig deep ◄◄◄

If someone **dips into** their **pocket** or **digs into** their **pocket** in order to pay for something, they pay for it with their own money. You can also say that someone **dips** their **hand into** their **pocket**.

The Government has decided to chase errant fathers and get them to dip into their pockets and provide for their children.

Potential lenders will need to be persuaded that the government is tackling its economic problems before they dig into their pockets again.

What this club needs is for the directors to dip their hands in their pockets.

□ If you say that someone **digs deep into** their **pocket** in order to pay for something, you mean that they use a lot of their own money to pay for it. If they **dig deeper into** their **pocket**, they use more of their own money.

Adrian dug deep into his own pocket and published the book himself.

The other countries are hoping that the West will dig deeper into its pockets than it has already promised.

□ You can just say that someone **digs deep**, or that they **dig deeper**.

At Christmas, most will dig deep and spend more than last year.

France would step up the pressure on its rich colleagues to dig deeper.

in someone's pocket

If you are **in** someone's **pocket**, they control you or have power over you and so you do everything that they tell you.

Surely there was a judge somewhere who wasn't in Jason's pocket.

The Labour party suffered badly in the election from Conservative claims that it was in the pockets of the unions.

out of pocket: 1 ◄◄

If you are left **out of pocket**, you have less money than you should have or than you intended, for example because something was more expensive than you expected or because of a mistake.

The promoter claims he was left £36,000 out of pocket.

I did make an offer through solicitors that if Mr Reynolds felt he was out of pocket we would be prepared to look at it.

As he'd been paid half his fee in advance he wouldn't be out of pocket.

□ You can use **out-of-pocket** before a noun to describe someone who is in this situation.

Mr Lilley does not want the public purse to

be used permanently to compensate out-of-pocket pensioners.

out of pocket: 2 ◄◄

Out-of-pocket expenses are expenses which someone pays out of their own money, and which are normally paid back later.

I charge twenty dollars an hour plus out-of-pocket expenses.

□ In American English, if you **pay out of pocket**, you pay for something yourself and claim the money back later.

As long as people have to pay out of pocket to see a physician, there will be a deterrent to seeking necessary care.

pockets

line your pockets ◄◄

If you accuse someone of **lining** their **pockets**, you are accusing them of making a lot of money in a dishonest or unfair way. If you say that they **are lining** another person's **pockets**, you mean that they are making a lot of money for the other person in a dishonest or unfair way.

He has been lining his pockets for 27 years while his country has festered in poverty.

Prosecutors say Morris lined his own pockets with most of the cash, buying a Mercedes Benz, jewelry and paying off credit card debts as well.

This is a government that ignores the needs of the majority in order to line the pockets of the favoured few.

live in each other's pockets

If you say that two or more people **live in each other's pockets**, you mean that they spend a great deal of time together. You usually use this expression to suggest that this is a bad thing, because they do not have enough time on their own or with other people as a result. You can use another verb instead of 'live'. This expression is used mainly in British English.

Just because you're married doesn't mean you have to live in each other's pockets.

This is insufficient to explain how the two of them survived 23 years in each other's pockets.

point

boiling point ◄◄

If a situation reaches **boiling point**, it becomes very tense or dangerous because the people involved are so angry that they are likely to go out of control.

As the debts piled up, hostilities reached boiling point.

Tempers were already close to boiling point as the dispute remained deadlocked for the ninth day.

not to put too fine a point on it ◄

You say **'not to put too fine a point on it'** in order to indicate that what you are about to say may sound unpleasant, unkind, or critical. This expression is used in British English.

We didn't meet. In fact, not to put too fine a point on it, I was warned off.

Sun City has had, not to put too fine a point on it, a slightly tacky reputation.

a sticking point ◄◄◄

A **sticking point** is a problem which stops you from achieving something, especially in a series of negotiations or a discussion.

Sources say a Republican call for a cut in the capital gains tax is the main sticking point in budget negotiations.

The sticking point is the method by which millionaires will be made to pay more taxes.

points

score points: 1 ◄◄◄

If someone **scores points** off you, they gain an advantage over you, especially in a discussion or argument. This expression is often used to suggest that they are not really interested in the issues being discussed, but are just trying to show that they are better than you.

They're not remotely concerned about the disabled. They're concerned about trying to score points off Willie Brown, the Democratic speaker of the State Assembly.

The Shadow Cabinet are a talented group of people and right up to the election they were constantly scoring points off the government.

He has been trying hard not to appear as though he was using the situation to score political points.

□ You can refer to this type of behaviour as **point-scoring**.

We shan't succeed if we indulge in self-righteous point-scoring for the benefit of audiences and voters at home.

We can see our leaders looking shifty in close-up every night on television. There is no frankness, only point-scoring.

score points: 2

If you **score points** with someone, you do something that impresses them or makes them think favourably of you.

Again, Laine paused, clearly confident in his arguments. He was scoring points with the judge and the spectators. The momentum was clearly with him. The judge kept nodding in agreement.

pole

the greasy pole ◄

In British English, if you say that someone is moving up **the greasy pole**, you mean that they are reaching a more successful position as a result of working very hard and dealing with all the difficulties they meet. This expression is often used disapprovingly, to suggest that their ambitions are wrong or their methods are dishonest.

Michael's ambition was focused: he would impress the boss and start up the greasy pole.

He was just another, albeit particularly hardworking, local politician climbing assiduously up the greasy pole.

The way has now been eased to allow other women of courage and commitment to follow me up the greasy pole of promotion.

pole position

If you are in **pole position**, you are in a very strong position in a competition or competitive situation, and are likely to win or be successful. This expression is used mainly in British English.

They've been favourites all season and are in pole position now.

The winners would be in pole position to bid to run the station, expected to come on air in spring 1995.

□ This expression comes from motor racing, where the driver who starts the race in front of all the other drivers is said to start in **pole position**. This is the more frequent use of this expression, and occurs in both British and American English.

□ Some people use the word 'poll' instead of 'pole' in this expression, but it is generally considered incorrect.

wouldn't touch something with a barge pole
wouldn't touch something with a ten-foot pole ◄

If you say that you **wouldn't touch** something or someone **with a barge pole**, you mean that you do not want to have anything to do with them, because you do not trust them or like them. This form of the expression is used in British English; in American English, the form is **wouldn't touch** something or someone **with a ten-foot pole**.

The history of the place kept the price down. No one would touch it with a barge pole.

Our message was: 'Don't touch this man with a bargepole.'

If it hadn't been for your wife, I wouldn't touch this stink with a ten-foot pole.

poles

poles apart ◄◄

If you say that two people, ideas, or systems are **poles apart**, you are emphasizing that they are very different.

In social and political terms, they were poles

apart. Haig was, for instance, especially dis-
dainful of French's persistent womanising.

The final goals of both sides are poles apart
and the negotiating path will be arduous.

The East seemed to be poles apart from the
capitalist West.

poor

poor as a church mouse

If you say that you are as **poor as a church
mouse**, you are emphasizing that you have
very little money. This is an old-fashioned expression.

I was as poor as a church mouse, but I
bought that wreck of a car.

I suspect we'll continue to be poor as church
mice.

port

a port in a storm

You can refer to a person, place, or organization where you can get help in a difficult
situation as **a port in a storm**.

She was sweet to take me in the way she did,
hardly any notice at all, just told me to come
right to her. A port in a storm is a welcome
thing.

Traders are still uncomfortable with a strong
yen, but analysts say a dearth of reasons to
buy the dollar leave the yen the safest port in
the current economic storm.

☐ You say **any port in a storm** when you
are in a position where you have to accept
help from anyone who will give it to you,
even if it is from someone who you do not
like or approve of.

Also with their basic vocational training year
nearly 50 percent of those who enter it end up
on the streets. There is an 'any port in a storm'
attitude.

possum

play possum

If someone **plays possum**, they try to make
people ignore them by pretending to be dead
or asleep. This expression is used mainly in
novels.

'Playing possum, huh?' said Joe. 'Right,' said
Frank. 'I figured it might be interesting to
hear what they had to say to each other when
they thought I was unconscious.'

post

first past the post

If you say that someone is **first past the
post** in a race or competitive situation, you
mean that they finish first or achieve something first.

Britain's bid to stage the Olympics in the
year 2000 failed to be the first past the post.

Manchester lost the race to host the biggest
sporting festival in the world. It was won by
Sydney, Australia.

☐ This expression is more commonly used in
talking about electoral systems. A **first-past-
the-post** electoral system is one in which the
candidate who gets the most votes wins.

pip someone at the post   ◄

If you **pip** someone **at the post** or **pip** them
to the post, you narrowly beat them in a
competition or race to achieve something.
This expression is used in British English.

Reg was pipped at the post twice before he
was appointed.

They were concerned that their rivals might
pip them to the post.

posted

keep someone posted   ◄◄

If someone asks you to **keep** them **posted**,
they are asking you to continue giving them
the latest information about a situation that
concerns them.

'Well, keep us posted.' 'I'll do that.'

She made me promise to keep her posted on
developments.

I'll keep you posted with what's happening.

pot

go to pot   ◄

If you say that something **is going to pot**,
you mean that its condition is becoming very
bad, because it has not been properly looked
after.

The neighbourhood really is going to pot.

I was able to keep my figure after Patrick,
but it went to pot after I had Daniel.

keep the pot boiling

If you do something in order to **keep the
pot boiling**, you do it in order to make sure
that a process does not stop.

I threw in a question, just to keep the pot
boiling while my brain caught up.

Recent inspections have been aimed simply at
keeping the pot boiling.

the pot calling the kettle black   ◄

When someone with a particular fault accuses someone else of having the same fault,
you can say this is a case of **the pot calling
the kettle black**.

In a prime case of the pot calling the kettle
black, 48-year-old Ian, whose recent loves included two 22-year-olds, asked a friend: 'Why
must she go for an older man? She should
know better than that.'

Ferguson publicly questioned the Leeds' players nerves before the weekend, which is a bit
like the pot calling the kettle black.

☐ People often vary this expression.

Pots should not call kettles black.

It is all very well for Washington State to assume moral superiority. There is a bit of pot-and-kettle about its outrage.

shit or get off the pot

If someone tells you to **shit or get off the pot**, they mean that you should either do something properly, or else let someone else do it. This is a very informal expression, which is used mainly in American English. Many people consider it offensive.

Time to shit or get off the pot, ain't it, Bud?

I thought Malcolm would be forced eventually either to shit or get off the pot.

a watched pot never boils

If you say **'a watched pot never boils'**, you mean that if you wait and watch anxiously to see something happen, it will seem to take a very long time, or it will not happen at all. This is an old-fashioned expression.

This strategy is doomed from the start because it is far too public: a watched pot never boils.

potato

drop something like a hot potato
drop something like a hot brick

If you **drop** something or someone **like a hot potato** or **drop** them **like a hot brick**, you get rid of them as quickly as possible because they are difficult to deal with, or because you do not want them any more.

It is a rule of the tourism business that clients must feel happy on holiday. If a place gains a reputation for being unwelcoming, the trade drops it like a hot potato.

He panicked and dropped his lover like a hot brick. But the scandal was already brewing.

a hot potato ◄◄

If you say that a subject or problem is **a hot potato**, you mean that it is very topical and controversial and most people would rather not have to deal with it.

When she is confronted with a political hot potato such as abortion or tightening the gun laws, she is not beyond voicing her opinion.

So the 'German question' is likely to continue to gain visibility here; a hot potato nobody wants to handle, but which will be increasingly hard to avoid.

potatoes

small potatoes ◄

If you say that something is **small potatoes**, you mean that it is not important or significant.

While a total tour attendance of around 20,000 is small potatoes by British standards, it is very big in this country.

They hope to get the rules changed, so they can negotiate the rights to make money from television reruns, no small potatoes when last year the rerun business was worth about $3 billion.

pot luck

be pot luck

If you ask someone to have a meal at your house and you tell them it will be **pot luck**, you mean that you have not planned it or prepared any special food.

'We'll just be casual and eat in the kitchen. It's just pot luck,' Moira said. 'Hope you don't mind.'

□ 'Pot luck' is usually written as 'potluck' in American English; a **potluck** is a meal at which different guests bring different parts of the meal.

take pot luck ◄◄

If you **take pot luck**, you make a choice from what is available, although you do not have any knowledge to help you, and so it is a matter of luck whether you get something good.

We'd take potluck at whatever restaurants might still be open.

Just leave the highway, drive out into the country, pick on a small town and take pot luck.

□ You can also say that something is **pot luck** when it is a matter of luck whether you get something good. You can also use **pot-luck** before a noun.

The major High Street electrical appliance retailers are offering interest-free credit but on ever-changing products, so finding good deals is pot luck.

Travel firms stuck with hundreds of unsold package holidays are offering great breaks on a pot-luck basis.

□ 'Pot luck' is usually written as 'potluck' in American English.

pottage

a mess of pottage

If you accuse someone of selling or exchanging something of lasting value for **a mess of pottage**, you mean that they have foolishly sold or exchanged it for something which has no lasting value at all. This is an old-fashioned, literary expression.

She was not going to lower herself for the sake of a fifty-dollar mess of pottage.

pound

your pound of flesh ◄

If you say that someone demands or gets their **pound of flesh**, you mean that they insist on getting something they are entitled to, even though they might not need it and it will cause problems for the people they are getting it from.

Banks are quick enough to demand their pound of flesh from the small businessman and other regular customers when overdrafts run a little over the limit.

They were still out for their pound of flesh and were not prepared to meet halfway.

powder

keep your powder dry

If someone **keeps** their **powder dry**, they are ready to take immediate action in case a situation suddenly gets worse.

The only course upon which the government could agree was to move cautiously, keep its powder dry, and await the outcome of events abroad.

powder keg

sit on a powder keg

If you say that someone **is sitting on a powder keg**, you mean that they are in a very dangerous situation, in which something could suddenly go seriously wrong at any time.

The Prime Minister was all too aware that he was sitting on a powder keg which could explode at any moment.

Is there a sense that you really are sitting there on a powder keg, that any one of these conflicts that we've been talking about could erupt at any moment and really engulf your country?

□ People often use **powder keg** to refer to a dangerous situation or to a place where disaster could suddenly happen.

The trial is viewed here as even more of a powder keg than the retrial of the policemen accused of beating Rodney King.

The region has long been regarded as the powder keg of Europe.

power

all power to your elbow
more power to your elbow ◄

People say '**all power to** your **elbow**' or '**more power to** your **elbow**', to wish someone luck and to encourage them to be successful. These expressions are used in spoken British English.

Bobby Gould is a good man and he's now paving the way for a very good third division campaign. So all power to his elbow.

It's nice talking to you, John, and more power to your elbow with your programme. It's absolutely super.

the power behind the throne ◄

If you refer to someone as **the power be-hind the throne**, you mean that although another person appears to have all the power and control in an organization, it is in fact the first person who has all the power and control.

Will the armed forces, which have been the power behind the throne for nearly thirty years, be prepared to take a back seat to a new civilian regime?

She was the real power behind the throne, a strong and single-minded woman manipulating a weaker husband for her own ends.

practise

practise what you preach ◄◄

If someone **practises what** they **preach**, they behave in the way that they encourage other people to behave.

Michael Blundell practised what he preached; having declared himself to be a Kenyan, he was one of the first British-born residents to apply for Kenyan citizenship.

Grown-ups don't know all the answers, don't practise what they preach, and must be held responsible for the poor state of society.

□ People sometimes vary this expression, for example by saying that someone **preaches what** they **practise**.

He is happy to preach what he practises.

The Bishop said the government had let the people down badly: it had preached love but practised hate.

□ The verb 'practise' is spelled 'practice' in American English.

praise

damn with faint praise ◄

If you **damn** someone **with faint praise**, you say something about them which sounds nice but which shows that you do not really have a high opinion of them. People occasionally say that someone **is damned by faint praise**.

In recent months he has consistently damned the government with faint praise, but earlier this week he issued an appeal for continuity.

Why you English seem oblivious to his talents and damn him with faint praise is totally beyond us.

□ You can also just talk about **faint praise**.

Mr Robinson acknowledged Mr Golub this week as 'the most obvious internal candidate'. That sounds like ominously faint praise.

praises

sing the praises of someone ◄◄◄

If you **sing the praises of** someone or something, you praise them in an enthusiastic way.

*Roxburgh, singing Durrant's praises, said:
'He's different, a real natural.'*

*This may sound like we're singing our own
praises here, but I honestly think most people
find our music irresistible.*

*All parties are singing the praises of the
multi-party system and the virtues of a market
economy.*

prawn

come the raw prawn

If you accuse someone of **coming the raw
prawn**, you are accusing them of trying to
cheat or trick you. This expression is used
mainly in Australian English.

*It pains me to say this but I'm afraid the
Italians were caught trying to come the raw
prawn, as it were.*

prayer

not have a prayer ◄

If you say that someone **does not have a
prayer** of achieving something, you mean
that it is impossible for them to achieve it.

*He did not seem to have a prayer of regain-
ing the world title.*

*He must know that he doesn't have a prayer
of beating the grand-theft and insurance-fraud
charges.*

pregnant

you can't be half pregnant

If you say **'you can't be half pregnant'**,
you are pointing out that it is often necessary
to commit yourself fully to an idea or project,
and you cannot keep changing your mind
about it.

*We did, however, pick up a valuable lesson:
you can't be half-pregnant. An entrepreneur
must be able to give his enterprise a full commitment.*

press

a bad press
a good press ◄◄◄

If someone or something gets **a bad press**,
they are repeatedly criticized, especially in
the newspapers, on television, or on radio.
This expression is often varied. For example,
you can talk about someone getting **bad
press**, or you can replace 'bad' with other adjectives.

*So-called 'arranged marriages', common in
many cultures, tend to get a bad press in the
West.*

*Not daunted by years of bad press and stereo-
typing, women drivers are steadily increasing
in number.*

*He often had such a terrible press, yet every-
one who met him liked him.*

☐ If someone or something gets **a good press**
or gets **good press**, they are praised a lot.

*Dublin's writers do not give the city an en-
tirely good press.*

*The auto maker has been getting some good
press lately for changes being made by its new
management team.*

a full-court press ◄

If there is **a full-court press** on something
or someone, people are making a lot of effort
and putting a lot of pressure on them in order
to get a particular result. This expression is
used in American English.

*The administration's full-court press on eco-
nomic remedies also includes moves by the
Treasury Secretary.*

*We put on what we think is a full-court press
in the Middle East to interest some of the airlines there in the 777 and in our other air-
planes too.*

*The administration steps up the full-court
press on the president's economic plan today.*

pretty

sit pretty ◄

If someone **is sitting pretty**, they are in a
good, safe, or comfortable situation.

*When the war started, they thought they were
sitting pretty, because they had all that extra
surplus grain.*

*If we'd let Mark have the statue for a cool
quarter of a million, we'd be sitting pretty by
now.*

price

at any price ◄◄◄

If you want something **at any price**, you
are determined to get it, even if unpleasant
things happen as a result of your actions.

*We obviously want to see the hostages home,
as quickly as we can get them, but not at any
price and I believe their families understand
that too.*

*They do not want to split their own ranks.
But they are not so desperate that they want a
deal at any price.*

*But they also worry that as negotiations pro-
ceed, there's likely to be more violence from rebel groups that are determined to stop the
peace process at any price.*

at a price: 1 ◄◄

If you say that something can be obtained **at
a price**, you mean that it is very expensive.

*Guests can always find a meal of sorts in the
hotel restaurant, but at a price.*

*War fears have faded and most goods are
available, but at a price.*

*She has been attempting to tell her side of the
story, at a price, to anybody in South Africa
who cares to telephone her.*

at a price: 2 ◄◄

If you get something you want **at a price**, you get it but you have to accept something unpleasant as well.

You can find uncertainty on those impudent features, turmoil and the growing realisation that fame comes at a price.

Among the various strands of opposition there are those who refuse all cooperation with the socialists, and those willing to cooperate, but at a price. The price is very high indeed: the Union of Democratic Forces is asking for six key cabinet posts.

everyone has their price
every man has his price ◄

If you say that **everyone has** their **price** or **every man has his price**, you mean that everyone can be persuaded to do something dishonest or immoral, if they are offered a large enough amount of money.

They say 'a million'. And then you say 'No'. And then they offer, because they think everybody has his price, three million. And then you say 'No' again. It feels good to know that you don't come cheap.

While it may not be true that every man has his price, there are always those who have.

prick

like a spare prick at a wedding

If you say that someone is **like a spare prick at a wedding**, you mean that they have no role in a particular situation or feel that they are being ignored. This is a very informal expression, which is used in British English. Many people consider it offensive.

The party conference exists only for Cabinet ministers to look good on television, and for party workers to rub shoulders with Cabinet ministers. Junior ministers and MPs here are like spare pricks at a wedding.

pricks

kick against the pricks

If someone **kicks against the pricks**, they show their opposition to people in authority. This is a literary expression, which is used mainly in British English.

Kicking against the pricks when you're 30 or 40 or more strikes me as a better test of one's convictions.

She is firmly foul-mouthed, ready to kick against every known prick.

pride

swallow your pride ◄◄

If you **swallow** your **pride**, you decide to do something even though it is shameful or embarrassing, and you would prefer not to.

However, if political compulsions demand, he can swallow his pride and ally himself with his political enemies.

States like Illinois have cut programs for the poor. They and members of their families are swallowing their pride and looking for charity.

print

the small print
the fine print ◄◄◄

If you refer to **the small print** or **the fine print** in a contract, agreement, or advertisement, you mean the part which contains important legal information, often in very small print. Most people do not read this information and so may not understand fully what their legal rights are.

Patients who thought they were fully covered are being hit by huge bills because they did not read the small print on their insurance forms.

I'm looking at the small print. I don't want to sign anything that I shouldn't sign.

The president said he'll wait to read the fine print of the still-secret trade agreement and see how the treaty might effect labor and the environment.

prisoners

take no prisoners ◄

If you say that someone **takes no prisoners** when they are carrying out a plan or an action, you mean that they do it in a very forceful and determined way, without caring if they harm or upset other people. This expression is used mainly in journalism.

You will have to fight for what you want and what you believe in and you should assume the attitude that you're taking no prisoners.

It's a team packed with experienced and mature professionals. They won't be taking prisoners.

□ You can also say that someone has a **take-no-prisoners** attitude or approach to something.

We had a take no prisoners attitude, which was we didn't care who we infuriated.

What these institutions do is embrace a particular agenda and they embrace it with a take-no-prisoners policy.

production

make a production of something

If you say that someone **is making a production of** something, you are criticizing them for doing it in a complicated or exaggerated way, when it could be done much more simply.

I don't know why we insisted on making such a production of these dinners, because by the time Julian arrived we were invariably nervous and exhausted.

He made a production of brushing his hands clean on his pant legs.

'Fasten your seat belt, love.' Her daughter complied, making a breathless production of it.

profile

a high profile   ◄◄◄

If someone has **a high profile**, people notice them and what they do.

He will be thinking about his future now that he has such a high profile in the cycling world.

She gained a high profile in Europe as a member of the European Union of Women, of which she is now the vice-chairperson.

It was expected that someone with a high profile would get the job.

□ You can also use **high-profile** before a noun.

Experience in Australia, which has the highest rate of skin cancer in the world, has shown how effective a high profile campaign can be in changing public attitudes and behaviour.

She works three days a week in a high-profile job as communications director for a top advertising agency.

keep a low profile   ◄◄◄

If someone **keeps a low profile**, they avoid doing things that will make people notice them.

The president continues to keep a low profile as he wraps up his weekend vacation in Maine.

The Home Secretary was keeping a low profile yesterday when the crime figures were announced in the House of Commons.

They have been dating for a month and have kept everything very low profile.

□ You can also use **low-profile** before a noun.

The President is pursuing a low-profile approach on difficult issues in order not to antagonise the parties involved.

There is no requirement for the presence of any police officers. This is a low-profile event.

proof

the proof of the pudding is in the eating   ◄

If you say that **the proof of the pudding is in the eating**, you mean that something new can only be judged to be good or bad after it has been tried or used.

With a lapse of almost 12 months since the changes were implemented, perhaps we can now apply the old maxim that 'the proof of the pudding is in the eating'.

Such therapies should not be dismissed out of hand, particularly when the proof of the pudding can be in the eating.

□ People often vary this expression, for example by just talking about **the proof of the pudding**.

The proof of the pudding, so to speak, will be if sales of English cheese hold up after the dispute is over.

The proof of a government policy is in its implementation.

pudding

over-egg the pudding

If you say that someone **over-eggs the pudding**, you are criticizing them for trying so hard to improve something that they spoil it, for example by making it seem exaggerated or extreme. Other nouns are sometimes used instead of 'pudding'. This expression is used mainly in British English.

The movie obviously over-eggs the glowing childhood pudding with lots of cuddles, warm milk and snow pattering against the window panes.

Supertramp certainly knew how to over-egg the cake, with no song being complete unless it underwent three tempo changes and a loud finale.

pull

pull the other one
pull the other one, it's got bells on it

If someone tells you something and you say **'pull the other one'**, you mean that you do not believe them. This expression is used in British English.

I saw him out, said goodbye, and he kissed me on both cheeks. The receptionist saw this and wanted to know who he was. I told her he had been a child in our care. She said: 'Pull the other one, kids in care never kiss anyone on both cheeks.'

□ People sometimes say **'pull the other one, it's got bells on it'**.

'The Duchess gave it to me.' 'Think I'd believe that? Pull the other one, there's bells on it.'

pulp

beat someone to a pulp   ◄

If you say that someone **was beaten to a pulp** or **was beaten to pulp**, you mean that they were injured very badly by someone hitting them repeatedly. Other verbs can be used instead of 'beat'.

I tried to talk myself out of a fight and got beaten to a pulp instead by three other boys.

Motorists were pulled from their cars, beaten and kicked to a pulp, and left to die in the road.

pump

prime the pump ◄◄

If someone **primes the pump**, they take action to help something succeed or grow, usually by spending money on it. This expression is used mainly in journalism.

Spring is the time when the government primes the pump to help farmers prepare their fields.

The budget in December is likely to prime the pump by tax cuts.

□ You can also talk about **pump-priming**, or say that someone **pump-primes** an economy or project.

I think we are going to have to do some more spending and some pump-priming in order to get the economy going.

The plan offers a way of pump-priming an economy which is growing at its slowest rate since 1981.

punch

pack a punch ◄◄

If something **packs a punch**, it has a very powerful effect. The noun 'wallop' is sometimes used instead of 'punch'.

The doctor objects to the innocuous-looking packaging for drinks that pack a punch.

Huge uniformed orchestras with vast brass sections packed a powerful punch and filled the dance halls during the depression years of the Thirties.

Scaring is easy, but creating a true chill is harder. Among the movies that still do that is 'Carrie' which, many years after it was made, still packs a wicked wallop.

pleased as punch

If you say that someone is as **pleased as punch** about something, you are emphasizing that they are very pleased about it.

He's obviously as pleased as punch about buying this timber firm of Coe's.

Branfoot announced he was as pleased as punch with his team's performance.

punches

not pull your punches
pull no punches ◄◄◄

If someone does **not pull** their **punches** or **pulls no punches**, they speak very frankly about something and do not moderate their comments or criticism in any way.

He had never lied to me in the past and he didn't pull his punches now. He told me that in his opinion, Robin would be dead in nine months.

I didn't pull any punches. We all knew we had a problem, a critical one, and that decisions would have to be reached quickly.

Chomsky pulls no punches in his attacks on

US foreign policy in Vietnam, Guatemala, El Salvador and East Timor.

roll with the punches

If someone **rolls with the punches**, they do not allow difficulties or criticism to discourage them or affect them badly.

He has impressed all sides by his ability to negotiate and willingness to roll with the punches.

As part of his success strategy Barnes is prepared to roll with the punches and appear 'raceless' to please the crowd.

pup

sell someone a pup

If someone **is sold a pup**, they buy or accept something and then feel deceived because it is not as good as they thought it would be. This expression is used in British English.

No-one is being sold a pup. What you see is what you get.

We were sold a pup with the exchange-rate mechanism. We're not going to be sold another pup with the Maastricht treaty.

purposes

at cross purposes ◄

If two people are **at cross purposes**, there is a misunderstanding between them because they think they are talking about or trying to do the same thing as each other, but they are actually talking about or trying to do different things.

They had been talking at cross purposes earlier, Enron realized. The Hungarian hadn't been offering Israel a slice of the deal at all.

Now that Council members are working together instead of at cross purposes, the chances for a third major project, Gateway 101, look considerably brighter.

The contract had been signed on his behalf by a new, inexperienced agent who was somehow working at cross-purposes with Faulkner's usual representative.

purse

hold the purse strings
tighten the purse strings
loosen the purse strings ◄◄◄

If someone **holds the purse strings**, they control the way that money is spent in a particular family, organization, or country. Other verbs can be used instead of 'hold'.

Six out of ten women think that financial institutions treat them like simpletons, even though they usually hold the domestic purse strings.

As higher education budgets have decreased, tension has increased between university offi-

cials and the political leaders who control the purse strings.

□ You can also say that someone **tightens the purse strings** when they reduce the amount of money that you can spend, or that they **loosen the purse strings** when they allow you to spend more money.

Grandiose election promises must be put on hold while the government tightens its purse strings.

If the Treasury loosens the purse strings, many authorities will be delighted to spend.

push

at a push

If you say that it is possible to do something **at a push**, you mean that it can be done if it is absolutely necessary to do it.

The only thing you didn't get in the village was milk and you could always, at a push, get some from the farm.

At a push, Ashley will concede that he's a bit bored by it all.

get the push
give someone the push ◄

If someone **gets the push** or **is given the push**, they lose their job. These are informal expressions, which are used in British English.

America's current economic downturn is markedly different from previous recessions. This time white-collar workers and professionals are getting the push, not just factory workers and low-level clerks.

The boss has been given the push in favour of his current number two.

when push comes to shove
if push comes to shove ◄◄

If you talk about what you will do **when push comes to shove** or **if push comes to shove**, you are talking about what you will do when a situation reaches a critical point and you must make a decision on how to progress. **When it comes to the crunch** means the same.

With the benefit of hindsight and with what we've learned from this war, the only thing we can do when push comes to shove is to try to save lives.

They knew they could sit back, and when push came to shove I'd do all the work.

They wouldn't back you, sir. If push came to shove. They wouldn't be behind you.

pusher

a pen pusher
a pencil pusher
a paper pusher ◄◄

If you refer to someone who works in an office as **a pen pusher**, **a pencil pusher**, or **a paper pusher**, you are expressing scorn for the sort of work which typically goes on in offices, in contrast to more active kinds of work. 'Pen pusher' is used mainly in British English; 'pencil pusher' is used only in American English; 'paper pusher' is used in both British and American English.

He already sees significant changes since the training was introduced. People who were called administrators, and perhaps seen as just pen pushers, have been transformed to proactive managers.

Many of the men who now sit on company boards are pencil pushers with PhDs and MBAs from top schools, but lack operating experience in business.

The bureaucrats, the paper-pushers, Lindsay feels, have succeeded in suffocating the spirit of the Bureau's street agents – driving the real cops who solve real crimes out of their minds and out of the Bureau.

□ You can refer to office work as **pen-pushing**, **pencil-pushing**, or **paper-pushing**. You can also say that office workers **push papers** or **push pens**.

I want our uniformed services freed from paper pushing, so that we can put police officers on the beat again.

It's very irritating hanging around while petty pen-pushing officials do their work.

I'm very thankful that I can scratch out a living surviving off my art and doing what I want to do, rather than working as a waiter or pushing papers eight hours a day.

putty

putty in your hands ◄

If you say that someone is **putty in** your **hands**, you mean that they will do anything you ask or tell them to do.

Simon proved to be putty in his hands.

I was completely in awe of him, I was putty in his hands.

□ You can also just say that someone **is putty**.

Sometimes he'd do something like bring her a box of chocolates and she would be putty for a week.

Q

QT

on the QT

If you do something **on the QT**, you do it secretly. This is an old-fashioned expression.

These two boys, on the QT, have bought up everything on both sides of the road, piece by piece. They've bought up that whole end of town.

Many of the companies in which he had a financial interest had been selling to the Russians for years, openly or on the q.t.

□ 'QT' is sometimes written as 'q.t.'. It is pronounced 'q t', as if you are spelling it out.

quantity

an unknown quantity ◄◄

If you say that someone or something is **an unknown quantity**, you mean that not much is known about what they are like or how they will behave.

She had known Max for some years now, but he was still pretty much an unknown quantity.

Belgium are something of an unknown quantity having, in recent years, played few games against leading countries.

Ballet was an unknown quantity in the United States at that time, and he himself admitted that music was quite foreign to him.

quart

a quart into a pint pot

In British English, if you say that someone is trying to get **a quart into a pint pot**, you mean that they are trying to put a large amount of something into a container or space that is too small.

In putting together a 'brief' article on the Tay Bridge Disaster, I was faced with the problem of fitting a quart into a pint pot, there being so much material available.

□ A quart is a unit of measure for liquids. It is equal to two pints.

quarterback

a Monday morning quarterback ◄

If you accuse someone of being a **Monday morning quarterback**, you mean that they are criticizing or judging something unfairly, because although they now have full knowledge of the way things happened, the people involved could not possibly have had that knowledge and so could not have behaved any differently. This expression is used in American English.

Some Monday-morning quarterbacks said the initial lower bid, without junk bonds, was a factor in his losing the company.

□ You can also accuse someone of **Monday morning quarterbacking**.

The Los Angeles County District Attorney rejects such Monday-morning quarterbacking, insisting that his lawyers did, quote, 'an excellent job'.

□ In the United States, most professional football games are played on Sunday. A **Monday morning quarterback** is someone, usually a man, who tells people what the coach should have done to win the game.

question

beg the question: 1 ◄◄◄

If you say that something **begs the question** or **begs** a particular **question**, you mean that it makes people want to ask that question.

Hopewell's success begs the question, why aren't more companies doing the same?

When pushed to explain, words – for once – failed the England manager, begging the obvious question: Does he really know?

beg the question: 2 ◄

If you say that someone's statement **begs the question**, you mean that they can only make that statement if they assume that a particular problem has already been dealt with. By using this expression, you are suggesting that the problem has not in fact been dealt with, and so their statement may not be valid or reasonable. This is a formal expression.

Even the New York Times in 1988 stated that 'the warming of the earth's climate is no longer in dispute', somewhat begging the question of whether or not that warming is a greenhouse effect or, indeed, necessarily part of a continuing long-range trend.

a question mark ◄◄◄

If you say that there is **a question mark** over something, you mean that there is doubt or uncertainty about it.

There's a big question mark over whether the two sides think they're in Freetown simply to negotiate a ceasefire or whether they're there to discuss the whole process of the political settlement.

Both riders have question marks over them due to ill-health and injury.

Multi-party democracy has arrived – albeit

with many question marks about its eventual form.

I am very pleased they have been acquitted. However it leaves a big question mark hanging over the original trial.

quick

cut someone to the quick

If something **cuts** you **to the quick**, it makes you very upset.

The naked ugliness of prejudice cut me to the quick when I heard it.

That tone of hers always cut him to the quick.

quick as a flash
quick as a wink
quick as lightning ◄

If you say that someone does something as **quick as a flash**, you are emphasizing that they do it very quickly. You can also say that someone does something as **quick as a wink** or as **quick as lightning**.

Harrison responded as quick as a flash.

She kissed him right on the lips and then turned to go. Like that, quick as a wink.

When Major Fox made his entrance, more champagne appeared as quick as lightning, as if the waiters had been cued in for that very moment.

quids

quids in ◄

If you are **quids in**, you make or have more money than you expected. This expression is used in British English.

Workers at a window factory were furious when they found German money in their wage packets. But they soon cheered up when they realised it left them quids in.

Still, we were quids in, we didn't care!

quiet

quiet as a lamb

If you say that someone is **quiet as a lamb**, you are emphasizing that they are very quiet, calm, or gentle.

She's fine, quiet as a lamb. You really mustn't worry.

As soon as the organ music began to play and people started going in to get their seats,

Ellie went quiet as a lamb.

quiet as a mouse

If you say that someone is **quiet as a mouse**, you are emphasizing that they are very quiet or silent.

During the day Mom was quiet as a mouse. She hardly said or did anything.

We were quiet as mice, hiding in there.

quits

call it quits ◄

If you say that you are going to **call it quits**, you mean that you have decided to stop doing something or stop being involved in something.

There is a disco called the Club Coqui, which stays open until the last customer is ready to call it quits.

He and Moira had finally called it quits.

quote

quote, unquote
quote, end quote ◄◄◄

If you use a word which someone else has used and you say **quote, unquote**, you are drawing attention to the word, and showing that it is not an accurate or precise way to describe the situation you are referring to. You sometimes use this expression to suggest that a word is being used with almost the opposite meaning to its normal meaning. This expression is used mainly in spoken American English. Compare **in inverted commas**; see **commas**.

What Clinton can do is convince enough people that these two quote unquote 'responsible' Democrats of the center are to be trusted with national office.

A spokesman said quote, 'a certain number', unquote of the men lost their lives that day.

She gathered around her a group of 'bodyguards', quote, unquote, who were essentially a bunch of thugs.

□ In American English, you can also say **quote, end quote**.

The book was given to several school libraries, and in every case a vice principal of the particular school took the book out and then reported it, quote, 'lost', end quote.

R

race

a race against time
race against time ◄◄◄

If you say that someone is in **a race against time,** you mean that they have only a very short time to finish a task and so they have to work very quickly.

The aid agencies have been in a race against time to get Bosnia equipped for winter.

Helicopters are being used to winch passengers to safety in the stormy weather. An air force spokesman said the rescue operation was a race against time.

Oldham's Ian Olney faces a race against time to be fit for tonight's Premier League match against Norwich.

□ You can also say that someone **is racing against time** to mean the same thing.

Irene Blanthorn is racing against time to save the life of a little boy on the other side of the world.

rack

on the rack
put someone on the rack ◄

If you say that someone is **on the rack,** you mean that they are in a state of anxiety, distress, or difficulty. You can also say that someone **puts** them **on the rack.** These expressions are used mainly in British English.

In the flat Vangelis waited, still on the rack, not daring to believe.

She and Michael listened closely, on the rack of apprehension.

John Major was put on the rack by his angry backbenchers yesterday.

rack and ruin

If you say that something is going to **rack and ruin,** you mean that it is falling into a very bad condition, because nobody is looking after it or dealing properly with it.

The country is going to rack and ruin. No one is discussing the economic crisis.

Your garden's fallen into rack and ruin.

□ The old-fashioned spelling 'wrack' is occasionally used instead of 'rack' in this expression.

rag

lose your rag

If you **lose** your **rag,** you suddenly lose your temper with someone and get very angry. This expression is used in British English.

Everyone said Wright did well simply because he didn't lose his rag with anyone.

The bloke pushed Melvin out of the way and he lost his rag and hit him.

ragged

run someone ragged ◄

If someone **runs** you **ragged,** they make you do so much that you get extremely tired.

He tends to produce his best football before half-time, though often coming back to run defenders ragged in the closing minutes.

Their defence was run ragged by a rampant Portsmouth in front of a crowd of 11,000.

They'd send me here, there and everywhere and I'd run myself ragged and get no place.

rags

rags to riches
riches to rags ◄◄

If you describe someone's life as a **rags to riches** story, you are saying that even though they were very poor when they were young, they became very rich and successful.

His life sounds to me like the classic rags to riches story. He married some money, I gather, but he made a lot more.

The company was created by rags-to-riches entrepreneur Albert Gubay, who nowadays deals in property.

□ You can also say that someone went **from rags to riches.**

When asked how he went from rags to riches, Plunkett said, 'I saw my opportunities and I took them.'

□ People sometimes use the expression **riches to rags** to mean that you have been very rich but have lost a lot of money and so have become very poor.

The country went from riches to rags in a generation.

rails

jump the rails

If something such as a plan or project **jumps the rails,** it suddenly goes wrong. This expression is used mainly in British English, especially in journalism.

You never know when or where you'll find examples of how life in this modern society has jumped the rails.

off the rails: 1 ◄◄◄

If someone goes **off the rails,** they start to behave in an unacceptable or peculiar way.

This expression is used mainly in British English.

Our family was so happy until our daughter went off the rails. She left school at 15, got in with the wrong crowd, left home, broke up the flat she found herself in, and now lives rough.

Sometimes, you drink too much and go off the rails.

Even the love that he found in his family didn't prevent him slipping off the rails and becoming a bit of a delinquent.

off the rails: 2 ◄

If something goes **off the rails**, it starts to go wrong. This expression is used mainly in British English.

By the Spring, the project seemed to be going off the rails. No major sponsor had come forward with the extra £1 million or so needed to fund her sailing programme and her pre-race running costs.

Clearly something has gone off the rails in the process of government when the leaders of the US government can't agree on providing money to keep the government going.

on the rails: 1 ◄

If something stays **on the rails**, it continues to be as successful as it has been in the past. If something is back **on the rails**, it is beginning to be successful again after a period when it almost failed. This expression is used mainly in British English.

Co-ordinated action is needed more than ever to put the European economy back on the rails.

Why have the tried and trusted companies remained on the rails while others have floundered?

on the rails: 2 ◄

If someone stays **on the rails**, they live and behave in a way which is acceptable and orderly. If someone is back **on the rails**, their life is going well again after a period when it was going badly.

Although my behavioural marks at school weren't particularly high, the one thing that kept me on the rails was realising that exams were quite important.

I was released from prison last year. I have managed to get part of my life back on the rails by finding a flat and a part-time job.

rain

it never rains but it pours

People say **'it never rains but it pours'** to comment on the fact that when one bad thing happens, other bad things often happen too and make the situation worse.

It never rains but it pours when you have a patient at home. You find yourself thinking 'What next?' and worrying about it. Thinking 'What's the next disaster?'

He had a legitimate goal disallowed for 'handball' and later had a shot handled by a defender, only to see no penalty given. It never rains but it pours.

rain or shine
come rain or shine ◄

If someone does something **rain or shine** or **come rain or shine**, they do it regularly, regardless of the weather or other circumstances.

He plays golf, come rain or shine, every Monday.

I'll come back to Umbria as soon as possible, rain or shine.

I'd been mailing checks to her every month, rain or shine, for three years.

take a rain check ◄

If you offer something to someone or invite them to do something, and they say that they will **take a rain check**, they are refusing your offer or invitation politely, or saying that they would like to accept it, but at a different time.

She says she'd like to take a rain check on it and do it in May.

I'm simply exhausted, Mimi. It's all been such a strain. Could I take a rain-check?

rainbow

at the end of the rainbow
the pot of gold at the end of the rainbow ◄

If you say that something is **at the end of the rainbow** or is **the pot of gold at the end of the rainbow**, you mean that although you dream of getting it, in reality it will be very difficult to achieve. Compare **a pot of gold**; see **gold**.

There's a great big prize at the end of the rainbow and we both want it.

Herbie promises to take us to the end of the rainbow, which would be a dream.

I would rather be honest with people than mislead them that there is going to be some pot of gold at the end of the rainbow.

rainbows

chase rainbows

If you say that someone **is chasing rainbows**, you mean that they are wasting their time by trying to get something which they can never have.

Only time will tell whether or not you're still chasing rainbows.

Kemp could see why there had been that open verdict, and why the police were having difficulty finding proof; they might as well be chasing rainbows.

ranch

bet the ranch

If you say that someone **bets the ranch**, you mean that they spend all the money they have in order to achieve something, and risk losing it if they fail. This expression is used in American English.

CBS Inc. agreed to pay $300 million to broadcast the 1994 Winter Olympics, further evidence that the network is betting the ranch on sports.

We thought that if we could do it, it would give us an important lead over our competition in future years. We've taken risks before and so we bet the ranch.

rank

pull rank ◄

If you say that someone in authority **pulls rank**, you disapprove of the fact that they make unfair use of their power or position to make people do what they want.

He was a chief superintendent and just occasionally he pulled rank.

The Federal Government threatened to pull rank and override the states with its own legislation.

ranks

break ranks
break rank ◄◄◄

If someone **breaks ranks**, they disobey the instructions of a group or organization of which they are a member, and express their own opinion. You can also say that someone **breaks rank**.

Would you break ranks with your party and vote against the president's tax bill?

A senior Scottish Labour MP has broken party ranks to attack the leadership's commitment to a referendum on Scotland's constitutional future.

Until Midland Bank broke rank in 1984, banks had charged for basic services such as cheque-processing and other sorts of money transmission. Midland made banking 'free' for customers whose accounts stayed in credit.

close ranks ◄◄◄

If the members of a group **close ranks**, they support each other totally and oppose any criticism or attacks from outside on individual members.

They would more likely close ranks and support their president rather than abandon him in an election year.

Most Conservative MPs intend to put aside their differences over Europe and close ranks behind the Prime Minister in today's debate over the government's handling of the sterling crisis.

ransom

hold someone to ransom ◄◄

If you say that one person **is holding** another **to ransom**, you mean that the first person is using their power or influence to force the second to do something they do not want to do. This expression is used in British English.

But who are the powerful men at the Bundesbank who have the power to hold Europe to ransom?

Giorgio Armani, the fashion guru, refused to be held to ransom by greedy catwalk supermodels.

a king's ransom ◄

If you refer to a sum of money as **a king's ransom**, you are emphasizing that it is very large. This expression is used mainly in British English.

Actress Julia Roberts is asking a king's ransom for her next film role.

Electricians, plumbers and central heating engineers regard themselves as the 'princes' of tradesmen and charge a king's ransom for their services.

rap

take the rap ◄

If someone **takes the rap**, they accept the blame or responsibility for something that has been done badly or has gone wrong, even if it is not their fault.

I myself am quite innocent, Joe. But, yes, my company – some over-enthusiastic juniors – was involved, so I must take the rap.

He had tried, and failed, to get someone to take the rap for a corruption scandal.

rat

look like a drowned rat

If you say that someone **looks like a drowned rat**, you mean that they are very wet, for example because they have been caught in the rain or because their hair is wet.

'Is there a swimming pool near where you work?' 'Oh there is, yes.' 'So you could nip out in your lunchtime and have a quick few lengths. Oh, and what a drowned rat you'd look like afterwards, wouldn't you?'

the rat race ◄◄

If you talk about getting out of **the rat race**, you are talking about giving up a job or way of life in which people compete aggressively with each other in order to be successful.

I had to get out of the rat race for a while and take a look at the real world again.

In the Seventies, when work, and the dole, were easier to come by, students could afford to dream about dropping out of the rat race when they graduated.

smell a rat   ◄◄

If you **smell a rat**, you suspect that something is wrong in a particular situation, for example that someone is trying to deceive you or harm you.

The public begins to smell a rat when scientists justify what they do by taking refuge in the law.

If only I'd used my head, I'd have smelt a rat straight away and never touched the proposition.

rate

at a rate of knots   ◄

If someone does something **at a rate of knots**, they do it very quickly. This expression is used in British English.

U2 worked at an incredible rate of knots on the LP, often flying back to Dublin after a European show, working all night on the album.

By 1935, Blyton was publishing at a rate of knots – adventures, fairy tales, mysteries.

ray

a ray of sunshine   ◄

If you describe someone or something as **a ray of sunshine**, you mean that they make you feel better because there is something positive and refreshing about them. This expression is sometimes used ironically, for example to describe someone who is depressing and miserable.

Kim is like a ray of sunshine, a wonderful and beautiful girl who has changed my life.

I am looking forward to the wedding, it's the one ray of sunshine for the future.

If the little ray of sunshine doesn't get himself killed he may turn into a fine bullfighter one of these days.

reap

reap the harvest   ◄

If you say that someone **reaps the harvest** of past actions, you mean that they suffer or benefit as a result of those actions.

Tonight we reap the bitter harvest of a decade of national indulgence.

Russia is reaping the vicious harvest of 74 years of Soviet rule.

Martin began work at Munich's best hotel, the Bayerischer, prior to a short spell at the Dorchester, then it was south to Bournemouth at the Carlton, where he began to reap the harvest of this sound training.

reap the whirlwind
sow the wind and reap the whirlwind
    ◄

If you say that someone **is reaping the whirlwind**, you mean that they are suffering

now because of mistakes that were made in the past. This is a literary expression.

Shortly thereafter we saw a doubling in the homicide rate with firearms, and we now see gun violence at all-time record highs. Because people turned to guns after the riots of '68, we're reaping the whirlwind now.

There has been a revulsion from authority and discipline. There has been a permissive revolution and now we all reap the whirlwind.

□ This expression comes from the proverb **sow the wind and reap the whirlwind**.

The new Chancellor has tended to flit from job to job, staying long enough to sow the wind but leaving someone else to reap the whirlwind.

Events beyond the Prime Minister's control mean that he is likely to reap the economic whirlwind he helped to sow.

you reap what you sow
as you sow, so shall you reap   ◄

You use the expression **you reap what you sow** to say that everything that happens is a result of things which you have done in the past.

It seems to me that if we create areas of such bleakness and social deprivation we should expect to reap what we sow.

The mother who repeatedly tells her little boy that he is naughty, for example, will reap what she sows.

□ People sometimes say '**as you sow, so shall you reap**'. This is a more formal form of the expression.

In the final analysis our future lies in our own hands. Let us ensure that it is ethically and spiritually orientated, for without doubt as we sow so shall we reap!

We will guarantee the rights of the Hungarian minority, according to how Hungarians respect the rights of Slovaks living in Hungary – exactly, no more, no less. As you sow, so shall you reap.

rearguard

fight a rearguard action   ◄◄◄

If you say that someone **is fighting a rearguard action**, you mean that they are trying hard to stop something happening, but you do not think that they will succeed. The verb 'mount' is sometimes used instead of 'fight'.

National telephone companies are fighting a rearguard action against competition from beyond their frontiers.

Senior civil servants are said to be mounting a rearguard action against a more enlightened attitude among a new generation of officials towards the release of records.

□ You can also just talk about **a rearguard action**.

The government move is being seen as a rear-

guard action to protect the corrupt among its own ranks.

record

off the record ◄◄◄

If you say that your remarks are **off the record**, you mean that you do not want anyone to report what you said.

I can't report what he said off the record at dinner the other evening.

Perhaps this should be off the record but I don't think it really matters.

That's off the record. You boys! I forgot you were here! Don't go repeating what I've said, you hear.

□ An **off-the-record** remark is one that you do not want anyone to report.

Downing Street was furious last night at further revelations of the Prime Minister's 'off-the-record' remarks to journalists.

on the record
go on record ◄◄◄

If you are **on the record** as saying something or if you **go on record**, you mean that you are willing for people to report and repeat what you are saying.

We are on the record as saying we will protect our friends in the war zone, and we mean that.

It's very hard to report a story here, because almost no one is willing to talk on the record.

Church leaders have gone on record saying they believe the authorities are losing the fight against the Mafia.

□ You can also use **on-the-record** before a noun.

He has never before given an on-the-record interview or been quoted in any media outlet.

I failed to get any on-the-record local authority line on the matter.

set the record straight
put the record straight ◄◄◄

If you **set the record straight** or **put the record straight**, you state that something is wrong and then correct the mistake or misunderstanding.

The investigation concluded that the basis of our article was wrong. This page sets the record straight.

But a company seeing wrong information about itself on a report can have a frustrating time setting the record straight.

I am amazed at the rubbish written about my alleged lack of fitness. Let me put the record straight.

red

in the red
into the red
out of the red ◄◄◄

If a person or organization is **in the red**, they owe money to someone or to another organization. Compare **in the black**; see **black**.

Banks are desperate to get your custom – even if you're in the red.

The company was already in the red to the extent of more than three million pounds.

□ You can also say that you go **into the red** when you start to owe money to the bank, or that you come **out of the red** when you have paid back your debt.

The network faces the prospect of falling back into the red for the first time in five years.

Life may be more complicated these days, but it means we're climbing out of the red.

red as a beetroot
red as a beet

If you say that someone goes as **red as a beetroot** or as **red as a beet**, you mean that their face goes very red, for example because they are very hot or very embarrassed. 'Red as a beetroot' is used in British English and 'red as a beet' is used in American English.

She ran her bath, then she plunged into the water and topped it up until it was as hot as she could bear. It would make her face as red as a boiled beetroot, but that was too bad.

He turned as red as beetroot when I told him.

a red letter day ◄

You refer to a day as **a red letter day** when something very important or exciting happens then.

Back in 1986 Jim had his first picture published in BBC Wildlife Magazine. 'That was a real red letter day for me!' he confesses.

Aleksandra loved her son-in-law and each time he came to see her was a red-letter day.

see red ◄◄◄

If you **see red**, you suddenly become very angry or annoyed because of something which has been said or done.

I cannot stand humiliation of any kind. I just see red. I could pick up a bottle and just smash it in someone's face because of it.

The programmes so far have simply reinforced negative stereotype images of young Black people. It makes me see red. What on earth do the producers of these programmes think they are doing?

red-handed

catch someone red-handed ◄◄

If someone is **caught red-handed**, they are caught while they are doing something illegal or wrong.

In fact, the burglar wasn't inside the flat, but on the roof and was caught red-handed by the police.

Three smugglers caught red-handed with several kilograms of uranium and other radioactive materials were detained last week in the southern Polish city of Rzeszow.

reed

a broken reed

If you refer to one of the members of a group as **a broken reed**, you mean that they are very weak and so you cannot depend on them in difficult situations. This is a literary expression, which is used in British English.

They recognized that their allies were a broken reed.

reign

a reign of terror ◄◄◄

A reign of terror is a period during which there is a lot of violence and killing, especially by people who are in positions of power.

The president last night dismissed the government, accusing it of maladministration, corruption and nepotism, and of having unleashed a reign of terror against its political opponents.

His victims during a four-month reign of terror included a schoolgirl and a student.

rein

give someone free rein
allow someone free rein ◄◄◄

If someone **is given free rein** or **is allowed free rein** to do something, they are given all the freedom they want or need to do it.

He was given free rein to manage the cavalry as he wished.

Much to her delight, she was given a free rein: her clients were keen that she should feature her own style and create ideas especially for them.

Most husbands, Barker discovered, insist that their tastes should dominate in areas like the living room. Their wives are allowed free rein only in private rooms like the bedroom.

keep a tight rein on someone
hold someone on a tight rein ◄◄

If you **keep a tight rein on** someone or something, you control them firmly. You can also say that you **hold** them **on a tight rein**.

It is said that you kept a very tight rein on your daughters, and that you were a very strict father. Is that true?

The recession has forced people to keep a very tight rein on their finances when on holiday.

I am holding my thoughts on a tight rein and refusing to allow myself to think ahead.

rhyme

without rhyme or reason ◄

If you say that something happens **without rhyme or reason**, you mean that there seems to be no logical or obvious reason for it to happen. You can also say that there is **no rhyme or reason** for it to happen.

Cuts are being made without rhyme or reason. The only motive is to save money to meet Treasury targets.

Sometimes I still get so depressed. There's no rhyme or reason for why all these awful things have happened.

rich

rich as Croesus

If you say that someone is as **rich as Croesus**, you mean that they are very rich. This expression is used in British English.

I made an awful lot of money. I was paying myself £40,000 in 1984, and with all the perks was living an £80,000 lifestyle. I was getting rich as Croesus.

He may be nearly as rich as Croesus, but that's still not rich enough for him.

strike it rich ◄

If you **strike it rich**, you suddenly earn or win a large amount of money.

She says the graduates' perception is that commerce offers more opportunities to strike it rich.

I've been thinking, prospecting might be just what we've been looking for: a quick way to strike it rich.

riddles

talk in riddles

If you say that someone is **talking in riddles**, you are accusing them of not saying clearly and directly what they mean. The verb 'speak' is sometimes used instead of 'talk'.

For several days, he dropped enigmatic clues to Ann, and talked in riddles about his unpredictable absences of the past months.

He seemed to be speaking in riddles when he added that anyone who studied the election law carefully would understand.

ride

a free ride ◄◄◄

If you say that someone is getting **a free ride** in a particular situation, you disapprove of the fact that they are getting some benefit from it without putting any effort into achieving it themselves.

I never wanted anyone to think I was getting a free ride or special treatment from the boss.

Tyrone will graduate soon and try to get his high school diploma. Many students like him are hoping to go to college. And then there are others who are just in for the free ride.

go along for the ride
come along for the ride

If you say that someone **is going along for the ride** or **is coming along for the ride**, you mean that they have decided to join in an activity but are not doing it seriously or getting deeply involved in it.

Your boyfriend is not likely to be serious about anything this week except having a good time. Go along for the ride.

'Who's that with you?' 'A friend of mine. He came along for the ride.'

a rough ride
a bumpy ride
an easy ride   ◄◄◄

If you say that someone will have **a rough ride** or **a bumpy ride**, you mean that they are likely to have a lot of problems and that it will be very difficult for them to achieve something.

The government is likely to face a rough ride in parliament.

The recession yesterday continued to provide a bumpy ride for the lower and middle range of the art market.

□ You can say that someone will have **an easy ride** if you think that they will achieve something without difficulty because they do not face much opposition.

You don't come into politics expecting an easy ride.

take someone for a ride   ◄◄

If you say that someone **has been taken for a ride**, you mean that they have been deceived or cheated.

You've been taken for a ride. Why did you give him five thousand francs?

Why do I have this sneaking suspicion that he is taking us all for a ride?

right

right as rain

If you say that someone is as **right as rain**, you mean that they are feeling well or healthy again after an illness or injury.

I am sure Graeme will come back as fit as ever. He's only in his late 30s. I was in my early 50s when I had the surgery and I feel as right as rain.

We put a bandage on his knee, gave him a biscuit and a cup of tea and he was right as rain.

your right-hand man
your right-hand woman   ◄◄◄

Someone's **right-hand man** is their close assistant and the person they trust to help and support them in everything they do. This ex-

pression is commonly used to talk about politics or business. People occasionally talk about someone's **right-hand woman** or their **right-hand person**.

Paddy Ashdown's speech to the Liberal Democrat conference yesterday was the last drafted for him by Alan Leaman, his right-hand man for the past 10 years.

He was always by her side and supported her in everything she did. He was her right-hand man, her business manager, and he travelled with her everywhere.

It's about time the Foundation started an art collection. But, besides that, you'd be Oliver's right-hand woman. He needs somebody he can really rely on, don't you, Oliver?

rights

bang to rights: 1
dead to rights

If you have got someone **bang to rights**, you have got enough evidence against them to accuse them of a crime and to prove that they are guilty. You can also have someone **dead to rights**. These expressions are used mainly in novels.

You've got your man – got him bang to rights – evidence, witnesses, the lot.

Now, Captain Millard, how do you intend to proceed in the Rafaelli case? I mean, you have him pretty well dead to rights.

bang to rights: 2
dead to rights

If someone gets you **bang to rights**, they show a good understanding of you and describe you accurately. You can also have someone **dead to rights**.

I read Matthew Sura's piece on you last month and I thought he got you bang to rights.

He is described as a debater, who made opponents feel personally responsible for everything. 'My wife thinks that gets me bang to rights.'

ringer

a dead ringer for someone   ◄◄

If you say that one person is **a dead ringer for** another, you mean that the first person looks or sounds exactly like the second.

The characters were led by Herman Munster, head of the household and a dead ringer for Frankenstein's monster.

She's throaty and suggestive, and a dead-ringer for Madonna.

An ordinary guy from Baltimore, Dave Kovic is extraordinary in one respect: he's a dead ringer for the US President.

rings

run rings round someone ◄

If someone **runs rings round** you or **runs rings around** you, they are much better at a particular activity than you and can beat or outwit you.

Mentally, he can still run rings round men half his age.

The permanent civil servants call the tune; they can run rings round the average minister.

Korean-born Jaechul Ahn, a Minneapolis-based exporter of timber products, says he's running rings around his larger American competitors in sales to Korea, Taiwan and Japan.

ringside

a ringside seat
a ringside view ◄

If you have **a ringside seat** or **a ringside view**, you have an excellent and clear view of what is happening somewhere.

From Arenal Lodge, a newly opened guest house to the south-east of Lake Arenal, you get a ringside seat at the volcano's performance.

The first US presidential election for which I had a ringside seat was that which brought John F. Kennedy to office over 30 years ago.

riot

read the riot act ◄

If someone in authority **reads the riot act**, they angrily tell someone off for having done something stupid or wrong.

I'm glad you read the riot act to Billy. He's still a kid, you know. He still needs to be told what to do.

The president read the riot act to his party, warning those who sought to preserve the old system that power was already slipping from their grasp.

run riot: 1 ◄◄◄

If someone **runs riot**, they get out of control.

Where my older sister Mandy had run riot, my parents doubled their efforts with me. They were far stricter with me about school work, for example.

Ignoring small crimes guarantees not only that they will carry on but that they will become big ones. Besides, there can be no parts of Britain which are no-go areas, where gangs run riot terrorising the innocent while the police stay safely away.

run riot: 2 ◄◄

If something such as imagination or speculation **runs riot**, it expresses itself or spreads in an uncontrolled way.

My imagination ran riot, visualising late nights, weekend parties, and irregular meals.

We have no proof and when there is no proof, rumour runs riot.

rip

let rip: 1 ◄◄

If you **let rip** or **let it rip**, you do something without restraint.

I give a dinner party for ten people about every three weeks. It's a big number where I can really let rip and make things look beautiful.

She will find that she does not ache after two days and by the end of her skiing holiday will be able to let rip on the mountains.

All of them know exactly when to let it rip and when to tread softly.

let rip: 2 ◄

If you say that someone **lets rip**, you mean that they suddenly start talking about something that they feel strongly about but that they had previously been quiet about.

He sometimes wondered if it wouldn't be better if she let rip as she used to do over his inadequacies in the past.

When he quit the Commons he let rip, claiming Parliament was 'a club for fat, tired, unfit old men'.

rise

get a rise out of someone ◄

If you **get a rise out of** someone, you deliberately make them angry by teasing them or making fun of them.

If he told Livvy he had my backing, my guess is he did it to taunt her, to get a rise out of her.

He decided to just go along with everything Johnson did and cater to him, on the theory that Johnson would quit bothering him once he saw he couldn't get a rise out of him.

take the rise out of someone

If you **take the rise out of** someone or something, you make fun of them.

That day they had the game won by half-time but they weren't satisfied with that. They were taking the rise out of us and my players won't forget that embarrassment in a hurry.

It should be fun taking the rise out of some love songs.

river

sell someone down the river ◄

If someone **sells** you **down the river**, they betray you or do something which harms you in order to gain an advantage for themselves.

He said he could not agree to measures which would sell British farmers down the river in order to keep smaller, less efficient farms in production.

He has been sold down the river by the people who were supposed to protect him. It had a devastating effect on his health.

road

down the road   ◄◄

If you talk about something happening a particular number of years or months **down the road**, you are talking about its happening after that amount of time. **Down the line** means the same.

Twenty-five years down the road from independence, we have to start making some new priorities.

The index is designed to predict economic performance six to nine months down the road.

Many authorities are concerned that long-term side effects will show up years down the road.

hit the road   ◄◄◄

If you **hit the road**, you begin a journey.

The band plan to release a new single and hit the road for a tour in November.

President Clinton hits the road again today, this time heading west; first to New Mexico, then on to California.

take the high road
take the low road   ◄

If you say that someone **takes the high road**, you mean that they follow the course of action which is the most moral or most correct and which is least likely to harm or upset other people. This expression is used in American English.

Carol stayed out of the crossfire and was perceived as taking a high road.

US diplomats say the president is likely to take the high road in his statements about trade.

□ You can say that someone **takes the low road** when they follow an immoral or dishonest course of action.

He was charged with taking the low road, which he seemed to do with relish.

robbery

highway robbery
daylight robbery   ◄

If you are charged a lot of money for something that should cost a lot less or even nothing at all, you can refer to it as **highway robbery** to express your outrage at it. In British English, the expression **daylight robbery** is also used.

They are charging three bucks for the comics, which sounds like highway robbery to us.

They're not doing a service, they're just taking the tickets away from the fans who have to

buy them back again later at triple the price. *They're just ripping the fans off; it's daylight robbery.*

rock

between a rock and a hard place   ◄

If you are caught **between a rock and a hard place**, you are in a difficult situation where you have to choose between two equally unpleasant courses of action.

We were caught between a rock and a hard place. Either we spend two months planning the operation and people say we are too late, or we come in and make it work on the ground.

Goss is caught between a rock and a hard place. If he bows to pressure and makes concessions on proposed cuts, middle-ground voters could see him as the typical Labor Premier in the grip of union bosses. If he ignores the unions he runs the risk of further alienating his traditional party supporters.

hit rock bottom: 1
reach rock bottom
at rock bottom   ◄◄◄

If something **hits rock bottom**, it is at an extremely low level and cannot go any lower. You can also say that it **reaches rock bottom** or is **at rock bottom**.

The UK motor industry slumped to one of its blackest days yesterday as new car sales hit rock bottom.

This is a good time to buy a house. Prices have reached rock-bottom in most areas.

Morale is at rock-bottom and constant talk of job losses does nothing to make them feel any safer in their jobs.

□ When people buy or sell things at **rock-bottom** prices, they buy or sell them when prices are extremely low.

He has been buying property at rock-bottom prices.

hit rock bottom: 2
reach rock bottom
at rock bottom   ◄

If someone **hits rock bottom**, they are in a hopeless or difficult situation, and so feel very depressed. You can also say that they **reach rock bottom** or they are **at rock bottom**.

When my girlfriend asked me to move out of our flat and end our relationship, I hit rock bottom.

I've reached rock bottom, time to call it quits.

She was at rock bottom. Her long-term love affair was breaking up and so was she.

rocker

off your rocker   ◄

If you say that someone is **off** their **rocker**, you mean that they are crazy or completely illogical. This is an informal expression.

I suppose they're saying that I'm past it at last – that the old so-and-so has either lost his touch or finally gone off his rocker.

Mrs. Stevens will think I'm off my rocker handing out my money like that before the bankruptcy business is even settled.

rocket

a rocket scientist
not rocket science ◄

You can use expressions such as 'it doesn't take **a rocket scientist**' to point out that doing a particular thing does not need much intelligence or skill, and is actually very easy or obvious. This expression is used mainly in American English, but is becoming more common in British English.

It doesn't take a rocket scientist to make a rock record.

You don't have to be a rocket scientist to understand that a wine at £3.99 is better value than a wine at £2.49. Most of the costs involved in making and selling wine are fixed so, in theory at least, the more you spend the better the wine.

☐ If you say that something **isn't rocket science**, you are emphasizing that it is very easy.

In 1981, it didn't take long for our people at CBS to learn these techniques. As I'd told Sauter, this isn't rocket science.

rocks

get your rocks off

If you say that someone **is getting** their **rocks off**, you mean that they are getting a lot of pleasure or satisfaction at someone else's expense. This is an informal expression, which many people find offensive.

You're getting your rocks off by pushing certain people way beyond their limits.

☐ This expression is often used to talk about a man getting sexual excitement or satisfaction without caring about his partner.

on the rocks ◄

If something such as a relationship or business is **on the rocks**, it is experiencing many difficulties and is likely to end or fail.

Their marriage was on the rocks, the husband had loved another woman for years; but they had determined not to divorce until the children were grown up.

Our film industry is on the rocks, reduced to a sad rump from the glory days when we could match Hollywood for talent.

rod

make a rod for your own back

If you say that someone **has made a rod for** their **own back**, you mean that they have

unintentionally done something which will cause them many problems. Verbs such as 'create' are sometimes used instead of 'make'. This expression is used in British English.

The transport secretary, who expects to be flooded with angry drivers dialling from car phones, said 'I know I am making a rod for my own back. But if people see examples where contractors have clearly got long stretches of cones with nothing happening, they should let me know.'

In a way, the company's success has created a rod for its own back, for the style is ceaselessly copied.

roll

on a roll ◄◄◄

If you say that you are **on a roll**, you mean that things are going very well for you, for example in your work or personal life, and you are making a lot of progress and having a lot of success.

We're on a roll and we're winning, which gives the players that extra belief in themselves.

Everything was going great for me. I made a name for myself and I was on a roll, I couldn't see anything going wrong.

When you start playing consistently, you get on a roll and you're harder to stop.

Rome

fiddle while Rome burns ◄

If you accuse someone of **fiddling while Rome burns**, you mean that they are doing nothing or are spending their time on unimportant things when they have very serious issues or problems to deal with.

He said that the Australian community did not realise the gravity of the situation. We think it does: it is the Federal Government that has been fiddling while Rome burns.

The Financial Times is also critical. It says the twelve leaders decided to fiddle in Rome, leaving the problem of farm reform to burn.

☐ This expression is very variable. For example, people sometimes replace 'Rome' with a different place name or other noun so that this expression is more relevant to the subject they are talking about.

People talk about choice, people talk about educational reform but while the politicians fiddle, Los Angeles and Chicago are burning and these kids' educational opportunities are going down in flames as well.

Far from fiddling while depositors got burnt, the Bank of England spent years containing BCCI's losses.

Rome was not built in a day

People say **'Rome was not built in a day'** to point out that it takes a long time to do a job or task properly, and you should not rush it or expect to do it quickly.

Only two shoppers I interviewed were charitable about the new government. 'Rome wasn't built in a day,' one man said 'Let's give them more time.'

I know Rome wasn't built in a day but I don't want to wait 200 years.

when in Rome
when in Rome, do as the Romans do

You say **'when in Rome'** to mean that people should follow the customs of the people they are visiting or living with.

'Aren't you meant to be at the Prado, not here?' 'I was, but there's a limit to art appreciation, however great the pictures may be. And there are better things to do of an afternoon. When in Rome. Isn't this how Spanish men spend the time from two till four?'

☐ This expression comes from the proverb **when in Rome, do as the Romans do**.

When in Rome (or Palo Alto) do as the Romans do. Close up shop for a month or so for vacation. That's why the restaurant has been quiet and empty for the last two weeks.

roof

go through the roof: 1
hit the roof
go through the ceiling   ◄◄

If the level of something such as the price of a product or the rate of inflation suddenly increases very rapidly, you can say that it **goes through the roof** or **hits the roof**. You can use 'ceiling' instead of 'roof'.

Interest rates were going through the roof.

In 1990, wool prices hit the roof.

Sales went through the ceiling and pharmacists began reporting shortages of the drug.

go through the roof: 2
hit the roof
hit the ceiling   ◄◄

If someone **goes through the roof** or **hits the roof**, they suddenly become very angry, and usually show their anger by shouting at someone. You can use 'ceiling' instead of 'roof'.

I admitted I had ordered a racing car, and found myself in terrible trouble. He went through the roof!

I don't know what to think. Everyone seems angry with me. My parents have hit the roof.

I hit the ceiling. I had wanted her sympathy, and I thought she was being really hard on me. I flounced out and drove home.

raise the roof
lift the roof   ◄

If a person or a crowd of people **raises the roof**, they make a very loud noise, for exam-

ple by cheering, singing, or shouting. In British English, you can also say that someone **lifts the roof**.

When the night staff came on, the infant was still raising the roof.

Best audience I've ever had in my life – they practically raised the roof.

The cheers and roars of approval lifted the pavilion roof.

rooftops

shout something from the rooftops   ◄

If you **shout** something **from the rooftops**, you let a lot of people know about something that you are particularly angry or excited about. Other verbs are sometimes used instead of 'shout'.

I would love to be able to shout our results from the rooftops.

I didn't want to shout about it from the rooftops because the tabloids would have made me out a lunatic.

Nobody has beaten Ferguson in the first round before. I am not going to brag about it from the rooftops, but I think I deserve a bit of credit for doing something no man has done.

room

a smoke-filled room   ◄◄

If someone says that a political or business decision is made in **a smoke-filled room**, they mean that it is made by a small group of people in a private meeting, rather than in a more democratic or open way.

Richards doesn't think that a return to the smoke-filled room, in which a few bosses make the decision, would be possible.

I would say that those 400 people do reflect a broad spectrum of expertise and interests, so we can't really say that just a small group is getting together in a small smoke-filled room.

roost

come home to roost
the chickens come home to roost   ◄◄

If someone has done something bad or unacceptable, and you say that it **has come home to roost**, you mean that they will now have to deal with the unpleasant consequences of their actions.

You ought to have known that your lies would come home to roost in the end.

The contradictions between the President's desire to be seen as the provider of a better life for all and harsh social and economic reality have now come home to roost.

☐ You can also say **the chickens are coming home to roost** to mean the same thing. People sometimes say 'pigeons' instead of 'chickens'.

Politicians can fool some people some of the time, but in the end, the chickens will come home to roost.

rule the roost ◄◄

If someone **rules the roost**, he or she is the most powerful and important person in a group.

In Germany, scientists will be found at the top of many manufacturing companies; in Britain, accountants rule the roost.

☐ People sometimes say that something **rules the roost** when it is more popular than the things that it is being compared to.

By now you would expect CD to rule the roost, having relegated the venerable black vinyl record to a dark and dusty corner of the Science Museum.

root

money is the root of all evil
the love of money is the root of all evil ◄

People say '**money is the root of all evil**' when they want to suggest that greed is the cause of a particular problem or the cause of society's problems in general. Other nouns are sometimes used instead of 'money' to suggest that these things are the cause of a problem.

From what I gather, Mr Smith owed Mr Morris some money. I believe the amount involved is a substantial sum and money is the root of all evil, as they say.

Greed may not be the root of all evil, but most certainly it is lurking behind many conflicts, from schoolyard spats to full-scale wars.

☐ This expression comes from the proverb **the love of money is the root of all evil**.

If ever we want evidence that the love of money is the root of all evil, we only have to look at the human cost of many monetary policies and decisions.

root and branch ◄◄

If something is changed or reformed **root and branch**, it is changed or reformed completely, so that none of the old or traditional parts remain.

These genuinely radical measures, in contrast to the half-measures of the previous reforms, should change our economic system root and branch.

It is common for such a discovery to prompt a determination to yank tradition out, root and branch.

☐ A **root-and-branch** reform or change is a complete reform or change.

To an independent outsider, the need for a root-and-branch reform of the administrative structure seemed absolutely essential and very long overdue.

take root ◄◄◄

If an idea, belief, or custom **takes root**, it becomes established or begins to develop.

When communism fell in Poland, it was said that time would be needed for democracy to take root.

The idea of starting up his own picture library began to take root.

Green politics have taken firm root in Alsace, where the Green Party have a chance of gaining two seats.

roots

put down roots: 1 ◄

If someone **puts down roots**, they make a place their home, for example by taking part in activities there or by making a lot of friends there.

Servicemen and women are seldom in the same place long enough to put down roots and buy their own home.

When they got to Montana they stayed, they put down roots, they built a life.

put down roots: 2

If something **puts down roots** somewhere, it becomes firmly established there, so that it is likely to last and to be successful in the future.

Not only did the party increase its share of the poll but it also put down roots in areas where it had previously been weak or even non-existent.

Despite evident parliamentary disarray, democracy is putting down roots.

rope

at the end of your rope

If you say that you are **at the end of your rope**, you mean that you feel desperate because you are in a difficult situation and do not know how to deal with it. You can also use this expression to show your impatience or annoyance with someone. This expression is used mainly in American English; the usual British expression is **at the end of your tether**.

Everything is dreadful and I am at the end of my rope.

He'd tried everything he could think of, and he was nearing the end of his rope.

give someone enough rope to hang themselves
give someone enough rope ◄

If you **give** someone **enough rope to hang** themselves, you give them the freedom to do something in the way they want to do it, usually in the hope that they will fail or become weak by doing it the wrong way.

The King has merely given the politicians enough rope to hang themselves, and once the party system has been discredited by political in-fighting, he will present himself once again as an absolute ruler.

The newspaper feared it was being manipulated by those who wanted greater controls on the press: 'We're worried that we're being set up. Being given enough rope to hang ourselves.'

□ If you **give** someone **enough rope** or **give** them **the rope** they need, you give them the freedom to do what they want in their own way.

He would give you enough rope and see what you did with it.

Seems to me they're already being given too much rope. The Commissioner and I are not at all happy about the way they're developing.

ropes

learn the ropes
know the ropes   ◄◄

If you **learn the ropes**, you learn how to do a particular job or task.

He tried hiring more salesmen to push his radio products, but they took too much time to learn the ropes.

By the time he was 34, he had learnt the ropes of the jewellery trade and developed ambition. He then took over as managing director of the family business.

□ You can also say that someone **knows the ropes** when they know how a particular job or task should be done.

He made her his secretary. That was the real beginning. The moment she got to know the ropes, there was no stopping her.

on the ropes   ◄◄

If you say that someone is **on the ropes**, you mean that they are very close to failing or being defeated.

The government we have now is on the ropes, as reviled as any in modern history. It soon faces another catastrophic by-election.

The Denver-based developer has been on the ropes because of depressed housing markets in Denver, Texas and Arizona.

show someone the ropes   ◄

If you **show** someone **the ropes**, you show them how to do a particular job or task. The verb 'teach' is sometimes used instead of 'show'.

We had a patrol out on the border, breaking in some young soldiers, showing them the ropes.

He guaranteed the kid was up to the job and he promised to work overtime teaching him the ropes.

roses

come up smelling of roses

If someone has been in a difficult situation and you say that they **have come up smelling of roses**, you mean that they are now in a better or stronger situation than they were before. You usually use this expression to show your surprise or resentment that this has happened.

Tom Ellis, who walked out on Monday after a boardroom row, has come up smelling of roses. He has been snapped up by a rival engineering company and the word is that his financial package is even healthier.

No matter the problem, he manages to wriggle out of it and come up smelling of roses.

everything is coming up roses   ◄

If you say that **everything is coming up roses** for someone, you mean that they are having a lot of success and everything is going well for them.

In the US suddenly, everything is coming up roses, with unemployment on a downward trend and industrial production on the way up.

For Rachel Ashwell, everything's coming up roses both in her home and her working life.

not a bed of roses
not all roses   ◄

If you say that a situation is **not a bed of roses** or **not all roses**, you mean that it is not all pleasant, and that there are some unpleasant aspects to it as well.

Life as a graduate is not a bed of roses.

I was angry with the world and with myself, and not without reason: my life had not been a bed of roses.

Inmates who have not considered their financial position are frequently shocked at the problems facing them on their release. The future's never all roses, and we make the men think about that.

rose-tinted

rose-tinted spectacles
rose-coloured glasses   ◄◄

If you say that someone looks at something through **rose-tinted spectacles** or **rose-coloured glasses**, you mean that they only notice the good things about it and so their view is unrealistic.

He accused diplomats of looking at the world through rose-tinted spectacles.

Even when I'd stopped looking at him through rose-coloured spectacles and I could see what he was, I was still tied to him.

Real estate broker Tom Foye believes that many buyers tend to look at houses with rose-colored glasses. Consequently, they end up feeling cheated.

☐ 'Rose-coloured' is spelled 'rose-colored' in American English.

rough

cut up rough

If you say that someone **cuts up rough**, you mean that they suddenly become extremely angry or violent. This expression is used in British English.

'Defenseless' stars Barbara Hershey as a defence lawyer whose fling with her client comes to a bloody end when he cuts up rough with her in his office one night.

I was detailed to take a revolver and accompany the sailor who brought him his meals in case he cut up rough.

rough and ready: 1   ◄◄◄

If you describe something as **rough and ready**, you mean that it is rather simple and basic, or it is not very exact, because it has been thought of or done in a hurry.

The rough and ready method used to limit total costs worked reasonably well.

We put up for the night at the town's only hostelry, a rough-and-ready bar with rooms attached.

These home-made jobs are rough and ready and are inferior to the real thing.

rough and ready: 2

If you describe someone as **rough and ready**, you mean that they are not very well-mannered or refined.

Some time ago I found myself temporarily in the employ of Joe Peters, a rough and ready but curiously sophisticated Canadian who came up the hard way.

At first the rough and ready sailors did not know what to make of the young cleric.

rough and tumble   ◄◄◄

You can use **rough and tumble** to refer to a situation in which the people involved try hard to get what they want, and do not worry about upsetting or harming others. You use this expression when you think that this is normal or acceptable behaviour.

Whoever expected leaders in the rough and tumble of electoral politics to be nice or fair?

Science is a rough-and-tumble activity that includes robust, healthy debate.

He cut his political teeth in the rough-and-tumble world of student politics at the University of Queensland.

take the rough with the smooth   ◄

If you **take the rough with the smooth**, you are willing to accept both the unpleasant and pleasant aspects of something. This expression is used in British English.

This is a camping trip, so if you can take a little rough with the smooth, we promise you an exciting and exhilarating trip.

You have to take the rough with the smooth. I never promised there would be no risk.

roughshod

ride roughshod over someone   ◄◄

If someone **rides roughshod over** other people, they pay no attention to what those people want, or they take decisions without considering their feelings or interests. The verb 'run' can be used instead of 'ride'.

Successive Secretaries of State for Education have arrogantly believed that they knew best, riding roughshod over parents and teachers.

Bosses nowadays seem to think they can ride roughshod over unions and I like to see them fighting back.

Beaverbrook had run roughshod over the British military establishment to accomplish his objectives.

☐ You can also say that someone **rides roughshod over** the rights or interests of other people.

This represents one of the few occasions in local government where voters can fight back and stop politicians riding roughshod over their wishes.

roulette

Russian roulette   ◄◄

If you say that someone is playing **Russian roulette**, you are critical of them for doing something which is very dangerous because it involves unpredictable risks. You can also say that a situation is like a game of **Russian roulette**.

One ex-employee said security was so lax that the airline was, in effect, playing Russian roulette with passengers' lives.

A concrete set of rules on which people can plan their financial future is necessary to stop the financial Russian roulette which people are being forced to play with their futures.

☐ If someone plays **Russian roulette**, they fire a gun containing only one bullet at their head without knowing whether the bullet will be released or not.

row

a hard row to hoe
a tough row to hoe

If you say that you have **a hard row to hoe** or **a tough row to hoe**, you mean that you are in a situation which is very difficult to deal with.

She is the first to admit that being a woman in politics has been a hard and sometimes isolated row to hoe.

I think, however, that in a criminal prosecu-

tion against the police, the prosecutor has a very tough row to hoe.

rub

don't rub it in ◄

You can say to someone **'don't rub it in'** when they are drawing attention to something that involves you and that you find embarrassing or unpleasant. When someone is doing this, you can say that they **are rubbing it in**. This expression is used mainly in spoken English.

'Beyond that, it was a matter of trust.' Her voice cracked on the word. 'Misplaced trust, it would seem.' 'Don't rub it in, Inspector.'

Of course too much good fortune could give rise to someone else's envy, so don't rub it in by boasting.

Thanks a lot, Meg. All I can hope is, maybe some day your heart will be broken and someone younger than you will start rubbing it in the way you're doing to me.

not have two pennies to rub together
not have two nickels to rub together ◄

If you say that someone **doesn't have two pennies to rub together**, you are emphasizing that they have very little money. You can replace 'pennies' with another word referring to coins, for example 'nickels' in American English, or 'halfpennies' or 'farthings' in old-fashioned British English.

And from all those interviews her family gave to the Press they sounded as if they hadn't two pennies to rub together.

He came here in 1980 from Vietnam. He didn't have two nickels to rub together. I think he's done pretty good for himself.

Kids didn't read books, and even if this one did, he didn't have two brass farthings to rub together to buy one.

☐ You can use other nouns in similar structures when you are emphasizing that someone or something has very little of a particular quality.

Out of 17 named singers there are not two true Rossini voices of international quality to rub together.

☐ You can also use these expressions without a negative when you are suggesting that someone or something has more of a quality than other people or things.

Anyone with two brain cells to rub together could have spotted she wasn't to be trusted.

the rub of the green

If you say that you have **the rub of the green** in an activity or sport, you mean that you have good luck. This expression is used mainly in British English.

Providing we have the rub of the green, there

is no reason why we can't do really well in the summer.

At this stage West would appreciate the rub of the green: the sort of luck that gave Bristol a penalty.

there's the rub
therein lies the rub ◄◄

You say **'there's the rub'** or **'therein lies the rub'** when you are commenting on a previous statement and drawing attention to a problem or contradiction which you think is difficult or impossible to deal with. You can also say **'here's the rub'** or **'there lies the rub'**.

'I am definitely not part of the club. I think they regard me as this ferocious feminist who doesn't approve of them.' And there's the rub. Women are much prone to imagining they are being criticised even when they are not.

'What we are asking for is a clarification of the current laws. We want to know what the law says is or is not pornography.' Ah, therein lies the rub. Porn, like beauty, is in the eye of the beholder.

Rubicon

cross the Rubicon ◄

If someone **has crossed the Rubicon**, they have made an important decision which cannot be changed and which will have very important consequences.

Mr Major's clear support for military action has come at a time when President Bush himself is said by his spokesmen to have crossed the Rubicon in his mind about the use of force.

No Rubicon has been crossed here. The decision to withdraw all treatment from him may look new and startling but this is something doctors already have to do every day.

☐ Sometimes this important decision is referred to as a person's **Rubicon**.

After the moment there would be no turning back; if he was making a big mistake, this was his Rubicon.

rug

pull the rug from under you
pull the rug from under your feet ◄◄

If someone **pulls the rug from under** you or **pulls the rug from under** your feet, they suddenly stop helping and supporting you. These expressions are often varied, for example by replacing 'pull' with another verb.

If the banks opt to pull the rug from under the ill-fated project, it will go into liquidation and be sold off.

Every time we have been close to saving the shipyard, the Government has pulled the rug from under our feet.

All at once they just yank the rug out from under you.

sweep something under the rug ◄

If you **sweep** something **under the rug**, you try to hide it and forget about it because you find it embarrassing or shameful. Other verbs such as 'brush' and 'push' are sometimes used instead of 'sweep'. This expression is used mainly in American English; the usual British expression is **sweep** something **under the carpet**.

By sweeping the wrongdoing under the rug, executives seek to avoid being accused of mismanagement by directors and shareholders.

The problem with all these responses is that they don't resolve the conflict. The issue is left up in the air, and your needs and feelings are pushed under the rug.

rule

a rule of thumb ◄◄◄

A **rule of thumb** is a general rule about something which you can be confident will be right in most cases.

As a rule of thumb, drink a glass of water or pure fruit juice every hour you are travelling.

A good rule of thumb for any type of studio photography is to use no more light sources than are strictly necessary.

rules

bend the rules
stretch the rules ◄◄◄

If someone **bends the rules**, they do something which is not allowed, either to help someone else or for their own advantage. You can also say that they **stretch the rules**.

The river authorities said they were willing to bend the rules for us and allowed us to go through the first lock.

He accused Benetton of stretching the sport's rules to the limit.

The rules are often bent at the organiser's discretion to ensure a good show.

run

a dummy run ◄

A **dummy run** is a trial or test procedure which you carry out in order to see if a plan or process will work properly. This expression is used in British English.

Before we started we did a dummy run, checking out all the streets and offices we would use, and planning our escape route.

If it is not possible to do a dummy run in the hire car, calculate how long the journey to the church will take on the day.

give someone a run for their money ◄◄◄

If you **give** someone **a run for their money**, you put up a very strong challenge in a contest which they are expected to win fairly easily.

The British team gave the host side a run for its money to finish a close second in the team competition.

We think the Irish will give the Welsh a good run for their money.

on the run ◄

If someone has an opponent **on the run**, they are in a stronger position than their opponent, so that they can control their actions and defeat them.

It is clear that the Opposition thinks it has him on the run.

We've got the Government on the run and we'll keep them on the run.

They sensed their opponents were on the run.

run before you can walk

If you say that someone is trying to **run before** they **can walk**, you mean that they are trying to do something which is very difficult or advanced before they have made sure that they can successfully achieve something simpler. This expression is used in British English.

They tried to run before they could walk. They made it too complicated.

I was running before I could walk. So I decided to go to Europe to do a second apprenticeship, almost to start again.

runaround

give someone the runaround
get the runaround ◄

If someone **gives** you **the runaround**, they deliberately try to mislead or confuse you and they do not tell you the truth about something which you need or want to know. You can also say that you **get the runaround** from them.

In early August, someone close could give you the runaround, especially where it concerns money or other joint matters.

In the early days of their questioning, they felt they were getting the runaround.

runes

read the runes

If someone **reads the runes**, they interpret a situation in a particular way and decide what is likely to happen. This is a literary expression, which is used in British English.

Of course, reading the runes on US interest rates may all seem irrelevant next month if the President goes to war.

The political assassin can be and often is an-

ticipated and intercepted by security teams who
have read the runes correctly before the trigger
is squeezed.

□ **Runes** were an alphabet used in northern
Europe until medieval times. The letters were
often thought to have magical properties.

running

in the running
out of the running ◄◄◄

If someone is **in the running** for a job or
prize, they have a good chance of getting it or
winning it. If they are **out of the running**,
they no longer have a chance of getting it or
winning it.

*Rumours that he is in the running for the job
of ITV's central scheduler are resurfacing.*

The US needs a win tonight to still be in the
running for the gold.

The ex-Communists are really out of the running for years to come.

rush

a rush of blood
a rush of blood to the head ◄

If you say that you have **a rush of blood** or
a rush of blood to the head, you mean that
you suddenly do something foolish or daring
which you would not normally do.

*Hughes' rush of blood may have cost United a
couple of million pounds.*

*You can't have a sudden rush of blood to the
head and speak about something which hasn't
been brought up before.*

S

sabre

sabre-rattling
rattle your sabre ◄◄

If you describe someone's behaviour as
sabre-rattling, you mean that they are behaving very aggressively and making threats,
often of military action, although it is not certain how serious they are or whether they
will actually carry out their threats.

*After more than a week of sabre-rattling, the
two countries have agreed to talk about their
differences.*

*A commission vice-president today accused the
Americans of sabre-rattling and taking the first
step in the trade war.*

□ You can also say that people **are rattling**
their **sabres**.

*There is a sliver of territory called Nakhiche-
van that several countries are rattling their
sabers over.*

□ 'Sabre' is spelled 'saber' in American English.

saddle

in the saddle ◄

You can say that someone is **in the saddle**
when they are in charge of their country's affairs, or when they make the important decisions in an organization.

*It is his bad luck to be in the saddle when
his country has to decide which road it is now
going to follow.*

*Their preliminary plan would sell 55 per cent
of the new stock to the company's majority
shareholders, putting them in the saddle.*

ride high in the saddle

If you say that someone **is riding high in**

the **saddle**, you mean that they are currently
very successful and are showing this in their
behaviour and attitudes.

*Australia are riding a little higher in the
saddle after their first Test victory.*

safe

play safe
play it safe ◄◄◄

If you **play safe** or **play it safe**, you do not
take any risks. The form 'play safe' is used
only in British English.

*If you want to play safe, cut down on the
amount of salt you eat.*

*Big tourist hotels and many restaurants play
safe with bland international menus, but traditional island cooking is also widely available
at good prices.*

*The pilot decided that Christchurch was too
far away, and played it safe and landed at
Wellington.*

safe as houses

If you say that something is as **safe as
houses**, you mean that it is very safe and reliable. This expression is used in British English.

*If you think building society cheques are as
safe as houses, think again.*

*Both managers can count on one thing –
their jobs are safe as houses.*

sailing

plain sailing
clear sailing
smooth sailing ◄◄◄

In British English, if you say that an activity or task will not be **plain sailing**, you

mean that it will be difficult to do or achieve. In American English, you say that it will not be **clear sailing, smooth sailing**, or **easy sailing**.

As Phillippa found, even with the ideal tenant it isn't all plain sailing. 'If you are used to having your home to yourself, it's difficult at first to get used to sharing the kitchen and the bathroom and so on,' she admits.

All of a sudden, my life just fell into place. Which is not to say that it was all smooth sailing from then on.

It's not going to be easy sailing. He's bound to come up with some tough opposition.

□ These expressions can also be used to say that an activity or task is easy to do or achieve. You can say, for example, that something is **plain sailing**.

Once I got used to the diet it was plain sailing. I lost 2 stones in weight over a four month period and the weight loss has been maintained.

The bill should have clear sailing because both the legislature and the governor, Democrat Bob Casey, are strongly anti-abortion.

sails

trim your sails

If you **trim** your **sails**, you adapt your behaviour to deal with a difficult situation, for example by limiting your demands, needs, or expectations.

Mr Lee, for his part, has already begun trimming his sails in preparation for dealing with the new government.

Would he trim his conservative sails to suit a Democratic Senate?

salad

your salad days   ◄

If you talk about your **salad days**, you are talking about the time when you were young and inexperienced. This is a literary expression.

I have now known you for over 30 years. I remember that in our salad days I shared many of your views on the economy while we were at Cambridge.

The Grand Hotel did not seem to have changed since her salad days.

saloon

the last chance saloon
drinking in the last chance saloon

If someone is doing something and you say that it is **the last chance saloon** for them, you mean that it is their final opportunity to succeed in what they are doing. You can also say that they **are drinking in the last**

chance **saloon**, with the same meaning. These expressions are used in British English.

Boxers Coetzer, 31, and Bruno, 30 and 11 months, understand one thing clearly. As far as the world title goes, Saturday is the last chance saloon for both of them.

David Mellor, who was the Cabinet minister in charge of media regulation, told the tabloid editors they were drinking in the last-chance saloon and to clean up their act or face government legislation.

salt

rub salt into the wound   ◄◄

If you are in an unpleasant situation and you accuse someone of **rubbing salt into the wound**, you are accusing them of making things even worse for you, for example by reminding you of your failures or faults or by increasing your difficulties. Other verbs can be used instead of 'rub'.

Labour lost half its 56 seats, and its former leader, Jim Anderton, who quit 18 months ago to form the New Labour Party, rubbed salt into the wound by holding his seat.

I believe such allegations are only putting salt into the wound.

the salt of the earth   ◄

If you describe someone as **the salt of the earth**, you are showing admiration for their honesty and reliability. This expression is used mainly by upper class people when talking about working people.

Excellent fellow, the Councillor. Salt of the earth. Few more like him on every council and our job would be a lot easier.

These are good people, rough-hewn, but the salt of the earth.

□ **Salt-of-the-earth** can be used before a noun.

Most of the people there are salt-of-the-earth, good, working-class people striving to improve themselves and to keep up their standards.

take something with a pinch of salt
take something with a grain of salt   ◄◄

If you say that a piece of information should **be taken with a pinch of salt**, you mean that it should not be relied on, because it may not be accurate or true. This form of the expression is used mainly in British English; in American English, the usual form is **take something with a grain of salt**.

The reports of calm and normality from various Russian cities should perhaps be taken with a pinch of salt.

You have to take these findings with a pinch of salt because respondents in attitude surveys tend to give the answers they feel they should.

The announcement that services to commuters would be improved dramatically by timetable alterations needs to be taken with a grain of salt if the experience of users of the Pinkenba line is anything to go by.

worth their salt ◄◄

If you say, for example, that no teacher **worth** their **salt** or no actor **worth** their **salt** would do a particular thing, you mean that no teacher or actor who was good at their job would consider doing that thing.

No racing driver worth his salt gets too sentimental about his cars.

No player worth his salt wants to play in the lower divisions.

□ Instead of 'no', you can use 'any' or 'every' with this expression. For example, if you say that any teacher **worth** their **salt** would do a particular thing, you mean that any teacher who was good at their job would do that thing.

Any policeman worth his salt would have made proper checks to find out exactly who this man was.

Twenty-five years ago every undergraduate worth his salt knew intimately many of Kipling's books, especially his early poems and stories about India.

sand

build something on sand

If you say that something **is built on sand**, you mean that it does not have a strong or proper basis, and so is likely to fail or come to an end.

Preference was to be given to temporary workers who could be dispensed with if the need arose. The experience of France indicates that such policies are built on sand. A temporary labour system seems impossible to achieve, at least under contemporary economic conditions.

He moved into the newspaper business in the Seventies. It was an empire built on sand. The newspapers folded, and in 1981 he was charged with fraudulent bankruptcy.

sands

shifting sands ◄

You can talk about the **shifting sands** of a situation when it keeps changing, and this makes it difficult to deal with.

Even his critics in the West have acknowledged his shrewd tactical skills in the shifting sands of Arab politics.

Arrogant and authoritarian he might be, but he had been a rock in the shifting sands of her existence.

All close relationships – with her mother, brother, son, old friends, and difficult new stepchildren – seem to be on shifting sands.

sandwich

the meat in the sandwich
the filling in the sandwich

If you say that you are **the meat in the sandwich** or **the filling in the sandwich**, you mean that you are in a very awkward position because you have been caught between two people or groups who are in conflict with each other. These expressions are used in British English.

She defended the police, adding: 'They are normally the meat in the sandwich and in the past they have been given precious little guidance.'

Previously, the idea of a closely united Europe was unpopular because Europeans feared being the filling in a superpower sandwich.

sardines

packed like sardines ◄

If a group of people are together in an enclosed space and you say that they **are packed like sardines**, you mean that there are far more of them than the space was intended to hold, and so they are very close to each other and cannot move about easily. Other verbs can be used instead of 'pack'.

The people are in an appalling condition. They're packed like sardines on the ship. They can barely move so the sanitary condition is very, very bad.

The male sauna was really packed. There were about five people squashed in there like sardines.

sauce

what's sauce for the goose is sauce for the gander

People say **'what's sauce for the goose is sauce for the gander'** when they are arguing that what applies to one person should apply to others, because people should be treated fairly and equally. This is a fairly old-fashioned expression.

There is no evidence that Newham is any more efficient than most other London Councils. Why should they be let off the hook so easily? Could it just be because they are Labour controlled? My view of this is simple and straightforward. What's sauce for the goose is sauce for the gander.

□ This expression is often shortened or varied.

If we're going to have equality, let's have real equality. There's been more male nudity in films lately and I think it's very refreshing – sauce for the goose and all that.

Obviously he didn't like the idea, any more than she'd liked the idea of their checking up on her social life. What's sauce for the goose is sauce for the gosling, she thought.

save

save someone's ass
save someone's butt ◄

If you do something to **save** someone's **ass** or to **save** their **butt**, you do it in order to save them from a dangerous or very unpleasant situation. You can also talk about **saving** your own **ass**. These are informal expressions, which are used mainly in American English. Many people consider them offensive.

Howard rushed up to me and said, 'Thank you, thank you, you saved my ass.'

I thought you'd want to know something, such as how I managed to save Grace's butt from Parish for this long.

Lenny said she climbed out the back of the car to get away, to save her own ass.

say

before you could say Jack Robinson
before you could say knife ◄◄

If you say that something happened **before you could say Jack Robinson** or **before you could say knife**, you are emphasizing that it happened very suddenly and quickly.

The pair of them were out of the door and down the steps before you could say Jack Robinson.

The money they'd sent their son for gold teeth had gone on booze before you could say knife.

□ People often change 'Jack Robinson' or 'knife' to a name or a word or expression that is relevant to the context they are talking about.

But before anyone can say 'soup kitchen', let alone open one, the mission gets bogged down in the harsh complexities of the Balkan conflict.

She was on the phone to New York before you could say long-distance.

scales

the scales fall from your eyes

When someone suddenly realizes the truth about something after a long period of not understanding it or of being deceived about it, you can say that **the scales have fallen from their eyes**. This is a literary expression.

It was only at that point that the scales finally fell from his eyes and he realised he had made a dreadful mistake.

The scales have fallen completely from her eyes, and like millions of others she's finally grasped the enormity of the lie.

scene

set the scene: 1 ◄◄◄

If you **set the scene**, you briefly tell people what they need to know about a subject or topic, so that they can understand what is going to happen or be said next.

To set the scene for this latest example of the improvement in East-West relations, here's Kevin Connolly from Moscow.

On Monday the G7 group of industrial nations will begin their annual summit, which this year is taking place in London. David Edmonds sets the scene by explaining what the G7 is and what it hopes to achieve.

□ Introducing a subject like this can be described as **scene-setting**.

The purpose of this chapter was scene-setting – to clarify our goals and the approach being taken.

set the scene: 2 ◄◄◄

If something **sets the scene** for an event, it creates the conditions in which that event is likely to happen. This expression is used mainly in journalism.

Some members feared that Germany might raise its interest rates. That could have set the scene for a confrontation with the US, which is concerned that increases could cut demand for its exports.

Democrats left New York full of hope after an unusually harmonious convention sent Bill Clinton surging past President Bush in the polls and set the scene for a ferocious election campaign in the autumn.

scenes

behind the scenes ◄◄◄

If something is done **behind the scenes**, it is done in private or in secret, rather than publicly.

Government officials have reacted by saying that Britain has been working behind the scenes just as strenuously as the United States to try to free the hostages.

The Prime Minister's remarks put in the public arena a debate which has been going on behind the scenes for months.

□ You can also talk about **behind-the-scenes** activities, deals, or negotiations.

The debate was postponed for a third time after another day of intensive behind-the-scenes negotiations.

scent

throw someone off the scent
put someone off the scent ◄

If you are looking for something or trying to find out the truth about something and someone **throws** you **off the scent** or **puts** you **off the scent**, they deliberately confuse or mislead you by making you believe something that is not true.

We decided that if anyone was following us, it

would be wiser if we split up to throw them temporarily off the scent.

The essence of the story was that it was not the KGB but the CIA that had sought to destroy me. Could anything be less likely, and better calculated to put me off the scent?

school

the old school   ◄◄◄

If you say that someone is of **the old school**, you mean that they have traditional ideas and values and are fairly old-fashioned. You can also say that they **come from the old school** or **belong to the old school**.

As a builder of the old school, he did not always see eye to eye with designers of new houses.

The mother may lean toward permissiveness; the stepfather may come from the old school and believe that children should be respectful and obedient.

Unlike the modern breed of film-makers, she belonged to the old school, observing the formality of surnames even with colleagues.

□ You can say that someone is an **old-school** type of person, especially when talking about the job that they do.

She is very much an old-school nurse and her outlook leads to clashes with other staff.

the old school tie   ◄

When people talk about **the old school tie**, they are referring to the belief that men who have been to the most famous British private schools use their positions of influence to help other men who went to the same school as themselves. This expression is used in British English.

As might be expected of such proud high-achievers, more than half claim that school made little difference to the professional paths they followed and most try to talk down the notion of the all-pervasive old school tie.

□ You can use **the old school tie** before a noun.

Ray Illingworth's appointment as chairman of selectors was a triumph of commonsense and a blow for sporting virtue ahead of the old school tie network.

the school of hard knocks

If you say that someone has graduated from **the school of hard knocks**, you mean that their life in the past has been very difficult or unpleasant.

He graduated from the school of hard knocks as well – most of his family perished in the war.

He certainly deserves a large measure of success, having reluctantly qualified with honours from the School of Hard Knocks.

science

blind someone with science

If someone **blinds** you **with science**, they tell you about something in a complex or technical way so that you have great difficulty in understanding it.

I must admit that as a young, teenage, amateur photographer I learned all the technical jargon so I could impress people by blinding them with science.

We want facts and figures but don't want to be blinded by science.

score

know the score   ◄◄

If you **know the score**, you know what the real facts of a situation are and how they affect you, even though you may not like them.

Now I know the score and know everything that's going on around there.

Taylor knows the score now, and what will happen if he fails.

When Robin died, I felt that, if nothing else, I was worldly-wise, I knew the score, I knew who my friends were.

settle a score
settle an old score   ◄◄◄

If someone **settles a score** or **settles an old score**, they take revenge for something that someone has done to them in the past.

The two players have been drawn to clash in the first game of the day. 'I've got a score to settle with him,' said Parrella. Parrella and Corsie have met twice, with Parrella yet to win.

The ethnic groups turned on each other to settle old scores, leaving millions dead.

□ You can talk about people or groups being involved in **score-settling** or **the settling of scores**.

What is happening now is score-settling and there is little hope of an end to it.

Some of the changes that have taken place since the war may amount to little more than the settling of scores.

scratch

from scratch   ◄◄◄

If you start **from scratch**, you create something completely new, rather than adding to something that already exists.

She moved to a strange place where she had to make new friends and start a new life from scratch.

He would rather start again from scratch with new rules, new members, and a new electoral system.

The Mlawa factory was one of the first in Poland to be built from scratch by a western investor.

not up to scratch
not come up to scratch   ◄◄◄

If you say that something or someone is **not up to scratch** or **does not come up to scratch**, you mean that they are not as good as they ought to be. These expressions are used in British English.

When services bought from the private sector are not up to scratch, the customer gets his money back.

Athletes have no one to blame but themselves if their performances are not up to scratch.

The Home Secretary wants better methods for dealing with police officers who do not come up to scratch.

screw

have a screw loose

If you say that someone **has a screw loose**, you mean that their behaviour is very strange or that they are slightly mad. This is an informal expression.

I'm sure some of my friends thought I had a screw loose during this period. It seemed to them that my life was all work and no play.

Do you honestly think if I had a screw loose, I would be allowed to work with the elderly?

turn the screw on someone
tighten the screw on someone   ◄◄◄

If someone **turns the screw on** you, they increase the pressure on you to make you do what they want. You can also say that they **tighten the screw** or **tighten the screws on** you.

Parisian taxi drivers were threatening to mount a blockade of their own to turn the screw on the administration of President François Mitterrand.

Perhaps it's a final attempt to turn the screw and squeeze a last concession out of us.

The BBC West Africa Correspondent, who is in Monrovia, says the attacks are tightening the screws still further on the government.

□ In a process like this, you can refer to each action that puts pressure on someone as **a turn of the screw**, **a twist of the screw**, or **a tightening of the screw**.

Every rebel raid, however small, is another turn of the screw, increasing the pressure on the President.

Opposition parties and immigrant organisations see the changes as a further tightening of the screw.

screws

put the screws on someone

If someone **puts the screws on** you, they use pressure or threats to make you do what they want.

They had to put the screws on Harper. So

far, he was the only person who might know something.

I can't understand why he isn't down there in Canberra putting the screws on his counterparts.

Scylla

between Scylla and Charybdis

If you are **between Scylla and Charybdis**, you have to choose between two possible courses of action, both of which seem equally bad. This is a literary expression.

We are between Scylla and Charybdis and we have little hope, but we cannot give up the struggle, even with little scope in which to find a solution.

The middle course was felt to be between the Scylla of democratic tyranny and the Charybdis of arbitrary rule.

sea

all at sea
at sea   ◄◄

If you say that someone is **all at sea** or is **at sea**, you mean that they are very confused by a situation and do not understand it. 'All at sea' is used only in British English.

While he may be all at sea on the economy, his changes have brought the West real and lasting political benefits.

Two recent items of research seem relevant. One suggested that primary school teachers are all at sea about what's what in the universe, although they are expected to teach the subject.

Most children aged between nine and ten were utterly at sea when faced with the problem as to how a shop functions; they thought, for example, that the shopkeeper buys at the same price as he sells.

a sea change   ◄◄◄

You can describe a complete change in someone's attitudes or behaviour as **a sea change**. This is a literary expression.

There has also been a sea-change in attitudes to drinking – a major cause of death on the roads – thanks to greater public awareness and the use of breathalysers.

Cook attributes the sea change that came over his writing to what had gone on before leaving London in the Seventies.

seams

burst at the seams   ◄◄

If you say that a place is **bursting at the seams**, you mean that it is very full of people or things.

The tiny Abbey Stadium was bursting at the seams with a capacity crowd of just under 10,000.

If your shed is bursting at the seams or you

can't get your car into the garage because of the clutter, it's time to get organised.

come apart at the seams: 1
fall apart at the seams ◀

If you say that a system or relationship is **coming apart at the seams** or is **falling apart at the seams**, you mean that it is in a very bad state, and is about to collapse and completely fail.

University lecturers have given a warning that Britain's university system is in danger of falling apart at the seams because of cuts in government funding.

Oliver and Jane began showing serious signs of stress; their relationship was coming apart at the seams. They seemed to be quarrelling all the time.

come apart at the seams: 2

If you say that someone is **coming apart at the seams**, you mean that they are behaving in a strange or illogical way, because they are under severe mental strain.

He stood for a moment, breathing deeply; he was coming apart at the seams, something he had never thought would happen to him.

season

open season ◀◀

If you say that it is **open season** on someone or something, you mean that a lot of people are currently criticizing or attacking them.

This case invites an open season on women employees.

Open season has been declared on the royal family.

It is always open season to attack a television documentary or a newspaper report.

seat

fly by the seat of your pants ◀

If you say that someone is **flying by the seat of** their **pants**, you mean that they are doing something difficult or dangerous using only their instincts, because they do not have the right kind of experience or information. You often use this expression to show disapproval of this situation.

The idea was that by opening up policy-making to outsiders the Treasury was taking on board the advice of its fiercest critics and not merely flying by the seat of its pants.

The truth is that neither experts nor mothers know as much as each might wish; to a great extent, all of us fly by the seat of our pants and try to learn quickly from experience.

☐ A **seat-of-the-pants** method of doing something depends on instinct rather than on careful planning or knowledge.

They're much more a seat-of-the-pants opera-

tion. Unlike the FBI and the Drug Enforcement Administration, ATF has traditionally operated without strict day-to-day supervision.

I don't know much law, never did. A seat-of-the-pants barrister, that's me.

in the driving seat
in the driver's seat ◀◀◀

If you say that someone is **in the driving seat**, you mean that they have control of a situation. This form of the expression is used in British English; in American English, the form is **in the driver's seat**.

The radicals were in the driving seat, much to the anxiety of the moderates.

The former Foreign Secretary, Sir Geoffrey Howe, has warned against Britain not being in the driving seat as Europe integrates further.

Those who had access to money were in the driver's seat.

in the hot seat ◀◀◀

If someone is **in the hot seat**, they are in a position where they have to make important or difficult decisions, or where they have to answer difficult questions. In American English, you can also say that they are **on the hot seat**.

'I'm always expecting trouble,' he explained. 'Anything from complaints about the food to breakage on the drill they're using to sink the shaft. Whatever happens, I'm in the hot seat.'

The club was formed in 1900 and since 1902 they have had only seven managers. Syd King was the longest-serving with 30 years in the hot seat from 1902.

She decided to end the interview by putting me in the hot seat. 'And you? What about your background?' I was stuck for words.

take a back seat: 1 ◀◀◀

If you **take a back seat**, you allow other people to have all the power, importance, or responsibility.

You will be aware that there are some situations when it is wise to take a back seat and some where it is appropriate to fight for your, and others', rights.

Jennifer felt trapped, not allowed to compete with her two older brothers and forced to take a back seat to a younger sister with greater social and physical graces.

take a back seat: 2 ◀

If one thing **takes a back seat** to another, people give the first thing less attention because they think that it is less important or less interesting than the other thing.

It is also true that in the Apollo programme science took a back seat to technology and engineering.

His own private life takes a back seat to the problems and difficulties of his patients.

Though Haig returned dutifully to India, his

heart was no longer in his work. Goings on at the War Office became an obsession, while Indian affairs took a back seat.

security

a security blanket ◄

If you refer to something as **a security blanket**, you mean that it provides someone with a feeling of safety and comfort when they are in a situation which worries them or makes them nervous.

He never gave a second thought to leaving behind the security blanket of his family and friends to head north.

For most of us, the lists we make act as security blankets, telling us what to do and how long to spend doing it.

☐ A young child's **security blanket** is a piece of cloth or clothing which the child holds and chews in order to feel comforted.

seed

go to seed: 1
run to seed

If you say that someone **has gone to seed**, you mean that they have allowed themselves to become unfit, untidy, or lazy as they have grown older. You can also say that they **have run to seed**.

He was big and fleshy, like an athlete gone to seed, with a pot belly that not even his expensively-tailored clothes could conceal.

Once he had carried a lot of muscle but now he was running to seed.

go to seed: 2
run to seed

If a place **has gone to seed** or **has run to seed**, it has become dirty and neglected because people have not bothered to care for it.

The report painted a grim picture of an America going to seed, its bridges and roads falling apart, its land scarred by dumps of untreated hazardous wastes, its national parks neglected.

When she died, the place lost its focus and went to seed.

seed corn
eat your seed corn ◄

If you refer to resources or people as **seed corn**, you mean that they will produce benefits in the future rather than immediately.

I regard the teachers as the people who are planting the seed corn for the future and therefore I regard their work as crucially important.

☐ If you say that people **are eating** their **seed corn**, you mean that they are using up their resources, and they will suffer for this in the future.

A society that's unwilling to invest in its future is a society that's living off capital. It's

eating its seed corn and I'm afraid that's what we're doing too much in the United States today.

☐ A farmer's **seed corn** is the grain that is used for planting rather than being sold or eaten.

seeds

sow the seeds of something
plant the seeds of something ◄◄

If something **sows the seeds of** a future problem, it starts the process which causes that problem to develop. You can also say that something **plants the seeds of** a future problem.

The birth of a second child may upset a previously satisfactory relationship between the mother and the first child and sow the seeds of a long-standing behaviour problem.

Shortly after that came foreign armies, foreign settlers and foreign apartheid, which planted the seeds of today's crises in Africa.

☐ You can also say **sow** or **plant the seeds of** something good.

The final communiqué adopted the main elements of Jacques Delors's proposals to sow the seeds of economic recovery.

Ministers had spent five years planting the seeds of reform.

send

send someone packing ◄◄◄

If someone **is sent packing**, they are told very forcefully or in an unsympathetic way to leave a place, or to leave their job or position.

Mr Cawley was sent packing from his home on the estate after 26 years as park manager.

We had an idyllic life in the country until I decided I wanted to live alone for the first time in my life and I sent him packing.

Jason Livingstone's attempt to make a comeback as a professional footballer ended yesterday when Cardiff City sent him packing.

shade

put someone in the shade ◄

If one person or thing **puts** another **in the shade**, they are so impressive that they make the other person or thing seem unimportant by comparison.

Joan Collins always stuns the crowds with her chic outfits and still manages to put younger women in the shade.

Amy Spielberg puts other Hollywood wives in the shade when it comes to taking a fortune from their famous husbands.

The celebrations put Mardi Gras in the shade.

shades

shades of ◄

If you have just mentioned a person or thing and you say **shades of** another person or thing, you mean that the first person or thing reminds you of the second one.

Andie MacDowell crops up again in the bizarre mystery thriller Ruby Cairo, as the wife of a crook who has faked his death (shades of The Third Man, perhaps?) and who tracks him down via his bank accounts around the world.

The debate had been brought forward by a week, in an effort to avert the protest planned for it by the school students' leaders. Shades of 1968, perhaps?

shadow

afraid of your own shadow

If you say that someone is **afraid of** their **own shadow**, you mean that are very timid or nervous. Words such as 'scared' or 'frightened' can be used instead of 'afraid'.

They're all afraid of their own shadows. Can't say I blame them. After all, this is a police state.

Used to be scared of his own shadow, you know. But they helped him greatly at the clinic.

a shadow of your former self ◄◄

If you say that someone or something is **a shadow of** their **former self**, you mean that they are much less powerful or capable than they used to be. This expression is used mainly in written English.

Our ninety-year-old dad was but a shadow of his former self.

The trouble with Kevin is that he dreaded going downhill as a player. He hated the thought of ending up a shadow of his former self.

The federal Communist party that resumed its Congress on Saturday after a break of four months was a pale shadow of its former self.

□ You sometimes use this expression simply to say that someone has lost a lot of weight.

She gradually turned into a strikingly slim shadow of her former self.

shakes

in two shakes of a lamb's tail
in two shakes

If you say that you will do something **in two shakes of a lamb's tail**, you mean that you will do it very soon or very quickly. Other words and phrases are sometimes used instead of 'lamb's tail'. You can also just say **in two shakes**. These are fairly old-fashioned expressions, which are used mainly in spoken English.

If you were an incompetent buffoon, I would have you out of office in two shakes of a lamb's tail.

I'll be back in two shakes of a leg.

I'll just dash up to the phone and be back in two shakes.

no great shakes ◄

If you say that someone or something is **no great shakes**, you mean that they are ineffective, useless, or of poor quality.

The protests have failed partly because the opposition politicians are no great shakes.

As a thriller, 'A Death in Paris' is no great shakes.

This restaurant is no great shakes gastronomically, but the portions are huge.

shape

knock something into shape
whip something into shape
lick something into shape ◄◄

If you **knock** something **into shape** or **whip** it **into shape**, you use whatever methods are necessary to change or improve it, so that it is in the condition that you want it to be in. In British English, 'lick' can be used instead of 'knock' or 'whip'.

Most experts agree that the country's agriculture can quickly be knocked into shape and be successful.

After a successful career at the Italian central bank, few people doubt his ability to whip the economy into shape.

We were licked into shape by the long-serving departmental managers to whom we reported.

shape up or ship out

If you tell someone to **shape up or ship out**, you are telling them that they should start behaving in a more reasonable or responsible way, or else leave the place where they are or give up what they are doing.

Out there, there are people who want to humiliate you. Grind you down, destroy you. You've either got to take all this, you've got to stomach it, join in, or you'll go under. Shape up or ship out.

shave

a close shave ◄

If you say that someone had **a close shave**, you mean that they very nearly had an accident or disaster, or very nearly suffered a defeat.

Admittedly you had a close shave, but you knew when you accepted this job that there would be risks involved.

You mentioned the close shave that Gingrich had in the 1990 general election. What are his chances in this general election?

sheep

the black sheep
the black sheep of the family ◄◄

If you describe someone as **the black sheep** or **the black sheep of the family**, you mean that they are very different from the other people in their family or group and are considered bad or worthless by them.

While to her family she might seem the rebellious black sheep, when Janet compared herself to friends like Nancy or Margaret, she saw herself as bourgeois, neat, and timid.

My aunt was very famous in those days, but because she was the black sheep of the family I was never encouraged to talk about her.

make sheep's eyes

If you **make sheep's eyes** at someone, you look at them in an adoring and admiring way. This is an old-fashioned expression.

I kissed her hand, made sheep's eyes and followed her, humming, up the winding stairs.

might as well be hanged for a sheep as a lamb

If someone says **'I might as well be hanged for a sheep as a lamb'**, they mean that they will suffer or be punished whatever they do, so they might as well do something really bad if they can get some enjoyment or profit from it. 'Hung' is sometimes used instead of 'hanged'.

If they are going to hang me for what has already been done why should I sue for peace? I might as well be hanged for a sheep as well as a lamb.

separate the sheep from the goats
sort out the sheep from the goats ◄

If you **separate the sheep from the goats** or **sort out the sheep from the goats**, you examine a group of things or people and decide which ones are good and which are bad.

It is getting harder and harder to sort out the sheep from the goats among the 4,000 or so titles for children that pour off the publishers' presses every year.

For the government, the first Chartermarks will be a chance to sort out the sheep from the goats, marking out the organisations able to embrace quality, choice, standards and value.

sheet

a clean sheet: 1
a clean sheet of paper

If you are allowed to start with **a clean sheet** or with **a clean sheet of paper**, you are allowed to forget previous debts or mistakes, and so are given a new chance to succeed at something.

The Christmas break has erased unhappy memories and allowed the Government to start the new year with a clean sheet.

Michael Lock, Triumph's marketing manager, said yesterday, 'We started with a clean sheet of paper. We put the past behind us, and looked at what the Japanese had done.'

a clean sheet: 2

In a football match, if a team keeps **a clean sheet**, no goals are scored against them. This expression is used in British journalism.

Tottenham's most successful campaign was 1944-45, when they lost only one League game and failed to score only three times. On twelve occasions they kept a clean sheet.

sheets

three sheets to the wind

If you say that someone is **three sheets to the wind** or **three sheets in the wind**, you mean that they are drunk. This is an old-fashioned expression.

He's probably three sheets to the wind down at Toby's, wondering where the hell he left his truck.

shelf

on the shelf ◄

In British English, when a woman is no longer young and has not married, people sometimes say that she is **on the shelf**, meaning that she will not get married because she is too old for men to find her attractive. Many people dislike this expression because of the attitude which it represents.

She had balanced the humiliation of being a spinster, left on the shelf, against the freedom to live a life of independence.

I certainly don't equate being single with being on the shelf!

shelf life ◄

If you say that something has a particular **shelf life**, you mean that it will only last for that length of time, rather than continuing indefinitely.

I was dismayed to read the comment 'all marriages have a shelf life' in the article 'When he walks out after 25 years'.

A large proportion of small businesses have a short shelf life.

Who knows, we could begin to build a policy that would have a shelf life of more than 30 months.

□ This expression is more commonly used in talking about food, drink, or medicine. The **shelf life** of a food, drink, or medicine is the length of time it can be kept before it is too old to sell or use.

shell

come out of your shell
go into your shell   ◄◄◄

If you **come out of** your **shell**, you become less shy and more talkative and friendly. Other verbs can be used instead of 'come'.

She used to be very timid and shy but I think she's come out of her shell.

I'm a fairly shy person but she has brought me out of my shell.

☐ If you **go into** your **shell**, you become more timid and less friendly. Verbs such as 'withdraw' and 'retreat' can be used instead of 'go'.

'After losing to Dennis I felt moments of disbelief for months but I never hid away,' he said. 'I never went into my shell to brood about it and that's the best therapy.'

Brian withdrew increasingly into his shell, inhibited by a growing but unrecognized sense of inferiority.

a shell game   ◄

If you say that someone is playing **a shell game**, you mean that they are deliberately deceiving people, for example by changing things or pretending to change things, in order to gain an advantage. This expression is used mainly in American English.

The union had accused the mine owners of playing a kind of corporate shell game, in which mines could be opened in the future under a variety of names with the intent of hiring non-union miners.

The Americans, who have still made no commitment to cut carbon-dioxide emissions, are scathing about pledges from other countries. Confidential instructions to the US delegation in Geneva say the pledges amount to a shell game without legal significance.

shine

take a shine to someone   ◄

If you **take a shine to** someone or something, you like them a lot from the very first time that you come into contact with them. This expression is used in British English.

Laura took a shine to her and offered her the job without any prompting from me.

James is not renowned for taking a shine to strangers.

take the shine off something   ◄

If something **takes the shine off** a pleasant event or achievement, it makes it less enjoyable than it should be. This expression is used mainly in British English.

There are two factors which may take the shine off the immediate euphoria following the end of the coup.

For Labour, their reverses in parts of London have taken the shine off what they otherwise

describe as their best local election performance ever.

ship

don't spoil the ship for a ha'porth of tar

People say **'don't spoil the ship for a ha'porth of tar'** when someone risks ruining something because they do not want to spend a relatively small amount of money on a necessity. This is an old-fashioned expression, which is used mainly in British English.

Don't spoil the ship for a ha'porth of tar. If you give away a miniature replica of a bottle that won a prize for design, you will attract more new customers than the same perfume in a plain bottle.

☐ A **ha'porth** is a 'halfpenny's worth'. A halfpenny was a British coin of very low value.

jump ship
abandon ship   ◄◄

If you accuse someone of **jumping ship** or of **abandoning ship**, you are accusing them of leaving an organization or cause, either because they think it is about to fail or because they want to join a rival organization.

Cheers rang out a week ago when the Liberal Democrat government lost a vote of confidence. Some ruling party members immediately jumped ship and created new parties.

I had a good contract with a rider which was legally binding and enforceable. However, the rider jumped ship and now rides for another team. I have taken legal advice, and am assured I will win the case against the rider.

For weeks he worked eighteen-hour days, pleading with his staff not to abandon ship.

run a tight ship   ◄

If you say that someone **runs a tight ship**, you mean that they keep firm control of the way their business or organization is run, so that it is well organized and efficient.

Shaona was running a tight ship and didn't waste time on pleasantries.

Harvard runs a tight ship: it spends less than a quarter of a percent of its portfolio on management, comfortably below many other universities.

a sinking ship
abandon a sinking ship
like a rat leaving a sinking ship   ◄

If you say that an organization or cause is **a sinking ship**, you mean that it is failing and unlikely to recover.

The television company is not a sinking ship. There is ample finance in the system to produce an original schedule which can be refreshed and renewed year-on-year with innovative new programmes.

☐ If you say that someone **is abandoning a**

sinking ship, you mean that they are leaving an organization or cause which is about to fail completely. You can use verbs such as 'leave' or 'desert' instead of 'abandon'. If you disapprove strongly of their behaviour, you can say that they are **like a rat leaving a sinking ship**.

It's looking more and more as though Communists across the country have realised this is the time to abandon their sinking ship.

He seems to be suggesting that we're deserting a sinking ship, but that's not the case.

I know people are saying things about rats deserting the sinking ship, but Tinsley was very junior. She hadn't the least idea of what was going on.

when your ship comes in ◄

When people talk about what they will do **when** their **ship comes in**, they are talking about what they will do if they become rich and successful.

Sims is convinced that one day his ship will come in, if only he waits long enough.

□ If someone suddenly becomes wealthy or successful, you can say that their **ship has come in**.

The ship has come in for Associated British Ports where profits have soared to £62.1 million after last year's loss of £36.6 million.

shirt

keep your shirt on
keep your pants on

If someone tells you to **keep** your **shirt on**, they are telling you to calm down and not be angry or impatient. 'Shirt' is sometimes replaced with 'pants'. This expression is used mainly in American English; the usual British expression is **keep** your **hair on**.

The doorbell rang. Helen told the caller to keep his shirt on – snappish because she felt the ringing had been excessive.

put your shirt on something
lose your shirt ◄

If you **put** your **shirt on** something, you bet or risk a large amount of money on it, because you are convinced that it will win or succeed. This expression is used mainly in British English.

I was just thinking you might put your shirt on Golden Boy. It's bound to be a winner, isn't it?

□ If you **lose** your **shirt**, you lose all your money on a bad investment or bet.

His father warned him that he knew nothing about shipping and could easily lose his shirt.

If you play cards with the big boys, you can lose your shirt.

a stuffed shirt ◄

If you refer to a man who has an important position as **a stuffed shirt**, you mean that he behaves in a very formal or pompous way.

His seminars work because he keeps things simple. He strides around talking like an ordinary person rather than a stuffed shirt.

He takes well-deserved credit for his pioneering stand against the stuffed-shirts of the organization.

□ You can use **stuffed-shirt** before a noun.

I have little patience with the dress rules of stuffed-shirt establishments.

shit

in the shit
in deep shit ◄

If you say that someone is **in the shit** or **in deep shit**, you are emphasizing that they are in a very difficult situation. These are very informal expressions, which many people find offensive.

He came and stood in front of her. 'They're serious. This is serious business. I am in deep shit.' He pulled her to her feet. 'I need your help. I've gotta have your help.'

No questions, and you get the cash. You cause me any trouble, and you'll be in the shit. You'll wish you'd never been born.

□ You can also say that someone **lands** you **in the shit** or **drops** you **in the shit** when they get you into trouble or into a very difficult situation. These are very informal expressions, which are used in British English. Many people find them offensive.

The treaty was supposed to protect us, not land us in the shit.

You're useful to us so we let you stay. But that doesn't mean I'll stand by and watch you drop other people in the shit to cover your own shabby name.

the shit hits the fan ◄

If someone talks about what will happen when **the shit hits the fan**, they are talking about what will happen when a situation becomes very bad or when some serious trouble begins. This is a very informal expression, which many people find offensive.

In addition to the jewelry fraud, Granger had been smuggling gold bars into India and finding devious ways to avoid paying tax. When customs officers called to examine his books, Granger panicked. 'The shit has hit the fan,' he told Davis.

There's so much shit going to hit the fan in the next few days, my getting fired won't matter a bit.

□ People sometimes use less offensive words instead of 'shit'.

The governor and his staff thought they'd be safely away when it hit the fan around here.

They had two boys and settled into domesti-

city. Then the brown stuff hit the fan. She looked at her life and pronounced it 'Boring!'

shoe

drop the other shoe

If someone **drops the other shoe**, they complete a task by doing the second and final part of it. This expression is used in American English.

Time Warner Inc. dropped the other shoe in its two-step $13.86 billion acquisition of Warner Communications Inc.

In 1972 the State Department was compelled to drop the other shoe.

People who have been successfully treated for cancer and return to work often find difficulties in being accepted as before; it is as though others were waiting for the other shoe to drop.

if the shoe fits

You can say **'if the shoe fits'** when you are telling someone that unpleasant or critical remarks which have been made about them are probably true or fair. This expression is used in American English; the British expression is **if the cap fits**.

'You said something about me being in a bad mood,' Jack said. 'What made you say that? If I wasn't in a bad mood before you said it, it's enough when you say it to put me in one.' 'If the shoe fits,' Mary said.

shoes

dead men's shoes

If you talk about **dead men's shoes**, you are talking about a situation in which people cannot make progress in their careers until someone senior to them retires or dies. This expression is used in British English.

We are sick of waiting to step into dead men's shoes.

At that particular time, jobs were rather difficult to obtain. It was more or less dead men's shoes.

in someone's shoes
in someone's boots   ◄◄

If you talk about being **in** someone's **shoes**, you are describing how you would feel or act if you were in the same situation as them.

I hope you'll stop and consider how you would feel if you were in my shoes.

You should be kinder when considering others, and put yourself in their shoes once in a while.

☐ If you say that you **wouldn't like to be in** someone's **shoes**, you mean that you would not like to be in the same situation as them.

He hasn't made any friends and has upset a lot of powerful people. I wouldn't like to be in his shoes if he comes back to work.

☐ You can also talk about being **in** someone's **boots**.

'I suppose Monsieur will start early.' Sharpe nodded. 'I would if I was in his boots.'

quake in your shoes

If you say that someone **is quaking in** their **shoes**, you mean that they are very frightened or anxious about something that is about to happen. Verbs such as 'shake' and 'tremble' are sometimes used instead of 'quake'. **Quake in** your **boots** means the same.

I chose to spend an evening at an Inner City Youth Club and was quaking in my shoes throughout the journey there.

I think I would be shaking in my shoes if I were cheating now because athletes who take drugs are being picked up in large numbers.

smudge your own shoes

If you **smudge** your **own shoes**, you damage your own reputation while trying to harm someone else's. This expression is used in British English.

He dishes the dirt on his buddies and smudges his own shoes with admissions of womanising, gambling and drugs.

step into someone's shoes
fill someone's shoes   ◄◄◄

If you **step into** someone's **shoes**, you take over their job or position. If you **fill** someone's **shoes**, you do their job or hold their position as well as they did. Compare **step into** someone's **boots**; see **boots**.

In America, if a president resigns or dies in office, the vice-president steps into his shoes.

Now that Chris is gone she wants me to step into his shoes.

It'll take a good man to fill her shoes.

shoestring

on a shoestring   ◄◄◄

If you do something **on a shoestring**, you do it using very little money.

The theatre will be run on a shoestring.

In contrast with the free-spending big parties, Mr Fujimori's political campaign has been run on a shoestring.

Newly divorced with two children to raise, she was living on a shoestring.

☐ You can use **shoestring** before a noun.

A British science fiction film made on a shoestring budget is taking America by storm.

Chris McNair says he will continue his shoestring campaign in every part of Alabama.

shoo-in

be a shoo-in   ◄

If you say that someone **is a shoo-in** for something such as an election or contest, you mean that they are certain to win. This expression is used mainly in American English.

The president seemed a shoo-in for a second term, even though the election was some 20 months away.

She seemed like a shoo-in. But in the past month she has seen her 20-point lead whittled down to a mere five percentage points.

The president looks as though he's a shoe-in for another four years.

□ 'Shoo-in' is sometimes spelled 'shoe-in'.

shop

all over the shop ◀

If you say that something is **all over the shop**, you mean that it is spread across a large area or over a wide range of things. This expression is used in British English; the American expression is **all over the lot**.

Big government majorities gave backbenchers the freedom to make trouble all over the shop without fear of retribution.

The problem is that this ambitious project roams around all over the shop and never quite settles into a coherent structure.

shut up shop
close up shop ◀

If a person or organization has to **shut up shop** or **close up shop**, they are forced to close their business, for example because of difficult economic conditions. 'Shut up shop' is used only in British English and 'close up shop' is used mainly in American English.

Unless business picks up soon, some of the 245 foreign-owned banks in Switzerland may have to shut up shop.

This year the opera house was forced to budget for a deficit and the deficit is now growing. If there is industrial action, the situation could become very serious indeed. It could mean shutting up shop.

Mr. Lemoyne had reluctantly closed up shop when the library had reached a rock-bottom membership of eleven.

a talking shop
a talk shop ◀◀

If you describe something such as a conference or an organization as **a talking shop** or **a talk shop**, you are being critical of it because you think that its discussions have no practical results. These expressions are used mainly in British English.

Governments which used to dismiss the UN as a mere 'talking shop' now see possibilities for the international body to act more as a world policeman.

They claim the Scottish Food Group, which has no government funding, will achieve little as it is nothing more than a talking shop.

Let's accept the fact that the committee is a

talk shop. *Let's try and get some form of executive group going which can actually make things happen.*

talk shop
shop talk ◀

If people who do the same kind of work **are talking shop**, they are talking to each other about their work. This expression is often used to suggest that this is boring for other people who are present and who do not do the same work.

Although I get on well with my colleagues, if you hang around together all the time you just end up talking shop. I think it's good to have a broader outlook and I've a lot of friends outside the Service.

With the pressures of the day behind them, they would gather in small, informal groups and talk shop.

□ Talking about your work like this can be referred to as **shop talk**.

Conversation over dinner began with catching up on family matters, then turned to shop talk.

shopping

a shopping list ◀

Someone's **shopping list** is a list of demands or requirements that they want to get from a particular person or organization.

Mr Baker presented a shopping list of additional help the United States was requiring from its allies.

The opposition Social Democratic Party has just held its annual conference and laid out a shopping list of changes that might make the treaty acceptable.

Mr Major has offered no shopping list of the old directives he wants scrapped.

short

by the short and curlies

If someone has you **by the short and curlies**, they have you completely in their power. This expression is used in British English. **By the short hairs** means the same.

The unions' chief negotiator last night said: 'We had the company by the short and curlies.'

From the poignant opening scene of a nostalgic middle-aged couple dancing cheek to cheek, the film has you by the emotional short and curlies.

one sandwich short of a picnic
several cards short of a full deck ◀

Short of is used in expressions such as 'one sandwich short of a picnic' or 'several cards short of a full deck' to indicate in a humorous way that you think someone is very stupid or is behaving very strangely. 'Short' is sometimes replaced with 'shy' in American English.

His daughter confirmed that her father was definitely one sandwich short of a picnic.

The guy was obviously several cards short of a full deck.

☐ This expression is used very creatively, and people often use it simply for the humorous effect of a new and amusing variation.

Miss Martin, who is clearly one tent peg short of a full set, felt they were communicating 'through some sort of telepathic link'.

He's also a few gallons shy of a full tank, if you catch my drift.

sell someone short ◄

If you accuse someone of **selling** you **short**, you are accusing them of failing to provide you with all the things which you think they ought to provide.

Students don't necessarily want to cope with too much complexity. But, on the other hand, if the tutor makes things too simple, that's selling them short too.

If a film is worth showing, it is worth showing as the full work it was intended to be. Anything less is selling us short.

sell yourself short ◄

If you **sell** yourself **short**, you are modest about your achievements and good qualities, so that other people do not realize just how good you are.

Deep down you know that you are someone of substance, and that many other people aren't. For many years you have been selling yourself short.

He had not risen to his lofty position by selling himself short or underestimating his own potential.

☐ You can also say that someone **sells** themselves **short** when they do something which is well below their capabilities.

Almond is an artist more than capable of scaling dizzying heights – here he is simply, woefully, selling himself short.

shot

by a long shot ◄

You can use **by a long shot** to add emphasis to a statement, especially a negative statement or one that contains a superlative. Compare **a long shot**.

We have to know what is going on, and we don't, not yet, not by a long shot.

The arms race isn't over by a long shot and there are no signs that the US and Russia plan to initiate another round of deep cuts anytime soon.

No city has escaped the ravages of recession, but Seattle has fared best by a long shot.

get shot of something
be shot of something ◄

If you want to **get shot of** someone or some-thing or to **be shot of** them, you want to get rid of them quickly. These expressions are used in British English.

He didn't want to be seen near me and couldn't wait to get shot of me.

City experts still reckon the company wants to get shot of its brewing division.

Financial institutions are now America's biggest hotel-owners – and most want to be shot of their investment.

give something your best shot ◄◄◄

If you **give** something your **best shot**, you try as hard as you can to achieve it, even though you know how difficult it is.

I don't think the Republic have enough quality players to become World Champions, but they'll give it their best shot.

As long as I play tennis, I'll keep coming back and giving Wimbledon my best shot.

I gave it my best shot, but I wasn't quite good enough. I may have lost, but I've learnt a lot from the whole thing.

☐ You can describe a course of action as someone's **best shot** when it is the best chance they have of achieving something.

Keep going in the direction I'm pointing. I think there's a highway over there. Five miles, something like that. I'm not sure. But it's your best shot.

Mazankowski and other analysts say Canada's best shot at economic recovery is continued growth in the United States.

like a shot ◄

If you do something **like a shot**, you do it immediately, because you are very eager to do it or because something forces you to do it.

If you heard noises downstairs and you'd put on the landing light and you shouted 'Who's there?', most burglars would be off like a shot.

They keep getting all sorts of opportunities to go to companies and exploit technology but they are back here like a shot because they can express their ideas.

a long shot ◄◄

If you describe a way of solving a difficulty or problem as **a long shot**, you mean that there is little chance that it will succeed, but you think it is worth trying. Compare **by a long shot**.

I'm betting Rafael knows where to find him. You might call it a long shot, but it's better than nothing.

Could he forestall a deal with Johnson? It was a long shot, but Bagley had little to lose.

☐ You can also say that something is **a long shot** when it is very unlikely to happen.

Observers say a deal between the White House and Congress is a long shot in an election year, when both political parties are trying to get the upper hand.

It seemed such a long shot, me walking over the hills, and seeing you at the end of it.

one shot in your locker

If you have only **one shot in** your **locker**, you have only one thing left that you can do in order to achieve success, and if this fails you will have to give up.

Few Australians believe that Paul Keating is finished. 'True,' he said, after Bob Hawke had beaten off his challenge on Monday, 'I had only one shot in the locker. I have fired it, and the result is there for all to see.' But the result that Australians see is that, although Mr Keating lost, he did not lose hopelessly.

It's hard to see what kind of concessions the government could make before it's too late to call off the strike. Having already offered talks and announced the wage rise, it can have few shots left in its locker.

a shot across someone's bows
a warning shot across someone's bows
a warning shot ◄◄

If you fire **a shot across** someone's **bows** or **a warning shot across** their **bows**, you do something which shows that you are prepared to oppose them strongly if they do not stop or change what they are doing.

Britain's agriculture minister departed from his prepared speech to fire a shot across Norway's bows.

The election result wasn't entirely responsible for the market's worries, but political analysts regard it as a warning shot across the government's bows.

As a warning shot across the bows of rivals the company is already setting aggressive prices.

□ 'Bows' is pronounced with the same vowel sound as the word 'how'.

□ You can also say simply that someone fires **a warning shot**.

The United States has fired a warning shot in its ongoing trade dispute with China.

Two days after that article appeared, they fired the first warning shot to us with a written, collective plea to abandon the tour and come home.

a shot in the arm ◄◄◄

If something gives you **a shot in the arm**, it gives you help and encouragement at a time when you badly need it.

Joe really helped us out of a hole and it was really exciting. It gave us a real shot in the arm at a time when we needed it most.

Last weekend's Gold Coast Boat Show, the first held at Royal Pines Resort, has proved a shot in the arm for the marine industry.

The remaining problems can be dealt with in weeks, and to risk further delay would be to

deny the world economy a desperately needed shot in the arm.

shots

call the shots ◄◄◄

If you **call the shots**, you are the person who makes all the important decisions in an organization or situation.

Is the military really the power behind the President now? Who really calls the shots?

The days of the empire are over. Britain must realise that she does not call the shots any more.

Christabel was calling the shots on who would be going and who wouldn't.

shoulder

give someone the cold shoulder
get the cold shoulder ◄◄◄

If someone deliberately ignores you, you can say that they **give** you **the cold shoulder** or that you **get the cold shoulder** from them.

He gives him the cold shoulder; he doesn't talk to him very much, if at all.

Her book is chilling in its description of what it feels like to be given the cold shoulder by Hollywood.

Nancy was sure she'd be getting the cold shoulder from a lot of people she'd thought were her friends.

□ You can also say that someone or something **is cold-shouldered** or talk about **cold-shouldering**. These forms are used mainly in journalism.

Even her own party considered her shrewish and nagging, and cold-shouldered her in the corridors.

Marketing has been cold-shouldered by hospitals, but managers are gradually accepting that it may genuinely be needed.

With Mr Yeltsin, Mr Major was able to go some way towards repairing the dents in the Russian leader's self-esteem caused by earlier western cold-shouldering.

put your shoulder to the wheel

If you **put** your **shoulder to the wheel**, you put a great deal of effort into a difficult task.

Is there anybody here that is not willing to put his or her shoulder to the wheel and do it?

Do not look back, look ahead. Keep your shoulder to the wheel, your feet on the ground. That is what I have done; it is how I have lived my life so far.

a shoulder to cry on
cry on someone's shoulder ◄◄

If you refer to someone as **a shoulder to cry on**, you mean that you can rely on them to give you emotional support when you are upset or anxious.

For a lot of new mums the health visitor becomes a real friend, full of sound advice and the perfect shoulder to cry on when it all gets too much.

Roland sometimes saw me as a shoulder to cry on. He certainly wasn't used to me being weak.

□ You can also say that one person **cries on** another's **shoulder**.

He had let her cry on his shoulder when she was upset, bringing her flowers and taking her on a late-night walk to help her feel better.

When I come off stage and things haven't gone well, there's no one whose shoulder I can cry on.

shoulder to shoulder　◄◄

If you stand **shoulder to shoulder** with a group of people, you work co-operatively with them to achieve a common aim.

Perreira, who had stood shoulder to shoulder with his players throughout the campaign, said 'I want to be with my players.'

He was working shoulder to shoulder with enthusiastic theatre folk for the first time in twenty-five years, and sharing in the creative spirit.

They were joined by leaders of all those nations who were shoulder-to-shoulder 50 years ago, including the Queen and Prince Philip.

straight from the shoulder

If you say something **straight from the shoulder**, you say it directly and with complete honesty.

He hasn't much good to say about the brotherhood of politicians he aspires to join. His opinions about top politicians in Washington and New York come straight from the shoulder. 'Bush,' he says, 'was out of touch with reality.'

□ You can use **straight-from-the-shoulder** before a noun.

Others came away thinking he had given something less than his usual straight-from-the-shoulder performance.

shoulders

rub shoulders with someone　◄◄◄

If you **rub shoulders with** someone important or famous, you associate with them for a while. This expression is used mainly in British English; the usual American expression is **rub elbows with** someone.

Johnson had always loved rubbing shoulders with celebrities.

She went to Cambridge before the First World War and rubbed shoulders with the likes of George Bernard Shaw and Sidney and Beatrice Webb.

Working on a ship can mean seeing the

world, rubbing shoulders with the rich and famous and partying nearly every night.

□ You can also say that two groups of people **rub shoulders**.

While there may be fewer poor people, the rich are also more visible, and in the cities the two rub shoulders, as Mercedes cars sweep past tin shacks.

Farmers, painters and retired colonels rub shoulders at an inn which used to entertain smugglers and coachmen.

show

get the show on the road
keep the show on the road　◄

If you **get the show on the road**, you put a plan or idea into action. If you **keep the show on the road**, you ensure that when a plan or idea has been put into action, it continues to operate successfully.

It was a British commander up at the front who suggested that we had better get this show on the road because people are getting tired of waiting.

He checked his watch. 'Shouldn't we get this show on the road, now that Rolfe's here?'

The government is going to have to find something to offer the unions if it is to keep the show on the road.

run the show　◄◄◄

If you say that someone **is running the show**, you mean that they are in control of an organization, event, or situation.

This is the first summit in which the Americans are just another player; Germany is now running the show.

The fear is that you have on paper the restoration of democracy, but in reality the military still run the show.

I wanted to run a record company so that I could have control. It feels wonderful to be running my own show. And now we're the most successful independent company in the country.

steal the show　◄◄◄

If you say that someone or something **steals the show**, you mean that they get more attention or praise than the other people or things in a show or other event.

It was Chinese women who stole the show on the first day of competition. Their swimmers are setting new Asian records in almost every race.

It's Jack Lemmon who finally steals the show, turning in his finest performance in years.

□ You can describe someone or something that gets more attention than other people or things as **a show-stealer**.

The latest Steven Spielberg epic, Jurassic Park, had theatre patrons squirming in their seats at a special preview in Hollywood this week. The show-stealer is Tyrannosaurus Rex, a 5 tonne dinosaur.

stop the show ◄◄

If you say that someone **stops the show**, you mean that they give an outstanding performance in a show or other event.

Twelve-year-old Reggie Jackson stopped the show last night with 'America the Beautiful'.

□ You can describe an impressive person, performance, or thing as **show-stopping** or say that they are **a show-stopper**.

She got a standing ovation for her show-stopping number 'And I'm Telling You I'm Not Going' and finished on a high note with 'Oh Happy Day'.

Her first encore was a real show-stopper, 'Je Suis Comme Je Suis'.

showers

send someone to the showers
a trip to the showers

If someone **is sent to the showers**, they are disqualified from a game or excluded from an activity, because of their bad behaviour or poor performance. You can also say that they earn **a trip to the showers**. These expressions are used in American English. Compare **an early bath**; see **bath**.

Investors, like savvy team owners, would be wise to weigh a variety of factors before sending a manager to the showers.

He declined to state which magic words Clemens uttered to earn his premature trip to the showers.

shrift

short shrift ◄◄◄

If someone or something gets **short shrift** or is given **short shrift**, they are treated very rudely or very little attention is paid to them.

Southerners are justifiably angry at the way their interests get short shrift.

Unions complain that this amounts to a transfer to employees of costs that employers used to bear. Such complaints are getting short shrift.

I worked as a waitress when I was a drama student and I gave short shrift to customers who got on my nerves.

shuffle

lost in the shuffle ◄

If you say that someone or something gets **lost in the shuffle**, you mean that nobody notices them or pays them any attention. This expression is used mainly in American English.

No one is lost in the shuffle. The staff is well trained in courteous and attentive service to each and every guest.

He worries campaign finance reform will get lost in the shuffle of White House priorities.

sick

sick as a dog

If you say that you are as **sick as a dog**, you are emphasizing that you feel very ill or upset.

A teacher says she was sick as a dog for three weeks last year after eating some imported soft cheese.

The superintendent had looked as sick as a dog when told of Jacobs's guilt.

sick as a parrot ◄

If you say that you are as **sick as a parrot**, you mean that you are very annoyed or disappointed about something. This expression is used in British English.

Sportsnight presenter Des Lynam will be as sick as a parrot if his new TV show fails to score with viewers.

sick as a pig

If you say that you are as **sick as a pig**, you mean that you are very annoyed and upset about something. This expression is used in British English.

I've had Les in my office and he's been disciplined the maximum. He's as sick as a pig.

side

let the side down ◄

If you accuse someone of **letting the side down**, you are criticizing them for disappointing people by doing something badly or by doing something which people do not approve of. This expression is used in British English.

The workers are the best in the world – it is the managements who let the side down.

She accused Andrew of letting the side down. 'I think it's very unfair that he's published this book,' she said.

look on the bright side ◄◄

If you try to **look on the bright side**, you try to be cheerful about a bad situation by concentrating on the few good things in it or by thinking about how it could have been even worse.

I tried to look on the bright side, to be grateful that I was healthy. I hid my feelings completely and didn't talk to other people at all about what was going on.

To repair the damage, the President should start by looking on the bright side. He still has a full year to recover before he faces the voters.

□ You can talk about **the bright side** of a bad situation.

If there is a bright side for the Prime Minister, however, it is that the elections were a judgment on the whole party, not just him.

In the overall scheme of things, the crisis in the European monetary system is not good news; but there is a bright side to the story, at least for one group of people: American tourists. They're getting more for their dollar right now.

on your side ◄

If you say that something is **on** your **side**, you mean that it gives you an advantage and helps you to achieve something.

Having time and money on your side helps, of course, but even if you have neither, it pays to know about all the options.

I have been very lucky this year. Luck seems to be on my side.

sunny side up

If you describe things or people as **sunny side up**, you mean that they are bright and cheerful. This expression is used mainly in British journalism.

Braden's consumer shows were fresh and friendly and sunny side up.

This book should keep you and your family feeling sunny-side-up throughout your vacation.

☐ In American English, if you ask for a fried egg to be cooked **sunny side up**, you want it to be cooked on one side only and not turned over in the pan.

to be on the safe side ◄◄

If you do something **to be on the safe side**, you do it as a precaution, although it is unlikely to be necessary.

When Alice went down with gastro-enteritis, she was admitted to hospital just to be on the safe side.

A solar panel for a typical house measures four square metres. You probably won't need to apply for planning permission, but to be on the safe side check with your local planning department.

sieve

a brain like a sieve

If you say that you have **a brain like a sieve**, you mean that you have a bad memory and often forget things. Nouns such as 'head' and 'mind' can be used instead of 'brain'.

He lost the key to his Ferrari but admitted that his brain was like a sieve.

My mind's like a sieve.

sight

at first sight ◄◄◄

You can say **at first sight** when you are describing your first impression of someone or something. You usually use this expression to indicate that this first impression was wrong or incomplete. **At first glance** means the same.

Edna O'Brien established her reputation with a series of novels in which Irish heroines battled against parental opposition, social convention and the Roman Catholic Church to achieve a measure of happiness or at least self-respect at the end of it. Her latest novel seems at first sight to be a reworking of similar themes.

His pictures can appear, at first sight, impenetrably obscure.

Nothing is ever quite as good or quite as bad as it looks at first sight.

lose sight of something ◄◄◄

If you do not **lose sight of** an important aspect of something, you do not forget it or ignore it, even though you have other things to think about.

The agreements we've reached cannot cause us to lose sight of some of the differences that remain.

We should not lose sight of the fact that, at times, depression is a perfectly normal reaction to marital problems, bereavement or job loss, for example.

As so often happened, Peter, Tommy and Henry had totally lost sight of their real objective.

out of sight, out of mind ◄

If you say **'out of sight, out of mind'**, you mean that it is easy to forget about someone or something, or to stop caring about them, when you have not seen them for a long time.

Because people think of Indians as being out of sight and out of mind, they feel that they can degrade and dehumanize our culture however they please.

After the drought is over, the systems are going to be out of sight, out of mind, They definitely will not be maintained after that, and yet there will be no mechanism for making sure they're removed.

☐ People often vary this expression.

You may miss out on promotion prospects too – out of sight may well mean out of mind.

In the years he spent imprisoned on Robben Island, Mandela was out of sight, but much in mind.

a sight for sore eyes

If you say that something is **a sight for sore eyes**, you mean that it gives you a lot of pleasure to look at it.

The sunset over the Strait of Malacca is a sight for sore eyes.

'We think the new headquarters is a sight for sore eyes,' he said. Others think the three-storey building is more of an eye sore.

☐ People sometimes say **'you're a sight for sore eyes'** when they are greeting someone who they have not seen for a long time.

Jack. You're a sight for sore eyes. It's been too long. Far too long.

sights

have something in your sights ◄◄◄

If you have something in your **sights**, you are aiming or trying hard to achieve it, and you have a good chance of success. If you have someone in your **sights**, you are determined to catch, defeat, or overcome them. You can use other verbs instead of 'have'.

Usually, at this stage of the season, Liverpool are lying first or second in the table and have the Championship firmly in their sights.

I am studying at university, with good job prospects firmly in my sights.

As Lehmann began to crumble, it was clear Boardman might catch him and, with just a couple of laps left, Boardman had him right in his sights.

Virgin Airlines earns just over half its revenues from the business travellers it has kept in its sights since it started in 1984.

☐ These expressions are often used more literally to say that someone is looking at a target through the sights of a gun.

set your sights on something
have your sights on something ◄◄◄

If you **set** your **sights on** something, you decide that you want it and try very hard to get it. Other verbs can be used instead of 'set'.

These days not all Russian girls are setting their sights on marriage to the boy next door.

Although she came from a family of bankers, Franklin set her sights on a career in scientific research.

Gareth Jenkins and his assistant, Alan Lewis, have clearly set their sights on winning the championship.

She could now fix her sights on continuing at school for another three years.

☐ If someone has made up their mind to try to get something, you can say that they **have** their **sights on** it.

Brand and Torrance now have their sights on the £111,000 first prize in the first qualifying event for next September's Ryder Cup.

And, proving she's just a kid at heart, she already had her sights on her next goal – hero Linford Christie's autograph.

☐ You can say that someone **sets** their **sights high** when they are trying to get something that is hard to achieve. If you say that someone **sets** their **sights low**, you mean that they are unambitious and do not achieve as much as they could.

Women tend to end up in low-status jobs with low pay. Often we only have ourselves to blame. We just do not set our sights high enough.

Don't go expecting Dannii to become a regular TV presenter. She has set her sights on higher things.

A joint study has criticized American car makers for setting their sights too low and with being content to build automobiles which are merely adequate.

signed

signed and sealed
signed, sealed, and delivered ◄◄

If you say that an agreement is **signed and sealed**, you mean that it is official and cannot be changed. You can also say that it is **signed, sealed, and delivered**.

Although a peace agreement has been signed and sealed, many of these villagers say they're afraid to return to their homes.

Well, it's all done, signed and sealed, and there's nothing you can do or say about it.

A government spokesman said the bill must be signed, sealed and delivered by tomorrow.

silk

you can't make a silk purse out of a sow's ear ◄

If you say that you **can't make a silk purse out of a sow's ear**, you mean that it is impossible to make something really successful or of high quality out of something which is unsuccessful or of poor quality.

'Some individuals say they want to become gorgeous, but to become gorgeous you really need a few basics,' she said. We presume she means you can't make a silk purse out of a sow's ear.

☐ People often vary this expression.

It takes more than a good swimming pool and an indoor tennis court or two to make a sow's ear of a resort into a silk purse.

Afterwards, Kendall made no attempt to describe this sow's ear as a silk purse.

silver

born with a silver spoon in your mouth ◄

If you say that someone **was born with a silver spoon in** their **mouth**, you mean that their family was very rich and they had a privileged upbringing. You usually use this expression to show resentment or disapproval.

People like Samantha and Timothy had been born with a silver spoon in their mouth; they hadn't a worry in the world, and there was always someone to pay their bills if their own inheritance was not sufficient.

☐ People sometimes vary this expression, for example by replacing 'silver' or 'mouth' with other words.

Henry Adams was born with a complete set of sterling silver in his mouth.

☐ You can use **silver-spoon** before a noun to describe a person like this or their lifestyle.

He reckons that, mentally at least, he dropped out of his silver-spoon existence at the age of about three.

a silver lining
every cloud has a silver lining ◄◄◄

If you say that a bad or unpleasant situation has **a silver lining**, you mean that there is a good or pleasant side-effect of it.

Richard Darman had trouble finding a silver lining in the report.

The fall in inflation is the silver lining of the prolonged recession.

☐ When you are using **a silver lining** in this way, you often refer to the bad or unpleasant situation as **the cloud**.

Even Kenneth Clarke, usually a man to find a silver lining in the blackest cloud, admitted that the government was in 'a dreadful hole'.

There's a bit of a silver lining in every cloud. I certainly can't say I'm sorry they abandoned the idea.

☐ These expressions come from the proverb **every cloud has a silver lining**, which is used to say that every bad or unpleasant situation has some benefits or pleasant side-effects.

As they say, every cloud has a silver lining. We have drawn lessons from the decisions taken.

☐ If you say that **every silver lining has a cloud**, you mean that every good or pleasant situation has an aspect which is bad or unpleasant.

We got on brilliantly; he was clever, sexy, funny – and leaving for New York on Tuesday. Every silver lining has a cloud, it seems.

sing

sing a different tune: 1
sing the same tune
sing the same song ◄

If you say that someone **is singing a different tune**, you mean that they are expressing ideas or opinions which are in complete contrast to the ones which they were expressing a short time ago. If you say that someone **is singing the same tune**, you mean that they are continuing to express the same ideas or opinions that they have expressed before. You can replace 'tune' with 'song' in these expressions.

Then he said: 'As employees of the county clubs, their first and only loyalty should be to English cricket.' Yesterday he was singing a different tune, hoping 'there is no acrimony from players who disagree with the decision'.

The president basically sent the signal that he's going to keep singing the same tune he's been singing.

sing a different tune: 2
sing the same tune
sing the same song ◄

If you say that a group of people **are singing the same tune**, you mean that they are all expressing the same opinions about something. You can also say that one person **is singing the same tune** as the others. If people **are singing a different tune**, they are expressing different opinions about something. You can replace 'tune' with 'song' in these expressions.

It doesn't help when politicians argue in public and so confuse our case. We should all be singing the same tune.

The burden of homelessness in Tower Hamlets is great enough without two Government departments singing different songs.

☐ You can also replace 'sing' with other verbs such as 'play'.

If Thailand is to join the other nations, it must play the same tunes.

If the vision is totally shared, the leader has done his job. He has succeeded in getting everyone to whistle the same tune.

sing from the same hymn sheet
sing from the same song sheet

In British English, if you say that two or more people **are singing from the same hymn sheet** or **are singing from the same song sheet**, you mean that they agree about something, and are saying the same things in public about it. You can replace 'sing' with 'read', and 'sheet' with 'book'.

The main theme is to bring together the departments so that we're all singing from the same hymn sheet.

As she and her husband face the latest controversy, they can be relied upon to sing from the same song-sheet.

sink

sink or swim ◄

If you say that someone will have to **sink or swim**, you mean that they are being left to do something on their own, and whether they succeed or not will depend entirely on their own efforts or abilities.

By some estimates, 70-80 per cent of the country's enterprises are technically bankrupt. Many will certainly fail once they are transferred to private ownership and forced to sink or swim on their own.

☐ You can use **sink-or-swim** before a noun.

Some institutions we visited deliberately follow a sink-or-swim approach. Others try hard to acclimatize students early to campus life.

sitting

at one sitting
in one sitting
at a single sitting   ◄◄

If you do something **at one sitting** or **in one sitting**, you do not stop doing it until you have finished it. You can also say that you do it **at a single sitting**.

The book does not have to be read at one sitting, but is broken conveniently into self-contained chapters.

Be as complete as possible, but go slowly. Don't expect to fill out these lists in one sitting.

She loved to go through a box of cookies at a single sitting.

six

knock someone for six
hit someone for six   ◄◄

If something **knocks** you **for six** or **hits** you **for six**, it gives you a surprise or shock which you have difficulty recovering from. These expressions are used mainly in British English.

Many people are very positive and see redundancy as a chance to start a new career, but the emotional impact of being made redundant can knock others for six.

We just cannot afford a wage rise as high as inflation. Double figures would just about hit us for six.

□ People occasionally use this expression to say that they are very impressed by someone or something.

One day Gary walked in with his sister. 'I was absolutely knocked for six. She's lovely, very caring, very supportive,' says Peter.

six of one and half a dozen of the other

If you describe two people, situations, or possible courses of action as **six of one and half a dozen of the other**, you mean that both are equally bad or equally good.

To me it was six of one and half a dozen of the other. They were both at fault.

Faced with a decision of six of one, half a dozen of the other, he put faith in his bowlers and was totally justified.

sixes

at sixes and sevens   ◄

If something or someone is **at sixes and sevens**, they are disorganized and confused. This expression is used mainly in British English.

They are at sixes and sevens over their tax and spending plans.

Of course everything in the place is at sixes and sevens. None of us know what we should be doing.

size

cut someone down to size   ◄◄

If you **cut** someone **down to size** when they are behaving arrogantly, you do or say something which shows that they are less important or impressive than they think they are.

It is time the big bosses were cut down to size. They are the ones to blame for much of the country's economic misery.

It may be that people are drawn to journalism because of the chance to cut everyone else down to size.

try something on for size
try something for size
try something out for size   ◄

If you **try** something **on for size**, you consider it carefully or try using it in order to decide whether you think it is any good or whether you believe it. You can also say that you **try** something **for size** or that you **try** it **out for size**.

We are able to a limited extent to try models on for size to see which may be compatible with us, but it is important to give time to the experiment.

'Jarvis killed Mr Rownall?' he said slowly, trying the idea for size and seeming to find it mildly attractive.

He makes conversation, trying you out for size. 'What do you think of the album?' he says.

skates

get your skates on

If someone tells you to **get** your **skates on**, they are telling you to hurry up. This expression is used mainly in British English.

You'll need to get your skates on before this unusually attractive offer ends a week tomorrow.

Bargain hunters had better get their skates on – the best properties are selling fast.

skeleton

a skeleton in the closet
a skeleton in the cupboard   ◄◄

If you say that someone has **a skeleton in the closet**, you mean that they are keeping secret something which would be scandalous or embarrassing for them if other people knew about it. In British English, you can also say that they have **a skeleton in the cupboard**.

But everybody's got vices, haven't they? There's always a skeleton in the closet somewhere.

Show me somebody with no skeletons in their cupboard, and I'll show you a skilful liar.

So far, little has been said to shift the presumption that if Mr Gates had any skeletons in his cupboard he would not have sought the nomination.

skid

skid row

You say that someone is on **skid row** when they have lost everything in their life, for example because they have become alcoholic or gone bankrupt.

The first pint of bitter at the village pub gives no indication that the drinker may have taken his first steps on the way to Skid Row.

Business is very tough right now, so if it wasn't for all my trinkets and paintings I would be on skid row.

□ **Skid row** is used, especially in American English, to refer a poor part of a city where many drunks and homeless people live.

skids

on the skids   ◄◄

If you say that something is **on the skids**, you mean that it is doing badly and is very likely to fail.

My marriage was on the skids.

It took Donny some time to realise his career was on the skids.

Buchanan was a Federalist at the time when the Federal Party was on the skids and about to vanish forever.

put the skids under something   ◄

If you **put the skids under** something or someone, you cause them to do badly or fail. This expression is used in British English.

Profits almost halved in the six months to end-August, from £16.7 million to £9.7 million, putting the skids under the share price, which dropped 21p to 88p.

Two new witnesses in the murder case have put the skids under his alibi.

skin

by the skin of your teeth   ◄◄

If you do something **by the skin of** your **teeth**, you just manage to do it but very nearly fail.

In the men's First Division, the champions, Cadbury's Kingston, survived by the skin of their teeth.

Premier John Major breathed a sigh of relief last night as he avoided a disastrous rise in interest rates by the skin of his teeth.

get under your skin: 1   ◄

If something **gets under** your **skin**, it annoys or worries you.

The continuing criticism, which is getting harsher, is getting under his skin a little bit.

Mothers should try not to be too irritated at the sudden demands made on them by

schoolchildren. 'Where's my football shorts?' for example, when they hadn't realized they'd be needed. Try not to let that kind of thing get under your skin.

get under your skin: 2

If someone or something **gets under** your **skin**, they begin to affect you in a significant way, so that you become very interested in them or very fond of them.

After a slow start, his play gets under your skin because of its affection for its characters and sympathy with the frustrations of small town life.

While you're here, take your shoes off. Feel the islands. Let the Galapagos get under your skin. You'll never forget them.

get under someone's skin: 3

If you try to **get under the skin of** someone, you try to find out how they feel and think, so that you are able to understand them better.

You are probably aware by now that it is only through getting right under the skin of your colleagues and loved ones that you will be able to relate to them as equals.

Geoffrey Beattie's book is presented as 'an attempt to get under the skin of the Protestant people of Ulster'.

it's no skin off my nose

If someone says '**it's no skin off my nose**' when something bad happens, they mean that they are not worried about it, because it only affects or harms other people, or because it is not their responsibility. This is an informal expression, which is used mainly in spoken British English.

When I heard she'd got the sack, I thought, no skin off my nose, she's not what you'd call a mate, and losing a lousy job like that's no big deal, is it? You've got to watch out for yourself these days, haven't you?

Let them publish it. It's no skin off my nose, if it turns out to be wrong. They wrote it, not me.

jump out of your skin   ◄

If you say that something made you **jump out of** your **skin**, you mean that it gave you a sudden unpleasant shock or surprise.

He nearly jumped out of his skin when he saw two rats in the wreckage of what a few years before had been a kitchen.

I'd never seen such large guns and everyone is armed. The first time I heard shots I jumped out of my skin, but now I hardly notice the continuous gunfire.

make your skin crawl

If you say that something **makes** your **skin crawl**, you mean that you find it unpleasant and it makes you frightened, distressed, or

uncomfortable. **Make** your **flesh creep** means
the same.

*He gave an amused snort that made my skin
crawl.*

*I hated this man, his very touch made my
skin crawl.*

save your skin
save your own skin   ◄◄

If someone tries to **save** their **skin** or **save**
their **own skin**, they try to save themselves
from something dangerous or unpleasant, often without caring what happens to anyone
else.

*He appeared to be condemning the entire
movement. Maybe this was because he was trying to save his skin.*

*It's an announcement that's got a lot more to
do with the government trying to save its own
skin than trying to help the victims.*

skin and bone
skin and bones   ◄◄

If you describe someone as **skin and bone**
or **skin and bones**, you mean that they are
very thin, because they have not had enough
to eat for a long time, or because they are suffering from a serious illness.

*A man like me can't live on beans – I'll soon
be skin and bone.*

*Many villages are deserted. In one we found
nomads looking for water. They were skin and
bones. They had no food.*

a thick skin   ◄◄

If you say that someone has **a thick skin**,
you mean that they are not easily hurt or
upset by criticism. Compare **a thin skin**.

*A woman who survives in politics needs a
thick skin.*

*Energy, self-confidence, an ability to get along
with people, and a thick skin to handle rejection, these are the primary ingredients in a
good salesperson.*

☐ You can also describe someone as being
thick-skinned.

*She worked as a nurse in a psychiatric emer-
gency clinic in South London, a job that made
her thick-skinned and able to handle abuse.*

a thin skin   ◄◄

If you say that someone has **a thin skin**,
you mean that they are very easily hurt or
upset by criticism. Compare **a thick skin**.

*Evidence of such a thin skin and lack of te-
nacity means that he is certainly not cut out to
be a journalist.*

☐ You can also describe someone as being
thin-skinned.

*At each level the judging gets more critical,
and if you're thin-skinned, it's better to start
slowly and build up your confidence.*

sky

blow something sky-high

If you **blow** someone's hopes or beliefs **sky-
high**, you do or say something which completely destroys them.

*They knew nothing about me, apart from
what I encouraged them to think. She could
have blown all that sky-high.*

out of a clear blue sky

If you describe something as happening **out
of a clear blue sky**, you mean that it happens completely unexpectedly. People sometimes omit 'clear' or 'blue'.

*It certainly cannot be bad news when, out of
a clear blue sky and after 34 months of successive increases, unemployment drops by 22,000.*

*The announcement that Mikhail Gorbachev
was 'ill' and that his duties had been taken
over by his vice-president came out of a blue
sky.*

the sky's the limit   ◄◄

You can say **'the sky's the limit'** when you
are talking about the possibility of someone
or something being very successful.

*'How much are you hoping to make for this
charity of yours?' 'Well loads hopefully. I mean
the sky's the limit.'*

*Asked how far Agassi could go, McEnroe said
simply: 'The sky's the limit.'*

slack

cut someone some slack

If you **cut** someone **some slack**, you make
things slightly easier for them than you normally would, because of their special circumstances or situation.

*When you're new at a job, colleagues and
bosses cut you a little slack. They forgive minor
mistakes because you're new.*

*But for me it was hate at first sight, this in-
truder in our midst. I was determined not to
cut him any slack.*

take up the slack
pick up the slack   ◄◄

If someone **takes up the slack** in an industry, economy, or organization, they start making full use of all its resources or potential.
You can also say that they **pick up the slack**.

*The export market has not taken up the
slack, so redundancies are coming thick and
fast.*

*Small investors still haven't returned in full
force, but the institutions are taking up much
of the slack.*

*That has prompted some steel marketers to
look elsewhere, including home and office furniture markets, to pick up the slack.*

slap

a slap in the face ◀◀

You can describe someone's behaviour as **a slap in the face** when they upset you by insulting you or appearing to reject you.

David Hart, the general secretary of the National Association of Head Teachers, described the report as a 'slap in the face' for pupils who had just received their results.

Mr Nakajima was the first Japanese to win a high UN office; if he were not re-elected, it would be a slap in the face.

a slap on the wrist ◀

You can refer to a very light punishment or reprimand as **a slap on the wrist**.

Most people say they gave her a suspension that's not really a suspension and the fine they gave her is just a slap on the wrist.

But other than a few slaps on the wrist, the General went unpunished.

slate

on the slate

If you buy something **on the slate**, you buy it on credit and will need to pay for it later. This expression is used in British English.

He'd call at the pub coming back from work and it was all put on the slate until Friday night.

wipe the slate clean: 1
a clean slate ◀◀

If you **wipe the slate clean**, you get rid of an existing system so that you can replace it with a new one. You can then say that you are beginning with **a clean slate**.

He wanted to wipe the slate clean of anything that had gone before. He wanted his new Council to make up its own mind about everything.

There's an equally strong desire to wipe the slate clean and call for early presidential and legislative elections.

The new chief executive has clearly decided to start with a clean slate as he embarks on one of the toughest jobs in British retailing.

wipe the slate clean: 2
a clean slate ◀

If you **wipe the slate clean**, you earn enough money to pay off your debts, so that you no longer owe money to anyone.

When his 1988 campaign ended he owed $4 million; after 12 weeks of hard work he was able to wipe the slate clean.

Over a decade he wiped the firm's slate clean of debt and brought it up to record earnings.

□ You can also say that someone **wipes the slate clean** when they agree to ignore money that you owe to them, so that you no longer owe them anything.

The ideal solution would be to wipe the slate

clean. To do this, the government would have to write off all the existing loans made by state-owned banks to state-owned enterprises.

□ When you begin something without owing any money, you can say that you are beginning with **a clean slate**.

The proposal is to pay everything you owe, so that you can start with a clean slate.

wipe the slate clean: 3 ◀

If you **wipe the slate clean**, you are punished for something wrong that you have done, or you make amends for it by your good behaviour, so that you can start your life again without feeling guilty about it.

Serving a prison sentence makes them believe they have 'wiped the slate clean', but the anger and hurt felt by those close to them remains long after their release.

sleep

not lose any sleep over something ◀◀

If you say that you **won't lose any sleep over** something, you mean that you will not worry about it at all.

I'd like to have a little more money – who wouldn't – but I won't lose any sleep over it.

People like to think that Peter is worried about not winning the race but I don't think he loses a lot of sleep over it.

sleeve

have something up your sleeve
have an ace up your sleeve
have a card up your sleeve ◀◀◀

If someone **has** something **up** their **sleeve**, they have a secret idea or plan which they can use to gain an advantage over other people.

The centre-forward insisted his team will use every trick up their sleeve to counter the physical threat posed by the Irish.

He's nothing if not a tough campaigner, and he has one final option up his sleeve.

The bank's strategy for improvement is simple, according to Mr Pearse: 'We've got nothing fancy up our sleeves. We just have to be better.'

□ The expressions **have an ace up** your **sleeve** and **have a card up** your **sleeve** mean the same.

The commission has another ace up its sleeve – it says tourist jobs will be created and estimates that the local economy will benefit to the tune of £2 million a year.

Even those who regard him as ruthless and brutal admit, however, that he seems always to have a card up his sleeve.

laugh up your sleeve

If you say that someone **is laughing up** their **sleeve**, you mean that they are secretly amused by something, for example because someone else has done something badly or because they know something that nobody else knows. This expression is usually used to show disapproval.

He wondered just how smugly she was laughing up her sleeve at his ineptitude.

He never left England. He's holed up somewhere in the countryside, laughing up his bloody sleeve.

sleeves

roll up your sleeves ◄

If you **roll up** your **sleeves**, you get ready to work hard, often as part of a group of people.

He was very much a team player, rolling up his sleeves and getting down to work.

Economic miracles are man-made. Let's roll up our sleeves and make unity work.

We will roll our sleeves up and get on with the job because we know what is expected of us.

sling

your ass in a sling

If someone has their **ass in a sling**, they are in a very difficult situation. Other words meaning 'bottom' are sometimes used instead of 'ass'. This is a very informal expression, which is used mainly in American English. Many people find it offensive.

His ass is in a sling. He's not afraid of us but he's afraid of the mud that's getting stirred up.

slings

slings and arrows ◄

If you talk about the **slings and arrows** of something, you are referring to the unpleasant things that it causes to happen to you and that are not your fault. This expression is used mainly in written English.

She had a significant personality disorder which reduced her ability to cope with the slings and arrows of life.

He received lectures on handling the press from his wife, who had suffered her own share of slings and arrows in the quest for publicity.

□ This expression comes from the line 'the slings and arrows of outrageous fortune', in Shakespeare's play 'Hamlet'. People sometimes use this line in full.

It may be difficult to forget the slings and arrows of outrageous fortune which the early Nineties fired at you, but now you really must resolve to let the past go.

slip

a slip of the tongue
a slip of the pen ◄

If you refer to something you said as **a slip**

of the tongue, you mean that you said it by mistake.

'Did you say Frank Sinatra?' 'Oh, did I? I'm sorry. That was a slip of the tongue. I don't know what got into me.'

At one stage he referred to her as James's fiancée but later said that was a slip of the tongue and said he did not believe they were formally engaged.

□ If you refer to something you wrote as **a slip of the pen**, you mean that you wrote it by mistake.

A slip of the editorial pen moved the celebrations forward 10 days. Please arrive on 29 August, not 19 August.

there is many a slip twixt cup and lip

If people say **'there is many a slip twixt cup and lip'**, they are warning that a plan may easily go wrong before it is completed, and they cannot be sure of what will happen. This is a literary expression.

Most Italians had thought it a foregone conclusion. But Mario Segni, the rebel Christian Democrat who first championed the referendum, fears the possibility of a slip twixt cup and lip.

□ People sometimes just say **'there's many a slip'**, or vary the second half of the expression.

He knows, too, after the much postponed title fight against Tyson, that there's many a slip between signing a contract and pulling on the gloves.

□ 'Twixt' is an old-fashioned word meaning 'between'.

slippery

slippery as an eel

If you say that someone is as **slippery as an eel**, you mean that it is very difficult to catch them or to get the information that you want from them.

The boy raided 36 homes. The judge said 'the invasion of homes by a boy as slippery as an eel' was a horrifying experience.

□ You can also describe someone as **a slippery eel**.

He himself concedes that he is regarded as a slippery eel – a man who constantly changes his mind.

slope

a slippery slope ◄◄◄

If someone is on **a slippery slope**, they are involved in a course of action that cannot be stopped and that will lead to failure or serious trouble.

They're opposed to all such government mandates. They see family leave as the first step down a slippery slope.

The new centre aims to help ex-offenders back into the community and guide young people who may already be on the slippery slope to criminality towards a better life.

The company started down the slippery slope of believing that they knew better than the customer, with the inevitable disastrous results.

small

make someone feel small
make someone look small   ◄

If you say that someone **makes** you **feel small** or **makes** you **look small**, you mean that they deliberately say or do something which makes you look or feel stupid, especially in front of other people.

He made me feel small, like an idiot.

When your children misbehave, tell them without making them feel small.

I could see he was going to do whatever he could to make me look small.

smoke

blow smoke
blow smoke in someone's face
blow smoke in someone's eyes   ◄

If you accuse someone of **blowing smoke** or of **blowing smoke in** your **face** or **eyes**, you are accusing them of deliberately confusing you or misleading you in order to deceive you. These expressions are used mainly in American English.

I just can't shake the feeling that he's up to something. Sounds to me like he's blowing smoke.

Everyone knew Philip Morris was growing faster than RJR. But now we know they've been growing faster than faster. RJR has been blowing smoke in our faces.

blow smoke up someone's ass

If someone praises you and you say they **are blowing smoke up** your **ass**, you mean that they are being insincere and just trying to please you. This is a very informal expression, which is used mainly in American English. Many people consider it offensive.

She would never blow smoke up my ass. Everybody tells you you're great, you're fabulous, when you're famous, but she'd always ask me, 'Hey, did you wash your underwear today?'

go up in smoke   ◄◄

If something that is important to you **goes up in smoke**, it fails or ends without anything being achieved.

For the president there is more at stake in the racial violence erupting all over America than burning streets – his whole political future could go up in smoke.

But with just eight minutes to go, their dreams of glory went up in smoke. Liverpool

scored twice within minutes and went three-two ahead.

smoke and mirrors   ◄

If you say that something is full of **smoke and mirrors**, you mean that it is full of things which are intended to deceive or confuse people. This expression is used mainly in American English.

The president and his aides claim that their economic plan is free of the gimmicks and smoke and mirrors that have characterized previous presidential budget proposals.

The so-called $28 billion aid package isn't really all aid – it's some smoke and mirrors and some items like postponement of debt repayment, which is not new money.

smoke signals   ◄

If someone sends out **smoke signals**, they give an indication of their views or intentions, often in an unclear or vague form which then needs to be interpreted.

I'll tell you exactly what I think we ought to do, but what kind of smoke signals ought to be sent by the White House is up to them to figure out.

Recent economic smoke-signals suggest that the economy began to pick up in May.

there's no smoke without fire
where there's smoke there's fire   ◄

If you say 'there's no smoke without fire' or 'where there's smoke there's fire' when you are referring to an unpleasant rumour or unlikely story, you mean that it is likely to be at least partly true, as otherwise nobody would be talking about it.

But what did upset me was the fact that it cast a slur on my character. The story was the main item on the news and people were bound to think there was no smoke without fire.

People were hardly likely to believe Rhonda's allegations. Still, the 'where there's smoke there's fire' adage held as true now as it ever had.

smooth

smooth the way
smooth the path   ◄◄◄

If someone or something **smooths the way** or **smooths the path** for something, they make it easier for it to happen or more likely to happen.

For several weeks now, the president has been trying to smooth the way for this package of spending cuts and tax increases.

The President said that if the talks took place without preconditions they could smooth the way to peace.

The current campaign against crime would play an important role in restoring social order and in smoothing the path of reform.

snail

at a snail's pace ◄◄

If you say that something is moving or developing **at a snail's pace** or **at snail's pace**, you mean that it is moving or developing very slowly. You usually use this expression when you think that it would be better if it went more quickly.

The vote counting continues at a snail's pace but our Latin America correspondent says clear trends are emerging.

The economy grew at a snail's pace in the first three months of this year.

She was driving at snail's pace, looking in every house.

☐ You can also use **snail's pace** before a noun.

Observers hope that the meeting will speed up two years of snail's-pace talks, marked by repeated breakdowns and little advance on issues of substance.

snake

a snake in the grass

If you describe someone as **a snake in the grass**, you are expressing strong dislike and disapproval of them because they pretend to be your friend while actually being an enemy and betraying you.

Sofia Petrovna would tell Kolya everything about that snake in the grass, the accountant's wife.

snake oil

a snake oil salesman ◄

You use **snake oil** to refer to something which someone is trying to sell you or make you believe in when you think that it is false and not to be trusted. This expression is used mainly in American English.

He's ready to be president. And he's a good salesman, even if he's selling snake oil.

It's a fine machine, but I've noticed that most of the similar devices already on the market give off a whiff of snake oil. There's nothing worse than having your product tainted by the hint of fraud.

☐ **A snake-oil salesman** is someone who tries to sell you something or make you believe in something like this.

This is the national headquarters for slick-talking snake-oil salesmen who use the telephone to extract money from the gullible and the greedy and then vanish.

snook

cock a snook at someone ◄

If you **cock a snook at** someone, you show your contempt or lack of respect for them by deliberately insulting or offending them. This is a fairly old-fashioned expression.

They drove around in Rolls-Royces, openly flaunting their wealth and cocking a snook at the forces of law and order.

The Danes cocked a snook in the vote at their own political establishment.

Terry Wogan is determined to cock a snook at the critics and go out on a high note.

snow

a snow job

You refer to what someone has said as **a snow job** to express your disapproval of the fact that it is full of lies and exaggerations, and was intended to deceive or flatter you. This expression is used mainly in American English.

They have the experience to know the difference between getting information and getting a snow job. You can lie to a member of Congress once, and that's it.

When he called me in London, he threw around a lot of names. A snow job. None of which checked out later, by the way.

snuff

up to snuff

If you say that something or someone is not **up to snuff**, you mean that they are not as good as they should be or as they normally are. This expression is considered old-fashioned in British English.

If the project goes ahead, Russia will spend ten years and at least $1 billion on technology and training to bring its banks and bankers up to snuff.

The hamburgers didn't come up to snuff.

snug

snug as a bug in a rug

If you say that someone is as **snug as a bug in a rug**, you are saying light-heartedly that they are in a very comfortable situation. This expression is considered old-fashioned in British English.

Jamieson went to the galley, ordered coffee for himself and his men and sat beside McKinnon. 'Ideal working conditions, you said. Snug as a bug in a rug, one might say.'

soap

no soap

You can say **'no soap'** to mean that you have tried to do something but have failed. This expression is used in American English.

I went out and wandered around the halls looking for him. Then finally I went home. I called him at home this morning. No soap.

sober

sober as a judge

If you say that someone is as **sober as a judge**, you are emphasizing that they are not drunk. This is an old-fashioned expression, which is used in British English.

After all, he was as sober as the proverbial judge. And when Tom was sober, they just couldn't find anything wrong with him.

sock

put a sock in it

If you tell someone to **put a sock in it**, you are rudely telling them to stop talking. This is an old-fashioned expression, which is used in British English.

'Can he not speak for himself?' 'He can,' Dermot said. 'Put a sock in it, all of you.'

socks

knock your socks off
knock the socks off someone ◄

If you say that something or someone **knocks** your **socks off**, you are saying in a light-hearted way that they are very good and that you are very impressed by them. If they **knock the socks off** other people or things, they are much better than the others. You can replace 'knock' with other verbs such as 'blow' or 'beat'.

I had heard he had some wonderful plans that he was going to bring forward. Someone told me that the economic plan would knock your socks off.

As a dancer he knocked the socks off everybody.

When his IQ was measured, he had beaten the socks off all the other kids in the compound.

pull your socks up

If someone tells you to **pull** your **socks up**, they want you to try hard to improve your behaviour or work. This expression is used in British English.

No matter how bad you think your problem is, they've probably heard worse – and more trivial, too. Nobody's going to say, 'Pull your socks up.'

In a way what happened last season gave us a necessary jolt. Maybe we needed to pull our socks up and we are trying to do just that.

work your socks off

If you **work** your **socks off**, you work as hard and as well as you can. You can use this expression with many other verbs, especially verbs related to performing such as 'dance', 'act', and 'play'.

I can see that the lecturers have really tried their hardest. They've worked their socks off to

produce something that's vivid and dynamic and vital.

'We're going to dance our socks off tonight,' said Chris de Burgh at the start of his show last Friday.

England will go into their World Cup qualifier against Holland tomorrow without Waddle, one of our most gifted footballers and currently playing his socks off for Sheffield Wednesday.

soft

soft as shit

If you accuse someone or something of being **soft as shit**, you are criticizing them for being very weak or sentimental. This is a very informal expression, which is used in British English. Many people consider it offensive.

When we came out we went up Strelley Woods, and everything started again. I'm as soft as shit where women are concerned.

When I heard that this album was inspired by your wedding, I feared it was gonna be soft as shite.

□ 'Shite' is a variation of 'shit' which is used in non-standard British English.

song

for a song ◄◄

If something is going **for a song**, it is being sold for an unexpectedly low price.

One marvellous touch of good fortune was to find a rug at Bennison in London, which was going for a song as it had been cut.

I know of good, solid, stone-built houses which have been sold by councils for a song.

Brandt was later to experiment with an ancient mahogany and brass camera which he picked up for a song in a Covent Garden shop.

make a song and dance about something ◄

If you accuse someone of **making a song and dance about** something, you mean that they are reacting in a very anxious, excited, or angry way to something that is not important. This expression is used mainly in British English.

The other 49 members made a great song and dance about it but they calmed down soon enough.

You'll be relieved to know I'm not going to make a song and dance about it.

□ You can also just talk about **a song and dance**.

You're within your rights to ask for the situation to be rectified. There's no need for a song and dance, but it shows you're prepared to be assertive.

on song ◄◄

If a sports player is **on song**, they are playing very well. This expression is used mainly in British journalism.

When I was on song, I knew opponents couldn't stop me. I felt I could take anyone on.

It only needs one or two players to malfunction and we'll be in trouble. The whole team must be on song.

sore

a sore point
a sore spot   ◄◄

You can say that a subject is **a sore point** with someone or **a sore spot** for them if it makes them feel angry, embarrassed, or upset.

The continuing presence of foreign troops remains a very sore point with these students.

We were approaching a sore spot for him, and we both knew it.

In the survey, the lack of access to sophisticated medical equipment was one of the sore points for Canadian physicians.

□ If you **touch** or **hit** someone's **sore point** or **sore spot**, you mention something which makes them feel angry, embarrassed, or upset.

The mention of Jim Kennerly had touched her sore spot.

His uneasiness increased when I asked about Dr. Guzman. In fact it was clear then, by the stiffening of the old priest's face, that my question hit a sore point.

sorrows

drown your sorrows   ◄

If someone **drowns** their **sorrows**, they drink a lot of alcohol in order to forget something sad or upsetting that has happened to them.

His girlfriend dumped him so he went off to the pub to drown his sorrows.

He could hardly bear to part with her, and drowned his sorrows in whisky on their last night together.

soul

bare your soul   ◄

If you **bare** your **soul** to someone, you tell them all the thoughts and feelings that are most important to you.

We all need someone we can bare our souls to, someone we can confide in.

Open to the point of indiscretion, he continues to bare his soul in public even though his frankness has caused grief.

sell your soul   ◄◄

If someone **sells** their **soul** for something, they do whatever they need to in order to get what they want, even if it involves abandon-

ing their principles or doing something they consider wrong.

As the Co-operative movement approaches its 150th anniversary, Clive Woodcock examines growing fears that it may have sold its soul to commercial pressures.

We have sold our soul to the devil, we do anything for money.

sound

sound as a bell

If you say that something is as **sound as a bell**, you mean that it is in a very good condition or is very reliable.

Timber that is as sound as a bell after 50 years under water or in dry air is quite capable of rotting completely in two years or less at the junction of soil and air.

soup

in the soup   ◄

If you are **in the soup**, you are in trouble.

She has a knack of landing herself right in the soup.

'It's not fair,' he grumbled to himself. 'They bring you back from London and second day on the job they drop you in the soup.'

A recession could put oil markets right back in the soup.

spade

call a spade a spade   ◄

If you **call a spade a spade**, you speak frankly and directly about something, especially if it is controversial or embarrassing, rather than being careful about what you say.

I'm not at all secretive, and I'm pretty good at calling a spade a spade.

The over-use of terms such as 'good judgments' or 'poor judgments' is weakening us. We are losing the capacity – and the courage – to call a spade a spade.

□ Sometimes people vary this expression, either to point out that a description of something is not as clear or as simple as it could be, or to indicate that someone is speaking frankly and directly about a particular issue.

Why call a spade a gardening implement when you can call it a spade?

□ If you want to say that someone is being extremely frank and direct about something, or more frank and direct than you think is necessary, you can say that they **call a spade a shovel**.

Nicola is refreshingly down-to-earth and not afraid to call a spade a bloody shovel if she has to.

spades

in spades ◄◄

If you have something **in spades**, you have a lot of it.

Consciously or not, if you're looking for trouble in love, chances are you'll find it. In spades.

All this effort has paid off in spades.

spanner

throw a spanner in the works
put a spanner in the works ◄◄

If someone or something **throws a spanner in the works**, they cause problems which prevent something from happening in the way that it was planned. This expression is used in British English; the American expression is **throw a wrench** or **a monkey wrench into the works**.

For Britain to throw a spanner in the works could damage the prospects of a treaty being successfully concluded.

The role of the US in throwing a spanner into the diplomatic works is a sore point with Tickell.

☐ This expression is often varied. For example, you can also say that someone or something **puts a spanner in the works**.

They will not want to risk a reversal of this process by putting a spanner in the works at this stage.

Apart from local objections to the planned visitors' centre, another possible spanner in the works is the Government's planned re-routing of the A303, which currently runs 200 yards from the site.

☐ Instead of saying 'in the works', people sometimes mention the process in which the problem is caused.

If you throw a spanner into the treaty negotiations, they will fail.

spark

a bright spark ◄

If you refer to someone as **a bright spark**, you mean that they are intelligent and lively. This expression is used mainly in British English.

It was totally demoralizing because in the third form we'd been real bright sparks.

☐ You usually use this expression ironically to criticize someone for being foolish, or to refer scornfully to someone.

You'd think the bright sparks who come up with these madcap ideas would have learned their lesson.

It never does to make jokes like that nowadays – some bright spark is bound to be listening.

sparks

sparks fly: 1 ◄

If **sparks fly** between two people, they discuss something in an angry or excited way.

From what I have seen of them on their regular magazine show This Morning, they are not afraid to tackle the issues or let the sparks fly when necessary.

France's bank may initially have to take an even harder line on interest rates than Germany's. Wait for the sparks to fly.

sparks fly: 2 ◄

You can say that **sparks fly** when you are describing a situation or relationship that is very exciting.

Whenever two such quality artists meet, you know sparks will fly.

Then, apparently without warning, he leaned over Serena to give her a tender kiss. Sparks were flying, I can tell you.

strike sparks off each other

If people who are trying to achieve something together **strike sparks** off each other, they react to each other in a very exciting or creative way. This expression is used mainly in British English.

It was to be a fertile association, the two men striking the creative sparks from each other that ensured whatever they did was an assault on traditional ideas of architectural propriety.

speed

bring someone up to speed: 1
get up to speed ◄

If you **bring** someone **up to speed**, you give them all the latest information about something. If you **get up to speed**, you make sure that you have all the latest information about something. You can then say that you **are up to speed**.

I guess I should bring you up to speed on what's been happening since I came to see you yesterday.

The president has been getting up to speed on foreign policy.

We have interviews, we have music, and generally keep people informed and entertained and thoroughly up to speed with what's going on in town.

bring something up to speed: 2
get up to speed ◄

If you **bring** something **up to speed** or if it **gets up to speed**, it reaches its highest level of efficiency. 'Come' is sometimes used instead of 'get', and you can also say that something **is up to speed**.

The fear is that the system will not be cheap to bring up to speed.

Grape production will decline steadily for the

next five years. It's not expected to get back up to speed until the year 2002.

Protected industries would have time to come up to speed before being exposed to market forces.

When up to speed in 1990, the plant will employ 3,000 people and create three times that number of jobs for parts suppliers in nearby communities.

spick

spick and span   ◄

If you say that a place or a person is **spick and span**, you mean that they are very clean, neat, and tidy.

When she arrived here this morning she had found Ann dusting the furniture, making sure her home was spick and span.

I busied myself sorting through and arranging the equipment. Our campsite was again spic and span.

☐ You can also use **spick-and-span** before a noun.

Its bright new buildings, where 2,000 people will eventually work, already resemble a spic-and-span Japanese car plant.

☐ 'Spick' is sometimes spelled 'spic'.

spin

in a spin
in a flat spin   ◄

If someone is **in a spin**, they are so angry, confused, or excited that they cannot act sensibly or concentrate on what they are doing. You can also say that they are **in a flat spin**. These expressions are used mainly in British English.

Perot started his morning each day reading the papers. 'It would put the guy in a spin all day long,' said one member of the staff. 'Whenever there was a comment from one of us in the paper, he would call up and say, "This is how you should have said it! This is how you should have done it differently!"'

The flautist's long blonde hair and sexy evening frocks have set the classical music world into a spin.

There's no need to go into a flat spin. It was a perfectly reasonable request to make.

spit

spit and polish   ◄

You can talk about **spit and polish** when you are talking about a place or person being very clean or being made very clean.

The bar, which had been open for two months now, was all spit and polish and good taste.

If you're in need of more than just a bit of

spit and polish, some body scrubs do offer extra help.

spit and sawdust

If you describe a place such as a pub or a bar as a **spit and sawdust** place, you mean that it looks dirty, untidy, and not very respectable. This expression is used in British English.

That night they squeezed into denim and leather to perform with their rock and roll band in the spit and sawdust Waterfront club.

There's the Compasses in the High Street if it's spit and sawdust you're after.

the spitting image
the spit and image
the dead spit   ◄

If you say that one person is **the spitting image** of another, you mean that the first person looks exactly like the second.

He is the spitting image of his father. He is going to be tall, just like his dad.

Now Nina looks the spitting image of Audrey Hepburn in Roman Holiday.

☐ People occasionally use **the spit and image** or **the dead spit** to mean the same thing.

They're crazy about six-month-old baby Caleb, who everybody says is the spit and image of his daddy.

He had a handsome face, the dead spit of Tikhonov, the film actor.

splash

make a splash   ◄◄◄

If someone **makes a splash**, they attract a lot of attention because of something successful that they do or by the way they behave on a particular occasion.

He loves playing there, he made his first big splash in the game there in 1977 when he made the semi-finals as a qualifier.

Japan has made a major splash here at the Earth Summit by demonstrating its technological prowess in the area of the environment.

Mrs Gorman has made quite a splash at Westminster with her outspoken views and colourful and expensive clothes.

spoke

put a spoke in someone's wheel

If you **put a spoke in** someone's **wheel**, you deliberately make it difficult for them to do what they are planning to do. This expression is used mainly in British English.

If she had known he was seeing Tinsley, she undoubtedly would have tried to put a spoke in his wheel.

Gurusinha and Ranatunga are brilliant players but they won't get far themselves – although they could put a spoke in someone else's wheel.

spoon

the wooden spoon　　　◄◄

If someone is last in a race or competition or is the worst at a particular activity, you can say that they get **the wooden spoon**. This expression is used in British English.

England must beat the defending champions Scotland today to avoid their first wooden spoon in the event's 49-year history.

Britain's bureaucrats won the EU's wooden spoon yesterday, as the worst linguists in Brussels.

☐ You can use **wooden spoon** before a noun.

The 32-year-old Scotland captain reacted sharply to questions about his intentions after today's Five Nations wooden spoon decider against France at Murrayfield.

Scotland, who finished second in the Five Nations Championship, have bagged eight places on the British team, while the wooden-spoon winners Wales have taken four.

spot

a blind spot　　　◄◄

If you describe something as **a blind spot** of yours, you mean that you do not understand it or know anything about it, although you feel that perhaps you should.

Computers are a blind spot with me.

My problem is that I don't really notice advertising pages. It's always been a blind spot of mine, so I can't comment on that.

His is a world of moral peaks and troughs; he is highly moral in some areas and has complete blind spots in others.

have a soft spot for someone　　　◄◄◄

If you say that you **have a soft spot for** someone or something, you mean that you like them or care about them a lot.

It looked to me as if he had a soft spot for Mrs Frazer and didn't like what was happening to her.

I've always had a very soft spot for hardy geraniums and although I have several dozen different varieties already, I am always delighted to try something new.

hit the spot　　　◄

If you say that something **hits the spot**, you mean that it is very good and succeeds in pleasing people.

Les Blair's improvised drama hits the spot, with an intelligent eye for detail which provides a refreshing and relaxed portrait of the chaos of real life.

She has worked for the company for 38 years and, despite the generation gap, when she was asked what she thought, she reckoned the advert hit the right spot perfectly.

on the spot: 1　　　◄◄◄

If an action is taken **on the spot**, it is carried out immediately.

Watch out for sales staff who say you'll get a special discount or prize if you sign on the spot.

Cissie's problem was that she had been sacked on the spot without a reference.

I was afraid they would kill me on the spot.

☐ You can also use **on-the-spot** before a noun.

Lady Porter, the leader of Westminster City Council, said the time had come for on-the-spot fines for litter louts.

on the spot: 2　　　◄◄◄

Someone who is **on the spot** is in the place where something that you are talking about is actually happening.

Park agents are on the spot to supervise cleaning and servicing between lettings and look after the people using the caravan.

The Guard has firefighters on the spot the minute a fire is sighted.

The first that reporters on the spot knew about the release of Mr. Mann was when they heard a news flash on a local radio station.

☐ You can use **on-the-spot** before a noun to say that something actually happens in the place that you are talking about.

The Austrian government has dispatched a group of experts to Thailand to begin an on-the-spot investigation.

There is little point in providing on-the-spot help while the fighting continues.

on the spot: 3　　　◄◄◄

If you say that someone puts you **on the spot**, you mean that they put you in a difficult situation which you cannot avoid, for example by making you answer difficult questions.

You shouldn't ask a player about how his manager is coping. You put Gary on the spot and that's very unfair.

If I was put on the spot in a witness box during a terrorist trial, I should certainly try to persuade the judge not to compel me to reveal my source.

It may be unexpected or come from people you feel self-conscious saying no to, and you may feel on the spot.

spots

knock spots off something　　　◄

If you say that one thing or person **knocks spots off** another, you mean that the first is much better than the second. This expression is used in British English.

I'm looking forward to the return of their chat show. It knocks spots off all the others.

Caroline didn't have much experience as a

nanny, but she knocked spots off everyone else I'd interviewed – she was so charming and friendly.

spout

up the spout: 1

If you say that something is **up the spout**, you mean that it is completely ruined or hopeless. This expression is used in British English.

The money's disappeared, so has he, and the whole bloody scheme's up the spout.

The economy's up the spout.

up the spout: 2

If someone says that a woman is **up the spout**, they mean that she is pregnant, and usually that this is a problem rather than a good thing. This is an informal expression, which is used in British English. Some people find it offensive.

There was always somebody up the spout, and there were some very strange marriages between young girls in the village and quite middle-aged farmers.

sprat

a sprat to catch a mackerel

If you describe something you do as **a sprat to catch a mackerel**, you mean that it involves a small sacrifice or a small amount of effort, but you are expecting that it will bring you great rewards or benefits. This is an old-fashioned expression, which is used in British English.

As a sprat to catch the American mackerel, MITI is now offering to share the patents resulting from the joint research with foreign participants.

spring

no spring chicken ◄

If you say that someone is **no spring chicken**, you mean that they are no longer young. You often use this expression when you think someone's behaviour is inappropriate or surprising for their age.

At 51, she's certainly no spring chicken.

At 85, he is no spring chicken, but Enrico Cuccia is busier than ever.

The idea of playing it up as a great romance was a mistake. Neither of them is a spring chicken.

☐ If you describe someone as **a spring chicken**, you mean that they are very young or seem younger than they really are.

Mick said the others are all spring chickens.

spur

on the spur of the moment ◄◄◄

If you do something **on the spur of the mo-**
ment, you do it suddenly and without planning it in advance.

He had decided on the spur of the moment to make the journey south to Newcastle.

This murder was done on the spur of the moment, and it was pure luck that there was no one around to see it.

☐ A **spur-of-the-moment** action or decision is sudden and has not been planned in advance.

Judges currently cannot reflect in their sentencing the difference between a planned killing and a spur-of-the-moment emotional crime.

spurs

earn your spurs
win your spurs ◄◄

If you say that someone **has earned** their **spurs** or **has won** their **spurs**, you mean that they have shown they are capable of doing something well, and can be relied on to do it well in the future. This expression is used mainly in British English.

How did he earn his spurs for the toughest police job in the country?

Kampelman had won his spurs as U.S. negotiator at the Madrid talks.

square

back to square one
back at square one
from square one ◄◄◄

If you say that someone is **back to square one**, you are emphasizing that they have failed completely in what they were trying to do, so that now they have to start again. You can also say that someone is **back at square one** or starts **from square one**.

So we are back to square one. Their costly intervention has been for nothing, a carefully-constructed peace process lies in ruins.

Defeat leaves Britain back at square one and with little still to show for the £55 million of investment in the infrastructure of the game over the past decade.

The new board will apparently be starting from square one.

on the square

If you say that someone is **on the square**, you mean that they are being totally honest with you. This expression is used mainly in American English.

Most say they plan to vote for the Clinton-Gore ticket. 'Anything is better than what we got. At least he's on the square.'

squib

a damp squib ◄◄

If you describe something as **a damp squib**, you are criticizing it for being much less impressive or exciting than you expected it to be. This expression is used mainly in British English.

As political scandals go it was a damp squib, and in Central Office it was greeted with hilarity and relief rather than indignation.

Those pictures we were promised turned out to be a damp squib – I thought they would be much more exciting.

stack

blow your stack

If you **blow** your **stack**, you become very angry with someone and shout at them. This expression is used mainly in American English.

'You told me that your parents were very forgiving. They let you do anything.' 'Yeah, that used to be true. But my father really blew his stack over this.'

Whenever I feel like I'm going to scream or blow my stack or punch Louise in the teeth, I head for my quiet place.

stack the deck
stack the cards ◄

If someone **stacks the deck** or **stacks the cards**, they arrange a situation unfairly against you, or in their own favour. 'Stack the deck' is used only in American English. Compare **not play with a full deck**; see **deck**.

There are many different ways an insurance company can fix it, stack the deck so that they don't sell insurance in an area where they don't want to have consumers.

The President is doing everything in his power to stack the cards in his favour and guarantee his regime's return to power.

stage

set the stage for something
the stage is set ◄◄◄

To **set the stage for** something means to make preparations so that the thing can happen. You can also say **the stage is set**.

Jamaica's prime minister set the stage for a snap election this month by announcing candidates for his People's National Party.

The agreement sets the stage for renewed nuclear arms reduction talks and paves the way for a superpower summit later this year.

Whatever the popular despondency at the slowing economy, one benefit has been to check inflation. Conceivably, therefore, the stage is set for economic recovery.

stake

go to the stake

If you say that you would **go to the stake** to defend something, you mean that you are

absolutely certain that you are right about it, and you are prepared to suffer the consequences of defending it. This is an old-fashioned expression, which is used mainly in British English.

Few universities would go to the stake to defend the National Union of Students; but, as debate at the Committee of Vice-Chancellors and Principals on July 3 showed, our own student unions are another matter.

He admitted several staff had keys but said: 'They are all trustworthy. I would go to the stake for all of them.'

stall

set out your stall ◄

If you **set out** your **stall** to achieve something, you make all the necessary plans or arrangements, and show that you are determined to achieve it. This expression is used in British English.

He has set out his stall to retain his place in Europe's Ryder Cup team.

He called on me over the weekend to set out his stall about a great annual festival to celebrate London's river.

I was lucky in that I was given a specific job to do. It helped because I could focus my thoughts on it and set my stall out accordingly.

stand

stand up and be counted ◄◄

If you are willing to **stand up and be counted**, you are willing to state publicly your support for or rejection of something, especially when this is difficult or controversial.

This kind of demonstration should not be necessary but we are here because we want to stand up and be counted.

Although she knew such measures would hurt sales from her state, Senator Kaffenbaum said the United States had to be prepared to stand up and be counted.

Will we, as members of the Senate and the House, have the guts to stand up and be counted on this issue or will we scurry and run and hide and say, 'Let the president do it'?

standard

the standard bearer ◄◄◄

If you say that someone is **the standard bearer** of an organization or a group of people who have the same aims or interests, you mean that they act as the leader or representative of the organization or group.

There is clearly a civil war going on for the ideological soul of the Tory Party and 41-year-old Portillo sees himself as the standard-bearer of the right.

Inevitably, the public perception of her is that of a standard-bearer for women jockeys.

stars

reach for the stars
reach for the sky
reach for the moon ◄◄

If you **reach for the stars** or **reach for the sky**, you are very ambitious and try hard to achieve something, even though it may be very difficult. You can also say that you **reach for the moon**. You can replace 'reach' with other verbs such as 'shoot' or 'aim'.

If you're ready to move on in your career, keep your feet firmly on the ground while reaching for the stars!

Liverpool have already reached for the skies and they have made it. But they can only go down now and my boys can still grow up.

It is better to succeed in changing your diet gradually, than to shoot for the moon and then give up and go back to your old habits because you couldn't meet your own aspirations.

stars in your eyes

If you say that someone has **stars in their eyes**, you mean that they are very hopeful and excited about things which they expect to happen to them in the future. You often use this expression to suggest that they are naive and their hopes are unlikely to come true.

We had stars in our eyes last weekend. Now we know what it is all about.

With stars in my eyes, I set about becoming a guitarist, singer and songwriter.

starter

under starter's orders

If you say that someone is **under starter's orders**, you mean that they are ready to do a task or job, and can begin doing it immediately if necessary. This expression is used in British English.

The Tories have been effectively put under starter's orders as they gather for tomorrow's party conference.

The Vice-President can hardly deny that he is under starter's orders since the need to provide for a legitimate successor if a president dies is the sole reason why his job exists.

□ This expression is more commonly used in talking about horse racing. When the horses in a race are **under starter's orders**, they are in the correct position at the start of the race, and are waiting for the signal for the race to begin.

state

the state of play ◄◄

If someone tells you what **the state of play** is, they tell you about the current situation. This expression is used in British English.

For a synopsis of the state of play in funda-

mental physics, his new book would be hard to better.

Ben Willmott gives you the state of play on marijuana and the law.

steam

full steam ahead ◄

If you go **full steam ahead** with a project, you start to carry it out in a thorough and determined way.

The Government was determined to go full steam ahead with its privatisation programme.

Mrs Thatcher declared it was full steam ahead for a fourth term of government.

let off steam
blow off steam ◄◄

If you **let off steam** or **blow off steam**, you do or say something which helps you to get rid of your strong feelings about something. 'Let off steam' is used mainly in British English and 'blow off steam' is used mainly in American English.

This special session will give politicians a chance to let off steam.

I was so frustrated I pulled the truck over to the side of the road, got out, and took a long walk. I just had to let off steam.

He may also experience reactions to stress, blowing off steam by turning violently on his wife and children.

pick up steam ◄

If something such as a process **picks up steam**, it starts to become stronger or more active.

Boskin said the economy should pick up steam next year.

Just as the presidential campaign was picking up steam, riots exploded in Los Angeles.

run out of steam

If something such as a process **runs out of steam**, it becomes weaker or less active, and often stops completely.

The US is in a triple dip of recession. The promised recovery ran out of steam, the economy is slowing sharply and consumer spending is falling.

A recent government study has confirmed that gold-panning and mahogany extraction are running out of steam in this area of eastern Amazonia.

under your own steam: 1

If you go somewhere **under your own steam**, you make your own arrangements for the journey, rather than letting someone else organize it for you.

Most hotels organise tours to inland beauty spots, but car hire is cheap enough to consider taking off into the hills under your own steam.

under your own steam: 2

If you do something **under** your **own steam**, you do it on your own and without help from anyone else.

He left the group convinced he could do better under his own steam.

stem

stem the tide
stem the flow   ◄◄◄

If you **stem the tide** or **stem the flow** of something undesirable which is happening on a large scale, you get control of it and stop it.

He argued that Germany already has enough to do to stem the tide of foreigners seeking political asylum.

The Kenyan authorities seem powerless to stem the rising tide of violence.

Mexico may have lost up to $2 billion in foreign-exchange reserves in June, before interest rates were raised to stem the flow.

stew

in a stew

If you say that someone is **in a stew**, you mean that they are very worried about something. This is a fairly old-fashioned expression.

He's been in a stew since early this morning.

'She was having trouble finding something, wasn't she?' 'Yeah, she was in a bit of a stew.'

let someone stew in their own juice
let someone stew
leave someone to stew   ◄

If you **let** someone **stew in** their **own juice** or **let** them **stew**, you deliberately leave them to worry about something, for example the consequence of their actions, and do not do anything to comfort or help them. You can also say that you **leave** someone **to stew**.

But what if the opposition leader refuses to take part in the elections? It will now be tempting for the government to let him stew in his own juice.

'I thought you might have pressed him on that, sir.' 'I'd rather let him stew,' said Thorne. 'We'll get more out of him that way in the end.'

The government should be left for a time to stew in its own problems.

stick

carry a big stick
wield a big stick   ◄

If someone **carries a big stick**, they have a lot of power, and so they can get what they want. If they **wield a big stick**, they have this power and use it. Compare **carrot and stick**; see **carrot**.

Delegates from the Organisation of American

States flew to Haiti to demand the return to power of President Jean-Bertrand Aristide. They carried a big stick. The OAS had mounted a trade blockade against the new regime. Haiti was fast running out of oil.

The company has a history of talking softly. But it wields a big stick. Over the past 107 years it has built itself up into the biggest brand in the world and now controls 44 per cent of the global market.

☐ **Big stick** is used in many other structures with a similar meaning.

President Clinton has presented his opponents with a big stick, and they have not hesitated to clobber him with it.

They wanted peace, he said, but this big stick policy was forcing them into war.

get a lot of stick
give someone stick   ◄◄◄

If you **get** a lot of **stick** or if someone **gives** you **stick**, you are criticized, often in an unfair way or for something that is not your fault. These expressions are used in British English.

I got a lot of stick when we returned from the India tour and some of it I deserved. I had a disastrous tour, the worst of all I have been on.

The critics gave me a lot of stick for some of my wooden performances but I gradually improved.

I am not one of these people who will change my views merely because I have been getting a bit of stick myself. My views would not be affected by that.

get the short end of the stick   ◄

If someone **gets the short end of the stick**, they end up in a worse position than other people in a particular situation, although this is not their fault. This expression is used mainly in American English.

Kids and young families get the short end of the stick because they don't get the kind of support that they need and the taxpayer ends up picking up the tab.

As usual it's the consumer who gets the short end of the stick.

get the wrong end of the stick
get hold of the wrong end of the stick   ◄

If someone **gets the wrong end of the stick** or **gets hold of the wrong end of the stick**, they completely misunderstand something, or completely miss someone's point.

Men are assigned the roles of heading their family, but unfortunately too many men have got the wrong end of the stick. They might perceive headship as meaning that they must be the main breadwinner for the family.

People are so easily confused, so readily get

hold of the wrong end of the stick, so easily miss the point.

in a cleft stick

If someone is **in a cleft stick**, they are in a difficult situation which they cannot get out of easily. This expression is used in British English.

Debbie now finds herself in a cleft stick. On the one hand, Social Security refuse to pay her more money. On the other hand, she is being pursued and hassled by debt collectors, wanting just that money which she doesn't have.

more things than you can shake a stick at ◄

If you say that you have **more** things **than** you **can shake a stick at**, you are emphasizing that you have a very large number of them.

I've replanted more geraniums than you can shake a stick at.

My daughter had more nappy rash creams than you could shake a stick at.

stick in your throat: 1 ◄

If something **sticks in** your **throat**, it makes you annoyed or impatient. 'Craw' and 'gullet' are sometimes used instead of 'throat'.

Smith is an excellent climber and it must have stuck in this throat to have had to sacrifice personal glory for the team.

But it sticks in my craw that such people think that they still have something to tell the rest of us about politics, economics, history or morality.

stick in your throat: 2

If you say that a particular word **sticks in** your **throat**, you mean that you cannot say it or dislike saying it, because it does not express your real feelings or because it makes you feel uncomfortable.

She found it impossible to utter the usual terms of maternal endearment: words such as 'darling' or 'pet' stuck in her throat.

She wanted to ask if he had news of Keith, but the words stuck in her throat.

a stick to beat someone with ◄◄

If you say that something is **a stick to beat** someone **with**, you mean that it can be used to cause embarrassment or difficulty for them. This expression is used in British English.

Surprisingly, the opposition, usually eager to find any stick to beat the government with, is refusing to comment on the affair.

The Greek prime minister is caught between ultra-nationalists on his right and a Socialist opposition that will use any stick to beat the government.

Reformers have been using the issue of corruption as a stick with which to beat the hardline old guard.

stiff

stiff as a board

If your body is very stiff, you can say that you are as **stiff as a board** or that your body is as **stiff as a board**.

Maxine emphasises that you can gain an amount of flexibility very quickly – even if you are as stiff as a board at your first session.

His lower back felt as stiff as a board.

sting

a sting in the tail ◄◄

If you say that something such as a remark or proposal has **a sting in the tail**, you mean that although most of it seems welcome or pleasing, it contains an unpleasant part at the end. This expression is used in British English.

Even the remark about Chomsky being 'arguably the most important intellectual alive' had a sting in its tail. The sentence read: 'arguably the most important intellectual alive, how can he write such nonsense about international affairs?'

The resolution had a sting in the tail. It said that the entire military aid package would be suspended if the country failed to make progress on the economic front.

take the sting out of something ◄

If something **takes the sting out of** an unpleasant situation, it makes it less unpleasant or painful.

His calmness surprised her and helped to take the sting out of her anger.

The most serious situation can be viewed with humour and that always helps to take the sting out of hard facts.

stitch

a stitch in time
a stitch in time saves nine

If someone says **'a stitch in time'**, they mean that it is better to deal with a problem in its early stages, in order to prevent it getting worse.

The adage 'a stitch in time' is never more true than with a steel boat's paintwork: one must be immediately ready to touch up the chips that inevitably occur in order to prevent a bigger job later.

□ This expression comes from the proverb **a stitch in time saves nine**.

stitches

in stitches ◄

If someone or something has you **in stitches**, they make you laugh a lot.

Outrageous American comedienne Thea Vidale plans to have the north of England in stitches as she tops the bill at the Liverpool Festival of Comedy.

If you have an unusual talent or a novel party piece that leaves your friends and family in stitches, then Clarke Television Productions want to hear from you.

stone

leave no stone unturned ◀◀

If you **leave no stone unturned** in your efforts to find something or achieve something, you consider or try every possible way of doing it.

In the difficult weeks ahead, we'll leave no stone unturned in our search for a peaceful solution of the crisis.

We will leave no stone unturned to keep our position as the world's number one football club.

They were contacted personally by telephone at their home by the New Zealand police minister, who promised no stone would be left unturned in the hunt for the killer.

not set in stone ◀

If you say that something such as an agreement, policy, or rule is **not set in stone**, you are pointing out that it is not permanent and that it can be changed. Other verbs such as 'carved' or 'cast' can be used instead of 'set'.

Promises made two or three years before an election are not set in stone and can be changed.

He is merely throwing the idea forward for discussion, it is not cast in stone.

Parents should not view a single IQ score as an indicator of their child's intelligence, carved in stone.

a rolling stone gathers no moss
a rolling stone
gather moss

People say **'a rolling stone gathers no moss'** when they want to point out that if a person keeps moving from one place to another, they will not get many friends or possessions. Some people use this proverb to say that it is a bad thing to keep moving like this, and it is better to be settled. Other people use this proverb to suggest that it is a good thing to keep moving and changing, and not be tied down.

If he was going to say that a rolling stone gathers no moss, that never having a family would be one of the penalties I would have to pay if I spent my life on the road, I was going to prove him wrong on that, too.

□ You can refer to a person who does not settle down as **a rolling stone**.

But throughout it all, Greta has found the desire and courage to keep in contact with her absentee father, who is a rolling stone to this day.

□ If you say that someone **is gathering moss**, you mean that they have stayed in the same place for a long time.

The old families die out or move on, or stay and gather moss.

a stone's throw ◀◀◀

If you describe one place as **a stone's throw** from another, you mean that the first place is very close to the second.

Burke found employment and rented a flat a stone's throw from their former, rather grand house.

The Diplomatic Service Wives Association is housed in a large room in the Foreign Office in London, a stone's throw away from Westminster.

Just a stone's throw away is the home he shares with his wife and daughter.

The cellars are within a stone's throw of the church where Dom Pérignon, the legendary creator of champagne, was buried.

stools

fall between two stools
caught between two stools ◀

If someone or something **falls between two stools**, they are in an unsatisfactory situation because they do not belong to either of two groups or categories, or because they are trying to do two different things at once and are failing at both. You can also say that someone **is caught between two stools**. These expressions are used mainly in British English.

Labour says that young people on waiting lists for youth training fall between two stools. They can't get unemployment benefit, nor can they get the allowance for the scheme they're waiting to get on.

Devo's problem remains the same: they are caught between the two stools of art and pop, operating on the fringes of both but easily dismissed by both for failing to be, respectively, serious or rampantly commercially successful.

□ This expression can be varied.

The album has fallen between stools to a certain extent.

The UN missions so far have fallen between all stools, and are in danger of merely prolonging the conflict.

stops

pull out all the stops ◀◀◀

If you **pull out all the stops**, you do everything you possibly can to make something happen in the way that you want it to.

Don't worry about taking foreign assignments, because if anything goes wrong, we're going to pull out all the stops to get you out.

We came so close at a time when everybody knew what the stakes were and the government had pulled out all the stops to try and ensure its own victory.

☐ This expression is very variable. For example, you can omit 'all' or 'the', or put an adjective before 'stops'.

The world's most gifted player, never afraid to speak his mind, added, 'When you are world champions, everyone pulls out the stops, everyone wants to beat you.'

Steven Pimlott's excellent new production gives the play fresh bite and urgency by clothing it in modern dress and by pulling out all the theatrical stops.

storage

into cold storage
in cold storage

If you put something **into cold storage**, you delay doing it or dealing with it, for example because other more important things need your attention or because you are not ready to do it. You can also say that something is **in cold storage**.

Talk of the pound rejoining the exchange-rate mechanism, which linked it to the Deutsch mark, has been put into cold storage.

A few years ago I was asked by a publisher to consider writing a novel with a motor racing background, and the idea has been in cold storage ever since.

storm

the calm before the storm
the lull before the storm ◄◄

If you describe a very quiet period as **the calm before the storm** or **the lull before the storm**, you mean that it is likely to be followed, or was followed, by a period of trouble or intense activity.

Things are relatively calm at the moment, but I think it probably is the calm before the storm.

Beneath the stillness of this city, there's foreboding that this is the calm before an approaching storm.

The fragile ceasefire in Croatia itself may only be the lull before another storm.

a storm in a teacup ◄

If you say that something is **a storm in a teacup**, you mean that it is not very important but people are making a lot of unnecessary fuss about it. This expression is used in British English; the American expression is **a tempest in a teapot**.

Ella likes you. I'm sure it's all a storm in a teacup. It'll blow over in no time.

It is frequently argued that such a small percentage of the countryside will disappear under housing development in the next ten years that conservationists' worries are a storm in a teacup.

take somewhere by storm ◄◄◄

If someone or something **takes** a place **by storm**, they are very successful or popular and make a good impression on people there.

Hailed as the next Sophia Loren, the dark-eyed Italian is set to take the fashion world by storm.

In 1991 many firms expected these computers to take the industry by storm.

It's nearly 12 months since the film took America by storm but it faces stiff competition for the Best Film nomination.

weather the storm
ride out the storm
ride the storm ◄◄◄

If you **weather the storm** or **ride out the storm**, you survive a difficult situation or period without being seriously harmed or affected very badly by it. You can also say that you **ride the storm**.

The General, who was appointed to office, not elected, insists he will not resign and will weather the storm.

Rover has weathered the storm of the current recession better than most. As car sales have plummeted, it's seen its share of the market actually increase.

By the late 1960s, there were three options for dealing with the crisis. The first option was to ride out the storm, and hope that the crisis would be dissipated through the beneficial effects of EU membership.

We are riding the storm at the moment but things are getting worse in the recession.

story

to cut a long story short
to make a long story short ◄◄

When you are giving an account of something, you can say **'to cut a long story short'** in British English or **'to make a long story short'** in American English to indicate that you are only going to mention the final result or point, without any further details.

To cut a long story short, a freak accident over four years ago left Paul prone to painful dislocations of the kneecaps.

One Sunday at two o'clock I went out to the airport, and this handsome man stepped off another airplane. I thought, Boy! I could go for him, and to make a long story short, we're getting married.

straight

the straight and narrow ◄◄

If someone keeps you on **the straight and narrow**, they help you to live an honest, decent life and prevent you from doing immoral or illegal things.

He depended on me when he was working to keep him on the straight and narrow, to keep some sense of perspective about what life was all about.

The Education Secretary, a devout Catholic, is determined to introduce a new classroom culture of morality to set youngsters on the straight and narrow.

The goal is to prevent them from straying from the straight and narrow.

□ Some people use the word 'strait' instead of 'straight' in this expression.

straight as a die: 1

If you say that someone is **straight as a die**, you mean that they are completely honest. This expression is used in British English.

But I got the impression that deviousness is not one of his characteristics. He is, as the English would say, as straight as a die.

straight as a die: 2

If you say that something is **straight as a die**, you are emphasizing that it is very straight. This expression is used in British English.

The streets are lined up, straight as a die, along the left bank of the Guadiana estuary.

He pauses to point out a trunk that rises straight as a die – an ash tree.

straw

draw the short straw ◄

If you **draw the short straw**, you are chosen from a number of people to perform a task or duty that nobody wants to do. Other verbs are sometimes used instead of 'draw'. This expression is used mainly in British English.

Brenner drained his glass with a sense of relief, thankful that it was someone else, probably Hean, who had drawn the short straw.

It sounds very much as though you pulled something of a short straw there, Jim. There's not very much we can do about it, I'm afraid.

the last straw
the final straw ◄◄◄

If you say that something is **the last straw** or **the final straw**, you mean it is the latest in a series of unpleasant or difficult events, and it makes you feel that you cannot tolerate a situation any longer. Compare **the straw that breaks the camel's back**.

Building societies have been under enormous pressure to increase savings rates to get the money they need. But that would mean putting mortgage rates up, and an increase now could be the last straw for thousands of borrowers.

The increased hardship caused by water and

power cuts appears to have been the last straw and provoked open rebellion.

Mr Elton was already distraught over his mother's death. The final straw came when his attractive wife asked for a divorce.

a man of straw
a straw man

If you say that a man is **a man of straw**, you mean that he does not have the ability or the courage necessary to carry out a particular task or fulfil a particular role. This is a fairly formal expression, which is used mainly in British English.

The problem of the Labour Party is that it is once again firmly in the grip of men of straw without guts and without principles.

□ You can also talk about **straw men**. This form of the expression is used in both British and American English, especially in journalism.

These also represent the reflex responses of straw men with straw policies.

the straw that breaks the camel's back
the last straw that breaks the camel's back ◄

You can say that something is **the straw that breaks the camel's back** when it is the latest in a series of unpleasant or difficult events, and it makes you feel that you cannot tolerate a situation any longer. Compare **the last straw**.

Last week, I broke my wrist skateboarding. I'm a good skateboard rider and love the sport – but that was the straw that broke the camel's back as far as my dad was concerned. He has ordered me to stay away from anything that could get me into an accident.

□ In British English, you can also say that something is **the last straw that breaks the camel's back**.

He tried to reassure my father, but said all the wrong things: 'I wouldn't worry about it. You've educated your daughter, she can work!' My father went berserk. This was the last straw that broke the camel's back. He ordered him out of the house.

straws

clutch at straws
grasp at straws
a drowning man will clutch at a straw ◄

If you say that someone **is clutching at straws** or **is grasping at straws**, you mean that they are relying on ideas, hopes, or methods which are unlikely to be successful, because they are desperate and cannot think of anything else to try. In American English 'grasp at straws' is more common.

This disparaging speech was made by a man

clutching at straws to gain much-desired publicity.

Whenever a new therapy or educational program seemed effective, the researchers scrambled for a new theory to explain its usefulness. Many parents followed blindly, grasping at straws in a desperate search for a cure.

☐ You can also say that an idea, hope, or method is **the straw** which someone **clutches at** or **the straw** which someone **grasps**.

The drop in bank base rates to their lowest levels since June 1988 may have given the property industry a much needed, if fragile, straw to clutch at.

Another straw the optimists grasp is that two trade disputes between the EU and the United States have been avoided.

☐ This expression comes from the proverb **a drowning man will clutch at a straw**.

People are still clinging to the hope that something will happen – but I think it's like a drowning man trying to clutch at a straw.

straws in the wind ◄

If you say that events are **straws in the wind**, you mean that they are signs of the way in which a situation may develop. This expression is used mainly in British English, especially in journalism.

They were straws in the wind, a foretaste of what was to come.

Day by day evidence mounts that the economy is starting to climb out of recession. The latest straw in the wind is a pick-up in sales among the nation's retail giants.

streak

talk a blue streak

If you say that someone **talks a blue streak**, you mean that they are talking a lot and very fast. Verbs such as 'scream' and 'spout' can be used instead of 'talk'. This expression is used in American English.

I was mostly shy, although they say I talked a blue streak from the time I opened my mouth.

I remember Malcolm screaming a blue streak that I was fired.

stream

on stream ◄◄◄

If a plan or a project comes **on stream**, it begins to operate fully. If it is **on stream**, it is operating fully. This expression is used mainly in British English; the usual American expression is **on line**.

Other new services from London City serve Stockholm and Rotterdam, and the airport's authorities say they expect new destinations to come on stream in the course of this summer.

Faults at Romania's first nuclear power plant must be repaired before it goes on stream.

The facility has been on stream since the early part of the year.

street

in Queer Street

If you say that someone is **in Queer Street**, you mean that they are having difficulties, especially financial difficulties. This is an old-fashioned expression, which is used in British English.

Had he spent more time then listening to the educators, he might not now be in Queer Street.

Beneath the glitzy surface, the financial whizzkids of the world are mostly on the road to alcoholism, loneliness, a bedsit in Queer Street, or sometimes all three.

the man in the street
the woman in the street ◄◄◄

When people talk about **the man in the street**, they mean ordinary, average people. Words such as 'woman' and 'person' are sometimes used instead of 'man'.

The man in the street will be able to buy all that he could reasonably need anywhere in Europe.

It was in terms that the more ordinary man and woman in the street could understand.

But how do these massive changes appear to people in the street? The general mood of the population seems to be contradictory.

right up your street
just up your street ◄

If you say that something is **right up your street** or **just up your street**, you mean that it is the kind of thing you like or know about. This expression is used mainly in British English. **Right up your alley** means the same.

There's a real quality and fighting spirit in this squad that's right up my street.

Actor Roy Barraclough has taken on a role that's right up his street – as Sherlock Holmes' bumbling sidekick Watson.

streets

streets ahead ◄◄

If you say that one person or thing is **streets ahead** of another, you are emphasizing that the first one is much better than the other one. This expression is used in British English.

Bill had a great imagination and was always streets ahead of his fellow clergy in seeing local needs and in arranging ways to meet them.

Even after its relative decline over the last three years, the South East is still streets ahead of the rest.

They are streets ahead in worldly wisdom, and not only where love and passion are concerned: they are hot on economics, too.

stretch

at full stretch   ◀◀

If someone or something is operating **at full stretch**, they cannot work any harder or more efficiently, because they are already using all their resources. This expression is used in British English.

Police are warning that emergency services are at full stretch and they are advising motorists to travel only if their journey is absolutely necessary.

A combination of record UK market share and increased export business kept our production plants at full stretch.

□ You can also say that someone or something is **fully stretched**.

Our services see a substantial number of children every day – we are already fully stretched. If we have any more coming along then that would be very worrying indeed.

stride

get into your stride
hit your stride   ◀◀◀

If you **get into** your **stride** or **hit** your **stride**, you start to do something easily and confidently, after being slow and uncertain at the beginning. 'Get into your stride' is used only in British English.

Once he had got into his stride, his capacity for informal decision taking and for doing what he regarded as right, without regard to the personal consequence, became remarkable.

The Government is getting into its stride and seems, for the moment, to be fulfilling its promises.

He's still learning and when he hits his stride, he'll be unstoppable.

put someone off their stride

If something **puts** you **off** your **stride**, it stops you from concentrating on what you are doing, so that you do not do it as well as usual. This expression is used in British English. **Put** someone **off** their **stroke** means the same.

His many opponents are suggesting that it is all a tactic designed to put his opponent off his stride.

□ The verbs 'knock' and 'throw' are sometimes used instead of 'put'.

Perhaps a few jokes during the game will knock Chris off his stride.

take something in your stride
take something in stride   ◀◀◀

If you are in a difficult situation and you **take** it **in** your **stride**, you deal with it calmly and successfully. This form of the expression is used in British English; the American form is **take** something **in stride**.

Ridley didn't start shouting, or anything like that. In fact, right until the end he seemed to be taking it all in his stride.

'Tim is absolutely dreading having to give a speech – he would rather have a tooth pulled!' said Christie, who takes such things in her stride.

Across the country, many people took yesterday's events in stride, while remaining generally uneasy about the stock market in general.

strikes

three strikes against someone
two strikes against someone

If there are **three strikes against** someone or something, there are three factors which make it impossible for them to be successful. This expression is used mainly in American English.

There was one lady that said to me, 'Listen young man, you got three strikes against you. You're black, you're poor, and you're blind.'

□ If there are **two strikes against** someone or something, there are two factors which make it difficult, but not impossible, for them to be successful, or they have only one more chance of succeeding.

The hotel has two strikes against it. One, it's an immense ugly concrete building. Second, it lies just inside the border so that all doorstep activities involve a fussy border crossing.

string

another string to your bow
many strings to your bow   ◀

If you have **another string to** your **bow**, you have more than one useful skill, ability, or thing you can use in case you are unsuccessful with your first attempt. If you have **many strings to** your **bow**, you have several skills, abilities, or things to use. These expressions are used in British English.

Looking, as it were, for another string to his bow, he turned to art and design, for which he had always shown a particular talent.

They should really develop a second string to their bow, so that they can make a little money in lean times.

Stephanie has many strings to her bow. Before opting for a career in interior design, she was a photographer and a Wall Street mergers specialist.

□ 'Bow' is pronounced with the same vowel sound as the word 'show'.

have someone on a string
keep someone on a string

If someone **has** you **on a string** or **keeps**

you **on a string**, they can make you do whatever they want, because they control you completely.

He was once again in serious difficulties. The Germans had him on a string.

For the rest of his life he kept her on a string, absorbing enormous amounts of her cash, and depending on her to edit his writing.

Nick had to end their relationship in the knowledge that he could no longer cope with the frustration of being kept dangling on a string.

strings

pull strings ◄◄◄

If someone **pulls strings** to get something they want, they get it by using their friendships with powerful and influential people, often in a way which is considered unfair.

Anyway, I'm not going to play in the tournament if it's part of a deal; it would look as if I was pulling strings.

As anywhere else, good managers are often thin on the ground, and organizing ability or being able to pull a few strings is useful.

□ You can also talk about **string-pulling**.

Recent news stories have raised questions about whether he engaged in the kind of string-pulling and backroom deal-making that he accuses his opponents of.

pull the strings ◄◄

If someone **pulls the strings**, they control everything that another person or an organization does.

Having engineered many of these political changes and pulled the strings from behind the stage, he now feels it's his due, as it were, to become national leader.

Mike worked sixteen hours a day, pulling the strings to make Apple a raging success.

Meanwhile, most of the city's administrative strings still have to be pulled from City Hall.

with no strings attached
without strings ◄◄◄

If you say that an offer of help comes **with no strings attached** or **without strings**, you mean that it has no unpleasant conditions which must be accepted as part of the offer, or that the person making it does not expect anything in return.

I think this is an extremely generous offer. There are no strings attached and I will recommend that everyone accepts.

I am grateful to them for their co-operation, which was also given with absolutely no strings attached.

He wanted aid quickly and without strings.

with strings
with strings attached ◄

You can say that an offer is **with strings** or **with strings attached** if it has unpleasant conditions which must be accepted as part of the offer, or if the person making it expects something in return.

We have very strict rules that we refuse to accept any donations with strings attached.

Western money came with strings such as commercial openings.

strip

tear a strip off someone
tear someone off a strip ◄

If you **tear a strip off** someone or **tear them off a strip**, you speak angrily or seriously to them, because they have done something wrong. This expression is used in British English.

After breakfast he heard Nora tearing a strip off an orderly for not returning the food bins to the kitchen soon enough.

We went along to the headmaster and he tore strips off both of us.

We turned up together on the first day and got torn off a strip for being late.

stroke

put someone off their stroke

If something **puts** you **off** your **stroke**, it stops you from concentrating on what you are doing, so that you do not do it as well as usual. This expression is used in British English. **Put** someone **off** their **stride** means the same.

'Is that what you wanted to tell me?' 'What? Oh no, sorry, this business of Ivor has quite put me off my stroke.'

strokes

broad strokes
broad brush strokes ◄

If someone describes something in **broad strokes** or in **broad brush strokes**, they describe it in general terms rather than giving details.

The speech will lay out in broad strokes the two candidates' differing approaches towards how best to stimulate the economy.

We had already come to an understanding with him, but it had been drawn in broad strokes. It was now necessary to get down to specifics.

In an interview yesterday in the daily Le Monde, he set out the broad brushstrokes of future French foreign policy.

different strokes for different folks

People say **'different strokes for different folks'** to point out that people are different, and some individuals or groups have different needs and wants from others. This expression is used more commonly in American English than British.

The federal government has, by tradition, been respectful of local standards in local communities, and therefore you had different strokes for different folks.

But no matter how much you spend on these clothes, you'll still look like a bum. It's different strokes for different folks, but it certainly isn't my cup of tea.

strong

strong as an ox
strong as a horse
strong as a bull ◄

If you say that someone is as **strong as an ox**, you are emphasizing that they are extremely strong. You can replace 'ox' with the name of another large animal. For example, you can say that someone is as **strong as a horse** or as **strong as a bull**.

Big Beppe, as everybody calls him, is enormous for his age and as strong as an ox.

He's as strong as a horse and he got better very quickly, but he could have died there in the square.

Despite his disabled arm, Tom was as strong as a bull.

stubborn

stubborn as a mule

If you say that someone is as **stubborn as a mule**, you mean that they are determined to do what they want and are unwilling to change their mind. This expression is usually used to show disapproval.

He is, without question, a man of his word, and he can certainly be stubborn as a mule. But he has been known to change his mind about all sorts of things.

Old Gregg is also stubborn as a mule. He won't say nothin', but he just goes on doin' what he planned.

stuff

strut your stuff ◄◄

If you **strut** your **stuff**, you do something which you know you are good at in a proud and confident way in order to impress other people.

He was the type of guy who liked to show off and strut his stuff.

This weekend, in parades across the nation, Irish Americans are strutting their stuff.

stuffing

knock the stuffing out of someone ◄

If you say that something **knocks the**

stuffing out of someone, you mean that it destroys all their energy and self-confidence, and leaves them feeling weak and nervous. Other verbs such as 'take' are sometimes used instead of 'knock'.

Bath knocked the stuffing out of us early on and we never got into the game.

Men have had a hard time for the last fifteen years. The women's movement knocked the stuffing out of them.

The drive from the airport always took the stuffing out of her.

stump

on the stump ◄◄◄

If politicians are **on the stump**, they are travelling to different places and speaking to voters as part of their election campaign. This expression is used mainly in American English, but is becoming more common in British English.

He began appearing frequently on the stump and in one celebrated incident mounted a soapbox and grabbed a megaphone to shout down hostile demonstrators.

Despite his falling popularity, the president braved it on the stump today on behalf of his fellow Republicans.

style

cramp someone's style ◄

If someone or something **cramps** your **style**, they prevent you from behaving freely in the way that you want.

Just imagine, no visitors allowed except in public rooms and all visitors to be off the premises by seven at night. It positively cramped a girl's style.

Like more and more women with good jobs, independent spirits and high standards, she believes wedlock would cramp her style.

suck

suck it and see

If you are considering doing something new and someone tells you to **suck it and see**, they mean that the only way to find out if it is a good idea and likely to be successful is to actually try it. This expression is used in British English.

These results do not mean, however, that the Japanese will automatically like Western products. The only sure way to prove that, says Prescott, is to suck it and see.

I don't see this interest-rate cut kick-starting the housing market, but it is very much a case of suck it and see.

□ You can also say that you have a **suck-it-and-see** approach or attitude to something.

As a result of the crude budgeting techniques

we use, we take a 'suck it and see' approach, i.e. try it and see what happens.

suit

follow suit   ◄◄◄

If someone **follows suit**, they do the same thing that someone else has just done.

He twisted himself free of his pack and laid his gun down. The others followed suit.

BP also make nursery provisions for the children of staff members. If only other employers would follow suit.

If Tim had a stack of pancakes for breakfast, Pam would follow suit.

your long suit

If you say that something is your **long suit**, you mean that you are good at it or know a lot about it, and this gives you an advantage.

Our long suit is our proven ability to operate power plants.

Dealing with suffering well was not their long suit.

suits

the men in suits
the men in grey suits   ◄◄

If you talk about **the men in suits** or **the men in grey suits**, you are referring to the men who are in control of an organization or company and who have a lot of power. These expressions are used mainly in British English.

Even if Prince Andrew wanted to put the clock back 30 months and restore happiness to his marriage, the men in suits who guide the monarchy would almost certainly rule against him.

A lot of young people feel detached from older, stereotype politicians – the men in grey suits.

summer

an Indian summer

If someone enjoys **an Indian summer** in their life or career, they have a period of great success late in their life or career, perhaps after a period of not being successful. This expression is used mainly in British English.

The Sixties revival in international fashion is proving an Indian summer for Mr Rabanne, better known for his perfumes in the Seventies and Eighties.

In this Indian summer of his life, he speaks openly of wanting to be remembered as a writer first and advocate second.

□ An **Indian summer** is a period of unusually warm sunny weather during the autumn. This use occurs in both British and American English.

supper

sing for your supper

If someone tells you that you will have to **sing for** your **supper**, they mean that you will have to do a particular job before you are allowed to do or have something that you want. This is a fairly old-fashioned expression.

'You only gave me the box number for that bureau, Jo,' I said. 'Is there more?' She took a while to answer. 'Very well,' she said finally. 'But you'll have to sing for your supper.'

Salter tried to sing for his supper by making conversation.

sure

sure as eggs is eggs
sure as eggs

If you say that something will happen as **sure as eggs is eggs** or **sure as eggs**, you are emphasizing that you are very certain it will happen. This expression is used in British English.

If when they leave church all the worried, anxious thoughts, which gave rise to the lack of peace in the first place, come back, then as sure as eggs is eggs, the feelings of peace will evaporate and the feelings of anxiety return.

The new magazine, out this month, will sell, sure as eggs.

surface

scratch the surface   ◄◄

If you only **scratch the surface** of something, you deal with or experience only a small part of it.

Officials say they've only scratched the surface of the drug problem for women in public housing.

This is the most exciting aspect of my career at present. I realise now I've only scratched the surface of what I can do.

November's trade surplus was down to just over four hundred million dollars. At such levels, even if the entire trade surplus were offset against debt, it would barely scratch the surface.

swallow

one swallow doesn't make a summer

People say **'one swallow doesn't make a summer'** when they want to point out that although something good has happened, the situation may not continue to be good, and you cannot rely on it.

Sales into the new year are also up about 1 percent, which is a sharp contrast to the 9 percent dive in the previous six months. One swallow, however, doesn't make a summer and close observers say that business at the 85

Debenhams stores and its 858 concessions could be a lot better.

sweat

by the sweat of your brow

If you do something such as earning your living **by the sweat of** your **brow**, you do it by means of hard physical work, without any help from anyone else. This is a literary expression.

There was no exploitation in what your father did. It was earned by the sweat of his brow.

in a cold sweat
in a sweat ◄

If someone is **in a cold sweat** or **in a sweat**, they feel very frightened, anxious, or embarrassed.

The paper says Britain's economic crisis is at the heart of the turmoil in the Tory party, with MPs in a cold sweat about an election occurring before the recession bottoms out.

She dialled his number every half-hour. No reply. Once it was engaged: excited, relieved, she tried it again five minutes later, once more without reply. By about two in the morning she was in a sweat of totally illogical jealousy.

sweep

make a clean sweep: 1 ◄◄◄

If someone wins something very easily, or wins a series of victories, you can say they **make a clean sweep** of it.

China were back on top again in the Women's Weightlifting. They have made a clean sweep of all nine titles in that event with three more gold medals today.

The RPR is ready to make a clean sweep of all constituencies in Paris where Mr Chirac is mayor.

☐ **A clean sweep** is used in many other structures with a similar meaning.

Pakistan are making a strong challenge to complete a clean sweep against New Zealand in the three match series.

The Italians look well placed to repeat their clean sweep of 1990.

make a clean sweep: 2

If someone who has just taken up a position of authority in an organization **makes a clean sweep**, they make a lot of changes, for example getting rid of a large number of employees, in order to make the organization more efficient or profitable. Compare **a new broom**; see **broom**.

When Don arrived he said he was going to make a clean sweep, but I didn't think he would go quite this far.

☐ **A clean sweep** is also used in other structures with a similar meaning.

They resented his youth and inexperience and worried about rumours that he planned a clean sweep of longtime employees. True to expectations, he fired the managers, one by one.

They're talking about a clean sweep of the entire cabinet.

sweet

cop it sweet

If you **cop it sweet**, you accept harsh treatment or a punishment without reacting violently or complaining. This expression is used mainly in Australian English.

Bullies tend to lose interest in a victim very quickly if that victim refuses to 'cop it sweet'.

keep someone sweet ◄◄

If you **keep** someone **sweet**, you do something to please them so that they will treat you well in return. This expression is used in British English.

Everyone knows the basic rules of prudent finance. Keep the tax man sweet while never letting him claim a penny he isn't entitled to.

Some firms even reserve boxes at football grounds and at theatres that can be used by high-flying staff they want to keep sweet.

sweet as pie

If you say that someone is as **sweet as pie**, you mean that they are very kind, friendly, and charming. If a situation is as **sweet as pie**, it is very satisfactory. This expression is used mainly in British English. Compare **nice as pie**; see **nice**.

In real life she's sweet as pie. She is original, honest and very funny. And she really is clever.

Everything was as sweet as pie, after that.

swing

get into the swing of something ◄

If you **get into the swing of** something, you get used to it and you start doing it well or start enjoying it. If you **get back into the swing of things**, you get used to something again after a period of not doing it.

I assumed everything would be okay once I got into the swing of college but I had no idea how emotionally blocked I was.

It didn't take people long to relax and get into the swing of things, with a little help from some champagne.

He added: 'The manager was first class. He said everyone understood how hard it was to get back into the swing of things after such a long absence.'

go with a swing ◄

If a party or other event **goes with a swing**, it happens in a lively and exciting way. This expression is used in British English.

Having a toast-master at a wedding reception

seems to be a good way of ensuring that a reception goes with a swing.

These impressive recipes are guaranteed to make the party go with a swing.

in full swing ◄◄◄

If something is **in full swing**, it is operating fully or has already been happening for some time, rather than being in its early stages.

Twelve days after Hurricane Andrew left its trail of destruction and misery across South Florida, officials say recovery efforts are at last in full swing.

With its mile-long beach and lively holiday air, Dieppe has plenty to attract cross-Channel visitors. While I was there, a national dog show and a jazz festival were in full swing.

At sunset the best free show in town is at Old Mallory Square as street musicians, fire eaters and jugglers perform for the crowds and Key West's lively nightlife gets into full swing.

swings

swings and roundabouts
what you lose on the swings you gain on the roundabouts ◄

If you say that a situation is **swings and roundabouts**, you mean that there are as many advantages as there are disadvantages in it. This expression is used in British English.

It's swings and roundabouts at Fuji, who have made welcome price reductions on its C-cassettes, but increased the cost of its 8mm tapes, without any significant changes to the product.

Without a doubt, you're going to pay extra for a set from a shop because of the VAT consideration. But it's swings and roundabouts, because if anything goes wrong, you've got somewhere to go back to and complain.

□ **Swings and roundabouts** can also be used before a noun.

Mr Beloff argued that the Lord Chancellor's decision was flawed because of the 'swings and roundabouts' approach to solicitors' pay. Solicitors would lose on some cases and gain on others.

□ This expression comes from the proverb **what you lose on the swings you gain on the roundabouts**. People sometimes use the full form of the proverb, or a variation of it.

The United States will gain far more on the swings than its loses on the roundabouts.

Since there were more positive swings than negative roundabouts in the year to May, pre-tax profits rose sharply from £89 million to £112.7 million.

Swiss cheese

more holes than Swiss cheese

If you say that something such as an argument or theory has **more holes than Swiss cheese**, you mean that it has so many faults that it cannot be taken seriously. This expression is used mainly in American English.

'The current laws,' he says, 'have more holes than Swiss cheese.'

□ **Swiss cheese** is used in various other ways to describe an argument or theory like this.

Admit it now, Sergeant, the case against Deirdre is a weak one. Deirdre may have had the opportunity, but so did three hundred others. So in my view it's a Swiss cheese you have there, not a case.

In the next few days it's possible that this document could be turned into diplomatic Swiss cheese as problematic language is cut out or weakened.

Paglia disparages Wolf as an ill-educated hustler peddling a Swiss-cheese thesis.

sword

a double-edged sword
a two-edged sword ◄◄

If you say that something is **a double-edged sword** or **a two-edged sword**, you mean that it has both a good and a bad side. People also sometimes talk about **a twin-edged sword** or **a dual-edged sword**. These are all literary expressions.

The strong yen is a double-edged sword for Japan. It increases the spending power of consumers and it helps the nation's banks, but it also raises the costs of exports for car and electronics manufacturers.

The change was a two-edged sword capable of being wielded by either party.

the Sword of Damocles ◄

If you say that someone has **the Sword of Damocles** hanging over their head, you mean that they are in a situation in which something very bad could happen to them at any time. This is a literary expression.

As a Grand Prix driver you have the Sword of Damocles hanging over your head at every moment.

Franco's power to fulfill or crush their hopes hung over the Spanish royal family like a Sword of Damocles.

This is a case where there is a sword of Damocles hanging over their lives.

swords

beat swords into ploughshares
turn swords into ploughshares ◄

If you talk about **beating swords into ploughshares** or **turning swords into ploughshares**, you are talking about plans or efforts to stop war or conflict and to use the resources and technology of warfare to do other things to improve people's lives.

We're going to have literally hundreds of military rockets that are going to be available for some sort of application. There are a lot of people in this country who think that it would be a good idea to beat those swords into plowshares and use them for launching small satellites into space.

Public opinion at the grassroots is now reacting with great warmth to the Gorbachev vision of a world that turns swords into ploughshares.

□ **Swords-into-ploughshares** can be used before a noun. This form of the expression is used mainly in journalism.

The industry grew first on Europe's need for gunpowder in the Napoleonic wars and then, in a sort of elemental swords-into-ploughshares conversion, from the demand for fertiliser.

'We want the soldiers to return to the factories.' The swords-into-ploughshares transformation has been actively encouraged by Belgrade.

□ 'Ploughshares' is spelled 'plowshares' in American English.

cross swords   ◄

If you **cross swords** with someone, you disagree and argue with them or oppose them.

He has perfected dissent as a tactic to further his political career. First, as a member of Indira Gandhi's Congress Party, he repeatedly crossed swords with Mrs Gandhi in the early 1970s.

Norman Fowler and Albert Booth had crossed swords on many occasions when their roles had been reversed in the closing months of the Callaghan Labour government.

In my career with Worcester City and then Yeovil Town I have crossed swords with the biggest and best in non-League football.

system

get something out of your system   ◄◄

If you **get** something **out of** your **system**, you say or do something that you have been wanting to for a long time, and so you begin to feel less worried or angry about it.

Go ahead and get it out of your system if you have to, but don't expect any of us to believe a word you say.

If something awful happens to you at least you can write about it. I'm sure you feel better if you get it out of your system.

systems

all systems go   ◄

You can say 'it's **all systems go**' when you want to indicate that people are very busy with a particular project, or that you expect there will be a lot of activity in a particular field.

Work started on the indoor arena at the beginning of the year and it's now all systems go for a full programme of events over the winter.

The Commonwealth has released its funds and it's all systems go.

T

tab

pick up the tab   ◄◄◄

If you **pick up the tab**, you pay a bill or pay the costs of something, often something that you are not responsible for.

Pollard picked up the tab for dinner.

Japan is already the biggest single aid donor in the world. But it has no intention of picking up the tab for everyone.

If she is always picking up the tab, the inequality in your relationship may be difficult for you both to handle.

table

drink someone under the table

If you say that someone can **drink** you **under the table**, you mean that they can drink much more alcohol than you can without getting drunk.

Donna is the only person I know who can drink me under the table.

They arrived back in the hotel room and the drink flowed even faster. His dad drank him under the table and then tucked him up in bed.

on the table   ◄◄◄

If you put a proposal, plan, or offer **on the table**, you present it formally to other people so it can be discussed and negotiated, in the hope that it will be accepted.

Most other delegations here said a few days' delay was of no matter – in any case the Americans and others had not yet put their proposals on the table.

The United States said Europe must put a new offer on the table to save the talks.

The offer on the table at present is part of the long-term movement to align and control indirect taxation within the EU.

under the table ◄

If you do something **under the table**, you do it secretly because it is dishonest or illegal. This expression is used mainly in American English; the usual British expression is **under the counter**.

Athletes sometimes cheated, sometimes lied, or took money under the table.

Their distributors are here selling their films at the festival's market but they're doing it under the table.

□ An **under-the-table** payment or deal is one that is secret and dishonest or illegal.

Charges flew about ineligible students and under-the-table payments.

There will be no more under-the-table cash.

tables

turn the tables ◄◄◄

If you **turn the tables** on someone, you do something to change a situation so that you gain an advantage over them or cause them problems, after a time when they have had the advantages or have been causing problems for you.

It's quite likely that the Prime Minister will want to turn the tables on his many enemies in the republics and give them something to worry about for a change.

In his response, Kissinger sought to turn the tables on his critics.

All of a sudden the tables are turned, and instead of being the person watching, he becomes the person that's being watched.

tabs

keep tabs on someone ◄◄◄

If someone **keep tabs on** you, they make sure that they always know where you are and what you are doing, often in order to control you.

The school is open to anyone over high school age and we don't keep close tabs on who's here or what they're working on.

It's obviously their job to keep tabs on the financial situation and my job to provide entertaining football on the pitch and win promotion.

We do know that somebody was keeping tabs on her. Perhaps we should have done the same.

tail

chase your own tail

If you say that someone **is chasing** their **own tail**, you are being critical of them for spending a lot of time and energy doing something, but achieving nothing.

Any striving for military superiority means chasing one's own tail.

Look at me, born right down the road, and

after all these years of chasing my tail doing nothing, here I still am.

on your tail ◄◄

If someone is **on** your **tail**, they are following you closely or are chasing you and trying to catch you.

Juarez entered the finishing lap with Zadrobilek right on his tail. Only three kilometres remained.

He heard the wail of sirens, loud and close by. They must be on his tail at last.

We couldn't get out from under the taxes. The IRS was on our tail and we had to do something.

the tail wags the dog ◄

If you say that **the tail is wagging the dog**, you are criticizing the fact that a small or unimportant part of something is becoming too important and is controlling the whole thing.

To avoid the impression of the tail wagging the dog, the Chancellor cannot be seen bending to the wishes of a minority party.

How much should the presentation of policy shape the policy itself? Or, as I heard too many disgruntled senior civil servants complain, how much should the tail wag the dog?

turn tail ◄

If you **turn tail**, you turn and run away from someone or something because you are frightened of them.

Rebels were forced back from position after position until they turned tail and fled.

My hair freezes on my neck to see her on the other side of the bar. I go weak all over. Stumbling, I almost turn tail. 'You have to face her,' I tell myself, trying to calm my heart.

with your tail between your legs ◄

If someone goes off **with** their **tail between** their **legs**, they go off feeling very ashamed, embarrassed, and humiliated, because of a defeat or foolish mistake that they have made.

Embarrassingly, the diplomats actually evacuated the country when there were fears about a possible communist attack. They came back a year or so later with their tails between their legs, having lost much face.

His team retreated last night with tails tucked firmly between their legs.

with your tail up

If you say that someone is doing something **with** their **tail up**, you mean that they seem to be very happy or confident about their chances of success.

We'll go to court with our tails up.

□ People sometimes vary this expression, for example by saying that someone **has** their **tail up** or that something **puts** their **tail up**.

There was no doubt that Mary Rand's out-

standing performance on the first day put everybody's tails up.

tale

live to tell the tale ◄

If you say that someone **has lived to tell the tale**, you mean that they have survived a dangerous or frightening experience.

Michael Sproule was attacked by a shark. He lived to tell the tale but underwent emergency surgery for multiple lacerations to his hands and legs.

At 20mph a pedestrian could escape death or serious injury, but at 30mph half of pedestrians are killed, and at 40mph the chances of living to tell the tale are negligible.

tell the tale
tell its own tale

If something **tells the tale** about a particular situation, it reveals the truth about it. You can also say that something **tells** its **own tale**.

Had he been fired from all of those jobs, or had he quit? I flipped through the papers again, looking for references that might tell the tale, but there weren't any.

The fact that yesterday's runner-up finished only a length in front of Contested Bid, the French Derby third, tells its own tale.

□ People also use the much more frequent adjective **tell-tale** to mean the same thing.

They would surprise the man and not give him time to hide any tell-tale evidence.

In every room are tell-tale signs of a once better life.

tales

dead men tell no tales

People say **'dead men tell no tales'** when they want to say that someone who is dead cannot reveal anything about the circumstances of their death.

Hanley told police the gun went off accidentally while Mr Khan was playing with it. 'These statements were a cover-up,' Mr Spencer told the jury. 'Mr Hanley did it on purpose, his thoughts being that dead men tell no tales.'

tell tales ◄

If you accuse someone of **telling tales**, you are accusing them of telling lies or revealing secrets about a person, so that the person gets into trouble.

She had no right to tell tales to his mother!

The usual pattern of criminal prosecutions is to get the already convicted to tell tales on their bosses in return for cuts in their own sentences.

talk

talk out of your arse

If you say that someone **is talking out of their arse**, you are saying rudely that they are talking complete nonsense. Other words such as 'backside' can be used instead of 'arse'. This is a very informal expression, which is used in British English. Many people consider it offensive.

tall

tall tales
tall stories ◄◄◄

Tall tales or **tall stories** are stories or statements which are difficult to believe because they are so exaggerated or unlikely.

Pollard was described as someone whose rich imagination and keen intellect were convincing, and some of his college chums believed his tall tales.

I have met older, more senior scientists who tell tall tales of the 'old days', 'the golden days' of research, when money was plentiful and there were lots of research jobs.

Sheila believes that children's lying can be taken too seriously. 'I think we need to be more sympathetic about tall stories, make-believe friends and other fibs,' she says.

tangent

go off on a tangent
go off at a tangent ◄

If someone **goes off on a tangent**, they start saying or thinking something that is not directly connected with what they were saying or thinking before. You can use other verbs instead of 'go'. In British English, you can also say that someone **goes off at a tangent**.

He would occasionally go off on a tangent totally unrelated to the textbook or curriculum.

Now and then the narrative goes off at a tangent, but it always seems to return to its theme.

□ These expressions are occasionally used to say that someone's behaviour changes, and they do something that is unconnected with the way they were behaving before.

I suppose I was trying to conform, but then I went off on a tangent.

'They start off with great enthusiasm and then they go off at a tangent.' 'Yes, and they leave the job half done.'

tango

it takes two to tango ◄

If you say that **it takes two to tango**, you mean that a situation or argument involves two people and they are both therefore responsible for it.

It would be very sad if we don't settle this. It

takes two to tango, however, and I suspect we'll still be here tomorrow discussing it.

I've tried everything to stop our marriage falling apart. But it takes two to tango and so far our relationship has been one-sided. At the moment the divorce is still going through.

tank

built like a tank

If you say that someone **is built like a tank**, you mean that they are very big and strong. If you say that an object **is built like a tank**, you mean that it has been constructed very well and very solidly, and will last a long time. Other nouns are sometimes used instead of 'tank'.

He was built like a tank, always sat alone in the bar, and only ever spoke to Nick the barman and then only to utter the same two words: 'Another beer.'

Once I had a Czechoslovakian motorbike. It was built like a tank, weighed a ton, went like a bomb and was pure joy to ride.

Built like a refrigerator and equipped with a formidable stage presence, the chief of the National Front party was in fine vitriolic form.

tap

on tap: 1 ◄◄

If something is **on tap**, it is available and ready for immediate use.

The enterprise agency's close links with the University of Sheffield as well as other business institutions provides local entrepreneurs with a wealth of knowledge and business expertise on tap.

The advantage of group holidays is company on tap but time alone if you want it.

People don't want to interest themselves in politics now, it's a bore. They've got escapist entertainment freely available: pop music, TV, videos on tap, they don't even have to read any more.

on tap: 2 ◄

If an event or activity is **on tap**, it is scheduled to happen very soon. This expression is used in American English.

More military and medical experiments are on tap for Atlantis astronauts today.

It's Detroit against Chicago and Dallas against Pittsburgh in the two pro football games on tap this afternoon.

tape

red tape ◄◄◄

People refer to official rules and procedures as **red tape** when they seem unnecessary and cause delay.

After dealing with all the red tape and finally getting approval we are told that none of the money is forthcoming.

Two lawyers have written a book in a bid to help people cut through the red tape when dealing with British immigration and nationality laws.

The Council said the little money that was available was tied up in bureaucratic red tape.

taped

have got something taped

If you think that you **have got** something **taped**, you think that you fully understand it and are in control of it. This expression is used in British English.

The one certainty of parenthood is that whenever you feel you've got it taped, something or someone will come along to throw you off balance!

China, who only returned to the Games in 1984 after a 28 year absence, rarely go in for anything until they have got it pretty much taped.

target

shoot for the same target

If two people **are shooting for the same target**, they are in agreement about what they are trying to achieve together.

Two brains are better than one in this area, especially when they're shooting for the same target.

Just so we can be sure we're both shooting at the same target, here's a summary of what will happen on Friday night.

taste

leave a bad taste in your mouth ◄

If you say that something someone does **leaves a bad taste in** your **mouth**, you mean that it makes you feel angry or disgusted with them because it was a very unpleasant thing to do. Adjectives such as 'nasty', 'bitter', and 'sour' can be used instead of 'bad'.

It has been called anti-Semitic, anti-feminist and homophobic. The charges are denied, but there's no doubt that some of the magazine's jokes about Jews, women and gays leave a bad taste in the mouth.

Some people are abusive in shops, in buses and on trains. They seem to think it is smart. For the victim it leaves a nasty taste in the mouth.

I'm not staying where I'm not wanted. The whole thing leaves a sour taste in my mouth.

tea

not for all the tea in China

If you say that you would **not** do something

for all the tea in China, you are emphasizing that you definitely do not want to do it.

I wouldn't go through that again for all the tea in China.

He would not change his job for all the tea in China.

tee

to a tee
to a T ◄◄

You can use **to a tee** or **to a T** to mean that something is perfectly or exactly right.

The police soon left, apologizing that they had just been responding to a call about robbers, whose description fit us to a tee.

Lucy was a stickler for perfection, and everything had to be exactly right, rehearsed down to a T.

It was incredibly well-organised, recalls William Boyd. 'He had it down to a tee, writing each contributor an individual letter about it all.'

teeth

armed to the teeth ◄

Someone who is **armed to the teeth** is armed with a lot of weapons or with very effective weapons.

They stationed themselves, armed to the teeth, at vantage points near the union hall.

The police are grossly underpaid and underequipped while the criminals are armed to the teeth with the most modern equipment.

cut your teeth ◄◄

If you do something new which gives you experience and helps you learn how to do more advanced or complicated things, you can say that you **cut** your **teeth** doing that thing.

For Dennis, the experience forms part of his plan to cut his teeth on demanding theatre parts before making the break for TV and film.

He cut his teeth in the sixties as director of Edinburgh's Traverse Theatre.

He had cut his editorial teeth on the London Evening Standard.

fed up to the back teeth
sick to the back teeth

If you are **fed up to the back teeth** with something or **sick to the back teeth** with it, you feel annoyed, irritated, or tired because it has been going on for a long time and you think it should be stopped or changed. These expressions are used in British English.

I've always been a very strong Conservative but I am fed up to the back teeth with them at the moment.

It also shows how frustrated and sick to the back teeth the US public is of big-time, big-money, slick Washington politics.

get your teeth into something
sink your teeth into something ◄◄

If you **get** your **teeth into** something or **sink** your **teeth into** it, you become deeply involved with it and do it with a lot of energy and enthusiasm.

Half the trouble is having nothing interesting to do. We've not had a case to get our teeth into for weeks.

When Jeff came to Britain in 1956 from his native Barbados, his welcome was harsh and so he wasted little time in sinking his teeth into combating prejudice.

gnashing of teeth
wailing and gnashing of teeth
weeping and gnashing of teeth ◄

When people become very worried or agitated by something unexpected or unnecessary that has happened, you can say that there is **gnashing of teeth** or **wailing and gnashing of teeth**, especially when you want to suggest that they are overreacting or showing their concern in an excessive way. You can also say that there is **weeping and gnashing of teeth**.

In times of widespread strife and much gnashing of teeth, a sense of community is needed to stop everyone plummeting into the dark depths of despair.

It was the biggest earthquake to hit LA in years. Radio preachers gibbered about the end of the world. There was a whole lot of wailing and gnashing of teeth.

Without this expert guidance, the gamut of amateur rug repairs often causes weeping and gnashing of teeth among professionals.

gnash your teeth ◄◄

If you say that someone **is gnashing** their **teeth**, you mean that they are showing their anger or annoyance about something in a very obvious way.

If Blythe heard that piece, I bet he was gnashing his teeth.

He naturally gnashes his teeth over the growing number of lawsuits that have made doing business in America increasingly expensive and unpredictable.

grind your teeth ◄

If someone **is grinding** their **teeth**, they are very angry or frustrated about something, but feel that they cannot say or do anything about it.

Men respond that if women are in charge they don't do anything for other women either. The predominantly female audience was grinding its teeth.

☐ You can also talk about **grinding of teeth**, **teeth-grinding**, and **tooth-grinding**.

There has been much grinding of teeth about what is seen by the government as the harsh-

ness of the European Community's decisions on the environment in relation to Britain.

When you are a little boy of nine, your father can seem like a hero one minute, only to cause you tooth-grinding embarrassment the next.

grit your teeth   ◄◄◄

If you **grit** your **teeth**, you decide to carry on even though the situation you are in is very difficult.

He says that there are no simple solutions, that it's going to take time, that there is going to be hardship, but we have to grit our teeth and get on with it.

We were very tired after Sunday which was understandable and we now face five games in nine days. The players gritted their teeth and kept going.

have teeth   ◄

If you say that an organization or law **has teeth**, you mean that it has the necessary authority or power to make people obey it.

Trade union committees should have teeth, and not be convenient partners for management.

Pro-democracy campaigners complain that the new assembly will have no teeth.

This legislation has teeth, but I am getting reports back that magistrates are not imposing the tougher penalties.

lie through your teeth   ◄

If you say that someone **is lying through** their **teeth** or **is lying in** their **teeth**, you mean that they are telling very obvious lies and do not seem to be embarrassed about this.

We ought to be mad that public officials lie through their teeth.

'We were on vacation in Barbados a few years ago and we met Freddie Mercury in a bar,' says Phil, lying through his teeth.

I should have known he was lying in his teeth when he said he would pay more than we were owed.

like pulling teeth

If you say that doing something is **like pulling teeth**, you mean that it is very difficult. This expression is used mainly in American English.

The whole scene over the last year is that people are just not buying. To get a car sold is like pulling teeth. And it's getting progressively worse.

Identifying excess and duplication of work is easy. Doing something about it is like pulling teeth.

set your teeth on edge   ◄

If something **sets** your **teeth on edge**, you find it extremely irritating or unpleasant.

He stood and took down the portrait. Some-

thing about it had lately been setting his teeth on edge.

His casual arrogance never failed to set my teeth on edge.

There is a long roof above the old body of the church and this roof has been re-tiled fairly recently in hard, livid-red shiny tiles which set the teeth on edge.

show your teeth

If you **show** your **teeth**, you show that you are capable of fighting or defending yourself.

The bureaucracy was still showing its teeth, resisting and trying to sabotage our efforts.

We need to show some teeth if we are going to solve the problems we have been experiencing.

teething

teething problems
teething troubles   ◄◄◄

If a project or new product has **teething problems** or **teething troubles**, there are problems in its early stages or when it first becomes available. These expressions are used in British English.

The Council has conceded there have been teething problems with the new voucher system but said these were being corrected.

Some teething troubles aside, it works – but not, it appears, significantly better than the old system.

tell

tell someone where to get off

If someone **tells** you **where to get off**, they are telling you in a rude and forceful way that they cannot accept what you are saying or doing.

But if somebody tried to do that to you, you'd just go right up to them and tell them where to get off.

Were she not Aubrey's niece, he would deal more sharply with her whining. He would tell her where to get off.

tempest

a tempest in a teapot

If you say that something is **a tempest in a teapot**, you mean that it is not very important but people are making a lot of unnecessary fuss about it. This expression is used in American English; the British expression is **a storm in a teacup**.

'It's a tempest in a teapot,' he said of the controversy over the painting.

He believed that the agency's clash with the company was, in effect, a tempest in a teapot and that they would take appropriate action to placate the agency.

tenterhooks

on tenterhooks ◄

If you are **on tenterhooks**, you are very nervous or excited, because you are keen to know what is going to happen.

Dealers said the market was on tenterhooks about the size of the German rate cut.

I know you're hanging on tenterhooks wanting to know what happened.

'It was a good match wasn't it? Very exciting.' 'Yes, we were on tenterhooks.'

territory

go with the territory

If you are talking about a particular situation or activity and you say that something **goes with the territory**, you mean that it often occurs in that kind of situation or activity, and so you have to be prepared for it.

At Arsenal, that kind of attention goes with the territory and I accept that I have to learn to live with it.

For Robbins, activism goes with the territory. 'Art and politics have always been connected,' he says.

test

stand the test of time ◄◄◄

If you say that something **has stood the test of time**, you mean that it has proved its value and has not failed or has not gone out of fashion since it first appeared. Verbs such as 'pass' and 'survive' are sometimes used instead of 'stand'.

Many people will be wary of the peace until it has stood the test of time.

The wit and wisdom of Oscar Wilde always seem to stand the test of time.

Fashions in floor coverings come and go, but wooden floors have stood the test of time.

Since it began manufacturing in 1933, Gossen has built easy-to-use, reliable equipment that has survived the test of time due to its robust design.

tether

at the end of your tether ◄◄

If you say that you are **at the end of** your **tether**, you mean that you feel desperate because you are in a difficult situation and you do not know how to deal with it. You can also use this expression to show your impatience or annoyance with someone. This expression is used mainly in British English; the usual American expression is **at the end of** your **rope**.

I'm at the end of my tether trying to find support and a cure for this condition which I have suffered from for 13 years.

She was in desperate straits, at the end of her tether. She needed someone she could talk to, someone she could trust.

We all reached the end of our tether. We snapped. It was spontaneous action but people are now saying they are not putting up with the appalling service any more.

there

not be all there

If you say that someone **is not all there**, you think that they are not very intelligent.

He wasn't all there, a bit mental or something.

But she wasn't all there and that's a fact. You could see it in those eyes, pretty and soft but more animal than human.

thick

in the thick of it
in the thick of something ◄◄◄

If you are **in the thick of it** or **in the thick of** an activity or situation, you are deeply involved in the activity or situation.

Although he was not a member of the Army Operational Staff, he soon put himself in the thick of it.

He suddenly found himself in the thick of desperate fighting.

He was in the thick of the action for the full 90 minutes of the game.

lay it on thick

If you say that someone **is laying it on thick**, you mean that they are exaggerating a statement, experience, or emotion in order to impress people. **Lay it on with a trowel** means the same.

Gerhardt explained the position to the Press Officer, laying it on thick about Adrian Winter's importance.

Very many people have written about this devastation, laying it on thick. But the real picture is more horrific.

thick as mince

If you say that someone is as **thick as mince**, you mean that they are very stupid. This expression is used mainly in Scottish English.

No point in expecting any real help from Personnel – most of them are as thick as mince.

Well, what do you expect? She's as thick as mince.

thick as shit

In British English, if you say that someone is as **thick as shit**, you mean that they are very stupid. This is a very informal expression, which many people find offensive.

After a few minutes browsing through these establishments, we can only conclude that the proprietors and their clientele are either thick as shit, blinded by racism, or both.

thick as thieves

If two or more people are as **thick as thieves**, they are very friendly with each other.

Jones and Cook had met at the age of ten when both had attended the Christopher Wren School in Shepherd's Bush. Now they were as thick as thieves.

Old man Grant went to school with Maloney, the other lawyer in town. They're thick as thieves. Maloney does all his business.

thick as two planks
thick as two short planks

If you say that someone is as **thick as two planks** or as **thick as two short planks**, you mean that they are very stupid. These expressions are used in British English.

His people regarded him as a great and wise monarch. In fact he was as thick as two planks.

He was convinced that private investigator Paul Crook was immature, inexperienced and as thick as two short planks.

through thick and thin ◄◄

If you do something **through thick and thin**, you continue doing it even when circumstances make it very difficult for you.

I will go on loving James through thick and thin no matter what happens.

Few things give me greater pleasure in my public life than the knowledge that I have supported the Open University, through thick and thin.

She has stuck with him through thick and thin, after everyone else thought he was a disgrace.

thin

spread yourself too thin ◄

If you **spread** yourself **too thin**, you try to do a lot of different things at the same time, with the result that you cannot do any of them properly. Other adverbs can be used instead of 'too'.

If you spread yourself too thin on the social circuit, you will not be able to keep up with everyone.

'There are 80 of us taking care of 117 cemeteries.' 'Isn't that spreading yourself a little thin?'

□ You can also say that someone **spreads** themselves **too thinly**.

Like so many businesses in the booming 1980s, the company grew too fast and spread itself too thinly across too many diverse areas.

thin as a rake
thin as a stick

If you say that someone is as **thin as a rake** or **thin as a stick**, you are emphasizing that they are very thin.

I was so shocked by his appearance, his face so gaunt, his eyes sunk in their sockets and his body thin as a rake as though he were suffering from some wasting disease.

I'd always been as thin as a stick but in London my weight went up to more than 12 stone.

□ Other nouns such as 'rail' or 'lath' can be used instead of 'rake' and 'stick'.

She was blue-eyed, tall, thin as a rail, pale as paper and very young.

She may be as thin as a lath, but single-handedly she swings a huge wheelbarrow on and off her little gray truck in one smooth motion.

thing

do your own thing ◄◄◄

If you **do** your **own thing**, you live, act, or behave in the way you want to, without paying attention to convention and without depending on other people.

She was allowed to do her own thing as long as she kept in touch by phone to say she was okay.

I made a point of doing my own thing on the pitch and ignored my coach's instructions. I must have been one of the most undisciplined players in Italy.

one thing leads to another ◄◄

If you are giving an account of something and you say **'one thing led to another'**, you mean that you do not think you need to give any details of events, because they happened in a fairly obvious way.

I never thought I'd be a president, but after they closed down the university where I was a professor, I emerged as a kind of spokesman. One thing led to another and so here I am today.

At the end of the evening, Mike said he'd drop me home and, you've guessed it, one thing led to another and we ended up in bed.

thorn

a thorn in your side
a thorn in your flesh ◄◄◄

If you describe someone or something as **a thorn in** your **side**, you mean that they continually annoy or irritate you. You can also say that they are **a thorn in** your **flesh**.

She has become a thorn in the side of the government since publishing a number of reports pointing out that public cash was being mishandled.

The council doesn't like organisations like ours because we're a thorn in their side.

She was regarded locally as an undoubted eccentric, and was, apparently, a thorn in the flesh of the Teignmouth police.

thread

hang by a thread: 1 ◄

If you say that something **hangs by a thread**, you mean that it is very likely to fail, although it has not failed yet.

It's clear that the ceasefire is hanging by a thread with as yet no appropriate impartial body to monitor or supervise it.

England's World Cup hopes hang by a thread and they must now rely on the results of the others in their group going their way.

hang by a thread: 2

If you say that someone's life **hangs by a thread**, you mean that they are seriously ill and are very likely to die.

The baby was delivered by emergency Caesarean and the life of her mother hung by a thread.

His kidneys had failed and his life was hanging by a thread.

throat

cut your own throat

If you say that someone **is cutting** their **own throat**, you mean that they are making a mistake by doing something which is going to result in disaster for them. The verb 'slit' is sometimes used instead of 'cut'.

I think the union is cutting its own throat because the fact of the matter is, if General Motors can't get its costs in line, then its market share will continue to fall, and there will be even more jobs lost.

Do they not care at all about the survival of the sport? They are slitting their own throats as they'll be the first to lose out when anglers start giving up.

grab someone by the throat: 1
take someone by the throat
have someone by the throat ◄

If you **grab** someone or something **by the throat** or **take** them **by the throat**, you make a determined attempt to control, defeat, or deal with them.

The French team grabbed the All Blacks by the throat and didn't let up the pressure on their players.

Instead of being passive because life won't come to you, you must get out there and grab life by the throat.

Gloucestershire took the game by the throat from the start.

□ If you are succeeding in dealing with some-one or something, you say that you **have** them **by the throat**.

He has his enemy by the throat and he is not about to let go.

grab someone by the throat: 2

If something **grabs** you **by the throat**, it is so powerful, interesting, or exciting that you are forced to pay attention to it.

A large animal had died, leaving a smell that grabs you by the throat.

The film still grabs you by the throat.

jump down someone's throat

If you say something to someone and you complain that they then **jump down** your **throat**, you are complaining that they react in a very impatient, angry, and unpleasant way which you consider unjustified and unreasonable.

If I even asked her about her day, she'd jump down my throat, as if I were interrogating her.

Is your boss more likely to jump down your throat than listen to your useful suggestions?

ram something down someone's throat ◄◄◄

If you accuse someone of trying to **ram** something **down** your **throat**, you mean that they are trying to force you to accept, believe, or learn something against your will. Verbs such as 'shove', 'force', and 'cram' are sometimes used instead of 'ram'.

I can't understand why we're trying to ram Shakespeare down their throat when they haven't got a basic education as regards reading and writing.

'In America, you get religion shoved down your throat as soon as you're born,' says Paul, disgusted.

I cannot force my beliefs down the throats of the Air Staff. I have to respond to the views of the Air Staff.

throats

at each other's throats
at one another's throats ◄◄

If you describe two people or groups as **at each other's throats**, you mean that they are continually arguing or fighting. You can also say that they are **at one another's throats**.

He and Stevens didn't get on, they'd been at each other's throats for years.

European partners, poised to sign a historic treaty for unity, were at each other's throats last night in some of the worst bickering since the Second World War.

MPs are at one another's throats all the time, and it's not functioning as a very effective government.

throes

in the throes of something ◄◄◄

If you are **in the throes of** doing or experiencing something, especially something difficult, you are busy doing it or are deeply involved in it.

The boy's parents are in the throes of moving house and it seems they completely forgot about the arrangement in all the upheaval.

The stock market is in the throes of its worst ever crisis. Amid rumours of brokers committing suicide and speculators going bankrupt, share prices have collapsed.

Earlier this year, the paper's future looked bleak. It was in the throes of a four-month-old strike and was losing nearly a million dollars a day.

throttle

at full throttle
in full throttle ◄

If someone does something **at full throttle**, they do it with all their energy and effort. When someone is behaving like this, you can say they are **at full throttle** or are **in full throttle**.

He started at full throttle, denouncing 'the poll tax which the Tories believe they can use to drive down living conditions and force poverty and suffering on working people'.

This was the actress whom I had seen in full throttle in performance, destroying all in her path.

□ You can use **full throttle** in other ways.

She was a high-powered Western businesswoman who went at things full throttle.

Robert Palmer turns on his oh-so-suave and silky touch and gives it full throttle on his latest album, Ridin' High.

□ **At full throttle** is often used literally to talk about an engine which is operating at its greatest speed.

thumb

have a green thumb ◄

If you say that someone **has a green thumb**, you mean that they are very good at gardening. This expression is used in American English; the British expression is **have green fingers**.

She had a green thumb and using only instinct and countless loads of cow manure, casually grew tomatoes, scallions, peonies, roses and bumper crops of fruit.

□ You can describe someone who is good at gardening as **green-thumbed**.

The green-thumbed gardeners will share the secrets of their success at a series of nine gardening workshops.

stick out like a sore thumb
stand out like a sore thumb ◄

If you say that someone or something **sticks out like a sore thumb** or **stands out like a sore thumb**, you mean that they are very noticeable because they are very different from the other people or things around them.

But the increase in armed robbery, that's a big problem. Foreigners are at somewhat greater risk because they are more wealthy and they stick out like a sore thumb.

'First impressions are very important,' says Baines. 'Does the new housing stick out like a sore thumb or blend into its surroundings?'

In that country a European stands out like a sore thumb.

under someone's thumb ◄◄

If you say that someone is **under** another person's **thumb**, you disapprove of the fact that the other person keeps them under their control or has a very strong influence on them.

'You mean he travels with his mother?' 'Incredible, isn't it? He's utterly under her thumb. It's a wonder he dared move out of his room without her permission.'

National television is firmly under the thumb of the hardline president.

Ian told the court how his wife kept him under the thumb during their seven-year marriage.

thumbs

all thumbs
all fingers and thumbs

If you do something in a clumsy way and keep making mistakes while you are doing it, you can say that you are **all thumbs**. In British English, you can also say that you are **all fingers and thumbs**.

Can you open this? I'm all thumbs.

I wish I had asked more questions in hospital. The staff made it look so easy but when I came to give Stephanie a bath, I was all fingers and thumbs.

the thumbs down ◄◄◄

If you give a plan, suggestion, or activity **the thumbs down**, you show that you do not approve of it and are not willing to accept it.

Out of 58,000 replies, 79 per cent gave the thumbs down to compulsory testing.

Unlicensed boxing should be illegal. It is dangerous for the individuals involved, dangerous for the sport and gets a firm thumbs down from me.

□ A **thumbs down** or a **thumbs-down sign** is a sign that you make by pointing your thumb downwards in order to show dissatisfaction or disagreement, or to show that things are going badly.

the thumbs up ◄◄◄

If you give a plan, suggestion, or activity **the thumbs up**, you show that you approve of it and are willing to accept it.

A big US oil company is giving the big thumbs-up to the president's energy plan.

The chairman of the Federal Communications Commission today gave a tentative thumbs-up to the alliance.

The ski school gets the thumbs up from visitors.

□ A **thumbs up** or a **thumbs-up sign** is a sign that you make by pointing your thumb upwards in order to show satisfaction or agreement, or to show that everything is all right.

twiddle your thumbs ◄

If you say that someone **is twiddling** their **thumbs,** you mean that they do not have anything to do or are wasting their time, and are not achieving anything useful.

The Government must address this problem. It cannot expect graduates who have invested time and their parents' money to go to university then to twiddle their thumbs on the dole.

I feel it's important to organise things for the children. You can't trust schools to do it, and if you leave children to themselves, they only twiddle their thumbs.

thunder

steal someone's thunder ◄

If someone **steals** your **thunder**, they stop you from getting attention or praise by doing something better or more exciting than you, or by doing what you had intended to do before you can do it. You can also say that someone **steals the thunder from** you.

Be wary. He's liable to be either a bad boss or an insecure one and afraid that you might steal some of his thunder.

He has begun to make a habit of stealing the thunder from his potential rivals.

ticket

a one-way ticket ◄

If you describe something as **a one-way ticket** to a particular situation or state, usually an undesirable or unpleasant one, you mean that it is certain to lead to that situation.

Having strong feelings for someone when those feelings aren't returned or even acknowledged can be difficult to cope with and very painful. It represents a one-way ticket to unhappiness.

She knew that the succession of secretarial jobs she'd picked up since leaving college were a one-way ticket to nowhere, professionally speaking.

tide

swim against the tide
swim with the tide ◄

If you say that someone **is swimming against the tide**, you mean that they are doing or saying something which is the opposite of what most other people are doing or saying.

Adenauer generally appeared to be swimming against the tide in international politics.

Smith New Court is swimming against the tide of financial forecasters and reckons inflation will fall over the next year.

□ If you say that someone **is swimming with the tide**, you mean that they are acting in the same way as most other people.

In promoting in Britain a more co-operative, less confrontational form of capitalism we are swimming with the tide of the future.

tight

sit tight ◄◄◄

If you decide to **sit tight**, you decide that the best way to deal with a difficult situation is to wait and see how it develops before taking any action.

The message is, those who want to sell their houses should sit tight for a couple of years if they can.

I think the Bundesbank is going to sit tight for a couple of months, at least until it sees good news on pay settlements and better signs on money supply growth.

They would be better off sitting tight in their cosy defended positions, holding fire until they saw their attackers' next move.

tightrope

walk a tightrope ◄◄◄

If you say that someone **is walking a tightrope**, you mean that they are in a difficult or delicate situation and need to be very careful what they do or say, because they need to take account of the interests of opposing groups.

He is walking a tightrope between the young activists and the more traditional elements within the democracy movement.

The government is walking a tightrope in trying to keep in balance all the various economic factors.

□ You can refer to someone's attempt to satisfy the interests of opposing groups as **a tightrope walk**.

The strategy is something of a tightrope walk.

tiles

on the tiles

If someone has a night **on the tiles**, they go

out in the evening, for example to a bar or disco, and do not return home until very late or until the following morning. This expression is used in British English.

Charlotte was dressed for a night on the tiles.

You look as though you've been out on the tiles, Ken.

till

have your hand in the till
have your fingers in the till ◄

If you say that someone **has had** their **hand in the till** or **has had** their **fingers in the till**, you mean that they have been caught stealing or doing something wrong. You can also talk about people being caught or found **with** their **hands in the till** or **with** their **fingers in the till**. These expressions are used mainly in British English; the usual American expression is **caught with** your **hand in the cookie jar**.

They have acknowledged that I did not have my hand in the till, I took no money for personal use and have not misappropriated any funds whatsoever.

Thirteen company directors were found with their hands in the till in the first quarter of this year.

He got caught with his fingers in the till once too often.

time

big time ◄

You can use **big time** to emphasize the importance or extent of something that is happening. This expression is used mainly in American English.

Wall Street does not like surprises and DEC is surprising Wall Street big time.

With a little luck we could make this thing work, and work big-time.

the big time
hit the big time ◄◄◄

The **big time** means fame and success. When someone becomes famous and successful, you can say that they **hit the big time**.

Sinclair now looks ready for a crack at the big time.

After a series of small but critically acclaimed roles in the Eighties, she has now moved into the big time.

He opened his own salon in 1923 and hit the big time in 1935, when he designed the wedding dress for the Duchess of Gloucester.

□ You can use **big-time** to describe someone or something that is very successful, powerful, or important.

He was a big-time drug trafficker who fled to Miami in 1986 to escape Colombian justice.

live on borrowed time
be on borrowed time ◄◄

If you say that someone or something **is living on borrowed time** or **is on borrowed time**, you mean that you do not expect them to survive for much longer.

The organization is living on borrowed time. Its state funding runs out in June of this year, and beyond that, the future is in doubt.

From this moment onwards, this government is on borrowed time.

mark time ◄◄

If you **mark time**, you do not do anything new or decisive, because you are waiting to see how a situation develops.

Today's gathering of European finance ministers in Bath can do little more than mark time pending the French referendum on September 20th.

The negotiations will resume next month at the State Department, but it could be an occasion for marking time, waiting for the Clinton administration to lean in one direction or the other.

play for time ◄◄◄

If you **play for time**, you try to delay doing or saying something definite until you have decided what is the best course of action to take.

He had to play for time, give himself a moment to think.

Pierce was playing for time, trying to decide if the call was genuine or some kind of hoax.

The republic's government is playing for time by asking for clarification of the nature of the economic sanctions.

time on your hands ◄◄◄

If you have **time on** your **hands**, you have a lot of free time and you do not know what to do with it.

Jimmy needed discipline and planned activities. He had too much time on his hands and that caused him to get into trouble.

There are one or two other people on the estate with time on their hands. I think they would all be eager to do something useful.

With more time on their hands, many people would like to become mature students but worry about whether they will be able to cope with the demands of studying while they still have mortgages and other commitments to attend to.

tin

have a tin ear for something

If you say that someone **has a tin ear for** something, you mean that they do not have any natural ability for it and cannot appreciate or understand it fully. Compare **have an ear for** something; see **ear**.

For a playwright specializing in characters

who use the vernacular, he has a tin ear for dialogue.

a tin god
a little tin god

If you accuse someone of behaving like **a tin god** or like **a little tin god**, you are accusing them of behaving as if they are much more important and powerful than they actually are. These expressions are used mainly in British English.

So what are his qualifications for acting like a little tin god?

In a country that has neither government nor political structure, he negotiated with tin-god warlords.

tinker

not give a tinker's damn
not give a tinker's cuss

If you say that you **don't give a tinker's damn** or **don't give a tinker's cuss** about something, you mean that you do not care about it at all. These are informal expressions, which are now old-fashioned.

The people in town did not seem to be as excited about it. I felt that day that most of them were uninformed and couldn't give a tinker's damn about the bowling alley or the students.

For 50 weeks of the year, give or take the odd Davis Cup disaster, the great British public couldn't give a tinker's cuss about tennis.

□ You can also say that someone or something is **not worth a tinker's damn** when you think they are useless or worthless.

The real truth is you haven't been worth a tinker's damn all week.

Worthless items are dismissed as not worth a tinker's damn.

tip

on the tip of your tongue: 1 ◄

If you say that a remark or question was **on the tip of** your **tongue**, you mean that you really wanted to say something but decided not to.

The worst happened: Amelia confirmed his fear that she didn't love him. At this point he could have easily counter-attacked. The words were on the tip of his tongue, but he took a deep breath, and instead said, 'Let's take some time out. I don't think I can talk about it right now without getting hostile myself.'

'What do you make of it?' he said after a while. It was on the tip of my tongue to tell him he'd have to ask Charlie. But I said nothing.

on the tip of your tongue: 2

If you say that something such as a word, answer, or name is **on the tip of** your **tongue**, you mean that you are sure you

know what it is even though you cannot remember it at the moment.

I know this, no, no, don't tell me, oh, it's on the tip of my tongue.

But it was no good trying to force recall. It would come to him eventually, like an elusive name on the tip of the tongue.

the tip of the iceberg ◄◄◄

If you describe something as **the tip of the iceberg**, you mean that it is part of a very large problem or a very serious situation, although the rest may not be obvious or fully known about.

We get about 2,000 complaints every year and we are just the tip of the iceberg. Most people just suffer in silence.

MPs Richard Burden and Lynne Jones claimed the case was the tip of a very large iceberg when they revealed the whole of the gruesome story.

Mr Gunn said the Fitzgerald inquiry only touched the tip of an iceberg of corruption.

tip the balance
tip the scales ◄◄◄

When two possible outcomes of a situation seem equally likely, and then something happens which is sufficient to produce one outcome rather than the other, you can say that this thing **tips the balance** or **tips the scales**.

As the election looms, the two main parties appear so evenly matched that just one issue could tip the balance.

Years later, she still believed it had been Howe's warnings, not the children's welfare or any residual love for her, that had finally tipped the scales against his leaving her for a new life with Lucy.

tod

on your tod

If you do something **on your tod**, you do it by yourself, without help from anyone else. If you are **on your tod**, you are alone. This expression is used in British English.

Oliver knows it's odds against me picking up his trail on my tod.

You're the talk of the Branch, the way you sussed things out all on your tod.

The main restaurant's OK. I use it every so often when I'm on my tod.

today

here today, gone tomorrow ◄

If you say that something or someone is **here today, gone tomorrow** or **here today and gone tomorrow**, you mean that they are only present for a short time. You often use this expression to suggest that this is a bad thing.

There have been numerous schemes designed to provide children who are here today, gone tomorrow with the same educational opportunities as settled children.

Well, I think it makes a big difference because the freedom that they have is not true freedom, and that's because it's here today and gone tomorrow.

□ Journalists sometimes use **here today, gone tomorrow** before a noun to describe a person or thing that is present for only a short time.

The defence secretary stormed off, throwing his microphone at Day, who had described him as a 'here today, gone tomorrow minister'.

Designers should be concentrating on creating beautiful, wearable clothes that flatter women and make them feel attractive. Here today, gone tomorrow fashion fads are passé.

toe

a toe in the water ◄

If you dip your **toe in the water**, you start slowly and carefully doing something that you have not done before, because you are not sure if you will like it or if it will be successful. This expression is used more commonly in British English than American. There are several variations of this expression; for example, you can say that you have your **toe in the waters**.

Last year, she finally dipped a toe in the commercial waters by hiring an agent.

Recently, judges have been encouraged to dip a cautious toe into the waters of public debate.

His company has recently opened offices in Taiwan and Spain, and has begun a joint venture in South Korea. 'We have our toes in the water,' Mr. Creedon says.

□ You can also use **toe in the water** before a noun.

We are taking a toe in the water approach, with a small gallery; but I think Paris has tremendous potential.

toe to toe ◄

If you go or stand **toe to toe** with someone, you fight, argue, or compete with them fiercely, openly, and directly. This expression is used mainly in American English, but it is also sometimes used in British journalism.

The company might seem to be strong enough to go toe-to-toe with their rivals. But Borden has no such intentions.

They do not stand toe to toe as enemies, as the relationship of so-called right- and left-wing Catholics is sometimes characterized. They are not necessarily opposed to each other at all.

He couldn't think of anything else. If it didn't work, he'd just fight it out toe to toe until there was nothing left to fight with. He wouldn't surrender.

□ You can also use **toe-to-toe** before a noun.

Toe-to-toe confrontations have plagued the project.

toes

keep you on your toes ◄◄◄

If you say that someone or something **keeps you on** your **toes**, you mean that they cause you or force you to be alert and ready for anything that might happen.

She kept us on our toes right from the moment she took command.

He is just back from his third nationwide campaign tour in a year and his fiery campaign rhetoric has kept opposition parties on their toes for months.

It's always good to have a little bit of apprehension, because it keeps you on your toes, doesn't it?

make your toes curl ◄

If something **makes** your **toes curl**, you react to it very strongly, and, for example, find it very embarrassing or very exciting.

He reminds us of every time our toes curled in the past watching TV presenters making idiotic comments or squirm-inducing jokes.

There are moments of tenderness and some very funny scenes in Nigel Charnock's direction. And there are scenes, too, that make your toes curl.

□ You can also talk about a **toe-curling** experience.

Movies about famous explorers rarely work, as some recent toe-curling efforts show.

step on someone's toes
tread on someone's toes ◄◄

If you **step on** someone's **toes** or **tread on** their **toes**, you offend them by criticizing the way they do something or by interfering in something that is their responsibility.

'Small shopkeepers know who sells what,' Sue explains, 'and so you don't step on one another's toes.'

Women often feel ridiculously inhibited and duty-bound not to antagonize the men they work with or tread on too many toes.

turn up your toes

In British English, if you say that someone or something **turns up** their **toes**, you mean that they die. This expression is used to refer to death in a light-hearted or humorous way.

Gardening is a joy for thousands of Britons, for most of the time. But then those little problems crop up. Pests and diseases turn great plans into dismal flops, healthy-looking plants turn up their toes, and crystal pools become smelly puddles.

toffee

can't do something for toffee

If you say, for example, that you **can't** dance **for toffee** or you **can't** sing **for toffee**, you are emphasizing that you are very bad at dancing or singing. This expression is used in British English.

We set off, and within a step or two it was clear she couldn't dance for toffee; she was as rigid as a telegraph pole and quite unwilling to be led.

Tom

every Tom, Dick, and Harry ◄

The expression **every Tom, Dick, and Harry** is used to refer informally or scornfully to ordinary people who do not have any special skills or qualities. In this expression, 'or' can be used instead of 'and', and 'Harriet' and various other names are sometimes used instead of 'Harry'.

In the last two years, the summer clientele going there has deteriorated. These days, they've been letting in every Tom, Dick and Harry.

You cannot sell a gun to any Tom Dick or Harry, can you? It's very difficult to obtain a legally held gun.

Any Tom, Dick or Harriet can put on a jacket and say, 'I'll be a producer.' I've just proved it.

tomorrow

like there's no tomorrow
as if there were no tomorrow ◄

If someone does something **like there's no tomorrow** or **as if there were no tomorrow**, they do it a lot, without thinking about the consequences of their behaviour.

Only one group is taking up smoking like there's no tomorrow, and that's teenage girls. One quarter of 15-year-old girls smoke now, averaging 50 cigarettes a week.

In the property boom of the 1980s, the banks lent to property companies in Britain as if there were no tomorrow.

tomorrow is another day

You say **tomorrow is another day** when you have just had an unhappy experience but you are confident or hopeful that your life will be much better in the future.

Smith told newspapers that his wife's killer was an evil woman, but that he fully intended to piece his life back together. 'I may take a walk down the fields and have a cry alone, but then I'll carry on. Tomorrow is another day.'

Everything went wrong. I didn't play well, but tomorrow is another day.

ton

come down on someone like a ton of bricks ◄

If you do something wrong and someone with authority **comes down on** you **like a ton of bricks**, they reprimand or punish you very severely. You can also say that someone **will be down on** you **like a ton of bricks**.

If you do something awful they all come down on you like a ton of bricks.

If I owed them any money, they'd be down on me like a ton of bricks.

□ The metric measurement **tonne** is occasionally used instead of **ton**.

like a ton of bricks

Like a ton of bricks is used to indicate that something happens very suddenly and dramatically. For example, if something hits you **like a ton of bricks**, you suddenly become aware of it. If you fall for someone **like a ton of bricks**, you fall suddenly and very deeply in love with them.

By mid-July, the dangers had hit Bobby like a ton of bricks.

She was twenty when Orpen met her and he fell for her like a ton of bricks.

tongue

bite your tongue
hold your tongue ◄◄◄

If you **bite** your **tongue** or **hold** your **tongue**, you do not say a particular thing, even though you want to or are expected to, because it would be the wrong thing to say in the circumstances, or because you are waiting for a more appropriate time to speak.

I'm perfectly prepared to bite my tongue until I've learned what the system is all about. Then when I've got something to contribute, they will hear from me.

Douglas held his tongue, preferring not to speak out on a politically sensitive issue he felt was best left to politicians.

find your tongue

If you **find** your **tongue**, you begin to talk, when you have previously been too shy, frightened, or embarrassed to say anything.

After a pause in which the gallery's distinguished visitor seemed lost for words, he eventually found his tongue.

get your tongue round something ◄

If you say that you cannot **get** your **tongue round** a word or phrase, you mean that you find it difficult to pronounce. This expression is used in British English.

He couldn't get his tongue round the word.

The Americans are as notorious as the British for their inability to get their tongues around foreign words.

give someone the rough side of your tongue
give someone the rough edge of your tongue

If you **give** someone **the rough side of** your **tongue** or **the rough edge of** your **tongue**, you speak angrily or harshly to them about something that they have done wrong. This is an old-fashioned expression, which is used in British English.

He's really going to give the boy the rough side of his tongue.

'Come on, Mrs Lorimer,' said Kemp, giving her the rough edge of his tongue, 'you surely knew before the police told you that Foster-Yates ran the Watlingford Motel.'

speak with forked tongue
talk with forked tongue ◄

If you accuse someone of **speaking with forked tongue** or of **talking with forked tongue**, you are accusing them of lying or of deliberately misleading people.

He speaks with forked tongue. I don't trust him and I don't like him.

Everybody in this business is talking with forked tongue.

tongue in cheek
with tongue in cheek ◄◄◄

If you describe a remark or piece of writing as **tongue in cheek**, you mean that it is meant to be funny and ironic, and is not meant to be taken seriously. You can also say that someone is talking or writing **with tongue in cheek**.

I think people are taking all this more seriously than we intended. It was supposed to be tongue in cheek.

If Howard has said that about Olney, it must have been with tongue in cheek.

Labour MPs, some with their tongue firmly in their cheeks, judged the overall result to have rewarded 'the competent and the loyal'.

□ **Tongue-in-cheek** can also be used before a noun.

We ran that ad just one time and it was meant to be a light-hearted, tongue-in-cheek approach. We never intended to offend anyone.

tongue-lashing ◄

If someone gives you **a tongue-lashing**, they speak harshly or angrily to you about something that you have done. You can also say that they **tongue-lash** you.

After a cruel tongue-lashing, he threw the girl out of the group, sending the boys onto the streets to search for a replacement.

The President of the EU Commission was given a tongue-lashing from Mr Major and told to drop his objections to a world trade deal.

He does not hesitate to tongue-lash anyone who crosses his path.

tongues
tongues are wagging
set tongues wagging ◄

If you say that **tongues are wagging**, you mean that people are gossiping as a result of someone's behaviour. You can also say that a person's behaviour **sets tongues wagging**.

They spent an evening together at his Knightsbridge flat. He said they played bridge but added: 'No doubt tongues will be wagging.'

Tongues started wagging when Claudia moved from her native Germany to Monaco earlier this year.

Pop singer Madonna set tongues wagging at a star-studded party by arriving with a mystery date.

tools
down tools
lay down tools ◄

If a group of people **down tools** or **lay down tools**, they stop working, for example in order to protest about something. These expressions are used in British English.

In August 1980, the workers at this shipyard downed tools and went on strike for pay increases.

Metal workers, engineers, dockers, chemical workers, waiters and cooks are among those who have laid down tools this week. They want their pay to be brought up to West German levels by next year.

the tools of the trade ◄

The tools of the trade or **the tools of** your **trade** are the skills and equipment which you need to do your job properly.

He was never a novelist in the conventional sense, having no use for the conventional tools of the trade such as plot and suspense; he wrote from experience first and imagination second.

Grace's fingers were the tools of her trade.

The peasants were deprived of their animals, the tools of their trade, and their land.

tooth
fight tooth and nail
fight tooth and claw ◄

If you **fight tooth and nail** for something, you make a determined effort to keep it or get it, when other people are trying to take it away from you or prevent you from having it. You can also say that you **fight tooth and claw** for something. Other verbs such as 'battle' can be used instead of 'fight'.

Our autonomous republics are fighting tooth and nail to preserve their special status.

The pair had fought tooth and claw for four hours and eight minutes until John McEnroe emerged the victor.

There are 12 League games to go and that's 36 points. We must battle tooth and nail for every one of them.

☐ If you **fight** something **tooth and nail** or **tooth and claw**, you make a determined effort to stop it.

Opponents in Parliament, which has to vote on the measure, vowed to fight it tooth and nail.

As a member of the council I fought the proposal tooth and claw.

long in the tooth ◄

If you describe someone as **long in the tooth**, you mean that they are getting old. If you describe something such as a machine or system as **long in the tooth**, you mean that it is old and outdated and should be replaced. This expression is sometimes used light-heartedly about a person or thing that is not really old at all.

'Why don't you enrol in the University and take a proper course?' 'Aren't I a bit long in the tooth to start being an undergraduate?'

Yet Porsche has other problems that look too big for it to solve on its own. The biggest is that its models are rather long in the tooth. The last really all-new Porsche was the 928, launched in 1978.

red in tooth and claw ◄

If you describe something as **red in tooth and claw**, you mean that it involves competitive and ruthless behaviour. This is a literary expression.

My wife and I both now work for companies that are red in tooth and claw.

His intention was to demonstrate that Labour is no longer red in tooth and claw, but a serious and sober political party.

☐ People sometimes talk about **nature red in tooth and claw** when they are describing the way wild creatures hunt and kill each other for food.

We had left orderly Canberra with its just-so boulevards and civic monuments and were heading into the bush to take on nature red in tooth and claw.

a sweet tooth ◄◄

If you have **a sweet tooth**, you like eating things that are sugary or taste sweet.

She has a sweet tooth for chocolate cake and peppermint creams.

The cream tea is especially authentic with its traditional fresh farmhouse clotted cream. For those without a sweet tooth, savoury snacks are also available.

top

blow your top ◄

If you **blow** your **top**, you become very angry with someone and shout at them. **Blow** your **stack** means the same.

It's a pent-up rage that I don't let out regularly enough. I blew my top recently and broke my right hand on a dustbin.

I wanted to talk to her about it, to understand her reasoning. But I never asked personal questions because she'd always blow her top.

from top to bottom ◄◄◄

If you say that you have cleaned, tidied, or examined something **from top to bottom**, you are emphasizing that you have done it completely and thoroughly.

She scrubbed the house from top to bottom.

She searched the apartment from top to bottom for the missing letters.

☐ You can also use **top to bottom** before a noun.

He called for a top to bottom review of existing regulations to see which of them could be eliminated.

from top to toe ◄◄

You can use **from top to toe** to emphasize that you are talking about the whole of someone's body. This expression is used mainly in British English. **From head to toe** and **from head to foot** mean the same.

Carefully, methodically, she began to wash her body from top to toe.

She was trembling from top to toe.

He's dressed from top to toe in black.

☐ You can also use **top-to-toe** before a noun.

Nothing beats a glass of mineral water for a top-to-toe great feeling.

A top to toe body treatment is just about the ultimate in luxury.

get on top of you ◄

If you say that something **is getting on top of** you, you mean that you are feeling depressed and helpless because it is very difficult or worrying, or because it involves more work than you can cope with.

I was depressed. I was fed up with everything. Everything was just getting on top of me.

Most of us from time to time will have been told by close friends or partners that we are irritable or bad-tempered when things get on top of us.

Things have been getting on top of me lately. Business hasn't been good, they're talking of firing some of us.

on top of something ◄◄◄

If you are **on top of** a task or situation, you are dealing with it successfully. If you are beginning to deal with it successfully, you can say that you **are getting on top of** it.

That's the job. You've got to be on top of the problems.

The headlines were mostly about the current unrest and the government's inability to get on top of the situation.

If we don't keep up with modern trends, we'll fail. We are getting on top of crime but there is much more to be done.

over the top: 1
OTT ◀◀◀

If you describe something as **over the top**, you are being critical of it because you think it is extreme and exaggerated.

At one point, which I think is a bit over the top, he talks about the collapse of civilisation.

Perhaps I was a bit over the top, accusing you at the inquiry of being a traitor.

When I look at models with all that over-the-top make-up, I think, 'What happens when you take your face off, when they see you in the morning?'

☐ In informal British English, you can also say that something is **OTT**. This is an abbreviation of 'over the top' and it is pronounced 'o t t', as if you are spelling it out.

Newcastle boss Keegan has vowed to appeal against his fine, imposed for comments to the referee after a flare-up at Derby last season. 'It's OTT,' said Keegan. 'I just feel it's severe.'

Each design is very different in style. Some are subtle, some gloriously OTT.

over the top: 2

In a competition or contest, if something puts someone **over the top**, it results in them winning. This expression is used in American English.

The Pepsi Challenge had pushed us over the top, allowing us to unseat Coke as the number-one soft drink in supermarkets.

Competitive schools receive applications from dozens of varsity players, newspaper editors, and class presidents, many of whom are 'A' students as well. An extracurricular may push a candidate over the top.

torch

carry a torch for someone

If you **carry a torch for** someone, you are in love with them but they do not love you or they are already involved with another person. The verb 'hold' is sometimes used instead of 'carry'.

What makes a woman so special that a man will carry a torch for her all his life?

As a child I was always having crushes on boys. I can still remember all their faces; sometimes I would carry a torch for years.

He never saw the woman again. And he went through the rest of his life holding a torch for her.

carry the torch ◀

If you **carry the torch** for something such as a political party or a particular belief, you support it very strongly and try to persuade other people to support it too. Other verbs can be used instead of 'carry'.

This group aims to carry the torch for the millions of people who demonstrated and the thousands who died.

I just want to thank all of you for carrying the torch, for being the grass roots that make our party what it is.

There's nobody left to take up the torch for the unity at national level.

toss

argue the toss ◀

If someone **argues the toss**, they waste their time by arguing about something which is not important or which cannot be changed anyway. This expression is used in British English.

Anyway, while London and Paris were still arguing the toss, the whole situation changed.

Dad would nudge him, and he would wake suddenly, bad-tempered, ready to argue the toss with anyone.

not give a toss ◀◀

⟩ If you say that you **don't give a toss** about something, you mean that you do not care about it at all. This is an informal expression, which is used in British English. Some people consider it offensive.

I didn't give a toss about society because it had never given a toss about me.

'We couldn't give a toss what journalists think,' says Dave Chambers, Cornershop's drummer.

The findings of a government inquiry may or may not, in three or four months' time, blame someone. But even if it does, who gives a toss?

toss-up

be a toss-up ◀◀

If two or more courses of action seem equally likely to succeed or fail, you can say **it's a toss-up** which one you choose. Similarly, if two or more things are equally likely to happen, you can say **it's a toss-up** which one will happen.

We could send you on to Scapa, but then she might come back here. Equally if you stay here, she might go to Scapa. Or Rosyth. Or anywhere. It's a toss-up really.

Some said it's a toss-up whether oil prices will go up or down over the days ahead.

touch

the common touch ◄◄

If you say that someone in a position of power has **the common touch**, you mean that they understand how ordinary people think and feel, and that they are able to communicate well with them.

The Home Secretary smiled. It was the easy expression of a man who, though born into wealth, prides himself on having the common touch.

Everyone agrees that he is one of the most talented politicians in Japan. But he lacks the common touch, and has little support outside his own faction.

The Bishop is said to have the common touch but his left-of-centre political views are said to weigh against him.

kick something into touch ◄

If you **kick** something **into touch**, you reject it or postpone it. This expression is used mainly in British English.

The prospect of an independent Bank of England voice in formulating economic policy was kicked into touch last night as Downing Street named Eddie George, the current deputy, as governor, making it plain that the Bank would remain strongly under Treasury influence.

She kicked the booze into touch, came back from the brink and emerged a whole person again.

Trish Johnson's challenge for the US Women's Open Championship was kicked into touch by a foot injury here yesterday.

a soft touch
an easy touch ◄◄

If you say that someone is **a soft touch** or **an easy touch**, you mean that it is easy to make them do what you want or agree with you.

He did not get where he is today by being either a soft touch or a poor judge of his core businesses.

The team still has a reputation for being a soft touch.

Pamela was an easy touch when she needed some cash.

touch and go ◄◄◄

If you say it is **touch and go** whether something will happen, you mean that you cannot be certain whether it will happen or not.

It was touch-and-go whether she would really go through with it up until she walked into court.

I thought I was going to win the race, but it was still touch and go.

Nancy nearly lost control of the craft. For a few moments it was touch and go.

touch paper

light the blue touch paper
light the touch paper

If you say that someone **lights the blue touch paper** or **lights the touch paper**, you mean that they do something which causes other people to react in an angry or aggressive way. These expressions are used in British English.

This kind of remark is guaranteed to light the blue touch paper with some Labour politicians.

He had heard ding-dong verbal battles there before, but nothing like as combative. Still, it had been building up for weeks. All it took was Mussonwell to light the blue touch paper and stand back.

tough

tough as old boots
tough as nails ◄

If you say that someone is **tough as old boots** or **tough as nails**, you are emphasizing that they have a strong and independent character. 'Tough as old boots' is only used in British English.

Barbara is tough as old boots and rules her husband with an iron hand.

This man was a very easy-going type of person in a large group, but across a negotiating table was just tough as nails.

towel

throw in the towel
throw in the sponge ◄◄◄

If someone **throws in the towel**, they stop trying to do something, because they know that they cannot succeed. Verbs such as 'chuck' and 'toss' are sometimes used instead of 'throw'.

Klara's support, when even her son's trainers wanted to throw in the towel, was crucial. At last, Garry won a game, the 32nd in the match.

One day I will be brave enough (or fed up enough) to chuck in the towel and start again.

□ You can also say that someone **throws in the sponge**. This expression is used mainly in British English.

You're not the kind of man who throws in the sponge. You're a fighter and it's your fighting spirit which is ultimately going to save you.

tower

a tower of strength
a pillar of strength ◄◄

If you say that someone was **a tower of strength** during a difficult period in your life, you mean that they gave you a lot of help or support and you are very grateful to them for this. You can also say that they were **a pillar of strength**.

My eldest daughter, Therese, who's six, was a tower of strength for me then. When I was sick she would clean up after me and look after the other kids.

In her terrible sadness she has found Charles to be a pillar of strength.

town

go to town ◄

If you say that someone **goes to town** on something or someone, you mean that they deal with them with a lot of enthusiasm or energy.

Johnny and one or two of the others went to town on the brandy.

You could really go to town and give her a night at the Sheraton at the Mother's Day rate of $120.

I felt I could go to town a bit more in here as it's a room we only use on special occasions.

paint the town red

If you **paint the town red**, you go out and enjoy yourself.

'Don't you and the other sisters ever paint the town red?' 'We sometimes go to the hotel and come back in a taxi. Just for a bit of fun.'

Preparing yourself to paint the town red on a Saturday night just doesn't have the same buzz without a suitable soundtrack to help you shower down, zip up and step out.

traces

kick over the traces

If someone **kicks over the traces**, they pay no attention to rules and conventions and behave exactly as they want to.

Harry had kicked over the traces when his father died, and quit going to church.

He could detect the same scent of rebellion, common to students the world over, smouldering beneath the surface: the desire to kick over the traces, the refusal to accept old values without question.

track

the fast track ◄◄◄

The fast track to something is the quickest way of achieving it. If you are on **the fast track** to a particular goal or state, you are likely to achieve it very soon or very easily.

The Clinton administration yesterday enthusiastically endorsed a family leave bill twice vetoed by President Bush, putting it on a fast track to becoming law.

Like many of his classmates, Chris Urwin believes a university degree will be his passport to the fast track into a company.

The water polo team is 12-1 and still atop the national rankings. And the school's cross-country teams are on the fast track to national prominence.

Those kids are on a fast track to becoming unhealthy adults.

□ You can also talk about a **fast-track** approach to something or a **fast-track** way of achieving something.

The fast-track process speeds up approval of international trade pacts in Washington.

They offer fast-track promotion schemes for promising young executives.

have the inside track ◄◄

If you say that someone **has the inside track**, you mean that they have an advantage, for example special knowledge about something. This expression is used mainly in American journalism.

Denver has the inside track among 10 sites being considered for the airline's new $1 billion maintenance facility.

As an agent, you may have an inside track, a first shot, when good deals become available.

keep track of something ◄◄◄

If you **keep track of** something or someone, you make sure that you have accurate and up-to-date information about them all the time.

I drank 20 shots of tequila and Georgina had 17. We were keeping track of how many we had each.

I could never keep track of all the visitors to the mansion.

The ability to keep track of time becomes one of the skills necessary to do well in the activity.

lose track of someone ◄◄◄

If you **lose track of** someone or something, you no longer know where they are or what is happening to them.

His family lost track of him under his new name.

You may have wondered how the administrators of the Social Fund can lose track of £20 million meant to help the poorest citizens.

He was asking us about our schoolwork, what it was like in school in Ireland, and it was interesting, and we just lost track of the time.

off the beaten track
off the beaten path ◄◄◄

If a place is **off the beaten track**, it is isolated and quiet, because it is far from large cities or their centres, and so few people go there or live there.

The house is sufficiently off the beaten track to deter all but a few tourists.

If you enjoy exploring off the beaten track, Sunmed is offering rambling holidays on the Greek island of Lesbos.

□ In American English, you can also say that somewhere is **off the beaten path**.

Rents at outlet malls, which are generally off the beaten path, are lower than at most suburban shopping centers.

on the right track ◄◄◄

If you are **on the right track**, you are acting or progressing in a way that is likely to result in success. **On the right lines** means the same.

We are finding that guests for lunch and dinner are returning in increasing numbers – a sure sign that we are on the right track.

We have taken action to put the industry back on the right track but we still have some way to go to return to full profitability.

on the wrong track ◄◄

If you are **on the wrong track**, you are acting or progressing in a way that is likely to result in failure.

Do you think the country is going in the right direction or is it headed on the wrong track?

The standard of careers advice given to school-leavers is generally appalling, setting us off on the wrong track from the start.

a track record ◄◄◄

If you talk about the **track record** of a person, company, or product, you are referring to the reputation they have, which is based on all their successes and failures in the past.

He joined the BBC as a general trainee in 1968, where he quickly developed a track record as an inventive programme maker.

Does this corporation have a high-quality management team with a good track record?

Glasgow Museums and Galleries have a proven track record of attracting very large audiences.

The region is known to have a poor track record in research.

tracks

cover your tracks ◄◄◄

If someone **covers** their **tracks**, they hide or destroy evidence of their identity or actions, because they want to keep them secret.

He was a very clever man, a very careful man who never took a chance, a man who totally covered his tracks.

The killer may have returned to the scene of the crime to cover his tracks.

from the wrong side of the tracks ◄

If you say that someone comes **from the wrong side of the tracks**, you mean that they come from a poor, unfashionable, and lower-class area of town.

I know kids back home who come from the wrong side of the tracks. When they go to

school, they haven't eaten and their clothes are all torn.

Black music, in the Western world, has always been considered to have emanated from the wrong side of the tracks.

make tracks ◄

If you **make tracks**, you leave the place where you are, usually in a hurry.

Webb looked at the bar clock. 'Ten past nine. We might as well be making tracks.'

Hawkins knew it was time to make tracks out of the country.

About 8pm, we decided it was time to start making tracks, but we all found it difficult to get going.

stop someone in their tracks: 1
stop someone dead in their tracks ◄◄◄

If something **stops** you **in** your tracks or **stops** you **dead in** your **tracks**, it makes you suddenly stop moving or doing something because you are very surprised, impressed, or frightened.

Seen across wide fields of corn this magnificent church cannot fail to stop you in your tracks.

They stopped in their tracks and stared at him in amazement.

They turned round. And then they stopped dead in their tracks, their hearts beating fast. Somebody was behind them.

stop something in its tracks: 2
stop something dead in its tracks ◄◄◄

If someone or something **stops** a process or activity **in** its **tracks** or **stops** it **dead in** its **tracks**, they make it immediately stop continuing or developing.

If the Chancellor pulls the plug on the £22 billion programme, the resulting job losses could stop Britain's economic revival dead in its tracks.

Francis felt he would like to stop this conversation in its tracks. He wished neither to confirm nor deny Cosmo's suspicions.

trail

blaze a trail ◄◄◄

If you say that someone **is blazing a trail**, you mean that they are the first person to do or discover something new and important, and this will make it easier for other people to do the same thing.

With his first book Parker has blazed a new trail in American literature.

The party is blazing the trail for the advancement of women in politics.

□ You can use **trail-blazing** to describe someone who does something new and important or you can refer to them as **a trail-blazer**. You can also describe what they do as **trail-blazing** or refer to it as **a trail-blazer**.

The other banks denied having plans to re-introduce charges for customers in credit but, behind the scenes, each would be only too happy to follow in the shadow of a trail-blazing competitor.

For many of those trail-blazers from the West, Hong Kong is the most practicable headquarters.

This trail-blazing study went into immense detail on the habits of pub-goers.

The magazine For Women was launched in April and branded as a trail-blazer for sexual equality.

trap

fall into the trap ◄◄◄

If someone **falls into the trap** of doing something, they make a very common mistake, or one that is very easy to make.

School administrators then fall into the trap of thinking that discipline problems, not unsatisfying education, are the cause of low levels of achievement.

Many of the world's economies were falling into the same trap as Australia in trying to boost their economy through government spending.

tree

bark up the wrong tree ◄

If you say that someone **is barking up the wrong tree**, you mean that they are following the wrong course of action because their beliefs or ideas about something are incorrect.

Scientists in Switzerland realised that most other researchers had been barking up the wrong tree.

They said we were barking up the wrong tree and then suddenly everyone came round to our point of view.

out of your tree

If you say that someone is **out of** their **tree**, you mean that they are crazy or behaving very strangely, perhaps because of alcohol or drugs. This is an informal expression.

'I'm going out of my tree with this.' 'Honey, don't let it get you down.'

It was obvious they were on something dodgy. They were both out of their tree.

the top of the tree ◄◄

If you say that someone is at **the top of the tree** or is **top of the tree**, you mean that they have reached the highest level in their career or profession. These expressions are used in British English.

She has been at the top of the acting tree for 35 years.

As a cricketer he is top of the tree and we will see that when the time comes, if he is picked for India.

trees

not grow on trees

If you say that people or things of a particular kind **do not grow on trees**, you are emphasizing that they are very difficult to obtain. This expression is used mainly in British English.

Mitchell could not be replaced in a hurry: agents with his expertise did not grow on trees.

Investments worth $1.75 billion do not grow on trees.

□ When people talk about money **growing on trees**, they are talking about situations in which it is possible to obtain or earn large amounts of money.

The merchant bank was purchased in 1987 for £777 million in hard cash at a time when money was growing on trees.

not see the wood for the trees
not see the forest for the trees ◄

If you say that someone **can't see the wood for the trees**, you mean that they are so involved in the details of something that they forget or do not realize the real purpose or importance of the thing as a whole. This form of the expression is used in British English; in American English, the form is **not see the forest for the trees**.

His fairness and clarity of vision often helped those who could not see the wood for the trees reach the correct decision.

We are so much involved in detail, which for the most part is no proper concern of the State, that we are reduced to almost total inability to see the wood for the trees.

Colonel Vardagas accused congressmen of looking at the problem simplistically. 'They failed to see the forest for the trees,' he said.

trial

a trial balloon ◄◄

A **trial balloon** is an idea or plan which is suggested in order to find out about public opinions on a controversial subject. This expression is used mainly in American English.

The administration has not officially released any of the specifics of the president's economic plan, although numerous trial balloons have been floated and hints have been dropped.

It's hard to say what's a trial balloon and what is a policy in a process of being formed.

trick

do the trick ◄◄◄

If something **does the trick**, it achieves what you want.

If these self-help remedies don't do the trick, consult a qualified homoeopath.

If you're not sure what your baby wants, then

try a cuddle; if all else fails, it usually does the trick.

every trick in the book   ◄

If you say that someone uses **every trick in the book**, you mean that they do everything they can think of in order to succeed in something.

Companies are using every trick in the book to stay one step in front of their competitors.

not miss a trick   ◄◄

If you say that someone **does not miss a trick**, you mean that they always know what is happening and take advantage of every situation.

When it comes to integrating their transport systems, the French don't miss a trick.

Matthews did not miss a trick, establishing a profitable connection with Adams, the powerful American boxing entrepreneur.

the oldest trick in the book

If someone has done something deceitful, dishonest, or unfair and you describe it as **the oldest trick in the book**, you mean that people should have expected it because it is a very common or obvious thing to do.

Well, that's the oldest trick in the book – to blame someone else for your problems.

That beggar's just collecting enough money to get drunk on. Using the children to persuade the gullible to part with their money. Oldest trick in the book.

tricks

up to your tricks
up to your old tricks   ◄◄

If you say that someone is **up to** their **tricks** or **up to** their **old tricks**, you mean that they are behaving in a deceitful, dishonest, or foolish way which is typical of them.

Homeowners wondering if estate agents are no longer up to their tricks should think again.

They seemed to be up to their old tricks of promising one thing and doing the opposite.

trim

in fighting trim

If someone or something is **in fighting trim**, they are in very good condition. This expression is used mainly in American English.

They argue that it isn't doing much to get Air France into fighting trim for the 1990s, when domestic competition may increase.

trolley

off your trolley   ◄

If you say that someone is **off** their **trolley**, you are saying in a light-hearted way that you think they are crazy or very foolish. This

is an informal expression, which is used in British English.

If they think officers are going to give up their cars, they're off their trolley.

Did you see Princess Di going on about how she likes fast food? Is she off her trolley or what?

trowel

lay it on with a trowel

If you say that someone is **laying it on with a trowel**, you mean that they are exaggerating a statement, experience, or emotion, in order to impress people. This expression is used in British English. **Lay it on thick** means the same.

The programme didn't lay it on with a trowel, starting gently with questions about lifestyles and aspirations, waiting till near the end to talk about violence and race.

There must have been some moments of comfort. Mr Harris skips them and lays on the squalor with a trowel.

truck

have no truck with something   ◄◄

If you **have no truck with** something or someone, you strongly disapprove of them and refuse to become involved with them. The verbs 'want' and 'hold' are sometimes used instead of 'have'.

As an American, she had no truck with the painful formality of English life.

Great efforts were made to get him on the side of the 'rebels'. He had no truck with them.

This is the most controversial area. Most mainstream doctors hold no truck with these ideas, while supporters insist they account for 99 per cent of cases.

true

ring true   ◄

If a statement or promise **rings true**, it seems to be true, sincere, or genuine. Compare **ring hollow**; see **hollow**.

It is Mandela's argument that rings true to American ears.

When I heard the initial reasons, they didn't ring true. It was only when Bill's statement came out it began to make sense.

trump

a trump card
play your trump card   ◄◄◄

Someone's **trump card** is something which gives them a decisive advantage over other people. You can say that someone holds **the trump card** when they have an advantage like this.

After only two days, the distribution of goods

was suffering: and that, ultimately is the railwaymen's trump card.

He said that the measure was his trump card in his plan to prevent electoral fraud.

In terms of passion and commitment, on the other hand, Ireland held every trump card.

Some nations, like Japan, seem content to keep their trump cards hidden.

☐ If someone **plays** their **trump card**, they do something unexpected which gives them a decisive advantage over other people.

If she wished, she could threaten to play her trump card, an autobiography of embarrassing disclosures.

trumpet

blow your own trumpet ◄◄

If you accuse someone of **blowing** their **own trumpet**, you are criticizing them for boasting about themselves. This expression is used in British English; the American expression is **blow** your **own horn**.

The three candidates traded insults and blew their own trumpets yesterday as each one claimed to be heading for victory.

Oscar winner Jodie Foster has few peers when it comes to blowing her own trumpet. 'You either have it or you don't,' says the star.

☐ You might say **'I'm not blowing my own trumpet'** when you are reporting something good about yourself but do not want other people to think you are boastful or vain.

I don't want to sound like I'm blowing my own trumpet, but musicians are much better advised now than they were in the '60s and '70s.

I am not blowing my own trumpet but I can claim I work a lot quicker than a lot of people.

trumps

come up trumps: 1 ◄◄

If you say that someone **has come up trumps**, you mean that they have achieved an unexpectedly good result. This expression is used in British English.

Sylvester Stallone has come up trumps at the US box office with his new movie Cliffhanger.

You came up trumps with the April issue. I've never received such good value for money from a magazine.

come up trumps: 2
turn up trumps

If you say that people or events **come up trumps** or **turn up trumps**, you mean that they unexpectedly help you with your problems. These expressions are used in British English.

Much of this luck will come from an unexpected direction. The most unlikely people or events will come up trumps.

In moments of crisis for me, you always turn up trumps!

truth

economical with the truth ◄◄

If you say that someone is being **economical with the truth**, you are criticizing them for deceiving people by deliberately not telling them the whole truth about something. People use this expression when they want to suggest that someone is being dishonest, but do not actually want to accuse them of lying.

In insisting that no changes had been made to the original plan, his team was being economical with the truth.

She asked repeated questions but was fobbed off with a series of misleading answers which were at best economical with the truth, at worst deliberately designed to deceive.

As campaigning in the Conservative leadership race in Britain draws to a climax, it's become clear that some MPs have been a little economical with the truth. For, if all the pledged votes are added up, they amount to far more than the number eligible to vote.

tub

tub-thumping
thump the tub ◄

In journalism, **tub-thumping** is used to describe people's attitudes or behaviour when they are supporting an idea or course of action in a very vigorous and sometimes aggressive way. This expression is usually used to show disapproval of this kind of behaviour. It is used in British English.

Conservatives know they still have a lot of hard work to do and the Environment Secretary rammed home their tax message in a tub-thumping speech.

We have reached the stage now where the players neither need, nor will respond to, tub-thumping.

☐ You can refer to someone who behaves in this way as **a tub-thumper**.

Marsh was far from being a woolly-minded idealist and tub-thumper.

☐ You can also say that someone **is thumping the tub**.

tune

call the tune ◄◄

If someone **calls the tune**, they are in control of a situation and make all the important decisions.

The government will thus reduce this country to one in which the claims of business, commerce and technology will call the tune.

If managers tried to get players to come back

in the afternoon they'd have a riot on their hands. The players call the tune these days.

□ This expression comes from the proverb **he who pays the piper calls the tune**; see **piper**.

change your tune
a change of tune ◄◄

If someone **changes** their **tune**, they express a different opinion about something from the one they had expressed previously, or they show a completely different attitude to something or someone.

Some see signs that the administration has not only changed its tune on the dollar, but is now resigned to higher short-term interest rates too.

He had maintained for many years that the Earl was dead. But these days he has changed his tune.

□ You can also talk about someone's **change of tune**.

The refugees, while welcoming the sudden change of tune, greeted this ploy with considerable reserve.

dance to someone's tune ◄

If you **dance to** someone else's **tune**, you do whatever they want or tell you to do, usually without challenging them or hesitating. This expression is often used to criticize someone for allowing themselves to be controlled in this way.

During my trip to the region, I reproached trade union leaders for pandering to managers, sometimes going so far as dancing to their tune.

I know the cathedral is desperate for money and has to raise cash somehow. But the danger of commercialism is that the churches end up dancing to the tune of their big business sponsors.

□ You can also say that someone **is dancing to** a particular **tune** when they are behaving in a particular way, especially if this is different from the way they were behaving before.

Change is never really easy and cannot be controlled and manipulated. It is a case of having to dance to a tune other than the one you are accustomed to.

With different circumstances in Germany and Britain, we cannot dance to the same tune.

tunnel

tunnel vision ◄◄

If you accuse someone of **tunnel vision**, you are accusing them of focusing all their energy and skill on the task which is most important to them and ignoring things that other people might consider important.

The implication of his letter is that only perfect human beings should be allowed to live in dignity in the community and gain self-respect. Such tunnel-vision appals me.

No marriage is risk-proof, unless people have absolute tunnel-vision about each other, isolate themselves and avoid any tempting situation.

□ This expression can also be used to show admiration for someone who has achieved a lot by concentrating on a single thing.

They always say that you have to have tunnel vision to be a champion. You can't have any outside distractions at all.

□ You can also use **tunnel-vision** before a noun.

The experts sometimes have a bureaucratic, tunnel-vision view of their mission.

The woman who won the world 10,000m title in Tokyo and the New York Marathon at the first attempt has a tunnel-vision attitude to her sport.

turkey

talk turkey ◄

If people **talk turkey**, they discuss something in a frank and serious way. This expression is used mainly in American English.

Suddenly government and industry are talking turkey. Last month the Prime Minister promised a partnership to improve the climate for business.

He worked with us very closely as a member of the Finance Committee, and he's got the credibility and the reputation, I think, to talk turkey.

a turkey shoot ◄

If someone refers to a battle or other conflict as **a turkey shoot**, they mean that one side is so much stronger or better armed than the other that the weaker side has no chance at all. This expression is usually used to suggest that the situation is unfair.

After weeks of bombing, it was a one-sided battle. The fighting stopped earlier than expected partly because of public disquiet at the 'turkey-shoot'.

The prospect of fishing for truly wild trout is very stimulating – but it's not a turkey shoot.

turkeys

like turkeys voting for Christmas

If you say that someone choosing to do a particular thing would be **like turkeys voting for Christmas**, you are emphasizing that they are very unlikely to do it because it would very obviously be bad for them. This expression is used mainly in British English.

To expect Lloyd's workers to vote against the status quo would be like expecting turkeys to vote for Christmas.

Most blacks regard supporting the 'Nats' as the equivalent of turkeys voting for Christmas, but some view the party as an attractive alternative.

☐ In Britain and some other countries, people traditionally eat turkey at Christmas.

turn

at every turn   ◄◄◄

If something happens **at every turn**, it happens very frequently or continuously, and usually prevents you from doing what you want to do.

Although the government has had a coherent economic plan, parliament has set out to block it at every turn.

I myself run a small business and it is my opinion that businesses such as mine are hampered at every turn by big business.

turn-up

a turn-up for the books

If you say that something is **a turn-up for the books**, you mean that it is very surprising and unexpected, and usually very pleasing. This expression is used in British English.

How about that for a turn-up for the books? I knew nothing about it, I can tell you.

This was a real turn up for the books, and is an observation still not accepted by all medical practitioners.

☐ You can also just say that something is **a turn-up**.

When I became middle-aged, I found myself unable to risk hurting animals. This came as something of a turn-up. I had loved shooting since I first got a shotgun in my hands at the age of 12.

turtle

turn turtle

If a boat **turns turtle**, it turns upside down when it is in the water.

The voyage took six months. The tug nearly turned turtle twice, but I managed to keep her upright.

twain

never the twain shall meet   ◄

People say **'never the twain shall meet'** when they believe that there are so many differences between two groups of people or two groups of things that they can never exist together in the same place or situation. People also say **'ne'er the twain shall meet'**. These

are rather literary expressions.

The British education system is notorious for separating the sciences and the humanities. This academic 'ne'er the twain shall meet' policy unfortunately does not always reflect the requirements of the real world.

☐ People often vary this expression. For example, they say that **the twain do meet** or **the twain are not supposed to meet**.

Although they recognised differences and that East is east and West is west, they would have gone on to argue not that the twain shall never meet but that the two should and must meet.

twist

round the twist

If you say that someone is **round the twist**, you mean that their ideas or behaviour are very strange or foolish. This is an informal expression, which is used in British English. **Round the bend** means the same.

You would have to be really round the twist to get pleasure out of this.

This man's round the twist.

☐ If you say that someone goes **round the twist**, you mean that they start behaving or thinking very strangely or foolishly. This is often as a result of being very frustrated or irritated by someone or something.

Most of them go round the twist in the end, you know. His predecessor killed himself.

I think that's why some people go round the twist. They get a religious mania and just get carried away, they go too far.

two

put two and two together   ◄◄

If you **put two and two together**, you correctly guess the truth about something from the information that you have. You can replace 'put' with 'add'.

He never came out and said, 'I am Jewish', but after a period of time, I put two and two together, and I assumed he was.

He knew perfectly well who her mother had been. He had only to think back to the time he'd dropped in on Grace and seen that book on pregnancy to put two and two together.

☐ If you say that someone **puts two and two together and makes five**, you mean that they reach the wrong conclusion about something.

Mr Lane's solicitor said after the case that police put two and two together and made five.

U

unbowed

bloodied but unbowed ◄

If you say that someone is **bloodied but unbowed** after a bad experience, you mean that they have not been defeated or destroyed, and they will be able to continue as they were. Adjectives such as 'battered' and 'bloody' can be used instead of 'bloodied'. This is a literary expression.

He went out there and worked for every single vote. It was a narrow victory but an important one. He is bloodied but unbowed.

Wolverhampton-based construction giant Tarmac has emerged from the recession battered but unbowed.

unglued

come unglued: 1 ◄

If you say that someone **has come unglued**, you mean that they have lost control of their emotions and are behaving in a strange or crazy way. This expression is used in American English.

She had apparently come unglued since losing her job as social columnist for Western Gentry magazine. Her life had been built around parties but the invitations had dried up months before.

We had just gotten him out of jail. He had come unglued over a girl who was pregnant with his child. She wouldn't marry him, and he had gone to her house with a sawed-off shotgun and threatened to shoot her.

come unglued: 2 ◄

If someone or something **comes unglued**, they fail. This expression is used in American English; the British expression is **come unstuck**.

Their marriage finally came unglued. Much of his behaviour had become unacceptable to her, and she had withdrawn more and more into herself.

They began to understand that everything was coming unglued.

unstuck

come unstuck ◄◄◄

If someone or something **comes unstuck**, they fail. This expression is used in British English; the American expression is **come unglued**.

Australia's Greg Norman came badly unstuck in the third round of the Memorial golf tournament yesterday.

With the end of the Cold War, everything has come unstuck and the refugee problem seems to be growing.

up

on the up
on the up and up ◄◄

If someone or something is **on the up**, they are becoming very successful and doing well. You can also say that they are **on the up and up**. These expressions are used in British English.

The East has an economy which is on the up, while the West's free market economy seems to be an unmitigated disaster.

I was pretty depressed sometimes at Dundee, but I never reached rock bottom. Now things are on the up.

Their career path has flattened out slightly rather than still being on the up and up.

on the up and up

To be **on the up and up** means to be honest or legal. This expression is used mainly in American English.

We'd like to know where the money came from. It may have been on the up-and-up. He was a frugal type, and he hit the lottery for twenty grand a while back.

swear up and down

If someone **swears up and down** that something is true, they insist that they are telling you the truth, even though you are not sure whether or not to believe them. This expression is used in American English; the usual British expression is **swear blind**.

He'd sworn up and down he was going to get the cash and bring it right back.

I couldn't get it out of my head that maybe it was all part of his plan, although he swore up and down it wasn't.

up and coming ◄◄◄

An **up and coming** person is someone who is likely to be successful in the future.

Beaton wants to help build up the pioneering 198 Gallery in Brixton which regularly exhibits up and coming artists.

He was one of our very up and coming young ministers and I feel he had a great future in front of him.

The magazine profiles the manager of the Toronto Blue Jays and two up-and-coming Canadian hockey stars.

up and running   ◄◄◄

If a system, business, or plan is **up and running**, it has started well and is working or functioning successfully.

We've invested in the people, tools, and technology to get your system up and running quickly and keep it that way.

Luton's first fully-fledged Business Centre – destined to play a leading role in the town's economic recovery – is up and running with good wishes from a Government Minister.

The project, once it was up and running, would be fraught with danger.

uppers

on your uppers
down on your uppers   ◄

If you say that a person or a company is **on** their **uppers** or **down on** their **uppers**, you mean that they have very little money. These expressions are used in British English.

The company is on its uppers and shareholders can forget about receiving dividends for a couple of years.

Galleries generally operate on a sale-or-return system but Simon pays cash upfront for his ceramics because he finds so many potters are down on their uppers.

upstairs

kick someone upstairs

If someone **is kicked upstairs**, they are given a job or position which appears to have a higher status but actually has less power or influence. This expression is used in British English.

A management shake-up is also underway. Peter Greenall becomes managing director succeeding Andrew Thomas, who is kicked upstairs to become deputy chairman.

The radicals kicked him upstairs to the then ceremonial job of president.

V

vacuum

in a vacuum   ◄◄◄

If something exists or happens **in a vacuum**, it seems to exist or happen separately from the things that you would expect it to be connected with.

Of course, much of that discussion takes place in a vacuum. The people do not yet have political power.

Property values do not exist in a vacuum. The market value of a well-maintained property can fall if the biggest employer in town closes or an all-night service station opens next door.

Such decisions do not occur in a political vacuum, but have serious political implications both at home and abroad.

variety

variety is the spice of life   ◄

If you say that **variety is the spice of life**, you are pointing out that doing and seeing a lot of different things makes life more enjoyable and interesting.

Families have discovered that variety is the spice of life and are switching to adventurous meals like home cooked curries, tacos and Chinese banquets.

It is important to vary the training program so that boredom is avoided. Exercise should be fun and variety is the spice of life.

veil

draw a veil over something   ◄

If you **draw a veil over** something, you deliberately do not talk about it or give any details, because you want to keep it private or because it is embarrassing.

It would be kinder, perhaps, to draw a veil over the party's career from 1906 to the outbreak of the War.

Of course you must not lie – a fraud on a CV can be grounds for cancelling a contract of employment – but most of us have something in our past career over which we choose to draw a veil.

She draws a veil of privacy over her life with him and discusses their relationship only in the abstract.

vessels

empty vessels make the most sound
empty vessels make the most noise

People say '**empty vessels make the most sound**' or '**empty vessels make the most noise**' to point out that people who talk a lot about their knowledge, talent, or experience are often not as knowledgeable, talented, or experienced as they claim to be. This is an old-fashioned expression.

There's a lot of truth in that old saying, 'Empty vessels make the most sound'. Those who are actually content with their choices are not usually interested in evangelising to the rest of us.

vest

play your cards close to the vest
keep your cards close to the vest ◄

If you **play** your **cards close to the vest** or **keep** your **cards close to the vest**, you do not tell anyone about your plans or thoughts. This expression is used in American English. **Play** your **cards close to** your **chest** means the same.

He plays his cards very close to the vest, leaving some attorneys with whom he's worked to describe him as secretive and manipulative.

They also are accused of keeping their cards too close to their vests. 'Some executives are not yet comfortable about sharing strategic information with their colleagues,' the researchers say.

□ 'Cards' is often replaced with other nouns.

The military's playing this whole operation pretty close to the vest – they generally don't like to talk about future operations.

view

a bird's-eye view ◄

If you have **a bird's-eye view** of a situation, you are able to form a clear impression of what is happening. Compare **a worm's eye view**.

Before I left England, I was a parliamentary lobby correspondent, getting a bird's eye view of the way politicians encourage people to believe in dreams.

□ People often change 'bird' to a word that is relevant to what they are talking about.

He seems to have a soldier's eye view.

He has a child's eye view of the war based on his own experiences.

□ The expression **a bird's-eye view** is more commonly used to indicate that someone who is looking down from a great height gets a clear view of everything below them. Similarly, you can use a variant to talk about someone having a clear view in a particular situation.

His pilot's licence enabled us to have a bird's-eye view of the beautiful countryside.

I remember with affection the splendid Glasgow 'blue trains' which gave the added bonus of a driver's eye view.

take a dim view of something
take a poor view of something ◄◄

If you **take a dim view of** something, you disapprove of it. In British English, you can also say that you **take a poor view of** it.

Back in 1989 he took a dim view of lotteries, and wrote to a proposer: 'I do not support your proposal for a lottery and would wish not to be involved at this stage.'

The French take a dim view of anyone who only snacks at lunchtime and it is usually best
to choose one of the set menus, chalked on boards outside.

Fellow critics took a poor view of a critic who reviewed Paramount films and accepted a fee from the studio.

a worm's eye view

If you say that someone has **a worm's eye view** of something, you mean that they are able to form an impression of what is happening in a situation, but that they have a low status, or are considered inferior in some way. Compare **a bird's-eye view**.

Let me offer, then, a worm's eye view of what Thatcherism was, and what its legacy may be.

They were considered to be leaders who, for the most part, 'were complete fools, with a worm's eye view of the world and a poor understanding of their jobs'.

□ This expression can also be used to indicate that something can be seen from very low on the ground, or from below the ground.

If only gardeners would care, occasionally, to get down and take a worm's eye view of their lawns, they would discover a mass of fascinating and horticulturally very useful information.

villain

the villain of the piece ◄◄

If you describe someone as **the villain of the piece**, you mean that they are responsible for all the trouble or all the problems in a situation. This expression is used in British English.

The real villains of the piece are the motor manufacturers. In a country where the top speed limit is 70mph, why do they make 140mph cars?

If he is indeed the villain of the piece, as the police claim he is, he should have been more carefully watched.

vine

wither on the vine
die on the vine ◄

If something **withers on the vine**, it dies or comes to an end because people show no enthusiasm for it or deliberately ignore it. You can also say that something **dies on the vine**. These are literary expressions.

The chance to make peace certainly exists, and has seldom been riper, but could still wither on the vine.

I talked to senior citizens and ordinary people all over this state who are worried that the American dream is dying on the vine.

violet

a shrinking violet
no shrinking violet ◄

If you describe someone as **a shrinking violet**, you mean that they are very shy and timid. If you say that someone is **no shrinking violet**, you mean that they are very self-confident.

Give him a tough assignment and he turns into a shrinking violet.

Amber is no shrinking violet. She is a brash colourful character.

None of the women he paints could be described as shrinking violets.

volumes

speak volumes ◄◄◄

If you say that something **speaks volumes**, you mean that it reveals or implies a lot about a situation.

His words speak volumes for the great divide in British politics.

Her background, while speaking volumes about her business acumen, could not convince the arts world that she was part of it.

What you wear speaks volumes, and it can lie, too. Remember the adage that you should dress for the job you aspire to.

wagon

hitch your wagon to someone
hitch your wagon to a star

If someone **hitches** their **wagon** to a particular person or policy, they try to become more successful by forming a relationship with someone who is already successful. You can also say that they **hitch** their **wagon to a star**.

The increasing power of the Pacific rim provides a reason why Russia should not hitch its wagon too closely to America.

Giammetti had the good fortune to hitch his wagon to a brilliant star – one that, without him, might just as easily have fallen as risen.

on the wagon
fall off the wagon ◄

If someone is **on the wagon**, they have given up drinking alcohol.

I'm on the wagon for a while. Cleaning out my system.

He was a teenage alcoholic, but he's been on the wagon for more than 30 years.

☐ You can say that someone **has fallen off the wagon** when they have begun to drink alcohol again after a period of not drinking it.

He has finally fallen off the wagon after 12 long, dry years. In 1982 doctors warned he would be dead within months if he didn't stop drinking.

wagons

circle the wagons
pull your wagons in a circle ◄

If a group of people who are in difficulty or danger **circle the wagons**, they unite in order to protect themselves and fight whoever is attacking them. You can also say that people **pull** their **wagons in a circle**.

Some African-Americans who initially opposed Thomas because of his politics are circling the wagons to support him because of his race.

When the overall budget shrinks, the services, by and large, pull their wagons in a circle around the next generation of hardware programs.

wake

in something's wake ◄◄◄

You say that an event leaves an unpleasant situation **in** its **wake** when that situation happens after that event or is caused by it.

A deadly cloud of gas swept along the valleys north of Lake Nyos in western Cameroon, leaving a trail of death and devastation in its wake.

Mr Stevens has disappeared, leaving in his wake debts of over £2 million.

in the wake of something ◄◄◄

If an event, especially an unpleasant one, follows **in the wake of** a previous event, it happens after the earlier event, often as a result of it.

The trouble at Shotts prison follows in the wake of unrest at several prisons in England.

He remained in office until 1985 when he resigned in the wake of a row with the Socialist government.

wake-up

a wake-up call ◄◄

You can refer to an event as **a wake-up call** when it shocks people into taking action about a difficult or dangerous situation. This expression is used mainly in American English.

The jury said the damages were intended to

send a wake-up call to the firm and other big companies that sexual harassment would not be tolerated.

Many church leaders have described last week's stabbing as a sort of wake-up call for the clergy. They hope tonight's meeting will be the start of a more concentrated effort to reach out to troubled kids.

□ If you have a **wake-up call**, you arrange for someone to telephone you at a certain time in the morning so that you are sure to wake up at that time.

walk

take a walk
take a hike

If someone tells you to **take a walk** or to **take a hike**, they are telling you very forcefully or angrily to go away or to stop interfering.

Some women editors on The Sunday Times Magazine tried to suppress my essay, arguing to the editor that it would be 'an indelible blot' on the magazine's reputation. He nobly told them to take a walk.

The Coastguard broke in almost immediately, asking if we required any assistance. 'Tell him to take a hike,' said Steve.

wall

bang your head against a brick wall
bang your head against a wall ◄

If you say that you **are banging** your **head against a brick wall** or **banging** your **head against a wall**, you mean that you feel frustrated because someone is stopping you from making progress in what you are trying to do. Other verbs are sometimes used instead of 'bang'. 'Bang your head against a brick wall' is used mainly in British English.

I was left out of the side and stuck in the reserves with no chance of playing for the first team again. I was banging my head against a brick wall.

It is a waste of valuable energy beating your head against a brick wall, wishing things were different.

come up against a brick wall

If you say that you **have come up against a brick wall**, you mean that something is stopping you from doing what you want and preventing you from making any progress. Verbs such as 'run' and 'go' are sometimes used instead of 'come'.

I was tired, I had been working real hard for a long time and I felt that I'd come up against a brick wall.

The system is loaded in favour of the accused, and investigators are coming up against a ˙rick wall again and again.

They have run up against a brick wall and the only increase in profits will come from a fall in bad debts.

drive someone up the wall ◄

If you say that something or someone is **driving** you **up the wall**, you mean that they are annoying and irritating you a lot.

The heat is driving me up the wall.

Yvonne said the pressure of living in squalor was threatening to split the family up. 'It drives you up the wall, you start taking it out on each other.'

He's so bloody unco-operative he's beginning to drive me up the wall.

go to the wall: 1 ◄◄

If a person or company **goes to the wall**, they lose all their money and their business fails. This expression is used in British English.

Over the last year, two football clubs have gone to the wall.

A total of 1,776 companies went to the wall in the three months to March – a drop of 14 per cent on the first three months of 1992.

go to the wall: 2

If you are willing to **go to the wall** for a person or a principle, you support them so strongly that you are prepared to suffer on their behalf. This expression is used in British English.

Above all, he prizes loyalty. He'll go to the wall for someone or something he believes in.

He did not have much of a ministerial future anyway and we won't go to the wall for him now.

hit the wall ◄

If you **hit the wall** when you are trying to do something, you reach a point where you cannot go any further or achieve any more.

To ensure their businesses do not hit the wall, operators must ensure their financial management is strong and streamlined.

The controversy shows feminism hitting the wall of its own broken promises.

nail someone to the wall

If someone **nails** you **to the wall**, they make you suffer, because they are very angry with you.

If he could not pay off his debt, they would nail him to the wall.

I hope to God he gets nailed to the wall for it.

off the wall ◄◄

If you describe something or someone as **off the wall**, you mean that they are unusual, unconventional, or eccentric. You can use this expression both when you like this kind of person or thing, and when you do not like them.

The new channel is so off-the-wall and unlike

anything we see at the moment that you really have to watch it to appreciate how it will be.

He kept saying he wanted to expose the beauty of opera to the public. I thought he was off the wall.

☐ You can use **off-the-wall** before a noun.

At other times the band plays a kind of off-the-wall lounge music, a kind of soundtrack to a hip science fiction movie.

the writing is on the wall
the handwriting is on the wall ◄◄◄

If you say that **the writing is on the wall** or **the handwriting is on the wall**, you mean that you have noticed things which strongly suggest that a situation is going to become difficult or unpleasant. The form with 'writing' is used mainly in British English and the form with 'handwriting' is used mainly in American English.

The writing is clearly on the wall. If we do nothing about it, we shall only have ourselves to blame.

The writing was on the wall for Capriati when she lost the first set 6-1 in less than 20 minutes.

The handwriting is on the wall: test the children for this major risk factor.

☐ You can refer to something as **the writing on the wall** or **the handwriting on the wall** when it seems to be a sign or warning of something unpleasant which is likely to happen in the future.

The Law Society has long seen the writing on the wall. In 1986, in an attempt to improve the profession's image, it set up the Solicitors' Complaints Bureau and laid down a code of practice.

Despite the president's wait-and-see attitude, his advisers have read the political handwriting on the wall. They are scrambling to come up with ways to revive the economy.

walls

climb the walls

If you say that you **are climbing the walls**, you are emphasizing that you feel very frustrated, nervous, or anxious.

I'm climbing the walls now because I have not got a job. I have been searching hard for six months without success.

Sitting at home would only have had him climbing the walls with worry and frustration.

walls have ears

You can say **'walls have ears'** in order to warn someone that they should be careful about what they are saying because people might be listening.

I shall give it to you and you will put it away quietly in your pocket and we will not discuss it. Walls have ears.

Take care. This place is like a village. Assume all walls have ears.

war

a war of words ◄◄◄

If two people or groups of people have **a war of words**, they argue or criticize each other because they strongly disagree about a particular issue. This expression is used mainly in journalism.

This latest move signals an escalation in the three-year-old war of words between the two countries.

A war of words has blown up over who is to blame for a confrontation between police and fans outside the venue.

The challenge from British favorite Liz McColgan, which descended into a bitter war of words before the race, failed to materialise.

warpath

on the warpath ◄

If you say that someone is **on the warpath**, you mean that they are very angry and getting ready for a fight or quarrel.

If only I had warned the children that daddy was on the warpath.

St Vincent and Grenadines' biggest businessmen are on the warpath after claims that foreign nationals are trying to con them out of thousands of dollars.

wars

in the wars

If you say that someone has been **in the wars**, you mean that they have been hurt or injured. You usually use this expression in a fairly light-hearted way.

Charlotte's four-year-old brother, Ben, has also been in the wars. He is still in plaster after breaking a leg.

We were in the wars a little with eight guys needing treatment afterwards.

warts

warts and all ◄◄

If you describe or accept someone or something **warts and all**, you describe or accept them as they are, including all their faults.

The Pill was welcomed as a major development 25 years ago. But 25 years later we are able to see it in a different perspective, warts and all.

Judith would not be the first wife to have got the measure of her husband and decided that he is still the man for her, warts and all.

☐ You can use **warts and all** before a noun.

'Jagger Unauthorised' is a sensational warts-and-all biography of the Rolling Stones' living legend.

The readable, 816-page book is a warts and all guide to every higher education institution in the country.

wash

come out in the wash: 1

If you say that something will **come out in the wash**, you mean that people will eventually find out the truth about it.

It will make great listening at an industrial tribunal. Everything will come out in the wash, and Flashman will deserve it all.

come out in the wash: 2

You can say that everything will **come out in the wash** when you want to reassure someone that everything will be all right.

That will be the end of that. This will all come out in the wash – I promise you.

waste

a waste of space

If you describe someone as **a waste of space**, you mean that they are completely useless. This expression is used in British English.

You've got another woman there in charge of administration. I talked to her – she's an absolute waste of space.

Even Sarah, a tall 13-year-old with a white face and black-ringed eyes, treated him as if he were a waste of space.

watch

on someone's watch   ◄◄

If something happens **on** someone's **watch**, it happens during a period when they are in a position of power, and are therefore considered to be responsible for it. This expression is used in American English.

The last two sitting Democratic presidents suffered enormous political damage from foreign policy reverses that occurred on their watch.

A leader is judged for what happens on his watch.

Mistakes were made on my watch, and accordingly I believe my decision to retire, while painful, is appropriate.

water

blow something out of the water   ◄

If something **is blown out of the water**, it is destroyed completely, suddenly, and violently.

The government is in a state of paralysis. Its main economic and foreign policies have been blown out of the water.

Butcher put paid to that. He blew our whole operation out of the water.

in deep water   ◄

If you are **in deep water**, you are in a difficult or awkward situation.

You certainly seem to be in deep water and doing your utmost to reverse the negative trends of the past couple of months or so.

It's the same in any business that gets into deep water. As soon as it becomes known that some outfit's down on its luck, all the creditors send in their bills.

in hot water   ◄◄

If you say that someone is **in hot water**, you mean that they have done something wrong and people are angry with them.

Debbie is in hot water when Rick discovers her attempt to sabotage his relationship with Sarah.

His forthright opinions have sometimes gotten him into hot water.

Buckingham Palace has warned a marketing firm it could land in hot water for using the name of the Princess Royal's daughter to promote a perfume.

like water off a duck's back

You can say that criticism is **like water off a duck's back** when it is not having any effect at all on the person being criticized.

We have heard a lot of comments over the years, so this is like water off a duck's back.

Every time you discipline him he will smile sweetly so that you may think your rebukes are streaming away like water off a duck's back.

not hold water   ◄◄

If you say that a theory or an argument **does not hold water,** you do not believe that it can possibly be true or right.

They make it clear that the British Government's argument does not hold water.

The reason given, that marks are just a guide and judges can make changes, does not hold water.

☐ You can say that a theory or an argument **holds water** when you think that it is true or right.

Your application will be scrutinized by a bank and passed on to the Department of Industry if it holds water.

If these arguments hold water, then British non-intervention policy in the 1860s and early 1870s was weak and inadequate.

of the first water

You can use **of the first water** after a noun to indicate that someone is very good at something or is an extreme example of something. This is a fairly old-fashioned expression.

Best of all there's a performance by M-People, proving themselves to be entertainers of the first water.

He was full of energy, Janet recalled, and an eccentric of the first water.

☐ Diamonds **of the first water** are very high-quality diamonds.

pour cold water on something
throw cold water on something ◄◄

If someone **pours cold water on** an idea or plan or **throws cold water on** it, they point out all its problems, rather than sharing other people's enthusiasm for it.

They poured cold water on the French proposal for a peace conference involving both the EU and the UN.

During the session, the Bank of Japan tried to pour cold water on expectations of early interest rate cuts.

This will simply throw cold water over all those plans and leave us with absolutely no energy policy in place.

talk under water

If you say that someone can **talk under water**, you mean that they always talk a lot in any situation, and it is sometimes difficult to stop them talking. This expression is used mainly in Australian English.

My friends tell me that I can talk under water.

What they didn't know was that she can also talk under water with a mouth full of marbles.

test the water
test the waters ◄◄◄

If you **test the water** or **test the waters**, you try to find out what the reaction to an idea or plan might be before taking action to put it into effect.

I was a bit sceptical. I decided to test the water before committing the complete management team.

Some European nations have been cautiously testing the water on visits to Vietnam and talking of upgrading relations. No one European country has yet leapt in with massive investment or aid packages, but there are signs that Europe's attitude to Vietnam may be warming.

I think the news might have been leaked by higher level officials as they test the waters to see how the press reacts to an idea of some sort of military intervention.

tread water ◄◄

If you say that someone **is treading water**, you mean that they are in an unsatisfactory situation where they are not progressing, but are just continuing doing the same things.

They're just going to have to do something to move it on, or they'll stand accused of treading water.

I could either tread water until I was promoted, which looked to be a few years away, or I could change what I was doing.

water under the bridge
water over the dam ◄

You say that an event or situation is **water under the bridge** when you want to say that it happened in the past and so it is no longer worth thinking about or worrying about. In American English, you can also say that something is **water over the dam**.

'I am sorry that I did not go to the 1992 Olympics,' says Timmis, 'but that is water under the bridge.'

Mr Bruce said that he was relieved it was over and that he regarded his time in jail as water under the bridge.

☐ You say things such as **'a lot of water has gone under the bridge'** when you want to say that a lot of time has passed or a lot of things have happened since the event that you are referring to.

It's almost two years since it happened. A lot of water has gone under the bridge but we're just about on speaking terms with Marcia.

waterfront
cover the waterfront

If you **cover the waterfront**, you cover a very wide range of things, or cover every aspect of something. This expression is used mainly in American English.

We have three partners and five employees looking after this whole category. They cover the entire waterfront: oil, real estate, high-tech, and everything else.

We wanted to cover – without covering the waterfront – as many issues as we could.

Waterloo
meet your Waterloo

If you say that someone **meets** their **Waterloo**, you mean that they suffer a very severe defeat or failure, especially one which causes them to finally give up what they are trying to do.

At the foot of the fourth pinnacle I met my Waterloo. The face of the fifth pinnacle rose sheer above us, and it was evident even to me that we would not be attempting it.

☐ In 1815, the French leader Napoleon suffered his final defeat at the Battle of Waterloo in Belgium.

waters
fish in troubled waters

If you say that someone **is fishing in troubled waters**, you mean that they are involved in a very difficult or delicate situation, which could cause them problems.

Mr Khan said firmly that Pakistan is not fishing in the troubled waters of Central Asia. 'It is not part of any of our policies,' he said, adding that the Central Asian region was far from Pakistan's borders.

muddy the waters ◄

If you accuse someone of **muddying the waters**, you mean that they are deliberately trying to make a situation or an issue more confusing and complicated than it really is.

'It's really difficult to see what they want,' said a Hong Kong source in London. 'They keep on muddying the waters by raising other political issues.'

Although he stands no chance of winning in November, he does have the potential to muddy the political waters and set the election on a perplexing new course.

This ruling seems only to have muddied the waters. It seems a bit confusing and we are seeking clarification.

still waters run deep

People say **'still waters run deep'** when they are talking about someone who seems to be unemotional or who is hard to get to know, to suggest that they are in fact interesting and complex.

He's extremely shy and withdrawn, though it may be that still waters run very deep.

For 25 years the orchestra's chief conductor was Haitink, for whom the phrase 'still waters run deep' might have been coined. Everyone expected his successor to be more fiery.

wave

catch the wave

If someone **catches the wave**, they seize an opportunity that is presented to them, especially an opportunity to do something new.

With parliamentary elections still officially scheduled for October, politicians are hoping to catch the wave of rising discontent.

I think that by concentrating on smaller companies you improve your chances of catching the next wave. You could be one of the guys riding the crest instead of one of those just trying to hang on.

wavelength

on the same wavelength ◄◄

If you say that two people are **on the same wavelength**, you mean that they understand each other well because they share the same attitudes, interests, and opinions.

We could complete each other's sentences because we were on the same wavelength.

Although I belonged to their children's generation I found myself very much on their wavelength, often exchanging friendly and amused glances with them.

waves

make waves ◄◄◄

If you say that someone is **making waves**, you mean that they are disturbing a situation by changing things or by challenging the way things are done. You sometimes use this expression to suggest that this is making things better or more exciting.

Manufacturers began shifting production to Taiwan, Korea, even the U.S. Apparently some workers felt this was no time to make waves by plunging into union organizing.

Maathai has a history of making waves. In 1971 she became the first woman in East and Central Africa to earn a PhD.

They are part of the new breed of furniture makers who are starting to make waves on the British scene.

way

the easy way out ◄◄◄

If you accuse someone of taking **the easy way out**, you are accusing them of doing what is easiest for themselves in a difficult situation, rather than dealing with the problem properly.

It is the easy way out to blame others for our failure, and this is bad practice. It is essential that we accept responsibility when things go wrong and endeavour to do something to correct the situation.

You've missed payments on the house, car, washing machine, furniture, TV, and credit card. Everything is an utter mess. There's no easy way out, you know that already. But you must do something or your debts will get worse.

go back a long way
go way back ◄

If you say that two or more people **go back a long way** or **go way back**, you mean that they have been friends or associates for a very long time. 'Go back a long way' is used mainly in British English and 'go way back' is used mainly in American English.

We go back quite a long way and we're very good mates.

We go back a long way, and she's always kept in touch, always been there for me.

'This here is Dr Gillespie, my horn player,' added Parker. 'We go way back.'

look the other way ◄◄◄

If you say that someone **looks the other way**, you mean that they deliberately ignore something unpleasant, immoral, or illegal that is happening when they should be trying to deal with it or stop it from happening. You usually use this expression to suggest that this is a bad thing to do.

Not all the homeland industries are polluting,

but those that are have been able to count on the government to look the other way.

Drugs are sold unashamedly in broad daylight but you tend to look the other way and mind your own business.

The flow of East Germans to Hungary swelled to a flood, and Hungarian border guards looked the other way as East Germans escaped to Austria.

pave the way ◄◄◄

If one thing **paves the way** for another, the first thing makes it easier for the second to happen.

A peace agreement last year paved the way for this week's elections.

The case may pave the way for legislation to lay down the circumstances in which doctors may withhold treatment from patients without hope of recovery.

The success of the new series could pave the way for the further growth of the channel.

She got a job as an assistant stage manager at the Cambridge Arts Festival Theatre, thinking that it might pave the way to a career as a playwright.

rub someone up the wrong way
rub someone the wrong way ◄

If you say that someone **rubs** you **up the wrong way**, you mean that you find them or their behaviour very annoying. This form of the expression is used in British English; in American English, the form is **rub** you **the wrong way**.

Ella Armstrong had an uncommon knack of rubbing everyone up the wrong way.

'I'm surprised at you for acting like that.' 'I know, and I'm sorry. But that woman just rubbed me the wrong way.'

ways

cut both ways
cut two ways ◄

If something **cuts both ways**, it has two different effects, usually one good and one bad. You can also say that something **cuts two ways**.

For Britain, the impact cuts both ways. The immediate effect of cheaper oil is to reduce North Sea oil revenue. But it also produces lower domestic inflation and stronger export markets.

This cuts two ways for the evicted homeowner. When he hands in his keys, he no longer owns the house; but he is still liable for interest on the loan, until the house is sold and the loan repaid.

mend your ways ◄◄

If someone **mends** their **ways**, they stop behaving badly or illegally and improve their behaviour.

He seemed to accept his sentence meekly, promising to work hard in prison and to mend his ways.

'At 34 I think I've done a lifetime of drinking. It's been made quite clear to me that if I carry on in this fashion I will die.' When asked if he intended to mend his ways, he told us 'I'll try my best.'

Complaining to the Commission does not usually bring a speedy result, but the mere fact that an investigation has begun can force a dominant company to mend its ways.

set in your ways ◄

If you describe someone as **set in** their **ways**, you mean that they have very fixed habits and ideas which they are unlikely or unwilling to change.

She knew that if the marriage was going to work it would have to be by her own efforts, her own painful adaptation. He was too set in his ways to make any real changes.

Perhaps you're worried that you may have become set in your ways. It's very easy to develop personal routines and not to accept that other people have other ways of doing things.

wayside

fall by the wayside ◄◄◄

If someone **has fallen by the wayside**, they have failed in something they were doing and have given up trying to achieve success in it. If an activity **has fallen by the wayside**, people have stopped doing it and forgotten about it. The noun 'way' is sometimes used instead of 'wayside'.

The average player's lifespan at the top is five years. You either play well, deal with the pressure, or you fall by the wayside.

With each year our birthday parties grow more and more polite. We still observe the cake and gift rites, but games are naturally out of the question, and even dancing seems to have fallen by the wayside.

Thousands of new diets are dreamed up yearly; many fall by the wayside, but a few are sufficiently effective to become popular.

wear

wear the trousers
wear the pants ◄

The person in a couple who **wears the trousers** or **wears the pants** is the one who makes all the important decisions. This expression is usually used about women who seem to dominate their husbands or partners. 'Wear the trousers' is used only in British English.

She may give the impression that she wears the trousers but it's Tim who makes the final decisions.

By coming across as the one who wears the

trousers, Glenys is sometimes in danger of making her husband seem hen-pecked.

For instance, salesmen may counter a man's objection that he wants to discuss an investment with his wife by asking, 'Who wears the pants in your family?'

weather

keep a weather eye on something ◄

If you **keep a weather eye on** something or someone, you watch them carefully so that you are ready to take action when difficulties arise or anything goes wrong. Other prepositions are sometimes used instead of 'on'. This expression is used in British English.

It is necessary always to keep a weather-eye on your symptoms and stay alert to the changes which occur.

Amy moved away from a neighbourhood where she'd kept a weather eye on an old lady.

Boat owners continue to use their boats, but at the same time they are keeping a weather eye out for surprises, especially in the field of taxation, that might surface in the next few months.

make heavy weather of something ◄

If you say that someone **is making heavy weather of** an activity or task, you are criticizing them for making it much more difficult or taking more time than it needs to. This expression is used in British English.

To an outsider, though, the surprising thing is not that Spain's conservatives are inching ahead but that they are making such heavy weather of it.

The League Cup may be Nottingham Forest's favourite competition – they have won it four times – but Brian Clough's troubled team made heavy weather of last night's tie at Stockport County.

under the weather ◄◄

If you are feeling **under the weather**, you do not feel very well.

If you're feeling a bit under the weather but can't work out what's wrong, try our DIY guide to self-diagnosis.

There are many things a child who is under the weather can do to stimulate his mind and imagination.

web

a tangled web ◄

If you refer to a situation as **a tangled web**, you mean that it is very confused and difficult to understand.

His literary life was a tangled web of frustrations, intrigues and reversals.

It is sometimes difficult to cut through the tangled web of government information in order to know the benefits you can claim.

wedge

drive a wedge between people ◄◄◄

If someone **drives a wedge between** two people who are close, they cause bad feelings between them in order to weaken their relationship. Prepositions such as 'into', 'in', and 'through' are sometimes used instead of 'between'.

I did try to reassure her, but that only seemed to irritate her more. That made me upset, and I started to feel Toby was driving a wedge between us.

He has set up a special radio station to beam propaganda to the Egyptian people. His aim is clearly to destabilise Egypt by driving a wedge between the people and their government. So far, he appears to have had little success.

They are very unlikely to drive a wedge within the Albanian community which seems now more united than ever before.

the thin end of the wedge ◄

If you refer to something as **the thin end of the wedge**, you mean that it is the beginning of something which seems harmless or unimportant at present but is likely to become important, serious, or harmful in the future. This expression is used in British English.

I think it's the thin end of the wedge when you have armed police permanently on patrol round a city.

Opponents of Sunday trading believe an exception made for the Christmas period would be the thin end of the wedge and then the major stores would soon be pressing – and allowed – to open at other times of the year as well.

weight

carry the weight of the world on your shoulders

If you say that someone **is carrying the weight of the world on** their **shoulders**, you mean that they have very many troubles or responsibilities. Other verbs are sometimes used instead of 'carry'.

You look as if you're carrying the weight of the world on those lovely shoulders.

You are the best qualified for this job but you might feel that the weight of the world has been placed on your shoulders.

carry weight ◄◄◄

If a person or their opinion **carries weight**, they are respected and are able to influence people.

It is the men who seem most often to be recognized and talk most in class. Not only do men talk more, but what they say often carries more weight.

El Tiempo is Colombia's leading newspaper.

Its opinions carry considerable weight in the country.

Even though the names of the alleged perpetrators won't be named and the findings will carry no legal weight, the report is expected to be politically explosive.

a dead weight ◄

If you talk about the **dead weight** of something, you are referring to the fact that it makes change or progress extremely difficult.

It's time for him to see that Labour must be free of the dead weight of union power.

I was floundering under the dead weight of a collapsed marriage.

As long as most firms remain nominally in state hands, they sit like a dead weight on Russia's struggling economy.

pull your weight ◄◄

If someone **pulls** their **weight**, they work as hard as everyone else who is involved in the same task or activity. This expression is often used in negative structures to suggest that someone is not working as hard as everyone else.

You must remember that your performance will be judged by the performance of your team, and you cannot afford to carry members who are not pulling their weight.

I'm angry with my mum. She expects me to do her shopping and give her a lot of my time, when I have a sister who doesn't pull her weight and has more free time than I do.

Socialism is about everyone making a contribution in one way or another, about being given a chance to pull your weight, about getting a fair reward for what you do.

throw your weight around
throw your weight about ◄◄

If you accuse someone of **throwing** their **weight around**, you are accusing them of behaving aggressively and of using their authority over other people more forcefully than they need to. In British English, you can also say that someone **is throwing** their **weight about**.

Some people regarded him as a bully who was inclined to throw his weight around, but others who worked more closely with him found the man to be totally uncomplicated if sometimes excessively forthright.

Jonathon Rose, defending, told the jury: 'My client is the sort of person who likes to throw his weight around when he has been drinking.'

They can get into difficult situations with superiors who are less intelligent than themselves or who satisfy their ego by throwing their weight about.

throw your weight behind something ◄◄◄

If you **throw** your **weight behind** a person, plan, or campaign, you do everything you can

to support them.

Shadow Chancellor Gordon Brown pulled out of the Labour leadership race last night to throw his weight behind Tony Blair.

The U.S. government is promising now to throw its weight behind the peace negotiations.

The President threw his weight behind a radical plan for economic reform – so placing him in opposition to his Prime Minister.

worth your weight in gold ◄

If you say that someone or something is **worth** their **weight in gold**, you mean that they are very useful, helpful, or valuable.

Successful television is about having ideas. It always has been and always will be. People with ideas are worth their weight in gold.

Francine was turning out to be worth her weight in gold. Many things that Bill hadn't the heart for these days, she attended to cheerfully and responsibly.

west

go west

When someone **goes west**, they die. When something **goes west**, it stops existing or working. This is an old-fashioned expression.

When he went west, he wanted to be remembered.

His hopes of a professional singing career long ago went west.

whale

have a whale of a time ◄

If you say that someone **is having a whale of a time**, you are emphasizing that they are enjoying themselves a lot.

Ferris wheels, helter skelters and roller coaster rides are the order of the day at Blackpool's world-famous Pleasure Beach. Here you'll find kids of all ages having a whale of a time.

I had a whale of a time in Birmingham.

wheel

a big wheel ◄

If you describe someone as **a big wheel** in an organization or society, you mean that they have an important and powerful position in it.

The general is a big wheel in the Directorate of Military Schools and Academies of the Russian Army.

They flew Robin to New York, where George's uncle was a big wheel at Memorial Hospital.

a fifth wheel
a third wheel

If you describe someone as **a fifth wheel** in a situation, you mean that they are unwanted, unimportant, out of place, or superfluous. You can also describe them as **a third wheel**. These expressions are used in American English.

Women really do suffer more as widows. The fifth woman at a couples dinner party is a fifth wheel; the fifth man is a social coup.

It prompts Miller to remark wryly: 'You know theatre today is the fifth wheel – it makes some noise but nothing rests on it.'

He says police and prosecutors did little to help the surviving family members stay informed, and generally treated him like a third wheel.

reinvent the wheel ◄

If you say that someone **is reinventing the wheel**, you are criticizing them for working on an idea or project that they consider new or different, when it is really no better than something that already exists.

Learn from the examples of the Netherlands and Scandinavia. We have created foundations for other countries to follow. Each country's organization does not need to reinvent the wheel.

Their tendency is to re-invent the wheel each time they are called upon to respond to a new refugee emergency.

□ People sometimes use this expression when someone has got a new idea or project that does improve on the thing that already exists.

It is new territory for the industry. We are reinventing the wheel here, and there is likely to be a massive change.

wheels

oil the wheels
grease the wheels ◄

If someone or something **oils the wheels** or **greases the wheels** of a process or system, they help things to run smoothly and successfully. The noun 'cogs' is sometimes used instead of 'wheels'. The forms with 'oil' are used only in British English.

There is a consensus that state planning should be greatly reduced and confined mainly to oiling the wheels of the market.

The best contribution you can make at this time is to support your wife emotionally and to oil the domestic wheels as much as possible.

Credit cards greased the wheels of the consumer boom by allowing us to buy what we want, when we want.

set the wheels in motion ◄

If you **set the wheels in motion** to carry out an important plan or project, you do what is necessary to start it. The verb 'put' is sometimes used instead of 'set', and you can also say that **the wheels are in motion**.

I have set the wheels in motion to sell Endsleigh Court: the sooner I get out of this block, the better.

It's time everyone else started believing it too and put the wheels of change into motion.

By the following February, all wheels are in motion for a city about to party with floats and costumes for an envious world to see.

spin your wheels ◄

If you accuse someone of **spinning** their **wheels**, you are criticizing them for failing to do or achieve anything satisfactory. This expression is used mainly in American English.

He is not getting anywhere. He's just spinning his wheels.

She admitted that she had been spinning her wheels for so long that she needed help in changing behaviors to get what she said she wanted.

the wheels are turning ◄

If you say that **the wheels are turning** in a process or situation, you mean that the process or situation is continuing to develop and progress.

The wheels continue to turn on plans to convert the building into a bookstore.

It is the small entrepreneurs of this country that keep the wheels of commerce turning and who create opportunity and employment.

A combination of craftsmanship and dedication has won much-needed orders and set the wheels turning once more.

wheels within wheels ◄

If you say that there are **wheels within wheels** in a situation, you mean that it is very complicated because many different things, which influence one another, are involved in it.

Our culture is more complex than he knows. Wheels within wheels. Hierarchies.

Moreover, there are wheels within wheels. Behind his apparent freedom as a director or a producer may lie the interest of the studio subsidising it.

There are wheels within wheels within wheels in the espionage game.

whip

crack the whip ◄

If a person in authority **cracks the whip**, they make people work very hard and treat them firmly, strictly, and perhaps harshly.

They run the chapel, I don't. They crack the whip and I have to jump to it.

Donna stayed at home and cooked and cracked the whip over her three girls and son.

□ When someone treats people in this way, you can talk about **the crack of** their **whip**.

It looked as though he had only acted under the crack of the whip of his Secretary of State.

a fair crack of the whip ◄

If you get **a fair crack of the whip**, you get

the chance to prove how good you are at something. This expression is used in British English.

None of them is expecting any favours, just a fair crack of the whip.

He is a first-rate actor who proved that he deserved a fair crack of the whip by turning in a good performance.

You could, given a fair crack of the whip, make a satisfying job out of this.

have the whip hand
hold the whip hand ◄

If you **have the whip hand** or **hold the whip hand** in a situation, you have more power than the other people involved, and so you have an advantage or control over them.

The biggest party in that government should have the whip hand in decision-making.

Consumers will be in the unusual position of having the whip hand over the agents.

As the Democrats have majorities in both Houses and therefore control the relevant committees, they now seem to hold the whip hand.

whirl

give something a whirl ◄

If you **give** something **a whirl**, you try it in order to see whether you like it or think you can be successful doing it.

Why not give acupuncture a whirl?

Paul confirmed that he, Ringo Starr and George Harrison were getting back together. 'For old time's sake we'll give it a whirl,' he said.

whisker

by a whisker ◄

If you succeed in doing something **by a whisker**, you almost fail. If you fail to do something **by a whisker**, you almost succeed.

The French government only scraped a Yes vote by a whisker.

At the end we lost by a whisker and I feel terribly disappointed.

within a whisker of something ◄◄

If you come **within a whisker of** doing something, you nearly succeed in doing it. If something is **within a whisker of** a particular amount, it is almost that amount.

He came within a whisker of scoring a spectacular goal.

The two firms are within a whisker of agreeing on a deal.

Unemployment, at 6.4 per cent of the labour force, is now within a whisker of the rate at which inflation has often started to climb.

whistle

blow the whistle on someone ◄◄◄

If you **blow the whistle on** someone who is doing something illegal, dishonest, or immoral, you tell the authorities about them because you feel strongly that what they are doing is wrong and they should be stopped.

The week he died, Foreign Minister Ouko was planning to blow the whistle on corrupt top-level officials.

Members of Queensland coastal communities are being asked to blow the whistle on activities that damage the marine environment.

□ You can refer to this activity as **whistle-blowing**.

It gives employees who wish to report unsafe practices a privileged route to go down without jeopardising their jobs. It makes whistle-blowing ultimately unnecessary.

As one whistle-blowing former drug salesperson said on the film: 'I sometimes wondered if people were dying as a result of what I was doing.'

□ A **whistle-blower** is someone who does this.

The department needs to protect whistle-blowers, health professionals who want and care to make a change in the system.

wet your whistle

If you **wet** your **whistle**, you have a drink, especially an alcoholic drink. This is a fairly old-fashioned expression.

Wine was the only thing available with which to wet your whistle, which might explain the rapid decline from civilised dinner to raucous riot.

Dine at the Griechenbeisel where Mozart, Strauss and Beethoven went to wet their whistles – see their signatures on the walls.

whistle for something

If you tell someone that they **can whistle for** something, you are telling them rudely that you will not give it to them.

Rejecting all overtures about the possibility of a compromise, she refused to open her books to the auditors, closed the show and told the city it could whistle for its money.

white

white as a sheet
white as a ghost ◄

If someone looks as **white as a sheet** or as **white as a ghost**, they look very pale and frightened.

There was another lady lorry driver who pulled in in front of me, who it affected badly. She was as white as a sheet.

In 30 years of marriage I have never seen my husband in such a state. He was as white as a ghost and trembling.

whys

white as snow

If you say that something is as **white as snow**, you are emphasizing that it is very white in colour.

When it's warm enough to go bare-legged but your skin's as white as snow, a fake tan's the answer.

whiter than white ◀

If you describe someone as **whiter than white**, you mean that their actions are always honest and moral. You usually use this expression when you are referring to doubts about the person's character or behaviour, or when you are being ironic and trying to suggest that the person is less honest or moral than they appear to be.

He is prepared to forgive Atherton's deceit this time, but has left him in no doubt that his behaviour must be whiter than white in future.

You can't pretend that somehow or other the police are whiter than white. We're living in a real world.

□ You can use **whiter than white** before a noun.

This brush with the law seems to have been the only taint in an otherwise whiter than white lifestyle.

whys

the whys and wherefores ◀

If you talk about **the whys and wherefores** of something, you are talking about the reasons for it.

Even successful bosses need to be queried about the whys and wherefores of their actions.

We may ask for whys and wherefores, but we don't really expect answers.

wick

get on someone's wick

If you say that someone or something **gets on** your **wick**, you mean that they irritate you a great deal. This is an informal expression, which is used in British English.

Let's face it, after three or four songs that voice really does get on your bloody wick.

wicket

on a sticky wicket
bat on a sticky wicket ◀

If you say that someone is **on a sticky wicket** or is **batting on a sticky wicket**, you mean that they are in a difficult situation, and they will find it hard to deal with their problems. These expressions are used in British English.

It seemed to me that we were on rather a sticky wicket. We couldn't admit that we had got the figures without provoking a major ex-plosion and the certain sacking of Mary Waller.

Mr Hughes is batting on a very sticky wicket indeed. Should he succeed in proving his outrageous claims, he would lay himself open to a charge of treason.

□ You can refer to a difficult situation as **a sticky wicket**.

Well, that's a really sticky wicket. As you know, the United Nations will be meeting again on that question later today.

wide

be wide open ◀

If a contest or competition **is wide open**, it is very difficult to say who will win because the competitors are all equally good.

The competition has been thrown wide open by the absence of the world champion.

The Tories breathed a sigh of relief last night as two polls showed the election race was still wide open.

blow something wide open: 1 ◀

If someone **blows** a way of doing things **wide open**, they change it completely by doing things in a totally different way. Verbs such as 'throw', 'bust', and 'split' are sometimes used instead of 'blow'.

Pamela has blown the old newsreader image wide open.

This means that any reopening of the debate could split the Italian political system wide open.

Reforms in the government-bond market will bust wide open the old monopoly on bond-price information.

blow something wide open: 2

If someone **blows** something **wide open**, they reveal something secret that other people have been trying to hide.

Yesterday morning, when Seb turned up, his nerve broke. He ran away, to London. He was going to blow the whole thing wide open.

Has it occurred to you that he can blow the operation wide open?

leave yourself wide open
lay yourself wide open ◀

If you **leave** yourself **wide open** to something such as criticism or ridicule, you make it very easy for other people to criticize or ridicule you, because you behave in a naive or foolish way. You can also say that you **lay** yourself **wide open** to something.

The statement leaves us wide open to attack.

The problem remains that a world-wide shortage of kidneys for transplantation has left the field wide open for the medical exploitation of poor people in less developed countries.

Presenting yourself as someone who is unable

to control their emotions lays you wide open to criticism.

wilderness

in the wilderness   ◄◄◄

If you refer to someone's time **in the wilderness**, you are referring to a part of their career when they are inactive and ignored, and do not have an influential role. This expression is used in British English, especially in journalism.

Dennis Skinner was voted back after two years in the wilderness.

He is delighted to get another chance to represent his country after a period in the wilderness.

After 10 years in the political wilderness the Danish Labour Party appeared yesterday to be on the verge of returning to power.

a voice crying in the wilderness
a lone voice in the wilderness   ◄

If you describe someone as **a voice crying in the wilderness** or **a lone voice in the wilderness**, you mean that they are pointing out the dangers in a situation or the truth about it, but nobody is paying any attention.

Ishmael Reed has been a frequent critic of television news coverage of African-Americans, but he says he considered himself a voice crying in the wilderness.

For years, he was a lone voice in the wilderness, and a lot of it came across as self-serving. But I'll tell you, the man was right.

wildfire

spread like wildfire   ◄◄

If something, especially news or a rumour, **spreads like wildfire**, it very quickly reaches or affects a lot of people. Other verbs such as 'sweep' and 'grow' are sometimes used instead of 'spread'.

When final confirmation of his release came, the news spread like wildfire.

Just about everybody I talked to had heard a story from a neighbor or friend or a relative about some terrible carnage at the front. And these stories are spreading like wildfire through the city.

The virus has forced us to isolate the players and our worry is that it will affect the remainder. It swept through the team like wildfire.

willies

give you the willies

If something **gives** you **the willies**, it makes you feel very nervous or frightened.

'I wonder how long this rain's going to keep up,' Tracy said. 'It's giving me the willies.'

Oh, living on the mountainside is enough to give anyone the willies – especially when the

wolves howl like the wind and the bobcats screech.

wind

blow in the wind

If something such as an idea or agreement **is blowing in the wind**, it is being thought about and discussed, but no decision has yet been taken about it.

The agreement blowing in the wind at Montreal signaled a change in business conditions, and du Pont decided to jump in.

Samaranch, sensing perhaps some difficulties blowing in the wind, withdrew, for the time being, the executive's proposal.

get wind of something
catch wind of something   ◄◄

If you **get wind of** something such as a plan or information, you get to know about it, often when other people did not want you to. You can also say that you **catch wind of** something.

I want nothing said about this until I give the word. I don't want the public, and especially not the press, to get wind of it at this stage.

It was at the end of July, five months into the company's year, that the market got wind of a problem, and Tom Farmer, chairman and chief executive, gave warning that sales were down.

in the wind   ◄

If something such as change is **in the wind**, it is likely to happen.

Change is in the wind and this England team will alter as the year unfolds.

Her intelligence, judgment and instinct, combined with her experience as a war correspondent, were all telling her the same thing. It was going to happen tonight. The crackdown that had been in the wind for days would be tonight.

it's an ill wind
it's an ill wind that blows nobody any good   ◄

People say **it's an ill wind** when they want to point out that unpleasant events and difficult situations often have unexpected good effects.

At the time I thought it a great misfortune indeed to have survived a war only to get an illness from my patients. But it's an ill wind – I recovered and married one of my nurses from that hospital.

It's an ill wind, of course, and what is bad for the oil companies is good for the consumer and inflation.

□ This expression comes from the proverb **it's an ill wind that blows nobody any good**.

There is nothing like a leadership contest for being able to lift stones up and look under

them again. It is an ill wind which blows no-
body any good. I welcome the fact that this is
being brought to the front again.

It's an ill wind that blows no good.

like the wind ◄

If you say that someone runs or moves **like
the wind**, you are emphasizing that they run
or move very quickly.

*She was a wonderful kid. Ran like the wind
on our track team.*

Out on the water, the boat goes like the wind.

put the wind up someone
get the wind up ◄

If someone or something **puts the wind up**
you, they make you scared or worried. This
expression is used mainly in British English.

*The front door was jammed and they couldn't
open it. The delay put the wind up me because,
by then, I knew something was very wrong.*

*He has already put the wind up his manage-
ment team by detailing his strategy of globali-
sation.*

□ If you become scared or worried, you can
say that you **get the wind up** or **have the
wind up**.

*She won't crack, but Denny might when he
gets the wind up.*

*As far as the real economy is concerned, it is
plain that despite all the encouraging noises
which have recently been emanating from the
Government it has the wind up about the recovery.*

sail close to the wind ◄

If you **sail close to the wind**, you take a
risk by doing or saying something which may
get you into trouble. This expression is used
mainly in British English.

*Max warned her she was sailing dangerously
close to the wind and risked prosecution.*

*Rogers has often railed against the transgres-
sions of businessmen who sometimes sail a bit
close to the wind for his liking.*

a second wind ◄

If you get **a second wind** when you are
tired or unsuccessful, you suddenly find the
strength or motivation to go on and succeed
in what you are doing.

*It was great tennis and it was fun. I got a se-
cond wind midway through the fourth set.*

*The president said today that this would be a
programme for the nineties, and give the party
a second wind.*

spit in the wind

If you say that someone **is spitting in the
wind**, you mean that they are wasting their
time by trying to do something which has little or no chance of success.

But the idea that you can talk about a single

*currency today is to spit in the wind of econom-
ic reality.*

take the wind out of someone's sails
take the wind out of someone's sail ◄

If something **takes the wind out of** your
sails or **takes the wind out of** your **sail**, it
makes you feel much less confident in what
you are doing or saying. The form with 'sail'
is used only in American English.

*We hit a bad patch after losing to Manchester
United in the Cup semi-final. We put everything
into those two games and it shows. The effort
and disappointment took the wind out of our
sails for a while.*

*This concession succeeded in taking much of
the wind out of the opposition's sails. Criticism
of the measure has been distinctly muted.*

*A year ago, had they offered them autonomy,
this would have taken the wind out of his sail
almost completely.*

twist in the wind
swing in the wind ◄

If you say that someone **is twisting in the
wind** or **is swinging in the wind**, you mean
that they have been left in a very difficult and
weak position, often by people who hope to
gain advantage from this for themselves. Other verbs such as 'hang' or 'turn' are sometimes used instead of 'twist' and 'swing'.
These expressions are used more commonly
in American English than British.

*For seven and a half months, it now seems
clear, she was left twisting mutely in the wind
to cover up a failed policy.*

*Critics accused the Prime Minister of leaving
the minister swinging in the wind, neither giving him unreserved backing, nor being prepared to end the agony by sacking him.*

which way the wind is blowing
how the wind is blowing ◄

If someone sees **which way the wind is
blowing**, they understand or realize how a
situation is developing and use this in deciding what to do. You can also say that someone sees **how the wind is blowing**.

*He wasn't one to make pronouncements before
he was sure which way the wind was blowing.*

*The Shadow Chancellor has sensed the way
the wind is blowing and is calling for a full
public inquiry into the activities of credit card
companies.*

*Well, I don't think he'd wait for anything. He
might jump in too quick – I don't think he'd
wait to see how the wind was blowing.*

whistle in the wind

If you say that someone **is whistling in the
wind**, you mean that what they are saying is
empty or pointless.

The leader of the Liberal Democrats accused

the Prime Minister of whistling in the wind to raise Conservative party morale.

Prior to going out, he had confided to some Spanish journalists that he was going to win the tournament, but that turned out to be whistling in the wind.

windmills

tilt at windmills   ◄

If you say that someone **is tilting at windmills**, you mean that they are wasting their time on problems or issues which in your opinion are not really problems at all.

The supporters of this act are tilting at windmills. They imagine that America is being leached of technology by predatory foreigners. That could not be further from the truth.

I have spent my life tilting at windmills. Will I never learn?

If they find it convenient to tilt at the windmill of Japanese exports rather than tackle their own fiscal disorders, they should remember that they are supposed to be serious governments.

window

go out the window
go out of the window   ◄◄◄

If something such as a plan or a particular way of thinking or behaving **has gone out the window** or **has gone out of the window**, it has disappeared completely. Other verbs such as 'fly' are sometimes used instead of 'go'. 'Out of the window' is used only in British English.

That theory has gone out the window with the last days of testimony.

It seems Britons are ready to sacrifice almost anything to have an annual holiday. Home improvements go out of the window and one in three people will even give up going to the pub to save for a break.

Three years later she met Mick, and her good intentions flew out the window.

Millions of pounds were recklessly and needlessly lost, wisdom and common sense thrown out of the window.

wing

on a wing and a prayer   ◄

If you do something **on a wing and a prayer**, you do it in the hope that you will succeed, even though you do not have the proper resources for it, or are not properly equipped or prepared.

Gay programmes and the gay press are run on a wing and a prayer.

Whatever the cause, large parts of the government seem to be running on a wing and a prayer.

Some rider and horse combinations are a joy to watch but others are simply not up to it. They get over the higher fences on a wing and a prayer.

take someone under your wing   ◄◄

If you **take** someone **under** your **wing**, you protect them and make sure that they are all right.

I let him tag along because he had not been too well recently. I took him under my wing and looked after him.

Food aid has already come from America and others. But it is Japan that seems most determined to take Mongolia under its wing.

under the wing of someone

If you are **under the wing of** someone, they control you or take responsibility for you.

If their problems are picked up at school and they come under the wing of an educational psychologist, they may be found a place in a special school.

What the government has not done, then or now, is to remove the office from under the wing of the economics ministry.

wings

clip someone's wings   ◄◄

If someone **clips** your **wings**, they limit your freedom to do what you want.

The opposition has been trying to clip his wings by making his actions and his appointments subject to parliamentary approval.

Congress tried to clip his wings and cancel his referendum.

Unfortunately, the race committee have seen fit to clip our wings in the race by banning the use of these sails in four of the six legs.

in the wings   ◄◄◄

If you say that someone is waiting **in the wings**, you mean that they are waiting for an opportunity to take action, especially to take over another person's job or position.

He was one of a number of young, up and coming American players who were waiting in the wings for the next Major Championship.

British Telecom has been attacked for excessive profits ever since it was privatised. But there are now more than 20 big companies waiting in the wings to take over some of its business.

□ You can also say that something is **in the wings** when it is about to happen or be made public.

More bad news could be in the wings in the form of more rises in licence fees.

spread your wings   ◄◄

If you **spread** your **wings**, you do something new that is more ambitious than anything you have done before.

I've always had a very strong musical direction and I was able to really flourish and spread my wings.

Given the firm's high profile in Scotland, it is perhaps surprising that it has not spread its wings across the border.

try your wings

If you **try** your **wings**, you try to do something new to see if you can succeed.

That's the other thing the school never teaches you. There's very little place to try your wings, to see how you do a particular task.

He was very keen to try his wings and be a deputy on his own.

wink

not sleep a wink
not get a wink of sleep ◄

If you say that you **did not sleep a wink** or that you **did not get a wink of sleep**, you mean that you tried to go to sleep but could not.

This was my first Grand Prix win of the season and I was so excited I couldn't sleep a wink that night.

Unfortunately, I didn't get a wink of sleep because the tablets I was given made me sick.

tip someone the wink

If you **tip** someone **the wink**, you quietly or secretly give them information that could be important or helpful to them. This is an old-fashioned expression, which is used in British English.

The commission may tip him the wink that certain compromises might prove acceptable to EU governments.

Back in Italy in 1945, he resolved to help them either by tipping them the wink to flee, or by fudging the evidence.

winks

forty winks ◄

If you have **forty winks**, you have a short sleep or rest. This is a fairly old-fashioned expression.

He's having his forty winks. It's a wonder you didn't hear his snores in the street.

There's nothing like 40 winks to ease away the tension and stresses of a hard day.

wire

down to the wire ◄◄

If you do something **down to the wire**, you continue doing it until the last possible moment. This expression is used mainly in American English.

As Congress worked down to the wire to reach a compromise, the president lectured a

group of White House interns on the budget crisis.

With two days to go, this means the parties will go down to the wire before a victor emerges.

Contract negotiations between General Motors and the United Auto Workers are going down to the wire in Detroit. The strike deadline is midnight tonight.

a live wire ◄

If you describe someone as **a live wire**, you mean that they are very lively and energetic.

She is a wonderful girl, a real live wire and full of fun.

under the wire

If you get in **under the wire**, you get in somewhere or do something at the last possible moment. This expression is used mainly in American English.

He has been running ads in publications like the Wall Street Journal, urging clients to get in under the wire.

On first reading it looks like they'll get under the wire because they have a US partner on the team.

wits

at your wits' end ◄◄

If you are **at your wits' end**, you are very worried and desperate about something and you do not know what to do about it.

Josh became very difficult after his father's death: he was rebellious and rude, and refused to go to school. I was at my wits' end.

We row a lot and we never have time on our own. I'm at my wit's end.

People are at their wits end about crime and they want to do something. They want action.

collect your wits
gather your wits

If you **collect** your **wits** or **gather** your **wits**, you make an effort to control yourself and become calm again, after you have had a frightening or shocking experience. These expressions are used mainly in novels.

For a bone-jarred moment all he knew was the shocked terror of being left in a hail of gunfire; then he collected his wits, scrambled up and fled.

Late that night, as we tried to gather our wits in a hotel, we sought to imagine what would have happened if, as so easily could have been the case, we had been on board the boat when the storm blew up.

have your wits about you
keep your wits about you
need your wits about you ◄

If you **have** your **wits about** you or **keep** your **wits about** you, you are alert and ready to take action in a difficult or new situation. If you **need** your **wits about** you, it is important for you to behave in this way.

You've got to have your wits about you when you're driving a car.

Obviously divers need to keep their wits about them.

It was a time when a woman needed her sharpest wits about her, a time to think clearly and keenly about escape.

pit your wits against someone ◄

If you **pit** your **wits against** someone, you use your intelligence to try and defeat them. This expression is used in British English.

I'm as ambitious as the next man. I'd like to manage a team at the very highest level and pit my wits against the best.

He has to pit his wits against an adversary who is cool, clever, cunning and desperate not to be caught.

scare someone out of their wits ◄

If something **scares** you **out of** your **wits**, it makes you very frightened or worried. You can also say that something **scares the wits out of** you. Verbs such as 'frighten' and 'startle' can be used instead of 'scare'.

'Oh, I'm so glad you're all right!' Bess exclaimed, hugging Nancy, and George added, 'You scared us out of our wits. We heard you had an accident.'

My people are actually getting frightened to go out into the field. Terrorists couldn't do it, civil wars didn't bother them, but a damned ghost is scaring the wits out of them.

The tree crashed through the conservatory and set off all the alarms, which joined with the sound of the gale to frighten me out of my wits.

□ You can also say that something **scares** you **witless**.

It was dark. Everybody was locked indoors, scared witless. Only a tiny minority know what happened.

The door used to blow open and startle me witless.

wives

an old wives' tale ◄◄

An old wives' tale is a commonly held belief that is based on traditional ideas, often ones which have been proved to be incorrect or inaccurate.

My mother used to tell me to feed a cold and starve a fever. Is it just an old wives' tale?

It's not just an old wives' tale, you know, that full moons and madness have an affinity. As a matter of fact, as recently as last year, at the University of Pennsylvania, an extremely interesting study was done along those lines.

wobbly

throw a wobbly
throw a wobbler ◄

If someone **throws a wobbly** or **throws a wobbler,** they lose their temper in a noisy, uncontrolled, and childish way, often about something unimportant. These expressions are used in British English.

I can't even lie in the bath without him throwing a wobbly because there are a few shampoo bottles with the lids off.

He saw no point in throwing a wobbler when his mum refused him his favourite pud: he reported her to the police instead.

wolf

cry wolf ◄◄

If you say that someone **is crying wolf,** you mean that they are continually asking for help when it is not needed, or warning about danger when it does not really exist. Because of this, people have stopped believing them and so will not help them when it is really necessary.

Knowing when to issue an evacuation order is crucial. If it is issued too early, the storm could veer off in another direction, then officials could be accused of crying wolf and future orders might not be taken seriously. On the other hand, if the order goes out too late, there may not be enough time for the residents to get out.

Wall Street analysts who have been telling clients to avoid Philadelphia Electric shares are starting to feel like the little boy who cried wolf. Nobody believes them.

□ In a story by Aesop, the little boy who looked after the sheep called for help so many times that, when a wolf really came and attacked the sheep, the villagers did not believe him and the sheep were killed.

keep the wolf from the door ◄

Something which **keeps the wolf from the door** provides you with enough money to live on.

Government pension provisions will keep the wolf from the door, but for a comfortable old age you need to make maximum use of the financial choices now open to you.

The finance we got then wasn't brilliant. A lot of the lads took small jobs to help keep the wolf from the door.

a lone wolf

If you refer to someone as **a lone wolf,** you mean that they are independent and like doing things on their own, rather than doing them with other people.

Among his peers, he is something of a lone wolf.

Furness was a maverick, a lone wolf. A wom-

an who didn't follow Standard Operating Procedures.

a wolf in sheep's clothing
a sheep in wolf's clothing ◄

If you refer to someone or something as a wolf in sheep's clothing, you mean that although they appear harmless or ordinary, they are really very dangerous or powerful.

John Major's grey image may disguise a wolf in sheep's clothing.

Calling it a wolf in sheep's clothing, Surgeon General Antonia Novello is stepping up her campaign against a high alcohol wine drink called Cisco.

□ People sometimes describe someone as a sheep in wolf's clothing to mean that the person seems dangerous or powerful, but is really harmless or ordinary.

His protruding jaw, combined with his teeth, gave him a vicious appearance. However, he was a sheep in wolf's clothing, a gentle, amiable parish priest, loved by his people in Aberconwy.

wolves
throw someone to the wolves ◄

If someone throws you to the wolves, they allow you to be criticized severely or treated roughly, and they do not try to protect you. Throw someone to the lions means the same.

What he feared even more than the isolation was the thought of being released into the general prison population. 'What will happen there?' he asked. 'I don't know what will happen if they throw me to the wolves.'

Suddenly he was thrown to the wolves with the stigma of being incompetent, no good, even a fool. It was a dreadful end to a distinguished career.

wonder
a one-day wonder
a nine-day wonder ◄

If you refer to something or someone as a one-day wonder or a nine-day wonder, you mean that they are interesting, exciting, or successful for only a very short time, and they do not have any lasting value. Other numbers can be used instead of 'one' or 'nine'.

If the goal was simply to make people aware of environmental problems it was a great success. The fear of environmentalists, though, is that this may prove to be a one-day wonder.

The other main theme that has wafted across the Atlantic this week, the vulnerability of brand leaders to price-cutting, shows no sign of passing away as a nine-day wonder.

The attitude of the majority of the people I've

spoken to is: 'So what? It's a seven-day wonder, people will forget it's there.'

wood
dead wood ◄

If you refer to someone or something as dead wood, you mean that they are no longer useful or effective in a particular organization or situation and you want to get rid of them.

Get rid of all the dross and dead wood. Recruit women and men who are lively, alert, imaginative and who want to teach.

Now is the time for the dead wood at the top of the party to be cut away. Since the elections, the leadership has received a great deal of criticism.

Mr Hill said the Government's policies, designed to streamline the industry and remove some of the dead wood, had 'gone too far'.

touch wood
knock on wood
knock wood ◄◄

When you are talking about how well things are going for you, you say 'touch wood', 'knock on wood', or 'knock wood' to mean that you hope the situation will continue to be good and that you will not have any bad luck. 'Touch wood' is used mainly in British English, and 'knock on wood' and 'knock wood' are used mainly in American English.

She's never even been to the doctor's, touch wood. She's a healthy happy child and anyone can see that.

'I really do not believe the things that are happening now. I have the potential at this point for the kind of career I could only have dreamed of. I'm knocking on wood because you never know.'

'And knock wood, I have been at the company for 13 years, and I have not missed one day's work through illness. Not one.'

□ People sometimes actually touch or knock on a wooden surface as they say this.

woods
out of the woods ◄◄

If someone or something is not yet out of the woods, they are still having difficulties with something or are still in a bad condition.

The Prime Minister is by no means out of the woods, and must fight to defend his leadership at a crisis Cabinet meeting to be called early today.

One economist warns the nation's economy is not out of the woods yet, that there has to be concern about financial shocks coming from abroad.

woodwork

come out of the woodwork ◄

You can say that people **are coming out of the woodwork** if they suddenly start publicly doing something or saying something, when previously they did nothing or kept quiet. You often use this expression when you are critical of them for not having done this earlier. You can replace 'come' with another verb such as 'crawl'.

People are starting to come out of the woodwork to talk about fraudulent practices in the industry.

The worst aspect of their decision for Britain is that it will now bring anti-Europeans crawling out of the woodwork once more.

wool

dyed-in-the-wool ◄◄

You use **dyed-in-the-wool** to describe a supporter of a particular philosophy or a member of a particular group to suggest that they have very strong beliefs or feelings about that philosophy or group, and are unlikely ever to change.

I am a dyed-in-the-wool Labour man. He'll not get my vote.

Mr Purves has made Hong Kong his home for the past 38 years but he remains a dyed-in-the-wool Scotsman.

Teaching literature to large groups of young people under school circumstances is almost doomed to failure. Earnest trendy teachers or dyed-in-the-wool traditionalists, you're bound to commit at least one of the main offences.

pull the wool over someone's eyes ◄

If you accuse someone of **pulling the wool over** your **eyes**, you mean that they are trying to deceive you, in order to get an advantage over you.

Parents who are mistreating their small children would find it much more difficult to pull the wool over her eyes.

'I just told them I was ten years younger than I really was,' says Liliana, speaking yesterday for the first time about how she pulled the wool over the medical profession's eyes.

word

a dirty word ◄◄◄

If you say that something is **a dirty word** to someone, you mean that they disapprove of it and do not want to have anything to do with it.

At the root of their problems was the misplaced belief that good products sell themselves. Marketing became a dirty word at the company.

A lot of younger women in the '80s and '90s somehow thought feminism was a dirty word.

Responsibility and duty are dirty words in progressive circles. That must change.

from the word go ◄◄

From the word go means from the very beginning of an activity.

Right from the word go, many of the players looked out of breath and out of their depth.

Pensions can be a money maze and it's essential you make the right decisions from the word go or you won't be able to enjoy your retirement.

get a word in edgeways
get a word in edgewise ◄

If you cannot **get a word in edgeways** or **get a word in edgewise** in a conversation, you find it difficult to say anything because someone else is talking so much. 'Get a word in edgeways' is used only in British English and 'get a word in edgewise' is used mainly in American English.

For heaven's sake, Sue, will you let me get a word in edgeways!

Ernest dominated the conversation. Zhou reportedly could hardly get a word in edgewise.

someone's word is law

If someone's **word is law** in an organization or group, everyone has to obey them. This expression is sometimes used to suggest that this kind of behaviour is unreasonable.

His word was law inside the firm, and subordinates literally trembled when he stalked into a room, waving one of his giant cigars.

His father was the kind of parent who saw no reason to discuss anything with his son; his word was law.

a word in someone's ear ◄

If you have **a word in** someone's **ear**, you speak to them quietly and privately about a delicate or difficult matter. This expression is used in British English.

I'll go and see Quennell. It won't be official, mind. Just a word in his ear over a drink.

We won't get away with that kind of display against Spain next month, and although I won't name names, I've had words in the right ears and told certain people they've got to show a big improvement.

words

eat your words ◄◄

If someone has given an opinion about something and is now proved to be wrong, you can say that they will have to **eat** their **words**.

England made Denmark eat their words with a brilliant victory in the European basketball championship. Danish coach Steen Knudsen had criticised England prior to their semi-final clash.

The company's embattled chairman has had to eat his words about the company being recession-proof. 'When I suggested that I saw no return to the dark days of recession, I was clearly wrong,' he acknowledges.

famous last words

If you claim that something will definitely happen in a certain way and then say **'famous last words'**, you are suggesting light-heartedly that it is quite possible that you will be proved wrong.

'There won't be any more positive drug tests from the ones completed in Britain before the Olympics,' he assured us. Then, he added: 'These might be famous last words.'

'All under control,' said Bertie. 'Famous last words,' added Idris with a wide grin.

□ You can also use **famous last words** to point out that you were in fact wrong about something.

When I set out from Birmingham I thought, at least I'm going to get an early finish. Famous last words.

in words of one syllable

If you say that you are going to tell someone something **in words of one syllable**, you mean that you are going to say it as simply and clearly as possible. You often use this expression to suggest that the other person is stupid or slow to understand something.

Then he wanted to know if I would help out, if it became necessary, by accepting the nomination for Vice-President. I told him in words of one syllable that I would not.

I'm sure I don't have to spell things out in words of one syllable to you.

lost for words
at a loss for words
stuck for words ◄◄◄

If you are **lost for words** or **at a loss for words**, you are so amazed, shocked, or moved by something that you do not know what to say or how to express your feelings in words. You can also say that you are **stuck for words**.

It has been a long time, a very long year since Anne was killed, and now at last we have justice. At a time like this, I have thought of so many things I wanted to say, but I'm lost for words.

I had the feeling they were all waiting for me to say something. But for the first time in my life I felt at a loss for words.

I was stuck for words when I heard the news. I couldn't believe it. I got a phone call from our assistant manager saying I had been picked and I thought he was winding me up.

not mince your words ◄◄◄

If you **do not mince** your **words** or **do not mince words** when you are giving an opin-

ion, you state it clearly and directly, even though you know that some people will not like what you are saying.

She did not mince her words when she came to the platform to demand a vote of no confidence in the president.

Ordinary people do not mince their words in expressing their worries about the effects of the price rises.

I tell it like it is. I don't mince words.

put words into someone's mouth ◄

If you accuse someone of **putting words into** your **mouth** or **in** your **mouth**, you mean that they are reporting opinions or statements which they claim are yours, but which you have never actually held or made.

You're trying to get me to say things and I'm rather annoyed with you! You're putting words into my mouth which have got nothing to do with me or my book!

At medical school, students are shown videos of bad doctors being arrogant, reaching for the prescription pad as soon as patients walk in, putting words in patients' mouths.

take the words out of someone's mouth

If you **take the words out of** someone's **mouth**, you say the thing that they were just about to say.

'Well, it's been amazing,' she said in closing. 'You took the words right out of my mouth, Lisa.'

work

do someone's dirty work ◄◄◄

If you **do** someone's **dirty work**, you do something unpleasant or difficult on their behalf because they do not want to do it themselves.

He's always got other people to do his dirty work for him.

He had offered me one hundred thousand dollars to do this. I had refused. So he did his own dirty work.

A lot of people feel that these people are death squads, doing the government's dirty work.

have your work cut out ◄◄◄

If you say that someone **has** their **work cut out** for them, you mean that they have a very big problem to deal with, and they will not find it easy to do.

The Prime Minister has his work cut out for him as most analysts see little chance of resolving the constitutional crisis.

A recent survey of 50 leading companies found that only one was able to respond promptly to an enquiry in French. Clearly language trainers have their work cut out.

a nasty piece of work ◄

If you say that someone is **a nasty piece of**

work, you mean that they are very unpleasant. Sometimes people use 'bit' instead of 'piece', or use another adjective instead of 'nasty'.

What about the husband, then. He's a real nasty piece of work.

He was a nasty bit of work, a demagogue, an admirer of the Fascists.

Anyone with eyes could have seen she was a dreadful piece of work.

works

in the works   ◄◄◄
If something is **in the works**, it is being planned or is in progress. This expression is used mainly in American English. **In the pipeline** means the same.

The Office of Development for the city says that a shopping center is in the works.

He said there were dozens of economic plans in the works.

He had a documentary film in the works.

the works
the whole works   ◄
When you are describing something, you can mention a number of things and then say **the works** or **the whole works** to refer to many other things of the same kind or to refer to all the other things which would normally be included.

Our agents are watching all exits from New York City – airports, train stations, bus stations, tunnels, bridges, the works.

Amazing place he's got there – squash courts, swimming pool, jacuzzi, the works.

There's a whole set of these dolls dressed like a wedding party: the bride, the groom, and the whole works!

world

come down in the world
If someone **has come down in the world**, they are not as rich as they used to be and have a lower social status. This is a fairly old-fashioned expression.

Young women of middle class families which had come down in the world also found work in the upper ranges of domestic service.

Jorg was behind the wheel, accompanied by Thomas, another Berliner who had come down in the world.

come up in the world
go up in the world
move up in the world   ◄
If someone **has come up in the world**, they are richer or more powerful than they used to be and have a higher social status. You can also say that they **have gone up in the world** or they **have moved up in the world**. These are all fairly old-fashioned expressions.

A well brought-up young man: he was said to have been an ordinary worker who had come up in the world. His hands were indeed rough as a workman's.

This was the rich man's end of town; Jerrold must be moving up in the world to live here.

dead to the world
If someone is **dead to the world**, they are sleeping very deeply.

Sarah was dead to the world and would probably sleep for twelve hours.

The kids were dead to the world, sprawled like rag dolls across their respective beds.

it's a small world
small world   ◄
You say **'it's a small world'** or **'small world'** to express your surprise when you unexpectedly meet someone you know in an unusual place. You can also use these expressions when you are talking to someone and are surprised to discover that you both know the same person.

He later became a surveyor and road engineer, and thirty years after leaving Sandwich I met him again in the Isle of Wight where he was Deputy County Surveyor. It is indeed a small world.

I'm only just recovering from the surprise of running into you like this. Small world.

I had no idea you knew the Proberts. Well, well, it's a small world.

not long for this world
If you say that someone **is not long for this world**, you mean that they are likely to die soon.

Peter Hastings asked Ian to become his assistant earlier that year, perhaps knowing that he was not long for this world. When he died in June, Ian's destiny was cast.

This had to be delicately handled. I mean you couldn't exactly barge in on Simon and Sam and say, 'Look guys, neither one of you are long for this world, so we think it might be a good time for you to sell the company.'

not set the world on fire
If you say that someone **won't set the world on fire**, you are saying in a light-hearted or ironic way that they are not very exciting and are unlikely to be very successful.

However, except for some time trial stage wins in the Tour of Vaucluse, the 29-year-old Frenchman hasn't exactly set the world on fire in this discipline.

But while Munton is a good, honest county medium fast bowler, hardly likely to set the world on fire, the selection of Salisbury is one of the most challenging moves by English cricket for two decades.

☐ You can replace 'the world' with **the Thames** or the name of another river.

None of these dishes would set the Thames on fire, but they were competently executed, and well set off our wines, which are really the whole point of the place.

They both had respectably successful careers in North America, without exactly setting the Hudson River on fire.

not the end of the world ◄◄◄

You can say **'it's not the end of the world'** when something bad happens, in order to console yourself or another person by suggesting that the consequences of the event are not as bad as they might seem at first.

If I make a mistake, it's not the end of the world. I can always go back and correct it.

I've enjoyed my time in international football, but it won't be the end of the world if I'm not selected again.

'So if you don't find the man of your dreams it's not the end of the world?' 'No, because you just keep going.'

on top of the world ◄◄

If you feel **on top of the world**, you feel extremely happy.

The combination of cold, crisp snow and warm sunshine makes you feel on top of the world.

When she came back from that holiday she was so happy, on top of the world.

out of this world ◄◄◄

If you say something is **out of this world**, you are emphasizing that you think it is very good or impressive.

The show was really good. The music was great and the costumes were out of this world.

Even the swankiest American hotels serve black bean soup with rice, the local staple, and the seafood is out of this world.

An Italian villa in Brentwood, which John Douglas himself has built for $7.3 million, is out of this world.

☐ You can also use **out-of-this-world** before a noun.

I can't think of a more skilful player in the First Division. He has out-of-this-world ability.

think the world of someone ◄

If you **think the world of** someone, you like and admire them very much or are very fond of them.

He is an involved and caring father, and Sam thinks the world of him.

One leading opposition woman politician said she'd thought the world of Mrs Thatcher while agreeing with hardly any of her policies.

the world is your oyster ◄

If someone says **'the world is** your **oyster'**,

they mean that you have the opportunity to achieve great success in your life.

When I was 29 I was a millionaire. You come from nothing and suddenly the world is your oyster.

You've got a wonderful watershed in your life, Johnny. If you don't like what the new situation is, somebody else will want you. You're young, you've got a lot of opportunity. The world is your oyster.

worlds

the best of both worlds ◄◄◄

If you have **the best of both worlds**, you are in a situation where you have all the benefits and advantages of two different things, without any of the problems or disadvantages. Compare **the worst of both worlds**.

There are surprising ways to get the best of both worlds: to enjoy the discounts package holidays make possible, and savour the untouched beauty usually only found on exclusive luxury hideaways.

These locations combine the best of both worlds. They're in the town yet close to the beautiful countryside of Worcestershire and Warwickshire and, thanks to the region's motorway network, with easy access to Birmingham for commuting.

the worst of both worlds ◄◄

If you have **the worst of both worlds**, you have all the problems and disadvantages of two different things without any of the benefits and advantages. Compare **the best of both worlds**.

And, of course, there are plenty of single women who, either through divorce or because they were never married in the first place, have the responsibilities of motherhood without the support of the partner and seem to have the worst of both worlds.

Fans got the worst of both worlds: higher prices and more low-quality football.

worm

the worm turns ◄

If someone who has tolerated a lot of bad treatment from other people without complaining unexpectedly changes their behaviour and starts to behave in a more forceful way, you can say that **the worm has turned**.

Then my mother came home and started bossing us around. She said, 'The worm has turned. Things are going to be different around here.'

For a moment last autumn it looked as if the worm might have turned when hundreds of thousands of ordinary folk marched against the grotesque vandalisation of the coal industry.

worms

a can of worms
a bag of worms   ◄◄

If you describe a situation as **a can of worms**, you mean that it is much more complicated, unpleasant, or difficult than it seems at first. If you say that someone is opening **a can of worms**, you mean that they are doing something which would be better left alone. 'Bag' is occasionally used instead of 'can'.

Now we have uncovered a can of worms in which there has not only been shameful abuse of power, but a failure of moral authority of the worst kind.

Attention has been switched to teaching English to Britain's diverse communities. But here a whole new can of worms is opened.

It really is a can of worms. Compensation is going to be a big practical problem.

Mary Ann rejected the idea with a frown. That would jeopardize things even more than the current bag of worms. It was better to stick with the whole truth.

worse

the worse for wear   ◄◄

If you say that someone is **the worse for wear**, you mean that they look tired or are in a bad state, especially because they have been working hard or drinking a lot of alcohol.

In the fourth round both fighters suffered cuts over the eyes, but the champion was beginning to look the worse for wear.

He turned up at important functions two hours late and noticeably the worse for wear.

wounds

lick your wounds   ◄◄

If you say that someone is **licking** their **wounds**, you mean that they are feeling sorry for themselves after being thoroughly defeated or humiliated.

England's cricketers are licking their wounds after being soundly defeated in the second Test against Australia at Melbourne.

The island has never supported a farming community, just a single farm doing the best it can. One by one the farmers have tried, failed and withdrawn to lick their financial wounds.

open old wounds
reopen old wounds   ◄

If you say that something **opens old wounds**, you mean that it reminds people of an unpleasant or embarrassing experience in the past that they would rather forget about. You can also say that something **reopens old wounds**.

But that afternoon my world was overturned. Ted's diagnosis had opened old wounds and I no longer felt secure.

Jean-Marie Le Pen, leader of the extreme-right National Front, has suggested that it is 'not a good idea to open old wounds. The past does not interest the French people, who are more concerned with unemployment, immigration problems, crime and AIDS.'

Our Political Correspondent, Andrew Whitehead, says the row is reopening old wounds among Conservative MPs.

wraps

keep something under wraps   ◄◄◄

If something **is kept under wraps**, it is kept secret and not revealed to anyone. Other verbs can be used instead of 'keep'.

The official report has been kept under wraps for months by legal objections from BA.

I know quite a lot of gay doctors and most are in stable relationships but feel they can't take their boyfriends to medical dinners or whatever. Everything is kept under wraps.

It was essential that the plans remained under wraps.

take the wraps off something
the wraps come off

If someone **takes the wraps off** something such as a proposal or a new product, they tell people about it for the first time. The verb 'pull' is sometimes used instead of 'take'.

The Clinton administration has taken the wraps off its proposals to enhance American technology.

Many of those who pulled the wraps off their plans before the Conservatives' election victory will be wishing they had pondered a little while longer.

□ You can also say that **the wraps come off**.

A breath of spring arrives today as the wraps come off the first Renault convertible to be sold in the UK for more than 20 years.

wrench

throw a wrench into the works
throw a monkey wrench into the works   ◄

If someone or something **throws a wrench into the works** or **throws a monkey wrench into the works**, they cause problems which prevent something from happening in the way that it was planned. These expressions are used in American English; the British expression is **throw a spanner in the works**.

When Elton was robbed it threw a monkey wrench into the works.

□ Instead of saying 'into the works', people often mention the problem in which the problem is caused.

The US delegation threw a giant monkey

wrench into the process this week by raising all sorts of petty objections.

The federal government has thrown a wrench in the multi-billion dollar Japanese buyout of an American company.

wringer

go through the wringer
be put through the wringer ◄

If you **go through the wringer** or **are put through the wringer**, you go through a very

difficult period or situation which upsets you greatly and makes you ill or unhappy.

Her laugh is that of a woman who went through the wringer attempting to please the man in charge.

I felt as though I'd been through a wringer. My life seemed a wreck.

With so much money around, there are bound to be plenty of unscrupulous people trying to get a slice. Think back to 1987 when Elton John was being put through a similar wringer by the tabloids.

YZ

yards

the whole nine yards ◄

If someone goes **the whole nine yards,** they do something to the fullest extent possible. People sometimes use this expression ironically to suggest that someone is being too extreme in their behaviour or actions. This expression is used in American English.

She's been the whole nine yards with the disease, has come through it, and has now taken up sailing.

There was a big protest to Chile, human rights complaints, the whole nine yards.

yesterday

not born yesterday ◄

You can use expressions such as **'I wasn't born yesterday'** to indicate that you are not as naive or as easily deceived as people seem to think.

He was rewarded with a disbelieving smirk. 'Now you really do sound like my father. I wasn't born yesterday, you know.'

'You mean you were only this far away and you couldn't smell the blood?' she challenged.

'Does anyone on this jury look like they were born yesterday?'

yonder

into the wide blue yonder
into the wild blue yonder

If someone goes **into the wide blue yonder**

or **into the wild blue yonder**, they go on a journey to a faraway place which is unfamiliar or mysterious. This is a literary expression.

Sailing into the wide blue yonder, Colin discovers his very own Treasure Island.

The boys, filled again with a sense of optimism and adventure, pack their bags and head for Heathrow and the wild blue yonder – to Nashville, Tennessee.

She made a graceless gesture in the general direction of Daly City. 'He is off in the wild blue yonder.'

zero-sum

a zero-sum game ◄

If you refer to a situation as **a zero-sum game,** you mean that if one person gains an advantage from it, someone else involved must suffer an equivalent disadvantage. Other nouns are sometimes used instead of 'game'. This expression is used mainly in journalism.

The idea that foreign investment is a zero-sum game – that one country's gain is another's loss – is mistaken.

In New York people pursue money, which is not a zero-sum game. No one has to lose money for you to make money.

According to Reed, employee benefits are a zero-sum gain. If costs for one benefit rise, it's often at the expense of another, such as paid vacation and health insurance.

How to use the index

This index includes every lexical word in every idiom in the dictionary, together with every major variation. That is, it includes entries for every word except grammatical words such as 'the', prepositions, or the very common verbs 'be' and 'have'. For example, if you are looking for *spill the beans* in the index, you can look it up under either 'spill' or 'beans', but not under 'the'. Note that because 'beans' in the idiom is always plural, you will find this idiom in the index under 'beans' rather than 'bean'. Hyphenated words are listed separately in the index, and so you will find separate entries for 'apple' and 'apple-pie'.

In the index, you will see that one of the words in each idiom is highlighted. This is the dictionary headword in the text where you will find the idiom. If the idiom is dealt with under a headword which is not one of the words in the idiom, there will be a cross-reference to the right headword.

right-hand — This is an index headword.
   your **right**-hand man
   your **right**-hand woman

rights — These are the idioms in the dictionary which contain 'rights'.
   bang to **rights**
   dead to **rights**

Riley
   live the **life** of Riley

ring — These are the dictionary headwords where you will find these idioms.
   alarm **bells** ring
   the **brass** ring
   have a **hollow** ring
   ring a **bell**
   ring **hollow**
   ring off the **hook**
   ring someone's **bell**
   ring the **changes**
   ring **true**
   a **three-ring** circus
   throw your cap into the ring: see **hat** — This is an index cross-reference. You will find the entry for the idiom under the dictionary headword 'hat'.
   throw your **hat** into the ring
   warning **bells** ring

ringer
   a dead **ringer** for someone

rings
   run **rings** round someone

ringside
   a **ringside** seat
   a **ringside** view

INDEX

have your **head** up your arse
lick someone's **arse**
not know your arse from your
  elbow
a **pain** in the arse
talk out of your arse
art
  have something down to a fine
    art
ashes
  rake over the ashes: see **coals**
ask
  ask for the **moon**
  a big **ask**
ass
  blow **smoke** up someone's ass
  chew your **ass**
  cover your ass
  get your ass in **gear**
  have your **head** up your ass
  kick ass
  kiss ass
  kiss someone's ass
  not know your ass from your
    elbow
  a **pain** in the ass
  put your ass on the **line**
  save someone's ass
  your ass in a **sling**
ate
  like the **cat** that ate the canary
atmosphere
  you could cut the atmosphere
    with a **knife**
attached
  with no **strings** attached
  with **strings** attached
automatic
  on automatic **pilot**
autopilot
  on autopilot: see **pilot**
avoid
  avoid something like the **plague**
awakening
  a rude **awakening**
ax: see **axe**
axe
  an **axe** hanging over something
  be given the **axe**
  get the **axe**
  have an **axe** to grind
babe
  a **babe** in arms
babes
  babes in the wood
baby
  leave someone holding the **baby**
  like taking **candy** from a baby
  throw the **baby** out with the bath
    water
back
  a back **number**
  back the wrong **horse**
  be glad to see the **back** of
    someone
  behind your **back**
  break the **back** of something
  break your **back**
  bring someone back to **earth**
  by the back **door**

cover your back
fed up to the back **teeth**
get off someone's **back**
get someone's **back** up
get the **monkey** off your back
get your own **back**
go behind someone's **back**
have a **monkey** on your back
have **eyes** in the back of your
  head
have your **back** to the wall
know something like the back of
  your **hand**
the last **straw** that breaks the
  camel's back
like **water** off a duck's back
make a **rod** for your own back
off the **back** of a lorry
on someone's **back**
on the back **burner**
on the **back** of an envelope
on the **back** of a postage stamp
a **pat** on the back
pat someone on the back
put someone's **back** up
put your **back** into something
sick to the back **teeth**
a **stab** in the back
stab someone in the **back**
the **straw** that breaks the camel's
  back
take a back **seat**
through the back **door**
turn your **back** on someone
turn your **back** on something
when your **back** is turned
with one **hand** tied behind your
  back
with your hands tied behind your
  back: see **hand**
you scratch my **back** and I'll
  scratch yours
backs
  live off the **backs** of someone
backside
  a boot up the backside: see **kick**
  a **kick** up the backside
backward
  bend over backward: see
    backwards
backwards
  bend over **backwards**
  know something **backwards**
  know something **backwards** and
    forwards
bacon
  bring **home** the bacon
  save someone's **bacon**
bad
  a bad **apple**
  a bad **apple** spoils the barrel
  bad **blood**
  a bad **press**
  come to a bad **end**
  in bad **odour**
  in someone's bad **books**
  leave a bad **taste** in your
    mouth
  throw good **money** after bad
  turn up like a bad **penny**

bag
  a bag of **nerves**
  a bag of **worms**
  be someone's **bag**
  can't fight your way out of a
    paper bag
  in the **bag**
  leave someone holding the **bag**
  let the **cat** out of the bag
  a mixed **bag**
  someone's **bag** of tricks
bags
  pack your **bags**
bait
  fish or cut **bait**
  rise to the **bait**
  take the **bait**
baited
  with baited **breath**
baker
  a **baker**'s dozen
balance
  in the **balance**
  throw off **balance**
  tip the balance
balancing
  a balancing **act**
ball
  a **ball** and chain
  the **ball** is in your court
  a crystal **ball**
  a different **ball** game
  drop the **ball**
  have a **ball**
  keep your **eye** on the ball
  a new **ball** game
  on the **ball**
  pick up the **ball** and run
  play **ball**
  set the **ball** rolling
  start the **ball** rolling
  take the **ball** and run with it
  take your **eye** off the ball
  throw someone a **curve** ball
  the whole **ball** of wax
ballistic
  go **ballistic**
balloon
  the **balloon** goes up
  go down like a **lead** balloon
  a **trial** balloon
ballpark
  a **ballpark** estimate
  a **ballpark** figure
  in the **ballpark**
  in the same **ballpark**
balls
  break someone's **balls**
  cold enough to freeze the balls off
    a **brass** monkey
  juggle **balls** in the air
  keep **balls** in the air
banana
  slip on a **banana** peel
  slip on a **banana** skin
band
  a one-man **band**
  a one-woman **band**
bandwagon
  jump on the **bandwagon**

bang
bang goes something
bang people's **heads** together
bang the **drum**
bang to **rights**
bang your head against a brick **wall**
bang your head against a **wall**
a bigger **bang** for the buck
more **bang** for the buck
not with a **bang** but a whimper

bangs
more bangs for your bucks: see **bang**

bank
break the **bank**
cry all the way to the **bank**
laugh all the way to the **bank**

baptism
a **baptism** of fire

bare
the bare **bones**
bare your **soul**
with your bare **hands**

barge
wouldn't touch something with a barge **pole**

bark
bark up the wrong **tree**
your **bark** is worse than your bite

barn
close the barn **door** after the horse has gone

barred
no-**holds**-barred

barrel
a bad **apple** spoils the barrel
have someone over a **barrel**
like shooting **fish** in a barrel
lock, stock, and barrel
on the barrel: see **barrelhead**
scrape the **barrel**
scrape the bottom of the **barrel**

barrelhead
on the **barrelhead**

barrels
give someone both **barrels**
with both **barrels**

base
get to first **base**
get to second **base**
off **base**
touch **base**

bases
cover all the **bases**
touch all the **bases**

basket
a **basket** case
put all your **eggs** in one basket

bat
bat on a sticky **wicket**
blind as a bat
go in to **bat** for someone
go to **bat** for someone
like a **bat** out of hell
not bat an **eye**
not bat an eyelash: see **eyelid**
not bat an **eyelid**
off your own **bat**

play a straight **bat**
right off the **bat**

bated
with bated **breath**

bath
an early **bath**
take a **bath**
throw the **baby** out with the bath water

baton
hand the **baton**
pass the **baton**
pick up the **baton**

bats
have **bats** in your belfry

batten
batten down the **hatches**

batteries
recharge your **batteries**

battle
the **battle** lines are drawn
a battle of **nerves**
a **battle** of wills
a **battle** of wits
fight a losing **battle**
join **battle**
lose the **battle**, win the war
a running **battle**
win the **battle**, lose the war

bay
bay at the **moon**
bay for **blood**
hold something at **bay**
keep something at **bay**

beach
not the only **pebble** on the beach

bead
draw a **bead** on
take a **bead** on

be-all
not the **be-all** and end-all

beam
be way off **beam**

bean
a **bean** counter
not have a **bean**

beans
count the beans: see **bean**
full of **beans**
know how many **beans** make five
not amount to a hill of **beans**
not worth a row of **beans**
spill the **beans**

bear
bear **fruit**
bear something in **mind**
bear the **brunt** of something
a **cross** to bear
grin and bear it
like a **bear** with a sore head
loaded for **bear**

bearer
the **standard** bearer

beast
the **nature** of the beast
no good to man or **beast**
no use to man or **beast**

beat
beat a dead **horse**
beat a path to someone's **door**

beat someone at their own **game**
beat someone **hands** down
beat someone **hollow**
beat someone to a **pulp**
beat something **hands** down
beat **swords** into ploughshares
beat the **bushes**
beat the **drum**
beat the living **daylights** out of someone
beat the **pants** off someone
beat your breast
beat your chest
march to the beat of a different drummer
miss a **beat**
not beat around the **bush**
a **stick** to beat someone with

beaten
off the beaten path: see **track**
off the beaten **track**

beaver
an eager **beaver**

beck
at someone's **beck** and call

bed
be in **bed** with someone
get into **bed** with someone
get out of **bed** on the wrong side
get out of **bed** the wrong side
not a bed of **roses**
put something to **bed**
you have made your **bed** and will have to lie on it

bedbug
crazy as a bedbug

bee
the **bee**'s knees
busy as a bee
a **busy** bee
have a **bee** in your bonnet

beeline
make a **beeline** for something

beer
not all **beer** and skittles
small **beer**

bees
the **birds** and the bees

beet
red as a beet

beetroot
red as a beetroot

beg
beg the **question**

beggars
beggars can't be choosers

begging
go **begging**

begin
charity begins at home

belfry
have **bats** in your belfry

bell
clear as a bell
ring a **bell**
ring someone's **bell**
saved by the **bell**
sound as a bell

bells
alarm **bells** ring

bells and whistles
pull the other one, it's got bells on it
warning **bells** ring
belly
  fire in your belly
bellyful
  have a **bellyful**
belly-up
  go **belly-up**
belt
  below the **belt**
  belt and braces
  tighten your **belt**
  under your **belt**
bend
  bend over backward: see **backwards**
  bend over **backwards**
  bend someone's **ear**
  bend the **rules**
  round the **bend**
bended
  on bended knee: see **knees**
benefit
  give someone the **benefit** of the doubt
berry
  brown as a berry
berth
  give someone a wide **berth**
best
  the best of both **worlds**
  the best thing since sliced **bread**
  give something your best **shot**
  put your best **foot** forward
  your best **bib** and tucker
bet
  bet the **ranch**
  bet your bottom **dollar**
  a good **bet**
  a safe **bet**
bets
  all **bets** are off
  hedge your **bets**
better
  better the **devil** you know
  better the **devil** you know than the devil you don't
  half a **loaf** is better than none
  have seen better **days**
  your better **half**
bib
  your best **bib** and tucker
big
  a big **ask**
  big as life: see **large**
  a big **cheese**
  a big **fish**
  a big **fish** in a small pond
  a big **frog** in a small pond: see **fish**
  a big **girl**'s blouse
  a big **gun**: see **guns**
  the big **guns**
  a big **hand** for someone
  big **time**
  the big **time**
  a big **wheel**
  carry a big **stick**

get too **big** for your boots
get too **big** for your britches
give someone a big **hand**
hit the big **time**
make a big **play** of something
wield a big **stick**
bigger
  a bigger **bang** for the buck
  bigger than life: see **larger**
  have bigger **fish** to fry
bike
  on your **bike**
bill
  bill and coo
  a clean **bill** of health
  fill the **bill**
  fit the **bill**
  foot the **bill**
  sell someone a **bill** of goods
bind
  a double **bind**
bird
  the **bird** has flown
  a **bird** in the hand
  a **bird** in the hand is worth two in the bush
  a **bird** of passage
  an early **bird**
  the early **bird** catches the worm
  eat like a **bird**
  free as a bird
  get the **bird**
  give someone the **bird**
  a little **bird** told me
  a rare **bird**
birds
  the **birds** and the bees
  birds of a feather
  birds of a feather flock together
  for the **birds**
  kill two **birds** with one stone
bird's-eye
  a bird's-eye **view**
biscuit
  take the **biscuit**
bit
  the **biter** gets bit
  champ at the **bit**
  chomp at the **bit**
  get the **bit** between your teeth
  a **hair** of the dog that bit you
bite
  bite off more than you can chew
  bite someone's **head** off
  bite the **bullet**
  bite the **dust**
  bite the **hand** that feeds you
  bite your **tongue**
  a second **bite** at the cherry
  take a **bite** out of something
  your **bark** is worse than your bite
biter
  the **biter** gets bit
bites
  two bites of the cherry: see **bite**
bitten
  bitten by the **bug**
  once **bitten**

once **bitten**, twice shy
bitter
  a bitter **pill** to swallow
  swallow a bitter **pill**
  to the bitter **end**
black
  black and blue
  black and white
  a black **box**
  a black **look**
  a black **mark**
  the black **sheep**
  the black **sheep** of the family
  give someone a black **eye**
  in **black** and white
  in the **black**
  not as **black** as you are painted
  the **pot** calling the kettle black
blank
  a blank **cheque**
  draw a **blank**
blanket
  a **security** blanket
  a wet **blanket**
blaze
  blaze a **trail**
blazing
  with all **guns** blazing
bleed
  bleed red **ink**
  bleed someone dry
  bleed someone white
  your **heart** bleeds for someone
bleeding
  a bleeding **heart**
blessing
  a **blessing** in disguise
blind
  a blind **alley**
  blind as a bat
  the **blind** leading the blind
  blind someone with **science**
  a blind **spot**
  fly **blind**
  swear **blind**
  turn a blind **eye** to something
blink
  on the **blink**
block
  a **chip** off the old block
  on the **block**
  put your head on the **block**
  put your neck on the **block**
  a stumbling **block**
blocks
  off the **blocks**
  off the starting **blocks**
  out of the **blocks**
blood
  after your **blood**
  bad **blood**
  bay for **blood**
  blood and thunder
  blood is shed
  blood is spilled
  blood is thicker than water
  blood, sweat, and tears
  flesh and **blood**
  fresh **blood**
  have **blood** on your hands

in cold **blood**
in your **blood**
like getting **blood** out of a stone
like getting **blood** out of a turnip
make your **blood** boil
make your **blood** freeze
make your **blood** run cold
new **blood**
out for **blood**
a **rush** of blood
a **rush** of blood to the head
scent **blood**
someone's **blood** boils
sweat **blood**
taste **blood**
young **blood**
bloodied
bloodied but **unbowed**
bloody
bloody someone's **nose**
get a bloody **nose**
give someone a bloody **nose**
have bloody hands: see **blood**
scream bloody **murder**
blot
a **blot** on the landscape
a **blot** on your escutcheon
blot your **copybook**
blouse
a big **girl**'s blouse
blow
blow a **fuse**
blow a **hole** in something
blow away the **cobwebs**
blow **hot** and cold
blow in the **wind**
blow off **steam**
blow **smoke**
blow **smoke** in someone's eyes
blow **smoke** in someone's face
blow **smoke** up someone's ass
blow someone to **kingdom** come
blow something out of the **water**
blow something **sky**-high
blow something **wide** open
blow the **gaff**
blow the **lid** off
blow the **whistle** on someone
blow up in your **face**
blow your **mind**
blow your own **horn**
blow your own **trumpet**
blow your **stack**
blow your **top**
a **body** blow
cushion the **blow**
a **death** blow
soften the **blow**
strike a **blow** against something
strike a **blow** for something
blowing
how the **wind** is blowing
which way the **wind** is blowing
blows
come to **blows**
it's an ill **wind** that blows nobody
  any good
blue
between the **devil** and the deep
  blue sea

black and blue
a **bolt** from the blue
into the wide blue **yonder**
into the wild blue **yonder**
light the blue **touch paper**
once in a blue **moon**
out of a clear blue **sky**
out of the **blue**
scream blue **murder**
talk a blue **streak**
until you are blue in the **face**
blue-arsed
like a blue-arsed **fly**
blue-eyed
your blue-eyed **boy**
bluff
call someone's **bluff**
blushes
save someone's **blushes**
spare someone's **blushes**
board
above **board**
across the **board**
back to the drawing **board**
go by the **board**
stiff as a board
sweep the **board**
take something on **board**
boards
go by the boards: see **board**
boat
float someone's **boat**
in the same **boat**
miss the boat
push the **boat** out
rock the **boat**
boats
burn your boats
Bob
Bob's your uncle
body
body and soul
a **body** blow
hold **body** and soul together
keep **body** and soul together
over my dead **body**
boggle
the **mind** boggles
boil
bring something to a **boil**
come to the **boil**
make your **blood** boil
off the **boil**
on the **boil**
someone's **blood** boils
a watched **pot** never boils
boiling
boiling **point**
keep the **pot** boiling
bold
bold as brass
bolt
a **bolt** from the blue
a **bolt** out of the blue
shoot your **bolt**
bolted
close the stable **door** after the
  horse has bolted
bolts
the **nuts** and bolts of something

bomb
go like a **bomb**
put a **bomb** under something
bombshell
drop a **bombshell**
bone
a **bone** of contention
close to the **bone**
cut to the **bone**
dry as a bone
have a **bone** to pick with
  someone
near to the **bone**
skin and bone
work your **fingers** to the bone
bones
the bare **bones**
feel something in your **bones**
have a feeling in your **bones**
make no **bones** about something
put **flesh** on the bones of
  something
skin and bones
bonnet
have a **bee** in your bonnet
boo
wouldn't say boo to a **goose**
book
bring someone to **book**
by the **book**
a closed **book**
close the **book** on something
every **trick** in the book
go by the **book**
in your **book**
the oldest **trick** in the book
an open **book**
play things by the **book**
read someone like a **book**
take a **leaf** out of someone's
  book
throw the **book** at someone
you can't judge a **book** by its
  cover
books
cook the **books**
in someone's bad **books**
in someone's good **books**
a **turn-up** for the books
boot
the boot is on the other **foot**
a boot up the backside: see **kick**
get the **boot**
give someone the **boot**
put the **boot** in
put the **boot** into someone
boots
die with your **boots** on
fill someone's **boots**
fill your **boots**
get too **big** for your boots
hang up your boots
in someone's boots: see **shoes**
lick someone's **boots**
quake in your **boots**
step into someone's **boots**
tough as old boots
bootstraps
pull yourself up by your
  bootstraps

to your **bootstraps**
bore
  bore the **pants** off someone
born
  born with a **silver** spoon in your
    mouth
  not born **yesterday**
borrowed
  be on borrowed **time**
  live on borrowed **time**
bothered
  hot and bothered
bottle
  the **genie** is out of the bottle
  hit the **bottle**
  let the **genie** out of the bottle
  put the **genie** back in the bottle
bottom
  at **rock** bottom
  at the bottom of your **heart**
  be at the **bottom** of something
  bet your bottom **dollar**
  the **bottom** drops out of
    something
  the **bottom** falls out of something
  the bottom **line**
  the bottom of the **heap**
  the bottom of the **pile**
  bump along the **bottom**
  from the bottom of your **heart**
  from **top** to bottom
  get to the **bottom** of something
  hit **rock** bottom
  lie at the **bottom** of something
  reach **rock** bottom
  scrape the bottom of the **barrel**
bound
  bound **hand** and foot
bounds
  by **leaps** and bounds
  in **leaps** and bounds
  out of **bounds**
bow
  another **string** to your bow
  bow and scrape
  many strings to your bow: see
    string
  take a **bow**
bowl
  life is a bowl of cherries
bows
  a **shot** across someone's bows
  a warning **shot** across someone's
    bows
box
  a black **box**
  box **clever**
  box someone into a **corner**
  out of the **box**
  out of your **box**
  a **Pandora**'s box
boy
  a whipping **boy**
  your blue-eyed **boy**
  your fair-haired **boy**
boys
  boys will be boys
  jobs for the boys
  one of the **boys**
  separate the **men** from the boys

sort out the **men** from the boys
braces
  belt and braces
brain
  a brain like a **sieve**
  get your brain into **gear**
  have your brain in **gear**
  pick someone's brain: see **brains**
  rack your brain: see **brains**
brains
  pick someone's **brains**
  rack your **brains**
branch
  an **olive** branch
  root and branch
brass
  bold as brass
  a **brass** farthing
  the **brass** ring
  cold enough to freeze the balls off
    a **brass** monkey
  get down to **brass** tacks
brave
  put a brave **face** on something
  put a brave front on something:
    see **face**
bread
  the best thing since sliced **bread**
  bread and butter
  bread and circuses
  cast your **bread** upon the waters
  the greatest thing since sliced
    bread
  know which side your **bread** is
    buttered
breadline
  on the **breadline**
breadth
  a **hair**'s breadth
break
  all **hell** breaks loose
  all **hell** breaks out
  break a **butterfly** on a wheel
  break a **leg**
  break a new **path**
  break **ground**
  break new **ground**
  break rank: see **ranks**
  break **ranks**
  break someone's **balls**
  break the **back** of something
  break the **bank**
  break the **ice**
  break the **mould**
  break your **back**
  break your **heart**
  get an even **break**
  give a sucker an even **break**
  give me a **break**
  give someone an even **break**
  the last **straw** that breaks the
    camel's back
  the **straw** that breaks the camel's
    back
breakfast
  a **dog**'s breakfast
breaking
  path-breaking
  you can't make an **omelette**
    without breaking eggs

breast
  beat your breast
  make a clean **breast** of something
breath
  a **breath** of fresh air
  hold your **breath**
  in the same **breath**
  take your **breath** away
  waste your **breath**
  with bated **breath**
breathe
  breathe down someone's **neck**
  breathe **fire**
  live and breathe something
breed
  familiarity breeds contempt
  familiarity breeds content
breeze
  shoot the **breeze**
brewery
  couldn't organize a piss-up in a
    brewery
brick
  bang your head against a brick
    wall
  built like a **brick** shithouse
  come up against a brick **wall**
  drop a **brick**
  drop something like a hot brick:
    see **potato**
  shit a **brick**
bricks
  a **cat** on hot bricks
  come down on someone like a **ton**
    of bricks
  like a **ton** of bricks
  make **bricks** without straw
bridge
  cross that **bridge** when you come
    to it
  water under the bridge
bridges
  build **bridges**
  burn your bridges
brief
  hold no **brief** for something
bright
  bright as a button
  a bright **spark**
  look on the bright **side**
bright-eyed
  bright-eyed and bushy-tailed
bring
  bring a **lump** to your throat
  bring **home** the bacon
  bring someone back to **earth**
  bring someone down a **peg** or two
  bring someone **face** to face with
    something
  bring someone in from the **cold**
  bring someone to **book**
  bring someone to **heel**
  bring someone to their **knees**
  bring someone up to **speed**
  bring something **home** to
    someone
  bring something out of the **closet**
  bring something to a **boil**
  bring something to a **head**
  bring something to its **knees**

bring something to the **party**
bring something up to **speed**
bring the **curtain** down on something
bring the **house** down
britches
get too **big** for your britches
broad
broad brush **strokes**
a broad **church**
broad **strokes**
in broad **daylight**
broke
go for **broke**
if it ain't **broke**, don't fix it
they broke the **mould** when they made someone
broken
a broken **heart**
a broken **reed**
broom
a new **broom**
a new **broom** sweeps clean
broth
too many **cooks** spoil the broth
brother
not your brother's **keeper**
brow
by the **sweat** of your brow
brown
brown as a berry
brownie
brownie points
brunt
bear the **brunt** of something
brush
broad brush **strokes**
daft as a brush
tar someone with the same **brush**
bubble
the **bubble** has burst
on the **bubble**
prick the **bubble**
buck
the **buck** stops here
the **buck** stops with someone
more **bang** for the buck
pass the **buck**
bucket
a **drop** in the bucket
kick the **bucket**
bucks
more bangs for your bucks: see **bang**
bud
nip something in the **bud**
buffers
hit the **buffers**
bug
bitten by the **bug**
snug as a bug in a rug
build
build **bridges**
build something on **sand**
built
built like a **brick** shithouse
built like a **tank**
Rome was not built in a day
bull
a **bull** in a china shop

a **cock** and bull story
a **cock** and bull tale
a red flag before a **bull**
a red rag to a **bull**
strong as a bull
take the **bull** by the horns
bullet
bite the **bullet**
get the **bullet**
give someone the **bullet**
bum
a **bum** steer
get the **bum**'s rush
give someone the **bum**'s rush
bump
bump along the **bottom**
come down to **earth** with a bump
bumpy
a bumpy **ride**
bums
bums on seats
bundle
a bundle of **nerves**
drop your **bundle**
burn
burn a **hole** in your pocket
burn the **candle** at both ends
burn the **midnight** oil
burn your boats
burn your bridges
burn your **fingers**
crash and burn
fiddle while **Rome** burns
have **money** to burn
burned
burned to a **crisp**
get your **fingers** burned
burner
on the back **burner**
on the front **burner**
burning
someone's **ears** are burning
burst
the **bubble** has burst
burst at the **seams**
bury
bury the **hatchet**
bury your **head** in the sand
bus
miss the bus
bush
a **bird** in the hand is worth two in the bush
the **bush** telegraph
not beat about the **bush**
not beat around the **bush**
bushel
hide your light under a **bushel**
bushes
beat the **bushes**
bushy-tailed
bright-eyed and bushy-tailed
business
business as usual
do a **land-office** business
in **business**
like nobody's **business**
mean **business**
monkey business

busman
a **busman**'s holiday
bust
bust a **gut**
busy
busy as a bee
a **busy** bee
butt
kick **butt**
a **kick** in the butt
save someone's butt
butter
bread and butter
butter wouldn't melt in your mouth
like a hot **knife** through butter
like a **knife** through butter
buttered
know which side your **bread** is buttered
butterflies
butterflies in your stomach
get **butterflies**
have **butterflies**
butterfly
break a **butterfly** on a wheel
button
at the touch of a **button**
bright as a button
button it: see **lip**
button your **lip**
have your **finger** on the button
a hot **button**
on the **button**
press the right **button**
push the right **button**
right on the **button**
buy
buy the **farm**
caboodle
the whole **caboodle**
the whole kit and **caboodle**
cackle
cut the **cackle**
cage
rattle someone's **cage**
Cain
raise **Cain**
cake
the frosting on the cake: see **icing**
have your **cake** and eat it
the **icing** on the cake
a **piece** of cake
take the **cake**
cakes
cakes and ale
go like **hot** cakes
sell like **hot cakes**
calf
kill the fatted **calf**
call
at someone's **beck** and call
call a **spade** a spade
call in your **chips**
call it a **day**
call it a night: see **day**
call it **quits**
call off the **dogs**
call someone **names**
call someone on the **carpet**

call someone's **bluff**
call someone to **heel**
call the **shots**
call the **tune**
a close **call**
he who pays the **piper** calls the
  tune
too **close** to call
a **wake-up** call
calling
  a calling **card**
  the **pot** calling the kettle black
calm
  the calm before the **storm**
camel
  the last **straw** that breaks the
    camel's back
  strain at a **gnat** and swallow a
    camel
  the **straw** that breaks the camel's
    back
camp
  a **camp** follower
  a **foot** in each camp
  pitch **camp**
camps
  a **foot** in both camps
can
  a can of **worms**
  carry the **can**
  in the **can**
canary
  like the **cat** that ate the canary
candle
  burn the **candle** at both ends
  can't hold a **candle** to someone
  the game is not worth the **candle**
  not worth the **candle**
candy
  like a kid in a **candy** store
  like taking **candy** from a baby
cannon
  cannon fodder
  a loose **cannon**
canoe
  paddle your own **canoe**
cap
  cap in hand
  a **feather** in your cap
  get your thinking **cap** on
  if the **cap** fits
  put your thinking **cap** on
  set your **cap** at someone
  throw your cap into the ring: see
    hat
capital
  Art with a **capital** A
  Life with a **capital** L
carbon
  a **carbon** copy
card
  a calling **card**
  have a card up your **sleeve**
  a **hole** card
  a **trump** card
  a **wild** card
cards
  a **house** of cards
  in the **cards**
  keep your cards close to the **vest**

keep your cards close to your
  chest
lay your **cards** on the table
on the **cards**
play your cards close to the **vest**
play your cards close to your
  chest
play your **cards** right
put your **cards** on the table
several cards **short** of a full deck
stack the cards
carpet
  call someone on the **carpet**
  on the **carpet**
  roll out the red **carpet**
  sweep something under the
    carpet
carrot
  carrot and stick
  dangle a **carrot** in front of
    someone
  offer someone a **carrot**
carry
  carry a big **stick**
  carry all before you
  carry a **torch** for someone
  carry the **can**
  carry the **day**
  carry the **torch**
  carry the **weight** of the world on
    your shoulders
  carry **weight**
cart
  put the **cart** before the horse
cartload
  a cartload of **monkeys**
carve
  carve a **niche**
case
  a **basket** case
  be on someone's **case**
  get off someone's **case**
  get on someone's **case**
  on the **case**
cash
  a **cash** cow
  cash in your **chips**
cast
  cast an **eye** on something
  cast a wide **net**
  cast **iron**
  cast **pearls** before swine
  cast the **net** wider
  cast your **bread** upon the waters
  cast your **eye** on something
  cast your **eye** over something
  cast your **eyes** on something: see
    eye
  cast your **lot** with someone
  the **die** is cast
cast-iron
  cast-**iron**
castle
  an **Englishman**'s home is his
    castle
castles
  castles in Spain
  castles in the air
cat
  cat and mouse

a **cat** on a hot tin roof
a **cat** on hot bricks
the **cat**'s whiskers
curiosity killed the cat
a fat **cat**
fight like **cat** and dog
a game of **cat** and mouse
grin like a Cheshire **cat**
let the **cat** out of the bag
like a scalded **cat**
like the **cat** that ate the canary
like the **cat** that got the cream
look like something the **cat**
  dragged in
look what the **cat**'s dragged in
no room to swing a **cat**
not a cat in hell's **chance**
put the **cat** among the pigeons
see which way the **cat** jumps
set the **cat** among the pigeons
there's more than one way to
  skin a **cat**
when the **cat**'s away, the mice
  will play
catbird
  in the **catbird** seat
catch
  a **Catch** 22
  catch **fire**
  catch someone **cold**
  catch someone **flat-footed**
  catch someone in the **act**
  catch someone **napping**
  catch someone off **guard**
  catch someone on the **hop**
  catch someone **red-handed**
  catch someone's **eye**
  catch someone with their **pants**
    down
  catch someone with their trousers
    down: see **pants**
  catch the **eye**
  catch the **wave**
  catch **wind** of something
  the early **bird** catches the worm
  a **sprat** to catch a mackerel
  when one person sneezes, another
    catches **cold**
cats
  fight like **Kilkenny** cats
  it's raining **cats** and dogs
cattle
  a cattle **market**
caught
  caught between two **stools**
  caught in the **crossfire**
  caught on the wrong **foot**
  caught with your hand in the
    cookie jar
  like a deer caught in the
    headlights
  like a rabbit caught in the
    headlights
  wouldn't be caught **dead**
caution
  throw **caution** to the wind
ceiling
  the **glass** ceiling
  go through the ceiling: see **roof**
  hit the ceiling: see **roof**

cent
  not a red cent
  not have a cent to your **name**
  not one red cent
center: see **centre**
centre
  centre stage
  left, right, and centre
cents
  your two **cents'** worth
chaff
  separate the grain from the **chaff**
  separate the wheat from the **chaff**
  sort the wheat from the **chaff**
chain
  a **ball** and chain
  pull someone's **chain**
  a weak **link** in the chain
  yank someone's **chain**
chair
  on the **edge** of your chair
chalice
  a poisoned **chalice**
chalk
  by a long **chalk**
  chalk and cheese
champ
  champ at the **bit**
chance
  a chance in a **million**
  chance your **arm**
  drinking in the last chance
    saloon
  an eye for the main **chance**
  the last chance **saloon**
  the main **chance**
  not a cat in hell's **chance**
  not a snowball's **chance** in hell
  not have a **chance** in hell
  a one in a **million** chance
  on the **off-chance**
change
  change **hands**
  change horses in **midstream**
  a **change** of heart
  a change of **tune**
  change your **tune**
  chop and change
  get no **change** out of someone
  a **leopard** does not change its
    spots
  a **sea** change
changes
  ring the **changes**
chapter
  chapter and verse
  a **chapter** of accidents
charity
  charity begins at home
charm
  charm the **pants** off someone
Charybdis
  between **Scylla** and Charybdis
chase
  chase **rainbows**
  chase your own **tail**
  cut to the **chase**
  lead you a merry chase: see
    dance
  a wild **goose** chase

check
  a blank check: see **cheque**
  take a **rain** check
cheek
  cheek by jowl
  tongue in cheek
  turn the other **cheek**
  with **tongue** in cheek
cheer
  cheer someone to the **echo**
cheese
  a big **cheese**
  chalk and cheese
  more holes than **Swiss cheese**
cheque
  a blank **cheque**
cherries
  life is a bowl of cherries
cherry
  a second **bite** at the cherry
  two bites of the cherry: see **bite**
Cheshire
  grin like a Cheshire **cat**
chest
  beat your **chest**
  get something off your **chest**
  keep your cards close to your
    chest
  play your cards close to your
    chest
  put hair on the chest: see **hairs**
  put **hairs** on your chest
chestnut
  a hoary old **chestnut**
  an old **chestnut**
chestnuts
  pull someone's **chestnuts** out of
    the fire
chew
  bite off more than you can chew
  chew the **fat**
  chew your **ass**
chicken
  chicken and egg
  chicken feed
  like a **chicken** with its head cut
    off
  like a headless **chicken**
  no **spring** chicken
chickens
  the chickens come home to **roost**
  don't count your **chickens** before
    they're hatched
  not count your **chickens**
chiefs
  too many **chiefs**
  too many **chiefs** and not enough
    Indians
child
  child's play
  like a child in a sweet shop: see
    candy
chilled
  chilled to the **marrow**
chin
  keep your **chin** up
  lead with your **chin**
  take it on the **chin**
china
  a **bull** in a china shop

  not for all the **tea** in China
chink
  a **chink** in someone's armour
chip
  a **chip** off the old block
  a **chip** on your shoulder
chips
  call in your **chips**
  cash in your **chips**
  the **chips** are down
  have had your **chips**
  when the **chips** are down
choice
  Hobson's choice
chomp
  chomp at the **bit**
choosers
  beggars can't be choosers
chop
  chop and change
  for the **chop**
  get the **chop**
chops
  lick your chops: see **lips**
chord
  strike a **chord**
  touch a **chord**
Christmas
  like **turkeys** voting for Christ-
    mas
church
  a broad **church**
  poor as a church mouse
cigar
  close but no **cigar**
  nice try but no **cigar**
circle
  circle the **wagons**
  come full **circle**
  pull your **wagons** in a circle
  square the **circle**
  turn full **circle**
  a vicious **circle**
  the wheel has come full **circle**
circles
  go around in **circles**
  go round in **circles**
  run around in **circles**
  run round in **circles**
circus
  a three-ring **circus**
circuses
  bread and circuses
clam
  happy as a clam
  shut up like a **clam**
clanger
  drop a **clanger**
Clapham
  the man on the Clapham
    omnibus
clappers
  like the **clappers**
class
  a class **act**
claw
  fight **tooth** and claw
  red in **tooth** and claw
claws
  get your **claws** into someone

clay
clay **feet**
have **feet** of clay
clean
clean as a whistle
a clean **bill** of health
a clean **sheet**
a clean **sheet** of paper
a clean **slate**
clean up your **act**
come **clean**
keep your **nose** clean
make a clean **breast** of something
make a clean **sweep**
a new **broom** sweeps clean
show a clean pair of **heels**
squeaky **clean**
wipe the **slate** clean
cleaners
take someone to the **cleaners**
clear
clear as a bell
clear as crystal
clear as day
clear as mud
clear **sailing**
clear the **air**
clear the deck: see **decks**
clear the **decks**
the **coast** is clear
the **dust** clears
in the **clear**
loud and clear
out of a clear blue **sky**
steer **clear**
steer someone **clear** of something
cleft
in a cleft **stick**
clever
box **clever**
climb
climb the **walls**
a **mountain** to climb
clip
clip someone's **wings**
cloak-and-dagger
cloak-and-dagger
clock
around the **clock**
round the **clock**
turn the **clock** back
clockwork
like **clockwork**
regular as **clockwork**
clogs
pop your **clogs**
close
as one **door** closes, another one opens
close but no **cigar**
a close **call**
close on the **heels** of something
close on your **heels**
close ranks
a close **shave**
close the barn door after the horse has gone
close the **book** on something
close the stable **door** after the horse has bolted

close to **home**
close to the **bone**
close to your **heart**
close up **shop**
cut it close: see **fine**
keep your cards close to the **vest**
keep your cards close to your **chest**
play your cards close to the **vest**
play your cards close to your **chest**
sail close to the **wind**
too **close** to call
closed
behind closed **doors**
a closed **book**
with your **eyes** closed
closet
bring something out of the **closet**
come out of the **closet**
a **skeleton** in the closet
cloth
cloth ears
cut from the same **cloth**
cut your **cloth**
cut your coat according to your **cloth**
whole **cloth**
clothes
steal someone's **clothes**
clothing
a sheep in **wolf**'s clothing
a **wolf** in sheep's clothing
cloud
every cloud has a **silver** lining
on **cloud** nine
under a **cloud**
clouds
have your **head** in the clouds
clover
in **clover**
club
join the **club**
clutch
clutch at **straws**
a drowning man will clutch at a straw: see **straws**
coach
drive a **coach** and horses through something
coalface
at the **coalface**
coals
coals to Newcastle
haul someone over the **coals**
rake over the **coals**
rake someone over the **coals**
coast
the **coast** is clear
coat
cut your coat according to your **cloth**
sugar-coat the **pill**
trail your **coat**
coat-tails
on the **coat tails** of someone
cobbler
let the cobbler stick to his **last**
cobwebs
blow away the **cobwebs**

cock
a **cock** and bull story
a **cock** and bull tale
cock a **snook** at someone
go off at **half** cock
cocked
knock something into a cocked **hat**
cockles
warm the **cockles** of your heart
coffee
wake up and smell the **coffee**
coffin
another **nail** in the coffin
the final **nail** in the coffin
the last **nail** in the coffin
coin
opposite sides of the same **coin**
the other side of the **coin**
pay someone back in their own **coin**
to coin a **phrase**
two sides of the same **coin**
cold
blow **hot** and cold
bring someone in from the **cold**
catch someone **cold**
cold as ice
cold **comfort**
cold enough to freeze the balls off a **brass** monkey
a cold **fish**
come in from the **cold**
get **cold** feet
get the cold **shoulder**
give someone the cold **shoulder**
have cold **feet**
hot and cold
in a cold **sweat**
in cold **blood**
in cold **storage**
in the cold **light** of day
into cold **storage**
leave someone **cold**
make your **blood** run cold
out in the **cold**
pour cold **water** on something
throw cold **water** on something
when one person sneezes, another catches **cold**
collar
hot under the **collar**
collect
collect your **wits**
color: see **colour**
colors: see **colours**
colour
the **colour** of someone's money
colours
nail your **colours** to the mast
sail under false **colours**
see someone in their true **colours**
show your true **colours**
with flying **colours**
comb
with a fine tooth **comb**
with a fine-toothed **comb**
come
blow someone to **kingdom** come
the chickens come home to **roost**

come a **cropper**
come along for the **ride**
come apart at the **seams**
come back from the **dead**
come **clean**
come down in the **world**
come down off your high **horse**
come down on someone like a **ton** of bricks
come down the **pike**
come down to **earth**
come down to **earth** with a bump
come **face** to face with someone
come **face** to face with something
come full **circle**
come **hell** or high water
come home to **roost**
come in from the **cold**
come knocking at your **door**
come off the **fence**
come out fighting
come out in the **wash**
come out of the **closet**
come out of the **woodwork**
come out of your **shell**
come out swinging
come **rain** or shine
come the raw **prawn**
come to a bad **end**
come to a **head**
come to a sticky **end**
come to **blows**
come to **grips** with something
come to the **boil**
come under **fire**
come **unglued**
come **unstuck**
come up against a brick **wall**
come up in the **world**
come up smelling of **roses**
come up **trumps**
come within an **ace** of something
come within an **inch** of doing something
cross that **bridge** when you come to it
the **crunch** comes
the **curtain** comes down
easy come, easy go
if **push** comes to shove
Johnny-come-lately
not come up to **scratch**
until the **cows** come home
what goes around comes around: see **go**
the wheel has come full **circle**
when it comes to the **crunch**
when **push** comes to shove
when your **ship** comes in
the **wraps** come off
comfort
cold **comfort**
comforts
creature comforts
coming
everything is coming up **roses**
have something coming out of your **ears**
have steam coming out of your **ears**

not **know** whether you are coming or going
up and coming
commas
in inverted **commas**
common
common as muck
the common **touch**
find common **ground**
on common **ground**
common-or-garden
common-or-**garden**
concrete
set in **concrete**
conjure
a **name** to conjure with
conquer
divide and conquer
contemplate
contemplate your **navel**
contemplation
navel-contemplation
contempt
familiarity breeds contempt
content
familiarity breeds content
contention
a **bone** of contention
converted
preach to the **converted**
coo
bill and coo
cook
cook the **books**
cook your **goose**
cookie
caught with your hand in the **cookie** jar
a smart **cookie**
that's the way the **cookie** crumbles
a tough **cookie**
cooks
too many **cooks**
too many **cooks** in the kitchen
too many **cooks** spoil the broth
cool
cool as a cucumber
a cool **head**
cool your **heels**
keep your **cool**
lose your **cool**
coop
fly the **coop**
cop
cop it **sweet**
not much **cop**
copy
a **carbon** copy
copybook
blot your **copybook**
cord
cut the **cord**
cut the umbilical **cord**
strike a cord: see **chord**
touch a cord: see **chord**
core
to the **core**
corn
earn your **corn**

eat your **seed** corn
seed corn
corner
box someone into a **corner**
fight your **corner**
hole-and-corner
hole-in-the-corner
in a **corner**
in a tight **corner**
in your **corner**
just around the **corner**
out of a **corner**
paint someone into a **corner**
turn the **corner**
corners
cut **corners**
the four **corners** of the earth
the four **corners** of the world
cost
cost an **arm** and a leg
count the **cost**
couch
a **couch** potato
count
count something on the **fingers** of one hand
count something on your **fingers**
count the beans: see **bean**
count the **cost**
don't count your **chickens** before they're hatched
down for the **count**
not count your **chickens**
out for the **count**
counted
stand up and be counted
counter
a **bean** counter
under the **counter**
country
go to the **country**
not your **line** of country
courage
Dutch **courage**
course
on **course** for
par for the course
run its **course**
stay the **course**
take its **course**
courses
horses for courses
court
the **ball** is in your court
a full-court **press**
hold **court**
laughed out of **court**
put out of **court**
ruled out of **court**
Coventry
send someone to **Coventry**
cover
cover all the **bases**
cover the **waterfront**
cover your ass
cover your back
cover your rear
cover your **tracks**
you can't judge a **book** by its cover

cow
a **cash** cow
have a **cow**
a sacred **cow**
cows
until the **cows** come home
crack
at the **crack** of dawn
crack the **whip**
a fair crack of the **whip**
have a **crack** at something
a sledgehammer to crack a
  nut
take a **crack** at something
a tough **nut** to crack
cracked
not all it's **cracked** up to be
cracking
get **cracking**
cracks
fall through the **cracks**
paper over the **cracks**
slip through the **cracks**
cradle
from the **cradle** to the grave
rob the **cradle**
cradle-snatching
cradle-snatching
cramp
cramp someone's **style**
crannies
the **nooks** and crannies
cranny
every nook and cranny: see
  nooks
crash
crash and burn
crawl
make your **flesh** crawl
make your **skin** crawl
crazy
crazy as a bedbug
go **ape** crazy
cream
the **cream** of the crop
like the **cat** that got the cream
creature
creature comforts
creek
up shit **creek**
up the **creek**
up the **creek** without a paddle
creep
make your **flesh** creep
crest
on the **crest** of a wave
ride the **crest** of the wave
cricket
it's just not **cricket**
crisp
burned to a **crisp**
critical
go **critical**
crock
a **crock** of shit
a crock of **gold**
crocodile
shed **crocodile** tears
Croesus
rich as Croesus

crook
by **hook** or by crook
crop
the **cream** of the crop
cropper
come a **cropper**
cross
at cross **purposes**
cross my **heart**
cross someone's **path**
cross **swords**
cross that **bridge** when you come
  to it
cross the **line**
cross the **Rubicon**
a **cross** to bear
cross your **fingers**
cross your **mind**
dot the **i**'s and cross the **t**'s
crossed
fingers crossed
get your lines **crossed**
get your wires **crossed**
keep your **fingers** crossed
crossfire
caught in the **crossfire**
crow
as the **crow** flies
eat **crow**
crown
the **jewel** in someone's crown
crumble
that's the way the **cookie**
  crumbles
crunch
the **crunch** comes
crunch time
when it comes to the **crunch**
crust
earn a **crust**
cry
cry all the way to the **bank**
cry for the **moon**
cry on someone's **shoulder**
cry **wolf**
cry your **heart** out
a far **cry** from something
a **hue** and cry
in full **cry**
a **shoulder** to cry on
crying
it's no use crying over spilled
  milk
a voice crying in the **wilderness**
crystal
clear as crystal
a crystal **ball**
cucumber
cool as a cucumber
cudgels
take up the **cudgels**
cuff
off-the-**cuff**
cup
not your **cup** of tea
there is many a **slip** twixt cup
  and lip
cupboard
cupboard love
a **skeleton** in the cupboard

curate
a **curate**'s egg
curiosity
curiosity killed the cat
curl
curl your **hair**
make your **hair** curl
make your **toes** curl
curlies
by the **short** and curlies
curtain
bring the **curtain** down on
  something
the **curtain** comes down
curtains
it's **curtains**
mean **curtains**
spell **curtains**
curve
throw someone a **curve**
throw someone a **curve** ball
cushion
cushion the **blow**
cuss
not give a **tinker**'s cuss
cut
cannot **cut** it
a **cut** above
a **cut** above the rest
cut a **dash**
cut and dried
cut and run
the **cut** and thrust
cut both **ways**
cut **corners**
cut from the same **cloth**
cut it close: see **fine**
cut it **fine**
cut **loose**
cut no **ice**
cut off your **nose** to spite your
  face
cut someone **dead**
cut someone down to **size**
cut someone some **slack**
cut someone to the **quick**
cut the **cackle**
cut the **cord**
cut the Gordian **knot**
cut the **ground** from under
  someone
cut the **ground** from under
  someone's feet
cut the umbilical **cord**
cut things **fine**
cut to the **bone**
cut to the **chase**
cut two **ways**
cut up **rough**
cut your **cloth**
cut your coat according to your
  cloth
cut your **losses**
cut your own **throat**
cut your **teeth**
does not **cut** it
fish or cut **bait**
have your **work** cut out
like a **chicken** with its head cut
  off

not **cut** out for something
not cut the **mustard**
to cut a long **story** short
you could cut the atmosphere
  with a **knife**
cutting
a cutting **edge**
the cutting **edge**
cylinders
fire on all **cylinders**
dab
a **dab** hand
daft
daft as a brush
dagger
cloak-and-**dagger**
daggers
at **daggers** drawn
look **daggers** at someone
shoot **daggers** at someone
daisies
push up the **daisies**
daisy
fresh as a daisy
dam
water over the dam
damn
damn with faint **praise**
not give a **tinker**'s damn
Damocles
the Sword of Damocles: see
  sword
damp
a damp **squib**
dampener
put a dampener on something: see
  damper
damper
put a **damper** on something
dance
dance to someone's **tune**
lead you a merry **dance**
make a **song** and dance about
  something
dancing
all-singing, all-dancing
dander
get someone's **dander** up
dangle
dangle a **carrot** in front of
  someone
Daniel
Daniel in the **lion**'s den
dark
a dark **horse**
in the **dark**
keep something **dark**
a leap in the **dark**
a shot in the **dark**
a stab in the **dark**
whistle in the **dark**
darken
not darken someone's **door**
dash
cut a **dash**
date
pass your sell-by **date**
past your sell-by **date**
dawn
at the **crack** of dawn

a false **dawn**
light dawns
day
all in a **day**'s work
at the end of the **day**
call it a **day**
carry the **day**
clear as day
the **day** of reckoning
don't give up the **day** job
every **dog** has its day
have a **field** day
have had your **day**
honest as the day is long
in the cold **light** of day
it's early in the day: see **days**
late in the **day**
make my **day**
make someone's **day**
a nine-day **wonder**
a one-day **wonder**
the **order** of the day
plain as day
put off the **evil** day
a **red** letter day
Rome was not built in a day
save for a rainy **day**
see the **light** of day
seize the **day**
tomorrow is another day
daylight
daylight **robbery**
in broad **daylight**
daylights
beat the living **daylights** out of
  someone
scare the living **daylights** out of
  someone
days
halcyon days
have seen better **days**
it's early **days**
someone's **days** are numbered
your **salad** days
dead
beat a dead **horse**
come back from the **dead**
cut someone **dead**
dead as a dodo
dead as a doornail
dead as mutton
a dead **duck**
a dead **end**
dead from the **neck** up
the dead **hand**
dead in the water
a dead **letter**
a dead **loss**
dead **meat**
dead men's **shoes**
dead men tell no **tales**
dead on your **feet**
a dead **ringer** for someone
the dead **spit**
dead to **rights**
dead to the **world**
a dead **weight**
dead **wood**
drop **dead**
flog a dead **horse**

knock 'em **dead**
knock someone **dead**
over my dead **body**
raise something from the **dead**
rise from the **dead**
stop someone dead in their
  tracks
stop something dead in its **tracks**
wouldn't be caught **dead**
wouldn't be seen **dead**
dead-end
dead-**end**
deaf
deaf as a post
fall on deaf **ears**
turn a deaf **ear** to something
deal
a done **deal**
get a raw **deal**
dear
dear to your **heart**
near and dear to your **heart**
death
at **death**'s door
a **death** blow
the death **knell** sounds
dice with **death**
fight to the **death**
the **kiss** of death
like **death** warmed over
like **death** warmed up
like grim **death**
a living **death**
sign someone's **death** warrant
sign your own **death** warrant
sound the death **knell**
to **death**
deck
all hands on **deck**
clear the deck: see **decks**
hit the **deck**
not play with a full **deck**
play with a loaded **deck**
play with a stacked **deck**
several cards **short** of a full
  deck
stack the deck
decks
clear the **decks**
deep
between the **devil** and the deep
  blue sea
dig deep: see **pocket**
dig deep into your **pocket**
go **deep**
go off the deep **end**
in at the deep **end**
in deep **shit**
in deep **water**
run **deep**
still **waters** run deep
deer
like a deer caught in the
  headlights
degree
give someone the third **degree**
deliver
deliver the **goods**
delivered
signed, sealed, and delivered

den
Daniel in the **lion**'s den
walk into the **lion**'s den
dent
make a **dent** in something
put a **dent** in something
department
be your **department**
not your **department**
depth
out of your **depth**
depths
plumb the **depths**
deserts
just **deserts**
designs
have **designs** on someone
have **designs** on something
desserts
just desserts: see **deserts**
devices
left to your own **devices**
devil
better the **devil** you know
better the **devil** you know than
the devil you don't
between the **devil** and the deep
blue sea
a **devil** of a job
the **devil**'s own job
the **devil** take the hindmost
every man for himself and the
devil take the hindmost
speak of the **devil**
talk of the **devil**
diamond
a **diamond** in the rough
a rough **diamond**
dice
dice with **death**
load the **dice** against someone
no **dice**
Dick
every **Tom**, Dick, and Harry
die
the **die** is cast
die like a **dog**
die on the **vine**
die with your **boots** on
old habits die **hard**
straight as a die
different
a different **ball** game
a different **kettle** of fish
different **strokes** for different
folks
march to a different drummer
march to a different tune
march to the beat of a different
drummer
sing a different tune
dig
dig deep: see **pocket**
dig deep into your **pocket**
dig for **dirt**
dig in your **heels**
dig the **dirt**
dig up **dirt**
dig your own **grave**

dilemma
the **horns** of a dilemma
dim
take a dim **view** of something
dime
a **dime** a dozen
nickel and dime
dinner
a **dog**'s dinner
done like a **dinner**
dinners
do something more than someone
has had hot **dinners**
dip
dip into your **pocket**
dirt
dig for **dirt**
dig the **dirt**
dig up **dirt**
dish the **dirt**
do someone **dirt**
do the **dirt** on someone
hit **pay dirt**
rub someone's **nose** in the dirt
strike **pay dirt**
dirty
air your **dirty** laundry in public
dirty laundry
dirty linen
a dirty **look**
a dirty **word**
dirty your **hands**
do someone's **dirty work**
do the **dirty** on someone
down and dirty
do your **dirty** washing in public
get your **hands** dirty
wash your **dirty** linen in public
disguise
a **blessing** in disguise
dish
dish the **dirt**
dishwater
dull as dishwater
distance
go the **distance**
go the full **distance**
within spitting **distance**
within striking **distance**
distraction
drive someone to **distraction**
ditch
last **ditch**
ditchwater
dull as ditchwater
divide
divide and conquer
divide and rule
dividends
pay **dividends**
Dixie
whistle **Dixie**
dizzy
the dizzy **heights**
dizzying
dizzying **heights**
do
can do something standing on
your **head**
can't do something for **toffee**

can't do something to save your
life
do a **job** on someone
do a **land-office** business
do a **number** on someone
do someone **dirt**
do someone's dirty **work**
do the **dirt** on someone
do the **dirty** on someone
do the **donkey** work
do the **trick**
do your **dirty** washing in public
do your **head** in
do your **nut**
do your own **thing**
not do things by **halves**
when in **Rome**, do as the Romans
do
doctor
just what the **doctor** ordered
dodo
dead as a dodo
dog
die like a **dog**
a **dog** and pony show
a **dog**'s breakfast
a **dog**'s dinner
every **dog** has its day
fight like **cat** and dog
a **hair** of the dog
a **hair** of the dog that bit you
it's a **dog**'s life
sick as a dog
a sleeping dog: see **dogs**
the **tail** wags the dog
you can't teach an old **dog** new
tricks
dog-eat-dog
dog-eat-dog
doghouse
in the **doghouse**
dog-in-the-manger
dog-in-the-manger
dogs
call off the **dogs**
go to the **dogs**
it's raining **cats** and dogs
let sleeping **dogs** lie
throw someone to the **dogs**
doldrums
in the **doldrums**
out of the **doldrums**
dollar
the 64,000 **dollar** question
bet your bottom **dollar**
dollars
dollars to doughnuts
feel like a million **dollars**
look a million **dollars**
domino
a **domino** effect
done
done and dusted
a done **deal**
done like a **dinner**
easier said than done
hard done by
donkey
donkey's years
do the **donkey** work

talk the hind **leg** off a donkey
don'ts
  the **dos** and don'ts
donuts
  dollars to donuts
door
  as one **door** closes, another one
    opens
  at **death's** door
  beat a path to someone's **door**
  by the back **door**
  close the barn **door** after the
    horse has gone
  close the stable **door** after the
    horse has bolted
  come knocking at your **door**
  a **foot** in the door
  keep the **wolf** from the door
  knock at your **door**
  knock on the **door**
  lay something at someone's **door**
  never darken someone's **door**
  not darken somewhere's **door**
  push at an open **door**
  the revolving **door**
  through the back **door**
doornail
  dead as a doornail
doors
  behind closed **doors**
dos
  the **dos** and don'ts
dose
  give someone a dose of their own
    medicine
dot
  dot the **i**'s and cross the **t**'s
  from the year **dot**
  on the **dot**
  since the year **dot**
dotted
  sign on the dotted **line**
double
  at the **double**
  a double **bind**
  on the **double**
double-edged
  a double-edged **sword**
doubt
  give someone the **benefit** of the
    doubt
doughnuts
  dollars to doughnuts
down
  down and dirty
  down and out
  down for the **count**
  down in the **dumps**
  down in the **mouth**
  down on your **knees**
  down on your **luck**
  down on your **uppers**
  down the drain
  down the **hatch**
  down the **line**
  down the pan
  down the **road**
  down the tubes
  down to **earth**
  down tools

down to the **wire**
have a **down** on someone
down-at-heel
  down-at-heel
down-at-the-heels
  down-at-the-heels
downer
  have a downer on someone: see
    down
dozen
  a **baker**'s dozen
  a **dime** a dozen
  six of one and half a dozen of the
    other
  talk **nineteen** to the dozen
drag
  drag someone through the mud
  drag your feet
  drag your heels
dragged
  look like something the **cat**
    dragged in
  look what the **cat**'s dragged in
drag-out
  a knock-down drag-out **fight**
drain
  down the drain
  laugh like a **drain**
drakes
  play **ducks** and drakes with
    someone
drape
  drape yourself in the **flag**
draw
  draw a **bead** on
  draw a **blank**
  draw a **line** under something
  draw a **veil** over something
  draw in your **horns**
  draw someone's **fire**
  draw the **line**
  draw the short **straw**
  the **luck** of the draw
drawer
  the top **drawer**
drawing
  back to the drawing **board**
drawn
  at **daggers** drawn
  the **battle** lines are drawn
dream
  a **dream** ticket
  like a **dream**
dreams
  beyond your wildest **dreams**
  never in your wildest **dreams**
  not in your wildest **dreams**
  the person of your **dreams**
  the thing of your **dreams**
dress
  dress to the **nines**
dressed
  all **dressed** up with nowhere to
    go
  dressed to kill
  mutton dressed as lamb
dried
  cut and dried
drink
  drink like a **fish**

drink someone under the **table**
meat and drink to someone
you can lead a **horse** to water but
  you can't make him drink
drinking
  drinking in the last chance
    saloon
drive
  drive a **coach** and horses through
    something
  drive a **wedge** between people
  drive someone to **distraction**
  drive someone up the **wall**
driver
  in the driver's **seat**
driving
  in the driving **seat**
drop
  at the **drop** of a hat
  the **bottom** drops out of
    something
  drop a **bombshell**
  drop a **brick**
  drop a **clanger**
  drop **dead**
  a **drop** in the bucket
  a **drop** in the ocean
  drop into your **lap**
  drop like **flies**
  drop something like a hot brick:
    see **potato**
  drop something like a hot **potato**
  drop the **ball**
  drop the other **shoe**
  drop your **bundle**
  drop your **guard**
  the **penny** drops
drop-dead
  drop-**dead**
drown
  drown your **sorrows**
drowned
  look like a drowned **rat**
drowning
  a drowning man will clutch at a
    straw: see **straws**
drum
  bang the **drum**
  beat the **drum**
drummer
  march to the beat of a different
    drummer
drunk
  drunk as a skunk
dry
  bleed someone dry
  dry as a bone
  dry as dust
  hang someone out to dry
  home and dry
  keep your **powder** dry
  leave someone **high** and dry
  watch **paint** dry
duck
  a dead **duck**
  a lame **duck**
  like **water** off a duck's back
  a sitting **duck**
  take to something like a **duck** to
    water

ducks
get your **ducks** in a row
play **ducks** and drakes with
someone
dudgeon
in high **dudgeon**
dull
dull as dishwater
dull as ditchwater
dummy
a dummy **run**
spit out the **dummy**
spit the **dummy**
dumps
down in the **dumps**
in the **dumps**
dust
bite the **dust**
dry as dust
the **dust** clears
the **dust** settles
eat someone's **dust**
gather **dust**
gold dust
not see someone for **dust**
shake the **dust** of somewhere
from your feet
dusted
done and dusted
dusty
a **dusty** answer
a **dusty** reply
Dutch
Dutch **courage**
a **Dutch** treat
go **Dutch**
in **Dutch**
dyed-in-the-wool
dyed-in-the-**wool**
eager
an eager **beaver**
eagle
an **eagle** eye
ear
bend someone's **ear**
a **flea** in your ear
go in one **ear** and out the
other
grin from **ear** to ear
half an **ear**
have an **ear** for something
have a **tin** ear for something
have someone's **ear**
have your **ear** to the ground
keep your **ear** to the ground
lend an **ear** to someone
make a **pig**'s ear of something
out on your **ear**
play it by **ear**
smile from **ear** to ear
turn a deaf **ear** to something
a **word** in someone's ear
you can't make a **silk** purse out
of a sow's ear
early
an **early** bath
an early **bird**
the early **bird** catches the worm
it's early **days**
it's early in the day: see **days**

earn
earn a **crust**
earn its **keep**
earn your **corn**
earn your **spurs**
ears
be all **ears**
between your **ears**
cloth ears
fall on deaf **ears**
have something coming out of
your **ears**
have steam coming out of your
ears
music to your ears
pin back your **ears**
pin someone's **ears** back
prick up your **ears**
someone's **ears** are burning
up to your **ears**
walls have ears
wet behind the **ears**
earth
bring someone back to **earth**
come down to **earth**
come down to **earth** with a
bump
down to **earth**
the four **corners** of the earth
go to **earth**
hell on earth
move **heaven** and earth
promise the **earth**
run someone to **earth**
the **salt** of the earth
easier
easier said than done
easy
easy as ABC
easy as falling off a **log**
easy as pie
easy come, easy go
an easy **ride**
an easy **touch**
the easy **way** out
go **easy** on someone
go **easy** on something
take it **easy**
take things **easy**
eat
dog-eat-dog
eat **crow**
eat humble **pie**
eat like a **bird**
eat like a **horse**
eat like a **pig**
eat someone **alive**
eat someone out of **house** and
home
eat someone's **dust**
eat your **hat**
eat your **heart** out
eat your **seed** corn
eat your **words**
have your **cake** and eat it
eating
have someone eating out of the
palm of your **hand**
have someone eating out of your
hand

the **proof** of the pudding is in the
eating
ebb
at a low **ebb**
at your lowest **ebb**
echo
cheer someone to the **echo**
eclipse
in **eclipse**
economical
economical with the **truth**
edge
a cutting **edge**
the cutting **edge**
give someone the rough edge of
your **tongue**
lose your **edge**
on a **knife**-edge
on **edge**
on the **edge** of your chair
on the **edge** of your seat
set your **teeth** on edge
take the **edge** off something
walk a **knife**-edge
edges
fray at the **edges**
rough **edges**
edgeways
get a **word** in edgeways
edgewise
get a **word** in edgewise
eel
slippery as an eel
effect
a **domino** effect
egg
chicken and egg
a **curate**'s egg
egg all over your face
egg on your face
kill the **goose** that lays the
golden egg
lay an **egg**
a **nest** egg
eggs
put all your **eggs** in one basket
sure as eggs is eggs
teach your **grandmother** to suck
eggs
walk on eggs: see **eggshells**
you can't make an **omelette**
without breaking eggs
eggshells
walk on **eggshells**
elbow
all **power** to your elbow
elbow grease
elbow room
more **power** to your elbow
not know your arse from your
elbow
not know your ass from your
elbow
elbows
rub **elbows** with someone
element
in your **element**
out of your **element**
elephant
a white **elephant**

eleventh
the eleventh **hour**
embarrassment
an **embarrassment** of riches
empty
empty **vessels** make the most noise
empty **vessels** make the most sound
run on **empty**
end
at a loose **end**
at the end of the **day**
at the end of the **rainbow**
at the end of your **rope**
at the end of your **tether**
at your **wits'** end
come to a bad **end**
come to a sticky **end**
dead-**end**
a dead **end**
end it all
the **end** of the line
the **end** of the road
get hold of the wrong end of the **stick**
get the short end of the **stick**
get the wrong end of the **stick**
go off the deep **end**
hold your **end** up
in at the deep **end**
keep your **end** up
the **light** at the end of the tunnel
make your **hair** stand on end
not see beyond the end of your **nose**
not the end of the **world**
on the wrong **end** of something
the pot of gold at the end of the **rainbow**
quote, end quote
the sharp **end**
someone's **hair** stands on end
the thin end of the **wedge**
to the bitter **end**
end-all
not the be-all and end-all
ends
at loose ends: see **end**
burn the **candle** at both ends
live on your nerve ends: see **nerves**
loose **ends**
make **ends** meet
play both **ends** against the middle
Englishman
an **Englishman's** home is his castle
enough
enough is as good as a **feast**
have enough on your **plate**
envelope
on the **back** of an envelope
envy
green with envy
error
the **error** of your ways
escutcheon
a **blot** on your escutcheon

estimate
a **ballpark** estimate
even
don't get mad, get **even**
get an even **break**
get **even**
give a sucker an even **break**
give someone an even **break**
on an even **keel**
everything
everything but the **kitchen** sink
everything is coming up **roses**
evil
the lesser evil: see **evils**
the love of money is the **root** of all evil
money is the **root** of all evil
put off the **evil** day
evils
the lesser of two **evils**
exception
the **exception** that proves the rule
expedition
a **fishing** expedition
expense
at someone's **expense**
explode
explode in your **face**
extra
go the extra **mile**
eye
the **apple** of your eye
a bird's-eye **view**
cast an **eye** on something
cast your **eye** on something
cast your **eye** over something
catch someone's **eye**
catch the **eye**
an **eagle** eye
an **eye** for an eye
an **eye** for an eye, a tooth for a tooth
an eye for the main **chance**
the **eye** of the storm
get your **eye** in
give someone a black **eye**
a gleam in your **eye**
have an **eye** for something
in the public **eye**
in your **mind's** eye
keep a **weather** eye on something
keep your **eye** on the ball
look someone in the **eye**
meet someone's eye: see **eyes**
the naked **eye**
not bat an **eye**
one in the **eye** for someone
out of the public **eye**
run your **eye** over something
see **eye** to eye with someone
spit in someone's **eye**
take your **eye** off the ball
there's less to something than meets the **eye**
there's more to something than meets the **eye**
turn a blind **eye** to something
with an **eye** for something
a worm's eye **view**

would give your **eye** teeth for something
eyeball
eyeball to eyeball
eyeballs
up to the **eyeballs**
eyebrows
raise **eyebrows**
eyelash
not bat an eyelash: see **eyelid**
eyelid
not bat an **eyelid**
eyes
all **eyes** are on someone
before your **eyes**
blow **smoke** in someone's eyes
can't keep your **eyes** off someone
can't take your **eyes** off someone
cast your eyes on something: see **eye**
feast your **eyes** on something
have **eyes** in the back of your head
in front of your **eyes**
keep your **eyes** open
keep your **eyes** peeled
keep your **eyes** skinned
look someone in the eyes: see **eye**
make **eyes** at someone
make **sheep's** eyes
meet someone's **eyes**
only have **eyes** for someone
only have **eyes** for something
open someone's **eyes**
open the **eyes** of someone
open your **eyes**
pull the **wool** over someone's eyes
the **scales** fall from your eyes
a **sight** for sore eyes
stars in your eyes
up to your **eyes**
with your **eyes** closed
with your **eyes** glued to something
with your **eyes** shut
face
at **face** value
blow **smoke** in someone's face
blow up in your **face**
bring someone **face** to face with something
come **face** to face with someone
come **face** to face with something
cut off your **nose** to spite your face
egg on your face
explode in your **face**
a **face** like thunder
face the **music**
fall **flat** on your face
fly in the **face** of something
get out of someone's **face**
in-your-**face**
keep a straight **face**
laugh on the other side of your **face**
a long **face**
look someone in the **face**
lose **face**

make a **face**
meet someone **face** to face
not have the **face**
plain as the nose on your face
pull a **face**
put a brave **face** on something
put a good **face** on something
save **face**
set your **face** against something
show your **face**
a **slap** in the face
stare someone in the **face**
stare something in the **face**
throw something back in
 someone's **face**
to someone's **face**
until you are blue in the **face**
with a straight **face**
written all over your **face**
faint
 damn with faint **praise**
fair
 all's **fair** in love and war
 by fair **means** or foul
 fair and square
 a fair crack of the **whip**
fair-haired
 your fair-haired **boy**
fall
 be headed for a **fall**
 be heading for a **fall**
 be riding for a **fall**
 the **bottom** falls out of something
 fall apart at the **seams**
 fall between two **stools**
 fall by the **wayside**
 fall **flat**
 fall **flat** on your face
 fall from **grace**
 fall **head** over heels
 fall into **place**
 fall into someone's **hands**
 fall into the **trap**
 fall into the wrong **hands**
 fall into your **lap**
 fall like **ninepins**
 fall off the **perch**
 fall off the **wagon**
 fall off your **perch**
 fall on deaf **ears**
 fall on stony **ground**
 fall on your **feet**
 fall through the **cracks**
 fall through the **net**
 the **scales** fall from your eyes
fallen
 a fallen **angel**
falling
 easy as falling off a **log**
 simple as falling off a **log**
false
 a false **dawn**
 sail under false **colours**
familiarity
 familiarity breeds contempt
 familiarity breeds content
family
 the black **sheep** of the family
famine
 feast or famine

famous
 famous last **words**
fan
 fan the **flames**
 the **shit** hits the fan
fancy
 flight of fancy
fancy-free
 footloose and fancy-free
far
 a far **cry** from something
 so **near** and yet so far
farm
 buy the **farm**
farthing
 a brass farthing
fashion
 after a **fashion**
 parrot fashion
fast
 the fast **lane**
 the fast **track**
 play **fast** and loose
 pull a **fast** one
fat
 chew the **fat**
 a fat **cat**
 the **fat** is in the fire
 the **fat** of the land
 it isn't over until the fat **lady**
 sings
fate
 seal someone's **fate**
 tempt **fate**
fatted
 kill the fatted **calf**
fault
 to a **fault**
fear
 fools rush in where angels fear to
 tread
feast
 enough is as good as a **feast**
 feast or famine
 feast your **eyes** on something
 the ghost at the **feast**
 the skeleton at the **feast**
 the spectre at the **feast**
feather
 birds of a feather
 birds of a feather flock together
 a **feather** in your cap
 feather your **nest**
 light as a feather
 you could have knocked me down
 with a **feather**
feathers
 ruffle someone's **feathers**
 smooth ruffled **feathers**
fed
 fed up to the back **teeth**
feed
 bite the **hand** that feeds you
 chicken feed
feeding
 a feeding **frenzy**
feel
 feel like a million **dollars**
 feel something in your **bones**
 feel the **pinch**

 make someone feel **small**
feelers
 put out **feelers**
feeling
 have a feeling in your **bones**
feet
 clay **feet**
 cut the **ground** from under
 someone's feet
 dead on your **feet**
 drag your feet
 fall on your **feet**
 feet on the ground
 find your **feet**
 get cold **feet**
 get your **feet** on the ground
 get your **feet** under the table
 get your **feet** wet
 have cold **feet**
 have **feet** of clay
 have your **feet** wet
 itchy **feet**
 land on your **feet**
 pull the **rug** from under your feet
 put your **feet** up
 rushed off your **feet**
 shake the **dust** of somewhere
 from your feet
 stand on your own **feet**
 stand on your own two **feet**
 sweep someone off their **feet**
 think on your **feet**
 under someone's **feet**
 vote with your **feet**
fence
 come off the **fence**
 the **grass** is always greener on
 the other side of the fence
 sit on the **fence**
fences
 mend **fences**
fever
 fever pitch
fiddle
 fiddle while **Rome** burns
 fit as a fiddle
 on the **fiddle**
 play second **fiddle**
field
 have a **field** day
 lead the **field**
 left-**field**
 a level **playing field**
 level the **playing field**
 out in left **field**
 out of left **field**
 play the **field**
fifth
 a fifth **wheel**
fig
 a fig **leaf**
fight
 can't fight your way out of a
 paper bag
 fight a losing **battle**
 fight a **rearguard** action
 fight **fire** with fire
 a fight for **life**
 fight for your **life**
 fight like a **lion**

fight like **cat** and dog
fight like **Kilkenny** cats
fight **tooth** and claw
fight **tooth** and nail
fight to the **death**
fight your **corner**
a knock-down drag-out **fight**
fighting
come out fighting
fighting **fit**
in fighting **trim**
figure
a **ballpark** figure
fill
fill someone's **boots**
fill someone's **shoes**
fill the **bill**
fill your **boots**
have had your **fill** of something
filling
the filling in the **sandwich**
filthy
a filthy **look**
final
the final **nail** in the coffin
the final **straw**
find
find common **ground**
find your **feet**
find your **tongue**
finders
finders keepers
fine
cut it **fine**
cut things **fine**
a fine **kettle** of fish
a fine **line**
the fine **print**
have something down to a fine
art
not to put too fine a **point** on it
fine-tooth
with a fine-tooth **comb**
fine-toothed
with a fine-toothed **comb**
finger
get your **finger** out
give someone the **finger**
have a **finger** in every pie
have a **finger** in the pie
have your **finger** on the button
have your **finger** on the pulse
keep your **finger** on the pulse
not lay a **finger** on someone
not lift a **finger**
not raise a **finger**
point the **finger** at someone
pull your **finger** out
put the **finger** on someone
put your **finger** on something
twist someone around your little
finger
wrap someone around your little
finger
fingernails
hang on by your fingernails: see
fingertips
fingers
all fingers and **thumbs**
burn your **fingers**

count something on the **fingers** of
one hand
count something on your **fingers**
cross your **fingers**
fingers crossed
get your **fingers** burned
have green **fingers**
have your fingers in the **till**
itchy **fingers**
keep your **fingers** crossed
slip through your **fingers**
work your **fingers** to the bone
fingertips
at your **fingertips**
hang on by your **fingertips**
fire
add **fuel** to the fire
a **baptism** of fire
be under **fire**
breathe **fire**
catch **fire**
come under **fire**
draw someone's **fire**
the **fat** is in the fire
fight **fire** with fire
fire from the **hip**
fire in your belly
fire on all **cylinders**
get on like a **house** on fire
hang **fire**
have a lot of **irons** in the fire
hold **fire**
hold your **fire**
in the **line** of fire
light a **fire** under someone
not set the **world** on fire
out of the **frying pan** into the
fire
play with **fire**
pull someone's **chestnuts** out of
the fire
set the **heather** on fire
there's no **smoke** without fire
where there's **smoke** there's fire
firing
in the firing **line**
out of the firing **line**
first
at first **glance**
at first **sight**
first off the **mark**
first past the **post**
get to first **base**
of the first **water**
fish
another **kettle** of fish
a big **fish**
a big **fish** in a small pond
a cold **fish**
a different **kettle** of fish
drink like a **fish**
a fine **kettle** of fish
fish in troubled **waters**
fish or cut **bait**
a **fish** out of water
have bigger **fish** to fry
have other **fish** to fry
like shooting **fish** in a barrel
neither **fish** nor fowl
a pretty **kettle** of fish

there are other **fish** in the sea
there are plenty more **fish** in the
sea
fishing
a **fishing** expedition
fist
hand over fist
an iron **fist**
an iron **fist** in a velvet glove
fit
fighting **fit**
fit as a fiddle
fit as a flea
fit like a **glove**
fit the **bill**
fit to be **tied**
fits
if the **cap** fits
if the **shoe** fits
in **fits** and starts
five
know how many **beans** make five
fix
if it ain't **broke**, don't fix it
no quick **fix**
flag
drape yourself in the **flag**
fly the **flag**
keep the **flag** flying
a red **flag**
a red flag before a **bull**
wrap yourself in the **flag**
flagpole
run something up the **flagpole**
flags
put the **flags** out
flame
like a **moth** to a flame
an old **flame**
flames
add **fuel** to the flames
fan the **flames**
go down in **flames**
go up in **flames**
shoot down in **flames**
flash
flash in the pan
quick as a flash
flat
fall **flat**
fall **flat** on your face
flat as a pancake
in a flat **spin**
flat-footed
catch someone **flat-footed**
flavor: see flavour
flavour
flavour of the month
flea
fit as a **flea**
a **flea** in your ear
flesh
flesh and blood
in the **flesh**
make your **flesh** crawl
make your **flesh** creep
put **flesh** on something
put **flesh** on the bones of
something
a **thorn** in your flesh

your **pound** of flesh
flex
  flex your muscle: see **muscles**
  flex your **muscles**
flick
  give someone the **flick**
  give someone the **flick** pass
flies
  as the **crow** flies
  drop like **flies**
  there are no **flies** on someone
flight
  flight of fancy
flip
  flip your lid
  flip your wig
float
  float on **air**
  float someone's **boat**
flock
  birds of a feather flock together
flog
  flog a dead **horse**
flood
  in full flood: see **flow**
floodgates
  the **floodgates** open
  open the **floodgates**
floor
  get in on the **ground** floor
  through the **floor**
  wipe the **floor** with someone
flow
  go with the **flow**
  in full **flow**
  stem the flow
flown
  the **bird** has flown
fly
  fly a **kite**
  fly **blind**
  fly by the **seat** of your pants
  fly in the **face** of something
  the **fly** in the ointment
  fly off the **handle**
  a **fly** on the wall
  fly the **coop**
  fly the **flag**
  fly the **nest**
  like a blue-arsed **fly**
  on the **fly**
  pigs might fly
  sparks fly
  when **pigs** fly
  wouldn't harm a **fly**
  wouldn't hurt a **fly**
flying
  the **fur** is flying
  keep the **flag** flying
  with flying **colours**
foam
  foam at the **mouth**
fodder
  cannon fodder
folks
  different **strokes** for different
    folks
follow
  follow in someone's **footsteps**
  follow **suit**

follow your **nose**
  a hard **act** to follow
follower
  a **camp** follower
food
  food for thought
fool
  a **fool** and his money are soon
    parted
  fool's gold
  live in a **fool's** paradise
  play someone for a fool
foolish
  penny-wise and pound-foolish
fools
  fools rush in
  fools rush in where angels fear to
    tread
foot
  the boot is on the other **foot**
  bound **hand** and foot
  caught on the wrong **foot**
  a **foot** in both camps
  a **foot** in each camp
  a **foot** in the door
  foot the **bill**
  from **head** to foot
  get off on the wrong **foot**
  not put a **foot** wrong
  one **foot** in the grave
  put your best **foot** forward
  put your **foot** down
  put your **foot** in it
  put your **foot** in your mouth
  the shoe is on the other **foot**
  shoot yourself in the **foot**
  start off on the right **foot**
  wait on someone **hand** and foot
  wouldn't touch something with a
    ten-foot **pole**
foot-in-the-door
  foot-in-the-door
footloose
  footloose and fancy-free
footsteps
  follow in someone's **footsteps**
forbidden
  forbidden **fruit**
force
  force someone's **hand**
forearmed
  forewarned is forearmed
forelock
  touch your **forelock**
  tug your **forelock**
forest
  not see the forest for the **trees**
forewarned
  forewarned is forearmed
forked
  speak with forked **tongue**
  talk with forked **tongue**
former
  a **shadow** of your former self
fort
  hold down the **fort**
  hold the **fort**
fortune
  a **hostage** to fortune
  a small **fortune**

forty
  forty **winks**
forward
  put your best **foot** forward
forwards
  know something **backwards** and
    forwards
foul
  by fair **means** or foul
  foul your own **nest**
foundations
  shake the **foundations**
four
  the four **corners** of the earth
  the four **corners** of the world
fowl
  neither **fish** nor fowl
frame
  in the **frame**
  the name in the **frame**
fray
  fray at the **edges**
frazzle
  wear yourself to a **frazzle**
free
  allow someone free **rein**
  footloose and fancy-free
  free as a bird
  free as the air
  a free **hand**
  a free **ride**
  give someone free **rein**
  there's no such thing as a free
    lunch
freefall
  go into **freefall**
  in **freefall**
freeze
  cold enough to freeze the balls off
    a **brass** monkey
  hell freezes over
  make your **blood** freeze
frenzy
  a feeding **frenzy**
fresh
  a **breath** of fresh air
  fresh as a daisy
  fresh as paint
  fresh **blood**
  fresh **pastures**
frighten
  frighten the **life** out of someone
frighteners
  put the **frighteners** on someone
fritz
  on the **fritz**
frog
  a big frog in a small pond: see
    fish
  a **frog** in your throat
front
  in the front **line**
  on the front **burner**
  on the front **line**
  put a brave front on something:
    see **face**
frosting
  the frosting on the cake: see **icing**
froth
  froth at the **mouth**

frozen
frozen to the **marrow**
fruit
bear **fruit**
forbidden **fruit**
fruitcake
nutty as a fruitcake
fry
have bigger **fish** to fry
have other **fish** to fry
frying
out of the **frying pan** into the
fire
fuel
add **fuel** to the fire
add **fuel** to the flames
full
at full **stretch**
at full **throttle**
come full **circle**
the full monte: see **monty**
the full **monty**
full of **beans**
full **steam** ahead
go the full **distance**
have your **hands** full
have your **plate** full
in full **cry**
in full flood: see **flow**
in full **flow**
in full spate: see **flow**
in full **swing**
in full **throttle**
not play with a full **deck**
several cards **short** of a full deck
turn full **circle**
the wheel has come full **circle**
your **hands** are full
full-court
a full-court **press**
full-time
a full-time **job**
funeral
it's your **funeral**
fur
the **fur** is flying
furniture
part of the **furniture**
furrow
plough a lone **furrow**
plough a lonely **furrow**
fury
hell hath no fury like a woman
scorned
fuse
blow a **fuse**
have a short **fuse**
light the **fuse**
on a short **fuse**
gab
the **gift** of gab
the **gift** of the gab
gaff
blow the **gaff**
gain
gain **ground**
what you lose on the **swings** you
gain on the roundabouts
gallery
play to the **gallery**

game
ahead of the **game**
beat someone at their own **game**
a different **ball** game
the game is not worth the **candle**
the **game** is up
a game of **cat** and mouse
a **game** plan
give the **game** away
the **name** of the game
a new **ball** game
new to the **game**
not play the **game**
the numbers **game**
the only **game** in town
on the **game**
play someone at their own **game**
play the **game**
a **shell** game
a waiting **game**
a **zero-sum** game
gamekeeper
poacher turned gamekeeper
games
play **games**
gander
what's **sauce** for the goose is
sauce for the gander
gangplank
walk the gangplank: see **plank**
garbage
garbage in, garbage out
garden
common-or-**garden**
lead someone down the **garden**
path
lead someone up the **garden** path
garden-variety
garden-variety
gas
run out of **gas**
gasp
last **gasp**
gather
gather **dust**
gather moss: see **stone**
gather your **wits**
a rolling **stone** gathers no moss
gauntlet
pick up the **gauntlet**
run the **gauntlet**
take up the **gauntlet**
throw down the **gauntlet**
gaze
gaze at your **navel**
gazing
navel-**gazing**
gear
get in **gear**
get into **gear**
get your arse in **gear**
get your ass in **gear**
get your brain into **gear**
have your brain in **gear**
in **gear**
genie
the **genie** is out of the bottle
let the **genie** out of the bottle
put the **genie** back in the
bottle

gentle
gentle as a lamb
get
the **biter** gets bit
don't get mad, get **even**
get a bloody **nose**
get a **grip**
get a **grip** on something
get a **grip** on yourself
get a **jump** on someone
get a **leg** up
get a **life**
get a **line** on someone
get a lot of **stick**
get an even **break**
get a raw **deal**
get a **rise** out of someone
get away with **murder**
get a **word** in edgeways
get a **word** in edgewise
get **butterflies**
get cold **feet**
get **cracking**
get down to **brass** tacks
get **even**
get hold of the wrong end of the
stick
get in **gear**
get in on the **act**
get in on the **ground** floor
get in over your **head**
get into **bed** with someone
get into **gear**
get into the **swing** of something
get into your **stride**
get it in the **neck**
get no **change** out of someone
get off on the wrong **foot**
get off someone's **back**
get off someone's **case**
get off the **ground**
get off the **mark**
get **one** over on someone
get **one** up on someone
get on like a **house** on fire
get on someone's **case**
get on someone's **nerves**
get on someone's **wick**
get on **top** of you
get on your high **horse**
get out of **bed** the wrong side
get out of **hand**
get out of someone's **face**
get **shot** of something
get someone's **back** up
get someone's **dander** up
get someone's **goat**
get something off the **ground**
get something off your **chest**
get something out of your **system**
get the **axe**
get the **bird**
get the **bit** between your teeth
get the **boot**
get the **bullet**
get the **bum**'s rush
get the **chop**
get the cold **shoulder**
get the **goods** on someone
get the **hang** of something

get the **hots** for someone
get the **hump**
get the **monkey** off your back
get the **nod**
get the **picture**
get the **push**
get the **runaround**
get the short end of the **stick**
get the **show** on the road
get the **wind** up
get the wrong end of the **stick**
get to first **base**
get to **grips** with something
get too **big** for your boots
get too **big** for your britches
get to second **base**
get to the **bottom** of something
get under someone's **skin**
get under your **skin**
get up someone's **nose**
get up to **speed**
get **wind** of something
get your **act** together
get your arse in **gear**
get your ass in **gear**
get your brain into **gear**
get your **claws** into someone
get your **ducks** in a row
get your **eye** in
get your **feet** on the ground
get your **feet** under the table
get your **feet** wet
get your **finger** out
get your **fingers** burned
get your **hands** dirty
get your **hands** on
get your **head** around something
get your **head** down
get your **hooks** into someone
get your **house** in order
get your **knickers** in a twist
get your **leg** over
get your **lines crossed**
get your mind around something:
  see **head**
get your own **back**
get your **rocks** off
get your **skates** on
get your **teeth** into something
get your thinking **cap** on
get your **tongue** round something
get your wires **crossed**
give as **good** as you get
if you can't stand the **heat**, get
  out of the kitchen
if you pay **peanuts**, you get
  monkeys
not get a **wink** of sleep
play **hard** to get
shit or get off the **pot**
tell someone where to get off
getting
be getting **past** it
like getting **blood** out of a stone
like getting **blood** out of a turnip
ghost
the ghost at the **feast**
give up the **ghost**
lay the **ghost** of something
lay to rest the **ghost** of something

white as a ghost
gift
the **gift** of gab
the **gift** of the gab
God's **gift**
God's **gift** to someone
God's **gift** to women
look a **gift horse** in the mouth
gild
gild the **lily**
gills
green around the **gills**
gilt
take the **gilt** off the gingerbread
gingerbread
take the **gilt** off the gingerbread
gird
gird your **loins**
girl
a big **girl's** blouse
girls
jobs for the girls
give
don't give up the **day** job
give and take
give as **good** as you get
give a sucker an even **break**
give **lip** service to something
give or take
give someone a big **hand**
give someone a black **eye**
give someone a bloody **nose**
give someone a dose of their own
  medicine
give someone a **leg** up
give someone an even **break**
give someone an **inch** and they'll
  take a mile
give someone a piece of your
  mind
give someone a **run** for their
  money
give someone a taste of their own
  medicine
give someone a wide **berth**
give someone both **barrels**
give someone enough **rope**
give someone enough **rope** to
  hang themselves
give someone free **rein**
give someone **hell**
give someone **stick**
give someone the **benefit** of the
  doubt
give someone the **bird**
give someone the **boot**
give someone the **bullet**
give someone the **bum's** rush
give someone the cold **shoulder**
give someone the **finger**
give someone the **flick**
give someone the **flick** pass
give someone their **head**
give someone the **nod**
give someone the **once-over**
give someone the **push**
give someone the rough edge of
  your **tongue**
give someone the rough side of

your **tongue**
give someone the **runaround**
give someone the third **degree**
give something a **whirl**
give something your best **shot**
give the **game** away
give the green **light**
give up the **ghost**
give with one **hand** and take
  away with the other
give your right **arm**
give you the **willies**
not give a **hoot**
not give a **monkey's**
not give a **tinker's** cuss
not give a **tinker's** damn
not give a **toss**
not give someone **house** room
not give two hoots: see **hoot**
would give your **eye** teeth for
  something
given
be given the **axe**
glad
be glad to see the **back** of
  someone
glance
at first **glance**
glass
the **glass** ceiling
people who live in **glass** houses
  shouldn't throw stones
glasses
rose-coloured glasses: see **rose-
  tinted**
gleam
a gleam in your **eye**
glister
all that glisters is not **gold**
glitter
all that glitters is not **gold**
gloss
put a **gloss** on something
glove
fit like a **glove**
hand in glove
an iron **fist** in a velvet glove
gloves
the **gloves** are off
handle someone with **kid** gloves
take the **gloves** off
treat someone with **kid** gloves
glued
with your **eyes** glued to
  something
glutton
a **glutton** for punishment
gnash
gnash your **teeth**
gnashing
wailing and gnashing of **teeth**
weeping and gnashing of **teeth**
gnat
strain at a **gnat**
strain at a **gnat** and swallow a
  camel
go
all **dressed** up with nowhere to
  go
all **systems** go

the **balloon** goes up
bang goes something
easy come, easy go
from the **word** go
go against the **grain**
go along for the **ride**
go **ape**
go **ape** crazy
go apeshit: see **ape**
go around in **circles**
go at it **hammer** and tongs
go at someone **hammer** and tongs
go back a long **way**
go **ballistic**
go **begging**
go behind someone's **back**
go **belly-up**
go by the **board**
go by the boards: see **board**
go by the **book**
go **critical**
go **deep**
go down in **flames**
go down like a **lead** balloon
go **Dutch**
go **easy** on someone
go **easy** on something
go for **broke**
go for the **jugular**
go for the **kill**
go for the throat: see **jugular**
go great **guns**
go **hog** wild
go in one **ear** and out the other
go in to **bat** for someone
go into **freefall**
go into **overdrive**
go into your **shell**
go like a **bomb**
go like **hot cakes**
go **nuclear**
go off at a **tangent**
go off at **half** cock
go off **half**-cocked
go off on a **tangent**
go off the deep **end**
go on **record**
go out of the **window**
go out the **window**
go out with the **ark**
go over someone's **head**
go **places**
go round in **circles**
go the **distance**
go the extra **mile**
go the full **distance**
go the whole **hog**
go through **hell**
go through the ceiling: see **roof**
go through the **hoops**
go through the **mill**
go through the **motions**
go through the **roof**
go through the **wringer**
go to **bat** for someone
go to **earth**
go to **ground**
go to **hell**
go to **hell** in a handbasket
go to **pieces**

go to **pot**
go to **seed**
go to the **country**
go to the **dogs**
go to the **mat**
go to the **stake**
go to the **wall**
go to **town**
go to your **head**
go up in **flames**
go up in **smoke**
go up in the **world**
go **way** back
go **west**
go whole **hog**
go with a **swing**
go with the **flow**
go with the **territory**
have a **go** at someone
if Mohammed will not go to the
   mountain, the mountain must
   go to Mohammed
pick up your **marbles** and go
   home
touch and go
what goes around comes around:
   see **go**
goal
   an own **goal**
goalposts
   move the **goalposts**
goat
   act the **goat**
   get someone's **goat**
goats
   separate the **sheep** from the
     goats
   sort out the **sheep** from the goats
god
   a little **tin** god
   a **tin** god
God
   God's **gift**
   God's **gift** to someone
   God's **gift** to women
   play **God**
gods
   in the **lap** of the gods
going
   not **know** whether you are
     coming or going
gold
   all that glisters is not **gold**
   all that glitters is not **gold**
   a crock of **gold**
   fool's gold
   gold dust
   good as gold
   a **heart** of gold
   a pot of **gold**
   the pot of gold at the end of the
     rainbow
   strike **gold**
   worth your **weight** in gold
golden
   kill the golden **goose**
   kill the **goose** that lays the
     golden egg
gone
   close the barn **door** after the

   horse has gone
   here **today**, gone tomorrow
good
   enough is as good as a **feast**
   for good **measure**
   give as **good** as you get
   good as gold
   good as new
   a good **bet**
   a good **press**
   have a good **innings**
   in good **odour**
   in someone's good **books**
   it's an ill **wind** that blows nobody
     any good
   no good to man or **beast**
   no **news** is good news
   put a good **face** on something
   the road to **hell** is paved with
     good intentions
   take something in good **part**
   throw good **money** after bad
   you can't keep a **good** man
     down
   you can't keep a **good** woman
     down
goodbye
   kiss **goodbye** to something
   say **goodbye** to something
good-for-nothing
   good-for-nothing
goods
   deliver the **goods**
   get the **goods** on someone
   have the **goods** on someone
   sell someone a **bill** of goods
goose
   cook your **goose**
   kill the golden **goose**
   kill the **goose** that lays the
     golden egg
   what's **sauce** for the goose is
     sauce for the gander
   a wild **goose** chase
   wouldn't say boo to a **goose**
   your **goose** is cooked
gooseberry
   play **gooseberry**
Gordian
   cut the Gordian **knot**
   a Gordian **knot**
gospel
   accept something as **gospel**
   the **gospel** truth
   take something as **gospel**
got
   got it in **one**
   have got something **taped**
   like the **cat** that got the cream
   pull the other one, it's got bells
     on it
grab
   grab someone by the **throat**
grabs
   up for **grabs**
grace
   fall from **grace**
   a saving **grace**
graces
   airs and graces

put on **airs** and graces
grade
  make the **grade**
grain
  go against the **grain**
  separate the grain from the **chaff**
  take something with a grain of
    salt
grandmother
  teach your **grandmother** to suck
    eggs
grapes
  sour **grapes**
grapevine
  hear something on the **grapevine**
  hear something through the
    grapevine
grasp
  grasp at **straws**
  grasp the **nettle**
grass
  the **grass** is always greener on
    the other side of the fence
  the **grass** roots
  green as grass
  the other man's **grass** is always
    greener
  put someone out to **grass**
  a **snake** in the grass
  watch **grass** grow
grasshopper
  knee-high to a grasshopper
grave
  dig your own **grave**
  from the **cradle** to the grave
  one **foot** in the grave
  turn in your **grave**
  turn over in your **grave**
gravy
  a **gravy** train
gray
  a gray **area**
  the men in gray **suits**
grease
  elbow grease
  grease someone's **palm**
  grease the **wheels**
greased
  like a greased **pig**
  like greased **lightning**
greasy
  the greasy **pole**
great
  go great **guns**
  great **oaks** from little acorns
    grow
  make great **play** of something
  no great **shakes**
greatest
  the greatest thing since sliced
    bread
Greek
  be all **Greek** to someone
  be **Greek** to someone
green
  give the green **light**
  green around the **gills**
  green as grass
  green with envy
  have a green **thumb**

have green **fingers**
the **rub** of the green
greener
  the **grass** is always greener on
    the other side of the fence
  greener **pastures**
  the other man's **grass** is always
    greener
grey
  a grey **area**
  the men in grey **suits**
grim
  like grim **death**
grin
  grin and bear it
  grin from **ear** to ear
  grin like a Cheshire **cat**
grind
  grind your **teeth**
  have an **axe** to grind
grinder
  the **organ** grinder's monkey
grindstone
  keep your **nose** to the grindstone
grip
  get a **grip**
  get a **grip** on something
  get a **grip** on yourself
  keep a **grip** on something
  keep a **grip** on yourself
  lose your **grip**
  take a **grip** on something
grips
  come to **grips** with something
  get to **grips** with something
grist
  grist for the mill
  grist to the mill
grit
  grit your **teeth**
groove
  in a **groove**
  in the **groove**
ground
  break **ground**
  break new **ground**
  cut the **ground** from under
    someone
  cut the **ground** from under
    someone's feet
  fall on stony **ground**
  feet on the ground
  find common **ground**
  gain **ground**
  get in on the **ground** floor
  get off the **ground**
  get something off the **ground**
  get your **feet** on the ground
  go to **ground**
  have your **ear** to the ground
  the high **ground**
  hit the **ground** running
  keep your **ear** to the ground
  lose **ground**
  make up lost **ground**
  the moral high **ground**
  on common **ground**
  on **home** ground
  prepare the **ground**
  run someone into the **ground**

run someone to **ground**
run something into the **ground**
run yourself into the **ground**
stamping **ground**
stomping **ground**
suit someone down to the **ground**
thick on the **ground**
thin on the **ground**
grow
  great **oaks** from little acorns
    grow
  not grow on **trees**
  watch **grass** grow
growing
  growing **pains**
guard
  catch someone off **guard**
  drop your **guard**
  let your **guard** down
  lower your **guard**
  off **guard**
  off your **guard**
  the old **guard**
  on **guard**
  on your **guard**
  take someone off **guard**
guest
  be my **guest**
guinea
  a **guinea pig**
gum
  up a **gum tree**
gun
  a big gun: see **guns**
  hold a gun to someone's **head**
  jump the **gun**
  put a gun to someone's **head**
  a smoking **gun**
  under the **gun**
guns
  the big **guns**
  go great **guns**
  spike someone's **guns**
  stick to your **guns**
  with all **guns** blazing
gut
  bust a **gut**
guts
  spill your **guts**
  work your **guts** out
habits
  old habits die **hard**
hackles
  raise someone's **hackles**
  someone's **hackles** rise
Hades
  hot as Hades
hair
  curl your **hair**
  a **hair** of the dog
  a **hair** of the dog that bit you
  a **hair's** breadth
  a **hair** shirt
  haven't seen **hide** nor hair of
    someone
  in your **hair**
  keep your **hair** on
  let your **hair** down
  make your **hair** curl
  make your **hair** stand on end

not a **hair** out of place
not turn a **hair**
out of someone's **hair**
pull your **hair** out
put hair on the chest: see **hairs**
someone's **hair** stands on end
tear your **hair** out
hairs
by the short **hairs**
put **hairs** on your chest
split **hairs**
halcyon
halcyon days
half
go off at **half** cock
half a **loaf** is better than none
half an **ear**
how the other **half** lives
six of one and half a dozen of the other
you can't be half **pregnant**
your better **half**
your other **half**
half-cocked
go off **half**-cocked
halfway
a halfway **house**
meet someone **halfway**
halves
not do anything by **halves**
not do things by **halves**
hammer
go at it **hammer** and tongs
go at someone **hammer** and tongs
hammer and tongs
under the **hammer**
hand
the **ace** in your hand
a big **hand** for someone
a **bird** in the hand
a **bird** in the hand is worth two in the bush
bite the **hand** that feeds you
bound **hand** and foot
cap in hand
caught with your hand in the **cookie** jar
count something on the **fingers** of one hand
a **dab** hand
the dead **hand**
force someone's **hand**
a free **hand**
get out of **hand**
give someone a big **hand**
give with one **hand** and take away with the other
hand in glove
hand in hand
hand over fist
hand someone something on a **plate**
hand the **baton**
hat in hand
have a **hand** in something
have someone eating out of the palm of your **hand**
have someone eating out of your **hand**
have the **whip** hand

have to **hand** it to someone
have your hand in the **till**
a heavy **hand**
hold someone's **hand**
hold the **whip** hand
in the hollow of your **hand**
in the palm of your **hand**
keep your **hand** in
know something like the back of your **hand**
lend a **hand**
lend someone a **hand**
live from **hand** to mouth
live **hand** to mouth
an old **hand**
out of **hand**
overplay your **hand**
the right **hand** doesn't know what the left hand is doing
show your **hand**
a steady **hand** on the tiller
take a **hand** in something
take someone in **hand**
throw in your **hand**
try your **hand** at something
turn your **hand** to something
the upper **hand**
wait on someone **hand** and foot
with one **hand** tied behind your back
your **right**-hand man
your **right**-hand woman
handbasket
go to **hell** in a handbasket
handle
fly off the **handle**
handle someone with **kid** gloves
too **hot** to handle
hands
all hands on **deck**
at the **hands** of someone
beat someone **hands** down
beat something **hands** down
change **hands**
dirty your **hands**
fall into someone's **hands**
fall into the wrong **hands**
get your **hands** dirty
get your **hands** on
have **blood** on your hands
have bloody hands: see **blood**
have your **hands** full
have your **hands** tied
in safe **hands**
in your **hands**
lay your **hands** on
off your **hands**
on your **hands**
out of your **hands**
play into someone's **hands**
putty in your hands
put your **life** in someone's hands
rub your **hands**
safe **hands**
a safe pair of **hands**
shake **hands** on something
sit on your **hands**
something ties your **hands**
sully your **hands**
take the **law** into your own hands

take your **life** in your hands
time on your hands
wash your **hands** of something
win **hands** down
with your bare **hands**
with your hands tied behind your back: see **hand**
wring your **hands**
your **hands** are full
your **hands** are tied
your **life** is in someone's hands
handsome
handsome is as handsome does
hand-to-mouth
hand-to-mouth
handwriting
the handwriting is on the **wall**
hang
get the **hang** of something
give someone enough **rope** to hang themselves
hang by a **thread**
hang **fire**
hang in the **air**
hang **loose**
hang on by your fingernails: see **fingertips**
hang on by your **fingertips**
hang over your **head**
hang someone out to dry
hang up your boots
let it all **hang** out
a **peg** on which to hang something
hanged
might as well be hanged for a **sheep** as a lamb
hanging
an **axe** hanging over something
be left hanging in the **air**
ha'porth
don't spoil the **ship** for a ha'porth of tar
happy
happy as a clam
happy as a lark
happy as a pig in muck
happy as a sandboy
happy as Larry
hard
between a **rock** and a hard place
a hard **act** to follow
hard as nails
hard done by
hard on the **heels** of something
hard on your **heels**
a hard **row** to hoe
old habits die **hard**
play **hard** to get
the **school** of hard knocks
hardball
play **hardball**
harden
your **heart** hardens
hare
run with the **hare** and hunt with the hounds
start a **hare**
harm
wouldn't harm a **fly**

harness
in **harness**

Harry
every **Tom**, Dick, and Harry

harvest
reap the harvest

hat
at the **drop** of a hat
eat your **hat**
hat in hand
keep something under your **hat**
knock something into a cocked
  hat
old **hat**
pass the **hat**
pass the **hat** around
pull a rabbit out of the **hat**
pull something out of the **hat**
take your **hat** off to someone
talk through your **hat**
throw your **hat** into the ring

hatch
down the **hatch**

hatched
don't count your **chickens** before
  they're hatched

hatches
batten down the **hatches**

hatchet
bury the **hatchet**
a **hatchet** job
a **hatchet** man

hath
hell hath no fury like a woman
  scorned

hats
hats off to someone: see **hat**

hatter
mad as a hatter

haul
haul someone over the **coals**
in something for the long **haul**
a long **haul**
over the long **haul**

hawk
watch someone like a **hawk**

hay
hit the hay
make **hay**
make **hay** while the sun shines

haystack
like looking for a **needle** in a
  haystack

head
bang your head against a brick
  wall
bang your head against a **wall**
be **head** over heels
be in over your **head**
be over someone's **head**
bite someone's **head** off
bring something to a **head**
bury your **head** in the sand
can do something standing on
  your **head**
cannot make **head** or tail of
  something
come to a **head**
a cool **head**
do your **head** in

fall **head** over heels
from **head** to foot
from **head** to toe
get in over your **head**
get your **head** around something
get your **head** down
give someone their **head**
go over someone's **head**
go to your **head**
hang over your **head**
have **eyes** in the back of your
  head
have your **head** in the
  clouds
have your **head** screwed on
have your **head** up your arse
have your **head** up your ass
head and shoulders above
  someone
a **head** of steam
head-to-head
hit the **nail** on the head
hold a gun to someone's **head**
keep your **head**
keep your **head** above water
keep your **head** below the
  parapet
keep your **head** down
knock something on the **head**
laugh your **head** off
like a **bear** with a sore head
like a **chicken** with its head cut
  off
lose your **head**
need something like a **hole** in the
  head
not right in the **head**
off the top of your **head**
off your **head**
on your **head**
out of your **head**
put a gun to someone's **head**
put your **head** above the parapet
put your **head** in a noose
put your head into the **lion's**
  mouth
put your head on the **block**
raise its **head**
rear its **head**
rear its ugly **head**
a **rush** of blood to the head
scratch your **head**
shout your **head** off
snap someone's **head** off
stand something on its **head**
stick your **head** in a noose
talk over someone's **head**
turn something on its **head**
with your **head** in the clouds

headed
be headed for a **fall**

heading
be heading for a **fall**

headless
like a headless **chicken**

headlights
like a deer caught in the
  headlights
like a rabbit caught in the
  headlights

heads
bang people's **heads** together
heads roll
knock people's **heads** together
put your **heads** together
turn **heads**

headway
make **headway**

health
a clean **bill** of health

heap
the bottom of the **heap**
the top of the **heap**

hear
hear something on the **grapevine**
hear something through the
  grapevine

heart
at the bottom of your **heart**
a bleeding **heart**
break your **heart**
a broken **heart**
a **change** of heart
close to your **heart**
cross my **heart**
cry your **heart** out
dear to your **heart**
eat your **heart** out
from the bottom of your **heart**
harden your **heart**
a **heart** of gold
in your **heart** of hearts
lose **heart**
lose your **heart**
near and dear to your **heart**
open your **heart**
pour out your **heart**
set your **heart** on something
take something to **heart**
warm the **cockles** of your heart
wear your **heart** on your sleeve
work your **heart** out
your **heart** bleeds for someone
your **heart** hardens
your **heart** is in the right place
your **heart** is in your mouth
your **heart** isn't in something

hearts
in your **heart** of hearts

heartstrings
tug at the **heartstrings**

heat
the **heat** is on
if you can't stand the **heat**, get
  out of the kitchen
in the **heat** of the moment
turn up the **heat** on someone

heather
set the **heather** on fire

heaven
in seventh **heaven**
move **heaven** and earth

heavens
the **heavens** open

heavy
a heavy **hand**
make heavy **weather** of
  something

hedge
hedge your **bets**

heel
  bring someone to **heel**
  call someone to **heel**
  down-at-heel
heels
  at your **heels**
  be **head** over heels
  close on the **heels** of something
  close on your **heels**
  cool your **heels**
  dig in your **heels**
  down-at-the-heels
  drag your heels
  fall **head** over heels
  hard on the **heels** of something
  hard on your **heels**
  hot on the **heels** of something
  hot on your **heels**
  kick up your **heels**
  kick your **heels**
  rock you back on your **heels**
  set you back on your **heels**
  show a clean pair of **heels**
  take to your **heels**
heights
  the dizzy **heights**
  dizzying **heights**
hell
  all **hell** breaks loose
  all **hell** breaks out
  come **hell** or high water
  from **hell**
  give someone **hell**
  go through **hell**
  go to **hell**
  go to **hell** in a handbasket
  hell for leather
  hell freezes over
  hell hath no fury like a woman
    scorned
  hell on earth
  hot as hell
  just for the **hell** of it
  like a **bat** out of hell
  a living **hell**
  not a cat in hell's **chance**
  not a snowball's **chance** in
    hell
  not have a **chance** in hell
  play **hell**
  play **hell** with something
  play merry **hell**
  play merry **hell** with something
  put someone through **hell**
  raise **hell**
  the road to **hell** is paved with
    good intentions
  shot to **hell**
  there'll be **hell** to pay
  there'll be merry **hell** to pay
  through **hell** and back
  through **hell** and high water
  to **hell** and back
hen
  rare as **hen**'s teeth
  scarce as **hen**'s teeth
herd
  ride **herd** on someone
here
  the **buck** stops here

  here **today**, gone tomorrow
  neither **here** nor there
herring
  a red **herring**
hidden
  a hidden **agenda**
hide
  haven't seen **hide** nor hair of
    someone
  hide your light under a **bushel**
hiding
  on a **hiding** to nothing
high
  blow something **sky**-high
  come down off your high **horse**
  come **hell** or high water
  for the high **jump**
  get on your high **horse**
  high as a kite
  the high **ground**
  a high **profile**
  hunt **high** and low for something
  in high **dudgeon**
  in high **places**
  knee-high to a grasshopper
  leave someone **high** and dry
  live high on the **hog**
  the moral high **ground**
  ride **high**
  ride high in the **saddle**
  search **high** and low for
    something
  take the high **road**
  through **hell** and high water
highway
  highway **robbery**
hike
  take a hike: see **walk**
hill
  not amount to a hill of **beans**
  over the **hill**
hills
  old as the hills
hilt
  to the **hilt**
  up to the **hilt**
hind
  talk the hind **leg** off a donkey
hindmost
  the **devil** take the hindmost
  every man for himself and the
    devil take the hindmost
hip
  fire from the **hip**
  joined at the **hip**
  shoot from the **hip**
history
  be **history**
  the rest is **history**
hit
  hit a **home** run
  hit and miss
  hit a **nerve**
  hit **home**
  hit it off
  hit it on the **nail**
  a **hit** list
  hit or miss
  hit **pay** dirt
  hit **rock** bottom

  hit someone for **six**
  hit the big **time**
  hit the **bottle**
  hit the **buffers**
  hit the ceiling: see **roof**
  hit the **deck**
  hit the **ground** running
  hit the hay
  hit the **jackpot**
  hit the **mark**
  hit the **nail** on the head
  hit the **road**
  hit the **roof**
  hit the sack
  hit the **spot**
  hit the **wall**
  hit your **stride**
  make a **hit**
  the **shit** hits the fan
hitch
  hitch your **wagon** to a star
  hitch your **wagon** to someone
hoary
  a hoary old **chestnut**
Hobson
  Hobson's choice
hoe
  a hard **row** to hoe
  a tough **row** to hoe
hog
  go **hog** wild
  go the whole **hog**
  go whole **hog**
  live high on the **hog**
hoist
  hoist by your own **petard**
hold
  can't hold a **candle** to someone
  get hold of the wrong end of the
    stick
  hold a gun to someone's **head**
  hold all the **aces**
  hold **body** and soul together
  hold **court**
  hold down the **fort**
  hold **fire**
  hold no **brief** for something
  hold someone on a tight **rein**
  hold someone's **hand**
  hold someone to **ransom**
  hold something at **bay**
  hold the **fort**
  hold the **purse** strings
  hold the **whip** hand
  hold your **breath**
  hold your **end** up
  hold your **fire**
  hold your **horses**
  hold your **own**
  hold your **tongue**
  not hold **water**
  on **hold**
holding
  leave someone holding the **baby**
  leave someone holding the **bag**
holds
  no-**holds**-barred
hole
  blow a **hole** in something
  burn a **hole** in your pocket

have an **ace** in the hole
a **hole** card
in a **hole**
in the **hole**
need something like a **hole** in the head
out of a **hole**
a square **peg** in a round hole
hole-and-corner
  hole-and-corner
hole-in-the-corner
  hole-in-the-corner
holes
  more holes than **Swiss cheese**
  pick **holes** in something
holiday
  a **busman**'s holiday
holies
  the **holy** of holies
hollow
  beat someone **hollow**
  have a **hollow** ring
  in the hollow of your **hand**
  ring **hollow**
  sound **hollow**
holy
  the **holy** of holies
home
  at **home**
  bring **home** the bacon
  bring something **home** to someone
  charity begins at home
  the chickens come home to **roost**
  close to **home**
  come home to **roost**
  eat someone out of **house** and home
  an **Englishman**'s home is his castle
  hit a **home** run
  hit **home**
  home and dry
  home and hosed
  the **home** straight
  the **home** stretch
  the **lights** are on but nobody is at home
  make yourself at **home**
  nothing to write **home** about
  on **home** ground
  pick up your **marbles** and go home
  something to write **home** about
  strike **home**
  until the **cows** come home
honest
  honest as the day is long
honey
  the land of **milk** and honey
  milk and honey
hoof
  on the **hoof**
hook
  by **hook** or by crook
  hook, line, and sinker
  off the **hook**
  on your own **hook**
  ring off the **hook**
  sling your **hook**

hooks
  get your **hooks** into someone
hoops
  go through the **hoops**
  jump through **hoops**
hoot
  not give a **hoot**
hoots
  not give two hoots: see **hoot**
hop
  catch someone on the **hop**
  have someone on the **hop**
  a **hop** and a skip
  a **hop**, skip, and a jump
  keep someone on the **hop**
horizon
  on the **horizon**
horn
  blow your own **horn**
hornet
  mad as a hornet
  stir up a **hornet**'s nest
horns
  draw in your **horns**
  the **horns** of a dilemma
  lock **horns**
  pull in your **horns**
  take the **bull** by the horns
horse
  back the wrong **horse**
  beat a dead **horse**
  close the barn **door** after the horse has gone
  close the stable **door** after the horse has bolted
  come down off your high **horse**
  a dark **horse**
  eat like a **horse**
  flog a dead **horse**
  from the **horse**'s mouth
  get on your high **horse**
  look a **gift horse** in the mouth
  a one-**horse** race
  a one-**horse** town
  put the **cart** before the horse
  a stalking **horse**
  strong as a horse
  a Trojan **horse**
  you can lead a **horse** to water but you can't make him drink
horses
  change horses in **midstream**
  drive a **coach** and horses through something
  hold your **horses**
  horses for courses
  ride two **horses** at once
  ride two **horses** at the same time
  switch horses in **midstream**
  wild **horses**
hosed
  home and hosed
hostage
  a **hostage** to fortune
hot
  blow **hot** and cold
  a **cat** on a hot tin roof
  a **cat** on hot bricks
  do something more than someone has had hot **dinners**

drop something like a hot brick: see **potato**
drop something like a hot **potato**
go like **hot cakes**
hot **air**
hot and bothered
hot and cold
hot as Hades
hot as hell
a hot **button**
hot on the **heels** of something
hot on your **heels**
a hot **potato**
hot under the **collar**
in hot **water**
in the hot **seat**
like a hot **knife** through butter
sell like **hot cakes**
strike while the **iron** is hot
too **hot** to handle
hotcakes
  sell like hotcakes: see **hot cakes**
hots
  get the **hots** for someone
  have the **hots** for someone
hounds
  run with the **hare** and hunt with the hounds
hour
  the eleventh **hour**
house
  bring the **house** down
  eat someone out of **house** and home
  get on like a **house** on fire
  get your **house** in order
  a halfway **house**
  a **house** of cards
  not give someone **house** room
  put your **house** in order
houses
  people who live in **glass** houses shouldn't throw stones
  round the **houses**
  safe as houses
howl
  howl at the **moon**
hue
  a **hue** and cry
huff
  in a **huff**
humble
  eat humble **pie**
hump
  get the **hump**
  over the **hump**
hunt
  hunt **high** and low for something
  run with the **hare** and hunt with the hounds
hurt
  wouldn't hurt a **fly**
hymn
  sing from the same hymn sheet
i
  dot the **i**'s and cross the t's
ice
  break the **ice**
  cold as ice
  cut no **ice**

on **ice**
put something on **ice**
skate on thin **ice**

iceberg
the **tip** of the iceberg

icing
the **icing** on the cake

ill
it's an ill **wind**
it's an ill **wind** that blows nobody
any good

image
the **spit** and image
the spitting image: see **spit**

inch
come within an **inch** of doing
something
give someone an **inch** and they'll
take a mile
to within an **inch** of your life

Indian
an Indian **summer**

Indians
too many **chiefs** and not enough
Indians

injury
add **insult** to injury

ink
bleed red **ink**

innings
have a good **innings**

ins
the **ins** and outs

inside
have the inside **track**
know something inside and out
know something inside out

insult
add **insult** to injury

intentions
the road to **hell** is paved with
good intentions

inverted
in inverted **commas**

in-your-face
in-your-**face**

iron
cast **iron**
an iron **fist**
an iron **fist** in a velvet glove
strike while the **iron** is hot

irons
have a lot of **irons** in the fire

itchy
itchy **feet**
itchy **fingers**

ivory
an **ivory** tower

jack
before you could **say** Jack
Robinson
a **jack** of all trades

jackpot
hit the **jackpot**

jam
jam today
jam tomorrow
money for jam

jar
caught with your hand in the

cookie jar

Jell-O
like trying to nail **Jell-O** to the
wall

jewel
the **jewel** in someone's crown

job
a **devil** of a job
the **devil's** own job
do a **job** on someone
don't give up the **day** job
a full-time **job**
a **hatchet** job
a **snow** job

jobs
jobs for the boys
jobs for the girls

Johnny-come-lately
Johnny-come-lately

join
join **battle**
join the **club**

joined
joined at the **hip**

joint
put someone's **nose** out of joint

joker
the **joker** in the pack

Joneses
keep up with the **Joneses**

jowl
cheek by jowl

judge
sober as a judge
you can't judge a **book** by its
cover

judgement: see **judgment**

judgment
sit in **judgment**

juggle
juggle **balls** in the air

jugular
go for the **jugular**

juice
let someone **stew** in their own
juice

jump
for the high **jump**
get a **jump** on someone
a **hop**, skip, and a jump
jump down someone's **throat**
jump on the **bandwagon**
jump out of your **skin**
jump **ship**
jump the **gun**
jump the **rails**
jump through **hoops**
jump up and down
see which way the **cat** jumps
take a running **jump**

jungle
the **law** of the jungle

jury
the **jury** is still out

just
just **deserts**

kangaroos
kangaroos in your top paddock

keel
on an even **keel**

keen
keen as mustard

keep
can't keep your **eyes** off someone
earn its **keep**
keep a **grip** on something
keep a **grip** on yourself
keep a low **profile**
keep a straight **face**
keep a tight **rein** on someone
keep a **weather** eye on something
keep **balls** in the air
keep **body** and soul together
keep someone in the **picture**
keep someone on a **string**
keep someone on the **hop**
keep someone **posted**
keep someone **sweet**
keep something at **bay**
keep something **dark**
keep something in **mind**
keep something under **wraps**
keep something under your **hat**
keep **tabs** on someone
keep the **flag** flying
keep the **lid** on something
keep the **pot** boiling
keep the **show** on the road
keep the **wolf** from the door
keep **track** of something
keep up with the **Joneses**
keep you on your **toes**
keep your cards close to the **vest**
keep your cards close to your
chest
keep your **chin** up
keep your **cool**
keep your **ear** to the ground
keep your **end** up
keep your **eye** on the ball
keep your **eyes** open
keep your **eyes** peeled
keep your **eyes** skinned
keep your **finger** on the pulse
keep your **fingers** crossed
keep your **hair** on
keep your **hand** in
keep your **head**
keep your **head** above water
keep your **head** below the
parapet
keep your **head** down
keep your **nose** clean
keep your **nose** out of something
keep your **nose** to the grindstone
keep your pants on: see **shirt**
keep your **pecker** up
keep your **powder** dry
keep your **shirt** on
keep your **wits** about you
you can't keep a **good** man down
you can't keep a **good** woman
down

keeper
not someone's **keeper**
not your brother's **keeper**

keepers
finders keepers

keg
sit on a **powder** keg

ken
beyond your **ken**
kettle
another **kettle** of fish
a different **kettle** of fish
a fine **kettle** of fish
the **pot** calling the kettle black
a pretty **kettle** of fish
kibosh
put the **kibosh** on something
kick
kick against the **pricks**
kick ass
kick butt
a **kick** in the butt
a **kick** in the teeth
kick over the **traces**
kick someone in the teeth
kick someone **upstairs**
kick someone when they are
down
kick something into **touch**
kick the **bucket**
a **kick** up the backside
kick up your **heels**
kick your **heels**
kicking
alive and kicking
kick-off
for a **kick-off**
kid
handle someone with **kid**
gloves
like a kid in a **candy** store
treat someone with **kid** gloves
Kilkenny
fight like **Kilkenny** cats
kill
dressed to kill
go for the **kill**
in at the **kill**
in on the **kill**
kill someone with **kindness**
kill the fatted **calf**
kill the golden **goose**
kill the **goose** that lays the
golden egg
kill two **birds** with one stone
move in for the **kill**
killed
curiosity killed the cat
killing
make a **killing**
kindness
kill someone with **kindness**
king
a king's **ransom**
live like a **king**
kingdom
blow someone to **kingdom** come
kiss
kiss and make up
kiss ass
kiss **goodbye** to something
the **kiss** of death
kiss someone's **ass**
kiss-and-tell
kiss-and-tell
kit
the whole kit and **caboodle**

kitchen
everything but the **kitchen** sink
if you can't stand the **heat**, get
out of the kitchen
too many **cooks** in the kitchen
kite
fly a **kite**
high as a kite
kittens
have **kittens**
knee
on bended knee: see **knees**
knee-high
knee-high to a grasshopper
knees
the **bee's** knees
be on its **knees**
be on your **knees**
bring someone to their **knees**
bring something to its **knees**
down on your **knees**
knell
the death **knell** sounds
sound the death **knell**
knickers
get your **knickers** in a twist
have your **knickers** in a twist
knife
before you could **say** knife
like a hot **knife** through butter
like a **knife** through butter
put the **knife** in
stick the **knife** in
twist the **knife**
twist the **knife** in the wound
you could cut the atmosphere
with a **knife**
knife-edge
on a **knife**-edge
walk a **knife**-edge
knight
a **knight** in shining armour
knitting
stick to your **knitting**
knives
have the **knives** out
the **knives** are out
knock
knock at your **door**
knock 'em **dead**
knock on the **door**
knock on **wood**
knock people's **heads** together
knock someone **dead**
knock someone for a **loop**
knock someone for **six**
knock someone off their **pedestal**
knock someone sideways
knock something into a cocked
hat
knock something into **shape**
knock something on the **head**
knock something sideways
knock **spots** off something
knock the **socks** off someone
knock the **stuffing** out of
someone
knock **wood**
knock you off your **perch**
knock your **socks** off

knock-down
a knock-down drag-out **fight**
knocked
you could have knocked me down
with a **feather**
knocking
come knocking at your **door**
knocks
the **school** of hard knocks
knot
cut the Gordian **knot**
a Gordian **knot**
tie the **knot**
knots
at a **rate** of knots
tie someone in **knots**
tie yourself in **knots**
know
better the **devil** you know
better the **devil** you know than
the devil you don't
know how many **beans** make five
know something **backwards**
know something **backwards** and
forwards
know something inside and out
know something inside out
know something like the back of
your **hand**
know the **ropes**
know the **score**
know which side your **bread** is
buttered
know your **onions**
not know someone from **Adam**
not know the **meaning** of the
word
not **know** whether you are
coming or going
not know your arse from your
elbow
not know your ass from your
elbow
the right **hand** doesn't know
what the left hand is doing
knuckle
near the **knuckle**
knuckles
rap someone on the **knuckles**
rap someone's **knuckles**
labor: see **labour**
labour
a **labour** of love
lads
one of the **lads**
lady
it isn't over until the fat **lady**
sings
lam
on the **lam**
lamb
gentle as a lamb
in two **shakes** of a lamb's tail
like a **lamb**
might as well be hanged for a
sheep as a lamb
mutton dressed as lamb
quiet as a lamb
lambs
like **lambs** to the slaughter

lame
a lame **duck**
land
the **fat** of the land
land in your **lap**
the land of **milk** and honey
land on your **feet**
the lay of the **land**
the lie of the **land**
land-office
do a **land-office** business
landscape
a **blot** on the landscape
lane
the fast **lane**
the slow **lane**
lap
be thrown into your **lap**
drop into your **lap**
fall into your **lap**
in the **lap** of luxury
in the **lap** of the gods
land in your **lap**
large
large as life
larger
larger than life
lark
happy as a lark
up with the **lark**
Larry
happy as Larry
lashing
tongue-lashing
last
drinking in the last chance
   saloon
famous last **words**
have the last **laugh**
the last chance **saloon**
last **ditch**
last **gasp**
the last **nail** in the coffin
the last **straw**
the last **straw** that breaks the
   camel's back
let the cobbler stick to his **last**
on your last **legs**
stick to your **last**
late
late in the **day**
lately
Johnny-come-lately
lather
in a **lather**
laugh
have the last **laugh**
laugh all the way to the **bank**
laugh like a **drain**
laugh on the other side of your
   face
laugh out of the other side of
   your **mouth**
laugh up your **sleeve**
laugh your **head** off
laughed
laughed out of **court**
laundry
air your **dirty** laundry in public
dirty laundry

a **laundry** list
laurels
look to your **laurels**
not rest on your **laurels**
law
the **law** of the jungle
a **law** unto yourself
lay down the **law**
the **letter** of the law
someone's **word** is law
take the **law** into your own hands
lay
kill the **goose** that lays the
   golden egg
lay an **egg**
lay down the **law**
lay down **tools**
lay it on the **line**
lay it on **thick**
lay it on with a **trowel**
the lay of the **land**
lay something at someone's **door**
lay something on the **line**
lay the **ghost** of something
lay your **cards** on the table
lay your **hands** on
lay yourself **wide** open
not lay a **finger** on someone
lead
go down like a **lead** balloon
have **lead** in your pencil
a **lead** balloon
lead someone by the **nose**
lead someone down the **garden**
   path
lead someone up the **garden** path
lead the **field**
lead with your **chin**
lead you a merry chase: see
   dance
lead you a merry **dance**
one **thing** leads to another
put **lead** in your pencil
swing the **lead**
you can lead a **horse** to water but
   you can't make him drink
leading
the **blind** leading the blind
a leading **light**
leaf
a **fig** leaf
take a **leaf** out of someone's book
turn over a new **leaf**
lean
lean on your **oars**
leap
a leap in the **dark**
leaps
by **leaps** and bounds
in **leaps** and bounds
learn
learn the **ropes**
lease
a new **lease** of life
a new **lease** on life
leash
a longer **leash**
on a short **leash**
on a tight **leash**
strain at the **leash**

least
least said, soonest mended
leather
hell for leather
leave
leave a bad **taste** in your mouth
leave a **mark**
leave no **stone** unturned
leave someone **cold**
leave someone **high** and dry
leave someone holding the **baby**
leave someone holding the **bag**
leave someone in the **lurch**
leave someone to **stew**
leave the **nest**
leave your **mark**
leave yourself **wide** open
leaving
like a rat leaving a sinking **ship**
left
be left hanging in the **air**
left and right
left, right, and centre
left to your own **devices**
out in left **field**
out of left **field**
the right **hand** doesn't know
   what the left hand is doing
left-field
left-**field**
leg
break a **leg**
cost an **arm** and a leg
get a **leg** up
get your **leg** over
give someone a **leg** up
have a **leg** up
not have a **leg** to stand on
pull someone's **leg**
talk the hind **leg** off a donkey
legs
have **legs**
on your last **legs**
with your **tail** between your legs
lend
lend a **hand**
lend an **ear** to someone
lend someone a **hand**
length
at **arm**'s length
leopard
a **leopard** does not change its
   spots
less
there's less to something than
   meets the **eye**
lesser
the lesser evil: see **evils**
the lesser of two **evils**
let
let it all **hang** out
let off **steam**
let **rip**
let sleeping **dogs** lie
let someone **stew**
let someone **stew** in their own
   juice
let the **cat** out of the bag
let the cobbler stick to his **last**
let the **genie** out of the bottle

let the **side** down
let your **guard** down
let your **hair** down
letter
a dead **letter**
the **letter** of the law
a **red** letter day
to the **letter**
level
a level **playing field**
level the **playing field**
on the **level**
licence
a **licence** to print money
license: see **licence**
lick
lick someone's **arse**
lick someone's **boots**
lick someone's shoes: see **boots**
lick something into **shape**
lick your chops: see **lips**
lick your **lips**
lick your **wounds**
lid
blow the **lid** off
flip your lid
keep the **lid** on something
lift the **lid** off
put the **lid** on something
put the tin **lid** on something
take the **lid** off
lie
let sleeping **dogs** lie
lie at the **bottom** of something
the lie of the **land**
lie through your **teeth**
live a **lie**
a living **lie**
nail a **lie**
therein lies the **rub**
a white **lie**
you have made your **bed** and will
    have to lie on it
life
big as life: see **large**
bigger than life: see **larger**
can't do something to save your
    life
fight for your **life**
frighten the **life** out of someone
get a **life**
it's a **dog**'s life
large as life
larger than life
the **life** and soul of the party
life is a bowl of cherries
the **life** of the party
live the **life** of Riley
a new **lease** of life
a new **lease** on life
put your **life** in someone's hands
risk **life** and limb
scare the **life** out of someone
shelf life
take your **life** in your hands
to within an **inch** of your life
variety is the spice of life
your **life** is in someone's hands
lift
lift the **lid** off

lift the **roof**
not lift a **finger**
light
give the green **light**
hide your light under a **bushel**
in the cold **light** of day
a leading **light**
light a **fire** under someone
light as a feather
the **light** at the end of the
    tunnel
light dawns
light the blue **touch paper**
light the **fuse**
light the **touch paper**
out like a **light**
see the **light**
see the **light** of day
lightning
lightning does not strike twice
a **lightning** rod for something
like greased **lightning**
like **lightning**
quick as lightning
lights
the **lights** are on but nobody is at
    home
like
like it or **lump** it
lily
gild the **lily**
limb
on a **limb**
out on a **limb**
risk **life** and limb
tear someone **limb** from limb
limit
the **sky**'s the limit
limits
off **limits**
line
all along the **line**
all the way down the **line**
along the **line**
be on the **line**
the bottom **line**
cross the **line**
down the **line**
draw a **line** under something
draw the **line**
the **end** of the line
a fine **line**
get a **line** on someone
have a **line** on someone
hook, line, and sinker
in the firing **line**
in the front **line**
in the **line** of fire
lay it on the **line**
lay something on the **line**
line your **pockets**
a narrow **line**
not your **line** of country
on **line**
on the front **line**
out of **line**
out of the firing **line**
put something on the **line**
put your ass on the **line**
put your neck on the **line**

shoot a **line**
sign on the dotted **line**
sign on the **line**
step out of **line**
a thin **line**
toe the **line**
way out of **line**
linen
dirty linen
wash your **dirty** linen in public
lines
along the right **lines**
the **battle** lines are drawn
get your lines **crossed**
on the right **lines**
read between the **lines**
lining
every cloud has a **silver** lining
a **silver** lining
link
a weak **link**
a weak **link** in the chain
lion
Daniel in the **lion**'s den
fight like a **lion**
the **lion**'s share
put your head into the **lion**'s
    mouth
walk into the **lion**'s den
lions
throw someone to the **lions**
lip
button your **lip**
give **lip** service to something
pay **lip** service to something
a stiff upper **lip**
there is many a **slip** twixt cup
    and lip
lips
lick your **lips**
on someone's **lips**
read someone's **lips**
seal someone's **lips**
someone's **lips** are sealed
list
a **hit** list
a **laundry** list
a **shopping** list
litmus
a **litmus** test
little
great **oaks** from little acorns
    grow
a little **bird** told me
little **love** lost
a little **tin** god
twist someone around your little
    finger
wrap someone around your little
    finger
live
live a **lie**
live and breathe something
live from **hand** to mouth
live **hand** to mouth
live high on the **hog**
live in a **fool**'s paradise
live in each other's **pockets**
live like a **king**
live off the **backs** of someone

live on borrowed **time**
live on your nerve ends: see
  nerves
live on your **nerves**
live the **life** of Riley
live to tell the **tale**
a live **wire**
people who live in **glass** houses
  shouldn't throw stones
lives
have nine **lives**
how the other **half** lives
living
beat the living **daylights** out of
  someone
a living **death**
a living **hell**
a living **lie**
scare the living **daylights** out of
  someone
load
a load off your **mind**
load the **dice** against someone
loaded
loaded for **bear**
play with a loaded **deck**
loaf
half a **loaf** is better than none
lock
lock **horns**
lock, stock, and barrel
locker
one **shot** in your locker
log
easy as falling off a **log**
simple as falling off a **log**
loggerheads
at **loggerheads**
loins
gird your **loins**
lone
a lone voice in the **wilderness**
a lone **wolf**
plough a lone **furrow**
lonely
plough a lonely **furrow**
long
by a long **chalk**
by a long **shot**
go back a long **way**
honest as the day is long
in something for the long **haul**
long as your arm
a long **face**
a long **haul**
long in the **tooth**
long on one thing and short on
  another
a long **shot**
not long for this **world**
over the long **haul**
to cut a long **story** short
to make a long **story** short
your long **suit**
longer
a longer **leash**
look
a black **look**
a dirty **look**
a filthy **look**

look after **number** one
look a **gift horse** in the mouth
look a million **dollars**
look **daggers** at someone
look down your **nose** at
  something
look like a drowned **rat**
look like something the **cat**
  dragged in
look on the bright **side**
look out for **number** one
look someone in the **eye**
look someone in the eyes: see **eye**
look someone in the **face**
look the other **way**
look the **part**
look to your **laurels**
look what the **cat's** dragged in
make someone look **small**
looked
have never **looked** back
looking
like looking for a **needle** in a
  haystack
loop
knock someone for a **loop**
throw someone for a **loop**
loose
all **hell** breaks loose
at a loose **end**
at loose ends: see **end**
cut **loose**
hang **loose**
have a **screw** loose
a loose **cannon**
loose **ends**
on the **loose**
play **fast** and loose
loosen
loosen the **purse** strings
lorry
off the **back** of a lorry
lose
lose **face**
lose **ground**
lose **heart**
lose **sight** of something
lose the **battle**, win the war
lose **track** of someone
lose your **cool**
lose your **edge**
lose your **grip**
lose your **head**
lose your **heart**
lose your **marbles**
lose your **rag**
lose your **shirt**
not lose any **sleep** over
  something
what you lose on the **swings** you
  gain on the roundabouts
win the **battle**, lose the war
losing
fight a losing **battle**
loss
at a **loss**
at a loss for **words**
a dead **loss**
losses
cut your **losses**

lost
little **love** lost
lost for **words**
lost in the **shuffle**
make up lost **ground**
no **love** lost
lot
all over the **lot**
cast your **lot** with someone
get a lot of **stick**
have a lot of **irons** in the fire
have a lot on your **plate**
throw in your **lot** with someone
loud
loud and clear
louder
actions speak louder than words
love
all's **fair** in love and war
cupboard love
for **love** nor money
a **labour** of love
little **love** lost
the love of money is the **root** of
  all evil
no **love** lost
low
at a low **ebb**
hunt **high** and low for something
keep a low **profile**
search **high** and low for
  something
take the low **road**
lower
lower your **guard**
lowest
at your lowest **ebb**
luck
be **pot** luck
down on your **luck**
the **luck** of the draw
take **pot** luck
lucky
strike **lucky**
lull
the lull before the **storm**
lump
bring a **lump** to your throat
have to **lump** it
like it or **lump** it
a **lump** in your throat
lunch
out to **lunch**
there's no such thing as a free
  lunch
lurch
leave someone in the **lurch**
luxury
in the **lap** of luxury
lying
not take something **lying** down
mackerel
a **sprat** to catch a mackerel
mad
don't get mad, get **even**
mad as a hatter
mad as a hornet
made
they broke the **mould** when they
  made someone

you have made your **bed** and will
have to lie on it
main
an eye for the main **chance**
the main **chance**
make
cannot make **head** or tail of
something
empty **vessels** make the most
noise
empty **vessels** make the most
sound
kiss and make up
know how many **beans** make five
make a **beeline** for something
make a big **play** of something
make a clean **breast** of something
make a clean **sweep**
make a **dent** in something
make a **face**
make a **hit**
make a **killing**
make a **mark**
make a **meal** of something
make a **monkey** out of someone
make a **mountain** out of a
molehill
make a **name** for yourself
make a **pig** of yourself
make a **pig**'s ear of something
make a **pitch**
make a **play** for
make a **production** of something
make a **rod** for your own back
make a **song** and dance about
something
make a **splash**
make **bricks** without straw
make **ends** meet
make **eyes** at someone
make great **play** of something
make **hay**
make **hay** while the sun shines
make **headway**
make heavy **weather** of
something
make **mincemeat** of someone
make my **day**
make no **bones** about something
make **noises**
make **sheep**'s eyes
make someone feel **small**
make someone look **small**
make someone's **day**
make the **grade**
make the right **noises**
make **tracks**
make up lost **ground**
make your **blood** boil
make your **blood** freeze
make your **blood** run cold
make your **flesh** crawl
make your **flesh** creep
make your **hair** curl
make your **hair** stand on end
make your **mark**
make your **mouth** water
make yourself at **home**
make your **skin** crawl
make your **toes** curl

make **waves**
one **swallow** doesn't make a
summer
to make a long **story** short
you can lead a **horse** to water but
you can't make him drink
you can't make an **omelette**
without breaking eggs
you can't make a **silk** purse out
of a sow's ear
man
a drowning man will clutch at a
straw: see **straws**
every man for himself and the
devil take the hindmost
every man has his **price**
a **hatchet** man
the man in the **street**
a man of **straw**
the man on the Clapham
omnibus
no good to man or **beast**
no use to man or **beast**
a one-man **band**
one man's **meat** is another man's
poison
the other man's **grass** is always
greener
a **straw** man
you can't keep a **good** man down
your **right**-hand man
manger
dog-in-the-manger
map
on the **map**
marbles
have all your **marbles**
lose your **marbles**
pick up your **marbles** and go
home
march
march to a different drummer
march to a different tune
march to the beat of a different
drummer
steal a **march**
marching
marching **orders**
mark
a black **mark**
first off the **mark**
get off the **mark**
hit the **mark**
leave a **mark**
leave your **mark**
make a **mark**
make your **mark**
mark **time**
off the **mark**
on the **mark**
overshoot the **mark**
overstep the **mark**
a **question** mark
quick off the **mark**
slow off the **mark**
up to the **mark**
wide of the **mark**
market
a cattle **market**
in the **market** for something

a meat **market**
marrow
chilled to the **marrow**
frozen to the **marrow**
to the **marrow**
mast
nail your **colours** to the mast
masters
not serve two **masters**
mat
go to the **mat**
match
meet your **match**
a shouting **match**
the whole shooting **match**
matter
mind over matter
McCoy
the real **McCoy**
meal
make a **meal** of something
a **meal** ticket
a square **meal**
mean
mean **business**
mean **curtains**
meaning
not know the **meaning** of the
word
means
by fair **means** or foul
measure
for good **measure**
have the **measure** of someone
meat
dead **meat**
meat and drink to someone
the meat in the **sandwich**
a meat **market**
one man's **meat** is another man's
poison
medicine
give someone a dose of their own
medicine
give someone a taste of their own
medicine
meet
make **ends** meet
meet someone **face** to face
meet someone **halfway**
meet someone's eye: see **eyes**
meet someone's **eyes**
meet your **match**
meet your **Waterloo**
never the **twain** shall meet
there's less to something than
meets the **eye**
there's more to something than
meets the **eye**
melt
butter wouldn't melt in your
mouth
melting
in the **melting pot**
men
dead men's **shoes**
dead men tell no **tales**
the men in grey **suits**
the men in **suits**
separate the **men** from the boys

sort out the **men** from the boys

mend
mend **fences**
mend your **ways**

mended
least said, soonest mended

merry
lead you a merry chase: see
dance
lead you a merry **dance**
play merry **hell**
play merry **hell** with something
there'll be merry **hell** to pay

mess
a mess of **pottage**

messenger
shoot the **messenger**

mice
when the **cat**'s away, the mice
will play

mick
take the mick: see **mickey**

mickey
take the **mickey**

middle
in the **middle** of nowhere
out in the **middle** of nowhere
the **piggy** in the middle
play both **ends** against the middle

middle-of-the-road
middle-of-the-road

midnight
burn the **midnight** oil

midstream
change horses in **midstream**
switch horses in **midstream**

mile
give someone an **inch** and they'll
take a mile
go the extra **mile**
a **mile** away
a **mile** off
run a **mile**

miles
miles away

milk
it's no use crying over spilled
milk
the land of **milk** and honey
milk and honey
milk and water

mill
go through the **mill**
grist for the mill
grist to the mill
put through the **mill**
run-of-the-**mill**

million
a chance in a **million**
feel like a million **dollars**
look a million **dollars**
one in a **million**
a one in a **million** chance

millstone
a **millstone** around your neck

mince
not mince your **words**
thick as mince

mincemeat
make **mincemeat** of someone

mind
bear something in **mind**
blow your **mind**
cross your **mind**
get your mind around something:
see **head**
give someone a piece of your
mind
have a one-track **mind**
in your **mind**'s eye
in your right **mind**
keep something in **mind**
a load off your **mind**
the **mind** boggles
mind over matter
mind your **p**'s and **q**'s
out of **sight**, out of mind
out of your **mind**
slip your **mind**
a weight off your **mind**

minds
in two **minds**
of two **minds**

mirrors
smoke and mirrors

misery
put someone out of their **misery**
put something out of its **misery**

miss
hit and miss
hit or miss
miss a **beat**
miss the boat
miss the bus
not miss a **trick**

mixed
a mixed **bag**

mockers
put the **mockers** on something

Mohammed
if Mohammed will not go to the
mountain, the mountain must
go to Mohammed

mold: see **mould**

molehill
make a **mountain** out of a
molehill

moment
in the **heat** of the moment
on the **spur** of the moment

Monday
a Monday morning **quarterback**

money
the **colour** of someone's money
a **fool** and his money are soon
parted
for **love** nor money
give someone a **run** for their
money
have **money** to burn
a **licence** to print money
the love of money is the **root** of
all evil
money for jam
money for old rope
money is the **root** of all evil
money talks
put your **money** where your
mouth is
right on the **money**

the smart **money**
spend **money** like water
throw good **money** after bad
throw **money** at someone
throw **money** at something

monkey
cold enough to freeze the balls off
a **brass** monkey
get the **monkey** off your back
have a **monkey** on your back
make a **monkey** out of someone
monkey business
not give a **monkey**'s
the **organ** grinder's monkey
throw a monkey **wrench** into the
works

monkeys
a cartload of **monkeys**
if you pay **peanuts**, you get
monkeys

monte
the full monte: see **monty**

month
flavour of the month
a **month** of Sundays

monty
the full **monty**

moon
ask for the **moon**
bay at the **moon**
cry for the **moon**
howl at the **moon**
once in a blue **moon**
over the **moon**
promise the **moon**
reach for the moon: see **stars**

moral
the moral high **ground**

morning
a Monday morning **quarterback**

moss
gather moss: see **stone**
a rolling **stone** gathers no moss

moth
like a **moth** to a flame

motion
set the **wheels** in motion

motions
go through the **motions**

mould
break the **mould**
they broke the **mould** when they
made someone

mountain
if Mohammed will not go to the
mountain, the mountain must
go to Mohammed
make a **mountain** out of a
molehill
a **mountain** to climb

mountains
move **mountains**

mouse
cat and mouse
a game of **cat** and mouse
poor as a church mouse
quiet as a mouse

mouth
all **mouth** and no trousers
all **mouth** and trousers

born with a **silver** spoon in your
   mouth
butter wouldn't melt in your
   mouth
down in the **mouth**
foam at the **mouth**
from the **horse**'s mouth
froth at the **mouth**
hand-to-mouth
laugh out of the other side of
   your **mouth**
leave a bad **taste** in your mouth
live from **hand** to mouth
live **hand** to mouth
look a **gift horse** in the mouth
make your **mouth** water
a **plum** in your mouth
put **words** into someone's mouth
put your **foot** in your mouth
put your head into the **lion**'s
   mouth
put your **money** where your
   mouth is
shoot your **mouth** off
speak out of both sides of your
   mouth
take the **words** out of someone's
   mouth
talk out of both sides of your
   mouth
your **heart** is in your mouth
move
move **heaven** and earth
move in for the **kill**
move **mountains**
move the **goalposts**
move up in the **world**
movers
the **movers** and shakers
much
much **ado** about nothing
not much **cop**
muck
common as muck
happy as a pig in muck
mud
clear as mud
drag someone through the mud
mud sticks
sling mud
a stick-in-the-**mud**
throw mud
your **name** is mud
muddy
muddy the **waters**
mule
stubborn as a mule
murder
get away with **murder**
scream bloody **murder**
scream blue **murder**
muscle
flex your muscle: see **muscles**
muscles
flex your **muscles**
music
face the **music**
music to your ears
mustard
keen as mustard

not cut the **mustard**
muster
pass **muster**
mutton
dead as mutton
mutton dressed as lamb
nail
another **nail** in the coffin
fight **tooth** and nail
the final **nail** in the coffin
hit it on the **nail**
hit the **nail** on the head
the last **nail** in the coffin
like trying to nail **Jell-O** to the
   wall
nail a **lie**
nail someone to the **wall**
nail your **colours** to the mast
on the **nail**
nails
hard as nails
tough as nails
naked
the naked **eye**
name
make a **name** for yourself
the name in the **frame**
the **name** of the game
a **name** to conjure with
not have a cent to your **name**
not have a penny to your **name**
take someone's **name** in vain
your **name** is mud
names
call someone **names**
napping
catch someone **napping**
narrow
a narrow **line**
the **straight** and narrow
nasty
a nasty piece of **work**
nature
the **nature** of the beast
navel
contemplate your **navel**
gaze at your **navel**
navel-contemplation
navel-contemplation
navel-gazing
navel-gazing
near
near and dear to your **heart**
near the **knuckle**
near to the **bone**
so **near** and yet so far
neck
breathe down someone's **neck**
dead from the **neck** up
get it in the **neck**
a **millstone** around your neck
neck and neck
a **pain** in the neck
put your neck on the **block**
put your neck on the **line**
risk your **neck**
stick your **neck** out
up to your **neck**
wring someone's **neck**
your **neck** of the woods

need
need something like a **hole** in the
   head
need your **wits** about you
needle
like looking for a **needle** in a
   haystack
needles
on **pins** and needles
sit on **pins** and needles
nellie: see **nelly**
nelly
not on your **nelly**
nerve
hit a **nerve**
live on your nerve ends: see
   nerves
strike a raw **nerve**
touch a **nerve**
nerves
a bag of **nerves**
a battle of **nerves**
a bundle of **nerves**
get on someone's **nerves**
live on your **nerves**
a war of **nerves**
nest
feather your **nest**
fly the **nest**
foul your own **nest**
leave the **nest**
a **nest** egg
stir up a **hornet**'s nest
net
cast a wide **net**
cast the **net** wider
fall through the **net**
slip through the **net**
nettle
grasp the **nettle**
new
break a new **path**
break new **ground**
good as new
a new **ball** game
new **blood**
a new **broom**
a new **broom** sweeps clean
a new **lease** of life
a new **lease** on life
new to the **game**
pastures new
turn over a new **leaf**
you can't teach an old **dog** new
   tricks
Newcastle
coals to Newcastle
news
be **news** to someone
no **news** is good news
nice
nice as pie
nice try but no **cigar**
niche
carve a **niche**
nick
in the **nick** of time
nickel
nickel and dime
a wooden **nickel**

nickels
not have two nickels to **rub**
 together
night
call it a night: see **day**
a **night** owl
nine
have nine **lives**
on **cloud** nine
a **stitch** in time saves nine
the whole nine **yards**
nine-day
a nine-day **wonder**
ninepins
fall like **ninepins**
nines
dress to the **nines**
nineteen
talk **nineteen** to the dozen
nip
nip and tuck
nip something in the **bud**
nits
pick **nits**
no-holds-barred
no-**holds**-barred
nobody
like nobody's **business**
nod
get the **nod**
give someone the **nod**
a **nod** and a wink
on the **nod**
nodding
a nodding **acquaintance**
noise
empty **vessels** make the most
 noise
noises
make **noises**
make the right **noises**
nook
every nook and cranny: see
 nooks
nooks
the **nooks** and crannies
noose
put your **head** in a noose
stick your **head** in a noose
nose
bloody someone's **nose**
cut off your **nose** to spite your
 face
follow your **nose**
from under your **nose**
get a bloody **nose**
get up someone's **nose**
give someone a bloody **nose**
it's no **skin** off my nose
keep your **nose** clean
keep your **nose** out of something
keep your **nose** to the grindstone
lead someone by the **nose**
look down your **nose** at
 something
a **nose** for something
not see beyond the end of your
 nose
not see beyond your **nose**
on the **nose**

pay through the **nose** for
 something
plain as the nose on your face
poke your **nose** into something
put someone's **nose** out of joint
rub someone's **nose** in it
rub someone's **nose** in the dirt
stick your **nose** into something
thumb your **nose** at someone
turn up your **nose** at something
under your **nose**
nosey
a nosey **parker**
nosy
a nosy **parker**
nothing
good-for-nothing
much **ado** about nothing
on a **hiding** to nothing
nowhere
from **nowhere**
in the **middle** of nowhere
out in the **middle** of nowhere
out of **nowhere**
nuclear
go **nuclear**
nudge
a **nudge** and a wink
nudge-nudge
nudge-nudge, wink-wink
number
a back **number**
do a **number** on someone
have someone's **number**
look after **number** one
look out for **number** one
someone's **number** is up
numbered
someone's **days** are numbered
numbers
the numbers **game**
nut
do your **nut**
a sledgehammer to crack a **nut**
a tough **nut**
a tough **nut** to crack
nuts
the **nuts** and bolts of something
nutshell
in a **nutshell**
nutty
nutty as a fruitcake
oaks
great **oaks** from little acorns
 grow
oar
put your **oar** in
oars
lean on your **oars**
rest on your **oars**
oats
sow your wild **oats**
ocean
a **drop** in the ocean
odds
at **odds** with someone
at **odds** with something
at **odds** with the world
at **odds** with yourself
pay over the **odds**

odor: see **odour**
odour
in bad **odour**
in good **odour**
off-chance
on the **off-chance**
offer
offer someone a **carrot**
office
do a **land-office** business
off-the-cuff
off-the-**cuff**
oil
burn the **midnight** oil
no **oil** painting
oil and water
oil the **wheels**
pour **oil** on troubled waters
snake oil
a **snake** oil salesman
strike **oil**
ointment
the **fly** in the ointment
old
a **chip** off the old block
a hoary old **chestnut**
money for old rope
old as the hills
an old **chestnut**
an old **flame**
the old **guard**
old habits die **hard**
an old **hand**
old **hat**
the old **school**
the old **school** tie
an old **wives'** tale
open old **wounds**
reopen old **wounds**
settle an old **score**
tough as old boots
up to your old **tricks**
you can't teach an old **dog** new
 tricks
oldest
the oldest **trick** in the book
olive
an **olive** branch
omelet: see **omelette**
omelette
you can't make an **omelette**
 without breaking eggs
omnibus
the man on the Clapham
 omnibus
once
once **bitten**
once **bitten**, twice shy
once in a blue **moon**
ride two **horses** at once
once-over
give someone the **once-over**
one
at one **sitting**
back at **square** one
back to **square** one
be **one** up on someone
from **square** one
get **one** over on someone
get **one** up on someone

got it in **one**
in one **sitting**
look after **number** one
look out for **number** one
one in a **million**
a one in a **million** chance
one in the **eye** for someone
one of the **boys**
one of the **lads**
pull a **fast** one
pull the other one
pull the other one, it's got bells
  on it
put **one** over on someone
six of one and half a dozen of the
  other
one-day
  a one-day **wonder**
one-horse
  a one-**horse** race
  a one-**horse** town
one-man
  a one-man **band**
one-track
  have a one-track **mind**
one-way
  a one-way **ticket**
one-woman
  a one-woman **band**
onions
  know your **onions**
open
  as one **door** closes, another one
    opens
  be **wide** open
  blow something **wide** open
  the **floodgates** open
  the **heavens** open
  keep your **eyes** open
  lay yourself **wide** open
  leave yourself **wide** open
  open and shut
  an open **book**
  open old **wounds**
  open **season**
  open someone's **eyes**
  open the **eyes** of someone
  open the **floodgates**
  open your **eyes**
  open your **heart**
  push at an open **door**
  with open **arms**
opposite
  opposite sides of the same **coin**
oranges
  apples and oranges
order
  get your **house** in order
  in **apple-pie** order
  the **order** of the day
  the **pecking** order
  put your **house** in order
  a tall **order**
ordered
  just what the **doctor** ordered
orders
  marching **orders**
  under **starter's** orders
organ
  the **organ** grinder's monkey

organize
  couldn't organize a piss-up in a
    brewery
OTT
  OTT: see **top**
out-and-out
  out-and-out
outs
  the **ins** and outs
over
  over the **hill**
  over the **hump**
  over the **moon**
  over the **top**
overdrive
  be in **overdrive**
  go into **overdrive**
over-egg
  over-egg the **pudding**
overplay
  overplay your **hand**
overshoot
  overshoot the **mark**
overstep
  overstep the **mark**
overtime
  work **overtime**
overturn
  overturn the **applecart**
owl
  a **night** owl
own
  hold your **own**
  off your own **bat**
  on your own **hook**
  an own **goal**
  under your own **steam**
ox
  strong as an ox
oyster
  the **world** is your oyster
p
  mind your **p's** and q's
  watch your **p's** and q's
pace
  at a **snail's** pace
  can't stand the **pace**
  can't take the **pace**
  set the **pace**
paces
  put someone through their **paces**
pack
  ahead of the **pack**
  the **joker** in the pack
  pack a **punch**
  pack your **bags**
packed
  packed like **sardines**
packing
  send someone packing
paddle
  paddle your own **canoe**
  up the **creek** without a paddle
paddock
  kangaroos in your top paddock
page
  on the same **page**
  turn the **page**
paid
  put **paid** to something

pain
  a **pain** in the arse
  a **pain** in the ass
  a **pain** in the neck
pains
  growing **pains**
paint
  fresh as paint
  paint someone into a **corner**
  paint the **town** red
  watch **paint** dry
painted
  not as **black** as you are painted
painting
  no **oil** painting
pair
  a safe pair of **hands**
  show a clean pair of **heels**
pale
  beyond the **pale**
palm
  grease someone's **palm**
  have someone eating out of the
    palm of your **hand**
  in the palm of your **hand**
pan
  down the pan
  flash in the pan
  out of the **frying pan** into the
    fire
pancake
  flat as a pancake
Pandora
  a **Pandora's** box
pants
  beat the **pants** off someone
  bore the **pants** off someone
  catch someone with their **pants**
    down
  charm the **pants** off someone
  fly by the **seat** of your pants
  keep your pants on: see **shirt**
  scare the **pants** off someone
  wear the pants
paper
  can't fight your way out of a
    paper bag
  a clean **sheet** of paper
  light the blue **touch paper**
  not worth the **paper** it's written
    on
  on **paper**
  paper over the **cracks**
  a paper **pusher**
  a **paper** tiger
  a **paper** trail
papers
  walking **papers**
par
  below **par**
  not up to **par**
  par for the course
  under **par**
parade
  rain on someone's **parade**
paradise
  live in a **fool's** paradise
parapet
  keep your **head** below the
    parapet

put your **head** above the parapet
parcel
  part and parcel
parker
  a nosey **parker**
parrot
  parrot fashion
  sick as a parrot
part
  look the **part**
  part and parcel
  part of the **furniture**
  take someone's **part**
  take something in good **part**
parted
  a **fool** and his money are soon
    parted
party
  bring something to the **party**
  the **life** and soul of the party
  the **life** of the party
pass
  give someone the **flick** pass
  pass **muster**
  pass the **baton**
  pass the **buck**
  pass the **hat**
  pass the **hat** around
  pass your sell-by **date**
  sell the **pass**
passage
  a **bird** of passage
passing
  a passing **acquaintance**
past
  be getting **past** it
  be **past** it
  first past the **post**
  past your sell-by **date**
  wouldn't put it **past** someone
pasture
  put someone out to **pasture**
pastures
  fresh **pastures**
  greener **pastures**
  pastures new
pat
  a **pat** on the back
  pat someone on the back
  stand **pat**
patch
  not a **patch** on someone
path
  beat a path to someone's **door**
  break a new **path**
  cross someone's **path**
  lead someone down the **garden**
    path
  lead someone up the **garden** path
  off the beaten path: see **track**
  smooth the path
path-breaking
  path-breaking
Paul
  rob **Peter** to pay Paul
pave
  pave the **way**
paved
  the road to **hell** is paved with
    good intentions

pay
  he who pays the **piper** calls the
    tune
  hit **pay** dirt
  if you pay **peanuts**, you get
    monkeys
  pay **dividends**
  pay **lip** service to something
  pay over the **odds**
  pay someone back in their own
    coin
  pay through the **nose** for
    something
  rob **Peter** to pay Paul
  strike **pay** dirt
  there'll be **hell** to pay
  there'll be merry **hell** to pay
paydirt
  hit paydirt: see **pay dirt**
  strike paydirt: see **pay dirt**
peanuts
  if you pay **peanuts**, you get
    monkeys
pearls
  cast **pearls** before swine
  pearls of wisdom
peas
  alike as two **peas** in a pod
  like two **peas** in a pod
pebble
  not the only **pebble** on the beach
pecker
  keep your **pecker** up
pecking
  the **pecking** order
pedestal
  be on a **pedestal**
  knock someone off their **pedestal**
  put someone on a **pedestal**
peel
  slip on a **banana** peel
peeled
  keep your **eyes** peeled
peg
  bring someone down a **peg** or
    two
  a **peg** on which to hang
    something
  a square **peg** in a round hole
  take someone down a **peg** or two
pegged
  have someone **pegged**
pen
  a pen **pusher**
  a **slip** of the pen
pencil
  have **lead** in your pencil
  a pencil **pusher**
  put **lead** in your pencil
pennies
  not have two pennies to **rub**
    together
  pinch **pennies**
penn'orth
  your two **penn'orth**
penny
  in for a **penny**, in for a pound
  not have a penny to your **name**
  the **penny** drops
  ten a **penny**

  turn up like a bad **penny**
  two a **penny**
penny-wise
  penny-wise and pound-foolish
people
  drive a **wedge** between people
  people who live in **glass** houses
    shouldn't throw stones
perch
  fall off the **perch**
  fall off your **perch**
  knock you off your **perch**
petard
  hoist by your own **petard**
Peter
  rob **Peter** to pay Paul
phrase
  to coin a **phrase**
pick
  have a **bone** to pick with
    someone
  pick **holes** in something
  pick **nits**
  pick someone's brain: see **brains**
  pick someone's **brains**
  pick up **steam**
  pick up the **ball** and run
  pick up the **baton**
  pick up the **gauntlet**
  pick up the **pieces**
  pick up the **slack**
  pick up the **tab**
  pick up your **marbles** and go
    home
picnic
  be no **picnic**
  one sandwich **short** of a picnic
picture
  get the **picture**
  in the **picture**
  keep someone in the **picture**
  out of the **picture**
  put someone in the **picture**
pie
  American as apple pie
  easy as pie
  eat humble **pie**
  have a **finger** in every pie
  have a **finger** in the pie
  in **apple-pie** order
  nice as pie
  pie in the sky
  sweet as pie
piece
  all of a **piece**
  give someone a piece of your
    mind
  a nasty piece of **work**
  a **piece** of cake
  a **piece** of piss
  a piece of the **action**
  say your **piece**
  the **villain** of the piece
pieces
  go to **pieces**
  pick up the **pieces**
  shot to **pieces**
pig
  eat like a **pig**
  a guinea **pig**

happy as a pig in muck
like a greased pig
make a pig of yourself
make a pig's ear of something
a pig in a poke
sick as a pig
squeal like a stuck pig
sweat like a pig
pigeon
be someone's pigeon
pigeons
put the cat among the
    pigeons
set the cat among the pigeons
piggy
the piggy in the middle
pigs
pigs might fly
when pigs fly
pike
come down the pike
pikestaff
plain as a pikestaff
pile
the bottom of the pile
the top of the pile
pill
a bitter pill to swallow
sugar-coat the pill
sugar the pill
swallow a bitter pill
sweeten the pill
pillar
from pillar to post
a pillar of strength: see tower
pillar to post
pilot
on automatic pilot
pin
pin back your ears
pin someone's ears back
pinch
at a pinch
feel the pinch
in a pinch
pinch pennies
take something with a pinch of
    salt
pink
in the pink
tickled pink
pins
for two pins
on pins and needles
sit on pins and needles
pint
a quart into a pint pot
pip
pip someone at the post
pipe
put that in your pipe and smoke
    it
pipeline
in the pipeline
piper
he who pays the piper calls the
    tune
piss
a piece of piss
take the piss

piss-up
couldn't organize a piss-up in a
    brewery
pit
pit your wits against someone
pitch
fever pitch
make a pitch
pitch camp
queer someone's pitch
place
between a rock and a hard place
fall into place
not a hair out of place
a place in the sun
put someone in their place
take second place
your heart is in the right place
places
go places
in high places
plague
avoid something like the plague
plain
plain as a pikestaff
plain as day
plain as the nose on your face
plain sailing
plan
a game plan
plank
walk the plank
planks
thick as two planks
thick as two short planks
plant
plant the seeds of something
plate
hand someone something on a
    plate
have a lot on your plate
have enough on your plate
have your plate full
platter
on a platter
on a silver platter
play
child's play
make a big play of something
make a play for
make great play of something
not play the game
not play with a full deck
play a straight bat
play ball
play both ends against the middle
play ducks and drakes with
    someone
play fast and loose
play for time
play games
play God
play gooseberry
play hardball
play hard to get
play hell
play hell with something
play into someone's hands
play it by ear
play it safe

play merry hell
play merry hell with something
play possum
play safe
play second fiddle
play someone at their own game
play someone for a fool
play the field
play the game
play things by the book
play to the gallery
play with a loaded deck
play with a stacked deck
play with fire
play your ace
play your cards close to the vest
play your cards close to your
    chest
play your cards right
play your trump card
the state of play
when the cat's away, the mice
    will play
playing
a level playing field
level the playing field
pleased
pleased as punch
plot
the plot thickens
plough
plough a lonely furrow
ploughshares
beat swords into ploughshares
turn swords into ploughshares
plowshares
beat swords into plowshares
turn swords into plowshares
pluck
pluck something from the air
plug
pull the plug on something
plum
a plum in your mouth
plumb
plumb the depths
plunge
take the plunge
poacher
poacher turned gamekeeper
pocket
burn a hole in your pocket
dig deep into your pocket
dip into your pocket
in someone's pocket
out of pocket
pockets
line your pockets
live in each other's pockets
pod
alike as two peas in a pod
like two peas in a pod
point
boiling point
not to put too fine a point on it
point the finger at someone
a sore point
a sticking point
points
brownie points

score **points**
poison
  one man's **meat** is another man's
    poison
poisoned
  a poisoned **chalice**
poke
  a **pig** in a poke
  poke your **nose** into something
pole
  the greasy **pole**
  pole position
  wouldn't touch something with a
    barge **pole**
  wouldn't touch something with a
    ten-foot **pole**
poles
  poles apart
polish
  spit and polish
poll
  poll position: see **pole**
pond
  a big **fish** in a small pond
  a big frog in a small pond: see
    fish
pony
  a **dog** and pony show
poor
  poor as a church mouse
  take a poor **view** of something
pop
  pop your **clogs**
port
  a **port** in a storm
position
  pole position
possum
  play **possum**
post
  deaf as a post
  first past the **post**
  from **pillar** to post
  pillar to post
  pip someone at the **post**
postage
  on the **back** of a postage stamp
posted
  keep someone **posted**
pot
  be **pot luck**
  go to **pot**
  in the **melting pot**
  keep the **pot** boiling
  the **pot** calling the kettle black
  a pot of **gold**
  the pot of gold at the end of the
    rainbow
  a **quart** into a pint pot
  shit or get off the **pot**
  take **pot luck**
  a watched **pot** never boils
potato
  a **couch** potato
  drop something like a hot **potato**
  a hot **potato**
potatoes
  small **potatoes**
potluck
  be potluck: see **pot luck**

take potluck: see **pot luck**
pottage
  a mess of **pottage**
pound
  in for a **penny**, in for a pound
  your **pound** of flesh
pound-foolish
  penny-wise and pound-foolish
pour
  it never rains but it pours: see
    rain
  pour cold **water** on something
  pour **oil** on troubled waters
  pour out your **heart**
powder
  keep your **powder** dry
  sit on a **powder** keg
power
  all **power** to your elbow
  more **power** to your elbow
  the **power** behind the throne
practice: see **practise**
practise
  practise what you preach
praise
  damn with faint **praise**
praises
  sing the **praises** of someone
prawn
  come the raw **prawn**
prayer
  not have a **prayer**
  on a **wing** and a prayer
preach
  practise what you preach
  preach to the **converted**
pregnant
  you can't be half **pregnant**
prepare
  prepare the **ground**
press
  a bad **press**
  a full-court **press**
  a good **press**
  press the right **button**
pretty
  pretty is as pretty does: see
    handsome
  a pretty **kettle** of fish
  sit **pretty**
price
  at any **price**
  at a **price**
  every man has his **price**
  everyone has their **price**
prick
  like a spare **prick** at a
    wedding
  prick the **bubble**
  prick up your **ears**
pricks
  kick against the **pricks**
pride
  swallow your **pride**
prime
  prime the **pump**
print
  the fine **print**
  a **licence** to print money
  the small **print**

prisoners
  take no **prisoners**
problems
  teething problems
production
  make a **production** of something
profile
  a high **profile**
  keep a low **profile**
promise
  promise the **earth**
  promise the **moon**
proof
  the **proof** of the pudding is in the
    eating
prove
  the **exception** that proves the
    rule
providence
  tempt providence: see **fate**
public
  air your **dirty** laundry in public
  do your **dirty** washing in public
  in the public **eye**
  out of the public **eye**
  wash your **dirty** linen in public
pudding
  over-egg the **pudding**
  the **proof** of the pudding is in the
    eating
pull
  not pull your **punches**
  pull a **face**
  pull a **fast** one
  pull a rabbit out of the **hat**
  pull in your **horns**
  pull no **punches**
  pull out all the **stops**
  pull **rank**
  pull someone's **chain**
  pull someone's **chestnuts** out of
    the fire
  pull someone's **leg**
  pull something out of the **air**
  pull something out of the **hat**
  pull **strings**
  pull the other one
  pull the other one, it's got bells
    on it
  pull the **plug** on something
  pull the **rug** from under you
  pull the **rug** from under your feet
  pull the **strings**
  pull the **wool** over someone's
    eyes
  pull your **finger** out
  pull your **hair** out
  pull yourself up by your
    bootstraps
  pull your **socks** up
  pull your **wagons** in a circle
  pull your **weight**
pulling
  like pulling **teeth**
pulp
  beat someone to a **pulp**
pulse
  have your **finger** on the pulse
pump
  prime the **pump**

punch
pack a **punch**
pleased as **punch**
punches
not pull your **punches**
pull no **punches**
roll with the **punches**
punishment
a **glutton** for punishment
pup
sell someone a **pup**
purposes
at cross **purposes**
purse
hold the **purse** strings
loosen the **purse** strings
tighten the **purse** strings
you can't make a **silk** purse out
of a sow's ear
push
at a **push**
get the **push**
give someone the **push**
if **push** comes to shove
push at an open **door**
push the **boat** out
push the right **button**
push up the **daisies**
when **push** comes to shove
pusher
a paper **pusher**
a pencil **pusher**
a pen **pusher**
put
be put through the **wringer**
not put a **foot** wrong
not to put too fine a **point** on it
put a **bomb** under something
put a brave **face** on something
put a brave front on something:
see **face**
put a dampener on something: see
damper
put a **damper** on something
put a **dent** in something
put a **gloss** on something
put a good **face** on something
put a gun to someone's **head**
put all your **eggs** in one basket
put a **sock** in it
put a **spanner** in the works
put a **spoke** in someone's wheel
put down **roots**
put **flesh** on something
put **flesh** on the bones of
something
put hair on the chest: see **hairs**
put **hairs** on your chest
put **lead** in your pencil
put off the **evil** day
put on **airs**
put on **airs** and graces
put **one** over on someone
put out **feelers**
put out of **court**
put **paid** to something
put someone in their **place**
put someone in the **picture**
put someone in the **shade**
put someone off their **stride**

put someone off their **stroke**
put someone off the **scent**
put someone on a **pedestal**
put someone on the **rack**
put someone out of their **misery**
put someone out to **grass**
put someone out to **pasture**
put someone's **back** up
put someone's **nose** out of joint
put someone through **hell**
put someone through their **paces**
put something on **ice**
put something on the **line**
put something out of its **misery**
put something to **bed**
put that in your **pipe** and smoke
it
put the **arm** on someone
put the **boot** in
put the **boot** into someone
put the **cart** before the horse
put the **cat** among the pigeons
put the **finger** on someone
put the **flags** out
put the **frighteners** on someone
put the **genie** back in the bottle
put the **kibosh** on something
put the **knife** in
put the **lid** on something
put the **mockers** on something
put the **record** straight
put the **screws** on someone
put the **skids** under something
put the tin **lid** on something
put the **wind** up someone
put through the **mill**
put **two** and two together
put **words** into someone's mouth
put your **ass** on the **line**
put your **back** into something
put your best **foot** forward
put your **cards** on the table
put your **feet** up
put your **finger** on something
put your **foot** down
put your **foot** in it
put your **foot** in your mouth
put your **head** above the parapet
put your **head** in a noose
put your head into the **lion's**
mouth
put your head on the **block**
put your **heads** together
put your **house** in order
put your **life** in someone's hands
put your **money** where your
mouth is
put your **neck** on the **block**
put your **neck** on the **line**
put your **oar** in
put your **shirt** on something
put your **shoulder** to the wheel
put your thinking **cap** on
wouldn't put it **past** someone
putty
putty in your hands
q
mind your **p's** and **q's**
QT
on the **QT**

quake
quake in your **boots**
quake in your **shoes**
quantity
an unknown **quantity**
quart
a **quart** into a pint pot
quarterback
a Monday morning **quarterback**
queer
in **Queer** Street
queer someone's **pitch**
question
the 64,000 **dollar** question
beg the **question**
a **question** mark
quick
cut someone to the **quick**
no quick **fix**
quick as a flash
quick as a wink
quick as lightning
quick off the **mark**
quids
quids in
quiet
quiet as a lamb
quiet as a mouse
quits
call it **quits**
quote
quote, end quote
quote, unquote
rabbit
like a rabbit caught in the
headlights
pull a rabbit out of the **hat**
race
a one-**horse** race
race against time
the **rat** race
rack
on the **rack**
put someone on the **rack**
rack and ruin
rack your brain: see **brains**
rack your **brains**
rag
lose your **rag**
a red rag to a **bull**
ragged
run someone **ragged**
rags
rags to riches
riches to **rags**
rails
jump the **rails**
off the **rails**
on the **rails**
rain
come **rain** or shine
it never rains but it pours: see
rain
rain on someone's **parade**
rain or shine
right as rain
take a **rain** check
rainbow
at the end of the **rainbow**

the pot of gold at the end of the
  rainbow
rainbows
  chase **rainbows**
raining
  it's raining **cats** and dogs
rainy
  save for a rainy **day**
raise
  not raise a **finger**
  raise **Cain**
  raise **eyebrows**
  raise **hell**
  raise its **head**
  raise someone's **hackles**
  raise something from the **dead**
  raise the **ante**
  raise the **roof**
rake
  rake over the ashes: see **coals**
  rake over the **coals**
  rake someone over the **coals**
  thin as a rake
ram
  ram something down someone's
    throat
ranch
  bet the **ranch**
rank
  break rank: see **ranks**
  pull **rank**
ranks
  break **ranks**
  close **ranks**
ransom
  hold someone to **ransom**
  a king's **ransom**
rap
  rap someone on the **knuckles**
  rap someone's **knuckles**
  take the **rap**
rare
  rare as **hen**'s teeth
  a rare **bird**
rat
  like a rat leaving a sinking **ship**
  look like a drowned **rat**
  the **rat** race
  smell a **rat**
rate
  at a **rate** of knots
rattle
  rattle someone's **cage**
  rattle your **sabre**
rattling
  sabre-rattling
raw
  come the raw **prawn**
  get a raw **deal**
  strike a raw **nerve**
ray
  a **ray** of sunshine
reach
  reach for the moon: see **stars**
  reach for the sky: see **stars**
  reach for the **stars**
  reach **rock** bottom
read
  read between the **lines**
  read someone like a **book**

read someone's **lips**
read the **riot** act
read the **runes**
ready
  rough and ready
real
  the real **McCoy**
reap
  as you sow, so shall you
    reap
  reap the harvest
  reap the whirlwind
  sow the wind and **reap** the
    whirlwind
  you **reap** what you sow
rear
  cover your rear
  rear its **head**
  rear its ugly **head**
rearguard
  fight a **rearguard** action
reason
  without **rhyme** or reason
recharge
  recharge your **batteries**
reckoning
  the **day** of reckoning
record
  go on **record**
  off the **record**
  on the **record**
  put the **record** straight
  set the **record** straight
  a **track** record
red
  bleed red **ink**
  in the **red**
  into the **red**
  not a red **cent**
  not one red **cent**
  out of the **red**
  paint the **town** red
  red as a beet
  red as a beetroot
  a red **flag**
  a red flag before a **bull**
  a red **herring**
  red in **tooth** and claw
  a **red** letter day
  a red rag to a **bull**
  red **tape**
  roll out the red **carpet**
  see **red**
red-handed
  catch someone **red-handed**
reed
  a broken **reed**
regular
  regular as **clockwork**
reign
  a **reign** of terror
rein
  allow someone free **rein**
  give someone free **rein**
  hold someone on a tight **rein**
  keep a tight **rein** on someone
reinvent
  reinvent the **wheel**
reopen
  reopen old **wounds**

reply
  a **dusty** reply
rest
  a **cut** above the rest
  lay to rest the **ghost** of something
  not rest on your **laurels**
  the rest is **history**
  rest on your **oars**
revolving
  the revolving **door**
rhyme
  without **rhyme** or reason
rich
  rich as Croesus
  strike it **rich**
riches
  an **embarrassment** of riches
  rags to riches
  riches to **rags**
riddles
  talk in **riddles**
ride
  a bumpy **ride**
  come along for the **ride**
  an easy **ride**
  a free **ride**
  go along for the **ride**
  ride **herd** on someone
  ride **high**
  ride high in the **saddle**
  ride out the **storm**
  ride **roughshod** over someone
  ride the **crest** of the wave
  ride the **storm**
  ride two **horses** at once
  ride two **horses** at the same time
  a rough **ride**
  take someone for a **ride**
riding
  be riding for a **fall**
right
  along the right **lines**
  give your right **arm**
  in your right **mind**
  left and right
  left, right, and centre
  make the right **noises**
  not right in the **head**
  on the right **lines**
  on the right **track**
  play your **cards** right
  press the right **button**
  right as rain
  the right **hand** doesn't know
    what the left hand is doing
  right off the **bat**
  right on the **button**
  right on the **money**
  right up your **alley**
  right up your **street**
  start off on the right **foot**
  your **heart** is in the right place
right-hand
  your **right**-hand man
  your **right**-hand woman
rights
  bang to **rights**
  dead to **rights**
Riley
  live the **life** of Riley

ring
alarm **bells** ring
the **brass** ring
have a **hollow** ring
ring a **bell**
ring **hollow**
ring off the **hook**
ring someone's **bell**
ring the **changes**
ring **true**
a **three-ring** circus
throw your cap into the ring: see
hat
throw your **hat** into the ring
warning **bells** ring

ringer
a dead **ringer** for someone

rings
run **rings** round someone

ringside
a **ringside** seat
a **ringside** view

riot
read the **riot** act
run **riot**

rip
let **rip**

rise
get a **rise** out of someone
rise from the **dead**
rise to the **bait**
someone's **hackles** rise
take the **rise** out of someone

risk
risk **life** and limb
risk your **neck**

river
sell someone down the **river**

road
down the **road**
the **end** of the road
get the **show** on the road
hit the **road**
keep the **show** on the road
middle-of-the-road
the road to **hell** is paved with
good intentions
take the high **road**
take the low **road**

rob
rob **Peter** to pay Paul
rob the **cradle**

robbery
daylight **robbery**
highway **robbery**

Robinson
before you could **say** Jack
Robinson

rock
at **rock** bottom
between a **rock** and a hard place
hit **rock** bottom
reach **rock** bottom
rock the **boat**
rock you back on your **heels**

rocker
off your **rocker**

rocket
not **rocket** science
a **rocket** scientist

rocks
get your **rocks** off
on the **rocks**

rod
a **lightning** rod for something
make a **rod** for your own back

roll
heads roll
on a **roll**
roll in the **aisles**
roll out the red **carpet**
roll up your **sleeves**
roll with the **punches**

rolling
a rolling **stone**
a rolling **stone** gathers no moss
set the **ball** rolling

Romans
when in **Rome**, do as the Romans
do

Rome
fiddle while **Rome** burns
Rome was not built in a day
when in **Rome**
when in **Rome**, do as the Romans
do

roof
a **cat** on a hot tin roof
go through the **roof**
hit the **roof**
lift the **roof**
raise the **roof**

rooftops
shout something from the
rooftops

room
elbow room
no room to swing a **cat**
not give someone **house** room
a smoke-filled **room**

roost
the chickens come home to **roost**
come home to **roost**
rule the **roost**

root
the love of money is the **root** of
all evil
money is the **root** of all evil
root and branch
take **root**

roots
the **grass** roots
put down **roots**

rope
at the end of your **rope**
give someone enough **rope**
give someone enough **rope** to
hang themselves
money for old rope

ropes
know the **ropes**
learn the **ropes**
on the **ropes**
show someone the **ropes**

rose-colored: see rose-tinted

rose-coloured
rose-coloured glasses: see **rose-
tinted**
rose-coloured spectacles: see
rose-tinted

roses
come up smelling of **roses**
everything is coming up **roses**
not a bed of **roses**
not all **roses**

rose-tinted
rose-tinted glasses
rose-tinted spectacles

rotten
a rotten **apple**

rough
cut up **rough**
a **diamond** in the rough
give someone the rough edge of
your **tongue**
give someone the rough side of
your **tongue**
rough and ready
rough and tumble
a rough **diamond**
rough **edges**
a rough **ride**
take the **rough** with the smooth

roughshod
ride **roughshod** over someone

roulette
Russian **roulette**

round
get your **tongue** round something
go round in **circles**
round the **bend**
round the **clock**
round the **houses**
round the **twist**
run **rings** round someone
run round in **circles**
a square **peg** in a round hole

roundabouts
swings and roundabouts
what you lose on the **swings** you
gain on the roundabouts

row
get your **ducks** in a row
a hard **row** to hoe
not worth a row of **beans**
skid row
a tough **row** to hoe

rub
don't **rub** it in
not have two nickels to **rub**
together
not have two pennies to **rub**
together
rub **elbows** with someone
the **rub** of the green
rub **salt** into the wound
rub **shoulders** with someone
rub someone's **nose** in it
rub someone's **nose** in the dirt
rub someone the wrong **way**
rub someone up the wrong **way**
rub your **hands**
therein lies the **rub**
there's the **rub**

Rubicon
cross the **Rubicon**

rude
a rude **awakening**

ruffle
ruffle someone's **feathers**

ruffled
smooth ruffled **feathers**
rug
pull the **rug** from under you
pull the **rug** from under your feet
snug as a bug in a rug
sweep something under the **rug**
ruin
rack and ruin
rule
divide and rule
the **exception** that proves the
rule
a **rule** of thumb
rule the **roost**
ruled
ruled out of **court**
rules
bend the **rules**
stretch the **rules**
run
cut and run
a dummy **run**
give someone a **run** for their
money
hit a **home** run
make your **blood** run cold
on the **run**
pick up the **ball** and run
run a **mile**
run around in **circles**
run a tight **ship**
run before you can walk
run **deep**
run its **course**
run on **empty**
run out of **gas**
run out of **steam**
run **rings** round someone
run **riot**
run round in **circles**
run someone into the **ground**
run someone **ragged**
run someone to **earth**
run someone to **ground**
run something into the **ground**
run something up the **flagpole**
run the **gauntlet**
run the **show**
run to **seed**
run with the **hare** and hunt with
the hounds
run your **eye** over something
run yourself into the **ground**
still **waters** run deep
take the **ball** and run with it
runaround
get the **runaround**
give someone the **runaround**
runes
read the **runes**
running
hit the **ground** running
in the **running**
out of the **running**
a running **battle**
take a running **jump**
up and running
run-of-the-mill
run-of-the-**mill**

rush
fools rush in
fools rush in where angels fear to
tread
get the **bum**'s rush
give someone the **bum**'s rush
a **rush** of blood
a **rush** of blood to the head
rushed
rushed off your **feet**
Russian
Russian **roulette**
saber: see **sabre**
sabre
rattle your **sabre**
sabre-rattling
sabre-rattling
sack
hit the sack
sacred
a sacred **cow**
sacrificed
sacrificed on the **altar** of
something
saddle
in the **saddle**
ride high in the **saddle**
safe
in safe **hands**
play it **safe**
play **safe**
safe as houses
a safe **bet**
safe **hands**
a safe pair of **hands**
to be on the safe **side**
said
easier said than done
least said, soonest mended
sail
sail close to the **wind**
sail under false **colours**
take the **wind** out of someone's
sail
sailing
clear **sailing**
plain **sailing**
smooth **sailing**
sails
take the **wind** out of someone's
sails
trim your **sails**
salad
your **salad** days
salesman
a **snake** oil salesman
saloon
drinking in the last chance
saloon
the last chance **saloon**
salt
rub **salt** into the wound
the **salt** of the earth
take something with a grain of
salt
take something with a pinch of
salt
worth their **salt**
sand
build something on **sand**

bury your **head** in the sand
sandboy
happy as a sandboy
sands
shifting **sands**
sandwich
the filling in the **sandwich**
the meat in the **sandwich**
one sandwich **short** of a picnic
sardines
packed like **sardines**
sauce
what's **sauce** for the goose is
sauce for the gander
save
can't do something to save your
life
save **face**
save for a rainy **day**
save someone's ass
save someone's **bacon**
save someone's **blushes**
save someone's butt
save your own **skin**
save your **skin**
a **stitch** in time saves nine
saved
saved by the **bell**
saving
a saving **grace**
sawdust
spit and sawdust
say
before you could **say** Jack
Robinson
before you could **say** knife
say **goodbye** to something
say your **piece**
wouldn't say boo to a **goose**
scalded
like a scalded **cat**
scales
the **scales** fall from your eyes
tip the scales
scarce
scarce as **hen**'s teeth
scare
scare someone out of their
wits
scare the **life** out of someone
scare the living **daylights** out of
someone
scare the **pants** off someone
scene
set the **scene**
scenes
behind the **scenes**
scent
put someone off the **scent**
scent **blood**
throw someone off the **scent**
school
the old **school**
the old **school** tie
the **school** of hard knocks
science
blind someone with **science**
not **rocket** science
scientist
a **rocket** scientist

score
know the **score**
score **points**
settle an old **score**
settle a **score**
scorned
hell hath no fury like a woman
scorned
scrape
bow and scrape
scrape the **barrel**
scrape the bottom of the **barrel**
scratch
from **scratch**
not come up to **scratch**
not up to **scratch**
scratch the **surface**
scratch your **head**
you scratch my **back** and I'll
scratch yours
scream
scream bloody **murder**
scream blue **murder**
screw
have a **screw** loose
tighten the **screw** on someone
turn the **screw** on someone
screwed
have your **head** screwed on
screws
put the **screws** on someone
Scylla
between **Scylla** and Charybdis
sea
all at **sea**
at **sea**
between the **devil** and the deep
blue sea
a **sea** change
there are plenty more **fish** in the
sea
seal
seal someone's **fate**
seal someone's **lips**
sealed
signed and sealed
signed, sealed, and delivered
someone's **lips** are sealed
seams
burst at the **seams**
come apart at the **seams**
fall apart at the **seams**
search
search **high** and low for
something
season
open **season**
seat
fly by the **seat** of your pants
in the **catbird** seat
in the **driver's** seat
in the driving **seat**
in the hot **seat**
on the **edge** of your seat
a **ringside** seat
take a back **seat**
seats
bums on seats
second
get to second **base**

play second **fiddle**
a second **bite** at the cherry
a second **wind**
take second **place**
security
a **security** blanket
see
be glad to see the **back** of
someone
not see beyond the end of your
nose
not see beyond your **nose**
not see someone for **dust**
not see the forest for the **trees**
not see the wood for the **trees**
see **eye** to eye with someone
see **red**
see someone in their true **colours**
see the **light**
see the **light** of day
see which way the **cat** jumps
suck it and see
seed
eat your **seed** corn
go to **seed**
run to **seed**
seed corn
seeds
plant the **seeds** of something
sow the **seeds** of something
seen
have seen better **days**
haven't seen **hide** nor hair of
someone
wouldn't be seen **dead**
seize
seize the **day**
self
a **shadow** of your former self
sell
sell like **hot cakes**
sell like hotcakes: see **hot cakes**
sell someone a **bill** of goods
sell someone a **pup**
sell someone down the **river**
sell someone **short**
sell the **pass**
sell yourself **short**
sell your **soul**
sell-by
pass your sell-by **date**
past your sell-by **date**
send
send someone packing
send someone to **Coventry**
send someone to the **showers**
separate
separate the grain from the **chaff**
separate the **men** from the boys
separate the **sheep** from the goats
separate the wheat from the
chaff
serve
not serve two **masters**
service
give **lip** service to something
pay **lip** service to something
set
not set in **stone**
not set the **world** on fire

set in **concrete**
set in your **ways**
set out your **stall**
set the **ball** rolling
set the **cat** among the pigeons
set the **heather** on fire
set the **pace**
set the **record** straight
set the **scene**
set the **stage** for something
set the **wheels** in motion
set **tongues** wagging
set you back on your **heels**
set your **cap** at someone
set your **face** against something
set your **heart** on something
set your **sights** on something
set your **teeth** on edge
the **stage** is set
settle
the **dust** settles
settle an old **score**
settle a **score**
sevens
at **sixes** and sevens
seventh
in seventh **heaven**
shade
put someone in the **shade**
shades
shades of
shadow
afraid of your own **shadow**
a **shadow** of your former self
shake
more things than you can shake a
stick at
shake **hands** on something
shake the **dust** of somewhere
from your feet
shake the **foundations** of
something
shakers
the **movers** and shakers
shakes
in two **shakes**
in two **shakes** of a lamb's tail
no great **shakes**
shape
knock something into **shape**
lick something into **shape**
shape up or ship out
whip something into **shape**
share
the **lion's** share
sharp
the sharp **end**
shave
a close **shave**
shed
blood is shed
shed **crocodile** tears
sheep
the black **sheep**
the black **sheep** of the family
like **sheep** to the slaughter: see
lambs
make **sheep's** eyes
might as well be hanged for a
sheep as a lamb

separate the **sheep** from the goats
a sheep in **wolf**'s clothing
sort out the **sheep** from the goats
a **wolf** in sheep's clothing

sheet
a clean **sheet**
a clean **sheet** of paper
sing from the same hymn sheet
sing from the same song sheet
white as a sheet

sheets
three **sheets** to the wind

shelf
on the **shelf**
shelf life

shell
come out of your **shell**
go into your **shell**
a **shell** game

shifting
shifting **sands**

shine
come **rain** or shine
make **hay** while the sun shines
rain or shine
take a **shine** to someone
take the **shine** off something

shining
a **knight** in shining armour

ship
abandon a sinking **ship**
abandon **ship**
don't spoil the **ship** for a ha'porth
of tar
jump **ship**
like a rat leaving a sinking **ship**
run a tight **ship**
shape up or ship out
a sinking **ship**
when your **ship** comes in

shirt
a **hair** shirt
keep your **shirt** on
lose your **shirt**
put your **shirt** on something
a stuffed **shirt**

shit
a **crock** of shit
in deep **shit**
in the **shit**
shit a **brick**
the **shit** hits the fan
shit or get off the **pot**
soft as shit
thick as shit
up shit **creek**

shithouse
built like a **brick** shithouse

shoe
drop the other **shoe**
if the **shoe** fits
the shoe is on the other **foot**

shoe-in: see **shoo-in**

shoes
dead men's **shoes**
fill someone's **shoes**
in someone's **shoes**
lick someone's shoes: see **boots**
quake in your **shoes**
smudge your own **shoes**

step into someone's **shoes**

shoestring
on a **shoestring**

shoo-in
be a **shoo-in**

shoot
shoot a **line**
shoot **daggers** at someone
shoot down in **flames**
shoot for the same **target**
shoot from the **hip**
shoot the **breeze**
shoot the **messenger**
shoot your **bolt**
shoot your **mouth** off
shoot yourself in the **foot**
a **turkey** shoot

shooting
like shooting **fish** in a barrel
the whole shooting **match**

shop
all over the **shop**
a **bull** in a china shop
close up **shop**
like a child in a sweet shop: see
candy
shop talk
shut up **shop**
a talking **shop**
talk **shop**

shopping
a **shopping** list

short
by the **short** and curlies
by the short **hairs**
draw the short **straw**
get the short end of the **stick**
have a short **fuse**
long on one thing and short on
another
on a short **fuse**
on a short **leash**
one sandwich **short** of a picnic
sell someone **short**
sell yourself **short**
several cards **short** of a full deck
short **shrift**
thick as two short planks
to cut a long **story** short
to make a long **story** short

shot
be **shot** of something
by a long **shot**
get **shot** of something
give something your best **shot**
like a **shot**
a long **shot**
one **shot** in your locker
a **shot** across someone's bows
a **shot** in the arm
a shot in the **dark**
shot to **hell**
shot to **pieces**
a warning **shot**
a warning **shot** across someone's
bows

shots
call the **shots**

shoulder
a **chip** on your shoulder

cry on someone's **shoulder**
get the cold **shoulder**
give someone the cold **shoulder**
put your **shoulder** to the wheel
a **shoulder** to cry on
shoulder to shoulder
straight from the **shoulder**

shoulders
carry the **weight** of the world on
your shoulders
head and shoulders above
someone
rub **shoulders** with someone

shout
shout something from the
rooftops
shout your **head** off

shouting
a shouting **match**

shove
when **push** comes to shove

show
a **dog** and pony show
get the **show** on the road
keep the **show** on the road
run the **show**
show a clean pair of **heels**
show someone the **ropes**
show your **face**
show your **hand**
show your **teeth**
show your true **colours**
steal the **show**
stop the **show**

showers
send someone to the **showers**
a trip to the **showers**

shrift
short **shrift**

shrinking
no shrinking **violet**
a shrinking **violet**

shuffle
lost in the **shuffle**

shut
open and shut
shut up like a **clam**
shut up **shop**
with your **eyes** shut

shy
once **bitten**, twice shy

sick
sick as a dog
sick as a parrot
sick as a pig
sick to the back **teeth**

side
from the wrong side of the **tracks**
get out of **bed** on the wrong side
get out of **bed** the wrong side
give someone the rough side of
your **tongue**
the **grass** is always greener on
the other side of the fence
know which side your **bread** is
buttered
laugh on the other side of your
face
laugh out of the other side of
your **mouth**

let the **side** down
look on the bright **side**
on the side of the **angels**
on your **side**
the other side of the **coin**
sunny **side** up
a **thorn** in your side
to be on the safe **side**
sides
  opposite sides of the same **coin**
  speak out of both sides of your
    mouth
  talk out of both sides of your
    mouth
  two sides of the same **coin**
sideways
  knock someone sideways
  knock something sideways
sieve
  a brain like a **sieve**
sight
  at first **sight**
  lose **sight** of something
  out of **sight**, out of mind
  a **sight** for sore eyes
sights
  have something in your **sights**
  have your **sights** on something
  set your **sights** on something
sign
  sign on the dotted **line**
  sign on the **line**
  sign someone's **death** warrant
  sign your own **death** warrant
signals
  smoke signals
signed
  signed and sealed
  signed, sealed, and delivered
silk
  you can't make a **silk** purse out
    of a sow's ear
silver
  born with a **silver** spoon in your
    mouth
  every cloud has a **silver** lining
  on a silver **platter**
  a **silver** lining
simple
  simple as falling off a **log**
sing
  it isn't over until the fat **lady**
    sings
  sing a different tune
  sing for your **supper**
  sing from the same hymn sheet
  sing from the same song sheet
  sing the **praises** of someone
  sing the same song
  sing the same tune
singing
  all-singing, all-dancing
single
  at a single **sitting**
sink
  everything but the **kitchen** sink
  sink or swim
  sink your **teeth** into something
sinker
  hook, line, and sinker

sinking
  abandon a sinking **ship**
  like a rat leaving a sinking **ship**
  a sinking **ship**
sit
  sit in **judgment**
  sit on a **powder keg**
  sit on **pins** and needles
  sit on the **fence**
  sit on your **hands**
  sit **pretty**
  sit **tight**
sitting
  at a single **sitting**
  at one **sitting**
  in one **sitting**
  a sitting **duck**
six
  hit someone for **six**
  knock someone for **six**
  six of one and half a dozen of the
    other
sixes
  at **sixes** and sevens
size
  cut someone down to **size**
  try something for **size**
  try something on for **size**
  try something out for **size**
skate
  skate on thin **ice**
skates
  get your **skates** on
skeleton
  the skeleton at the **feast**
  a **skeleton** in the closet
  a **skeleton** in the cupboard
skid
  skid row
skids
  on the **skids**
  put the **skids** under something
skin
  by the **skin** of your teeth
  get under someone's **skin**
  get under your **skin**
  it's no **skin** off my nose
  jump out of your **skin**
  make your **skin** crawl
  save your own **skin**
  save your **skin**
  skin and bone
  skin and bones
  skin someone **alive**
  slip on a **banana** skin
  there's more than one way to
    skin a **cat**
  a thick **skin**
  a thin **skin**
skinned
  keep your **eyes** skinned
skip
  a **hop** and a skip
  a **hop**, skip, and a jump
skittles
  not all **beer** and skittles
skull
  out of your skull: see **head**
skunk
  drunk as a skunk

sky
  out of a clear blue **sky**
  pie in the sky
  reach for the sky: see **stars**
  the **sky**'s the limit
sky-high
  blow something **sky**-high
slack
  cut someone some **slack**
  pick up the **slack**
  take up the **slack**
slap
  a **slap** in the face
  a **slap** on the wrist
slate
  a clean **slate**
  on the **slate**
  wipe the **slate** clean
slaughter
  like **lambs** to the slaughter
  like sheep to the slaughter: see
    lambs
sledgehammer
  a sledgehammer to crack a **nut**
sleep
  not get a **wink** of sleep
  not lose any **sleep** over
    something
  not sleep a **wink**
sleeping
  let sleeping **dogs** lie
  a sleeping dog: see **dogs**
sleeve
  have a card up your **sleeve**
  have an ace up your **sleeve**
  have something up your **sleeve**
  laugh up your **sleeve**
  wear your **heart** on your sleeve
sleeves
  roll up your **sleeves**
slice
  a slice of the **action**
sliced
  the best thing since sliced **bread**
  the greatest thing since sliced
    bread
sling
  sling **mud**
  sling your **hook**
  your ass in a **sling**
slings
  slings and arrows
slip
  a **slip** of the pen
  a **slip** of the tongue
  slip on a **banana** peel
  slip on a **banana** skin
  slip through the **cracks**
  slip through the **net**
  slip through your **fingers**
  slip your **mind**
  there is many a **slip** twixt cup
    and lip
slippery
  slippery as an eel
  a slippery **slope**
slope
  a slippery **slope**
slow
  the slow **lane**

slow off the **mark**

small
a big **fish** in a small pond
a big **frog** in a small pond: see
   fish
it's a small **world**
make someone feel **small**
make someone look **small**
small **beer**
a small **fortune**
small **potatoes**
the small **print**
small **world**

smart
a smart **alec**
a smart aleck: see **alec**
a smart **cookie**
the smart **money**

smell
smell a **rat**
wake up and smell the **coffee**

smelling
come up smelling of **roses**

smile
smile from **ear** to ear

smoke
blow **smoke**
blow **smoke** in someone's eyes
blow **smoke** in someone's face
blow **smoke** up someone's ass
go up in **smoke**
put that in your **pipe** and smoke
   it
smoke and mirrors
smoke signals
there's no **smoke** without fire
where there's **smoke** there's
   fire

smoke-filled
a smoke-filled **room**

smoking
a smoking **gun**

smooth
smooth ruffled **feathers**
smooth **sailing**
smooth the path
smooth the way
take the **rough** with the smooth

smudge
smudge your own **shoes**

snail
at a **snail**'s pace

snake
a **snake** in the grass
snake oil
a **snake** oil salesman

snap
snap someone's **head** off

snatching
cradle-**snatching**

sneeze
when one person sneezes, another
   catches **cold**

snook
cock a **snook** at someone

snow
a **snow** job
white as snow

snowball
not a snowball's **chance** in hell

snuff
up to **snuff**

snug
snug as a bug in a rug

soap
no **soap**

sober
sober as a judge

sock
put a **sock** in it

socks
knock the **socks** off someone
knock your **socks** off
pull your **socks** up
work your **socks** off

soft
have a soft **spot** for someone
soft as shit
a soft **touch**

soften
soften the **blow**

song
for a **song**
make a **song** and dance about
   something
on **song**
sing from the same song sheet
sing the same song

soonest
least said, soonest mended

sore
like a **bear** with a sore head
a **sight** for sore eyes
a **sore** point
a **sore** spot
stand out like a sore **thumb**
stick out like a sore **thumb**

sorrows
drown your **sorrows**

sort
sort out the **men** from the boys
sort out the **sheep** from the goats
sort the wheat from the **chaff**

soul
bare your **soul**
body and soul
hold **body** and soul together
keep **body** and soul together
the **life** and soul of the party
sell your **soul**

sound
the death **knell** sounds
empty **vessels** make the most
   sound
sound as a bell
sound **hollow**
sound the death **knell**

soup
in the **soup**

sour
sour **grapes**

sow
as you sow, so shall you **reap**
sow the **seeds** of something
sow the wind and **reap** the
   whirlwind
sow your wild **oats**
you can't make a **silk** purse out
   of a sow's ear
you **reap** what you sow

space
a **waste** of space

spade
call a **spade** a spade

spades
in **spades**

Spain
castles in Spain

span
spick and span

spanner
put a **spanner** in the works
throw a **spanner** in the works

spare
like a spare **prick** at a wedding
spare someone's **blushes**

spark
a bright **spark**

sparks
sparks fly
strike **sparks** off each other

spate
in full spate: see **flow**

speak
actions speak louder than
   words
speak of the **devil**
speak out of both sides of your
   mouth
speak **volumes**
speak with forked **tongue**

spectacles
rose-tinted **spectacles**

spectre
the spectre at the **feast**

speed
bring someone up to **speed**
bring something up to **speed**
get up to **speed**

spell
spell **curtains**

spend
spend **money** like water

spic: see **spick**

spice
variety is the spice of life

spick
spick and span

spike
spike someone's **guns**

spill
spill the **beans**
spill your **guts**

spilled
blood is spilled
it's no use crying over spilled
   milk

spin
in a flat **spin**
in a **spin**
spin your **wheels**

spit
the dead **spit**
the **spit** and image
spit and polish
spit and sawdust
spit in someone's eye
spit in the **wind**
spit out the **dummy**
spit the **dummy**

spite
cut off your **nose** to spite your
  face
spitting
the spitting image: see **spit**
within spitting **distance**
splash
make a **splash**
split
split **hairs**
spoil
a bad **apple** spoils the barrel
don't spoil the **ship** for a ha'porth
  of tar
too many **cooks** spoil the broth
spoke
put a **spoke** in someone's wheel
sponge
throw in the sponge: see **towel**
spoon
born with a **silver** spoon in your
  mouth
the wooden **spoon**
spot
a blind **spot**
have a soft **spot** for someone
hit the **spot**
on the **spot**
a **sore** spot
spots
knock **spots** off something
a **leopard** does not change its
  spots
spout
up the **spout**
sprat
a **sprat** to catch a mackerel
spread
spread like **wildfire**
spread yourself too **thin**
spread your **wings**
spring
no **spring** chicken
spur
on the **spur** of the moment
spurs
earn your **spurs**
win your **spurs**
square
back at **square** one
back to **square** one
fair and square
from **square** one
on the **square**
a square **meal**
a square **peg** in a round hole
square the **circle**
squeaky
squeaky **clean**
squeal
squeal like a stuck **pig**
squib
a damp **squib**
stab
a stab in the **back**
a stab in the **dark**
stab someone in the **back**
stable
close the stable **door** after the
  horse has bolted

stack
blow your **stack**
stack the cards
stack the deck
stacked
play with a stacked **deck**
stage
centre stage
set the **stage** for something
the **stage** is set
stake
go to the **stake**
stalking
a stalking **horse**
stall
set out your **stall**
stamp
on the **back** of a postage stamp
stamping
stamping **ground**
stand
can't stand the **pace**
if you can't stand the **heat**, get
  out of the kitchen
make your **hair** stand on end
not have a **leg** to stand on
someone's **hair** stands on end
stand on your own two **feet**
stand out like a sore **thumb**
stand **pat**
stand something on its **head**
stand the **test** of time
stand up and be counted
standard
the **standard** bearer
standing
can do something standing on
  your **head**
star
hitch your **wagon** to a star
stare
stare someone in the **face**
stare something in the **face**
stars
reach for the **stars**
stars in your eyes
start
start a **hare**
start off on the right **foot**
start the **ball** rolling
starter
under **starter's** orders
starting
off the starting **blocks**
starts
in **fits** and starts
state
the **state** of play
stay
stay the **course**
steady
a steady **hand** on the tiller
steal
steal a **march**
steal someone's **clothes**
steal someone's **thunder**
steal the **show**
steam
blow off **steam**
full **steam** ahead

have steam coming out of your
  ears
a **head** of steam
let off **steam**
pick up **steam**
run out of **steam**
under your own **steam**
steer
a **bum** steer
steer **clear**
steer someone **clear** of something
stem
stem the flow
stem the tide
step
step into someone's **boots**
step into someone's **shoes**
step on someone's **toes**
step out of **line**
stew
in a **stew**
leave someone to **stew**
let someone **stew**
let someone **stew** in their own
  juice
stick
carrot and stick
carry a big **stick**
get a lot of **stick**
get hold of the wrong end of the
  stick
get the short end of the **stick**
get the wrong end of the **stick**
give someone **stick**
in a cleft **stick**
let the cobbler stick to his **last**
more things than you can shake a
  stick at
mud sticks
stick in your throat
stick out like a sore **thumb**
stick the **knife** in
a **stick** to beat someone with
stick to your **guns**
stick to your **knitting**
stick to your **last**
stick your **head** in a noose
stick your **neck** out
stick your **nose** into something
thin as a stick
wield a big **stick**
sticking
a sticking **point**
stick-in-the-mud
a stick-in-the-**mud**
sticky
bat on a sticky **wicket**
come to a sticky **end**
on a sticky **wicket**
stiff
stiff as a board
a stiff upper **lip**
still
the **jury** is still out
still **waters** run deep
sting
a **sting** in the tail
take the **sting** out of something
stir
stir up a **hornet's** nest

stitch
a **stitch** in time
a **stitch** in time saves nine

stitches
in **stitches**

stock
lock, stock, and barrel

stomach
butterflies in your stomach

stomping
stomping **ground**

stone
kill two **birds** with one stone
leave no **stone** unturned
like getting **blood** out of a stone
not set in **stone**
a rolling **stone**
a rolling **stone** gathers no moss
a **stone**'s throw

stones
people who live in **glass** houses
 shouldn't throw stones

stony
fall on stony **ground**

stools
caught between two **stools**
fall between two **stools**

stop
stop someone dead in their
 tracks
stop someone in their **tracks**
stop something dead in its **tracks**
stop something in its **tracks**
stop the **show**

stops
the **buck** stops here
the **buck** stops with someone
pull out all the **stops**

storage
in cold **storage**
into cold **storage**

store
like a kid in a **candy** store

stories
tall stories

storm
the calm before the **storm**
the **eye** of the storm
the lull before the **storm**
a **port** in a storm
ride out the **storm**
ride the **storm**
a storm in a teacup
take somewhere by **storm**
weather the **storm**

story
a **cock** and bull story
to cut a long **story** short
to make a long **story** short

straight
the **home** straight
keep a straight **face**
play a straight **bat**
put the **record** straight
set the **record** straight
the **straight** and narrow
a straight **arrow**
straight as a die
straight from the **shoulder**
with a straight **face**

strain
strain at a **gnat**
strain at a **gnat** and swallow a
 camel
strain at the **leash**

strait
the strait and narrow: see
 straight

straw
draw the short **straw**
a drowning man will clutch at a
 straw: see **straws**
the final **straw**
the last **straw**
the last **straw** that breaks the
 camel's back
make **bricks** without straw
a man of **straw**
a **straw** man
the **straw** that breaks the camel's
 back

straws
clutch at **straws**
grasp at **straws**
straws in the wind

streak
talk a blue **streak**

stream
on **stream**

street
in Queer **Street**
just up your **street**
the man in the **street**
right up your **street**
the woman in the **street**

streets
streets ahead

strength
a pillar of strength: see **tower**
a **tower** of strength

stretch
at full **stretch**
the **home** stretch
stretch the **rules**

stride
get into your **stride**
hit your **stride**
put someone off their **stride**
take something in **stride**
take something in your **stride**

strike
lightning does not strike
 twice
strike a **blow** against something
strike a **blow** for something
strike a **chord**
strike a raw **nerve**
strike **gold**
strike **home**
strike it **rich**
strike **lucky**
strike **oil**
strike **pay** dirt
strike **sparks** off each other
strike while the **iron** is hot

strikes
three **strikes** against someone
two **strikes** against someone

striking
within striking **distance**

string
another **string** to your bow
have someone on a **string**
keep someone on a **string**

strings
apron strings
hold the **purse** strings
loosen the **purse** strings
many strings to your bow: see
 string
pull **strings**
pull the **strings**
tighten the **purse** strings
with no **strings** attached
without **strings**
with **strings**
with **strings** attached

strip
tear a **strip** off someone
tear someone off a **strip**

stroke
put someone off their **stroke**

strokes
broad brush **strokes**
broad **strokes**
different **strokes** for different
 folks

strong
strong as a bull
strong as a horse
strong as an ox

strut
strut your **stuff**

stubborn
stubborn as a mule

stuck
squeal like a stuck **pig**
stuck for **words**

stuff
strut your **stuff**

stuffed
a stuffed **shirt**

stuffing
knock the **stuffing** out of
 someone

stumbling
a stumbling **block**

stump
on the **stump**

style
cramp someone's **style**

suck
suck it and see
teach your **grandmother** to suck
 eggs

sucker
give a sucker an even **break**

sugar
sugar the **pill**

sugar-coat
sugar-coat the **pill**

suit
follow **suit**
suit someone down to the **ground**
your long **suit**

suits
the men in grey **suits**
the men in **suits**

sully
sully your **hands**

sum
  a **zero-sum** game
summer
  an Indian **summer**
  one **swallow** doesn't make a
    summer
sun
  make **hay** while the sun shines
  a **place** in the sun
Sundays
  a **month** of Sundays
sunny
  sunny **side** up
sunshine
  a **ray** of sunshine
supper
  sing for your **supper**
sure
  sure as eggs
  sure as eggs is eggs
surface
  scratch the **surface**
swallow
  a bitter **pill** to swallow
  one **swallow** doesn't make a
    summer
  strain at a **gnat** and swallow a
    camel
  swallow a bitter **pill**
  swallow your **pride**
swear
  swear **blind**
  swear **up** and down
sweat
  blood, sweat, and tears
  by the **sweat** of your brow
  in a cold **sweat**
  in a **sweat**
  sweat **blood**
  sweat like a **pig**
sweep
  make a clean **sweep**
  a new **broom** sweeps clean
  sweep someone off their **feet**
  sweep something under the
    carpet
  sweep something under the **rug**
  sweep the **board**
sweet
  cop it **sweet**
  keep someone **sweet**
  like a child in a sweet shop: see
    candy
  sweet as pie
  a sweet **tooth**
sweeten
  sweeten the **pill**
swim
  sink or swim
  swim against the **tide**
  swim with the **tide**
swine
  cast **pearls** before swine
swing
  get into the **swing** of something
  go with a **swing**
  in full **swing**
  no room to swing a **cat**
  swing in the **wind**
  swing the **lead**

swinging
  come out swinging
swings
  swings and roundabouts
  what you lose on the **swings** you
    gain on the roundabouts
Swiss
  more holes than **Swiss cheese**
switch
  switch horses in **midstream**
sword
  a double-edged **sword**
  the **Sword** of Damocles
  a two-edged **sword**
swords
  beat **swords** into ploughshares
  cross **swords**
  turn **swords** into ploughshares
syllable
  in **words** of one syllable
system
  get something out of your **system**
systems
  all **systems** go
t
  dot the **i**'s and cross the **t**'s
  to a T: see **tee**
tab
  pick up the **tab**
table
  drink someone under the **table**
  get your **feet** under the table
  lay your **cards** on the table
  on the **table**
  under the **table**
tables
  turn the **tables**
tabs
  keep **tabs** on someone
tacks
  get down to **brass** tacks
tail
  cannot make **head** or tail of
    something
  chase your own **tail**
  in two **shakes** of a lamb's tail
  on your **tail**
  a **sting** in the tail
  the **tail** wags the dog
  turn **tail**
  with your **tail** between your legs
  with your **tail** up
tails
  on the **coat-tails** of someone
take
  can't take the **pace**
  can't take your **eyes** off someone
  the **devil** take the hindmost
  every man for himself and the
    devil take the hindmost
  give and take
  give or take
  give someone an **inch** and they'll
    take a mile
  give with one **hand** and take
    away with the other
  it takes two to **tango**
  not take no for an **answer**
  not take something **lying** down
  take a back **seat**

take a **bath**
take a **bead** on
take a **bite** out of something
take a **bow**
take a **crack** at something
take a dim **view** of something
take a **grip** on something
take a **hand** in something
take a hike: see **walk**
take a **leaf** out of someone's book
take a poor **view** of something
take a **rain** check
take a running **jump**
take a **shine** to someone
take a **walk**
take it **easy**
take it on the **chin**
take its **course**
take no **prisoners**
take **pot** luck
take **root**
take second **place**
take someone by the **throat**
take someone down a **peg** or two
take someone for a **ride**
take someone in **hand**
take someone off **guard**
take someone's **name** in vain
take someone's **part**
take someone to the **cleaners**
take someone under your **wing**
take something as **gospel**
take something in good **part**
take something in **stride**
take something in your **stride**
take something on **board**
take something to **heart**
take something with a grain of
  salt
take something with a pinch of
  salt
take somewhere by **storm**
take the **bait**
take the **ball** and run with it
take the **biscuit**
take the **bull** by the horns
take the **cake**
take the **edge** off something
take the **gilt** off the gingerbread
take the **gloves** off
take the high **road**
take the **law** into your own hands
take the **lid** off
take the low **road**
take the mick: see **mickey**
take the **mickey**
take the **piss**
take the **plunge**
take the **rap**
take the **rise** out of someone
take the **rough** with the smooth
take the **shine** off something
take the **sting** out of something
take the **wind** out of someone's
  sail
take the **wind** out of someone's
  sails
take the **words** out of someone's
  mouth
take the **wraps** off something

take things **easy**
take to something like a **duck** to water
take to your **heels**
take up the **cudgels**
take up the **gauntlet**
take up the **slack**
take your **breath** away
take your **eye** off the ball
take your **hat** off to someone
take your **life** in your hands
taking
  like taking **candy** from a baby
tale
  a **cock** and bull tale
  live to tell the **tale**
  an old **wives'** tale
  tell its own **tale**
  tell the **tale**
tales
  dead men tell no **tales**
  tall tales
  tell **tales**
talk
  money talks
  shop talk
  talk a blue **streak**
  talk in **riddles**
  talk **nineteen** to the dozen
  talk of the **devil**
  talk out of both sides of your **mouth**
  talk out of your arse
  talk over someone's **head**
  talk **shop**
  talk the hind **leg** off a donkey
  talk through your **hat**
  talk **turkey**
  talk under **water**
  talk with forked **tongue**
talking
  a talking **shop**
tall
  a tall **order**
  tall stories
  tall tales
tangent
  go off at a **tangent**
  go off on a **tangent**
tangled
  a tangled **web**
tango
  it takes two to **tango**
tank
  built like a **tank**
tap
  on **tap**
tape
  red **tape**
taped
  have got something **taped**
tar
  don't spoil the **ship** for a ha'porth of tar
  tar someone with the same **brush**
target
  shoot for the same **target**
taste
  give someone a taste of their own **medicine**

leave a bad **taste** in your mouth
taste **blood**
tea
  not for all the **tea** in China
  not your **cup** of tea
teach
  teach your **grandmother** to suck eggs
  you can't teach an old **dog** new tricks
teacup
  a **storm** in a teacup
teapot
  a **tempest** in a teapot
tear
  tear a **strip** off someone
  tear someone **limb** from limb
  tear someone off a **strip**
  tear your **hair** out
tears
  blood, sweat, and tears
  shed **crocodile** tears
tee
  to a **tee**
teeth
  armed to the **teeth**
  by the **skin** of your teeth
  cut your **teeth**
  fed up to the back **teeth**
  get the **bit** between your teeth
  get your **teeth** into something
  gnashing of **teeth**
  gnash your **teeth**
  grind your **teeth**
  grit your **teeth**
  have **teeth**
  a **kick** in the teeth
  kick someone in the teeth
  lie through your **teeth**
  like pulling **teeth**
  rare as **hen's** teeth
  scarce as **hen's** teeth
  set your **teeth** on edge
  show your **teeth**
  sick to the back **teeth**
  sink your **teeth** into something
  wailing and gnashing of **teeth**
  weeping and gnashing of **teeth**
  would give your **eye** teeth for something
teething
  teething problems
  teething troubles
telegraph
  the **bush** telegraph
tell
  dead men tell no **tales**
  live to tell the **tale**
  tell its own **tale**
  tell someone where to get off
  tell **tales**
  tell the **tale**
tempest
  a **tempest** in a teapot
tempt
  tempt **fate**
  tempt providence: see **fate**
ten
  ten a **penny**

ten-foot
  wouldn't touch something with a ten-foot **pole**
tenterhooks
  on **tenterhooks**
territory
  go with the **territory**
terror
  a **reign** of terror
test
  the **acid** test
  a **litmus** test
  stand the **test** of time
  test the **water**
  test the waters: see **water**
tether
  at the end of your **tether**
there
  neither **here** nor there
  not be all **there**
thick
  in the **thick** of it
  in the **thick** of something
  lay it on **thick**
  thick as mince
  thick as shit
  thick as thieves
  thick as two planks
  thick as two short planks
  thick on the **ground**
  a thick **skin**
  through **thick** and thin
thicken
  the **plot** thickens
thicker
  blood is thicker than water
thieves
  thick as thieves
thin
  from thin **air**
  into thin **air**
  out of thin **air**
  skate on thin **ice**
  spread yourself too **thin**
  thin as a rake
  thin as a stick
  the thin end of the **wedge**
  a thin **line**
  thin on the **ground**
  a thin **skin**
  through **thick** and thin
thing
  the best thing since sliced **bread**
  do your own **thing**
  the greatest thing since sliced **bread**
  one **thing** leads to another
  there's no such thing as a free **lunch**
things
  cut things **fine**
  not do things by **halves**
  play things by the **book**
  take things **easy**
think
  think on your **feet**
  think the **world** of someone
thinking
  get your thinking **cap** on
  put your thinking **cap** on

third
give someone the third **degree**
a third **wheel**
thorn
a **thorn** in your flesh
a **thorn** in your side
thought
food for thought
thread
hang by a **thread**
three
three **sheets** to the wind
three **strikes** against someone
three-ring
a three-ring **circus**
throat
bring a **lump** to your throat
cut your own **throat**
a **frog** in your throat
go for the throat: see **jugular**
grab someone by the **throat**
have someone by the **throat**
jump down someone's **throat**
a **lump** in your throat
ram something down someone's **throat**
stick in your throat
take someone by the **throat**
throats
at each other's **throats**
throes
in the **throes** of something
throne
the **power** behind the throne
throttle
at full **throttle**
in full **throttle**
throw
people who live in **glass** houses shouldn't throw stones
a **stone's** throw
throw a monkey **wrench** into the works
throw a **spanner** in the works
throw a wobbler: see **wobbly**
throw a **wobbly**
throw a **wrench** into the works
throw **caution** to the wind
throw cold **water** on something
throw down the **gauntlet**
throw good **money** after bad
throw in the sponge: see **towel**
throw in the **towel**
throw in your **hand**
throw in your **lot** with someone
throw **money** at someone
throw **money** at something
throw **mud**
throw off **balance**
throw someone a **curve**
throw someone a **curve** ball
throw someone for a **loop**
throw someone off the **scent**
throw someone to the **dogs**
throw someone to the **lions**
throw someone to the **wolves**
throw something back in someone's **face**
throw the **baby** out with the bath water

throw the **book** at someone
throw your cap into the ring: see **hat**
throw your **hat** into the ring
throw your **weight** about
throw your **weight** around
throw your **weight** behind something
thrown
be thrown into your **lap**
thrust
the **cut** and thrust
thumb
have a green **thumb**
a **rule** of thumb
stand out like a sore **thumb**
stick out like a sore **thumb**
thumb your **nose** at someone
under someone's **thumb**
thumbs
all fingers and **thumbs**
all **thumbs**
the **thumbs** down
the **thumbs** up
twiddle your **thumbs**
thump
thump the **tub**
thumping
tub-thumping
thunder
blood and thunder
a **face** like thunder
steal someone's **thunder**
ticket
a **dream** ticket
a **meal** ticket
a one-way **ticket**
tickled
tickled **pink**
tide
stem the tide
swim against the **tide**
swim with the **tide**
tie
the old **school** tie
something ties your **hands**
tie someone in **knots**
tie the **knot**
tie yourself in **knots**
tied
fit to be tied
have your **hands** tied
with one **hand** tied behind your back
with your hands tied behind your back: see **hand**
your **hands** are tied
tiger
a **paper** tiger
tight
hold someone on a tight **rein**
in a tight **corner**
keep a tight **rein** on someone
on a tight **leash**
run a tight **ship**
sit **tight**
tighten
tighten the **purse** strings
tighten the **screw** on someone
tighten your **belt**

tightrope
walk a **tightrope**
tiles
on the **tiles**
till
have your fingers in the **till**
have your hand in the **till**
tiller
a steady **hand** on the tiller
tilt
tilt at **windmills**
time
be on borrowed **time**
big **time**
the big **time**
crunch time
a full-time **job**
have a **whale** of a time
hit the big **time**
in the **nick** of time
live on borrowed **time**
mark **time**
play for **time**
race against time
ride two **horses** at the same time
stand the **test** of time
a **stitch** in time
a **stitch** in time saves nine
time on your hands
tin
a **cat** on a hot tin roof
have a **tin** ear for something
a little **tin** god
put the tin **lid** on something
a **tin** god
tinker
not give a **tinker's** cuss
not give a **tinker's** damn
tip
on the **tip** of your tongue
the **tip** of the iceberg
tip someone the **wink**
tip the balance
tip the scales
tod
on your **tod**
today
here **today**, gone tomorrow
jam today
toe
from **head** to toe
from **top** to toe
a **toe** in the water
toe the **line**
toe to toe
toes
keep you on your **toes**
make your **toes** curl
step on someone's **toes**
tread on someone's **toes**
turn up your **toes**
toffee
can't do something for **toffee**
told
a little **bird** told me
Tom
every **Tom**, Dick, and Harry
tomorrow
as if there were no **tomorrow**
here **today**, gone tomorrow

jam tomorrow
like there's no **tomorrow**
tomorrow is another day
ton
come down on someone like a **ton**
of bricks
like a **ton** of bricks
tongs
go at it **hammer** and tongs
go at someone **hammer** and tongs
hammer and tongs
tongue
bite your **tongue**
find your **tongue**
get your **tongue** round something
give someone the rough edge of
your **tongue**
give someone the rough side of
your **tongue**
hold your **tongue**
on the **tip** of your tongue
a **slip** of the tongue
speak with forked **tongue**
talk with forked **tongue**
tongue in cheek
with **tongue** in cheek
tongue-lashing
tongue-lashing
tongues
set **tongues** wagging
tongues are wagging
tonne: see **ton**
tools
down **tools**
lay down **tools**
the **tools** of the trade
tooth
an **eye** for an eye, a tooth for a
tooth
fight **tooth** and claw
fight **tooth** and nail
long in the **tooth**
red in **tooth** and claw
a sweet **tooth**
with a fine-tooth **comb**
top
blow your **top**
from **top** to bottom
from **top** to toe
get on **top** of you
kangaroos in your top paddock
off the top of your **head**
on **top** of something
on top of the **world**
over the **top**
the top **drawer**
the top of the **heap**
the top of the **pile**
the top of the **tree**
torch
carry a **torch** for someone
carry the **torch**
toss
argue the **toss**
not give a **toss**
toss-up
be a **toss-up**
touch
at the touch of a **button**
the common **touch**

an easy **touch**
kick something into **touch**
light the blue **touch paper**
light the **touch paper**
a soft **touch**
touch a **chord**
touch all the **bases**
touch and go
touch a **nerve**
touch **base**
touch **wood**
touch your **forelock**
wouldn't **touch** something with a
barge **pole**
wouldn't **touch** something with a
ten-foot **pole**
tough
tough as nails
tough as old boots
a tough **cookie**
a tough **nut**
a tough **nut** to crack
a tough **row** to hoe
tow
tow the **line**
towel
throw in the **towel**
tower
an **ivory** tower
a **tower** of strength
town
go to **town**
a one-**horse** town
the only **game** in town
paint the **town** red
traces
kick over the **traces**
track
the fast **track**
have a one-track **mind**
have the inside **track**
keep **track** of something
lose **track** of someone
off the beaten **track**
on the right **track**
on the wrong **track**
a **track** record
tracks
cover your **tracks**
from the wrong side of the **tracks**
make **tracks**
stop someone dead in their
tracks
stop someone in their **tracks**
stop something dead in its **tracks**
stop something in its **tracks**
trade
the **tools** of the trade
trades
a **jack** of all trades
trail
blaze a **trail**
a **paper** trail
trail your **coat**
train
a gravy **train**
trap
fall into the **trap**
tread
fools rush in where angels fear to

tread
tread on someone's **toes**
tread **water**
treat
a **Dutch** treat
treat someone with **kid** gloves
tree
bark up the wrong **tree**
out of your **tree**
the top of the **tree**
up a **gum tree**
trees
not grow on **trees**
not see the forest for the **trees**
not see the wood for the **trees**
trial
a **trial** balloon
trick
do the **trick**
every **trick** in the book
not miss a **trick**
the oldest **trick** in the book
tricks
someone's **bag** of tricks
up to your old **tricks**
up to your **tricks**
you can't teach an old **dog** new
tricks
trim
in fighting **trim**
trim your **sails**
trip
a trip to the **showers**
Trojan
a Trojan **horse**
trolley
off your **trolley**
troubled
fish in troubled **waters**
pour **oil** on troubled waters
troubles
teething troubles
trousers
all **mouth** and no trousers
all **mouth** and trousers
catch someone with their trousers
down: see **pants**
wear the trousers
trowel
lay it on with a **trowel**
truck
have no **truck** with something
true
ring **true**
see someone in their true **colours**
show your true **colours**
trump
play your **trump** card
a **trump** card
trumpet
blow your own **trumpet**
trumps
come up **trumps**
turn up **trumps**
truth
economical with the **truth**
the **gospel** truth
try
nice **try** but no **cigar**
try something for **size**

try something on for **size**
try something out for **size**
try your **hand** at something
try your **wings**
trying
  like trying to nail **Jell-O** to the wall
tub
  thump the **tub**
tubes
  down the tubes
tub-thumping
  tub-thumping
tuck
  nip and tuck
tucker
  your best **bib** and tucker
tug
  tug at the **heartstrings**
  tug your **forelock**
tumble
  rough and tumble
tune
  call the **tune**
  a change of **tune**
  change your **tune**
  dance to someone's **tune**
  he who pays the **piper** calls the tune
  march to a different tune
  sing a different tune
  sing the same tune
tunnel
  the **light** at the end of the tunnel
  tunnel vision
turkey
  talk **turkey**
  a **turkey** shoot
turkeys
  like **turkeys** voting for Christmas
turn
  at every **turn**
  not turn a **hair**
  turn a blind **eye** to something
  turn a deaf **ear** to something
  turn full **circle**
  turn **heads**
  turn in your **grave**
  turn over a new **leaf**
  turn over in your **grave**
  turn something on its **head**
  turn **swords** into ploughshares
  turn **tail**
  turn the **clock** back
  turn the **corner**
  turn the **heat** on someone
  turn the other **cheek**
  turn the **page**
  turn the **screw** on someone
  turn the **tables**
  turn **turtle**
  turn up like a bad **penny**
  turn up the **heat** on someone
  turn up **trumps**
  turn up your **nose** at something
  turn up your **toes**
  turn your **back** on someone
  turn your **back** on something
  turn your **hand** to something
  the **worm** turns

turned
  poacher turned gamekeeper
  when your **back** is turned
turning
  the **wheels** are turning
turnip
  like getting **blood** out of a turnip
turn-up
  a **turn-up** for the books
turtle
  turn **turtle**
twain
  never the **twain** shall meet
twice
  lightning does not strike twice
  once **bitten**, twice shy
twiddle
  twiddle your **thumbs**
twist
  get your **knickers** in a twist
  round the **twist**
  twist in the **wind**
  twist someone around your little **finger**
  twist someone's **arm**
  twist the **knife**
  twist the **knife** in the wound
twixt
  there is many a **slip** twixt cup and lip
two
  alike as two **peas** in a pod
  a **bird** in the hand is worth two in the bush
  bring someone down a **peg** or two
  caught between two **stools**
  cut two **ways**
  fall between two **stools**
  for two **pins**
  in two **minds**
  in two **shakes**
  in two **shakes** of a lamb's tail
  it takes two to **tango**
  kill two **birds** with one stone
  the lesser of two **evils**
  like two **peas** in a pod
  not give two hoots: see **hoot**
  not have two nickels to **rub** together
  not have two pennies to **rub** together
  not serve two **masters**
  of two **minds**
  put **two** and two together
  ride two **horses** at once
  ride two **horses** at the same time
  stand on your own two **feet**
  take someone down a **peg** or two
  thick as two planks
  thick as two short planks
  two a **penny**
  two bites of the cherry: see **bite**
  two sides of the same **coin**
  two **strikes** against someone
  your two **cents'** worth
  your two **penn'orth**
two-edged
  a two-edged **sword**
ugly
  rear its ugly **head**

umbilical
  cut the umbilical **cord**
unbowed
  bloodied but **unbowed**
uncle
  Bob's your uncle
under
  under a **cloud**
  under **par**
  under someone's **feet**
  under someone's **thumb**
  under the **counter**
  under the **gun**
  under the **hammer**
  under the **table**
  under the **weather**
  under the **wing** of someone
  under the **wire**
  under your **belt**
  under your **nose**
  under your own **steam**
unglued
  come **unglued**
unknown
  an unknown **quantity**
unquote
  quote, unquote
unstuck
  come **unstuck**
unto
  a **law** unto yourself
unturned
  leave no **stone** unturned
up
  on the **up**
  on the **up** and up
upper
  a stiff upper **lip**
  the upper **hand**
uppers
  down on your **uppers**
  on your **uppers**
upset
  upset the **applecart**
upstairs
  kick someone **upstairs**
use
  it's no use crying over spilled **milk**
  no use to man or **beast**
usual
  business as usual
vacuum
  in a **vacuum**
vain
  take someone's **name** in vain
value
  at **face** value
variety
  garden-variety
  variety is the spice of life
veil
  draw a **veil** over something
velvet
  an iron **fist** in a velvet glove
verse
  chapter and verse
vessels
  empty **vessels** make the most noise

empty **vessels** make the most
sound
vest
keep your cards close to the **vest**
play your cards close to the **vest**
vicious
a vicious **circle**
view
a bird's-eye **view**
a **ringside** view
take a dim **view** of something
take a poor **view** of something
a worm's eye **view**
villain
the **villain** of the piece
vine
die on the **vine**
wither on the **vine**
violet
no shrinking **violet**
a shrinking **violet**
vision
tunnel vision
voice
a lone voice in the **wilderness**
a voice crying in the **wilderness**
volumes
speak **volumes**
vote
vote with your **feet**
voting
like **turkeys** voting for Christmas
wag
the **tail** wags the dog
wagging
set **tongues** wagging
tongues are wagging
wagon
fall off the **wagon**
hitch your **wagon** to a star
hitch your **wagon** to someone
on the **wagon**
wagons
circle the **wagons**
pull your **wagons** in a circle
wailing
wailing and gnashing of **teeth**
wait
wait on someone **hand** and foot
waiting
a waiting **game**
wake
in something's **wake**
in the **wake** of something
wake up and smell the **coffee**
wake-up
a **wake-up** call
walk
run before you can walk
take a **walk**
walk a **knife**-edge
walk a **tightrope**
walk into the **lion**'s den
walk on **air**
walk on eggs: see **eggshells**
walk on **eggshells**
walk the gangplank: see **plank**
walk the **plank**
walking
walking **papers**

wall
bang your head against a brick
wall
bang your head against a **wall**
come up against a brick **wall**
drive someone up the **wall**
a **fly** on the wall
go to the **wall**
the handwriting is on the **wall**
have your **back** to the wall
hit the **wall**
like trying to nail **Jell-O** to the
wall
nail someone to the **wall**
off the **wall**
the writing is on the **wall**
walls
climb the **walls**
walls have ears
war
all's **fair** in love and war
lose the **battle**, win the war
a war of **nerves**
a **war** of words
win the **battle**, lose the war
warm
warm the **cockles** of your heart
warmed
like **death** warmed over
like **death** warmed up
warning
warning **bells** ring
a warning **shot**
a warning **shot** across someone's
bows
warpath
on the **warpath**
warrant
sign someone's **death** warrant
sign your own **death** warrant
wars
in the **wars**
warts
warts and all
wash
come out in the **wash**
wash your **dirty** linen in public
wash your **hands** of something
washing
do your **dirty** washing in public
waste
a **waste** of space
waste your **breath**
watch
on someone's **watch**
watch **grass** grow
watch **paint** dry
watch someone like a **hawk**
watch your **p's** and **q's**
watched
a watched **pot** never boils
water
blood is thicker than water
blow something out of the **water**
come **hell** or high water
dead in the water
a **fish** out of water
in deep **water**
in hot **water**
keep your **head** above water

like **water** off a duck's back
make your **mouth** water
milk and water
not hold **water**
of the first **water**
oil and water
pour cold **water** on something
spend **money** like water
take to something like a **duck** to
water
talk under **water**
test the **water**
through **hell** and high water
throw cold **water** on something
throw the **baby** out with the bath
water
a **toe** in the water
tread **water**
water over the dam
water under the bridge
you can lead a **horse** to water but
you can't make him drink
waterfront
cover the **waterfront**
Waterloo
meet your **Waterloo**
waters
cast your **bread** upon the waters
fish in troubled **waters**
muddy the **waters**
pour **oil** on troubled waters
still **waters** run deep
test the waters: see **water**
wave
catch the **wave**
on the **crest** of a wave
ride the **crest** of the wave
wavelength
on the same **wavelength**
waves
make **waves**
wax
the whole **ball** of wax
way
all the way down the **line**
be way off **beam**
can't fight your way out of a
paper bag
cry all the way to the **bank**
the easy **way** out
go back a long **way**
go **way** back
laugh all the way to the **bank**
look the other **way**
a one-way **ticket**
pave the **way**
rub someone the wrong **way**
rub someone up the wrong
way
see which way the **cat** jumps
smooth the way
that's the way the **cookie**
crumbles
there's more than one way to
skin a **cat**
way out of **line**
which way the **wind** is blowing
ways
cut both **ways**
cut two **ways**

the **error** of your ways
mend your **ways**
set in your **ways**
wayside
fall by the **wayside**
weak
a weak **link**
a weak **link** in the chain
wear
wear yourself to a **frazzle**
wear the pants
wear the trousers
wear your **heart** on your sleeve
the **worse** for wear
weather
keep a **weather** eye on something
make heavy **weather** of
something
under the **weather**
weather the **storm**
web
a tangled **web**
wedding
like a spare **prick** at a wedding
wedge
drive a **wedge** between people
the thin end of the **wedge**
weeping
weeping and gnashing of **teeth**
weight
carry the **weight** of the world on
your shoulders
carry **weight**
a dead **weight**
pull your **weight**
throw your **weight** about
throw your **weight** around
throw your **weight** behind
something
a weight off your **mind**
worth your **weight** in gold
west
go **west**
wet
get your **feet** wet
have your **feet** wet
wet behind the **ears**
a wet **blanket**
wet someone's **appetite**
wet your **whistle**
whale
have a **whale** of a time
wheat
separate the wheat from the **chaff**
sort the wheat from the **chaff**
wheel
a big **wheel**
break a **butterfly** on a wheel
a fifth **wheel**
put a **spoke** in someone's wheel
put your **shoulder** to the wheel
reinvent the **wheel**
a third **wheel**
the wheel has come full **circle**
wheels
grease the **wheels**
oil the **wheels**
set the **wheels** in motion
spin your **wheels**
the **wheels** are turning

wheels within wheels
wherefores
the **whys** and wherefores
whet
whet someone's **appetite**
whimper
not with a **bang** but a whimper
whip
crack the **whip**
a fair crack of the **whip**
have the **whip** hand
hold the **whip** hand
whip something into **shape**
whipping
a whipping **boy**
whirl
give something a **whirl**
whirlwind
reap the whirlwind
sow the wind and **reap** the
whirlwind
whisker
by a **whisker**
within a **whisker** of something
whiskers
the **cat's** whiskers
whistle
blow the **whistle** on someone
clean as a whistle
wet your **whistle**
whistle **Dixie**
whistle for something
whistle in the **dark**
whistle in the **wind**
whistles
bells and whistles
white
black and white
bleed someone white
in **black** and white
white as a ghost
white as a sheet
white as snow
a white **elephant**
a white **lie**
whiter than **white**
whiter
whiter than **white**
whole
go the whole **hog**
go whole **hog**
the whole **ball** of wax
the whole **caboodle**
whole **cloth**
the whole kit and **caboodle**
the whole nine **yards**
the whole shooting **match**
the whole **works**
whys
the **whys** and wherefores
wick
get on someone's **wick**
wicket
bat on a sticky **wicket**
on a sticky **wicket**
wide
be **wide** open
blow something **wide** open
cast a wide **net**
give someone a wide **berth**

into the wide blue **yonder**
lay yourself **wide** open
leave yourself **wide** open
wide of the **mark**
wider
cast the **net** wider
wield
wield a big **stick**
wig
flip your wig
wild
go **hog** wild
into the wild blue **yonder**
sow your wild **oats**
a wild **card**
a wild **goose** chase
wild **horses**
wilderness
in the **wilderness**
a lone voice in the **wilderness**
a voice crying in the **wilderness**
wildest
beyond your wildest **dreams**
never in your wildest **dreams**
wildfire
spread like **wildfire**
willies
give you the **willies**
wills
a **battle** of wills
win
lose the **battle**, win the war
win **hands** down
win the **battle**, lose the war
win your **spurs**
wind
blow in the **wind**
catch **wind** of something
get the **wind** up
get **wind** of something
how the **wind** is blowing
in the **wind**
it's an ill **wind**
it's an ill **wind** that blows nobody
any good
like the **wind**
put the **wind** up someone
sail close to the **wind**
a second **wind**
sow the wind and **reap** the
whirlwind
spit in the **wind**
straws in the wind
swing in the **wind**
take the **wind** out of someone's
sail
take the **wind** out of someone's
sails
three **sheets** to the wind
throw **caution** to the wind
twist in the **wind**
which way the **wind** is blowing
whistle in the **wind**
windmills
tilt at **windmills**
window
go out of the **window**
go out the **window**
wing
on a **wing** and a prayer

take someone under your **wing**
under the **wing** of someone
wings
  clip someone's **wings**
  in the **wings**
  spread your **wings**
  try your **wings**
wink
  a **nod** and a wink
  not get a **wink** of sleep
  not sleep a **wink**
  a **nudge** and a wink
  quick as a wink
  tip someone the **wink**
winks
  forty **winks**
wink-wink
  nudge-nudge, wink-wink
wipe
  wipe the **floor** with someone
  wipe the **slate** clean
wire
  down to the **wire**
  a live **wire**
  under the **wire**
wires
  get your wires **crossed**
wisdom
  pearls of wisdom
wise
  penny-wise and pound-foolish
wither
  wither on the **vine**
wits
  at your **wits'** end
  a **battle** of wits
  collect your **wits**
  gather your **wits**
  have your **wits** about you
  keep your **wits** about you
  need your **wits** about you
  pit your **wits** against someone
  scare someone out of their
    wits
wives
  an old **wives'** tale
wobbler
  throw a wobbler: see **wobbly**
wobbly
  throw a **wobbly**
wolf
  cry **wolf**
  keep the **wolf** from the door
  a lone **wolf**
  a sheep in **wolf's** clothing
  a **wolf** in sheep's clothing
wolves
  throw someone to the **wolves**
woman
  hell hath no fury like a woman
    scorned
  a one-woman **band**
  the woman in the **street**
  you can't keep a **good** woman
    down
  your **right**-hand woman
women
  God's **gift** to women
wonder
  a nine-day **wonder**

a one-day **wonder**
wood
  babes in the wood
  dead **wood**
  knock on **wood**
  knock **wood**
  not see the wood for the **trees**
  touch **wood**
wooden
  a wooden **nickel**
  the wooden **spoon**
woods
  out of the **woods**
  your **neck** of the woods
woodwork
  come out of the **woodwork**
wool
  dyed-in-the-**wool**
  pull the **wool** over someone's
    eyes
word
  a dirty **word**
  from the **word** go
  get a **word** in edgeways
  get a **word** in edgewise
  not know the **meaning** of the
    word
  someone's **word** is law
  a **word** in someone's ear
words
  actions speak louder than words
  at a loss for **words**
  eat your **words**
  famous last **words**
  in **words** of one syllable
  lost for **words**
  not mince your **words**
  put **words** into someone's mouth
  stuck for **words**
  take the **words** out of someone's
    mouth
  a **war** of words
work
  all in a **day's** work
  do someone's dirty **work**
  do the **donkey** work
  have your **work** cut out
  a nasty piece of **work**
  work **overtime**
  work your **fingers** to the bone
  work your **guts** out
  work your **heart** out
  work your **socks** off
works
  in the **works**
  put a **spanner** in the works
  throw a monkey **wrench** into the
    works
  throw a **spanner** in the works
  throw a **wrench** into the works
  the whole **works**
  the **works**
world
  at **odds** with the world
  carry the **weight** of the world on
    your shoulders
  come down in the **world**
  come up in the **world**
  dead to the **world**
  the four **corners** of the world

go up in the **world**
it's a small **world**
move up in the **world**
not long for this **world**
not set the **world** on fire
not the end of the **world**
on top of the **world**
out of this **world**
small **world**
think the **world** of someone
the **world** is your oyster
worlds
  the best of both **worlds**
  the worst of both **worlds**
worm
  the early **bird** catches the worm
  a worm's eye **view**
  the **worm** turns
worms
  a bag of **worms**
  a can of **worms**
worse
  the **worse** for wear
  your **bark** is worse than your
    bite
worst
  the worst of both **worlds**
worth
  a **bird** in the hand is worth two
    in the bush
  the game is not worth the **candle**
  not worth a row of **beans**
  not worth the **candle**
  not worth the **paper** it's written
    on
  worth their **salt**
  worth your **weight** in gold
  your two **cents'** worth
wound
  rub **salt** into the wound
  twist the **knife** in the wound
wounds
  lick your **wounds**
  open old **wounds**
  reopen old **wounds**
wrack
  wrack and ruin: see **rack**
  wrack your brain: see **brains**
  wrack your **brains**
wrap
  wrap someone around your little
    finger
  wrap someone's **knuckles**
  wrap yourself in the **flag**
wraps
  keep something under **wraps**
  take the **wraps** off something
  the **wraps** come off
wrench
  throw a monkey **wrench** into the
    works
  throw a **wrench** into the works
wring
  wring someone's **neck**
  wring your **hands**
wringer
  be put through the **wringer**
  go through the **wringer**
wrist
  a **slap** on the wrist

write
  nothing to write **home** about
  something to write **home** about
writing
  the writing is on the **wall**
written
  not worth the **paper** it's written
    on
  written all over your **face**
wrong
  back the wrong **horse**
  bark up the wrong **tree**
  caught on the wrong **foot**
  fall into the wrong **hands**
  from the wrong side of the
    tracks

get hold of the wrong end of the
  stick
get off on the wrong **foot**
get out of **bed** on the wrong
  side
get out of **bed** the wrong side
get the wrong end of the **stick**
not put a **foot** wrong
on the wrong **end** of something
on the wrong **track**
rub someone the wrong **way**
rub someone up the wrong **way**
wrote
  that's **all** she wrote
yank
  yank someone's **chain**

yards
  the whole nine **yards**
year
  from the year **dot**
  since the year **dot**
years
  donkey's years
yesterday
  not born **yesterday**
yonder
  into the wide blue **yonder**
  into the wild blue **yonder**
young
  young **blood**
zero-sum
  a **zero-sum** game

Collins COBUILD Idioms Workbook

The Collins COBUILD Idioms Workbook focuses on 250 of the most common idioms in current use in British and American English. It is organized in 30 chapters, each of which looks at a group of idioms centring around a particular theme. The material is suitable for both class work and self-study.

Collins COBUILD English Dictionary

This is a major new edition, containing a wealth of information on meaning, usage, and grammar. For the first time, word frequency information is included. There is a workbook to accompany the dictionary.

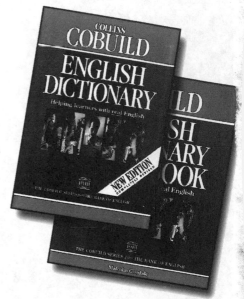

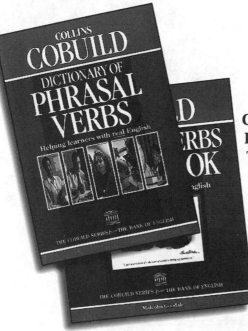

Collins COBUILD Dictionary of Phrasal Verbs

The Dictionary of Phrasal Verbs gives detailed explanations of the meanings, usage, and grammatical behaviour of more than 3000 phrasal verbs.
The unique Particles Index deals with the adverbs and prepositions used in phrasal verbs, and shows the common meanings that they have in these combinations. There is a workbook to accompany the dictionary.